The Government Contracts Reference Book

A Comprehensive Guide to the Language of Procurement

FIFTH EDITION

Ralph C. Nash, Jr.
Steven L. Schooner
Karen R. O'Brien-DeBakey
Vernon J. Edwards

Copyright © 2021 CCH Incorporated. All Rights Reserved.

No part of this publication may be reproduced or transmitted in any form or by any means, including electronic, mechanical, photocopying, recording, or utilized by any information storage or retrieval system, without written permission from the publisher. For information about permissions or to request permissions online, visit us at *www.WoltersKluwerLR.com/policies/permissions-reprints-and-licensing*, or email us at *LRUSpermissions@wolterskluwer.com*.

Published by Wolters Kluwer in New York.

Wolters Kluwer Legal & Regulatory U.S. serves customers worldwide with CCH, Aspen Publishers and Kluwer Law International products.

Printed in the United States of America

ISBN: 978-1-4548-9730-9

2 3 4 5 6 7 8 9 0

Library of Congress Cataloging-in-Publication Data

Names: Nash, Ralph C., Jr., 1928- author. | Schooner, Steven L., author.
  O'Brien-DeBakey, Karen R., author. | Edwards, Vernon J., 1947- author.
Title: The government contracts reference book : a comprehensive guide to
  the language of procurement / Ralph C. Nash, Jr., Steven L. Schooner,
  Karen R. O'Brien-DeBakey, Vernon J. Edwards.
Description: Fifth edition. | Chicago, IL : Wolters Kluwer, [2021] |
  Includes bibliographical references. | Summary: "The Government
  Contracts Reference Book provides clear explanations of both general and
  agency-specific federal contracting terms from the Department of
  Defense, General Services Administration, Department of Energy, NASA and
  others followed by a summary of where the term is used in the statutes
  or regulations dealing with the procurement process. Organized in an
  easy-to-use alphabetical format and fully cross-referenced, this
  essential resource to today's government contract terminology will help
  you procure goods and services efficiently and with confidence"—
  Provided by publisher.
Identifiers: LCCN 2021009489 | ISBN 9781454897309 (paperback) | ISBN
  9781454897309 (ebook)
Subjects: LCSH: Public contracts—United States—Encyclopedias. | Letting
  of contracts—United States—Encyclopedias. | Government purchasing—Law
  and legislation—United States—Encyclopedias.
Classification: LCC KF847.5 .N37 2021 | DDC 346.7302/303—dc23
LC record available at https://lccn.loc.gov/2021009489

SUSTAINABLE FORESTRY INITIATIVE
Certified Sourcing
www.sfiprogram.org
SFI-01051

Contents

Preface to the Fifth Edition

Since our first publication of *The Government Contracts Reference Book*, the policies and practices of government contracting have continued to change with the result that the terminology of this field has also changed. This fifth edition reflects the new terminology and updated references throughout.

The purpose of the book remains the same: to give concise, comprehensive information to the practitioner of the art of government contracting. Looking up a key term, the reader can find a definition, followed by a summary of where the term is used in the statutes or regulations dealing with the procurement process. We have also included references to those places in the literature where the term is more fully discussed. The book is not designed to stand alone: it is a *first* reference, pointing the user to additional sources as needed. The book makes it clear what we have known for a long time: government contracting is complex, and the rules cannot be gleaned from a single source such as the Federal Acquisition Regulation. They can only be learned from constant reading of reference materials and textbooks—not to mention decisions of the courts, boards of contract appeals, and the Government Accountability Office. Navigating the waters of government procurement is an arduous task, and this book is intended as an aid in that journey.

The one thing that we have learned in updating and revising the book is that it is impossible to make it fully comprehensive. While the book is significantly expanded, we are sure that there are additional terms that could be added. We urge our readers to let us know of terms that we have omitted so that they can be included in the next edition.

About the Authors

Ralph C. Nash, Jr., is a widely recognized author and lecturer in the government contracts field. A professor emeritus of law at The George Washington University Law School, he founded the University's Government Contracts Program in 1960 and served as its director from 1960 to 1966 and from 1979 to 1984. In addition to teaching, he does consulting work for government agencies, private corporations, and law firms. He is a member of the Procurement Round Table, and is a fellow and serves on the board of advisers of the National Contract Management Association. He served as a member of the Department of Defense Advisory Panel on streamlining and codifying Acquisition laws (Section 800 Panel). Professor Nash is the coauthor of *Government Contract Changes, Formation of Government Contracts, Administration of Government Contracts, Cost-Reimbursement Contracting, Competitive Negotiation: The Source Selection Process*, and *Intellectual Property in Government Contracts*. He received an A.B., magna cum laude, from Princeton University and a J.D. from The George Washington University Law School.

Vernon J. Edwards is a former U.S. Air Force and U.S. Department of Energy contracting official. He is a monthly contributor to *The Nash & Cibinic Report* and an occasional contributor to other publications, such as *Contract Management, The Government Contractor*, and *Briefing Papers*. He has written more than 200 published articles on various topics in acquisition in addition to books and monographs. He founded The FAR Bootcamp® and The Source Selection Bootcamp® and authored *The Source Selection Answer Book*. He is a 1974 graduate of the University of California at Los Angeles.

Karen R. O'Brien-DeBakey is a Vice-President at Jefferson Consulting Group where she provides expert assistance to government agencies in a wide range of acquisition services. Prior to joining Jefferson, she was Of Counsel to the firm of McCarthy, Sweeney and Harkaway, P.C., where she practiced government contract law. Prior to that, Ms. O'Brien-DeBakey was at ESI International managing the Government Contracts publications program of the George Washington University Law School. She began her career as a procurement law attorney in the Army Judge Advocate General's Corps. She also served as a staff attorney for the DOD Advisory Panel on Streamlining and Codifying the Acquisition Process (Section 800 Panel). She is coauthor of *Competitive Negotiation: The Source Selection Process* with John Cibinic, Jr. and Ralph C. Nash, Jr., and *ILI/JCG Guide to Millennium Challenge Indicators and Source Data* with Allan V. Burman. She received a B.A. in accounting, magna cum laude, from Niagara University and a J.D., cum laude, from Vermont Law School.

Steven L. Schooner is Nash & Cibinic Professor of Government Procurement Law, and Co-Director of the Government Procurement Law Program at the George Washington University Law School. Before joining the faculty, he served as the Associate Administrator for Procurement Law and Legislation at the Office of Federal Procurement Policy. He also served as a trial attorney in the Commercial

Litigation Branch of the Department of Justice, practiced with private law firms and, as an Active Duty Army Judge Advocate, served as a Commissioner at the Armed Services Board of Contract Appeals. As an Army Reserve officer, he taught for more than 20 years as an Adjunct Professor at the Judge Advocate General's School of the Army. His dispute resolution experience includes service as an arbitrator, mediator, neutral, and ombudsman. He serves on the Board of Directors of the Procurement Round Table and is a Fellow of the National Contract Management Association, a Member of the Board of Advisors, and a Certified Professional Contracts Manager. He is the Faculty Advisor to the American Bar Association's Public Contract Law Journal and a member of the Government Contractor Advisory Board. Professor Schooner received his B.A. from Rice University, J.D. from the College of William and Mary, and LL.M. from the George Washington University.

Note on References

DAU GLOSSARY refers to the DEFENSE ACQUISITION UNIVERSITY GLOSSARY OF DEFENSE ACQUISITION ACRONYMS AND TERMS, an online resource: www.dau.edu/tools/t/DAU-Glossary.

DOD 5000 Series refers to the directives (DoDD) and instructions (DoDI) that describe The Defense Acquisition System, beginning with DOD Directive (DoDD) 5000.01, *The Defense Acquisition System*. The current directives and instructions are maintained by the DOD Executive Services Directorate and may be accessed at https://www.esd.whs.mil/DD/Dod-Inssuances. Documents referenced in this book as the DOD 5000 Series include the following:

- DOD Directive 5000.01, The Defense Acquisition System, Sept. 9, 2020
- DOD Instruction 5000.02, Operation of the Adaptive Acquisition Framework, Jan. 23, 2020
- DOD Instruction 5000.02T, Operation of the Defense Acquisition System, Jan. 23, 2020
- DOD Instruction 5000.74, Defense Acquisition of Services, Jan. 10, 2020
- DOD Instruction 5000.75, Business Systems Requirements and Acquisition, Jan. 24, 2020
- DOD Instruction 5000.81, Urgent Capability Acquisition, Dec. 31, 2019
- DOD Instruction 5000.80, Operation of the Middle Tier of Acquisition (MTA), Dec. 30, 2019
- DOD Instruction 5000.85, Major Capability Acquisition, Aug. 6, 2020
- DOD Instruction 5000.87, Operation of the Software Acquisition Pathway, Oct. 2, 2020

A

A-76 POLICY   The policy of the executive branch that the government should generally rely on the private sector for commercially available goods and services. See COMPETITIVE SOURCING. Detailed guidance on determining whether commercially available services should be performed under contract with commercial sources or in-house using government facilities and personnel is contained in OMB Circular No. A-76 (revised), *Performance of Commercial Activities*, Aug. 16, 1983, most recently amended May 29, 2003; its *Revised Supplemental Handbook* (June 14, 1999); and FAR Subpart 7.3. The policy recognized that some functions are inherently governmental (see INHERENTLY GOVERNMENTAL FUNCTIONS) and must be performed by government personnel. However, the government should contract for commercially available services ("contract out") if certain criteria are met and consider relative cost in deciding between government performance and performance under contract. The revised Circular provides that contractors will compete against the government agency in a single competition with an AGENCY TENDER OFFICIAL representing the MOST EFFICIENT ORGANIZATION (MEO) being proposed by the agency. See FAR Subpart 7.3. A-76 competitions were conducted regularly until Congress imposed a moratorium on DOD competitions in 2008. See Cong. Research Serv. R40854, Circular A-76 and the Moratorium on DOD Competitions: Background and Issues for Congress (Jan. 16, 2013) and A-76 Competitions in the Department of Defense (June 2, 2020).

ABILITY ONE   The central NONPROFIT ORGANIZATION that coordinates the mandatory purchase requirements from organizations that employ BLIND OR SEVERELY DISABLED employees. It publishes a PROCUREMENT LIST of all supplies and services required to be purchased from these organizations (http://www.abilityone.gov/index.html). This policy is implemented in FAR Subpart 8.7. See BLIND OR SEVERELY DISABLED. See Memorandum by the National Council on Disability (NCD) (Feb. 22, 2019), which provides an initial report of the AbilityOne Program that assesses various aspects of the Program in the context of broader federal disability policy.

ABSTRACT OF BIDS   See ABSTRACT OF OFFERS.

ABSTRACT OF OFFERS   The record of all BIDS received on an unclassified sealed bid (see SEALED BIDDING) procurement. FAR 14.403 requires the BID OPENING officer to personally and publicly open all bids received and have them recorded on Standard Form 1409, Abstract of Offers, FAR 53.301-1409, or Optional Form 1419, Abstract of Offers—Construction, FAR 53.302-1419. The BID OPENING officer must complete the abstract and certify its accuracy as soon after bid opening as possible. Because they are available for public inspection, abstracts will not contain information about failure to meet minimum standards of RESPONSIBILITY, apparent collusion of bidders (see COLLUSIVE BIDDING), or other matters properly exempt from public disclosure. When bid items are too numerous to warrant complete recording, abstract entries for individual bids may be limited to item numbers and corresponding prices.

ACAT   See ACQUISITION CATEGORIES.

ACCELERATED PROCEDURE   A procedure for the accelerated disposition of appeals before an agency BOARD OF CONTRACT APPEALS (BCA) that is required by the CONTRACT DISPUTES ACT OF 1978 at 41 U.S.C. § 7106(a). The accelerated procedure may be elected only by the contractor and originally applied to claims of $50,000 or less. This limit was raised to claims of $100,000 by the FEDERAL ACQUISITION STREAMLINING ACT OF 1994, Pub. L. No. 103-355. The appellant must make the election to proceed within 30 days of receipt of the notice of docketing. See Rule 53 Rules of Procedure for the Civilian Board of Contract Appeals. The BCA has 180 days after the election to issue a decision on the appeal. Under this procedure the parties are encouraged to waive pleadings, discovery and briefs; and a concise written decision will normally be rendered by a single judge with such concurrence as may be required by the rules. The decision may be given orally at the close of the hearing followed by the written decision. For claims of $50,000 or less, a contractor may elect an alternate expedited procedure (see EXPEDITED PROCEDURES). Neither procedure is available if the contractor appeals the DECISION OF THE CONTRACTING OFFICER to the U.S. COURT OF FEDERAL CLAIMS. See Schaengold, Prusock, Muenzfeld & Straus, *Choice of Forum for Federal Government Contract Claims: Court of Federal Claims vs. Board of Contract Appeals/Edition III*, BRIEFING PAPERS No. 19-3 (Feb. 2019).

ACCELERATION   Speeding up work to complete performance earlier than anticipated. If a contractor accelerates on its own initiative to ensure completion within the contract schedule, the additional costs of that acceleration are not recoverable from the government. In addition, the Schedules for Construction Contracts clause at FAR 52.236-15 permits the contracting officer to order acceleration without compensation if the contractor has fallen behind schedule. Compensable acceleration occurs when the government orders accelerated performance that is not required to meet the current contract schedule. This generally occurs constructively (as a type of CONSTRUCTIVE CHANGE) when the government requires the contractor to meet the current contract schedule in the face of a delay to which the contractor is entitled such as an EXCUSABLE DELAY or a delay pursuant to a contract clause calling for a time extension such as the Changes clause. Such a delay entitles the contractor to a schedule extension, and an order to meet the original schedule is equivalent to an order to complete the work in advance of schedule. A constructive acceleration thus typically entails an excusable delay, government knowledge of the delay, some government statement or act construed as an acceleration order, notice by the contractor that the order is a constructive change, and incurring of additional costs of accelerated effort. See Nash & Feldman, 1 GOVERNMENT CONTRACT CHANGES §§ 15:1–15:25 (3d ed. 2006–2020); Cibinic, Nash & Nagle, ADMINISTRATION OF GOVERNMENT CONTRACTS 402–13 (5th ed. 2016). See also Dale & D'Onofrio, *Reconciling Concurrency in Schedule Delay and Constructive Acceleration*, 39 PUB. CONT. L.J. 161 (2010); Gourlay, *Constructive Acceleration and Concurrent Delay: Is There a "Middle Ground"?*, 39 PUB. CONT. L.J. 231 (2010).

ACCEPTABLE ACCOUNTING SYSTEM *Official:* A system that complies with the system criteria in paragraph (c) of this clause to provide reasonable assurance that—(i) Applicable laws and regulations are complied with; (ii) The accounting system and cost data are reliable; (iii) Risk of misallocations and mischarges are minimized; and (iv) Contract allocations and charges are consistent with billing procedures. *Source:* The Accounting System Administration clause in DFARS 252.242-7006. This clause contains 18 requirements necessary to meet the system criteria. If the ACCOUNTING SYSTEM contains a SIGNIFICANT DEFICIENCY, the contractor is subject to a withholding of payments penalty.

ACCEPTABLE CONTRACTOR BUSINESS SYSTEMS *Official:* CONTRACTOR BUSINESS SYSTEMS that complies with the terms and conditions of the applicable business system clauses listed in the definition of "contractor business systems" in this clause. *Source:* The Contractor Business Systems clause in DFARS 252.242-7005. A requirement that the Department of Defense adopt a rule requiring major contractors to have acceptable business systems was included in Section 893 of the National Defense Authorization Act for FY 2011, Pub. L. No. 111-383. This requirement is implemented in DFARS Subpart 242.70. Failure to maintain an acceptable contractor business system may result in disapproval of the system by the CONTRACTING OFFICER and the withholding of payments. Mandatory withholding of payments is not applicable to SMALL BUSINESSES because they are exempt from COVERED CONTRACTS. To meet the requirement of an acceptable business system a contractor must have an ACCEPTABLE ACCOUNTING SYSTEM, an ACCEPTABLE EARNED VALUE MANAGEMENT SYSTEM, an ACCEPTABLE ESTIMATING SYSTEM, an ACCEPTABLE MATERIAL MANAGEMENT AND ACCOUNTING SYSTEM, an ACCEPTABLE PROPERTY MANAGEMENT SYSTEM, and an ACCEPTABLE PURCHASING SYSTEM. See DCAA Memorandum 12-PAS-012(R), "Audit Guidance on Auditing Contractor Business Systems and Contractor Compliance with DFARS 252.242-7006," Accounting System Administration (Apr. 24, 2012); U.S. GOV'T ACCOUNTABILITY OFFICE, CONTRACTOR BUSINESS SYSTEMS: DOD NEEDS BETTER INFORMATION TO MONITOR AND ASSESS REVIEW PROCESS, GAO-19-212 (Feb. 2019); MCKENNA LONG & ALDRIDGE LLP, GOVERNMENT CONTRACTOR BUSINESS SYSTEMS COMPLIANCE GUIDE (2011); Manos, *Contractor Business Systems Audits: The Coming Train Wreck*, 5 CP&A Rep. ¶ 52 (Nov. 9, 2010).

ACCEPTABLE EARNED VALUE MANAGEMENT SYSTEM *Official:* An EARNED VALUE MANAGEMENT SYSTEM that complies with paragraph (b) of this clause. *Source:* The Earned Value Management System clause in DFARS 252.234-7002. The clause requires that the system comply with the AMERICAN NATIONAL STANDARDS INSTITUTE/ELECTRONIC INDUSTRIES ALLIANCE STANDARD 748 and contain management procedures that provide for the generation of timely, reliable, and verifiable information required by the contract performance report and integrated master schedule. It cannot contain a SIGNIFICANT DEFICIENCY. See Department of Defense, *Earned Value Management Implementation Guide* (Jan. 18, 2019); and Department of Defense, Office of Performance Assessments and Root Cause Analyses, *Earned Value Management Interpretation Guide* (Feb. 1, 2018).

ACCEPTABLE ESTIMATING SYSTEM *Official:* An ESTIMATING SYSTEM that an estimating system that complies with the system criteria in paragraph (d) of this clause, and provides for a system that—(1) Is maintained, reliable, and consistently applied; (2) Produces verifiable, supportable, documented, and timely cost estimates that are an acceptable basis for negotiation of fair and reasonable prices; (3) Is consistent with and integrated with the Contractor's related management systems; and (4) Is subject to applicable financial control systems. *Source:* The Cost Estimating System Requirements clause in DFARS 252.215-7002. Such systems must (1) be disclosed to the ACO in writing, (2) accurately describe those policies, procedures, and practices that the Contractor currently uses in preparing cost proposals, (3) provides sufficient detail for the Government to reasonably make an informed judgment regarding the acceptability of the Contractor's estimating practices, and (4) provide for the use of appropriate source data, utilize sound estimating techniques and good judgment, maintain a consistent approach, and adhere to established policies and procedures. If the ESTIMATING SYSTEM contains a SIGNIFICANT DEFICIENCY, the contractor is subject to a withholding of payments penalty.

ACCEPTABLE MATERIAL MANAGEMENT AND ACCOUNTING SYSTEM   *Official:* A MATERIAL MANAGEMENT AND ACCOUNTING SYSTEM that generally complies with the system criteria in paragraph (d) of this clause. *Source:* The Material Management and Accounting System clause in DFARS 252.242-7004. A contractor's MMAS must have adequate internal controls to ensure system and data integrity by incorporating the ten criteria provided in paragraph (d) of the clause. If the MATERIAL MANAGEMENT AND ACCOUNTING SYSTEM contains a SIGNIFICANT DEFICIENCY, the contractor is subject to a withholding of payments penalty.

ACCEPTABLE PURCHASING SYSTEM   *Official:* A PURCHASING SYSTEM that complies with the system criteria in paragraph (c) of this clause. *Source:* The Contractor Purchasing System Administration clause in DFARS 252.244-7001. The clause contains 24 criteria which must be met. If the PURCHASING SYSTEM contains a SIGNIFICANT DEFICIENCY, the contractor is subject to a withholding of payments penalty.

ACCEPTABLE QUALITY LEVEL (AQL)   Generally, in QUALITY ASSURANCE, the worst quality that will be accepted. In PERFORMANCE-BASED CONTRACTING, the maximum percent defective, the maximum number of defects per hundred units, or the number of defects in a lot that can be considered satisfactory on the average. The allowable leeway or variance from a standard before the government will reject the specific service. An AQL does not say that the contractor may knowingly offer defective service. It implies that the government recognizes that defective performance sometimes happens unintentionally. As long as the percent of defective performance does not exceed the AQL, the service will not be rejected by the government. The contractor, however, must reperform the defective service when possible. See OFFICE OF FEDERAL PROCUREMENT POLICY PAMPHLET NO. 4, SUPPLEMENT NO. 2 TO OMB CIRCULAR NO. A-76: A GUIDE FOR WRITING AND ADMINISTERING PERFORMANCE STATEMENTS OF WORK FOR SERVICE CONTRACTS (1980). See also Edwards, *Service Contract Quality: We've Got More Thinking to Do*, 22 N&CR ¶ 20 (Mar. 2008) and *Postscript: Proposals and Promises*, 15 N&CR ¶ 3 (Jan. 2001).

ACCEPTANCE   See ACCEPTANCE OF OFFER and ACCEPTANCE OF WORK.

ACCEPTANCE OF OFFER   The formal act of the recipient of an OFFER, typically the government, that results in a legally binding contract. The standard forms (SFs) for issuing solicitations—SF 33, Solicitation, Offer, and Award, FAR 53.301-33 and SF 1442, Solicitation, Offer, and Award (Construction, Alteration, or Repair), FAR 53.301-1442—contain a block for the signature of the CONTRACTING OFFICER signifying acceptance. Acceptance is also made by sending a NOTICE OF AWARD. When the government issues a

PURCHASE ORDER, under SIMPLIFIED ACQUISITION PROCEDURES, acceptance is made by the contractor, either by signing the purchase order or by beginning performance. FAR 13.302-3. Acceptance is generally binding at the time of transmission of the acceptance document (the MAILBOX RULE). See Cibinic, Nash & Yukins, FORMATION OF GOVERNMENT CONTRACTS 241–52 (4th ed. 2011).

ACCEPTANCE OF WORK   *Official:* The act of an AUTHORIZED REPRESENTATIVE of the government by which the government, for itself or as an agent of another, (1) assumes ownership of existing identified supplies tendered or (2) approves specific services rendered as partial or complete performance of a contract. *Source:* FAR 46.101. Acceptance of supplies or services is the responsibility of the CONTRACTING OFFICER. FAR 46.502. Acceptance constitutes acknowledgment that the supplies or services conform to applicable contract quality and quantity requirements. FAR 46.501. Acceptance may take place before delivery, at the time of delivery, or after delivery, depending on the TERMS AND CONDITIONS of the contract. Neither supplies nor services are ordinarily accepted before completion of government contract QUALITY ASSURANCE actions. Acceptance is usually evidenced by execution of an acceptance certificate on an inspection and receiving report (see MATERIAL INSPECTION AND RECEIVING REPORT) or commercial shipping document/packing list. FAR 46.501. Acceptance has unusual legal significance in government contracting because the Inspection of Supplies—Fixed-Price clause (FAR 52.246-2) and the Inspection of Construction clause (FAR 52.246-12) make acceptance conclusive on the government except for LATENT DEFECTs, FRAUD, GROSS MISTAKEs AMOUNTING TO FRAUD, or any right of the government under warranties (see WARRANTY). See Cibinic, Nash & Nagle, ADMINISTRATION OF GOVERNMENT CONTRACTS 748–55 (5th ed. 2016).

ACCORD AND SATISFACTION   A method of resolving an issue whereby the parties (1) agree (enter into an EXECUTORY ACCORD) to give and accept something ("satisfaction") in settlement of the issue and (2) perform the agreement. If the performance is not rendered, the other party has the election to pursue its rights under the original contract. If the performance is rendered, the new contract discharges the original contract. RESTATEMENT (SECOND) OF CONTRACTS § 281 (1981). In an alternative form of settlement agreement, the SUBSTITUTED CONTRACT, the old contract is discharged at the time of entering into the new contract. RESTATEMENT (SECOND) OF CONTRACTS § 279 (1981). Decisions on government contracts frequently do not distinguish between these two types of settlement agreements but refer to them both as accord and satisfaction. Accord and satisfaction is normally accomplished by execution of a bilateral MODIFICATION and payment by the government in accordance with the modification. See Cibinic, Nash & Nagle, ADMINISTRATION OF GOVERNMENT CONTRACTS 1113–15 (5th ed. 2016). See also Ganderson, et al., *Information and Analysis on Legal Aspects of Procurement*, 59 The Gov't Contractor ¶ 64 (Mar. 2017); Nash, *Postscript V: The Plain Meaning Rule*, 23 N&CR ¶ 49 (Sept. 2009).

ACCOUNTING CLASSIFICATION REFERENCE NUMBER (ACRN)   *Official:* Any combination of a two-position alpha/numeric code used as a method of relating the accounting classification citation to detailed line item information contained in the schedule. *Source:* DFARS 204.7101. The ACRN may be any discrete two-position alphanumeric code assigned to each accounting classification within each contract (except that the letters "I" and "O" are not used). The code is shown as a detached prefix to the long-line accounting classification number, usually in the Accounting and Appropriation Data block of the contract. DOD PGI 204.7107. The same ACRNs cannot be assigned to more than one accounting classification citation and each accounting classification citation can have only one ACRN assigned to it.

ACCOUNTING SYSTEM   *Official:* The contractor's system or systems for accounting methods, procedures, and controls established to gather, record, classify, analyze, summarize, interpret, and present accurate and timely financial data for reporting in compliance with applicable laws, regulations and management decisions, and may include subsystems for specific areas such as indirect and other direct costs, compensation, billing, labor, and general information technology. *Source:* The Accounting System Administration clause in DFARS 252.242-7006. This clause is required to be used in DoD cost-reimbursement, incentive, time-and-materials and labor-hour contracts and contracts with PROGRESS PAYMENTS based on costs or percentage of completion. DFARS 242.7503. It specifies 18 requirements for an ACCEPTABLE ACCOUNTING SYSTEM.

ACCRUAL BASIS ACCOUNTING   An accounting method in which revenue is recorded when earned and costs and BALANCE SHEET items are recorded when commitments are made. The accrual basis of accounting, rather than the CASH BASIS ACCOUNTING method, is used by organizations with more complex dealings. Under the accrual basis, costs are incurred when an obligation to pay arises, and such costs are recorded as accrued even though actual payment is not required until later. The overwhelming majority of government contractors use the accrual basis.

ACCRUAL OF A CLAIM   *Official:* The date when all events, that fix the alleged liability of either the Government or the contractor and permit assertion of the claim, were known or should have been known. For liability to be fixed, some injury must have occurred. However, monetary damages need not have been incurred. *Source:* FAR 33.201. This date is the beginning of the running of a STATUTE OF LIMITATIONS, which for most contract claims is six years. See Cibinic, Nash & Nagle, ADMINISTRATION OF GOVERNMENT CONTRACTS 1184–87 (5th ed. 2016).

ACCUMULATING COSTS   *Official:* Collecting cost data in an organized manner, such as through a system of accounts. *Source:* FAR 31.001. CAS 401, Consistency in Estimating, Accumulating, and Reporting Costs, 48 C.F.R. § 9904.401-20, requires that a contractor's practices in estimating costs in order to price a proposal be consistent with the COST ACCOUNTING PRACTICEs the contractor uses in accumulating contract costs, and that, conversely, the contractor's practices in accumulating actual contract costs be consistent with practices used in pricing the related proposal.

ACCURATE, COMPLETE, AND CURRENT   The standard that CERTIFIED COST OR PRICING DATA must meet when submitted in accordance with FAR 15.403 (implementation of TRUTH IN NEGOTIATIONS ACT, 10 U.S.C. § 2306a and 41 U.S.C. chapter 35). When a contracting officer requires an offeror or contractor to submit certified cost or pricing data, the firm must certify that, to the best of their knowledge and belief, the data were accurate, complete, and current as of the date the parties agreed on a price or another date agreed to by the parties. FAR 15.403-4; FAR 15.406-2. If the data were not, in fact, accurate or complete or current as of the date stipulated they are said to have been "defective." In that case, if the defective data led the government to agree to a higher price than it otherwise would have, the government is entitled to a price reduction in the amount of "overpricing." See FAR 15.407-1(b) and the Price Reduction for Defective Cost or Pricing Data clause at FAR 52.215-10. See also Bodenheimer, DEFECTIVE PRICING HAND-BOOK (2019–2020 Edition); Cibinic, Nash & Nagle, ADMINISTRATION OF GOVERNMENT CONTRACTS 134–35 (5th ed. 2016); and Manos, GOVERNMENT CONTRACT COSTS & PRICING (Apr. 2020).

ACQUISITION   *Official:* Acquiring by contract, with appropriated funds, supplies or services (including construction) by and for the use of the federal government through purchase or LEASE, whether the supplies or services already exist or must be created, developed, demonstrated, and evaluated. Acquisition begins at the point when agency needs are established and includes the description of requirements to satisfy agency needs, solicitation and selection of sources, AWARD of contracts, contract financing, contract performance, contract administration, and those technical and management functions directly related to the process of fulfilling agency needs by contract. *Source:* FAR 2.101. The procurement statutes generally use the synonymous term PROCUREMENT. However, "acquisition" is generally used in the FAR to describe this activity. See Cibinic, Nash & Yukins, FORMATION OF GOVERNMENT CONTRACTS 3–4 (4th ed. 2011); Nagle, HISTORY OF GOVERNMENT CONTRACTING (2d ed. 1999); Edwards, *The Dawn of the Modern Acquisition Era*, 23 N&CR ¶62 (Nov. 2009); Przemieniecki, ed., ACQUISITION OF DEFENSE SYSTEMS (1993).

ACQUISITION ADVISORY PANEL   A panel of experts established by Congress through the SERVICES ACQUISITION REFORM ACT (SARA), Section 1423 of the National Defense Authorization Act for FY 2006, Pub. L. No. 109-163. Also known as the "SARA Advisory Panel" and the "1423 Advisory Panel." The law directed the panel to review federal acquisition laws, regulations, and policies "with a view toward ensuring effective and appropriate use of commercial practices and performance-based contracting" and to make recommendations for improvements. The 14 panel members from government, academia, and the private sector were appointed by the Office of Management and Budget on February 1, 2005. The panel held numerous public hearings in 2005 and 2006. Originally tasked with reporting its findings within one year, the panel sought and received an extension. The Panel published its findings in a report titled *"Report of the Acquisition Advisory Panel to the Office of Federal Procurement Policy and United States Congress"* (Jan. 2007).

ACQUISITION CATEGORIES (ACATs)   The division by DOD of its major programs into categories, ACAT I through ACAT III, each based on acquisition objectives and dollar values, and each with its own procedures and corresponding levels of scrutiny. See DOD 5000 Series.

ACQUISITION CENTER OF EXCELLENCE (ACE)   [1] Generally, a multi-functional organizational unit or team with a mandate to improve acquisition processes or techniques. The term appears to date from the late 1990s and to have originated in the Department of Defense. [2] A website, https://www.dau.edu/cop/ace/SitePages/About.aspx, that is a repository of service contracting best practices. The website was established in September 2004 by the OFFICE OF FEDERAL PROCUREMENT POLICY in cooperation with the DEFENSE ACQUISITION UNIVERSITY and the FEDERAL ACQUISITION INSTITUTE as mandated by Section 1431(b) of the Services Acquisition Reform Act of 2003, Pub. L. No. 108-136, Title XIV.

ACQUISITION INSTRUMENT IDENTIFICATION   A system of identifying numbers to be assigned to NASA contracts and related instruments. NFS Subpart 18-4.71. The basic number will remain unchanged throughout the life of the instrument. It consists of no more than 11 alphanumeric characters. A five-position prefix combines "NAS" (except for certain reimbursable contracts, which use "DEN") with a two-position identifier of the installation responsible for the contract. A hyphen is inserted after the prefix and is followed by a six-position set of serial numbers assigned by each installation, without regard to fiscal year or type of contract. (As an exception, "(F)" appears in the final position for facilities contracts.) The two-position installation identifier used in the prefix is also used to begin solicitation numbers, but the rest of the solicitation identifying numbers are installation-unique. PUR-CHASE ORDERs, including blanket purchase orders, use a simplified identification system. NFS 18-4.7103. See also PROCUREMENT INSTRUMENT IDENTIFICATION NUMBERS.

ACQUISITION LIFE CYCLE   See ACQUISITION PROCESS.

ACQUISITION MANAGEMENT SYSTEM   The document providing guidance on the Federal Aviation Administration's acquisition policies and management of resources to fulfill its mission. (http://fast.faa.gov/) It was adopted when the Agency was given the authority to conduct its procurement operations without following the FEDERAL PROPERTY AND ADMINISTRATIVE SERVICES ACT and the FEDERAL ACQUISITION REGULA-TION. See Department of Transportation Appropriations Act for FY 1996, Pub. L. No. 104-50, 109 Stat. 436, § 348 and 49 U.S.C. § 46101 et seq. The system calls for a progressive procurement process that allows for sequential SCREENING of potential contractors through the issuance of SCREENING INFORMATION REQUESTs. This allows the elimination of potential contractors that are judged not to have the capability to perform the required work. See Cibinic, Nash & Yukins, FORMATION OF GOVERNMENT CONTRACTS 1011–15 (4th ed. 2011).

ACQUISITION PLAN   A plan addressing all technical, business, management, and other significant considerations that will control an acquisition. It summarizes ACQUISITION PLANNING deliberations and must identify milestones for decisions in the ACQUISITION PROCESS. FAR 7.105 contains detailed guidance on the contents of written acquisition plans. See also DFARS 207.105; GSAR 507.105; NFS 18-7.105. See Feldman, GOVERNMENT CONTRACT AWARDS: NEGOTIATION AND SEALED BIDDING § 3:13 (2019–2020 ed.); Cibinic, Nash & Yukins, FORMATION OF GOVERNMENT CONTRACTS 279–93 (4th ed. 2011). See also Nash, *Postscript: Negotiation Instead of Sealed Bidding*, 23 N&CR ¶ 56 (Oct. 2009); Gohl, *Acquisition Planning in the United States Army Reserve*, The Army Lawyer (Feb. 2008), at 1; Edwards, *The Decision to Use Negotiation Instead of Sealed Bidding: Is It Entirely Discretionary?*, 21 N&CR ¶ 73 (Dec. 2007).

ACQUISITION PLANNING   *Official:* The process by which the efforts of all personnel responsible for an acquisition are coordinated and integrated through a comprehensive plan for fulfilling the agency need in a timely manner and at a reasonable cost. It includes developing the overall strategy for managing the acquisition. *Source:* FAR 2.101. This planning process is conducted pursuant to the statutory requirement in 10 U.S.C. § 2305(a)(1)(A)(ii) and 41 U.S.C. § 3306(a)(1)(B) that agencies conduct advance procurement planning. Its purpose is to ensure that FULL AND OPEN COMPETITION is obtained to the greatest extent feasible and that COMMERCIAL ITEMs are procured to the maximum extent practicable. FAR Part 7 prescribes policies and procedures for (1) developing ACQUISITION PLANs, (2) determining whether to use commercial or government resources for acquisition of supplies or services, (3) deciding whether it is more economical to lease equipment than to purchase it, and (4) determining whether functions are inherently governmental (see INHERENTLY GOVERNMENTAL FUNCTIONS). Some agencies prescribe extensive additions or modifications to the FAR guidance. See, for example, DFARS Subpart 207.1 and NFS Subpart 18-7.1. See Cibinic, Nash & Yukins, FORMATION OF GOVERNMENT CONTRACTS, chap. 3 (4th ed. 2011); DOD, Source Selection Procedures (Mar. 31, 2016). See also U.S. GOV'T ACCOUNTABILITY OFFICE, ACQUISITION PLANNING: OPPORTUNITIES TO BUILD STRONG FOUNDATIONS FOR BETTER SERVICES CONTRACTS, GAO-11-672 (Aug. 2011); Nash, *Postscript III: Weapon System Acquisition Planning*, 22 N&CR ¶ 21 (Mar. 2008); Edwards, *The Decision to Use Negotiation Instead of Sealed Bidding: Is It Entirely Discretionary?*, 21 N&CR ¶ 73 (Dec. 2007); Nash, *Acquisition Planning: The Missing Link*, 21 N&CR ¶ 7 (Mar. 2007).

ACQUISITION SAVINGS *Official:* Savings resulting from the application of a VALUE ENGINEERING CHANGE PROPOSAL to contracts awarded by the same contracting office or its successor for essentially the same unit. Acquisition savings include (1) INSTANT CONTRACT SAVINGS, (2) CONCURRENT CONTRACT SAVINGS, and (3) FUTURE CONTRACT SAVINGS. *Source:* FAR 48.001. Savings of the government are called COLLATERAL SAVINGS. See Nash & Feldman, 1 GOVERNMENT CONTRACT CHANGES §§ 9:1–9:15 (3d ed. 2006–2020); Cibinic, Nash & Nagle, ADMINISTRATION OF GOVERNMENT CONTRACTS 371–85 (5th ed. 2016).

ACQUISITION SERVICES FUND *Official:* A revolving fund in the DEPARTMENT OF THE TREASURY that can be used by the GENERAL SERVICES ADMINISTRATION to procure for other agencies personal property, nonpersonal services, personal services related to the provision of INFORMATION TECHNOLOGY, repair, rehabilitation and conversion of personal property, and the management of personal property and nonpersonal services provided by GSA. *Source:* 40 U.S.C. § 321. This fund was established by the General Services Administration Modernization Act, Pub. L. No. 109-313, 120 Stat. 1724 (Oct. 6, 2006). The fund assumed the assets and liabilities of the INFORMATION TECHNOLOGY FUND. Agencies pay for property and services procured plus a fee established by the Administrator of GSA for work procured through the fund.

ACQUISITION STRATEGY A top-level plan for conducting an ACQUISITION. As applied to MAJOR SYSTEMS it describes the Program Manager's plan to achieve program execution and programmatic goals across the entire program life cycle. Summarizes the overall approach to acquiring the capability (to include the program schedule, structure, risks, funding, and the business strategy). Contains sufficient detail to allow senior leadership and the Milestone Decision Authority (MDA) to assess whether the strategy makes good business sense, effectively implements laws and policies, and reflects management's priorities. Once approved by the MDA, the Acquisition Strategy provides a basis for more detailed planning. The strategy evolves over time and should continuously reflect the current status and desired goals of the program. DAU GLOSSARY. The strategy is documented in an ACQUISITION PLAN prepared in accordance with FAR Subpart 7.1.

ACQUISITION STREAMLINING *Official:* Any effort that results in more efficient and more effective use of resources to design, develop, produce, or deploy quality systems. This includes ensuring that only necessary and cost-effective requirements are included, at the most appropriate time in the acquisition cycle, in solicitations and resulting contracts for the design, development, and production of new systems, or for modifications to existing systems that involve redesign of systems or subsystems. *Source:* FAR 7.101. The objective of acquisition streamlining is to reduce the time and cost required for acquiring systems and to improve the quality of those systems by ensuring that solicitations and contracts contain only those necessary SPECIFICATIONs, STANDARDs, and related documents that have been tailored (see TAILORING) for application at the most appropriate time in the acquisition cycle. FAR 10.002. A streamlined technique is available in FAR Subpart 12.6 for the acquisition of COMMERCIAL ITEMs. Acquisition streamlining has also been addressed to shortening the time for and reducing the resources used in the SOURCE SELECTION process.

ACQUISITION STREAMLINING AND STANDARDIZATION INFORMATION SYSTEM (ASSIST)   Websites that provide access to DOD specifications and standards that are maintained by the DEFENSE STANDARDIZATION PROGRAM (DSP). ASSIST Online is the portal for DOD users and requires registration. ASSIST Quicksearch provides registration-free access.

ACTIVITY BASED COSTING (ABC)   A set of managerial accounting methods used to identify and describe COST OBJECTIVEs, the activities they create and the amount of resources the activities consume. It is a technique to quantitatively measure the cost and performance of activities, resources, and cost objects, including, when appropriate, OVERHEAD. ABC identifies organizational activities, traces costs to these activities, and then uses various cost drivers to trace the cost of activities to products. These cost drivers, such as the number of persons performing work or the number of setups required per product, reflect the consumption of activities by the products. ABC is a tool for management designed to translate cost data and provide a reliable information source on which to base managerial decisions. See Kaplan & Anderson, TIME-DRIVEN ACTIVITY BASED COSTING (2007); Whittaker, *Five Keys To Deploying Activity-Based Costing, The Armed Forces Comptroller* (Vol. 50, No. 1, 2005); Turney, COMMON CENTS: THE ACTIVITY-BASED COSTING AND ACTIVITY-BASED MANAGEMENT PERFORMANCE BREAKTHROUGH (2005).

ACTUAL CASH VALUE   *Official:* The cost of replacing damaged property with other property of like kind and quality and in the physical condition of the damaged property immediately before the damage. *Source:* FAR 31.001. CAS 416, Accounting for Insurance Costs, 48 C.F.R. § 9904.416-50(a)(3), states that in measuring actual losses to be covered by a contractor's SELF INSURANCE program, the amount of loss must be measured, in part, by the actual cash value of the property destroyed.

ACTUAL COSTS   *Official:* An amount determined on the basis of incurred costs, as distinguished from forecasted costs, including STANDARD COSTs properly adjusted for applicable VARIANCE. *Source:* 48 C.F.R. § 9904.401-30; FAR 31.001. They are those costs sustained in fact, on the basis of costs incurred, as distinguished from projected or estimated costs. The actual cost history of producing the same or a similar product is a fact taken into account when COST ANALYSIS is performed. Actual costs are also the preferred data for establishing the amount of an EQUITABLE ADJUSTMENT when it is determined after the work has been performed. See HISTORICAL COST. See Nash & Feldman, 2 GOVERNMENT CONTRACT CHANGES §§ 19:6–19:9 (3d ed. 2006–2020); Cibinic, Nagle & Nash, ADMINISTRATION OF GOVERNMENT CONTRACTS 622–23 (5th ed. 2016).

ACTUARIAL ACCRUED LIABILITY   *Official:* Pension cost attributable, under the ACTUARIAL COST METHOD in use, to years prior to the current period considered by a particular actuarial valuation. As of such date, the actuarial liability represents the excess of the present value of future benefits and administrative expenses over the present value of future normal costs for all plan participants and beneficiaries. The excess of the actuarial accrued liability over the actuarial value of the assets of a PENSION PLAN is the unfunded actuarial liability. The excess of the actuarial value of the assets of a pension plan over the actuarial accrued liability is an actuarial surplus and is treated as a negative unfunded actuarial liability. *Source:* FAR 31.001. Pension plan costs applicable to prior years that were specifically unallowable (see ALLOWABLE COST) under then-existing government contracts must be separately identified and excluded from unfunded actuarial liability. 48 C.F.R. § 9904.412-40(b)(2). See U.S. Gov't Accountability Office, Pension Costs on DOD Contracts: Additional Guidance Needed to Ensure Costs are Consistent and Reasonable, GAO-13-158 (Jan. 2013); Briggerman, *155 CAS 413: Determining Segment Closing Adjustments Triggered by Sale of a Segment—Part II*, 24 N&CR ¶ 15 (Apr. 2010); Briggerman, *Cost Accounting Standards: Liability for Interest Under CAS 413 When Terminating A Pension Plan*, 24 N&CR ¶ 1 (Jan. 2010).

ACTUARIAL ASSUMPTION   *Official:* An estimate of future conditions affecting pension costs; e.g., mortality rate, employee turnover, compensation levels, earnings of pension plan assets, and changes in values of pension plan assets. *Source:* FAR 31.001. CAS 412, Cost Accounting Standard for Composition and Measurement of Pension Cost, 48 C.F.R. § 9904.412-40(b)(2), provides that, in accounting for pension costs and allocating them to COST OBJECTIVEs, actuarial assumptions must be separately identified and take into account past experience and reasonable expectations. It also states that their validity shall be evaluated solely with respect to these assumptions. See U.S. Gov't Accountability Office, Pension Costs on DOD Contracts: Additional Guidance Needed to Ensure Costs are Consistent and Reasonable, GAO-13-158 (Jan. 2013); Pompeo, *COFC Addresses Actuarial Assumptions for Segment Closing Adjustment*, 49 Gov't Contractor ¶ 389 (Oct. 2007).

ACTUARIAL COST METHOD   *Official:* A technique which uses ACTUARIAL ASSUMPTIONs to measure the present value of future pension benefits and pension fund administrative expenses, and that assigns the cost of such benefits and expenses to cost accounting periods. The actuarial cost method includes the asset valuation method used to determine the actuarial value of the assets of a pension plan. *Source:* FAR 31.001. Under CAS 412, Cost Accounting Standard for Composition and Measurement of Pension Cost. Under CAS 412, Cost Accounting Standard for Composition and Measurement of Pension Cost, 48 C.F.R. § 9904.412-40, a cost method used in determining and measuring component costs of a defined-benefit PENSION PLAN must measure separately (1) the normal cost of the cost accounting period, (2) a part of any unfunded ACTUARIAL LIABILITY, (3) an interest equivalent on the unamortized portion of such liability, and (4) an adjustment for any ACTUARIAL GAIN AND LOSS. An actuarial cost method under which units of benefits are assigned to each cost accounting period and are valued as they accrue are called accrued benefits. CAS 413, Adjustment and Allocation of Pension Cost, 48 C.F.R. § 9904.413-30. See Cooke, ERISA Practice and Procedure § 5:14 (May 2011).

ACTUARIAL GAIN AND LOSS   *Official:* The effect on PENSION COST resulting from differences between ACTUARIAL ASSUMPTIONs and actual experience. *Source:* FAR 31.001. CAS 413, Adjustment and Allocation of Pension Cost, 48 C.F.R. § 9904.413-20, provides guidance on adjusting pension costs by measuring actuarial gains and losses and assigning them to cost accounting periods. It requires that actuarial gains and losses be (1) calculated annually and assigned to the cost accounting period for which the actual valuation is made and to subsequent periods, and (2) identified separately from unfunded actuarial liabilities. It permits them to be amortized through subsequent pension contributions or offset by gains and losses in subsequent cost accounting periods. 48 C.F.R. § 9904.413-50(a)(1). See Manos, 2 GOVERNMENT CONTRACT COSTS & PRICING § 74:6 (2d ed. 2009–2020).

ADDITIONAL DATA REQUIREMENTS The FAR technique for obtaining additional DATA that was not ordered from a contractor in the original contract. FAR 27.406-2 contains guidance on the use of the optional Additional Data Requirements clause in FAR 52.227-16, which allows the ordering of "any data first produced or specifically used" in the performance of the contract if the order is issued within 3 years of final acceptance. See DEFERRED ORDERING.

ADEQUATE EVIDENCE *Official:* Information sufficient to support the reasonable belief that a particular act or omission has occurred. *Source:* FAR 2.101. FAR 9.407-1(b) permits SUSPENSION of a contractor if an agency official finds adequate evidence to show that the contractor has committed one of the acts listed in the regulation to constitute grounds for suspension. See Robbins, et al., *Path of an Investigation: How Major Contractor's Ethics Office and Air Force Procurement Fraud and Suspension/Debarment Apparatus Deal with Allegations of Potential Fraud and Unethical Conduct,* 40 PUB. CONT. L.J. 595 (2011); Canni, *Debarment Is No Longer Private World Bank Business: An Examination of the Bank's Distinct Debarment Procedures Used for Corporate Procurements and Financed Projects,* 40 PUB. CONT. L.J. 147 (2010).

ADEQUATE PRICE COMPETITION The degree of competition that precludes the contracting officer from obtaining CERTIFIED COST OR PRICING DATA under the TRUTH IN NEGOTIATIONS ACT. FAR 15.403-1(c)(1)(i) provides that adequate price competition exists when (1) two or more responsible (see RESPONSIBILITY) offerors, competing independently, submit priced offers responsive to the SOLICITATION's expressed requirements; (2) award is to be made to the offeror with the greatest value or the lowest evaluated price; and (3) there is no finding that the price is unreasonable. FAR 15.403-1(c)(1)(ii) provides that adequate price competition exists when only one offer was received, if it is determined by the contracting officer and approved at a level above the contracting officer that (1) there was a reasonable expectation, based on MARKET RESEARCH, that two or more responsible offerors, competing independently, would submit priced offers responsive to the solicitation's requirements; (2) the single offer was submitted in the expectation of competition; and (3) the determination that the proposed price is based on adequate price competition is reasonable and made at a level above the CONTRACTING OFFICER. FAR 15.403-1(c)(1)(iii) provides that adequate price competition exists when PRICE ANALYSIS clearly demonstrates that a proposed price is reasonable in comparison with current prices or recent prices for the same or similar items purchased in comparable quantities, under comparable terms and conditions of contracts that resulted from adequate price competition. When adequate price competition exists and CERTIFIED COST OR PRICING DATA is not required, generally no DATA OTHER THAN CERTIFIED COST OR PRICING DATA is required. FAR 15.403-3(b). DOD has adopted special requirements for the determination of when adequate price competition has been achieved. DFARS 215.403-1. See Cibinic, Nash & Yukins, FORMATION OF GOVERNMENT CONTRACTS 1452–56 (4th ed. 2011); Edwards, *Agency Policy Memos,* 25 N&CR ¶9 (Feb. 2011).

ADJECTIVAL RATINGS (SCORES)   In SOURCE SELECTION, a method of declaring the evaluated merits of an offeror and its offer by using adjectives organized on a word scale such as Outstanding, Good, Acceptable, Marginal, and Unacceptable. See RATING. See Nash, *Postscript: Scoring Systems*, 24 N&CR ¶ 13 (Mar. 2010); Nash & Edwards, *Scoring Systems: Are They Useful?*, 23 N&CR ¶ 61 (Nov. 2009); Edwards, *Postscript II: Scoring or Rating in Source Selection*, 23 N&CR ¶ 2 (Jan. 2009).

ADMINISTRATIVE CHANGE   *Official:* A unilateral contract change, in writing, that does not affect the substantive rights of the parties (e.g., a change in the paying office or the appropriation data). *Source:* FAR 43.101. Administrative changes are made by UNILATERAL MODIFICATIONs. FAR 43.103(b). See also MODIFICATION.

ADMINISTRATIVE COMMITMENT   See COMMITMENT.

ADMINISTRATIVE CONTRACTING OFFICER (ACO)   *Official:* A CONTRACTING OFFICER who is administering contracts. *Source:* FAR 2.101 (in the definition of contracting officer). An ACO does most of his or her work after the PROCURING CONTRACTING OFFICER has awarded the contract but generally has only limited authority to enter into MODIFICATIONs. An ACO functions at and through a contract administration office and performs contract administration functions involving, among other things, contractors' employee compensation structures and insurance plans, postaward orientation, FORWARD PRICING RATE AGREEMENTs, ADVANCE AGREEMENTs, ALLOWABLE COSTs, DISPUTEs, COST ACCOUNTING STANDARDS, PROGRESS PAYMENTs, COST OVERRUNs, modifications, traffic management, tax exemption and duty-free entry certificates, LABOR RELATIONS, QUALITY ASSURANCE, safety requirements, property administration, engineering surveillance, acceptance and rejection of WAIVERs and DEVIATIONs, VALUE ENGINEERING programs, CONTRACTOR PURCHASING SYSTEM REVIEW, consent to subcontracts, and monitoring of small business subcontracting plan compliance. FAR 42.302(a). Additional functions that may be delegated to ACOs are contained in FAR 42.302(b). A number of agencies do not separate the procuring and administrative contracting officer functions, but hold a single contracting officer responsible for both the award and administration of a contract. FAR 42.6 covers CORPORATE ADMINISTRATIVE CONTRACTING OFFICERs, which deal with corporate management and perform contract administration on a corporate-wide basis. See Nash & Feldman, 1 GOVERNMENT CONTRACT CHANGES § 5:8 (3d ed. 2006–2020); Cibinic, Nagle & Nash, ADMINISTRATION OF GOVERNMENT CONTRACTS 27–36 (5th ed. 2016).

ADMINISTRATIVE DISPUTE RESOLUTION ACT   A 1990 Act, 5 U.S.C. § 571 et seq., of five years' duration, that required all federal agencies to adopt a policy favoring the use of ALTERNATIVE DISPUTE RESOLUTION (ADR) procedures, in lieu of litigation, to settle claims and disputes. One such procedure, ARBITRATION, was allowed, for the first time, in situations in which all parties agreed to its use but the government was given the right to reject the arbitration award. The Act also amended the CONTRACT DISPUTES ACT OF 1978 to authorize contracting officers to use ADR. The Act was made permanent in 1996 by the ADMINISTRATIVE DISPUTE RESOLUTION ACT OF 1996. At that time the provision permitting arbitration was amended to allow government agencies to use binding arbitration. Feldman, GOVERNMENT CONTRACT GUIDEBOOK, §§ 23:22–23:25 (4th ed. 2019–2020). See also Section of Public Contract Law, ALTERNATIVE DISPUTE RESOLUTION: A PRACTICAL GUIDE FOR RESOLVING GOVERNMENT CONTRACT CONTROVERSIES, THIRD

EDITION, ABA Book Publishing (July 2014); Arnavas & Victorino, *Litigation or ADR?: Choosing The Right Dispute Resolution Process*, BRIEFING PAPERS No. 09-8 (July 2009).

ADMINISTRATIVE DISPUTE RESOLUTION ACT OF 1996 A 1996 Act, Pub. L. No. 104-320, that made the procedures of the ALTERNATIVE DISPUTE RESOLUTION ACT permanent. In addition, section 12 of the Act enlarged the BID PROTEST jurisdiction of the U.S. COURT OF FEDERAL CLAIMS, granting the court jurisdiction to hear both pre- and post-award protests. Further, section 12 of the Act statutorily provided jurisdiction to the district courts to hear protests (see SCANWELL ACTION) only until January 1, 2001.

ADMINISTRATIVE JUDGE *Official:* A member of the CIVILIAN BOARD OF CONTRACT APPEALS (CBCA) functioning under the CONTRACT DISPUTES ACT (CDA) OF 1978. *Source:* 41 U.S.C. § 607(b)(1). Commonly confused with the title "administrative law judge" (see Keyes, GOVERNMENT CONTRACTS UNDER THE FEDERAL ACQUISITION REGULATION (2d ed. 1997)) the position of administrative judge was created by the CDA under Title 41, not by the Administrative Procedure Act under Title 5. While administrative judges must be appointed in the same manner as administrative law judges, they must also have five years or more of public contract law experience and are not subject to reassignment by the Office of Personnel Management. See 9271.1B ADM Procedures for Selection of U.S. Civilian Board of Contract Appeals Members.

ADMINISTRATIVE SETOFF See SETOFF.

ADVANCE AGREEMENT An agreement as to the reasonableness, allocability, or allowability of costs, negotiated by a contracting officer and a contractor before the costs are incurred. See ALLOWABLE COST. FAR 31.109 provides guidance on the negotiation of such agreements and suggests their use to avoid possible subsequent DISALLOWANCE or DISPUTE based on unreasonableness or nonallocability (see REASONABLENESS OF COST and ALLOCABLE COST) of special or unusual costs. Advance agreements may be negotiated either before or during a contract. The advance agreement must be (1) in writing, (2) executed by both contracting parties, and (3) incorporated into applicable current and future contracts. It must contain a statement of its applicability and duration. Advance agreements may be negotiated with a particular contractor for a single contract, for a group of contracts, or for all contracts with a contracting office, an agency, or several agencies. Advance agreements are not required and their absence does not affect the reasonableness, allocability, or allowability of costs. FAR 31.109(h) provides examples for which advance agreements can be particularly important. See Manos, 1 GOVERNMENT CONTRACT COSTS & PRICING § 7:13 (2d ed. 2009–2020); Cibinic & Knight, COST-REIMBURSEMENT CONTRACTING 654 (4th ed. 2014).

ADVANCE APPROPRIATION Appropriations that are enacted normally in the current year, scored after the budget year (for example, in each one, two, or more later years, depending on the language), and available for obligation in the year scored and subsequent years if specified in the language. Advance appropriations may be accompanied by regular annual appropriations to provide funds available for obligation in the budget year as well as in subsequent years. See also MULTIYEAR APPROPRIATION. U.S. GOV'T ACCOUNTABILITY OFFICE, GLOSSARY OF TERMS USED IN THE FEDERAL BUDGET PROCESS, GAO-05-734SP (2005), at 8. See Tollestrup & McClanahan, CONG. RESEARCH SERV., Report No. R43482, ADVANCE APPROPRIATIONS, FORWARD FUNDING, AND ADVANCE FUNDING: CONCEPTS, PRACTICE AND BUDGET CONSIDERATIONS (June 10, 2019).

ADVANCE FUNDING   BUDGET AUTHORITY provided in an APPROPRIATION ACT to OBLIGATE and disburse (outlay) in the current FISCAL YEAR funds from a succeeding year's APPROPRIATION. Advance funding is a means to avoid making supplemental requests late in the fiscal year for certain entitlement programs in cases where the appropriations for the current year prove to be insufficient. When such budget authority is used (i.e., funds obligated), the budget records an increase in the budget authority for the fiscal year in which it is used and a reduction in the budget authority for the following fiscal year. U.S. GOV'T ACCOUNTABILITY OFFICE, GLOSSARY OF TERMS USED IN THE FEDERAL BUDGET PROCESS, GAO-05-734SP (Sept. 2005), at 8. See Tollestrup & McClanahan, CONG. RESEARCH SERV., Report No. R43482, ADVANCE APPROPRIATIONS, FORWARD FUNDING, AND ADVANCE FUNDING: CONCEPTS, PRACTICE AND BUDGET CONSIDERATIONS (June 10, 2019).

ADVANCE PAYMENT   *Official:* Advances of money by the government to a prime contractor before, in anticipation of, and for the purpose of complete performance under one or more contracts. *Source:* FAR 32.102(a). Such payments are expected to be liquidated from payments due on the contract or contracts for which they made. Agencies may authorize advance payments in negotiated and sealed bid contracts if appropriate under the procurement statutes (41 U.S.C. §§ 4501 & 4503 and 10 U.S.C. § 2307) or under Pub. L. No. 85-804, 50 U.S.C. §§ 1431–1435, which provides for EXTRAORDINARY CONTRACTUAL ACTIONs. FAR 32.401. Agencies should authorize advance payments sparingly, as they are the least preferred method of contract FINANCING. See FAR 32.402(b). However, advance payments may be appropriate for research and development with educational institutions and for the management and operation of government-owned plants. FAR 31.403. For advance payments to be authorized, the statutes provide that (1) the contractor must give adequate security, (2) the payments must not exceed the unpaid contract price, and (3) the agency head or a designee must determine that advance payment is in the public interest or facilitates the NATIONAL DEFENSE. FAR 32.402 contains detailed guidance on these requirements. When advance payments are used, the Advance Payments clause in FAR 52.232-12 is required. FAR 32.412.

ADVANCE PROCUREMENT   *Official:* An exception to the FULL FUNDING policy that allows acquisition of LONG-LEAD-TIME ITEMS (advanced long lead acquisition) or economic order quantities (see ECONOMIC ORDER QUANTITY) of items (advance EOQ) acquisition in a FISCAL YEAR in advance of that in which the related end item is to be acquired. Advance procurements may include materials, parts, components, and effort that must be funded in advance to maintain a planned production schedule. *Source:* DFARS 217.103. DOD is authorized to make use of this technique in multiyear procurement by 10 U.S.C. § 2306b(h)(2). See DFARS 217.172(f)(2).

ADVANCED NOTICE OF PROPOSED RULEMAKING (ANPR)   A public notice of a regulation at an early stage before the agency has arrived at even a tentative decision on a regulatory change. ANPRs generally provide the text of a regulation that is under consideration and invite comments from industry either in writing or at a public meeting. They differ from PROPOSED REGULATIONs in that they do not begin the running of the mandatory comment period before the issuance of a FINAL REGULATION.

ADVERTISEMENT   *Official:* Any single message prepared for placement in communications media, regardless of the number of placements. *Source:* FAR 5.501. FAR Subpart 5.5 provides guidance on the use of paid advertisements by government agencies as a means of informing potential offerors of contracting opportunities with the government. NASA does not permit the use of paid advertisements for procurement purposes. NFS 18-5.502. FAR 31.205-1 places strict limitations on the allowability of the ADVERTISING costs incurred by contractors. See ALLOWABLE COST and RECRUITMENT COSTS.

ADVERTISING   *Official:* The use of media to promote the sale of products or services and to accomplish the activities referred to in FAR 31.205-1(d), regardless of the medium employed, when the advertiser has control over the form and content of what will appear, the media in which it will appear, and the time when it will appear. Advertising media include but are not limited to conventions, exhibits, free goods, samples, magazines, newspapers, trade papers, direct mail, dealer cards, window displays, outdoor advertising, radio, and television. *Source:* FAR 31.205-1. Advertising costs are allowable in contracts with commercial organizations only when specifically required by the contract or used to recruit personnel for a contract, acquire scarce items, dispose of scrap or promote foreign sales of products normally sold domestically. FAR 31.205-1(d). See Manos, 1 GOVERNMENT CONTRACT COSTS & PRICING § 8:1 (2d ed. 2009–2020); Cibinic, Knight & Nash, COST-REIMBURSEMENT CONTRACTING 644 (4th ed. 2014).

ADVERTISING MATERIAL   *Official:* Material designed to acquaint the government with a prospective contractor's present products, services, or potential capabilities, or designed to stimulate the government's interest in buying such products or services. *Source:* FAR 15.601. FAR 15.603(b) provides that such materials are not UNSOLICITED PROPOSALs.

ADVISORY AND ASSISTANCE SERVICES   *Official:* Those services provided under contract by nongovernmental sources to support or improve: organizational policy development; decision-making; management and administration; program and/or project management and administration; or R&D activities. It can also mean the furnishing of professional advice or assistance rendered to improve the effectiveness of Federal management processes or procedures (including those of an engineering and technical nature). In rendering the foregoing services, outputs may take the form of information, advice, opinions, alternatives, analyses, evaluations, recommendations, training and the day-to-day aid of support personnel needed for the successful performance of ongoing Federal operations. All advisory and assistance services are classified in one of the following definitional subdivisions: MANAGEMENT AND PROFESSIONAL SUPPORT SERVICES, STUDIES, ANALYSIS AND EVALUATIONS, and ENGINEERING AND TECHNICAL SERVICES. *Source:* FAR 2.101. Acquisition of advisory and assistance services is a legitimate way to improve government services and operations. Such services may be used at all organizational levels to help managers achieve maximum effectiveness or economy in their operations. FAR 37.203. However, the acquisition of such services shall not be used to (1) perform work of a policy, decisionmaking or management nature, (2) bypass personnel ceilings or competitive employment practices, (3) give preference to former government employees, (4) aid or influence legislation, or (5) obtain professional or technical advice that is readily available within the federal government. FAR 37.203(c). 41 U.S.C. § 1709 also limits the use of advisory and assistance services for the evaluation or analysis of PROPOSALs. See FAR 37.204. Such services are treated in OFPP Policy Letter No. 93-1 (Reissued) May 18, 1994, *Management Oversight of Service Contracting*; and DOD Directive 4205.2, *Acquiring and Managing Contracted and Assistance Services*, Feb. 10, 1992. The FEDERAL ACQUISITION STREAMLINING ACT OF 1994 added 10 U.S.C. § 2304b and 41 U.S.C. § 4105, limiting the use of TASK

ORDER CONTRACTs for advisory and assistance services. These provisions preclude the award of such contracts for a period longer than five years and require multiple award contracts for contracts that exceed three years in duration or $10,000,000. FAR 16.504(c)(2). FAR 16.506(g) requires the use of the Multiple Awards for Advisory and Assistance Services clause in FAR 52.216-28 when multiple awards will be made. Contracts for advisory and assistance services are generally subject to special scrutiny and oversight because the services are closely related to INHERENTLY GOVERNMENTAL FUNCTIONs. See OFPP Policy Letter 11-01, *Performance of Inherently Governmental and Critical Functions*, Sept. 12, 2011; Cibinic, Nash & Yukins, FORMATION OF GOVERNMENT CONTRACTS 9–10 (4th ed. 2011); U.S. GOV'T ACCOUNTABILITY OFFICE, CONGRESSIONAL ACTION NEEDED TO ADDRESS LONG-STANDING PROBLEMS WITH REPORTING OF ADVISORY AND ASSISTANCE SERVICES, GAO-08-319 (Mar. 2008).

ADVISORY MULTI-STEP PROCESS A competitive negotiation procedure where the agency provides a general description of the scope and purpose of an acquisition and allows potential offerors to submit statements of their qualifications. In this procedure, the agency must advise those respondents considered not to be viable competitors of the basis for such an opinion, but the respondent may still participate in the resulting acquisition if it so chooses. FAR 15.202.

AEROSPACE INDUSTRIES ASSOCIATION OF AMERICA (AIA) A nonprofit trade association representing the nation's manufacturers of commercial, military, and business aircraft, helicopters, aircraft engines, missiles, spacecraft, and related components and equipment. AIA's professional staff works through councils and committees made up of volunteers from member companies who develop policy on significant issues and present industry's point of view. AIA speaks for industry on such issues as procurement policy, legislative affairs, civil aviation, environmental concerns, technology development, and internationalization of the industry. [AIA, 1000 Wilson Boulevard, Suite 1700, Arlington, VA 22209-3901; (703) 358-1000; www.aia-aerospace.org.]

AFFILIATES *Official:* Associated business concerns or individuals if, directly or indirectly, either one controls or can control the other; or a third party controls or can control both. *Source:* FAR 2.101. See also FAR 9.403 and 19.101. See Cibinic, Nash & Yukins, FORMATION OF GOVERNMENT CONTRACTS 1575–79 (4th ed. 2011).

AFFIRMATIVE ACTION A contractual requirement under the Equal Opportunity clause, FAR 52.222-26, to take positive steps to ensure that applicants and employees are given equal opportunity without regard to their race, color, religion, sex, sexual orientation, gender identity or national origin. Detailed requirements for steps to be taken in a company's hiring practices to ensure that its workforce is representative of the local area are set forth in DEPARTMENT OF LABOR (DOL) regulations at 41 C.F.R. § 60-2. Generally, a contractor must (1) make a utilization analysis of its workforce, (2) determine that there is underutilization of minority groups that are not employed in representative percentages, (3) establish a set of goals and timetables to reach representative percentages, and (4) adopt policies for recruitment and training that will assist in achieving the goals. See CONG. RESEARCH SERV., Rep. No. RS22256, FEDERAL AFFIRMATIVE ACTION LAW: A BRIEF HISTORY (Oct. 19, 2015).

AFFIRMATIVE ACTION PROGRAM *Official:* A contractor's program that complies with DEPARTMENT OF LABOR regulations in 41 C.F.R. § 60-1 and § 60-4 to ensure equal employment opportunity in employment to minorities and women. *Source:* FAR 22.801.

Under such program a contractor must use best efforts to bring its employment of minorities and women to a level commensurate with the number of minorities and women in the community through AFFIRMATIVE ACTION. Such efforts include establishing employment goals, adopting a timetable for reaching such goals, and recruiting and training minorities and women. See Cibinic, Nash & Yukins, FORMATION OF GOVERNMENT CONTRACTS 1638–43 (4th ed. 2011).

AGENCY   *Official:* Any executive department, military department or defense agency, or other agency or independent establishment of the executive branch. *Source:* FAR 9.403. This definition pertains to DEBARMENT and SUSPENSION procedures. The term has a variety of meanings depending on the context in which it is used. See Cibinic, Nash & Yukins, FORMATION OF GOVERNMENT CONTRACTS 30–31 (4th ed. 2011). See FAR 24.101 for a slightly different and potentially broader definition of the term as it is used in regulations protecting the privacy of individuals.

AGENCY HEAD   See HEAD OF THE AGENCY.

AGENCY RECORD   Information in any format in the possession of a government agency that is subject to the provisions of the FREEDOM OF INFORMATION ACT. The Electronic Freedom of Information Act of 1996, Pub. L. No. 104-231, amended 5 U.S.C. § 552(f)(2) to include records kept in electronic format. The Act contains no definition of "agency record," but the term has been interpreted broadly in litigation. DOD defines the term in 32 C.F.R. § 286.3 as "The products of data compilation, such as all books, papers, maps, and photographs, machine readable materials, inclusive of those in electronic form or format, or other documentary materials, regardless of physical form or characteristics, made or received by an agency of the United States Government under Federal law in connection with the transaction of public business and in Department of Defense possession and control at the time the FOIA request is made." See Nash & Rawicz, INTELLECTUAL PROPERTY IN GOVERNMENT CONTRACTS, chap. 9 (6th ed. 2008). See also Meagher & Bareis, *The Freedom of Information Act*, BRIEFING PAPERS No. 10-12 (Nov. 2010); Abbott & Bohn, *Disputes Involving Access to National Security Information*, BRIEFING PAPERS No. 10-9 (Aug. 2010).

AGENCY REPORT   A mandatory report that an agency is required to file within 30 calendar days of receiving notice of a PROTEST at the GOVERNMENT ACCOUNTABILITY OFFICE. 4 C.F.R. § 21.3. The report must include the contracting officer's statement of the relevant facts (including a best estimate of the contract value), a memorandum of law, and a list and a copy of all relevant documents, or portions of documents, not previously produced, including, as appropriate: the bid or proposal submitted by the protester; the bid or proposal of the firm which is being considered for award, or whose bid or proposal is being protested; all evaluation documents; the solicitation, including the specifications; the abstract of bids or offers; and any other relevant documents. 4 C.F.R. § 21.3(d).

AGENCY TENDER OFFICIAL   The official representing the agency employees in an A-76 competition with private companies. FAR 7.302(b)(4) provides that this official will be considered to have the right to file a protest with the GOVERNMENT ACCOUNTABILITY OFFICE contesting the conduct and results of the competition in accordance with 31 U.S.C. § 3551 and § 3553.

AGILE DEVELOPMENT   *Official:* A development methodology that uses an iterative approach to deliver solutions incrementally through close collaboration and frequent reassessment. *Source:* OMB Circular A-130. This term is most frequently used with regard to contracting for SOFTWARE. OMB Circular A-130 requires agencies to consider the use of this technique when planning INFORMATION TECHNOLOGY projects. The developers work to stated goals but not rigidly defined specifications. Government agencies have increasingly used this process as a means of improving their software. See the GSA 18F An Agile Software Development Solicitation Guide, Aug. 20, 2019.

AGGREGATION   See BUNDLING.

AGREEMENT   A written instrument of understanding, negotiated between an agency or contracting activity and a contractor, containing contract clauses that will apply to future contracts. See FAR Subpart 16.7. The two types of agreements described in the FAR are BASIC AGREEMENTs and BASIC ORDERING AGREEMENTs (BOAs). Agreements are not contracts that are legally binding on the parties because the government makes no promise to purchase any supplies or services. However, agreements facilitate the making of future contracts because they spell out all standard TERMS AND CONDITIONS of such future contracts. The term also is generically to mean any contractually binding agreement between contracting parties. See Nash, *Reaching a Binding Agreement,* 24 N&CR ¶ 56 (Nov. 2010); Nash, *Agreements to Agree: What Is a Breach?,* 21 N&CR ¶ 12 (Apr. 2007).

AIR FORCE INSTITUTE OF TECHNOLOGY (AFIT)   The major educational institution of the United States Air Force (www.afit.edu/). It contains a Graduate School of Engineering and Management, a School of Systems and Logistics, a Civil Engineering School, a School of Strategic Force Studies and a number of Civilian Institution Programs. Its headquarters are at the Wright Patterson Air Force Base in Dayton, Ohio.

AIR FREIGHT FORWARDER   *Official:* An indirect air carrier that is responsible for the transportation of property from the point of receipt to the point of destination, and utilizes for the whole or any part of such transportation the services of a direct air carrier or its agent, or of another air freight forwarder. *Source:* FAR 47.401. Agencies may use air freight forwarders that are engaged in international air transportation for U.S. Government-financed movements of property. See FAR 47.404.

ALASKA NATIVE   A citizen of the United States who is a person of one-fourth degree or more Alaska Indian (including Tsimshian Indians not enrolled in the Metlaktla Indian Community), Eskimo, or Aleut blood, or a combination of those bloodlines. Alaska Native Claims Settlement Act, 43 U.S.C. § 1602. The term includes, in the absence of proof of a minimum blood quantum, any citizen whom a Native village or Native group regards as an Alaska Native. 13 C.F.R. § 124.3.

ALASKA NATIVE CORPORATION (ANC)   *Official:* Any Regional, Village, Urban or Group Corporation organized under the laws of the State of Alaska, in accordance with the Alaska Native Claims Settlement Act, as amended (43 U.S.C. § 1601 et seq.), and which is considered a minority and ECONOMICALLY DISADVANTAGED concern under the criteria at 43 U.S.C. § 1626(e)(1). This definition also includes ANC direct and indirect subsidiary corporations, joint ventures, and partnerships that meet the requirements of 43 U.S.C. § 1626(e)(2). *Source:* FAR 19.701. SMALL BUSINESS CONCERNS owned and controlled by ANCs are eligible for participation in the 8(a) PROGRAM if they meet the criteria set forth in 13 C.F.R. § 124.109 and 13 C.F.R. § 112. When they are admitted to this program, they may be awarded sole source contracts for unlimited dollar amounts because they are not subject to the competition requirements in FAR 19.805-1. However, awards over $25 million must be justified in accordance with FAR 19.808-1. See Buchanan, Note, *One Company, Two Worlds: The Case For Alaska Native Corporations*, 27 ALASKA L. REVIEW 297 (2010); Yang, Note, *Small Business, Rising Giant: Policies and Costs of Section 8(a) Contracting Preferences For Alaska Native Corporations*, 23 ALASKA L. REVIEW 315 (2006).

ALL-DISPUTES CLAUSE   A disputes clause that gives the BOARDs OF CONTRACT APPEALS (BCAs) jurisdiction to hear all disputes "RELATING TO THE CONTRACT." The current Disputes clause in FAR 52.233-1 is an all-disputes clause. The adoption of such a clause was one of the major innovations included in the CONTRACT DISPUTES ACT OF 1978. Its main benefit is that it precludes the contractor from having to file CLAIMs on one contract in both the agency BCA and the court (called FRAGMENTATION OF REMEDIES). See Cibinic, Nagle & Nash, ADMINISTRATION OF GOVERNMENT CONTRACTS 1135–36 (5th ed. 2016).

ALL-ENCOMPASSING DISCUSSIONS   DISCUSSIONS conducted during SOURCE SELECTION in which an AGENCY points out and tells an OFFEROR how to improve every feature in its PROPOSAL that did not receive the highest possible RATING or SCORE, no matter how insignificant. If an agency conducts discussion in a source selection, it must conduct MEANINGFUL DISCUSSIONS, but they need not conduct all-encompassing discussions. The GOVERNMENT ACCOUNTABILITY OFFICE and the U.S. COURT OF FEDERAL CLAIMS use the term in their PROTEST decisions to set a limit on an agency's obligations during discussions to give offerors an opportunity to improve their proposals. See *TriCenturian, Inc.*, Comp. Gen. Dec. B-406032, 2012 CPD ¶ 52 and *Wackenhut Services, Inc. v. United States*, 85 Fed. Cl. 273 (2008).

ALLOCABLE COST   A cost that is assignable or chargeable to one or more COST OBJEC-TIVEs in accordance with the relative benefits received or other equitable relationships defined or agreed upon by contractual parties. FAR 31.201-4 provides that a cost is allocable to a government contract if it (1) is incurred specifically for the contract, (2) benefits both the contract and other work and can be distributed in reasonable proportion to the benefits received, or (3) is necessary to the overall operation of the business, although a direct rela-tionship to any particular cost objective cannot be shown. Substantial guidance on the treat-ment of allocable costs is contained in the COST ACCOUNTING STANDARDS at 48 C.F.R. chap. 99. See Manos, 2 GOVERNMENT CONTRACT COSTS & PRICING §§ 63:1–63:4 (2d ed. 2009–2020); Cibinic, Knight & Nash, COST-REIMBURSEMENT CONTRACTING 590–632 (4th ed. 2014).

ALLOCATE   *Official:* To assign an item of cost, or a group of items of cost, to one or more COST OBJECTIVEs. This term includes both direct assignment of cost and the reassign-ment of a share from an INDIRECT COST POOL. *Source:* FAR 31.001. See ALLOCA-TION OF COSTS. See Manos, 2 GOVERNMENT CONTRACT COSTS & PRICING §§ 63:1–63:4 (2d ed. 2009–2020).

ALLOCATED CONFIGURATION IDENTIFICATION (ACI)   A DOD term for currently approved performance-oriented specifications governing the development of CONFIGURA-TION ITEMs (CIs) that are part of a higher-level CI, in which each specification defines the functional characteristics that are allocated from those of the higher-level CI; establishes the tests required to demonstrate achievement of its allocated functional characteristics;

delineates necessary interface requirements with other CIs; and establishes design constraints, if any, such as component or part standardization, use of inventory items, and logistic support requirements. DAU GLOSSARY.

ALLOCATION See ALLOCATION OF COSTS and ALLOCATION OF WORK.

ALLOCATION BASE A numerical measure to which costs can be assigned in a methodical fashion from an indirect pool to COST OBJECTIVEs. FAR 31.203 provides general guidance on the selection of allocation bases. CAS 410, Allocation of Business Unit General and Administrative Expenses to Final Cost Objectives, 48 C.F.R. § 9904.410-40, provides guidance on the calculation of the allocation base for GENERAL AND ADMINISTRATIVE EXPENSEs, stating a preference for a cost input base. See Cibinic & Nash, COST-REIMBURSEMENT CONTRACTING 607–16 (4th ed. 2014).

ALLOCATION OF COSTS The assignment of costs to a COST OBJECTIVE such as a contract or profit center. Sound accounting practices require contractors to ALLOCATE costs so that no cost objective is unfairly assigned costs. Substantial guidance on the proper allocation of costs is contained in the COST ACCOUNTING STANDARDS at 48 C.F.R. chap. 99. See ALLOCABLE COST. See also DCAA CAM 8-418 Cost Accounting Standard 418 – Allocation of Direct and Indirect Costs. See Manos, 2 GOVERNMENT CONTRACT COSTS & PRICING §§ 71:1–71:7 (2d ed. 2009–2020).

ALLOCATION OF WORK The assignment of work by a government agency to a source without following the normal competitive processes. Allocation is generally disfavored but can be used to preserve a company for INDUSTRIAL MOBILIZATION purposes. FAR Subpart 8.7 requires the allocation of certain specified work to nonprofit agencies for the BLIND OR SEVERELY DISABLED.

ALLOWABLE COST A cost that the government will permit to be recovered (reimbursed by the government) for the performance of a contract. FAR 31.201-2 provides that the factors to be considered in determining whether a cost is allowable include (1) reasonableness (see REASONABLENESS OF COST), (2) allocability (see ALLOCABLE COST), (3) standards promulgated by the COST ACCOUNTING STANDARDS BOARD, (4) GENERALLY ACCEPTED ACCOUNTING PRINCIPLES and practices appropriate to the particular circumstances, (5) the terms of the contract, and (6) any limitations set forth in FAR Subpart 31.2. FAR 31.205 contains detailed guidance on the allowability of 46 categories of "selected costs." Costs, including directly associated costs, that are unallowable must, in almost all cases, be identified and excluded from any billing, claim, or proposal applicable to a government contract. FAR 31.201-6; Cost Accounting Standard 405 – Accounting for Unallowable Costs. Many EXPRESSLY UNALLOWABLE COSTS are subject to a penalty in the amount of the claimed costs, 10 U.S.C. § 2324, 41 U.S.C. § 4303 and FAR 42.709. See FAR 31.105 for special rules applicable to CONSTRUCTION and ARCHITECT-ENGINEER contracts. FAR 31.6 provides principles for determining allowable costs under contracts with State, local, and Indian tribal governments. See generally Cibinic & Nash, COST-REIMBURSEMENT CONTRACTING, chap. 9 (4th ed. 2014) and Manos, 2 GOVERNMENT CONTRACT COSTS & PRICING Part II (2d ed. 2009–2020). See also Nash, *The Burden of Proving Allowable Costs: Additional Guidance*, 33 N&CR ¶ 15 (Mar. 2019); Willard, *Allowability of Legal Costs*, BRIEFING PAPERS No. 10-5 (Apr. 2010); Nash, *Postscript V: Unallowable Claims Costs vs. Allowable Contract Administration Costs*, 23 N&CR ¶ 30 (June 2009); Calhoon & McDonald, *Excessive Pass-Through Charges: Brass Tacks and Booby Traps*, 3 CPA&R ¶ 40 (July 2008).

ALTERNATIVE DISPUTE RESOLUTION (ADR)   *Official:* Any type of procedure or combination of procedures voluntarily used to resolve issues in controversy. These procedures may include, but are not limited to, conciliation, facilitation, MEDIATION, fact-finding, MINITRIALs, ARBITRATION, and use of ombudsmen. *Source:* FAR 33.201. ADR is used when the contracting officer and the contractor cannot resolve a dispute through normal contracting procedures. These techniques are now recognized and encouraged by the ADMINISTRATIVE DISPUTE RESOLUTION ACT, 5 U.S.C. §§ 571–584, as implemented by FAR Subpart 33.2. The techniques are intended to resolve disputes without the time, expense, and cost of formal litigation, whether before a court or an agency BOARD OF CONTRACT APPEALS. ADR is sometimes called alternate dispute resolution. It includes any alternative to full-scale litigation, whether mandatory or voluntary, binding or nonbinding, structured or unstructured. ADR is often conducted with the understanding that the record of the proceeding will be kept confidential and that—if the selected method's conclusions are not acceptable to either party—the normal litigation process may be begun or resumed. See Section of Public Contract Law, ALTERNATIVE DISPUTE RESOLUTION: A PRACTICAL GUIDE FOR RESOLVING GOVERNMENT CONTRACT CONTROVERSIES, THIRD EDITION, ABA Book Publishing (July 2014); Arnavas & Victorino, *Litigation or ADR: Choosing the Right Dispute Resolution Process,* BRIEFING PAPERS No. 09-81 (July 2009). See "Electronic Guide to Federal Procurement ADR" at https://www.adr.gov/adrguide/home.html.

AMBIGUITY   Contract language that is capable of being understood to have more than one meaning. The test for determining whether the language is ambiguous is whether reasonable persons would find the contract subject to more than one interpretation. A PATENT AMBIGUITY is obvious, since it arises from defective, contradictory, obscure, or senseless language. In contrast, a LATENT AMBIGUITY arises from language that appears clear and intelligible but that—because of some extrinsic fact or extraneous evidence—requires interpretation or a choice between two or more possible meanings. BLACK'S LAW DICTIONARY 100 (11th ed. 2019). See also CONTRA PROFERENTEM. Contractors frequently receive EQUITABLE ADJUSTMENTs for latent ambiguities, but they are held to a DUTY TO SEEK CLARIFICATION of patent ambiguities. See Cibinic, Nagle & Nash, ADMINISTRATION OF GOVERNMENT CONTRACTS 211–24 (5th ed. 2016). See also Ellis, *Toward a Nuanced Plain Language Approach in Federal Contract Interpretation: What Do Bell BCI, States Roofing, and LAI Services Imply?,* 39 PUB. CONT. L.J. 821 (2010); Stubbs, *The Federal Circuit and Contract Interpretation: May Extrinsic Evidence Ever Be Used to Show Unambiguous Language is Ambiguous,* 39 PUB. CONT. L.J. 785 (2010).

AMENDMENT   An alteration to a SOLICITATION. See FAR 14.208 and FAR 15.206. The FAR distinguishes between amendments and MODIFICATIONs: amendments alter solicitations and modifications alter contracts. Standard Form 30, Amendment of Solicitation/ Modification of Contract, FAR 53.301-30, must be used to change sealed bid solicitations, FAR 14.208(a), and may be used to change negotiated solicitations, FAR 15.210. Detailed instructions on the proper response upon receipt of an amendment are set forth in the solicitation provisions Amendments to Invitation for Bids in FAR 52.214-3 and Instructions to Offerors—Competitive Acquisition in FAR 52.215-1. In normal legal terminology an amendment is a formal legal document altering a contract by mutual agreement (hence signed by both parties). FAR 43.103 discusses such documents using the terms "bilateral modification" (see MODIFICATION) and SUPPLEMENTAL AGREEMENT. See Cibinic, Nash & Yukins, FORMATION OF GOVERNMENT CONTRACTS 741–49 (4th ed. 2011).

AMENDMENT WITHOUT CONSIDERATION   A contract alteration that benefits the contractor but contains no CONSIDERATION to the government. Authority to make such alterations is conferred by Pub. L. No. 85-804, 50 U.S.C. §§ 1431–1435, as implemented by Exec. Order No. 10789, 23 Fed. Reg. 8897 (Nov. 14, 1958), as amended. Procedures for use of this authority are set forth in FAR Part 50, EXTRAORDINARY CONTRACTUAL ACTION.

AMERICAN INSTITUTE OF ARCHITECTS (AIA)   A national professional society, founded in 1857, whose members are licensed architects, graduate architects, and retired architects. AIA promotes design excellence and fosters professionalism and accountability through professional development programs and achievement awards. It also maintains a 30,000-volume library and publishes reference books and standard documents on legal, contract, and accounting forms. The organization maintains a Government Affairs department.

AMERICAN NATIONAL STANDARDS INSTITUTE/ELECTRONIC INDUSTRIES ALLIANCE STANDARD 748 (ANSI/EIA-748)   A standard defining 32 criteria required for ACCEPTABLE EARNED VALUE MANAGEMENT SYSTEMs. ANSI/EIA-748 was first approved May 19, 1998 and was reaffirmed on August 28, 2002. It has been adopted by the government in FAR Subpart 34.2 and DFARS Subpart 234.2.

AMERICAN RECOVERY AND REINVESTMENT ACT   A statute enacted in February 2009, Pub. L. No. 111-5, to stimulate the economy to overcome the recession of 2008. It provided funding for a number of acquisition projects in the area of construction, energy, housing and research. Briggerman, *Buy American Requirements Under the Recovery Act: The Final Rules*, 25 N&CR ¶1 (Jan. 2011); Barsalona, Koos & Meene, *Managing Compliance with ARRA in the Context of Lessons Learned from Previous Emergency Federal Procurements*, BRIEFING PAPERS No. 10-8 (July 2010).

AMERICAN SUBCONTRACTORS ASSOCIATION (ASA)   A national trade association, founded in 1966, whose members are construction subcontractors of trades and specialties such as foundations, concrete, masonry, steel, mechanical, drywall, electrical, painting, plastering, roofing, and acoustical. ASA works with other segments of the construction industry to promote ethical practices, beneficial legislation, and business education. It maintains a Government Relations committee.

AMORTIZATION   *Official:* An accounting procedure that gradually reduces the cost value of a limited-life or intangible asset through periodic charges to income. *Source:* BARRON'S FINANCE AND INVESTMENT HANDBOOK (3d ed. 1990). When the purchase method of accounting for a BUSINESS COMBINATION is used, allowable amortization is limited to the amounts that would have been allowed had the combination not taken place. FAR 31.205-52. In measuring and allocating the COST OF CAPITAL COMMITTED TO FACILITIES in accordance with CAS 414, 48 C.F.R. § 9904.414, contractors must take into account INTANGIBLE CAPITAL ASSETs subject to amortization.

ANNOUNCEMENT OF OPPORTUNITY (AO)   A NASA BROAD AGENCY ANNOUNCEMENT generally used to solicit PROPOSALs for on-board flight experiments. Special proposal preparation, evaluation, and selection regulations are found in NFS Subpart 1872.3, NASA Acquisitions of Investigations. AOs are publicized in the same manner as other solicitations and also through a mailing list maintained by the Office of External Relations at NASA Headquarters.

ANNUAL APPROPRIATION   See APPROPRIATION.

ANNUAL BID BOND   See BID BOND.

ANNUAL FUNDING   The current congressional practice of including in authorizations and APPROPRIATIONs authority and funds to cover the needs of an agency for only one fiscal year at a time. This practice is used, with rare exceptions, for all types of appropriations. It can lead to inefficient procurement on a year-to-year basis but can be overcome by the use of OPTIONs, multiple year contracting (see MULTIPLE YEAR CONTRACT) or MULTIYEAR CONTRACTING. See U.S. Gov't Accountability Office, Principles of Federal Appropriations Law: Annual Update to the Third Edition, chap. 7, GAO-15-303SP (Washington, D.C.: Mar. 2015)

ANNUAL PERFORMANCE BOND   See PERFORMANCE BOND.

ANNUAL RECEIPTs   The average annual gross revenue of a concern. In some instances, the qualification of a company as a SMALL BUSINESS CONCERN is determined by its annual receipts. For companies in business over three years, the amount is determined by averaging the receipts for the last three fiscal years. For a company in business for less than three complete fiscal years, total receipts for the period it has been in business are divided by the number of weeks including fractions of a week that it has been in business, and multiplied by 52. FAR 19.101 contains a detailed definition of the types of revenues that are included in annual receipts. See also STANDARD INDUSTRIAL CLASSIFICATION. See Cibinic, Nash & Yukins, Formation of Government Contracts 1573–74 (4th ed. 2011).

ANSWER   In a contract DISPUTE, a formal pleading presented to a court by the DEFENDANT, or to a BOARD OF CONTRACT APPEALS by the RESPONDENT, in response to a COMPLAINT filed by the PLAINTIFF, or appellant (see APPELLANT BEFORE BOARD OF CONTRACT APPEALS and APPELLANT BEFORE FEDERAL CIRCUIT COURT OF APPEALS). This statement is normally filed by the government because the plaintiff, or appellant, is normally the contractor.

ANTICIPATORY REPUDIATION   Statements or acts of a contractor before an actual BREACH OF CONTRACT that indicate that the contractor does not intend or is unable to complete, or continue to perform under the contract. Black's Law Dictionary 1560 (11th ed. 2019). Anticipatory repudiation is sometimes called "anticipatory breach." It will generally not be found unless the contractor, by statements, actions, or refusal to provide adequate assurance of performance, clearly manifests the intention not to perform. Generally in this case, the government need not wait for the performance period to run in order to terminate the contract for default (see TERMINATION FOR DEFAULT). See Cibinic, Nagle & Nash, Administration of Government Contracts 835–42 (5th ed. 2016); U.C.C. § 2-610, § 2-611.

ANTI-DEFICIENCY ACT   A statute prohibiting government agencies from obligating the government, by contract or otherwise, in excess of or in advance of appropriations, unless authorized by some specific statute. Codified at 31 U.S.C. § 1341 et seq. since 1982, the Act prevents government employees from involving the government in expenditures or liabilities beyond those contemplated and authorized by Congress. As a result, the government uses clauses such as the Limitation of Cost clause at FAR 52.232-20 to limit its liability in COST-REIMBURSEMENT CONTRACTs. 31 U.S.C. § 1350 provides that government officers and employees can be fined and/or imprisoned for violating the Act. The Act's salient features include (1) prohibitions against authorizing or incurring OBLIGATIONs or expenditures in excess of the appropriation of funds for the expenditure or obligation or before an appropriate is made, unless authorized by law; and (2) establishment of procedures for determining responsibility for violations and for reporting them to the Congress and, through OMB, to the President. See Manos, 2 GOVERNMENT CONTRACT COSTS AND PRICING § 85:1 (2d ed. 2009–2020); U.S. GOV'T ACCOUNTABILITY OFFICE, PRINCIPLES OF FEDERAL APPROPRIATIONS LAW: ANNUAL UPDATE TO THE THIRD EDITION, chap. 6, GAO-15-303SP (Washington, D.C.: Mar. 2015); Allen, The Obsolete Services Restrictions Of The Antideficiency Act-Still The Law, BRIEFING PAPERS No. 17-12 (Nov. 2017).

ANTI-KICKBACK ACT OF 1986 An Act, 41 U.S.C. §§ 8701–8707, to deter subcontractors from making payments and contractors from accepting payments for the purpose of improperly obtaining or rewarding favorable treatment. FAR 3.502-2. The Act prohibits any person from providing KICKBACKs, soliciting kickbacks, or including the amount of the kickback in the contract price. It imposes criminal penalties for engaging in these prohibited practices, provides for recovery of civil penalties by the United States, requires the reporting of suspected violations, and calls for the inclusion of contract provisions regarding the Act. FAR 3.502-2. The Act is implemented through the use of the Anti-Kickback Procedures clause in FAR 52.203-7. See Manos, 3 GOVERNMENT CONTRACT COSTS AND PRICING §§ 91:22–91:24 (2d ed. 2009–2020); Ifrah, *Board Procedures Involving Fraud Counterclaims Against Contractors*, BRIEFING PAPERS No. 07-10 (Sept. 2007). See also COPELAND ANTI-KICKBACK ACT.

ANTI-LOBBYING ACT A 1919 Act, 18 U.S.C. § 1913, providing that no money appropriated by Congress may be used to pay for any personal service, ADVERTISEMENT, communication, or other device intended or designed to influence a member of Congress to favor or oppose any legislation or APPROPRIATION. The Act does not prohibit requests, through proper official channels, for legislation and appropriations deemed necessary for the efficient conduct of the public business. The Act includes criminal fines and imprisonment as penalties for violations. The BYRD AMENDMENT, an Act passed in 1989, 31 U.S.C. § 1352, prohibits the use of appropriated funds to influence government personnel (in both the legislative and executive branches). This Act, implemented in FAR Subpart 3.8, requires certifications and disclosures on contracts exceeding $150,000, as required by the Certification and Disclosure Regarding Payments to Influence Certain Federal Transactions clause in FAR 52.203-11. See also LOBBYING COSTS.

ANTITRUST VIOLATION A violation of a U.S. law intended to ensure that markets operate competitively. 10 U.S.C. § 2305(b)(9) and 41 U.S.C. § 3707 require that such violations be reported to the Attorney General. Any agreement or mutual understanding among competing firms that restrains the natural operation of market forces is suspect. FAR 3.203. See Kovacic, *"Panel III: Antitrust and the Obama Administration: U.S. Convergence with International Competition Norms: Antitrust Law and Public Restraints on Competition" (Antitrust Conference in Honor of Joseph Brodley)*, 90 BOSTON UNIV. L. REV. 1555–1610 (2010). See CLAYTON ACT; SHERMAN ACT.

APPARENT AUTHORITY Obvious, evident, or manifest authority that a reasonably prudent person, using diligence and discretion, would, in view of a principal's conduct, naturally suppose the principal's agent to possess. BLACK'S LAW DICTIONARY 164 (11th ed. 2019). The federal government is not bound by unauthorized agents with apparent authority; only properly designated CONTRACTING OFFICERs, or their representatives acting within the limits of their designated authority, can obligate the government. Therefore, anyone dealing with the government should ascertain whether a person who purports to act for the government has the authority to do so, and not rely on a mere appearance of authority. BOARDs OF CONTRACT APPEALS and courts frequently found that government employees had IMPLIED AUTHORITY but this holding was greatly restricted by *Winter v. Cath-dr/Balti Joint Venture*, 497 F.3d 1339 (Fed. Cir. 2007). See Nash & Feldman, 1 GOVERNMENT CONTRACT CHANGES § 5:1 (3d ed. 2006–2020); Cibinic, Nagle & Nash, ADMINISTRATION OF GOVERNMENT CONTRACTS 28–29 (5th ed. 2016). See also Nash, *Postscript II: Contracting Officer Authority*, 25 N&CR ¶ 30 (June 2011); Pachter, *The Incredible Shrinking Contracting Officer*, 39 PUB. CONT. L.J. 705 (2010).

APPARENT CLERICAL MISTAKE   See CLERICAL MISTAKE.

APPEAL FILE   A file containing all documents pertaining to a DISPUTE before a BOARD OF CONTRACT APPEALS (BCA), which Uniform Rule 4 (see UNIFORM RULES) requires the CONTRACTING OFFICER to assemble. Frequently called the RULE 4 FILE, it represents one of the more significant differences between appeals before BCAs and litigation before the U.S. COURT OF FEDERAL CLAIMS. The Rule 4 procedure, applying only to BCA appeals, is intended to make all pertinent documents immediately available to the contractor and the BCA. The rule gives the contractor an opportunity to supplement this appeal file. Rule 4 requires and encourages both parties to present relevant documents in support of their respective cases and facilitates the production of documents as an aid to further discovery. It operates as an automatic, first-round discovery order without eliminating customary discovery proceedings; documents contained in the appeal file are considered, without further action by the parties, as part of the record on which the BCA will render its decision. See Feldman, GOVERNMENT CONTRACT GUIDEBOOK, § 23:13 (4th ed. 2019–2020).

APPEAL FROM A CONTRACTING OFFICER'S DECISION   The document that a contractor must file before a BOARD OF CONTRACT APPEALS (BCA) to obtain review of a DECISION OF THE CONTRACTING OFFICER. Contractors must file their appeals with the agency BCA and furnish a copy to the contracting officer within 90 days of receiving a contracting officer's decision. 41 U.S.C. § 7104(a); FAR 33.211. The notice of appeal should include (1) a statement of intent to appeal, (2) reference to a contract and the agency involved so that the BCA can identify the DISPUTE, and (3) signature by an authorized representative of the contractor. The contractor may begin an appeal on the basis of DEEMED DENIAL jurisdiction; if the contracting officer fails to render a decision within 60 days of submission of a CLAIM for $100,000 or less, or within a reasonable time for greater claims, the CONTRACT DISPUTES ACT OF 1978 deems that the contracting officer has denied the claim, and the contractor may appeal. 41 U.S.C. § 7103(f)(5). In lieu of appealing to the BCA, the contractor may bring a DIRECT ACCESS suit within 12 months in the U.S. COURT OF FEDERAL CLAIMS. See Cibinic, Nagle & Nash, ADMINISTRATION OF GOVERNMENT CONTRACTS 1214–16 (5th ed. 2016). See also COMPLAINT.

APPEAL FROM THE RULING OF A COURT OR BOARD   A document, filed by either the contractor or the government, requesting that the U.S. COURT OF APPEALS FOR

THE FEDERAL CIRCUIT review a decision of a BOARD OF CONTRACT APPEALS (BCA) or of the U.S. COURT OF FEDERAL CLAIMS. A BCA's decision against the government is final unless either the HEAD OF THE AGENCY (with prior approval of the Attorney General) or a contractor appeals the decision within 120 days after receipt of a copy. 41 U.S.C. § 7105. Appeals from rulings of the U.S. COURT OF FEDERAL CLAIMS must be filed within 60 days. 28 U.S.C. § 2107. Under the EQUAL ACCESS TO JUSTICE ACT, 5 U.S.C. § 504, the government cannot appeal a BCA's award of ATTORNEY'S FEES. See Somers, *The Boards of Contract Appeals: A Historical Perspective*, 60 AM. U.L. REV. 745 (2011); Schaengold & Brams, *Choice of Forum for Government Contract Claims: Court of Federal Claims vs. Board of Contract Appeals*, 17 Fed. Cir. B.J. 279 (2008); McGovern III, Graham & Nibley, *A Level Playing Field: Why Congress Intended the Boards of Contract Appeals to Have Power Over Both Contractors and the Government*, 36 PUB. CONT. L.J. 495 (2007); Schaengold & Brams, *A Guide to the Civilian Board of Contract Appeals*, BRIEFING PAPERS No. 07-8 (July 2007).

APPELLANT BEFORE BOARD OF CONTRACT APPEALS   The contractor who files an APPEAL FROM A CONTRACTING OFFICER'S DECISION before a BOARD OF CONTRACT APPEALS (BCA). Since all appeals are from a DECISION OF THE CONTRACTING OFFICER, regardless of whether the DISPUTE arises from a contractor or a government CLAIM, the contractor is always the appellant. The government thus becomes the RESPONDENT. In spite of the use of these titles, the Board conducts a DE NOVO review of the dispute. The contractor, or appellant, may be represented before the BCA by an attorney, by a corporate officer, or, in some instances, by himself or herself. See, for example, ARMED SERVICES BOARD OF CONTRACT APPEALS Rule 26. Sole-proprietor contractors can handle their own appeals, partnerships can be represented by a partner, and corporations can be represented by a corporate officer. Of course, any of these types of contractors may retain an attorney, provided that the attorney has been admitted to practice in a state's highest court. See Schaengold & Brams, *A Guide to the Civilian Board of Contract Appeals*, BRIEFING PAPERS No. 07-8 (July 2007).

APPELLANT BEFORE FEDERAL CIRCUIT COURT OF APPEALS   The party bringing an appeal before the U.S. COURT OF APPEALS FOR THE FEDERAL CIRCUIT, the court authorized by the CONTRACT DISPUTES ACT OF 1978 to review the decisions of the BOARDs OF CONTRACT APPEALS or the U.S. COURT OF FEDERAL CLAIMS. The appellant must have been one of the litigants in the forum from which the appeal is taken. If the appellant is the government, it will be represented by the DEPARTMENT OF JUSTICE, even if agency counsel represented it before the BCA.

APPLICABLE CONDITIONS   Those conditions that could significantly affect an acquisition, such as requirements for compatibility with existing or future systems or programs and any cost, schedule, and capability or performance constraints. See FAR 7.105(a)(2). Applicable conditions are a mandatory element of the ACQUISITION PLAN prepared by the CONTRACTING OFFICER, and they identify the constraints that must be imposed on the end product of the procurement. Precise identification of such constraints early in the procurement process enables the agency to explore options to reduce or eliminate them if they appear detrimental to the planned procurement. Many constraints, however, must be accepted as an inherent element of a procurement. See Trakman, *The Boundaries of Contract Law in Cyberspace*, 38 PUB. CONT. L.J. 187 (2008).

APPLIED RESEARCH   *Official:* The effort that (1) normally follows BASIC RESEARCH, but may not be severable from the related basic research; (2) attempts to determine and exploit the potential of scientific discoveries or improvements in technology, materials, processes, methods, devices or techniques; and (3) attempts to advance the state of the art. When being used by contractors in cost principle applications, this term does not include efforts whose principal aim is the design, development, or testing of specific items or services to be considered for sale; these efforts are within the definition of development, given below. *Source:* FAR 35.001. It is a systematic study to understand the means to meet a recognized and specific need. *DOD Financial Management Regulation* 7000.14-R, v. 2B, chap. 5 (Sept. 2012). Applied research does not include DEVELOPMENT—those efforts whose principal aim is design, development, or test of specific items or services to be considered for sale.

APPORTIONMENT   A periodic distribution made by the OFFICE OF MANAGEMENT AND BUDGET of amounts available for OBLIGATION in an APPROPRIATION or fund account. Apportionments divide amounts available for obligation by specific time periods (usually quarters), activities, projects, or objects, or by a combination of these. The amounts so apportioned limit the amount of obligations that may be incurred during the segment. Apportionment is intended to prevent the need for deficiency or supplemental appropriations and to ensure that there is no need for drastic curtailment of the activity for which the appropriation is made. That is, apportionment should prevent an agency from spending its entire appropriation before the end of the FISCAL YEAR and requiring Congress to grant an additional appropriation or else allow activity to be suspended. U.S. Gov't Accountability Office, Principles of Federal Appropriations Law: Annual Update to the Third Edition, chap. 6, GAO-15-303SP (Washington, D.C.: Mar. 2015).

APPROPRIATED FUNDS   Funds made available by Congress for specific purposes, including formation of contracts. See APPROPRIATION.

APPROPRIATION   An act of Congress permitting federal agencies to incur OBLIGATIONs and to make payments out of the Treasury for specified purposes. Appropriation acts make funds available for obligation for one FISCAL YEAR (annual appropriations), for a specified number of years (multiyear appropriations), or for an unlimited period (no-year appropriations). General appropriations are for broad categories of work (such as research and development, procurement, operation and maintenance), while specific appropriations are for specific projects (most frequently construction projects). Contractors are limited by the amounts in a specific appropriation but not by those in a general appropriation. See 31 U.S.C. § 1301 et seq.; U.S. Gov't Accountability Office, Principles of Federal Appropriations Law, 4th ed. 2016 rev., chap. 2, GAO-16-463SP (Washington, D.C.: Mar. 2016). An appropriation bill is a measure before a legislative body to authorize the expenditure of public moneys and to stipulate the amount, manner, and purpose of the various items of expenditure. Black's Law Dictionary 127 (11th ed. 2019). See Cibinic, Nash & Yukins, Formation of Government Contracts 39–58 (4th ed. 2011). See also DAU, *Allocation of Appropriated Funds* (May 2010); Durkee, *The Proper Obligation and Use of Appropriated Funds in Interagency Contracting Under Non-Economy Act Authorities: Have We Got It Right Yet?*, 38 Pub. Cont. L.J. 317 (2009); Mansfield, *Appropriations Law: Obligations vs. Contingent Liabilities*, 22 N&CR ¶ 41 (July 2008); Alinger, *The Impact of Procurement Provisions in Appropriations Acts on the Federal Acquisition System*, 36 Pub. Cont. L.J. 583 (2007).

APPROVAL *Official:* A contracting officer's written notification to a contractor accepting the test results of the FIRST ARTICLE. *Source:* FAR 9.301. This definition is limited in that it only relates to the acceptance of test results when the contract requires FIRST ARTICLE TESTING. A more generic definition would be consent to an action or statement of another party.

APPROVED PURCHASING SYSTEM *Official:* A contractor's purchasing system that has been reviewed and approved in accordance with the CONTRACTOR PURCHASING SYSTEM REVIEW. *Source:* FAR 44.101. A contractor with an approved purchasing system is required to get far less prior consent of the contracting officer for subcontracts that it issues during contract performance. See FAR 44.201. See also ACCEPTABLE PURCHASING SYSTEM.

APPROVING AUTHORITY *Official:* An agency official or CONTRACT ADJUSTMENT BOARD authorized to approve EXTRAORDINARY CONTRACTUAL ACTIONs under Pub. L. No. 85-804, 50 U.S.C. § 1431 et seq., and Exec. Order No. 10789, 23 Fed. Reg. 8897 (Nov. 14, 1958), as amended. *Source:* FAR 50.100. For most actions this authority may not be delegated below the secretarial level in the department. FAR 50.102-1.

ARBITRATION A dispute resolution technique whereby parties voluntarily refer disputes to an impartial third party (an arbitrator or panel of arbitrators, typically made up of experts in the field) for a decision based on the presentation of evidence and arguments. Arbitration frequently proves more expeditious and less expensive than litigation. In binding arbitration, the parties agree in advance to be bound by the arbitrator's determination and award. Nonbinding arbitration differs in that the parties may consider the determination a recommendation rather than a binding decision. Arbitration, binding and nonbinding, has frequently been used between contractors and subcontractors. The government, however, was not permitted to use binding arbitration (31 U.S.C. § 3702(a); 8 Comp. Gen. 96 (1928)) until 1990, when such use was authorized by the ADMINISTRATIVE DISPUTE RESOLUTION ACT (with the proviso that the HEAD OF THE AGENCY be permitted to vacate any arbitration award). 5 U.S.C. § 580(c). The Act was amended in 1996 to permit an agency to use binding arbitration after the head of the agency, in consultation with the Attorney General, has issued guidance. 5 U.S.C. § 575(c). See also ALTERNATIVE DISPUTE RESOLUTION.

ARCHITECT-ENGINEER (A-E) CONTRACT A government contract for ARCHITECT-ENGINEER SERVICES. Such contracts are entered into using special SOURCE SELECTION procedures as required by the BROOKS ACT (ARCHITECT-ENGINEER PROCUREMENT). See FAR Subpart 36.6. These procedures are conducted in two phases. In the first phase, the agency prepares a "final selection list" of firms, in order of preference, that are considered the most qualified to perform the services based on all relevant criteria except the fee to be paid for the services. In the second phase, the contracting officer negotiates the contract with the most preferred firm on the selection list. If a satisfactory contract cannot be negotiated with this firm, the contracting officer is then permitted to negotiate with the next firm in the rankings. A-E Contracts for military CONSTRUCTION are governed by DFARS Part 236. See Feldman, GOVERNMENT CONTRACT AWARDS: NEGOTIATION AND SEALED BIDDING, chap. 22 (2019–2020 ed.); Cibinic, Nash & Yukins, FORMATION OF GOVERNMENT CONTRACTS 1059–75 (4th ed. 2011). See also Branca, et al., FEDERAL GOVERNMENT CONSTRUCTION CONTRACTS 79–95 (2d ed. 2010).

ARCHITECT-ENGINEER (A-E) SERVICES   *Official:* (1) Professional services of an architectural or engineering nature, as defined by State law, if applicable, that are required to be performed or approved by a person licensed, registered, or certified to provide those services; (2) Professional services of an architectural or engineering nature that are associated with research, planning, development, design, construction, alteration, or repair of real property; and (3) Those other professional services of an architectural or engineering nature, or incidental services, that members of the architectural or engineering professions (and individuals in their employ) may logically or justifiably perform, including studies, investigations, surveying and mapping, tests, evaluations, consultations, comprehensive planning, program management, conceptual designs, plans and specifications, value engineering, construction phase services, soils engineering, drawing reviews, preparation of operating and maintenance manuals, and other related services. *Source:* FAR 2.101. If these services are acquired under a separate contract, the procedures set forth in the BROOKS ACT (ARCHITECT-ENGINEER PROCUREMENT) must be followed. See FAR Subpart 36.6. However, such services can also be acquired as part of a DESIGN-BUILD contract. DFARS Subpart 236.6 provides guidance for procuring A-E services in military CONSTRUCTION. See also ARCHITECT-ENGINEER CONTRACT.

ARCHITECTURAL WORK   *Official:* The design of a building as embodied in any tangible medium of expression, including a building, architectural plans, or drawings. The work includes the overall form as well as the arrangement and composition of spaces and elements in the design, but does not include individual standard features. *Source:* 17 U.S.C. § 101. Under COPYRIGHT law, this type of work is unique in that protection is granted for some elements of the design of a building as well as for the drawings and SPECIFICATIONs. See Nash & Rawicz, INTELLECTUAL PROPERTY IN GOVERNMENT CONTRACTS, chap. 1 (6th ed. 2008).

AREAWIDE CONTRACT   *Official:* A contract entered into between the GENERAL SERVICES ADMINISTRATION and a utility service supplier to cover utility service needs of federal agencies within the franchise territory of the supplier. Each areawide contract includes an "authorization" form for requesting service, connection, disconnection, or change in service. *Source:* FAR 41.101. Such contracts are entered into under the authority of 40 U.S.C. § 501, to cover the utility service to all federal agencies from that supplier for a period not to exceed 10 years. Federal agencies, including DOD, are covered when an authorization attached to the area wide contract is completed and accepted by the supplier and executed by the agency and the supplier. FAR 41.204. See FAR Subpart 41.2 for procedures to be followed in contracting for utility services when an areawide contract is in place and when there is no such contract.

"ARISING UNDER THE CONTRACT"   Falling within the scope of a contract clause and therefore providing a REMEDY (usually an EQUITABLE ADJUSTMENT) for some event that occurred during contract performance. Prior to the enactment of the CONTRACT DISPUTES ACT (CDA) OF 1978, BOARDs OF CONTRACT APPEALS (BCAs) had jurisdiction only over DISPUTEs that were found to arise under the contract. Other cases were required to be resolved by the Court of Claims. The CDA abolished this rule by granting the BCAs jurisdiction over all disputes "RELATING TO THE CONTRACT." "Arising under the contract" still has significance, however, because the standard Disputes clause in FAR 52.233-1 provides that the contractor has a DUTY TO PROCEED only with regard to claims that meet the "arising under" test. See Cibinic, Nagle & Nash, ADMINISTRATION

OF GOVERNMENT CONTRACTS 1135–36 (5th ed. 2016). See also Nash, *Postscript II: "Disputes" Clause Duty to Proceed*, 21 N&CR ¶ 29 (July 2007).

ARMED SERVICES BOARD OF CONTRACT APPEALS (ASBCA)   DOD's BOARD OF CONTRACT APPEALS (BCA). As the largest BCA, the ASBCA employees 24 ADMINISTRATIVE JUDGEs and maintains a pending docket of approximately 900 cases annually as compared with approximately 3100 cases in the 1980s. In addition to formal litigation of disputes, the Board makes ALTERNATIVE DISPUTE RESOLUTION procedures available at the request of the parties. The ASBCA has a chairman and two vice chairs. The ASBCA has resolved disputes involving a number of agencies other than DOD but beginning in 2007, with the establishment of the CIVILIAN BOARD OF CONTRACT APPEALS, it has jurisdiction over disputes of DOD and NASA. Although ASBCA offices are located in Falls Church, Virginia, the Board's administrative judges travel across the country and around the world to give contractors the opportunity to litigate their disputes. See Somers, *The Boards of Contract Appeals: A Historical Perspective*, 60 AM. U. L. REV. 745 (2011); Ting, *2009 Practice Pointers: A Primer on Effective Presentation of an Appeal Before the Armed Services Board of Contract Appeals*, 44 The Procurement Lawyer 3 (Spring 2009); Ting & Page, *Practice Pointers: A Short Primer on the Effective Preparation and Use of Rule 4 Files*, 43 The Procurement Lawyer 4 (Summer 2008); Shackleford, *2008 Effective Practice Under ASBCA Rule 11, Submission Without a Hearing*, 43 Procurement Lawyer 20 (Spring 2008).

ARMED SERVICES PRICING MANUAL (ASPM)   A two-volume manual, issued in 1986 and 1987, based on the policies and procedures of the FAR and the DFARS, which contained instructional material covering the entire range of CONTRACT PRICING. The ASPM has been replaced by a series of five CONTRACT PRICING REFERENCE GUIDES. See FAR 15.404-1(a)(7). The ASPM used detailed discussions and examples to illustrate the application of pricing policies to pricing problems, but it was not directive in nature. The first volume dealt with contract pricing in general, whereas the second focused specifically on PRICE ANALYSIS. The ASPM contained a topical index, appendices, a list of acronyms, and a short glossary. It was used for training in classrooms and on the job and also as a reference. Murphy, GUIDE TO CONTRACT PRICING: COST AND PRICE ANALYSIS FOR CONTRACTORS (5th ed. 2009).

ARMED SERVICES PROCUREMENT ACT (ASPA)   The statute governing the procurement procedures followed by DOD, NASA, and the Coast Guard. It was originally enacted in 1947 and is now codified at 10 U.S.C. § 2302 et seq. It has been modified numerous times, with the most sweeping changes enacted in the COMPETITION IN CONTRACTING ACT in 1984 and the FEDERAL ACQUISITION STREAMLINING ACT OF 1994. See Cibinic, Nash & Yukins, FORMATION OF GOVERNMENT CONTRACTS 29 (4th ed. 2011). NASA derives its procurement authority from the ASPA, but that does not modify its civilian agency role as established by the Space Act. 51 U.S.C. § 10101.When sections of the Act state that "the agency head shall" they apply to DOD, NASA and the Coast Guard. When they state "the Secretary of Defense shall" they apply only to DOD. Alinger, *The Impact of Procurement Provisions in Appropriations Acts on the Federal Acquisition System*, 36 PUB. CONT. L.J. 583 (2007).

ARMED SERVICES PROCUREMENT REGULATION (ASPR)   The original regulation issued under the ARMED SERVICES PROCUREMENT ACT (ASPA) to promulgate the procedures to be followed by DOD. During its existence the ASPR was a top-level regulation that was by far the most complete procurement regulation in the federal government. It was in effect from 1948 to 1978. It was renamed the DEFENSE ACQUISITION REGULA-TION (DAR) in 1978. In 1984, the DAR was replaced by the current FEDERAL ACQUI-SITION REGULATION (FAR) SYSTEM combining defense and civilian agency regulations. Many of the DAR/ASPR clauses, provisions, and textual explanations survived the merger and were incorporated in simplified form into the FAR; many of those that failed to survive were put in the original DOD FAR SUPPLEMENT.

AS-BUILT DRAWINGS   See RECORD DRAWINGS.

AS-PLANNED DRAWINGS   Drawings that show how a construction contractor or subcon-tractor plans to perform the work under contract. Such drawings are updated as changes, delays, and other eventualities occur during performance and thus eventually take the form of "as-built" or RECORD DRAWINGS. They are often used, in conjunction with record drawings, to prove DELAY.

ASIAN-PACIFIC AMERICANS   U.S. citizens whose origins are in Burma, Thailand, Malaysia, Indonesia, Singapore, Brunei, Japan, China (including Hong Kong), Taiwan, Laos, Cambodia (Kampuchea), Vietnam, Korea, the Philippines, the U.S. Trust Territory of the Pacific Islands (Republic of Palau), Republic of the Marshall Islands, Federated States of Micronesia, the Commonwealth of the Northern Mariana Islands, Guam, Samoa, Macao, Figi, Tonga, Kiribati, Tuvalu, or Nauru. 13 C.F.R. § 124.103(b). There is a rebuttable presumption that these persons are SOCIALLY DISADVANTAGED INDIVIDUALS for the purpose of determining the ownership of a SMALL DISADVANTAGED BUSINESS CONCERN. They must then demonstrate to the SMALL BUSINESS ADMINISTRATION that are ECONOMICALLY DISADVANTAGED INDIVIDUALS. Businesses owned by such individuals are given special preferences in government procurement. See SMALL DISADVANTAGED BUSINESS CONCERN.

ASSET   An amount recorded on a contractor's BALANCE SHEET representing the value of property owned by or debts owed to the contractor. Assets may be cash, near-cash (accounts receivable, temporary investments, notes receivable), or nonmonetary. Nonmonetary assets consumed in the creation of goods and services have limited lives, while others, such as land, have unlimited lives. CAPITAL ASSETs are long-term assets that are not bought or sold in the normal course of business. Such assets may be further classified as TANGIBLE CAPI-TAL ASSETs and INTANGIBLE CAPITAL ASSETs.

ASSET ACCOUNTABILITY UNIT   *Official:* A TANGIBLE CAPITAL ASSET which is a component of plant and equipment that is capitalized (see CAPITALIZATION) when acquired or whose replacement is capitalized when the unit is removed, transferred, sold, abandoned, demolished, or otherwise disposed of. *Source:* CAS 404, 48 C.F.R. § 9904.404-30. A contractor's capitalization policy must provide for identification of asset accountability units to the maximum extent practical. 48 C.F.R. § 9904.404-40(b)(3).

ASSIGNEE   A person or entity to whom all or part of one's property, interest, or rights are transferred. BLACK'S LAW DICTIONARY 145 (11th ed. 2019). In most cases, the assignee of a contract or a claim is an organization to which a contractor transfers its rights and/or obliga-tions. See ASSIGNMENT OF CONTRACT and ASSIGNMENT OF CLAIMS; FAR Subpart 32.8.

ASSIGNMENT OF CLAIMS   *Official:* The transfer or making over by the contractor to a bank, trust company, or other financing institution, as security for a loan to the contractor, of its right to be paid by the government for contract performance. *Source:* FAR 2.101. Under the Assignment of Claims Act, 31 U.S.C. § 3727, a contractor may assign moneys due after a claim has been allowed and a warrant for payment issued or moneys due—or to become due—under a contract, if (1) the contract specifies payments aggregating $1,000 or more; (2) the assignment is made to a bank, trust company, or other financing institution, including any federal lending agency; (3) the contract does not prohibit the assignment; (4) the assignment covers all unpaid amounts payable under the contract, is made to only one party, and is not subject to further assignment; and (5) the ASSIGNEE sends a written notice of the assignment to the contracting officer, to the SURETY on any BOND applicable to the contract, and to the DISBURSING OFFICER designated in the contract to make payment. 41 U.S.C. § 6305 contains a similar provision. See FAR Subpart 32.8. Once a proper assignment of claims has occurred, the government will be liable to the financing institution if it pays the contractor. See Manos, 2 GOVERNMENT CONTRACT COSTS AND PRICING § 85:18 (2d ed. 2009–2020).

ASSIGNMENT OF CONTRACT   Transfer of the rights and obligations under a contract to another party. When such assignment occurs, the ASSIGNOR (the original contractor) remains liable to the government if the ASSIGNEE fails to complete performance of the contract. 41 U.S.C. § 6305 prohibits contractors from assigning contracts; however, assignment of contracts may be made with the consent of the CONTRACTING OFFICER. *Tuftco Corp. v. United States*, 222 Ct. Cl. 277, 614 F.2d 740 (1980). Such assignments are called NOVATIONs in FAR Subpart 42.12, which contains procedures for entering into such agreements.

ASSIGNMENT OF COST TO COST ACCOUNTING PERIODS   *Official:* A method or technique used in determining the amount of cost to be assigned to individual cost accounting periods. Examples of COST ACCOUNTING PRACTICEs that involve the assignment of cost to cost accounting periods are requirements for the use of specified ACCRUAL BASIS ACCOUNTING or CASH BASIS ACCOUNTING for a cost element. *Source:* 48 C.F.R. § 9903.302-1.

ASSIGNOR   A person or entity "who assigns or transfers property to an ASSIGNEE." BLACK'S LAW DICTIONARY 149 (11th ed. 2019). In most cases, the assignor of a CONTRACT or a CLAIM is a contractor. See ASSIGNMENT OF CONTRACT and ASSIGNMENT OF CLAIMS; FAR Subpart 32.8.

ASSIST   See ACQUISITION STREAMLINING AND STANDARDIZATION INFORMATION SYSTEM.

ASSIST AUDIT   An AUDIT performed by one audit office at the request of another. The assist audit is usually an adjunct to or an integral part of an audit being performed by the requesting audit office. The DEFENSE CONTRACT AUDIT AGENCY (DCAA) CONTRACT AUDIT MANUAL explains that the prime contractor is primarily responsible for awarding subcontracts, monitoring their performance, and paying each subcontractor for the work accomplished under the subcontract's terms. Accordingly, the prime contractor is also responsible for audits of its subcontractors. However, it is DCAA's policy to perform assist audits of incurred costs whenever such audits are determined to be of potential benefit to the government and necessary to ensure adequate and effective review of a contractor's operations or cost representations. *DCAA Contract Audit Manual* ¶ 6-801.1.

ASSISTANCE SERVICES   See ADVISORY AND ASSISTANCE SERVICES.

ASSISTED ACQUISITION   *Official:* A type of INTERAGENCY ACQUISITION where a SERVICING AGENCY performs acquisition activities on a REQUESTING AGENCY's behalf, such as awarding and administering a contract, task order, or delivery order. *Source:* FAR 2.101. Agencies can only use an assisted acquisition when they have made a determination that this procedure is the best procurement approach and have obtained concurrence from the servicing agency. FAR 17.502-1(a)(1). The two agencies must then enter into an INTERAGENCY AGREEMENT establishing their relationship. FAR 17.502-1(b)(1). See Cibinic, Nash & Yukins, FORMATION OF GOVERNMENT CONTRACTS 1130–35 (4th ed. 2011).

ASSOCIATED GENERAL CONTRACTORS OF AMERICA (AGC)   A national trade association, founded in 1918, whose members include general contractors, subcontractors, industry suppliers, and service firms. AGC conducts seminars and conferences, provides tax services, compiles statistics on job accidents, and bestows safety and outstanding achievement awards. It represents over 2600 firms and publishes manuals, studies and model contract documents.

ATTACHMENT   *Official:* Any documentation, appended to a contract or incorporated by reference, which does not establish a requirement for deliverables. *Source:* DFARS 204.7101. See EXHIBIT. Guidance on the use of exhibits and attachments is contained in DOD PGI 204.7105.

ATTEMPTING TO INFLUENCE   See INFLUENCING OR ATTEMPTING TO INFLUENCE.

ATTORNEY WORK-PRODUCT PRIVILEGE   An exemption under the FREEDOM OF INFORMATION ACT that protects documents prepared by an agency's attorney which reveal the theory of a case or proposed litigation from release. 5 U.S.C. § 552(b)(5). This privilege does not extend to routine reports in the ordinary course of business but is limited to documents prepared in anticipation of a particular litigation or related to a specific claim which is likely to lead to litigation. See Nash & Rawicz, INTELLECTUAL PROPERTY IN GOVERNMENT CONTRACTS, chap. 9 (6th ed. 2008). See also PRIVILEGED INFORMATION.

ATTORNEY'S FEES   Compensation, at an hourly rate, fixed rate, or CONTINGENT FEE, for the performance of professional legal services. Most attorney's fees in government contract litigation are paid at an hourly rate for time reasonably expended. In government contracts, contractors generally cannot recover their attorney's fees for litigation against the government. Under the EQUAL ACCESS TO JUSTICE ACT, however, small contractors that meet prescribed standards can recover their attorney's fees and expenses in litigation before the U.S. COURT OF FEDERAL CLAIMS and the BOARDs OF CONTRACT APPEALS under the CONTRACT DISPUTES ACT OF 1978. Costs related to legal proceedings are unallowable if the proceedings result in a criminal conviction, a finding of contractor liability where there are allegations of FRAUD or similar misconduct, imposition of a monetary penalty, DEBARMENT or SUSPENSION, or termination or voiding of the contract. FAR 31.205-47(b). Costs related to legal proceedings are also unallowable if they are incurred in connection with (1) prosecution or defense of claims or appeals against the government; (2) organization, reorganization (including mergers and acquisitions), or resisting

mergers and acquisitions; (3) defense of antitrust suits; (4) defense of QUI TAM PRO-
CEEDINGS when the contractor is found liable or has settled; (5) prosecution or defense
of lawsuits or appeals between contractors concerning arrangements of shared interest such
as JOINT VENTUREs or teaming agreements unless agreed to by the contracting officer;
(6) PATENT INFRINGEMENT; (7) representation of individuals, groups or legal entities,
which the contractor is not legally obligated to provide, where the participant was convicted
or found civilly liable for a violation of law or regulation; and (8) PROTESTs of federal government SOLICITATIONs or CONTRACT AWARDs, or the defense against such protests of such solicitations or contract awards. FAR 31.205-47(f). See Manos, 1
GOVERNMENT CONTRACT COSTS AND PRICING §§ 54:1–54:11 (2d ed. 2009–2020).

AUCTION A buying or selling technique whereby open bidding is continued until no competitor is willing to submit a better bid. Prior to FAC 97-02, September 30, 1997, FAR Part
15 prohibited such auction techniques as (1) indicating to an offeror a cost or price that it
must meet to obtain further consideration, or (2) advising an offeror of its price standing relative to another offeror. FAR 15.306(e) now provides only that the government may not
reveal an offeror's price without that offeror's permission. However, the contracting officer
may inform an offeror that its price is too high or too low, and reveal the results of the analysis supporting that conclusion. It is also permissible to indicate to all offerors the cost or
price that the government's PRICE ANALYSIS, MARKET RESEARCH, and other reviews
have identified as reasonable. Dekel, *The Legal Theory of Competitive Bidding for Government
Contracts*, 37 PUB. CONT. L.J. 237 (2008). See also REVERSE AUCTION.

AUDIT The systematic examination of records and other documents and the securing of
evidence—by confirmation, physical inspection, or otherwise—for one or more of the following purposes: determining the propriety or legality of proposed or consummated transactions; ascertaining whether all transactions have been recorded and are reflected accurately in
accounts; determining the existence of recorded assets and the inclusiveness of recorded liabilities; determining the accuracy of financial or statistical statements or reports and the fairness of the facts they present; determining the degree of compliance with established policies
and procedures of financial transactions and business management; and appraising an
accounting system and making recommendations concerning it. Contract audit is an integral
part of procurement by NEGOTIATION. Its purpose is to assist in achieving prudent contracting by having government AUDITORs provide government procurement personnel
with financial information and advice on contractual matters and the effectiveness, efficiency,
and economy of the contractor's operations. *DCAA Contract Audit Manual* ¶ 1-104.2. On
COST-REIMBURSEMENT CONTRACTS, audit ensures that a contractor has incurred
all costs claimed for reimbursement. In conducting a contract audit before award of a contract or negotiation of a CLAIM, the auditor must examine or develop sufficient evidence
to support a valid opinion of the extent to which costs or estimates contained in a contractor's claim or PROPOSAL are (1) reasonable as to nature and amount, (2) allocable, (3) measurable by the application of duly promulgated COST ACCOUNTING STANDARDS
(CAS) and GENERALLY ACCEPTED ACCOUNTING PRINCIPLES (GAAP) and prac-
tices appropriate to the particular circumstances, and (4) in accordance with applicable cost
limitations or exclusions as stated in the contract or in the FAR. Although the detection of
FRAUD or similar unlawful activity is not a primary function of contract audit, the auditor
must constantly be alert to situations or transactions that may indicate such activity. *DCAA*

Contract Audit Manual ¶ 1-102. See Cibinic, Knight & Nash, Cost-Reimbursement Contracting, 849–86 (4th ed. 2014).

AUDITOR   A person conducting AUDIT activities. Broad authority to audit government programs is vested in the Comptroller General of the United States (see GOVERNMENT ACCOUNTABILITY OFFICE). The Comptroller General also has authority under the EXAMINATION OF RECORDS clause to audit government contractors. Most contract audit is performed by agency auditors, who are generally assigned to the agency INSPECTOR GENERAL, except in DOD where they are assigned to the DEFENSE CONTRACT AUDIT AGENCY. Auditors perform work for other agencies through CROSS-SERVICING arrangements. See FAR Subpart 42.1. Agencies also obtain audit services by contracting with professional accounting firms.

AUTHORITY FOR SYSTEMS ACQUISITION   An umbrella term used by DOD to describe the framework granting authority for it to develop, produce, and field weapon systems. This authority emanates from two sources: the law (legal basis) and executive branch policy that includes EXECUTIVE ORDERS, Office of Management and Budget Circulars and National Security Council Directives, and other regulations and directives. DAU Glossary.

AUTHORIZATION   Legal authority to carry out a program. Statutes granting authorization are initiated in the legislative committees of Congress having cognizance over the agency involved. Generally, they are a prerequisite to an APPROPRIATION for that program or agency. The purpose of the authorization process is to ensure that the legislative committees have reviewed and approved the current programs of their respective agencies before the appropriations committees make the final decisions on the amount of funds that should be provided to carry out agency missions. See Cibinic, Nash & Yukins, Formation of Government Contracts 42 (4th ed. 2011).

AUTHORIZATION AND CONSENT   Authorization by the government for a contractor to use an invention that has been patented but to which the government has no rights. Under 28 U.S.C. § 1498(a), when such authorization and consent has been granted, the owner of the PATENT can sue only the government in the U.S. COURT OF FEDERAL CLAIMS (it cannot sue the contractor for damages or obtain an injunction against the contractor to block use of the patent). The government grants such authorization and consent in order to further the progress of work on its contracts—to obtain the performance of the work in the most effective manner without the need to create new technology. FAR 27.201-2 provides for the use of three different Authorization and Consent clauses. The clause in FAR 52.227-1 is used in supply and service contracts (including CONSTRUCTION contracts) and gives authorization and consent to use all patents necessary to perform the specified work or required to be used by the contracting officer. This clause is optional in simplified acquisitions. FAR 27.201-1(a)(1)(i). The Alternate I clause in FAR 52.227-1 is used in RESEARCH AND DEVELOPMENT contracts and gives blanket authorization and consent to use any invention. The Alternate II clause in FAR 52.227-1 is used in contracts for communication services with a common carrier. Neither FAR Part 12 nor the Contract Terms and Conditions—Commercial Items clause in FAR 52.212-4 call for the granting of authorization and consent when the government procures a commercial item. See Nash & Rawicz, Intellectual Property in Government Contracts, chaps. 4 & 7 (6th ed. 2008); Nash, *Authorization* *and Consent: Its Role in Private Litigation,* 20 N&CR ¶ 31 (July 2006); Nash, *Authorization and Consent: Inappropriate on Contracts for Commercial Items?,* 19 N&CR ¶ 59 (Dec. 2005).

AUTHORIZED INDIVIDUAL   *Official:* A person who has been granted authority, in accordance with agency procedures, to acquire supplies and services in accordance with FAR Part 13 SIMPLIFIED ACQUISITION PROCEDURES. *Source:* FAR 13.001. In the context of simplified acquisition under FAR Part 13, such individuals are CONTRACTING OFFICERs except for MICRO-PURCHASEs where non-contracting officers are authorized to make purchases.

AUTHORIZED OFFICIAL OF AN AGENCY   *Official:* An officer or employee responsible for contracting, program management, audit, inspection, investigation, or enforcement of any law or regulation relating to government procurement or the subject matter of a contract. *Source:* FAR 3.901. FAR Subpart 3.9 implements the provisions of 10 U.S.C. § 2409 and 41 U.S.C. § 4705 that bar contractors from discharging, demoting or discriminating against WHISTLEBLOWERS when they have disclosed information about potential violations of law to such authorized officials.

APPROVED PROGRAM   *Official:* A program determined as necessary or appropriate for priorities and allocations support to promote the national defense by the Secretary of Defense, the Secretary of Energy, or the Secretary of Homeland Security, under the authority of the Defense Production Act, the Stafford Act, and Executive Order 12919, or the Selective Service Act and related statutes and Executive Order 12742. *Source:* FAR 11.601. Under the DEFENSE PRIORITIES AND ALLOCATIONS SYSTEM (DPAS), such programs are assigned a RATED ORDER giving them priority over other work. Such programs are listed in Schedule I of the DPAS. See FAR Subpart 11.6.

AUTHORIZED REPRESENTATIVE   An employee of a CONTRACTING ACTIVITY with the authority to perform CONTRACT ADMINISTRATION activities. Both FAR 2.101 and the Definitions clause in FAR 52.202-1 state that "certain" authorized representatives are CONTRACTING OFFICERs. However, it is generally recognized that they do not have the authority to enter into agreements or MODIFICATIONs that alter the terms of existing contracts. See FAR 1.602-2(d)(5) stating this rule with regard to CONTRACTING OFFICER REPRESENTATIVEs. When authorized representatives act within the scope of their express authority, the government agency will be bound by their actions under the doctrine of IMPLIED AUTHORITY. The authority of authorized representatives has been severely limited by the FEDERAL CIRCUIT. See Nash & Feldman, 1 GOVERNMENT CONTRACT CHANGES §§ 5:9–5:10 (3d ed. 2006–2020); Cibinic, Nagle & Nash, ADMINISTRATION OF GOVERNMENT CONTRACTS 36–41 (5th ed. 2016); Pachter, *The Incredible Shrinking Contracting Officer,* 39 PUB. CONT. L.J. 705 (2010); Nash, *Postscript: Contracting Officer Authority,* 22 N&CR ¶ 33 (June 2008); Nash, *Contracting Officer Authority: A Strict Requirement,* 21 N&CR ¶ 58 (Nov. 2007).

AUTOMATIC STAY (GAO PROTEST FILING)   A mechanism by which contract AWARD is withheld or further performance of a contract is suspended when a disappointed bidder or offeror files a timely PROTEST with the COMPTROLLER GENERAL. This authority derives from the COMPETITION IN CONTRACTING ACT. 31 U.S.C. § 3553(c) and (d). It is implemented in FAR 33.104 and 4 C.F.R. § 21.4. When an agency is notified that a protest has been filed prior to contract award, the agency is required by law not to make award before the protest is resolved, unless the HEAD OF THE CONTRACTING

ACTIVITY decides that urgent and compelling circumstances significantly affecting the interests of the United States will not permit waiting for the decision. Similarly, when an agency is notified of a protest within 10 calendar days after award has been made, the law requires the agency to direct the contractor to suspend performance until the protest is resolved. See Schooner, *Postscript III: Challenging an Override of a Protest Stay*, 26 N&CR ¶ 25 (May 2012); Roberts, *Does Automatic Mean Automatic? The Applicability of the CICA Automatic Stay to Task and Delivery Order Bid Protests*, Note, 39 PUB. CONT. L.J. 641 (2010); Sacilotto, *Is the Game Worth the Candle? The Fate of the CICA Override*, 45 The Procurement Lawyer 1 (Fall 2009).

AUTOMATIC SUSPENSION   See AUTOMATIC STAY.

AVAILABILITY OF APPROPRIATIONS   Appropriations are available for OBLIGATION only in the budget year of the appropriation, unless the language in the appropriation act specifies a longer period. If the language specifies that the funds are to remain available until the end of a certain year beyond the budget year, the availability is said to be multiyear. If the language specifies that the funds are to remain available until expended, the availability is said to be no-year. Appropriations for major procurements and construction projects are typically made available for multiple years or until expended. U.S. GOV'T ACCOUNTABILITY OFFICE, PRINCIPLES OF FEDERAL APPROPRIATIONS LAW: ANNUAL UPDATE TO THE THIRD EDITION, chaps. 4 & 5, GAO-15-303SP (Washington, D.C.: Mar. 2015); Solomson, Miller & Demory, *Fiscal Matters: An Introduction to Federal Fiscal Law & Principles*, BRIEFING PAPERS No. 10-7 (June 2010).

AVERAGE PROCUREMENT UNIT COST (APUC) OBJECTIVES   A DOD projected all-encompassing measure of per-item cost. APUC includes recurring flyaway (e.g., for an aircraft program), rollaway, sailaway costs (including nonrecurring production costs) adjusted for data, training, support equipment, and initial spares costs. Design to average unit procurement COST OBJECTIVEs, expressed in constant dollars, are established within DOD as part of obtaining approval to begin a new ACQUISITION PROGRAM. DAU GLOSSARY.

AVOIDANCE OF CONTRACT   The withdrawal by one party from a contract or contract MODIFICATION without performance because of a defect in the process of entering into the contract or contract modification. The most common grounds for avoidance are ECONOMIC DURESS, FRAUD, illegality, MUTUAL MISTAKE, and UNCONSCIONABILITY. When one party to a contract finds that any of these things has occurred in the formation of a contract or a modification, it has the right of avoidance without recourse by the other party. See Cibinic, Nagle & Nash, ADMINISTRATION OF GOVERNMENT CONTRACTS 311–14 (5th ed. 2016).

AWARD (OF A CONTRACT)   The act by a CONTRACTING OFFICER of entering into a contract by accepting an OFFER (BID or PROPOSAL). The award may be made by sending a written notice of award (acceptance). See FAR 14.408, *Award*, and 15.504, *Award to successful offeror*. Alternatively, it may be done by sending an executed contract document, see FAR 4.201. FAR Part 53 prescribes a number of forms that may be used to notify the contractor of the government's acceptance.

AWARD FEE   The FEE that a contractor receives above the BASE FEE in a COST-PLUS-AWARD-FEE CONTRACT. The total amount of fee available to be awarded is set forth in the original contract in an award fee plan and should be an amount that is sufficient to provide motivation for excellence in such areas as cost, schedule, and technical performance. FAR 16.405. The award fee plan must include criteria for contractor performance evaluation, provide for evaluation periods, prohibit the contractor from earning an award fee if performance is below satisfactory, and define the total award fee pool. FAR 16.401(e)(3). The determination and methodology for determining the award fee are made at the discretion of the government. Award fees can also be used on fixed price contracts. FAR 16.404. In DOD contracts, award fees must be tied to identifiable outcomes, discrete events, or milestones as much as possible. Normally, an award fee is not earned when the fee-determining official has determined that contractor performance has been submarginal or unsatisfactory. DOD PGI 216.405-2. See Cibinic, Nash & Yukins, FORMATION OF GOVERNMENT CONTRACTS 1291–1300 (4th ed. 2011); Cibinic, Knight & Nash, COST-REIMBURSEMENT CONTRACTING 74-80 (4th ed. 2014). See also Edwards, *Award-Fee Contracting*, BRIEFING PAPERS No. 10-3 (Mar. 2010); U.S. GOV'T ACCOUNTABILITY OFFICE, *Use of Award Fees for Achieving Program Outcomes Should Be Improved*, GAO-07-58 (Jan. 2007), Edwards, *Award-Fee Contracts: What Should They Say About the Government's Internal Organization and Processes?*, 21 N&CR ¶ 8 (Mar. 2007); Edwards, *Award-Fee Incentives: Do They Work? Do Agencies Know How to Use Them?*, 20 N&CR ¶ 26 (June 2006).

AWARD FEE DETERMINATION OFFICIAL (FDO)   See FEE DETERMINATION OFFICIAL.

AWARD ON INITIAL PROPOSALS   Award of a competitively negotiated contract (see NEGOTIATION) on the basis of the initial proposals received, without conducting DISCUSSIONs with the OFFERORs in a COMPETITIVE RANGE. Such awards can be made whenever the contracting officer determines that discussions are not necessary and the solicitation contains a clause stating that the agency intends to award without discussions. FAR 15.306(a)(3). CLARIFICATIONs are permitted with this type of award. FAR 52.215-1 contains two clauses to be used depending on whether the contracting officer decides that discussions will be necessary or that award on initial proposals will probably be possible. See Feldman, GOVERNMENT CONTRACT AWARDS: NEGOTIATION AND SEALED BIDDING, chap. 14 (2019–2020 ed.); Cibinic, Nash & Yukins, FORMATION OF GOVERNMENT CONTRACTS 868–69 (4th ed. 2011).

AWARD TERM INCENTIVE   A contract incentive providing that the contractor can earn additional periods of performance instead of, or in addition to, an AWARD FEE or incentive fee. Under an award term contract the government monitors and evaluates the contractor's performance, and if a government TERM DETERMINING OFFICIAL decides that the contractor's performance was excellent, the contractor earns an extension. If the extension is required by the contract, it must be conditioned upon the government's continuing need for the service and the availability of funds. However, most award term contracts have called for the award of one or more OPTION years which can be exercised at the sole discretion of the government.

AWARD WITHOUT DISCUSSIONS   See AWARD ON INITIAL PROPOSALS.

B

BACK PAY Payment to employees of previously earned compensation. Back pay may result from a negotiated settlement, order, or court decree that resolves a violation of federal labor laws or the Civil Rights Act of 1964. It falls into two categories: (1) payment of additional compensation to employees for work performed for which they were underpaid, and (2) payment resulting from such violations as improper discharge or discrimination. Back pay resulting from underpaid work is compensation for the work performed and is an ALLOWABLE COST; all other back pay resulting from violation of federal labor laws or the Civil Rights Act is unallowable. FAR 31.205-6(h). See Cibinic, Knight & Nash, Cost-Reimbursement Contracting 676–78 (4th ed. 2014).

BACKGROUND RIGHTS Intellectual property rights in PATENTs, COPYRIGHTs, TECHNICAL DATA or COMPUTER SOFTWARE that have been perfected by a contractor prior to entering into a contract. The government generally does not take these rights when it contracts for research and development. FAR 27.306 contains restrictions on the use of contract clauses requiring a contractor to give the government background patent rights. However, 28 U.S.C. § 1498(a) permits the government to use background patents and to pay the owner of the patent reasonable compensation. There is no similar policy with regard to background rights in technical data and computer software. However, such technical data and computer software may fall into the DEVELOPED AT PRIVATE EXPENSE category with the government obtaining a LIMITED RIGHTS or RESTRICTED RIGHTS license. Background rights in copyrights are obtained when the government procures EXISTING WORKS. In addition, the Rights in Data—General clause in FAR 52.227-14, the Rights in Technical Data—Noncommercial Items clause in DFARS 252.227-7013, and the Rights in Noncommercial Computer Software and Noncommercial Computer Software Documentation clause in DFARS 252.227-7014 permit the contractor to obtain background copyrights in technical data and computer software by negotiating a license with the owner of the rights. See Nash & Rawicz, Intellectual Property in Government Contracts, chaps. 2 & 8 (6th ed. 2008); Nash, *Government Use of Private Patents: A License to Steal*, 24 N&CR ¶ 12 (Mar. 2010); Nash, *Recovering for Government Use of a Private Patent: An Uphill Battle*, 23 N&CR ¶ 32 (June 2009).

BAD DEBTS Losses arising from uncollectible accounts receivable due from customers. FAR 31.205-3 makes such losses, whether actual or estimated, and any associated costs, such as collection efforts and LEGAL FEES, UNALLOWABLE COSTs. See Manos, 1 Government Contract Costs & Pricing §§ 10:1–10:2 (2d ed. 2009–2020); Cibinic, Knight & Nash, Cost-Reimbursement Contracting 721 (4th ed. 2014).

BAD FAITH   Acting with malice or intent to harm the other party to a contract. In order to prove that the government acted in bad faith, it is necessary to prove by clear and convincing evidence that a government official had a specific intent to harm the contractor. *Am-Pro Protective Agency, Inc. v. United States*, 281 F.3d 1234 (Fed. Cir. 2002). Bad faith is sometimes equated with "lack of good faith" but, generally, it has not been necessary to prove bad faith in order to prove that the government breached its DUTY OF GOOD FAITH AND FAIR DEALING. See Nash, *Postscript VIII: Breach of the Duty of Good Faith and Fair Dealing*, 33 N&CR ¶ 3 (Jan. 2019); Nash, *The Government's Duty of Good Faith and Fair Dealing: Proving a Breach*, 23 N&CR ¶ 66 (Dec. 2009); Nash, *Agreements to Agree: What Is a Breach?*, 21 N&CR ¶ 12 (Apr. 2007); Johnson, *Still Needed: Augmentation of Government Ethics Standards to Embrace "Square Dealing" With Contractors—And A Possible Resolution*, 20 N&CR ¶ 60 (Dec. 2006); Armstrong, Pupko & Yenovkian II, *Federal Procurement Ethical Requirements and the Good Faith Presumption*, 20 N&CR ¶ 29 (June 2006); Nash, *Nondisclosure of Superior Knowledge: The Scope of the Government's Duty*, 20 N&CR ¶ 1 (Jan. 2006).

BALANCE OF PAYMENTS PROGRAM   A nonstatutory program giving preference to American products over foreign products. See DFARS Subpart 225.75. The program applies to acquisitions of supplies to be used or construction to be performed outside of the United States. It provides that, unless an exception applies, the foreign offer must be increased for evaluation purposes by a factor of 50% (excluding duty). DFARS 225.7502. Examples of the proper evaluation of offers subject to the balance of payment procedures are set forth in DOD PGI 225.504. The program was more widely used until the TRADE AGREEMENTS ACT OF 1979 became the controlling law dealing with the purchase of foreign products. It is now only used by DOD in narrow circumstances. See Feldman, GOVERNMENT CONTRACT GUIDEBOOK, § 8:32 (4th ed. 2019–2020); Cibinic, Nash & Yukins, FORMATION OF GOVERNMENT CONTRACTS 1632 (4th ed. 2011).

BARGAINING NEGOTIATIONs   with an offeror including persuasion, alteration of assumptions and positions, give-and-take, that apply to price, schedule, technical requirements, type of contract, or other terms and conditions. FAR 15.306(d). Bargaining may occur in sole source procurements or during competitive negotiations. When it occurs in the competitive negotiation process after establishment of the COMPETITIVE RANGE, it is called DISCUSSIONs. FAR 15.306(d)(4) indicates that, in this situation, bargaining may include negotiation with an offeror to increase performance beyond mandatory minimums or suggesting to an offeror that they have exceeded mandatory minimums in a way that makes their offer noncompetitive. See Cibinic, Nash & Yukins, FORMATION OF GOVERNMENT CONTRACTS 888–90 (4th ed. 2011).

BASE   The numerical measure, such as costs, hours of LABOR, or hours of machine usage, to which INDIRECT COSTs are allocated (see ALLOCATION OF COST). The base must be selected to permit allocation of indirect costs on the basis of the benefits accruing to all COST OBJECTIVEs within the base. FAR 31.203(c). Once an appropriate base has been selected, individual elements may not be removed; thus, all items within the base should bear their pro rata share of indirect costs. FAR 31.203(d). See Cibinic, Knight & Nash, COST-REIMBURSEMENT CONTRACTING 607–09 (4th ed. 2014).

BASE FEE   A fixed dollar amount established at the inception of a COST-PLUS-AWARD-FEE CONTRACT as the amount of PROFIT the contractor will receive under the contract if the work is successfully completed. FAR 16.305. In addition to this base fee, the contractor receives an AWARD FEE in an amount that reflects the government's periodic judgmental evaluation of contractor performance. The base fee is established, administered, and paid like a fixed fee under a COST-PLUS-FIXED-FEE CONTRACT. See Cibinic, Knight & Nash, COST-REIMBURSEMENT CONTRACTING 75 (4th ed. 2014).

BASE PERIOD *Official:* The cost accounting period during which INDIRECT COSTs are incurred and accumulated for allocation to work performed in that period. *Source:* FAR 31.203(g). For contracts subject to the COST ACCOUNTING STANDARDS, CAS 406, Cost Accounting Period, 48 C.F.R. § 9904.406, provides guidance for selecting the base period. CAS 406 requires that contractors use the same fiscal year for cost accounting purposes, subject to several limited exceptions. 48 C.F.R. § 9904-406.40(a). For contracts not subject to the Cost Accounting Standards, the COST PRINCIPLES indicate that the contractor's fiscal year is normally the appropriate base period, but the use of a shorter period is permitted (1) for contracts in which performance involves only a minor portion of the fiscal year, or (2) when it is general practice in the industry to use a shorter period. FAR 31.203(e). See Cibinic, Knight & Nash, COST-REIMBURSEMENT CONTRACTING 610–12 (4th ed. 2014).

"BASED ON" PRICE A price that was comparable to a previous price that was an ESTABLISHED CATALOG OR MARKET PRICE or a price established through ADEQUATE PRICE COMPETITION. When a "based on" price was submitted in a negotiated procurement, the contracting officer did not need to obtain CERTIFIED COST OR PRICING DATA. With the new policies on COST OR PRICING DATA adopted in 1995 and 1996, this concept is one means of determining that there is adequate price competition. FAR 15.403-1(c)(1)(iii).

BASIC AGREEMENT *Official:* A written instrument of understanding negotiated between a procuring activity and a contractor, that (1) contains contract clauses applying to future procurements between the parties during its term and (2) contemplates separate future contracts that will incorporate by reference or attachment the required and applicable clauses agreed upon in the basic agreement. A basic agreement is not a CONTRACT. *Source:* FAR 16.702. Basic agreements are used to expedite future procurement when there is a likelihood that a substantial number of future contracts will be issued. Basic agreements must be revised annually to incorporate contract clauses that are currently applicable. FAR 16.702(b)(3).

BASIC ASSUMPTION A matter that is a significant part of the bargaining process in the formation of a contract. To be a basic assumption, the facts on which the assumption is based must have been knowable at the time the contract was formed; events that could not be foreseen cannot be considered a basic assumption. If there is a MUTUAL MISTAKE as to a basic assumption in a contract, relief may be granted where, had the parties known the correct information at the time the contract was formed, they would have altered the contract. Cibinic, Nagle & Nash, ADMINISTRATION OF GOVERNMENT CONTRACTS 297–301 (5th ed. 2016).

BASIC ORDERING AGREEMENT (BOA) *Official:* A written instrument of understanding, negotiated between an agency, contracting activity, or contracting office and a contractor, that contains—(1) terms and clauses applying to future contracts (orders) between the parties during its term, (2) a description, as specific as practicable, of supplies or services to be provided, and (3) methods for pricing, issuing, and delivering future orders under the basic ordering agreement. A basic ordering agreement is not a contract. *Source:* FAR 16.703.

BOAs may be used to expedite contracting for supplies or services when specific items, quantities, and prices are not known but a substantial number of requirements are anticipated. They are frequently issued to multiple contractors and may not be used to avoid the requirements for competition. FAR 16.703(d). See Seto, *Basic Ordering Agreements: The Catch-22 Chameleon of Government Contract Law*, 55 SMU L. REV. 427 (Spring 2002).

BASIC RESEARCH   *Official:* That research directed toward increasing knowledge in science. The primary aim of basic research is a fuller knowledge or understanding of the subject under study, rather than any practical application of that knowledge. *Source:* FAR 2.101. It is the first stage of the RESEARCH AND DEVELOPMENT process and is followed by APPLIED RESEARCH. Most basic research is acquired through the BROAD AGENCY ANNOUNCEMENT process. See Cibinic, Nash & Yukins, FORMATION OF GOVERNMENT CONTRACTS 1083 (4th ed. 2011).

BAYH-DOLE ACT   The Act giving small businesses and nonprofit organizations the right to elect to retain title to SUBJECT INVENTIONs. The Act was enacted in 1980 as the Patent and Trademark Law Amendments Act, Pub. L. No. 96-517, and amended in 1984 by the Trademark Clarification Act of 1984, Title V of Pub. L. No. 98-620. It is implemented by the Department of Commerce in 37 C.F.R. § 401 and in FAR Subpart 27.3. See PATENT RIGHTS. See Nash & Rawicz, INTELLECTUAL PROPERTY IN GOVERNMENT CONTRACTS, chap. 2 (6th ed. 2008).

BENCHMARK   Any test conducted on computer hardware, software, or telecommunications equipment to determine (1) that the configuration performs in accordance with vendor-published PERFORMANCE SPECIFICATIONS; (2) that the configuration satisfies certain functional requirements that cannot be measured in terms of performance and/or design criteria; (3) the estimated annual costs to an agency for teleprocessing services; and (4) the size system that must be purchased (e.g., how many components are needed to process the anticipated workload). The term has been broadly interpreted to include evaluation exercises of varying degrees of complexity. In general, there are two types of benchmarks: operational capability demonstrations (OCDs) and live test demonstrations (LTDs), the latter being the more rigorous. See CAPABILITY VALIDATION.

BENCHMARK COMPENSATION AMOUNT   *Official:* The median amount of the compensation provided for all SENIOR EXECUTIVEs of all BENCHMARK CORPORA-TIONs for the most recent year for which data is available at the time the determination of the Administrator of the Office of Federal Procurement Policy is made. *Source:* 41 U.S.C. § 1127. This is the ceiling amount of compensation that may be treated as an ALLOWABLE COST in accordance with 10 U.S.C. § 2324(e)(1)(P) and 41 U.S.C. § 4304(a)(16). See FAR 31.205-6(p). This amount applies equally to both defense and civilian procurement agencies. See *Regulations in Brief*, 49 Gov't Contractor ¶ 140 (2007). The amount applies to all employees (not just senior executives) starting on January 1, 2012 for DOD, NASA, and the Coast Guard and on June 24, 2014 for all other executive agencies. See 10 U.S.C. § 2324(e)(1)(P), 41 U.S.C. § 4304(a)(16), and FAR 31.205-6(p)(2)–(4). The amount is determined by a statutory formula which was revised in 2014 and has risen since then from $487,000 in 2015 to $555,000 in year ending December 31, 2020.

BENCHMARK CORPORATION   *Official:* A publicly-owned United States corporation that has annual sales in excess of $50,000,000 for the fiscal year. *Source:* 41 U.S.C. § 1127. Such corporations are subject to the limitations on the compensation of SENIOR EXECUTIVEs and all employees after 2011 or 2014 (see BENCHMARK COMPENSATION AMOUNT) pursuant to 10 U.S.C. § 2324(e)(1)(P) and 41 U.S.C. § 4304(a)(16). See FAR 31.205-6(p). See BENCHMARK COMPENSATION AMOUNT.

BERNE CONVENTION *Official:* The Convention for the Protection of Literary and Artistic Works, signed at Berne, Switzerland, on September 9, 1886, and all acts, protocols, and revisions thereto. *Source:* 17 U.S.C. § 101. This is the major international agreement providing the basic terms governing COPYRIGHT protection in all countries that enter into the convention. The United States joined the convention in 1988 and adopted required changes, effective on March 1, 1989, in the Berne Convention Implementation Act of 1988, Pub. L. No. 100-568. The fundamental premise of the convention is that there should be no formal requirements to obtain copyright protection. Thus, under the convention no notice of authorship need be placed on a work and the work is not required to be registered in the country of authorship. However, 17 U.S.C. § 401 allows the use of a notice and contains guidance on the form of the notice. In addition, 17 U.S.C. § 407 allows registration of a work in the Copyright Office of the Library of Congress and 17 U.S.C. § 411(a) requires registration of United States works as a prerequisite to bringing a suit for copyright infringement. See Nash & Rawicz, INTELLECTUAL PROPERTY IN GOVERNMENT CONTRACTS, chap. 1 (6th ed. 2008); Ginsburg, *The U.S. Experience with Mandatory Copyright Formalities: A Love/Hate Relationship*, 33 COLUM. J.L. & ARTS 311 (2010).

BERRY AMENDMENT A statute requiring the DEPARTMENT OF DEFENSE to give preference in procurement to domestically produced, manufactured, or home grown products, notably food, clothing, fabrics, and specialty metals. It was first enacted into law on April 5, 1941 and subsequently codified in 10 U.S.C. § 2533a. It is implemented in DFARS Subpart 225.70. The Berry Amendment differs from the BUY AMERICAN ACT (BAA), another domestic preference statute, in that the BAA governs most procurement by the federal government, while the Berry Amendment governs DOD procurement only. Further, the BAA requires that substantially all of the costs of foreign components not exceed 50% of the cost of all components (thus, an item can be 51% domestic content and still be in compliance with the BAA) while the Berry Amendment requires, with limited exceptions, that items be 100% domestic in origin. Domestic nonavailability exceptions to the Berry Amendment are found in DFARS 225-7002-2. See Feldman, GOVERNMENT CONTRACT GUIDEBOOK, § 8:34 (4th ed. 2019–2020). See also Kerlin, *1,000 Trucks Can't All Be Wrong: The Untenable Reality of the Specialty Metals Requirement*, 38 PUB. CONT. L.J. 237 (2008); Churchill & Weinberg, *Domestic Specialty Metals Restrictions: A Bumper Crop of Fresh Berry Issues*, BRIEFING PAPERS No. 07-4 (Mar. 2007); Pavlick & Pearson, *New DOD Guidance on the Berry Amendment: Still Berry After All These Years*, 42 The Procurement Lawyer 1 (Winter 2007).

BEST AND FINAL OFFER (BAFO) An OFFER submitted to the government in a competitive negotiated procurement (see NEGOTIATION) after written or oral DISCUSSIONs have been conducted. FAC 97-02, Sept. 30, 1997, changed this term to FINAL PROPOSAL REVISION. Under the prior FAR, the contracting officer would issue a request for BAFOs to all offerors still within the COMPETITIVE RANGE. The request included (1) notice that discussions are concluded, (2) notice that the offeror has the opportunity to submit a BAFO, (3) a common cutoff date and time allowing a reasonable opportunity for submission of BAFOs, and (4) notice of the ramifications of late submission. Following evaluation of the BAFOs, the contracting officer selected the source whose offer was most advantageous to the government, considering price and the other factors included in the solicitation. See Cibinic, Nash & Yukins, Formation of Government Contracts 925–37 (4th ed. 2011).

BEST EFFORTS   A contractual obligation to *attempt* to meet a goal—as, for example, under the LIMITATION OF COST CLAUSE, which requires contractors to use their best efforts to perform the work within the estimated cost of the contract. Under the Utilization of Indian Organizations and Indian-Owned Economic Enterprises clause at FAR 52.226.1, the contractor must agree to use its best efforts to give Indian organizations and Indian-owned economic enterprises the maximum practicable opportunity to participate in the subcontracts it awards to the fullest extent consistent with efficient performance of its contract if subcontracting possibilities exist for such organizations and funds are available for any increased costs. FAR 26.104. See Nash & Cibinic, *The Ubiquitous "Best Efforts" Term: Does It Mean Anything?*, 15 N&CR ¶45 (Aug. 2001).

BEST PRACTICES GUIDES   A series of guidebooks on best practices developed by the OFFICE OF FEDERAL PROCUREMENT POLICY. (As government agencies implement reinvention policies, they may develop promising practices that may be applied by other organizations, thus becoming best practices.) Guides are currently available addressing: PERFORMANCE-BASED SERVICE ACQUISITION; MODULAR CONTRACTING; and EMERGENCY ACQUISITION. These best practices illustrate increased efficiencies and savings in time and costs that agencies have experienced as they adopt innovative measures to communicate their acquisition needs. The GOVERNMENT ACCOUNTABILITY OFFICE has also issued best practices guides on Cost Estimating and Assessment, Schedule Assessment, and Technology Readiness Assessment.

BEST VALUE   *Official:* The expected outcome of an acquisition that, in the government's estimation, provides the greatest overall benefit in response to the requirement. *Source:* FAR 2.101. This term was added to the FAR by FAC 97-02, Sept. 30, 1997, as part of the rewrite of FAR Part 15. While the above FAR definition appears to apply to all types of procurement, the term has traditionally been used to describe the TRADEOFF PROCESS that is used in the competitive negotiation process. See Nash, *Best Value: Does It Mean High Price?*, 24 N&CR ¶9 (Feb. 2010); Nash, *Best Value Procurement: A Flawed Process?*, 20 N&CR ¶34 (July 2006).

BEST VALUE CONTINUUM   A variety of techniques that can be used in conducting competitive procurement in accordance with the procedures in FAR Part 15. FAR 15.101 describes the "best value continuum" as any one or a combination of source selection approaches that are used to obtain BEST VALUE. Two specific techniques are described: (1) the TRADEOFF PROCESS, and (2) the LOWEST PRICE TECHNICALLY ACCEPTABLE source selection process. However, by describing these practices as a "continuum," the FAR gives contracting offices the authority to use other practices that meet the requirements of the procurement statutes. See Cibinic, Nash & Yukins, Formation of Government Contracts 676–86 (4th ed. 2011).

BETE.SAM.GOV   The GOVERNMENTWIDE POINT OF ENTRY (GPE) for federal government procurement opportunities over $25,000. See FAR 5.101(a). Opportunities are posted under "Contract Opportunities." Through this one portal vendors seeking federal markets for their products and services can search, monitor and retrieve opportunities solicited by the entire federal contracting community.

BIAS A prejudice that prevents fair consideration of an issue. Government decisions with regard to contractors are expected to be made with integrity, fairness, and openness. FAR 1.102-2(c)(3) requires that all contractors "be treated fairly and impartially but need not be treated the same." CONFLICT OF INTEREST is a key reason for findings of bias. See FAR 9.505. Agencies are also normally expected to write their WORK STATEMENTs to avoid bias, and contractors who assist in the creation of work statements are prohibited, absent limited circumstances, from supplying systems or services required by the statement. In PROTESTs strong evidence is required to prove biased decisionmaking in the source selection process. See Cibinic, Nash & Yukins FORMATION OF GOVERNMENT CONTRACTS 947–48 (4th ed. 2011). For discussion of an infamous case of bias involving a senior government official, Darlene Druyun, see *Lockheed Martin Aeronautics Co., L-3 Communications Integrated Systems L.P.*, Comp. Gen. Dec. B-295401, 2005 CPD ¶ 4 Johnson, *Needed: A Government Ethics Code and Culture Requiring Its Officials to Turn "Square Corners" When Dealing with Contractors*, 19 N&CR ¶ 47 (Oct. 2005); Branstetter, *Darlene Druyun: An Evolving Case Study in Corruption, Power, and Procurement*, 34 PUB. CONT. L.J. 443 (2005).

BIASED GROUND RULES A type of ORGANIZATIONAL CONFLICT OF INTEREST where an organization has participated substantially in the writing of a specification for a future procurement. FAR 9.505-2 states that contractors that prepare "complete specifications" for NONDEVELOPMENTAL ITEMS may not be allowed to furnish those items. This is one of the categories of OCIs that GAO has identified in its protest decisions.

BID *Official:* An OFFER submitted to the government in response to an INVITATION FOR BIDS (IFB) that, if accepted, would bind the BIDDER to perform the resultant contract. *Source:* FAR 2.101 (in the definition of OFFER). Bidders must be given a reasonable time (generally at least 30 days) to prepare and submit bids, consistent with the needs of the government. FAR 14.202-1. Bids must conform in all material respects to the IFB in order to be responsive (see RESPONSIVENESS) and thus eligible for award. See Cibinic, Nash & Yukins, FORMATION OF GOVERNMENT CONTRACTS 503 (4th ed. 2011). See also Edwards, *Postscript: Electronic Bids and Proposals*, 25 N&CR ¶ 28 (June 2011); Bezer, *The Inadequacy of Surety Bid Bonds in Public Construction Contracting*, 40 PUB. CONT. L.J. 87 (2010).

BID AND PROPOSAL (B&P) COSTS *Official:* The costs incurred in preparing, submitting, and supporting BIDs and PROPOSALs (whether or not solicited) on potential government or non-government contracts. The term does not include the costs of efforts sponsored by a GRANT or COOPERATIVE AGREEMENT, or required in the performance of a contract. *Source:* FAR 31.205-18. Generally discussed in conjunction with INDEPENDENT RESEARCH AND DEVELOPMENT (IR&D) costs, B&P costs receive extensive treatment as a SELECTED COST under FAR 31.205-18 and under CAS 420, Accounting for Independent Research and Development Costs and Bid Proposal Costs, 48 C.F.R. § 9904.420, which also provides criteria for the ALLOCATION of these costs to COST OBJECTIVEs. B&P costs are ALLOWABLE COSTs as indirect expenses to the extent they are ALLOCABLE and reasonable (see REASONABLENESS OF COST) except as provided otherwise in agency regulations (see, e.g., DEAR 970.3102-05-18). DOD is authorized to implement regulations limiting the allowability of B&P costs to work the Secretary of Defense determines is of potential interest to the DOD. 10 U.S.C. § 2372. See DFARS 231.205-18. See Cibinic, Knight & Nash, COST-REIMBURSEMENT CONTRACTING 645–55 (4th ed. 2014); Nash, *Bid and Proposal Costs: Are They Excessive?*, 31 N&CR ¶ 18 (Mar. 2017). Recovery of bid or proposal costs represents a potential monetary remedy for a successful protester before the GOVERNMENT ACCOUNTABILITY OFFICE (GAO) or the U.S. COURT OF FEDERAL CLAIMS. See 31 U.S.C. § 3554(c)(1)(B) for the authority of the GAO to award such costs. If the protester prevails in the protest action and had a substantial chance for award of the contract but does not receive the award, the protester may recover the costs of preparing the bid or proposal. Typically, however, the protest forums will not award bid or proposal costs if the successful protester gains the opportunity to compete for the procurement. See Cibinic, Nash & Yukins, FORMATION OF GOVERNMENT CONTRACTS 1744–46, 1794–97 (4th ed. 2011).

BID BOND   A BOND that serves as a BID GUARANTEE. Such bonds are used frequently in public construction projects and sometimes, but rarely, in nonconstruction contracts. Annual bid bonds are bonds that secure all nonconstruction contract bids during a specific fiscal year. FAR 28.001. Agencies may specify that only separate bid bonds are acceptable for construction projects. FAR 28.101-1(b). See Bezer, *The Inadequacy of Surety Bid Bonds in Public Construction Contracting*, 40 Pub. L. Cont. L.J. 87 (2010).

BID GUARANTEE   *Official:* A form of security assuring that the BIDDER (1) will not withdraw a BID within the period specified for acceptance and (2) will execute a written contract and furnish required BONDs, including any necessary coinsurance or reinsurance agreements, within the time specified in the bid, unless a longer time is allowed, after receipt of the specified forms. *Source:* FAR 28.001. FAR 28.101-1(a) permits the use of bid guarantees *only* when a PERFORMANCE BOND or a PAYMENT BOND is required. Such guarantees must be in an amount adequate to protect the government from loss and must be at least 20% of the bid price, but not more than $3 million. FAR 28.101-2(b). A bidder's failure to comply with bid guarantee requirements results in rejection of the bid unless narrow WAIVER exceptions apply. FAR 28.101-4. The Bid Guarantee solicitation provision at FAR 52.228-1 states that bid guarantees must be "in the form of a firm commitment, such as a bid bond, postal money order, certified check, or, under Treasury Department regulations, certain bonds or notes of the United States." See Cibinic, *Bid Bonds and Bid Guarantees: That Tail Is Still Wagging*, 16 N&CR ¶ 12 (Mar. 2002).

BID OPENING   The public opening of BIDs submitted to the government in a sealed bid procurement (see SEALED BIDDING). The INVITATION FOR BIDS specifies an exact date and time for opening of bids. When the set time arrives, the bid opening officer informs those present of that fact and then (1) personally and publicly opens all bids received before the set time, (2) if practical, reads the bids aloud to the persons present, and (3) has the bids recorded. FAR 14.402-1. However, the general public may not have access to the opening of classified bids (see CLASSIFIED ACQUISITION). FAR 14.402-2. Bid openings may be postponed if the CONTRACTING OFFICER has reason to believe that the bids of an important segment of bidders have been delayed for causes beyond the bidders' control, or in the case of an emergency or unanticipated event that interrupts normal government processes. FAR 14.402-3. Bids are recorded on an ABSTRACT OF OFFERS. See Cibinic, Nash & Yukins, FORMATION OF GOVERNMENT CONTRACTS 515–18 (4th ed. 2011).

BID PROTEST   See PROTEST.

BID SAMPLE   *Official:* A product sample required to be submitted by an offeror to show characteristics of the offered product that cannot adequately be described in SPECIFICATIONs, PURCHASE DESCRIPTIONs, or the solicitation (e.g., balance, facility of use, or pattern). *Source:* FAR 2.101. Bid samples are used only to determine the RESPONSIVENESS of the bid, not to determine a bidder's ability to produce the required items. They provide the government extra assurance that a bidder has submitted a bid that is responsive on its face can actually provide a product that meets the government's requirements. FAR 14.202-4(b) provides that the use of bid samples is appropriate for products that must be suitable from the standpoint of balance, facility of use, general feel, color, pattern, or other characteristic that cannot be described adequately in the specification. A standard Bid Samples solicitation provision to be used when bid samples are required is provided in FAR 52.214-20.

BIDDER *Official*: Any entity that is responding to a solicitation, including an offeror under a negotiated acquisition. *Source:* FAR 28.001. This is a generic definition used in FAR Part 28 with regard to bonds and insurance. A more accurate and limited definition is one who submits a BID on a sealed bid procurement (see SEALED BIDDING). However, the term is frequently used to refer to any offeror on a government procurement—whether sealed bid, competitive NEGOTIATION, or otherwise.

BIDDER (UNCITRAL) Persons or groups of persons who participate in the selection proceedings. This term includes those parties who have sought an invitation to take part in pre-selection proceedings and those who have submitted a proposal in response to a contracting authority's REQUEST FOR PROPOSAL. See *UNCITRAL, Model Legislative Provisions on Privately Financed Infrastructure Projects*, 6 (2004).

BIDDERS' CONFERENCE See PRE-BID CONFERENCE and PRE-PROPOSAL CONFERENCE.

BIDDERS MAILING LIST See SOLICITATION MAILING LIST.

BIDDING TIME The time allowed prospective BIDDERs to prepare and submit their BIDs—the time between SOLICITATION issuance and BID OPENING. All INVITATION FOR BIDS (IFBs) must allow a reasonable bidding time, consistent with the needs of the government; bidding time of at least 30 calendar days must be provided when a SYNOPSIS is required by the SMALL BUSINESS ACT, 15 U.S.C. § 637(e), and the OFFICE OF FEDERAL PROCUREMENT POLICY ACT, 41 U.S.C. § 1708. If bidding time were unduly limited, some potential sources might be precluded from bidding, and others might be forced to raise their bids by including amounts to cover otherwise avoidable contingencies. Thus, to avoid unduly restricting competition or paying higher than necessary prices, consideration must be given to the following factors in establishing a reasonable bidding time: (1) the degree of urgency, (2) the complexity of the requirement, (3) the anticipated extent of subcontracting, (4) whether a PRE-SOLICITATION NOTICE was issued, (5) the geographic distribution of bidders, and (6) normal transmittal time for both IFBs and bids. FAR 14.202-1; FAR 36.213-3 (construction contracts).

BIFURCATION OF ENTITLEMENT AND QUANTUM A distinction between the *right* to recover additional compensation under a contract and the *amount* of compensation to be recovered; the separation of issues of ENTITLEMENT (referring to whether a party prevails) and QUANTUM (referring to the amount a party recovers) in the hearing of a DISPUTE before a BOARD OF CONTRACT APPEALS (BCA). (The U.S. COURT OF FEDERAL CLAIMS does not follow this procedure.) BCAs generally prefer to hear only entitlement issues initially, assuming that, in most cases, the parties will be able to negotiate quantum successfully if the contractor is held to be entitled to compensation. The facts relating to entitlement are often simple, whereas the quantum issues may be complex; if the contractor fails to establish a right to recover, the BCA and the parties need not invest time and energy in calculating how much the contractor will *not* recover. Thus, prehearing instructions often explain that quantum will not be heard unless the BCA has expressly agreed to hear it, full cost, schedule and supporting information have been furnished, and the government has had an opportunity to conduct an AUDIT. When a case has been bifurcated and a contractor's claim to entitlement is sustained, the BCA remands the negotiation of quantum to the contracting officer and closes the file. If the parties fail to agree, the contractor must request a DECISION OF THE CONTRACTING OFFICER on quantum. Upon receipt of this decision, or after sufficient time passes for DEEMED DENIAL jurisdiction, the contractor can file a new notice of appeal with the BCA.

BILATERAL CONTRACT   A contract in which parties exchange promises to perform reciprocal obligations in the future. Except for contracts using SIMPLIFIED ACQUISITION PROCEDURES, where the contracting officer must decide whether to use a bilateral PURCHASE ORDER (see FAR 13.302), virtually all government contracts are bilateral contracts. Bilateral contracts are contrasted with UNILATERAL CONTRACTs. See Nash, *The Common Law of Contracts: It Sometimes Applies to Government Contract Disputes*, 22 N&CR ¶74 (Dec. 2008).

BILATERAL MODIFICATION   *Official:* A CONTRACT MODIFICATION that is signed by the contractor and the contracting officer. Bilateral modifications are used to (1) make negotiated equitable adjustments resulting from the issuance of a CHANGE ORDER, (2) definitize LETTER CONTRACTs, and (3) reflect other agreement of the parties modifying the terms of the contract. *Source:* FAR 43.103(a). See SUPPLEMENTAL AGREEMENT. The alternative to a bilateral modification is a UNILATERAL MODIFICATION. See Nash & Feldman, GOVERNMENT CONTRACT CHANGES, chap. 7 (3d ed. 2006–2020).

BILL OF LADING   *Official:* A transportation document used as a receipt of goods, as documentary evidence of title, for clearing customs, and generally used as a contract of carriage. (1) Commercial bill of lading (CBL), unlike the Government bill of lading, is not an accountable transportation document. (2) Government bill of lading (GBL) is an accountable transportation document, authorized and prepared by a Government official. *Source:* FAR 47.001. See also U.C.C. § 1-201(6). A bill of lading is the standard form of contract between a COMMON CARRIER and a party shipping goods. In government contracting this form of contract can be used by the government (a government bill of lading) or a contractor (a commercial bill of lading). Guidance on the use of bills of lading is found in FAR Part 47. FAR 9.403 provides that firms shipping goods for the government on either government or commercial bills of lading are contractors and are subject to DEBARMENT and SUSPENSION.

BILL OF MATERIALS   A list of the quantities of various materials required to produce a product. A bill of materials is the normal format used to summarize the material costs a contractor has included in its estimate of the contract price. Table 15-2 in FAR 15.408 calls for the submission of a bill of materials, including the source, quantity and price of each item, accompanying CERTIFIED COST OR PRICING DATA when it is required. See Cibinic, Nash & Yukins, FORMATION OF GOVERNMENT CONTRACTS 1502–04 (4th ed. 2011).

BILLING RATE   *Official:* An INDIRECT COST rate established temporarily for interim reimbursement of incurred indirect costs and adjusted as necessary pending establishment of a FINAL INDIRECT COST RATE. *Source:* FAR 42.701. The contracting officer establishes a billing rate on the basis of information resulting from recent review, previous AUDITs or experience, or similar reliable data or experience of other contracting activities. Once established, billing rates may be prospectively or retroactively revised by mutual agreement of the contracting officer or AUDITOR and the contractor, at either party's request, to prevent substantial overpayment or underpayment. The elements of indirect cost and the base used in computing billing rates must not be construed as determining either the indirect costs to be distributed or the bases for distribution in the final settlement. FAR 42.704. Billing rates and final indirect cost rates are used in reimbursing indirect costs under COST-REIMBURSEMENT CONTRACTs and in determining cost-based progress payments under FIXED-PRICE CONTRACTs. FAR 42.703-1. Manos, 2 GOVERNMENT CONTRACT COSTS AND PRICING § 86:15 (2d ed. 2009–2020).

BLACKLIST   See DE FACTO DEBARMENT.

BLANKET PURCHASE AGREEMENT (BPA)   *Official:* A simplified method of filling the government's anticipated repetitive needs for supplies or services by establishing charge accounts with qualified sources of supply. *Source:* FAR 13.303. BPAs are not contracts. BPAs are designed to reduce administrative costs in accomplishing SIMPLIFIED ACQUISITIONs by eliminating the need for individual purchase documents. BPAs must contain the following terms and conditions: (1) a description of the agreement, (2) the extent of obligation, (3) purchase limitation, which includes pricing, (4) notice of individuals authorized to purchase under the BPA, and dollar limitations by title of position and name, (5) delivery tickets, and (6) INVOICEs. FAR 13.303-3. Individual purchases under BPAs may not exceed the dollar limitation for simplified acquisitions, and the existence of a BPA does not justify sole source purchasing (see SOLE SOURCE). FAR 13.303-5. BPAs are also authorized for use with vendors that have products or services on a FEDERAL SUPPLY SCHEDULE. FAR 8.405-3. Such BPAs are designed to be a flexible and streamlined contracting mechanism for meeting repetitive procurement needs and require agencies to seek discounts. They are permitted to be with multiple sources or with a single source, may be used by multiple agencies, and may be for five years. They are required to be reviewed at least once a year to ensure that they will still result in BEST VALUE. FAR 8.405-3 also provides criteria for COMPETITIVE PROCEDURES, which varies depending on whether the supplies or services require a STATEMENT OF WORK or not. Within DOD, BPAs are issued on DD Form 1155, DFARS 213.203-1. See DOD PGI 208.405-70 for additional guidance for DOD schedule BPAs. See Nash, *BPAs or IDIQs: An Interesting Choice*, 24 N&CR ¶ 26 (June 2010); Nash, *Postscript II: Blanket Purchase Agreements*, 23 N&CR ¶ 64 (Dec. 2009).

BLENDED FEDERAL WORKFORCE   A workforce in a government office comprised of both government and contractor personnel. The workforce may be so situated that it is difficult to distinguish between the government and the contractor employees. Also referred to as "mixed workforce." A blended workforce can potentially create issues with respect to the proper roles of and the relationship between federal employees and contractors, especially regarding INHERENTLY GOVERNMENTAL FUNCTIONS. U.S. Gov't ACCOUNTABILITY OFFICE, OVERSIGHT PLAN NEEDED TO HELP IMPLEMENT ACQUISITION ADVISORY PANEL RECOMMENDATIONS, GAO-08-160 (Dec. 2007). See Schooner & Swan, *Suing the Government as a 'Joint Employer'—Evolving Pathologies of the Blended Workforce*, 52 Gov't Contractor ¶ 341 (2010); Edwards, *Contracting for Services: Challenges for the Next Generation*, 24 N&CR ¶ 59 (2010); Nash, *Postscript IV: Mixed Workforce Questions*, 22 N&CR ¶ 36

(2008); Edwards, *The Blended Workforce: Another Concern*, 21 N&CR ¶9 (2007); Nash, *Postscript II: Mixed Workforce Questions*, 21 N&CR ¶3 (2007); Thompson & Mastracci, *The Blended Workforce: Maximizing Agility Through Nonstandard Work Arrangements* (Apr. 2005).

BLIND OR SEVERELY DISABLED *Official:* **Blind** An individual or class of individuals whose central visual acuity does not exceed 20/200 in the better eye with correcting lenses or whose acuity, if better than 20/200, is accompanied by a limit to the field of vision in the better eye to such a degree that its widest diameter subtends an angle of no greater than 20 degrees. **Severely disabled** An individual or class of individuals with a physical or mental disability, other than blindness, which (according to criteria established by the Committee after consultation with appropriate entities of the Federal Government and taking into account the views of non-Federal Government entities representing the disabled) constitutes a substantial handicap to employment and is of a nature that prevents the individual from currently engaging in normal competitive employment. *Source:* 41 U.S.C. § 8501. The JAVITS-WAGNER-O'DAY ACT ("the JWOD Act"), 41 U.S.C. §§ 8501–8506, requires government entities to purchase certain supplies and services from JWOD PARTICIPATING NONPROFIT AGENCIES for people who are blind or severely disabled, if the supplies or services are available when required. FAR Subpart 8.7 prescribes policies and procedures for implementing the Act and the rules of the Committee for Purchase from People Who Are Blind or Severely Disabled. The central agency administering this program is ABILITY ONE. It publishes a PROCUREMENT LIST of all supplies and services required to be purchased from these agencies (http://www.abilityone.gov /index.html). Feldman, Government Contract Awards: Negotiation and Sealed Bidding § 3:25 (2019–2020 ed.).

BLOCK BUY CONTRACTING A technique that permits DOD to use a single contract for more than one year's worth of procurement of a given kind of item without having to exercise a contract option for each year after the first year. There is no permanent statute authorizing the use of this technique but DOD must obtain Congressional approval for its use. It is more flexible than the use of a MULTI-YEAR CONTRACT but has been used infrequently. See "Multiyear Procurement (MYP) and Block Buy Contracting in Defense Acquisition: Background and Issues for Congress" (R41909) (Mar. 17, 2020).

BOARD OF CONTRACT APPEALS (BCA) An administrative board established in a procuring agency to hear and decide DISPUTEs under the CONTRACT DISPUTES ACT (CDA) OF 1978. There are presently four BCAs. The CDA established the BCAs at 41 U.S.C. § 7105(c) and defined their jurisdiction over federal contract performance disputes at 41 U.S.C. § 7105(e)(1)(A)–(B). The BCAs resolve disputes, as distinguished from PROTEST actions, between the federal government and contractors. The ARMED SERVICES BOARD OF CONTRACT APPEALS is the largest BCA with 24 ADMINISTRATIVE JUDGEs. The second largest, the CIVILIAN AGENCY BOARD OF CONTRACT APPEALS, which hears appeals from the General Services Administration, and the Departments of Agriculture, Energy, Homeland Security, Housing and Urban Development, Interior, Labor, Transportation, and Veterans Affairs, has 14 administrative judges. The Postal Service and Tennessee Valley Authority have their own boards of contract appeals, and the Federal Aviation Administration resolves its contract disputes in its OFFICE OF DISPUTE RESOLUTION FOR ACQUISITION. The personnel, rules of procedure, and decisions of the BCAs are published in the *Contract Appeals Decisions Reporter*, CCH, 4025 Peterson

Ave., Chicago, IL 60646. See Cibinic, Nagle & Nash, ADMINISTRATION OF GOVERNMENT CONTRACTS 1319–22 (4th ed. 2006); Somers, *The Boards of Contract Appeals: A Historical Perspective*, 60 AMULR 745 (2011); Schaengold & Brams, *Choice of Forum for Government Contract Claims: Court of Federal Claims vs. Board of Contract Appeals*, 17 FED. CIR. B.J. 279 (2008); Schaengold & Brams, *A Guide to the Civilian Board of Contract Appeals*, BRIEFING PAPERS No. 07-8 (July 2007); McGovern III, Graham & Nibley, *A Level Playing Field: Why Congress Intended the Boards of Contract Appeals to Have Power Over Both Contractors and the Government*, 36 PUB. CONT. L.J. 495 (2007). See also APPEAL FROM A CONTRACTING OFFICER'S DECISION and APPEAL FROM THE RULING OF A COURT OR BOARD.

BOILERPLATE Standard contract language that is used by a party on all contracts of a certain type. This standardized language is generally relatively nonnegotiable. Black's Law Dictionary 216 (11th ed. 2019). In government procurement this term is generally used to describe the GENERAL PROVISIONS that are included in contracts pursuant to FAR Part 52.

BONA FIDE AGENCY *Official:* An established commercial or selling agency, maintained by a contractor for the purpose of securing business, that neither exerts nor proposes to exert IMPROPER INFLUENCE to solicit or obtain government contracts nor holds itself out as being able to obtain any government contract or contracts through improper influence. *Source:* FAR 3.401. Payments to such an agency are not improper under the contract provisions barring CONTINGENT FEEs. See Cibinic, Nash & Yukins, FORMATION OF GOVERNMENT CONTRACTS 176–78 (4th ed. 2011).

BONA FIDE EMPLOYEE *Official:* A person, employed by a contractor and subject to the contractor's supervision and control as to time, place, and manner of performance, who neither exerts nor proposes to exert improper influence to solicit or obtain government contracts nor holds out as being able to obtain any government contract or contracts through improper influence. *Source:* FAR 3.401. Payments to such employees are not improper under the contract provisions barring CONTINGENT FEEs. See Cibinic, Nash & Yukins, FORMATION OF GOVERNMENT CONTRACTS 176–78 (4th ed. 2011).

BONA FIDE NEEDS RULE A rule established in case law by the Comptroller General of the United States, based on statutory analysis, which holds that appropriated funds may be obligated only to meet a legitimate need arising in, or in some cases arising prior to but continuing to exist in, the fiscal year(s) for which the appropriation was made. This concept of this rule is codified in 31 U.S.C. § 1502(a). The bona fide needs rule applies to all government activity carried out with appropriated funds, including CONTRACTs, GRANTs, COOPERATIVE AGREEMENTs, and INDEFINITE DELIVERY CONTRACTS. A "bona fide need" depends largely on the facts and circumstances of the particular case. See GAO, PRINCIPLES OF FEDERAL APPROPRIATIONS LAW, chap. 5 (3d ed. 2004; Annual Update Mar. 2015); Cibinic, Nash & Yukins, FORMATION OF GOVERNMENT CONTRACTS 50–52 (4th ed. 2011); Nash, *Funding Overruns: The Evolving Bona Fide Needs Rule*, 23 N&CR ¶ 52 (Oct. 2009).

BOND *Official:* A written instrument executed by a BIDDER or contractor (the principal) and a second party (the SURETY or sureties) to assure fulfillment of the principal's obligations to a third party (the obligee or the government) identified in the bond. If the principal's obligations are not met, the bond assures payment, to the extent stipulated, of any loss sustained by the obligee. Types of bonds discussed in the FAR include: (1) ADVANCE PAYMENT bonds, which secure fulfillment of the contractor's obligations under an advance payment provision; (2) BID BONDs, a form of BID GUARANTEE ensuring that the bidder will not withdraw a bid within the period specified and will execute a written contract within the time specified in the bid; (3) PERFORMANCE BONDs, which secure performance and fulfillment of the contractor's obligations under the contract; (4) PATENT INFRINGEMENT bonds, which secure fulfillment of the contractor's obligations under a PATENT provision; and (5) PAYMENT BONDs, which ensure payments as required by law to all persons supplying LABOR or MATERIAL in the prosecution of the work required by the contract. *Source:* FAR 28.001. Mentioned but not discussed in the FAR are fidelity bonds, used for ensuring the faithful performance of employees to their employers and their employers' clients (e.g., to cover losses by theft or embezzlement).

BONDING COSTS   The cost incurred by a contractor when the government requires assurance against financial loss to itself or others stemming from an act or default of the contractor, or when the contractor requires similar assurance. Included are the costs of such BONDs as bid, performance, payment, ADVANCE PAYMENT, PATENT INFRINGEMENT, and fidelity bonds. Costs of bonding required by the terms of the contract are ALLOWABLE COSTs. FAR 31.205-4. See Manos, 1 GOVERNMENT CONTRACT COSTS & PRICING §§ 11:1–11:2 (2d ed. 2009–2020); Cibinic, Knight & Nash, COST-REIMBURSEMENT CONTRACTING 721 (4th ed. 2014). Costs of bonding required by the contractor in the general conduct of its business are allowable to the extent that (1) such bonding is in accordance with sound business practice and (2) the rates and premiums are reasonable under the circumstances.

BONUS   A payment of extra compensation to an employee. FAR 31.205-6(f) specifies when the costs of such payments by contractors may be treated as ALLOWABLE COSTs. See Manos, 1 GOVERNMENT CONTRACT COSTS & PRICING § 13.8 (2d ed. 2009–2020); Cibinic, Knight & Nash, COST-REIMBURSEMENT CONTRACTING 672 (4th ed. 2014).

BORROWER   *Official:* A contractor, subcontractor (at any tier), or other supplier who receives a GUARANTEED LOAN. *Source:* FAR 32.301. This is a narrow definition applied only when the government guarantees a loan pursuant to FAR Subpart 32.3. A more generic definition would be any recipient of a loan.

BRAND NAME DESCRIPTION   A PURCHASE DESCRIPTION or specification that calls for a particular brand-name product, or a feature of a product, that is peculiar to one manufacturer, and which does not permit the offer or delivery of an equal. See BRAND-NAME-OR-EQUAL DESCRIPTION. The use of such a specification is discouraged because it constitutes a SOLE SOURCE ACQUISITION. See FAR 11.105. FAR 6.302-1(c) provides guidance on the JUSTIFICATION AND APPROVAL for acquisitions using these descriptions.

BRAND-NAME-OR-EQUAL DESCRIPTION   A PURCHASE DESCRIPTION that identifies a product by its brand name and model or part number or other appropriate nomenclature by which it is offered for sale and permits offers on products essentially equal to the specified brand name product. A brand-name-or-equal description must include those salient physical, functional, or other characteristics of the brand name product that are deemed essential in meeting the government's needs. FAR 11.104(b). This is generally the minimum acceptable description in government contracting; prospective contractors must be allowed to offer products other than those named by brand if those other products will meet the needs of the government in essentially the same manner. This policy is incorporated in all construction contracts in paragraph (a) of the Material and Workmanship clause at FAR 52.236-5, which permits contractors to furnish equal items whenever an item is specified by trade name, make, or catalog number. Use of these descriptions provides for FULL AND OPEN COMPETITION and does not require JUSTIFICATION AND APPROVAL. FAR 6.302-1(c). See Cibinic, Nagle & Nash, ADMINISTRATION OF GOVERNMENT CONTRACTS 834–35 (5th ed. 2016); Edwards, *Postscript: A Case of Poor Draftsmanship*, 22 N&CR ¶ 10 (2008).

BREACH OF CONTRACT   Failure, without legal excuse, to perform any promise that forms the whole or part of a contract. Breach can be found of both express promises in a contract and IMPLIED PROMISEs that are inherent in the transaction. "Breach" also means the unequivocal, distinct, and absolute refusal to perform under the agreement. It may also entail the prevention or hindrance by a party to the contract of any occurrence or performance required under the contract for the creation or continuance of a right in favor of the other party or for the discharge of a duty by that party. Constructive breach, also known as an anticipatory breach, which entails the concept of REPUDIATION, takes place when a party disables itself from performance by some act or declares unequivocally, before the time of performance comes, that it does not intend to perform. BLACK'S LAW DICTIONARY 232 (11th ed. 2019). Traditionally, in government contract law, breach of contract by the government meant the government's failure to perform one of its contractual obligations that was not redressable under a contract clause (thus not a CONSTRUCTIVE CHANGE). Prior to the CONTRACT DISPUTES ACT OF 1978, appeals boards could not award damages for such breaches of contract. However, under the Act they now have the authority to award such damages. See Cibinic, Nagle & Nash, ADMINISTRATION OF GOVERNMENT CONTRACTS 1137 (5th ed. 2016). See also Nash, *Agreements to Agree: What Is a Breach?*, 21 N&CR ¶ 12 (Apr. 2007).

BREAK-EVEN ANALYSIS   The study of cost-volume-profit (C-V-P) relationships, or the analysis of proposed procurement and facilitization to compare potential costs of establishing a second source with potential savings due to competitive pressure from the second source. DAU GLOSSARY. Historically establishing a second source has led to lower prices in future procurements because of the continuing competition between the sources. Thus, when a procuring agency intends to procure a product over many years, it can justify a relatively high cost to establish the second source. Two ways to accomplish this are LEADER-COMPANY CONTRACTING and DIRECT LICENSEs. See Cafferky & Wentworth, BREAKEVEN ANALYSIS: THE DEFINITIVE GUIDE TO COST-VOLUME-PROFIT ANALYSIS (2010).

BREAK-EVEN POINT   In a business enterprise, the point at which revenues from sales exactly equal total INCURRED COST (revenues = variable costs + fixed costs). In decisionmaking (such as MAKE OR BUY), the point of indifference; that level of activity where either method results in exactly the same cost. These types of break-even decisions often involve making assumptions about levels of activity such as the number of units needed. DAU GLOSSARY. See BREAK-EVEN ANALYSIS.

BREAKOUT   A government decision to procure a component or part directly from its manufacturer rather than from a systems contractor. DAU GLOSSARY. DFARS 207.171 articulates DOD's policy for breaking out COMPONENTs during the manufacturing process (involving furnishing the components to the systems contractor as GOVERNMENT-FURNISHED MATERIAL); DOD PGI 217.7506 addresses breakout during the procurement of replenishment parts. The purpose of breakout is to acquire the components or parts at a reduced price by avoiding the need to pay a systems contractor's overhead and PROFIT when the contractor is not the actual manufacturer of the part or requiring competitive acquisition of a component previously purchased noncompetitively. Breakout is also loosely used to mean obtaining additional competition, especially from small businesses. See FAR 19.403. See also BREAKOUT ADVOCATE.

BREAKOUT ADVOCATE   An employee of the SMALL BUSINESS ADMINISTRATION specifically assigned the task of seeking opportunities to reduce government expenditures by using BREAKOUT. Section 403 of Pub. L. No. 98-577 requires the SBA to assign breakout advocates called breakout PROCUREMENT CENTER REPRESENTATIVEs to each major procurement center. Breakout PCRs advocate COMPETITION by identifying items being procured on a sole source basis (see SOLE SOURCE) and the factors that prevent competitive procurement of those items. In other words, breakout PCRs advocate breaking the item out for competition and encourage small business concerns to participate in future competitive procurements for those items. See FAR 19.403.

BRIBERY   The crime of offering, giving, receiving, or soliciting anything of value to influence action as an official or in discharge of a public duty. 18 U.S.C. § 201 makes bribery a criminal offense on the part of "any officer or employee or person acting for or on behalf of the United States, or any department or agency or branch of government thereof, . . . in any official function." See Cibinic, Nash & Yukins, FORMATION OF GOVERNMENT CONTRACTS 148–51 (4th ed. 2011); Cibinic, Nagle & Nash, ADMINISTRATION OF GOVERNMENT CONTRACTS 83–85 (5th ed. 2016). See also Tillipman & Mahini, *Government Lawyering*, BRIEFING PAPERS No. 11-3 (Feb. 2011); Kathuria, *Best Practices for Compliance with the New Government Contractor Compliance and Ethics Rules Under the Federal Acquisition Regulation*, 38 PUB. CONT. L.J. 803 (2009); Tillipman, *Foreign Corrupt Practices Act Fundamentals*, BRIEFING PAPERS No. 08-10 (Sept. 2008).

BRIDGE CONTRACT   A contract extension, typically through a MODIFICATION of an existing contract. A bridge contract with the incumbent contractor is often required when, for example, a BID PROTEST or disappointed-offeror suit results in a STAY of the award or performance of the follow-on contract. Bridge contracts may be awarded noncompetitively in certain circumstances, particularly when they fall between two competitively awarded contracts, when the bridge contract is necessary to avoid disruption of necessary services, and the bridge contract was not necessitated because of the lack of advance planning.

BROAD AGENCY ANNOUNCEMENT (BAA)   *Official:* A general announcement of an agency's RESEARCH interest including criteria for selecting proposals and soliciting the participation of all offerors capable of satisfying the government's needs. *Source:* FAR 2.101. Under 10 U.S.C. § 2302(2) and 41 U.S.C. § 152 the solicitation of research proposals through BAAs is one of the COMPETITIVE PROCEDURES meeting the statutory requirement for FULL AND OPEN COMPETITION. However, BAAs may be used only when meaningful proposals with varying scientific or technical approaches can reasonably be expected. BAAs should (1) describe the agency's research interest; (2) describe the criteria for selecting the proposals, their RELATIVE IMPORTANCE, and the method of evaluation; (3) specify the period of time during which proposals will be accepted; and (4) contain instructions for the preparation and submission of proposals. Proposals are evaluated by PEER OR SCIENTIFIC REVIEW. The primary bases for award are technical excellence, importance to agency programs, and fund availability. FAR 35.016. Contracts are awarded until the agency has utilized its research funds in the area of interest. See Cibinic, Nash & Yukins, FORMATION OF GOVERNMENT CONTRACTS 1083–91 (4th ed. 2011). See also RESEARCH AND DEVELOPMENT.

BROOKS ACT (ARCHITECT-ENGINEER PROCUREMENTS)   A 1972 Act, 40 U.S.C. § 1101 et seq., requiring the use of special procedures to procure ARCHITECT-ENGINEER (A-E) SERVICES. The procedures to be followed are set forth in FAR Subpart 36.6. They call for the selection of A-Es based on qualifications (as stated in Standard Form 330, Architect-Engineer Qualifications, FAR 53.301-330 and assessed during discussions) without evaluation of the proposed price for the work to be accomplished. Contract negotiations must be conducted with the highest-ranked offeror, and award must be made to that firm unless a reasonable price cannot be agreed upon. See Cibinic, Nash & Yukins, FORMATION OF GOVERNMENT CONTRACTS 1059–75 (4th ed. 2011).

BUDGET AUTHORITY   *Official:* The authority provided by federal law to incur financial obligations, as follows: (i) provisions of law that make funds available for OBLIGATION and expenditure (other than borrowing authority), including the authority to obligate and expend the proceeds of offsetting receipts and collections; (ii) borrowing authority, which means authority granted to a Federal entity to borrow and obligate and expend the borrowed funds, including through the issuance of promissory notes or other monetary credits; (iii) contract authority, which means the making of funds available for obligation but not for expenditure; and (iv) offsetting receipts and collections as negative budget authority, and the reduction thereof as positive budget authority. *Source:* 2 U.S.C. § 622(2). Budget authority is that authority required to enter into a binding obligation in accordance with the ANTI-DEFICIENCY ACT. With regard to government contracts, budget authority is conferred by the enactment of (1) an APPROPRIATION act or (2) a statute conferring CONTRACT AUTHORITY. See Cibinic, Nash & Yukins, FORMATION OF GOVERNMENT CONTRACTS 41 (4th ed. 2011). See also Solomsom, Miller & Demory, *Fiscal Matters: An Introduction to Federal Fiscal Law and Principles*, BRIEFING PAPERS No. 10-7 (June 2010).

BUDGET ENFORCEMENT ACT OF 1990 (BEA)   Pub. L. No. 101-508, title XII, 104 Stat. 1388-573. A law designed to limit discretionary spending while ensuring that any new entitlement program or tax cuts did not make the federal budget deficit (when spending exceeds revenues) worse. The law set annual limits on total discretionary spending and created pay-as-you-go rules for any changes, such as increases in entitlements or decreases in taxes. The pay-as-you-go rules required that new spending proposals or suggested tax reductions had to be offset by cuts in other entitlements or by other tax increases.

BUDGETING AND FUNDING   A required element of the Plan of Action in the written ACQUISITION PLAN which describes how budget estimates for the procurement were derived and discusses the schedule for obtaining adequate funds at the time they are required. FAR 7.105(b)(6). Generally, the ANTI-DEFICIENCY ACT, 31 U.S.C. § 1341, requires that contracts be fully funded. Under MULTIPLE YEAR CONTRACTs, INCREMENTALLY FUNDED CONTRACTs, and contracts conditioned on the availability of funds, however, contracts can be awarded without full funds.

BUILDING   *Official:* Construction activity as distinguished from manufacturing, furnishing of materials, or servicing and maintenance work. The term includes, without limitation, buildings, structures, and improvements of all types, such as bridges, dams, plants, highways, parkways, streets, subways, tunnels, sewers, mains, power lines, pumping stations, heavy generators, railways, airports, terminals, docks, piers, wharves, ways, lighthouses, buoys, jetties, breakwaters, levees, canals, dredging, shoring, rehabilitation and reactivation of plants, scaffolding, drilling, blasting, excavating, clearing, and landscaping. The manufacture or furnishing of materials, articles, supplies, or equipment (whether or not a Federal or State agency acquires title to such materials, articles, supplies, or equipment during the course of the manufacture or furnishing, or owns the materials from which they are manufactured or furnished) is not "building" within the meaning of this definition unless, conducted in connection with, and at the site of such building as is described in the foregoing sentence, or under the United States Housing Act of 1937 and the Housing Act of 1949 in the construction or development of the project. *Source:* FAR 2.101. Contracting for building-type work is called CONSTRUCTION and is subject to the DAVIS-BACON ACT and the procedures in FAR Part 36.

BULK FUNDING   *Official:* A system whereby the contracting officer receives authorization from a fiscal and accounting officer to obligate funds on purchase documents, against a specified lump sum of funds reserved for the purpose for a specified period of time rather than obtaining individual obligational authority on each purchase document. *Source:* FAR 13.101(b)(4). It is particularly appropriate if numerous purchases using the same type of funds are to be made during a given period. Agencies are required to use bulk funding to the maximum extent practicable to increase the efficiency of SIMPLIFIED ACQUISITION PROCEDURES. FAR 13.101(b)(4).

BUNDLING   *Official:* (1) A subset of consolidation that combines two or more requirements for SUPPLIES or SERVICES, previously provided or performed under separate smaller contracts, into a solicitation for a single contract, a multiple-award contract, or a task or delivery order that is likely to be unsuitable for award to a SMALL BUSINESS CONCERN (even if it is suitable for award to a small business with a Small Business Teaming Arrangement) due to—(i) The diversity, size, or specialized nature of the elements of the performance specified; (ii) The aggregate dollar value of the anticipated award; (iii) The geographical dispersion of the contract performance sites; or (iv) Any combination of the factors described in paragraphs (1)(i), (ii), and (iii) of this definition. (2) "Separate smaller contract" as used in this definition, means a contract that has been performed by one or more small business concerns or that was suitable for award to one or more small business concerns. (3) This definition does not apply to a contract that will be awarded and performed entirely outside of the United States. *Source:* FAR 2.101. Section 413 of the Small Business Reauthorization Act of 1997, Pub. L. No. 105-135, 111 Stat. 2592 (codified as amended at 15 U.S.C. § 644(e)) requires the head of the agency to conduct MARKET RESEARCH before proceeding with an ACQUISITION STRATEGY that could lead to bundling of contract requirements. 15 U.S.C. § 644(a) & (e) and FAR 7.104(d) require bundling to be addressed during ACQUISITION PLANNING and require coordination with small business specialists prior to bundling of contracts over stated dollar thresholds. In addition, FAR 7.107-3 precludes bundling unless "measurable substantial benefits" are obtained (defined as a savings of 10% on contracts of $94 million or less and 5% on contracts over $94 million). See Feldman, GOVERNMENT CONTRACT GUIDEBOOK, § 8:14 (4th ed. 2019–2020).

BURDEN OF PROOF   The obligation of a litigant to prove its allegations, such as the allegation in a CLAIM that an act of the government caused an increase in the contractor's costs. It includes (1) the burden of producing enough evidence to enable a judge or jury to determine the facts (the burden of production) and (2) the burden of persuading the judge or jury to determine the facts in a way that favors the party making the allegation (the burden of persuasion). When one side of an issue makes a prime facie case in support of its allegation, the burden of proof is said to shift to the other side. *Source:* BLACK'S LAW DICTIONARY 244 (11th ed. 2019). See Cibinic, Nagle & Nash, ADMINISTRATION OF GOVERNMENT CONTRACTS 619–28 (5th ed. 2016). See also Cibinic, *Cost Issues: Who Has the Burden of Proof?*, 17 N&CR ¶ 54 (Oct. 2003); Terrence, Rosenthal & Alter, *Clear & Convincing to Whom? The False Claims Act & Its Burden of Proof Standard: Why the Government Needs a Big Stick*, 75 NOTRE DAME L. REV. 1405 (May 2000). See STANDARD OF PROOF.

BUREAU OF STANDARDS   See NATIONAL INSTITUTE OF STANDARDS AND TECHNOLOGY.

BUSINESS CASE 1.   An analysis of the factors affecting and affected by a capital investment or other acquisition decision. Such factors could include cost/benefit, cash flow, and cost and schedule risk. Business case analysis is intended to determine a best-value solution for product support. DAU GLOSSARY. **2.**   A document containing a report of a business case analysis. See OMB, *OMB Circular A-11, Planning, Budgeting, Acquisition and Management of Capital Assets* (June 2006); Schmidt, *Business Case Essentials: A Guide to Structure and Content*, Revised October 2005, available from Solution Matrix Ltd., http://www.solution matrix.com; U.S. GOV'T ACCOUNTABILITY OFFICE, NASA'S SPACE VISION: BUSINESS CASE FOR PROMETHEUS 1 NEEDED TO ENSURE REQUIREMENTS MATCH AVAILABLE RESOURCES, GAO-05-242 (Feb. 2005).

BUSINESS CASE ANALYSIS   See BUSINESS CASE.

BUSINESS CLEARANCE MEMORANDUM (BCM)   A memorandum that documents the rationale for a decision concerning a NEGOTIATED CONTRACT, such as a PRENEGOTIATION OBJECTIVE, a COMPETITIVE RANGE DETERMINATION, a contractor selection, or a price agreement. The purpose of the BCM is to show that a prospective business decision represents good business judgment and that it conforms to federal or agency acquisition policies, and to seek higher-level approval of the decision. The term is not used by all agencies. Some agencies may refer to a BCM as a PRENEGOTIATION OBJECTIVE memorandum, a SOURCE SELECTION decision memorandum, or a similar name. See, e.g., *Navy Marine Corps Acquisition Guide* G5215.406-90, Nov. 2003 (Rev. Dec. 14, 2006). See FAR 15.406-1 requiring that contracting officers establish "prenegotiation objectives" and FAR 15.406-3 requiring the preparation of a PRICE NEGOTIATION MEMORANDUM.

BUSINESS COMBINATION   The legal bringing together under common control of a corporation and one or more incorporated or unincorporated firms, generally into a single organization. The single organization carries on the activities of the previously separate, independent enterprises. There are two basic approaches to obtaining control over assets owned and used by other firms. The acquiring firm may buy the desired assets and thereby obtain title to their use directly, or it may obtain an ownership interest in the common stock of another company, enabling the acquiring firm to exercise indirect control over the other firm's assets. The two basic approaches can be adopted in various forms: (1) acquisition of assets, (2) acquisition of stock, (3) statutory merger, (4) statutory consolidation. There are two methods of accounting for a business combination: the purchase method and the pooling-of-interest method. All business combinations initiated after June 30, 2001 must be accounted for using the purchase method. Any excess in fair value of assets and liabilities assumed and the amount paid is GOODWILL and an UNALLOWABLE COST. *DCAA Selected Area of Cost Guidebook*, chap. 8. FAR 31.205-52 limits the allowability of AMORTIZATION, cost of money (see COST OF MONEY FACTORS), and DEPRECIATION when the purchase method is used. See ALLOWABLE COST. FAR Subpart 42.12 contains procedures for recognizing business combinations by processing CHANGE OF NAME AGREEMENTs or NOVATIONs. See McGladrey & Pullen, LLP, A Guide to Accounting for Business Combinations (2d ed. 2012); Deloitte LLP, A Roadmap to Accounting for Business Combinations and Related Topics (Updated Dec. 2009); Dover, Horan, Jr. & Overman, *Mergers & Acquisitions—Special Issues When Purchasing Government Contractor Entities/Edition II*, Briefing Papers No. 09-7 (June 2009); Dover, *Mergers & Acquisitions—Special Issues When Purchasing Government Contractor Entities*, Briefing Papers No. 04-8 (July 2004).

BUSINESS UNIT   *Official:* Any SEGMENT of an organization, or an entire business organization, that is not divided into segments. *Source:* FAR 2.101. To ensure consistency and efficiency, single OVERHEAD RATEs must be established for all contracts held by a contractor business unit. FAR 42.703. This is accomplished by designating a single contracting agency to negotiate or determine such rates. CAS 410, Allocation of Business Unit General and Administrative Expenses to Final Cost Objectives, 48 C.F.R. § 9904-410, requires a business unit's GENERAL AND ADMINISTRATIVE EXPENSE to be grouped in a separate INDIRECT COST POOL that will be allocated only to its final COST OBJECTIVEs.

BUY AMERICAN ACT   An Act, 41 U.S.C. §§ 8301–05, formerly 41 U.S.C. §§ 10a–10d, originally enacted in 1933, that generally requires that only DOMESTIC END PRODUCTs may be procured in purchasing supplies and CONSTRUCTION MATERIALS for public use in contracts over the MICRO-PURCHASE threshold, unless the items (1) are for use outside the United States, (2) would be unreasonable in cost, or (3) are not mined, produced, or manufactured domestically in sufficient and reasonably available commercial quantities of satisfactory quality. Additional exemptions include information technology that is a commercial item, items purchased for commissary resale and items for which the HEAD OF THE AGENCY determines that domestic preference would be inconsistent with the public interest. FAR 25.103. The FAR contains separate regulations for supplies (FAR Subpart 25.1) and construction materials (FAR Subpart 25.2). With regard to supplies, it provides a preference evaluation system for domestic end products over foreign end products as defined in FAR 25.101. Foreign offers are evaluated by including duty, whether or not actually paid, and adding 6% to the total (or 12% if the domestic offeror is a SMALL BUSINESS CONCERN). When they exceed these margins, domestic prices are deemed unreasonable and competing foreign offers may be accepted. FAR 25.105. FAR 25.104 lists approximately 100 articles, materials, and supplies excepted from application of the Buy American Act. DOD has also created exceptions to the Act by negotiating memoranda of understanding with foreign governments. DFARS 225.802, DOD PGI 225.802(b). Agencies are required to submit annual reports to Congress on their purchases of non-domestic articles and all waivers to the Buy American Act. 41 U.S.C. § 8302(b). The Buy American Act does not apply to products covered by the TRADE AGREEMENTS ACT, NORTH AMERICAN FREE TRADE AGREEMENTS ACT, or other free trade agreements acts. FAR 25.402. See Feldman, Government Contract Guidebook, § 8:31 (4th ed. 2019–2020). See also Briggerman, *Buy American Requirements Under the Recovery*

Act: The Final Rules, 25 N&CR ¶1 (Jan. 2011); Osei, *The Best of Both Worlds: Reciprocal Preference and Punitive Retaliation in Public Contracts*, 40 PUB. CONT. L.J. 715 (2011); Belkin & Brown, *The Buy American Act Information Technology Exception: Should It Apply to the Trade Agreement Act-Covered Contracts?*, 24 No. 6 WESTLAW J. GOV'T CONT. 3 (2010); Luckey, CONG. RESEARCH SERV., Report No. 7-5700, THE BUY AMERICAN ACT: REQUIRING GOVERNMENT PROCUREMENTS TO COME FROM DOMESTIC SOURCES (Mar. 13, 2009); Kessler, *Protection and Protectionism: The Practicalities of Offshore Software Development in Government Procurement*, 38 PUB. CONT. L.J. 1 (2008).

BUY INDIAN ACT   An Act, 25 U.S.C. § 47, authorizing the Secretary of the Interior to SET ASIDE procurements for Indian-owned and controlled enterprises. In 1976, the Bureau of Indian Affairs formally adopted the policy that purchases and contracts be made with qualified Indian contractors to the maximum practicable extent. Buy Indian procurements are conducted in much the same way as other procurements, the primary difference being that only Indian-owned or controlled enterprises are eligible for award. See Feldman, GOVERNMENT CONTRACT AWARDS: NEGOTIATION AND SEALED BIDDING § 18:31 (2019–2020 ed.).

BUY ITEM   An item or work effort to be produced or performed by a firm other than the CONTRACTOR. Such items are reviewed by the contracting officer when FAR 15.407-2 requires review of a contractor's MAKE-OR-BUY PROGRAM. See also MAKE ITEM.

BUYING-IN   *Official:* Submitting an OFFER below anticipated costs, expecting to (1) increase the contract amount after award (e.g., through unnecessary or excessively priced change orders); or (2) receive FOLLOW-ON CONTRACTs at artificially high prices to recover LOSSes incurred on the buy-in contract. *Source:* FAR 3.501-1. Because buying-in may decrease competition or result in poor contract performance, the contracting officer is directed to take "appropriate action" to ensure that losses are not recovered by the contractor. FAR 3.501-2. This can be accomplished by seeking a price commitment covering as much of the program as is practical by using MULTIYEAR CONTRACTING or priced OPTIONs for additional quantities that, together with the firm contract quantity, equal the program requirements. The government can also employ other safeguards, such as amortizing NONRECURRING COSTS or determining that the offered price is unreasonable. See Feldman, GOVERNMENT CONTRACT AWARDS: NEGOTIATION AND SEALED BIDDING §§ 3:73–3:74 (2019–2020 ed.); Cibinic, Nagle & Nash, ADMINISTRATION OF GOVERNMENT CONTRACTS 142 (5th ed. 2016). See also Nash, *Postscript II: Buying-In as Fraud*, 21 N&CR ¶67 (2007).

BYRD AMENDMENT   A provision in the Department of the Interior Appropriations Act for FY 1990, Pub. L. No. 101-121, 31 U.S.C. § 1352, that imposes lobbying restrictions on all government contractors. These restrictions, which became effective in December 1989, prohibit recipients of appropriated federal funds (that is, recipients of contracts, GRANTs, loans, or COOPERATIVE AGREEMENTs) from using those funds to pay persons to attempt to influence members of Congress or their staffs or members of the executive branch in connection with the award, extension, or MODIFICATION of a contract, grant, or other funding instrument. The provisions, which flow down to subcontracts exceeding $100,000 regardless of tier, carry civil penalties of $10,000 to $100,000. This act is implemented by FAR Subpart 3.8, which requires the use of the solicitation provision Certification and Disclosure Regarding Payments to Influence Certain Federal Transactions in FAR 52.203-11 in all solicitations for contracts exceeding the SIMPLIFIED ACQUISITION THRESHOLD.

C

CABLE TELEVISION FRANCHISE AGREEMENTS   See FRANCHISE AGREEMENTS.

CAD/CAM   Software computer programs that integrate COMPUTER-AIDED DESIGN with COMPUTER-AIDED MANUFACTURING to enable the manufacture of a product by feeding digital design information directly into manufacturing equipment controlled by computers. See www.compinfo-center.com/cad/cam.htm.

CALS   See CONTINUOUS ACQUISITION AND LI

FE-CYCLE SUPPORT.

CANCELLATION   *Official:* The cancellation (within a contractually specified time) of the total requirements of all remaining program years. Cancellation results when the contracting officer (1) Notifies the contractor of nonavailability of funds for contract performance for any subsequent program year, or (2) Fails to notify the contractor that funds are available for performance of the succeeding program year requirement. *Source:* FAR 17.103. This term is used in conjunction with MULTIYEAR CONTRACTs and describes the government rights in such contracts. Such cancellation permits the contractor to recover costs in accordance with the Cancellation of Items clause in FAR 52.217-2, up to the amount of the CANCELLATION CEILING. See Cibinic, Nash & Yukins, FORMATION OF GOVERNMENT CONTRACTS 1380–86 (4th ed. 2011).

CANCELLATION CEILING   *Official:* The maximum cancellation charge that the contractor can receive in the event of cancellation. *Source:* FAR 17.103. This amount is included in a MULTIYEAR CONTRACT. See CANCELLATION. Under 10 U.S.C. § 2306b(c), both RECURRING COSTS and NONRECURRING COSTS may be included in this ceiling. However, recurring costs are only included in the cancellation ceiling when approved by the HEAD OF THE AGENCY. FAR 17.106-3. 41 U.S.C. § 3903 permits the civilian agencies to use multiyear contracts but contains no guidance on the costs to be included in cancellation ceilings. FAR 17.106-1(c) provides that the contracting officer will establish a cancellation ceiling, in diminishing amounts, for each program year and that it will include a reasonable estimate of the nonrecurring costs that will not have been recovered if the contract is canceled. The amount that is actually paid to the contractor upon settlement for unrecovered costs (which cannot exceed the ceiling) is referred to as the cancellation charge. See Cibinic, Nash & Yukins, FORMATION OF GOVERNMENT CONTRACTS 1380–86 (4th ed. 2011).

CANCELLATION OF CONTRACT   Notification to a contractor that the government considers the contract null and void and will not be bound by its terms. Cancellation is generally proper only when the contractor has violated a criminal statute or committed some other gross impropriety. *United States v. Mississippi Valley Generating Co.*, 364 U.S. 520 (1961). Cancellation for BRIBERY, gratuities (see GRATUITY), or CONFLICT OF INTEREST is permitted by 18 U.S.C. § 218. See FAR Subpart 3.7. See AVOIDANCE OF CONTRACT.

CANCELLATION OF SOLICITATION   Notification to potential offerors, before AWARD, that a procurement will be permanently or temporarily stopped. Cancellation of an INVITATION FOR BIDS (IFB) involves a loss of time, effort, and money spent by the government and bidders. Therefore, IFBs should not be canceled unless cancellation is clearly in the public interest (for instance, when the supplies or services are no longer required or when amendments to the IFB would be of such magnitude that a new IFB is desirable). FAR 14.209. When an IFB is canceled, bids that have been received must be returned unopened to the bidders and a notice of cancellation must be sent to all prospective bidders to which IFBs were issued. For bids received electronically, the data received must not be viewed and must be purged from primary and backup storage systems. Cancellation of IFBs after BID OPENING is to be avoided even more than cancellation before bid opening because at that time all of the bids have been exposed. Therefore, FAR 14.404-1 prohibits cancellation after bid opening unless there is a compelling reason to reject all bids and cancel the invitation. See Cibinic, Nash & Yukins, FORMATION OF GOVERNMENT CONTRACTS 741–45 (4th ed. 2011). With regard to competitive proposals solicited in contracting by NEGOTIATION, the contracting officer is to cancel the original REQUEST FOR PROPOSALS (RFPs) and issue a new one, regardless of the stage of the acquisition, if a change is so substantial that it warrants complete revision of the RFP. FAR 15.206(e).

CAPABILITY   The ability of a prospective contractor to perform a contract. In procurement using SEALED BIDDING, capability is assessed by making a RESPONSIBILITY determination. In procurement using COMPETITIVE NEGOTIATION, capability is assessed by using one or more capability EVALUATION FACTORs as well as making a responsibility determination.

CAPABILITY FACTORS   In SOURCE SELECTION, evaluation factors that bear on the offerors' relative ability to perform the contract. Such factors include experience, past performance, qualifications of proposed key personnel, facilities, and understanding of the work. Such factors are used to determine relative degrees of capability in order to compare offerors to each other, and must be distinguished from responsibility factors used on a pass/fail basis to determine if an offeror is a RESPONSIBLE PROSPECTIVE CONTRACTOR. See Cibinic, Nash & Yukins, FORMATION OF GOVERNMENT CONTRACTS 701–16 (4th ed. 2011).

CAPABILITY OR PERFORMANCE   One of eight required elements of the Acquisition Background and Objectives in the written ACQUISITION PLAN prepared by the contracting agency. FAR 7.105(a)(4) provides that the acquisition should specify the required capabilities or performance characteristics of the supplies or services being acquired and state how they are related to the need. The requirement for a specific statement of the key performance characteristics of the proposed acquisition should assist the agency in identifying restrictive provisions in the STATEMENT OF WORK that may preclude potential contractors from participating in the procurement. When such provisions are identified, an agency can address options to eliminate them.

CAPITAL ASSET   An ASSET of a contractor that has been capitalized. With regard to contractor assets, see CAPITALIZATION and TANGIBLE CAPITAL ASSET. With regard to government assets, this term means land, structures, equipment, and intellectual property (including software) that are used by the federal government and have an estimated useful life of two years or more. Capital assets include leasehold improvements and lease rights, assets owned by the federal government but located in a foreign country, and assets whose ownership is shared by the federal government with other entities. Capital assets include all additions, improvements, replacements, rearrangements, reinstallations, and major repairs made to the asset. The cost of a capital asset includes both its purchase price and all other costs incurred to bring it to a form and location suitable for its intended use. CAS 417, Cost of Money as an Element of the Cost of Capital Assets Under Construction, 48 C.F.R. § 9904.417-20, establishes criteria for measuring the cost of money attributable to capital assets under construction, fabrication, or development as an element of the cost of those assets.

CAPITAL INVESTMENTS   The amount of funds a contractor has invested in FACILITIES and equipment that contributes to efficient and economic contract performance. Capital investments are one of the six factors agencies must consider in developing their PROFIT OBJECTIVE when they use the structured approach to profit determination, and contracting officers must also consider them in analyzing profit whether or not they are using a structured approach. FAR 15.404-4(d). The agencies have developed various systems for determining the amount of profit that should be attributed to capital investments. See NFS 18-15.970-2 and GSAR 515.905-1(c)(4). DOD has a rather precise mathematical method which gives far greater weight to this segment of the profit objective. See DFARS 215.404-71-4. See Cibinic, Nash & Yukins, FORMATION OF GOVERNMENT CONTRACTS 1555–60 (4th ed. 2011).

CAPITALIZATION   Setting up expenditures as ASSETs rather than treating them as current expenses. General accounting practices require contractors to capitalize the costs of tangible assets when they exceed predetermined amounts. CAS 404, 48 C.F.R. § 9904.404, sets forth principles governing such capitalization. Once assets are capitalized, their cost is charged to contracts through DEPRECIATION. See Cibinic, Knight & Nash, COST-REIMBURSEMENT CONTRACTING 709 (4th ed. 2014).

CARDINAL CHANGE   An order directing a contractor to perform additional work that is not a CHANGE because it is beyond the SCOPE OF THE CONTRACT and, thus, cannot be ordered legally by the contracting officer under the contract's Changes clause. Cardinal changes are BREACHES OF CONTRACT. In determining whether a change is beyond the scope of the contract, courts and boards compare the total work performed by the contractor with the work called for by the original contract. Work lies within the scope of contract if it can fairly and reasonably be regarded as within the contemplation of the parties when the contract was entered into or if it is essentially the same work that the parties bargained for when the contract was awarded. See Nash & Feldman, 1 GOVERNMENT CONTRACT CHANGES §§ 4:2–4:9 (3d ed. 2006–2020); Cibinic, Nagle & Nash, ADMINISTRATION OF GOVERNMENT CONTRACTS 345–49 (5th ed. 2016). See also Backus, *The Cumulative Impact Claim: Where Do We Stand in 2010?*, 77 DEF. COUNS. J. 206 (Apr. 2010).

CARGO PREFERENCE ACTS   Acts giving preference to U.S.-owned vessels in the shipment of work under government contracts. See FAR Subpart 47.5. The Cargo Preference Act of

1904, 10 U.S.C. § 2631, requires that DOD use only U.S.-FLAG VESSELs for ocean transportation of supplies for the Army, Navy, Air Force, or Marine Corps, unless those vessels are not available at fair and reasonable rates. Under the Cargo Preference Act of 1954, 46 U.S.C. § 1241(b), government agencies acquiring supplies that require ocean transportation must ensure that at least 50% of the gross tonnage of the supplies is transported in privately-owned U.S.-flag commercial vessels, to the extent that such vessels are available at fair and reasonable rates. This Act may be temporarily waived when the Congress, the President, or the Secretary of Defense declares the existence of an emergency that justifies a temporary waiver. 46 U.S.C. § 1241(c)(1). When this Act is applicable, the clause at FAR 52.247-64 is used. See Bloom, *The Cargo Preference Act of 1954 and Related Legislation*, 39 J. Mar. L. & Com. 289 (2008).

CARIBBEAN BASIN COUNTRY   *Official:* Any of the following countries: Antigua and Barbuda, Aruba, Bahamas, Barbados, Belize, Bonaire, British Virgin Islands, Curacao, Dominica, Grenada, Guyana, Haiti, Jamaica, Montserrat, Saba, St. Kitts and Nevis, St. Lucia, St. Vincent and the Grenadines, Sint Eustatius, Sint Maarten, or Trinidad and Tobago. *Source:* FAR 25.003.

CARIBBEAN BASIN COUNTRY END PRODUCT   *Official:* An article that—(i)(A) is wholly the growth, product, or manufacture of a Caribbean Basin country, or (B) in the case of an article consisting in whole or in part of materials from another country, has been substantially transformed in a Caribbean Basin country into a new and different article of commerce with a name, character, or use distinct from that of the article or articles from which it was transformed, and (ii) is not excluded from duty-free treatment for Caribbean countries under 19 U.S.C. § 2703(b). (A) For this reason, the following articles are not Caribbean Basin country end products: (1) Tuna, prepared or preserved in any manner in airtight containers. (2) Petroleum, or any product derived from petroleum. (3) Watches and watch parts (including cases, bracelets, and straps) of whatever type including, but not limited to, mechanical, quartz digital, or quartz analog, if such watches or watch parts contain any material that is the product of any country to which the Harmonized Tariff Schedule of the United States (HTSUS) column 2 rates of duty apply (i.e., Afghanistan, Cuba, Laos, North Korea, and Vietnam). (4) Certain of the following: textiles and apparel articles; footwear, handbags, luggage, flat goods, work gloves, and leather wearing apparel; or hand loomed, handmade, and folklore articles. (B) Access to the HTSUS to determine duty-free status of articles of the types listed in paragraph (ii)(A)(4) of this definition is available via the Internet at http://www.usitc.gov/tata/hts/index.htm. In particular see the following (1) General Note 3(c), Products Eligible for Special Tariff treatment. (2) General Note 17, Products of Countries Designated as Beneficiary Countries under the United States – Caribbean Basin Trade Partnership Act of 2000. (3) Section XXII, Chapter 98, Subchapter II, Articles Exported and Returned, Advanced or Improved Abroad, U.S. Note 7(b). (4) Section XXII, Chapter 98, Subchapter XX, Goods Eligible for Special Tariff Benefits under the United States-Caribbean Basin Trade Partnership Act; and (2) Refers to a product offered for purchase under a supply contract, but for purposes of calculating the value of the acquisition, includes services (except transportation services) incidental to the article, provided that the value of those incidental services does not exceed that of the article itself. *Source:* FAR 25.003. These products are subject to the TRADE AGREEMENTS ACT. FAR 25.405. See United States International Trade Commission, *Caribbean Basin Economic Recovery Act: Impact on U.S. Industries and Consumers and on Beneficiary Countries*, 22nd Report 2013–14 (Sept. 2015).

CARIBBEAN BASIN ECONOMIC RECOVERY ACT   A 1983 Act, 19 U.S.C. § 2701 et seq., making certain CARIBBEAN BASIN COUNTRIES eligible for the TRADE AGREEMENTS ACT OF 1979 exceptions to the BUY AMERICAN ACT. These countries are in addition to those designated in the Trade Agreements Act itself. FAR 25.405 makes these countries, which the President designated as beneficiaries under the Act, eligible for this preference. The U.S. Trade Representative has determined that these countries provide appropriate reciprocal, competitive government procurement opportunities for U.S. products and suppliers. The FAR contains a list of products excluded from duty-free treatment for Caribbean countries, such as (1) certain textiles and apparel, (2) leather wearing apparel (footwear, gloves, luggage), (3) tuna (in airtight containers), (4) petroleum goods, and (5) watches and watch parts. FAR 25.003. See Feldman, GOVERNMENT CONTRACT GUIDEBOOK, § 8:36 (4th ed. 2019–2020). See also United States International Trade Commission, *Caribbean Basin Economic Recovery Act: Impact on U.S. Industries and Consumers and on Beneficiary Countries,* 22nd Report 2013–14 (Sept. 2015).

CARRIER (TELECOMMUNICATIONS)   A COMMON CARRIER, foreign carrier, or noncommon carrier engaged in providing TELE-COMMUNICATIONS SERVICES. "Common carrier" means any entity engaged in the business of providing telecommunications services that is regulated by the Federal Communications Commission or other governmental body. "Noncommon carrier" means any entity other than a common carrier offering telecommunications facilities, services, or equipment for lease. "Foreign carrier" means any person, partnership, association, joint-stock company, trust, governmental body, or corporation not subject to regulation by a U.S. governmental body and not doing business as a citizen of the United States, providing telecommunications services outside the territorial limits of the United States. DFARS 239.7401. DFARS Subpart 239.74 states DOD policy on acquiring telecommunications services from common, noncommon, and foreign carriers. Trakman, *The Boundaries of Contract Law in Cyberspace,* 38 PUB. CONT. L.J. 187 (2008).

CARRIER (TRANSPORTATION)   *Official:* A COMMON CARRIER or a contract carrier. *Source:* FAR 47.001. "Common carrier" means an entity holding itself out to the general public to provide transportation for compensation. "Contract carrier" means an entity providing transportation for compensation under a continuing agreement with one party or a number of parties. FAR 47.001. Guidance on contracts for transportation is contained in FAR Subpart 47.2.

CASCADING SET-ASIDE   An acquisition procedure in which the government makes a decision whether to set it aside for a class of small businesses only after proposals have been solicited and received from designated classes of SMALL BUSINESS offerors, sometimes including large businesses. Also called TIERED EVALUATION OF OFFERS. For example, proposals are solicited from all businesses, and a firm must submit a proposal in order to be considered for award. But if the agency receives at least two proposals from HUBZone small businesses, it sets the acquisition aside for the HUBZone small businesses and the proposals from other firms are not considered. If the agency does not receive two proposals from HUBZone small businesses, but receives two proposals from the members of any other class of small businesses, it sets the acquisition aside for small businesses and the proposals from other firms are not considered. If the agency does not receive two proposals from small business, it opens the acquisition to all businesses that submitted proposals. There are many possible variations. The procedure is not mentioned in or authorized by FAR or the regulations of the Small Business Administration, but the GAO has accepted it as legitimate, *The Urban*

Group, Inc., Comp. Gen. Dec. B-281352, 99-1 CPD ¶ 25. Many, including the National Defense Industries Association and the Professional Services Council, consider the procedure to be unfair because it requires firms to prepare and submit proposals in order to be considered for award, but does not guarantee that their proposals will receive consideration. See Nash, *Postscript III: Cascading Set-Asides*, 33 N&CR ¶ 27 (May 2019).

CAS-COVERED CONTRACT   Any negotiated contract or subcontract that is subject to full, modified, or other type of COST ACCOUNTING STANDARDS (CAS) coverage. 48 C.F.R. § 9903.201-2 provides that such contracts are subject to either full or modified coverage of the Cost Accounting Standards requirements in accordance with the rules in 48 C.F.R. § 9903.201-1, which provide exemptions for small businesses and twelve other contract and subcontract types. See Cibinic, Knight & Nash, Cost-Reimbursement Contracting 523–30 (4th ed. 2014).

CASH BASIS ACCOUNTING   An accounting method in which revenue, expense, and BALANCE SHEET items are recorded only when cash is paid or received. See Black's Law Dictionary 25 (11th ed. 2019). Although there is no specific prohibition against the use of the cash basis in government contract accounting, most government contractors use the ACCRUAL BASIS.

CATALOG PRICE   *Official:* A price included in a catalog, price list, schedule, or other form that is regularly maintained by the manufacturer or vendor, is either published or otherwise available for inspection by customers, and states prices at which sales are currently, or were last, made to a significant number of buyers constituting the general public. *Source:* FAR 2.101 (in the definition of COMMERCIAL ITEM). Such a price permits an agency to treat a STAND-ALONE COMMERCIAL SERVICE as a COMMERCIAL ITEM if other requirements are met. See also ESTABLISHED CATALOG OR MARKET PRICE.

CATALOGING AND STANDARDIZATION ACT   A statute requiring the DEPARTMENT OF DEFENSE to maintain a single catalog system and related program of standardizing supplies. Pub. L. No. 85-861 § 33(a)(13), amended by Pub. L. No. 108-136 § 341, 10 U.S.C. § 2451. The system is maintained by the DEFENSE STANDARDIZATION PROGRAM (DSP).

CATEGORY MANAGEMENT   A strategic purchasing practice through which Government agencies categorize, consolidate, and coordinate their purchases of common goods and services in order to gain economies of scale, eliminate redundancies, and increase purchasing efficiency. The practice was mandated by the OFFICE OF MANAGEMENT AND BUDGET (OMB) in its Memorandum M-19-13, *Category Management: Making Smarter Use of Common Contract Solutions and Practices*, dated March 20, 2019 and addressed to heads of executive departments and agencies, which directed them to: (1) establish annual purchasing plans, (2) develop effective vendor management strategies, (3) implement demand management strategies, (4) share purchasing data across the Federal government, and (5) train and develop the workforce in category management principles and practices. See O'Brien, Category Management in Purchasing (4th ed. 2019).

CATEGORY OF MATERIAL   *Official:* A particular kind of goods, comprised of identical or interchangeable units, acquired or produced by a contractor, that are intended to be sold or consumed or used in the performance of either direct or indirect functions. *Source:* 48 C.F.R. § 9904.411-30(a)(3). Under CAS 411, 48 C.F.R. § 9904.411-50(a), contractors must adjust the purchase price of a category of material by extra charges incurred, or discounts and credits earned, when accounting for the acquisition costs of material. See Cibinic, Knight & Nash, COST-REIMBURSEMENT CONTRACTING 732–33 (4th ed. 2014).

CATEGORY I CONDITION   *Official:* A subsurface or latent physical conditions at the site which differ materially from those indicated in this contract. *Source:* FAR 52.236-2(a)(1). This type of DIFFERING SITE CONDITION entitles a construction contractor to an EQUITABLE ADJUSTMENT if its claim contains the following elements: (1) the contract documents must have affirmatively indicated or represented the subsurface conditions that form the basis of the claim; (2) the contractor must have acted with reasonable prudence in interpreting the contract documents; (3) the contractor must have reasonably relied on the indications of subsurface conditions in the contract; (4) the subsurface conditions actually encountered, within the contract site area, must have differed materially from the subsurface conditions indicated in the same contract area; (5) the actual subsurface conditions encountered must have been reasonably unforeseeable; and (6) the contractor's claimed excess costs must be shown to be solely attributable to the materially different subsurface conditions within the contract site. *Weeks Dredging & Contracting, Inc. v. United States*, 13 Cl. Ct. 193 (1987), *aff'd*, 861 F.2d 728 (Fed. Cir. 1988). See Cibinic, Nagle & Nash, ADMINISTRATION OF GOVERNMENT CONTRACTS 446–60 (5th ed. 2016).

CATEGORY II CONDITION   *Official:* An unknown physical condition at the site, of an unusual nature, which differs materially from those ordinarily encountered and generally recognized as inhering in work of the character provided for in the contract. *Source:* FAR 52.236-2(a)(1). This type of DIFFERING SITE CONDITION entitles a construction contractor to an EQUITABLE ADJUSTMENT if its claim identifies a condition that was unknown, unforeseeable, and unusual. *Lathan Co. v. United States*, 20 Cl. Ct. 122 (1990). In asserting a Category II claim, the contractor faces a relatively heavy burden of proof, and the court has stated that "[a]s a general matter, it is more difficult to establish a Type II differing site condition," *CCI Contractors, Inc.*, AGBCA 84-314-1, 91-3 BCA ¶ 24,225, *aff'd*, 979 F.2d 216 (Fed. Cir. 1992). See Cibinic, Nagle & Nash, ADMINISTRATION OF GOVERNMENT CONTRACTS 461–64 (5th ed. 2016). See also Dale & D'Onofrio, *Reconciling Concurrency in Schedule Delay and Constructive Acceleration*, 39 PUB. CONT. L.J. 161 (2010); Gourlay, *Constructive Acceleration and Concurrent Delay: Is There a "Middle Ground"?*, 39 PUB. CONT. L.J. 231 (2010); Kelleher, Nelson & Miller, *The Resurrection of Rice? The Evolution (And De-evolution) of the Ability of Contractors to Recover Delay Damages on Federal Government Construction Contracts*, 39 PUB. CONT. L.J. 305 (2010).

CDA CLAIM   See CLAIM.

CEILING PRICE   A price negotiated by the parties that is the maximum price that the government will pay regardless of the cost of performance. Ceiling prices are included in all FIXED-PRICE-INCENTIVE CONTRACTs (FAR 16.403(a)) and FIXED-PRICE REDETERMINATION—RETROACTIVE CONTRACTs (see FAR 16.206) and may be used in FIXED-PRICE REDETERMINATION—PROSPECTIVE CONTRACTs (see FAR 16.205). They are also included in COST-REIMBURSEMENT CONTRACTs on occasion. Ceiling prices are subject to revision under all contract clauses calling for EQUITABLE ADJUSTMENT or PRICE ADJUSTMENT. The Payments Under Time-and-Materials and Labor-Hour Contracts clause in FAR 52.232-7 uses the term "ceiling price" to describe an amount over which the government does not have to pay and that excuses the contractor's performance if completion would exceed the amount. The contractor cannot exceed this ceiling price without prior written approval from the contracting officer notifying the contractor of a new ceiling price (the same as a LIMITATION OF COST clause in cost-reimbursement contracts).

CENTER FOR STRATEGIC AND INTERNATIONAL STUDIES (CSIS) A private, nonpartisan, tax-exempt organization. CSIS addresses the full spectrum of new challenges to national and international security, maintains resident experts on all of the world's major geographical regions, and is committed to helping to develop new methods of governance for the global age; to this end, CSIS has programs on technology and public policy, international trade and finance, and energy.

CENTRAL CONTRACTOR REGISTRATION (CCR) DATABASE This government repository for contractor information was replaced by the SYSTEM FOR AWARD MANAGEMENT.

CENTRAL NONPROFIT AGENCY *Official:* National Industries for the Blind (NIB), which has been designated to represent people who are blind; or NISH, which has been designated to represent AbilityOne participating nonprofit agencies serving people with severe disabilities other than blindness. *Source:* FAR 8.701. These two nonprofit agencies create employment opportunities for the blind and for the severely disabled (NISH is not an acronym.) They work in conjunction with the Committee for Purchase from People Who Are Blind or Severely Disabled under the Javits-Wagner-O'Day Act. FAR Subpart 8.7. See ABILITY ONE.

CERCLA See COMPREHENSIVE ENVIRONMENTAL RESPONSE, COMPENSATION, AND LIABILITY ACT.

CERTIFICATE OF APPOINTMENT See WARRANT.

CERTIFICATE OF COMMERCIAL PRICING See COMMERCIAL PRICING CERTIFICATE.

CERTIFICATE OF COMPETENCY (COC) Certification by the SMALL BUSINESS ADMINISTRATION (SBA) under the Small Business Act, 15 U.S.C. § 637(b)(7), that a SMALL BUSINESS CONCERN meets the standard of RESPONSIBILITY with regard to performing a particular government contract. The issuance of a COC overrides a determination of nonresponsibility made by a contracting officer. When a contracting officer determines that a small business concern is nonresponsible, the matter be referred to the SBA, which will offer the small business an opportunity to apply for a COC. An SBA decision to issue a COC can be appealed by the contracting officer to the SBA Central Office. See FAR Subpart 19.6. Application for a COC consists of three forms to be completed by the small business contractor: SBA Form 1531, Application for Certificate of Competency, and SBA Form 355, Application for Small Business Size Determination and SBA Form 74B, Monthly cash flow. See Efron & Muchmore, *Certificates of Competency*, BRIEFING PAPERS No. 87-11 (Oct. 1987).

CERTIFICATE OF CONFORMANCE A certification of a contractor that contractual supplies or services are of the quality specified and conform in all respects to the contract requirements. This certificate may be required of contractors and is used as a substitute for full inspection by the government. FAR 46.504. The submission of a certificate is required by the Certificate of Conformance clause in FAR 52.246-15. A certificate of conformance may increase a contractor's liability for defective work. See Cibinic, Nagle & Nash, ADMINISTRATION OF GOVERNMENT CONTRACTS 771–73 (5th ed. 2016).

CERTIFICATE OF COST OR PRICING DATA   Certification by a successful offeror on a negotiated procurement that the CERTIFIED COST OR PRICING DATA submitted to the government was, to the best of its knowledge and belief, ACCURATE, COMPLETE, AND CURRENT as of the date when price agreement was reached or a cutoff date agreed to by the parties. FAR 15.406-2 contains a copy of the certificate and requires that it be submitted as soon as practicable after price agreement is reached. This certificate must also be submitted when a contractor is required to submit certified cost or pricing data in support of a modification of a negotiated contract or of a SEALED BID contract if no exception applies and the amount is over the $2,000,000 threshold (adding the cost increases and the cost decreases), FAR 15.403-4(a)(1)(iii). See FAR 15.208(m) requiring the use of the Requirements for Certified Cost or Pricing Data and Data Other Than Certified Cost or Pricing Data—Modifications clause in FAR 52.215-21 in specified negotiated contracts and FAR 14.201-7(b) requiring the use of the Price Reduction for Defective Certified Cost or Pricing Data—Modifications—Sealed Bidding clause in FAR 52.215-21 in specified sealed bidding contracts). The certificate must also be submitted by subcontractors in specified situations, FAR 15.403-4(a)(1)(ii). See the clauses at FAR 52.214-28 and 52.215-12(d) and (e). See Manos, 2 GOVERNMENT CONTRACT COSTS & PRICING § 84:12 (2d ed. 2009–2020).

CERTIFICATION   A signed representation that certain facts are accurate. A certification can entail either (1) an explicit representation of fact requiring the inclusion of data and signature by the contractor ("The contractor hereby certifies that . . ." or "This is to certify that . . ."), or (2) a deemed representation of a particular fact without execution of a specific certification document or use of specific certification language. All certifications required by solicitations are included in Section K of the UNIFORM CONTRACT FORMAT. FAR 14.201-5, FAR 15.204-5. Contractors are required to submit certifications and representations to the SYSTEM FOR AWARD MANAGEMENT and to update this submission "as necessary but at least annually." FAR 4.1201(a). The government has traditionally used certifications in such matters as contractor status; truth of a matter; origin of a component; compliance with specifications; compliance with applicable laws; accuracy, currency, and completeness of cost or pricing data (see CERTIFIED COST OR PRICING DATA); and good faith, accuracy, and completeness in reflecting the amount owed with regard to claims, past contractual performance, and other matters. False claims have also been based on an IMPLIED CERTIFICATION that the contractor has met contract requirements when submitting an INVOICE. See Mitchell, et al., *Implied Certification Liability Under the False Claims Act,* BRIEFING PAPERS No. 11-4 (Mar. 2011); Levy, et al., *The Implied Certification Theory, When Should The False Claims At Reach Statements Never Spoken or Communicated, But Only Implied?,* 38 PUB. CONT. L.J. 131 (2008). Nash, *False Claims Flowing Out of False Statements: Certification Doesn't Matter,* 22 N&CR ¶ 54 (Sept. 2008).

CERTIFICATION OF CLAIM   A certification by a contractor under the CONTRACT DISPUTES ACT (CDA) that (1) a claim is made in good faith, (2) the supporting data are accurate and complete to the best of the certifier's knowledge and belief, (3) the amount requested accurately reflects the contract adjustment for which the contractor believes the government is liable, and (4) the signer is duly authorized to certify the claim on behalf of the contractor. This certification is required by 41 U.S.C. § 7103(b) for all claims over $100,000. FAR 33.207(e) allows this certification to be executed by any person duly authorized to bind the contractor with respect to the claim. DEFECTIVE CERTIFICATIONs can be corrected during litigation. FAR 33.207(f). However, a claim over $100,000 with no certification will deprive a board or court of jurisdiction to hear the claim. See Cibinic, Nagle & Nash, ADMINISTRATION OF GOVERNMENT CONTRACTS 1173–79 (5th ed. 2016). See also Nash, *Defense to a Government Claim is a Contractor Claim: A Weird Thought*, 24 N&CR ¶ 42 (Sept. 2010).

CERTIFICATION OF REQUEST FOR EQUITABLE ADJUSTMENT A certification by a contractor under 10 U.S.C. § 2410(a) that the request is made in good faith and that the supporting data are ACCURATE and COMPLETE. This certification requirement is applicable only to REQUESTS FOR EQUITABLE ADJUSTMENTs over the SIMPLIFIED ACQUISITION THRESHOLD submitted to DOD, DFARS 243.204-71. However, in determining the amount of the REA, the amount of cost increases claimed and the amount of cost decreases claimed must be added. This requirement is implemented by the inclusion in DOD contracts of the Requests for Equitable Adjustment clause in DFARS 252.243-7002. This certification is in addition to the CERTIFICATION OF CLAIM requirement and if no settlement is reached and the contractor subsequently submits a CLAIM, that additional certification requirement applies. DFARS 243.204-71(c).

CERTIFIED COST OR PRICING DATA *Official:* COST OR PRICING DATA that were required to be submitted in accordance with FAR 15.403-4 and 15.403-5 and have been certified, or are required to be certified, in accordance with 15.406-2. This certification states that, to the best of the person's knowledge and belief, the cost and pricing data are ACCURATE, COMPLETE, AND CURRENT as of a date certain before contract award. Cost or pricing data are required to be certified in certain procurements (10 U.S.C. § 2306a and 41 U.S.C. chapter 35. *Source:* FAR 2.101. Unless an exemption applies, the Act requires such submission for negotiated procurement actions (see NEGOTIATION) expected to exceed $2,000,000. FAR 15.403-4. Exempt are actions (1) where a waiver has been granted; (2) modification to a contract for commercial items; or (3) whose prices are (A) based on ADEQUATE PRICE COMPETITION, (B) for COMMERCIAL ITEMs, or (C) set by law or regulation. FAR 15.403-1(b). The contracting officer may require submission of cost or pricing data in the format indicated at Table 15-2 of FAR 15.408, specify an alternative format, or permit submission in the contractor's format. FAR 15.403-5. After price agreement is reached on a contract, modification or subcontract that requires submission of certified cost or pricing data, the contractor must submit a CERTIFICATE OF COST OR PRICING DATA. See also DEFECTIVE COST OR PRICING DATA. See Manos, 2 GOVERNMENT CONTRACT COSTS & PRICING §§ 84:10–84:13 (2d ed. 2009–2020).

CERTIFIED PROFESSIONAL CONTRACTS MANAGER (CPCM) An individual who has attained certain levels of education, experience, and knowledge pertaining to contracts management. To be eligible, candidates must have a degree from a regionally accredited institution at a higher level than a bachelor's; five years of experience and 120 hours of continuing professional education. Waivers to the advanced degree requirement will be considered for those candidates who have a Bachelor's degree and ten years of experience who present a letter from a supervisor supporting their candidacy. Candidates must pass three examination modules: one for general business knowledge, one for federal contracting knowledge, and one for commercial contracting knowledge. The examinations are administered by the NATIONAL CONTRACT MANAGEMENT ASSOCIATION (NCMA). See http://www.ncmahq.org/certification/.

CERTIFYING OFFICER *Official:* A government officer or employee whose job is or includes certifying VOUCHERs (including voucher schedules or INVOICEs used as vouchers) for payment. *Source:* U.S. Gov't Accountability Office, Principles of Federal Appropriations Law: Annual Update to the Third Edition, Ch. 9, GAO-15-303SP (Washington, D.C.: Mar. 2015). Certifying officers can be personally liable for incorrect vouchers (see 31 U.S.C. § 3541) but the COMPTROLLER GENERAL has the authority to relieve them of liability. 31 U.S.C. § 3528. See Cibinic, Nagle & Nash, Administration of Government Contracts 1034–35 (5th ed. 2016).

CHALLENGE PROCEDURE A nondiscriminatory, timely, transparent, and effective procedure required by the WORLD TRADE ORGANIZATION (WTO) that enables suppliers to challenge alleged breaches of agreements arising out of the context of procurements in which they have or have had an interests. Each WTO member must develop their own challenge procedures. However, all challenge procedures must be heard by a court or impartial and independent review body that is subject to judicial review and provide for (1) rapid interim measures to correct breaches in agreements and preserve commercial opportunities, (2) an assessment and a possibility for a decision on the justification of the challenged, and (3) correction of the breach of the Agreement or compensation for the loss suffered. Suppliers can likely invoke challenge procedures based on substantive obligations of the Agreement on Government Procurement only to the extent they have been implemented in the WTO member's domestic law. It is unclear who can invoke challenge procedures, whether they are reserved to entities seeking to be parties to a contract or whether they are available to any firm in the supply chain. See Gao, *The Bid Challenge Procedures Under the WTO Government Procurement Agreement: A Critical Study of the Hong Kong Experience*, P.P.L.R. 2007, 4, 211-54 (2007).

CHANGE Any alteration to a contract under the Changes clause that is within the general SCOPE OF THE CONTRACT. Contract changes may be bilateral (signed by both the contractor and the contracting officer) or unilateral (signed only by the contracting officer). A bilateral change is issued by a BILATERAL MODIFICATION and is often referred to as a supplemental agreement. A UNILATERAL CHANGE is issued by a UNILATERAL MODIFICATION and is generally called a CHANGE ORDER. FAR 43.103. Following receipt of a unilateral change, to receive an EQUITABLE ADJUSTMENT, a contractor must submit a proposal and negotiate a bilateral modification with the contracting officer. See also CONSTRUCTIVE CHANGE. See generally Nash & Feldman, Government Contract Changes (3d ed. 2006–2020). See also Cibinic, Nagle & Nash, Administration of Government Contracts, chap. 4 (5th ed. 2016).

CHANGE-OF-NAME AGREEMENT *Official:* A legal instrument executed by the contractor and the government that recognizes the legal change of name of the contractor without disturbing the original contractual rights and obligations of the parties. *Source:* FAR 2.101. FAR 42.1205 contains guidance on when such an agreement should be used and provides a model agreement. See also NOVATION.

CHANGE ORDER *Official:* A written order, signed by the contracting officer, directing the contractor to make a CHANGE that the Changes clause authorizes the contracting officer to order without the contractor's consent. *Source:* FAR 2.101. Generally, government contracts contain one of the Changes clauses in FAR 52.243-1 through -6 permitting the contracting officer to make UNILATERAL CHANGEs, in designated areas, within the general SCOPE OF THE CONTRACT. These changes are accomplished by issuing written orders on Standard Form 30, Amendment of Solicitation/Modification of Contract, FAR 53.301-30. Change orders must be issued by the contracting officer, except when authority to issue such orders is delegated to an administrative contracting officer. FAR 43.202. Upon receipt of a change order, the contractor must continue performance of the contract as changed, except that, in cost-reimbursement or incrementally funded contracts, the contractor is not obligated to continue performance or incur costs beyond the established funding limits. FAR 43.201 and 52.243-1 through -6. FAR 43.102(b) discourages the use of unilateral change orders and calls for establishing a ceiling price when they are used and could result in significant cost increases. For contracts with the DOD, unpriced change orders must include a not-to-exceed price. DFARS 243.204-70-2. See Nash & Feldman, 1 GOVERNMENT CONTRACT CHANGES §§ 7:1–7:20 (3d ed. 2006–2020); Cibinic, Nagle & Nash, ADMINISTRATION OF GOVERNMENT CONTRACTS 360–71 (5th ed. 2016). See also Nash, *Unpriced Changes: In DOD They're Now Undefinitized Contract Actions*, 24 N&CR ¶ 60 (Dec. 2010).

CHANGE TO COST ACCOUNTING PRACTICE *Official:* Any alteration in a COST ACCOUNTING PRACTICE, as defined in 9903.302-1, whether or not such practices are covered by a DISCLOSURE STATEMENT, except the following: (a) the initial adoption of a cost accounting practice when a cost is first incurred or a function is first created is not a change in cost accounting practice. The partial or total elimination of a cost or the cost of a function is not a change in cost accounting practice. As used here, function is an activity or group of activities that is identifiable in scope and has a purpose or end to be accomplished, (b) the revision of a cost accounting practice for a cost that previously had been immaterial is not a change in cost accounting practice. *Source:* 48 C.F.R. § 9903.302-2. 48 C.F.R. § 9903.302-3 contains illustrations of changes that meet this definition and 48 C.F.R. § 9903.302-4 describes changes that do not. The COST ACCOUNTING STANDARDS clause in FAR 52.230-3 requires that the parties negotiate an EQUITABLE ADJUSTMENT if the price is affected by a change to the contractor's cost accounting practice. Guidance on processing and negotiating changes is contained in FAR 30.603 and 30.604. Changes to cost accounting practices are sometimes the result of REQUIRED CHANGES. See Manos, 2 GOVERNMENT CONTRACT COSTS & PRICING § 60:16 (2d ed. 2009–2020); Cibinic, Knight & Nash, COST-REIMBURSEMENT CONTRACTING 513–22 (4th ed. 2014).

CHANGED CONDITIONS Conditions at the site of a CONSTRUCTION project that the government agreed were subject to price adjustment. In 1969 this term was changed to DIFFERING SITE CONDITIONS.

CHARTER Authorization to establish an acquisition organization for a specific purpose, containing instructions about function and authority of the organization and the resources available to it. In DOD, charters are used to establish programs, OVERARCHING INTEGRATED PRODUCT TEAMs (OIPTs), COST ANALYSIS IMPROVEMENT GROUPs, and other special acquisition organizations. Specific types of charters include Joint Program Manager's Charters, which are formal document prepared by the lead Service with approval of the participating Services that delineates the Program Manager's responsibility, authority, and major functions, and describes relationships with other organizations that will use and/or support the program, and that describes and assigns responsibility for satisfying unique management requirements of participating Services, and Program Manager's Charters, which confers authority to conduct the program within cost, schedule, and performance constraints approved by the decision authority, establishes manpower resources for the Program Office (PO) and includes assignment of personnel to perform the functions of technical management/systems engineering, logistics, business and financial management, as well as the designation of a contracting officer, and defines the PM's line of authority and reporting channels. See DAU GLOSSARY.

CHERRY PICKING   A contractor's decision to perform work that may yield intellectual property rights with funds outside of contract funding in order to deny contractual rights to the government. In order to prevent this practice the 1988 DOD TECHNICAL DATA policy gave the government UNLIMITED RIGHTS to data that resulted from development of items, components or processes "required for the performance of a government contract or subcontract." See the definition of "Developed Exclusively with Government Funds" in the Rights in Technical Data and Computer Software clause in DFARS 252.227-7013 (pre-1995 version). This policy was reversed in the 1995 technical data policy which gives the government only LIMITED RIGHTS to technical data pertaining to items, components or processes that was developed "entirely with costs charged to indirect cost pools, costs not allocated to a government contract, or any combination thereof." See the definition of "Developed exclusively at private expense" in the Rights in Technical Data—Noncommercial Items clause in DFARS 252.227-7013 and the Rights in Noncommercial Computer Software and Noncommercial Computer Software Documentation clause in DFARS 252.227-7014. See Nash & Rawicz, INTELLECTUAL PROPERTY IN GOVERNMENT CONTRACTS, chap. 4 (6th ed. 2008).

CHIEF ACQUISITION OFFICER   *Official:* An executive level acquisition official responsible for agency performance of acquisition activities and acquisition programs created pursuant to 41 U.S.C. § 1702. *Source:* FAR 2.101. Chief acquisition officers are non-career employees of each agency except DOD appointed by the head of the agency to have acquisition management as his or her primary duty and to advise and assist the head of the EXECUTIVE AGENCY and other agency officials to ensure that the mission of the executive agency is achieved through the management of the agency's acquisition activities. 41 U.S.C. § 1702. Agency heads can appoint the SENIOR PROCUREMENT EXECUTIVE to this position or, alternatively, have the Senior Procurement Executive report directly to the Chief Acquisition Officer.

CHIEF ACQUISITION OFFICERS COUNCIL (CAOC)   An advisory group of agency CHIEF ACQUISITION OFFICERs, which was chartered by the OFFICE OF MANAGEMENT AND BUDGET in 2004 to provide acquisition information and advice to the OMB Director and OFPP Administrator. 41 U.S.C. §§ 131–132. They meet every three months or as needed. The CAOC promotes effective business practices and advises the Administrator, Office of Federal Procurement Policy, and the Federal Acquisition Regulatory Council concerning acquisition policy. Formerly the Procurement Executives Council (PEC). The Council's website is at http://caoc.gov/.

CHIEF INFORMATION OFFICER (CIO)   An executive level official responsible for information policies and information resources management. Each agency is required to appoint a CIO, 44 U.S.C. § 3506(a)(2). The responsibilities of CIOs are set forth in 44 U.S.C. § 3501 and § 3506.

CHIEF INFORMATION OFFICERS (CIO) COUNCIL.   The principal interagency forum to improve agency practices on such matters as the design, acquisition, development, modernization, use, operation, sharing, and performance of agency information resources. 44 U.S.C. § 3603. The Council is expected to: (1) develop recommendations for overall federal INFORMATION TECHNOLOGY management policy and requirements; (2) share experiences, ideas, and promising practices to improve the management of information resources; (3) identify, develop, and coordinate multiagency projects and other initiatives to improve government performance through the use of information technology; (4) promote the development and use of commoner performance measures for agency information resources management; and (5) make recommendations and provide advice to appropriate executive agencies, organizations related to information resources management. The CIO Council is composed of the deputy director for management of the OMB, the administrators of the Office of Electronic Government and Office of Information and Regulatory Affairs, the CIOs and Deputy CIOs of the Departments and of numerous other agencies and other federal employees designated by the chairperson.

CHOICE OF FORUM   See ELECTION DOCTRINE.

CHRISTIAN DOCTRINE   A legal rule providing that clauses required by regulation to be included in government contracts will be read into a contract whether or not physically included in the contract, unless a proper DEVIATION from the regulations has been obtained. The doctrine derives from the case of *G. L. Christian & Assoc. v. United States*, 312 F.2d 418, 320 F.2d 345 (Ct. Cl. 1963), *cert. denied*, 375 U.S. 954 (1963), 170 Ct. Cl. 902, *cert. denied*, 382 U.S. 821 (1965), in which it was held that the TERMINATION FOR CONVENIENCE clause applied even though it had been omitted from the contract, because the procurement regulations required its inclusion. The Christian doctrine should not, however, be read to mean that *all* procurement regulations have the force and effect of law; it applies only to those regulations that implement fundamental procurement policy. See Cibinic, Nash & Yukins, FORMATION OF GOVERNMENT CONTRACTS 76–79 (4th ed. 2011). See also Darst, *The Christian Doctrine at 50: Unravelling The Federal Procurement System's Gordian Knot*, BRIEFING PAPERS No. 13-11 (Oct. 2013).

CICA OVERRIDE   The common name for a decision by an agency head of a contracting activity, pursuant to 31 U.S.C. § 3553(d)(3)(c), to proceed with contract performance notwithstanding receipt of timely notification of a protest to the GAO. See COMPETITION IN CONTRACTING ACT and CICA STAY. FAR 33.104(c)(2) implements the statute and prescribes limitations and procedures. See Roberts, *Does Automatic Mean Automatic? The Applicability of the CICA Automatic Stay to Task and Delivery Order Bid Protests*, 39 PUB. CONT. L.J. 641 (2010); Sacilotto, *Is the Game Worth the Candle? The Fate of the CICA Override*, 45 The Procurement Lawyer 3 (Fall 2009); Boland, *CICA Override Practice—The Case Against Injunctive Relief*, 50 Gov't Contractor ¶ 1 (2008); Pompeo, *Establishing Trends in Override Case Law*, 49 Gov't Contractor ¶ 87 (2007); Cho, *Judicial Review of "Best Interest of the United States" Justification for CICA Overrides: Overstepping Boundaries or Giving the Bite Back?*, 34 PUB. CONT. L.J. 337 (2005); Nash *Postscript II: Challenging an Override of a Protest Stay*, 18 N&CR ¶ 54 (Dec. 2004).

CICA STAY   The common name for the requirement in 31 U.S.C. § 3553(c) that agencies suspend contract performance upon receipt of timely notification of a PROTEST to the GAO. FAR 33.104(c) implements the statute. See COMPETITION IN CONTRACTING ACT and CICA OVERRIDE. See Wilkinson & Page, *CICA Stay Revisited: Keys to Successful Overrides*, 66 A.F.L. Rev. 135 (2010); Roberts, *Does Automatic Mean Automatic? The Applicability of the CICA Automatic Stay to Task and Delivery Order Bid Protests*, 39 Pub. Cont. L.J. 641 (2010).

CIVIL DEFENSE COSTS   Costs incurred by a contractor in planning for, and protecting life and property against, the possible effects of enemy attack. FAR 31.205-5 (pre 1999). This definition was removed from the FAR in 1998. It included the costs of civil defense measures (including costs in excess of normal plant protection costs, first-aid training and supplies, fire-fighting training and equipment, posting of additional exit notices and directions, and other approved civil defense measures) undertaken on the contractor's premises pursuant to suggestions or requirements of civil defense authorities. Such costs were allowable (see ALLOWABLE COST) when allocated to all work of the contractor. Costs of capital ASSETs acquired for civil defense purposes were allowable through depreciation. Contributions to local civil defense funds and projects were unallowable.

CIVIL FALSE CLAIMS ACT   See FALSE CLAIMS ACT.

CIVIL JUDGMENT   *Official:* A judgment or finding of a civil offense by any court of competent jurisdiction. *Source:* FAR 9.403. FAR 9.406-2 states that a contractor can be debarred (see DEBARMENT) on the basis of civil judgments for (1) commission of fraud or a criminal offense in connection with obtaining, attempting to obtain or performing a government contract or subcontract; (2) violating antitrust statutes relating to submission of offers; (3) commission of embezzlement, theft, forgery, bribery, falsification, or destruction of records, making false statements, tax evasions, violating Federal criminal tax laws, or receiving stolen property; (4) intentionally affixing a "Made in America" inscription on a product sold or shipped to the United States that was not made in the United States; and (5) commission of any other offense that evidences a lack of business honesty that affects a contractor's present RESPONSIBILITY can all be causes for debarment.

CIVIL INVESTIGATIVE DEMAND   A demand by the DOJ that a person (1) produce any documentary material for inspection and copying, (2) answer any written INTERROGATORY with respect to such material, or (3) give oral testimony concerning such material. Such demands may be made in the course of any false claims investigation prior to filing suit (See FALSE CLAIMS ACT). 31 U.S.C. § 3733. See Laemmle-Weidenfeld & Schaengold, *The Impact of the Fraud Enforcement and Recovery Act of 2009 on the Civil False Claims Act*, 51 Gov't Contractor ¶ 224 (2009).

CIVILIAN AGENCY ACQUISITION COUNCIL (CAAC)   The government body that, with the DEFENSE ACQUISITION REGULATORY COUNCIL, prepares and issues revisions to the FEDERAL ACQUISITION REGULATION (FAR) through coordinated action. FAR 1.201-1. Each council maintains cognizance over specified portions of the FAR and is responsible for (1) agreeing with the other council on all revisions, (2) submitting to the FAR Secretariat information required for publishing a FEDERAL REGISTER notice soliciting comments, (3) considering all comments received, (4) arranging for public meetings, (5) preparing any final revision in the appropriate FAR format and language, and (6) submitting any final revision to the FAR Secretariat for publication in the Federal

Register and printing. Members of the CAAC (1) represent their agencies on a full-time basis, (2) are selected for their superior qualifications in terms of acquisition experience and demonstrated professional expertise, and (3) are funded by their respective agencies. The chairperson of the CAAC is the representative of the Administrator of General Services Administration; the other members represent the Departments of Agriculture, Commerce, Energy, Health and Human Services, Homeland Security, Interior, Labor, State, Transportation, Treasury, and Veterans Affairs, as well as the Environmental Protection Agency, the Social Security Administration and the Small Business Administration.

CIVILIAN BOARD OF CONTRACT APPEALS A consolidated BOARD OF CONTRACT APPEALS (BCA) established by the National Defense Authorization Act for FY 2006, Pub. L. No. 109-163, § 847, that began operations in January 2007. The board has jurisdiction of DISPUTEs of all EXECUTIVE AGENCIES except those within the jurisdiction of the ARMED SERVICES BOARD OF CONTRACT APPEALS, the Federal Aviation Administration, the Postal Service and the Tennessee Valley Authority. It consolidates the previous agency boards of the General Services Administration and the Departments of Agriculture, Commerce, Energy, Interior, Labor, Transportation and Veterans Affairs. Its members are appointed by the Administrator of General Services in consultation with the Administration for Federal Procurement Policy. It is located at 1800 M St., N.W., 6th Floor, Washington, DC 20036. See McGovern III, Graham, & Nibley, *A Level Playing Field: Why Congress Intended the Boards of Contract Appeals to Have Power Over Both Contractors and the Government*, 36 Pub. Cont. L.J. 495 (2007); Schaengold & Brams, *A Guide to the Civilian Board of Contract Appeals*, Briefing Papers No. 07-8 (July 2007).

CLAIM *Official:* A written demand or written assertion by one of the contracting parties seeking, as a matter of right, the payment of money in a sum certain, the adjustment or interpretation of contract terms, or other relief arising under, or relating to, the contract. However, a written demand or written assertion by the contractor seeking the payment of money exceeding $100,000 is not a claim under the Contract Disputes Act of 1978 until certified as required by the Act. A voucher, invoice, or other routine request for payment that is not in dispute when submitted is not a claim. The submission may be converted to a claim, by written notice to the contracting officer as provided in 33.206(a), if it is disputed either as to liability or amount or is not acted upon in a reasonable time. *Source:* FAR 2.101. This is the definition of a claim asserted pursuant to the CONTRACT DISPUTES ACT OF 1978 and FAR 33.207. A claim ARISING UNDER THE CONTRACT is a claim that can be resolved under a contract CLAUSE providing for relief sought by the claimant; a claim RELATING TO THE CONTRACT is one for which no specific contract clause provides such relief. The cost of preparing a claim is not an allowable cost, FAR 31.205-47(f)(1), but INTEREST on an amount recovered is paid from the date the CONTRACTING OFFICER receives the claim until the date of payment. See Cibinic, Nagle & Nash, Administration of Government Contracts 1156–84 (5th ed. 2016). See also Nash, *Postscript: Defense to a Government Claim is a Contractor Claim*, 32 N&CR ¶ 4 (Jan. 2018); Nash, *Defining Contract Disputes Act Claims: A Requirement for Complete Disclosure*, 25 N&CR ¶ 43 (Sept. 2011); Nash, *Contract Disputes Act "Claims": Routine Requests for Payment Don't Qualify*, 25 N&CR ¶ 42 (Sept. 2011); Willard, *Appeal of Government "Cost" Claims*, Briefing Papers No. 11-8 (July 2011); Nash, *Government Collection of Claims: A District Court Is the Place to Go*, 25 NCR ¶ 17 (Apr. 2011); Seiden, *Defenses: CBCA Says Appellant's 14-Year Unexcused Delay in Submitting Claims Was Unreasonable*, Fed. Cont.

Rep. (BNA) (Feb. 22, 2011); Huttmacher, *Government Contracting Disputes: It's Not All About the Money*, 2009 Army Law. 31 (Aug. 2009); See Zupa, *When Is A Claim Not A Claim?*, PUBLIC CONTRACT LAW JOURNAL, No. 22 (Summer 1993); Johnson, *A Retrospective on the Contract Disputes Act*, PUBLIC CONTRACT LAW JOURNAL No. 28 (Summer 1999); Nash & Edwards, *Requests for Equitable Adjustments vs. Claims: Is There A Difference?* 26 N&CR ¶ 10 (Feb. 2012); Nash & Edwards, *Postscript: Requests for Equitable Adjustments vs. Claims*, 26 N&CR ¶ 42 (Aug. 2012); Nash & Edwards, *Postscript II: Requests for Equitable Adjustments vs. Claims*, 26 N&CR ¶ 51 (Oct.2012); Nash, *Postscript III: Requests for Equitable Adjustments vs. Claims* (Nov. 2012); Nash, *Postscript IV: Requests for Equitable Adjustments vs. Claims*, 30 N&CR ¶ (Feb. 2016); Nash, *Postscript V: Requests for Equitable Adjustment vs. Claims*, 33 NCR-NL ¶ 58 (Oct. 2019); Edwards, *Postscript VI: Request for Equitable Adjustment vs. Claim*, 33 NCR-NL ¶ 65 (Nov. 2019).

CLAIMS COURT See COURT OF FEDERAL CLAIMS.

CLARIFICATION A government communication with an offeror on a competitively negotiated procurement (see NEGOTIATION) that is a limited exchange, between the government and an offeror, that occurs when AWARD ON INITIAL PROPOSALS is contemplated. FAR 15.306(a). Clarification may be used to resolve minor or clerical errors or "certain aspects of proposals." FAR 15.306(a)(2). The government is not obligated to seek clarification from all offerors. Prior to FAC 97-02, September 30, 1997, clarification was defined as communication with an offeror for the sole purpose of eliminating minor irregularities, informalities, or apparent CLERICAL MISTAKEs in a proposal. Under that definition, clarification was accomplished by explanation or substantiation, either in response to government inquiry or as initiated by the offeror, and unlike DISCUSSION, clarification did not give the offeror an opportunity to revise or modify its proposal, except to the extent that correction of apparent clerical mistakes resulted in a revision. The term "clarification" is also used to describe an inquiry by a contractor regarding ambiguous specifications. See DUTY TO SEEK CLARIFICATION. See Nash, *Postscript VII: Clarifications vs. Discussions*, 26 N&CR ¶ 11 (Mar. 2012).

CLASS DETERMINATIONS AND FINDINGS (D&Fs) A DETERMINATION AND FINDING providing authority for a class of contracting actions. A class of contracting actions typically entails the same or related supplies or services or other contracting actions that require essentially identical justification. FAR 1.703. This authority is for a specified period of time, with an expiration date stated in the document.

CLASS DEVIATION A DEVIATION from the FAR that affects more than one contracting action. FAR 1.404. See also DFARS 201.404; GSAR 501.404. When an agency requires a class deviation on a permanent basis, it should propose a FAR revision. The authority to approve class deviations is limited to higher-level officials in accordance with the FAR Supplements of each agency. FAR 1.405 contains special rules for class deviations that pertain to treaties and executive agreements.

CLASSIFIED ACQUISITION *Official:* An ACQUISITION in which offerors must have access to CLASSIFIED INFORMATION in order to properly submit an OFFER or QUOTATION, to understand the performance requirements, or to perform the contract. *Source:* FAR 2.101. FAR Subpart 4.4 provides guidance on such acquisitions. See also DFARS Subpart 204.4; DEAR Subpart 904.4; NFS Subpart 1804.4.

CLASSIFIED CONTRACT   *Official:* Any contract in which the contractor or its employees must have access to CLASSIFIED INFORMATION during contract performance. A contract may be a classified contract even though the contract document is not classified. *Source:* FAR 2.101. Such contracts may be awarded only to contractors that have complied with the security requirements of DOD or any other agency that has classified necessary information.

CLASSIFIED INFORMATION   *Official:* Any knowledge that can be communicated or any documentary material, regardless of its physical form or characteristics, that (1)(i) Is owned by, produced by or for, or under the control of the U.S. Government; or (ii) Has been classified by DOE as privately generated restricted data in accordance with the procedures at 10 C.F.R. § 1045.21, and (2) Must be protected against unauthorized disclosure according to Exec. Order No. 12958, Classified National Security Information, April 17, 1995, or classified in accordance with the Atomic Energy Act of 1954. *Source:* FAR 2.101. The fundamental document establishing rules about classified information is Exec. Order No. 12958, which has been amended by Exec. Order No. 13292, 68 Fed. Reg. 15315 (Mar. 25, 2003). Information is classified as Confidential, Secret, or Top Secret. See Department of Defense, DOD 5220.22-M § 4-100, *National Industrial Security Program Operating Manual.* FAR Subpart 4.4 provides guidance on safeguarding classified information within industry. See also DFARS Subpart 204.4. FAR 14.409-2 provides guidance on the disposal of classified information that has been furnished to unsuccessful bidders.

CLAUSE   *Official:* A term or condition used in CONTRACTs—or in both SOLICITATIONs and contracts—and applying after contract award, or both before and after award. *Source:* FAR 2.101. This term has the same meaning as "contract clause" in the FAR. A term used only in solicitations is called a SOLICITATION PROVISION or a PROVISION. FAR Subpart 52.2 sets forth the texts of all standard FAR clauses (as does DFARS Subpart 252.2 for DOD contracts), each in its own separate subsection. The subpart is arranged by subject matter in the same order as, and keyed to, the parts of the FAR. All FAR clause numbers begin with "52.2." The next two digits correspond to the number of the FAR part in which the clause is prescribed. The number is completed by a hyphen and a sequential number assigned within each section of FAR Subpart 52.2. The FAR clause number will be followed by the clause's title and—in contracts—by its effective date (e.g., FAR 52.203-3, Gratuities (Apr. 1984)). FAR Subpart 52.1 contains instructions for using clauses, and FAR Subpart 52.3 contains an extensive PROVISION AND CLAUSE MATRIX.

CLAUSE MATRIX   See PROVISION AND CLAUSE MATRIX.

CLAYTON ACT   An antitrust statute, 15 U.S.C. § 12 et seq., first enacted in 1914, that, among other things, prohibits mergers or acquisitions that may substantially lessen competition or tend to create a monopoly. 15 U.S.C. § 18. Mergers and acquisitions are subject to antitrust review by the DEPARTMENT OF JUSTICE and the Federal Trade Commission. The reviewer's goal is to prevent mergers or acquisitions that would hinder or terminate price competition in an industry over a long period of time. The Clayton Act plays a role in the debate over federal intrusion in defense industry mergers. See RUANE, PRE-MERGER REVIEW AND CHALLENGES UNDER THE CLAYTON ACT AND THE FEDERAL TRADE COMMISSION ACT (Sept. 27, 2017).

CLERICAL ERROR   An undefined term that describes a type of MISTAKE in a negotiated procurement than can be addressed through CLARIFICATIONs. FAR 15.306(a) permits correction of clerical errors prior to AWARD ON INITIAL PROPOSALS. The GAO and the Court of Federal Claims are not in total agreement on the meaning of this term. Compare *Enterprise Solutions Realized, Inc.*, Comp. Gen. Dec. B-409642, 2014 CPD 201, with *Griffy's Landscape Maintenance, L.L.C. v. United States*, 51 Fed. Cl. 667 (2001).

CLERICAL MISTAKE A mistake of a contractor in a BID that can be corrected before award. FAR 14.407-2(a) states that examples of such apparent clerical mistakes are obvious misplacement of decimal points, incorrect discounts, reversal of prices and misdesignation of units. When such mistakes are apparent on the face of a bid, the contracting officer must request verification (see DUTY OF VERIFICATION). FAR 14.407-1. Such mistakes may be routinely corrected by contracting officers in accordance with the procedures set forth in FAR 14.407-2. Other mistakes in bids alleged before contract award are dealt with under more elaborate procedures in accordance with FAR 14.407-3. See Cibinic, Nash & Yukins, FORMATION OF GOVERNMENT CONTRACTS 627–28, 784 (4th ed. 2011).

CLICK WRAP LICENSE A license to use a COMPUTER PROGRAM that is downloaded from the INTERNET that is entered into by clicking a button that appears on the screen that signifies agreement to the license terms. The terms of the license usually provide that the user is not the owner of the copy of the OBJECT CODE which is downloaded, that title to the object code is retained by the program proprietor, and that the user will not reverse engineer, decompile or disassemble the object code. Such provisions give the purchaser of the license fewer rights than would be obtained under the Copyright Act if the purchaser was the owner of the program. The comparable SHRINK WRAP LICENSE has been held to be a valid contract in *ProCD v. Zeidenberg*, 86 F.3d 1447 (7th Cir. 1996). See Nash & Rawicz, INTELLECTUAL PROPERTY IN GOVERNMENT CONTRACTS, chap. 5 (6th ed. 2008).

CLIN Acronym for CONTRACT LINE ITEM.

CLINGER-COHEN ACT A 1996 act that made a number of significant changes to the federal procurement system and totally revised the rules and procedures governing the procurement of INFORMATION TECHNOLOGY. The Act was originally enacted as Divisions D (the FEDERAL ACQUISITION REFORM ACT OF 1996) and E (the INFORMATION TECHNOLOGY MANAGEMENT REFORM ACT OF 1996) of the Fiscal Year 1996 Defense Authorization Act, Pub. L. No. 104-106. Section 808 of the Omnibus Consolidated Appropriations Act of 1996, renamed these divisions to honor retiring members of Congress, Representative William Clinger and Senator William Cohen.

CLOSEOUT The process of settling all outstanding contractual issues to ensure that each party has met all of its obligations, and documenting the contract file accordingly. The primary objectives of contract closeout are (1) to identify and resolve, before memories fade, any uncompleted obligations or pending liabilities on the part of either the government or the contractor; and (2) to ensure that contract-related decisions and actions have been properly documented. FAR 4.804-1 through -5 provides instructions for the closeout of contract files. FAR 42.708 contains "quick closeout procedures" for contracts where the amount of unsettled INDIRECT COSTs are relatively insignificant.

CLOUD COMPUTING *Official:* A model for enabling ubiquitous, convenient, on-demand network access to a shared pool of configurable computing resources (e.g., networks, servers, storage, applications, and services) that can be rapidly provisioned and released with minimal management effort or service provider interaction. This includes other commercial terms, such as on-demand self-service, broad network access, resource pooling, rapid elasticity, and measured service. It also includes commercial offerings for software-as-a-service, infrastructure-as-a-service, and platform-as-a-service. *Source:* DFARS 239.7601. Government agencies are increasingly procuring the services of contractors to host their data on a cloud. This allows multiple employees and contractors to access and modify the data as necessary to meet agency needs. DFARS Subpart 239.76 contains the DOD policies on cloud computing.

CODE As used with reference to the UNITED STATES CODE and the CODE OF FEDERAL REGULATIONS, a topically organized compilation of the laws enacted by Congress or the regulations promulgated by the EXECUTIVE BRANCH. The United States Code and the Code of Federal Regulations are comprised of topical sets called titles, e.g., Title 10 of the United States Code, "Armed Forces," contains the laws that pertain to the Department of Defense and the military departments. See How Our Laws Are Made, available at the Library of Congress website, http://thomas.loc.gov/home/lawsmade.toc.html.

CODE OF ETHICS A written code, adopted by a government contractor, setting forth the basic ethical rules that the contractor follows. FAR Subpart 3.10 FAR 3.1002 provides guidance on written code of business ethics and conduct for contractors. FAR 52.203-13, Contractor Code of Business Ethics and Conduct, is included in contracts that exceed $5,500,000 and have a performance period of 120 days or more. It requires contractors to have a written code of business ethics and conduct that is made available to all employees within 30 days of contract award. This clause is also applicable to subcontracts that meet the dollar and performance time criteria. As part of the code of business ethics, contractors subject to this clause are required to (1) exercise due diligence to prevent and detect criminal conduct and otherwise promote an organizational culture that encourages ethical conduct and compliance with the law and (2) timely disclose credible evidence that a principal, employee, agent, or subcontractor to the contract has violated criminal laws involving FRAUD, BRIBERY, or GRATUITY violations or the FALSE CLAIMS ACT. A contractor shall also develop a business ethics awareness and compliance program. (See PROCUREMENT INTEGRITY). A code of ethics serves as a mechanism by which questionable activities can be brought to the attention of management and places the contractor's corporate seal on compliance with government antifraud initiatives. The code of ethics gains effectiveness if (1) the policy is communicated to employees in writing, (2) employees certify that they have read the code and understand it, and (3) individuals found violating the code are disciplined. See Cibinic, Nash & Yukins, FORMATION OF GOVERNMENT CONTRACTS 142–48 (4th ed. 2011).

CODE OF FEDERAL REGULATIONS (C.F.R.) A government codification of the general and permanent rules published in the FEDERAL REGISTER by the executive departments and agencies of the federal government. The Code is divided into 50 titles, each representing a broad area subject to federal regulation. Each title is subdivided into chapters, which usually bear the name of the issuing agency. Each chapter is further subdivided into parts covering specific regulatory areas. For example, Title 48 contains the Federal Acquisition Regulation System (Chapter 1 contains the FAR, Chapter 2 contains the DFARS, and following chapters include other supplemental regulations). The C.F.R. is updated annually and is issued on a quarterly basis. It is available from the U.S. Government Printing Office, 732 North Capital Street, NW, Washington, DC 20401 and online at http://www.gpoaccess.gov/cfr/.

COLLATERAL COSTS   *Official:* Agency costs of operation, maintenance, logistic support, or GOVERNMENT-FURNISHED PROPERTY. *Source:* FAR 48.001. If these costs are reduced as a result of a VALUE ENGINEERING CHANGE PROPOSAL, the contractor is entitled to a share of the resulting COLLATERAL SAVINGS. Collateral costs also refer to expenses associated with getting materials into the offeror's plant, such as inbound transportation. FAR 31.205-26.

COLLATERAL SAVINGS   *Official:* Those measurable net reductions resulting from a VALUE ENGINEERING CHANGE PROPOSAL in the agency's overall projected COLLATERAL COSTS, exclusive of ACQUISITION SAVINGS, whether or not the ACQUISITION COST changes. *Source:* FAR 48.001. FAR 48.104-3 and the Value Engineering clauses in FAR 52.248-1 and -3 provide that a percentage of such savings (between 20 and 100%) is awarded to the contractor based solely on the calculation of the CONTRACTING OFFICER and may not exceed $100,000 or the contract price or cost, whichever is greater. See 1 Nash & Feldman, GOVERNMENT CONTRACT CHANGES § 9:16 (3d ed. 2006–2020); Cibinic, Nagle & Nash, ADMINISTRATION OF GOVERNMENT CONTRACTS 376 (5th ed. 2016).

COLLECTIVE WORK   See COMPILATION.

COLLUSIVE BIDDING   A fraudulent agreement between OFFERORs to eliminate competition or restrain trade. FAR 3.301(a). Generally, such bidding involves exchanging information before bidding or agreeing which offeror will submit the low bid. Collusive bidding violates antitrust laws and must be reported to the Attorney General by the procuring agency. FAR 3.303. See SEYFARTH SHAW LLP, THE GOVERNMENT CONTRACT COMPLIANCE HANDBOOK Part IV (5th ed. 2014–2019).

COLOR CODING   A NOTATIONAL SCORING SYSTEM in which colors are used to describe the quality of elements of an offeror's proposal. See DOD Source Selection Procedures, March 4, 2011, http://www.acq.osd.mil/dpap/ policy/policyvault/USA007183-10-DPAP.pdf. which sets forth a description of color coding systems which are mandatory for defense agencies. See Nash, *Source Selection Procedures: New DOD Guidance*, 25 N&CR ¶ 29 (June 2011); Nash, *Postscript: Scoring Systems*, 24 N&CR ¶ 13 (Mar. 2010); Nash, *Scoring Systems: Are They Useful?*, 23 N&CR ¶ 61 (Nov. 2009). See also ADJECTIVAL RATINGS.

COMBINED SYNOPSIS/SOLICITATION   A procedure which combines the SYNOPSIS required by FAR 5.203 and the issuance of the SOLICITATION into a single document with a response time no longer than is necessary to give potential offerors a reasonable opportunity to respond to the solicitation. This allows greatly shortening the statutory requirements for standard procurement that require a 15-day synopsis period and a 30-day offer period. This combined synopsis/solicitation is only appropriate when COMMERCIAL ITEMs are being procured. FAR 12.603. See Cibinic, Nash & Yukins, FORMATION OF GOVERNMENT CONTRACTS 1010–13 (4th ed. 2011).

COMMERCIAL   In the context of criteria for the establishment of contract quality requirements, a contract item that is described in commercial catalogs, drawings, or industrial standards. FAR 46.203(a).

COMMERCIAL BILL OF LADING   See BILL OF LADING.

COMMERCIAL COMPUTER SOFTWARE   *Official:* Software developed or regularly used for non-governmental purposes that (1) has been sold, leased, or licensed to the public; (2) has been offered for sale, lease, or license to the public; (3) has not been offered, sold, leased, or licensed to the public but will be available for commercial sale, lease, or license in time to satisfy the delivery requirements of the contract; or (4) satisfies the requirements of (1), (2), or (3) of this clause and would require only minor modifications to meet the requirements of this contract. *Source:* DFARS 252.227-7014. This definition is not stated in FAR 12.212 but is implicit in that regulation since the DOD definition is modeled on the definition of COMMERCIAL ITEM in FAR 2.101. Such software should be acquired under licenses customarily provided to the public unless they are inconsistent with federal procurement law. FAR 12.212; DFARS 227.7202-1(a). Such software is frequently procured using Schedule 70 of the Federal Supply Schedule. FAR 27.405-3 provides additional guidance on the procurement of commercial computer software and permits the use of the Commercial Computer Software—Restricted Rights clause in FAR 52.227-19 when the procuring agency is unsure whether a commercial license is consistent with federal procurement law. This clause specifies the RESTRICTED RIGHTS that pertain to such software. See Nash & Rawicz, INTELLECTUAL PROPERTY IN GOVERNMENT CONTRACTS, chap. 5 (6th ed. 2008). See also DeVecchio, *Licensing Commercial Computer Software*, BRIEFING PAPERS No. 04-3 (Feb. 2004); Anderson, *Comparative Analysis of Intellectual Property Issues Relating to the Acquisition of Commercial and Noncommercial Items by the Federal Government*, 33 PUB. CONT. L.J. 37 (2003).

COMMERCIAL IMPRACTICABILITY   See   IMPRACTICABILITY   OF PERFORMANCE.

COMMERCIAL ITEM   *Official:* (1) Any item, other than real property, that is of a type customarily used by the general public or by non-governmental entities for purposes other than governmental purposes, and (i has been sold, leased, or licensed to the general public or (ii) has been offered for sale, lease, or license to the general public; (2) Any item that evolved from an item described in paragraph (1) of this definition through advances in technology or performance and that is not yet available in the commercial marketplace, but will be available in the commercial marketplace in time to satisfy the delivery requirements under a government solicitation; (3) Any item that would satisfy the criterion expressed paragraphs (1) and (2) of this definition but for (i) modifications of a type customarily available in the commercial marketplace, or (ii) minor modifications of a type not customarily available in the commercial marketplace made to meet federal government requirements. Minor modifications means modifications that do not significantly alter the nongovernmental function or essential physical characteristics of an item or component, or change the purpose of a process. Factors to be considered in determining whether a modification is minor include the value and size of the modification and the comparative value and size of the final product. Dollar values and percentages may be used as guideposts, but are not conclusive evidence that a modification is minor; (4) Any combination of items meeting the requirements of paragraphs (1), (2), (3), or (5) of this definition that are of a type customarily combined and sold in combination to the general public; (5) Installation services, maintenance services, repair services, training services, and other services, if (i) Such services are procured for support of an item referred to in paragraphs (1), (2), (3), or (4) of this definition, regardless of whether such services are provided by the same source or at the same time as the item; and (ii) The source of such services provides similar services contemporaneously to the general public under terms and conditions similar to those offered to the federal government; (6) Services of a type offered and sold competitively in substantial quantities in the commercial marketplace based on established catalog (see CATALOG PRICE) or MARKET PRICES for specific tasks performed under standard commercial terms and conditions, not including services that are sold based on hourly rates without an established catalog or market price for a specific service performed (see STAND-ALONE COMMERCIAL SERVICES); (7) Any item, combination of items, or service referred to in paragraphs (1) through (6) of this definition, notwithstanding the fact that the item, combination of items, or service is transferred between or among separate divisions, subsidiaries, or affiliates of a contractor; or (8) A nondevelopmental item, if the procuring agency determines the item was developed exclusively at private expense and sold in substantial quantities, on a competitive basis to multiple state and local governments. *Source:* FAR 2.101. Note that this definition uses the word "item" to mean a product and both products and services. This confusing language was cleared up by changing the terms to COMMERCIAL PRODUCT and COMMERCIAL SERVICE. Title VIII of the FEDERAL ACQUISITION STREAMLINING ACT OF 1994, Pub. L. No. 103-355, contains detailed provisions stating a preference for commercial items and establishing acquisition policies for commercial items more closely resembling those of the commercial marketplace. These policies are set forth in FAR Part 12. See STREAMLINED PROCEDURES FOR COMMERCIAL ITEMS. See SEYFARTH SHAW LLP, THE GOVERNMENT CONTRACT COMPLIANCE HANDBOOK, chap. 10 (5th ed. 2014–2019); Cibinic, Nash & Yukins, FORMATION OF GOVERNMENT CONTRACTS 995–1027 (4th ed. 2011). See also Castellano, Blanchard, Casimir & Valle, *The Federal Circuit Addresses Commercial Item Contracting: Palantir & K-Con*, BRIEFING PAPERS 18-12 (Nov. 2018); Nash, *Postscript: Termination for Convenience of FAR Part 12 Commercial Item Contracts*, 25 N&CR ¶ 37 (Aug. 2011); Seidman, *Termination for Convenience of FAR Part 12 Commercial Item Contracts: Is Fair Compensation Required?*, 24 N&CR ¶ 37 (Aug. 2010).

COMMERCIAL ITEM DESCRIPTION (CID)   An indexed, simplified product description managed by the General Services Administration that describes, by functional or performance characteristics, the available, acceptable commercial products that will satisfy the government's needs. GSA, *Federal Standardization Manual* (2000); DOD 4120.3-M, *DoD Standardization Program (DSP) Policies and Procedures*, AP1.1.8; 41 C.F.R. § 101-29.208. Instructions for the preparation of CIDs are in the *Federal Standardization Manual*, Ch. 4. Government policy is to acquire commercial items when they meet agency needs. FAR 12.101(b). CIDs for items bought by the government are listed in the General Services Administration (GSA) Index of Federal Specifications, Standards and Commercial Item Descriptions, http://apps.fss.gsa.gov/pub/fedspecs/, and the DOD Index of Specifications and Standards (DODISS), http://dodssp.daps.dla.mil/dodiss_index.htm. See Nash, *Commercial Item Determination: A Matter of Discretion?*, 23 N&CR ¶ 10 (Feb. 2009).

COMMERCIAL ITEM EXCEPTION   An exception to the requirement for the submission of CERTIFIED COST OR PRICING DATA under the TRUTH IN NEGOTIATIONS ACT. This exception was added to 10 U.S.C. § 2306a(b)(1)(B) and 41 U.S.C. § 3503 by the FEDERAL ACQUISITION STREAMLINING ACT OF 1994, Pub. L. No. 103-355. It became the sole exception for commercial items when the standard catalog or market price exception was repealed in 1996 by the CLINGER-COHEN ACT OF 1996, Pub. L. No. 104-106. It is implemented in FAR 15.403-1. In negotiating contracts covered by this exception, the contracting officer must obtain, at a minimum, prices at which the same or similar item has been offered in the commercial market, and may obtain additional data, necessary to determine that the price is fair and reasonable. FAR 15.403-3(c). See Cibinic, Nash & Yukins, FORMATION OF GOVERNMENT CONTRACTS 1457-61 (4th ed. 2011). The "exception" is actually a prohibition because a contracting officer may not require the submission of CERTIFIED COST OR PRICING DATA for an acquisition of any item that meets the definition of COMMERCIAL ITEM in FAR 2.101.

COMMERCIAL ITEM OFFER   *Official:* An OFFER of a COMMERCIAL ITEM that the vendor wishes to see introduced in the government's supply system as an alternate or a replacement for an existing supply item. This term does not include innovative or unique configurations or uses of commercial items that are being offered for further development and that may be submitted as an unsolicited proposal. *Source:* FAR 15.601. Such offers may not be submitted as UNSOLICITED PROPOSALs because they do not include innovative or unique configurations or uses of commercial items that are being offered for further development. FAR 15.603(b).

COMMERCIAL GOODS OR SERVICES (GPA CONTEXT)   GOODS or SERVICES of a type generally sold or offered for sale in the commercial marketplace to, and customarily purchased by, non-governmental buyers for non-governmental purposes. World Trade Organization, Revision of the Agreement on Government Procurement, art. I (Dec. 13, 2010). A procuring entity seeking these goods or services may reduce the time period for tendering (see TENDER) required for other procurements if the procurement is published electronically. See also COMMERCIAL PRODUCT. Other trade agreements contain similar provisions regarding the procurement of commercial goods or services that are found in the GOVERNMENT PROCUREMENT AGREEMENT. See, e.g., United States—Chile Free Trade Agreement, art. 9.5 (2003). See Reich, *The New Text of the Agreement on Government Procurement: An Analysis and Assessment,* 12 J. INT'L ECON. L. 989 (2009).

COMMERCIAL MARKET REPRESENTATIVE (CMRs)   The SMALL BUSINESS ADMINISTRATION's subcontracting specialists who are responsible for (1) facilitating the matching of large prime contractors with SMALL BUSINESS CONCERNs; (2) counseling large prime contractors on their responsibilities to maximize subcontracting opportunities for small business concerns; (3) instructing prime contractors on identifying small business concerns through electronic and other means; (4) counseling small business concerns on how to market themselves to large prime contractors; (5) maintaining a portfolio of large prime contractors and conducting Subcontracting Orientation and Assistance Reviews (SOARS) to assist prime contractors in complying with their small business subcontracting responsibilities; and (6) conducting periodic reviews. 13 C.F.R. § 125.3(e).

COMMERCIAL OR FINANCIAL INFORMATION   Information concerning the business dealing of an organization. Such information falls within Exemption 4 of the FREEDOM OF INFORMATION ACT if it is privileged or confidential. It is confidential if disclosure would impair the government's ability to obtain such information in the future or would cause substantial harm to the person from whom the information was obtained. The TRADE SECRETS ACT makes it a crime for a government employee to disclose such information. See Nash & Rawicz, INTELLECTUAL PROPERTY IN GOVERNMENT CONTRACTS, chap. 9 (6th ed. 2008).

COMMERCIAL PRODUCT   *Official:* Any of the following: (1) A product, other than real property, that—(A) is of a type customarily used by the general public or by nongovernmental entities for purposes other than governmental purposes; and (B) has been sold, leased, or licensed, or offered for sale, lease, or license, to the general public. (2) A product that—(A) evolved from a product described in paragraph (1) through advances in technology or performance; and (B) is not yet available in the commercial marketplace but will be available in the commercial marketplace in time to satisfy the delivery requirements under a Federal Government solicitation. (3) A product that would satisfy the criteria in paragraph (1) or (2) were it not for—(A) modifications of a type customarily available in the commercial marketplace; or (B) minor modifications made to meet Federal Government requirements. (4) Any combination of products meeting the requirements of paragraph (1), (2), or (3) that are of a type customarily combined and sold in combination to the general public. (5) A product, or combination of products, referred to in paragraphs (1) through (4), even though the product, or combination of products, is transferred between or among separate divisions, subsidiaries, or affiliates of a contractor. (6) A nondevelopmental item if the procuring agency determines, in accordance with conditions in the Federal Acquisition Regulation, that—(A) the product was developed exclusively at private expense; and (B) has been sold in substantial quantities, on a competitive basis, to multiple State and local governments or to multiple foreign governments. *Source:* 41 U.S.C. § 103. This definition will replace the term COMMERCIAL ITEM when the FAR implements this statutory change.

COMMERCIAL SERVICE   *Official:* Any of the following: (1) Installation services, maintenance services, repair services, training services, and other services if—(A) those services are procured for support of a COMMERCIAL PRODUCT, regardless of whether the services are provided by the same source or at the same time as the commercial product; and (B) the source of the services provides similar services contemporaneously to the general public under terms and conditions similar to those offered to the Federal Government; (2) Services of a type offered and sold competitively, in substantial quantities, in the commercial marketplace—(A) based on established catalog (see CATALOG PRICE) or MARKET PRICES; (B) for specific tasks performed or specific outcomes to be achieved (see STAND-ALONE COMMERCIAL SERVICES); and (C) under standard commercial terms and conditions. (3) A service described in paragraph (1) or (2), even though the service is transferred between or among separate divisions, subsidiaries, or affiliates of a contractor. *Source:* 41 U.S.C. § 103. This definition will replace the term COMMERCIAL ITEM when the FAR implements this statutory change.

COMMERCIAL SOLUTIONS OPENING (CSO)   A publication seeking innovative commercial items, technologies or services that directly fulfill requirements, close capability gaps, or provide potential technological advances. It is similar to a BROAD AGENCY ANNOUNCEMENT but allows for acquiring technology directly relevant to a specific program unlike BAAs which are restricted to only basic and applied research and that portion of development not related to a specific system or hardware program. CSOs focus on businesses or institutions that have not traditionally done business with the government. They were authorized by § 879 and § 880 of Pub. L. No. 114-328. See the GSA *Commercial Solutions Opening Guide*, June 1, 2018.

COMMERCIALLY AVAILABLE OFF-THE-SHELF (COTS) ITEM   *Official:* (1) Any ITEM of supply (including construction material) that is—(i) a COMMERCIAL ITEM; (ii) sold in substantial quantities in the commercial marketplace; and (iii) offered to the Government, under a contract or SUBCONTRACT at any tier, without modification, in the same form in which it is sold in the commercial marketplace; and (2) does not include bulk cargo, as defined in section 3 of the Shipping Act of 1984 (46 U.S.C. App. § 1702) such as agricultural products and petroleum products. *Source:* FAR 2.101. In addition to laws inapplicable to commercial items (see FAR 12.503 to 12.504), the BUY AMERICAN ACT-supplies component test and the Estimate and Percentage of Recovered Material Act (see 42 U.S.C. § 6962(c)(3)(A)) are waived for COTS items. FAR 12.505. See Shepphard Mullin, *New Rules for Commercial Off-the-Shelf Products Exempts BAA Components and Exempts Recycled Content Reporting Requirement,* Government Contracts, Investigations, & International Trade Blog (Feb. 17, 2009).

COMMISSION ON GOVERNMENT PROCUREMENT (COGP)   Commission that studied federal procurement and recommended to Congress methods to promote the economy, efficiency, and effectiveness of procurement by the executive branch. Created by Pub. L. No. 91-129 in 1969, the Commission, made up of 12 members (two congressmen, two senators, the Comptroller General, two executive branch officials, and five non-government persons), submitted its findings and recommendations in 1972. The Commission's four-volume report included a Blueprint for Action that outlined an integrated system for the federal procurement process, addressing policy control, the statutory framework, the workforce, funding, contracting officer authority, contract administration and AUDIT, disputes and protests, and the uses of commercial products and services. The recommendations of the Commission led to significant statutory changes including the creation of the OFFICE OF FEDERAL PROCUREMENT POLICY in 1974 (Pub. L. No. 93-400), the enactment of the CONTRACT DISPUTES ACT of 1978 (Pub. L. No. 95-563), and the enactment of the COMPETITION IN CONTRACTING ACT in 1984 (Div. B., Title VII, Pub. L. No. 98-369).

COMMITMENT (OF FUNDS)   An accounting procedure whereby an agency administratively reserves or "earmarks" allotted funds, or other funds, in anticipation of their OBLIGATION. A PURCHASE REQUEST sent to a contracting officer should include documentation by an agency financial official to the effect that funds have been committed (or "administratively committed") for the acquisition. U.S. Gov't Accountability Office, A Glossary of Terms Used in the Federal Budget Process, GAO-05-734SP (Sept. 2005), at 32 and U.S. Gov't Accountability Office, Policies and Procedures Manual for Guidance of Federal Agencies, 7 PPM § 3.5F. Commitment is also defined as an administrative reservation of funds by the comptroller in anticipation of their obligation based upon firm procurement directives, orders, requisitions, authorizations to issue travel orders, or requests.

COMMITTEE FOR PURCHASE FROM PEOPLE WHO ARE BLIND OR SEVERELY DISABLED   A committee established under the JAVITS-WAGNER-O'DAY ACT (JWOD), 41 U.S.C. § 8502-04. Its job is to compile a procurement list of commodities and services that the government must procure from JWOD PARTICIPATING nonprofit agencies and to oversee the JWOD program. 41 C.F.R. § 51-2.2. Its membership is comprised of 15 persons appointed by the President of the United States from government and the private sector. See FAR Subpart 8.7. The Committee operates as the U.S. AbilityOne Commission and maintains a website at http://www.abilityone.gov/abilityone/.

COMMON CARRIER   An entity that, without right of refusal, provides services to the general public as required by law. Black's Law Dictionary 264 (11th ed. 2019). See also CARRIER (TELECOMMUNICATIONS) and CARRIER (TRANSPORTATION).

COMMON ITEM   *Official:* Material that is common to the applicable government contract and to the contractor's other work. *Source:* FAR 2.101. In contract terminations, the costs of common items reasonably usable on the contractor's other work are not allowable unless the contractor submits evidence that the items could not be retained at cost without sustaining a loss. FAR 31.205-42. The term is used in the *Reporting Nonconforming Items* clause in FAR 52.246-26 to mean "an item that has multiple applications versus a single or peculiar application." See Cibinic, Nagle & Nash, Administration of Government Contracts 1024–25 (5th ed. 2016); Cibinic, Knight & Nash, Cost-Reimbursement Contracting 747 (4th ed. 2014).

COMMON RULE   See OMB UNIFORM GUIDANCE

COMPARABILITY   The condition that exists when an offered price can be compared with some other price in the process of PRICE ANALYSIS. This condition, necessary for effective price comparison, exists when all price-related differences have been identified and accounted for so that the prices being compared are based on relatively equal assumptions. A practical definition of "comparable" is "having enough similar characteristics or qualities to make comparison useful." The government has two choices if it cannot establish comparability in price analysis: it can disregard the data, or it can discount them. See DAU, *Contract Pricing Reference Guide* v. I, chap. 6 (Feb. 21, 2012).

COMPENSABLE DELAY   A DELAY, incurred by a contractor in contract performance, for which the government is required to give compensation. The government must have been the sole cause of the delay, that is there must be no other cause of delay on the CRITICAL PATH during the time of the government delay (See CONCURRENT DELAY). There are two standard clauses providing for such compensation: (1) the Suspension of Work clause in FAR 52.242-14, which must be used in all fixed-price construction and architect-engineer contracts; and (2) the Government Delay of Work clause in FAR 52.242-17, which must be used in all fixed-price supply contracts except those for commercial or modified-commercial items. These clauses give a PRICE ADJUSTMENT (excluding PROFIT) when an unreasonable delay is caused by an act (or failure to act) of the contracting officer in the administration of the contract. If a clause of this nature is not included in the contract, the contractor may obtain compensation for a delay caused by the government under a BREACH OF CONTRACT theory. See Cibinic, Nagle & Nash, Administration of Government Contracts 521–51 (5th ed. 2016). See also Dale & D'Onofrio, *Reconciling Concurrency in Schedule Delay and Constructive Acceleration*, 39 Pub. Cont. L.J. 161 (2010).

COMPENSATED PERSONAL ABSENCE   *Official:* Any absence from work for reasons such as illness, vacation, holidays, jury duty, military training, or personal activities for which an employer pays compensation directly to an employee in accordance with a plan or custom of the employer. *Source:* FAR 31.001. CAS 408, Accounting Costs for Compensated Personal Absence, 48 C.F.R. § 9904.408-40(a) requires that such costs be assigned to the accounting period in which the entitlement was earned and § 9904.408-50 provides guidance on the interpretation of this requirement. FAR 31.205-6(m) provides that such costs incurred by a contractor are allowable (see ALLOWABLE COST) to the extent that they are reasonable and required by law, an employer-employee agreement, or an established policy of the contractor. See Cibinic, Knight & Nash, Cost-Reimbursement Contracting 687–88(4th ed. 2014).

COMPENSATION FOR PERSONAL SERVICES   All remuneration paid by a contractor currently or accrued, in whatever form and whether paid immediately or deferred, for services rendered by employees to the contractor during the period of contract performance (with some exceptions with regard to severance pay costs and pension costs). FAR 31.205-6. Such compensation is generally an ALLOWABLE COST subject to the detailed guidance in FAR 31.205-6. See Manos, 1 GOVERNMENT CONTRACT COSTS & PRICING §§ 13:1–13:22 (2d ed. 2009–2020). Compensation for personal services includes, but is not limited to, salaries; wages; directors' and executive committee members' fees; bonuses (including stock bonuses); incentive awards; employee stock options, stock appreciation rights and stock ownership plans; employee insurance; fringe benefits; contributions to pension, annuity, and management-employee incentive compensation plans; and allowances for off-site pay, incentive pay, location allowances, hardship pay, severance pay, and cost-of-living differentials. Congress has enacted ceilings on executive compensation paid to SENIOR EXECUTIVEs. 10 U.S.C. § 2324(e)(1)(P) and 41 U.S.C. § 4304(a)(16). See FAR 31.205-6(p). This ceiling is established as a BENCHMARK COMPENSATION AMOUNT by the Administrator of the Office of Federal Procurement Policy in accordance with 41 U.S.C. § 1127.

COMPENSATORY DAMAGES   See DAMAGES.

COMPETING CONTRACTOR   Any entity that is, or is reasonably likely to become, a competitor for or recipient of a contract or subcontract under any procurement of property or services; or any person acting on behalf of such an entity. Competing contractors were subject to many of the provisions governing PROCUREMENT INTEGRITY until the law was changed in 1996. Contracts signed before Jan. 1, 1997, will have imposed these rules on competing contractors. FAR 3.104-4(b), prior to its revision on Jan. 2, 1997, contained additional guidance on the meaning of "competing contractor."

COMPETITION [1]   Generally, the struggle for commercial advantage; the effort or action of two or more commercial interests to obtain the same business from third parties. BLACK'S LAW DICTIONARY 355 (11th ed. 2019). **[2]** A contract formation procedure in which the government solicits or entertains offers from two or more competitors, compares them, and accepts one based on its relative value. FAR Part 6. The FAR makes a distinction between the government's *pursuit* of competition, i.e., full and open competition, full and open competition after exclusion of sources, or other than full and open competition, and the *market's response* to the government's pursuit, i.e., ADEQUATE PRICE COMPETITION or EFFECTIVE COMPETITION. See COMPETITION IN CONTRACTING ACT. See Cibinic, Nash & Yukins, FORMATION OF GOVERNMENT CONTRACTS 293–94 (4th ed. 2011).

COMPETITION ADVOCATE   An employee of a CONTRACTING ACTIVITY specifically assigned the task of challenging barriers to competition and promoting FULL AND OPEN COMPETITION. 41 U.S.C. § 1705, requires that each EXECUTIVE AGENCY and each contracting activity appoint a competition advocate. Such advocates are generally high-ranking employees reporting directly to the heads of their agency or activity. 41 U.S.C. § 1705 requires that they report their activities and remaining barriers to the SENIOR PROCUREMENT EXECUTIVE of the agency on an annual basis. FAR 6.501 requires that they must be in a position other than that of the agency senior procurement executive, must not be assigned any duties inconsistent with those of competition advocate, and must be provided with necessary staff or assistance. Competition advocates are charged with

(1) promoting full and open competition and challenging barriers to it; (2) reviewing contracting operations to identify (a) opportunities and actions necessary to achieve full and open competition and (b) the conditions that unnecessarily restrict it; (3) preparing annual reports; (4) recommending goals and plans for increasing competition; and (5) recommending a system of personal and organizational accountability—one that motivates individuals to promote competition and recognizes those who do. FAR 6.502. See U.S. Gov't Accountability Office, Federal Contracting: Opportunities Exist To Increase Competition And Assess Reasons When Only One Offer Is Received, GAO-10-833 (July 2010); Nash, *Dateline December 2010*, 24 N&CR ¶ 12 (2010).

COMPETITION IN CONTRACTING ACT (CICA) A 1984 Act that amended the two basic procurement statutes (the ARMED SERVICES PROCUREMENT ACT, 10 U.S.C. § 2304 et seq., and the FEDERAL PROPERTY AND ADMINISTRATION SERVICES ACT OF 1949, 41 U.S.C. § 3101 et seq.) in order to enhance competition, grant statutory authorization for the Government Accountability Office's PROTEST function, create protest jurisdiction for federal information processing resources procurement at the GENERAL SERVICES ADMINISTRATION BOARD OF CONTRACT APPEALS, and revise protest procedures. CICA was the first major revision to the procurement statutes since the 1940s. It introduced the phrase FULL AND OPEN COMPETITION, replaced the term "formal advertising" with "SEALED BIDDING," and authorized contracting by COMPETITIVE PROPOSALS (i.e., competitive NEGOTIATION) when sealed bidding is not practical. Recognizing that negotiation could be as competitive as sealed bidding, CICA eliminated the requirement to execute a DETERMINATION AND FINDINGS to justify use of negotiation. It established a requirement to execute a justification—and obtain approval of it—for any procurement in which full and open competition cannot be obtained. See Cibinic, Nash & Yukins, Formation of Government Contracts 293–98 (4th ed. 2011); Cong. Research Serv., Report No. RL40516, Competition in Federal Contracting: Legal Overview (Jan. 21, 2015); Cohen, *The Competition in Contracting Act*, Public Contract Law Journal, Vol. 14, No. 1 (Oct. 1983), pp. 1–39.

COMPETITIVE ADVANTAGE An advantage of one competitor over another. Normally, the government is not concerned with competitive advantages held by one competitor in the procurement process because many advantages are inherent in a free economy. For example, a competitor may have an advantage because of its superior design capabilities, its geographic location (resulting in lower transportation costs), its lower taxes (because its state has low tax rates), or its more productive employees. However, it is the policy of the government to attempt to overcome UNFAIR COMPETITIVE ADVANTAGEs. The government also attempts to compensate for the advantage gained by manufacturing materials and products in a foreign country. See BUY AMERICAN ACT.

COMPETITIVE ALTERNATIVE SOURCE See DUAL SOURCE.

COMPETITIVE COPYING The furnishing of a product to a potential contractor to allow that contractor to replicate the product by REVERSE ENGINEERING. This is a common technique for an agency to obtain competition for the production of defense products, particularly replenishment parts. 10 U.S.C. § 2320(d) requires defense agencies to allow such competitors to "purchase or borrow replenishment parts" for this purpose. See Nash & Rawicz, Intellectual Property in Government Contracts, chap. 8 (6th ed. 2008).

COMPETITIVE NEGOTIATION See COMPETITIVE PROPOSALS.

COMPETITIVE PROCEDURES   Contracting procedures that meet the statutory requirement for FULL AND OPEN COMPETITION in government procurement. 10 U.S.C. § 2304(a)(2) and 41 U.S.C. § 3301(b), cite two major types of competitive procedures: SEALED BIDDING and COMPETITIVE PROPOSALS. 10 U.S.C. § 2302(2) and 41 U.S.C. § 152, list five additional types of competitive procedures: (1) BROOKS ACT (ARCHITECT-ENGINEER (A-E) PROCUREMENT) procedures, (2) BROAD AGENCY ANNOUNCEMENT, (3) MULTIPLE-AWARD SCHEDULE contracting, (4) procurement under 15 U.S.C. § 644 (small business SET-ASIDE), and (5) SMALL BUSINESS INNOVATIVE RESEARCH contracting. See also OTHER THAN FULL AND OPEN COMPETITION. See Cibinic, Nash & Yukins, FORMATION OF GOVERNMENT CONTRACTS 331 (4th ed. 2011). See also Manuel, CONG. RESEARCH SERV., Report No. R40516, COMPETITION IN FEDERAL CONTRACTING: AN OVERVIEW OF THE LEGAL REQUIREMENTS (Aug. 20, 2009); Dekel, *The Legal Theory Of Competitive Bidding For Government Contracts*, 37 PUB. CONT. L.J. 237 (2008); Dekel, *Modification Of A Government Contract Awarded Following A Competitive Procedure*, 38 PUB. CONT. L.J. 401 (2009); Nash, *Postscript II: The Competition Cure All*, 22 N&CR ¶ 53 (Sept. 2008); Edwards, *Competition: Is it the Cure All That Everyone Seems to Think It Is?*, 21 N&CR ¶ 36 (July 2007).

COMPETITIVE PROPOSALS   See FAR Subpart 6.4, *Sealed Bidding and Competitive Proposals*, FAR Subpart 15.3, *Source Selection*, and SOURCE SELECTION.

COMPETITIVE PROTOTYPES   Initial models of a proposed new weapon system or subsystem that are submitted by competing contractors to demonstrate through side-by-side testing that their technical solution is the superior solution. The competitive prototyping acquisition strategy has been used sporadically for many years in an attempt to improve the weapon system acquisition process. The concept of competitive prototyping is to gain more precise information on system or subsystem capabilities than can be obtained from competing technical proposals in order to permit a more technically sound decision on proceeding to the ENGINEERING AND MANUFACTURING DEVELOPMENT PHASE of a weapon system project. See Drezner & Huang, ON PROTOTYPING (Rand Corp. 2009). See also PROTOTYPE OTHER TRANSACTION.

COMPETITIVE RANGE   In SOURCE SELECTION, the set of proposals that are most highly rated, unless the fewer proposals are included for purposes of efficiency. FAR 15.306(c), *Competitive range*. FAR 15.306(c) that a contracting officer establish the competitive range on the basis of the ratings of each proposal against all evaluation criteria. After evaluating all proposals, the contracting officer may determine that the number of most highly rated proposals exceeds the number at which an efficient competition can be conducted. In that case, and if the solicitation notified prospective offerors of the possibility, the contracting officer may limit the number of proposals in the competitive range to the greatest number that will permit an efficient competition among the most highly rated proposals. FAR 15.306(c)(2). The contracting officer must then conduct DISCUSSIONS with all offerors in the competitive range in accordance with FAR 15.306(d). If, after discussions, the contracting officer decides that a particular offeror should no longer be included in the competitive range, the offeror must be eliminated from further consideration and notified in writing to that effect. FAR 15.306(d)(5) and FAR 15.503. Offerors excluded or otherwise eliminated from the competitive range may request a DEBRIEFING. FAR 15.306(d)(4) and 15.505. See Cibinic, Nash & Yukins, FORMATION OF GOVERNMENT CONTRACTS 875–88 (4th ed. 2011); Craig, *Note, Searching For Clarity: Completing the Unfinished FAR Part 15*

Rewrite, 39 Pub. Cont. L.J. 661 (2010); Nash, *Postscript: Communications With Offeror Before Establishing A Competitive Range*, 24 N&CR ¶ 47 (Oct. 2010); Nash, *Discussions After Establishing the Competitive Range: Are They Mandatory?*, 22 N&CR ¶ 34 (June 2008).

COMPETITIVE SOURCING The act of exposing government activities to competition with the private sector following the A-76 POLICY. Competitive sourcing calls for conducting public-private competitions as a way of improving performance and efficiency in the government. A competition involves comparing the performance of the government organization with that of a private sector organization using cost, quality and/or other criteria. A competition determines if agency business requirements can be met at a minimum cost to taxpayers without compromise to quality or performance. Competitive Sourcing is not the same as OUTSOURCING which assumes that the private sector can perform activities more efficiently that the government and does not allow the government organization the opportunity to compete. The FEDERAL ACTIVITIES INVENTORY REFORM ACT (FAIR) of 1998 requires that federal agencies annually provide the OMB and the Congress with a list of commercial functions performed by the government. OMB CIRCULAR A-76 sets forth procedures that federal agencies must use for the competition of commercial activities. Competitive sourcing competitions were conducted regularly until Congress imposed a moratorium on DOD competitions in 2008 and on all competitions in 2009. See Gov't Accountability Office, Competitive Sourcing: Greater Emphasis Needed on Increasing Efficiency and Improving Performance, GAO-04-367 (Fed. 2004); Federal Acquisition Council, *Manager's Guide to Competitive Sourcing* (Oct. 2, 2003); Schooner, *Competitive Sourcing Policy: More Sail Than Rudder?*, 33 Pub. Cont. L.J. 263 (2004).

COMPILATION *Official:* A WORK, formed by the collection and assembling of preexisting materials or of data that are selected, coordinated, or arranged in such a way that the resulting work as a whole constitutes an original work of authorship. The term "compilation" includes collective works. *Source:* 17 U.S.C. § 101. "Collective works" that are defined as "a work, such as a periodical issue, anthology, or encyclopedia, in which a number of contributions, constituting separate and independent works in themselves, are assembled into a collective whole." 17 U.S.C. § 101. An author of a compilation (the owner of the work or another author with permission of the owner) may obtain a copyright on material contributed by that author. 17 U.S.C. § 103. Authors of the material in the compilation retain the copyright on the material they have contributed unless it is assigned to the compiler. See Nash & Rawicz, Intellectual Property in Government Contracts, chap. 1 (6th ed. 2008).

COMPLAINT In a contract DISPUTE, a written statement in which a PLAINTIFF before the U.S. COURT OF FEDERAL CLAIMS or an APPELLANT BEFORE a BOARD OF CONTRACT APPEALS giving a direct statement of each of its claims, the bases for these claims, and the dollar amount claimed to the extent known.

COMPLETION BOND See PERFORMANCE BOND.

COMPLETION FORM CONTRACT A COST-PLUS-FIXED-FEE CONTRACT that describes the work by stating a definite goal or target and specifying an end product. FAR 16.306(d)(1). This is contrasted with a TERM CONTRACT where the contractor's obligation is stated in terms of a specified level of effort for a stated period of time. In the completion form contract, the contractor does not earn the full FIXED FEE until the work, as specified, has been satisfactorily completed. If completion within the estimated cost is not possible, the government may require more effort without an increase in the fixed fee as long as the estimated cost is increased. While these terms are defined as applying to cost-plus-fixed-fee contracts, they are also relevant in describing the variable forms of other types of COST-REIMBURSEMENT CONTRACTS. See Cibinic, Knight & Nash, COST-REIMBURSEMENT CONTRACTING 47–49 (4th ed. 2014).

COMPLEX ITEMS   In the context of criteria for the establishment of CONTRACT QUALITY REQUIREMENTS, a contract item that has characteristics not wholly visible in the end item, for which contractual conformance must be established progressively through precise measurements, tests, and controls applied during purchasing, manufacturing, performance, assembly, and functional operation either as an individual item or in conjunction with other items. FAR 46.203(b)(1). FAR 46.202-4 states that it is appropriate to impose HIGHER-LEVEL CONTRACT QUALITY REQUIREMENTS when procuring complex items.

COMPONENT   *Official:* Any item supplied to the government as part of an END ITEM or of another component (with Buy American exceptions). *Source:* FAR 2.101. When the BUY AMERICAN ACT is applicable, a component is an article, material, or supply incorporated directly into an END PRODUCT or CONSTRUCTION MATERIAL. FAR 25.003. In such cases, over 50% of the cost of the components must be of domestic origin for the end product to qualify as a DOMESTIC END PRODUCT. When applying the TECHNICAL DATA statutes, 10 U.S.C. § 2320 and 41 U.S.C. § 2302, a component is included in the definition of ITEM, item of supply, or supplies. 10 U.S.C. § 2302(3); 41 U.S.C. §§ 105 and 108.

COMPONENT ACQUISITION EXECUTIVE   Secretaries of the military departments or heads of agencies with the power of re-delegation. In the military departments, the officials delegated as CAEs (also called Service Acquisition Executives (SAEs)) are respectively, the Assistant Secretary of the Army for Acquisition, Logistics, and Technology (ASA(AL&T)), the Assistant Secretary of the Navy for Research, Development and Acquisition (ASN(RD&A)), and the Assistant Secretary of the Air Force for Acquisition (ASAF(A)). The CAEs are responsible for all acquisition functions within their Components. This includes both the SAEs for the military departments and acquisition executives in other DoD Components, such as the U.S. Special Operations Command (SOCOM) and Defense Logistics Agency (DLA), which also have acquisition management responsibilities. DAU GLOSSARY.

COMPREHENSIVE ENVIRONMENTAL RESPONSE, COMPENSATION, AND LIABILITY ACT (CERCLA)   A statute permitting the government to clean up environmentally hazardous materials that have been left on sites throughout the United States. 42 U.S.C. chapter 103. The money available to finance such cleanup activities is commonly known as the "Superfund." Organizations that have owned or controlled the sites at the time the materials were disposed of are required to reimburse the superfund for the cost of the cleanup work. See EPA, *CERCLA Overview*, http://www.epa.gov/superfund/policy/cercla.htm.

COMPTROLLER GENERAL (COMP. GEN.)   The government officer, appointed by the President of the United States to serve a 15-year term as head of the GOVERNMENT ACCOUNTABILITY OFFICE (GAO). The GAO is part of the legislative branch of the government. 31 U.S.C. § 712 requires the Comptroller General to investigate all matters relating to the receipt, disbursement, and application of public funds. The Comptroller General also has the power to examine the records of contractors doing business with the government (see EXAMINATION OF RECORDS CLAUSE), evaluate and assess the results of government programs (and typically issue reports), and evaluate and issue recommendations on PROTESTs pursuant to the COMPETITION IN CONTRACTING ACT. FAR 33.104.

COMPULSORY LICENSE   See MARCH-IN.

COMPUTER   A data processing device capable of accepting data, performing prescribed operations on the data, and supplying the results of these operations (for example, a device that operates on discrete data by performing arithmetic and logic processes on the data, or a device that operates on analog data by performing physical processes on the data). This definition was included in the 1988 DOD policy on TECHNICAL DATA at DFARS 227.471 but was omitted from the 1995 DFARS policy. Neither is the term defined in the FAR.

COMPUTER-AIDED DESIGN   Design of a product using COMPUTER SOFTWARE as the primary tool to create the design. This software creates accurate drawings and permits changes with minimal effort. It can be linked to COMPUTER-AIDED MANUFACTURING software to produce products without drawings. See CAD/CAM. A comprehensive website is www.caddprimer.com/library/.

COMPUTER-AIDED MANUFACTURING   The process of using a COMPUTER to control machine tools and other manufacturing equipment. The software permits precise manufacturing and allows changes to be introduced with a minimum of effort. When COMPUTER-AIDED DESIGN information is fed directly into the computer, the product can be manufactured without intervening drawings. See CAD/CAM. A comprehensive website is www.compinfo-center.com/cad/cam.htm.

COMPUTER DATABASE   *Official:* A collection of recorded information in a form capable of, and for the purpose of, being stored in, processed, and operated on by a COMPUTER. The term does not include COMPUTER SOFTWARE. *Source:* FAR 2.101. A shorter but essentially the same definition is in DFARS 252.227-7013. Under the 2007 FAR policy and the 1995 DOD policy on TECHNICAL DATA and COMPUTER SOFTWARE, computer databases are considered to be technical data not computer software. Under prior policies on technical data and computer software, computer databases were considered to be computer software. See Nash & Rawicz, INTELLECTUAL PROPERTY IN GOVERNMENT CONTRACTS, chap. 5 (6th ed. 2008).

COMPUTER PROGRAM 1.   *Official:* A set of statements or instructions to be used directly or indirectly in a computer in order to bring about a certain result. *Source:* 17 U.S.C. § 101. This definition in the Copyright Act, which appears to include both object code and source code, as well as information on the design of the program, is not used in the contracting process. Rather the procuring agencies use the term COMPUTER SOFTWARE to describe the operation of a computer both directly and indirectly. **2.** *Official:* A set of instructions, rules, or routines recorded in a form that is capable of causing a computer to perform a specific operation or series of operations. *Source:* FAR 52.227-14 and DFARS 252.227-7013. The 1988 DOD policy on COMPUTER SOFTWARE contained a more complete definition stating that computer programs include operating systems, assemblers, compilers, interpreters, data management systems, utility programs, sort-merge programs, and ADPE maintenance/ diagnostic programs, as well as applications programs such as payroll, inventory control, and engineering analysis programs; and that they may be either machine-dependent or machine-independent and may be general-purpose in nature or designed to satisfy the requirements of a particular user. DFARS 227.471 (pre-1995 version). Under these FAR and DFARS definitions, computer programs are one element of computer software since they appear to include only OBJECT CODE. See Nash & Rawicz, INTELLECTUAL PROPERTY IN GOVERNMENT CONTRACTS, chap. 5 (6th ed. 2008); Nash, *Computer Programs: Are They Products?*, 21 N&CR ¶71 (Dec. 2007).

COMPUTER SOFTWARE   *Official:* (1) Means (i) COMPUTER PROGRAMs that comprise a series of instructions, rules, routines, or statements, regardless of the media in which recorded, that allow or cause a computer to perform a specific operation or series of operations; and (ii) Recorded information comprising source code listings, design details, algorithms, processes, flow charts, formulas, and related material that would enable the computer program to be produced, created, or compiled. (2) Does not include COMPUTER DATABASEs or COMPUTER SOFTWARE DOCUMENTATION. *Source:* FAR 2.101. This term has had a different meaning in the evolving policies on TECHNICAL DATA and computer software. In the 1995 DOD policy, it means computer programs, SOURCE CODE, source code listings, object code listings, design details, algorithms, processes, flowcharts, formulae, and related material that would enable the software to be produced, created, or compiled; but not computer databases and computer software documentation, DFARS 252.227-7013. In the pre-2007 FAR policy, it meant computer programs, computer databases, and computer software documentation, FAR 27.401 (pre-2007 version). In the 1988 DOD policy, it meant computer programs and computer databases but not computer software documentation. DFARS 227.471 (pre-1995 version). In general, both the FAR and the DFARS regulations grant the government only RESTRICTED RIGHTS to software that is DEVELOPED AT PRIVATE EXPENSE. See Nash & Rawicz, INTELLECTUAL PROPERTY IN GOVERNMENT CONTRACTS, chap. 5 (6th ed. 2008); DeVecchio, *Taking the Mystery Out Of Data Rights*, BRIEFING PAPERS No. 18-8 (July 2018).

COMPUTER SOFTWARE DOCUMENTATION   *Official:* Owner's manuals, user's manuals, installation instructions, operating instructions, and other similar items, regardless of storage medium, that explain the capabilities of the computer software or provide instructions for using the software. *Source:* FAR 2.101. This term has had a different meaning in the evolving policies on TECHNICAL DATA and COMPUTER SOFTWARE. The current definition applies to the 2007 FAR policy and the 1995 DOD policy. In the 1988 DOD policy, it meant TECHNICAL DATA, including computer listings and printouts, in human-readable form which (a) documents the design or details of computer software, (b) explains the capabilities of the software, or (c) provides operating instructions for using the software to obtain desired results from a computer. DFARS 227.471 (pre-1995 version). This appeared to include the SOURCE CODE. The term was undefined in the pre-2007 FAR but it appeared to mean any written material relating to a COMPUTER PROGRAM or a COMPUTER DATABASE. For the purposes of allocating the rights of the contracting parties to the information, this documentation is technical data under the current FAR policy and the DOD policies and computer software under pre-2007 FAR Subpart 27.4. See Nash & Rawicz, INTELLECTUAL PROPERTY IN GOVERNMENT CONTRACTS, chap. 5 (6th ed. 2008).

COMPUTER SOFTWARE LICENSE　A license to use COMPUTER SOFTWARE for purposes designated in the license. Under the FAR policy, the government gets an UNLIMITED RIGHTS license in software first produced in the performance of the contract and a RESTRICTED RIGHTS license in software developed at PRIVATE EXPENSE that is a TRADE SECRET if the contract contains Alternate III to the Rights in Data—General clause in FAR 52.227-14. Alternatively, the government gets only restricted rights if the contract contains the Commercial Computer Software—Restricted Rights clause in FAR 52.227-19. Under the DOD policy, the government gets an unlimited rights license in software developed exclusively with government funds, a GOVERNMENT PURPOSE license in software developed with MIXED FUNDING and a restricted rights license in software developed exclusively at private expense if the contract contains the Rights in Noncommercial Computer Software and Noncommercial Computer Software Documentation clause in DFARS 252.227-7014. If the software is commercial, the DFARS prescribes no clause but permits the government's license to be of the same scope as the contractor's commercial license. DFARS 227.7202-3. Most commercial software is subject to a SHRINKWRAP LICENSE or a CLICKWRAP LICENSE. See Nash & Rawicz, INTELLECTUAL PROPERTY IN GOVERNMENT CONTRACTS, chap. 5 (6th ed. 2008). See also DeVecchio, *Taking the Mystery Out Of Data Rights*, BRIEFING PAPERS No. 18-8 (July 2018).

COMPUTER SOFTWARE REPOSITORY　See DATA REPOSITORY.

CONCEPT EXPLORATION　*Historical.* See MATERIAL SOLUTION ANALYSIS PHASE.

CONCEPT REFINEMENT　*Historical.* See MATERIAL SOLUTION ANALYSIS PHASE.

CONCEPTION　The formation in the mind of an inventor of a definite idea of a complete and operative invention as it is thereafter to be reduced to practice. Conception of a patentable idea is the act of invention that entitles an inventor to a PATENT. If the conception of an invention occurs during the performance of a government contract containing a Patent Rights clause, the invention will be classified as a SUBJECT INVENTION and the government will obtain rights (at least a royalty-free license) in any patent that issues on that invention. See Nash & Rawicz, INTELLECTUAL PROPERTY IN GOVERNMENT CONTRACTS, chaps. 2 and 3 (6th ed. 2008).

CONCERN　*Official:* Any business entity organized for PROFIT (even if its ownership is in the hands of a nonprofit entity) with a place of business located in the United States or its outlying areas and that makes a significant contribution to the U.S. economy through payment of taxes and/or use of American products, material and/or LABOR, etc. "Concern" includes, but is not limited to, an individual, partnership, corporation, JOINT VENTURE, association, or cooperative. For the purpose of making affiliation findings (see 19.101), include any business entity, whether organized for profit or not, and any foreign business entity, i.e., any entity located outside the United States and its outlying areas. *Source:* FAR 19.001. This term is used in the FAR Part 19 guidance on determining whether potential contractors are eligible for the benefits of the SMALL BUSINESS ACT.

CONCURRENT CONTRACT SAVINGS　*Official:* Net reductions in the prices of other contracts that are definitized and ongoing at the time the VALUE ENGINEERING CHANGE PROPOSAL is accepted. *Source:* FAR 48.001 (in the definition of ACQUISITION SAVINGS). FAR 48.104-1 contains guidance on government-contractor sharing arrangements for such savings. Under the Value Engineering clause in FAR 52.248-1, these savings are shared with the contractor only if they pertain to contracts issued by the same contracting office or its successor for essentially the same unit. Concurrent contract savings are calculated by subtracting any government COSTs from the reduction in price negotiated on the concurrent contract and multiplying the result by the contractor's rate in the SHARING ARRANGEMENT. See Nash & Feldman, 1 GOVERNMENT CONTRACT CHANGES § 9:12 (3d ed. 2006–2020); Cibinic, Nagle & Nash, ADMINISTRATION OF GOVERNMENT CONTRACTS 374 (5th ed. 2016).

CONCURRENT DELAY   A DELAY incurred by a contractor in contract performance in which (1) the government's causal responsibility cannot be separated from otherwise intertwined causes for which the government is not responsible, see *Commerce Int'l Co. v. United States*, 338 F. 2d 81 (Ct. Cl. 1964), or (2) both parties were at fault for the delay. Delays are not concurrent unless both causes for delay impact the CRITICAL PATH. In such cases, the general rule is that neither party can use the other party's delay to recover compensation from the other party. Thus, if there are concurrent government and contractor delays, the government cannot recover LIQUIDATED DAMAGES from the contractor and the contractor cannot receive a PRICE ADJUSTMENT under the Suspension of Work clause. However, there are a few instances when DAMAGEs have to be apportioned according to the degree of fault both parties were at fault. See *E.H. Marhoefer, Jr. Co.*, DOTCAB 70-17, 70-1 BCA ¶ 8177 (1970). See also Cibinic, Nagle & Nash, ADMINISTRATION OF GOVERNMENT CONTRACTS 515 (5th ed. 2016); Dale & D'Onofrio, *Reconciling Concurrency in Schedule Delay and Constructive Acceleration*, 39 PUB. CONT. L.J. 161 (2010); Dale & Muldoon, *A Government Windfall: ASBCA's Attack On Concurrent Delays As A Basis For Constructive Acceleration*, 44 The Procurement Lawyer 4 (Summer 2009); Bidgood, Reed & Taylor, *Cutting the Knot on Concurrent Delay*, CONSTR. BRIEFINGS No. 2008-2 (Feb. 2008); Nash, *Concurrent Delays: The Apportionment Logic*, 19 N&CR ¶ 42 (2005).

CONFIDENTIALITY CLAUSE   A stipulation commonly attached to research grants or contracts with the government that seeks to restrict the researcher's ability to publish or otherwise disseminate research results. See the Rights in Data—Special Works clause at FAR 52.227-17(d) providing that the contractor may not release, reproduce, distribute, or publish any data first produced in the performance of the contract without written permission of the contracting officer. The Department of Health and Human Services Regulation Subpart 324.1 and the Confidentiality of Information clause at HHSAR 352.224-70 require contractors to handle disclosure of certain types of information prudently and address the kinds of data that are considered confidential and how they should be treated. HHSAR 324.103. A similar clause used by DOD is the Disclosure of Information clause in DFARS 252.204-7000.

CONFIGURATION   The characteristics of a product (such as a weapon or a software package) as described by specifications, drawings and other data. Although these characteristics can be expressed in functional terms, such as describing the performance the item is expected to achieve, the term is generally used to describe the precise details of a product that would enable its manufacture. See CONFIGURATION CONTROL; CONFIGURATION MANAGEMENT.

CONFIGURATION CONTROL   The process of establishing a baseline CONFIGURATION of a product and controlling changes to that product by requiring approval at various levels depending on the impact and complexity of the proposed change. Such control ensures that the specifications and drawings depicting the product accurately reflect the product that is actually delivered to the government. This process establishes a complete audit trail documenting the extent of each change to the configuration and when it occurred. Agencies generally establish Configuration Control Boards to manage this process. DOD, *Military Handbook Configuration Management Guidance* MIL-HDBK 61-A(SE) (Feb. 7, 2001). See CONFIGURATION MANAGEMENT.

CONFIGURATION MANAGEMENT   A systems engineering management process for establishing and maintaining the consistency of a system's performance, functional, and physical attributes with its requirements, design and operational information throughout its life. Department of Defense, Military Handbook (MIL-HDBK) 61-A(SE), *Configuration Management Guidance* (2001). The process manages CONFIGURATION CONTROL activities. The objective of configuration management is to ensure that the current configuration of a hardware or software system is known and properly documented to reflect all changes. The principal activities of configuration management are: (1) planning, (2) configuration identification, (3) configuration control, (4) configuration status accounting, and (5) configuration verification and audit. See also ANSI/EIA-649.

CONFLICT OF INTEREST   A clash between the public interest and the private interest of an individual or organization. The term is typically used in regard to public officials and their relationship to matters of private interest or private gain; see PERSONAL CONFLICT OF INTEREST. It is also used in regard to persons who have left government employment; see REVOLVING DOOR. The term also identifies those situations in which contractors or prospective contractors have some bias relating to a procurement or would gain a competitive advantage from a procurement; see ORGANIZATIONAL CONFLICT OF INTEREST. The term is also used in the context of prohibiting contracting officers from knowingly awarding contracts to government employees or to business concerns owned or controlled by government employees. FAR 3.601. This policy seeks to avoid any conflict of interest that might arise between the employees' interest and their government duties, and any appearance of favoritism or preferential treatment. See also PROCUREMENT INTEGRITY. See Geldon & Caitlin Conroy, *Organizational Conflicts Of Interest / Edition VI: Is The OCI Pendulum Swinging Back At The GAO?*, Briefing Papers No. 18-13 (Dec. 2018); Geldon, *"Organizational Conflict of Interest Challenges: Thirty-Nine in a Row!" Public Contracting Institute* (Aug. 22, 2014), http://publiccontractinginstitute.com/organizational-conflict-of-interest-challenges/.

CONSEQUENTIAL DAMAGES   Those losses, injuries, or damages that do not flow directly and immediately from the improper act of a party but flow instead from some of the consequences or results of that party's act. Consequential damages resulting from a seller's BREACH OF CONTRACT, for example, include (1) any loss resulting from general or particular requirements and needs that the seller at the time of contracting had reason to know of and that could not reasonably be prevented by COVER or otherwise, and (2) any injury to persons or property proximately resulting from any breach of warranty. U.C.C. § 2-715(2). Contractors generally cannot recover consequential damages from the government and this policy is explicitly stated in FAR 49.202 with regard to the compensation allowed in a TERMINATION FOR CONVENIENCE. The government also limits its ability to recover consequential damages from a contractor in FAR Subpart 46.8 providing that it is the policy of the government to relieve contractors from liability for government property that is damaged after acceptance of items delivered on contracts. See the Limitation of

Liability clauses in FAR 52.246-23 through -25. However, FAR 12.403 permits the government to recover any incidental or consequential damages incurred because of any termination for cause of a contract for commercial items.

CONSIDERATION   A performance or return promise that is the inducement to a contract because it is sought by the PROMISOR in exchange for his promise and is given by the PROMISEE in exchange for that promise. RESTATEMENT (SECOND) CONTRACTS § 71 (1981). A binding contract requires an OFFER, ACCEPTANCE of the offer, and consideration. Consideration generally requires two elements: (1) something must be given that the law regards as of sufficient legal value for the purpose—either a benefit to the seller or a detriment to the buyer, and (2) that benefit or detriment of legal value must be dealt with by the parties as the agreed-upon price or exchange for the promise—there must be a "bargained-for exchange." The requirement for consideration does not require that what is relied upon for consideration be equivalent in value to the promise; the consideration need only have "some value." MURRAY ON CONTRACTS 55 (3d ed. 1990). See Cibinic, Nash & Yukins, FORMATION OF GOVERNMENT CONTRACTS 264–74 (4th ed. 2011).

CONSISTENCY IN ALLOCATING COSTS   The allocation of each type of contract cost on the same basis. CAS 402, 48 C.F.R. § 904.402, requires such consistency and gives detailed guidance on the interpretation of this rule. See COST ACCOUNTING STANDARDS. See Cibinic, Knight & Nash, COST-REIMBURSEMENT CONTRACTING 622–25 (4th ed. 2014).

CONSISTENCY IN ESTIMATING, ACCUMULATING, AND REPORTING COSTS   The treating of comparable transactions in the same manner for cost accounting purposes whether a contractor is estimating costs or accumulating and reporting costs. CAS 401, 48 C.F.R. § 9904.401, requires such consistency and gives detailed guidance on the interpretation of this rule. See COST ACCOUNTING STANDARDS.

CONSORTIUM   See OTHER TRANSACTIONS CONSORTIUM

CONSTANT DOLLARS   A method of relating dollars from several FISCAL YEARs by removing the effects of inflation and showing all dollars at the value they would have in a selected base year. When used in the procurement process, this method is generally called the PRESENT VALUE method. Constant dollar series are derived by dividing current dollar estimates by appropriate price indices, a process generally known as deflating. The result is a time series as it would presumably exist if prices were the same throughout all years as in the base year. In other words, constant dollars reflect what a present cost would be if the dollar had constant purchasing power. Any changes in such a series would reflect only changes in the real (physical) volume of output. Constant dollar figures are commonly used for gross domestic product and its components. DAU GLOSSARY.

CONSTANT YEAR DOLLARS   See CONSTANT DOLLARS.

CONSTRUCTION   *Official:* Construction, alteration, or repair (including dredging, excavating, and painting) of buildings, structures, or other REAL PROPERTY. For purposes of this definition, the terms "buildings, structures, or other real property" include, but are not limited to, improvements of all types, such as bridges, dams, plants, highways, parkways, streets, subways, tunnels, sewers, mains, power lines, cemeteries, pumping stations, railways, airport facilities, terminals, docks, piers, wharves, ways, lighthouses, buoys, jetties, breakwaters, levees, canals, and channels. Construction does not include the manufacture, production, furnishing, construction, alteration, repair, processing, or assembling of vessels, aircraft, or other kinds of PERSONAL PROPERTY (except that for use in subpart 22.5, see the definition at 22.502). *Source:* FAR 2.101. FAR Part 36 contains guidance on the procedures to be followed in buying construction, and FAR Subpart 22.4 covers the procedures for paying workers required by the DAVIS-BACON ACT. The FAR contains special clauses for construction contracts. See the PROVISION AND CLAUSE MATRIX in FAR Subpart 52.3. See also Branca, et al., FEDERAL GOVERNMENT CONSTRUCTION CONTRACTS (2d ed. 2010).

CONSTRUCTION ACTIVITY   *Official:* An activity at any organizational level of DOD that (1) is responsible for the architectural, engineering, and related technical aspects of the planning, design, and CONSTRUCTION of FACILITIES; and (2) receives its technical guidance from the Army Office of the Chief of Engineers, Naval Facilities Engineering Command, or Air Force Directorate of Civil Engineering. *Source:* DFARS 236.102. DFARS Part 236 contains special requirements that apply to these activities.

CONSTRUCTION, ALTERATION, OR REPAIR   See CONSTRUCTION.

CONSTRUCTION MANAGEMENT   A method of acquiring CONSTRUCTION in which the government contracts with a construction manager to assist in project design and construction. During the design phase the construction manager monitors the design for constructability and conformance with the project budget. During the construction phase, the construction manager acts as the agent of the government in assisting in the award of contracts for elements of the project and/or as a GENERAL CONTRACTOR to coordinate the construction process. See Douthwaite, *Why Procure Construction by Negotiation?*, 25 PUB. CONT. L.J. 423 (1996).

CONSTRUCTION MANAGEMENT ASSOCIATION OF AMERICA (CMAA)   A national trade association, founded in 1982, that encourages the growth of construction management as a professional service and promotes ethical standards. CMAA presents seminars, forums, and awards, and it publishes a Standards of Practice manual and model contract documents, as well as providing scholarships and administering the Certified Construction Manager Program which is accredited by the American National Standards Institute. The organization also provides telephone referral services on technical and legal issues. [CMAA, 7926 Jones Branch Drive, Suite 800, McLean, VA 22102; (703) 356-2622, http://cmaanet.org]

CONSTRUCTION MATERIAL   *Official:* An article, material, or supply brought to the construction site by a contractor or subcontractor for incorporation into the building or work. The term also includes an item brought to the site preassembled from articles, materials, or supplies. However, emergency life safety systems, such as emergency lighting, fire alarm, and audio evacuation systems, that are discrete systems incorporated into a public building or work and that are produced as complete systems, are evaluated as a single and distinct construction material regardless of when or how the individual parts or components of those systems are delivered to the construction site. Materials purchased directly by the government are supplies, not construction material. *Source:* FAR 25.003. Such materials are either DOMESTIC CONSTRUCTION MATERIALs or FOREIGN CONSTRUCTION MATERIALs for purposes of the BUY AMERICAN ACT. See Cibinic, Nash & Yukins, FORMATION OF GOVERNMENT CONTRACTS 1614–24 (4th ed. 2011).

CONSTRUCTIVE CHANGE   An oral or written communication, act or omission by the contracting officer or other authorized government official that is construed as having the same effect as a written CHANGE ORDER. A constructive change consists of two elements:

(1) a change element, which calls for examination of the work done by the contractor to determine whether it went beyond the minimum standards demanded by the contract; and (2) a government causation element (either an order or fault), which required the contractor to perform work that was not a necessary part of its contract. If the causation element is in the form of an order, it must be traced to a contracting officer or some other government employee acting with authority. Fault has been found most frequently in issuing the contract, such as by using defective specifications (see IMPLIED WARRANTY OF SPECIFICATIONS) or failing to disclose vital information (see SUPERIOR KNOWLEDGE). Claims for constructive changes are the primary means used by contractors to obtain additional compensation for performing fixed-price contracts. Included are claims concerning CONTRACT INTERPRETATION, defective specifications, nondisclosure of information, IMPRACTICABILITY OF PERFORMANCE, breach of the DUTY TO COOPERATE, and ACCELERATION. See Nash & Feldman, 1 GOVERNMENT CONTRACT CHANGES §§ 10:1–10:20 and §§ 15:1–15:27 (3d ed. 2006–2020); Cibinic, Nagle & Nash, ADMINISTRATION OF GOVERNMENT CONTRACTS 386–424 (5th ed. 2016). See also Backus, *The Cumulative Impact Claim: Where Do We Stand in 2010?*, 77 DEF. COUNS. J. 206 (2010); Dale & D'Onofrio, *Reconciling Concurrency in Schedule Delay and Constructive Acceleration*, 39 PUB. CONT. L.J. 161 (2010); Gourlay, *Constructive Acceleration and Concurrent Delay: Is There a "Middle Ground"?*, 39 PUB. CONT. L.J. 231 (2010); Kelleher, Nelson & Miller, *The Resurrection of Rice? The Evolution (And De-evolution) of the Ability of Contractors to Recover Delay Damages on Federal Government Construction Contracts*, 39 PUB. CONT. L.J. 305 (2010); Dale & D'Onofrio, *Reconciling Concurrency in Schedule Delay and Constructive Acceleration*, 39 PUB. CONT. L.J. 161 (2010); Nash, *Constructive Changes: Can They Be Prevented by Contract Language*, 22 N&CR ¶ 52 (Sept. 2008).

CONSTRUCTIVE REDUCTION TO PRACTICE   Disclosure in a patent application of a practical use of an INVENTION. The U.S. Patent Office accepts such disclosure as meeting the reduction to practice requirement for the granting of a PATENT. This concept does not apply to the PATENT RIGHTS granted by the clauses used in government contracts because they confer rights based on FIRST ACTUAL REDUCTION TO PRACTICE. See Nash & Rawicz, INTELLECTUAL PROPERTY IN GOVERNMENT CONTRACTS, chaps. 2 and 3 (6th ed. 2008).

CONSULTANTS   See ADVISORY AND ASSISTANCE SERVICES; EXPERTS; PROFESSIONAL AND CONSULTANT SERVICES.

CONTIGUOUS UNITED STATES (CONUS)   *Official:* The 48 contiguous states and the District of Columbia. *Source:* FAR 2.101. The policies in FAR 47.304 for the shipment of supplies are different for shipments within the contiguous United States than for shipments from CONUS for overseas delivery and shipments originating outside CONUS.

CONTINGENCY   *Official:* A possible future event or condition arising from presently known or unknown causes, the cost outcome of which is indeterminable at the present time. *Source:* FAR 31.205-7(a). Costs of allowances for contingencies are generally considered UNALLOWABLE COSTs for historical costing purposes because historical costing deals with costs incurred and recorded on the contractor's books. FAR 31.205-7(b). See Manos, 1 GOVERNMENT CONTRACT COSTS & PRICING §§ 14:1–14:2 (2d ed. 2009–2020). However, in some cases (for example, contract terminations), a contingency factor applicable to a past period may be recognized in the interest of expediting settlement. FAR 49.201(c). In connection with estimates of future costs, contingencies fall into two categories: (1) those that may arise from presently known and existing conditions, the effects of which are foreseeable within reasonable limits of accuracy (for example, anticipated costs of rejects and defective work); and (2) those that may arise from presently known or unknown conditions, the effects of which cannot be anticipated so precisely (the results of pending litigation, for example). In negotiating contract prices, contracting officers generally are willing to include the first category but attempt to exclude the second category from the price. FAR 15.402(c) prohibits contractors from including in a contract price any amount for a specified contingency if the contract also provides for a PRICE ADJUSTMENT based on the occurrence of that contingency. When ECONOMIC PRICE ADJUSTMENT clauses are used, contingencies covered by those clauses must be excluded from the original contract price, FAR 16.203-2(a). See Nagle, *Contingency Costs: Why All the Confusion?*, 20 N&CR ¶ 12 (Mar. 2006).

CONTINGENCY CONTRACTING   *Official:* Contracting to provide supplies, services, and construction to support mission objectives during contingency operations and other emergency operations as determined by the president or the Congress. Emergency acquisitions support several different types of operations: • CONTINGENCY OPERATIONS • HUMANITARIAN OR PEACEKEEPING OPERATIONS • Defense or recovery from certain attacks, as described in FAR 18.202 and Defense Federal Acquisition Regulation Supplement (DFARS) 218.202 • Emergency declarations or major disaster declarations, as described in FAR 18.203 and DFARS 218.203. *Source:* DEPARTMENT OF DEFENSE, DEFENSE CONTINGENCY CONTRACTING HANDBOOK 87 (April 2017). This handbook contains extensive guidance on the procedures to be followed in contingency contracting, See U.S. GOV'T ACCOUNTABILITY OFFICE, CONTINGENCY CONTRACTING: IMPROVEMENTS NEEDED IN MANAGEMENT OF CONTRACTORS SUPPORTING CONTRACT AND GRANT ADMINISTRATION IN IRAQ AND AFGHANISTAN, GAO-10-357 (Apr. 2010). For disposal of real property in contingency operations see Olson, *Herding Cats I: Disposal of DoD Real Property and Contractor Inventory in Contingency Operations*, The Army Lawyer (Apr. 2010), at 5.

CONTINGENCY CONTRACTING CORPS   A government-wide group of contract specialists that have volunteered to be available to be deployed to respond to an emergency, major disaster or contingency, 41 U.S.C. § 2312. The GENERAL SERVICES ADMINISTRATION is responsible for establishing the Corps and for establishing educational and training standards for the members of the Corps. See CONTINGENCY CONTRACTING CORPS PROGRAM GUIDE (http://www.fai.gov/drupal/training/contingency- contracting- corps-program-guide.

CONTINGENCY OPERATION   *Official:* A military operation that (1) is designated by the Secretary of Defense as an operation in which members of the armed forces are or may become involved in military actions, operations, or hostilities against an enemy of the United States or against an opposing military force; or (2) results in the call or order to, or retention on, active duty of members of the uniformed services under 10 U.S.C. §§ 688, 12301(a), 12302, 12304–06, or any other provision of law during a war or a national emergency declared by the President or Congress. *Source:* FAR 2.101; 10 U.S.C. § 101(a)(13). See also CONTINGENCY CONTRACTING. For acquisitions in contingency operations the MICRO-PURCHASE THRESHOLD is increased to $20,000 for domestic purchases and $35,000 for purchases outside of the United States. FAR 13.201(g). Similarly, the SIMPLIFIED ACQUISITION THRESHOLD is increased to $800,000 for domestic purchases and $1.5 million for purchases outside of the United States. FAR 2.101 (in the definition of simplified acquisition threshold).

CONTINGENT FEE   *Official:* Any commission, percentage, brokerage, or other fee that is contingent upon the success that a person or concern has in securing a government contract. *Source:* FAR 3.401. Such fees are prohibited by 10 U.S.C. § 2306(b) and 41 U.S.C. § 3901(b)(1). Contractors' arrangements to pay contingent fees for soliciting or obtaining government contracts have long been considered contrary to public policy because such arrangements may lead to attempted or actual exercise of IMPROPER INFLUENCE (which is *any* influence that induces or tends to induce a government employee or officer to give consideration or to act regarding a government contract on any basis other than the merits of the matter). Negotiated solicitations and contracts must contain a warranty by the contractor against contingent fees. FAR 52.203-5, Covenant Against Contingent Fees. As an exception to the warranty, contingent fee arrangements between a contractor and a BONA FIDE EMPLOYEE or a BONA FIDE AGENCY are permitted. For breach of the contractor's warranty, the government may annul the contract or recover the full amount of the contingent fee. FAR 3.402. FAR 31.205-33(b) also precludes the allowability of the cost of consultants when they are contingent on the recovery of costs. See Manos, 3 GOVERNMENT CONTRACT COSTS AND PRICING § 91:29 (2d ed. 2009–2020).

CONTINGENT LIABILITY   An existing condition, situation, or set of circumstances that poses the possibility of a loss to an agency that will ultimately be resolved when one or more events occur or fail to occur. U.S. GOV'T ACCOUNTABILITY OFFICE, GLOSSARY OF TERMS USED IN THE FEDERAL BUDGET PROCESS, GAO-05-734SP (Sept. 2005), at 35. A contingent liability has not ripened into a definite OBLIGATION and thus is not recordable as such. However, funds must be COMMITTED (or "administratively committed") to cover the liability in the event that the contingency ripens, so as to avoid a violation of the ANTI-DEFICIENCY ACT. An example of a contingent liability is the amount of available, but unearned, award fee under a COST-PLUS-AWARD-FEE or FIRM-FIXED-PRICE CONTRACT WITH AWARD FEE. The contingent liability ripens into an obligation when the FEE DETERMI-NATION OFFICIAL makes an award fee determination. See Mansfield, *Appropriations Law: Obligations vs. Contingent Liability*, 22 N&CR ¶ 41 (July 2008); U.S. GOV'T ACCOUNTABILITY OFFICE, PRINCIPLES OF FEDERAL APPROPRIATIONS LAW, 4th ed. 2016 rev., Ch. 2, GAO-16-463SP (Washington, D.C.: Mar. 2016).

CONTINUED PORTION OF THE CONTRACT   *Official:* The portion of a contract that the contractor must continue to perform following a partial termination of the contract. *Source:* FAR 2.101. A contractor is entitled to equitably adjust the price of a continued portion of a contract when the termination results in increased costs. See paragraph (l) of the Termination for Convenience of the Government clause in FAR 52.249-2.

CONTINUING RESOLUTION   Legislation enacted by Congress to provide BUDGET AUTHORITY for specific ongoing activities in cases where the regular FISCAL YEAR appropriation has not been enacted by the beginning of the fiscal year. For example, a continuing resolution permits avoidance of ANTI-DEFICIENCY ACT violations and provides for some amount of necessary services when Congress and the President cannot agree on the budget. A continuing resolution usually specifies a designated period and maximum rate at which the agency may incur obligations, based on the rate of the prior year, the President's budget request, or an appropriation bill passed by either or both Houses of Congress. Normally, new programs cannot be started under a continuing resolution. U.S. GOV'T ACCOUNTABILITY OFFICE, PRINCIPLES OF FEDERAL APPROPRIATIONS LAW: ANNUAL UPDATE TO THE THIRD EDITION, Ch. 8, GAO-15-303SP (Washington, D.C.: Mar. 2015).

CONTINUOUS ACQUISITION AND LIFE-CYCLE SUPPORT (CALS)   A former DOD initiative for electronically capturing military documentation and linking related information. The initiative had developed a number of standard specification protocols for the exchange of electronic data with commercial suppliers which were often referred to as CALS. CALS standards were adopted by several other allied nations. CALS was formerly known as "Computer-aided Acquisition and Logistics Support." See JOINT COMPUTER-AIDED ACQUISITION AND LOGISTICS SUPPORT.

CONTINUOUS COMPETITION   The process of planning an acquisition program so that two or more contractors or products are retained in competition over the life of the program. Such avoidance of SOLE SOURCE ACQUISITION is intended to achieve lower prices by keeping competitive pressure on the contractors during each year that the product is procured. Gansler, *The Future of Acquisition*, Compusearch (Dec. 1, 2010); Gansler, *Competition in Defense Acquisitions*, Center for Public Policy and Private Enterprise (Feb. 2009).

CONTRA PROFERENTEM   A rule of contract interpretation that imposes the risk of ambiguous contract language on the party that drafted the language. In most cases, the rule applies against the government; as the customary drafter, the government bears the responsibility for using language that permits only one reasonable interpretation. The rule is not applied against the government, however, if the contractor has failed to meet its DUTY TO SEEK CLARIFICATION. The rule also does not apply when the language is drafted by both parties. See Cibinic, Nagle & Nash, ADMINISTRATION OF GOVERNMENT CONTRACTS 211–26 (5th ed. 2016).

CONTRACT   *Official:* A mutually binding legal relationship obligating the seller to furnish the supplies or services (including construction) and the buyer to pay for them. It includes all types of commitments that obligate the Government to an expenditure of appropriated funds and that, except as otherwise authorized, are in writing. In addition to bilateral instruments, contracts include (but are not limited to) awards and NOTICEs OF AWARDs; job orders or task letters issued under BASIC ORDERING AGREEMENTs; LETTER CONTRACTs; orders, such as PURCHASE ORDERs, under which the contract becomes effective by written acceptance or performance; and bilateral contract modifications (see MODIFICATIONS). Contracts do not include GRANTS and COOPERATIVE AGREEMENTS covered by 31 U.S.C. § 6301 et seq. For discussion of various types of contracts, see part 16. *Source:* FAR 2.101. This is actually a definition of a PROCUREMENT CONTRACT as distinguished from other types of government contracts such as a contract for employment or for sale of property. A more generic definition of contract would be an agreement, enforceable by law, between two or more competent parties, to do or not to do something not prohibited by law, for a legal CONSIDERATION. See generally Cibinic, Nash & Yukins, FORMATION OF GOVERNMENT CONTRACTS 221–32 (4th ed. 2011).

CONTRACT ACTION   [1] For SYNOPSIS requirements. *Official:* An action resulting in a CONTRACT, as defined in subpart 2.1, including actions for additional supplies or services outside the existing contract scope, but not including actions that are within the scope and under the terms of the existing contract, such as CONTRACT MODIFICATIONs issued pursuant to the Changes clause, or funding and other administrative changes. *Source:* FAR 5.001; FAR 32.001. FAR 5.2 covers the requirements or agencies to provide notices of contract actions. [2] For DOD policies regarding UNDEFINITIZED CONTRACT ACTIONs: *Official:* An action that results in a contract. It includes (a) contract modifications for additional supplies and services, and (b) task orders and delivery orders. (c) It does not include change orders, administrative changes, funding modifications, or any other contract modifications that are within the scope and under the terms of the contract, e.g., engineering change proposals, value engineering change proposals, and over and above work requests as described in subpart 217.77. *Source:* DFARS 217.7401. [3] For GSA contracts, a contract action, for the purpose of determining whether an individual or class deviation is appropriate, has the same meaning as that used for reporting contract actions to Federal Procurement Data System—Next Generation (FPDS-NG). A contract action includes, but is not limited to, any of the following: (a) Initial letter contract. (b) Definitive contract superseding letter contract. (c) New definitive contract. (d) Purchase order/BPA calls using simplified acquisition procedures. (e) Orders under single award indefinite delivery contracts. (f) Orders under BOA. (g) Order/modification under federal schedule contract. (h) Modification. (i) Termination for Default. (j) Termination for Convenience. (k) Order under multiple award contract. (l) Initial load of federal schedule contract. GSAR 501.404-70.

CONTRACT ADJUSTMENT   The modification of a contract under the authority of Public Law No. 85-804. FAR 50.103-2 describes three types of contract adjustments: (1) AMEND-MENTs WITHOUT CONSIDERATION, (2) correction of a mistake, and (3) FORMAL-IZATION OF INFORMAL COMMITMENTs. FAR 50.103-3 through -7 contain the procedures that are used to process these adjustments. Because they are EXTRAORDI-NARY CONTRACTUAL ACTIONs, these procedures are not used frequently. Rather correction of mistakes and formalization of informal commitments are generally handled under the CONTRACT DISPUTES ACT OF 1978, FAR 50.101-2(a)(2) and (c).

CONTRACT ADJUSTMENT BOARD   A board established within an agency to make decisions pertaining to EXTRAORDINARY CONTRACTUAL ACTIONS under Public Law No. 85-804. An AGENCY HEAD may establish a contract adjustment board with authority to approve, authorize, and direct appropriate action under FAR Subpart 50.1 and to make all appropriate determinations and findings. When a board is established, its decisions must not be subject to appeal; however, it may reconsider and modify, correct, or reverse its previous decisions. The board must be allowed to determine its own procedures and have authority to take all action necessary or appropriate to conduct its functions. FAR 50.102-2. See generally FAR Subpart 50.1

CONTRACT ADMINISTRATION   Any administrative activity undertaken by either the government or the contractor during the time from contract AWARD to contract CLOSE-OUT. More specifically, the term refers to steps taken by the government representatives responsible for ensuring government and contractor compliance with the TERMS AND CONDITIONS of the contract. Such steps include routine tasks such as monitoring contractor progress, reviewing INVOICEs, processing payments, inspecting deliverables, and closing out the contract file; they also include problem-solving activities that are necessitated by unforeseeable circumstances—changes, problems, and disagreements—that arise following contract award. FAR Part 42 contains general guidance on these activities, including a long list of functions that are generally considered to be part of the contract administration process. See generally Cibinic, Nagle & Nash, ADMINISTRATION OF GOVERNMENT CONTRACTS (5th ed. 2016). See also Davison & Sebastian, *A Detailed Analysis of the Relationship Between Contract Administration Problems and Contract Types*, 11 J. OF PUB. PROCUREMENT 108 (2011); Irwin & Navarre, *Selected Compliance and Contract Administration Issues in*

Contingency Contracting, BRIEFING PAPERS No. 09-13 (Dec. 2009); Davison & Sebastian, *The Relationship Between Contract Administration Problems and Contract Type*, 9 J. of Pub. Procurement 262 (2009).

CONTRACT ADMINISTRATION OFFICE   *Official:* An office that performs (1) assigned postaward functions related to the administration of contracts, and (2) assigned preaward functions. *Source:* FAR 2.101. The office also maintains CONTRACT ADMINISTRATION OFFICE CONTRACT FILEs.

CONTRACT ADMINISTRATION OFFICE CONTRACT FILE   The file maintained by the government CONTRACT ADMINISTRATION OFFICE that documents actions reflecting the basis for and the performance of CONTRACT ADMINISTRATION responsibilities. FAR 4.802(a)(2). Typical contents are described at FAR 4.803(b).

CONTRACT AUDIT MANUAL   See DCAA CONTRACT AUDIT MANUAL.

CONTRACT AUTHORITY   A form of BUDGET AUTHORITY under which contracts or other obligations may be entered into in advance of an APPROPRIATION or in excess of amounts otherwise available in a revolving fund. Legislation providing new contract authority must also provide that it will be effective for any fiscal year only to such extent or in such amounts as provided in appropriations acts. 2 U.S.C. § 651(a). When an agency has contract authority, it may enter into contracts without an appropriation without violating the ANTIDEFICIENCY ACT. Since contract authority itself is not an appropriation—it provides authority to enter into binding contracts rather than the funds to make payments under them—a contractor cannot be paid until the obligation is funded by a subsequent appropriation or by the use of a revolving fund. See Cibinic, Nash & Yukins, FORMATION OF GOVERNMENT CONTRACTS 38 (4th ed. 2011); U.S. Gov't Accountability Office, PRINCIPLES OF FEDERAL APPROPRIATIONS LAW, 4th ed. 2016 rev., Ch. 2, GAO-16-463SP (Washington, D.C.: Mar. 2016).

CONTRACT AWARD   See AWARD.

CONTRACT BUNDLING   See BUNDLING.

CONTRACT CARRIER   See CARRIER (TRANSPORTATION).

CONTRACT CLAUSE   See CLAUSE.

CONTRACT COST PRINCIPLES   See COST PRINCIPLES.

CONTRACT DATA REQUIREMENTS LIST (CDRL)   A list of all technical data to be delivered on a contract with DOD, prepared using DD Form 1423, DFARS 253.303-1423. The purpose of this list is to identify, in a single document, all technical data ordered under a contract in order to permit the management of such data. Detailed guidance on the preparation and use of this form was contained in DOD Instruction 5010.12-M (May 1993) (this document is not in the current DOD database but can be found on the internet). DFARS 215.470 provides that when data are required to be delivered under a contract, the solicitation must include DD Form 1423 which requires prospective contractors to state the portion of the proposed price that is attributable to the production or delivery of the listed data and contains guidance on the computation of such prices. See Nash & Rawicz, INTELLECTUAL PROPERTY IN GOVERNMENT CONTRACTS, chap. 6 (6th ed. 2008).

CONTRACT DEBT   An amount of money owed to the government by a contractor because of one or more occurrences in the performance of a contract. FAR 32.601(b) gives the following examples of causes of contract debts: (1) price redeterminations; (2) reductions from DEFECTIVE CERTIFIED COST OF PRICING DATA; (3) excess FINANCING PAYMENTs, PROGRESS PAYMENTs, or PERFORMANCE-BASED PAYMENTs; (4) increases in financing payment liquidation rates; (5) overpayments; (6) PRICE ADJUSTMENTs from CHANGEs TO COST ACCOUNTING PRACTICEs; (7) reinspection costs for nonconforming supplies or services; (8) duplicate payments; (9) DAMAGEs or from TERMINATIONs FOR DEFAULT; (10) BREACH OF CONTRACT; (11) defective goods or services; (12) overpayments due to errors in billing; (13) delinquency in contractor payments; and (14) reimbursement of amounts due because the government paid PROTEST costs and the awardee was guilty of misrepresentation. FAR Subpart 32.6 provides guidance on collection of contract debts through techniques such as WITHHOLDING (see FAR 32.606) and SETOFF (see FAR 32.604).

CONTRACT DISPUTES ACT (CDA) OF 1978   An Act, Pub. L. No. 95-563, 41 U.S.C. §§ 7101-09, that establishes the procedures to be used by contractors and contracting officers in resolving DISPUTEs ARISING OUT OF and RELATING TO contracts. The Act contains detailed provisions for handling contract CLAIMs by and against the government, including (1) certification of contractor claims of $100,000 or more (see CERTIFICATION OF CLAIM), (2) contractor and government claims as the subject of a DECISION OF THE CONTRACTING OFFICER, (3) APPEAL FROM A CONTRACTING OFFICER'S DECISION to a BOARD OF CONTRACT APPEALS (BCA) within 90 days or to the U.S. COURT OF FEDERAL CLAIMS within 12 months, (4) appeals of decisions of either the BCAs or the Court of Federal Claims to the COURT OF APPEALS FOR THE FEDERAL CIRCUIT, (5) establishment of the BCAs and ADMINISTRATIVE JUDGEs (members of BCAs), (6) SMALL CLAIMS PROCEDUREs and ACCELERATED PROCEDUREs before the BCAs, (7) payment of INTEREST on claims to contractors, (8) BCA subpoena power, (9) penalties for submission of fraudulent claims, and (10) payment of claims. The Act is implemented by FAR Subpart 33.2 and the Disputes clause at FAR 52.233-1. See Cibinic, Nagle & Nash, ADMINISTRATION OF GOVERNMENT CONTRACTS, chap. 13 (5th ed. 2016); Nash, *Contract Disputes Act Claims: Minimal Requirements*, 33 N&CR ¶ 32 (June 2019); Willard, *Limitations Of Actions Under The Contract Disputes Act*, BRIEFING PAPERS NO. 13-9 (Aug. 2013).

CONTRACT DISTRIBUTION   The act by the government of distributing copies of a signed ("executed") contract document to all interested parties. Contracting officers are required to distribute copies of contracts or modifications within 10 working days after execution by all parties. See FAR Subpart 4.2.

CONTRACT EXECUTION   The act of signing a CONTRACT. Only CONTRACTING OFFICERs have the legal authority to sign contracts on behalf of the United States. The contracting officer's name and official title must be typed, stamped, or printed on the contract. The contracting officer normally signs the contract after it has been signed by the contractor. FAR 4.101. Contract execution does not necessarily complete the process of offer and acceptance, which under the MAILBOX RULE would not be completed until transmission of a signed document in the CONTRACT DISTRIBUTION process. See SIGNATURE. See also Cibinic, Nash & Yukins, FORMATION OF GOVERNMENT CONTRACTS

257–64 (4th ed. 2011). The term contract execution is also used occasionally to mean the performance of the contract after it is issued.

CONTRACT FILE   An organized collection of documents that constitutes a complete history of a contractual action for the purpose of (1) providing a complete background as a basis for informed decisions at each step in the acquisition process; (2) supporting actions taken; (3) providing information for reviews and investigations; and (4) furnishing essential facts in the event of litigation or congressional inquiries. A contract file may consist of paper or electronic records. FAR 4.802 prescribes three standard contract files: (1) the contracting office contract file, (2) the contract administration office contract file, and (3) the paying office contract file. FAR 4.803 describes the typical contents of each file. FAR 4.804 prescribes procedures for the CLOSEOUT of contract files. FAR 4.805 prescribes the storage, handling, and disposal of contract files.

CONTRACT FINANCING   The obtaining by a contractor of the money necessary for performance of a contract. FAR Part 32 governs contract financing. FAR 32.106 states the following order of preference for obtaining financing: (1) private financing without government guarantee on reasonable terms (the contractor is not required to obtain private financing from other agencies), (2) customary contract financing (see FAR 32.113), (3) loan guarantees, (4) unusual contract financing (see FAR 32.114), and (5) ADVANCE PAYMENTs (see FAR 32.402(d) for exceptions). FAR 32.104 states that government financing should be provided only to the extent actually needed for prompt and efficient performance, considering the availability of private financing. FAR 32.107, however, provides that if a contractor or offeror meets the RESPONSIBILITY standards prescribed for prospective contractors, the contracting officer shall not treat the contractor's need for contract financing as a handicap for a contract award. See Chierchella & Gallacher, *Financing Government Contracts/Edition II –Part I*, BRIEFING PAPERS No. 04-12 (Nov. 2004); Chierchella & Gallacher, *Financing Government Contracts/Edition II—Part II*, BRIEFING PAPERS No. 04-13 (Dec. 2004).

CONTRACT FINANCING PAYMENT   *Official:* An authorized government disbursement of monies to a contractor prior to acceptance of supplies or services by the Government. (1) Contract financing payments include—(i) Advance payments; (ii) Performance-based payments; (iii) Commercial advance and interim payments; (iv) Progress payments based on cost under the clause at 52.232-16, Progress Payments; (v) Progress payments based on a percentage or stage of completion (see 32.102(e)), except those made under the clause at 52.232-5, Payments Under Fixed-Price Construction Contracts, or the clause at 52.232-10, Payments Under Fixed-Price Architect-Engineer Contracts; and (vi) Interim payments under a cost reimbursement contract, except for a cost reimbursement contract for services when Alternate I of the clause at 52.232-25, Prompt Payment, is used. (2) Contract financing payments do not include—(i) Invoice payments; (ii) Payments for partial deliveries; or (iii) Lease and rental payments. *Source:* FAR 32.001. Such payments are not subject to the PROMPT PAYMENT ACT. FAR 32.901(b). Thus, no interest penalty is paid to a contractor as a result of delayed contract financing payments. See Cibinic, Nagle & Nash, ADMINISTRATION OF GOVERNMENT CONTRACTS 1018–25 (5th ed. 2016); *OMB Circular No. A-125, Prompt Payment*, Aug. 19, 1982.

CONTRACT INTERPRETATION   The process of determining what the parties agreed to in their bargain. Contract interpretation involves determining the meaning of words, supplying missing terms and filling in gaps, and resolving ambiguities. The basic objective of contract interpretation is to determine the intent of the parties based on the PLAIN MEANING of the contract language. Various rules of interpretation define contract terms, determine ORDER OF PRECEDENCE among the various parts of the contract, or seek to read the contract as a whole, interpreting it so as to (1) avoid rendering its terms meaningless, (2) avoid conflict, and (3) fulfill the principal purpose of the parties. See Nash & Feldman, 1 GOVERNMENT CONTRACT CHANGES §§ 11:1–11:21 (3d ed. 2006–2020); Cibinic, Nagle & Nash, ADMINISTRATION OF GOVERNMENT CONTRACTS, chap. 2 (5th ed. 2016). See also Allen, *Government Contract Interpretation: A Comprehensive Overview*, BRIEFING PAPERS No. 15-4 (Mar. 2015); Nash, *Postscript VIII: The Plain Meaning Rule*, 26 N&CR ¶ 68 (Dec. 2012); Stubbs, *The Federal Circuit and Contract Interpretation: May Extrinsic Evidence Ever Be Used to Show Unambiguous Language Is Ambiguous?*, 39 PUB. CONT. L.J. 785 (2010); Ellis, *Toward a Nuanced Plain Language Approach in Federal Contract Interpretation: What Do Bell BCI, States Roofing, and LAI Services Imply?*, 39 PUB. CONT. L.J. 821 (2010); Nash, *The Government Contract Decisions of the Federal Circuit*, 78 GEO. WASH. L. REV. 586 (2010); Nash, *Reading Contract Language: Strict Construction*, 23 N&CR ¶ 40 (Aug. 2009); Claybrook, *It's Patent that "Plain Meaning" Dictionary Definitions Shouldn't Dictate: What Phillips Portends for Contract Interpretation*, 16 FED. CIR. BAR. J. 92 (2006).

CONTRACT LINE ITEM   A separate listing of a supply or service that is set forth in Section B of a SOLICITATION or CONTRACT following the UNIFORM CONTRACT FORMAT. Contract line items are usually priced separately but they can be designated NSP (not separately priced) if their price is included in another line item. DFARS 204.7103-1(a)(1). DFARS Subpart 204.71 encourages the use of separate contract line items and contains guidance on numbering contract line items. See UNIFORM CONTRACT LINE ITEM NUMBERING SYSTEM.

CONTRACT MODIFICATION   *Official:* Any written change in the terms of a contract. *Source:* FAR 2.101. There are BILATERAL MODIFICATIONS and UNILATERAL MODIFICATIONS. FAR 43.103. Only a CONTRACTING OFFICER acting within the scope of his or her authority is empowered to execute contract modifications on behalf of the government. FAR 43.102. See Dekel, *Modification of a Government Contract Awarded Following a Competitive Procedure*, 38 PUB. CONT. L.J. 401 (2009). See also CHANGE and EQUITABLE ADJUSTMENT.

CONTRACT NUMBER   A number assigned by a contracting agency to identify a procurement action and provide the most efficient point of reference in correspondence dealing with the action. In DOD contracting actions, uniform PROCUREMENT INSTRUMENT IDENTIFICATION NUMBERS are assigned to all contracts and related instruments. DFARS 204.7000. NASA has a uniform ACQUISITION INSTRUMENT IDENTIFICATION system covering solicitations and contracts. NFS Subpart 18-4.71.

CONTRACT PRICING   The function that gathers, assimilates, evaluates, and, in establishing objectives, brings to bear all the skills and techniques needed to shape a specific PRICING ARRANGEMENT. Those skills and techniques include PRICE ANALYSIS, COST ANALYSIS, and use of accounting and technical evaluations and systems analysis techniques to facilitate the negotiation of realistic pricing arrangements. DAU, *Contract Pricing Reference Guides* v. I (Feb. 21, 2012). See FAR Subpart 15.4 for guidance on contract pricing. Pricing policy guidance for the DOD is found in DOD PGI 215.402. See Cibinic, Nash & Yukins,

FORMATION OF GOVERNMENT CONTRACTS, chap. 10 (4th ed. 2011); Nash, *Guidance on Contract Pricing: A Substantive Addition*, 21 N&CR ¶41 (Aug. 2007).

CONTRACT PRICING PROPOSAL COVER SHEET   A document (Standard Form 1411) formerly prescribed by FAR 15.804-6(b) for contractors' use in submitting pricing proposals for negotiated procurements when CERTIFIED COST OR PRICING DATA is required. This form is no longer used. Contracting officers may now require submission of cost or pricing data in the format indicated at Table 15-2 of FAR 15.408 (which includes all of the information on the SF 1411), specify an alternative format, or permit submission in the contractor's format. FAR 15.403-5.

CONTRACT PRICING REFERENCE GUIDES   Five manuals: *Price Analysis, Quantitative Techniques for Contract Pricing, Cost Analysis, Advanced Issues in Contract Pricing*, and *Federal Contract Negotiation Techniques* developed by the FEDERAL ACQUISITION INSTITUTE (FAI) and the AIR FORCE INSTITUTE OF TECHNOLOGY (AFIT) to provide instruction and professional guidance for contracting personnel. The Guides are now maintained by the Deputy Director of Defense Procurement for Cost, Pricing and Finance (https://dau.edu/tools/p/cprg). They provide the most complete guidance in the government for analyzing costs and prices in order to determine that an offeror has submitted a FAIR AND REASONABLE PRICE.

CONTRACT QUALITY REQUIREMENTS   *Official:* The technical requirements in the contract relating to the quality of the product or service and those contract clauses prescribing inspection, and other quality controls incumbent on the contractor, to assure that the product or service conforms to the contractual requirements. *Source:* FAR 46.101. Contract quality requirements fall into four general categories, depending on the extent of quality assurance needed by the government for the acquisition involved: (1) reliance on contractors' existing quality assurance systems on contracts for commercial items, (2) government reliance on inspection by the contractor, (3) standard inspection requirements, and (4) higher-level contract quality requirements. FAR 46.202-1 through -4. The extent of contract quality requirements, including contractor inspection, required under a contract is usually based on the classification of the contract item (supply or service) as determined by its technical description, its complexity, and the criticality of its application. FAR 46.203. See Cibinic, Nagle & Nash, ADMINISTRATION OF GOVERNMENT CONTRACTS, chap. 9 (5th ed. 2016).

CONTRACT SCOPE   See SCOPE OF THE CONTRACT.

CONTRACT SPECIALIST   An employee of a CONTRACTING ACTIVITY in the GS 1102 personnel series. This series also includes procurement analysts, contract negotiators, cost/price analysts, and contract administrators. This series of employees forms the pool that is the main source of CONTRACTING OFFICERs.

CONTRACT TYPE   See TYPE OF CONTRACT.

CONTRACT WORK HOURS AND SAFETY STANDARDS ACT (CWHSSA)   A 1962 Act, 40 U.S.C. §§ 3701–3708, that regulates the wages and working conditions of LABORERS OR MECHANICS performing work under certain government contracts. The Act requires that at least time-and-a-half overtime be paid to any such laborer or mechanic who works more than 40 hours in a week. Any contractor or subcontractor who violates these requirements is liable to the employee for unpaid wages and to the government for liquidated damages of $10 for each calendar day in violation. Intentional violations of this

Act can result in criminal penalties. 40 U.S.C. § 3708. FAR Subpart 22.3 implements the CWHSSA requirements.

CONTRACTED ADVISORY AND ASSISTANCE SERVICES (CAAS) See ADVISORY AND ASSISTANCE SERVICES.

CONTRACTING *Official:* Purchasing, renting, leasing, or otherwise obtaining supplies or services from non-federal sources. Contracting includes description (but not determination) of supplies and services required, selection and solicitation of sources, preparation and award of contracts, and all phases of contract administration. It does not include making GRANTs or COOPERATIVE AGREEMENTs. *Source:* FAR 2.101. Contracting is a subset of ACQUISITION and PROCUREMENT.

CONTRACTING ACTIVITY *Official:* An element of an agency designated by the agency head and delegated broad authority regarding acquisition functions. *Source:* FAR 2.101. In NASA regulations, the term is synonymous with "NASA Headquarters," "installation," and "field installation." NFS 1802.101. DOD contracting activities are listed at DFARS 202.101. When an agency determines the amount of compensation due for a VALUE ENGINEERING CHANGE PROPOSAL, the term "contracting activity" means "any contracting office that the acquisition is transferred to, such as another branch of the agency or another agency's office that is performing a joint acquisition action."

CONTRACTING METHODS See METHODS OF PROCUREMENT.

CONTRACTING OFFICE *Official:* An office that awards or executes a CONTRACT for supplies or services and performs postaward functions not assigned to a CONTRACT ADMINISTRATION OFFICE. *Source:* FAR 2.101. The office also maintains CONTRACTING OFFICE CONTRACT FILEs.

CONTRACTING OFFICE CONTRACT FILE The file maintained by the original government CONTRACTING OFFICE to document the basis for the acquisition and the award, the assignment of CONTRACT ADMINISTRATION (including payment responsibilities) and any subsequent actions taken by the contracting officer. FAR 4.802(a)(1). Typical contents are described at FAR 4.803(a).

CONTRACTING OFFICER (CO) *Official:* A person with the authority to enter into, administer, and/or terminate contracts and make related DETERMINATIONs AND FINDINGS. The term includes certain AUTHORIZED REPRESENTATIVEs of the contracting officer acting within the limits of their authority as delegated by the contracting officer. "Administrative contracting officer (ACO)" refers to a contracting officer who is administering contracts. "Termination contracting officer (TCO)" refers to a contracting officer who is settling terminated contracts. A single contracting officer may be responsible for duties in any or all of these areas. Reference in this regulation (48 C.F.R. chap. 1) to administrative contracting officer or termination contracting officer does not—(1) Require that a duty be performed at a particular office or activity; or (2) Restrict in any way a contracting officer in the performance of any duty properly assigned. *Source:* FAR 2.101 See FAR 1.602-1(a) stating: "Contracting officers may bind the Government only to the extent of the authority delegated to them. Contracting officers shall receive from the appointing authority (see 1.603-1) clear instructions in writing regarding the limits of their authority. Information on the limits of the contracting officer's authority shall be readily available to the public and agency personnel." Contracting officers are responsible for ensuring performance of all necessary actions for effective contracting, for ensuring compliance with the terms of the contract, and for safeguarding the interest of the government in its contractual relationships. FAR 1.602-2.Contracting officers are appointed in writing, on Standard Form 1402, Certificate of Appointment (see WARRANT). FAR 53.301-1402. In selecting contracting officers, the appointing official must consider the complexity and dollar value of the acquisitions to be assigned and the candidates' training, education, business acumen, judgment, character, and reputation. FAR 1.603-2. However, FAR 1.601(a). points out that "In some agencies, a relatively small number of high level officials are designated contracting officers solely by virtue of their positions." In some agencies, such as DOD, there are three types of contracting officers, each with different responsibilities in contract procurement, management, and execution. A purchasing or PROCURING CONTRACTING OFFICER has authority to enter into a contract; an ADMINISTRATIVE CONTRACTING OFFICER administers the performance of the contract; and a TERMINATION CONTRACTING OFFICER is responsible for contract termination. See Nash & Feldman, 1 GOVERNMENT CONTRACT CHANGES §§ 5:2–5:8 (3d ed. 2006–2020); Cibinic, Nagle & Nash, ADMINISTRATION OF GOVERNMENT CONTRACTS 31–35 (5th ed. 2016); Cibinic, Nash & Yukins, FORMATION OF GOVERNMENT CONTRACTS, 81–114 (4th ed. 2011). See also Nash, *Postscript II: Contracting Officer Authority*, 25 N&CR ¶ 30 (June 2011); Pachter, *The Incredible Shrinking Contracting Officer*, 39 PUB. CONT. L.J. 705 (2010); Edwards & Nash, *Postscript II: The Role of the Contracting Officer*, 24 N&CR ¶ 14 (Mar. 2010).

CONTRACTING OFFICER'S REPRESENTATIVE (COR)   *Official:* An individual, including a contracting officer's technical representative (COTR), designated and authorized in writing by the CONTRACTING OFFICER to perform specific technical or administrative functions. *Source:* FAR 2.101. CORs "assist in the technical monitoring and administration" of contracts and maintain the CONTRACT ADMINISTRATION OFFICE CONTRACT FILE. FAR 1.604. Their duties are specified by the contracting officer but they may not be given the authority "to make any commitments or changes that affect price, quality, quantity, delivery or other terms and conditions of the contract." FAR 1.602-2(d)(5). See Cibinic, Nagle & Nash, ADMINISTRATION OF GOVERNMENT CONTRACTS 36–39 (5th ed. 2016); Cibinic, Nash & Yukins, FORMATION OF GOVERNMENT CONTRACTS, 81–114 (4th ed. 2011).

CONTRACTING OFFICER'S TECHNICAL REPRESENTATIVE (COTR)   An employee of a CONTRACTING ACTIVITY designated by a CONTRACTING OFFICER to perform CONTRACT ADMINISTRATION activities in regard to technical issues. A COTR is an AUTHORIZED REPRESENTATIVE of a contracting officer but is rarely given the authority to enter into contractual agreements or MODIFICATIONs. Frequently the authority of COTRs is delineated by TECHNICAL DIRECTION clauses. Not all of the agencies use the term COTR, but some of their regulations contain guidance on the functions of such employees. See, for example, NFS 18-42.270 and 18-53.242-70. See Cibinic, Nagle & Nash, ADMINISTRATION OF GOVERNMENT CONTRACTS 36–39 (5th ed. 2016).

CONTRACTING OFFICER'S DECISION   See DECISION OF THE CONTRACTING OFFICER.

CONTRACTING OUT   See A-76 POLICY.

CONTRACTOR   Usually denotes a party that enters into a CONTRACT with the government. However, the FAR contains several different definitions. [1] In the context of DEBARMENT or SUSPENSION: *Official:* Any individual or other legal entity that—(1)

Directly or indirectly (e.g., through an affiliate), submits offers for or is awarded, or reasonably may be expected to submit offers for or be awarded, a Government contract, including a contract for carriage under Government or commercial bills of lading, or a subcontract under a Government contract; or (2) Conducts business, or reasonably may be expected to conduct business, with the Government as an agent or representative of another contractor. *Source:* FAR 9.403. [2] In regard to subcontracting: *Official:* The total contractor organization or a separate entity of it, such as an affiliate, division, or plant, that performs its own purchasing. *Source:* FAR 44.101. [3] In regard to EQUAL EMPLOYMENT OPPORTUNITY: *Official:* Contractor includes the terms "prime contractor" and "SUBCONTRACTOR." *Source:* FAR 22.801. [4] In regard to the Service Contract Act: *Official:* Contractor includes a subcontractor at any tier whose subcontract is subject to the provisions of the Act. *Source:* FAR 22.1001.

CONTRACTOR-ACQUIRED PROPERTY   *Official:* Property acquired, fabricated or otherwise provided by a contractor for performing a contract and to which the government has title. *Source:* FAR 45.101. Contractor-acquired property is treated as GOVERNMENT PROPERTY for the purpose of management and control under the provisions of the Government Property clause in FAR 52.245-1. This clause gives the government title to contractor-acquired property on fixed-price contracts with financing provisions or that direct a contractor to purchase property for which the costs will be directly reimbursed and on all cost-reimbursement contracts. The government asserts that this title pertains not only to property that is charged directly to a contract but also to property that is purchased through indirect cost accounts. DOD PGI 245.402-70 states the DOD's policy on contractor-acquired property. See Cibinic, Nagle & Nash, ADMINISTRATION OF GOVERNMENT CONTRACTS, chap. 7 (5th ed. 2016).

CONTRACTOR BUSINESS SYSTEMS   Systems that provides timely, reliable information for the management of DOD programs. The six contractor business systems are the contractor's accounting system, EARNED VALUE MANAGEMENT SYSTEM, estimating system, MATERIAL MANAGEMENT AND ACCOUNTING SYSTEM, PROPERTY MANAGEMENT SYSTEM, and PURCHASING SYSTEM when the appropriate contract clauses are used. DFARS 252.242-7005. In a COVERED CONTRACT, when any of the contractor's business systems contain a SIGNIFICANT DEFICIENCY, the CONTRACTING OFFICER must withhold a percentage of payments under certain conditions. DFARS 252.242-7005. See GAO-19-212, CONTRACTOR BUSINESS SYSTEMS: DOD NEEDS BETTER INFORMATION TO MONITOR AND ASSESS REVIEW PROCESS (Feb. 2019).

CONTRACTOR BID OR PROPOSAL INFORMATION   *Official:* Any of the following information submitted to a federal agency as part of or in connection with a BID or PROPOSAL to enter into a FEDERAL AGENCY PROCUREMENT CONTRACT, if that information has not been previously made available to the public or disclosed publicly: (1) COST OR PRICING DATA; (2) INDIRECT COSTs and direct labor rates; (3) proprietary information about manufacturing processes, operations, or techniques marked by a contractor as proprietary in accordance with applicable law or regulation; (4) information marked as "contractor bid or proposal information" in accordance with applicable law or regulation; and (5) information marked in accordance with the Instructions to Offerors— Competitive Acquisition clause in FAR 52.215-1. *Source:* FAR 3.104-1. This class of information may not be disclosed or obtained under the current PROCUREMENT INTEGRITY rules. The synonymous term under the old rules was PROPRIETARY

INFORMATION. Guidance on the treatment of this information is contained in FAR 3.104-4. See Cox, *Is the Procurement Integrity Act "Important" Enough for the Mandatory Disclosure Rule? A Case for Inclusion*, 40 PUB. CONT. L.J. 347 (2010); Kathuria, *Best Practices for Compliance with the New Government Contractor Compliance and Ethics Rules Under the Federal Acquisition Regulation*, 38 PUB. CONT. L.J. 803 (2009); Vacketta & Curley, *An Effective Compliance Program: A Necessity for Government Contractor Under IDIQ Contracts and Beyond*, 37 PUB. CONT. L.J. 593 (2008).

CONTRACTOR CODE OF BUSINESS ETHICS AND CONDUCT   A written set of ethical rules that contractors doing business with the government are expected to have to ensure that their employees conduct themselves ethically. FAR 3.1004 requires such a code if a company receives a contract or subcontract expected to exceed $5.5 million with a performance period exceeding 120 days. In such cases, the Contractor Code of Business Ethics and Conduct clause in FAR 52.203-13 is included in solicitations and contracts. This clause contains a set of detailed requirements for this code which are not applicable if a company is a small business or a contract is for a COMMERCIAL ITEM. A significant requirement in this clause is the MANDATORY DISCLOSURE of criminal conduct or conduct amounting to civil fraud. Contractors under these thresholds are also expected to follow the prescribed procedures and are subject to SUSPENSION or DEBARMENT if they fail to meet the mandatory disclosure requirement. FAR 3.1003(a)(2).

CONTRACTOR COST AND SOFTWARE DATA REPORTING (CSDR)   The DoD system for collecting actual costs and software data and related business data. The resulting repository serves as the primary contract cost and software data (CSD) repository for most DoD resource analysis efforts, including cost database development, applied cost estimating, cost research, program reviews, Analysis of Alternatives (AoA), and life cycle cost estimates. DAU GLOSSARY. See DOD 5000 Series.

CONTRACTOR DATA REPOSITORY   See DATA REPOSITORY.

CONTRACTOR INSURANCE/PENSION REVIEW (CIPR)   An in-depth evaluation of a contractor's insurance program, pension plans, other deferred compensation plans, and related policies, procedures, practices, and costs. The Defense Contract Management Agency (DCMA) is the designated DOD executive agency for CIPRs. ADMINISTRATIVE CONTRACTING OFFICERs (ACOs) are responsible for determining the allowability of government contractors' insurance/pension costs and for determining the need for a CIPR. DCMA insurance/pension specialists and DCAA auditors assist ACOs in making these determinations, conduct CIPRs when needed, and perform other routine audits. DFARS 242.7301. If any organization believes that additional reviews of the contractor's insurance/pension program should be performed, that request should be conveyed to the ACO. DFARS 242.7302. The procedures for conducting a CIPR can be found at DOD PGI 242.7303 See also INSURANCE and PENSION PLAN.

CONTRACTOR INVENTORY   *Official:* (1) Any property acquired by and in the possession of a contractor or subcontractor under a contract for which title is vested in the Government and which exceeds the amounts needed to complete full performance under the entire contract; (2) Any property that the Government is obligated or has the option to take over under any type of contract, e.g., as a result either of any changes in the specifications or plans thereunder or of the termination of the contract (or subcontract thereunder), before completion of the work, for the convenience or at the option of the Government; and (3) government-furnished property that exceeds the amounts needed to complete full performance under the entire contract. *Source:* FAR 45.101. The procedures for reporting, reutilization and disposal of contractor INVENTORY to which the government has title but which is no longer required for contract performance are set forth in FAR Subpart 45.6. The most common form of inventory requiring disposal under government procurement is TERMINATION INVENTORY.

CONTRACTOR PAST PERFORMANCE   See PAST PERFORMANCE.

CONTRACTOR PERFORMANCE ASSESSMENT REPORTING SYSTEM (CPARS)
The government-wide evaluation reporting tool for all PAST PERFORMANCE reports on contracts and orders. FAR 42.1502(a). Reports must be submitted at least annually and at the completion of contract performance. Contractors are given access to these reports and can submit comments which are included. The reports are entered into the FAPISS and are available to all government agencies but not to the general public. Procedures for filling out the reports are contained in FAR 42.1503. See https://www.cpars.gov. See Lee, *Death By CPAR: Is There a Remedy*, 33 N&CR ¶ 60 (Oct. 2019).

CONTRACTOR PURCHASING SYSTEM REVIEW (CPSR)   *Official:* The complete evaluation by the government of a contractor's purchasing of material and services, subcontracting, and subcontract management from development of the requirement through completion of subcontract performance. *Source:* FAR 44.101. The objective of a CPSR is to evaluate the efficiency and effectiveness with which the contractor spends government funds and complies with government policy when subcontracting. The review provides the ADMINISTRATION CONTRACTING OFFICER with a basis for granting, withholding, or withdrawing approval of the contractor's purchasing system. FAR 44.301. Contractors are subject to a CPSR if their expected sales to the government under other than sealed bid procedures are expected to exceed $25 million during the next 12 months. FAR 44.302. The review specifically focuses on (1) the results of market research accomplished, (2) the degree of price competition obtained, (3) pricing policies and techniques, (4) methods of evaluating subcontractors' responsibility, (5) treatment accorded affiliates, (6) policies and procedures regarding small business concerns, (7) planning, award, and postaward management of major subcontract programs, (8) compliance with Cost Accounting Standards in awarding subcontracts, (9) appropriateness of types of contracts used, and (10) management control systems to administer progress payments to subcontractors. FAR 44.303. See DFARS Subpart 244.3 and appendix C.

CONTRACTOR TEAM ARRANGEMENT   *Official:* An arrangement in which—(1) Two or more companies form a partnership or joint venture to act as a potential prime contractor; or (2) A potential prime contractor agrees with one or more other companies to have them act as its subcontractors under a specified government contract or acquisition program. *Source:* FAR 9.601. It is the government's policy to recognize team arrangements that are disclosed in OFFERs. FAR 9.603. See TEAM AGREEMENT.

CONTRACTOR VERSUS GOVERNMENT PERFORMANCE   See A-76 POLICY.

CONTRACTOR WEIGHTED AVERAGE SHARE (CWAS)   A DOD system, used in the late 1960s and 1970s, for reduced government oversight when a contractor's business was predominantly commercial or competitive fixed-priced work. DOD considered it desirable (1) to measure the cost-risk motivation imposed on individual contractors (as evidenced by the nature and type of the contracts), and (2) whenever practicable, to eliminate administrative controls and overhead AUDITs on those contractors that attained a verifiable "weighted average share" or risk that met a prescribed threshold. The CWAS concept was based on the premise that companies would exercise good management to be cost-conscious under contracts for commercial work or entered into on a competitive fixed-price basis—with the result that detailed review, control, and overhead audit by government personnel was not necessary. ASPR 3-1001. DOD eliminated the program in 1983.

CONTRACTOR'S DEVELOPMENT AND IMPLEMENTATION COSTS   *Official:* Those costs the contractor incurs on a VECP specifically in developing, testing, preparing, and submitting the VECP, as well of those costs the contractor incurs to make the contractual changes required by government acceptance of a VECP. *Source:* FAR 48.001. In calculating the savings resulting from a VALUE ENGINEERING CHANGE PROPOSAL, these costs are deducted from the gross amount saved to arrive at the INSTANT CONTRACT SAVINGS. See Nash & Feldman, 1 GOVERNMENT CONTRACT CHANGES § 9:10 (3d ed. 2006–2020); Cibinic, Nagle & Nash, ADMINISTRATION OF GOVERNMENT CONTRACTS 380–81 (5th ed. 2016).

CONTRACTUAL RELIEF   See EXTRAORDINARY CONTRACTUAL ACTION.

CONTRIBUTION   See DONATION.

CONTROLLED SUBSTANCE   *Official:* A controlled substance, schedules I through V of section 202 of the Controlled Substances Act (21 U.S.C. § 812), and as further defined in regulation at 21 C.F.R. §§ 1308.11–1308.15. *Source:* FAR 23.503. See www.deadiversion. usdoj.gov/schedules.htm. Under the DRUG-FREE WORKPLACE program described in FAR Subpart 23.5, companies with government contracts that meet the applicability criteria in FAR 23.501 must establish programs to ensure that their workplace is free of abuses of controlled substances, i.e., "drugs." Failure to comply with program requirements can result in suspension of payment, termination for default, and SUSPENSION or DEBARMENT.

CONTROLLED UNCLASSIFIED INFORMATION (CUI)   *Official:* Information that requires safeguarding or dissemination controls pursuant to and consistent with law, regulations, and Government-wide policies, excluding information that is classified under Executive Order 13526 of December 29, 2009, or the Atomic Energy Act, as amended. *Source:* Executive Order No. 13556, Nov. 4, 2010. This order establishes a uniform system for dealing with CUI under the direction of the National Archives and Records Administration. The policy for agencies on designating, safeguarding, disseminating, marking, decontrolling, and disposing of CUI, self-inspection and oversight requirements, and other facets of the program is set forth in 32 C.F.R. part 2002. DOD policy is contained in DOD Instruction 5200.48, March 6, 2020. See COVERED DEFENSE INFORMATION.

CONVENIENCE TERMINATION   See TERMINATION FOR CONVENIENCE.

CONVERSION DIRECT LABOR   A PROFIT analysis subfactor that measures the contribution of direct engineering, manufacturing, and other LABOR to converting the raw materials, data, and subcontracted items into the contract items using the theory that such labor should yield the highest rates of profit. Considerations include the diversity of engineering, scientific, and manufacturing labor skills required and the amount and quality of supervision and coordination needed to perform the contract task. FAR 15.404-4(d)(1)(i)(B). This factor is no longer used by DOD or NASA but is an element of most civilian agency

STRUCTURED PROFIT APPROACHES. See Cibinic, Nash & Yukins, FORMATION OF GOVERNMENT CONTRACTS 1546–47 (4th ed. 2011).

CONVERSION-RELATED INDIRECT COSTS   A PROFIT analysis subfactor that measures how much the INDIRECT COSTs contribute to contract performance. The LABOR elements in the allocable indirect costs should be given the profit consideration they would receive if treated as direct labor. The other elements of indirect costs should be evaluated to determine whether they merit only limited profit consideration because of their routine nature, or are elements that contribute significantly to the proposed contract. FAR 15.404-4(d)(1)(i)(C). This factor is no longer used by DOD or NASA but is an element of most civilian agency STRUCTURED PROFIT APPROACHES. See Cibinic, Nash & Yukins, FORMATION OF GOVERNMENT CONTRACTS 1546–47 (4th ed. 2011).

CONVICTION   *Official:* A judgment or conviction of a criminal offense by any court of competent jurisdiction, whether entered upon a verdict or a plea, and includes a conviction entered upon a plea of nolo contendere. *Source:* FAR 2.101. FAR 9.406-2 permits DEBARMENT of contractors if they have been convicted of acts that indicate they lack business integrity. For the purposes of implementing the DRUG FREE WORKPLACE ACT OF 1988, conviction means a finding of guilt (including a plea of nolo contendere) or imposition of sentence, or both, by any judicial body charged with the responsibility to determine violations of the Federal or State criminal drug statutes. FAR 23.503.

COOPERATIVE AGREEMENT   A legal instrument used principally for transferring a thing of value to a state or local government or to another recipient in order to accomplish a public purpose of support or stimulation where substantial involvement is expected between the government agency and the recipient. 31 U.S.C. § 6305. See Riley, *III Federal Contracts, Grants and Assistance* 85 (1984). A cooperative agreement is frequently similar to a COST-SHARING CONTRACT. However, a cost-sharing contract is subject to the FEDERAL ACQUISITION REGULATION, whereas a cooperative agreement is not. Thus, agencies entering into cooperative agreements generally have substantial freedom to structure the terms and conditions of the agreement. In DOD and DOE cooperative agreements are dealt with in the regulations governing TECHNOLOGY INVESTMENT AGREEMENTs. Other regulatory guidance is issued by agencies in the form of assistance regulations, in cooperation with the OFFICE OF MANAGEMENT AND BUDGET. However, statutes establishing specific programs, as well as certain other regulations, may contain requirements for cooperative agreements that differ from the usual assistance regulations or even resemble ACQUISITION approaches. For example, the Cooperative Agreement with Canada is a MEMORANDUM OF UNDERSTANDING that does not fall within the scope of 31 U.S.C. § 6305. See Cibinic, Nash & Yukins, FORMATION OF GOVERNMENT CONTRACTS 16–20 (4th ed. 2011). See also Nash, *Cooperative Agreements: A Possible Remedy*, 33 N&CR ¶ 16 (Mar. 2019).

COOPERATIVE PROGRAMS   Programs that comprise one or more specific cooperative projects conducted under an international agreement and that are implemented under the ARMS EXPORT CONTROL ACT, including specific provisions of 22 U.S.C. § 2767, regarding cooperative projects with friendly foreign countries, or 10 U.S.C. § 2350a, regarding cooperative RESEARCH AND DEVELOPMENT programs with allied countries. Cooperative programs exclude programs that entail acquisition for solely foreign military requirements, as distinct from joint U.S.-foreign military requirements. (Acquisition for solely foreign military requirements will be satisfied through either FOREIGN MILITARY SALES or direct commercial transactions with U.S. contractors.) Cooperative programs may also comprise one or more specific cooperative projects whose arrangements are defined in a written agreement between the parties and that involve: (1) research, development, testing, and evaluation (RDT&E) of defense articles, joint production of a defense article that was developed by one or more of the participants, and procurement by the United States of a foreign defense article, technology, or service that are implemented under 22 U.S.C. § 2767, to promote the rationalization, standardization, and interoperability of NATO armed forces or to enhance the ongoing efforts of non-NATO countries to improve their conventional defense capabilities; (2) cooperative research and development with NATO and major non-NATO allies implemented under 10 U.S.C. § 2350a, to improve the conventional defense capabilities of NATO and enhance rationalization, standardization, and interoperability; (3) data, information, and personnel exchange activities conducted under approved DOD programs; or (4) testing and evaluation of conventional defense equipment, munitions, and technologies developed by allied and friendly nations to meet valid existing U.S. military requirements. DAU GLOSSARY.

COOPERATIVE PURCHASING   Two or more organizations purchasing under the same contract; the organizations can be a mixture of state or local government agencies, or a combination of federal agencies. In addition to the advantage of achieving better prices, organizations may participate in cooperative purchasing arrangements to reduce possible duplication of effort, attract a larger number of bidders, or share information regarding specific items. 48 C.F.R. Subpart 538.70 prescribes policies and procedures that implement statutory provisions authorizing cooperative purchasing by non-federal organizations. See INTERAGENCY ACQUISITION. See also Miller & McConnell, MODEL PROCUREMENT CODE FOR STATE AND LOCAL GOVERNMENTS § 10-201 (2000).

COOPERATIVE RESEARCH AND DEVELOPMENT AGREEMENT (CRADA)   Agreement between a government laboratory or government-owned, contractor-operated laboratory and a private organization to conduct RESEARCH AND DEVELOPMENT jointly. Such an agreement combines the resources of the private sector, state and local governments, universities, or consortia with those of the federal government. CRADAs are authorized by 15 U.S.C. § 3701 et seq. They are a means of FEDERAL TECHNOLOGY TRANSFER whereby the government may share its research resources but may not use appropriated funds to conduct joint research projects. See Nash & Rawicz, INTELLECTUAL PROPERTY IN GOVERNMENT CONTRACTS, chap. 7 (6th ed. 2008). See also Nash, *Cooperative Research and Development Contracts: An Egregious Breach*, 23 N&CR ¶ 23 (May 2009).

COPELAND ANTI-KICKBACK ACT   A 1934 Act, 18 U.S.C. § 874, 40 U.S.C. § 3145, that contains provisions to prevent KICKBACKs by construction workers to contractors or subcontractors on projects financed in whole or in part by the government. This act is implemented by 29 C.F.R. part 3 and FAR 22.403-2 which calls for the use of the clause at FAR 52.222-10.

COPYRIGHT   The exclusive rights of an author in WORKs (literary, musical, dramatic, choreographic, pictorial, graphic, sculptural, audio-visual, sound recordings or architectural) that he or she has created. The rights are (1) reproduction, (2) preparation of DERIVATIVE WORKs, (3) distribution by sale or leasing, (4) performance, and (5) public display. Title 17 of the United States Code governs these rights. Authors obtain the rights at the time the work is first created (without regard to publication) and may register their works in the Copyright Office of the Library of Congress, 17 U.S.C. § 407. Copyright has become an important facet of government contracting because most SOFTWARE is copyrighted by its creators. Contractual provisions governing the ownership and use of copyrights are contained in the Rights in Data—General clause in FAR 52.227-14, the Rights in Technical Data—Noncommercial Items clause in DFARS 252.227-7013 and the Rights in Noncommercial Computer Software and Noncommercial Computer Software Documentation clause in DFARS 252.227-7014. See Nash & Rawicz, INTELLECTUAL PROPERTY IN GOVERNMENT CONTRACTS, chaps. 1 & 4 (6th ed. 2008). See also Nash, *Copyright Protection: The Inadequate Regulations*, 24 N&CR ¶ 2 (Jan. 2010); Littman, *Lessons From The Procurement World: Understanding Why the Government Denies its Employees Recovery After Infringing Their Copyrighted Works*, 39 PUB. CONT. L.J. 879 (2010); Nash, *Government Hacking Into Copyrighted Material: A Proper Act*, 22 N&CR ¶ 55 (Sept. 2008).

CORPORATE ADMINISTRATIVE CONTRACTING OFFICER (CACO)   An ADMINISTRATIVE CONTRACTING OFFICER (ACO) assigned to a corporation that has more than one location with resident ACOs. FAR 42.602. The AGENCY HEAD can approve the need for a CACO in other circumstances. CACOs deal with corporate management and perform contract administration functions on a corporate-wide basis. FAR 42.601. Typical CACO functions include (1) determining final INDIRECT COST rates for cost-reimbursement contracts, (2) establishing ADVANCE AGREEMENTs or recommendations on corporate/HOME OFFICE expense allocations, and (3) administering COST ACCOUNTING STANDARDS applicable to corporate-level and corporate-directed accounting practices. FAR 42.603.

CORRECTIVE ACTION   Action taken by an agency to correct a problem in a procurement when it determines that it is likely to lose a PROTEST or has lost a protest. Data provided by the GOVERNMENT ACCOUNTABILITY OFFICE indicates that agencies frequently take corrective action during a protest rather than waiting for a decision. When informed that an agency is taking corrective action, GAO will dismiss the protest. If the scope of corrective action is protested to the COURT OF FEDERAL CLAIMS, the court can enjoin the action only if it finds that the action has no rational basis (rather than requiring that it be "narrowly tailored" to resolve the grounds for granting a protest). *Dell Federal Systems, L.P. v. United States*, 906 F.3d 982 (Fed. Cir. 2018).

COST   The sacrifice incurred in economic activities such as the value of cash or other resources given in exchange for a resource or the expiration of benefits caused by using a resource in production. Financial Accounting Standards Board Concept No. 6. The government recognizes only ALLOWABLE COSTs in computing the costs that it will reimburse under COST-REIMBURSEMENT CONTRACTs and in pricing actions under FIXED-PRICE CONTRACTs. See Cibinic, Knight & Nash, COST-REIMBURSEMENT CONTRACTING, chap. 9 (4th ed. 2014).

COST ACCOUNTING   The area of accounting that focuses on the method and system used to compile and analyze the costs of selling and manufacturing products and services. It includes the method for classifying, summarizing, recording, and allocating the ACTUAL COSTs incurred and comparing them with the historical costs that have been established by a contractor. BLACK'S LAW DICTIONARY 25 (11th ed. 2019). See generally Cibinic, Knight & Nash, COST-REIMBURSEMENT CONTRACTING (4th ed. 2014).

COST ACCOUNTING PERIOD   See BASE PERIOD.

COST ACCOUNTING PRACTICE   *Official:* Any disclosed or established accounting method or technique which is used for allocation of cost to cost objectives, assignment of cost to cost accounting periods, or measurement of cost. *Source:* 48 C.F.R. § 9903.302-1. This regulation contains detailed guidance on the treatment of cost accounting practices. The determination of the amount paid or a change in the amount paid for a unit of goods and services is not a cost accounting practice. CAS 402, Consistency in Allocating Costs Incurred for the Same Purpose, 48 C.F.R. § 9904.402, requires that contractors follow consistent cost accounting practices. Contractors subject to the COST ACCOUNTING STANDARDS must disclose their cost accounting practices on DISCLOSURE STATE-MENTs. See Cibinic, Knight & Nash, COST-REIMBURSEMENT CONTRACTING 513–35 (4th ed. 2014).

COST ACCOUNTING STANDARDS (CAS)   A series of accounting standards originally issued by the COST ACCOUNTING STANDARDS BOARD under Pub. L. No. 91-379, 50 U.S.C. App. § 2168, to achieve uniformity and consistency in measuring, assigning, and allocating costs to contracts with the federal government. The 19 standards that were issued between 1970 and 1980 are now incorporated in FAR appendix B and 48 C.F.R. part 9904. The standards apply to contracts issued by all agencies of the government. The standards do not apply to (1) sealed bid contracts, (2) negotiated contracts under the TINA threshold, (3) contracts or subcontracts with SMALL BUSINESS CONCERNs, (4) contracts or subcontracts with foreign firms, (5) contracts or subcontracts where the price is set by law or regulation, (6) contracts or subcontracts for COMMERCIAL ITEMS, (7) contracts or subcontracts of less than $7.5 million, (8) subcontracts under the NATO PHM Ship program to be performed outside the United States by a foreign concern, and (9) firm-fixed-price contracts or subcontracts awarded on the basis of adequate price competition without submission of CERTIFIED COST OR PRICING DATA. 48 C.F.R. § 9903.201-1. Each of the 19 standards consists of 6 parts: purpose, fundamental requirement, technique for application, illustration, interpretation, and exemption. 48 C.F.R. part 9904 lists each of the standards that deal with consistency in estimating, accumulating, and reporting costs (CAS 401); consistency in allocating costs incurred for the same purpose (CAS 402); allocation of HOME OFFICE expenses (CAS 403); capitalization of tangible assets (CAS 404); accounting for unallowable costs (CAS 405); selection of cost accounting periods (CAS 406); use of standard costs for direct material and direct labor (CAS 407); accounting for costs of compensated personal absence (CAS 408); depreciation of TANGIBLE CAPITAL ASSETs (CAS 409); allocation of BUSINESS UNIT general and administrative expenses to final cost objectives (CAS 410); accounting for acquisition costs of material (CAS 411); composition and measurement of pension cost (CAS 412); adjustment and allocation of pension cost (CAS 413); cost of money as an element of the cost of facilities capital (CAS 414); accounting for the cost of deferred compensation (CAS 415); accounting for insurance costs (CAS 416); cost of money as an element of the cost of capital assets under construction (CAS 417); allocation of direct and indirect costs (CAS 418); and accounting for independent research and development and bid and proposal costs (CAS 420). Cost accounting standards administration is covered in FAR Part 30. See Feldman, GOVERNMENT CONTRACTS GUIDEBOOK §§ 9:54–9:63 (4th ed. 2019–2020); Manos, 2 GOVERNMENT CONTRACT COSTS & PRICING, chaps. 60–81 (2d ed. 2009–2020); Cibinic, Knight & Nash, COST-REIMBURSEMENT CONTRACTING 523–35 (4th ed. 2014).

COST ACCOUNTING STANDARDS (CAS) BOARD   The governmental entity with the exclusive authority to make, promulgate, amend, and rescind COST ACCOUNTING STANDARDS and interpretations of them. The CAS Board was originally established in 1970 by Pub. L. No. 91-379, 50 U.S.C. App. § 2168. That Board, which promulgated the current 19 standards, was part of the legislative branch and was chaired by the Comptroller General. Its jurisdiction was limited to national defense contracts, and it was abolished in 1980 after Congress failed to provide an appropriation. Section 5 of Pub. L. No. 100-679, 41 U.S.C. § 1501 et seq., the Office of Federal Procurement Policy Act Amendments of 1988, reestablished the CAS Board as an independent board within the Office of Management and Budget's OFFICE OF FEDERAL PROCUREMENT POLICY (OFPP). By law, the Board consists of five members. The Administrator of OFPP chairs the Board. The other four members, each experienced in government contract cost accounting, are as follows: two representatives of the federal government, one representing DOD and the other representing GSA; and two individuals from the private sector (both appointed by the Administrator of OFPP), one representing industry and one who is particularly knowledgeable about cost accounting problems and systems. 41 U.S.C. § 1501(b). Rules and regulations promulgated by the CAS Board are presently incorporated in 48 C.F.R. chap. 99 and in FAR appendix B. See Manos, 1 GOVERNMENT CONTRACT COSTS & PRICING, §§ 2:6–2:10 (2d ed. 2009–2020). See also Thomas, *The Case For A Reactivated CASB: Critical Accounting Issues For Government Contracts*, BRIEFING PAPERS NO. 16-5 (Apr. 2016).

COST ANALYSIS   *Official:* The review and evaluation of any separate cost elements and PROFIT or FEE in an offeror's or contractor's proposal, as needed to determine a FAIR AND REASONABLE PRICE or to determine COST REALISM and the application of judgment to determine how well the proposed costs represent what the cost of the contract should be, assuming reasonable economy and efficiency. *Source:* FAR 15.404-1(c). Cost analysis is used to establish the basis for negotiating contract prices when PRICE COMPETITION is inadequate or lacking altogether and when PRICE ANALYSIS, by itself, does not ensure price reasonableness. FAR 16.104(c). The contracting officer uses the following techniques and procedures, as appropriate, to perform cost analysis: (1) verification of cost or pricing data and evaluation of cost elements; (2) evaluation of the effect of current practices on future costs; (3) comparison of costs proposed for individual cost elements with previously incurred ACTUAL COSTs, previous cost estimates, independent government estimates, and forecasts; (4) verification of compliance with the FAR COST PRINCIPLES and applicable COST ACCOUNTING STANDARDS; (5) identification of any COST OR PRICING DATA needed to make the proposal ACCURATE, COMPLETE, AND CURRENT; and (6) analysis of the results of MAKE-OR-BUY PROGRAM reviews. FAR 15.404-1(c)(2). The contracting officer should also perform cost analysis in selecting and negotiating a contract type in the absence of effective price competition and when price analysis is insufficient. FAR 16.104(c). See Cibinic, Nash & Yukins, FORMATION OF GOVERNMENT CONTRACTS 1487–1533 (4th ed. 2011); DAU, *Contract Pricing Reference Guides* v. III (Feb. 22, 2012). See also Shearer, *How Could It Hurt to Ask? The Ability to Clarify Cost/Price Proposals Without Engaging in Discussions*, 39 PUB. CONT. L.J. 583 (2010).

COST AS AN INDEPENDENT VARIABLE (CAIV)   A methodology used by DOD to acquire and operate affordable systems by setting aggressive, achievable LIFE-CYCLE COST objectives and managing achievement of these objectives by trading off performance and schedule, as necessary. Cost objectives balance mission needs with projected out-year resources, taking into account anticipated process improvements in both DoD and industry. DAU GLOSSARY. See Kaye, et al., *Cost As An Independent Variable: Principles and Implementation*, ACQUISITION REVIEW QUARTERLY, Fall 2000.

COST BASE   See BASE.

COST BENEFIT ANALYSIS   (also Benefit-Cost Analysis) "An analytic technique that compares the costs and benefits of investments, programs, or policy actions in order to determine which alternative or alternatives maximize net profits. Net benefits of an alternative are determined by subtracting the present value of costs from the present value of benefits." The results are used to inform a decision maker. See also OFFICE OF MANAGEMENT AND BUDGET Circular A-94, *Guidelines and Discount Rates for Benefit-Cost Analysis of Federal Programs* (1992): "A systematic quantitative method of assessing the desirability of government projects or policies when it is important to take a long view of future effects and a broad view of possible side effects." Requirements to conduct a cost-benefit analysis are stated in many places in the CODE OF FEDERAL REGULATIONS. The FAR and agency supplements mention cost-benefit analysis in connection with many contracting decisions. See, for example, FAR 16.401(e)(1)(iii) concerning the use of award fee-contracts and DFARS 234.201(1)(iii)(C) concerning the use of EARNED VALUE MANAGEMENT SYSTEMS. Cost-benefit analysis should not be confused with TRADEOFF ANALYSIS, which is a different process. See Edwards, *Tradeoff Analysis vs. Cost-Benefit Analysis in Source Selection: How Do They Differ?*, 24 N&CR ¶ 32 (July 2010).

COST CONTRACT   *Official:* A COST-REIMBURSEMENT CONTRACT in which the contractor receives no fee. *Source:* FAR 16.302. It can also be referred to as a cost-no-fee contract. The FAR states that such a contract may be appropriate for RESEARCH AND DEVELOPMENT work, particularly with nonprofit educational institutions or other nonprofit organizations but they have rarely been used in these situations. Cost contracts were used for FACILITIES CONTRACTs before the guidance on these contracts was deleted from the FAR in 2007. See Cibinic, Knight & Nash, COST-REIMBURSEMENT CONTRACTING 92–93 (4th ed. 2014).

COST ELEMENT BREAKDOWN   A listing of the COST ELEMENTS that a contractor has incurred or believes it will incur in the performance of a contract. When a contractor is required to submit CERTIFIED COST OR PRICING DATA, Table 15-1 in FAR 15.408 requires the submission of cost element breakdowns as the top level of information that must be submitted. The submission of cost element breakdowns is also necessary when submitting a proposal for a COST-REIMBURSEMENT CONTRACT in order to permit the government to perform the required COST REALISM ANALYSIS. See Cibinic, Knight & Nash, COST-REIMBURSEMENT CONTRACTING 456–77 (4th ed. 2014).

COST ELEMENTS   The types of costs that a contractor will incur in the performance of a contract. When a contractor is required to submit CERTIFIED COST OR PRICING DATA, Table 15-1 in FAR 15.408 requires information on an enumerated set of cost elements: MATERIALs and services, DIRECT LABOR, INDIRECT COSTS, other costs, ROYALTIES, and the FACILITIES CAPITAL COST OF MONEY. However, contractors may use other categories of cost elements depending on their accounting system. Cost elements are generally depicted in a COST ELEMENT BREAKDOWN.

COST IMPACT PROPOSAL   The documentation of the estimated increased or decreased costs resulting from a change in accounting practices. Whenever a contractor makes a change to disclosed or established accounting practices or is determined to be in noncompliance, the Administration of Cost Accounting Standards clause at FAR 52.230-6 calls for the submission of a cost impact proposal and provides detailed guidance on the contents of such a proposal. *DCAA Contract Audit Manual* ¶ 8-500 Section 5 contains guidance to auditors on obtaining and auditing such proposals. See Cibinic, Knight & Nash, COST-REIMBURSEMENT CONTRACTING 533–34 (4th ed. 2014).

COST INCENTIVE   A contract term that provides for an upward adjustment of PROFIT or FEE for performance at a cost to the government that is lower than the TARGET COST (a "positive" incentive), or for a downward adjustment of profit or fee for performance at a cost that is higher than the target cost (a "negative" incentive). See FAR 16.402-1. Such an incentive might be a PREDETERMINED, FORMULA-TYPE INCENTIVE or an AWARD FEE incentive. See DOD, *Contract Pricing Reference Guides* v. 4, chap. 1 (Sept. 9, 2014); Cibinic, Knight & Nash, COST-REIMBURSEMENT CONTRACTING 49–69 (4th ed. 2014); Cibinic, Nash & Yukins, FORMATION OF GOVERNMENT CONTRACTS 1256–88 (4th ed. 2011).

COST INCURRED   See INCURRED COST.

COST INPUT   *Official:* The cost, except GENERAL AND ADMINISTRATIVE (G&A) EXPENSEs, which for contract costing purposes is allocable (see ALLOCABLE COST) to the production of goods and services during a cost accounting period. *Source:* FAR 31.001. The cost input is usually the COST BASE to which G&A expenses are allocated.

COST OBJECTIVE   *Official:* A function, organizational subdivision, contract, or other work unit for which cost data are desired and for which provision is made to accumulate and measure the cost of processes, products, jobs, capitalized projects, etc. *Source:* FAR 31.001. A final cost objective is a cost objective that has allocated to it both DIRECT COSTs and INDIRECT COSTs and, in the contractor's accumulation system, is one of the final accumulation points. This definition is not applicable to contracts with state, logical and Indian tribes which are subject to different allowable cost rules in accordance with FAR Subpart 31.6. See Cibinic, Knight & Nash, COST-REIMBURSEMENT CONTRACTING 590–616 (4th ed. 2014).

COST OF CAPITAL COMMITTED TO FACILITIES   See FACILITIES CAPITAL COST OF MONEY.

COST OF MONEY AS A COST OF CAPITAL ASSETS UNDER CONSTRUCTION   An IMPUTED COST of the capital assets a contractor has used to construct, fabricate, or develop new FACILITIES. 48 C.F.R. § 9904.417-40. This cost is computed in accordance with CAS 417, Cost of Money as an Element of the Cost of Capital Assets Under Construction, 48 C.F.R. § 9904.417. It is added to the capitalized acquisition cost of the facilities when they are placed on the contractor's BALANCE SHEET as an ASSET. It is an allowable cost in accordance with FAR 31.205-10(b). See Cibinic, Knight & Nash, COST-REIMBURSEMENT CONTRACTING 723 (4th ed. 2014).

COST OF MONEY FACTORS (CMF)   Factors developed by overhead pools at contractors' BUSINESS UNITs, using Form CASB CMF (48 C.F.R. § 9904.414, Appendix A, Facilities Capital Cost of Money Factors Computation), to measure a contractor's FACILITIES

CAPITAL COST OF MONEY. Three elements are required: (1) business unit facilities capital data (the NET BOOK VALUE for each cost accounting period), (2) overhead allocation bases (the same as the bases used to compute the proposed overhead rates), and (3) the TREASURY INTEREST RATE. Cost of money factors are also used to develop the "facilities capital employed" base used in prenegotiation profit objectives under the DOD WEIGHTED GUIDELINES METHOD. DFARS 215.404-71-4. Actual CFMs are required when it is necessary to determine final allowable costs for cost settlement or repricing in accordance with CAS 414, Cost of Money as an Element of the Cost of Facilities Capital, 48 C.F.R. § 9904.414 and with FAR 31.205-10. See Manos, 2 GOVERNMENT CONTRACT COSTS & PRICING §§ 75:1–75:7 (2d ed. 2009–2020).

COST OF REPROCUREMENT   See EXCESS COST OF REPROCUREMENT.

COST OR PRICING DATA   *Official:* All facts that, as of the date of price agreement or, if applicable, an earlier date agreed upon between the parties that is as close as practicable to the date of agreement on price, prudent buyers and sellers would reasonably expect to affect price negotiations significantly. Cost or pricing data are factual, not judgmental; and are verifiable (see FACT and JUDGMENT IN PRICING). While they do not indicate the accuracy of the prospective contractor's judgment about estimated future costs or projections, they do include the data forming the basis for that judgment. Cost or pricing data are more than historical accounting data; they are all the facts that can be reasonably expected to contribute to the soundness of estimates of future costs and to the validity of determinations of costs already incurred. They also include, but are not limited to, such factors as—(1) Vendor quotations; (2) Nonrecurring costs; (3) Information on changes in production methods and in production or purchasing volume; (4) Data supporting projections of business prospects and objectives and related operations costs; (5) Unit-cost trends such as those associated with labor efficiency; (6) Make-or-buy decisions; (7) Estimated resources to attain business goals; and (8) Information on management decisions that could have a significant bearing on costs. *Source:* FAR 2.101. 10 U.S.C. § 2306a(h)(1) and 41 U.S.C. § 3501(a)(2) contain a shorter definition. See Nash & Feldman, 2 GOVERNMENT CONTRACT CHANGES §§ 21:4–21:12 (3d ed. 2006–2020); Feldman, GOVERNMENT CONTRACT AWARDS: NEGOTIATION AND SEALED BIDDING § 11:19 (2019–2020 ed.); Cibinic, Nash & Yukins, FORMATION OF GOVERNMENT CONTRACTS 1493–1500 (4th ed. 2011). See also CERTIFIED COST OR PRICING DATA.

COST OVERRUN   The excess of ALLOWABLE COSTs incurred by a contractor on a COST-REIMBURSEMENT CONTRACT over the ESTIMATED COST or TARGET COST of the contract. Under the LIMITATION OF COST CLAUSE, contractors are not obligated to incur such overruns and the government is not obligated to reimburse such costs. However, if the government provides additional funds, the contractor is required to incur the overrun. This term is also used, on occasion, to refer to the incurrence of more costs than predicted in the performance of FIXED-PRICE CONTRACTs. See CAS 405, Accounting for Unallowable Costs, 48 C.F.R. § 9904.405-40, which requires cost overruns that are not compensated by the government to be allocated to the contract cost objective to which they pertain. See Cibinic, Knight & Nash, COST-REIMBURSEMENT CONTRACTING 978–1018 (4th ed. 2014). See also Edwards, *Cost Overrun v. Cost Growth: Is There a Difference? Does It Matter?*, 22 N&CR ¶ 27 (June 2008).

COST PERFORMANCE INDEX (CPI)   A key indicator used to analyze cost and schedule performance data reported by defense contractors. This figure informs the agency of the contractor's efficiency and whether the contractor is above or below cost. It is computed by dividing the budgeted cost for work performed by the corresponding actual cost of work performed. The cost performance index is an EARNED VALUE MANAGEMENT performance factor.

COST PERFORMANCE REPORT (CPR)   *Historical.* A primary means of communication between the contractor and the procuring agency to report cost and schedule performance and trends. The CPR serves to alert the agency of any problems arising with cost or schedule and demonstrates the results of any corrective action taken to address earlier deficiencies. CPRs were required on all DOD contracts that required compliance with Cost/Schedule Control Systems Criteria but agencies were encouraged to permit contractors to use their own systems if they provide accurate and timely information. They have since been deleted from the DOD 5000 Series. DOD now requires reporting using the COST AND SOFTWARE DATA REPORTING SYSTEM.

COST-PLUS-A-PERCENTAGE-OF-COST   (CPPC)   CONTRACT A COST-REIMBURSEMENT CONTRACT that obligates the government to pay the contractor some amount that is undetermined at the time the contract is made and to be incurred in the future, based on a percentage of future costs. *Muschany v. United States*, 324 U.S. 49, 61–62 (1944). The use of a cost-plus-a-percentage of cost system of payment is prohibited by 10 U.S.C. § 2306(a) and 41 U.S.C. § 3905(a). The COMPTROLLER GENERAL OF THE UNITED STATES has stated that a CPPC arrangement exists when the following are present: (1) payment of some amount is to be calculated at a predetermined rate; (2) the pre-determined rate is to be applied to actual performance costs; (3) the contractor's entitlement is uncertain at the time of contract formation; and (4) the contractor's entitlement increases commensurately with increased performance costs. See *Mr. James K. White; Assistant General Counsel for Finance and Litigation; Office of the General Counsel; Department of Commerce*, Comp. Gen. Dec. B-252378, Sept. 21, 1993. The prohibition against a CPPC arrangement applies regardless of the stated contract type. The purpose of the prohibition is to prohibit contracts that motivate a contractor to increase its profits by increasing its costs of performance. The inclusion of a CEILING PRICE does not make CPPCs acceptable. See Cibinic, Knight & Nash, Cost-Reimbursement Contracting 42–47 (4th ed. 2014); Cibinic, Nash & Yukins, Formation of Government Contracts 1206–12 (4th ed. 2011).

COST-PLUS-AWARD-FEE (CPAF) CONTRACT   A COST-REIMBURSEMENT CONTRACT that provides for a fee consisting of (1) a BASE FEE (which may be zero) fixed at the inception of the contract and (2) an AWARD FEE, based upon a periodic judgmental evaluation by the government, sufficient to provide motivation for excellence in such areas as quality, timeliness, technical ingenuity, and cost-effective management during contract performance. FAR 16.305. CPAF contracts are INCENTIVE CONTRACTs. A DETERMINATION AND FINDING must be completed for CPAF contracts justifying that such a contract is in the best interest of the government. FAR 16.401(d). CPAF contracts are appropriate when the work to be performed is such that it is neither feasible nor effective to devise predetermined objective incentive targets applicable to cost, schedule, and technical performance; the likelihood of meeting acquisition objectives will be enhanced by using a contract that effectively motivates the contractor toward exceptional performance and provides the government with the flexibility to evaluate both actual performance and the conditions under which it was achieved; and any additional administrative effort and cost required to monitor and evaluate performance are justified by the expected benefits as documented by a risk and cost benefit analysis. FAR 16.401(e). The contractor may earn the award amount in whole or in part. FAR 16.405-2 states that the determination of the award fee is made unilaterally by the government but it is subject to the CONTRACT DISPUTES ACT. *Burnside-Ott Aviation Training Center v. Dalton*, 107 F.3d 854 (Fed. Cir. 1997). CPAF contracts have been widely used to contract for services and research and development but their use has been discouraged in recent years. One of their major features is that they require the government to give contractors regular evaluations of their performance (usually every three to six months) and these evaluations are now subject to a mandatory scheme set forth in Figure 16-1 in FAR 16.401(e)(3). For contracts with DOD, CPAFs are suitable for LEVEL-OF-EFFORT CONTRACTs where mission feasibility is established but measurement of achievement must be by subjective evaluation rather than objective measurement. It is DOD's policy to utilize objective criteria, whenever possible, to measure contract performance. DOD PGI § 216.405-2. See Cibinic, Knight & Nash, COST-REIMBURSEMENT CONTRACTING 70–91 (4th ed. 2014); Cibinic, Nash & Yukins, FORMATION OF GOVERNMENT CONTRACTS 1288–1314 (4th ed. 2011). See also Nash, *Selection of Contract Type: Ensuring That Contractors Do Not Earn Excessively High Profits*, 25 N&CR ¶ 55 (Nov. 2011); Edwards, *Award-Fee Contracting*, BRIEFING PAPERS No. 10-3 (Feb. 2010); Edwards & Nash *The End of a Love Affair: New Policies About Incentive Contracts*, 23 N&CR ¶ 63 (Dec. 2009); Edwards & Nash, *Postscript: Award-Fee Incentives*, 21 N&CR ¶ 24 (June 2007); Edwards, *Award-Fee Contracts: What Should They Say About the Government's Internal Organization and Processes?*, 21 N&CR ¶ 8 (Mar. 2007); Edwards, *Award-Fee Incentives: Do They Work? Do Agencies Know How to Use Them?*, 20 N&CR ¶ 26 (June 2006).

COST-PLUS-FIXED-FEE (CPFF) CONTRACT A COST-REIMBURSEMENT CONTRACT that provides for payment to the contractor of a negotiated FEE (profit) that is fixed at the inception of the contract. FAR 16.306(a). This fixed fee does not vary with ACTUAL COST but may be adjusted as a result of changes in the work to be performed under the contract. The CPFF type of contract permits contracting for efforts that might otherwise present too great a risk to contractors, but it is thought to give the contractor less incentive to control costs than does a FIXED-PRICE CONTRACT. FAR 16.306(b) limits its use to those situations where the contract is for performance of research or study and either the level of effort is unknown or a COST-PLUS-INCENTIVE CONTRACT is not practical. There are two forms of CPFF contracts: (1) the COMPLETION FORM CONTRACT, in which the work is described by stating a definite goal or target and an end product (frequently a report); and (2) the TERM CONTRACT, in which the contract calls for a stated level of effort (usually hours or days of specified classes of LABOR) over a stated period of time. FAR 16.306(d). The amount of the fixed fee is subject to FEE LIMITATIONs. 10 U.S.C. § 2306(d); 41 U.S.C. § 3905(b). See Cibinic, Knight & Nash, COST-REIMBURSEMENT CONTRACTING 47–49 (4th ed. 2014); Cibinic, Nash & Yukins, FORMATION OF GOVERNMENT CONTRACTS 1245–47 (4th ed. 2011).

COST-PLUS-INCENTIVE-FEE (CPIF) CONTRACT A COST-REIMBURSEMENT CONTRACT that provides for the initially negotiated TARGET FEE to be adjusted later by a formula based on the relationship of total ALLOWABLE COSTs (with some exclusions as stated in the Incentive Fee clause at FAR 52.216-10) to total TARGET COSTs. FAR 16.304. This contract type specifies a target cost, a target fee, a MINIMUM FEE, a

MAXIMUM FEE, and a fee adjustment formula. After contract performance, the fee payable to the contractor is determined in accordance with the formula. FAR 16.405-1. To encourage the contractor to manage the contract effectively, the formula provides, within limits, for increases in fee above target fee, when total allowable costs are less than target costs, and decreases in fee below target fee, when total allowable costs exceed target costs. When the total allowable cost is greater or less than the range of costs (the RANGE OF INCENTIVE EFFECTIVENESS) within which the fee adjustment formula operates, the contractor is paid total allowable costs plus the minimum or maximum fee. CPIF contracts are subject to the same limitations as other cost-reimbursement contracts found in FAR 16.301-3. See Manos, 1 GOVERNMENT CONTRACT COSTS AND PRICING § 4:6 (2d ed. 2009–2020); Cibinic, Knight & Nash, COST-REIMBURSEMENT CONTRACTING 49–69 (4th ed. 2014); Cibinic, Nash & Yukins, FORMATION OF GOVERNMENT CONTRACTS 1257–69 (4th ed. 2011).

COST POOL See INDIRECT COST POOL.

COST PRINCIPLES The rules promulgated by the government in FAR Part 31 that define which costs are allowable (see ALLOWABLE COST) in the negotiation and administration of government contracts. This part of the FAR contains contract cost principles and procedures for (1) the pricing of contracts, subcontracts, and contract modifications whenever cost analysis is performed and (2) the determination, negotiation, or allowance of costs when required by a contract clause. These principles are made a part of all COST-REIMBURSEMENT CONTRACTs by incorporation by reference in the Allowable Cost and Payment clause at FAR 52.216-7. See Manos, 1 GOVERNMENT CONTRACT COSTS & PRICING, Part II. (2d ed. 2009–2020); Cibinic, Knight & Nash, COST-REIMBURSEMENT CONTRACTING 513–22 (4th ed. 2014).

COST-REALISM *Official:* The costs in an offeror's proposal (1) are realistic for the work to be performed; (2) reflect a clear understanding of the requirements; and (3) are consistent with the various elements of the offeror's technical proposal. *Source:* FAR 2.101. See COST REALISM ANALYSIS.

COST-REALISM ANALYSIS *Official:* The process of independently reviewing and evaluating specific elements of each offeror's proposed cost estimate to determine whether the estimated proposed COST ELEMENTS are realistic for the work to be performed; reflect a clear understanding of the requirements; and are consistent with the unique methods of performance and materials described in the offeror's technical proposal. *Source:* FAR 15.404-1(d)(1). Cost realism analysis is required on COST-REIMBURSEMENT CONTRACTs to determine the PROBABLE COST of performance of the contract, which is used as the evaluation factor in selecting the winning contractor. FAR 15.305(a)(1), FAR 15.404-1(d)(2). However, it can also indicate that an offeror does not understand the technical requirements or that it has a superior method of accomplishing the required work. A cost realism analysis may also be made in limited circumstances on FIXED-PRICE CONTRACTs for purposes of determining whether a contractor understands the work or is a responsible contractor (see PRICE REALISM ANALYSIS and RESPONSIBILITY). FAR 15.404-1(d)(3). In such cases, the proposed prices are not adjusted for purposes of evaluation. Although it is generally believed that cost realism analysis is performed in order to determine whether a cost or price is unrealistically low, FAR 15.402(a)(3) states that cost realism can also be used, in addition to PRICE and COST ANALYSIS, to establish a FAIR

AND REASONABLE PRICE. See Feldman, GOVERNMENT AWARDS: NEGOTIATION AND SEALED BIDDING § 11:16 (2019–2020 ed.); Cibinic, Knight & Nash, COST-REIMBURSEMENT CONTRACTING 431–80 (4th ed. 2014); DAU, *Contract Pricing Reference Guides* v.4, chap. 8 (Feb. 22, 2012). See also Edwards, *Cost Realism: A Challenge for Both Industry and Government*, 25 N&CR ¶ 53 (Nov. 2011).

COST-REIMBURSEMENT CONTRACT A contract that provides for payment to the contractor of ALLOWABLE incurred COSTs to the extent provided in the contract. FAR 16.301-1. Cost-reimbursement contracts are distinguished from FIXED-PRICE CONTRACTs, under which payment is made to the contractor on the basis of pre-established prices. Cost-reimbursement contracts are suitable for use only when the uncertainties involved in an agency's requirements cannot be sufficiently defined or contract performance does not permit costs to be estimated with sufficient accuracy to use any type of fixed-price contract. FAR 16.301-2. They may be used only when (1) the factors in FAR 16.104 have been considered, (2) a written acquisition plan has been approved and signed by at least one level above the contracting officer, (3) the contractor's accounting system is adequate for determining applicable costs, and (4) adequate government resources are available to award and manage a contract other than a FIRM-FIXED-PRICE CONTRACT, including a qualified CONTRACTING OFFICER'S REPRESENTATIVE (COR) and appropriate surveillance during performance that will provide reasonable assurance that efficient methods and effective cost controls are used. FAR 16.301-3(a). The use of cost-reimbursement contracts is prohibited for the acquisition of COMMERCIAL ITEMs. FAR 16.301-3(b). In order to avoid violation of the ANTI-DEFICIENCY ACT, all cost-reimbursement contracts must contain the LIMITATION OF COST CLAUSE. This clause limits the government's obligation by stipulating that it will pay only the amount contained in the contract's ESTIMATED COST or TARGET COST (plus any prescribed FEE). FAR 7.103 provides that the HEAD OF THE AGENCY require a written acquisition plan for cost-reimbursement contracts. Cost-reimbursement pricing arrangements include COST CONTRACTs, COST-SHARING CONTRACTs, COST-PLUS-INCENTIVE-FEE CONTRACTs, COST-PLUS-AWARD-FEE CONTRACTs, and COST-PLUS-FIXED-FEE CONTRACTs. COST-PLUS-A-PERCENTAGE-OF-COST CONTRACTs are prohibited. See Manos, 1 GOVERNMENT COSTS & PRICING § 4:3 (2d ed. 2009–2020); Cibinic, Knight & Nash, COST-REIMBURSEMENT CONTRACTING, chap. 2 (4th ed. 2014).

COST RISK An assessment of possible monetary loss or gain in light of the work to be done under a contract. It is one of the elements to be considered in negotiating a FAIR AND REASONABLE PRICE, as well as in determining the TYPE OF CONTRACT to be used. See FAR 16.104. Cost risk is assessed so that the contractor can be compensated commensurately with the extent of risk assumed. Factors included in a cost risk assessment are the reliability of the contractor's proposed costs; the extent of contingency factors included in the proposed costs; the relative firmness or uncertainty of the estimated costs for major components, subcontracts, etc.; and the contractor's prior profit experience with the same or similar supplies or systems. *DCAA Contract Audit Manual* ¶ 9-906.2.

COST TO THE GOVERNMENT The amount to be paid to the contractor and other costs that the government incurs in procuring and using articles or services. In cost-reimbursement contracts, the amount to be paid to the contractor is the estimated or TARGET COST plus the fee. In fixed-price contracts, this amount is the contract price. Cost to the government is a mandatory EVALUATION FACTOR when an agency is soliciting COMPETITIVE PROPOSALS. See 10 U.S.C. § 2305(a)(3)(A); 41 U.S.C. § 3306(c).

COST UNDERRUN   The incurrence of costs less than those in the contract's TARGET COST (in a FIXED-PRICE-INCENTIVE CONTRACT or a COST-PLUS-INCENTIVE-FEE CONTRACT), ESTIMATED COST (in any other COST-REIMBURSEMENT CONTRACT), or a redeterminable price (in a FIXED-PRICE REDETERMINATION—PROSPECTIVE CONTRACT or FIXED-PRICE REDETERMINATION—RETROACTIVE CONTRACT). An underrun is caused by the contractor's ACTUAL COSTs being under target or under anticipated contract costs, but not for reasons such as quantity changes, engineering changes, or economic changes.

COST/SCHEDULE CONTROL SYSTEM   *Historical.* A management system requiring the contractor to establish a WORK BREAKDOWN STRUCTURE for all work to be performed on the contract and to record performance and costs for each element of that structure as the work progresses. The purpose of such systems is to track the contractor's performance at a level of detail that will provide early information if a contractor is not performing on schedule or at the predicted costs. Guidance on such systems has been rescinded. C/SCS requirements have been replaced by requirements for EARNED VALUE MANAGEMENT SYSTEMs.

COST-SHARING   *Official:* An explicit arrangement under which the contractor bears some of the burden of reasonable, allocable, and allowable contract costs. *Source:* FAR 2.101. See COST-SHARING CONTRACT.

COST-SHARING CONTRACT   *Official:* A COST-REIMBURSEMENT CONTRACT in which the contractor receives no FEE and is reimbursed only for an agreed-upon portion of its ALLOWABLE COSTs. *Source:* FAR 16.303. Such a contract may be used only when the contractor agrees to absorb a portion of the costs in the expectation of substantial compensating benefits. Cost-sharing arrangements may call for the contractor to participate in the costs of the contract by accepting INDIRECT COST rates lower than the anticipated actual rates. In such cases, a negotiated indirect cost rate ceiling may be incorporated into the contract for prospective application. FAR 42.707. Another common form of cost sharing is the award of a FIXED-PRICE CONTRACT at less than the contractor's estimated costs of performance. See Cibinic, Knight & Nash, *Cost-Reimbursement Contracting* 93–98 (4th ed. 2014). For contracts with the HHS, cost-sharing contracts are appropriate where there is a probability that the contractor will receive present or future benefits from participation, such as training for employees, acquisition of equipment, and use of background knowledge in future contracts. Cost-sharing is intended to ensure efficient utilization of the resources available for the conduct of RESEARCH AND DEVELOPMENT projects and to promote sound planning and prudent fiscal policies of the performing organization. 48 C.F.R. § 335.070-1.

COSTS CONTINUING AFTER TERMINATION   Costs that cannot be discontinued immediately after the effective date of TERMINATION FOR CONVENIENCE despite all reasonable efforts. These costs are generally allowable; however, any costs that continue after the effective date of the termination due to the negligent or willful failure of the contractor to discontinue the costs are unallowable. FAR 31.205-42(b). Costs continuing after termination are often associated with a contractor's facilities, such as contractor-owned and contractor-leased buildings, machinery, and equipment. Recovery for the loss of useful value of facilities is covered under FAR 31.205-42(d) and rental costs under unexpired leases is dealt with under FAR 31.205-42(e). Neither the cost of work performed on the contract after termination nor the cost of UNABSORBED OVERHEAD are includable in these costs. See Manos, 1 GOVERNMENT COST & PRICING § 49:4 (2d ed. 2009–2020); Cibinic, Nash & Nagle, ADMINISTRATION OF GOVERNMENT CONTRACTS 983–85 (5th ed. 2016); Cibinic & Nash, COST-REIMBURSEMENT CONTRACTING 748–50 (3d ed. 2014).

COSTS RELATED TO LEGAL AND OTHER PROCEEDINGS   *Official:* The costs of administrative and clerical expenses, the costs of legal services whether performed by in-house and private counsel, the costs of the services of accountants, consultants, or others retained by the contractor to assist it, costs of employees, officers, directors, and any similar costs incurred before, during, and after commencement of a judicial or administrative proceeding which bears a direct relationship to the proceeding. *Source:* FAR 31.205-47. This COST PRINCIPLE provides that such costs are UNALLOWABLE in most circumstances—most notably in the prosecution of defense of CLAIMs. However, SMALL BUSINESSES may recover such costs under the EQUAL ACCESS TO JUSTICE ACT. See Manos, 1 GOVERNMENT COSTS & PRICING §§ 54:1–54:11 (2d ed. 2009–2020); Cibinic, Knight & Nash, COST-REIMBURSEMENT CONTRACTING 694–96 (4th ed. 2014).

COUNCIL OF DEFENSE AND SPACE INDUSTRY ASSOCIATIONS (CODSIA)   An association formed in 1964 by industry associations with common interests in the defense and space fields. DOD encouraged formation of this organization to provide a vehicle to obtain broad industry reactions to procurement regulations, policies, and procedures. CODSIA currently is composed of seven associations, including the AEROSPACE INDUSTRY ASSOCIATION, the American Council of Engineering Companies, the ASSOCIATED GENERAL CONTRACTORS, the Information Technology Information Council, the NATIONAL DEFENSE INDUSTRIAL ASSOCIATION, the Professional Services Council, and the U.S. Chamber of Commerce. [CODSIA, 4401 Wilson Boulevard, Suite 1110, Arlington, VA 22203; (703) 243-2020]

COURSE OF DEALING   See PRIOR COURSE OF DEALING.

COURT OF APPEALS FOR THE FEDERAL CIRCUIT (CAFC or Fed. Cir.)   The appellate (reviewing) court for both the U.S. COURT OF FEDERAL CLAIMS and the BOARDs OF CONTRACT APPEALS. 28 U.S.C. § 1295(a)(3), (a)(10); 41 U.S.C. § 7107(a). Because the Supreme Court rarely considers decisions regarding government contract disputes, the Court of Appeals for the Federal Circuit typically provides the last opportunity for their review. The Federal Courts Improvement Act of 1982 created the U.S. Court of Appeals for the Federal Circuit from the Appellate Division of the Court of Claims and the Court of Customs and Patent Appeals. See generally West's FEDERAL FORMS, NATIONAL COURTS, Chapter 186 (discussing the jurisdiction, rules and procedures applicable to Federal Circuit). See Cibinic, Nagle & Nash, ADMINISTRATION OF GOVERNMENT CONTRACTS 1218–20 (5th ed. 2016). See also Huffman, *Litigating Appeals in the Court of Appeals for the Federal Circuit: Insights from the 2017 Roundtable*, 32 N&CR ¶ 14 (Mar. 2018).

COURT OF CLAIMS   The original court, established in 1855, to hear and decide claims against the government. The court was divided into a trial division and an appellate division with the result that most cases were subject to decision by two sets of judges. The court was split in 1982, by the Federal Courts Improvement Act, into the COURT OF APPEALS FOR THE FEDERAL CIRCUIT and the Claims Court (subsequently named the COURT

OF FEDERAL CLAIMS). The Court of Claims frequently took a broad view of the obligations of the government—regarding itself as the "conscience of the nation."

COURT OF FEDERAL CLAIMS (COFC or Fed. Cl.)   A court of the United States established especially to hear and decide legal claims against the government. It is an Article I court with judges appointed for 15-year terms. Its basic jurisdiction is conferred by 28 U.S.C. § 1491(a), but it has a variety of additional jurisdictional statutes. Under the CONTRACT DISPUTES ACT OF 1978, 41 U.S.C. §§ 7101–7109, as amended, this court shares concurrent jurisdiction with the BOARDs OF CONTRACT APPEALS (BCAs) over government contract DISPUTEs (each contractor appealing a DECISION OF THE CONTRACTING OFFICER must elect either the appropriate BCA or the Court of Federal Claims). The other jurisdiction of the Court of Federal Claims most relevant to government procurement concerns PROTESTs, 28 U.S.C. § 1491(b), disputes concerning fraud or forfeiture, 41 U.S.C. § 7103(c)2, and PATENT and COPYRIGHT disputes, 28 U.S.C. § 1498. The Federal Courts Improvement Act of 1982 created this court (called the Claims Court until 1992) from the Trial Division of the Court of Claims. See Feldman, GOVERNMENT CONTRACT GUIDEBOOK, §§ 7:16–7:29 (4th ed. 2019–2020); Manos, 3 GOVERNMENT CONTRACT COSTS AND PRICING §§ 90:3–90:6 (2d ed. 2009–2020); Cibinic, Nagle & Nash, ADMINISTRATION OF GOVERNMENT CONTRACTS 1216, 1218 (5th ed. 2016). See also Schaengold, Prusock, Muenzfeld & Straus, *Choice of Forum for Federal Government Contract Claims: Court of Federal Claims vs. Board of Contract Appeals/Edition III*, BRIEFING PAPERS No. 19-3 (Feb. 2019).

COVER   The common-law right of a buyer, after BREACH OF CONTRACT by a seller, to purchase goods in substitution for those due from the seller if such purchase is made in good faith and without unreasonable delay. The buyer may then recover as DAMAGES the difference between the cost of such cover and the contract price, plus any incidental and CONSEQUENTIAL DAMAGES but less expenses saved. U.C.C. § 2-712(1), (2). The DEFAULT clause in government contracts gives the government the equivalent right to recover the EXCESS COST OF REPROCUREMENT after a TERMINATION FOR DEFAULT.

COVERED CONTRACT   *Official:* A contract that is subject to the COST ACCOUNTING STANDARDS under 41 U.S.C. chapter 15, as implemented in regulations found at 48 C.F.R. § 9903.201-1 (see the FAR Appendix). (10 U.S.C. § 2302 note, as amended by section 816 of Pub. L. No. 112-81). *Source:* DFARS 242.7000. Such contracts are subject to withholding provisions of the CONTRACTOR BUSINESS SYSTEMS clause if data produced by a contractor business system has a SIGNIFICANT DEFICIENCY. Covered contracts include COST-REIMBURSEMENT CONTRACTs, incentive-type contracts, TIME-AND-MATERIALS CONTRACTs, and LABOR-HOUR CONTRACTs. Covered contracts do not apply to small businesses. See Cibinic, Knight & Nash, COST-REIMBURSEMENT CONTRACTING 524–30 (4th ed. 2014).

COVERED DEFENSE INFORMATION   *Official:* Unclassified controlled technical information or other information (as described in the CONTROLLED UNCLASSIFIED INFORMATION (CUI) Registry at http://www.archives.gov/cui/registry/category-list.html) that requires safeguarding or dissemination controls pursuant to and consistent with law, regulations, and Governmentwide policies, and is—(1) Marked or otherwise identified in the contract, task order, or delivery order and provided to the contractor by or on behalf of DoD in support of the performance of the contract; or (2) Collected, developed, received, transmitted, used, or stored by or on behalf of the contractor in support of the performance of the contract. *Source:* DFARS 204.7301. Contractors and subcontractors are required to provide adequate security on all covered contractor information systems. DFARS 204.7304 implements this policy by requiring the use of the Compliance with Safeguarding Covered Defense Information Controls solicitation provision at DFARS 252.204-7008, and the Safeguarding Covered Defense Information and Cyber Incident Reporting clause at DFARS 252.204-7012, in all solicitations and contracts, including solicitations using FAR Part 12 procedures for the acquisition of commercial items, except for solicitations solely for the acquisition of commercially available off-the-shelf (COTS) items.

COVERED GOVERNMENT SUPPORT CONTRACTOR *Official:* A contractor under a contract the primary purpose of which is to furnish independent and impartial advice or technical assistance directly to the Government in support of the Government's management and oversight of a program or effort (rather than to directly furnish an end item or service to accomplish a program or effort), which contractor—(1) is not affiliated with the prime contractor or a first-tier subcontractor on the program or effort, or with any direct competitor of such prime contractor or any such first-tier subcontractor in furnishing end items or services of the type developed or produced on the program or effort and (2) agrees that it will protect proprietary information to which it obtains access. *Source:* 10 U.S.C. § 2320(g). DoD agencies may give these contractors LIMITED RIGHTS TECHNICAL DATA but they must sign NONDISCLOSURE AGREEMENTs and take all reasonable steps to protect the data.

CRADLE-TO-GRAVE A representation of the total life cycle of a given system, from concept through development, acquisition, operations phases, and final disposition. Also called womb-to-tomb.

CREDIT CARD See GOVERNMENT-WIDE COMMERCIAL PURCHASE CARD.

CREDITS Decreases in the amount of the government's preliminarily or previously determined liability to a contractor. FAR 31.201-5 states that such amounts that are received or accrued by the contractor must be credited to the government either as a cost reduction or by cash refund. However, this may be dependent on the status of the contract at the time of receipt of the credit and whether the contractor has agreed to pay credits to the government. The Allowable Cost and Payment clause, FAR 52.216-7, provides that a contractor must execute and deliver an assignment to the government of credits. See Manos, 1 GOVERNMENT COSTS & PRICING § 7:11 (2d ed. 2009–2020).

CRITICAL APPLICATION OF AN ITEM For the purposes of determining contract terms for QUALITY ASSURANCE, a use of an item of supply in which the failure of the item could injure personnel or jeopardize a vital agency mission. FAR 46.203(c)(1). When an item being procured will have a critical application, it can be expected that the agency will require a higher level QUALITY REQUIREMENT in the contract.

CRITICAL DESIGN REVIEW (CDR) A multidisciplined technical review to ensure that a system can proceed into fabrication, demonstration, and test, and can meet stated performance requirements within cost, schedule, risk, and other system constraints. Generally, this review assesses the system's final design as captured in product specifications for each Configuration Item (CI) in the system's product baseline, and ensures that each CI in the product baseline has been captured in the detailed design documentation. Normally conducted during the Engineering and Manufacturing Development (EMD) phase. DAU GLOSSARY.

CRITICAL FUNCTION   *Official:* A function that is necessary to the agency being able to effectively perform and maintain control of its mission and operations. Typically, critical functions are recurring and long-term in duration. *Source:* OFPP Policy Letter 11-01, *Performance of Inherently Governmental and Critical Functions*, 76 Fed. Reg. 562267 (Sept. 12, 2011). The policy letter requires that these functions be performed by government personnel "to the extent necessary for the agency to operate effectively and maintain control of its mission and operations."

CRITICAL INFRASTRUCTURE INFORMATION ACT OF 2002   An Act, passed on November 25, 2002 as subtitle B of Title II of the Homeland Security Act, Pub. L. No. 107-296, codified at 6 U.S.C. §§ 131–134, which regulates the use and disclosure of information submitted to the DEPARTMENT OF HOMELAND SECURITY about vulnerabilities and threats to critical infrastructure. This Act consists of a group of provisions that addresses the circumstances under which the Department of Homeland Security may obtain, use, and disclose critical infrastructure information as part of a critical infrastructure protection program. It establishes several limitations on the disclosure of critical infrastructure information voluntarily submitted to DHS. It was enacted, in part, to respond to the need for the federal government and owners and operators of the nation's critical infrastructures to share information on vulnerabilities and threats, and to promote information sharing between the private and public sectors in order to protect critical assets.

CRITICAL NONCONFORMANCE   *Official:* A nonconformance that is likely to result in hazardous or unsafe conditions for individuals using, maintaining, or depending upon the supplies or services; or is likely to prevent performance of a vital agency mission. *Source:* FAR 46.101. FAR 46.407(c)(1) requires contracting officers to reject supplies or services when their nonconformance is critical unless conditional acceptance is in the best interest of the government.

CRITICAL PATH   The longest chain of interrelated activities in the project schedule diagram that is created when using the CRITICAL PATH METHOD. This path controls the contractor's ability to complete a construction project because any delay in completing an item on this path delays the entire project. See DAU GLOSSARY.

CRITICAL PATH METHOD (CPM)   A network scheduling technique used by contractors to plan, coordinate, and control work activities so as to complete contract work as quickly and economically as possible. The technique plots the time needed to complete each activity required for a project and the dependencies between the activities. It then determines the longest time required for the interrelated activities which is defined as the CRITICAL PATH. The Schedules for Construction Contracts clause in FAR 52.236-15 requires construction contractors to provide a schedule of anticipated performance to the contracting officer shortly after award of the contract. CPM has become an accepted means of substantiating delay CLAIMs before the courts and boards of contract appeals because it demonstrates which delays impact the critical path. Proving delay typically entails comparing AS-PLANNED DRAWINGS or CPM diagrams with RECORD (as-built) DRAWINGS or CPM diagrams. See Nash, Nagle & Cibinic, ADMINISTRATION OF GOVERNMENT CONTRACTS, 519–21 (5th ed. 2016).

CRITICALITY   One of three criteria used in determining the extent of contract quality requirements to be used in the quality assurance and inspection sections of the REQUEST FOR PROPOSALS and the contract. FAR 46.203 states that a critical application of an item is one in which the failure of the item could injure personnel or jeopardize a vital agency mission. A critical item may be either peculiar, meaning it has only one application, or common, meaning it has multiple applications. The remaining two criteria are technical description and complexity. See CRITICAL APPLICATION OF AN ITEM.

CROSS-SERVICING   An arrangement between federal agencies where one agency will make or oversee an AUDIT for another agency that is unable to perform the audit needed by a contracting officer or other official. Federal regulatory policy strongly encourages the use of cross-servicing to conserve staff resources, promote efficiency, and minimize the impact of audits on the operations of the organizations subject to audit. See OMB Circular No. A-73, *Audit of Federal Operations and Programs;* OFPP Policy Letter No. 78-4, *Field Contract Support Cross-Servicing Program,* Aug. 8, 1978; and FAR Subpart 42.1. Because of its greater resources, the DEFENSE CONTRACT AUDIT AGENCY (DCAA) performs most of the work done under cross-servicing arrangements. *DCAA Contract Audit Manual* ¶ 1-303 contains guidance on when DCAA will perform an audit under a cross-servicing agreement.

CURE NOTICE   A delinquency notice that must be issued by the government prior to TERMINATION FOR DEFAULT of a supply or service contract before the contract's delivery date. See ¶ (a)(2) of the Default (Fixed-Price Supply and Service) clause in FAR 52.249-8. FAR 49.607(a) contains a suggested form of the notice. FAR 49.402-3 contains the procedures that must be followed by contracting officers in determining whether to terminate for default. FAR 49.402-3(d) provides that, if the time remaining does not permit a "cure" period of 10 days or more, the cure notice should not be issued. Failure to issue a cure notice when required will result in an invalid termination for default, with the result that the termination will be converted to a TERMINATION FOR CONVENIENCE. See also SHOW CAUSE NOTICE. See Cibinic, Nagle & Nash, Administration of Government Contracts 871–75 (5th ed. 2016).

CUSTODIAL RECORDS   Written memoranda of any kind, such as requisitions, issue hand receipts, tool checks, and stock record books, used to control items from tool cribs, tool rooms, and stockrooms. This term was defined in FAR 45.501 prior to the issuance of FAC 2005-17, May, 15, 2007. FAR 45.505-3(c) required that the contractor maintain such records of tool crib items, guard force items, protective clothing, and other items issued to employees when these items were GOVERNMENT-FURNISHED MATERIAL or material to which the government has title. The term is no longer used in the FAR but the Government Property clause in FAR 52.245-1 requires the contractor to maintain appropriate records of government property.

CUSTOMARY CONTRACT FINANCING   *Official:* That financing deemed by an agency to be available for routine use by contracting officers. Most customary contract financing arrangements should be usable by contracting officers without specific reviews or approvals by higher management. *Source:* FAR 32.001. FAR 32.113 provides that customary financing consists of: (a) Financing of shipbuilding, or ship conversion, alteration, or repair, when agency regulations provide for progress payments based on a percentage or stage of completion. (b) Financing of construction or architect-engineer services purchased under the authority of part 36. (c) Financing of contracts for supplies or services awarded under the sealed bid method of procurement in accordance with part 14 through PROGRESS PAYMENTS BASED ON COSTS in accordance with subpart 32.5. (d) Financing of contracts for supplies or services awarded under the competitive negotiation method of procurement in accordance with part 15, through either progress payments based on costs in accordance with subpart 32.5, or PERFORMANCE-BASED PAYMENTS in accordance with subpart 32.10 (but not both). (e) Financing of contracts for supplies or services awarded under a sole-source acquisition as defined in 2.101 and using the procedures of part 15, through either progress payments based on costs in accordance with subpart 32.5, or performance-based payments in accordance with subpart 32.10 (but not both). (f) Financing of contracts for supplies or services through ADVANCE PAYMENTS in accordance with subpart 32.4. (g) Financing of contracts for supplies or services through GUARANTEED LOANs in accordance with subpart 32.3. (h) Financing of contracts for supplies or services through any appropriate combination of advance payments, guaranteed loans, and either performance-based payments or progress payments (but not both) in accordance with their respective subparts. Any other type of financing is UNUSUAL CONTRACT FINANCING.

CYBERSECURITY   The state of being protected against the criminal or unauthorized use of electronic data, or the measures taken to achieve this. The government is in the process of adopting increasingly stringent standards to protect FEDERAL CONTRACT INFORMATION and COVERED DEFENSE INFORMATION from attacks by third parties. Thus, FAR 4.1903 requires the inclusion of the Basic Safeguarding of Covered Contractor Information Systems, in 52.204-21, in solicitations and contracts when the contractor or a subcontractor at any tier may have federal contract information residing in or transiting through its information system. Similarly, DFARS 204.7304 requires the inclusion of the Safeguarding Covered Defense Information and Cyber Incident Reporting clause at DFARS 252.204-7012, in all solicitations and contracts, including solicitations using FAR Part 12 procedures for the acquisition of commercial items, except for solicitations solely for the acquisition of commercially available off-the-shelf (COTS) items. These clauses require contractors to have systems providing cybersecurity and the DFARS clause requires reporting of cyber incidents. Basic requirements for cybersecurity are set forth in National Institute of Standards and Technology (NIST) Special Publication (SP) 800-171, "Protecting Controlled Unclassified Information in Nonfederal Information Systems and Organizations" (see http:// dx.doi.org/10.6028/NIST.SP.800-171). In addition, DOD is in the process of issuing a CYBERSECURITY MATURITY MODEL.

CYBERSECURITY MATURITY MODEL   A detailed set of standards and best practices promulgated by DOD for contractors to follow to achieve CYBERSECURITY. Contractors will be required to obtain third party certification that their systems meet prescribed levels of security. The system is expected to be implemented in 2020.

D

DAMAGES   Monetary compensation that one contracting party is entitled to for BREACH OF CONTRACT by the other party. Contractors may claim damages for breach from contracting agencies or, after a CONTRACTING OFFICER DECISION, in the U.S. COURT OF FEDERAL CLAIMS or the appropriate BOARD OF CONTRACT APPEALS. Compensatory damages compensate the injured party for the injury sustained and for nothing more. CONSEQUENTIAL DAMAGES do not flow directly and immediately from the act of the other party but, rather, from the consequences or results of the act. PUNITIVE (or exemplary) DAMAGES are generally not included in contract damages. Damages are infrequently awarded in government contracts because of the large number of contract clauses giving EQUITABLE ADJUSTMENTs and PRICE ADJUSTMENTs. See Cibinic, Nagle & Nash, Administration of Government Contracts 612–18 (5th ed. 2016).

DATA   *Official:* Recorded information, regardless of form or the media on which the information is recorded. The term includes TECHNICAL DATA and COMPUTER SOFTWARE. The term does not include information incidental to contract administration, such as financial, administrative, cost or pricing, or management information. *Source:* FAR 27.401. When this type of information is created by contractors in the performance of contracts, it is subject to LIMITED RIGHTS, RESTRICTED RIGHTS, or UNLIMITED RIGHTS as specified in contract clauses. This term is not used in the 1995 DOD policy on technical data and computer software. It was used in the 1988 DOD policy with essentially the same meaning as in the FAR. See Nash & Rawicz, Intellectual Property in Government Contracts, chap. 4 (6th ed. 2008).

DATA ITEM DESCRIPTION (DID)   A description of a TECHNICAL DATA item to be provided under a contract with DOD. The form used for this description is DD Form 1664, DFARS 253.303-1664. DIDs are listed on the CONTRACT DATA REQUIREMENTS LIST that is incorporated into contracts. See Nash & Rawicz, Intellectual Property in Government Contracts, chap. 6 (6th ed. 2008).

DATA OTHER THAN CERTIFIED COST OR PRICING DATA   *Official:* Pricing data, cost data, and JUDGMENTAL INFORMATION necessary for the CONTRACTING OFFICER to determine a FAIR AND REASONABLE PRICE or to determine COST REALISM. Such data may include the identical types of data as CERTIFIED COST OR PRICING DATA, consistent with Table 15-2 of 15.408, but without the certification. The data may also include, for example, sales data and any information reasonably required to explain the offeror's estimating process, including, but not limited to—(1) The judgmental factors applied and the mathematical or other methods used in the estimate, including those used in projecting from known data; and (2) The nature and amount of any contingencies included in the proposed price. *Source:* FAR 2.101. FAR 15.403-3 provides guidance on obtaining this information and provides that the contracting officer should not obtain from a contractor more information than is necessary to determine a FAIR AND REASONABLE PRICE if data from other sources other than the offeror are not available. FAR 15.402(a)(2) provides a preference for types of data the contracting officer can obtain. This term replaced "information other than cost or pricing data" in the FAR.

DATA PROCESSING EQUIPMENT See AUTOMATIC DATA PROCESSING EQUIPMENT.

DATA REPOSITORY An office with the responsibility for the storage and maintenance of TECHNICAL DATA necessary to support government programs. DOD agencies and contracting activities generally maintain data repositories and this function has, on occasion, been given to contractors. DFARS 227.7108 provides guidance on the contractual provisions that should be used when establishing contractor data repositories. DFARS 227.7207 states that this guidance is applicable when the government establishes a contractor COMPUTER SOFTWARE repository. See Nash & Rawicz, INTELLECTUAL PROPERTY IN GOVERNMENT CONTRACTS, chap. 6 (6th ed. 2008).

DATA UNIVERSAL NUMBERING SYSTEM (DUNS) NUMBER The 9-digit number assigned by Dun and Bradstreet, Inc. to identify unique business entities. This number has been used as the UNIQUE ENTITY IDENTIFIER for federal contractors but is being replaced in the SYSTEM FOR AWARD MANAGEMENT.

DATA WARRANTY A promise that all data delivered under a contract will be in conformance with the specifications and other contract requirements. 10 U.S.C. § 2320(b)(8) and 41 U.S.C. § 2302(e)(8) require that, when issuing contracts calling for delivery of TECHNICAL DATA, agencies consider including provisions establishing remedies when the data is incomplete or inadequate. DFARS 227.7103-14(c) implements this statute by providing guidance on when the Warranty of Data clause in DFARS 252.246-7001 should be used. The FAR does not implement the statute except when an agency is procuring a MAJOR SYSTEM in which case FAR 27.409(j) requires the use of the Technical Data Declaration, Revision, and Withholding of Payment—Major Systems clause in FAR 52.227-21 which requires the contractor to submit a declaration that the technical data "are complete, accurate, and comply with the requirements of the contract." General guidance on the use of warranties is contained in FAR 46.703. See Nash & Rawicz, INTELLECTUAL PROPERTY IN GOVERNMENT CONTRACTS, chap. 6 (6th ed. 2008).

DAVIS-BACON ACT An Act, 40 U.S.C. § 3141 et seq., passed in 1931, requiring payment of not less than PREVAILING WAGE RATEs to workers at the site of the work on federal or federally funded CONSTRUCTION projects of over $2,000. FAR 22.403-1. See the Construction Wage Rate Requirements clause at FAR 52.222-6. WAGE DETERMINATIONs, issued by the DOL, must be included in construction contracts for such projects. FAR 22.404-2. See Feldman, GOVERNMENT CONTRACT GUIDEBOOK §§ 30:2–30:10 (4th ed. 2019–2020).

DAY *Official:* Unless otherwise specified, a calendar day. *Source:* FAR 2.101. With regard to protests and debriefing, FAR 33.101 and FAR 15.501 add: *Official:* In the computation of any period—(1) The day of the act, event, or default from which the designated period of time begins to run is not included; and (2) The last day after the act, event, or default is included unless—(i) The last day is a Saturday, Sunday, or federal holiday; or (ii) In the case of a filing of a paper at any appropriate administrative forum, the last day is a day on which weather or other conditions cause the closing of the forum for all or part of the day, in which event the next day on which the appropriate administrative forum is open is included.

DCAA CONTRACT AUDIT MANUAL (CAM)   A publication of the DEFENSE CON-TRACT AUDIT AGENCY (DCAA) (sometimes referred to as the *Defense Contract Audit Manual*, or DCAM) containing detailed guidance on auditing policies and procedures followed by DCAA AUDITORs. The manual is instructive rather than directive in nature, and its contents apply to the AUDIT of all types of contracts. The manual is available at https://www.dcaa.mil/Guidance/CAM-Contract-Audit-Manual/.

DE FACTO DEBARMENT   A refusal of the government to deal with a contractor that is construed by a court to constitute a DEBARMENT, even though formal debarment procedures are not used. Generally, de facto debarment has been found in cases where a government agency refuses to award one or more contracts on the basis that the OFFEROR does not meet the requisite standards of RESPONSIBILITY. See *Old Dominion Dairy Prod., Inc. v. Secretary of Defense*, 631 F.2d 953 (D.C. Cir. 1980), where de facto debarment was found when the agency refused to award a contract because of a perceived lack of integrity. The court held the contractor was entitled to the DUE PROCESS OF LAW accorded by the debarment procedures to protect its constitutional liberty interest. De facto debarments will also be found when an agency declares an offeror nonresponsible on repeated occasions without instituting formal debarment procedures. The FAR contains no guidance on de facto debarments. See Cibinic, Nash & Yukins, FORMATION OF GOVERNMENT CONTRACTS 496–98 (4th ed. 2011). See also Nash, *De Facto Debarment: Can Congress Avoid It?*, 32 N&CR ¶7 (Jan. 2018).

DE NOVO   Considering a matter without regard to prior procedures. When a contractor files an APPEAL FROM A CONTRACTING OFFICER'S DECISION under the CON-TRACT DISPUTES ACT OF 1978, the BOARD OF CONTRACT APPEALS (BCA) or the U.S. COURT OF FEDERAL CLAIMS will rehear the case completely and decide it on the basis of the evidence heard. Thus, the prior decision of the contracting officer is not binding on the BCA or U.S. Court of Federal Claims in any way, and the proceeding before the BCA or U.S. Court of Federal Claims is in the nature of a new trial, not a review of the record made by the contracting officer. See Cibinic, Nagle & Nash, ADMINISTRATION OF GOVERNMENT CONTRACTS 1207–08 (5th ed. 2016).

DEBARMENT   *Official:* Action taken by a DEBARRING OFFICIAL under FAR 9.406 to exclude a contractor from government contracting and government-approved subcontracting for a reasonable, specified period: a contractor that is excluded is "debarred." *Source:* FAR 2.101. FAR Subpart 9.4 contains the policies and procedures governing debarment of contractors. When a contractor is proposed for debarment, it is excluded from the award of contracts by being placed on the Excluded list in the SYSTEM FOR AWARD MAN-AGEMENT. FAR 9.404. Causes for debarment include (1) conviction of or civil judgment for (a) commission of a FRAUD or criminal offense related to obtaining or performing a public contract, (b) ANTITRUST VIOLATION, (c) commission of embezzlement, theft, forgery, BRIBERY, making FALSE STATEMENTs, or the like, (d) intentionally affixing a label bearing a "Made in America" inscription to a product sold in or shipped to the United States, when the product was not made in the United States, or (e) commission of any other offense indicating a lack of business integrity or business honesty that seriously and directly affects the contractor's present RESPONSIBILITY; (2) based upon a preponderance of evidence (a) violation of the terms of a government contract so serious as to justify debarment, such as (i) willful failure to perform or (ii) a history of failure to perform or unsatisfactory performance; (b) violations of the Drug-Free Workplace Act of 1988 (see DRUG-FREE WORKPLACE); (c) intentionally affixing a label bearing a "Made in America" inscription to a product sold in or shipped to the United States, when the product was not made in the United States, (d) commission of an unfair trade practice as defined in FAR 9.403; (e) delinquent federal taxes in an amount over $3,000; or (3) any other cause of so serious or compelling a nature that it affects the present responsibility of a government contractor or subcontractor; or (4) knowing nondisclosure of credible evidence of (i) violation of federal criminal law, (ii) violation of the CIVIL FALSE CLAIMS ACT, or (iii) significant overpayments on a contract; or (3) employment of illegal immigrants. FAR 9.406-2. Remedial measures and mitigating factors for debarring officials to consider in making debarment decisions are set forth at FAR 9.406-1(a). See Cibinic, Nash & Yukins, FORMATION OF GOVERNMENT CONTRACTS 457–98 (4th ed. 2011); Nash, *Suspension and Debarment: Is More Desirable*, 26 N&CR ¶4 (Jan. 2012); U.S. GOV'T ACCOUNTABILITY OFFICE, SUSPENSION AND DEBARMENT: SOME AGENCY PROGRAMS NEED GREATER ATTENTION, AND GOVERNMENTWIDE OVERSIGHT COULD BE IMPROVED, GAO-11-739 (Aug. 2011); Madsen, et al., *Suspension and Debarment: Past Performance/Suspension and Debarment: How Would Performance Data Be Obtained and Used?*, 95 Fed. Cont. Rep. (BNA) 423 (Apr. 19, 2011); Robbins, et al., *Path of An Investigation: How Major Contractor's Ethics Office and Air Force Procurement Fraud and Suspension/Debarment Apparatus Deal with Allegations of Potential Fraud and Unethical Conduct*, 40 PUB. CONT. L.J. 595 (2011); Canni, *Debarment Is No Longer Private World Bank Business: An Examination of the Bank's Distinct Debarment Procedures Used for Corporate Procurements and Financed Projects*, 40 PUB. CONT. L.J. 147 (2010); Davidson & Longmeyer-Wood, *The Ice Suspension and Debarment Program Heats Up*, 46 The Procurement Lawyer 1 (Fall 2010).

DEBARRING OFFICIAL   *Official:* An AGENCY HEAD or a designee authorized by the agency head to impose debarment. *Source:* FAR 9.403. Almost all agencies have delegated this function to a designated person with various levels of staff support. See U.S. GOV'T ACCOUNTABILITY OFFICE, SUSPENSION AND DEBARMENT: SOME AGENCY PROGRAMS NEED GREATER ATTENTION, AND GOVERNMENTWIDE OVERSIGHT COULD BE IMPROVED, GAO-11-739 (Aug. 2011). These officials are given a considerable degree of discretion in determining whether to debar a contractor. See FAR 9.406-1(a). See Nash, *Suspension and Debarment: Is More Desirable*, 26 N&CR ¶4 (Jan. 2012).

DEBRIEFING   Explanation by a procuring agency of why an offeror did not win a competition for a negotiated contract (see NEGOTIATION). Debriefings are required by 10 U.S.C. § 2305(b) and 41 U.S.C. §§ 3704–3705. Offerors excluded from the COMPETITIVE RANGE or otherwise excluded from the competition before award may request a debriefing either before or after award of the contract. FAR 15.505–06. For preaward debriefings, requests must be received within three days after the offeror receives notice of exclusion from competition. FAR 15.505(a)(1). The debriefing must include (1) the agency's evaluation of significant elements in the offeror's proposal; (2) a summary of the rationale for elimination from the competition; and (3) reasonable responses to relevant questions about whether source selection procedures contained in the solicitation, applicable regulations, and other applicable authorities were followed. FAR 15.505(e). For postaward debriefings, requests must be received within three days after the offeror receives notice of contract award. FAR 15.506(a)(1). At a minimum, the debriefing information must include: (1) the government's evaluation of the significant weaknesses or deficiencies in the offeror's proposal; (2) the overall evaluated cost or price and technical ratings of successful and debriefed offeror, and past performance information on the debriefed offeror; (3) the overall ranking of all offerors; (4) a summary of the rationale for award; (5) for acquisitions of commercial items, the make and model of the selected item; and (6) reasonable responses to relevant questions about whether source selection procedures, regulations, and authorities were followed. FAR 15.506(d). The debriefing must not include point-by-point comparisons or any information exempt from release under the FREEDOM OF INFORMATION ACT, including: TRADE SECRETs; privileged or confidential manufacturing processes and techniques, privileged or confidential commercial and financial information, and the names of individuals providing reference information on PAST PERFORMANCE. FAR 15.506(e). The contracting officer must include an official summary of the debriefing in the contract file. FAR 15.506(f). The 2018 NDAA requires DOD to conduct ENHANCED DEBRIEFINGS. See Cibinic, Nash & Yukins, FORMATION OF GOVERNMENT CONTRACTS 985–90 (4th ed. 2011); Sturgis, *Note, The Illusory Debriefing: A Need For Reform*, 38 PUB. CONT. L.J. 469 (2009).

DEBT COLLECTION ACT   31 U.S.C. § 3701 et seq. Originally the FEDERAL CLAIMS COLLECTION ACT OF 1966, the Act provides the basic legal framework for agency collection of debts owed to the United States, with oversight by the Treasury Department and the Department of Justice. The Act authorizes compromise, suspension, or termination of collection action in limited circumstances—with the U.S. Attorney General's approval for debts exceeding $100,000. The Act is implemented by the Federal Claims Collection Standards, issued jointly by the Treasury Department and the DOJ, 31 C.F.R. chap. 9. Agency collection action should be aggressive and timely with effective follow-up, using all reasonable means of collection consistent with good business practice and the debtor's ability to pay. Agencies that cannot compromise debts after using all reasonable means of collection are required to promptly refer them to the DOJ for litigation. GAO, PRINCIPLES OF FEDERAL APPROPRIATIONS LAW: ANNUAL UPDATE TO THE THIRD EDITION, Ch. 14, GAO-15-303SP (Washington, D.C.: Mar. 2015). Most claims collection is performed by accounting officials from government agencies. However, procedures for collecting claims on contracts are set forth in FAR Subpart 32.6. See Cibinic, Nagle & Nash, ADMINISTRATION OF GOVERNMENT CONTRACTS 1079 (5th ed. 2016).

DEBT COLLECTION IMPROVEMENT ACT OF 1996 (DCIA)   Pub. L. No. 104–134, § 31001. A law amending the DEBT COLLECTION ACT designed to improve the collection of debts owed to the government. Among its many requirements, it directs agencies to obtain the TAXPAYER IDENTIFICATION NUMBER of every contractor and to pay contractors by electronic funds transfer. The Financial Management Service is responsible for Treasury's implementation of the debt collection provisions of the DCIA.

DECISION OF THE CONTRACTING OFFICER   A written document signed by a CONTRACTING OFFICER ruling on a CLAIM by or against the government. Under the CONTRACT DISPUTES ACT OF 1978, all claims by a contractor against the government relating to a contract must be in writing and must be submitted to the contracting officer for a decision. All claims by the government against a contractor relating to a contract must also be the subject of a decision by the contracting officer. 41 U.S.C. § 7103. This decision describes the claim, references pertinent contract terms, states areas of factual agreement and disagreement, states the reasons for the decision reached, and informs the contractor of its rights to challenge the decision through an APPEAL FROM A CONTRACTING OFFICER'S DECISION. FAR 33.211(a)(4). Contracting officers' decisions, often called "final decisions," must inform the contractor that it may either appeal the decision to a BOARD OF CONTRACT APPEALS within 90 days or bring an action directly in the U.S. COURT OF FEDERAL CLAIMS within 12 months. If the contracting officer fails to render a decision, the board and court may deem the claim denied (see DEEMED DENIAL) 60 days after its submission. Procedures for issuing decisions are contained in FAR 33.211 and the Disputes clause at FAR 52.233-1. See Cibinic, Nagle & Nash, ADMINISTRATION OF GOVERNMENT CONTRACTS 1192–1216 (5th ed. 2016). See also Nash, *Contracting Officer Decisions During Litigation: Are They Valid?*, 22 N&CR ¶ 13 (Feb. 2008). Nash, *Contracting Officer Decisions: Required to Be Personal and Independent*, 21 N&CR ¶ 20 (May 2007); Nash, *The Contracting Officer Decisions: A Negotiating Ploy?*, 21 N&CR ¶ 34 (July 2007).

DECISIONAL RULE   The section of the SOURCE SELECTION PLAN that outlines the fundamental basis that will be used to make the source selection decision in a procurement using competitive negotiation. There are two decisional rules described in FAR 15.101: (1) discretionary tradeoff analysis (see TRADEOFF PROCESS) and (2) LOWEST PRICE TECHNICALLY ACCEPTABLE proposal. When the tradeoff analysis decisional rule is used, the agency makes the award decision by comparing the marginal differences in price/cost with the marginal differences in the other EVALUATION FACTORs. If the lowest price technically acceptable proposal rule is used, the non-price factors of a proposal are evaluated to determine which proposals are "technically acceptable" and award is made to the offeror with the technically acceptable proposal with the lowest price. FAR 15.101 permits agencies to use other decisional rules. See Cibinic, Nash & Yukins, FORMATION OF GOVERNMENT CONTRACTS 676–86 (4th ed. 2011).

DECOMPILE   Analysis of the OBJECT CODE of a COMPUTER PROGRAM to recreate the SOURCE CODE of the program. This is a form of REVERSE ENGINEERING that is generally prohibited by SHRINKWRAP LICENSEs and CLICKWRAP LICENSEs. However, it is a permissible process by the owner of a computer program under the COPYRIGHT ACT. See Nash & Rawicz, INTELLECTUAL PROPERTY IN GOVERNMENT CONTRACTS 686–88 (6th ed. 2008).

DECREMENT   The amount of a reduction or price reduction. A decrement factor may represent a percentage by which a subcontractor has agreed to reductions in past quoted prices or has agreed to if the contractor purchases more than a specified amount of supplies. Subcontractors may also use a decrement to compensate for the amount of profit generated in an INTER-ORGANIZATIONAL TRANSFER. See *Grumman Aerospace Corp.*, ASBCA 35188, 90-2 BCA ¶ 22,842. The *Defense Contract Audit Manual* ¶ 9-404.6 directs AUDITORs to review the methodologies used by contractors in arriving at subcontractor price reductions, to ensure that the data used for decrements were reasonably accurate, current, and representative. The manual explains that information concerning patterns of reductions from quotes to actual prices paid may be useful in evaluating a cost estimate. Briggerman, *Postscript: U.S. v. United Technologies Corp.*, 25 N&CR ¶ 14 (Mar. 2011).

DECREMENT FACTOR   See DECREMENT.

DEDUCTIVE CHANGE   A unilateral action by the contracting officer or other procurement official that reduces the amount of work required or the quantity of products procured by the contract. Deductive changes entitle the government to an EQUITABLE ADJUSTMENT reducing the contract price by the amount the reduced work would have cost plus a reasonable profit on that amount if the contract is profitable. See Nash & Feldman, 1 GOVERNMENT CONTRACT CHANGES § 4:15 (3d ed. 2006–2020); Cibinic, Nagle & Nash, ADMINISTRATION OF GOVERNMENT CONTRACTS 602–09 (5th ed. 2016).

DEEMED DENIAL   A legal rule under the CONTRACT DISPUTES ACT (CDA) OF 1978 permitting a contractor to appeal (see APPEAL FROM THE CONTRACTING OFFICER'S DECISION) the failure of a contracting officer to issue a decision (see DECISION OF THE CONTRACTING OFFICER). See 41 U.S.C. § 7103(f)(5). If the contractor submits a CLAIM and the contracting officer fails to render a decision within 60 days of receiving the claim (or within a reasonable time for claims over $100,000), the Act provides that this failure will be deemed a decision of the contracting officer to deny the claim and will authorize the commencement of an appeal or suit on the claim. This "deemed denial" jurisdiction confers upon the contractor all rights that flow from receipt of a contracting officer's decision. Although the CDA provides limited time period for filing appeals (90 days to an agency BOARD OF CONTRACT APPEALS or one year to the U.S. COURT OF FEDERAL CLAIMS) when the contractor has received a decision of the contracting officer, no similar provision exists when the contracting officer fails to render a decision on a valid claim and thereby prompts "deemed denial" jurisdiction. However, a contractor will lose appeal rights if it files no claim for over six years from the time the cause of action has accrued pursuant to the STATUTE OF LIMITATIONS in 41 U.S.C. § 7103(a)(4)(A). See Cibinic, Nagle & Nash, ADMINISTRATION OF GOVERNMENT CONTRACTS 1195 (5th ed. 2016).

DEEMED EXPORT LICENSE   See EXPORT CONTROL

DEFAULT   The omission or failure to perform a legal or contractual duty, to observe a promise or discharge an obligation, or to perform an agreement. BLACK'S LAW DICTIONARY 526 (11th ed. 2019). The government has the right to terminate the contract when a contractor is found to be in default in the performance of a contract. See TERMINATION FOR DEFAULT. See also Cibinic, Nagle & Nash, ADMINISTRATION OF GOVERNMENT CONTRACTS, chap. 10 (5th ed. 2016).

DEFAULT TERMINATION   See TERMINATION FOR DEFAULT.

DEFECT   An aspect of the supplies or services to be delivered on a contract that does not comply with the contract requirements. Under the UNIFORM COMMERCIAL CODE, a product is defective if it is not fit for the ordinary purposes for which it is sold and used. U.C.C. § 2-314. In government contracts, the government is entitled to strict compliance—hence any noncompliance with the contract requirements, no matter how inconsequential, is a defect. A LATENT DEFECT is a defect that would not be apparent to the buyer by reasonable observation or INSPECTION. A PATENT DEFECT, in contrast, is a defect that would be apparent to the buyer by normal inspection. Defective performance by a contractor may result in the government's rejection of a contractor's supplies or services, a reduction in the contract price or a contract's TERMINATION FOR DEFAULT. See Cibinic, Nagle & Nash, ADMINISTRATION OF GOVERNMENT CONTRACTS 732–40, 762–66 (5th ed. 2016).

DEFECTIVE CERTIFICATION   *Official:* A certificate which alters or otherwise deviates from the language in 33.207(c) or which is not executed by a person duly authorized to bind the contractor with respect to the claim. Failure to certify shall not be deemed to be a defective certification. *Source:* FAR 33.201. FAR 33.207(f) allows for correction of defection certifications of CLAIMs prior to entry of judgment by a court or a decision by a BOARD OF CONTRACT APPEALS. See CERTIFICATION OF CLAIM.

DEFECTIVE CERTIFIED COST OR PRICING DATA   CERTIFIED COST OR PRICING DATA found to be or have been inaccurate, incomplete, or noncurrent. 10 U.S.C. § 2306a(e); 41 U.S.C. § 3506. If the CONTRACTING OFFICER finds such defective data, he or she is required to bring the defect to the attention of the prospective contractor. FAR 15.407-1(a). After a contract is entered into, under the TRUTH IN NEGOTIATIONS ACT the government is entitled to an adjustment of the negotiated price, including PROFIT or FEE, to exclude any significant sum by which the price was increased because of defective data, provided the government had relied on the data. See FAR 15.407-1(b) for guidance on the computation of the adjustment. The government's entitlement to a reduction in price is ensured by the inclusion in the contract of one of the clauses prescribed in FAR 15.408(b) and (c), such as Price Reduction for Defective Cost or Pricing Data in FAR 52.215-10 and Price Reduction for Defective Cost or Pricing Data—Modifications in FAR 52.215-11. These clauses give the government the right to a unilateral PRICE ADJUSTMENT for defects in cost or pricing data submitted by the contractor or by a prospective or actual subcontractor. The DCAA CAM § 14-109 states that there is a rebuttable presumption that the natural and probable consequences of defective cost or pricing data is an increase in the contract price of the defective amount, plus related burden and profit or fee. See Manos, 2 GOVERNMENT COSTS AND PRICING § 84:16 (2d ed. 2009–2020); Cibinic, Nagle & Nash, ADMINISTRATION OF GOVERNMENT CONTRACTS 669–77 (5th ed. 2016). See also Bodenheimer, *Litigation & Proof In Defective Pricing Cases*, BRIEFING PAPERS No. 15-5 (Apr. 2015); Bodenheimer, *Calculating Defective Pricing Damages*, BRIEFING PAPERS No. 11-7 (June 2011).

DEFECTIVE PRICING   See DEFECTIVE CERTIFIED COST OR PRICING DATA.

DEFECTIVE SPECIFICATIONS   See IMPLIED WARRANTY OF SPECIFICATIONS.

DEFENDANT   The party against whom a suit is filed in court. In the U.S. COURT OF FEDERAL CLAIMS, the government is always the defendant even though the suit may be based on a government CLAIM under the CONTRACT DISPUTES ACT OF 1978. In such cases the contractor is referred to as the PLAINTIFF. If such cases are appealed to a BOARD OF CONTRACT APPEALS, the contractor is referred to as the appellant (see APPELLANT BEFORE BOARD OF CONTRACT APPEALS) and the government is called the RESPONDENT.

DEFENSE ACQUISITION BOARD (DAB)   The DAB is DoD's senior-level forum for advising the Under Secretary of Defense for Acquisition and Sustainment (USD(A&S)) on critical decisions concerning ACQUISITION CATEGORY (ACAT) ID programs, and selected ACAT IA programs. The DAB is composed of the DoD's senior executives. The DAB is chaired by the Under Secretary of Defense (Acquisition & Sustainment). Other executive members of the DAB include: • Vice Chairman, Joint Chiefs of Staff (VCJCS) • Secretaries of the Military Departments • Under Secretary of Defense (Research & Engineering) • Under Secretary of Defense (Comptroller) • Under Secretary of Defense

(Policy) • Under Secretary of Defense (Personnel and Readiness) • Under Secretary of Defense (Intelligence) • Chief Information Officer of DoD • Director of Operational Test and Evaluation • Director, Cost Assessment and Program Evaluation • Director, Acquisition Resources and Analysis (executive secretary of the DAB). An Acquisition Decision Memorandum (ADM) will document decisions resulting from DAB reviews. DAU GLOSSARY.

DEFENSE ACQUISITION CIRCULARS (DAC) Government publications that revise, amend, and supplement the DOD FAR SUPPLEMENT. DACs are approved and issued by the DEFENSE ACQUISITION REGULATORY COUNCIL—in most cases, after a period of public notice and comment that begins with publication in the FEDERAL REGISTER. See DFARS 201.304. DACs are numbered sequentially by edition (for example, 91-1, 91-2).

DEFENSE ACQUISITION GUIDEBOOK (DAG) A guide to discretionary best practices that the DOD acquisition workforce may use to implement the DOD 5000 Series. Available online or as a downloadable pdf at www.dau.edu/tools/dag.

DEFENSE ACQUISITION REGULATION (DAR) The regulation that controlled DOD procurement from 1978 until early 1984 and was replaced by the FEDERAL ACQUISITION REGULATION (FAR) and the DEPARTMENT OF DEFENSE FEDERAL ACQUISITION REGULATION SUPPLMENT (DFARS). Prior to 1978 it was known as the Armed Services Procurement Regulation (ASPR). In 1984, the DAR and the Federal Procurement Regulations were replaced by the current regulatory system, based on the FEDERAL ACQUISITION REGULATION (FAR). Many of the DAR/ASPR clauses, provisions, and textual explanations survived and were incorporated into the FAR in simplified form. Many of the DAR/ASPR remnants that were not incorporated in the FAR were retained in the DOD FAR SUPPLEMENT (DFARS). The DFARS applies specifically to procurement involving the Office of the Secretary of Defense; the Departments of the Army, Navy, and Air Force; the Defense Logistics Agency; and other defense agencies.

DEFENSE ACQUISITION REGULATORY (DAR) COUNCIL The organization in DOD responsible for issuing procurement regulations. The DAR Council and the CIVILIAN AGENCY ACQUISITION COUNCIL prepare and issue revisions to the FAR through coordinated action. See FAR 1.201-1. The DAR Council also maintains the DOD FAR SUPPLEMENT. See DFARS 201.201-1. Each council maintains cognizance over specified portions of the FAR and is responsible for (1) agreeing on all revisions with the other council, (2) submitting to the FAR SECRETARIAT information required for publishing a FEDERAL REGISTER notice soliciting comments, (3) considering all comments received, (4) arranging for public meetings, (5) preparing any final revision in the appropriate FAR format and language, and (6) submitting any final revision to the FAR Secretariat for publication in the Federal Register and for printing and distribution. The Director of the DAR Council represents the Secretary of Defense. The Council's membership includes representatives of the military departments, the Defense Logistics Agency, and NASA. See DOD 5000 Series.

DEFENSE ACQUISITION UNIVERSITY (DAU) An organization established by Congress in 1990 to provide a global learning environment to support a mission-ready Defense Acquisition Workforce that develops, delivers, and sustains effective and affordable warfighting capabilities. See DOD Instruction 5000.57, *Defense Acquisition University*, May 7, 2019. DAU aims to impact acquisition excellence through: (1) Acquisition certification and leadership training, (2) Mission assistance to acquisition organizations and teams, (3) Improving the Core Technical Competence of the Defense Workforce, (4) Online knowledge-sharing resources, and (5) Continuous learning assets. DAU headquarters is at Fort Belvoir, Virginia. It has five regional campuses located throughout the United States.

DEFENSE ACQUISITION WORKFORCE IMPROVEMENT ACT (DAWIA)   A statute that requires the Secretary of Defense to establish policies and procedures for effective management of persons serving in acquisition positions in DOD. The Act provides for establishment of certain minimum education, training, and experience requirements for individuals filling acquisition positions. The Act concentrates on the professionalism of the workforce rather than on organizational structure or process and addresses acquisition positions rather than acquisition personnel in recognition of the fact that acquisition is a multi-disciplinary or multi-functional career field. For the purposes of this statute, the acquisition discipline includes such functions as: program management; systems planning, research, development, engineering, and testing; procurement, including contracting; industrial property management; logistics; quality control and assurance; manufacturing and production; business, cost estimating, financial management and auditing; education, training, and career development; construction; and joint development and production with other government agencies and foreign countries. The Act also identifies education and training requirements, education assistance, increasing other acquisition training opportunities, and establishing a DEFENSE ACQUISITION UNIVERSITY structure. See 10 U.S.C. § 1701 et seq.

DEFENSE ADVANCED RESEARCH PROJECTS AGENCY (DARPA)   The special research and development organization located in the Office of the Secretary of Defense. It was established in 1958 to explore technology beyond the immediate and specific requirements of the military services. It manages and directs selected basic, advanced, and applied research, development and prototype projects for DOD where the risk and payoff are both very high and where success may provide dramatic advances in capability. Its prime responsibility is to enter into and administer contracts, grants, and cooperative agreements, directly or through a military department, in pursuit of its research and development mission. 10 U.S.C. § 2358. Further, 10 U.S.C. § 2371 and § 2371a authorize DARPA to enter into OTHER TRANSACTIONS, which are not procurement contracts, grants or cooperative agreements, when such innovative arrangements are in the best interests of the government. Primarily, DARPA solicits research and development work through advertising in SAM. These solicitations are primarily in the form of BROAD AGENCY ANNOUNCEMENTS but also may be SMALL BUSINESS INNOVATION RESEARCH PROGRAM solicitations, REQUESTS FOR PROPOSALS, Sources-Sought Announcements, or Special Research Announcements. [Internet site at www.darpa.mil/]

DEFENSE ARTICLE   *Official:* Any item or technical data designated in § 121.1 of this subchapter. The policy described in § 120.3 is applicable to designations of additional items. This term includes technical data recorded or stored in any physical form, models, mockups or other items that reveal technical data directly relating to items designated in § 121.1 of this subchapter. It also includes forgings, castings, and other unfinished products, such as extrusions and machined bodies, that have reached a stage in manufacturing where they are clearly identifiable by mechanical properties, material composition, geometry, or function as defense articles. It does not include basic marketing information on function or purpose or general system descriptions. *Source:* 22 C.F.R. § 120.6. Any item or technical data listed in § 121.1 has been designated by the DEPARTMENT OF STATE with the concurrence of DOD as subject to EXPORT CONTROL. The list of articles is referred to as the

United States Munitions List. These articles have a military application which is sufficiently sensitive as to require their export to be controlled. See DEFENSE SERVICE.

DEFENSE CONTRACT ADMINISTRATIVE SERVICE (DCAS)   An organization within the Defense Logistics Agency that performed CONTRACT ADMINISTRATION on assigned contracts at contractor plants. It was renamed the DEFENSE CONTRACT MANAGEMENT COMMAND which was subsequently replaced by the DEFENSE CONTRACT MANAGEMENT AGENCY.

DEFENSE CONTRACT AUDIT AGENCY (DCAA)   A DOD agency responsible for performing contract AUDIT services for the department. The DCAA was established by DOD Directive 5105.36, *Defense Contract Audit Agency*, June 8, 1978, to perform all contract auditing for DOD and to provide all DOD procurement and contract administration activities with accounting and financial advisory services in connection with negotiating, administering, and settling contracts and subcontracts. DCAA also furnishes contract audit services to other government agencies. *DCAA Contract Audit Manual* ¶ 1-102. DCAA is a separate DOD agency under the direction, authority, and control of the Assistant Secretary of Defense (Comptroller). *DCAA Contract Audit Manual* ¶ 1-103. See Feldman, Government Contract Guidebook § 9:78 (4th ed. 2019–2020); Manos, 2 Government Contract Costs & Pricing § 86:10 (2d ed. 2009–2020).

DEFENSE CONTRACT AUDIT MANUAL (DCAM)   See DCAA CONTRACT AUDIT MANUAL.

DEFENSE CONTRACT MANAGEMENT AGENCY (DCMA)   An independent organization within DOD that performs CONTRACT ADMINISTRATION services for all parts of DOD and other agencies. DOD activities must use DCMA for contract administration unless they fall within the list of exceptions in DFARS 242.202(a). The services performed are described at FAR 42.302 and DFARS 242.302. Contract administration services include all actions accomplished in or near a contractor's plant for the government's benefit that are necessary to the performance of a contract or in support of the buying offices, system and project managers, and other organizations. Guidance on procedures and practices are set forth in the DCMA Instructions/DCMA Guidebook at http://guidebook.dcma.mil/.

DEFENSE COOPERATION   A generic term for the range of activity undertaken by DOD with its allies and other friendly nations to promote international security. Such activity includes, but need not be confined to, security assistance, industrial cooperation, armaments cooperation, FOREIGN MILITARY SALES, training, logistics cooperation, cooperative RESEARCH AND DEVELOPMENT, Foreign Comparative Testing, and host nation support. A defense cooperation country is a "qualifying country" that has a defense cooperation agreement with the United States and for which a DETERMINATION AND FINDINGS has been made by the Secretary of Defense waiving the BUY AMERICAN ACT restrictions for a list of mutually agreed-upon items (see DFARS Subparts 225.871 & .872). DAU Glossary.

DEFENSE PRIORITIES AND ALLOCATIONS SYSTEM (DPAS)   A system controlling the usage of critical materials and facilities to ensure that they will be used for national defense in the event of an emergency. See FAR Subpart 11.6. Certain contracts and orders are accorded preferential treatment by being designated as RATED ORDERs under the Defense Priorities and Allocations System regulation, 15 C.F.R. part 700, which guides the

Department of Commerce's Office of Industrial Resource Administration in developing, coordinating, and administering a system of priorities and allocations with respect to industrial resources, pursuant to Title I of the DEFENSE PRODUCTION ACT OF 1950. See FAR Subpart 11.6. The DPAS legislation also provides that programs that maximize domestic energy supplies are eligible for priorities and allocations support. Rated orders placed in support of authorized energy programs are equivalent to orders placed in support of authorized defense programs under the DPAS; they receive the same preferential treatment throughout the industrial supply chain. DEAR 911.602(d). The Secretary of Homeland Security authorizes certain national defense programs for priorities and allocations support. 15 C.F.R. § 700.2. See Efron & Ebert, *Defense Priorities & Allocation System*, BRIEFING PAPERS No. 01–12 (Nov. 2001).

DEFENSE PROCUREMENT AND ACQUISITION POLICY (DPAP)   A website providing an easy-to-use, automated information retrieval system and real-time access to the most current DOD acquisition information at www.acq.osd.mil/dpap.

DEFENSE PRODUCTION ACT OF 1950   An Act, 50 U.S.C. App. § 2061 et seq., that authorizes the President to require that contracts in support of the national defense be accepted and performed on a preferential or priority basis over all other contracts; and to allocate materials and facilities in such a manner as to promote the national defense. See DEFENSE PRIORITIES AND ALLOCATIONS SYSTEM and FAR 11.602.

DEFENSE PRODUCTION POOL   A POOL of SMALL BUSINESS CONCERNs or other concerns that have joined together to submit offers on one or more defense production contracts; that have entered into an agreement governing their organization, relationship, and procedures; and that have gained approval from the SMALL BUSINESS ADMINISTRATION or a designated official under Executive Order No. 10480, Aug. 14, 1953. FAR 9.701. FAR 9.702 provides that government agencies must treat such pools as they treat any other government contractor. Thus, these pools are entitled to have the status of a JOINT VENTURE.

DEFENSE RESEARCH AND DEVELOPMENT POOL   A POOL of SMALL BUSINESS CONCERNs or other concerns that have joined together to submit offers on one or more defense RESEARCH AND DEVELOPMENT contracts; that have entered into an agreement governing their organization, relationship, and procedures; and that have gained approval from the SMALL BUSINESS ADMINISTRATION or a designated official under Executive Order No. 10480, Aug. 14, 1953. FAR 9.701. FAR 9.702 provides that government agencies must treat such pools as they treat any other government contractor. Thus, these pools are entitled to have the status of a JOINT VENTURE.

DEFENSE SERVICE   *Official:* (1) The furnishing of assistance (including training) to foreign persons, whether in the United States or abroad in the design, development, engineering, manufacture, production, assembly, testing, repair, maintenance, modification, operation, demilitarization, destruction, processing or use of DEFENSE ARTICLEs; (2) The furnishing to foreign persons of any technical data controlled under this subchapter (see § 120.10), whether in the United States or abroad; or (3) Military training of foreign units and forces, regular and irregular, including formal or informal instruction of foreign persons in the United States or abroad or by correspondence courses, technical, educational, or information publications and media of all kinds, training aid, orientation, training exercise, and military advice. *Source:* 22 C.F.R. § 120.9. These services are subject to the EXPORT CONTROL regulations of the DEPARTMENT OF STATE. 22 C.F.R. Subchapter M.

DEFENSE STANDARDIZATION PROGRAM (DSP) An activity within the DEPARTMENT OF DEFENSE, mandated by the Cataloging and Standardization Act, 10 U.S.C. § 2451, that identifies, influences, develops, manages, and provides access to standardization processes, products, and services for the acquisition and logistics communities in order to promote interoperability, reduce total ownership costs, and sustain readiness. The program is managed by the DEFENSE STANDARDIZATION PROGRAM OFFICE (DSPO). DSPO is in charge of standardization throughout DOD to reduce costs and improve operational effectiveness and is governed by DOD Instruction 4120.24, *Defense Standardization Program Procedures* (Sept. 24, 2014, ch. 2, Oct. 15, 2018). There are standardization offices in several DOD components. DSP maintains a website at https://www.dsp.dla.mil.

DEFENSE STANDARDIZATION PROGRAM OFFICE (DSPO) The office that manages the DEFENSE STANDARDIZATION PROGRAM (DSP), located at Fort Belvoir, Virginia. The Director, Defense Standardization Program Office, serves as the DOD Executive Agent for the DEFENSE STANDARDIZATION PROGRAM and publishes DOD Instruction 4120.24-M. DSPO supports the Defense Standardization Executive, carries out the day-to-day management of the DSP, and promulgates DSP policies and procedures.

DEFENSE SYSTEMS MANAGEMENT COLLEGE (DSMC) A school within the DEFENSE ACQUISITION UNIVERSITY (DAU), located at Fort Belvoir, Virginia, and chartered to provide executive level and international program management training, consulting, acquisition leadership training and research. Founded in 1971, it was incorporated into DAU upon its creation in 1992.

DEFERMENT AGREEMENT A debt collection procedure where the government agrees to delayed payment of debts owed by a contractor if it is unable to pay or if the amount is in dispute. FAR 32.607-2 contains detailed guidance for deferment of collection actions. At a minimum, a deferment agreement must contain: (1) a description of the debt, (2) the date of first demand for payment, (3) a notice of an interest charge, (4) identification of the office to which the contractor is to send debt payments, (5) a requirement for the contractor to submit financial information requested by the government and for reasonable access to the contractor's records and property, (6) provision for the government to terminate the deferment agreement and accelerate the maturity of the debt if the contractor defaults or if bankruptcy or insolvency proceedings are instituted, and (7) protective requirements that are considered by the government to be prudent and feasible in the specific circumstances. FAR 32.607-2(g). FAR 32.607 directs CONTRACTING OFFICERs to develop a recommendation on whether a deferment agreement should be entered into and to refer that recommendation to an office "designated in agency procedures" to make the final decision and enter into the agreement. See Cibinic, Nagle & Nash, ADMINISTRATION OF GOVERNMENT CONTRACTS 1077 (5th ed. 2016).

DEFERRAL OF BUDGET AUTHORITY *Official:* The (A) withholding or delaying the obligation or expenditure of BUDGET AUTHORITY (whether by establishing reserves or otherwise) provided for projects or activities; or (B) any other type of Executive action or inaction which effectively precludes the obligation or expenditures of budget authority, including authority to obligate by contract in advance of appropriations as specifically authorized by law. *Source:* 2 U.S.C. § 682. Budget authority may be deferred to provide for contingencies, to achieve savings or greater efficiency in the operations of government, or as otherwise specified by law. Budget authority may not be deferred in order to effect a policy in lieu of one established by law or for any other reason. Deferrals must be communicated to the Congress by the President in a special message. The special message must state (1) the amount of the budget authority proposed to be deferred; (2) any account, department, or establishment which such budget authority is available for obligation; (3) the period of time during which the budget authority is proposed to be deferred; (4) the reasons for the proposed deferral; (5) the estimated fiscal, economic, and budgetary effect of the proposed deferral; and (6) all facts bearing on the proposed deferral. A deferral may not be proposed for any period of time extending beyond the end of the fiscal year in which the message proposing the deferral is transmitted to Congress. 2 U.S.C. § 684. See IMPOUNDMENT; RESCISSION OF BUDGET AUTHORITY.

DEFERRED COMPENSATION   *Official:* An award made by an employer to compensate an employee in a future cost accounting period or periods for services rendered in one or more cost accounting periods before the date of the receipt of compensation by the employee. This definition shall not include the amount of year-end accruals, for salaries, wages, or bonuses that are to be paid within a reasonable period of time after the end of a cost accounting period. *Source:* FAR 31.001. The costs of such compensation are generally considered to be ALLOWABLE COSTs pursuant to FAR 31.205-6(k), if the costs are accounted for in accordance with CAS 415, 48 C.F.R. § 9904-415. See Manos, 1 GOVERNMENT CONTRACT COSTS & PRICING § 13.15 (2d ed. 2009–2020); Cibinic, Knight & Nash, COST-REIMBURSEMENT CONTRACTING 686 (4th ed. 2014).

DEFERRED DELIVERY   A DOD technique for deferring the time of delivery of TECHNI-CAL DATA or COMPUTER SOFTWARE until any time up to two years after acceptance of all other items on a contract. DFARS 227.7103-8(a) and 227.7203-8(a). This right pertains only to technical data and software called out on the CONTRACT DATA REQUIRE-MENTS LIST. The procedure is implemented by the inclusion in a contract of the Deferred Delivery of Technical Data or Computer Software clause in DFARS 252.227-7026. There is no similar procedure in the FAR. See Nash & Rawicz, INTELLECTUAL PROPERTY IN GOVERN-MENT CONTRACTS, chap. 6 (6th ed. 2008).

DEFERRED ORDERING   A DOD technique allowing the government to order any TECH-NICAL DATA or COMPUTER SOFTWARE generated in the performance of the contract or its subcontracts until any time up to three years after acceptance of all other items on a contract. DFARS 227.7103-8(b) and 227.7203-8(b). This gives the government the right to order technical data and software that was not called out on the CONTRACT DATA REQUIREMENTS LIST. The procedure is implemented by the inclusion in a contract of the Deferred Ordering of Technical Data or Computer Software clause in DFARS 252.227-7027. A similar procedure is included in FAR 27.409(d), which calls for the use of the Additional Data Requirements clause in FAR 52.227-16 in research, development and demonstration contracts except those not exceeding $500,000 with educational institutions. This clause allows the government to order any data first produced or specifically used in the performance of the contract. These clauses do not alter the license rights to the data. However, they give the government a very broad right to call for the delivery of technical data and computer software and are subject to negotiation if the contractor does not want to deliver such data. Section 815 of the National Defense Authorization Act for FY 2012 adds 10 U.S.C. § 2320(b)(9) requiring the inclusion of a deferred ordering requirement in contracts and altering the scope of the technical data that can be ordered. See Nash & Raw-icz, INTELLECTUAL PROPERTY IN GOVERNMENT CONTRACTS, chap. 6 (6th ed. 2008); Nash, *New Technical Data Legislation: Revisions to the DOD Statutes*, 26 N&CR ¶ 18 (Apr. 2012).

DEFICIENCY *Official:* A material failure of a proposal to meet a government requirement or a combination of significant weaknesses in a proposal that increases the risk of unsuccessful contract performance to an unacceptable level. *Source:* FAR 15.001. When an agency conducts DISCUSSIONs after establishing a COMPETITIVE RANGE in a competitively negotiated procurement, all deficiencies must be identified. FAR 15.306(d)(3). This permits each offeror to submit a FINAL PROPOSAL REVISION that maximizes the government's ability to obtain the BEST VALUE. See Cibinic, Nash & Yukins, FORMATION OF GOVERN-MENT CONTRACTS 888–06 (4th ed. 2011); Edwards, *Meaningful Discussions: What is the Standard?*, 24 N&CR ¶ 5 (Feb. 2010); Edwards, *Meaningful Discussions: The Unending Quest for Clarity and Sound Policy*, 22 N&CR ¶ 57 (Sept. 2009).

DEFINITE-QUANTITY CONTRACT *Official:* A type of contract providing for delivery of a definite quantity of specific supplies or services for a fixed period, with deliveries of performance to be scheduled at designated locations upon order. *Source:* FAR 16.502. Definite-quantity contracts are one of the three types of INDEFINITE-DELIVERY CONTRACTs. They may be used when it can be determined in advance that (1) a definite quantity of supplies or services will be required during the contract period, and (2) the supplies or services are regularly available or will be available after a short lead-time. By buying a stated quantity for delivery on a deferred basis, the government seeks to induce contractors to submit low prices and to reduce its costs of maintaining high levels of inventory.

DEFINITIZATION *Official:* The agreement on, or determination of, contract terms, specifications, and price, which converts the UNDEFINITIZED CONTRACTUAL ACTION to a definitive contract. *Source:* DFARS 217.7401. 10 U.S.C. § 2326 places strict requirements on the definitization of such actions. This term is generally used with regard to LETTER CONTRACTs. Cibinic, Nash & Yukins, FORMATION OF GOVERNMENT CONTRACTS 1213–17 (4th ed. 2011); Nash, *Unpriced Changes: In DOD They're Now Undefinitized Contract Actions*, 24 N&CR ¶ 60 (Dec. 2010).

DEFINITIZED ITEM *Official:* An item for which a firm price has been established in the basic contract or by MODIFICATION. *Source:* DFARS 204.7101. DFARS 204.7106 contains criteria on the use of CONTRACT LINE ITEMs when a CONTRACT MODIFICATION effects a definitized item. See UNIFORM CONTRACT LINE ITEM NUMBERING SYSTEM.

DELAY An event that slows the performance of the work by a government contractor. In government contracts, the contractor generally bears the RISK of both time and cost for delays caused by the contractor, within the contractor's control, or reasonably avoidable by the contractor. However, the contractor is generally entitled to a time extension if there is an EXCUSABLE DELAY and to additional compensation if there is a COMPENSABLE DELAY. See Cibinic, Nagle & Nash, ADMINISTRATION OF GOVERNMENT CONTRACTS, chap. 6 (5th ed. 2016); Nash, *No Damages for Delay: A Rare Clause in Federal Contracting*, 24 N&CR ¶ 51 (Oct. 2010); Dale & D'Onofrio, *Reconciling Concurrency in Schedule Delay and Constructive Acceleration*, 39 PUB. CONT. L.J. 161 (2010); Kelleher, *The Resurrection of Rice? The Evolution (And De-Evolution) of the Ability of Contractors to Recover Delay Damages on Federal Government Construction Contracts*, 39 PUB. CONT. L.J. 305 (2010).

DELEGATE AGENCY   *Official:* A Government agency authorized by delegation from the Department of Commerce to place priority ratings on contracts or orders needed to support approved programs. *Source:* FAR 11.601. Schedule I of the DEFENSE PRIORITIES AND ALLOCATIONS SYSTEM lists the delegate agencies. See 15 C.F.R. § 700.10.

DELEGATION OF CONTRACTING OFFICER AUTHORITY   The granting of authority to act as a CONTRACTING OFFICER for an EXECUTIVE AGENCY. FAR 1.603-1 requires that each agency establish a system for the selection, appointment, and termination of appointment of contracting officers. Agency procedures for delegating contracting officer authority are found in each agency FAR Supplement. Each contracting officer with delegated authority is given a WARRANT using the Certificate of Appointment in Standard Form 1402, FAR 53.301-1402. See Nash & Feldman, 1 GOVERNMENT CONTRACT CHANGES §§ 5:9–5:12 (3d ed. 2006–2020); Cibinic, Nagle & Nash, ADMINISTRATION OF GOVERNMENT CONTRACTS 30–39 (5th ed. 2016); Cibinic, Nash & Yukins, FORMATION OF GOVERNMENT CONTRACTS 81–111 (4th ed. 2011); Nash, *Postscript: Contracting Officer Authority*, 22 N&CR ¶ 33 (June 2008); Nash, *Contracting Officer Authority: A Strict Requirement*, 11 N&CR ¶ 58 (Nov. 2007).

DELIBERATIVE PROCESS EXEMPTION   An exemption under the FREEDOM OF INFORMATION ACT from the disclosure of internal government memorandums or letters that constitute advice, recommendations or opinions concerning a prospective government decision. See EXECUTIVE PRIVILEGE. See Nash & Rawicz, INTELLECTUAL PROPERTY IN GOVERNMENT CONTRACTS, chap. 9 (6th ed. 2008).

DELINQUENCY NOTICE   A notice from a contracting officer to a contractor asserting that contract performance is delinquent and requesting that the contractor provide information as to the delinquency. FAR 49.607 discusses two types of delinquency notices: (1) CURE NOTICEs and (2) SHOW CAUSE NOTICEs. See Cibinic, Nagle & Nash, ADMINISTRATION OF GOVERNMENT CONTRACTS 871–75 (5th ed. 2016).

DELIVERY OR PERFORMANCE PERIOD REQUIREMENTS   One of the eight required elements of the Acquisition Background and Objectives section of the written ACQUISITION PLAN that outlines the timing requirements for contract performance or supply delivery. FAR 7.105(a)(5). FAR Subpart 11.4 gives contracting officers a number of factors to consider in establishing the delivery schedule or performance period. Contracting officers must ensure that delivery or performance schedules are realistic and meet the requirements of the acquisition. Schedules that are unreasonably tight or difficult of attainment tend to restrict competition, are inconsistent with small business policies, and may result in higher contract prices. FAR 11.401.

DELIVERY OR PERFORMANCE SCHEDULE   The contract provision setting forth the time of delivery or performance. This provision is included in Section F of the UNIFORM CONTRACT FORMAT. FAR 14.201-1; FAR 15.204-1. FAR 11.401 requires that contracting officers ensure that delivery schedules are realistic, meet the requirements of the acquisition, and are clearly stated in the SOLICITATION. Schedules that are unreasonably tight tend to restrict competition, are inconsistent with small business policies, and may result in higher contract prices. When establishing contract delivery schedules for supply or service contracts, the contracting officer must consider factors such as urgency of the need, production time, market conditions, transportation time, industry practices, capabilities of small business concerns, administrative time for obtaining and evaluating offers and awarding contracts, time for contractors to comply with any conditions precedent to contract performance, and time for the government to perform its obligations under the contract. Scheduling the completion date for construction contracts requires consideration of the nature and complexity of the project, construction seasons involved, required completion date, availability of materials and equipment, capacity of the contractor to perform, and advisability of multiple completion dates. FAR 11.402. A contractor must be able to comply with the required or proposed schedule to be RESPONSIBLE. FAR 9.104-1(b).

DELIVERY INCENTIVE A contract term that financially rewards a contractor for delivery or completion before a target date (a "positive" incentive), or that reduces a contractor's compensation for delivery or completion after a target date (a "negative" incentive). FAR 16.402-3. Such an incentive might be a PREDETERMINED, FORMULA-TYPE INCENTIVE or an AWARD FEE incentive. Delivery incentives are not considered to be a type of LIQUIDATED DAMAGES. See Cibinic, Nash & Yukins, FORMATION OF GOVERNMENT CONTRACTS 1276–88 (4th ed. 2011); Edwards, *Contract Pricing Arrangements: A Primer-Part II*, BRIEFING PAPERS No. 09-12 (Nov. 2009).

DELIVERY ORDER *Official:* An order for supplies placed against an established contract or with government sources. *Source:* FAR 2.101. Delivery orders can be placed on DELIVERY-ORDER CONTRACTS, FEDERAL SUPPLY SCHEDULES and SIMPLIFIED ACQUISITIONs. Delivery orders placed on delivery-order contracts must be issued in accordance with the procedures in FAR 16.505. For delivery order competitions exceeding $100,000, the RULE OF TWO applies. *Delex Sys., Inc.*, Comp. Gen. B-400403, Oct. 8, 2008, 08-2 CPD ¶ 181. 10 U.S.C. § 2304c(b) and 41 U.S.C. § 4106(c) provide requirements for enhanced competition for delivery orders in excess of $3,500. See FAIR OPPORTUNITY. In addition, 10 U.S.C. § 2304c(d) and 41 U.S.C. § 4106(d) contain more stringent notice requirements for delivery orders in excess of $5.5 million. The GOVERNMENT ACCOUNTABILITY OFFICE currently has jurisdiction to hear protests of delivery order awards in excess of $10 million by civilian agencies, 41 U.S.C. § 4106(f)(3), and in excess of $25 million by DOD, NASA and the Coast Guard, 10 U.S.C. § 2304c(e)(1)(B). Delivery orders issued against Federal Supply Schedule contracts must comply with the procedures in FAR 8.405. FAR 13.307 provides that delivery orders for simplified acquisitions may be issued using Standard Form 1449, Solicitation/Contract/Order for Commercial Items, Optional Form 347, Order for Supplies or Services, or Optional Form 348, Order for Supplies or Services Schedule—Continuation, which are set forth at FAR 53.302-347 and -348. Delivery orders can also be placed using a GOVERNMENTWIDE COMMERCIAL PURCHASE CARD. FAR 13.031.

DELIVERY-ORDER CONTRACT *Official:* A contract for supplies that does not procure or specify a firm quantity of supplies (other than a minimum or maximum quantity) and that provides for the issuance of orders for the delivery of supplies during the period of the contract. *Source:* FAR 16.501-1. Under 10 U.S.C. § 2304a and 41 U.S.C. § 4103, delivery-order contracts must contain (1) the period of the contract, including options; (2) the maximum quantity or dollar value of the supplies to be procured; and (3) a STATEMENT OF WORK that reasonably describes the general scope, nature, complexity, and purposes of the supplies being procured. See FAR 16.505. 10 U.S.C. § 2304a(d) and 41 U.S.C. § 4103(d)(4)(A) require that such contracts be issued to multiple contractors whenever practicable (see MULTIPLE AWARD PREFERENCE). Although REQUIREMENTS CONTRACTs can be considered delivery order contracts, the term generally refers to

INDEFINITE-QUANTITY CONTRACTs. FAR 16.501-2(a). Delivery order contracts with the DOD awarded under 10 U.S.C. § 2304a cannot exceed five years, but may contain options to extend the contract to up to 10 years. DFARS 217.204. See Cibinic, Nash & Yukins, FORMATION OF GOVERNMENT CONTRACTS 1386–1406 (4th ed. 2011); Alinger, *Recent Developments in Task and Delivery Order Contracting*, 39 PUB. CONT. L.J. 839 (2010), Mansfield, *Task and Delivery Orders: Are They "Contracts"?*, 24 N&CR ¶ 50 (Oct. 2010).

DEMOBILIZATION   The effort of a construction contractor in leaving the site after the contract work is completed. In major construction contracts agencies frequently pay for the cost of this effort as a separate pay item. DFARS 236.570(b)(2)(ii) requires the use of the Payment for Mobilization and Demobilization clause in DFARS 252.236-7004 in these circumstances.

DEPARTMENT OF AGRICULTURE (USDA)   Government agency created by act of May 15, 1862, 7 U.S.C. § 2201. USDA works to improve and maintain farm income and to develop and expand markets abroad for agricultural products. USDA also helps to curb and cure poverty, hunger, and malnutrition. Through its rural development, credit and conservation programs, it works to enhance the environment and maintain production capacity. Further, it safeguards and ensures standards of quality in the daily food supply through inspection and grading services. USDA contracts fall under the coverage of the FEDERAL ACQUISITION REGULATION and the Agriculture Acquisition Regulation (AGAR), 48 C.F.R. chap. 4. See the U.S. Government Manual, https://www.usgovernmentmanual.gov. [USDA, 14th Street and Independence Avenue, S.W., Washington, DC 20250; www.usda.gov.]

DEPARTMENT OF COMMERCE   Government agency created by act of February 14, 1903, 15 U.S.C. § 1501. The agency was established to promote American businesses and trade. Its broad range of responsibilities includes expanding U.S. exports, developing innovative technologies, gathering and disseminating statistical data, measuring economic growth, granting patents, registering trademarks, promoting minority entrepreneurship, and predicting the weather. Department of Commerce contracts fall under the coverage of the FEDERAL ACQUISITION REGULATION and the Department of Commerce Acquisition Regulation (CAR), 48 C.F.R. chap. 13. See the U.S. Government Manual, https://www. usgovernmentmanual.gov. [Department of Commerce, 14th Street and Constitution Avenue, N.W., Washington, DC 20230; www.doc.gov.]

DEPARTMENT OF DEFENSE (DOD)   The Office of the Secretary of Defense, the military departments, and the defense agencies. The military departments include the Departments of the Army, the Navy, and the Air Force (the Marine Corps is a part of the Department of the Navy and the Space Corps is a part of the Department of the Air Force). The defense agencies are listed in DFARS 202.101. DOD contracts fall under the coverage of the FEDERAL ACQUISITION REGULATION (FAR) and the DOD FAR SUPPLEMENT (DFARS), as well as lower-level supplemental regulations for the military services and defense agencies. Before the FAR went into effect in 1984, DOD contracts were governed by the DEFENSE ACQUISITION REGULATION and its predecessor, the ARMED SERVICES PROCUREMENT REGULATION. See the U.S. Government Manual, https://www.us governmentmanual.gov. [DOD, 1000 Defense Pentagon, Washington, DC 20301-1000. Nash, *Postscript: Department of Defense Acquisition Guidance*, 23 N&CR ¶ 8 (Feb. 2009)]

DEPARTMENT OF DEFENSE DIRECTIVES SYSTEM   A single, uniform system governing the coordination, publication, dissemination, implementation, and biennial review of issuances maintained within DOD. The system includes (1) DOD Directives (DODDs), which establish or describe Secretary of Defense policies, programs and major activities, and organizations; define missions; delegate authority; and assign responsibility, (2) DOD Instructions (DODIs), which implement policy, or prescribe a uniform method or delineate a specific plan of action for carrying out the policy, or provide directions or details for operating a program or activity; and assign responsibilities, (3) DOD Publications, which implement or supplement DODDs and DODIs by providing uniform procedures for management or operational systems and by disseminating administrative information (these publications include handbooks and manuals, designated by the suffixes "H" and "M," respectively), and (4) DOD transmittals, which change or cancel DOD issuances. When directive-type memoranda of continuing application issued by principal staff assistants cannot, because of time constraints, be published in the DOD Directives System at the time of signature, they are to be reissued as DOD issuances as soon as practicable. Directive-type memoranda of a one-time nature are not issued in the DOD Directives System. DOD Instruction 5025.01, *DoD Directives Program*, May 22, 2019. Although all procurement regulations are required to be included in the FAR and the DFARS, the DOD Directives System contains a significant amount of information bearing directly on the procurement process. Unclassified documents in the system are available at https://www.esd.whs.mil/Directives/issuances/dodd/. Other documents are published on a classified website.

DEPARTMENT OF DEFENSE FAR SUPPLEMENT (DFARS)   The procurement regulation applicable to DOD that implements and supplements the FEDERAL ACQUISITION REGULATION (FAR). It applies specifically to procurement involving the Office of the Secretary of Defense; the Departments of the Army, Navy, and Air Force; the Defense Logistics Agency (DLA) and other defense agencies. The DFARS contains requirements of law, DOD-wide policies, delegations of FAR authorities, deviations from FAR requirements, and policies or procedures that have a significant effect beyond internal operating procedures or impose a significant cost on contractors. DFARS 201.301. It is supplemented by the DFARS PROCEDURES, GUIDANCE AND INFORMATION (DOD PGI). The DFARS is not a stand-alone document; it must be read in conjunction with the FAR and the DOD PGI. The DFARS is amended through the use of DEFENSE ACQUISITION CIRCULARS, which are issued by the DEFENSE ACQUISITION REGULATORY COUNCIL and resemble FEDERAL ACQUISITION CIRCULARS. DFARS 201.301. Implementing coverage in the DFARS is numbered in the same way as the FAR material it implements, except for the addition of a "2" or "20" prefix (the DFARS is Chapter 2 of Title 48 of the CODE OF FEDERAL REGULATIONS). Thus, DFARS Parts 201 through 253 corresponds to FAR Parts 1 through 53, DFARS Subpart 252.1 parallels FAR Subpart 52.1, and DFARS 201.101 implements FAR 1.101. Supplementary coverage, for which there is no parallel in the FAR, is distinguished by using numbers 70 and above (e.g., Part 270, Subpart 245.73). Supplementary numbering is used only when the DFARS text cannot be integrated intelligibly with counterpart text in the FAR. DFARS 201.303. The DFARS can be purchased in paperback from Commerce Clearing House, Inc., 4025 West Peterson Avenue, Chicago, IL 60646, or as part of the loose-leaf-bound subscription edition of the FEDERAL ACQUISITION REGULATIONS SYSTEM available from the U.S. Government Printing Office, Washington, DC 20402; www.acq.osd.mil/dpap/dars/index.htm.

DEPARTMENT OF EDUCATION   Government agency created by the Department of Education Organization Act of May 4, 1980, 20 U.S.C. § 3411. The agency establishes policy for, administers, and coordinates most federal assistance to education. The Department of Education operates more than 200 programs that cover every area of education and range from preschool education through postdoctoral research. The Department's contracts fall under the coverage of the FEDERAL ACQUISITION REGULATION and the Department of Education Acquisition Regulation (EDAR), 48 C.F.R. chap. 34. See the U.S. Government Manual, https://www.usgovernmentmanual.gov. [Department of Education, 600 Independence Avenue, S.W., Washington, DC 20202; www.ed.gov]

DEPARTMENT OF ENERGY (DOE)   Government agency established by the Department of Energy Organization Act, 42 U.S.C. § 7131, effective Oct. 1, 1977, pursuant to Exec. Order No. 12009, 42 Fed. Reg. 46267 (Sept. 13, 1977). The Act consolidated the major federal energy functions into one cabinet-level department, transferring to the department all the responsibilities of several components of the Department of the Interior, as well as the Energy Research and Development Administration and the Federal Energy Administration. DOE is responsible for long-term, high-risk research and development of energy technology; the marketing of federal power; energy conservation; the nuclear weapons program; energy regulatory programs; and a central energy data collection and analysis program. DOE contracts fall under the coverage of the FEDERAL ACQUISITION REGULATION and the DEPARTMENT OF ENERGY ACQUISITION REGULATION (DEAR), 48 C.F.R. chap. 9. See the U.S. Government Manual, https://www.usgovernmentmanual.gov. [DOE, 1000 Independence Avenue, S.W., Washington; DC 20585: www.doe.gov]

DEPARTMENT OF ENERGY ACQUISITION REGULATION (DEAR)   The DOE regulation that implements and supplements the FEDERAL ACQUISITION REGULATION (FAR). The DEAR is not a stand-alone document but must be read in conjunction with the FAR. DEAR 901.101. It is divided into the same parts, subparts, sections, subsections, and paragraphs as the FAR. The implementing passages of the DEAR are numbered the same as the FAR to the extent possible, except that they are preceded with a "9" or a "90" because the DEAR is Chapter 9 of Title 48 of the CODE OF FEDERAL REGULATIONS. DEAR 901.104-2. The DEAR is revised by acquisition letters issued by the DOE SENIOR PROCUREMENT EXECUTIVE. DEAR 901.301-70. The DEAR is supplemented by the DOE Acquisition Guide. The DEAR is available from the U.S. Government Printing Office, Washington DC 20402, as part of the loose-leaf-bound subscription edition of the FEDERAL ACQUISITION REGULATIONS SYSTEM.

DEPARTMENT OF HEALTH AND HUMAN SERVICES (HHS)   Government agency created on April 11, 1953, as the Department of Health, Education, and Welfare. It was redesignated as the Department of Health and Human Services by the Department of Education Organization Act, 20 U.S.C. § 3508, effective May 4, 1980. HHS is the government's principal agency for protecting the health of all Americans and providing essential human services. It operates more than 300 programs covering a wide spectrum of activities, including: medical and social science research, preventing outbreak of infectious disease, assuring food and drug safety, Medicare and Medicaid, financial assistance for low-income families (AFDC), child-support enforcement, improving maternal and infant health, Head Start, prevention of child abuse and domestic violence, substance abuse treatment and prevention, and services for older Americans. HHS contracts fall under the coverage of the FEDERAL ACQUISITION REGULATION, the Department of Health and Human Services Acquisition Regulation (HHSAR), 48 C.F.R. chap. 3, and the HHS Acquisition Policies and Guidance. See the U.S. Government Manual, https://www.usgovernmentmanual.gov. [HHS, 200 Independence Avenue, S.W., Washington DC 20201; www.hhs.gov]

DEPARTMENT OF HOMELAND SECURITY (DHS)   Government agency created by the Homeland Security Act of 2002, 6 U.S.C. § 111, effective January 24, 2003. DHS is responsible for programs to prevent and deal with terrorist attacks, to deal with natural disasters, to secure the borders, to secure cyberspace and critical infrastructure, to interdict illegal drug trafficking and to perform emergency planning. DHS is to generally follow existing, government-wide procurement laws, but also has broad authority to deviate from those rules if they would "impair" the agency's missions or operations. DHS possesses special authority to use OTHER TRANSACTIONS in the same manner as DOD. DHS contracts fall under the coverage of the FEDERAL ACQUISITION REGULATION, the Department of Homeland Security Acquisition Regulation (HSAR), 48 C.F.R. chap. 30, and the Homeland Security Acquisition Manual. See the U.S. Government Manual, https://www.us governmentmanual.gov. See Zenner, Handwerker & Catoe, *Fundamentals of Contracting with the Department of Homeland Security*, BRIEFING PAPERS No. 03–4 (Mar. 2003).

DEPARTMENT OF HOUSING AND URBAN DEVELOPMENT (HUD)   Government agency created by the Department of Housing and Urban Development Act, 42 U.S.C. §§ 3532–3537, effective November 9, 1965. HUD is responsible for programs concerned with the Nation's housing needs, fair housing opportunities, and improvement and development of the nation's communities. HUD administers a wide variety of programs, including federal housing administration mortgage insurance programs, rental assistance programs, the government National Mortgage Association mortgage-backed securities program, programs to combat housing discrimination, programs that aid community and neighborhood development and preservation, and programs to protect the homebuyer in the marketplace. HUD contracts fall under the coverage of the FEDERAL ACQUISITION REGULATION and the Department of Housing and Urban Development Acquisition Regulation (HUDAR), 48 C.F.R. chap. 24. See the U.S. Government Manual, www.gpoaccess.gov/gmanual/index.html. [HUD, 451 Seventh Street, S.W., Washington, DC 20410; http:/www.hud.gov]

DEPARTMENT OF JUSTICE (DOJ)   Government agency established by act of June 22, 1870, 28 U.S.C. §§ 501, 503, with the Attorney General as its head. DOJ serves as counsel for the nation's citizens, representing them in enforcing the law in the public interest. DOJ's roles include protection against criminals and subversion; ensuring healthy competition in business; safeguarding the consumer; and enforcing drug, immigration, and naturalization laws. It also protects citizens through its efforts for effective law enforcement, crime prevention, crime detection, and prosecution and rehabilitation of offenders. DOJ conducts all suits in the Supreme Court in which the United States is concerned and represents the government in legal matters generally. DOJ contracts fall under the coverage of the FEDERAL ACQUISITION REGULATION and the Department of Justice Acquisition Regulation (JAR), 48 C.F.R. chap. 28. See the U.S. Government Manual, www.gpoaccess.gov/gmanual/index.html. [DOJ, 10th Street and Constitution Avenue, N.W., Washington, DC 20530; http:/www.usdoj.gov]

DEPARTMENT OF LABOR (DOL)   Government agency created by act of March 4, 1913, 42 U.S.C. § 551. The Department of Labor administers a variety of federal labor laws; protects workers' pension rights; provides job training programs; helps workers find jobs; works to strengthen free collective bargaining; and keeps track of changes in employment, prices, and other national economic measurements. DOL contracts fall under the coverage of the FEDERAL ACQUISITION REGULATION and the Department of Labor Acquisition Regulation (DOLAR), 48 C.F.R. chap. 29. See the U.S. Government Manual, www.gpoaccess.gov/gmanual/index.html. [DOL, 200 Constitution Avenue, N.W., Washington, DC 20210; www.dol.gov]

DEPARTMENT OF STATE   The senior government agency created by act of July 27, 1789, 1 Stat. 28, as the Department of Foreign Affairs and renamed Department of State by act of September 15, 1789, 1 Stat. 68. The Department of State advises the President in the formulation and execution of foreign policy. The Department of State determines and analyzes the facts relating to American overseas interests, makes recommendations on policy and future action, and takes the necessary steps to carry out established policy. In doing so, the department engages in consultations with the American public, Congress, other U.S. departments and agencies, and foreign governments; negotiates treaties and agreements with foreign nations; speaks for the United States in the United Nations and in more than 50 international organizations; and represents the United States at more than 800 international conferences annually. The department operates more than 250 diplomatic and consular posts around the world, including embassies, consulates, and delegations and missions to international organizations. Department of State contracts fall under the coverage of the FEDERAL ACQUISITION REGULATION and the Department of State Acquisition Regulation (SAR), 48 C.F.R. chap. 6. See the U.S. Government Manual, www.gpoaccess.gov/gmanual/index.html. [Department of State, 2201 C Street, N.W., Washington, DC 20520; www.state.gov]

DEPARTMENT OF THE INTERIOR (DOI)   Government agency created by act of March 3, 1849, 43 U.S.C. § 1451. As the nation's principal conservation agency, DOI has responsibility for most nationally owned public lands and natural resources. These responsibilities include: fostering sound use of land and water resources; protecting fish, wildlife, and biological diversity; preserving and operating national parks and historical places; and providing for the enjoyment of life through outdoor recreation. DOI also has a major responsibility for American Indian reservation communities and for people who live in island territories under U.S. administration. DOI contracts fall under the coverage of the FEDERAL ACQUISITION REGULATION and the Department of the Interior Acquisition Regulation (DIAR), 48 C.F.R. chap. 14. See the U.S. Government Manual, www.gpoaccess.gov/gmanual/index.html. [DOI, 1849 C Street, N.W. Washington, DC 20240; www.doi.gov]

DEPARTMENT OF THE TREASURY   Government agency created by act of September 2, 1789, 31 U.S.C. § 1001. The Department of the Treasury performs four basic functions: formulating and recommending economic, financial, tax, and fiscal policies; serving as financial agent for the U.S. Government; enforcing the law; and manufacturing coins and currency. Department of the Treasury contracts fall under the coverage of the FEDERAL ACQUISITION REGULATION and the Treasury Acquisition/Procurement Regulation (TAPR), 48 C.F.R. chap. 10. See the U.S. Government Manual, www.gpoaccess.gov/gmanual/index.html. [Department of the Treasury, 1500 Pennsylvania Avenue, N.W., Washington, DC 20220; www.ustreas.gov]

DEPARTMENT OF TRANSPORTATION (DOT)   Government agency established by act of October 15, 1966, 49 U.S.C. App. § 1651 note. DOT establishes the nation's overall transportation policy. It operates 10 administrations whose jurisdictions include highway planning, development, and construction; urban mass transit; railroads; aviation; and the safety of waterways, ports, highways, and oil and gas pipelines. Except for contracts of the FEDERAL AVIATION ADMINISTRATION, DOT contracts fall under the coverage of the FEDERAL ACQUISITION REGULATION, the Transportation Acquisition Regulation (TAR), 48 C.F.R. chap. 12, and the Transportation Acquisition Manual. See the U.S. Government Manual, www.gpoaccess.gov/gmanual/index.html. [DOT, 400 Seventh Street, S.W., Washington DC 20590; www.dot.gov]

DEPARTMENT OF VETERANS AFFAIRS (VA)   Government agency established in 1988 as an executive department by the Department of Veterans Affairs Act, Pub. L. No. 100-527. The Department's predecessor, the Veterans Administration, had been established as an independent agency by Exec. Order No. 5398 of July 21, 1930, in accordance with the act of July 3, 1930, 46 Stat. 1016. The Department operates programs to benefit veterans and their families, including: compensation payments for disabilities or death related to military service; pensions; education and rehabilitation; home loan guaranty; and a medical care program incorporating nursing homes, clinics, and medical centers. VA contracts fall under the coverage of the FEDERAL ACQUISITION REGULATION and the Veterans Affairs Acquisition Regulation (VAAR), 48 C.F.R. chap. 8. See the U.S. Government Manual, www.gpoaccess.gov/gmanual/index.html. [VA, 810 Vermont Avenue, N.W., Washington, DC 20420; www.va.gov] See Yesner & Ruscus, *Selling Medical Supplies and Services Through the Department of Veterans Affairs Federal Supply Schedule Program*, 37 Pub. Cont. L.J. 489 (2008).

DEPOSITION   The examination of a potential witness in writing or in person about information concerning a pending litigation by a party to the litigation. Rule 27 of the Federal Rules of Civil Procedure permits depositions to be taken for the purpose of gathering evidence (discovery depositions) and requires the other party to a litigation to make its employees and witnesses available for such depositions. Rule 32 of the Federal Rules of Civil Procedure permits depositions to be used for evidentiary purposes. Rule 14 of the UNIFORM RULES (before the BOARDs OF CONTRACT APPEALS) permits the use of depositions for both discovery and evidentiary purposes (if the witness is not present at the hearing).

DEPOT MAINTENANCE AND REPAIR   *Official:* Material maintenance or repair requiring the overhaul, upgrading, or rebuilding of parts, assemblies, or subassemblies, and the testing and reclamation of equipment as necessary, regardless of the source of funds for the maintenance or repair or the location at which the maintenance or repair is performed. The term includes (1) all aspects of software maintenance classified by the Department of Defense as of July 1, 1995, as depot-level maintenance and repair, and (2) interim contractor support or contractor logistics support (or any similar contractor support), to the extent that such support is for the performance of services described in the preceding sentence. The term does not include the procurement of major modifications or upgrades of weapon systems that are designed to improve program performance or the nuclear refueling or defueling of an aircraft carrier and any concurrent complex overhaul. A major upgrade program covered by this exception could continue to be performed by private or public sector activities. he term also does not include the procurement of parts for safety modifications. However, the term does include the installation of parts for that purpose. *Source:* 10 U.S.C. § 2460. 10 U.S.C.

§ 2466 requires that "not more than 50% of the funds made available in a fiscal year to a military department or a Defense Agency for depot-level maintenance and repair workload may be used to contract for the performance by non-Federal Government personnel." See www.acq.osd.mil/log/mpp/depot.html. Alinger, *The Impact of Procurement Provisions in Appropriations Acts on the Federal Acquisition System*, 36 PUB. CONT. L.J. 583 (2007).

DEPRECIATION   *Official:* A charge to current operations that distributes the cost of a TAN-GIBLE CAPITAL ASSET, less estimated RESIDUAL VALUE, over the estimated useful life of the ASSET in a systematic and logical manner. It does not involve a process of valuation. Useful life refers to the prospective period of economic usefulness in a particular contractor's operations as distinguished from physical life; it is evidenced by the actual or estimated retirement and replacement practice of the contractor. *Source:* FAR 2.101. CAS 409, Depreciation of Tangible Capital Assets, 48 C.F.R. § 9904-409, provides guidance on the computation of depreciation and generally requires that the costs be distributed equally over the years of use of the asset. FAR 31.205-11 provides that depreciation is an ALLOWABLE COST unless the cost of depreciation would significantly reduce the book value of a tangible capital asset below its residual value or other stated conditions apply. See Manos, 2 GOVERN-MENT CONTRACT COSTS AND PRICING §§ 70:1–70:10 (2d ed. 2009–2020); Cibinic, Knight & Nash, COST-REIMBURSEMENT CONTRACTING 708–12 (4th ed. 2014).

DERIVATIVE WORK   *Official:* A WORK based on one or more preexisting works, such as a translation, musical arrangement, dramatization, fictionalization, motion picture version, sound recording, art reproduction, abridgment, condensation, or any other form in which a work may be recast, transformed, or adapted. A work consisting of editorial revisions, annotations, elaborations, or other modifications which, as a whole, represent an original work of authorship, is a "derivative work." *Source:* 17 U.S.C. § 101. The owner of a COPY-RIGHT has the exclusive right to prepare derivative works of the work covered by the copy-right. 17 U.S.C. § 106. An author of a derivative work (the owner of the work or another author with permission of the owner) may obtain a copyright on material contributed by that author. 17 U.S.C. § 103. Under the Rights in Data—General clause in FAR 52.227-14, the Rights in Technical Data—Noncommercial Items clause in DFARS 252.227-7013, and the Rights in Noncommercial Computer Software and Noncommercial Computer Software Documentation clause in DFARS 252.227-7014 the government has the right to make derivative works through its LIMITED RIGHTS or RESTRICTED RIGHTS, which permit modification of the technical data or computer software. See Nash & Rawicz, INTELLECTUAL PROPERTY IN GOVERNMENT CONTRACTS, chap. 5 (6th ed. 2008).

DESCRIPTION OF WORK   See STATEMENT OF WORK.

DESCRIPTIVE LITERATURE   *Official:* Information provided by an offeror, such as cuts, illustrations, drawings, and brochures that shows a product's characteristics or construction of a product or explains its operation. The term includes only that information needed to evaluate the acceptability of a product and excludes other information for operating or maintaining the product. *Source:* FAR 2.101. When required by the Descriptive Literature solicitation provision in FAR 52.214-21, descriptive literature is furnished by bidders as part of their bids to describe the products offered. FAR 14.202-5(b) states that the government should not require bidders to furnish descriptive literature unless the contracting office needs it before award to determine whether the products offered meet the SPECIFICATION and to establish exactly what the bidder proposes to furnish. However, requiring descriptive literature is a means that contracting officers use to determine whether bidders actually intend to meet the contract SPECIFICATIONs and to identify bids that are not responsive (see RESPONSIVENESS). See Cibinic, Nash & Yukins, FORMATION OF GOVERNMENT CONTRACTS 559–61 (4th ed. 2011).

DESIGN (in construction contracting)   *Official:* Defining the construction requirement (including the functional relationships and technical systems to be used, such as architectural, environmental, structural, electrical, mechanical, and fire protection), producing the technical SPECIFICATIONs and DRAWINGS, and preparing the construction cost estimate. *Source:* FAR 36.102. This work is the major part of ARCHITECT/ENGINEER (A-E) SERVICES. It can be created by government personnel or procured under a single ARCHITECT/ENGINEER CONTRACT or as part of a DESIGN-BUILD contract.

DESIGN (in research and development contracting)   The preparation of DRAWINGS and SPECIFICATIONs for a product. Design is one of the major tasks in the DEVELOPMENT process.

DESIGN-BID-BUILD   *Official:* The traditional delivery method [for construction projects] where design and construction are sequential and contracted for separately with two contracts and two contractors. *Source:* FAR 36.102. This is contrasted with DESIGN-BUILD contracting where a single contract is used. In design-bid-build contracting the drawings and specifications created under an initial ARCHITECT/ENGINEER CONTRACT are used as the bid documents in the following CONSTRUCTION contract. This permits competition among construction contractors on a project that has a quite complete design. However, the government bears the risk that the drawings and specifications are defective (see IMPLIED WARRANTY OF SPECIFICATIONS). Procedures to be used for design-bid-build contracting are set forth in FAR Subpart 36.2.

DESIGN-BUILD   *Official:* Combining DESIGN and construction in a single contract with one contractor. *Source:* FAR 36.102. Under such an agreement, the owner contracts with a single entity; the contractor providing the end product is responsible for both design and construction. Section 4105 of the CLINGER-COHEN ACT OF 1996 adds 10 U.S.C. § 2305a and 41 U.S.C. § 3309 to authorize the use of two-phase design-build procedures, limiting the competition in the second phase to five contractors or less. FAR Subpart 36.3 implements this statute by providing guidance on this two-phase procedure. Phase one is aimed to limit the number of contractors. Phase two identifies the best-qualified contractor with whom to negotiate. The FAR is silent on the procurement of a design-build contract in a single phase but this technique was widely used prior to the passage of the statutes and is still used by some agencies. In design-build contracting, the contractor is responsible for any deficiencies or defects in the design, except to the extent that such responsibility is specifically waived or limited by the contract. This format is widely used in the commercial sector. It is sometimes called "turnkey" construction because, at least in theory, the owner presents its requirements to a design/build organization and, at some later date, the designer/builder simply hands over the keys to the building to the owner. Guidance and model documents are provided by the DESIGN BUILD INSTITUTE OF AMERICA. See Gadbois, et al., *Turning a Battleship: Design-Build on Federal Construction Projects*, 31 CONSTR. LAW 6 (Winter 2011); *Design/Build Construction Contracts*, 27 Corp. Couns. Quarterly 5 (Jan. 2011); Nash, *Postscript: Design-Build Contracting*, 20 N&CR ¶ 19 (Apr. 2006).

DESIGN BUILD INSTITUTE OF AMERICA   An organization of over 5,000 members that promotes the use of DESIGN-BUILD contracting by providing courses, sponsoring conferences and providing model documents to be used to write design-build contracts. It is located at 1331 Pennsylvania Ave NW Ste 4, Washington, DC 20004.

DESIGN SPECIFICATIONS   Specifications that set forth precise measurements, tolerances, materials, in-process and finished-product tests, quality control measures, inspection requirements, and other specific information. The government uses design specifications in solicitations when the technical requirements are definite and can be communicated clearly to potential offerors. Design specifications permit the government to award solely on the basis of price and offeror CAPABILITY FACTORS or RESPONSIVENESS, since very little flexibility in the design is allowed. Design specifications increase the government's liability for claims that arise during contract performance regarding design defects, since the government generally assumes responsibility for the correctness and adequacy of design specifications (see IMPLIED WARRANTY OF SPECIFICATIONS). FAR 11.002 requires that contract requirements be stated in terms of FUNCTIONAL SPECIFICATIONS, PERFORMANCE SPECIFICATIONS, and essential physical characteristics and that they permit the acquisition of COMMERCIAL ITEMS; and FAR 11.101 states a preference for performance-oriented requirements documents over design-oriented requirements documents to describe an agency's needs. See Cibinic, Nash & Yukins, FORMATION OF GOVERNMENT CONTRACTS 364 (4th ed. 2011).

DESIGN-TO-COST   *Historical.* Management concept that historically emphasized cost-effective design (minimizing cost while achieving performance) and targeting an Average Unit Procurement Cost (AUPC). DTC concentrated on the contractors' activities associated with tracking/controlling costs and performing cost-performance analyses/tradeoffs. Cost as an Independent Variable (CAIV) has refocused DTC to consider cost objectives for the total life cycle of the program and to view CAIV with the understanding it may be necessary to trade off performance to stay within cost objectives and constraints. DTC now is those explicit design actions undertaken to meet cost objectives. Contractual implementation of DTC should go beyond simply incentivizing the contractor to meet cost commitments—it should also incentivize the contractor to seek out additional cost reduction opportunities.

DESIGNATED BILLING OFFICE   *Official:* The office or person (governmental or nongovernmental) designated in the contract where the contractor first submits INVOICEs and contract financing requests. The contract might designate different offices to receive invoices and contract financing requests. The designated billing office might be—(1) The government disbursing office; (2) The contract administration office; (3) The office accepting the supplies delivered or services performed by the contractor; (4) The contract audit office; or (5) A nongovernmental agent. Source: FAR 32.001. When payments are subject to the PROMPT PAYMENT ACT, receipt of a proper invoice in this office starts the running of the time for payment without incurring interest. FAR 32.905.

DESIGNATED PAYMENT OFFICE   *Official:* The office designated in the contract to make INVOICE PSYMENTs or CONTRACT FINANCING PAYMENTs. Normally, this will be the government disbursing office. *Source:* FAR 32.001. See also DISBURSING OFFICER.

DETAILED COST IMPACT PROPOSAL   See COST IMPACT PROPOSAL.

DETERMINATION AND FINDINGS (D&Fs)   *Official:* A special form of written approval by an authorized official that is required by statute or regulation as a prerequisite to taking certain contracting actions. The "determination" is a conclusion or decision supported by the "findings." The findings are statements of fact or rationale essential to support the determination and must cover each requirement of the statute or regulation. *Source:* FAR 1.701. FAR 1.704 requires that D&Fs set forth enough facts and circumstances to justify the specific determination clearly and convincingly. At a minimum, a D&F must include (1) identification of the agency and the contracting activity and of the document as a D&F; (2) a description of the contracting action; (3) citation of the appropriate statute and/or regulation; (4) findings that detail the particular circumstances, facts, or reasoning essential to support the determination; (5) a determination based on the findings; (6) the expiration date of the D&F, if required; and (7) the date and signature of the official authorized to sign the D&F. Further requirements may apply in a given situation; for example, FAR 14.407-4 lists specific types of statements that a D&F must contain in documenting the contracting officer's handling of a MISTAKE in A bid that the contractor discovers and asks to correct following contract award.

DEVELOPED   (1) With regard to rights in TECHNICAL DATA pertaining to NONCOMMERCIAL ITEMS procured by DOD. *Official:* An item, component, or process exists and is workable. Thus, the item or component must have been constructed or the process practiced. Workability is generally established when the item, component, or process has been analyzed or tested sufficiently to demonstrate to reasonable people skilled in the applicable art that there is a high probability that it will operate as intended. Whether, how much, and what type of analysis or testing is required to establish workability depends on the nature of the item, component, or process, and the state of the art. To be considered "developed," the item, component, or process need not be at the stage when it could be offered for sale or sold on the commercial market, nor must the item, component, or process be actually reduced to practice within the meaning of Title 35 of the United States Code. *Source:* The Rights in Technical Data—Noncommercial Items clause at DFARS 252.227-7013. (2) With regard to rights in COMPUTER SOFTWARE procured by DOD. *Official:* (1) A COMPUTER PROGRAM has been successfully operated in a computer and tested to the extent sufficient to demonstrate to reasonable persons skilled in the art that the program can reasonably be expected to perform its intended purpose, (2) COMPUTER SOFTWARE, other than computer programs, has been tested or analyzed to the extent sufficient to demonstrate to reasonable persons skilled in the art that the software can reasonably be expected to perform its intended purpose, or (3) COMPUTER SOFTWARE DOCUMENTATION required to be delivered under a contract has been written, in any medium, in sufficient detail to comply with the requirements under the contract. *Source:* The Rights in Noncommercial Computer Software and Noncommercial Computer Software Documentation clause at DFARS 252.227-7014. This condition is part of the determination of intellectual property rights in FAR Subpart 27.4 and DFARS Subparts 227.71 and 227.72 in that rights are given to the government only with regard to funds used in the development process. Although this is also a prerequisite for the government's obtaining of rights in the Rights in Data–General clause in FAR 52.227-14, the FAR contains no definition of this term. See Nash & Rawicz, INTELLECTUAL PROPERTY IN GOVERNMENT CONTRACTS, chaps. 4 & 5 (6th ed. 2008).

DEVELOPED AT PRIVATE EXPENSE   A condition of an item, component, or process wherein no part of the cost of development was paid for by the government. This term is used, without definition, in the policy on rights to TECHNICAL DATA in FAR Subpart 27.4. It was also used in the DOD clause prior to the enactment of 10 U.S.C. § 2320 in 1984. It was generally believed that private expense includes all costs not charged as DIRECT COSTs to a contract. See Nash & Rawicz, INTELLECTUAL PROPERTY IN GOVERNMENT CONTRACTS, chap. 4 (6th ed. 2008).

DEVELOPED EXCLUSIVELY AT PRIVATE EXPENSE   *Official:* Development was accomplished entirely with costs charged to indirect costs pools, costs not allocated to a government contract, or any combination thereof. (i) Private expense determinations should be made at the lowest practicable level. (ii) Under fixed-price contracts when total costs are greater than the firm-fixed-price or CEILING PRICE of the contract, the additional development costs necessary to complete development shall not be considered in determining whether development was at government, private, or mixed expense. *Source:* DFARS 252.227-7013 and -7014. This DOD definition pertains to the 1995 TECHNICAL DATA and COMPUTER SOFTWARE policy. The term was defined more restrictively in the 1988 DOD technical data and software policy where it meant that no part of the cost of development was paid for by the government and the development was not REQUIRED FOR PERFORMANCE of a government contract or subcontract. DFARS 252.227-7013 (pre-1995 version). Under this definition, INDEPENDENT RESEARCH AND DEVELOPMENT (IR&D) costs and BID AND PROPOSAL COSTS as defined in FAR 31.205-18, whether or not included in a formal IR&D program, were considered to be private expenses, but all other indirect costs of development were considered government funded when development was required for the performance of a government contract or subcontract. This definition is important because 10 U.S.C. § 2320(a)(2)(B) provides that, with certain exceptions, TECHNICAL DATA pertaining to items or processes developed exclusively at private expense may be submitted to the government with LIMITED RIGHTS markings prohibiting their disclosure except in specified circumstances. DFARS 227.7103-4(a)(1) Similarly, under the DOD computer software policy, software meeting this definition can generally be marked with RESTRICTED RIGHTS legends. DFARS 227.7203-4(a). See Nash & Rawicz, INTELLECTUAL PROPERTY IN GOVERNMENT CONTRACTS, chaps. 4 & 5 (6th ed. 2008).

DEVELOPED EXCLUSIVELY WITH GOVERNMENT FUNDS   *Official:* Development was not accomplished exclusively or partially at private expense. *Source:* DFARS 252.227-7013 and -7014. The term was defined more broadly in the 1988 DOD technical data and software policy. See DEVELOPED EXCLUSIVELY AT PRIVATE EXPENSE.

DEVELOPMENT   *Official:* The systematic use of scientific and technical knowledge in the design, development, testing, or evaluation of a potential new product or service (or of an improvement in an existing product or service) to meet specific performance requirements or objectives. It includes the functions of design engineering, prototyping, and engineering testing; it excludes subcontracted technical effort that is for the sole purpose of developing an additional source for an existing product. *Source:* FAR 35.001. It generally follows APPLIED RESEARCH in the RESEARCH AND DEVELOPMENT process. In the context of INDEPENDENT RESEARCH AND DEVELOPMENT, FAR 31.205-18 contains a similar definition with the additional exclusion of development effort for manufacturing or production of materials, systems, processes, methods, equipment, tools, and techniques not intended for sale. This excludes engineering work for the purpose of enhancing manufacturing processes from the IR&D COST PRINCIPLE. *DOD Financial Management Regulation* 7000.14-R, v. 2B, chap. 5 (Sept. 2012) breaks development into seven categories: basic research, applied research, advanced technology development, advanced component development and prototypes, system development and demonstration, management support, and operational system development.

DEVELOPMENTAL TEST AND EVALUATION (DT&E)   Testing and evaluation conducted throughout the life cycle of a program to (1) identify potential operational and technological capabilities and limitations of the alternative concepts and design options being pursued; (2) support the identification of cost-performance tradeoffs by providing analyses of the capabilities and limitations of alternatives; (3) support the identification and description of design technical risks; (4) assess progress toward meeting critical operational issues, mitigation of acquisition technical risk, achievement of manufacturing process requirements, and system maturity; (5) assess the validity of assumptions and conclusions from the analysis of alternatives; (6) provide data and analysis in support of the decision to certify the system ready for operational test and evaluation; and (7) in the case of automated information systems, support an information systems security certification prior to processing classified or sensitive data and ensure a standards conformance certification. DAU GLOSSARY. Such testing during the DEVELOPMENT process is contrasted with OPERATIONAL TEST AND EVALUATION which is conducted after the completion of development.

DEVIATION (FROM REGULATIONS)   *Official:* Any one or combination of the following: (a) The issuance or use of a policy, procedure, SOLICITATION PROVISION, contract CLAUSE, method, or practice of conducting acquisition actions of any kind, at any stage of the ACQUISITION PROCESS, that is inconsistent with the FAR; (b) The omission of any solicitation provision or contract clause when its prescription requires its use; (c) The use of any solicitation provision or contract clause with modified or alternate language not authorized by the FAR (see definition of "modification" in 52.101(a) and definition of "alternate" in 2.101(a); (d). The use of a solicitation provision or contract clause prescribed by the FAR on a "substantially as follows" or "substantially the same as" basis (see definitions in 2.101 and 52.101(a)), if such use is inconsistent with the intent, principle, or substance of the prescription or related coverage on the subject matter in the FAR; (e) The authorization of lesser or greater limitations on the use of any solicitation provision, contract clause, policy, or procedure prescribed by the FAR; and (f) The issuance of policies or procedures that govern the contracting process or otherwise control contracting relationships that are not incorporated into agency acquisition regulations in accordance with 1.301(a). *Source:* FAR 1.401. FAR Subpart 1.4 sets forth the procedures to be used in obtaining the authority to deviate from the FAR. FAR 52.107 requires contracting officers to use the Authorized Deviations in Provisions clause in FAR 52.252-5 and the Authorized Deviations in Clauses clause in FAR 52.252-6 to notify offerors and contractors when a solicitation or contract contains solicitation provisions or clauses that deviate from the FAR. See DFARS Subpart 201.4 for DOD's policy on deviations. Mandatory clauses that are omitted from a contract without a proper deviation are read into the contract following the CHRISTIAN DOCTRINE. See Cibinic, Nash & Yukins, FORMATION OF GOVERNMENT CONTRACTS 69–71 (4th ed. 2011).

DEVIATION (FROM SPECIFICATIONS)   A specific written authorization to depart from a particular requirement(s) of an item's current approved configuration documentation for a specific number of units or a specified period of time, and to accept an item which is found to depart from specified requirements, but nevertheless is considered suitable for use "as is" or after repair by an approved method. (A deviation differs from an engineering change in that an approved engineering change requires corresponding revision of the item's current approved configuration documentation, whereas a deviation does not.) DAU GLOSSARY.

DFARS PROCEDURES, GUIDANCE AND INFORMATION (DOD PGI) The supplement to the DFARS which publishes procedures, guidance and information that does not meet the standards established for inclusion of material in the DEPARTMENT OF DEFENSE FAR SUPPLEMENT (DFARS). DFARS 201.301(a)(2). This information should be read in conjunction with the DFARS to understand the full impact of DOD policy. It is available at www.acq.osd.mil/dpap/dars/index.htm.

DHS See DEPARTMENT OF HOMELAND SECURITY.

DIFFERING SITE CONDITIONS *Official:* (1) Subsurface or LATENT physical conditions at a site which differ materially from those indicated in the contract; or (2) unknown physical conditions at the site, of an unusual nature, which differ materially from those ordinarily encountered and generally recognized as inhering in work of the character provided for in the contract. *Source:* Differing Site Conditions clause in FAR 52.236-2. This standard clause in CONSTRUCTION contracts provides for an EQUITABLE ADJUSTMENT when the contractor encounters such conditions. The first category is commonly referred to as a "Type I" condition and the second category is commonly referred to as a "Type II" condition. The clause serves to take some of the risk out of bidding. For example, bidders do not have to take their own soil borings or consider how large a contingency allowance should be added to the bid price to cover the risk of unanticipated, unfavorable subsurface conditions. The government benefits from more accurate bidding, without inflation for potentially nonexistent risks, and pays for difficult subsurface or hidden work only when such work is found to be necessary but could not reasonably have been anticipated. See Cibinic, Nagle & Nash, ADMINISTRATION OF GOVERNMENT CONTRACTS, chap. 5 (5th ed. 2016).

DIGITAL MILLENNIUM COPYRIGHT ACT An Act providing sanctions for the circumvention of technological measures used to protect COPYRIGHTed works and tampering with copyright management information. The Act was enacted in 1998 in Pub. L. No. 105-304 and is codified in 17 U.S.C. § 1201 et seq. See Nash & Rawicz, INTELLECTUAL PROPERTY IN GOVERNMENT CONTRACTS, chap. 1 (6th ed. 2008).

DIRECT ACQUISITION *Official:* A type of INTERAGENCY ACQUISITION where a REQUESTING AGENCY places an order directly against a SERVICING AGENCY's indefinite-delivery contract. The servicing agency manages the indefinite-delivery contract but does not participate in the placement or administration of an order. *Source:* FAR 2.101. Agencies can only use direct acquisitions when they have made a determination that this procedure is the best procurement approach. FAR 17.502-1(a)(2). These acquisitions are conducted using FEDERAL SUPPLY SCHEDULES, GOVERNMENTWIDE ACQUISITION CONTRACTS and ECONOMY ACT orders. See Cibinic, Nash & Yukins, FORMATION OF GOVERNMENT CONTRACTS, chap. 8 (4th ed. 2011).

DIRECT COST *Official:* Any cost that is identified specifically with a particular final COST OBJECTIVE. Direct costs are not limited to items that are incorporated in the end product as MATERIAL or LABOR. Costs identified specifically with a contract are direct costs of that contract. All costs identified specifically with other final cost objectives of the contractor are direct costs of those cost objectives. *Source:* FAR 2.101. FAR 31.202(a) provides that no final cost objective may have any cost allocated to it (see ALLOCATION OF COST) as a direct cost if other costs incurred for the same purpose in like circumstances have been included in any INDIRECT COST POOL to be allocated to that or any other final cost objective. FAR 31.202(b) provides that for practical reasons, direct costs of minor dollar amounts may be treated as indirect costs if the accounting treatment is consistently applied and the results achieved are substantially the same as treating them as direct costs. 48 C.F.R. § 9904.418-50, Techniques for Application, provides guidance to account for direct costs. See Cibinic, Knight & Nash, COST-REIMBURSEMENT CONTRACTING 592–96 (4th ed. 2014); DAU, *Contract Pricing Reference Guides* v. III (Feb. 22, 2012).

DIRECT LABOR   Labor specifically identified with a particular final COST OBJECTIVE. Manufacturing direct labor includes fabrication, assembly, inspection, and testing of the end product. Engineering direct labor consists of reliability, quality assurance, test, design, and other engineering work readily identified with the end product. DAU GLOSSARY. Direct labor should be distinguished from indirect labor, which is labor assigned to an INDIRECT COST pool because it is identified with two or more cost objectives but not specifically allocable to any final cost objective.

DIRECT LICENSE   A LICENSE to use TECHNICAL DATA granted by the owner of the rights in that data directly to the party that will use the data. Direct licenses are permitted by DFARS 227.7103-5(d)(2)(ii), but the regulation gives no guidance on their use. They have an advantage over GOVERNMENT PURPOSE RIGHTS in that they establish a direct contractual relationship between the owner of the proprietary right and the user, without interjecting the government agency between the two parties. 10 U.S.C. § 2320(a)(1) requires that DOD regulations permit a contractor or subcontractor that directly licenses its technical data to receive a "fee or royalty." DOD PGI 217.7504(3)(i) states that direct licensing is one of the means of obtaining competition for REPLENISHMENT PARTS. One way to encourage direct licensing is to use the LEADER-COMPANY CONTRACTING process. See Nash & Rawicz, INTELLECTUAL PROPERTY IN GOVERNMENT CONTRACTS, chap. 8 (6th ed. 2008).

DIRECTIVE   A DEPARTMENT OF DEFENSE (DOD) issuance that transmits information required by law, the President, or the Secretary of Defense that applies to all branches of DOD. Directives establish or describe policy, programs, and organizations; define missions; provide authority; and assign responsibilities, but do not prescribe one-time tasks or deadline assignments. DOD Instruction 5025.01, *DOD Directives Program* (Aug. 1, 2016, ch. 3 May 22, 2019). See also DOD DIRECTIVES SYSTEM.

DISADVANTAGED BUSINESS   See SMALL DISADVANTAGED BUSINESS CONCERN (SCBC).

DISALLOWANCE   The refusal of the government to recognize a cost as an ALLOWABLE COST. FAR Subpart 42.8 prescribes policies and procedures for issuing notices of intent to disallow costs and disallowing costs already incurred during the course of performance. DOD has a form for this purpose: DCAA Form 1, Notice of Contract Costs Suspended and/or Disapproved. DFARS 242.803. FAR 42.801 provides that at any time during the performance of a COST-REIMBURSEMENT CONTRACT, FIXED-PRICE INCENTIVE CONTRACT, FIXED-PRICE REDETERMINATION—PROSPECTIVE CONTRACT, or FIXED-PRICE REDETERMINATION—RETROACTIVE CONTRACT, the contracting officer responsible for administering the contract may issue the contractor a written notice of intent to disallow specified costs incurred or planned for incurrence. The purpose of the notice is to inform the contractor of this intent as early as practicable and provide for timely resolution of any resulting disagreement. See the Notice of Intent to Disallow Costs clause in FAR 52.242-1. FAR 42.803 provides that under cost-reimbursement contracts, TIME AND MATERIALS, and LABOR-HOUR CONTRACTs, costs can be disallowed after incurrence and deducted from current payments. If a contractor disagrees with a post-incurrence disallowance, the contractor may request discussions with the contracting officer or file a CLAIM under the Disputes clause at FAR 52.233-1.

DISASTER RESPONSE REGISTRY   *Official:* A voluntary registry of contractors who are willing to perform debris removal, distribution of supplies, reconstruction, and other disaster or emergency relief activities established in accordance with 6 U.S.C. § 796, Registry of Disaster Response Contractors. The Registry contains information on contractors who are willing to perform disaster or emergency relief activities within the United States and its outlying areas. The Registry is accessed via https://www.sam.gov, Search Records, Advanced Search, Disaster Response Registry Search (See 26.205.) *Source:* FAR 2.101. Contracting officers are required to consult this registry when they are issuing EMERGENCY RESPONSE CONTRACTS for disaster and emergency assistance. FAR 26.205.

DISBURSING OFFICER (DO)   *Official:* A government officer or employee designated to pay out monies and render accounts in accordance with laws and regulations governing the disbursement of public funds. The disbursing officer must (1) disburse monies only upon, and in strict accordance with, VOUCHERs duly certified by the head of the agency or by an officer or employee duly authorized in writing to certify them; (2) examine vouchers as necessary to ascertain whether they are in proper form, duly certified and approved, and correctly computed on the basis of the facts certified; and (3) be held accountable accordingly, except that accountability for the correctness of the computations of certified vouchers lies with the CERTIFYING OFFICER and not the disbursing officer. *Source:* U.S. Gov't Accountability Office, Principles of Federal Appropriations Law: Annual Update to the Third Edition, Ch. 9, GAO-15-303SP (Washington, D.C.: Mar. 2015). See also 31 U.S.C. §§ 3322(a) and 3325(a); Cibinic, Nagle & Nash, Administration of Government Contracts 1034–35 (5th ed. 2016).

DISCLAIMER   See EXCULPATORY CLAUSE.

DISCLOSURE STATEMENT   *Official:* A written description of a contractor's cost accounting practices and procedures. The submission of a new or revised Disclosure Statement is not required for any non-CAS-covered contract or from any small business concern. *Source:* 48 C.F.R. § 9903.202-1. These statements are required by the COST ACCOUNTING STANDARDS and filed with the cognizant ADMINISTRATIVE CONTRACTING OFFICER, with a copy to the cognizant contract auditor. 48 C.F.R. § 9903.202-5. In general, a disclosure statement, on Form CASB-DS-1 or DS-2, must be submitted by any company or educational institution receiving CAS-COVERED CONTRACTs or subcontracts totaling $50 million or more in a cost accounting period. (Submission may also be required in certain other circumstances.) The presumed or anticipated presence of a competitive environment does not create an exemption from the requirement to submit a disclosure statement. 48 C.F.R. § 9903.202-1. After submission, disclosure statements are reviewed for adequacy by the cognizant auditor and the administrative contracting officer. FAR 30.202-7. Thereafter, the disclosed cost accounting practices must be followed or a change to the disclosure statement must be requested. See Cibinic, Knight & Nash, COST-REIMBURSEMENT CONTRACTING 531–33 (4th ed. 2014).

DISCOUNT FOR PROMPT PAYMENT   *Official:* An INVOICE PAYMENT reduction offered by the contractor for payment prior to the due date. *Source:* FAR 32.902. The Discounts for Prompt Payment clause at FAR 52.232-8 is included in fixed price contracts for supplies and services. FAR 32.111(b)(1). It provides that discounts are not taken into consideration in evaluating offers but will be taken in making payments. FAR 32.906(e) directs DESIGNATED PAYMENT OFFICEs to make payment as close as possible to the end of the discount period. See also PROMPT PAYMENT ACT.

DISCOVERY   The process of gathering and assessing evidence that the other party to a litigation has or intends to use. Generally, discovery is either in the form of a DEPOSITION or an INTERROGATORY. When the information to be discovered is privileged, it may be released subject to a PROTECTIVE ORDER. See Fed. R. Civ. P. 26(c). Discovery is permitted in appeals before the BOARDs OF CONTRACT APPEALS. See Uniform Rules 14 and 15. See McGovern, et al., *A Level Playing Field: Why Congress Intended the Boards of Contract Appeal to have Enforceable Subpoena Power Over Both Contractors and the Government*, 36 PUB. CONT. L.J. 495 (2007).

DISCREPANCIES INCIDENT TO SHIPMENT   *Official:* Any differences (e.g, count or condition) between the items documented to have been shipped and items actually received. *Source:* FAR 45.101. The Government Property clause in FAR 52.245-1 requires the contractor to adjust for such discrepancies in CONTRACTOR ACQUIRED PROPERTY during performance of its contract.

DISCRETION   A power or right to utilize judgment to take an action or arrive at a decision, without being constrained by a mandatory rule or procedure. To perform the actions necessary for effective contracting, ensuring compliance with the terms of contracts and safeguarding the interests of the United States in its contractual relationships, contracting officers are allowed wide latitude to exercise business judgment. FAR 1.602-2. FAR 1.102-2(c)(3) provides that "the Government shall exercise discretion, use sound business judgment, and comply with applicable laws and regulations in dealing with contractors and prospective contractors." Situations in which contracting officers are called on to exercise discretion include determining which PROPOSALs are in the COMPETITIVE RANGE (FAR 15.306), selecting the source for award of a contract (FAR 15.308), selecting the appropriate TYPE OF CONTRACT (FAR 16.104), deciding and settling CLAIMs (FAR 33.210), and determining when TERMINATION FOR DEFAULT or TERMINATION FOR CONVENIENCE is in the best interest of the government (FAR Part 49).

DISCRETIONARY FUNCTION   An act or decision of an official of the federal government which is of a discretionary nature and therefore exempts the government from TORT liability under the Federal Tort Claims Act, 28 U.S.C. § 2680(a). This act provides that the government is not liable for any claim based upon the execution in due care of a statute or regulation as well as exercise or performance of any discretionary function or duty, whether or not the discretion is abused. See FEDERAL TORT CLAIMS ACT.

DISCUSSION   An EXCHANGE in a procurement using COMPETITIVE PROPOSALS procedures, between the government and an offeror in the COMPETITIVE RANGE undertaken with the intent of allowing the offeror to revise its proposal. Discussions include

BARGAINING. FAR 15.306(d). The primary objective of discussions is to maximize the government's ability to obtain best value, based on the requirements and the evaluation factors set forth in the solicitation. FAR 15.306(d)(2). The contracting officer must discuss with each and every offeror still being considered for award, significant weaknesses, deficiencies, and adverse past performance information to which the offeror has not yet had an opportunity to respond. The contracting officer is encouraged to discuss other aspects of the proposal that could be altered or explained to enhance materially the proposal's potential for award. FAR 15.306(d)(3). If, after discussions have begun, an offeror in the competitive range is no longer considered to be among the most highly rated offerors being considered for award, that offeror may be eliminated from the competitive range whether or not all material aspects of the proposal have been discussed, or the offeror has been afforded an opportunity to submit a PROPOSAL REVISION. FAR 15.306(d)(5). At the conclusion of discussions, each offeror still in the competitive range must be given an opportunity to submit a FINAL PROPOSAL REVISION. FAR 15.307(b). Discussions must not (1) favor one offeror over another, (2) reveal an offeror's technical solution, including technology, innovative and unique uses of COMMERCIAL ITEMs, or any information that would compromise an offeror's intellectual property to another offeror, (3) reveal an offeror's price without that offeror's permission, nor (4) reveal the names of individuals providing information about an offeror's past performance. FAR 15.306(e). If discussions are held with one offeror, they must be held with all offerors in the COMPETITIVE RANGE. See Cibinic, Nash & Yukins, FORMATION OF GOVERNMENT CONTRACTS 888–25 (4th ed. 2011). See also Nash, *Misleading Discussions: A Disturbing New Rule*, 33 N&CR ¶ 8 (Feb. 2019); Nash, *Robust Discussions: Is There A Risk of Too Much Discretion?*, 26 N&CR ¶ 20 (Apr. 2012); Shearer, *How Could It Hurt To Ask? The Ability To Clarify Cost/Price Proposals Without Engaging In Discussions*, 39 PUB. CONT. L.J. 583 (2010); Nash, *Postscript: Communications With Offerors Before Establishing A Competitive Range*, 24 N&CR ¶ 47 (Oct. 2010); Edwards, *Meaningful Discussions: What Is The Standard?*, 24 N&CR ¶ 5 (Feb. 2010); Nash, *Discussions After Establishing The Competitive Range: Are They Mandatory?*, 22 N&CR ¶ 34 (June 2008).

DISMISSAL WAGES   See SEVERANCE PAY.

DISPUTE   A disagreement between the contractor and the contracting officer regarding the rights of the parties under a contract. Under the CONTRACT DISPUTES ACT (CDA) OF 1978, 41 U.S.C. §§ 7101–7109, contractors are permitted to submit CLAIMs (demands for a sum certain) against the government. Conversely, the government may make claims against contractors. There is no requirement that there be a dispute prior to the filing of a proper claim except where the issue is nonpayment of a VOUCHER, INVOICE, or routine request for payment. In normal circumstances, disputes are resolved through negotiation or by the use of ALTERNATIVE DISPUTE RESOLUTION procedures. FAR 33.204. If this is not possible, the dispute must become the subject of a DECISION OF THE CONTRACTING OFFICER with further resolution subject to the CDA. FAR Subpart 33.2 provides guidance to contracting officers on the handling of disputes. A dispute should be distinguished from a PROTEST: a dispute arises between a contractor and the government during or after the performance of a contract, whereas a protest involves an offeror or prospective contractor and contests the award of the contract or the conduct of the solicitation process itself. See Cibinic, Nagle & Nash, ADMINISTRATION OF GOVERNMENT CONTRACTS, chap. 13 (5th ed. 2016). See also Feldman & Fioravanti, *Contract Dispute or Bid Protest? The Delex Systems Dilemma*, 39 PUB. CONT. L.J. 483 (2009).

DISQUALIFICATION Exclusion of an offeror from a procurement because of an impropriety in the competitive process. Offerors have been disqualified by contracting officers or by the GOVERNMENT ACCOUNTABILITY OFFICE (GAO) because of a CONFLICT OF INTEREST, improper obtaining of information, or MISREPRESENTATION. See Cibinic, Nash & Yukins, FORMATION OF GOVERNMENT CONTRACTS 826–31 (4th ed. 2011). See also Nash, *Postscript: Material Misrepresentation*, 33 N&CR ¶ 64 (Nov. 2019).

DISTRIBUTION BASE A type of recorded accounting or other data common to all COST OBJECTIVEs to which costs accumulated in indirect cost pools are to be assigned. The most common bases are recorded accounting data such as DIRECT LABOR hours and direct labor dollars. Acceptable distribution bases may also consist of nonaccounting data such as floor space or meter readings. See Cibinic, Knight & Nash, COST-REIMBURSEMENT CONTRACTING 607–14 (4th ed. 2014). FAR 31.203(c) contains guidance for selecting a distribution base. See also BASE.

DIVERTING *Official:* Redirecting materials that might otherwise be placed in the waste stream to recycling or recovery, excluding diversion to waste-to-energy facilities. *Source:* FAR 36.001. It is the government's goal to divert at least 50% of construction and demolition materials and debris by the end of fiscal year 2015 to ensure pollution prevention and eliminate waste. FAR 36.104(b)(5). This policy was adopted in response to Executive Order No.13514, Federal Leadership in Environmental, Energy, and Economic Performance, 74 Fed. Reg. 52117 (Oct. 8, 2009).

DO RATING The lower of two priority ratings that can be assigned to a contract or order under the DEFENSE PRIORITIES AND ALLOCATIONS SYSTEM (DPAS), the higher rating being the DX RATING. A contractor or subcontractor receiving a contract or order with a DO Rating must give it a higher performance priority than all non-rated contracts or orders. Under Title I of the Defense Production Act of 1950, as amended, 50 U.S.C. § 2061 et seq., 15 C.F.R. §§ 700.70 and 700.74, willful failure to comply with the prioritization obligations under a rated order is punishable by fine, imprisonment, or both. See FAR Subpart 11.6; 15 C.F.R. part 700; DOD 4400.1-M, *Department of Defense Priorities and Allocations Manual*, Feb. 21, 2002.

DOCUMENTATION See COMPUTER SOFTWARE DOCUMENTATION.

DOD See DEPARTMENT OF DEFENSE.

DOD FAR SUPPLEMENT (DFARS) See DEPARTMENT OF DEFENSE FAR SUPPLEMENT.

DOD INDEX OF SPECIFICATIONS AND STANDARDS (DODISS) A list of SPECIFICATIONs and STANDARDs used by the DEPARTMENT OF DEFENSE. It comes in four parts, the first is an alphabetical list, the second is a numerical list, the third is a list of Federal Supply Classes, and the fourth is a list of cancelled documents. Most of the documents listed are available through DOD's Acquisition Streamlining and Standardization Information System (ASSIST), https://www.dau.edu/tools/t/Acquisition-Streamlining-and-Standardization-Information-System-(ASSIST) and www.assistdocs.com.

DOD GRANT AND AGREEMENT REGULATIONS (DODGARS) Regulations in 32 C.F.R. part 21 through part 37 prescribing rules and procedures for the award of GRANTs, COOPERATIVE AGREEMENTs, and some OTHER TRANSACTIONS by DOD agencies. Since these types of contracts are not PROCUREMENT CONTRACTs, the regulations give agencies more discretion than the FAR. Under this regulation, cooperative agreements and research other transactions are called TECHNOLOGY INVESTMENT AGREEMENTs and are covered in 32 C.F.R. part 37. See Nash & Rawicz, Intellectual Property in Government Contracts, chap. 7 (6th ed. 2008).

DOD PRIVACY PROGRAM   DOD's implementation of the PRIVACY ACT. See DOD Directive 5400.11, *DOD Privacy Program*, Oct. 29, 2014.

DOE   See DEPARTMENT OF ENERGY.

DOI   See DEPARTMENT OF THE INTERIOR.

DOJ   See DEPARTMENT OF JUSTICE.

DOL   See DEPARTMENT OF LABOR.

DOLLAR THRESHOLD   A dollar amount that determines the applicability of a law, regulation, or policy to an acquisition based on whether the dollar value of the acquisition is expected to be less than, equal to, or more than the amount. FAR 1.108(c) states that dollar thresholds apply to "the final anticipated dollar value" of a contract, including OPTIONs, unless a law or regulation specifies otherwise. FAR 1.108(c) also states that if a contract will set a maximum amount of supplies or services to be purchased either in terms of quantity or dollar value, or if it will set a ceiling price, then the dollar threshold applies to the maximum or the ceiling. The most well-known examples of dollar thresholds are the MICRO-PURCHASE THRESHOLD and the SIMPLIFIED ACQUISITION THRESHOLD, which are defined in FAR 2.101, and the threshold for requiring submission of CERTIFIED COST OR PRICING DATA, which is defined in FAR 15.403-4(a)(1). 41 U.S.C. § 1908 requires periodic adjustment for inflation of certain acquisition related dollar thresholds. See FAR 1.109. The adjustments are to be made every five years using the Consumer Price Index for all urban consumers.

DOMESTIC CONSTRUCTION MATERIAL   (1) Under the BUY AMERICAN ACT: *Official:* (a) An unmanufactured CONSTRUCTION MATERIAL mined or produced in the United States; (b) A construction material manufactured in the United States, if—(i) The cost of the COMPONENTs mined, produced, or manufactured in the United States exceeds 50% of the cost of all its components. Components of foreign origin of the same class or kind for which nonavailability determinations have been made are treated as domestic; or (ii) The construction material is a COTS item. *Source:* FAR 25.003. The policies applicable to these materials are set forth in FAR Subpart 25.2. The cost of each component includes cost of transportation to the place of incorporation into the construction material and any applicable duty (whether or not a duty-free entry certificate is issued). Components of foreign origin are treated as domestic if they are of the same class or kind for which it has been determined that the material is not mined, produced, or manufactured in the United States in sufficient and reasonably available commercial quantities of a satisfactory quality. The components requirement is waived if the construction material is a commercially available off the shelf item. FAR 25.003. Exceptions to the required use of domestic construction materials include when: 1) their use would be impracticable or inconsistent with the public interest; 2) domestic materials are not available; 3) the cost would be unreasonable; or 4) the material is information technology that is a commercial item. FAR 25.202. (2) Under the AMERICAN RECOVERY AND REINVESTMENT ACT: *Official:* (1) An unmanufactured construction material mined or produced in the United States. (The Buy American Act applies.) (2) A manufactured construction material that is manufactured in the United States and, if the construction material consists wholly or predominantly of iron or steel, the iron or steel was produced in the United States. (Section 1605 of the Recovery Act applies.) *Source:* FAR 25.601. The narrower rules for procurements under this Act are set forth in FAR Subpart 25.6. See Cibinic, Nash & Yukins, FORMATION OF GOVERNMENT CONTRACTS 1614–24 (4th ed. 2011).

DOMESTIC END PRODUCT *Official:* (1) An unmanufactured end product mined or produced in the United States; (2) An end product manufactured in the United States, if—(i) the cost of its components mined, produced, or manufactured in the United States exceeds 50% of the cost of all its components. Components of foreign origin of the same class or kind as those that the agency determines are not mined, produced, or manufactured in sufficient and reasonably available commercial quantities of a satisfactory quality are treated as domestic. Scrap generated, collected, and prepared for processing in the United States is considered domestic; or (ii) the end product is a COTS item. *Source:* FAR 25.003. These products are given preference under the BUY AMERICAN ACT as implemented in FAR Subparts 25.1 and 25.2. The cost of each component includes cost of transportation to the place of incorporation into the end product and any applicable duty (whether or not a duty-free certificate is issued). The cost of components manufacturer by the contractor includes all costs associated with manufacture including indirect costs but excluding profit. Components of foreign origin are treated as domestic if they are of the same class or kind for which it has been determined either (1) that domestic preference would be inconsistent with the public interest; or (2) that they are not mined, produced, or manufactured in the United States in sufficient and reasonably available commercial quantities of a satisfactory quality. FAR 25.103. See Cibinic, Nash & Yukins, FORMATION OF GOVERNMENT CONTRACTS 1614–24 (4th ed. 2011).

DOMESTIC MANUFACTURING REQUIREMENT A requirement of the BAYH-DOLE ACT that SMALL BUSINESS CONCERNs and NONPROFIT ORGANIZATIONs that receive title to a PATENT will not grant to any person the exclusive right to use or sell any SUBJECT INVENTION unless that person agrees that any product embodying the invention will be manufactured substantially in the United States. 35 U.S.C. § 204. This requirement is implemented in the PATENT RIGHTS clauses. See Nash & Rawicz, INTELLECTUAL PROPERTY IN GOVERNMENT CONTRACTS, chap. 2 (6th ed. 2008).

DOMESTIC OFFER *Official:* An offer of a DOMESTIC END PRODUCT. When the solicitation specifies that award will be made on a group of line items, a domestic offer means an offer where the proposed price of the D0MESTIC END PRODUCTs exceeds 50% of the total proposed price of the group. *Source:* FAR 25.003. When a procurement is subject to the BUY AMERICAN ACT, the government may accept only domestic offers unless an exception applies. See Cibinic, Nash & Yukins, FORMATION OF GOVERNMENT CONTRACTS 1614–24 (4th ed. 2011).

DOMESTIC PREFERENCE See BALANCE OF PAYMENTS PROGRAM; BUY AMERICAN ACT; CARGO PREFERENCE ACTS; CARIBBEAN BASIN ECONOMIC RECOVERY ACT; DOMESTIC END PRODUCT; TRADE AGREEMENTS ACT OF 1979.

DONATION A gift of cash, property, or services to a charitable organization. FAR 31.205-8 provides that the costs of donations are UNALLOWABLE COSTs unless they are PUBLIC

RELATIONS costs incurred from participation in community service activities, such as blood bank drives, charity drives, or disaster assistance. See Cibinic, Knight & Nash, COST-REIMBURSEMENT CONTRACTING 722 (4th ed. 2014).

DOT See DEPARTMENT OF TRANSPORTATION.

DOWN-SELECT A two-step procurement technique where, as a first step, the number of competitors is reduced by preliminary screening, and in the second step, a competitively negotiated procurement is conducted between the remaining competitors. FAR 15.202 provides for the use of an ADVISORY MULTI-STEP SOURCE SELECTION when appropriate. FAR Subpart 9.2 provides for a more formal type of PRE-QUALIFICATION. The FEDERAL AVIATION ADMINISTRATION also uses a SCREENING procedure to make down selects.

DRAWINGS A set of documents giving the details of manufacture or construction. Drawings typically contain dimensions and tolerances to be followed, materials or components to be used, testing requirements, and other specific information. They are frequently called DESIGN SPECIFICATIONS. See Nash & Feldman, 1 GOVERNMENT CONTRACT CHANGES § 4:11 (3d ed. 2006–2020).

DRUG-FREE WORKPLACE *Official:* The site(s) for the performance of work done by a contractor in connection with a specific contract where employees of the contractor are prohibited from engaging in the unlawful manufacture, distribution, dispensing, possession, or use of a CONTROLLED SUBSTANCE. *Source:* FAR 2.101. FAR Subpart 23.5 implements the Drug-Free Workplace Act of 1988, 41 U.S.C. § 8102 et seq., and applies to domestic government contracts above the SIMPLIFIED ACQUISITION THRESHOLD that do not procure COMMERCIAL PRODUCTs or COMMERCIAL SERVICEs. To ensure compliance the Drug-Free Workplace clause in FAR 52.223-6 is included in all contracts to which the Act applies. This clause requires, among other things, posting notices to employees, establishing drug-free awareness programs, requiring notification by employees of related convictions, and making a good-faith effort to maintain a drug-free workplace. Failure to comply may result in suspension of payments, TERMINATION FOR DEFAULT, or SUSPENSION or DEBARMENT of the contractor. See Feldman, GOVERNMENT CONTRACT GUIDEBOOK, § 8:45 (4th ed. 2019–2020); Cibinic, Nash & Yukins, FORMATION OF GOVERNMENT CONTRACTS 1669–71 (4th ed. 2011).

DRY BULK CARRIER *Official:* A vessel used primarily for the carriage of shipload lots of homogeneous unmarked nonliquid cargoes such as grain, coal, cement, and lumber. *Source:* FAR 47.501. This term is used in connection with implementing the policies of the CARGO PREFERENCE ACTS and the Merchant Marine Act of 1936, which give preference to U.S.-FLAG VESSELs when ocean transportation of supplies is required. See the Preference for Privately Owned U.S.-Flag Commercial Vessels clause in FAR 52.247-64, which requires contractors to compute shipments in such vessels separately in determining whether they have met the requirement that at least 50% of the gross tonnage shipped be in U.S.-flag vessels.

DRY CARGO LINER *Official:* A vessel used for the carriage of heterogeneous marked cargoes in parcel lots. However, any cargo may be carried in these vessels, including part cargoes of dry bulk items or, when carried in deep tanks, bulk liquids such as petroleum and vegetable oils. *Source:* FAR 47.501. This term is used in connection with implementing the policies of the CARGO PREFERENCE ACTS and the Merchant Marine Act of 1936, which give preference to U.S.-FLAG VESSELs when ocean transportation of supplies is required. See the Preference for Privately Owned U.S.-Flag Commercial Vessels clause in FAR 52.247-64, which requires contractors to compute shipments in such vessels separately in determining whether they have met the requirement that at least 50% of the gross tonnage shipped be in U.S.-flag vessels.

DSP   See DEFENSE STANDARDIZATION PROGRAM.

DUAL SOURCE   The existence of two or more sources for the same product or service. DFARS 215.403-1(c) provides that the determination that ADEQUATE PRICE COMPETITION exists in dual source programs, in order to avoid obtaining CERTIFIED COST OR PRICING DATA, must be made on a case-by-case basis. However, it provides that adequate price competition normally exists when prices are solicited across the full range of quantities from at least two offerors and PRICE ANALYSIS establishes that the prices are reasonable.

DUE DATE   The date when payment is due in order to avoid the payment of interest by the government pursuant to the PROMPT PAYMENT ACT. Due dates for INVOICE PAYMENTs must be specified in contracts in accordance with the guidance in FAR 32.904. As a general rule, payments are not to be made earlier than seven days prior to the due date. FAR 32.906(a).

DUE PROCESS OF LAW   A guarantee, found in the Fifth and Fourteenth amendments of the U.S. Constitution, of fundamentally fair treatment by the government. *Substantive* due process requires that no person be arbitrarily denied life, liberty, or property by government action. *Procedural* due process includes notice by the government and an opportunity to be heard by the government prior to the infringement of a liberty or property interest by the government. Procedural requirements increase with the importance of the interest taken. BLACK'S LAW DICTIONARY 632 (11th ed. 2019). In government contracting, the issue of due process arises whenever a contractor claims that it has been denied a liberty or property right without proper procedures. Such claims may arise in DEBARMENT and SUSPENSION actions, TERMINATION FOR DEFAULT, and nonresponsibility (see RESPONSIBILITY) determinations. See, for example, *Old Dominion Dairy Products, Inc. v. Secretary of Defense*, 631 F.2d 953 (D.C. Cir. 1980), in which the court found that a liberty interest was infringed without due process in a nonresponsibility determination.

DURESS   A condition in which one party is induced by a wrongful act or threat of another party to enter into a contract under circumstances depriving the first party of the exercise of its free will. Like "undue influence," duress includes conduct that overpowers a party's will and coerces or constrains performance of an act that otherwise would not have been performed. BLACK'S LAW DICTIONARY 636 (11th ed. 2019). Duress is also known as business compulsion. The elements of duress in government contracting are (1) threat of economic harm which is improper as a violation of the contracting officer's DUTY OF GOOD FAITH AND FAIR DEALING; and (2) a showing that the contractor's will was overborne (i.e., that the contractor accepted contract terms because circumstances permitted no alternative). See Cibinic, Nagle & Nash, ADMINISTRATION OF GOVERNMENT CONTRACTS 1125–26 (5th ed. 2016). Theoretically, duress, UNCONSCIONABILITY, and undue influence may differ, but all are aimed at unconscionable conduct by one party that may permit the other party to avoid a contract (see AVOIDANCE OF CONTRACT).

DURING THE CONDUCT OF A PROCUREMENT   The period that begins on the earliest date on which an identifiable, specific action is taken for a particular procurement and concludes on the AWARD or MODIFICATION of a contract or the cancellation of the procurement. The term included evaluation of OFFERs, SOURCE SELECTION, and conduct of NEGOTIATIONs. It defined the period during which the PROCUREMENT INTEGRITY rules applied before the Procurement Integrity Act was amended in 1996, but it no longer has any relevance. Under that Act, each award or each modification constituted a separate procurement action—that is, a separate period during which the prohibitions and requirements regarding procurement integrity applied. Some agencies promulgated additional guidance on the determination of the beginning date of this period.

DUTY OF GOOD FAITH AND FAIR DEALING   An implied obligation of all contracting parties to treat each other fairly during the performance and enforcement of a contract. RESTATEMENT (SECOND) OF CONTRACTS § 205 (1981). "Good faith" is defined at U.C.C. § 1-201 as "honesty in fact in the conduct or transaction concerned." The *Restatement* describes "good faith performance" as follows: "Subterfuges and evasions violate the obligation of good faith in performance even though the actor believes his conduct to be justified. But the obligation goes further: bad faith may be overt or may consist of inaction, and fair dealing may require more than honesty. A complete catalogue of types of bad faith is impossible, but the following types are among those which have been recognized in judicial decisions: evasion of the spirit of the bargain, lack of diligence and slacking off, willful rendering of imperfect performance, abuse of a power to specify terms, and interference with or failure to cooperate in the other party's performance." When this implied duty is discussed in the context of a government contract dispute, it is usually in reference to the government's DUTY TO COOPERATE. See Nash & Feldman, 1 GOVERNMENT CONTRACT CHANGES §§ 12:1–12:14 (3d ed. 2006–2020); Cibinic, Nagle & Nash, ADMINISTRATION OF GOVERNMENT CONTRACTS 272–88 (5th ed. 2016). See also Nash, *Postscript VIII: Breach of the Duty of Good Faith and Fair Dealing*, 33 N&CR ¶ 3 (Jan. 2019).

DUTY OF VERIFICATION   The contracting officer's obligation, when a MISTAKE in a BID is suspected, to call the mistake or the affected portion of the bid to the offeror's attention, ask for verification that no mistake was made and allow the offeror either to correct the bid before award is made or to withdraw it altogether if a mistake is identified. FAR 14.407 discusses the procedures to be followed in SEALED BIDDING. FAR Part 15 contains no explicit verification requirement in conducting COMPETITIVE NEGOTIATIONs, but FAR 15.306(b) references FAR 14.407 for the procedures to be followed when a mistake in a proposal is suspected. Requests for verification must inform the offeror of the facts that led the contracting officer to suspect a mistake. If the contracting officer fails to seek verification, the government may be subject to claims for PRICE ADJUSTMENT through contract reformation or the contractor may use a claimed mistake as a basis for avoiding performance obligations. See Cibinic, Nash & Yukins, FORMATION OF GOVERNMENT CONTRACTS 630–34 and 783–96 (4th ed. 2011). See also Nash, *Postscript: Verification of Proposals When Mistakes Are Suspected*, 17 N&CR ¶ 56 (Nov. 2003).

DUTY TO COOPERATE   An implied duty of a contracting party to cooperate with the other party to facilitate the performance of the contract. This duty is most frequently used to hold the government liable for a CONSTRUCTIVE CHANGE when the government does not assist the contractor. Under RESTATEMENT (SECOND) OF CONTRACTS § 205 (1981), this duty is defined as one aspect of the DUTY OF GOOD FAITH AND FAIR DEALING. See

Nash & Feldman, 1 GOVERNMENT CONTRACT CHANGES §§ 12:1–12:13 (3d ed. 2006–2020); Cibinic, Nagle & Nash, ADMINISTRATION OF GOVERNMENT CONTRACTS 276–82 (5th ed. 2016). See also Nash, *Postscript: Breach of the Duty of Good Faith and Fair Dealing*, 24 N&CR ¶ 22 (May 2010); Nash, *The Government's Duty of Good Faith and Fair Dealing: Proving a Breach*, 23 N&CR ¶ 66 (Dec. 2009); Ramos, *Never Say Die: The Continued Existence of the Government Officials' Good Faith Presumption in Federal Contracting Law and the Well-Nigh Irrefragable Proof Standard After Tecom*, 63 A.F.L. REV. 163 (2009).

DUTY TO DISCLOSE INFORMATION   See SUPERIOR KNOWLEDGE.

DUTY TO INQUIRE   See DUTY TO SEEK CLARIFICATION.

DUTY TO PROCEED   The obligation of a government contractor to continue to prosecute work under a government contract or risk TERMINATION FOR DEFAULT (see FAILURE TO MAKE PROGRESS). The Disputes clause in FAR 52.233-1 states that the contractor "shall proceed diligently with performance of this contract, pending final resolution of any request for relief, claim, appeal, or action ARISING UNDER THE CONTRACT, and comply with any decision of the Contracting Officer." Alternate I to that clause, used in MAJOR SYSTEM contracts, requires the contractor to proceed in the face of disputes arising under the contract or RELATING TO THE CONTRACT. With regard to a CHANGE ORDER, the contractor must, except under cost or fund limitations, continue performance of the contract as changed. The Changes—Fixed-Price clause in FAR 52.243-1 (for supply and services contracts) states: "Failure to agree to any adjustment shall be a dispute under the Disputes clause. However, nothing in this clause shall excuse the Contractor from proceeding with the contract as changed." See also the Commencement, Prosecution, and Completion of Work clause in FAR 52.211-10. Exceptions to the duty to proceed are BREACH OF CONTRACT by the government, CARDINAL CHANGE, and IMPRACTICABILITY. However, it is uncertain whether these exceptions apply to the Alternate I clause. See Nash & Feldman, 1 GOVERNMENT CONTRACT CHANGES §§ 6:1– 6:9 (3d ed. 2006–2020); Cibinic, Nagle & Nash, ADMINISTRATION OF GOVERNMENT CONTRACTS 823–34 (5th ed. 2016); Nash, *Postscript II: "Disputes" Clause Duty to Proceed*, 21 N&CR ¶ 29 (July 2007).

DUTY TO SEEK CLARIFICATION   The duty of an offeror to request the guidance of the contracting officer when competing for a contract that contains a patent AMBIGUITY, obvious omission, or drastic conflict. The offeror's failure to seek clarification in such circumstances is a valid government defense to a CLAIM for EQUITABLE ADJUSTMENT because of ambiguous specifications. See Nash & Feldman, 1 GOVERNMENT CONTRACT CHANGES § 11:20 (3d ed. 2006–2020); Cibinic, Nagle & Nash, ADMINISTRATION OF GOVERNMENT CONTRACTS 219–24 (5th ed. 2016).

DX RATING   The higher of two priority ratings that can be assigned to a contract or order under the DEFENSE PRIORITIES AND ALLOCATIONS SYSTEM, the lower rating being the DO Rating. A contractor or subcontractor receiving a contract or order with a DX Rating must give it a higher performance priority than all lower-rated and non-rated contracts or orders. Under Title I of the Defense Production Act of 1950, as amended, 50 U.S.C. § 2061 et seq., 15 C.F.R. §§ 700.70 and 700.74, willful failure to comply with the prioritization obligations under a rated order is punishable by fine, imprisonment, or both. See FAR Subpart 11.6; 15 C.F.R. part 700; DOD 4400.1-M, *Department of Defense Priorities and Allocations Manual*, Feb. 21, 2002.

E

EARNED VALUE   In an EARNED VALUE MANAGEMENT SYSTEM (EVMS), the value of completed work expressed in terms of the budget assigned to that work, also referred to as the BUDGETED COST OF THE WORK PERFORMED (BCWP). Government Electronics and Information Technology Association, *GEIA Standard: Earned Value Management Systems*, ANSI/EIA-748-B-2007 (Sept. 2007) and DOD, *Earned Value Management Implementation Guide* (Jan. 2018). The BCWP is compared to the BUDGETED COST OF THE WORK SCHEDULED and the ACTUAL COST OF THE WORK PERFORMED (ACWP) in order to determine the schedule and cost status of a project.

EARNED VALUE MANAGEMENT SYSTEM (EVMS)   *Official:* A project management tool that effectively integrates the project scope of work with cost, schedule, and performance elements for optimum project planning and control. The qualities and operating characteristics of an earned value management system are described in American National Standards Institute /Electronics Industries Alliance (ANSI/EIA) Standard-748, *Earned Value Management Systems*. (See OMB Circular A-11, Part 7.) *Source:* FAR 2.101. It is a method of comparing accomplishment to the plan for performance in order to determine project status and predict expected outcomes based on progress to date. Earned value management is based primarily on a STATEMENT OF WORK, a WORK BREAKDOWN STRUCTURE, a structure of cost accounts, and four key parameters: BUDGETED COST OF THE WORK SCHEDULED, BUDGETED COST OF THE WORK PERFORMED (EARNED VALUE), ACTUAL COST OF THE WORK PERFORMED, and ESTIMATE AT COMPLETION (EAC). BCWS—BCWP indicates schedule status. BCWP—ACWP indicates cost status. In formal earned value management systems, earned value is determined through one of three methods: Discrete Effort, Apportioned Effort, and Level of Effort. FAR 34.201 requires use of EVMS for major acquisitions in accordance with OMB Circular A-11. This requirement is implemented by the Notice of Earned Value Management System—Pre-Award IBR solicitation provision in FAR 52.234-2, the Notice of Earned Value Management System—Post-Award IBR solicitation provision in FAR 52.234-3, and the Earned Value Management System clause in FAR 52.234-4 or agency variations and applies to contractors and to subcontractors in accordance with specified criteria. When an EVM system is required, FAR 34.202 requires the conduct of an INTEGRATED BASELINE REVIEW, which is jointly conducted by an offeror or contractor and the government to determine the soundness of the contractor's system. Because EVMS are costly to establish and administer, agencies generally use them only for relatively large acquisitions that meet certain criteria. See, e.g., DFARS 234.201 and NFS 1834.201. See also Government Electronics and

Information Technology Association, *GEIA Standard: Earned Value Management Systems*, ANSI/EIA-748-B-2007 (Sept. 2007); LeeVan & Willard, *A Beginner's Guide To Program Metrics*, BRIEFING PAPERS No. 06-7 (June 2006); and DOD, *Earned Value Management Systems Interpretation Guide* (Apr. 2, 2015).

E-COMMERCE   See ELECTRONIC COMMERCE

ECONOMIC DURESS   See DURESS.

ECONOMIC ESPIONAGE ACT OF 1996   Pub. L. No. 104-294, 18 U.S.C. §§ 1831(a) and 1832. A law that makes it a crime to steal a TRADE SECRET either for the benefit of a foreign entity or any other person that will use it to place a product in interstate commerce. The law provides for imprisonment of persons for significant periods of time and for substantial monetary penalties for organizations. See Manos, 3 GOVERNMENT CONTRACT COSTS AND PRICING § 91:25 (2d ed. 2009–2020); Nash & Rawicz, INTELLECTUAL PROPERTY IN GOVERNMENT CONTRACTS, chap. 1 (6th ed. 2008).

ECONOMIC ORDER QUANTITY (EOQ)   A quantity of SUPPLIES that will result in a TOTAL COST and UNIT COST most advantageous to the government, where practicable, and does not exceed the quantity reasonably expected to be required by the agency. 10 U.S.C. § 2384a and 41 U.S.C. § 3310 require agencies to procure economic order quantities and to include a provision in solicitations inviting offerors to state an opinion on whether the quantity of supplies being procured is economically advantageous to the government. This requirement is implemented by FAR Subpart 7.2 and the Economic Purchase Quantity—Supplies solicitation provision at FAR 52.207-4. Economic order quantities can also be procured by the DOD in advance of the procurement of multiyear items under the advance acquisition procedures used in MULTIYEAR CONTRACTING. See DFARS 217.174. In the field of inventory management, economic order quantity has long been a topic of intensive study, and there is considerable literature about it. Operations research analysts have developed elaborate mathematical models for determining economic order quantities. See Roach, *Origins of the Economic Order Quantity Formula*, Working Paper Series No. 37 (Washburn University School of Business, Jan. 2005).

ECONOMIC PLANNING COSTS   *Official:* The costs of general long-range management planning that is concerned with the future overall development of the contractor's business and that may take into account the eventual possibility of economic dislocations or fundamental alterations in those markets in which the contractor currently does business. *Source:* FAR 31.205-12. Economic planning costs do not include ORGANIZATION COSTS or reorganization costs. Economic planning costs are ALLOWABLE COSTs. See Manos, 2 GOVERNMENT CONTRACT COSTS & PRICING § 74:6 (2d ed. 2009–2020); Cibinic, Knight & Nash, COST-REIMBURSEMENT CONTRACTING 656 (4th ed. 2014).

ECONOMIC PRICE ADJUSTMENT (EPA)   See FIXED-PRICE CONTRACT WITH ECONOMIC PRICE ADJUSTMENT.

ECONOMICALLY DISADVANTAGED INDIVIDUALS   *Official:* SOCIALLY DISADVANTAGED INDIVIDUALS whose ability to compete in the free enterprise system has been impaired due to diminished opportunities to obtain capital and credit as compared with others in the same or similar line of business who are not socially disadvantaged. *Source:* 13 C.F.R. § 124.104. Persons who certify that they are members of named groups (Black Americans, Hispanic Americans, NATIVE AMERICANS, ASIAN-PACIFIC AMERICANS,

SUBCONTINENT-ASIAN AMERICANS) are presumed to be socially disadvantaged. 13 C.F.R. § 124.103. They must then demonstrate to the SMALL BUSINESS ADMINIS-TRATION that they are economically disadvantaged. Businesses owned by such individuals are given special preferences in government procurement. See SMALL DISADVANTAGED BUSINESS CONCERN. See Cibinic, Nash & Yukins, FORMATION OF GOVERNMENT CON-TRACTS 1600–08 (4th ed. 2011); Taylor, *The End of an Era? How Affirmative Action in Government Contracting Can Survive After Rothe*, 39 PUB. CONT. L.J. 853 (2010); Hewitt, Williams & Alba, *Small Business Contracting Programs—Part II*, BRIEFING PAPERS No. 10-13 (Dec. 2010).

ECONOMICALLY DISADVANTAGED WOMEN-OWNED SMALL BUSINESS (EDWOSB)
Official: A SMALL BUSINESS CONCERN that is not less than 51% unconditionally and directly owned and controlled by one or more women who are United States citizens and are economically disadvantaged. *Source:* 13 C.F.R. § 127.200. A woman is economically disadvantaged if she can demonstrate that her ability to compete in the free enterprise system has been impaired due to diminished capital and credit opportunities as compared to others in the same or similar line of business and meet the other criteria in 13 C.F.R. § 127.203. See Cibinic, Nash & Yukins, FORMATION OF GOVERNMENT CON-TRACTS 1612–14 (4th ed. 2011); Hewitt, *Small Business Contracting Programs: An Update*, BRIEFING PAPERS No. 12-8 (July 2012); Meagher, *The Women-Owned Small Business Federal Contract Program: Ten Years In The Making*, 46 The Procurement Lawyer 1 (Winter 2011); Hewitt, Williams & Alba, *Small Business Contracting Programs-Part II*, BRIEFING PAPERS No. 10-13 (Dec. 2010); Hewitt, Williams & Alba, *Small Business Contracting Programs—Part I*, BRIEFING PAPERS No. 10-11 (Oct. 2010). See also www.sba.gov/WOSB.

ECONOMIES OF SCALE   Factors that enable a business to reduce the average cost of producing a product by increasing the volume of its output. Such factors include increased labor efficiency, volume price discounts for materials, and a broader base of allocation for fixed costs. The benefits are most commonly reflected in a reduction in unit cost. Economies of scale can be offset by diseconomies of scale if a business's size makes it less efficient. See Chandler, *Scale and Scope: The Dynamics of Industrial Capitalism* (Harvard 1994); Stigler, *The Economies of Scale*, 1 J.L. ECON. 54 (Oct. 1958).

ECONOMIES OF SCOPE   Factors that enable a business to reduce product costs by producing two or more products simultaneously. Such factors include the sharing of inputs such as productive capacity and administrative services. Economies of scope can be offset by diseconomies of scope to the extent that simultaneous production is more costly. See Chandler, *Scale and Scope: The Dynamics of Industrial Capitalism* (Harvard 1994); Panzar & Willig, *Economies of Scope,* 71 Am. Econ. Rev. 268 (May 1981).

ECONOMY ACT   A law that permits agencies to obtain supplies or services from other agencies through INTERAGENCY ACQUISITION and to place orders between major organizational units within an agency. 31 U.S.C. § 1535. Agencies must comply with FAR 17.502 and 17.503 in order to proceed with an interagency acquisition pursuant to the Economy Act. See Cibinic, Nash & Yukins, FORMATION OF GOVERNMENT CONTRACTS 1135–36 (4th ed. 2011); U.S. GOV'T ACCOUNTABILITY OFFICE, PRINCIPLES OF FEDERAL APPROPRIATIONS LAW: ANNUAL UPDATE TO THE THIRD EDITION, Ch. 12, GAO-15-303SP (Washington, D.C.: Mar. 2015); Edwards, *Obligating Funds Under the Economy Act: A Clarification*, 20 N&CR ¶8 (Feb. 2006).

EDUCATION COSTS   Costs of education that are related to the field in which a bona fide employee is working or may reasonably be expected to work. FAR 31.205-44 specifies that such costs are ALLOWABLE COSTs with some limitations. See also TRAINING COSTS. See Manos, 1 GOVERNMENT CONTRACT COSTS & PRICING §§ 51:1–51:3 (2d ed. 2009–2020); Cibinic, Knight & Nash, COST-REIMBURSEMENT CONTRACTING 707–08 (4th ed. 2014).

EFFECTIVE COMPETITION   *Official*: A market condition that exists when two or more contractors, acting independently, actively contend for the government's business in a manner that ensures that the government will be offered the lowest cost or price alternative or best technical design meeting its minimum needs. *Source:* FAR 34.001. In MAJOR SYSTEM ACQUISITION, the program manager is required to both promote FULL AND OPEN COMPETITION and sustain effective competition between alternative major system concepts and sources, as long as it is economically beneficial and practicable to do so. FAR 34.005-1. The term is used informally and without specific meaning in FAR 5.101(b)(4)(i). It is also used informally and without specific meaning in various publications to denote a degree of competition that is generally effective in producing a good result for the government, but that is less exacting than FULL AND OPEN COMPETITION. See Schank, et al., *Acquisition and Competition Strategy Options for the DD(X), The U.S. Navy's 21st Century Destroyer* (RAND Corp. 2006); Nash, *Postscript IV: The Competition Cure-All*, 23 N&CR ¶ 48 (Sept. 2009).

EFFECTIVE DATE   (OF A CONTRACT) The date on which the parties to a contract become bound by its terms and on which the contract becomes enforceable. It is the date of CONTRACT FORMATION unless the parties stipulate a different date in a clause such as Approval of Contract clause in FAR 52.204-1 or the Availability of Funds clause in FAR 52.232-18. STANDARD FORMS 26 *Award/Contract*, 1447 *Solicitation/Contract*, and 1449 *Solicitation/Contract/Order for Commercial Items* contain spaces for the insertion of the effective date, but SFs 33 *Solicitation, Offer and Award* and 1442 *Solicitation, Offer, and Award (Construction, Alteration, or Repair)* do not. The effective date determines what laws and regulations apply to the contract. See Cibinic, Nash & Yukins, FORMATION OF GOVERNMENT CONTRACTS 244–50 (4th ed. 2011); Cibinic, *Determining Applicable Statutes Or Regulations: What Date Governs?* 18 N&CR ¶ 10 (Mar. 2004).

EFFECTIVE DATE (OF OTHER ACTIONS)   *Official:* (1) For a solicitation amendment, change order, or administrative change, the effective date shall be the issue date of the amendment, change order, or administrative change. (2) For a supplemental agreement, the effective date shall be the date agreed upon by the contracting parties. (3) For a modification issued as a confirming notice of termination for the convenience of the government, the effective date of the confirming notice shall be the same as the effective date of the initial notice. (4) For a modification converting a termination for default to a termination for the convenience of the government, the effective date shall be the same as the effective date of the termination for default. (5) For a modification confirming the termination contracting officer's previous letter determination of the amount due in settlement of a contract termination for convenience, the effective date shall be the same as the effective date of the previous letter determination. *Source:* FAR 43.101. Standard Form 30 Amendment of Solicitation/ Modification of Contract contains a space for the insertion of the effective date.

EFFECTIVE DATE (OF A REGULATION)   The date on which a regulation becomes enforceable and applicable to ACQUISITIONs as provided in a FINAL RULE published in the FEDERAL REGISTER. FAR 1.108(d) states that changes to the FEDERAL ACQUI-SITION REGULATION apply to SOLICITATIONS issued on or after the effective date of the change, which is stated in the issue of the Federal Register in which the regulation is published. Agencies may include FAR changes in solicitations issued before the effective date of the change only if the resulting contract will be awarded after the effective date of the change. Contracting officers may include a FAR change in an existing contract if the contractor will agree and if consideration is furnished. See Cibinic, *Determining Applicable Statutes Or Regulations: What Date Governs?* 18 N&CR ¶ 10 (Mar. 2004); *Dyncorp Information Systems, LLC v. U.S.,* 58 Fed. Cl. 446 (2003).

EFFECTIVE DATE OF TERMINATION   *Official:* The date on which the notice of termination requires the contractor to stop performance under the contract. If the contractor receives the termination notice after the date fixed for termination, then the effective date of termination means the date the contractor receives the notice. *Source:* FAR 2.101. FAR 49.102 prescribes the requirements for termination notices, including the statement of an effective date.

E-GOVERNMENT ACT   A law enacted in 2002 and subsequently reauthorized to improve the management and promotion of the government's use of information technology to provide government functions and services. 44 U.S.C. § 3601 et seq. It created an Office of Electronic Government within OMB headed by an Administrator and a Chief Information Officers Council and imposed management and reporting requirements on government agencies. See ELECTRONIC GOVERNMENT. See also Seifert, Cong. Research Serv., Report No. RL34492, Reauthorization of the E-Government Act: A Brief Overview (May 14, 2008); OMB, *Implementation Guidance for the E-Government Act of 2002* (Aug. 2003).

EICHLEAY FORMULA   The prevalent method for calculating extended and unabsorbed HOME OFFICE overhead when the government has delayed the work on CONSTRUCTION contracts. In *Eichleay Corp.,* ASBCA 5183, 60-2 BCA ¶ 2688, *mot. for recons.,* 61-1 BCA ¶ 2894, the ARMED SERVICES BOARD OF CONTRACT APPEALS found the formula a "realistic method of allocation of continuing home office expenses." To recover under the Eichleay formula, a contractor generally must show (1) that the government caused a delay, (2) the contractor was required to stand by during the delay (see STAND-BY), and (3) it was unable to do additional work while standing by. Application of the formula entails a three-step process. First, the ratio of contract billings to total billings for the actual contract period is multiplied by the total overhead for the contract period to arrive at the overhead, or INDIRECT COST, allocable to the contract. Next, the allocable overhead is divided by the number of days of actual performance to determine the daily contract overhead. Finally, the daily contract overhead is multiplied by the number of days of government caused delay to arrive at the amount claimed for UNABSORBED OVERHEAD. This formula is used in lieu of computing the actual costs incurred. A contractor must separate government-caused delays from its own delays. There has been considerable dispute and litigation on the conditions that must be proved to justify recovery of costs using this formula. See Nash & Feldman, 2 Government Contract Changes §§ 17:9–17:16 (3d ed. 2006–2020); Cibinic, Nagle & Nash, Administration of Government Contracts 647–53 (5th ed. 2016); Eclavea & Shampo, *Unabsorbed Overhead Costs or "Eichleay" Damages,* 64 Am. Jur. 2d Public Works & Contracts § 157 (May 2011); Nash, *Postscript: Unabsorbed Overhead and the "Eichleay" Formula,* 17 N&CR ¶ 33 (June 2003).

8(a) PROGRAM   A program authorized by 15 U.S.C. § 637(a) that permits the U.S. SMALL BUSINESS ADMINISTRATION (a) to provide business development assistance to SMALL BUSINESS CONCERNS that are SOCIALLY AND ECONOMICALLY DISADVANTAGED, (b) to enter into contracts with government agencies to provide supplies and services, (c) to then subcontract with socially and economically disadvantaged small business concerns for the performance of the work, and (d) to delegate contract administration to the government agency that awarded the prime contract. The program is implemented in 13 C.F.R. part 124 and FAR Subpart 19.8. 8(a) subcontracts valued at $7.5 million or less may be awarded without competition. 8(a) subcontracts that exceed $7.5 million must be awarded competitively if two or more 8(a) small businesses are capable of performing at a FAIR MARKET PRICE. 13 C.F.R. § 124.506 and FAR 19.805. The program has been used extensively by government agencies. It has long been controversial with respect to its constitutionality and its effectiveness in enabling socially and economically disadvantaged small business concerns to become economically viable without further government assistance and underwent a major statutory reform in 1988. See Cibinic, Nash & Yukins, FORMATION OF GOVERNMENT CONTRACTS 1603–07 (4th ed. 2011). See also Oakes, *Inching Toward Balance: Reaching Proper Reform of the Alaska Native Corporations' 8(a) Contracting Preferences*, 40 PUB. CONT. L.J. 777 (2011); Noon, *The Use of Racial Preferences in Public Procurement for Social Stability*, 38 PUB. CONT. L.J. 611 (2009); Zehrt, *A Decade Later: Adarand and Croson and the Status of Minority Preferences in Government Contracting*, 21 NAT'L BLACK LAW JOURNAL 1 (2009).

ELECTION DOCTRINE   A legal doctrine established by the former Court of Claims in *Tuttle/White Constructors, Inc. v. United States*, 656 F.2d 644 (Ct. Cl. 1981), which provides that a contractor's election of a litigation forum, either a BOARD OF CONTRACT APPEALS or the UNITED STATES COURT OF FEDERAL CLAIMS, is binding and may not be changed. The doctrine applies only if the elected forum possesses subject matter jurisdiction over the claim or appeal, and the contractor's choice of forum is informed, knowing, and voluntary. See Manos, 3 GOVERNMENT CONTRACT COSTS AND PRICING § 89:12 (2d ed. 2009–2020); Cibinic, Nagle & Nash, ADMINISTRATION OF GOVERNMENT CONTRACTS 1208–09 (5th ed. 2016).

ELECTION OF FORUMS   See ELECTION DOCTRINE.

ELECTION OF REMEDIES DOCTRINE   The legal doctrine that the choice of one of two or more inconsistent remedies is binding on the party that elected to make the choice. An example would be a government decision to permit a contractor that is in default to continue performance instead of terminating the contract for default. The Election of Remedies Doctrine is related to the doctrines of ESTOPPEL and WAIVER. See Cibinic, Nagle & Nash, ADMINISTRATION OF GOVERNMENT CONTRACTS 849–51 (5th ed. 2016). Some authors have used the term election of remedies in the sense of election of forum.

ELECTRONIC AND INFORMATION TECHNOLOGY (EIT)   *Official:* This term has the same meaning as INFORMATION TECHNOLOGY, except EIT also includes any equipment or interconnected system or subsystem of equipment that is used in the creation, conversion, or duplication of data or information. The term EIT includes, but is not limited to, telecommunication products (such as telephones), information kiosks and transaction machines, worldwide websites, multimedia, and office equipment (such as copiers and fax machines). *Source:* FAR 2.101. Policies for the acquisition of EIT are set forth in FAR Part 39.

ELECTRONIC COMMERCE (E-COMMERCE)   *Official:* Electronic techniques for accomplishing business transactions including electronic mail or messaging, World Wide Web technology, electronic bulletin boards, PURCHASE CARDs, ELECTRONIC FUNDS TRANSFER, and ELECTRONIC DATA INTERCHANGE. *Source:* FAR 2.101. 41 U.S.C. § 2301 requires agencies to use electronic commerce to the maximum extent that it is practicable and cost-effective in the conduct and administration of their acquisitions. In using electronic commerce techniques, agencies must apply nationally and internationally recognized standards that broaden INTEROPERABILITY and ease the electronic interchange of information. See FAR Subpart 4.5. See Edwards, *Postscript: Electronic Bids and Proposals*, 25 N&CR ¶ 28 (June 2011).

ELECTRONIC FUNDS TRANSFER (EFT)   *Official:* Any transfer of funds, other than a transaction originated by cash, check, or similar paper instrument, that is initiated through an electronic terminal, telephone, computer, or magnetic tape, for the purpose of ordering, instructing, or authorizing a financial institution to debit or credit an account. The term includes Automated Clearing House transfers, Fedwire transfers, and transfers made at automated teller machines and point-of-sale terminals. For purposes of compliance with 31 U.S.C. § 3332 and implementing regulations at 31 C.F.R. part 208, the term "electronic funds transfer" includes a GOVERNMENTWIDE COMMERCIAL PURCHASE CARD transaction. *Source:* FAR 2.101. 31 U.S.C. § 3332(e) and FAR 32.1101 make payment by EFT mandatory with limited exceptions. If a contractor is registered in SAM, its contracts are to include the Payment by Electronic Funds Transfer—System for Award Management clause in FAR 52.232-33. See Department of the Treasury Financial Management Service, *Electronic Funds Transfer*, available at http://www.fms.treas.gov/eft/index.html. If the contractor is not registered in SAM, its contracts are to include the Payment by Electronic Funds Transfer—Other Than System for Award Management clause in FAR 52.232-34.

ELECTRONIC FUNDS TRANSFER INFORMATION (EFT)   *Official:* Information necessary for making payment by EFT through specified EFT mechanisms. *Source:* FAR 32.1102. FAR 32.1104 requires agencies to protect this information from "improper" disclosure.

ELECTRONIC GOVERNMENT   *Official:* The use by the Government of web-based Internet applications and other information technologies, combined with processes that implement these technologies, to—(A) enhance the access to and delivery of Government information and services to the public, other agencies, and other Government entities; or (B) bring about improvements in Government operations that may include effectiveness, efficiency, service quality, or transformation. *Source:* 44 U.S.C. § 3601. This term is used in the E-GOVERNMENT ACT.

ELECTRONIC INDUSTRIES ASSOCIATION (EIA)   A national trade organization representing a variety of companies. It was instrumental in government procurement by establishing standards such as the EARNED VALUE ANSI/EIA-748 standard. EIA was dissolved in 2011, and its standard setting activity was transferred to the Electronic Components Industry Association.

E-MARKETPLACE   A GSA pilot program that will allow PURCHASE CARD holders to obtain standard products under the MICRO-PURCHASE THRESHOLD from a group of commercial vendors. This program was mandated by § 846 of the 2018 NDAA, Pub. L. No. 115-91. Contracts are expected to be awarded in 2020.

EMERGENCY ACQUISITION   An ACQUISITION for which statute or regulation permit the use of certain "flexibilities," i.e., departures from ordinarily prescribed procedures. As listed in FAR 18.001, they include acquisitions (a) in support of a CONTINGENCY OPERATION, (b) to facilitate the defense against or recovery from cyber. nuclear, biological, chemical, or radiological attack against the United States, (c) in support of a request from the Secretary of State or the Administrator of the United States Agency for International Development to facilitate the provision of international disaster assistance; and (d) conducted when the president declares an incident of national significance, emergency declaration, or a major disaster declaration. See EMERGENCY ACQUISITION FLEXIBILITIES.

EMERGENCY ACQUISITION FLEXIBILITIES.   *Official:* Flexibilities provided with respect to any ACQUISITION of SUPPLIES or services by or for an EXECUTIVE AGENCY that, as determined by the head of an executive agency, may be used—(a) In support of a CONTINGENCY OPERATION as defined in 2.101; (b) To facilitate the defense against or recovery from cyber, nuclear, biological, chemical, or radiological attack against the United States; (c) In support of a request from the Secretary of State or the Administrator of the United States Agency for International Development to facilitate the provision of international disaster assistance; or (d) When the President issues an emergency declaration, or a MAJOR DISASTER declaration. *Source:* FAR 18.001. A "flexibility" is a departure from ordinarily prescribed procedure. Substantial emergency acquisition authority was added to 41 U.S.C. § 1903 in 2004 by Pub. L. No. 108-375. FAR Part 18 describes the emergency acquisition flexibilities that are available under various circumstances. The DOD is also authorized to use emergency procurement in HUMANITARIAN or PEACEKEEPING MISSIONs by raising the SIMPLIFIED ACQUISITION THRESHOLD for purchases awarded or made outside of the United States in support of the operations. DFARS 218.270.

EMERGENCY RESPONSE CONTRACT   *Official:* A contract with private entities that supports assistance activities in a MAJOR DISASTER OR EMERGENCY AREA, such as debris clearance, distribution of supplies, or reconstruction. *Source:* FAR 26.201. FAR Subpart 26.2 provides mandatory procedures applying to these contracts.

EMINENT DOMAIN   The power of the government to take private property for public use. The Fifth Amendment of the Constitution of the United States prohibits the government from taking private property without just compensation. When the government takes REAL PROPERTY, it generally attempts to negotiate a reasonable price, but the owner can sue if agreement cannot be reached. See Hudson, *Eminent Domain Due Process*, 119 YALE L.J. 1280 (Apr. 2010); Simpson, *Constitutionalizing the Right of Property: The U.S., England and Europe*, 31 U. HAW. L. REV. 1 (2008); Garden, *Fifth Amendment Takings of Rights Arising from Agreements with the Federal Government*, 29 PUB. CONT. L.J. 187 (2000). 28 U.S.C. § 1498(a) has been construed as an eminent domain statute giving the government or its contractors with AUTHORIZATION AND CONSENT the right to take PATENT rights. Suit for reasonable compensation in such cases is in the COURT OF FEDERAL CLAIMS. See Nash & Rawicz, INTELLECTUAL PROPERTY IN GOVERNMENT CONTRACTS, chap. 8 (6th ed. 2008). See also Nash, *Government Use of Private Patents: A License to Steal*, 24 N&CR ¶ 12 (Mar. 2010); Nash, *Recovering for Government Use of a Private Patent: An Uphill Battle*, 23 N&CR ¶ 32 (June 2009); Svetz, *The Government's Patent Policy: The Bayh-Dole Act & "Authorization & Consent,"* BRIEFING PAPERS No. 02-08 (July 2002).

EMPLOYEE IN A SENSITIVE POSITION   *Official:* An employee who has been granted access to classified information; or employees in other positions that the contractor determines involve national security, health or safety, or functions other than the foregoing requiring a high degree of trust and confidence. *Source:* DFARS 252.223-7004(a)(1). See also *Official:* A contractor or subcontractor employee who has been granted access to classified information; a contractor or subcontractor employee in other positions that the contractor or subcontractor determines could reasonably be expected to affect safety, security, National security, or functions other than the foregoing requiring a high degree of trust and confidence; and includes any employee performing in a position designated "mission critical" pursuant to the clause at 1852.246–70. *Source:* NFS 1823.570-1. Contractors must test such employees for drug usage under the *Drug-Free Work Force* clause in DFARS 252.223-7004.

EMPLOYEE, MORALE, HEALTH, WELFARE, FOOD SERVICE, AND DORMITORY COSTS AND CREDITS   *Official:* Aggregate costs incurred on activities designed to improve working conditions, employer-employee relations, employee morale, and employee performance, less the income generated by these activities. *Source:* FAR 31.205-13(a). These costs are allowable, with the exception of the costs of gifts and the costs of recreation (except for the costs of employees' participation in company-sponsored sports teams or employee organizations designed to improve company loyalty, teamwork, or physical fitness). FAR 31.205-13(b) and (c). Losses from operating food and dormitory services are allowable only if the contractor's objective is to operate them on a break-even basis. FAR 31.205-13(d). See Manos, 1 Government Contract Costs & Pricing §§ 20:1–20:3 (2d ed. 2009–2020); Cibinic, Knight & Nash, Cost-Reimbursement Contracting 704 (4th ed. 2014).

EMPLOYEE STOCK OWNERSHIP PLAN (ESOP)   A stock bonus plan designed to invest primarily in the stock of the employer corporation. The contractor's contributions to an Employee Stock Ownership Trust (ESOT) may be in the form of cash, stock, or property. FAR 31.205-6(q)(1) Costs for ESOPs satisfying the criteria in FAR 31.205-6(q)(2) are allowable. See Manos, 1 Government Contract Costs & Pricing § 13:14 (2d ed. 2009–2020); Cibinic, Knight & Nash, Cost-Reimbursement Contracting 683–84 (4th ed. 2014).

EMPLOYMENT CONTRACT   A contract between an employer and employee for the personal services of the employee. Such contracts may be formal, i.e., written, or informal (unwritten), and definite term or indefinite term. Most are informal and indefinite. Historically, employers have been able to terminate informal and indefinite employment contracts "at will"; however, the state courts have increasingly constrained the employer's rights in that regard. Cibinic, Nash & Yukins, Formation of Government Contracts 22–25 (4th ed. 2011); Nash, *Personal Services Contracts: Is the Federal Acquisition Regulation Guidance Valid?*, 21 N&CR ¶ 16 (Apr. 2007).

END PRODUCT   *Official:* Supplies delivered under a line item of as Government contract except for use in Part 25. *Source:* FAR 2.101. With regard to the BUY AMERICAN ACT, *Official:* Those articles, materials, and supplies to be acquired for public use. *Source:* FAR 25.003. Such end products are either DOMESTIC END PRODUCTs or FOREIGN END PRODUCTs. See Cibinic, Nash & Yukins, Formation of Government Contracts 1614–24 (4th ed. 2011).

END ITEM   Generally, a specific product or service identified for delivery or performance by a line item in a government contract. The precise meaning of the term is thus largely contract-specific. A DELIVERABLE. This term is not defined in the FEDERAL ACQUISITION REGULATIONS SYSTEM but is used in a number of different contexts.

ENERGY-EFFICIENT PRODUCT   *Official*: A product that—(i) meets Department of Energy and Environmental Protection Agency criteria for use of the Energy Star trademark label; or (ii) is in the upper 25% of efficiency for all similar products as designated by the Department of Energy's Federal Energy Management Program. As used in this definition, the term "product" does not include any energy-consuming product or system designed or procured for combat or combat-related missions (42 U.S.C. § 8259b). *Source:* FAR 2.101. FAR 23.203(a) states that agencies must buy energy-efficient products when acquiring supplies that consume energy and when specifying products that consume energy for service and construction contracts.

ENERGY-EFFICIENT STANDBY POWER DEVICES   *Official:* Products that use—(1) external standby power devices, or that contain an internal standby power function; and (2) no more than one watt of electricity in their standby power consuming mode or meet recommended low standby levels as designated by the Department of Energy Federal Energy Management Program. *Source:* FAR 2.101. FAR 23.203(a) states that agencies must buy energy-efficient standby power devices when acquiring supplies that consume power in a standby mode.

ENERGY-SAVINGS PERFORMANCE CONTRACT   *Official*: A contract that requires the contractor to—(1) Perform services for the design, acquisition, financing, installation, testing, operation, and where appropriate, maintenance and repair, of an identified energy conservation measure or series of measures at one or more locations; (2) Incur the costs of implementing the energy savings measures, including at least the cost (if any) incurred in making energy audits, acquiring and installing equipment, and training personnel in exchange for a predetermined share of the value of the energy savings directly resulting from implementation of such measures during the term of the contract; and (3) Guarantee future energy and cost savings to the government. *Source:* FAR 2.101. Guidance on the use of these contracts is set forth in FAR 23.205. See Frenkil, *Energy Saving Performance Contracts: Assessing Whether to "Retrofit" and Effective Contracting Vehicle for Improving Energy Efficiency in Federal Government Facilities*, 39 Pub. Cont. L.J. 331 (2010); Toomey, *Energy Savings Performance Contracting: Will the Demand Remain High Despite Dropping Energy Prices?*, 44 WTR Procurement Law 1 (2009).

ENGINEERING AND MANUFACTURING DEVELOPMENT PHASE   The third phase of the DOD MAJOR SYSTEM ACQUISITION process under the DOD 5000 Series. In this phase, the military service awards a contract to design a weapon system and prove that it is manufacturable. The phase generally includes the production of prototypes and can include the production of a LOW-RATE INITIAL PRODUCTION quantity. See DAU, Defense Acquisition Guidebook (2010); Schwartz, Cong. Research Serv., Report No. RL34026, Defense Acquisitions: How DOD Acquires Weapon Systems and Recent Efforts to Reform the Process (Apr. 23, 2010).

ENGINEERING AND TECHNICAL SERVICES   *Official:* Contractual services that provide assistance, advice, or training for the efficient and effective management and operation of organizations, activities (including management and support services for R&D activities), or systems. These services are normally closely related to the basic responsibilities and mission of the agency originating the requirement for the acquisition of services by contract. Included are efforts that support or contribute to improved organization of program management, logistics management, project monitoring, and reporting, data collection, budgeting, accounting, performance auditing, and administrative technical support for conferences and training programs. *Source:* FAR 2.101 (in definition of ADVISORY AND ASSISTANCE SERVICES). This is one of the three types of advisory and assistance services that are subject to statutory limitations.

ENGINEERING CHANGE PROPOSAL (ECP)   A proposed engineering change and the documentation by which the change is described, justified, and submitted to the procuring activity for approval or disapproval. Both DOD and NASA had Engineering Change Proposal clauses, which allowed either party to initiate an ECP and specified the information that had to be included documenting the impact of a proposed change. These clauses have been deleted from the procurement regulations, but agencies still request contractors to prepare ECPs. See the guidance in MIL-HDBK-61A(SE), *Configuration Management Guidance* (2001). See Nash & Feldman, 1 GOVERNMENT CONTRACT CHANGES §§ 7:2–7:6 (3d ed. 2006–2020); Cibinic, Nagle & Nash, ADMINISTRATION OF GOVERNMENT CONTRACTS 376–85 (5th ed. 2016).

ENHANCED DEBRIEFINGS   More robust post-award DEBRIEFINGs by DOD activities required by § 818 of the 2018 NDAA. The key additional requirement was the opportunity for a disappointed offeror to submit, within two business days after receiving a post-award debriefing, additional questions related to the debriefing and the requirement that the agency respond to these questions within five business days. This requirement was implemented by a class deviation issued on March 22, 2018.

ENTERPRISE ARCHITECTURE [1]   Generally, the conceptual design or blueprint of a computer network that will serve an entire organization (enterprise), including the hardware, software, data resources, communications infrastructure, their interrelationships, and the organizational component that will manage the network. Office of Management and Budget (OMB) Circular A-130 Revised, *Managing Information As a Strategic Resource* (July 2016), requires that agencies develop and document an enterprise architecture as part of their strategic plan for managing information technology. **[2]** A blueprint for organizational transformation and IT modernization. Generally speaking, it consists of "snapshots" of the enterprise's current, or "as-is," operational and technological environment and its target, or "to-be," environment, and contains a capital investment road map for transitioning from the current to the target environment. These snapshots consist of "views," which are basically one or more architecture products that provide conceptual, logical, or physical representations of the enterprise. Further, these views or representations are not static but rather will evolve and change over time, making the EA a "living document." U.S. GOV'T ACCOUNTABILITY OFFICE, A FRAMEWORK FOR ASSESSING AND IMPROVING ENTERPRISE ARCHITECTURE MANAGEMENT (VERSION 2.0), GAO-10-846G (Aug. 2010). See FEDERAL ENTERPRISE ARCHITECTURE PROGRAM.

ENTERTAINMENT COSTS   The costs of amusement, diversions, social activities, and any directly associated costs such as tickets to shows or sports events, meals, lodging, rentals, transportation, and gratuities. FAR 31.205-14. Such costs are specifically unallowable and are not allowable under any other COST PRINCIPLE. See Manos, 1 GOVERNMENT

CONTRACT COSTS §§ 21:1–21:3 (2d ed. 2009–2020); Cibinic, Knight & Nash, COST-REIMBURSEMENT CONTRACTING 656 (4th ed. 2014).

ENTITLEMENT The right of a contractor to compensation, such as an EQUITABLE ADJUSTMENT or recovery of damages for BREACH OF CONTRACT, for an injury that it suffered during contract performance. In order to be entitled to compensation, a contractor must show that an event caused it to suffer an injury for which the government was liable either by operation of a CONTRACT CLAUSE or on grounds of breach of contract. See *The Redland Co. v. United States*, 97 Fed. Cl. 736 (2011). In order to conserve resources, BOARDs OF CONTRACT APPEALS frequently permit the parties to litigate only entitlement initially. See BIFURCATION OF ENTITLEMENT AND QUANTUM.

ENTITY OF THE GOVERNMENT *Official:* Any entity of the legislative or judicial branch, any EXECUTIVE AGENCY, military department, government corporation, or independent establishment; the U.S. Postal Service; or any NONAPPROPRIATED-FUND INSTRUMENTALITY of the Armed Forces. *Source:* FAR 8.701. This definition is used in FAR Subpart 8.7, which requires such entities to purchase supplies and services from nonprofit agencies employing people who are BLIND OR SEVERELY DISABLED. The common dictionary definition of "entity" refers to a discrete or distinct thing. Thus, an "entity of the Government" or "Government entity" is a discrete or distinct organizational unit.

ENVIRONMENTAL *Official:* Environmental aspects of internal agency operations and activities, including those aspects related to energy and transportation functions. *Source:* FAR 23.001. The government policies for protecting and improving the environment in the acquisition process are set forth in FAR Part 23. In a written acquisition plan, the contracting officer must discuss all applicable environmental objectives associated with the acquisition, the proposed resolution of environmental issues, and any environmental requirements to be included in the solicitations or contracts. FAR 7.105(a)(17). FAR 42.302(a)(68) allows the CONTRACTING OFFICER to delegate the responsibility to monitor the contractor's environmental practices for adverse impact on contract performance or contract cost and for compliance with environmental requirements specified in the contract to the CONTRACT ADMINISTRATION officer, whose responsibilities include requesting environmental technical assistance if needed and monitoring contractor compliance with specifications or other contractual requirements requiring the delivery or use of environmentally preferable products, energy-efficient products, products containing recovered materials, and biobased products. This must occur as part of the quality assurance procedures set forth in Part 46.

EQUAL ACCESS TO JUSTICE ACT (EAJA) A law, 5 U.S.C. § 504 and 28 U.S.C. § 2412, that permits small contractors to recover ATTORNEY'S FEES and expenses in litigation against the government. Under what is called the AMERICAN RULE, the parties to a litigation must pay their own litigation expenses, and the rule applies generally when contractors litigate contract disputes. The EAJA is an exception to the American Rule. It permits small contractors to recover if (1) the contractor prevails before a BOARD OF CONTRACT APPEALS or the U.S. COURT OF FEDERAL CLAIMS (see PREVAILING PARTY), (2) the government's position is not SUBSTANTIALLY JUSTIFIED, and (3) no special circumstances make an award unjust. The remedies provided by the boards of contract appeals are addressed in 5 U.S.C. § 504, whereas the remedies given by courts,

including the Court of Federal Claims, are covered by 28 U.S.C. § 2412. See Feldman, Gov-
ernment Contract Guidebook, §§ 8:15–8:19 (4th ed. 2019–2020); Nash & Feldman,
Government Contract Changes §§ 16:36–16:41 (3d ed. 2006–2020); Standard, *The
Equal Access to Justice Act: Practical Applications to Government Contract Litigation*, The Army
Lawyer (Apr. 2012), at 4.

EQUAL EMPLOYMENT OPPORTUNITY (EEO)   Government policies and procedures
that are designed to ensure that government contractors and subcontractors do not improperly discriminate against employees and applicants and that they take AFFIRMATIVE
ACTION against such discrimination. EEO policies and procedures are implemented in
Title 29 of the Code of Federal Regulations and FAR Subpart 22.8. The EEO obligations
of firms seeking government contracts and of government contractors and subcontractors
are stated in SOLICITATION PROVISIONs and CONTRACT CLAUSEs prescribed by
FAR 22.810. Policy exemptions are listed in FAR 22.807. A firm seeking a government contract must make representations about the conduct of its business and their compliance with
EEO clauses under other government contracts and submit to compliance evaluations by the
OFFICE OF FEDERAL CONTRACT COMPLIANCE PROGRAMS. Contractors must
agree not to maintain segregated facilities or improperly discriminate against employees and
applicants for employment and to prepare and submit specified reports. The Secretary of
Labor bears primary responsibility for enforcement and sole authority to resolve disputes.
Violations can result in TERMINATION FOR DEFAULT and DEBARMENT. See Feld-
man, Government Contract Guidebook, chap. 8 (4th ed. 2019–2020); Cibinic, Nash &
Yukins, Formation of Government Contracts 1638-45 (4th ed. 2011). See also Everitt,
*Promoting Equal Access to Employment and Achieving Discrimination Fee Workplaces: Recent
Guidance from the Equal Employment Opportunity Commission*, 34 FALL Vt. B.J. 23 (2008).

EQUIPMENT   *Official:* A tangible item that is functionally complete for its intended purpose,
durable, nonexpendable, and needed for the performance of a contract. Equipment is not
intended for sale and does not ordinarily lose its identity or become a component part of
another article when put into use. Equipment does not include material, real property,
special test equipment, or special tooling. *Source:* FAR 45.101. Equipment is one type of
GOVERNMENT PROPERTY subject to FAR Part 45.

EQUITABLE ADJUSTMENT   A fair price adjustment under a contract clause for changed
work, including an adjustment in profit, a change in the delivery schedule, if appropriate,
and a change in any other affected terms of the contract. Equitable adjustments can result
in price increases for the contractor for increased work, price reductions for the government
for reduced work, or an increase or decrease due to substitution of one item of work for
another. The major contract clause that calls for equitable adjustments is the Changes clause,
FAR 52.243-1 through -5. However, the term is a standard contract term that is used in
many other clauses. Equitable adjustments are distinguished from DAMAGES, which are
given in the absence of a contract clause calling for an equitable adjustment. The basic formula for an equitable adjustment is an estimate of the difference between (1) what it would
have reasonably cost to perform the work as originally required and (2) what it will reasonably cost to perform the work as changed. See Nash & Feldman, Government Contract
Changes, chap. 16 through 19 (3d ed. 2006–2020); Cibinic, Nagle & Nash, Administration of Government Contracts 593–612 (5th ed. 2016). See also Nash, *Proving
Equitable Adjustment Costs: How Much Detail is Required?*, 33 N&CR ¶ 31 (June 2019);
Nash, *"Equitable Adjustment": A Term Of Art?*, 30 N&CR ¶ 8 (Feb. 2016).

EQUITABLE ALLOCATION   Allocation of INDIRECT COSTs so that each COST OBJECTIVE bears a share of the cost on the basis of the benefits accruing to it. See FAR 31.203(c). An allocation method that causes the government to bear a greater portion of the contractor's costs than is attributable to government work is considered inequitable, and although a contractor has considerable discretion in selecting a method for allocating indirect costs, the method selected will be rejected by the boards or courts if the results are inequitable to the government. See COST ACCOUNTING STANDARD 418, Allocation of Direct and Indirect Costs, 48 C.F.R. § 9904.418. See also Manos, 1 GOVERNMENT CONTRACT COSTS & PRICING § 7:3 (2d ed. 2009–2020); Cibinic, Knight & Nash, COST-REIMBURSEMENT CONTRACTING 604–16 (4th ed. 2014).

ERRORS OR OMISSIONS   See OMISSIONS AND MISDESCRIPTIONS.

ESCALATION   See FIXED-PRICE CONTRACT WITH ECONOMIC PRICE ADJUSTMENT.

ESCROW AGREEMENT   An agreement with a third party to hold property of a contracting party and to release it to another party under specified conditions. Such agreements are frequently used with banks or other financing institutions to ensure that funds are used for contractual performance. See Nash, *Third Party Beneficiaries: Unpaid Subcontractors,* 19 N&CR ¶ 19 (Apr. 2005); Nash, *Postscript: Subcontractors As Third Party Beneficiaries,* 19 N&CR ¶ 51 (Nov. 2005). They are also used to protect proprietary TECHNICAL DATA or COMPUTER SOFTWARE when a buyer is willing to forego immediate delivery but desires protection in the event that the seller becomes unable to continue to perform its contractual obligations. Agreements of this type are not covered in the procurement regulations but are recommended in the DOD training guide, *Intellectual Property: Navigating Through Commercial Waters* (Oct. 2001) and the report of the SECTION 813 PANEL.

ESTABLISHED CATALOG OR MARKET PRICE   *Historical.* A price that established an exemption from the requirements for submission of CERTIFIED COST OR PRICING DATA by an offeror on a negotiated procurement (see NEGOTIATION). This exemption was removed from 10 U.S.C. § 2306a(b) and 41 U.S.C. § 3503 by the CLINGER-COHEN ACT OF 1996, Pub. L. No. 104-106. The exemption applied if the prices were, or were based on, established catalog prices or established market prices of commercial items sold in substantial quantities to the general public (see COMMERCIALITY). The exemption was burdensome because the offeror had to claim it by providing detailed sales information on Standard Form 1412, Claim for Exemption from Submission of Certified Cost or Pricing Data, FAR 53.301-1412. The exemption was replaced by the COMMERCIAL ITEM EXEMPTION. See 41 U.S.C. § 103. A contractor may be required to provide data related to established catalog or market prices as DATA OTHER THAN CERTIFIED COST OR PRICING DATA. FAR 15.402. See Cibinic, Nash & Yukins, FORMATION OF GOVERNMENT CONTRACTS 1457–61 (4th ed. 2011); Nash, *Pricing Policy: New Federal Acquisition Regulation Guidance,* 24 N&CR ¶ 46 (Oct. 2010).

ESTIMATE AT COMPLETION (EAC)   In an EARNED VALUE MANAGEMENT SYSTEM, the current estimated total cost for program authorized work. It includes actual cost to a point in time plus the ESTIMATE TO COMPLETE. See EARNED VALUE MANAGEMENT SYSTEM.

ESTIMATE TO COMPLETE   In an EARNED VALUE MANAGEMENT SYSTEM, the estimate of costs to complete all work from a point in time to the end of the program. Government Electronics and Information Technology Association, *GEIA Standard: Earned Value Management Systems*, ANSI/EIA-748-B-2007 (Sept. 2007) and DOD, *Earned Value Management Implementation Guide* (Jan. 2018).

ESTIMATED COST   In COST, COST-PLUS-FIXED-FEE, COST-PLUS-AWARD-FEE, and COST-SHARING contracts, the amount stated as the estimate to complete specified work. The estimated cost does not include FEE. Pursuant to the Limitation of Cost clause at FAR 52.232-20, the estimated cost marks the absolute limit of the parties' obligations under the contract. When the allowable incurred cost equals the estimated cost, the contractor is not obligated to continue working, and the government is not obligated to reimburse the contractor for costs in excess of that amount unless and until the contracting officer notifies that contractor that the estimated cost has been increased and modifies the contract accordingly. The estimated cost is negotiated in accordance with the procedures in FAR Subpart 15.4 or established competitively in accordance with those in FAR Subpart 15.3. The estimated cost may be changed, either increased or decreased, pursuant to any of the CONTRACT CLAUSEs that provide for a cost adjustment, e.g., the CHANGES CLAUSE. See Cibinic, Knight & Nash, COST-REIMBURSEMENT CONTRACTING 431–80 (4th ed. 2014).

ESTIMATING COSTS   *Official:* The process of forecasting a future result in terms of cost, based upon information available at the time. *Source:* FAR 31.001. FAR 31.102 states that the COST PRINCIPLES "shall be used" in the pricing of FIXED-PRICE CONTRACTs when COST ANALYSIS is performed or a clause requires the negotiation of costs. Thus, contracting officers are required to estimate costs following this guidance.

ESTIMATING SYSTEM   *Official:* The contractor's policies, procedures, and practices for budgeting and planning controls and generating estimates of costs and other data included in proposals submitted to customers in the expectation of receiving contract awards. Estimating system includes the Contractor's—(1) Organizational structure; (2) Established lines of authority, duties, and responsibilities; (3) Internal controls and managerial reviews; (4) Flow of work, coordination, and communication; and (5) Budgeting, planning, estimating methods, techniques, accumulation of historical costs, and other analyses used to generate cost estimates. *Source:* The Cost Estimating System Requirements clause at DFARS 252.215-7002. Estimating systems with SIGNIFICANT DEFICIENCIES subject the contractor to withholding of payments. The government policy is to review contractor's estimating systems to verify their reliability. FAR 15.407-5. To be considered acceptable, a contractor's estimating system must be maintained, reliable, and consistently applied; must produce verifiable, supportable, and documented cost estimates; be integrated with other CONTRACTOR BUSINESS SYSTEMs and subjected to applicable financial controls. DFARS 215.407-5-70 and 252.215-7002 provide further guidance on the acceptability of a system. CAS 401, Consistency in Estimating, Accumulating, and Reporting Costs, 48 C.F.R. § 9904.401, requires contractors to follow estimating practices that are consistent with their cost accumulation and reporting practices. See *DCAA Contract Audit Manual* ¶ 5-1200. See Manos, 2 GOVERNMENT CONTRACT COSTS & PRICING §§ 62:1–62:6 (2d ed. 2009–2020).

ESTIMATING SYSTEM SURVEY REPORT   A report containing (1) the results of reviews of ESTIMATING SYSTEMs or estimating methods designed to reduce reviews of individual proposals, expedite the negotiating process, and increase the reliability of the proposals and

(2) any SIGNIFICANT DEFICIENCIES that must be corrected. When a government auditor has completed an audit of a contractor's estimating system, this report must be sent to all contracting officers having substantial business with the contractor. See FAR 15.407-5; *DCAA Contract Audit Manual* ¶ 5-1215; Cibinic, Knight & Nash, Cost-Reimbursement Contracting 479–80 (4th ed. 2014).

ESTOPPEL   A legal doctrine preventing a party from asserting a right to the detriment of the other party, when the first party has acted or made statements contrary to the right asserted, and the other party has reasonably relied on such conduct. The Supreme Court has strictly limited the use of estoppel against the government, *Schweiker v. Hansen*, 450 U.S. 785 (1981), but government contractors are still permitted to use the doctrine when they can prove affirmative misconduct by an officer of the government with the authority to bind the government. *Zacharin v. United States*, 213 F.3d 1366 (Fed. Cl. 2000). See Cibinic, Nagle & Nash, Administration of Government Contracts 63–70 (5th ed. 2016). The most common form of estoppel against the government that is not subject to these strict requirements occurs when the government fails within a reasonable period to terminate a contractor for default because of a late delivery and the contractor continues to work in reliance on the government's actions. See WAIVER. In this situation, it is often held that the government has effectively waived the delivery date and may be estopped from terminating the contract for failure to deliver. *DeVito v. United States*, 188 Ct. Cl. 979, 413 F.2d 1147 (1969).

ETHICS   Principles of proper personal and organizational conduct. They include principles such as honesty, compliance with law and regulation, good faith and fair dealing, avoidance of conflicts or interest, etc. Members of the government acquisition workforce must adhere to specified STANDARDS OF CONDUCT in the performance of their duties. See FAR 3.101. FAR 3.1001 states that government contractors must conduct themselves with the highest degree of integrity and business ethics and should have a written code of business ethics and conduct. A series of CONTRACT CLAUSES stipulating contractual ethics requirements are contained in FAR 52.203-13 through FAR 52.203-19. See generally Seyfarth Shaw LLP, The Government Contract Compliance Handbook (5th ed. 2014–2019). See also Cibinic, Nagle & Nash, Administration of Government Contracts 75–149 (5th ed. 2016).

ETHICS ADVISORY OPINION   An opinion from an AGENCY ETHICS OFFICIAL, made in response to a written request, that advises an active or former government official whether, as a former official, he or she would or would not be prohibited by the PROCUREMENT INTEGRITY ACT from becoming an employee and accepting compensation from a particular contractor. FAR 3.104-6(a). Good faith reliance by a former official and a contractor will preclude a finding that they knowingly violated the Act by accepting and providing such compensation. FAR 3.104-6(d)(3). See REVOLVING DOOR. See also DOD, *Ethics Counselor's Deskbook* (July 15, 2010).

EVALUATION   See PROPOSAL EVALUATION.

EVALUATION CRITERIA   See EVALUATION FACTORS.

EVALUATION FACTORS (FOR AWARD)   In a COMPETITIVE PROPOSALS ACQUISITION (i.e., a SOURCE SELECTION conducted pursuant to FAR Part 15), the criteria used by the government to determine the relative value of competing proposals and to determine which proposal offers the best value. 10 U.S.C. § 2305(a)(2)(A), 41 U.S.C. § 3306(b)(1)(A) and FAR 15.304(d) require that the government's REQUEST FOR PROPOSALS clearly identify the factors and significant subfactors that will be considered in evaluating proposals and state their RELATIVE IMPORTANCE in specified terms. The government has broad discretion in the selection of evaluation factors. However, FAR 15.304(b) states that the factors chosen must reflect considerations of importance to the source selection decision and enable the government to make meaningful comparisons and distinctions among competing proposals. Moreover, FAR 15.304(c) prescribes the following factors: (1) the evaluation of price or cost to the government, (2) consideration of product or service quality (this has not been interpreted to be a firm requirement to evaluate quality), (3) evaluation of past performance when the criteria in 15.304(c)(3) are met, and (4) proposed small business subcontracting in acquisitions that involve BUNDLING. Agencies may not evaluate an offeror unfavorably because it proposes telecommuting when telecommuting is not prohibited unless the contracting officer signs a determination in accordance with FAR 7.108(b). See Feldman, GOVERNMENT CONTRACT AWARDS: NEGOTIATION AND SEALED BIDDING § 6:11 (2019–2020 ed.); Cibinic, Nash & Yukins, FORMATION OF GOVERNMENT CONTRACTS 686–726 (4th ed. 2011). See also Edwards, *A Primer On Source Selection Planning: Evaluation Factors And Rating Methods*, BRIEFING PAPERS No. 17-8 (July 2017); Nash, *Unstated Evaluation Factors: Innovative Solutions Are Implicit*, 29, N&CR ¶ 14 (Mar. 2015).

EXAMINATION OF RECORDS   The examination by the COMPTROLLER GENERAL or the GOVERNMENT ACCOUNTABILITY OFFICE of a contractor's books, documents, papers, or other records that directly pertain to transactions under the contract. 10 U.S.C. § 2313(c) and 41 U.S.C. § 3901 & 3905(d) require that the government have the right to make such examination in all negotiated contracts, with the exception of contracts for utility services at established rates, contracts, or subcontracts for an amount not greater than the SIMPLIFIED ACQUISITION THRESHOLD, and contracts with foreign contractors for which the agency head authorized omission. The policy is implemented by inclusion in contracts of the Audit and Records—Negotiation clause at FAR 52.215-2 and the Audit and Records—Sealed Bidding clause at FAR 52.214-26. The right to examine and audit records may be exercised until three years after final payment or for any shorter period specified for a particular type of record in FAR Subpart 4.7. It also continues until the disposal of any claim, appeal, or litigation or any GAO exception to a contractor's costs or expenses.

EXCESS COSTS OF REPROCUREMENT   Costs incurred by the government in excess of the contract price of a contract that has been terminated for default (see TERMINATION FOR DEFAULT). The standard Default clauses, FAR 52.249-8 through -10, provide that these costs may be recovered from the defaulted contractor if the government repurchases the supplies or services or completes the work at a price exceeding the price under the terminated contract. FAR 49.402-6 requires the contracting officer, after the default termination, to repurchase against the account of the contractor as soon as practicable at a reasonable price and, after payment for the work to complete the contract, make a written demand on the terminated contractor for the total amount of the excess. For the defaulted contractor to be charged for the excess costs of reprocurement (1) the reprocured supplies, services, or work must be the same as or similar to the original; (2) the government must actually incur the costs; and (3) the government must reasonably minimize the excess costs (e.g., by obtaining maximum feasible competition). In addition to any difference in price incurred by the government, the government may also seek additional costs necessary for contract completion, such as interest, removing defective items, and necessary administrative costs. The government cannot obtain these costs for work it prevented the contractor from completing. See Feldman, GOVERNMENT CONTRACT GUIDEBOOK § 19:21 (4th ed. 2019–2020); Feldman, GOVERNMENT CONTRACT AWARDS: NEGOTIATION AND SEALED BIDDING §§ 26:1–26:13 (2019–2020 ed.); Cibinic, Nagle & Nash, ADMINISTRATION OF GOVERNMENT CONTRACTS 882–918 (5th ed. 2016). See also Feldman, *Reprocurement And Termination For Default*, BRIEFING PAPERS No. 17-5 (Apr. 2017).

EXCESS PERSONAL PROPERTY   *Official:* Any personal property under the control of a federal agency that the agency head determines is not required for its needs or for the discharge of its responsibilities. *Source:* FAR 2.101. FAR 8.102 provides that it is the policy of the government to use such property as the first source of supply for itself and cost-reimbursement contractors. Guidance on the abandonment, destruction, or donation of excess personal property is contained in FAR 45.603. See SURPLUS PROPERTY.

EXCISE TAX   A tax on the sale or use of a particular supply or service, levied by the federal government and by state and local governments. FAR 31.205-41 specifies the rules governing whether such taxes paid by contractors are ALLOWABLE COSTs. See Cibinic, Knight & Nash, COST-REIMBURSEMENT CONTRACTING 741–45 (4th ed. 2014). Contractors are frequently not subject to such taxes imposed by the federal government. See FAR Subpart 29.2. Contractors bear the risk of determining which excise taxes apply to their contracts but are given PRICE ADJUSTMENTs for changes in such taxes under the Federal, State, and Local Taxes clause in FAR 52.229-3. See STATE AND LOCAL TAXES.

EXCLUDED PARTIES LIST SYSTEM   An electronic database maintained and posted by the GENERAL SERVICES ADMINISTRATION that contained the list of all parties SUSPENDED, proposed for debarment, DEBARRED, declared INELIGIBLE, or excluded or disqualified under the NONPROCUREMENT COMMON RULE by AGENCIES, GOVERNMENT CORPORATIONS, or by the GOVERNMENT ACCOUNTABILITY OFFICE. This list is now included in the SYSTEM FOR AWARD MANAGEMENT. Contracting officers are required to review the list after opening bids or receipt of proposals and again immediately before award to ensure that a contract is not awarded to contractors that are listed. FAR 9.405. See Cibinic, Nash & Yukins, FORMATION OF GOVERNMENT CONTRACTS 485–89 (4th ed. 2011); Robbins, et al., *Path of an Investigation: How Major Contractor's Ethics Office and Air Force Procurement Fraud and Suspension/Debarment Apparatus Deal with Allegations of Potential Fraud and Unethical Conduct*, 40 PUB. CONT. L.J. 595 (2011); Albright, *Strengthening the Excluded Parties List System*, 40 PUB. CONT. L.J. 849 (2011).

EXCULPATORY CLAUSE   A contract clause stating that one of the contracting parties is not liable upon the occurrence of some specified event. These clauses are most frequently used by the government in an attempt to relieve itself of liability for defective specifications (see IMPLIED WARRANTY OF SPECIFICATIONS). Such clauses are not against public policy but are carefully scrutinized by the courts and BOARDs OF CONTRACT APPEALS to ensure that they are applicable to the specific problem that has been encountered by the contractor. See Nash & Feldman, 1 GOVERNMENT CONTRACT CHANGES §§ 13:23–13:29 (3d ed. 2006–2020); Cibinic, Nagle & Nash, ADMINISTRATION OF GOVERNMENT CONTRACTS 322–28, 480–81 (5th ed. 2016).

EXCUSABLE DELAY   A delay in the performance of a contract that is caused by an event that is beyond the control of and without the fault or negligence of the contractor or its subcontractors at any tier. The TERMINATION FOR DEFAULT clauses indicate that a contractor will not be held liable if its failure to perform a contract arises from such delays. The Excusable Delays clause at FAR 52.249-14, used in cost-reimbursement contracts, identifies the typical excusable delays found in the default clauses for all contract types. Such delays include (1) acts of God or of the public enemy, (2) acts of the government in either its sovereign or its contractual capacity, (3) fires, (4) floods, (5) epidemics, (6) quarantine restrictions, (7) strikes, (8) freight embargoes, and (9) unusually severe weather. The fixed-price construction Default clause at FAR 52.249-10 adds as excusable delays the following: (1) acts of another contractor in the performance of a contract with the government and (2) delays of subcontractors or suppliers at any tier, arising from unforeseeable causes beyond the control and without the fault or negligence of the contractor and its subcontractors or suppliers. See issued by the DOL, must be included in construction contracts for such projects. FAR 22.404-2. See Feldman, GOVERNMENT CONTRACT GUIDEBOOK §§ 29:11–29:16 (4th ed. 2019–2020); Cibinic, Nagle & Nash, ADMINISTRATION OF GOVERNMENT CONTRACTS 487–512 (5th ed. 2016); Nash, *Excusable Delays Under Commercial Item Contracts: Are Subcontractor Delays Excusable?*, 21 N&CR ¶ 22 (May 2007). Excusable delays are typical of the situations described in FORCE MAJEURE clauses in commercial contracts.

EXECUTIVE AGENCY   *Official:* An executive department, a military department, or any independent establishment within the meaning of 5 U.S.C. §§ 101, 102, and 104(1), respectively, and any wholly owned government corporation within the meaning of 31 U.S.C. § 9101. *Source:* FAR 2.101. Executive agencies include the executive departments (State, Justice, Treasury, Defense, Interior, Agriculture, Commerce, Labor, Health and Human Services, Housing and Urban Development, Transportation, Energy, Education, Veterans Affairs and Homeland Security), 5 U.S.C. § 101; the military departments (Army, Navy, and Air Force), 5 U.S.C. § 102; any independent establishment, 5 U.S.C. § 104(1); and any wholly owned government corporation within the meaning of 31 U.S.C. § 9101 (such as the Export-Import Bank of the United States, the Federal Crop Insurance Corporation, FEDERAL PRISON INDUSTRIES, INC., and the Pension Benefit Guaranty Corporation). See Cibinic, Nash & Yukins FORMATION OF GOVERNMENT CONTRACTS 25–34 (4th ed. 2011).

EXECUTIVE COMPENSATION   The compensation paid to a contractor's senior executives. FAR 31.205-6(p)(2)(ii) defines senior executive as including the five most highly compensated employees in management positions at each home office and each segment of a contractor. FAR 31.205-6(p)(2)(i) defines compensation as including the total amount of wages, salary, bonuses, deferred compensation, and employer contributions to defined contribution pension plans for the fiscal year, whether paid, earned, or otherwise accruing, as recorded in the contractor's cost accounting records for the fiscal year. 10 U.S.C. § 2324(e)(1)(p), 41 U.S.C. § 4304(a)(16), and FAR 31.205-6(p)(2) limit the allowability of such senior executive compensation to the BENCHMARK COMPENSATION AMOUNT determined applicable for the contractor fiscal year by the Administrator, OFFICE OF FEDERAL PROCUREMENT POLICY pursuant to 41 U.S.C. § 1127. Payments to senior executives in excess of the benchmark compensation amount are unallowable. The limitation on senior executive compensation should not be construed to mean that compensation up to the limit is *prima facie* reasonable. The Federal Funding Accountability and Transparency Act of 2006, Pub. L. No. 109-282, as amended by § 6202 of the

Government Funding Transparency Act of 2008, Pub. L. No. 110-252, as implemented by FAR Subpart 4.14, requires contractors to report senior executive compensation for all contracts with a value of $30,000 or more. See Manos, 1 GOVERNMENT CONTRACT COSTS & PRICING §§ 13:1–13:22 (2d ed. 2009–2020); Cibinic, Knight & Nash, COST-REIMBURSEMENT CONTRACTING 688 (4th ed. 2014); Owren-Wiest & O'Keefe, Jr., *Handle With Care' –ASBCA Finds Unreasonable DCAA's Misuse Of Statistics In Evaluating Reasonableness Of Executive Compensation*, 7 CP&A Rep. ¶ 15 (Mar. 2012); O'Keeffe, Jr., *Compensation Is Not a Four-Letter Word: Coping with a DCAA Executive Compensation Review*, 45 The Procurement Lawyer 1 (Fall 2009).

EXECUTIVE PRIVILEGE   An exemption under the FREEDOM OF INFORMATION ACT which protects inter-agency or intra-agency memorandums or letters which would not be available by law to a party other than an agency in litigation with the agency from release. 5 U.S.C. § 552(b)(5). This exemption is designed to protect the decision-making process of government agencies, which require the open exchange of ideas and opinions among government employees. See Nash & Rawicz, INTELLECTUAL PROPERTY IN GOVERNMENT CONTRACTS, chap. 9 (6th ed. 2008). See also PRIVILEGED INFORMATION.

EXECUTORY ACCORD   See ACCORD AND SATISFACTION.

EXHIBIT   *Official:* A document, referred to in a contract, which is attached to the contract and establishes requirements for deliverables. The term shall not be used to refer to any other kind of attachment to a contract. The DD Form 1423, Contract Data Requirements List, is always an exhibit rather than an attachment. *Source:* DFARS 204.7101. While this is a DOD definition, the term is commonly used by all agencies.

EXISTING WORKS   Existing motion pictures, television recordings, and other audiovisual works; sound recordings; musical, dramatic, and literary works; pantomimes and choreographic works; pictorial, graphic, and sculptural works; and works of a similar nature that are procured without modification. FAR 27.405-2; DFARS 227.7105. Such works are procured using the Rights in Data–Existing Works clauses in FAR 52.227-18 and DFARS 252.227-7021. These clauses give the government a royalty-free copyright license for government purposes. They also require the contractor to indemnify the government from a variety of claims that might arise from the use of such work. See Nash & Rawicz, INTELLECTUAL PROPERTY IN GOVERNMENT CONTRACTS, chap. 4 (6th ed. 2008).

EXPECTANCY DAMAGES   A monetary measure of DAMAGES in the amount a party would have benefited had the other party not breached the contract. This is the preferred measure of damages. To recover such damages, the nonbreaching party must show that they were unavoidable (see MITIGATION OF DAMAGES), foreseeable, and provable with a degree of certainty. See Cibinic, Nagle & Nash, ADMINISTRATION OF GOVERNMENT CONTRACTS 614–16 (5th ed. 2016).

EXPECTED MONETARY VALUE (EMV)   In DECISION ANALYSIS, a criterion of choice for a decision involving only money—the monetary value of the payoff of a course of action determined by multiplying the payoff by the probability of its occurrence. For example, if one choice of a course of action would offer a 20% chance of earning $100,000, the expected monetary value of that choice would be $20,000. When using expected monetary value criterion in conducting a decision analysis, the decision maker would be expected to choose the course of action that offers the highest expected monetary value. See Clemen, MAKING HARD

DECISIONS: AN INTRODUCTION TO DECISION ANALYSIS 105–09 (2d ed. 1996). The EMV criterion is also used in risk analysis.

EXPEDITED PROCEDURES Procedures used by the BOARDs OF CONTRACT APPEALS (BCAs) for the expedited disposition of any APPEAL FROM A CONTRACTING OFFICER'S DECISION, if the amount in dispute is $50,000 or less. These "small claims (expedited)" procedures are required by 41 U.S.C. § 7106(b)(1) and are often referred to as Rule 12.2 procedures because they are discussed in Uniform Rule 12.2 (see UNIFORM RULES). They apply at the sole election of the contractor. Uniform Rule 12.1(c) explains that the contractor must elect to proceed pursuant to Rule 12 within 60 days of receipt of the notice of docketing "unless such period is extended by the BCA for good cause." The government is not only unable to choose the expedited procedure should it so desire, but it is also, for the most part, powerless to stop the contractor from electing it in appropriate circumstances. Under the expedited procedure, appeals may be decided by a single member of the agency BCA, with such concurrences as may be required by rule or regulation. Appeals must be resolved, whenever possible, within 120 days after the contractor elects to use the procedure. A decision against either party reached under the procedure is final and conclusive and may be set aside only in cases of fraud. Administrative determinations and final decisions under expedited procedures have no value as precedent for future cases. Alternatively, contractors with small claims may elect the ACCELERATED PROCEDURE.

EXPENSING OF COSTS Charging the full acquisition cost of tangible capital assets to current accounts, as opposed to CAPITALIZATION. Expensing of costs permits a contractor to charge the full cost of an asset to the year it is acquired—thus maximizing its recovery. CAS 404, Capitalization of Tangible Assets, 48 C.F.R. § 9904.404-40, permits expensing of CAPITAL ASSETs with a value not exceeding $5,000, but a lesser amount may be used by contractors. See Manos, 2 GOVERNMENT CONTRACT COSTS & PRICING §§ 65:1–65:9 (2d ed. 2009–2020).

EXPERTS See INDIVIDUAL EXPERTS AND CONSULTANTS.

EXPIRED APPROPRIATION An appropriation that is no longer available for new obligations because the time available for incurring such obligations has expired. Expired appropriations are maintained by FISCAL YEAR identity for five years. During this period, obligations may be adjusted if otherwise proper, and outlays are made from these accounts. Unobligated balances may not be withdrawn from expired accounts. After the five-year period has elapsed, all obligated and unobligated balances are canceled, and the expired account is closed. U.S. GOV'T ACCOUNTABILITY OFFICE, PRINCIPLES OF FEDERAL APPROPRIATIONS LAW: ANNUAL UPDATE TO THE THIRD EDITION, Ch. 5, GAO-15-303SP (Washington, D.C.: Mar. 2015). See Nash, *Settlement Without Funds: Life Without An "M" Account*, 8 N&CR ¶ 17 (Mar. 1994).

EXPORT ADMINISTRATION REGULATIONS (EAR) Regulations in 15 C.F.R. part 740 that are promulgated and administered by the Department of Commerce, Bureau of Industry & Security to control export and reexport of items and activities within the bureau's jurisdiction. These regulations are located at 15 C.F.R. Subchapter C. (available at www.bis.doc.gov/).

EXPORT CONTROL The control of sensitive technologies by limiting the export of products, services, or technical information containing such technologies. The framework for export control is set forth in the EXPORT CONTROL REFORM ACT OF 2018. Export licenses are obtained from either the DEPARTMENT OF STATE (defense items) or the DEPARTMENT OF COMMERCE (commercial and dual use items). Licenses are required to release a controlled technology to a foreign national working in the United States (a "deemed export"). Guidance on export control is contained in 15 C.F.R. § 30.16 and DFARS Subpart 225.79. See U.S. Gov't Accountability Office, Export Controls: Challenges Exist in Enforcement of an Inherently Complex System, GAO-07-265 (Dec. 2006); Barker, *Export Controls, Compliance & National Security Concerns: Recent Developments & Current Trends*, Briefing Papers No. 18-3 (Feb. 2018); Best, et al., *DOJ Export Controls And Economic Sanctions Enforcement Guidance Likely To Impact Government Contractors, Parallels FCPA Pilot Program*, Briefing Papers No. 16-12 (Nov. 2016); Baj, et al., *Export Control Reform: Implementation & Implications*, Briefing Papers No. 14-13 (Dec. 2014).

EXPORT CONTROL REFORM ACT OF 2018   An Act, adopted at § 1741 et seq. of Pub. L. No. 115-232, setting forth the U.S. policy of restricting the export of products and technology through the requirement for mandatory licensing of exports, to friendly countries only, of data, research, development, production, procurement, and LOGISTICS support. This Act provides statutory authority for the EXPORT CONTROL activities of the DEPARTMENT OF COMMERCE. It is implemented by the Export Administration Regulation in 15 C.F.R. § 30.16.

EXPORT LICENSE   See EXPORT CONTROL.

EXPRESSLY UNALLOWABLE COST   *Official:* A particular item or type of cost which, under the express provisions of an applicable law, regulation, or contract, is specifically named and stated to be unallowable. *Source:* FAR 31.001. FAR 31.201-6 requires that contractors identify such costs and exclude them from any billing, CLAIM, or PROPOSAL submitted to the government. 10 U.S.C. § 2324(b) and 41 U.S.C. § 4303(b) call for penalties in the amount of the claimed costs to be assessed if expressly unallowable costs are included in indirect cost proposals. See FAR 42.709 and the Penalties for Unallowable Costs clause at FAR 52.242-3, also applying these penalties to final proposals under the Incentive Price Revision clause in FAR 52.216-16. 10 U.S.C. § 2324(e) and 41 U.S.C. § 4304(a) declare certain specific costs to be unallowable. See also SELECTED COSTS. See Manos, 1 Government Contract Costs & Pricing § 7:12 (2d ed. 2009–2020); Cibinic, Knight & Nash, Cost-Reimbursement Contracting, chap. 10 (4th ed. 2014).

EXTENDED OVERHEAD   See UNABSORBED OVERHEAD.

EXTRAORDINARY CONTRACTUAL ACTION   An action taken to enter into or amend a contract without regard to other provisions of law pursuant to the authority of Pub. L. No. 85-804, as amended by Pub. L. No. 93-155, 50 U.S.C. §§ 1431–1435. FAR Part 50 discusses extraordinary contractual actions and prescribes policies and procedures for the government to use to enter into, amend, or modify contracts in order to facilitate the national defense. This power is used to give contractors additional compensation, without regard to their legal entitlement, when an actual or threatened loss under a defense contract, however caused, will impair the productive ability of a contractor whose continued performance on any defense contract or whose continued operation as a source of supply is found to be essential to the national defense. In such cases, the contract may be amended without CONSIDERATION, but only to the extent necessary to avoid impairing the contractor's productive ability. An amendment without consideration may also be appropriate when a contractor suffers a loss because of government action, in which case the contract may be adjusted in the interest of fairness. FAR 50.103-2(a). Contracts may also be amended or modified to correct mistakes or formalize informal commitments. FAR 50.102(c) notes that certain kinds of contractual relief formerly available only under Pub. L. No. 85-804 (such as rescission or reformation for mutual mistake) are now available under the authority of the CONTRACT DISPUTES ACT OF 1978; it also provides that this authority should be relied on in preference to Pub. L. No. 85-804. Providing indemnification to contractors is another significant use of this authority. The clause at FAR 52.250-1, Indemnification Under Pub. L. No. 85-804 is inserted in a contract whenever the approving authority determines that the contractor must be indemnified against unusually hazardous or nuclear risks. FAR 50.104-4. issued by the DOL, must be included in construction contracts for such projects. FAR 22.404-2. See Feldman, GOVERNMENT CONTRACT GUIDEBOOK §§ 21:12–21:16 (4th ed. 2019–2020). See also Nash, *Indemnification Clauses: Litigation Breeders*, 20 N&CR ¶ 42 (Sept. 2006).

EXTRAORDINARY CONTRACTUAL RELIEF   See EXTRAORDINARY CONTRACTUAL ACTION.

EXTRINSIC EVIDENCE   Evidence proffered for contract interpretation other than the words of the contract itself. The most common types of extrinsic evidence are communications and negotiations prior to the signing of the contract, actions of the contracting parties before and after the contract is signed, and trade usage or practice. The admission of extrinsic evidence in a board or court proceeding has been significantly limited by the PAROL EVIDENCE RULE. Furthermore, such evidence should not be used to interpret words of the contract that have a PLAIN MEANING. Nash & Feldman, 1 GOVERNMENT CONTRACT CHANGES §§ 11:12–11:17 (3d ed. 2006–2020); Cibinic, Nagle & Nash, ADMINISTRATION OF GOVERNMENT CONTRACTS 177–211 (5th ed. 2016); 20 WILLISTON ON CONTRACTS § 55:23 (4th ed. 2011); Stubbs, *The Federal Circuit and Contract Interpretation: May Extrinsic Evidence Ever Be Used To Show Unambiguous Language Is Ambiguous?*, 39 PUB. CONT. L.J. 785 (2010); *Postscript VI: The Plain Meaning Rule*, 25 N&CR ¶ 16 (Mar. 2011); *Reading Contract Language: Strict Construction*, 23 N&CR ¶ 40 (Aug. 2009); Nash, *Incorporation By Reference: Be Explicit!*, 22 N&CR ¶ 72 (Dec. 2008).

F

FACILITIES Property used for production, maintenance, research, development, or testing. This term was defined in FAR 45.301 prior to the issuance of FAC 2005-17, May 15, 2007. The term was used to describe property provided to contractors but is no longer used in the FAR and FAR Part 45 (as rewritten) no longer contains any special policies regarding providing facilities to contractors, except for the general guidance in FAR Subpart 45.3. Such property also is subject to the provisions of the Government Property clause in FAR 52.245-1. See Cibinic, Nagle & Nash, ADMINISTRATION OF GOVERNMENT CONTRACTS 565 (5th ed. 2016).

FACILITIES CAPITAL *Official:* The NET BOOK VALUE of TANGIBLE CAPITAL ASSETS and of those INTANGIBLE CAPITAL ASSETS that are subject to AMORTIZA-TION. *Source:* CAS 414, Cost of Money as an Element of Facilities Capital, 48 C.F.R. § 9904.414-30. This amount is one of the key elements in the computation of the FACILI-TIES CAPITAL COST OF MONEY and the COST OF CAPITAL COMMITTED TO FACILITIES. Manos, 2 GOVERNMENT CONTRACT COSTS AND PRICING §§ 75:1–75:7 (2d ed. 2009–2020).

FACILITIES CAPITAL COST OF MONEY (FCCM) *Official:* Cost of money as an element of the cost of FACILITIES CAPITAL as used at 48 C.F.R. § 9904.414—Cost Accounting Standard—Cost of Money as an Element of Facilities Capital. *Source:* FAR 2.101. This is an imputed cost of money committed to the contractor's facilities employed in contract performance. FAR 31.205-10(a). The amount of imputed cost is calculated using the TREASURY INTEREST RATE. The costs are allowable and must be measured and allocated according to CAS 414, Cost of Money as an Element of the Cost of Facilities Capital, 48 C.F.R. § 9904.414, or CAS 417, Cost of Money as an Element of the Cost of Capital Assets Under Construction, 48 C.F.R. § 9904.417, whether or not the contract is otherwise subject to CAS. FAR 31.205-10(b). The provisions of the Facilities Capital Cost of Money clause, FAR 52.215-16, provide that if a prospective contractor does not propose this cost in its offer, the resulting contract will include the clause at FAR 52.215-17, Waiver of Facilities Capital Cost of Money. FAR 15.404-4 requires that, in establishing the PROFIT or FEE portion of the contract, the contracting officer must exclude any facilities capital cost of money included with the COST OBJECTIVE amounts. However, this exclusion is not required for DOD contracts where the WEIGHTED GUIDELINES are used. DAU, *Contract Pricing Reference Guides* v. III, chap. 10 (Feb. 22, 2012) provides guidance for analyzing facilities capital cost of money. See Manos, 2 GOVERNMENT CONTRACT COSTS AND PRICING §§ 75:1–75:7 (2d ed. 2009–2020); Cibinic, Nash & Yukins, FORMATION OF GOVERNMENT CONTRACTS 1563–64

(4th ed. 2011); Cibinic, Knight & Nash, Cost-Reimbursement Contracting 556–57 (4th ed. 2014). See also COST OF CAPITAL COMMITTED TO FACILITIES.

FACILITIES CONTRACT   A contract under which the government provides FACILITIES to a contractor or subcontractor for use in performing one or more related contracts for supplies or services. This term was defined in FAR 45.301 prior to the issuance of FAC 2005-17, May 15, 2007. The term is no longer used in the FAR and FAR Part 45 (as rewritten) no longer contains any special policies regarding facilities contracts. Rather they are governed by the general guidance in FAR Subpart 45.3. Under the prior FAR Subpart 45.3, facilities contracts could take any of the following forms: (1) facilities acquisition contracts for the acquisition, construction, and installation of facilities; (2) facilities use contracts for the use, maintenance, accountability, and disposition of facilities; or (3) consolidated facilities contracts for both facilities acquisition and use. Facilities contracts were required to be COST CONTRACTs with the contractor receiving no FEE. FAR 45.302-3 specified that facilities could be provided as part of another contract when one of the following exceptions applied: (1) the actual or estimated cumulative acquisition cost of the facilities provided by the contracting activity to the contractor at one plant or general location does not exceed $1 million, (2) the number of items of plant equipment provided is 10 or fewer, (3) the contract performance period is 12 months or less, (4) the contract is for construction, (5) the contract is for services and the facilities are to be used in connection with the operation of a government-owned plant or installation, or (6) the contract is for work within an establishment or installation operated by the government.

FACSIMILE (FAX)   Electronic equipment that communicates and reproduces both printed and handwritten material. If used in conjunction with a reference to a document; e.g., facsimile bid, the terms refers to a document (in the example given, a bid) that has been transmitted to and received by the government via facsimile. This term was previously defined in FAR 2.101. Facsimile BIDs OR PROPOSALs can be considered if permitted by the SOLICITATION. FAR 14.301(c); FAR 15.203(d). Offerors are informed that such bids or proposals may be submitted by inclusion in the solicitation of the Facsimile Bids provision in FAR 52.214-31 or the Facsimile Proposals provision in FAR 52.215-5.

FACT   An event that has occurred. Under the TRUTH IN NEGOTIATIONS ACT (TINA), the CERTIFIED COST OR PRICING DATA that a contractor must submit to the government must include all facts that a prudent buyer or seller would reasonably expect to affect price negotiations significantly. In this regard, facts are distinguished from judgments. A fact is objectively verifiable by AUDIT or technical evaluation; a judgment is subjective and cannot be verified except in hindsight. While vendor quotations, nonrecurring costs, information on changes in production methods, management decisions impacting costs, data supporting projections of business prospects, unit-cost trends, and the like are considered facts, a pure estimate of the cost of future contract performance based on these facts is considered a judgment. In the application of TINA, contractors and contracting officers have encountered continuing difficulties in drawing a firm line between facts and judgments. See Cibinic, Nagle & Nash, Administration of Government Contracts 1165–67 (5th ed. 2016); Nash, *Postscript: Cost or Pricing Data*, 15 N&CR ¶ 47 (Sept. 2001).

FAILURE TO DISCLOSE INFORMATION   See SUPERIOR KNOWLEDGE.

FAILURE TO MAKE A GOOD FAITH EFFORT TO COMPLY WITH THE SUBCONTRACTING PLAN   *Official:* Willful or intentional failure to perform in accordance with the requirements of the SUBCONTRACTING PLAN, or willful or intentional action to frustrate the plan. *Source:* FAR 19.701. FAR Subpart 19.7 addresses subcontracting with SMALL BUSINESS CONCERNs, VETERAN-OWNED SMALL BUSINESS CONCERNs, SERVICE-DISABLED VETERAN-OWNED SMALL BUSINESS CONCERNs, HUBZONE small business concerns, small disadvantaged business, and WOMEN-OWNED SMALL BUSINESS CONCERNs, including the requirement that specified contractors have subcontracting plans. When a contractor fails to make a good faith effort to comply with a subcontracting plan, the contractor can be held liable for LIQUIDATED DAMAGES. FAR 19.705-7; 15 U.S.C. § 637(d)(4)(F). See Hewitt, *Small Business Contracting Programs-Part II*, BRIEFING PAPERS No. 10-13 (Dec. 2010).

FAILURE TO MAKE PROGRESS   A failure of a contractor to perform the work required by a government supply or service contract in a manner that provides reasonable assurance to the government that the contract schedule will be met. The Default (Fixed-Price Supply and Service) clause in FAR 52.249-8 provides that the government may terminate the contract for default before the completion date if the contractor's failure to make progress is such that the performance of the contract is endangered. Terminations based on failure to make progress require that the contracting officer give the contractor notice and an opportunity to "cure" the failure (a minimum of 10 days) before the government exercises its right to terminate the contract for default. This type of TERMINATION FOR DEFAULT is distinguished from terminations based on failure to deliver supplies or perform services within the time specified in the contract, which require no CURE NOTICE. FAR 49.402-3. See Cibinic, Nagle & Nash, ADMINISTRATION OF GOVERNMENT CONTRACTS 813–19 (5th ed. 2016).

FAILURE TO PROSECUTE THE WORK   Failure of a contractor to perform the work, or any part thereof, under a construction contract with sufficient diligence to ensure completion by the contract date. The Default (Fixed-Price Construction) clause in FAR 52.249-10 provides that the government may terminate the contract for default before the completion date if the contractor fails to prosecute the work. No CURE NOTICE is required for this type of TERMINATION FOR DEFAULT, but a SHOW CAUSE NOTICE is usually issued prior to termination. The Default (Fixed-Price Research and Development) clause in FAR 52.249 also contains this ground for default termination but requires the issuance of a CURE NOTICE prior to making the termination decision.

FAIR AND REASONABLE PRICE   A price that is fair to both parties, considering the agreed-upon conditions, including the promised quality and time of contract performance. FAR 15.402(a) requires contracting officers to ensure that supplies and services are purchased under negotiated contracts (see NEGOTIATION) at fair and reasonable prices. FAR 15.405(a) provides that price negotiation is the means to be used by contracting officers to arrive at this result, while FAR 15.404-1(b)(2) suggests the use of PRICE ANALYSIS to determine whether the price is fair and reasonable. FAR 14.408-2 requires contracting officers to ensure that sealed bid contracts (see SEALED BIDDING) are awarded at "reasonable" prices. It also suggests that price analysis be used to determine whether the offered price is reasonable. All of this guidance is addressed, primarily, to the issue of whether the price is too high; whereas, COST REALISM is generally addressed to the issue of whether the cost estimate is too low. See Cibinic, Nash & Yukins, FORMATION OF GOVERNMENT CONTRACTS 1476–87 (4th ed. 2011). See also Nash & Cibinic, *Contract Prices: What Is a "Fair and Reasonable Price"?*, 15 N&CR ¶ 22 (Apr. 2001); Nash, *Guidance on Contract Pricing: A Substantive Addition*, 21 N&CR ¶ 41 (Aug. 2007).

FAIR LABOR STANDARDS ACT (FLSA)   29 U.S.C. § 201 et seq. A 1938 Act commonly known as the "Federal Wage and Hour Law." The FLSA establishes minimum-wage and maximum-hour standards. However, if an employee is entitled under state law to higher wages or better hours than those mandated by the FLSA, the state law controls. The FLSA applies to industry generally rather than to government contractors specifically. Federal agencies must encourage contractors to enforce FLSA requirements when applicable. Supply contractors subject the WALSH-HEALEY ACT must pay the minimum wages specified by the FLSA. See the Walsh-Healey Public Contracts Act clause in FAR 52.222-20. SERVICE CONTRACTs in excess of $2,500 must contain mandatory provisions regarding minimum wage and fringe benefits, safe and sanitary working conditions, and other statutory requirements. See FAR 22.1002-1. FAR 22.1002-4 states that no contractor or subcontractor holding a service contract for any dollar amount shall pay any of its employees less than the minimum wage specified in § 6(a)(1) of the FLSA. FAR 22.1003-3 lists contracts exempt from the FLSA. See Cibinic, Nash & Yukins, FORMATION OF GOVERNMENT CONTRACTS 1653–66 (4th ed. 2011).

FAIR MARKET PRICE   *Official:* A price based on reasonable costs under normal competitive conditions and not on lowest possible cost (see 19.202-6). *Source:* FAR 19.001. The expectation that awards will be made at fair market prices is one of the conditions that must be met in order to SET ASIDE an acquisition or class of acquisitions for exclusive small business participation. FAR 19.502-2(b). In DOD, the expectation that award will be made at not more than 10% above fair market price is one of the expectations that must be met in order for an acquisition to be set aside for HISTORICALLY BLACK COLLEGES AND UNIVERSITIES and MINORITY INSTITUTIONs. DFARS 226.370-4. See Cibinic, Nash & Yukins, FORMATION OF GOVERNMENT CONTRACTS 1590–95 (4th ed. 2011).

FAIR MARKET VALUE   The price at which supplies would change hands between a willing buyer and a willing seller in the open market in an arm's-length transaction. BLACK'S LAW DICTIONARY 1865 (11th ed. 2019). The term arises in discussions of REASONABLENESS OF COST. In *Bruce Constr. Corp. v. United States*, 163 Ct. Cl. 97, 324 F.2d 516 (1963), in reference to the amount of an EQUITABLE ADJUSTMENT, it was held that HISTORICAL COST, rather than fair market value, is the proper measure of cost reasonableness. However, 10 U.S.C. § 2324(j) and FAR 31.201-3(a) state that contractors have the burden of proving that the costs they incurred were reasonable. Fair market value is also used to determine allowable portion of losses for impairing depreciable PROPERTY or CAPITAL ASSETs. FAR 31.205-16.

FAIR OPPORTUNITY (TO BE CONSIDERED)   Under a multiple-award indefinite-delivery indefinite-quantity (IDIQ) contract, a process in which the government gives each of the contractors a chance to win the award of a delivery order or a task order. FAR 16.505(b)(1)(ii) states that the process used need not conform to the requirements or procedures for sealed bidding or competitive negotiation (source selection). However, there are stringent notice requirements in FAR 16.505(b)(1) to ensure that competition is obtained to the maximum extent practicable. See Nash, *Postscript II: Breach of the Loss of the Fair Opportunity to Compete*, 22 N&CR ¶ 39 (July 2008).

FAIR USE   Use of a WORK that is not an infringement of a COPYRIGHT because it is used for the purpose of criticism, comment, news reporting, teaching, scholarship, or research. 17 U.S.C. § 107. In determining whether a use is fair, a court must consider: (1) the purpose and character of the use, including whether it is commercial or educational; (2) the nature of the copyrighted work; (3) the amount and substantiality of the use in relation to the whole work; and (4) the effect of the use on the potential market for or value of the copyrighted work. See Nash & Rawicz, INTELLECTUAL PROPERTY IN GOVERNMENT CONTRACTS, chap. 1 (6th ed. 2008).

FALSE CLAIMS ACT   An Act giving the government remedies against parties that process false claims. It was originally passed at the time of the Civil War and has now been divided into two sections: the Civil False Claims Act, 31 U.S.C. § 3729 et seq., and the Criminal False Claims Act, 18 U.S.C. § 287. These acts are commonly used to address fraudulent conduct by contractors. To establish a violation of either statute, the government must prove that (1) the contractor made or presented a claim for payment to the government; (2) the claim was asserted against the government; (3) the claim was false, fictitious, or fraudulent; and (4) the contractor knew that the claim was false, fictitious, or fraudulent when presenting it. The primary differences between the civil statute and the criminal statute are the level of intent required, the standard of proof the government must meet, and the penalties the government can inflict. Contractors can be found liable for both criminal and civil penalties. In addition, Congress has enacted a qui tam statute (see QUI TAM PROCEEDINGS) authorizing private individuals to bring actions for violations of the Civil False Claims Act. See generally Boese, CIVIL FALSE CLAIMS AND QUI TAM ACTIONS (5th ed. 2020) and Sylvia, THE FALSE CLAIMS ACT: FRAUD AGAINST THE GOVERNMENT (3d ed. 2016–2020). See also Schooner, *False Claims Act: Greater DOJ Scrutiny of Frivolous Qui Tam Actions?*, 32 N&CR ¶ 20 (Apr. 2018); Mitchell, Krigsten & Grandt, *Lowering The Bar: Courts Continue To Narrow The Scope Of The False Claims Act's Public Disclosure Rule*, BRIEFING PAPERS NO. 15-12 (Nov. 2015); Cone, Rhoad & Sneckenberg, *Negotiating False Claims Act Settlements*, BRIEFING PAPERS NO. 14-3 (Feb. 2014). See also PROGRAM FRAUD CIVIL REMEDIES ACT.

FALSE STATEMENTS ACT   An Act, 18 U.S.C. § 1001, that prohibits any person, in any matter under the government's jurisdiction, from "knowingly and willfully" falsifying, concealing, or covering up a material fact, or making a false, fictitious, or fraudulent statement. Considerably broader in scope than the FALSE CLAIMS ACT, the False Statements Act has been held to cover all false statements that might support fraudulent claims or that might pervert or corrupt the authorized functions of a government agency to which the statements were made. It covers oral as well as written statements and unsworn as well as sworn statements. It also covers the omission of information on a certified statement when the information should have been included. The Act applies to matters that involve a government agency's activity even though the false statement is not made directly to the government. The courts have required that a statement must be material to fall within the scope of the Act; that is, it must have a natural tendency to influence or be capable of influencing the actions of a federal agency. See Sylvia, THE FALSE CLAIMS ACT: FRAUD AGAINST THE GOVERNMENT (3d ed. 2016–2020). See also Cibinic, Nagle & Nash, ADMINISTRATION OF GOVERNMENT CONTRACTS 120–24 (5th ed. 2016); Cibinic, Nash & Yukins, FORMATION OF GOVERNMENT CONTRACTS 191–95 (4th ed. 2011).

FAR   See FEDERAL ACQUISITION REGULATION.

FAR PROHIBITION ON TEXTING   A government policy, established in Executive Order No. 13513 (Oct. 2009), to encourage contractors and subcontractors to adopt and enforce policies that ban text messaging while driving rented, contractor-owned, or government-owned vehicles or privately owned vehicles when performing work on behalf of the government. The prohibition on text messaging includes reading or entering data into a handheld or other electronic device, which includes email, text message services, and obtaining navigational information (the term does not include glancing or listening to a navigational device as long as the route is programmed before driving or while stopped). FAR Subpart 23.11 implements the ban on text messaging while driving.

FAR SECRETARIAT   The government organization, housed in the GENERAL SERVICES ADMINISTRATION, that maintains, prints, publishes, and distributes the FEDERAL ACQUISITION REGULATION. The FAR Secretariat provides the DEFENSE ACQUISITION REGULATORY COUNCIL and the CIVILIAN AGENCY ACQUISITION COUNCIL with centralized services for keeping a synopsis of current FAR cases (proposed FAR changes) and their status, assigning FAR case numbers, maintaining official case files, assisting parties interested in reviewing the files on completed cases, and performing miscellaneous administrative tasks pertaining to the maintenance of the FAR. See FAR 1.201-2.

FAR SYSTEM   See FEDERAL ACQUISITION REGULATIONS SYSTEM.

FAST PAYMENT PROCEDURE   A payment procedure that allows payment to a contractor, under limited conditions (such as individual orders not exceeding $35,000, unless the agency authorizes exceptions), before the government verifies that supplies have been received and accepted. See FAR Subpart 13.4. When the government intends to use the procedure, the procuring agency will include the Fast Payment Procedure clause in FAR 52.213-1 in the solicitation and contract. Under the procedure, payment may be made on the basis of the contractor's submission of an INVOICE constituting a representation that (1) the supplies have been delivered to a post office, common carrier (see CARRIER (TRANSPORTATION)), or point of first receipt by the government; and (2) the contractor agrees to replace, repair, or correct supplies not received at destination, damaged in transit, or not conforming to purchase agreements. FAR 13.402(c) provides that title to supplies vests in the government upon delivery to a post office or common carrier for mailing or shipment, or upon receipt by the government if the shipment is by means other than Postal Service or common carrier. See Cibinic, Nagle & Nash, ADMINISTRATION OF GOVERNMENT CONTRACTS 1048 (5th ed. 2016).

FAST-TRACK CONSTRUCTION   A method of CONSTRUCTION contracting under which the contractor begins building as soon as the foundation plans are ready and a foundation permit has been issued, despite the fact that the architect-engineer has not finished designing the project. Throughout performance, the architect-engineer must keep ahead of the contractor's progress in order to supply the necessary plans and drawings before each stage of the construction is reached. This is a method of shortening the time to complete a construction project but it increases the risk of DEFECTIVE SPECIFICATIONS.

FEDBIZOPPS   See **FEDERAL BUSINESS OPPORTUNITIES**

FEDERAL ACQUISITION CIRCULAR (FAC)   A publication of the government that revises, amends, and/or updates the FEDERAL ACQUISITION REGULATION. Revisions to the FAR are prepared and issued through the coordinated action of the DEFENSE ACQUISITION REGULATORY COUNCIL and the CIVILIAN AGENCY ACQUISITION COUNCIL. Each council maintains cognizance over specified portions of the FAR and is responsible for agreeing with the other council on revisions. Revisions to the FAR are submitted to the FAR SECRETARIAT and pass through a period of public notice and comment begun by publication in the FEDERAL REGISTER. See FAR Subpart 1.2. FACs were numbered sequentially (84-1 through 84-60) from the original promulgation of the FAR in 1984 until the issuance of the 1990 version of the FAR. FACs were then numbered sequentially (90-1 through 90-46) until the issuance of the 1997 version of the FAR. FACs were then numbered sequentially (97-1 through 97-26) until the issuance of the 2001 version of the FAR. FACs were then numbered sequentially (01-1 through 01-27) until the issuance of the 2005 version of the FAR. FACs were then numbered sequentially (05-1 through 05-101) until the issuance of the 2019 version of the FAR. They are now being issued sequentially under that version.

FEDERAL ACQUISITION INSTITUTE (FAI)   A research and management facility dedicated to promoting government-wide career management programs for a professional procurement workforce. Originally an organization within the OFFICE OF FEDERAL PROCUREMENT POLICY (OFPP), FAI was transferred to the GENERAL SERVICES ADMINISTRATION (GSA) in January 1984, with OFPP retaining a "policy oversight role." FAI conducts courses in government procurement and maintains a list of organizations providing such training. It also administers certification programs for civilian agency personnel. See www.fai.gov. It released the five–volume set of CONTRACT PRICING REFERENCE GUIDES jointly with the AIR FORCE INSTITUTE OF TECHNOLOGY.

FEDERAL ACQUISITION REFORM ACT OF 1996 (FARA)   A 1996 Act, enacted as Division D of the Fiscal Year 1996 Defense Authorization Act, Pub. L. No. 104-106. The Act provides for government-wide acquisition reform, including the adoption of a two-phase DESIGN-BUILD procedure, revision of the TRUTH IN NEGOTIATIONS ACT, revision of the rules on the acquisition of COMMERCIAL ITEMS, elimination of a number of CERTIFICATION requirements, revision of the PROCUREMENT INTEGRITY ACT, and adoption of new rules concerning the acquisition workforce. The provisions of this Act are codified in the ARMED SERVICES PROCUREMENT ACT, the FEDERAL PROPERTY AND ADMINISTRATIVE SERVICES ACT, and the OFFICE OF FEDERAL PROCUREMENT POLICY ACT. The Act was renamed the CLINGER-COHEN ACT OF 1996.

FEDERAL ACQUISITION REGULATION (FAR)   The primary document in the FEDERAL ACQUISITION REGULATIONS SYSTEM, containing uniform policies and procedures that govern the ACQUISITION activity of all federal agencies that do not have a specific exemption (such as the FEDERAL AVIATION ADMINISTRATION and the POSTAL SERVICE). The FAR is prepared, issued, and maintained jointly by the Secretary of Defense, the Administrator of General Services, and the NASA Administrator. FAR 1.103. It is published in Title 48 of the CODE OF FEDERAL REGULATIONS and in a commercial version published by Commerce Clearing House, 4025 West Peterson Avenue, Chicago, IL 60646-6085, www.cch.com. In addition, the GSA has made the FAR available on the Internet at www.acquisition.gov Changes to the FAR are made through FEDERAL ACQUISITION CIRCULARS. The FAR has 53 parts, which are grouped in 8 subchapters: General, ACQUISITION PLANNING, Contracting Methods and Contract Types, Socioeconomic Programs, General Contracting Requirements, Special Categories of Contracting, Contract Management, and Clauses and Forms. See Nash, *The Federal Acquisition Regulation: It Doesn't Resolve Problems*, 20 N&CR ¶ 6 (Jan. 2006).

FEDERAL ACQUISITION REGULATIONS SYSTEM   The system of regulations that governs the acquisition by contract of supplies and services needed by federal agencies. The system consists of the FEDERAL ACQUISITION REGULATION (FAR), which is the primary document, and supplementary regulations issued by individual agencies. Such supplements (for example, the DOD FAR SUPPLEMENT and the NASA FAR SUPPLEMENT) contain regulations limited (in theory, at least) to those needed to implement FAR policies and procedures within the agency or supplement the FAR to satisfy agency-specific needs. Implementation (agency treatment expanding on FAR material) is numbered parallel to the FAR. Supplementation (agency-peculiar material with no FAR counterpart) is given numbers of 70 and up. The FAR System does not include purely internal agency guidance that does not have a significant effect beyond the internal operating procedures of the agency and does not have a significant cost or administrative impact on contractors or offerors. FAR 1.301(a)(2). Part 1 of the FAR sets forth the rules governing the issuance of regulations in the FAR System, including administration (Subpart 1.2), agency acquisition regulations (Subpart 1.3), DEVIATIONs (Subpart 1.4), and agency and public participation (Subpart 1.5). The regulations making up the FAR system are published in Title 48 of the CODE OF FEDERAL REGULATIONS. Many of the FAR regulations are available on the Internet, including the FAR at www.acquisition.gov; the DFARS at http://www.acq.osd.mil/dpap/dars/dfarspgi/current/index.html; and the NFS at http://www.hq.nasa.gov/office/procurement/regs/nfstoc.htm. See *Overview of Federal Acquisition Regulation System*, 15A Fed. Proc., L. Ed. § 39.1 (June 2011); Cibinic, Nash & Yukins, Formation of Government Contracts 34–37 (4th ed. 2011).

FEDERAL ACQUISITION REGULATORY (FAR) COUNCIL   The government organization, established by 41 U.S.C. § 1302, that is charged with assisting in the direction and coordination of government-wide procurement policy and regulatory activities. It is made up of the Administrator of the OFFICE OF FEDERAL PROCUREMENT POLICY (OFPP), the Secretary of Defense, and the administrators of GSA and NASA. DOD, GSA, and NASA are represented, through delegation, by their officials in charge of acquisition policy. The council, in a very broad sense, manages, coordinates, controls, and monitors maintenance of, issuance of, and changes in the FEDERAL ACQUISITION REGULATION (FAR). The OFPP Administrator, in conjunction with the FAR Council, ensures that procurement regulations promulgated by an EXECUTIVE AGENCY are consistent with the FAR and are limited to regulations essential to implement government-wide policies and procedures within the agency and additional policies and procedures required to satisfy the agency's specific and unique needs. Written justification by the council and statutory authority are the only means of including CERTIFICATION requirements for contractors or offerors. See FAR 1.107. See www.whitehouse.gov/omb/procurement_far_council.

FEDERAL ACQUISITION SERVICE   The office in the GENERAL SERVICES ADMINISTRATION that procures on a government-wide basis commercial products and services, INFORMATION TECHNOLOGY, the FEDERAL TELECOMMUNICATIONS SYSTEM, and other services related to information technology. 40 U.S.C. § 303. This service was created in 2006 by merging the FEDERAL SUPPLY SERVICE and the FEDERAL TECHNOLOGY SERVICE. See www.gsa.gov/fas.

FEDERAL ACQUISITION STREAMLINING ACT (FASA) OF 1994   An Act, Pub. L. No. 103-355, that substantially revised federal procurement law. The Act sought to reduce paperwork, encourage the acquisition of commercial items, raise the threshold for SIMPLIFIED

ACQUISITION PROCEDURES (previously called "small purchases") to $100,000, promote electronic commerce, and achieve greater efficiency and uniformity among the agencies in their procurement practices.

FEDERAL ACTIVITIES INVENTORY REFORM ACT (FAIR ACT)   Pub. L. No. 105-270. An Act which requires the OFFICE OF MANAGEMENT AND BUDGET to publish each fiscal year an announcement of public availability of agency inventories of activities that are not inherently governmental. The purpose is to enhance A-76 policy. Guidance on the preparation of these inventories is provided by memoranda from the Administrator of the OFFICE OF FEDERAL PROCUREMENT POLICY. See OFPP M-12-09, Mar. 26, 2012. Agencies are required to make their inventories public after reviewing and consulting with OMB. Agencies also include activities that are inherently governmental. Interested parties who disagree with the agency's initial judgment can challenge the inclusion or the omission of an activity, and may demand a higher agency review.

FEDERAL AGENCY   *Official:* Any EXECUTIVE AGENCY or any independent establishment in the legislative or judicial branch of the government (except the Senate, the House of Representatives, the Architect of the Capitol, and any activities under the Architect's direction). *Source:* FAR 2.101. For the purpose of Right-To-Know laws and Pollution Prevention requirements in FAR Subpart 23.10, the term means only an executive agency. FAR 23.1003.

FEDERAL AGENCY PROCUREMENT   *Official:* The acquisition (by using competitive procedures and awarding a contract) of goods and services (including construction) from non-federal sources by a federal agency using appropriated funds. For BROAD AGENCY ANNOUNCEMENTs and small business innovative research programs (see SMALL BUSINESS INNOVATIVE RESEARCH CONTRACT), each proposal received by an agency constitutes a separate procurement for purposes of the Act. *Source:* FAR 3.104-1. The new PROCUREMENT INTEGRITY rules regarding disclosure and receipt of information and employment contracts apply only to conduct relating to federal agency procurement contracts. This is a substantial limitation of these rules because only competitive contracts are included in this definition (excluding sole source procurement and contract modifications). See Cibinic, Nash & Yukins, FORMATION OF GOVERNMENT CONTRACTS 170–72, 212–16 (4th ed. 2011).

FEDERAL AVIATION ADMINISTRATION (FAA)   An organization within the DEPARTMENT OF TRANSPORTATION responsible for the control and safety of civil aviation with the United States. Section 348 of the Department of Transportation Appropriations Act of 1996, Pub. L. No. 104-50, directed the FAA to develop and implement a new acquisition management system and provided that it was not subject to the major laws governing procurements of the Department of Transportation. As a result, the FAA is not subject to the FEDERAL ACQUISITION REGULATION but performs its procurements under the FEDERAL AVIATION ADMINISTRATION ACQUISITION MANAGEMENT SYSTEM.

FEDERAL AVIATION ADMINISTRATION ACQUISITION MANAGEMENT SYSTEM (AMS)   The regulation issued by the FEDERAL AVIATION ADMINISTRATION on April 1, 1996 to establish the procedures for conducting procurement under its independent authority. The most current version of the AMS was issued in October 2019. Under this regulation, the FAA does not use SEALED BIDDING but conducts all procurements under a

SCREENING procedure, soliciting information or offers through one or more SCREEN-ING INFORMATION REQUESTs (SIRs). The regulation also establishes an independent system for resolving PROTESTs and DISPUTEs (not following the procedures of the GOVERNMENT ACCOUNTABILITY OFFICE or the CONTRACT DISPUTES ACT). See Cibinic, Nash & Yukins, FORMATION OF GOVERNMENT CONTRACTS 1111–15 (4th ed. 2011).

FEDERAL AWARDEE PERFORMANCE AND INTEGRITY INFORMATION SYSTEM (FAPIIS) A government database of information regarding the integrity and performance of contractors and grantees with awards over $500,000 required to be compiled by § 872 of the National Defense Authorization Act for FY 2009, Pub. L. No. 110-417 (Oct. 14, 2008). FAPIIS includes PAST PERFORMANCE information and information on defective COST OR PRICING DATA, DEFAULT TERMINATIONs, civil and criminal fraud proceedings, SUSPENSIONs and DEBARMENTs, and non-responsibility determinations. FAR 42.1503 provides that agencies will report much of this information with reporting instructions in www.ppirs.gov/fapiis.html. Contractors are required to update information in FAPIIS on a semi-annual basis by the Updates of Publicly Available Information Regarding Responsibility Matters clause in FAR 52.209-9. Section 3010 of the Supplemental Appropriations Act for FY 2010, Pub. L. No. 111-212, requires that all of the information in FAPIIS except past performance information be made publicly available. (See www.fapiis.gov) Contracting officers awarding contracts over the SIMPLIFIED ACQUISITION THRESHOLD must review FAPIIS before award. FAR 9.104-6.

FEDERAL BUSINESS OPPORTUNITIES (FEDBIZOPPS) A single GOVERNMENT-WIDE POINT OF ENTRY (GPE) for federal government procurement opportunities over $25,000—used until 2019. It has been replaced by beta.SAM.gov—Contract Opportunities. Government buyers are required to publicize proposed CONTRACT ACTIONs over $25,000 by posting information directly to beta.SAM.gov via the Internet. FAR 5.101(a)(1). See Feldman, GOVERNMENT CONTRACT AWARDS: NEGOTIATION AND SEALED BIDDING §§ 3:3–3:8 (2019–2020 ed.).

FEDERAL CIRCUIT COURT See COURT OF APPEALS FOR THE FEDERAL CIRCUIT.

FEDERAL CLAIMS COLLECTION ACT The original debt collection statute that was enacted in 1966 and renamed under the DEBT COLLECTION ACT OF 1982, Pub. L. No. 97–365.

FEDERAL CONTRACT INFORMATION *Official:* Information, not intended for public release, that is provided by or generated for the government under a contract to develop or deliver a product or service to the government, but not including information provided by the government to the public (such as that on public Web sites) or simple transactional information, such as that necessary to process payments. *Source:* FAR 4.1901. Contractors must protect this information from cyber attacks. Thus, FAR 4.1903 requires the inclusion of the Basic Safeguarding of Covered Contractor Information Systems, in 52.204-21, in solicitations and contracts when the contractor or a subcontractor at any tier may have federal contract information residing in or transiting through its information system. See CYBERSECURITY.

FEDERAL COURTS ADMINISTRATION ACT OF 1992 An Act, Pub. L. No. 102-572, that, among other things, made improvements in the U.S. Claims Court, renamed by this

Act to be the U.S. COURT OF FEDERAL CLAIMS. Title IX of the Act clarified the proceedings and powers of the court, as well as made certification of CLAIMs under the CONTRACT DISPUTES ACT nonjurisdictional. See House Rept. 102-1006, 102d Congress, 2d Sess. (Oct. 3, 1992); Senate Rept. 102-342 (July 27, 1992).

FEDERAL COURTS IMPROVEMENT ACT (FCIA) 28 U.S.C. § 171 et seq., 791, 794–98, 1491–92, 1494–1503, 1505, 1507–1509. A 1982 act that reorganized the courts dealing with government procurement by eliminating the Court of Claims and creating the U.S. Claims Court (subsequently renamed the U.S. COURT OF FEDERAL CLAIMS) and the U.S. COURT OF APPEALS FOR THE FEDERAL CIRCUIT. The Act also conferred new jurisdiction on the Claims Court to hear preaward protests. See 28 U.S.C. § 1491(b)(1). See Hrabik, *Federal Courts Improvement Act*, 24 Duq. L. Rev. 945 (1986); Anthony & Smith, *The Federal Courts Improvement Act of 1982: Its Impact on the Resolution of Federal Contract Disputes*, 13 Pub. Cont. L.J. 201 (1983).

FEDERAL HELIUM SUPPLIER *Official:* A private helium vendor that has an in-kind crude helium sales contract with the Bureau of Land Management, and that is on the BLM Amarillo Field Office's Authorized List of Federal Helium Suppliers available via the Internet at http://blm.gov/8pjd. *Source:* FAR 8.501. See FAR Subpart 8.5 implementing the HELIUM ACT, 50 U.S.C. § 167a et seq., which concerns the acquisition of liquid or gaseous helium by federal agencies or by government contractors or subcontractors for use in the performance of a government contract. Contracts requiring a major supply of helium must contain the Required Sources for Helium and Helium Usage Data clause, FAR 52.208-8.

FEDERAL INFORMATION PROCESSING STANDARDS PUBLICATIONS (FIPS PUBS) Official government publications relating to standards adopted and issued under the provisions of § 5131 of the Information Technology Management Reform Act of 1996, 40 U.S.C. § 1441. FIPS PUBS, issued by the National Institute of Standards and Technology (NIST), fall into two general categories: standards, which are mandatory, and guidelines, which are informational documents. Agencies are required to follow the FIPS PUBS guidance when selecting specifications for information technology. FAR 11.102. The Government Information Services Board was established by Exec. Order No. 13011, 61 Fed. Reg. 37657 (July 16, 1996), to assist NIST in developing standards and guidelines for federal information systems.

FEDERAL LABORATORY CONSORTIUM (FLC) FOR TECHNOLOGY TRANSFER The organization that carries out the formal mission of promoting and strengthening TECHNOLOGY TRANSFER across the federal research system under 15 U.S.C. § 3701 et seq. Membership is mandatory for most federal laboratories. The FLC was created in 1971 to facilitate technology transfer between DOD and state and local governments. In 1974, the FLC was expanded to include other federal agencies on a voluntary basis. See Nash & Rawicz, Intellectual Property in Government Contracts, chap. 7 (6th ed. 2008).

FEDERAL MANAGEMENT REGULATION (FMR) The successor to the FEDERAL PROPERTY MANAGEMENT REGULATION (FPMR), promulgated by the General Services Administration (GSA) pursuant to 40 U.S.C. § 486(c) in order to establish rules for the management of Federal property and associated administrative matters. 41 C.F.R., chapter 102. It contains updated regulatory policies originally in the FPMR, but does not contain material describing how to do business with the GSA. 41 C.F.R. § 102-2.5. It applies to all executive agencies with some provisions applying to all federal agencies. 41 C.F.R. § 102-2.20.

FEDERAL PRISON INDUSTRIES, INC. (FPI)   A self-supporting, wholly owned government corporation of the District of Columbia; also referred to as UNICOR. FAR 8.601. Through the sale of its products and services to government agencies, Federal Prison Industries provides training and employment for prisoners confined in federal penal and correctional institutions. 18 U.S.C. §§ 4121–4129. Federal Prison Industries maintain a list of supplies manufactured and services performed by FPI (www.unicon.gov). See FAR 8.601(d). FAR 8.602 requires agencies to conduct MARKET RESEARCH to determine if the FPI price is comparable to private MARKET PRICEs and to purchase from FPI if the price is comparable. FAR 8.601(c) states that Federal Prison Industries diversify its products and services to prevent private industry from experiencing unfair competition from prison workshops or activities. See McDonald, *Federal Prison Industry Reform: The Demise of Prison Factories?*, 35 Pub. Cont. L.J. 675 (2006).

FEDERAL PRIZE COMPETITION   See PRIZE COMPETITION

FEDERAL PROCUREMENT DATA SYSTEM (FPDS)   A system for collecting and compiling data on federal procurement. The FPDS provides a comprehensive mechanism for assembling, organizing, and presenting contract placement data for the federal government. FAR 4.602. Federal agencies report data directly to the Federal Procurement Data System—Next Generation (FPDS-NG), which collects, processes, and disseminates official statistical data on federal contracting. The data provide (1) a basis for recurring and special reports to the President, the Congress, the Government Accountability Office, federal executive agencies, and the general public, (2) a means of measuring and assessing the impact of federal contracting on the nation's economy and the extent to which small, veteran-owned small, service-disabled veteran-owned small, HUBZone small, small disadvantaged, and women-owned small business concerns are sharing in federal contracts, and (3) information for other policy and management control purposes.

FEDERAL PROCUREMENT REGULATIONS (FPR)   The federal regulation that sets forth uniform policies and procedures applicable to federal agencies, other than DOD and NASA, in the procurement of supplies and nonpersonal services, including construction. The FPR was superseded by the FEDERAL ACQUISITION REGULATION in 1984. The FPR was issued by the Administrator of General Services under the FEDERAL PROPERTY AND ADMINISTRATIVE SERVICES ACT OF 1949.

FEDERAL PROPERTY AND ADMINISTRATIVE SERVICES ACT (FPASA) OF 1949
An Act, 40 U.S.C. § 471 et seq. and 41 U.S.C. § 3101 et seq., containing policies and procedures for the use and disposal of GOVERNMENT PROPERTY by all agencies and for the procurement of supplies and services, including CONSTRUCTION, by almost all federal agencies except DOD, NASA, and the Coast Guard. See 41 U.S.C. § 3101 for a description of the agencies covered. This Act is one of the two major acts prescribing procurement policies and procedures—the other being the ARMED SERVICES PROCUREMENT ACT. Both acts were significantly amended in 1984 by the COMPETITION IN CONTRACTING ACT and in 1994 by the FEDERAL ACQUISITION STREAMLINING ACT. See Cibinic, Nash & Yukins, Formation of Government Contracts 27–33 (4th ed. 2011).

FEDERAL PROPERTY MANAGEMENT REGULATION (FPMR)   The regulation that guides and governs the federal agencies in their management of property and records. 41 C.F.R., chapter 101. It is issued by the General Services Administration.

FEDERAL REGISTER   A daily publication of the Office of the Federal Register, established in 1935 by the Federal Register Act, 44 U.S.C. § 1501 et seq., as part of a central publications system for promulgating the detailed regulations issued by federal agencies. The Federal Register is the medium for notifying the public of official agency actions. Agencies' regulatory documents are filed with the Office of the Federal Register, placed on public inspection, published in the Federal Register, and then permanently codified (numerically arranged) in the CODE OF FEDERAL REGULATIONS. Publication in the Federal Register gives a regulation the force of law. In 1948, the ADMINISTRATIVE PROCEDURE ACT, 5 U.S.C. § 551 et seq., introduced the requirement that the public have an opportunity to comment on most proposed regulations (excluding procurement regulations). It stated that, absent good cause, no regulation would become final less than 30 days from its publication in the Federal Register. 5 U.S.C. § 553(d). It also provided for publication in the Federal Register of agency statements of organization and procedural rules. Proposed procurement regulations are required to be published in the Federal Register by 41 U.S.C. § 1707. See the Office of the Federal Register publication *The Federal Register: What It Is and How to Use It* (available from the U.S. Government Printing Office, Washington, DC 20402), which provides comprehensive information on how to obtain Federal Register documents. The *Federal Register* is available on the Internet at a variety of sites, including the Government Printing Office at www.gpo.gov/fdsys and www.regulations.gov.

FEDERAL SPECIFICATION   A specification issued in the federal series that is available for use by all federal agencies and that describes the essential technical requirements for purchased material. These documents are issued or controlled by the GENERAL SERVICES ADMINISTRATION and are listed in the GSA INDEX OF FEDERAL SPECIFICATIONS, STANDARDS AND COMMERCIAL ITEM DESCRIPTIONS. Such specifications generally need not be furnished in SOLICITATIONs. FAR 11.201(a). See Cibinic, Nash & Yukins, FORMATION OF GOVERNMENT CONTRACTS 369–70 (4th ed. 2011).

FEDERAL STANDARDS   A STANDARD issued in the federal series that establishes engineering and technical requirements for items, processes, procedures, practices, and methods that have been adopted as customary and are available for use by all federal agencies. These documents are issued or controlled by the General Services Administration (GSA) and listed in the GSA INDEX OF FEDERAL SPECIFICATIONS, STANDARDS AND COMMERCIAL ITEM DESCRIPTIONS. See fedspecs.gsa.gov. Such standards generally need not be furnished in SOLICITATIONs. FAR 11.201(a). See Cibinic, Nash & Yukins, FORMATION OF GOVERNMENT CONTRACTS 369–70 (4th ed. 2011).

FEDERAL SUPPLY SCHEDULES (FSS)   A series of schedules, compiled by the GENERAL SERVICES ADMINISTRATION (GSA), of commonly used supplies and services available to government agencies (and some cost-reimbursement contractors) at specified prices or labor rates. The schedules are nonmandatory sources of supply that are available to agencies as a simplified process for obtaining commercial supplies or services. This process permits contracting officers outside GSA to acquire items covered by such schedules without engaging in the time-consuming process of issuing INVITATION FOR BIDS or REQUESTS FOR PROPOSALS. The schedules, often referred to as GSA schedules or MULTIPLE-AWARD SCHEDULEs, allow ordering offices to issue delivery orders or task orders directly to listed contractors, receive direct shipments, make payment directly to contractors, and administer the orders. See FAR Subpart 8.4 and Part 38; and the FPMR at 41 C.F.R. chap. 101, Subchapter E, Part 101-26. GSA can authorize other agencies to award schedule contracts and publish schedules; the DEPARTMENT OF VETERANS AFFAIRS, for example, awards schedule contracts for medical and nonperishable subsistence items. FAR 38.101(d). See Feldman, GOVERNMENT CONTRACT AWARDS: NEGOTIATION AND SEALED BIDDING §§ 23:1–23:21 (2019–2020 ed.); Cibinic, Nash & Yukins, FORMATION OF GOVERNMENT CONTRACTS 1143–88 (4th ed. 2011).

FEDERAL SUPPLY SERVICE   The office in the GENERAL SERVICES ADMINISTRATION that procured on a government-wide basis commercial products and services by establishing FEDERAL SUPPLY SCHEDULES. This service was merged in 2006 with the FEDERAL TECHNOLOGY SERVICE to become the FEDERAL ACQUISITION SERVICE.

FEDERAL TECHNOLOGY TRANSFER   The process of shifting federally generated technology and technical know-how to state and local governments or the private sector for development and commercialization. This program was established by the STEVENSON-WYDLER ACT. The term "technology transfer" is used to describe the process by which technology or know-how developed for a particular purpose by one organization can be transferred to another organization for use in another area. The goal of federal technology transfer is to make technology developed in federal laboratories available to non-federal organizations to promote economic growth through commercialization of new products or processes and improvement of existing techniques. Companies interested in a particular technology can contact a state technology transfer program, the OFFICE OF RESEARCH AND TECHNOLOGY APPLICATION of a local laboratory, the FEDERAL LABORATORY CONSORTIUM FOR TECHNOLOGY TRANSFER, or the NATIONAL INSTITUTE OF STANDARDS AND TECHNOLOGY in Washington, DC. The party contacted will try to identify a knowledgeable source within the federal network. Types of assistance available include technical assistance; access to nonclassified work; use of federal laboratory facilities or equipment; access to federal patented inventions for licensing; participation in COOPERATIVE RESEARCH AND DEVELOPMENT AGREEMENTS; and access to information, databases, and publications. See Nash & Rawicz, INTELLECTUAL PROPERTY IN GOVERNMENT CONTRACTS, chap. 7 (6th ed. 2008).

FEDERAL TECHNOLOGY TRANSFER ACT   See STEVENSON-WYDLER ACT and FEDERAL TECHNOLOGY TRANSFER.

FEDERAL TORT CLAIMS ACT (FTCA)   A 1946 Act, 28 U.S.C. §§ 1346(b), 2401–2402, 2671–2672, 2674–2680, permitting persons injured by negligent conduct of the government to sue for damages in U.S. District Courts. Prior to suit, 28 U.S.C. § 2675(a) requires that the injured person file for administrative relief with the agency involved. Thereafter, if relief is not granted, suit in court is permitted. 28 U.S.C. § 2680(a) precludes recovery if the government action is the result of a DISCRETIONARY FUNCTION. Recovery under the FTCA is limited to actual damages; punitive damages and interest prior to judgment are barred by 28 U.S.C. § 2674. See Cibinic, Nash & Yukins, FORMATION OF GOVERNMENT CONTRACTS 1801–02 (4th ed. 2011). See also TORT.

FEDERAL TRAVEL REGULATION (FTR)   A regulation promulgated by the General Services Administration pursuant to the authority of several federal statutes in order to establish rules for official travel by federal civilian employees. 41 C.F.R., chapters 300 to 304. It applies to both agencies and individual federal employees.

FEDERALLY CONTROLLED FACILITY   *Official:* (1) Federally owned buildings or leased space, whether for single or multi-tenant occupancy, and its grounds and approaches, all or any portion of which is under the jurisdiction, custody, or control of a department or agency; (2) Federally controlled commercial space shared with non-government tenants. For example, if a department or agency leased the 10th floor of a commercial building, the Directive applies to the 10th floor only; (3) Government-owned, contractor-operated facilities, including laboratories engaged in national defense research and production activities; and (4) Facilities under a management and operating contract, such as for the operation, maintenance, or support of a Government-owned or Government-controlled research, development, special production, or testing establishment. *Source:* FAR 2.101. Contractors with physical access to these facilities must meet the PERSONAL IDENTITY VERIFICATION requirements in FAR Subpart 4.13.

FEDERALLY CONTROLLED INFORMATION SYSTEM   *Official:* an information system (44 U.S.C. § 3502(8) used or operated by a Federal agency, or a contractor or other organization on behalf of the agency (44 U.S.C. § 3544(a)(1)(A)). Source: FAR 2.101. Contractors with access to these systems must meet the PERSONAL IDENTITY VERIFICATION requirements in FAR Subpart 4.13.

FEDERALLY FUNDED RESEARCH AND DEVELOPMENT CENTER (FFRDC)   *Official:* Activities that are sponsored under a broad charter by a government agency (or agencies) for the purpose of performing, analyzing, integrating, supporting, and/or managing basic or applied research and/or development, and that receive 70% or more of their financial support from the government; and—(1) A long-term relationship is contemplated; (2) Most or all of the facilities are owned or funded by the government; and (3) The FFRDC has access to government and supplier data, employees, and facilities beyond that common in a normal contractual relationship. *Source:* FAR 2.101. FFRDCs enable agencies to use private-sector resources to accomplish RESEARCH AND DEVELOPMENT tasks that are integral to agency missions and operations. FFRDCs are operated, managed, and/or administered by either a university or a consortium of universities, another not-for-profit organization, or an industrial firm as an autonomous firm or as an identifiable separate operating unit of a parent organization. FAR 35.017(a). FFRDCs have access to government and supplier data, including PROPRIETARY DATA beyond a normal contractual relationship with the government and accordingly must operate in the public interest with objectivity and independence, without ORGANIZATIONAL CONFLICTs OF INTEREST, and with full disclosure of their affairs to the sponsoring agency. FAR 35.017(a). The government may enter into contracts with an FFRDC to facilitate long-term relationships and establish the FFRDC's mission, but an FFRDC may not compete with non-FFRDCs on agency-issued REQUESTs FOR PROPOSALS for work other than operation of the FFRDC. FAR 35.017-1(c)(4). The National Science Foundation maintains a master list of FFRDCs. FAR 35.017-6.

FEE   The amount paid to a contractor beyond allowable costs under a COST-REIMBURSEMENT CONTRACT. In government contracting, "fee" is the term of art for PROFIT the government agrees to pay on a cost-reimbursement contract. ("Profit" is used when the contract is a fixed-price type.) In most instances, fee reflects a variety of factors, including RISK. The FIXED FEE on COST-PLUS-FIXED-FEE CONTRACTs may not exceed certain statutory limitations. See FAR 15.404-4(c)(4)(i). The fee may be fixed at the outset of performance, as in a cost-plus-fixed-fee contract, or it may vary within a contractually specified range (see RANGE OF INCENTIVE EFFECTIVENESS), as in a COST-PLUS-INCENTIVE-FEE CONTRACT or a COST-PLUS-AWARD-FEE CONTRACT. The fee represents the total remuneration that a contractor may receive for contract performance over and above ALLOWABLE COSTs, not necessarily net income. FAR 15.404-4(a)(1). See Cibinic, Knight & Nash, COST-REIMBURSEMENT CONTRACTING, chap. 2 (4th ed. 2014).

FEE DETERMINATION OFFICIAL (FDO)   The individual responsible for reviewing the recommendations of the Performance Evaluation Board and making the final determination of the amount of AWARD FEE to be awarded to the contractor. EPAR 1516.405-270; AGAR 416.405-2. This is usually the third and last step in the procedure of establishing an award on a COST-PLUS-AWARD-FEE CONTRACT. Contract clauses frequently stated that the FDO's determination is binding on both parties and is not subject to appeal under the Disputes clause or any other appeal clause, but the COURT OF APPEALS FOR THE FEDERAL CIRCUIT has ruled that courts may review such fee determinations to determine if they are arbitrary or capricious, *Burnside-Ott Aviation Training Center v. Dalton*, 107 F.3d 854 (Fed. Cir. 1997). DEAR 916.405. In major procurement, this official should be at the management level of the procuring agency, while in small contracts the contracting officer might perform this task. See Cibinic, Knight & Nash, COST-REIMBURSEMENT CONTRACTING 87–90 (4th ed. 2014); Cibinic, Nash & Yukins, FORMATION OF GOVERNMENT CONTRACTS 1309–12 (4th ed. 2011).

FEE FOR PROFESSIONAL SERVICES   The amount paid to a member of a profession for the performance of services. Used in this sense, the "fee" is the PRICE to be paid under a contract for PROFESSIONAL AND CONSULTANT SERVICES when the work is satisfactorily performed. 10 U.S.C. § 2306(d) and 41 U.S.C. § 254(b) (pre-2011 codification) provide that the fee paid for ARCHITECT-ENGINEER SERVICES may not exceed 6% of the estimated cost of construction of the work designed by the A-E. There the term "fee" describes the total amount paid to the contractor. See FAR 15.404-4(c)(4)(i)(B) implementing the 6% limitation following these statutes but not using the term "fee." The 2011 codification of Title 41 mistakenly uses the term "fee" ambiguously, 41 U.S.C. § 3905(b)(3). See FEE LIMITATION. See also Cibinic, Nash & Yukins, FORMATION OF GOVERNMENT CONTRACTS 1801-02 (4th ed. 2011). Neither the statutes nor the procurement regulations limit the fees paid to other professionals.

FEE LIMITATION [1]   Statutory limitation on the amount of fee that the government may pay under a COST-PLUS-FIXED-FEE CONTRACT. If the contract was for experimental, developmental, or research work, the limitation is 15% of the contract's ESTIMATED COST. For all other contracts, the limitation is 10% of the estimated cost. 10 U.S.C. § 2306(d) and 41 U.S.C. § 3905(b); FAR 15.404-4(c)(4)(i)(A) and (C). These limitations do not apply to cost-plus-incentive-fee or cost-plus-award-fee contracts. **[2]** Statutory limitation on the amount of professional fee (cost plus profit) that the government may pay for ARCHITECT-ENGINEER (A-E) SERVICES to produce and deliver designs, plans, drawings, and specifications for public works or utilities. The limitation is 6% of the estimated cost of construction of the public work or utility, exclusive of fee. 10 U.S.C. § 2306(d) and 41 U.S.C. § 3905(b); FAR 15.404-4(c)(4)(i)(B). There is considerable confusion about the fee limitation for architect-engineer services: (a) the "fee" is not just profit, but the entire compensation to be paid, i.e., costs plus profit; (b) although 41 U.S.C. § 3905(b) explicitly applies the limitation only to services procured under cost-plus-fixed-fee contract, it has been well-established that the limitation applies to A-E services procured under contracts of all types; and (c) the limitation applies whether the contract is exclusively for A-E services or only partially so. The 2011 codification of title 41 of the U.S.C. adds to the confusion because the codified 41 U.S.C. § 3905(b) is substantively different than the prior 41 U.S.C. § 254(b). See Cibinic, Knight & Nash, Cost-Reimbursement Contracting 76 (4th ed. 2014); Cibinic, Nash & Yukins, Formation of Government Contracts 1069–73 (4th ed. 2011).

FIELD PRICING ASSISTANCE   A review and evaluation of the contractor's or subcontractor's proposal by any or all field pricing support personnel. FAR 15.404-2(a)(2). Such personnel may include plant representatives, ADMINISTRATIVE CONTRACTING OFFICERS, contract AUDITORs, price analysts, QUALITY ASSURANCE personnel, engineers, and small business and legal specialists. FAR 15.404-2(a) states that a contracting officer should request field pricing assistance when the information available at the buying activity is inadequate to determine a fair and reasonable price. Such requests must be tailored to reflect the minimum essential supplementary information needed to conduct a technical or cost or pricing analysis. When field pricing assistance is requested, contracting officers are encouraged to team with appropriate field experts throughout the ACQUISITION PROCESS, including negotiations. FAR 15.404-2(a)(3). See Cibinic, Knight & Nash, Cost-Reimbursement Contracting 855–56 (4th ed. 2014).

FINAL COST OBJECTIVE   See COST OBJECTIVE.

FINAL DECISION   See DECISION OF THE CONTRACTING OFFICER.

FINAL INDIRECT COST RATE   *Official:* The INDIRECT COST RATE established and agreed upon by the government and the contractor as not subject to change. It is usually established after the close of the contractor's fiscal year (unless the parties decide upon a different period) to which it applies. For cost-reimbursement research and development contracts with educational institutions, it may be predetermined; that is, established for a future period on the basis of cost experience with similar contracts, together with supporting data. *Source:* FAR 2.101. FAR 42.703-1 requires that a single agency must establish the indirect cost rates for each BUSINESS UNIT of a contractor. This provides (1) uniformity of approach when more than one contract or agency is involved, (2) economy of administration, and (3) timely settlement under cost-reimbursement contracts. FAR 42.702. The FAR requires that final indirect cost rates be established on the basis of either a contracting officer's or an auditor's determination procedure. FAR 42.705. These rates are binding on all cost-reimbursement contracts at the business unit. Established final indirect cost rates are used in negotiating the final price of FIXED-PRICE INCENTIVE and FIXED-PRICE REDETERMINABLE CONTRACTs. FAR 42.703-1. See Cibinic, Knight & Nash, Cost-Reimbursement Contracting 895–98 (4th ed. 2014).

FINAL PAYMENT   The last payment the government makes on a contract when the parties believe all obligations under the contract have been closed out. The government makes final payment upon completion and acceptance of all work required under a contract, once the disbursing officer receives a properly executed and duly certified VOUCHER or INVOICE showing the total amount agreed upon, less amounts previously paid. The contract may require the contractor to give a RELEASE of CLAIMs and liabilities before the government makes final payment. The various Changes clauses in FAR 52.243-1 et seq., the Suspension of Work clause, FAR 52.242-14, and the Government Delay of Work clause, FAR 52.242-17, expressly bar proposals for EQUITABLE ADJUSTMENT or PRICE ADJUSTMENT not asserted by the contractor before final payment. Whether final payment has occurred for the purposes of these clauses depends on the totality of the facts and circumstances of a particular case. See Cibinic, Nagle & Nash, ADMINISTRATION OF GOVERNMENT CONTRACTS 1106–11 (5th ed. 2016).

FINAL PROPOSAL REVISION   An offer in writing from which an award may be made without further revisions submitted to the government in a competitive negotiated procurement (see NEGOTIATION) after DISCUSSIONs have been conducted. FAR 15.307(b). The contracting officer is required to request such revisions from all offerors still in the COMPETITIVE RANGE and to establish a common cut-off date for receipt of final proposal revisions. Prior to FAC 97-02, September 30, 1997, final proposal revisions were called BEST AND FINAL OFFERS. See Feldman, GOVERNMENT CONTRACT GUIDEBOOK, §§ 6:18–6:23 (4th ed. 2019–2020); Cibinic, Nash & Yukins, FORMATION OF GOVERNMENT CONTRACTS 925–31 (4th ed. 2011). See also Nash, *Postscript: Late Final Proposal Revisions*, 21 N&CR ¶ 60 (2007).

FINAL REGULATION   A revision to the FAR or a FAR Supplement issued in accordance with the procedures prescribed in 41 U.S.C. § 1707. Except in urgent circumstances, final regulations cannot be issued until the issuance of a PROPOSED REGULATION with a 60-day period to receive comments from the public. These regulations must be published in the FEDERAL REGISTER where they are preceded by responses to the comments that have been submitted. These responses frequently are helpful in understanding the regulation.

FINANCIAL ACCOUNTING STANDARDS BOARD (FASB)   A private organization that establishes standards of financial accounting and reporting. Those standards govern the preparation of financial reports and provide for the guidance and education of the public, including issuers, auditors, and users of financial information. The FASB follows certain precepts in conducting its activities: objectivity in decisionmaking, careful weighing of the views of its constituents, promulgation of standards only when expected benefits exceed perceived costs, introduction of changes in ways that least disrupt the continuity of reporting practice, and review of the effects of past decisions (www.fasb.org).

FINANCIAL INABILITY   A contractor's lack of capacity to perform for economic reasons: the contractor cannot buy materials, pay its workforce, keep its plant open, or prevent foreclosure. Such inability is generally the responsibility of the contractor, but it may be excusable if caused by an event outside the control of the contractor and may even be compensable if the government caused it. Financial inability is distinguished from "financial difficulty" (which means economic hardship, but not to the level of incapacity) and from "commercial impracticability" (see IMPRACTICABILITY OF PERFORMANCE). If financial inability is excusable, it may be raised as a defense against TERMINATION FOR DEFAULT or as an excuse for failing to continue performance.

FINANCING   See CONTRACT FINANCING.

FINANCING INSTITUTION   An institution dealing in money—as distinguished from other commodities—as the primary function of its business activity. A financing institution may be an individual or a partnership as well as a corporate organization, but it may not be a SURETY, a trust, or an ordinary corporation that incidentally provides financing to its suppliers or to others with whom it deals. The ASSIGNMENT OF CLAIMS Act permits the assignment of contract proceeds only to a bank, trust company, or other financing institution. See FAR Subpart 32.8; U.S. Gov't Accountability Office, Principles of Federal Appropriations Law: Annual Update to the Third Edition, Ch. 12, GAO-15-303SP (Washington, D.C.: Mar. 2015).

FINANCING PAYMENT See CONTRACT FINANCING PAYMENT.

FINE A payment required to be made as a result of violating or failing to comply with applicable laws and regulations. FAR 31.205-15 makes fines UNALLOWABLE COSTs. Fines are generally specified as criminal sanctions under Title 18 of the United States Code or state law. See Cibinic, Knight & Nash, Cost-Reimbursement Contracting 727 (4th ed. 2014); *Ingalls Shipbuilding, Inc. v. Dalton*, 119 F.3d 972 (Fed. Cir. 1997).

FIRM-FIXED-PRICE (FFP) CONTRACT A FIXED-PRICE CONTRACT providing for a price that is not subject to adjustment on the basis of the contractor's cost experience in performing the contract. FAR 16.202-1. FFP contracts are generally subject to adjustment in accordance with contract clauses providing for EQUITABLE ADJUSTMENTs or PRICE ADJUSTMENTs. They place maximum RISK and full responsibility on the contractor for all performance costs and resulting profit or loss. FAR 16.101(b). They provide maximum incentive for the contractor to control costs and perform effectively and impose a minimum administrative burden upon the contracting parties unless changes are issued or unforeseen events occur during performance. FAR 16.103(b) provides that FFP contracts are the preferred type of contract when the risk involved is minimal or can be predicted with an acceptable degree of certainty. FAR 16.104(e) requires that the CONTRACTING OFFICER consider whether or not a portion of the contract can be established on an FFP basis if the entire contract cannot be FFP. See Cibinic, Nash & Yukins, Formation of Government Contracts 1218–19 (4th ed. 2011).

FIRM-FIXED-PRICE LEVEL-OF-EFFORT TERM CONTRACT A FIRM-FIXED PRICE CONTRACT requiring (1) the contractor to provide a specified level of effort over a stated period of time, on work that can be stated only in general terms; and (2) the government to pay the contractor a fixed dollar amount. FAR 16.207-1. Such a contract is suitable for investigation or study in a specific research and development area. The product of the contract is usually a report showing the results achieved through application of the required level of effort. Payment, however, is based on the effort expended rather than the results achieved. FAR 16.207-2. Fixed-price level-of-effort contracts may be used only when (1) the work required cannot otherwise be clearly defined, (2) the required level of effort is identified and agreed upon in advance, (3) there is a reasonable assurance that the intended result cannot be achieved by expending less than the stipulated effort, and (4) the contract price is $150,000 or less (unless higher level approval is obtained). FAR 16.207-3. See Cibinic, Nash & Yukins, Formation of Government Contracts 1330 (4th ed. 2011); Edwards, *The Firm-Fixed-Price Level-of-Effort Contract: A Mystery in an Enigma*, 26 N&CR ¶ 35 (July 2012); Nash, *Dateline November 2008*, 22 N&CR (Nov. 2008); Manos, *Estimates in Level of Effort Contracts: Wrong Contract Type, Wrong Breach*, 19 N&CR ¶ 29 (June 2005).

FIRMWARE A COMPUTER PROGRAM that is embedded in a hardware device that allows reading and executing the program but does not allow modification. Under the Rights in Data—General clause at FAR 52.227-14 and the Rights in Noncommercial Computer Software and Noncommercial Computer Software Documentation clause at DFARS 252.227-7014, firmware is a form of COMPUTER SOFTWARE.

FIRST ACTUAL REDUCTION TO PRACTICE   The initial embodiment of an INVENTION in a physical form and the demonstration of workability by subsequent testing. The amount of testing is dependent on the complexity of the invention and the environment in which it is claimed to work. Thus, the testing necessary to establish reduction to practice may be mere observation, laboratory testing, or testing in an actual operational environment. If first actual reduction to practice of an invention occurs in the performance of a government contract containing a Patent Rights clause, the invention will be a SUBJECT INVENTION and the government will get rights (at least a royalty-free license) to any PATENT that issues on the invention. See Nash & Rawicz, INTELLECTUAL PROPERTY IN GOVERNMENT CONTRACTS, chaps. 2 & 3 (6th ed. 2008).

FIRST ARTICLE   *Official:* A preproduction model, initial production sample, test sample, first lot, pilot lot, or pilot models. *Source:* FAR 2.101. Contractors are required to provide first articles when FIRST ARTICLE TESTING is called for to ensure that the contractor can furnish a product that meets the contract requirements.

FIRST ARTICLE TESTING   *Official:* Testing and evaluating the FIRST ARTICLE for conformance with specified contract requirements before or in the initial stage of production. *Source:* FAR 2.101. The procedures governing first article testing are set forth in FAR Subpart 9.3. First article testing and approval ensures that the contractor can furnish a product that conforms to all contract requirements for acceptance. Contracts imposing a first article testing requirement upon the contractor will contain the First Article Approval—Contractor Testing clause at FAR 52.209-3 or the First Article Approval—Government Testing clause at FAR 52.209-4. Failure to deliver or gain approval of first articles may result in TERMINATION FOR DEFAULT.

FIRST IN, FIRST OUT (FIFO)   An INVENTORY costing method in which stock acquired earliest is assumed to be sold first, leaving stock acquired more recently in inventory. Under FIFO, inventory is valued near current replacement costs. CAS 411, Accounting for Acquisition Cost of Material, 48 C.F.R. § 9904.411, identifies FIFO as one of the inventory costing methods that a contractor must use in accounting for the ACQUISITION COST of material. See Cibinic, Knight & Nash, COST-REIMBURSEMENT CONTRACTING 732–33 (4th ed. 2014).

FISCAL YEAR (FY) For contractors—*Official:*   The accounting period for which annual financial statements are regularly prepared, generally a period of 12 months, 52 weeks, or 53 weeks. *Source:* FAR 31.001. CAS 406, Cost Accounting Period, 48 C.F.R. § 9904.406, provides criteria for selecting the time periods to be used as cost accounting periods for contract cost estimating, accumulating, and reporting. The standard is intended to reduce the effects of variations in the flow of costs within each cost accounting period; enhance objectivity, consistency, and verifiability; and promote uniformity and comparability in contract cost measurements. **For the government—**The period running from October 1 to September 30. Thus, the period running from October 1, 2019 to September 30, 2020 is designated FY 2020. Generally, APPROPRIATIONs are made for each fiscal year.

FIXED-CEILING-PRICE CONTRACT   See FIXED-PRICE REDETERMINATION—RETROACTIVE CONTRACT.

FIXED COSTS   Costs whose values do not fluctuate with changes in output or business activity, such as rent, salaries, and DEPRECIATION. BLACK'S LAW DICTIONARY 436 (11th ed.

2019). Fixed costs are generally compared to VARIABLE COSTS when analyzing INDIRECT COSTs of a contractor. If the fixed costs comprise a large part of such indirect costs, the contractor's OVERHEAD RATEs can be expected to increase if the amount of work performed declines or decrease if the amount of work performed increases.

FIXED FEE   The FEE agreed upon for the performance of a COST-PLUS-FIXED-FEE CONTRACT. 10 U.S.C. § 2306(d) and 41 U.S.C. § 3905 provide that fixed fees may not exceed 10% of the ESTIMATED COST except in the case of contracts for experimental, developmental, or research work, where the limitation is 15%. Fixed fees are negotiated in accordance with FAR 15.404-4 as supplemented by agency FAR supplements. See Cibinic, Nash & Yukins, FORMATION OF GOVERNMENT CONTRACTS 1534–65 (4th ed. 2011); Cibinic, Knight & Nash, COST-REIMBURSEMENT CONTRACTING 47–49 (4th ed. 2014).

FIXED-PRICE CONTRACT   A type of contract providing for a firm pricing arrangement established by the parties at the time of contracting. The policies on the use of this type of contract are set forth in FAR Subpart 16.2. Whereas a FIRM-FIXED-PRICE CONTRACT is not subject to adjustment on the basis of the contractor's cost experience in performing the contract, other types of fixed-price contracts are subject to PRICE ADJUSTMENT on the basis of economic conditions or the contractor's performance of the contract. These types of contracts are FIXED-PRICE CONTRACTs WITH ECONOMIC PRICE ADJUSTMENT, FIXED-PRICE-INCENTIVE CONTRACTs, FIXED-PRICE REDETERMINATION—PROSPECTIVE CONTRACTs, and FIXED-PRICE REDETERMINATION—RETROACTIVE CONTRACTs. See Manos, 1 GOVERNMENT CONTRACT COSTS AND PRICING § 4:2 (2d ed. 2009–2020); Cibinic, Nash & Yukins, FORMATION OF GOVERNMENT CONTRACTS 1218–42 (4th ed. 2011); Nash, *Selecting the Correct Type of Contract: A Smart Contracting Officer*, 23 N&CR ¶ 45 (Aug. 2009); Edwards, *Contract Pricing Arrangements: A Primer –Part 1*, BRIEFING PAPERS No. 09-11 (2009).

FIXED-PRICE CONTRACT WITH ECONOMIC PRICE ADJUSTMENT   A FIXED-PRICE CONTRACT providing for upward or downward revision of the stated contract price upon the occurrence of specified contingencies. FAR 16.203-1. Adjustments may reflect increases or decreases in established prices for specific items, in the contractor's actual costs of LABOR or material, or in specific indexes of labor or material costs. FAR 16.203-2 provides that a fixed-price contract with economic price adjustment may be used when (1) there is serious doubt that market or labor conditions will remain stable during an extended period of contract performance, and (2) contingencies (see CONTINGENCY) that would otherwise be included in the contract price can be identified and covered separately in the contract. FAR 14.408-4 provides that when the government proposes inclusion of an economic price adjustment clause in the INVITATION FOR BID (IFB), bids will be evaluated on the basis of the quoted prices without adding any amount for price adjustment. However, if no such clause is included in the IFB, the FAR provides that bids proposing economic price adjustment must be rejected unless they propose a ceiling price—in which case they will be evaluated at the ceiling. Economic price adjustment is sometimes called "escalation," but that is a misnomer because the price can be lowered as well as raised. See Feldman, GOVERNMENT CONTRACT AWARDS: NEGOTIATION AND SEALED BIDDING § 4:8 (2019–2020 ed.); Cibinic, Nash & Yukins, FORMATION OF GOVERNMENT CONTRACTS 1219–39 (4th ed. 2011).

FIXED-PRICE-INCENTIVE (FPI) CONTRACT   A FIXED-PRICE CONTRACT that provides for adjusting PROFIT and establishing the final contract price by a formula based on the relationship of final negotiated TOTAL COST to total TARGET COST. FAR 16.403(a). The final price is subject to a CEILING PRICE negotiated at the outset. Fixed-price incentive contracts are appropriate when (1) a FIRM-FIXED-PRICE CONTRACT is not suitable, (2) the nature of the supplies or services being acquired are such that the contractor's assumption of a degree of cost responsibility will provide a positive profit incentive for effective cost control and performance, and (3) the performance requirements provide a reasonable opportunity for the incentives to have a meaningful impact on the contractor's management of the work if the contract also includes incentives on technical performance and/or delivery. FAR 16.403(b). See *Guidance on Using Incentive and Other Contract Types*, March 2016, stating DOD's preference for using incentive contracts and providing detailed guidance on their use. There are two forms of fixed-price-incentive contracts: firm target and successive target. FAR 16.403-1 provides that a firm target is appropriate when the parties can negotiate at the outset a firm target cost, a TARGET PROFIT, a profit adjustment formula, and a ceiling price that will both give the contractor a fair and reasonable incentive and ensure that the contractor assumes an appropriate share of the RISK. FAR 16.403-2(b) provides that successive targets are appropriate when available cost or pricing information is not sufficient to permit the negotiation of a realistic firm target cost and profit before award; sufficient information is available to permit negotiation of the initial targets; and there is reasonable assurance that information will be available early into contract performance to negotiate a firm fixed price, or firm targets and incentive formula that will provide a fair and reasonable incentive. Standard clauses are provided for these types of contracts: the Incentive Price Revision—Firm Target clause in FAR 52.216-16 and the Incentive Price Revision—Successive Targets clause in FAR 52.216-17. See Cibinic, Nash & Yukins, FORMATION OF GOVERNMENT CONTRACTS 1269–88 (4th ed. 2011); Edwards, *Increased Use of Fixed-Price Incentive Contracts: The Way to Greater Efficiency and Productivity?*, 25 N&CR ¶ 21 (Apr. 2011).

FIXED-PRICE LEVEL-OF-EFFORT CONTRACT   See FIRM-FIXED-PRICE LEVEL-OF-EFFORT TERM CONTRACT.

FIXED-PRICE REDETERMINATION—PROSPECTIVE (FPRP) CONTRACT   A FIXED-PRICE CONTRACT that contains a firm-fixed-price for an initial period of contract delivery or performance and provides for the negotiation of a new firm-fixed-price for subsequent contract work. FAR 16.205-1. The contract specifies the time or times when new prices will be negotiated. FPRP contracts may be used to acquire production or services in quantity in cases when it is possible to negotiate a firm-fixed-price for an initial period but not for the entire amount of goods or services needed. The initial period should be as long as possible, and each subsequent period should be at least 12 months. FAR 16.205-2. An FPRP contract may be used only when (1) a FIRM-FIXED-PRICE CONTRACT is not feasible and a FIXED-PRICE-INCENTIVE CONTRACT would not be more appropriate, (2) the contractor's accounting system will permit price redetermination, (3) the prospective pricing periods can be made to conform with operation of the contractor's accounting system, and (4) there is reasonable assurance that price redetermination will take place promptly at the specified times. FAR 16.205-3. See Feldman, GOVERNMENT CONTRACT AWARDS: NEGOTIATION AND SEALED BIDDING § 4:10 (2019–2020 ed.); Cibinic, Nash & Yukins, FORMATION OF GOVERNMENT CONTRACTS 1240–41 (4th ed. 2011).

FIXED-PRICE REDETERMINATION–RETROACTIVE (FPRR) CONTRACT   A FIXED-PRICE CONTRACT under which a CEILING PRICE is negotiated before contract performance and a final fixed price within that ceiling is determined, based on an assessment of the contractor's performance and its actual audited costs, after the work is completed. Because FPRR contracts provide no positive incentive for the contractor to control costs (other than the ceiling price, which may contain a sizable margin for error and uncertainty), FAR 16.206-2 limits their use. They may be used only for research and development estimated at $150,000 or less when a FIRM-FIXED-PRICE CONTRACT cannot be negotiated and the dollar amount involved and short performance period make any other fixed-price contract type impracticable. FAR 16.206-3 further narrows the conditions for use to situations in which the contractor's accounting system is adequate for price redetermination, there is reasonable assurance that price redetermination will take place promptly as specified, and the head of the contracting activity or a higher level official grants approval in writing. See Cibinic, Nash & Yukins, FORMATION OF GOVERNMENT CONTRACTS 1241–42 (4th ed. 2011).

FLOW-DOWN CLAUSES   Clauses prescribed by the government for inclusion in PRIME CONTRACTS that a PRIME CONTRACTOR incorporates into SUBCONTRACTs. These clauses "flow down" rights and responsibilities of the contractor to the subcontractor. They are also known as pass-through or conduit clauses. Mandatory flow-down clauses are those contract clauses that specifically require the inclusion of their text in subcontracts entered into in support of the contract. Other clauses, although not mandatory, should be flowed down to ensure that the subcontractor will provide adequate assistance or cooperation to enable the contractor to meet its contractual requirements with the government. Failure to flow down certain clauses may expose the contractor to financial risk if the government takes certain actions under the contract and the subcontract does not obligate the subcontractor to respond in accordance with those actions. See Feldman, GOVERNMENT CONTRACT GUIDEBOOK §§ 26.5–26.7 (4th ed. 2019–2020).

FLY AMERICA ACT   An Act, Section 5 of the International Air Transportation Fair Competitive Practices Act of 1974, 49 U.S.C. § 40118, requiring federal employees and their dependents, consultants, contractors, grantees, and others to use U.S.-flag air carriers for U.S. government-financed international air travel and transportation of their personal effects or property, to the extent that service by these carriers is available. FAR 47.402. "International air transportation" means transportation by air between a place in the United States and a place outside the United States, or between two places both of which are outside the United States. FAR 47.401. Contracting officers must insert the clause at FAR 52.247-63, Preference for U.S. Flag Air Carriers, in solicitations and contracts unless the contract is awarded under simplified acquisition procedures or is a contract for commercial items.

FLYAWAY COSTS   A DOD term that attempts to encompass the total acquisition cost of an aircraft program. It includes costs related to the development and production of a useable end item of military hardware, as well as the cost of creating the basic unit (airframe, hull, chassis, etc.), an allowance for CHANGES, propulsion equipment, electronics, armament, and other installed GOVERNMENT-FURNISHED EQUIPMENT, and nonrecurring "start-up" production costs. The term equates to rollaway and sailaway costs for non-aircraft programs. See also AVERAGE UNIT PROCUREMENT COST OBJECTIVES. DAU GLOSSARY.

F.O.B.   *Official:* Free on board. This term is used in conjunction with a physical point to determine—(1) The responsibility and basis for payment of freight charges; and (2) Unless otherwise agreed, the point where TITLE for goods passes to the buyer or consignee. *Source:*

FAR 2.101. The policies on designation of contracts as F.O.B. ORIGIN or F.O.B. DESTI-NATION are set forth in FAR Subpart 47.3. Contract clauses providing a variety of payment and evaluation arrangements for transportation costs are set forth in FAR 52.247-29 through 52.247-62. See U.C.C. § 2-319.

F.O.B. DESTINATION *Official:* Free on board at destination, i.e., the seller or consignor delivers the goods on the seller's or consignor's conveyance at destination. Unless the contract provides otherwise, the seller or consignor is responsible for the cost of shipping and risk of loss. For use in the clause at 52.247-34, see the definition at 52.247-34(a). *Source:* FAR 2.101. Guidance on the use of this technique is set forth in FAR 47.303-6 and -7. Various clauses are provided for this type of arrangement in FAR 52.247-34, -35, -41, -42, -45, and -48.

F.O.B. ORIGIN *Official:* Free on board at origin; i.e., the seller or consignor places the goods on the conveyance. Unless the contract provides otherwise, the buyer or consignee is responsible for the cost of shipping and risk of loss. For use in the clause at 52.247-29, see the definition at 52.247-29(a). *Source:* FAR 2.101. Guidance on the use of this technique is set forth in FAR 47.303-1 through -5. Various clauses are provided for this type of arrangement in FAR 52.247-29 through -33, -45, -46, -47, and -59.

FOLLOW ON CONTRACT A type of sole source award made to a contractor that has previously been awarded a design or manufacturing contract for the same item or who has previously performed the services being procured. 41 U.S.C. § 253(d)(1)(B) and 10 U.S.C. § 3304(b)(2) specifically permit sole source contracting for follow-on contracts for the continued development or production of a major system or highly specialized equipment when it is likely that award to a source other than the original source would result in substantial duplication of cost to the government, which is not expected to be recovered through competition, or unacceptable delays in fulfilling the agency's needs. See Cibinic, Nash & Yukins, Formation of Government Contracts 311–13 (4th ed. 2011).

FOLLOWER COMPANY See LEADER-COMPANY CONTRACTING.

FORBEARANCE The postponement of the decision to terminate for default (see TERMINA-TION FOR DEFAULT) while the contracting officer is investigating the reasons for the contractor's failure to meet the contract requirements. With regard to the government's WAIVER of its right to terminate a contract for late delivery, the contracting officer has a reasonable period of forbearance to investigate the facts and determine what course of action best serves the government's interests. During the forbearance period, the government may terminate at any time, without prior notice. The facts and circumstances of each case determine the length of time constituting a reasonable forbearance period; no clear demarcation exists between reasonable forbearance and waiver. Once the forbearance period expires, the government waives its right to terminate for default and must reestablish a delivery schedule if it wishes to terminate for default. See Cibinic, Nagle & Nash, Administration of Government Contracts 848–49 (5th ed. 2016).

FORCE AND EFFECT OF LAW A term applied to a regulation, such as the FEDERAL ACQUISITION REGULATION, meaning that it has the same binding effect as a statute. As a general rule, regulations promulgating substantive rules have the force and effect of law, whereas, regulations providing administrative procedures may not have the force and effect of law. If a contract does not comply with a regulation with the force and effect of law it may be held to be void or a contract clause may be unenforceable. Further, under the CHRISTIAN DOCTRINE, a contract clause required by a regulation with the force and effect of law will be included in the contract even though the parties omitted it, unless a DEVIATION has been granted. Cibinic, Nash & Yukins, FORMATION OF GOVERNMENT CONTRACTS 69–81 (4th ed. 2011).

FORCE MAJEURE A term, derived from insurance law, meaning superior or irresistible force, such as lightning, earthquakes, storms, flood, sunstroke, and freezing. Force majeure is at times thought of as an "act of God"—one occasioned exclusively by violence of nature without the interference of any human agency. Force majeure clauses are common in commercial construction contracts to protect the parties if part of the contract cannot be performed as a result of causes that are outside the control of the parties and could not have been avoided by the exercise of due care. In government contracting, the clauses granting the government the right to terminate for default (see TERMINATION FOR DEFAULT) generally contain EXCUSABLE DELAY provisions that are in the nature of force majeure clauses.

FOREIGN CARRIER See CARRIER (TELECOMMUNICATIONS).

FOREIGN CONSTRUCTION MATERIAL *Official:* A CONSTRUCTION MATERIAL other than a DOMESTIC CONSTRUCTION MATERIAL. *Source:* FAR 25.003. When a contract is subject to the BUY AMERICAN ACT, the contractor may not meet the contract requirements by furnishing a foreign construction material. See Cibinic, Nash & Yukins, FORMATION OF GOVERNMENT CONTRACTS 1614–24 (4th ed. 2011).

FOREIGN CORRUPT PRACTICES ACT (FCPA) 15 U.S.C. § 78dd-1, et seq. A 1977 Act that prohibits the payment of bribes by United States companies and nationals to foreign officials to obtain or attempt to retain business. The penalties for criminal violations may reach $2 million for companies and $100,000 or more, with up to five years' imprisonment, for individuals. The FCPA also requires that publicly held companies maintain certain books and records to reflect certain transactions and dispositions of assets. 15 U.S.C. § 78m. FCPA issues often arise with regard to agents or foreign sales representatives -2. See O'MELVENY & MYERS LLP, FOREIGN CORRUPT PRACTICES ACT HANDBOOK (6th ed. 2009). See also Manos, 3 GOVERNMENT CONTRACT COSTS AND PRICING § 91:26 (2d ed. 2009–2020); Williams, Caccia, Volkmar, & Sharma, *The Foreign Corrupt Practices Act & Unique Risks For Government Contractors*, BRIEFING PAPERS No. 14-12 (Nov. 2014).

FOREIGN END PRODUCT *Official:* An END PRODUCT other than a DOMESTIC END PRODUCT. *Source:* FAR 25.003. When a contract is subject to the BUY AMERICAN ACT, the contractor may not meet the contract requirements by furnishing a foreign end product. See Cibinic, Nash & Yukins, FORMATION OF GOVERNMENT CONTRACTS 1614–24 (4th ed. 2011).

FOREIGN-FLAG VESSEL *Official:* Any vessel of foreign registry including vessels owned by U.S. citizens but registered in a nation other than the United States. *Source:* FAR 47.501. Such a vessel is subject to the limitations on use specified in the CARGO PREFERENCE ACTS and the Merchant Marine Act of 1936, which give preference to U.S.-FLAG VESSELs when ocean transportation of supplies is required. See the Preference for Privately Owned U.S.-Flag Commercial Vessels clause in FAR 52.247-64, which requires contractors to compute shipments in such vessels separately in determining whether they have met the requirement that at least 50% of the gross tonnage shipped be in U.S.-flag vessels.

FOREIGN MILITARY FINANCING PROGRAM   The program through which the United States provides funds to its allies to purchase American military articles and services. Foreign military financing funds purchases are made through the FOREIGN MILITARY SALES program, which manages government-to-government sales.

FOREIGN MILITARY SALES (FMS)   Government-to-government sales of U.S. defense items and services (including training), as authorized under the Foreign Assistance Act of 1961 and the ARMS EXPORT CONTROL ACT. In the normal situation, FMS transactions involve DOD contracts with U.S. contractors for the furnishing of military equipment to a foreign government. Although recipient governments generally pay cash for the full costs associated with such sales, some programs involve loans or other arrangements to permit the purchase. A MEMORANDUM OF UNDERSTANDING may be established to define the relationship between the foreign government and the United States. The process typically entails a letter of request from the foreign country and either pricing and availability information or a letter of offer and acceptance from the government, which may require congressional approval. See DOD Manual 5015.38-M, Security Assistance Management Manual, April 30, 2012. The Arms Export Control Act requires that FMS activities be conducted at no cost to the U.S. Government, that all costs be collected from the recipient government, and, generally, that payments be made in advance of delivery. See 22 U.S.C. § 2761. FMS are considered a component of the U.S. Security Assistance Program, which provides defense articles, defense services, and military training to U.S. allies and friendly foreign nations. See DFARS Subpart 225.73; DOD Manual 7290.3-M. See U.S. Gov't Accountability Office, FOREIGN MILITARY SALES: DOD Should Further Strengthen Financial Oversight of Transportation Fees, GAO-20-386 (May 2020); U.S. Gov't Accountability Office, FOREIGN MILITARY SALES: Observations on DOD's Approach to Developing Price and Availability Estimates for Foreign Customers, GAO-19-214 (Feb. 2019).

FOREIGN OFFER   *Official:* Any offer other than a DOMESTIC OFFER. *Source:* FAR 25.003. When a procurement is subject to the BUY AMERICAN ACT, the government may not accept a foreign offer unless an exception applies. See Cibinic, Nash & Yukins, Formation of Government Contracts 1614–24 (4th ed. 2011).

FOREIGN OWNERSHIP, CONTROL, OR INFLUENCE (FOCI)   *Official:* The situation where the degree of ownership, control, or influence over an offeror(s) or a contractor by a foreign interest is such that a reasonable basis exists for concluding that compromise of CLASSIFIED INFORMATION or special nuclear material may possibly result. *Source:* DEAR 904.7002. DOE has procedures that require certain offerors, bidders, contractors, or subcontractors to submit information that helps in determining whether award of a contract, or continued performance of a contract, may pose an undue risk to the common defense and security because of FOCI. DEAR Subpart 904.70; DEAR 952.204-74. DOD has implemented this policy of ensuring that FOCI contractors can be given access to classified information in the National Industrial Security Program Operating Manual. The procedures in this manual have been adopted by almost all government agencies except DOE.

FORFEITURE   The loss of benefits received under a contract as a result of illegal conduct. For example, in one case of BRIBERY and CONFLICT OF INTEREST, the contractor was required to forfeit the entire contract price after completion of the work. *K & R Eng'g Co. v. United States*, 616 F.2d 469 (Ct. Cl. 1980). 18 U.S.C. § 218 permits the voiding or rescission of a contract where there has been a violation of the criminal law against BRIBERY, the giving or receiving of GRATUITIES, or a CONFLICT OF INTEREST. This statute is implemented in FAR Subpart 3.7. 28 U.S.C. § 2514 also requires forfeiture of any claim filed in the courts that is tainted with FRAUD. See Nash, *Postscript II: Forfeiture of Claims*, 23 N&CR ¶ 15 (Apr. 2009); Stouck & Caplen, *The Forfeiture of Claims Act Today*, BRIEFING PAPERS No. 07-9 (Aug. 2008).

FORM, FIT, AND FUNCTION DATA *Official:* Data relating to items, components, or processes that are sufficient to enable physical and functional interchangeability, and data identifying source, size, configuration, mating and attachment characteristics, functional characteristics, functional characteristics, and performance requirements. For COMPUTER SOFTWARE, it means data identifying source, functional characteristics, and performance requirements but specifically excludes the source code, algorithm, processes, formulas, and flow charts of the software. *Source:* FAR 27.401. The term has a slightly different meaning in DFARS 252.227-7013 where it is defined as "TECHNICAL DATA that describes the required overall physical, functional, and performance characteristics (along with the qualification requirements, if applicable) of an item, component, or process to the extent necessary to permit identification of physically and functionally interchangeable items." Pursuant to 10 U.S.C. § 2320, the Rights in Technical Data—Noncommercial Items clause in DFARS 252.227-7013 provides that the government acquires UNLIMITED RIGHTS in form, fit, and function data prepared in the performance of a contract. Under the Rights in Data—General clause at FAR 52.227-14, such data are furnished with unlimited rights and the contractor may protect qualifying LIMITED RIGHTS DATA and RESTRICTED RIGHTS computer software by withholding them from delivery to the government and delivering form, fit, and function data instead (unless the agency includes Alternates II and/or III in the contract). FAR 27.404. See Nash & Rawicz, INTELLECTUAL PROPERTY IN GOVERNMENT CONTRACTS, chaps. 4 & 5 (6th ed. 2008).

FORMAL ADVERTISING The term used, before the COMPETITION IN CONTRACTING ACT (CICA) of 1984, to describe the procurement technique now referred to as SEALED BIDDING. Under the statutes and regulations preceding passage of CICA, there was an expressed preference for formal advertising. Formal advertising, like sealed bidding, entailed drafting and publicizing an INVITATION FOR BIDS, holding a public BID OPENING, and awarding the contract to the lowest responsive and responsible bidder (see RESPONSIVENESS and RESPONSIBILITY).

FORMS Government documents used in the procurement process and governed by the policies in FAR Part 53. This Part gives rules for using forms, prescribes STANDARD FORMS (SFs), references OPTIONAL FORMS (OFs) and agency-prescribed forms used in acquisition, and illustrates all these forms (SFs in 53.301, OFs in 53.302, and selected agency forms in 53.303, in numerical order). Forms may be copied from the FAR. Executive agencies obtain forms (both SFs and OFs) from the General Services Administration; contractors and other parties can obtain them from the U.S. Government Printing Office, Washington, DC 20402. Agency forms can be obtained from the prescribing agency. FAR 53.107 or through the GSA Forms Library at www.gsa.gov/reference/forms.

FORWARD PRICING RATE AGREEMENT *Official:* A written agreement negotiated between a contractor and the government to make certain rates available during a specified period for use in pricing contracts or modifications. These rates represent reasonable projections of specific costs that are not easily estimated for, identified with, or generated by a specific contract, contract end item, or task. These projections may include rates for such things as labor, indirect costs, material obsolescence and usage, spare parts provisioning, and material handling. *Source:* FAR 2.101. In determining whether to establish such an agreement, the ADMINISTRATIVE CONTRACTING OFFICER should consider whether the benefits to be derived from it are commensurate with the effort of establishing and monitoring it. FAR 42.1701(a). FAR 15.407-3(a) provides guidance on forward pricing rate agreements when CERTIFIED COST OR PRICING DATA is required, DFARS 215.407-3 directs the use of the rates in forward pricing rate agreements when such rates are available unless waived. See Manos, 2 GOVERNMENT CONTRACT COSTS AND PRICING § 84:11 (2d ed. 2009–2020); Cibinic, Nash & Yukins, FORMATION OF GOVERNMENT CONTRACTS 1532 (4th ed. 2011).

FRAGMENTATION OF A BASE   The removal of individual elements from an appropriate base for distributing INDIRECT COSTs that has been accepted by the government. The fragmentation of a base is prohibited. FAR 31.203(d). This requires contractors to allocate indirect costs to UNALLOWABLE COSTs as well as ALLOWABLE COSTs. See Cibinic, Knight & Nash, COST-REIMBURSEMENT CONTRACTING 604–18 (4th ed. 2014).

FRAGMENTATION OF REMEDIES   A requirement that a contractor obtain remedies from different administrative agencies or courts for events that have occurred on a single contract. One of the major difficulties that led to the passage of the CONTRACT DISPUTES ACT (CDA) OF 1978 was the complaint that disputes "ARISING UNDER THE CONTRACT" had to be appealed to BOARDs OF CONTRACT APPEALS (BCAs), while claims for government BREACH OF CONTRACT could be taken only to the Court of Claims. This problem was resolved in the CDA by permitting contractors to elect to take all claims arising under the contract or "RELATING TO THE CONTRACT" to either the appropriate BCA or the CLAIMS COURT (now the U.S. COURT OF FEDERAL CLAIMS). Fragmentation of remedies still exists with regard to some claims of contractors involving both contract breach and tortious conduct (see TORT) by the government. In such cases, contract claims must be processed under the CDA while tort claims must be taken to a U.S. District Court pursuant to the FEDERAL TORT CLAIMS ACT. See Cibinic, Nagle & Nash, ADMINISTRATION OF GOVERNMENT CONTRACTS 1209 (5th ed. 2016).

FRANCHISE AGREEMENTS   Typically refers to a special privilege conferred by a government on an individual or corporation, which would not otherwise belong to citizens as a common right. The term also refers to the selling or granting of the privilege to use a name or to sell products or services. Franchises typically entail elaborate agreements under which franchisees conduct business in accordance with methods prescribed by the franchiser, and the franchiser assists through promotion, advertising, and advisory services. Pursuant to a U.S. COURT OF FEDERAL CLAIMS advisory opinion, cable television franchise agreements for the construction, installation, or capital improvement of cable systems at military installations were required to be considered contracts for purposes of the FEDERAL ACQUISITION REGULATION. Pub. L. No. 104-201, § 833; *In the Matter of the Dep't of Defense Cable Television Franchise Agreements*, 36 Fed. Cl. 171 (1996).

FRAUD   An intentional perversion of truth for the purpose of inducing someone to rely upon it and part with something of value or surrender a legal right. The three necessary elements of a cause of action for fraud are (1) false representation of a present or past fact on the part of the defendant, (2) a plaintiff's action in reliance upon that misrepresentation, and (3) damage resulting to the plaintiff from the action that was based on the misrepresentation. BLACK'S LAW DICTIONARY 803 (11th ed. 2019). A fraudulent representation is a FALSE STATE-MENT as to a material fact that another party believes and relies upon, and that induces that other party to act to his or her injury. The speaker must know the statement to be false or must make the statement with utter disregard for its truth or falsity and must intend that the other party will rely upon the statement. Fraud and corruption offenses, typically characterized as white-collar crimes, fall into two main areas: (1) fraud and false statement offenses, which involve deceptive conduct (see FALSE CLAIMS ACT and FALSE STATEMENTS ACT); and (2) public corruption offenses, which involve BRIBERY or illegal gratuities (see GRATUITY). See Cibinic, Nagle & Nash, ADMINISTRATION OF GOVERNMENT CONTRACTS 109-43 (5th ed. 2016); Cibinic, Nash & Yukins, FORMATION OF GOVERNMENT CONTRACTS 178-95 (4th ed. 2011).

FREE ON BOARD   See F.O.B.

FREEDOM OF INFORMATION ACT (FOIA)   An Act, 5 U.S.C. § 552, part of the Administrative Procedure Act, passed in 1966, that provides a mechanism for members of the public (including contractors) to gain access to AGENCY RECORDs maintained by the government. The Act requires public disclosure unless records fall within any of nine exemptions listed in the Act. The exemption most relevant to information submitted by contractors is Exemption 4, covering "TRADE SECRETs and commercial or financial information obtained from a person and privileged or confidential." Even if information falls within this exemption, an agency may release it unless such release would constitute an abuse of discretion. However, an abuse of discretion would normally be found if the information fell within the scope of the TRADE SECRETS ACT. Exec. Order No. 12600, 52 Fed. Reg. 23781 (June 23, 1987) requires agencies to notify persons that have submitted information to the government when a FOIA request for that information is received. This is implemented in 12 C.F.R. § 4.16. See Adler, LITIGATION UNDER THE FEDERAL OPEN GOVERNMENT LAWS (17th ed. 1992); DOJ *Freedom of Information Guide* at www.usdoj.gov/oip. The FAR's limited treatment of FOIA is in Subpart 24.2. DOD and NASA, however, provide expanded FOIA coverage. See 32 C.F.R. § 286.3, and NFS Subpart 18-24.2. See also Nash & Rawicz, INTELLECTUAL PROPERTY IN GOVERNMENT CONTRACTS, chap. 9 (6th ed. 2008). See Nash, *Postscript IV: Exemption 4 of the Freedom of Information Act*, 33 N&CR ¶ 47 (Aug. 2019); Turner & Castellano, *FOIA Exemption 4*, BRIEFING PAPERS No. 17-7 (June 2017); Meagher & Bareis, *The Freedom of Information Act*, BRIEFING PAPERS No. 10-12 (Nov. 2010).

FRICTIONLESS ACQUISITION   A cross-agency priority (CAP) management initiative launched in 2019 by the ADMINISTRATOR OF FEDERAL PROCUREMENT POLICY in furtherance of the President's Management Agenda. The goal is for the government to acquire commercial items at marketplace speed using innovative processes. See Frictionless Acquisition https://www.performance.gov/CAP/frictionless-acquisition/.

FRINGE BENEFIT   *Official:* Allowances and services provided by the contractor to its employees as compensation in addition to regular wages and salaries. Fringe benefits include, but are not limited to, the cost of vacations, sick leave, holidays, military leave, employee insurance, and supplemental unemployment benefit plans. *Source:* FAR 31.205-6(m)(1). Fringe benefits are ALLOWABLE COSTs to the extent that they are reasonable and required by law, agreement, or established policy. See Manos, 1 GOVERNMENT CONTRACT

Costs & Pricing § 13:17 (2d ed. 2009–2020); Cibinic, Knight & Nash, Cost-Reimbursement Contracting 687 (4th ed. 2014).

FRONT-END LOADING   The inclusion in a BID or PROPOSAL of inflated prices on items to be delivered early in the performance of the contract and unduly low prices on later items. Front-end loading, or front loading, is a form of unbalanced bidding (see UNBALANCED BID) that is aimed at enabling the bidder to recover money in advance of the performance of the work. Front-end loading may be permissible so long as the bid will clearly result in the lowest overall cost to the government. But it will cause a bid to be found nonresponsive (see RESPONSIVENESS) if it cannot be justified on the basis of substantial mobilization or equipment costs or when it is so egregious as to amount, substantively, to an ADVANCE PAYMENT. See Cibinic, Nash & Yukins, Formation of Government Contracts 578–81 (4th ed. 2011).

FRUSTRATION OF PURPOSE   A legal doctrine that excuses a party to a contract from performing its contractual obligations in situations when the objectives of the contract have been utterly defeated by circumstances arising after the contract was formed. In such situations, performance is excused even though there is no impediment to actual performance. Black's Law Dictionary 812 (11th ed. 2019). This doctrine is rarely used in government contracting.

FULFORD DOCTRINE   A legal rule that permits a contractor's APPEAL FROM A CONTRACTING OFFICER'S DECISION assessing EXCESS COSTS OF REPROCUREMENT following a TERMINATION FOR DEFAULT to "revive" the issue of the propriety of the default termination itself, even though the contractor failed to file a timely appeal of the default termination. The name is derived from the decision of the ARMED SERVICES BOARD OF CONTRACT APPEALS in *Fulford Manufacturing Co.*, ASBCA 2144 (May 20, 1955). The result of the rule is that, upon default of a contract, a contractor may choose not to litigate the issue of whether the government properly terminated the contract. But if the government later charges the contractor for the excess costs of reprocurement, the contractor may appeal that cost assessment and simultaneously challenge the government's termination action. See Cibinic, Nagle & Nash, Administration of Government Contracts 884–85 (5th ed. 2016).

FULL AND OPEN COMPETITION   *Official:* All responsible sources (see RESPONSIBILITY) are permitted to compete. *Source:* FAR 2.101. Under 10 U.S.C. § 2304(a) and 41 U.S.C. § 3301, full and open competition is the established norm in government contracting. However, 10 U.S.C. § 2304(c) and 41 U.S.C. § 3301, provide for seven circumstances permitting OTHER THAN FULL AND OPEN COMPETITION: (1) only one responsible source (see RESPONSIBILITY); (2) UNUSUAL AND COMPELLING URGENCY; (3) INDUSTRIAL MOBILIZATION, or the need to maintain engineering, developmental, or research capability; (4) international agreement; (5) statutory authorization or requirement; (6) risk of compromising the national security; and (7) protecting the public interest. See FAR 6.302 for additional guidance on these exceptions to the full and open competition rule. The statutes and regulations also provide substantial guidance on the type of COMPETITIVE PROCEDURES that meet the requirement for full and open competition. See FAR 6.102. FAR Subpart 6.1 prescribes the policy and procedures to be used to promote and provide for full and open competition. FAR Subpart 6.2 describes limited exceptions for full and open competition after exclusion of sources. FAR 6.303 provides guidance on the preparation of justifications and on obtaining approvals (see JUSTIFICATION AND APPROVAL) when full and open competition is not obtained. See Feldman, GOVERNMENT CONTRACT AWARDS: NEGOTIATION AND SEALED BIDDING §§ 3:27–3:33 (2019–2020 ed.); Cibinic, Nash & Yukins, FORMATION OF GOVERNMENT CONTRACTS 293–331 (4th ed. 2011). See also Manuel, CONG. RESEARCH SERV., Report No. R40516, COMPETITION IN FEDERAL CONTRACTING: AN OVERVIEW OF THE LEGAL REQUIREMENTS (Aug. 20, 2009); U.S. GOV'T ACCOUNTABILITY OFFICE, OPPORTUNITIES EXIST TO INCREASE COMPETITION AND ASSESS REASONS WHEN ONLY ONE OFFER IS RECEIVED, GAO-10-833, (July 26, 2010).

FULL COVERAGE   A type of COST ACCOUNTING STANDARDS coverage that requires that the contractor comply with all cost accounting standards in effect on the date of contract award. This coverage is required if the contractor receives a single CAS-covered contract award of $50 million or more or receives $50 million or more in net CAS-covered contract awards in its preceding cost accounting period. 48 C.F.R. § 9903.201-2(b)(1). See Cibinic, Knight & Nash, COST-REIMBURSEMENT CONTRACTING 523–30 (4th ed. 2014).

FULL FUNDING   With regard to APPROPRIATIONS, an appropriation that is sufficient in total to complete a useful segment of a capital project before any obligations may be incurred for that segment (as opposed to INCREMENTALLY FUNDING). With regard to contracts, the OBLIGATION, at the time of contract award, of all of the funds believed to be necessary to perform the contract. Fully funded contracts are contrasted with INCREMENTALLY FUNDED CONTRACTs. Full funding is frequently required before a contract may be awarded. DFARS Subpart 232.7. See O'Bourke, CONG. RESEARCH. SERV., Report No. RL31404, DEFENSE PROCUREMENT: FULL FUNDING POLICY—BACKGROUND, ISSUES, AND OPTIONS FOR CONGRESS (June 2006).

FULL-SCALE DEVELOPMENT   The final development phase of a MAJOR SYSTEM. This is the term in the FAR that is synonymous with the DOD term ENGINEERING AND MANUFACTURING DEVELOPMENT. FAR 34.005-5 provides that, whenever practicable, full-scale development contracts should require contractors to submit priced proposals for production that are based on the latest quantity, schedule, and LOGISTICS requirements and other considerations that will be used in making the production decision.

FULL-SCALE ENGINEERING DEVELOPMENT (FSED)   The third phase in the pre-1995 DOD MAJOR SYSTEM ACQUISITION process, in which the SYSTEM and the principal items necessary for its support were fully developed, engineered, designed, fabricated, tested, and evaluated. Systems in this phase had to be approved before entering the production phase. This phase is now known as the ENGINEERING AND MANUFACTURING DEVELOPMENT phase.

FUNCTION   A task that must be performed by an agency of the government. An INHERENTLY GOVERNMENTAL FUNCTION must be performed by government personnel. See OFPP Policy Letter 11-01, *Performance of Inherently Governmental and Critical Functions,* 76 Fed. Reg. 562267 (Sept. 12, 2011). The policy letter does not define the word "function," leaving it to the discretion of each agency as to the breadth of the task that is being analyzed.

FUNCTIONAL CONFIGURATION AUDIT   The formal examination of functional characteristics of a configuration item, or system to verify that the item has achieved the requirements specified in its functional and/or allocated configuration documentation.

MIL-HDBK-61A, *Configuration Management Guidance*, Feb. 7, 2001, provides guidance on conducting these audits during the phases of the development and deployment of new WEAPON SYSTEMs.

FUNCTIONAL SPECIFICATIONS   Specifications that describe work to be performed in terms of the end purpose or the government's ultimate objective, rather than in terms of the way in which the work is to be performed. Functional specifications are broader descriptions of the work than PERFORMANCE SPECIFICATIONS and are aimed at permitting more open competition on the ways of accomplishing the government's purpose. 10 U.S.C. § 2305(a)(1) and 41 U.S.C. § 3701 state a preference for functional specifications. See FAR 11.002(a). A functional specification may include a statement of the qualitative nature of the product and, when necessary, will contain the minimum essential characteristics the product must exhibit in order to satisfy its intended use. See Cibinic, Nash & Yukins, FORMATION OF GOVERNMENT CONTRACTS 362–67 (4th ed. 2011).

FUND CITATION   An account number, used to identify the agency financial account from which appropriated funds to be obligated on a contract are to be drawn. Also called "fund cite." The contracting officer obtains the account number from a purchase request document that has been signed by an agency financial officer, thereby indicating funds are available for obligation and that the financial official has made an ADMINISTRATIVE COMMITMENT of the funds.

FUNDED PENSION COST   *Official:* The portion of pension cost for a current or prior cost accounting period that has been paid to a funding agency. *Source:* FAR 31.001. FAR 31.205-6(j) provides detailed guidance on the allowability of pension costs and generally requires that such costs be funded to be allowable. See Cibinic, Knight & Nash, COST-REIMBURSEMENT CONTRACTING 678 (4th ed. 2014).

FUNDING AGREEMENT   *Official:* Any CONTRACT, GRANT or COOPERATIVE AGREEMENT entered into between any federal agency, other than the Tennessee Valley Authority, and any contractor for the performance of experimental, developmental, or research work funded in whole or in part by the federal government. Such term includes any assignment, substitution of parties, or subcontract of any type entered into for the performance of experimental, developmental, or research work under a funding agreement as herein defined. *Source:* 35 U.S.C. § 201. This is the type of agreement subject to the BAYH-DOLE ACT. The term "contract" is generally construed to mean PROCUREMENT CONTRACT with the result that this Act is held not applicable to OTHER TRANSACTIONS. See Nash & Rawicz, INTELLECTUAL PROPERTY IN GOVERNMENT CONTRACTS, chap. 2 (6th ed. 2008).

FUTURE CONTRACT SAVINGS   *Official:* The product of the FUTURE UNIT COST REDUCTION multiplied by the number of future contract units in the sharing base. On an instant contract, future contract savings include savings on increases in quantities after VECP acceptance that are due to contract modifications, exercise of options, additional orders, and funding of subsequent year requirements on a multiyear contract. *Source:* FAR 48.001 (in the definition of ACQUISITION SAVINGS). These are generally the savings resulting from a VALUE ENGINEERING CHANGE PROPOSAL on future contract units scheduled for delivery during the three-year period following acceptance of the first unit incorporating the VECP. FAR 48.104-1 contains guidance on government-contractor sharing arrangements for such savings. The calculation of these savings is either (1) based on an estimate made by the CONTRACTING OFFICER as prescribed in ¶ (i)(4) of the Value Engineering clause in FAR 52.248-1; or (2) shared in a series of payments over time as future contracts are awarded. If the INSTANT CONTRACT is a multiyear contract (see MULTIYEAR CONTRACTING), future contract savings include savings on quantities funded after VECP acceptance. Like CONCURRENT CONTRACT SAVINGS, these savings are only shared with the contractor if they pertain to contracts issued by the same contracting office or its successor for essentially the same unit. See Nash & Feldman, 1 GOVERNMENT CONTRACT CHANGES §§ 9:13–9:15 (3d ed. 2006–2020); Cibinic, Nagle & Nash, ADMINISTRATION OF GOVERNMENT CONTRACTS 374–75 (5th ed. 2016).

FUTURE YEARS DEFENSE PROGRAM (FYDP) An official DOD document (formerly the Five-Year Defense Program) that summarizes forces and resources associated with programs approved by the Secretary of Defense. Its three parts entail the organizations affected, appropriations accounts (such as RESEARCH, DEVELOPMENT, TEST, AND EVALUATION, OPERATIONS AND MAINTENANCE, etc.), and the eleven major force programs (such as strategic forces, airlift/sealift, research and development, etc.). Under the current DOD PLANNING, PROGRAMMING, AND BUDGETING SYSTEM cycle, the FYDP is updated when the services submit their program objective memoranda to the Office of the Secretary of Defense (OSD), when the services submit their budgets to OSD, and when the President submits the national budget to Congress. See DAU GLOSSARY. U.S. GOV'T ACCOUNTABILITY OFFICE, FUTURE YEARS DEFENSE PROGRAM: OPERATION AND MAINTENANCE AND PROCUREMENT PROGRAMS, GAO-01-33 (Oct. 2000).

FUTURE UNIT COST REDUCTION *Official:* The instant unit cost reduction adjusted as the contracting officer considers necessary for projected learning or changes in quantity during the sharing period. It is calculated at the time the VECP is accepted and applies either (1) throughout the sharing period, unless the contracting officer decides that recalculation is necessary because conditions are significantly different from those previously anticipated or (2) to the calculation of a lump-sum payment that cannot later be revised. *Source:* FAR 48.001. This amount is used to calculate FUTURE COST SAVINGS when the government has accepted a VALUE ENGINEERING CHANGE PROPOSAL. See Nash & Feldman, 1 GOVERNMENT CONTRACT CHANGES §§ 9:13–9:15 (3d ed. 2006–2020); Cibinic, Nagle & Nash, ADMINISTRATION OF GOVERNMENT CONTRACTS 374 (5th ed. 2016).

G

GATEWAY AIRPORT ABROAD *Official:* The airport from which the traveler last embarks en route to the United States or at which the traveler first debarks incident to travel from the United States. *Source:* FAR 47.401. This term is used in the FAR Subpart 47.4 implementation of the FLY AMERICA ACT, which requires that federal employees and their dependents, consultants, contractors, grantees, and others use U.S.-flag air carriers for U.S. Government-financed international air travel and transportation of their property or personal effects, to the extent that service by these carriers is available. Availability of service between gateway airports is subject to the conditions in FAR 47.403-1(d).

GATEWAY AIRPORT IN THE UNITED STATES *Official:* The last U.S. airport from which the traveler's flight departs or the first U.S. airport at which the traveler's flight arrives. *Source:* FAR 47.401. This term is used in the FAR Subpart 47.4 implementation of the FLY AMERICA ACT.

GENERAL ACCOUNTING OFFICE The former title of the GOVERNMENT ACCOUNTABILITY OFFICE.

GENERAL AGREEMENT ON TARIFF AND TRADE (GATT) An agreement among nations to provide an international forum that encourages free trade between member states by regulating and reducing tariffs on traded goods and by providing a common mechanism for resolving trade disputes. GATT was originated in 1947 and now has over 110 member states. The United States joined in 1994, becoming a member of the WORLD TRADE ORGANIZATION, and implemented the agreement in 19 U.S.C. § 3511 et seq. This Act adopted a Government Procurement Agreement that provided for waiver of the BUY AMERICAN ACT in certain situations. See FAR Subpart 25.4. Title V of this Act made changes to COPYRIGHT law to conform to GATT. See Nash & Rawicz, INTELLECTUAL PROPERTY IN GOVERNMENT CONTRACTS, chap. 1 (6th ed. 2008).

GENERAL AND ADMINISTRATIVE (G&A) EXPENSE *Official:* Any management, financial, and other expense which is incurred by or allocated to a BUSINESS UNIT and which is for the general management and administration of the business unit as a whole. G&A expense does not include those management expenses whose beneficial or causal relationship to COST OBJECTIVEs can be more directly measured by a base other than a cost input base representing the total activity of a business unit during a cost accounting period. *Source:* FAR 2.101. G&A expenses commonly include expenses of a company's general and executive offices; executive compensation; the cost of staff services such as legal, accounting, public relations, financial, and similar expenses; and other miscellaneous expenses related to the overall business. CAS 410, 48 C.F.R. § 9904.410, deals with the allocation of business unit G&A expenses to FINAL COST OBJECTIVEs. When CAS 410 does not apply, DCAA CAM 6-606.4 provides audit guidelines. See Cibinic, Knight & Nash, Cost-Reimbursement Contracting 612–15 (4th ed. 2014). See also ALLOCATION OF COST.

GENERAL APPROPRIATION   See APPROPRIATION.

GENERAL CONTRACTOR   A contractor with the entire responsibility for performing a contract for CONSTRUCTION. This term is used in the construction industry to designate the contractor that bids for a construction contract and bears the risk if the contract is for a firm fixed-price and cannot be performed at the contract price unless events occur that are the responsibility of the owner.

GENERAL PROVISIONS   The standard clauses that are used by government agencies in various types of contracts. Most of these clauses are set forth in FAR Part 52, and guidance on their use is set forth in the PROVISION AND CLAUSE MATRIX in FAR Part 52.301. The term also includes clauses specified in FAR Supplements for agency-wide use. FAR 52.102-1 provides that general provisions will be incorporated by reference to the regulations "to the maximum practical extent" rather than by placing the full text of the clauses in the contract document.

GENERAL PUBLIC   Buyers other than a federal entity. General public is an important term that is used in several places in the FEDERAL ACQUISITION REGULATION without official definition. See, e.g., the definition of COMMERCIAL ITEM in FAR 2.101 and the new definition of COMMERCIAL PRODUCT. The term was originally defined in FAR 15.804-3(c)(5) as follows: "The 'general public' is a significant number of buyers other than the Government or affiliates of the offeror; the item involved must not be for Government end use. For the purpose of this subsection 15.804-3, items acquired for "Government end use" include items acquired for foreign military sales." 48 Fed. Reg. 42102, 42207. However, the definition was subsequently moved to FAR 15.804-1(b)(2)(v) and changed to read as follows: "The general public ordinarily consists of buyers other than the U.S. Government or its instrumentalities, e.g., U.S. Government corporations. Sales to the general public do not include sales to affiliates of the offerors or purchases by the U.S. Government on behalf of foreign governments, such as for Foreign Military Sales." That definition was eliminated from the FAR with the publication of Federal Acquisition Circular 90-45, 61 Fed. Reg. 224, in implementation of the Clinger-Cohen Act of 1996, which replaced the catalog or market price "exemption" under the TRUTH IN NEGOTIATIONS ACT with the COMMERCIAL ITEMS "exception." Apparently, the definition was thought to be unnecessary for the new commercial items exception although it requires that such items be "of a type customarily used by the general public."

GENERAL SCOPE   See SCOPE OF THE CONTRACT.

GENERAL SERVICES ADMINISTRATION (GSA)   An agency in the executive branch with the function of acquiring supplies and services (including construction) that are used in common by many agencies. The agency is comprised of the Federal Acquisition Service, the Public Building Service, and several staff offices. The Federal Acquisition Service includes acquires products and services and manages programs in information technology, telecommunications, professional services, supplies, motor vehicles, travel and transportation, charge cards, and personal property utilization and disposal. The Public Building Service designs, builds, leases, manages, and maintains space in office buildings, courthouses, laboratories, border stations, data processing centers, warehouses, and child care centers. It also repairs, alters, and renovates existing facilities and disposes of surplus government properties. With DOD and NASA, GSA has responsibility for the promulgation of the FEDERAL ACQUISITION REGULATION. GSA also supports the FAR Secretariat, the focal point for managing the FAR. See National Archives and Records Administration, U.S. Government Manual Office of the Federal Register (GPO 2006/07).

GENERAL SERVICES ADMINISTRATION ACQUISITION MANUAL (GSAM)   The GENERAL SERVICES ADMINISTRATION supplement to the FEDERAL ACQUISITION REGULATION which contains both the General Services Administration Acquisition Regulation (GSAR), designated 48 C.F.R. chap. 5, which is regulatory, and nonregulatory internal agency policy and guidance. In the online edition, GSAR regulatory content is shaded to distinguish it from nonregulatory content. www.acquisition.gov/gsam/gsam.html.

GENERAL SERVICES ADMINISTRATION BOARD OF CONTRACT APPEALS (GSBCA)   The BOARD OF CONTRACT APPEALS for the GENERAL SERVICES ADMINISTRATION (GSA) and certain other federal agencies that was merged into the CIVILIAN AGENCY BOARD OF CONTRACT APPEALS, effective January 7, 2007.

GENERAL STANDARDS OF RESPONSIBILITY   The seven standards of RESPONSIBILITY listed in FAR 9.104-1, which are, in brief: (1) adequate financial resources to perform the contact, or the ability to obtain them; (2) ability to comply with the required or proposed delivery schedule; (3) a satisfactory performance record; (4) a satisfactory record of integrity and business ethics; (5) possession of the necessary organization, experience, accounting and operational controls, and technical skills, or the ability to obtain them; (6) possession of the necessary production, construction, and technical equipment and facilities, or the ability to obtain them; and (7) other qualifications and eligibility under applicable laws and regulations. Offerors must meet these standards to be eligible for award of a contract. See Cibinic, Nash & Yukins, Formation of Government Contracts 409–28 (4th ed. 2011).

GENERAL WAGE DETERMINATION   See WAGE DETERMINATION.

GENERALLY ACCEPTED ACCOUNTING PRINCIPLES (GAAP)   Accounting principles that are generally accepted by commercial organizations doing business in the United States. Under FAR 31.201-2, such principles are a factor to be considered in determining whether a cost is an ALLOWABLE COST, if none of the COST ACCOUNTING STANDARDS apply. In such cases, unless the FAR's selected COST PRINCIPLES applying to commercial contractors in FAR 31.205 specifically deal with an accounting issue, the GAAP will likely prevail. Thus, pronouncements of the FINANCIAL ACCOUNTING STANDARDS BOARD and the extensive body of uncodified GAAP found in general practice or individual industry practice are used in determining the allowable costs of government contracts. See generally Cibinic, Knight & Nash, Cost-Reimbursement Contracting 513–22 (4th ed. 2014).

GENERALLY ACCEPTED AUDITING STANDARDS (GAAS)   Audit standards that articulate the minimum requirements (as opposed to aspirational goals) for the work of auditors, both government and private. There are 10 generally accepted auditing standards, which are promulgated by the American Institute of Certified Public Accountants: three general standards, which require minimum training and proficiency, independence, and due professional care; three field work standards, which mandate adequate planning, understanding of the internal control structure, and the need for sufficient competent evidential matter; and four reporting standards, which require stating whether the financial statements comply with the GENERALLY ACCEPTED ACCOUNTING PRINCIPLES (GAAP), identifying where GAAP has not been consistently followed, regarding informative disclosures as adequate, and containing an expression of opinion regarding the financial statement. Auditing standards are distinct from auditing procedures; procedures dictate acts to be performed whereas standards assess the quality of the performance of those acts and auditing objectives to be achieved. Standards for DEFENSE CONTRACT AUDIT AGENCY auditors are found in Chapter 2 of the DCAA CONTRACT AUDIT MANUAL.

GIFT   *Official:* Any GRATUITY, favor, discount, entertainment, hospitality, loan, forbearance, or other item having monetary value. It includes services as well as gifts of training, transportation, local travel, lodgings and meals, whether provided in-kind, by purchase of a ticket, payment in advance, or reimbursement after the expense has been incurred. It does not include: (1) Modest items of food and refreshments, such as soft drinks, coffee and donuts, offered other than as part of a meal; (2) Greeting cards and items with little intrinsic value, such as plaques, certificates, and trophies, which are intended solely for presentation; (3) Loans from banks and other financial institutions on terms generally available to the public; (4) Opportunities and benefits, including favorable rates and commercial discounts, available to the public or to a class consisting of all Government employees or all uniformed military personnel, whether or not restricted on the basis of geographic considerations; (5) Rewards and prizes given to competitors in contests or events, including random drawings, open to the public unless the employee's entry into the contest or event is required as part of his official duties; (6) Pension and other benefits resulting from continued participation in an employee welfare and benefits plan maintained by a former employer; (7) Anything which is paid for by the Government or secured by the Government under Government contract; NOTE: An employee may accept and retain travel promotional items, such as frequent flyer miles, received as a result of her official travel, to the extent permitted by 5 U.S.C. § 5702, note, and 41 C.F.R. part 301-53. (8) Free attendance to an event provided by the sponsor of the event to: (i) An employee who is assigned to present information on behalf of the agency at the event on any day when the employee is presenting; (ii) An employee whose presence on any day of the event is deemed to be essential by the agency to the presenting employee's participation in the event, provided that the employee is accompanying the presenting employee; and (iii) The spouse or one other guest of the presenting employee on any day when the employee is presenting, provided that others in attendance will generally be accompanied by a spouse or other guest, the offer of free attendance for the spouse or other guest is unsolicited, and the agency designee, orally or in writing, has authorized the presenting employee to accept; (9) Any gift accepted by the Government under specific statutory authority, including: (i) Travel, subsistence, and related expenses accepted by an agency under the authority of 31 U.S.C. § 1353 in connection with an employee's attendance at a meeting or similar function relating to his official duties which takes place away from his duty station, provided that the agency's acceptance must be in accordance with the implementing regulations at 41 C.F.R. part 304-1; and (ii) Other gifts provided in-kind which have been accepted by an agency under its agency gift acceptance statute; or (10) Anything for which market value is paid by the employee. *Source:* 5 C.F.R. § 2635.203(b). The federal STANDARDS OF CONDUCT, 5 C.F.R. part 235, Subpart

B, contain extensive guidance on gifts from contractors to government employees and, generally, prohibit gifts of any magnitude. In addition, the Gratuities clause in FAR 52.203-3 gives the government the right to terminate a contract if gratuities are given to government employees. See Cibinic, Nagle & Nash, ADMINISTRATION OF GOVERNMENT CONTRACTS 86–88 (5th ed. 2016); Cibinic, Nash & Yukins, FORMATION OF GOVERNMENT CONTRACTS 151–57 (4th ed. 2011); Tillipman, *Gifts, Hospitality & The Government Contractor*, BRIEFING PAPERS No. 14-7 (June 2014); Tillipman & Mahini, *Government Lawyering*, BRIEFING PAPERS No. 11-3 (Feb. 2011); Kathuria, *Best Practices for Compliance with the New Government Contractor Compliance and Ethics Rules Under the Federal Acquisition Regulation*, 38 PUB. CONT. L.J. 803 (2009).

GLOBAL SETTLEMENT   A settlement between a contractor and the government resolving criminal, civil, and administrative disputes with the government through simultaneous, coordinated, comprehensive agreements. The term is generally used to describe the settlement of administrative proceedings involving a SUSPENSION or DEBARMENT as well as the settlement of any criminal charges arising out of a contractor's actions. See Stubbs, *Fighting Fraud Illustrated: The Robins AFB Case*, 38 A.F. L. Rev. 141 (1994); D'Aloisio, *Accusations of Criminal Conduct by Government Contractors: The Remedies, Problems, and Solutions*, 17 PUB. CONT. L.J. 265, 300–10 (1987).

GOALS AND TIMETABLES   A series of annual goals by LABOR category that a contractor establishes in an attempt to increase its minority employment as part of its AFFIRMATIVE ACTION commitment to the government. 41 C.F.R. § 60-2.16 now describes these as "placement goals." These goals are not a firm contractual commitment but, rather, are an agreement to use best efforts to meet them. See FAR Subpart 22.8; 41 C.F.R. § 60-1 and 60-2. See also DFARS Subpart 222.8; DEAR Subpart 922.8; GSAR Subpart 522.8; NFS Subpart 18-22.8.

GOLDEN PARACHUTE COSTS   Costs paid to an employee of a contractor in excess of normal severance pay and contingent on, and following, a change in management control over, or ownership of, the contractor or a substantial portion of the contractor's assets. Such costs are UNALLOWABLE COSTs under 10 U.S.C. § 2324(e)(1)(K) and 41 U.S.C. § 4304(a)(11). See FAR 31.205-6(l); Cibinic, Knight & Nash, COST-REIMBURSEMENT CONTRACTING 686 (4th ed. 2014).

GOOD FAITH AND FAIR DEALING   See DUTY OF GOOD FAITH AND FAIR DEALING.

GOODS   All things (including specially manufactured goods) which are movable at the time of identification to the contract for sale other than the money in which the price is to be paid, investment securities (Article 8), and things in action. A purported present sale of future goods or of any interest therein operates as a contract to sell. U.C.C. § 2-105. Article 2 of the UNIFORM COMMERCIAL CODE governs contracts for the sale of goods throughout the United States, except in Louisiana. Government contracts for goods are called "supply contracts" and generally are not subject to Article 2 of the U.C.C. See SUPPLIES.

GOODWILL   An intangible ASSET resulting when the price paid by an acquiring company exceeds the sum of the identifiable individual assets acquired less liabilities assumed, based upon their fair values. FAR 31.205-49 specifies that costs resulting from such goodwill are UNALLOWABLE COSTs. See Manos, 1 GOVERNMENT CONTRACT COST AND PRICING

§§ 56.1–53-3 (2d ed. 2009–2020); Cibinic, Knight & Nash, Cost-Reimbursement Contracting 720 (4th ed. 2014).

GOVERNMENT ACCOUNTABILITY OFFICE (GAO)   (Formerly the GENERAL ACCOUNTING OFFICE (prior to July 7, 2004).) A government agency that is part of the legislative branch and that investigates matters relating to the receipt, disbursement, and application of public funds. Headed by the COMPTROLLER GENERAL, GAO evaluates the performance of government programs (and typically issues reports when the assessment is negative), and issues decisions concerning PROTESTs against award. See FAR Subpart 33.1. See also United States Government Accountability Office, BID PROTESTS AT GAO: A Descriptive Guide, GAO-18-510SP (May 2018, 10th ed.); Nash, *The Protest Role of the Government Accountability Office: An Assessment*, 22 N&CR ¶ 27 (Apr. 2008). GAO has broad powers to AUDIT contractors under the EXAMINATION OF RECORDS provisions and occasionally investigates contractors in the course of auditing government programs. GAO maintains a network of 11 regional and field offices and has 15 mission teams that assess program performance. The name of this office was changed by the GAO Human Capital Reform Act of 2004, Pub. L. No. 108-271, 118 Stat. 811 (2004). Besides the name change, the law decouples GAO from the federal employee pay system, establishes a compensation system that places greater emphasis on job performance while protecting the purchasing power of employees who are performing acceptably, gives GAO permanent authority to offer voluntary early retirement opportunities and voluntary separation payments (buy-outs), provides greater flexibility for reimbursing employees for relocation benefits, allows certain employees and officers with less than three years of federal service to earn increased amounts of annual leave, and authorizes an exchange program with private sector organizations.

GOVERNMENT BILL OF LADING   See BILL OF LADING.

GOVERNMENT CLAIM   See CLAIM.

GOVERNMENT CONTRACT QUALITY ASSURANCE   *Official:* The various functions, including inspection, performed by the government to determine whether a contractor has fulfilled the contract obligations pertaining to quality and quantity. *Source:* FAR 46.101. See QUALITY ASSURANCE.

GOVERNMENT CONTRACTOR DEFENSE   A legal defense to a product liability claim (brought by or on behalf of a person injured by the product) that is available to government contractors under certain scenarios. The defense permits the contractor to enjoy the government's SOVEREIGN IMMUNITY from liability for the injury. The contractor escapes liability if (1) the government approved reasonably precise specifications for the contractor, (2) the contractor's equipment conformed to those specifications, and (3) the contractor warned the government about the dangers in the use of the equipment that were known to the contractor but not to the government. See Coleman and Moore, *Government Contractor Defense: Military and Non-Military Applications* (ABA Sept. 12, 2016).

GOVERNMENT DELAY OF WORK   See COMPENSABLE DELAY.

GOVERNMENT-FURNISHED EQUIPMENT (GFE)   Various types of property in the possession of, or acquired by the government, and delivered or otherwise made available to a contractor for use in performing a contract. This term was not used or defined in the FAR but was commonly used in dealing with GOVERNMENT-FURNISHED PROPERTY under FAR Part 45. FAR 45.101 now defines EQUIPMENT and treats it as an element of GOVERNMENT PROPERTY. Generally, government-furnished equipment by the DOD may be required to be reported in the Item Unique Identification Registry. DFARS 211.274-4. See Cibinic, Nagle & Nash, ADMINISTRATION OF GOVERNMENT CONTRACTS, chap. 7 (5th ed. 2016).

GOVERNMENT-FURNISHED PROPERTY (GFP)   *Official:* Property in the possession of, or directly acquired by, the government and subsequently furnished to the contractor for performance of a contract. Government-furnished property includes, but is not limited to, spares and property furnished for repair, maintenance, overhaul, or modification. Government-furnished property also includes CONTRACTOR-ACQUIRED PROPERTY if the contractor-acquired property is a deliverable under a COST CONTRACT when accepted by the government for continued use under the contract. *Source:* FAR 45.101. FAR 47.305-12 provides guidance on delivering GFP. GFP is included in the broad term GOVERNMENT PROPERTY, which is subject to the policies and procedures of FAR Part 45. The Government Property clause, FAR 52.245-1 includes provisions covering GFP. See Cibinic, Nagle & Nash, ADMINISTRATION OF GOVERNMENT CONTRACTS 553–57 (5th ed. 2016). See also GOVERNMENT-FURNISHED MATERIAL.

GOVERNMENT-OWNED, CONTRACTOR-OPERATED PLANT (GOCO)   An industrial or research and development facility that is owned by the government but operated by a contractor. The procedures used in contracting for the operation of GOCOs are set forth in FAR Subpart 17.6 dealing with MANAGEMENT AND OPERATING CONTRACTs. ADVANCED AGREEMENTs can be particularly significant for GENERAL AND ADMINISTRATIVE COSTs in GOCO contracts. FAR 31.109(h)(13). Guidance for INDIRECT COSTs in GOCO contracts is found in FAR 31.203(h).

GOVERNMENT PERFORMANCE AND RESULTS ACT OF 1993   31 U.S.C. § 1115 et seq. and 39 U.S.C. § 2801 et seq. An Act that seeks to improve the efficiency and effectiveness of federal programs, eliminate wasteful management and performance practices, and establish accountability for results. The Act mandates that, beginning in Fiscal Year 1994, various agencies must establish pilot programs aimed toward program performance measurement, reporting, and goal setting. The Act requires agency heads to submit strategic plans to the OFFICE OF MANAGEMENT AND BUDGET, then requires annual performance plans and reports on program performance. According to Senate Report 103-58, this Act will provide the information necessary to strengthen program management in the federal government. U.S. GOV'T ACCOUNTABILITY OFFICE, THE RESULTS ACT: AN EVALUATOR'S GUIDE TO ASSESSING AGENCY ANNUAL PERFORMANCE PLANS, GAO/GGD-10.1.20 (Apr. 1998).

GOVERNMENT PRINTING   *Official:* Printing, binding, and blankbook work for the use of an executive department, independent agency, or establishment of the government. *Source:* FAR 8.801. 44 U.S.C. § 501 et seq. requires that such printing be done by the GOVERNMENT PRINTING OFFICE with specified exceptions. See FAR 8.802.

GOVERNMENT PRINTING OFFICE (GPO)   The entity that handles all printing, binding, and blankbook work for Congress, the Executive Office of the President, the Judiciary (except the Supreme Court), and every executive department, independent office, and establishment of the government. Among its major publications are the *Congressional Record* and the FEDERAL REGISTER. In addition, the GPO sells government publications and documents in printed and electronic formats through its Washington, DC and regional bookstores. For information about obtaining publications, contact GPO, North Capitol & H Streets, Washington, DC 20401; (202) 512-1800, www.access.gpo.gov.

GOVERNMENT PROPERTY   *Official:* All property owned by or leased to the government. Government property includes both GOVERNMENT-FURNISHED PROPERTY and CONTRACTOR-ACQUIRED PROPERTY. Government property includes material, EQUIPMENT, SPECIAL TOOLING, SPECIAL TEST EQUIPMENT and REAL PROPERTY. Government property does not include intellectual property and software. *Source:* FAR 45.101. FAR Part 45 was totally revised by FAC 2005-17, May 17, 2007 to simplify the coverage of government property. Contractors are generally required to furnish all property necessary to perform contracts, but they can use government property if (1) it is in the best interests of the government; (2) the overall benefit outweighs the increased cost of administration; (3) the government's assumption of risk is not substantially increased; and (4) government requirements cannot otherwise be met. FAR 45.102. FAR 45.103 sets forth the following general principles that agencies should follow with regard to government property: (1) allow and encourage contractors to use voluntary consensus standards and industry-leading practices and standards to manage government property in their possession; (2) eliminate to the maximum practical extent any competitive advantage a prospective contractor may have by using government property; (3) ensure maximum practical reutilization of contractor inventory for government purposes; (4) require contractors to use government property already in their possession to the maximum extent practical in performing government contracts; (5) charge appropriate rentals when the property is authorized for use on other than a rent-free basis; and (6) require contractors to justify retaining government property not needed for contract performance and to declare property as excess when no longer needed for contract performance. FAR Subpart 45.6 contains detailed guidance on the reporting, reutilization and disposal of government property. A single Government Property clause, containing all of the responsibilities of contractors for government property, is set forth in FAR 52.245-1. DFARS Part 245 contains guidance on government property furnished by the DOD. Instructions for audit responsibilities in connection to government property are found in the *DCAA Contract Audit Manual* ¶ 14-400. See Feldman, GOVERNMENT CONTRACT GUIDEBOOK §§ 14:1–14.8 (4th ed. 2019–2020); Cibinic, Nagle & Nash, ADMINISTRATION OF GOVERNMENT CONTRACTS, chap. 7 (5th ed. 2016).

GOVERNMENT-PURPOSE   *Official:* Any activity in which the United States Government is a party, including cooperative agreements with international or multi-national defense organizations, or sales or transfers by the United States Government to foreign governments or international organizations. Government purposes include competitive procurement, but do not include the rights to use, modify, reproduce, release, perform, display, or disclose technical data for commercial purposes or authorize others to do so. *Source:* DFARS 252.227-7013 and DFARS 252.227-7014. When the government has GOVERNMENT PURPOSE RIGHTS in TECHNICAL DATA or COMPUTER SOFTWARE these are the purposes for which it can be used. See Nash & Rawicz, INTELLECTUAL PROPERTY IN GOVERNMENT CONTRACTS, chaps. 4 & 5 (6th ed. 2008).

GOVERNMENT-PURPOSE LICENSE RIGHTS (GPLR)   The right to use, duplicate, and disclose TECHNICAL DATA, in whole or in part and in any manner, for government purposes only, and to have or permit others to do so for government purposes only. This right was included in the DOD data policy from 1988 to 1995 when it was replaced by

GOVERNMENT PURPOSE RIGHTS. See Nash & Rawicz, INTELLECTUAL PROPERTY IN GOVERNMENT CONTRACTS, chaps. 4 & 5 (6th ed. 2008).

GOVERNMENT PURPOSE RIGHTS (GPR)   *Official:* The rights to (1) Use, modify, reproduce, release, perform, display or disclose TECHNICAL DATA or COMPUTER SOFTWARE or COMPUTER SOFTWARE DOCUMENTATION within the government without restriction; and (2) Release or disclose technical data or computer software or computer software documentation outside the government and authorize persons to whom release or disclosure has been made to use, modify, reproduce, release, perform, display or disclose that data or software or documentation for United States GOVERNMENT PURPOSEs. *Source:* DFARS 252.227-7013 and DFARS 252.227-7014. This right was included in the DOD data and software policy in 1995 to replace GOVERNMENT-PURPOSE LICENSE RIGHTS. Under GPR, the government obtains the right to use technical data and computer software for all government purposes, including competitive procurement but not for commercial purposes. Under the Rights in Technical Data—Noncommercial Items clause in DFARS 252.227-7013 and the Rights in Noncommercial Computer Software and Noncommercial Computer Software Documentation clause in DFARS 252.227-7014, the government obtains GPR to all technical data and computer software developed with MIXED FUNDING if the contractor marks the data with a legend denoting such rights. These clauses provide that such rights expire at the end of five years after execution of the development contract, with the government obtaining UNLIMITED RIGHTS thereafter. However, either party may request a different period and longer periods are encouraged when the contractor needs more time to apply the data or software to commercial products, DFARS 227.7103-5(b)(2) and 227.7203-5(b)(2). This regulation permits the negotiation of such longer periods during contract performance without CONSIDERATION from either party. See Nash & Rawicz, INTELLECTUAL PROPERTY IN GOVERNMENT CONTRACTS, chaps. 4 and 5 (6th ed. 2008).

GOVERNMENT TECHNICAL MONITOR   An occasionally used term for CONTRACTING OFFICER REPRESENTATIVE.

GOVERNMENT VERSUS CONTRACTOR PERFORMANCE   See A-76 POLICY.

GOVERNMENT VESSEL   *Official:* A vessel owned by the U.S. Government and operated directly by the government or for the government by an agent or contractor, including a privately owned U.S.-flag vessel under bareboat charter to the government. *Source:* FAR 47.501. Such a vessel is included in the definition of U.S.-flag vessel for the purpose of the cargo preference regulations in FAR Subpart 47.5.

GOVERNMENTWIDE ACQUISITION CONTRACT (GWAC)   *Official:* A task-order or delivery-order contract for work related to INFORMATION TECHNOLOGY established by one agency for governmentwide use that is operated—(1) By an EXECUTIVE AGENCY designated by the OFFICE OF MANAGEMENT AND BUDGET pursuant to 40 U.S.C. § 11302(e); or (2) Under a delegation of procurement authority issued by the General Services Administration (GSA) prior to August 7, 1996, under authority granted GSA by former section 40 U.S.C. § 759, repealed by Pub. L. 104-106. The Economy Act does not apply to orders under a Governmentwide acquisition contract. *Source:* FAR 2.101. These contracts were created by § 5124 of the CLINGER-COHEN ACT OF 1996. See 40 U.S.C. § 11314(a)(2). The host agency normally adds a small administrative fee. Multi-agency contracts permit AGGREGATION of agency demand to encourage vendors to offer the best possible prices, while reducing the overhead associated with multiple acquisitions, particularly by smaller agencies. Each GWAC has its own particular rules and conditions. See INDEFINITE-DELIVERY CONTRACTS. See Cibinic, Nash & Yukins, FORMATION OF GOVERNMENT CONTRACTS 1189–97 (4th ed. 2011).

GOVERNMENTWIDE COMMERCIAL PURCHASE CARD   *Official:* A purchase card, similar in nature to a commercial credit card, issued to authorized agency officials to use to acquire and to pay for SUPPLIES and SERVICES. *Source:* FAR 13.001. These cards are given to agency officials who are not CONTRACTING OFFICERs, with limitations on their use. FAR 13.301(a). FAR 13.003(e) encourages their use on simplified acquisitions (see SIMPLIFIED ACQUISITION PROCEDURES) to the maximum extent practicable, and they are also used by some agencies for purchases of larger dollar amounts or making payments in larger amounts. FAR 13.301(c) explicitly allows the cards to be used to (1) make MICRO-PURCHASEs; (2) place TASK or DELIVERY ORDERs, and (3) make payments. Payments made by purchase cards satisfy any requirement that payment be made by ELEC-TRONIC FUNDS TRANSFER. FAR 32.1102. Guidance on the use of these cards is set forth in FAR 32.1108.

GOVERNMENTWIDE POINT OF ENTRY (GPE)   *Official:* The single point where government business opportunities greater than $25,000, including synopses of proposed contract actions (see SYNOPSIS), SOLICITATIONs, and associated information can be accessed electronically by the public. The GPE is located at http://www.fbo.gov. *Source:* FAR 2.101. The site has been moved to BETA.SAM.GOV. FAR 5.003 requires the contracting officer to transmit notices to the government point of entry for any requirement in the FAR to publish notice. See Cibinic, Nash & Yukins, FORMATION OF GOVERNMENT CONTRACTS 390–401 (4th ed. 2011).

GOVERNMENT WORK   See WORK OF THE UNITED STATES GOVERNMENT.

GRANT   A legal instrument for transferring money, property, or services to the recipient in order to accomplish a public purpose of support or stimulation where there will be no substantial involvement between the federal agency and the recipient during performance. Federal Grant and Cooperative Agreement Act of 1977, 31 U.S.C. § 6304. This act distinguishes federal assistance relationships, or grants and COOPERATIVE AGREE-MENTs, from procurement relationships, or PROCUREMENT CONTRACTs. Unlike a procurement contract, which is a legal instrument for acquiring supplies or services for the direct benefit of or use by the federal government, a grant—like a cooperative agreement—has, as its main purpose, support or stimulation. A grant differs from a cooperative agreement in that, under a cooperative agreement, there is substantial involvement between the federal agency and the recipient during performance of the contemplated activity, whereas under a grant there is not. Cappalli, *I Federal Grants and Cooperative Agreements* 1-136 and 1-137 (1982). Grants are not subject to the FEDERAL ACQUISITION REGULATION. The term "grant" is an ambiguous term in that it is used to refer to agreements with private organizations (such as research grants) as well as arrangements where the federal government provides funds to state and local governments. With regard to the latter use, there are three general types of grants: (1) categorical grants, (2) block grants, and (3) revenue-sharing grants (currently not in use). See Allen, *Grantee Contracting–What Grantees And Their Lawyers Need To Know*, BRIEFING PAPERS NO. 18-10 (Sept. 2018); Allen, *Federal Grants: A Comprehensive Overview And Comparison To Federal Contracting*, BRIEFING PAPERS NO. 16-6 (May 2016).

GRATUITY   Anything of value given to a public official for or because of an act by the recipient. 18 U.S.C. § 201(c) makes it a crime to offer or solicit GIFTs, as well as to accept a gift, and, for practical purposes, prohibits all gifts to public officials made to influence or appear to influence acts. The statute requires only a showing of wrongful purpose in offering or accepting a thing of value for or because of an official act. FAR 3.101-2 and Subpart 3.2 spell out the government's policy on gratuities offered to or solicited by contracting personnel. See Manos, 2 GOVERNMENT CONTRACT COSTS & PRICING, chap. 91 (2d ed. 2009–2020); Cibinic, Nagle & Nash, ADMINISTRATION OF GOVERNMENT CONTRACTS 86–90 (5th ed. 2016); Cibinic, Nash & Yukins, FORMATION OF GOVERNMENT CONTRACTS 151–57 (4th ed. 2011). See Kathuria, *Best Practices for Compliance with the New Government Contractor Compliance and Ethics Rules Under the Federal Acquisition Regulation,* 38 PUB. CONT. L.J. 803 (2009).

GREENHOUSE GASES   *Official:* Carbon dioxide, methane, nitrous oxide, hydrofluorocarbons, perfluorocarbons, and sulfur hexafluoride. *Source:* FAR 23.001. It is the government's policy to acquire supplies and services that reduce greenhouse gas emissions from direct and indirect federal activities. FAR 23.202.

GROSS MISTAKE AMOUNTING TO FRAUD   A mistake so serious or uncalled for as not to be reasonably expected, or justifiable, in the case of a responsible contractor; a mistake that cannot be reconciled in good faith. *Catalytic Eng'g & Manufacturing Corp.,* ASBCA 15257, 72-1 BCA ¶ 9342. This type of mistake overcomes the finality of ACCEPTANCE OF WORK in the Inspection of Supplies—Fixed-Price clause, FAR 52.246-2, and the Inspection of Construction clause, FAR 52.246-12. See Cibinic, Nagle & Nash, ADMINISTRATION OF GOVERNMENT CONTRACTS 768–70 (5th ed. 2016).

GSA   See GENERAL SERVICES ADMINISTRATION.

GSA ADVANTAGE!   An electronic catalog intended to maximize item visibility, facilitate customer learning about available products, and simplify the ordering process. GSA Advantage! is an on-line ordering system that allows agencies to search through all General Services Administration sources of supply and select the item that is the best value for their requirements, without having to know a complex paperwork or logistics system. This on-line catalog can be found on the Internet at www.gsaadvantage.com.

GSA INDEX OF SPECIFICATIONS, STANDARDS AND COMMERCIAL ITEM DESCRIPTIONS   A list of federal SPECIFICATIONs and STANDARDs, and COMMERCIAL ITEM DESCRIPTIONs. The documents are listed alphabetically, numerically, and by FEDERAL SUPPLY CLASSIFICATION. The list may be searched at www.apps.fss.gsa.gov/pub/fedspecs/.

GSA MOTORPOOLS   See INTERAGENCY FLEET MANAGEMENT SYSTEM.

GSA SCHEDULE   See FEDERAL SUPPLY SCHEDULES.

GSA STORES STOCK   Supply distribution facilities operated by the General Services Administration (GSA) that maintain an inventory of stock items that constitute a mandatory source for executive agencies located within the United States. See 41 C.F.R. § 101-26.301. FAR 8.001(a)(1) requires agencies to requisition supplies from GSA stock before taking other procurement action. See Cibinic, Nash & Yukins, FORMATION OF GOVERNMENT CONTRACTS 358 (4th ed. 2011).

GUARANTEED LOAN   *Official:* A loan, revolving credit fund, or other financial arrangement made pursuant to Regulation V of the Federal Reserve Board, under which the guaranteeing agency is obligated, on demand of the lender, to purchase a stated percentage of the loan and to share any losses in the amount of the guaranteed percentage. *Source:* FAR 32.301. These are sometimes called "V loans." The loans are originally made by commercial lending institutions and government funds are not involved except for the purchase of the guaranteed portion of the loan for the settlement of losses. Section 301 of the Defense Production Act of 1950, 50 U.S.C. app. § 2061 et seq., authorizes loan guarantees for contract performance or other operations related to the national defense, subject to amounts annually authorized by Congress. FAR 32.106 states that guaranteed loans are a preferred form of FINANCING over UNUSUAL CONTRACT FINANCING and ADVANCE PAYMENTs.

GUIDELINES FOR THE ACQUISITION OF INVESTIGATIONS   See ANNOUNCEMENT OF OPPORTUNITY.

H

HAMILTON STIPULATION   A stipulation, relating to an uncertified CLAIM before a BOARD OF CONTRACT APPEALS (BCA), that the contracting officer was aware of the claim, considered it, and would have denied it formally had it been properly certified at the time of submission. The CONTRACT DISPUTES ACT (CDA) OF 1978 states that a contractor's demand or assertion seeking payment of a sum exceeding $100,000 does not become a claim until certified. However, in *United States v. Hamilton Enterprises*, 711 F.2d 1038 (Fed. Cir. 1983), the U.S. COURT OF APPEALS FOR THE FEDERAL CIRCUIT held that "there was substantial compliance with the certification requirements" of the CDA, even though the contractor had not certified and therefore had not formally asserted its claim until it appealed the contracting officer's denial. Thus, the stipulation generates a sufficient basis for jurisdiction by a BCA to overcome the untimely certification and the lack of a final DECISION OF THE CONTRACTING OFFICER. Because of the statutory change to the certification requirement by Pub. L. No. 102-572, § 907, it is unlikely that the Hamilton stipulation will be used in the future. See CERTIFICATION OF CLAIM.

HEAD OF THE AGENCY   *Official:* The Secretary, Attorney General, Administrator, Governor, Chairperson, or other chief official of an EXECUTIVE AGENCY, unless otherwise indicated, including any deputy or assistant chief official of an executive agency. *Source:* FAR 2.101. Some statutes and regulations provide that actions may only be taken by heads of agencies. For example, FAR DEVIATIONs must be approved by heads of an agency. FAR 1.403; FAR 1.404. Heads of agencies can also waive the applicability of COST ACCOUNTING STANDARDs. FAR 30.201-5.

HEAD OF THE CONTRACTING ACTIVITY (HCA)   *Official:* The official who has overall responsibility for managing the CONTRACTING ACTIVITY. *Source:* FAR 2.101. Examples of contracting activities are the Naval Sea Systems Command, the Air Force Material Command, NASA's Goddard Space Flight Center, and General Service Administration's Federal Acquisition Service. Some actions in the procurement process may be taken only by the HCA (not a CONTRACTING OFFICER). See, for example, FAR 1.602-3(b) permitting RATIFICATION of UNAUTHORIZED COMMITMENTs by an HCA with the caveat that the power may be delegated no lower than the chief of the contracting office.

HEALTH CARE SERVICES   See NONPERSONAL HEALTH CARE SERVICES.

HHS   See DEPARTMENT OF HEALTH AND HUMAN SERVICES.

HIGH PERFORMANCE SUSTAINABLE BUILDING   A building or the design, CON-
STRUCTION, renovation, repair, or deconstruction of Federal buildings that conforms to
the Guidance Principles for Federal Leadership in High Performance and Sustainable Buildings. FAR 7.103(p)(3). The Energy Independence and Security Act of 2007, Pub. L. No.
110-140, added a number of requirements to 42 U.S.C. § 8251 et seq., that must be met
by Federal buildings to reduce their energy and water consumption. FAR 36.104(b) states
that the goals of high performance sustainable building are to (1) ensure compliance with
the guiding principles; (2) pursue cost-effective, innovative strategies to minimize consumption of energy, water, and materials; (3) identify alternatives to renovation that reduce existing assets' deferred maintenance costs; (4) ensure that rehabilitation of Federally-owned
historic buildings utilizes best practices and technologies in retrofitting to promote long-
term viability of the buildings; and (5) ensure the diverting of construction and demolition
materials and debris. Each federal agency is responsible for prioritizing and monitoring its
compliance with the guidance principles. See Millan, *Far in the LEED in Going Green*, 46
The Procurement Lawyer 7 (2011); Millan, *Far in the LEED: Taking Green Buildings Out
of the Black Box*, 57 FED. LAW. 47 (2010); U.S. GOV'T ACCOUNTABILITY OFFICE, AGENCIES
ARE TAKING STEPS TO MEETING HIGH-PERFORMANCE FEDERAL BUILDING REQUIREMENTS, BUT
FACE CHALLENGES, GAO-10-22 (Oct. 2009).

HIGH-VALUE ITEM   *Official:* A contract end item that (1) has a high cost (normally exceeding $100,000 per unit), such as an aircraft, an aircraft engine, a communication system, a
computer system, a missile, or a ship; and (2) is designated by the contracting officer as a
high-value item. *Source:* FAR 46.802. FAR 46.803 states the government policy to relieve
the contractor of liability for loss of or damage to such items. This is done by including in
the contract the Limitation of Liability—High-Value Item clause in FAR 52.246-24.

HIGHER-LEVEL CONTRACT QUALITY REQUIREMENTS   Contractual quality requirements that are greater than the normal requirements in standard INSPECTION clauses.
FAR 46.202-4. These are used for COMPLEX ITEMs and items that have a critical application. FAR 46.202-4(b) gives examples of such quality requirements including ISO 9001,
9002 and 9003. Agencies impose these requirements by using the Higher-Level Contract
Quality Requirement clause in FAR 52.246-11.

HISPANIC AMERICANS   Individuals that are presumed to be SOCIALLY DISADVAN-
TAGED INDIVIDUALS for the purpose of determining the ownership of a SMALL DIS-
ADVANTAGED BUSINESS CONCERN. 13 C.F.R. § 124.103. They must then
demonstrate to the SMALL BUSINESS ADMINISTRATION that are ECONOMICALLY
DISADVANTAGED INDIVIDUALS. Businesses owned by such individuals are given spe-
cial preferences in government procurement. See FAR Subparts 19.8 and 19.11.

HISTORICAL COST   The ACTUAL COST incurred by a contractor in performing the
work. In *Bruce Constr. Corp. v. United States*, 163 Ct. Cl. 97, 324 F.2d 516 (1963), it was
held that the measure for determining the amount of an EQUITABLE ADJUSTMENT is
reasonable cost (see REASONABLENESS OF COST) plus an allowance for profit, and that
historical cost, rather than FAIR MARKET VALUE, was presumed to be the proper measure of reasonable cost. This rule gives greater weight to a particular contractor's actual cost
than to the determination of what the cost would have been to other contractors in general.
10 U.S.C. § 2324(j) overcame the presumption of validity of historical costs with regard to
indirect cost rulings by providing that contractors have the burden of proof of reasonableness

when litigating such costs. FAR 31.201-3(a) carries this logic further by stating that contractors have the burden of proof when any cost is challenged as unreasonable. See Nash & Feldman, 2 GOVERNMENT CONTRACT CHANGES § 16:2 (3d ed. 2006–2020); Cibinic, Nagle & Nash, ADMINISTRATION OF GOVERNMENT CONTRACTS 622 (5th ed. 2016); Nash, *Allowability of Subcontractor Prices: A Surprising Decision*, 26 N&CR ¶ 58 (Nov. 2012).

HISTORICALLY BLACK COLLEGES AND UNIVERSITIES (HBCU)   *Official:* An institution determined by the Secretary of Education to meet the requirements of 34 C.F.R. § 608.2. *Source:* FAR 2.101. Executive Order 12928, September 16, 1994, requires all agencies to promote participation of HBUCs and MIs in federal procurement. This policy is stated in FAR Subpart 26.3 with no guidance on how it is to be achieved. Agency participation has occurred by encouraging these institutions to respond to BROAD AGENCY ANNOUNCEMENTs for research work. See Matthews, CONG. RESEARCH SERV., Report No. RL34435, FEDERAL RESEARCH AND DEVELOPMENT FUNDING AT HISTORICALLY BLACK COLLEGES AND UNIVERSITIES (Sept. 26, 2008).

HISTORICALLY UNDERUTILIZED BUSINESS ZONE   See HUBZONE.

HOME OFFICE   *Official:* An office responsible for directing or managing two or more, but not necessarily all, SEGMENTs of an organization. A home office typically establishes policy for, and provides guidance to, the segments in their operations. It usually performs management, supervisory, or administrative functions and may also perform service functions in support of the operations of the various segments. An organization that has intermediate levels, such as groups, may have several home offices that report to a common home office. An intermediate organization may be both a segment and a home office. *Source:* FAR 31.001. CAS 403, Allocation of Home Office Expenses to Segments, 48 C.F.R. § 9904.403-40, requires that, to the maximum extent practicable, home office expenses must be allocated directly to segments on the basis of the beneficial or causal relationship between supporting and receiving activities. If these expenses are not allocated directly to segments, they are to be grouped in logical and homogeneous expense pools and allocated in accordance with detailed rules in the standard. When CAS 403 does not apply, *DCAA Contract Audit Manual* ¶ 6-606.5 provides guidelines for allocation of home office expenses. See Cibinic, Knight & Nash, COST-REIMBURSEMENT CONTRACTING 615–16 (4th ed. 2014). In pricing claims for government delay, home office expenses are generally computed using the EICHLEAY FORMULA.

HOMELAND SECURITY ACQUISITION MANUAL (HSAM)   A supplement to both the FEDERAL ACQUISITION REGULATION and the HOMELAND SECURITY ACQUISITION REGULATION, the HSAM was issued on December 19, 2003 by the DEPARTMENT OF HOMELAND SECURITY. The HSAM focuses on procedural and administrative aspects of implementing the HSAR. HSAM is not promulgated through the regulatory process and thus its policies and procedures do not have the force and effect of law and may be given less deference by the courts.

HOMELAND SECURITY ACQUISITION REGULATION (HSAR)   The DEPARTMENT OF HOMELAND SECURITY supplement to the FEDERAL ACQUISITION REGULATION, designated 48 C.F.R. chap. 30, which contains the department-wide acquisition policy and regulation for all DHS contracting activities. While the TRANSPORTATION SECURITY ADMINISTRATION was initially exempt from the HSAR, on July 22, 2008 that agency also became subject to its regulations. The HSAR contains both department-wide guidance as well as specific guidance that applies only to particular elements within the department. The HSAR can be found at www.dhs.gov.

HORIZONTAL MERGER GUIDELINES   A document issued August 19, 2010 by the DEPARTMENT OF JUSTICE (DOJ) and the Federal Trade Commission (FTC) detailing the agencies' enforcement policies regarding horizontal mergers in the private sector and describing how the federal antitrust laws (§ 7 of the CLAYTON ACT, § 1 of the Sherman Act, and § 5 of the FTC Act) can impact them. It also outlines the analytical framework the government will utilize in determining whether or not to challenge a horizontal merger. The guidelines are available at https://www.ftc.gov/public-statements/2010/08/horizontal-merger-guidelines-united-states-department-justice-federal. See Brandenburger & Matelis, *The 2010 U.S. Horizontal Merger Guidelines: A Historical & International Perspective*, 25 ANTITRUST 8 (Sum. 2011); Fullerton, *Introduction: 2010 Horizontal Merger Guidelines*, 25 Antitrust 8 (Fall 2010).

HOTLINE   A toll-free telephone line which can be used to report activity that requires investigation. Agency INSPECTORs GENERAL have hotlines that can be used by agency employees and outside personnel to report suspected instances of improper conduct. Information on the use of these hotlines is contained on hotline posters which are displayed in government agencies and must be displayed by contractors with contracts over $5 million in some instances. See FAR 3.1003(c) and DFARS 203.1004(b)(2)(i). Contractors generally have hotlines, as part of their business ethics programs that allow their employees to report suspected instances of improper conduct.

HUBZONE   *Official:* An historically underutilized business zone that is an area located within one or more qualified census tracts, qualified non-metropolitan counties, lands within the external boundaries of an Indian reservation, qualified base closure areas, or (5) redesignated areas, as defined in 13 C.F.R. § 126.103. *Source:* FAR 2.101. These areas tend to be low income and have high poverty or unemployment rates. See Dilger, CONG. RESEARCH SERV., Report No. R41268, SMALL BUSINESS ADMINISTRATION HUBZONE PROGRAM (July 5, 2010). See HUBZONE PROGRAM.

HUBZONE CONTRACT   *Official:* A contract awarded to a Small Business Administration certified HUBZONE SMALL BUSINESS CONCERN through any of the following procurement methods: (1) A sole source award to a HUBZone small business concern. (2) Set-aside awards based on competition restricted to HUBZone small business concerns. (3) Awards to HUBZone small business concerns through full and open competition after a price evaluation preference in favor of HUBZone small business concerns. These contracts are intended to provide contracting assistance to qualified small business concerns in HUBZONEs in an effort to increase employment opportunities, investment and economic development in those areas. FAR 19.1301. Unless a set-aside is made for another small business program in parity with the HUBZone program, acquisitions over the SIMPLIFIED ACQUISITION THRESHOLD must be set aside for such firms if the contracting officer believes that there will be two or more such firms competing for the work and a fair market price can be achieved. FAR 19.1305. FAR 19.1306 states that contracting officer shall issue sole source contracts to HUBZone contractors if competition is anticipated for manufacturing contracts for no more than $7 million and other contracts for no more than $4 million. HUBZone contractors are also entitled to a price evaluation preference of 10% on contracts where there is FULL AND OPEN COMPETITION. FAR 19.1307. Complete guidance on

HUBZone contracts is set forth in 13 C.F.R. part 126. See Cibinic, Nash & Yukins, FORMATION OF GOVERNMENT CONTRACTS 1608–11 (4th ed. 2011); Dilger, CONG. RESEARCH SERV., Report No. R41268, SMALL BUSINESS ADMINISTRATION HUBZONE PROGRAM (Nov. 9, 2010); Hewitt, *Small Business Contracting Programs-Part II*, BRIEFING PAPERS No. 10-13 (2010).

HUBZONE SMALL BUSINESS CONCERN   *Official:* A small business concern that appears on the List of Qualified HUBZone Small Business Concerns maintained by the Small Business Administration (13 C.F.R. § 126.103). *Source:* FAR 2.101. Only firms that are certified by the SBA are eligible for participating in the HUBZONE PROGRAM, FAR 19.1303. See http://www.sba.gov/hubzone.

HUD   See DEPARTMENT OF HOUSING AND URBAN DEVELOPMENT.

HUMANITARIAN OR PEACEKEEPING OPERATION   *Official:* A military operation in support of the provision of humanitarian or foreign disaster assistance or in support of a peacekeeping operation under chapter VI or VII of the Charter of the United Nations. The term does not include routine training, force rotation, or stationing (10 U.S.C. § 2302(8) and 41 U.S.C. § 153(2)). *Source:* FAR 2.101. When a contract for these operations is awarded and performed outside of the United States, the SIMPLIFIED ACQUISITION THRESHOLD is double the normal threshold. Minimal guidance on such contracts is in FAR Subpart 25.3.

I

IDENTICAL BIDS *Official:* Bids for the same LINE ITEM that are determined to be identical as to unit price or total line item amount, with or without the application of evaluation factors (*e.g.*, discount or transportation cost). *Source:* FAR 3.302. FAR 3.303(d) requires the reporting of such bids as possible ANTITRUST VIOLATIONS when there is some reason to suspect collusion between the bidders.

IDIQ CONTRACT See INDEFINITE-QUANTITY CONTRACT.

IDLE CAPACITY *Official:* The unused capacity of partially used facilities. It is the difference between that which a facility could achieve under 100% operating time on a one-shift basis, less operating interruptions resulting from time lost for repairs, setups, unsatisfactory materials, and other normal delays; and the extent to which the facility was actually used to meet demands during the cost accounting period. A multiple-shift basis may be used in the calculation instead of a one-shift basis if it can be shown that this amount of usage could normally be expected for the type of facility involved. *Source:* FAR 31.205-17. Costs of idle capacity are costs of doing business and are a factor in the normal fluctuations of use or overhead rates from period to period. Such costs are ALLOWABLE COSTs, provided the capacity is necessary or was originally reasonable and is not subject to reduction or elimination by subletting, renting, or sale, in accordance with sound business, economic, or security practices. See Manos, 1 GOVERNMENT CONTRACT COSTS AND PRICING §§ 24:1–24:4 (2d ed. 2009–2020); Cibinic, Knight & Nash, COST-REIMBURSEMENT CONTRACTING 716 (4th ed. 2014).

IDLE FACILITIES *Official:* Completely unused FACILITIES that are excess to the contractor's current needs. *Source:* FAR 31.205-17. The costs of idle facilities are UNALLOWABLE COSTs unless the facilities (1) are necessary to meet fluctuations in workload; or (2) were necessary when acquired and are now idle because of changes in requirements, production economies, reorganization, termination, or other causes that could not reasonably have been foreseen. When they are allowable, the period of allowability is generally limited to one year. See Manos, 1 GOVERNMENT CONTRACT COSTS AND PRICING §§ 24:1–24:4 (2d ed. 2009–2020); Cibinic, Knight & Nash, COST-REIMBURSEMENT CONTRACTING 714–16 (4th ed. 2014).

"ILITIES" A slang term commonly used within DOD for the operational and support requirements a program must address (such as availability, maintainability, vulnerability, reliability, and logistic supportability). DAU GLOSSARY.

ILLEGAL DRUGS *Official:* CONTROLLED SUBSTANCES included in Schedules I and II, as defined by section 802(6) of title 21 of the United States Code, the possession of which is unlawful under chapter 13 of that Title. The term "illegal drugs" does not mean the use of a controlled substance pursuant to a valid prescription or other uses authorized by law. *Source:* DFARS 252.223-7004. DOD policy to ensure that its contractors have a DRUG-FREE WORKPLACE requires contractors to have a program to work with employees in sensitive positions to assist them in desisting in the use of illegal drugs. See DFARS Subpart 223.5.

IMMEDIATE-GAIN ACTUARIAL COST METHOD   *Official:* Any of several ACTUARIAL COST METHODs under which actuarial gains and losses are included as part of the unfunded ACTUARIAL LIABILITY of a PENSION PLAN, rather than as part of the normal cost of the plan. *Source:* FAR 31.001. Actuarial gains and losses under a pension plan whose costs are measured by this actuarial cost method must be amortized over a 15-year period in equal annual installments, beginning with the date of the actuarial valuation. CAS 413, Adjustment and Allocation of Pension Costs, 48 C.F.R. § 9904.413-50(a)(2).

IMPAIRED OBJECTIVITY   A type of ORGANIZATIONAL CONFLICT OF INTEREST where an organization has a relationship that would call into question its objectivity in performing a contract. FAR 9.505-3 precludes the award of a contract for evaluation services if the contract calls for the evaluation of its own or its competitors' products or services. This is one of the categories of OCIs that GAO has identified in its protest decisions.

IMPAIRMENT OF LONG-LIVED ASSETS   Loss of value of long-lived assets to the extent that their value may not be recoverable. Long-lived assets include land, buildings, and equipment that are held for use and, as such, are subject to the write-down provisions of the Statement of Financial Accounting Standards (SFAS) No. 121, *Accounting for the Impairment of Long-Lived Assets and for Long-Lived Assets to be Disposed Of* (Mar. 1995). When events and circumstances indicate that the value in the financial statements may not be fully recoverable, SFAS No. 121 requires that the asset be written down to its fair value. Once an impaired asset has been written down under the provisions of SFAS No. 121, GENERALLY ACCEPTED ACCOUNTING PRINCIPLES do not permit the subsequent write up of a previously impaired asset, even if that asset later recovers any part of its value. The impairment losses recognized for financial accounting purposes pursuant to SFAS No. 121, are not ALLOWABLE COSTs for government contract costing purposes. FAR 31.205-16(i). CAS 409, 48 C.F.R. § 9904.409, Depreciation of Tangible Capital Assets, recognizes gains and losses for government contract purposes only upon the disposition of the asset. Accordingly, the allowable cost attributed to the loss upon disposition of an impaired long-lived asset must be the amount that would have been allowed had the asset not been written down for financial accounting purposes.

IMPLIED AUTHORITY CONTRACTING OFFICER   Authority that is implied from the facts of the transaction rather than delegated in writing in accordance with FAR Subpart 1.6. Implied authority is found by the courts and boards when they determine that the government should be bound by the acts of agency employees who do not have formal contracting officer authority. It generally flows from acts of which a contracting officer was, or should have been, aware. Finding such authority has been greatly limited by the decision in *Winter v. Cath-dr/Balti Joint Venture*, 497 F.3d 1339 (Fed. Cir. 2007). See Nash & Feldman, GOVERNMENT CONTRACT CHANGES §§ 5:14–5:16 (3d ed. 2006–2020); Cibinic, Nagle & Nash, ADMINISTRATION OF GOVERNMENT CONTRACTS 41–44 (5th ed. 2016); Nash, *The Government Contract Decisions of the Federal Circuit*, 78 GEO. WASH. L. REV. 593-98 (2010); Nash, *Postscript II: Contracting Officer Authority*, 25 N&CR ¶30 (June 2011).

IMPLIED CONTRACT   A contract not created or evidenced by an explicit agreement of the parties, but inferred, as a matter of reason and justice, from the parties' acts or conduct (the circumstances surrounding the transaction making it reasonable or even necessary to assume that a contract existed between the parties by tacit understanding). Implied contracts are sometimes divided into two categories: (1) those implied in fact, which derive from the above definition; and (2) those implied in law, often referred to as "quasi-contracts." Quasi-contracts derive from obligations imposed on a person by the law, not pursuant to the person's intention and agreement, either expressed or implied, and even against the person's will and design, because circumstances between the parties are such as to render it just that one party should have a right and the other party a corresponding liability, similar to those that would arise from a contract between them. BLACK'S LAW DICTIONARY 407 (11th ed. 2019). The U.S. COURT OF FEDERAL CLAIMS has jurisdiction over contracts implied in fact but not over contracts implied in law. 28 U.S.C. § 1491(a)(1). The BOARDs OF CONTRACT APPEALS also have jurisdiction over implied in fact contracts under the CONTRACT DISPUTES ACT. See Cibinic, Nash & Yukins, FORMATION OF GOVERNMENT CONTRACTS 252–56 (4th ed. 2011). See also Nash, *Postscript III: The Implied Contract to Fairly and Honestly Consider an Offer*, 26 N&CR ¶ 17 (Apr. 2012).

IMPLIED DUTY   See IMPLIED PROMISE.

IMPLIED PROMISE   A promise of a contracting party that is implied from the facts of the transaction. There are a number of implied promises that attach to most contracts, such as the implied DUTY OF GOOD FAITH AND FAIR DEALING and the implied DUTY TO COOPERATE. The government is also held to an IMPLIED WARRANTY OF SPECIFICATIONS when it furnishes design specifications to a contractor and to an implied duty to disclose information (see SUPERIOR KNOWLEDGE) when it has vital information needed by a contractor to permit successful performance. See Nash & Feldman, GOVERNMENT CONTRACT CHANGES, chaps. 12, 13 & 14 (3d ed. 2006–2020); Cibinic, Nagle & Nash, ADMINISTRATION OF GOVERNMENT CONTRACTS 272–88 (5th ed. 2016).

IMPLIED RATIFICATION   RATIFICATION of an UNAUTHORIZED COMMITMENT by the actions of a government official rather than by the issuance of a formal document. This can occur if an official with the authority to ratify assures a contractor that he or she is processing the documents needed to ratify an unauthorized commitment. See Cibinic, Nagle & Nash, ADMINISTRATION OF GOVERNMENT CONTRACTS 45 (5th ed. 2016); Nash, *Implied Ratification A Rare Result*, 34 N&CR ¶ 5 (Jan. 2020).

IMPLIED WARRANTY OF SPECIFICATIONS   The warranty of the government that its DESIGN SPECIFICATIONs can be successfully used to perform a contract. When a contractor fails to perform because such specifications are defective, it can assert a CONSTRUCTIVE CHANGE claim in order to obtain an EQUITABLE ADJUSTMENT in the contract price. See Feldman, GOVERNMENT CONTRACT GUIDEBOOK, §§ 13:2–13:4 (4th ed. 2019–2020); Cibinic, Nagle & Nash, ADMINISTRATION OF GOVERNMENT CONTRACTS 251–72 (5th ed. 2016); Nash, *Does the Implied Warranty of Specifications Attach to Cooperative Agreements?: A Surprising Answer*, 22 N&CR ¶ 71 (Dec. 2008).

IMPORTANCE WEIGHTS   See WEIGHTS.

IMPOSSIBILITY OF PERFORMANCE   A legal doctrine deriving from the concept that an implied condition exists under which the parties to a contract intended to dissolve their contractual obligations upon an individual's death or incapacity or upon the destruction or loss of vital and irreplaceable materials. Thus, a party encountering impossibility of performance will have a defense against a suit for BREACH OF CONTRACT. Discussion of impossibility of performance typically references concepts of IMPRACTICABILITY OF PERFORMANCE and FRUSTRATION OF PURPOSE. "Impossibility" generally means technical or physical impossibility—that is, on the basis of all human experience, a thing clearly cannot be done; "impracticability of performance" typically includes unforeseen cost increases, extreme financial difficulty, illegality, or other situations in which a court may excuse lack of performance. The term "existing impossibility" refers to an impossibility of performance existing when the contract was entered into, so that the contract was to do something that was impossible from the outset; "supervening impossibility" refers to impossibility that developed after the inception of the contract. BALLENTINE'S LAW DICTIONARY (3d ed. 1969). If a party has assumed the risk of impossibility, it will be denied the use of the defense and will be held liable for breach of contract. Existing impossibility (or impracticability) infrequently has been treated as a type of CONSTRUCTIVE CHANGE. See Feldman, GOVERNMENT CONTRACT GUIDEBOOK, § 13:6 (4th ed. 2019–2020); Cibinic, Nagle & Nash, ADMINISTRATION OF GOVERNMENT CONTRACTS 289–94 (5th ed. 2016).

IMPOUNDMENT   An action by the President that prevents the obligation or expenditure of BUDGET AUTHORITY. 2 U.S.C. § 681 et seq. Deferrals and rescissions are the two types of presidential impoundment. Whenever all or part of any budget authority provided by Congress is deferred or rescinded, the President must transmit a message to Congress describing the deferral or rescission. In the case of a deferral, either house of Congress may, at any time, pass an impoundment resolution disapproving this DEFERRAL OF BUDGET AUTHORITY, thus requiring that the funds be made available for obligation. When no congressional action is taken, deferrals may remain in effect until, but not beyond, the end of the FISCAL YEAR. If the funds remain available beyond the end of a fiscal year and continued deferral of their use is desired, the President must transmit a new special message to Congress. In the case of a rescission (see RESCISSION OF BUDGET AUTHORITY), any amount of budget authority proposed to be rescinded must be made available for obligation unless, within the prescribed 45-day period, Congress has completed action on a rescission bill rescinding all or part of the amount proposed to be rescinded. See U.S. GOV'T ACCOUNTABILITY OFFICE, PRINCIPLES OF FEDERAL APPROPRIATIONS LAW, 4th ed. 2016 rev., Ch. 1 (Washington, D.C.: Mar. 2016).

IMPRACTICABILITY OF PERFORMANCE   Extreme and unreasonable difficulty, expense, injury, or loss to a contracting party. RESTATEMENT (SECOND) OF CONTRACTS § 261 (1981) cmt. d. See also U.C.C. § 2-615. The Restatement gives as examples severe shortages of raw materials or supplies due to war, embargo, local crop failure, or unforeseen shutdown of major sources of supply, all of which cause a marked increase in costs. It warns, however, that a mere change in the degree of difficulty due to such causes as increased wages, prices of raw materials, or costs of construction, unless well beyond the normal range, does not amount to impracticability. The term derives from the legal concept of IMPOSSIBILITY OF PERFORMANCE and has the same legal effect: it excuses a party from performing a contract unless that party has assumed the risk of the event. In government contracting, impracticability infrequently has also been treated as a type of CONSTRUCTIVE

CHANGE giving a contractor that has incurred extra costs an EQUITABLE ADJUST-MENT. See Nash & Feldman, GOVERNMENT CONTRACT CHANGES § 13:3 (3d ed. 2006–2020); Cibinic, Nagle & Nash, ADMINISTRATION OF GOVERNMENT CONTRACTS 289–94 (5th ed. 2016).

IMPREST FUND *Official:* A cash fund of a fixed amount established by an advance of funds, without charge to an APPROPRIATION, from an agency finance or disbursing officer to a duly appointed cashier, for distribution as needed from time to time in making payment in cash for relatively small amounts. *Source:* FAR 13.001. Imprest funds are also known as "petty cash." Imprest funds may be used when (a) the transaction does not exceed $500 or another limit approved by the HEAD OF THE AGENCY, (b) the use of imprest funds is considered to be advantageous to the government, and (c) the use of imprest funds complies with any additional conditions established by agencies and certain Department of the Treasury and Government Accountability Office manuals. FAR 13.305-3; DFARS 213.305. The use of imprest funds has been largely displaced by the use of GOVERNMENT-WIDE COMMERCIAL PURCHASE CARDs. FAR 13.301.

IMPROPER BUSINESS PRACTICES A broad range of activities forbidden or limited by FAR Part 3 with regard to the award and performance of government contracts. The prohibitions and guidelines are based on the premise that government business must be conducted in a manner above reproach and, except as otherwise authorized by statute or regulation, with complete impartiality and preferential treatment for none. Transactions relating to the expenditure of public funds should merit the highest degree of public trust and reflect an impeccable standard of conduct. FAR 3.101-1. The FAR discusses the following improper or potentially improper business practices: contractor gratuities (see GRATUITY) to government personnel (FAR Subpart 3.2); ANTITRUST VIOLATIONs (FAR Subpart 3.3); CONTINGENT FEEs (FAR Subpart 3.4); BUYING IN (FAR 3.501); KICKBACKs (FAR 3.502); unreasonable restrictions on subcontractor sales (FAR 3.503); and contracts with government employees or organizations owned or controlled by them (FAR Subpart 3.6). It also discusses the voiding and rescinding of contracts in relation to which improper business practices have been found (FAR Subpart 3.7), limitations on payments to influence federal transactions (FAR Subpart 3.8), WHISTLEBLOWER protection (FAR Subpart 3.9), and PROCUREMENT INTEGRITY (FAR 3.104). In 2007, the FAR Subpart 3.10 was added to require contractors to adopt a Contractor Code of Business Ethics and Conduct. FAR 3.1004 requires the inclusion of the Code of Business Ethics & Conduct clause at FAR 52.203-13 in solicitations and contracts expected to exceed $5.5 million and with a performance period greater than 120 days. Also, the Display of Hotline Poster(s) clause at FAR 52.203-14 must be included in any contract, not for commercial items or to be performed outside the U.S., which exceeds $5.5 million. FAR 3.1004. FAR Part 3, while containing some specific guidance, is incomplete in terms of total coverage of improper business practices. See STANDARDS OF CONDUCT for other applicable coverage. See Feldman, GOVERNMENT CONTRACT GUIDEBOOK, chap. 12 (4th ed. 2019–2020); Cibinic, Nagle & Nash, ADMINISTRATION OF GOVERNMENT CONTRACTS 75–149 (5th ed. 2016); Cibinic, Nash & Yukins, FORMATION OF GOVERNMENT CONTRACTS 136–75 (4th ed. 2011).

IMPROPER INFLUENCE *Official:* Any influence that induces or tends to induce a government employee or officer to give consideration to or act regarding a government contract on any basis other than the merits of the matter. *Source:* FAR 3.401. FAR Subpart 3.4 discusses the "improper influence" that may occur because of the payment of CONTINGENT

FEEs. See Cibinic, Nagle & Nash, ADMINISTRATION OF GOVERNMENT CONTRACTS, 97–107 (5th ed. 2016); Cibinic, Nash & Yukins, FORMATION OF GOVERNMENT CONTRACTS 175–78 (4th ed. 2011).

IMPROVEMENT CURVE   See LEARNING CURVE.

IMPUTED COSTS   A cost that does not entail actual dollar outlays. In some circumstances, contractors are permitted to recover imputed costs. Under CAS 416, Accounting for Insurance Costs, 48 C.F.R. § 9904-416, a contractor's reserves for self-insurance may be recognized as costs even though there is neither actual payment nor the incurrence of an obligation to make payment. A specific imputed cost that is recognized throughout the government is FACILITIES CAPITAL COST OF MONEY, CAS 414, Cost of Money as an Element of the Cost of Facilities Capital, 48 C.F.R. § 9904-414. See Cibinic, Knight & Nash, COST-REIMBURSEMENT CONTRACTING 556–59 (4th ed. 2014).

IMPUTED INTEREST   An amount that is added to a contractor CLAIM under the CONTRACT DISPUTES ACT. 41 U.S.C. § 7109. The amount is simple interest computed using the TREASURY INTEREST RATE from the date the CONTRACTING OFFICER receives the claim until the date of payment. This interest applies whether the claim has resulted from a board or court decision or as a result of a negotiated settlement. It also applies even though the contractor has submitted a DEFECTIVE CERTIFICATION. FAR 33.208(c). See Nash & Feldman, GOVERNMENT CONTRACT CHANGES §§ 16:26–16.30 (3d ed. 2006–2020); Cibinic, Nagle & Nash, ADMINISTRATION OF GOVERNMENT CONTRACTS 692–93 (5th ed. 2016).

IMPUTED KNOWLEDGE   Knowledge possessed by a government employee that is ascribed to a CONTRACTING OFFICER by virtue of the relationship presumed to exist between the employee and the contracting officer. The principle of imputed knowledge is based on the common-law concept that a principal is charged with knowledge that an agent has a duty to deliver to the principal. Courts and boards of contract appeals frequently assume that responsible government employees will convey their knowledge to the contracting officer. The imputed knowledge issue arises, for example, in cases in which a contractor has failed to give formal notice of an event as required by one of the contract's adjustment clauses (such as the CHANGES, DIFFERING SITE CONDITIONS, or SUSPENSION OF WORK clauses) but has made a government employee aware of the event. In such a case, the courts and BCAs frequently refuse to deny, solely on grounds that formal notice was not given to the contracting officer, contractor CLAIMs for price adjustment. See Nash & Feldman, 1 GOVERNMENT CONTRACT CHANGES § 5:22 (3d ed. 2006–2020); Cibinic, Nagle & Nash, ADMINISTRATION OF GOVERNMENT CONTRACTS 52–55 (5th ed. 2016); Cibinic, Nash & Yukins, FORMATION OF GOVERNMENT CONTRACTS 108–11 (4th ed. 2011).

IN-KIND CONTRIBUTIONS   *Official:* Non-cash contributions provided by the performing contractor which would normally be a charge against the contract. While in-kind contributions are an acceptable method of cost-sharing, should the booked costs of property appear unrealistic, the fair market value of the property shall be determined pursuant to 1516.303-74 of this chapter. *Source:* EPAAR 1516.303-73(b). Such contributions may be used to fulfill the contractor's obligation to share the costs of performance. In-kind contributions may be in the form of personal property (equipment or supplies) or services. Such contributions must be directly beneficial, specifically identifiable, and necessary to the performance of the project or program. They must (1) be verifiable from the performer's books and records; (2) not be included as contributions under any other federal contract; (3) be necessary to accomplishment project objectives; (4) provide for types of charges that would otherwise be allowable under applicable federal cost principles appropriate to the contractor's organization; and (5) not be paid for by the federal government under any contract, AGREEMENT, or GRANT. EPAAR 1516.303-73(c).

IN-SOURCING   Pursuing a policy to turn work that is being performed by contractors over to federal employees. As a result of the new policies on INHERENTLY GOVERNMENTAL FUNCTIONS, government agencies have been directed to ensure that they had sufficient staff to perform critical functions as well as inherently governmental functions. This has resulted in decisions to hire more federal employees to replace contractors. See U.S. Gov't Accountability Office, DOD Needs to Better Oversee In-sourcing Data and Align In-sourcing Efforts with Strategic Workforce Plans, GAO-12-319 (Feb. 9, 2012); Manual & Maskell, Cong. Research Serv., Report No. R41810, Insourcing Functions Performed by Federal Contractors: An Overview of the Legal Issues (May 7, 2012); U.S. Gov't Accountability Office, Initial Agency Efforts to Balance the Government to Contractor Mix in the Multisector Workforce, GAO-10-744T (May 20, 2010); Stiens & Turley, *Uncontracting: The Move Back to Performing In-House*, 65 A.F. L. Rev. 145 (2010).

IN WRITING   *Official:* Any worded or numbered expression that can be read, reproduced, and later communicated, and includes electronically transmitted and stored information. *Source:* FAR 2.101. This term defines the conditions that must be met when the FAR specifies that a contract action must be in writing as contrasted with "oral."

INCENTIVE COMPENSATION   Compensation paid to an employee to motivate good performance. FAR 31.205-6(f) specifies when the cost of such compensation by a contractor may be treated as an ALLOWABLE COST. See Manos, 1 Government Contract Cost and Pricing § 13.8 (2d ed. 2009–2020); Cibinic, Knight & Nash, Cost-Reimbursement Contracting 672–73 (4th ed. 2014).

INCENTIVE CONTRACT   A negotiated pricing arrangement that gives the contractor higher PROFITs or FEEs for better performance and/or lower profits for worse performance in prescribed areas (cost, delivery, or technical performance). They are appropriate when there are cost and technical uncertainties, making a FIRM-FIXED-PRICE CONTRACT inappropriate, and the government believes it is able to acquire the contractor's performance at a lower cost by relating the contractor's profits to the performance of the contract. FAR 16.401(a). FAR 16.401(d) requires the contracting officer to prepare determinations and findings justifying that the use of incentive contracts is in the best interest of the government. However, under the DOD "Guidance on Using Incentive and Other Contract Types," March 2016, incentive contracts are preferred in many situations. The standard types of incentive contracts are prescribed in FAR Subpart 16.4. These include (1) contracts where the profit adjustment is made in accordance with a preestablished formula, such as FIXED-PRICE-INCENTIVE CONTRACTs (with firm or successive targets) and COST-PLUS-INCENTIVE-FEE CONTRACTs; and (2) contracts where the profit adjustment is made by unilateral determination of an officer of the government, such as COST-PLUS-AWARD-FEE CONTRACTs. A non-FAR incentive contract, the AWARD TERM CONTRACT, has also been used widely in recent years. Incentive contracts are designed to achieve specific acquisition objectives by (1) establishing reasonable and attainable targets that are clearly communicated to the contractor and (2) including appropriate incentive arrangements designed to motivate contractor efforts and discourage contractor inefficiency and waste. FAR 16.401(a). See Manos, GOVERNMENT CONTRACT COST AND PRICING §§ 4:4–4:7 (2d ed. 2009–2020); Cibinic, Nash & Yukins, FORMATION OF GOVERNMENT CONTRACTS 1256–1317 (4th ed. 2011). See also Nash, *Postscript: Fixed-Price Incentive Contracts*, 25 N&CR ¶ 54 (Nov. 2011); Edwards, *Fixed-Price Incentive Contracts: A Primer*, 25 N&CR ¶ 44 (Sept. 2011); Edwards, *Increased Use of Fixed-Price Incentive Contracts: The Way to Greater Efficiency and Productivity?*, 25 N&CR ¶ 21 (Apr. 2011); Edwards, *Contract Pricing Arrangements: A Primer—Part II*, 09-12 BRIEFING PAPERS (Oct. 2009); U.S. GOV'T ACCOUNTABILITY OFFICE, DOD HAS PAID BILLIONS IN AWARD AND INCENTIVE FEES REGARDLESS OF ACQUISITION OUTCOMES, GAO-06-66 (Dec. 2005).

INCREMENTAL DEVELOPMENT   *Historical.* The development over time of mature technologies which will meet identified requirements of a system with desired capabilities. This was one of the EVOLUTIONARY ACQUISITION strategies. The theory of incremental development was that a WEAPON SYSTEM consists of "increments" which are independently useful to the military and that deferring buying of these increments until they are based on mature technology is a more effective acquisition technique.

INCREMENTALLY FUNDED CONTRACTS   Contracts for which the funds needed to pay for the work are obligated in increments, rather than in full at the time of contract award, and under which the contractor's duty to perform is limited to the amount allotted. Incrementally funded contracts are usually COST-REIMBURSEMENT CONTRACTs, but some agencies permit incremental funding of FIXED-PRICE CONTRACTs, as well. Such contracts are used mainly in RESEARCH, DEVELOPMENT, TEST AND EVALUATION programs. The FAR contains no guidance on when an agency may use an incrementally funded contract. FAR 32.705-2(c) calls for the use of the LIMITATION OF FUNDS CLAUSE in FAR 52.232-22 when an incrementally funded cost-reimbursement contract is used. NASA specifies a Limitation of Funds clause for use in incrementally funded fixed-price research and development contracts in NFS 1852.232-77. DOD's policy on the use of incrementally funded fixed-price contracts is located at DFARS 232.703-1. The Limitation of Government's Obligation clause for use in such contracts is in DFARS 252.232-7007. See O'Rourke & Daggett, CONG. RESEARCH SERV., Report No. RL31404, DEFENSE PROCUREMENT: FULL FUNDING POLICY—BACKGROUND, ISSUES, AND OPTIONS FOR CONGRESS (June 2007).

INCURRED COST   A cost identified through the use of ACCRUAL BASIS ACCOUNTING, or otherwise actually paid. Such costs include some IMPUTED COSTS and do not include CONTINGENCIES. Although a commercial definition of incurred costs would include all costs actually paid or properly accrued, the government guidance may limit the definition to include only ALLOWABLE COSTs. See ALLOCABLE COST. The *DCAA Contract Audit Manual* ¶ 6-102.1, in discussing AUDIT objectives for and approaches to incurred costs, explains that the AUDITOR's objective is to examine the contractor's cost representations, in whatever form they may be presented, and express an opinion whether the incurred costs (1) are reasonable, applicable to the contract, and determined according to GENERALLY ACCEPTED ACCOUNTING PRINCIPLES and COST ACCOUNTING STANDARDS applicable in the circumstances; and (2) are not prohibited by the contract, by government statute or regulation, or by previous agreement with or decision of a government contracting officer. See Cibinic, Knight & Nash, COST-REIMBURSEMENT

CONTRACTING 553–62 (4th ed. 2014). See also Nash, *Postscript: Auditing Incurred Costs*, 32 N&CR ¶ 9 (Feb. 2018).

INDEFINITE-DELIVERY CONTRACT   A type of contract in which the time of delivery is unspecified in the original contract but established by the contracting officer during performance. FAR Subpart 16.5 contains guidance on three types of indefinite-delivery contracts: (1) DEFINITE-QUANTITY CONTRACTs, (2) REQUIREMENTS CONTRACTs, and (3) INDEFINITE-QUANTITY CONTRACTs. FAR 16.501-2 states that the appropriate type of indefinite-delivery contract may be used when the exact times and/or quantities of future deliveries are not known at the time of contract award. Indefinite-delivery contracts permit maintenance of government stocks at minimum levels and direct shipment to users. Indefinite-delivery contracts may provide for any appropriate cost or pricing arrangement under FAR Part 16. For the acquisition of commercial items, indefinite-delivery contracts may be used when prices are established based on a firm-fixed-price or fixed-price with economic price adjustment; or rates are established for commercial services acquired on a time-and-materials or labor-hour basis. FAR 12.207(c). DOD notes that for items with a shelf life of less than six months, consideration should be given to use of these contracts with orders placed directly by users. DFARS 216.501. See Manos, 1 GOVERNMENT CONTRACT COST & PRICING § 4:8 (2d ed. 2009–2020); Cibinic, Nash & Yukins, FORMATION OF GOVERNMENT CONTRACTS 1331–63, 1386–1406 (4th ed. 2011).

INDEFINITE-QUANTITY CONTRACT   A contract providing for an indefinite quantity, within stated maximum or minimum limits, of specific supplies or services to be furnished during a fixed period, with deliveries to be scheduled by placing orders for individual requirements with the contractor. FAR 16.504(a). Such contracts are commonly referred to as IDIQ contracts. The contractor is legally bound to such a contract because the government promises to procure, as CONSIDERATION, a MINIMUM QUANTITY that is more than a nominal quantity. The contract requires the government to order at least the quantity designated as the minimum and requires the contractor to furnish, when ordered, supplies or services up to and including the quantity designated as the maximum. FAR 16.504(a)(4) provides that the solicitation for IDIQ contracts must specify the period of the contract; the minimum and maximum quantities; a STATEMENT OF WORK or specifications that reasonably describe the general scope, nature, complexity, and purpose of the supplies or services the government will acquire under the contract; and the procedures for issuing orders. The contract may also specify maximum or minimum quantities that the government may order under each TASK ORDER or DELIVERY ORDER and the maximum that it may order during a specific period of time. An indefinite-quantity contract should be used only when a recurring need above the specified minimum is anticipated. FAR 16.504(b). There is a MULTIPLE AWARD PREFERENCE in awarding such contracts and each awardee is entitled to a FAIR OPPORTUNITY to compete for task and delivery orders. Funds for other than the stated minimum quantity are obligated by each task or delivery order, not by the contract itself. See Feldman, GOVERNMENT CONTRACT AWARDS: NEGOTIATION AND SEALED BIDDING § 4:25 (2019–2020 ed.); Cibinic & Nash, FORMATION OF GOVERNMENT CONTRACTS 1386–1406 (4th ed. 2011). See also Nash, *Evaluating Price in an IDIQ Contract: A New Slant*, 25 N&CR ¶ 10 (Mar. 2011); Yukins, *Are IDIQs Inefficient? Sharing Lessons with European Framework Contracting*, 37 PUB. CONT. L.J. 545 (2008); Kipa, Szeliga, & Aronie, *Conquering Uncertainty in an Indefinite World: A Survey of Disputes Arising Under IDIQ Contracts*, 37 PUB. CONT. L.J. 415 (2008); Nash, *Fixed-Price IDIQ Contracts: High-*

Risk Ventures, 21 N&CR ¶ 43 (Sept. 2007); Edwards, *Obligating Funds for Services under IDIQ Contracts that Cross Fiscal Years: What Are the Rules?*, 21 N&CR ¶ 42 (Aug. 2007).

INDEMNIFICATION   The agreement of a contracting party to hold the other party harmless, to secure the other party against loss or damage, or to give security for the reimbursement of the other party in case of an anticipated loss. See BLACK'S LAW DICTIONARY 918 (11th ed. 2019). The government does not generally require contractors to indemnify the government or protect the government from liability, but a similar result is achieved in those cases where the government requires the contractor to purchase INSURANCE or protect itself through SELF-INSURANCE. See, for example, the Insurance—Liability to Third Persons clause in FAR 52.228-7. FAR 31.205-19 contains the cost principle on insurance and indemnification. See Manos, 1 GOVERNMENT CONTRACT COSTS AND PRICING §§ 26:1–26:6 (2d ed. 2009–2020); Cibinic, Knight & Nash, COST-REIMBURSEMENT CONTRACTING 844–47 (4th ed. 2014). The government does require contractors selling commercial items to indemnify it against PATENT INFRINGEMENT. See FAR 27.201-1(d) and paragraph (h) of the Contract Terms and Conditions—Commercial Items clause at FAR 52.212-4. See Nash & Rawicz, INTELLECTUAL PROPERTY IN GOVERNMENT CONTRACTS 1123–35 (6th ed. 2008). The government indemnifies contractors against losses only in unusual circumstances. FAR Subpart 50.4 and the Indemnification under Pub. Law No. 85-804 clause at FAR 52.250-1 contain guidance on indemnifying contractors against unusually hazardous or nuclear risks. See Nash, *Indemnification Clauses: Litigation Breeders*, 20 N&CR ¶ 42 (Sept. 2006).

INDEPENDENT CONTRACTOR   A person who, "in exercise of an independent employment, contracts to do a piece of work according to his own methods and is subject to his employer's control only as to end product or final result of his work." An independent contractor is contrasted to an employee, where the employer exercises detailed control over the employee's activities. An independent contractor who commits a wrong while carrying out the work usually does not create liability for the one who did the hiring. BLACK'S LAW DICTIONARY 413 (11th ed. 2019). Government contractors are almost always independent contractors even when they enter into COST-REIMBURSEMENT CONTRACTs.

INDEPENDENT RESEARCH AND DEVELOPMENT (IR&D)   *Official:* A contractor's INDEPENDENT RESEARCH & DEVELOPMENT COST that consists of projects falling within the four following areas: (1) Basic research, (2) applied research, (3) development, and (4) systems and other concept formulation studies. The term does not include the costs of effort sponsored by a grant or required in the performance of a contract. IR&D effort shall not include technical effort expended in developing and preparing technical data specifically to support submitting a bid or proposal. *Source:* FAR 31.205-18(a). The development effort in IR&D does not include (a) subcontracted technical effort to develop an additional source for an existing product; or (b) manufacturing engineering effort to develop or improve manufacturing or production materials, systems, processes, methods, equipment, tools, and techniques not intended for sale. Contractors are encouraged to conduct IR&D by the fact that its costs are treated as PRIVATE EXPENSE for the determination of PATENT RIGHTS, RIGHTS IN TECHNICAL DATA and RIGHTS IN COMPUTER SOFTWARE. See Nash & Rawicz, INTELLECTUAL PROPERTY IN GOVERNMENT CONTRACTS 1123–35 (6th ed. 2008).

INDEPENDENT RESEARCH AND DEVELOPMENT COST   *Official:* The cost of effort that is neither sponsored by a grant, nor required in performing a contract, and which fall within any of the following four areas: (a) BASIC RESEARCH, (b) APPLIED RESEARCH, (c) DEVELOPMENT, and (d) systems and other concept formulation studies. *Source:* FAR 31.001. IR&D costs, together with BID AND PROPOSAL COSTS, are generally ALLOWABLE COSTs under FAR 31.205-18, subject to proper allocation under CAS 420, Accounting for Independent Research and Development Costs and Bid Proposal Costs, 48 C.F.R. § 9904.420. Allowable IR&D costs on DOD contracts are limited to costs for projects that are of potential interest to DOD. DFARS 231.205-18. See Manos, 1 Government Cost and Pricing §§ 25:1–25:7 (2d ed. 2009–2020); Cibinic, Knight & Nash, Cost-Reimbursement Contracting 645–52 (4th ed. 2014). See also Nash, *Postscript IV: Independent Research and Development Costs*, 30 N&CR ¶ 9 (Feb. 2016).

INDIAN PREFERENCE　A policy established in 1975 by § 7(b) of the Indian Self-Determination and Education Assistance Act, 25 U.S.C. §§ 450–450n, 455–458e, for contracts and subcontracts entered into under the Act, as well as other contracts or subcontracts with Indian organizations or for the benefit of Indians. The policy requires that (1) preference and training/education opportunities in contract administration be given to Indians, and (2) preference in SUBCONTRACTing be given to Indian organizations and Indian-owned economic enterprises. The Indian Preference Program is used primarily by the Bureau of Indian Affairs and the Indian Health Service but may be used by other contracting activities. 25 U.S.C. § 1544 allows contractors on federal contracts to pay up to 5% more to INDIAN ORGANIZATIONs and INDIAN-OWNED ECONOMIC ENTERPRISEs serving as subcontractors. This policy is implemented in FAR Subpart 26.1. See also BUY INDIAN ACT.

INDIAN ORGANIZATION　*Official:* The governing body of any INDIAN TRIBE or entity established or recognized by the governing body of an Indian tribe for the purposes of 25 U.S.C., chapter 17. *Source:* FAR 26.101. INDIAN-OWNED ECONOMIC ENTERPRISES of these organizations are entitled to preferred treatment in the procurement process. These organizations are subject to special COST PRINCIPLES in FAR Subpart 31.6.

INDIAN-OWNED ECONOMIC ENTERPRISE　*Official:* Any Indian-owned (as determined by the Secretary of Interior) commercial, industrial, or business activity established or organized for the purpose of profit, provided the Indian ownership constitutes not less than 51% of the enterprise. *Source:* FAR 26.101. These enterprises are excepted from the requirement that contracts with the SMALL BUSINESS ADMINISTRATION under the 8(a) program over specified dollar amounts must be subjected to competition. See FAR 19.805-1(b)(2). They also are entitled to a 5% incentive as subcontractors. See FAR 26.102.

INDIAN TRIBE　*Official:* Any Indian tribe, band, group, pueblo, or community, including native villages and native groups (including corporations organized by Kenai, Juneau, Sitka, and Kodiak) as defined in the Alaska Native Claims Settlement Act, that is recognized by the Federal Government as eligible for services from BIA in accordance with 25 U.S.C. § 1452(c). *Source:* FAR 26.101. Slightly different definitions are included in the SMALL BUSINESS ADMINISTRATION regulations at 13 C.F.R. § 124.3 and FAR 19.701. Indian tribes are entitled to the benefits of the INDIAN PREFERENCE. See also NATIVE AMERICANS.

INDICTMENT　*Official:* Indictment for a criminal offense. An information or other filing by competent authority charging a criminal offense is given the same effect as an indictment. *Source:* FAR 9.403. Contractors or contractor employees that had been indicted are subject to SUSPENSION. FAR 9.407-2(b).

INDIRECT COST   *Official:* Any cost not directly identified with a single, final COST OBJECTIVE, but identified with two or more final cost objectives or with at least one intermediate cost objective. *Source:* FAR 2.101. This term is also referred to as "overhead" or "burden." FAR 31.203 provides that after direct costs have been determined and charged directly to the contract or other work, indirect costs are those remaining to be allocated to the several cost objectives. An indirect cost must not be allocated to a final cost objective if other costs incurred for the same purpose in like circumstances have been included as a direct cost of that or any other final cost objective. FAR Subpart 42.7 deals with establishing an indirect cost rate (see OVERHEAD RATE): the percentage or dollar factor that expresses the ratio of the indirect expense incurred in a given period to the direct labor cost, manufacturing cost, or other appropriate base for the same period. Procedures are prescribed to ensure that a single agency is responsible for negotiating BILLING RATEs and FINAL INDIRECT COST RATEs for each BUSINESS UNIT of a contractor, which shall be used in reimbursing indirect costs under COST-REIMBURSEMENT CONTRACTs and in determining progress payments made under FIXED-PRICE CONTRACTs. Indirect costs that are EXCESSIVE PASS-THROUGH CHARGEs are not allowable. See Cibinic, Knight & Nash, COST-REIMBURSEMENT CONTRACTING 598–604 (4th ed. 2014). See also Nash, *Indirect Costs: Conflicting Policies Raise Some Questions*, 26 N&CR ¶ 36 (June 2012).

INDIRECT COST POOLS   *Official:* Groupings of INCURRED COSTs identified with two or more COST OBJECTIVEs but not specifically identified specifically with any final cost objective. *Source:* FAR 31.001. This definition does not apply to FAR Subparts 31.3 and 31.6. FAR 31.203 requires that indirect costs be accumulated by logical cost groupings, with due consideration of the reasons for incurring those costs. Each grouping should be determined to permit distribution of the grouping on the basis of the benefits accruing to the several cost objectives. In most circumstances, manufacturing OVERHEAD, selling expenses, and GENERAL AND ADMINISTRATIVE EXPENSEs are separately grouped. The contractor must select a distribution base common to all cost objectives to which the grouping is to be allocated. The contractor's method of allocating indirect costs must comply with CAS 418, Allocation of Direct and Indirect Cost, 48 C.F.R. § 9904.418, if applicable, or GENERALLY ACCEPTED ACCOUNTING PRINCIPLES. CAS 418 distinguishes homogeneous indirect cost pools, which contain activities that have a similar beneficial or causal relationship to cost objectives, from not homogenous indirect cost pools See also ALLOCABLE COST. See Manos, 2 GOVERNMENT COST AND PRICING §§ 79:1–79:4 (2d ed. 2009–2020); Cibinic, Knight & Nash, COST-REIMBURSEMENT CONTRACTING 605–07 (4th ed. 2014).

INDUSTRIAL BASE   The manufacturing industry that produces consumer products, including components and parts, and that represents the basic capability available in the United States in the event of an INDUSTRIAL MOBILIZATION during a national emergency. The "mobilization base" consists of those companies that have entered into agreements with the government to produce specific defense items in the event the government declares a state of national emergency or war and the economy is mobilized for war. The industrial base supports the mobilization-base planned producers and, more importantly, must expand its capability to meet the large demands DOD would make in order to defend the country. See CONG. RESEARCH SERV., *Defense Primer: U.S. Industrial Base* (Updated Feb. 6, 2020); Brown, *Legal Propriety of Protecting Defense Industrial Base Information Infrastructure*, 64 A.F. L. REV. 211 (2009); Watts, *The US Defense Industrial Base: Past, Present and Future* (Center for Strategic and Budgetary Assessments, 2008).

INDUSTRIAL ENGINEERING   The art and science of determining the utilization of personnel, equipment, and materials, as well as the coordination of activities and events, that will attain a desired quantity of output at a specified time and at an optimum cost. Industrial engineering may include gathering, analyzing, and acting on facts pertaining to buildings and facilities, layouts, personnel organization, operating procedures, methods, processes, schedules, time standards, wage rates, wage payment plans, costs, and systems for controlling the quality and quantity of goods and services. DAU Glossary. The techniques of industrial engineering are used when the government makes a SHOULD-COST ANALYSIS of a contractor's proposed cost of performance pursuant to FAR 15.407-4.

INDUSTRIAL MOBILIZATION   The use of American industry to produce supplies and services in the event of a national emergency. 10 U.S.C. § 2304(c)(3) and 41 U.S.C. § 3304(a)(3)(A) permit the awarding of contracts without FULL AND OPEN COMPETITION when it is necessary to maintain sources in order to achieve such mobilization capability. See FAR 6.302-3. See INDUSTRIAL BASE.

INDUSTRIAL PLANT EQUIPMENT   See PLANT EQUIPMENT.

INDUSTRY [1]   *Official:* All CONCERNs primarily engaged in similar lines of activity, as listed and described in the North American Industrial Classification system (NAICS) manual. *Source:* FAR 19.001. **[2]** As used generally, a group of entities that constitute a particular sector of the economy and that are engaged in similar activities. See, e.g., FAR 11.302(b)(2): "When acquiring commercial items, the contracting officer must consider the customary practices in the industry for the item being acquired," and FAR 11.701(b): "The overrun or underrun permitted in each contract should be based upon the normal commercial practices of a particular industry for a particular item." **[3]** More generally, the universe of entities that do business or might do business with the government. See, e.g., FAR 5.404: "To assist industry planning and to locate additional sources of supply, it may be desirable to publicize estimates of unclassified long-range acquisition requirements," and FAR 27.302(a): "[I]t is the policy and objective of the government to (1) Use the patent system to promote the use of inventions arising from federally supported research or development; (2) Encourage maximum participation of industry in federally supported research and development efforts."

INELIGIBLE   *Official:* Excluded from government contracting (and subcontracting, if appropriate) pursuant to statutory, Executive order, or regulatory authority other than [the FAR] and its implementing and supplementing regulations; for example, pursuant to the DAVIS-BACON ACT and its related statutes and implementing regulations, the SERVICE CONTRACT ACT, the EQUAL EMPLOYMENT OPPORTUNITY Acts and Executive orders, the WALSH-HEALEY PUBLIC CONTRACTS ACT, the BUY AMERICAN ACT, or the Environmental Protection Acts and Executive orders. *Source:* FAR 2.101. Although the FAR makes this distinction between "debarred" contractors and "ineligible" contractors, all such contractors are commonly referred to as having been debarred and are included in the SAM Exclusions list. FAR 9.404. See Cibinic, Nash & Yukins, Formation of Government Contracts 467–70 (4th ed. 2011). See also Robbins, et al., *Path of An Investigation: How Major Contractor's Ethics Office and Air Force Procurement Fraud and Suspension/ Debarment Apparatus Deal with Allegations of Potential Fraud and Unethical Conduct,* 40 Pub. Cont. L.J. 595 (2011).

INFLUENCING OR ATTEMPTING TO INFLUENCE   *Official:* Making, with the intent to influence, any communication or appearance before an officer or employee of any agency, a Member of Congress, an officer or employee of Congress or an employee of a Member of Congress in connection with any covered Federal action. *Source:* FAR 3.801. Actions covered by this definition are the awarding, making, entering into, extension, renewal, AMEND-MENT, or MODIFICATION of any federal contract, GRANT, loan, or COOPERATIVE AGREEMENT. This is commonly referred to as "lobbying." A recipient of a federal contract, grant, loan, or cooperative agreement is prohibited from using APPROPRIATED FUNDS to pay any person for influencing or attempting to influence such government officers or employees in connection with any of these actions. FAR 3.802; 31 U.S.C. § 1352. See ANTI-LOBBYING ACT; LOBBYING COSTS.

INFORMATION ASSURANCE　　*Official:* Measures that protect and defend information, that is entered, processed, transmitted, stored, retrieved, displayed, or destroyed, and information systems, by ensuring their availability, integrity, authentication, confidentiality, and non-repudiation. This includes providing for the restoration of information systems by incorporating protection, detection, and reaction capabilities. *Source:* DFARS 239.7101. DFARS Subpart 239.71 contains the DOD policy on providing such assurance when acquiring INFORMATION TECHNOLOGY.

INFORMATION OTHER THAN COST OR PRICING DATA　　This term described cost or pricing information that could be obtained from offerors when an agency was prohibited from obtaining COST OR PRICING DATA. It was replaced by the term DATA OTHER THAN CERTIFIED COST OR PRICING DATA by FAC 2005-45, 75 Fed. Reg. 53135, Aug. 30, 2010.

INFORMATION RESOURCES MANAGEMENT (IRM)　　*Official:* The process of managing information resources to accomplish agency missions and to improve agency performance, including the reduction of information collection burdens on the public. *Source:* 44 U.S.C. § 3502(7). Such management is accomplished by the OFFICE OF INFORMATION AND REGULATORY AFFAIRS which reviews and approves the collection of information from the public, oversees the compilation of statistics, and oversees federal INFORMATION TECHNOLOGY programs. 44 U.S.C. § 3503.

INFORMATION SECURITY　　*Official:* Protecting information and information systems from unauthorized access, use, disclosure, disruption, modification, or destruction in order to provide—(1) Integrity, which means guarding against improper information modification or destruction, and includes ensuring information nonrepudiation and authenticity; (2) Confidentiality, which means preserving authorized restrictions on access and disclosure, including means for protecting personal privacy and proprietary information; and (3) Availability, which means ensuring timely and reliable access to, and use of, information. *Source:* FAR 2.101. 44 U.S.C. § 3553 assigns responsibility for information security to the Director of OMB, the Secretary of Homeland Security, the Secretary of Defense and the Director of National Intelligence. Guidance on preserving information security during the release of information is contained in FAR Subpart 5.4.

INFORMATION TECHNOLOGY (IT)　　*Official:* Any equipment, or any interconnected system(s) or subsystem(s) of equipment, that is used in the automatic acquisition, storage, analysis, evaluation, manipulation, management, movement, control, display, switching, interchange, transmission, or reception of data or information by the agency. (1) For purposes of this definition, equipment is used by an agency if the equipment is used by the agency directly or is used by a contractor under a contract with the agency that requires—(i) Its use; or (ii) To a significant extent, its use in the performance of a service or the furnishing of a product. (2) The term "information technology" includes computers, ancillary equipment (including imaging peripherals, input, output, and storage devices necessary for security and surveillance), peripheral equipment designed to be controlled by the central processing unit of a computer, software, firmware and similar procedures, services (including support services), and related resources. (3) The term "information technology" does not include any equipment that—(i) Is acquired by a contractor incidental to a contract; or (ii) Contains imbedded information technology that is used as an integral part of the product, but the principal function of which is not the acquisition, storage, analysis, evaluation, manipulation, management, movement, control, display, switching, interchange, transmission, or reception of data or information. For example, HVAC (heating, ventilation, and air conditioning) equipment, such as thermostats or temperature control devices, and medical equipment where information technology is integral to its operation, are not information technology. *Source:* FAR 2.101. FAR Part 39 provides policies and procedures to be used in the acquisition of information technology. The CLINGER-COHEN ACT OF 1996 repealed the BROOKS ACT (AUTOMATED DATA PROCESSING PROCUREMENT) and substituted §§ 5001–5703 of the INFORMATION TECHNOLOGY MANAGEMENT REFORM ACT OF 1996.

INFORMATION TECHNOLOGY MANAGEMENT REFORM ACT (ITMRA)   A 1996 Act, part of the CLINGER-COHEN ACT OF 1996 (originally included as Division E of Pub. L. No. 104-106), that repealed the BROOKS ACT (AUTOMATED DATA PROCESSING PROCUREMENT) and substitutes new guidance on the procurement of INFORMATION TECHNOLOGY (IT). The Act is codified in 40 U.S.C. § 11101 et seq., § 11301 et seq., § 11311 et seq., and § 11501 et seq. as well as 41 U.S.C. § 2308. The Act provides that the director of the OFFICE OF MANAGEMENT AND BUDGET will (1) promote and improve the acquisition, use, and disposal of IT by administering a capital planning and investment system (40 U.S.C. § 11302) and (2) encourage the use of performance-based and results-based management (40 U.S.C. § 11303). It provides that agencies will (1) implement capital planning and investment programs (40 U.S.C. § 11312), (2) use performance-based and results-based management procedures in the acquisition of IT (40 U.S.C. § 11313), (3) promote multiagency acquisitions of IT (40 U.S.C. § 11314), (4) appoint a Chief Information Officer (40 U.S.C. § 11315), (5) ensure that there is accountability that IT systems are effective (40 U.S.C. § 11316), and (6) use MODULAR CONTRACTING to the maximum extent practicable in acquiring IT (41 U.S.C. § 2308). See Cong. Research Serv., Report No. R44843, The Current State of Federal Information Technology Acquisition Reform and Management (Feb. 2020).

INHERENTLY GOVERNMENTAL FUNCTIONS   *Official:* As a matter of policy, a function that is so intimately related to the public interest as to mandate performance by government employees. This definition is a policy determination, not a legal determination. An inherently governmental function includes activities that require either the exercise of discretion in applying government authority, or the making of value judgments in making decisions for the government. Governmental functions normally fall into two categories: the act of governing, i.e., the discretionary exercise of government authority, and monetary transactions and entitlements. (1) An inherently governmental function involves, among other things, the interpretation and execution of the laws of the United States so as to—(i) Bind the United States to take or not to take some action by contract, policy, regulation, authorization, order, or otherwise; (ii) Determine, protect, and advance United States economic, political, territorial, property, or other interests by military or diplomatic action, civil or criminal judicial proceedings, contract management, or otherwise; (iii) Significantly affect the life, liberty, or property of private persons; (iv) Commission, appoint, direct, or control officers or employees of the United States; or (v) Exert ultimate control over the acquisition, use, or disposition of the property, real or personal, tangible or intangible, of the United States, including the collection, control, or disbursement of Federal funds. (2) Inherently governmental functions do not normally include gathering information for or providing advice, opinions, recommendations, or ideas to government officials. They also do not include functions that are primarily ministerial and internal in nature, such as building security, mail operations, operation of cafeterias, housekeeping, facilities operations and maintenance, warehouse operations, motor vehicle fleet management operations, or other routine electrical or mechanical services. *Source:* FAR 2.101. Inherently governmental functions cannot be performed by contractors. FAR 7.503. See also A-76. FAR 7.503(c) contains an extensive list of inherently governmental functions, which includes, among others, criminal investigations, command of military forces, foreign relations, and contract award, administration, and termination. See generally, FAR Subpart 7.5, FAR 37.102(c); OFPP Policy Letter No. 11-01, Performance of Inherently Governmental and Critical Functions, 76 Fed. Reg. 56227, Sept. 12, 2011. Agencies must distinguish between inherently governmental functions and commercial functions when publishing the inventories required by the FEDERAL ACTIVITIES INVENTORY REFORM ACT. See Manuel, CONG. RESEARCH SERV., REPORT NO. R42325, DEFINITIONS OF "INHERENTLY GOVERNMENTAL FUNCTION" IN FEDERAL PROCUREMENT LAW AND GUIDANCE (Dec. 2014).

INITIAL COSTS   Preproduction and startup costs, including costs such as preproduction engineering, production planning, special plant rearrangement, training programs, and such nonrecurring costs as initial rework, initial spoilage, and pilot runs, which are not fully recovered because of a TERMINATION FOR CONVENIENCE. Such costs are generally allowable TERMINATION COSTS subject to the guidance in FAR 31.205-42. See Manos, 1 GOVERNMENT CONTRACT COSTS AND PRICING § 49:5 (2d ed. 2009–2020); Cibinic, Nagle & Nash, ADMINISTRATION OF GOVERNMENT CONTRACTS 985 (5th ed. 2016).

INSPECTION   *Official:* Examining and testing supplies or services (including, when appropriate, raw materials, components, and intermediate assemblies) to determine whether they conform to contract requirements. *Source:* FAR 2.101. TESTING is the part of inspection that determines the properties or elements, including the functional operation of supplies or their components, by the application of established scientific principles and procedures. Although contracts generally make contractors responsible for performing inspection before tendering supplies to the government, there are situations in which contracts will provide for specialized inspection to be performed solely by the government. FAR 46.201. The standard inspection clauses in FAR 52.246-2 through -8 and -10 require the contractor to (1) provide and maintain an inspection system that is acceptable to the government, (2) give the government the right to perform reviews and evaluations as reasonably necessary, and (3) keep complete records of its inspection work and make them available to the government. Regulatory guidance on inspection is contained in FAR Part 46 covering QUALITY ASSURANCE. See Cibinic, Nagle & Nash, ADMINISTRATION OF GOVERNMENT CONTRACTS 698–729 (5th ed. 2016).

INSPECTOR GENERAL (IG)   An officer of the United States, appointed by the President and confirmed by the Senate, to serve in each major department of the government to independently audit and investigate the activities of that department. The Inspector General Act of 1978, 5 U.S.C. app. 3, created Inspector General offices for government agencies in order to establish independent and objective units to (1) conduct and supervise audits and investigations relating to the programs and operations of the agencies and organizations; (2) provide leadership and coordination and recommend policies for activities designed to promote administrative economy, efficiency, and effectiveness and to prevent and detect fraud and abuse; and (3) provide a means for keeping the head of the establishment and Congress informed about administrative problems and deficiencies and about the necessity for and progress of corrective action. 5 U.S.C. App. 3 § 2. IGs are authorized to (1) have access to records, reports, and audits; (2) make investigations and reports; (3) request information and assistance from federal, state, and local governments; (4) require production of documents by subpoena; (5) administer oaths; (6) have direct access to the head of the agency or organization; (7) select employees as necessary; (8) obtain services; and (9) enter into contracts and other arrangements for audits, studies, and analyses with public agencies and private persons. 5 U.S.C. App. 3 § 6.

INSTANT CONTRACT   *Official:* The contract under which the VALUE ENGINEERING CHANGE PROPOSAL (VECP) is submitted. It does not include increases in quantities made to the contract after acceptance of the VECP that are due to contract modification, exercise of options, or additional orders. If the contract is a multiyear contract (see MULTIYEAR CONTRACTING), the term does not include quantities funded after VECP acceptance. In a FIXED-PRICE REDETERMINATION—PROSPECTIVE CONTRACT, the term refers to the period for which firm prices have been established. *Source:* FAR 48.001. Contractors share in INSTANT CONTRACT SAVINGS under the Value Engineering clauses for supplies and services and construction, FAR 52.248-1 and FAR 52.248-3. See Nash & Feldman, 2 GOVERNMENT CONTRACT CHANGES, chap. 9 (3d ed. 2006–2020);

INSTANT CONTRACT SAVINGS   *Official:* The net cost reductions on contract under which the VALUE ENGINEERING CHANGE PROPOSAL (VECP) is submitted and accepted, and that are equal to the INSTANT UNIT COST REDUCTION multiplied by the number of INSTANT CONTRACT units affected by the VECP, less the contractor's allowable development and implementation costs. *Source:* FAR 48.001 (in the definition of ACQUISITION SAVINGS). FAR 48.104-1 contains guidance on such savings; their calculation is prescribed in ¶ (g) of the Value Engineering clause in FAR 52.248-1. See also NEGATIVE INSTANT CONTRACT SAVINGS. In construction contracts, using the Value Engineering—Construction clause in FAR 52.248-3, instant contract savings include all cost savings of the contractor (not just unit cost reductions). See Nash & Feldman, 2 GOVERNMENT CONTRACT CHANGES § 9:8 (3d ed. 2006–2020); Cibinic, Nagle & Nash, ADMINISTRATION OF GOVERNMENT CONTRACTS 374 (5th ed. 2016).

INSTANT UNIT COST REDUCTION   *Official:* The amount of the decrease in unit cost of performance (without deducting any contractor's development or implementation costs) resulting from using the VALUE ENGINEERING CHANGE PROPOSAL (VECP) on the INSTANT CONTRACT. In service contracts, the instant unit cost reduction is normally equal to the number of hours per line-item task saved by using the VECP on the instant contract, multiplied by the appropriate contract labor rate. *Source:* FAR 48.001. The concept of instant unit cost reduction is contrasted with that of future unit cost reduction, just as INSTANT CONTRACT SAVINGS are contrasted with FUTURE CONTRACT SAVINGS. See Nash & Feldman, 2 GOVERNMENT CONTRACT CHANGES, chap. 9 (3d ed. 2006–2020).

INSURANCE   *Official:* A contract that provides that for a stipulated consideration, one party undertakes to indemnify another against loss, damage, or liability arising from an unknown or contingent event. *Source:* FAR 2.101. FAR 31.205-19 specifies that most normal costs of insurance incurred by a contractor are ALLOWABLE COSTs. See Manos, 1 GOVERNMENT CONTRACT COSTS AND PRICING §§ 26:1–26:6 (2d ed. 2009–2020); Cibinic, Knight & Nash, COST-REIMBURSEMENT CONTRACTING 728 (4th ed. 2014). CAS 416, Accounting for Insurance Costs, 48 C.F.R. § 9904.416, governs the accounting techniques that are to be used by contractors for insurance costs and permits SELF-INSURANCE in lieu of the purchase of insurance policies. See *DCAA Contract Audit Manual* ¶ 8-416. See also Manos, 2 GOVERNMENT COST AND PRICING §§ 77:1–77:7 (2d ed. 2009–2020). FAR Subpart 28.3 sets forth the policies of the government in dealing with insurance by contractors.

INTANGIBLE CAPITAL ASSET   *Official:* An asset that has no physical substance, has more than minimal value, and is expected to be held by an enterprise for continued use or possession beyond the current accounting period for the benefits it yields. *Source:* FAR 31.001. The value of such assets lies in the use that can be made of them, although they cannot be seen. Examples are GOODWILL and patent rights. DEPRECIATION on intangible capital assets is not an ALLOWABLE COST because FAR 31.205-11 allows depreciation only on TANGIBLE CAPITAL ASSETs.

INTEGRATED AGREEMENT   A writing or writings constituting a final expression of one of more terms of an agreement. RESTATEMENT (SECOND) CONTRACTS § 209 (1981). When an agreement is found to be integrated, the PAROL EVIDENCE RULE applies. Integrated agreements are found to be "complete" or "partial" depending on the circumstances. RESTATEMENT (SECOND) CONTRACTS § 210 (1981). If an agreement that is reduced to writing appears to be complete, it is assumed to be an integrated agreement unless proven otherwise. When the parties include a clause stating that the agreement is completely integrated, there is a strong presumption to that effect. See Cibinic, Nagle & Nash, ADMINISTRATION OF GOVERNMENT CONTRACTS 191 (5th ed. 2016).

INTEGRATED ASSESSMENT   A PROPOSAL evaluation during SOURCE SELECTION that takes into account all price and nonprice EVALUATION FACTORS in order to identify the proposal that offers the BEST VALUE. Such assessments are made in TRADEOFF PROCESS source selections conducted pursuant to FAR 15.101-1 and entail the conduct of a TRADEOFF ANALYSIS. REQUESTS FOR PROPOSALS commonly state that the government will determine which proposal represents the best value on the basis of an integrated assessment. See, e.g., the SOLICITATION PROVISIONs prescribed in the Department of Commerce FAR Supplement, 48 C.F.R. § 1352.215-74 and 1352.215-75. In other fields, the term integrated assessment broadly refers to analyses of cause or estimates of value that take all relevant considerations into account.

INTEGRATED MASTER PLAN (IMP)   A part of a contract that describes the plan for the execution of a Department of Defense program. It is officially defined as follows: "An event-based plan consisting of a hierarchy of program events, with each event being supported by specific accomplishments, and each accomplishment associated with specific criteria to be satisfied for its completion. The IMP is normally part of the contract and thus contractually binding. The IMP is a narrative explaining the overall management of the program." See Department of Defense, Integrated Master Plan and Integrated Master Schedule Preparation and Use Guide, Ver. 0.9 (Oct. 2005).

INTEGRATED MASTER SCHEDULE (IMS)   A document used in conjunction with an INTEGRATED MASTER PLAN (IMP) to specify the sequence of, and relationship among, events in the execution of a contract for a DEPARTMENT OF DEFENSE program. It is officially defined, in part, as follows: "An integrated, networked schedule containing all the detailed discrete work packages and planning packages (or lower level tasks or activities) necessary to support the events, accomplishments, and criteria of the IMP (if applicable). The IMP events, accomplishments, and criteria are duplicated in the IMS. Detailed tasks are added to depict the steps required to satisfy criterion. The result is a fully networked 'bottoms up' schedule that supports critical path analysis." See Department of Defense, Integrated Master Plan and Integrated Master Schedule Preparation and Use Guide, Ver. 0.9 (Oct. 2005).

INTEGRITY   See PROCUREMENT INTEGRITY.

INTELLECTUAL PROPERTY   The legal rights which result from intellectual activity in the industrial, scientific, literary and artistic fields. The WORLD INDUSTRIAL PROPERTY ORGANIZATION divides intellectual property into two categories: "industrial property" and "COPYRIGHT." Industrial property includes PATENTs, TRADEMARKs, industrial designs, and geographic indications of source. See WIPO Industrial Property Handbook: Policy, Law and Use, WIPO Publication No. 489 (2d ed. Reprinted 2008). The government's policies regarding intellectual property are dealt with in Nash & Rawicz, Intellectual Property in Government Contracts (6th ed. 2008). See also Masiello, Bareis & Pratt, *Managing Intellectual Property Issues With The U.S. Government: A User's Guide*, Briefing Papers No. 16-3 (Feb. 2016).

INTERAGENCY ACQUISITION   *Official:* A procedure by which an agency needing supplies or services (the REQUESTING AGENCY) obtains them from another agency (the SERVICING AGENCY), by an ASSISTED ACQUISITION or a DIRECT ACQUISITION. The term includes—(1) Acquisitions under the ECONOMY ACT (31 U.S.C. § 1535); and (2) Non-Economy Act acquisitions completed under other statutory authorities (*e.g.*, General Services Administration FEDERAL SUPPLY SCHEDULES in subpart 8.4 and GOVERNMENTWIDE ACQUISITION CONTRACTS (GWACS)). *Source:* FAR 2.101. Guidance on interagency acquisitions is set forth in FAR Subpart 17.5. Interagency acquisitions are commonly conducted through INDEFINITE-DELIVERY CONTRACTs. The Economy Act authorizes agencies to enter into mutual agreements and obtain supplies and services by interagency acquisition. The Act may not be used by an agency to circumvent conditions and limitations imposed on the use of funds. FAR 17.501(b). Each Economy Act order must be supported by a DETERMINATION AND FINDINGS (D&F). The D&F must state that (1) the use of an interagency acquisition is in the best interest of the government, and (2) the supplies and services cannot be obtained as conveniently or economically by contracting directly with a private source. FAR 17.502-2(c). Agencies are forbidden to use interagency acquisition as a means of avoiding the requirement to obtain FULL AND OPEN COMPETITION. FAR 6.002. See Cibinic, Nash & Yukins, Formation of Government Contracts, chap. 8 (4th ed. 2011). See also Manual & Yeh, Cong. Research Serv., Report No. R40814, Interagency Contracting: An Overview of

Federal Procurement and Appropriations Law (Aug. 30, 2010); U.S. Gov't Accountability Office, Interagency Contracting: Need for Improved Information and Policy Implementation at the Department of State, GAO-08-578 (May 8, 2008).

INTERAGENCY AGREEMENT An agreement between a REQUESTING AGENCY and a SERVICING AGENCY containing the terms and conditions that will govern an ASSISTED ACQUISITION. These agreements are required by FAR 17.502-1(b)(1). Guidance on the preparation of these agreements is contained *Department of the Treasury Interagency Agreement Guide* (2d ed. 2013).

INTERAGENCY FLEET MANAGEMENT SYSTEM (IFMS) A pool of vehicles and service facilities maintained by the General Services Administration for the use of federal agencies in a given area. FAR 51.201 provides that, if it is in the government's interest, the contracting officer may authorize the contractor under a COST-REIMBURSEMENT CONTRACT to obtain, for official purposes only, IMFS vehicles and related services, including (1) fuel and lubricants, (2) vehicle inspection, maintenance, and repair, (3) vehicle storage, and (4) commercially rented vehicles for short- term use. Complete rebuilding of major components of contractor-owned or contractor-leased vehicles requires the approval of a contracting officer. The contractor must, among other things, (1) obtain vehicle liability insurance covering bodily injury and property damage protecting the contractor and the government against third-party claims, and (2) establish and enforce penalties for its employees who use or authorize the use of government vehicles for other than performance of government contracts. FAR 51.202. When a contractor is authorized to follow these procedures, the solicitation and the contract will contain the Interagency Fleet Management System Vehicles and Related Services clause in FAR 52.251-2. Detailed regulations on these systems are contained in 41 C.F.R. Part 101-39.

INTEREST An amount paid for the use of money. Interest on borrowings by a contractor (however represented) is not an ALLOWABLE COST under a contract. FAR 31.205-20. See Manos, 1 Government Contract Costs and Pricing §§ 27:1–27:3 (2d ed. 2009–2020); Cibinic, Knight & Nash, Cost-Reimbursement Contracting 724–27 (4th ed. 2014). However, interest imputed to the cost of facilities is allowable. See COST OF CAPITAL COMMITTED TO FACILITIES. The PROMPT PAYMENT ACT requires payment of an interest penalty for late government payment of contractor INVOICEs. FAR 32.903; OMB Circular No. A-125, Prompt Payment, Aug. 18, 1982. FAR 32.407 requires that the contracting officer charge interest on the daily unliquidated balance of ADVANCE PAYMENTs made to the contractor. The Interest clause at FAR 52.232-17 requires that all amounts payable by the contractor to the government bear simple interest from the date due unless paid within 30 days of becoming due. Each clause requiring the payment of interest specifies how the rate will be calculated (several different ways). The CONTRACT DISPUTES ACT OF 1978, at 41 U.S.C. § 7109, provides for the payment of IMPUTED INTEREST on the amount found due and unpaid on contractor claims, running from the date the contracting officer receives the CLAIM (or the due date, if later) until the date the government pays the contractor. When interest is paid under the CDA, it is paid at the TREASURY INTEREST RATE. See Cibinic, Nagle & Nash, Administration of Government Contracts 1009–16 (5th ed. 2016). See also Edwards, *A Mystery: When Does Interest Begin to Accrue on a Contractor's Claim?*, 23 N&CR ¶ 6 (Feb. 2009); Nash, *Interest on Borrowings: A Legitimate Cost in Damages Calculations*, 21 N&CR ¶ 69 (Dec. 2007); Hanson & Jackson, *Interest In & On Claims*, Briefing Papers No. 06-4 (Mar. 2006).

INTEREST RATE   See TREASURY INTEREST RATE.

INTERESTED PARTY   *Official:* An actual or prospective offeror whose direct economic interest would be affected by the award of a contract or by the failure to award a contract. *Source:* 31 U.S.C. § 3551(2); FAR 33.101. Interested parties are parties entitled to bring PROTESTs—either to the awarding agency directly, before the GOVERNMENT ACCOUNTABILITY OFFICE (GAO), or to the U.S. COURT OF FEDERAL CLAIMS. The "interested party" standard was first applied to the courts by the addition of 28 U.S.C. § 1491(b) in 1996, Pub. L. No. 104-320. An interested party is encouraged to seek resolution within the agency before going before the GAO. FAR 33.102. To determine whether a protester is an interested party, many factors are considered, including the protester's status in relation to the procurement (prospective offeror, offeror eligible for award, nonofferor, etc.), the nature of the issues raised, and the direct or indirect benefit or relief sought by the protester. See UNITED STATES GOVERNMENT ACCOUNTABILITY OFFICE, BID PROTESTS AT GAO: A DESCRIPTIVE GUIDE, GAO-18-510SP (10th ed. May 2018). See also Cibinic, Nash & Yukins, FORMATION OF GOVERNMENT CONTRACTS 1693–1700, 1767–69 (4th ed. 2011).

INTERFACE DATA   TECHNICAL DATA and COMPUTER SOFTWARE necessary to permit segregation and reintegration of an ITEM or process with other items or processes. See SEGREGATION AND REINTEGRATION DATA. Such data describing components is required to be obtained when using the MODULAR OPEN SYSTEM APPROACH. 10 U.S.C. § 2320(a)(2)(D)(i)(II) permits the Government to release this type of data outside of the Government even though it is subject to LIMITED RIGHTS. This statute has not been implemented in the DFARS. The Rights in Data—General clause in FAR 52.227-14 requires the submission of interface data as part of FORM, FIT AND FUNCTION DATA with UNLIMITED RIGHTS.

INTERIM FEDERAL SPECIFICATION   *Official:* A potential FEDERAL SPECIFICATION issued in temporary form for optional use by all federal agencies. Interim amendments to federal specifications and amendments to interim federal specifications are included in this definition. These documents are issued or controlled by the General Services Administration and are listed in the GSA Index of Federal Specifications, Standards and Commercial Item Descriptions. *Source:* 41 C.F.R. § 101-29.204. Guidance on the promulgation and use of these specifications is contained in 41 C.F.R. part 101-29.

INTERIM PAYMENTS   Payments made by the government to a contractor periodically during performance of a COST-REIMBURSEMENT CONTRACT. These payments are generally made on a provisional basis to provide the contractor with a flow of funds that can be used to finance contract performance. Through these payments, contractors are reimbursed for COSTS, and, if any, FEE, as performance progresses. Requests for interim payments are made on public voucher forms Standard Form 1034, FAR 53.301-1034, and Standard Form 1035, FAR 53.301-1035. DCAA Pamphlet 7641.90, June 26, 2012, gives guidance to contractors on the preparation of vouchers. Interim payments are CONTRACT FINANCING PAYMENTS which are not subject to the interest provisions of the PROMPT PAYMENT ACT, FAR 32.001. However, if the contract is for services, FAR 32.908(c)(3) requires the use of Alternate I to the Prompt Payment clause, FAR 52.232-25, which makes these payments subject to the Prompt Payment Act requirements. FAR 32.202-1 states the limited circumstances when interim payments can be made for

COMMERCIAL ITEMs. Interim payments can be withheld if one of a CONTRACTOR's BUSINESS SYSTEMs contains a SIGNIFICANT DEFICIENCY. See DFARS 252.242-7005. See Cibinic, Knight & Nash, Cost-Reimbursement Contracting 889–901 (4th ed. 2014).

INTERIM RATE   See BILLING RATE.

INTERMEDIATE COST OBJECTIVE   A COST OBJECTIVE to which costs are allocated for purposes of accumulating similar costs. Once accumulated, the costs are allocated to another intermediate cost objective or to a FINAL COST OBJECTIVE. CAS 502, Consistency in Allocating Costs Incurred for the Same Purpose by Educational Institutions, 48 C.F.R. § 9905.502-30. An example of an intermediate cost objective is a contractor's BUSINESS UNIT, to which is allocated HOME OFFICE expense. Subsequently, the business unit allocates the cost to a contract or other cost objective. See Manos, 2 Government Cost and Pricing §§ 71.1–71:7 (2d ed. 2009–2020).

INTERNATIONAL TRAFFIC & ARMS REGULATION (ITAR)   Regulation promulgated by the DEPARTMENT OF STATE in accordance with the ARMS EXPORT CONTROL ACT, 22 U.S.C. § 2778, and implemented in 22 C.F.R. Parts 120 through 130, for the control of the permanent and temporary export and temporary import of DEFENSE ARTICLES and DEFENSE SERVICES. Part 121 of the ITAR (the MUNITIONS LIST) lists all articles subject to EXPORT CONTROL. See Tschetter and Titus, *Export Controls Compliance Manual Digital Version*, North Dakota State University (Apr. 26, 2017).

INTERORGANIZATIONAL TRANSFER   A transaction between a contractor and a sister division, an affiliate (see AFFILIATES), or a subsidiary. Allowance for all materials, supplies, and services that are sold or transferred between any divisions, subdivisions, subsidiaries, or affiliates of the contractor under common control are required to be on the basis of cost incurred in accordance with FAR 31.205-26(e). However, allowance may be at price (1) when it is the established practice of the transferring organization to price interorganizational transfers at other than cost for commercial work of the contractor or any division, subsidiary, or affiliate of the contractor under a common control; and (2) when the item being transferred qualifies for an exception under FAR 15.403-1 and the contracting officer has not determined the price to be unreasonable. FAR 31.205-26(e); FAR Table 15-2 at FAR 15.408. The Defense Contract Audit Agency (DCAA) instructs its auditors to give "careful consideration" to transactions between affiliated concerns. *DCAA Contract Audit Manual* ¶ 6-313.1.

INTERPRETATION   See CONTRACT INTERPRETATION.

INTERROGATORY   A written question submitted to the other party to a litigation. Rule 33 of the Federal Rules of Civil Procedure and Rule 15 of the UNIFORM RULES (before the BOARDs OF CONTRACT APPEALS) permit the use of written interrogatories and require that they be answered or objected to within 30 days. Such written interrogatories are one of the major forms of DISCOVERY.

INTERVENOR   A person who voluntarily interposes in an action or other proceeding with the permission of the forum or court. Intervention is a procedure by which a third person, not originally a party to a suit but claiming an interest in the subject matter, comes into the dispute in order to protect its own right or interpose its own claim. Black's Law Dictionary 983 (11th ed. 2019). In PROTEST proceedings before the GOVERNMENT

ACCOUNTABILITY OFFICE (GAO) an intervenor is an awardee if the award has been made or, if no award has been made, any bidder or offeror who appears to have a substantial prospect of receiving an award if the protest is granted. 4 C.F.R. § 21.0(b). In GAO protests, agencies must notify all potential intervenors when a protest is filed, and intervenors must enter the case as soon as practicable. 4 C.F.R. § 21.3. Rule 24 of the U.S. COURT OF FEDERAL CLAIMS permits intervention when a party has an interest in a transaction which will be impaired but for intervention. Intervenors are rarely permitted to participate in disputes in the BOARDs OF CONTRACT APPEALS.

INTRINSIC EVIDENCE   The words of the contractual document that must be interpreted to determine the understanding reached by the contracting parties. These words are analyzed using dictionaries and evidence of trade usage. Courts and boards also follow common rules to determine the meaning of contract language such as searching for PLAIN MEANING, reading the contract as a whole, interpreting to avoid conflict, give meaning to all of the words and fulfill the principal purpose of the contract. The FEDERAL CIRCUIT has held that if the plain meaning of a contract can be ascertained by a review of the intrinsic evidence, a judge should not review any EXTRINSIC EVIDENCE to determine the meaning of the contract language, *Coast Federal Bank, FSB v. United States*, 323 F.3d 1035 (Fed. Cir. 2003). See Cibinic, Nagle & Nash, ADMINISTRATION OF GOVERNMENT CONTRACTS 177–211 (5th ed. 2016).

INVENTION   A new idea that is susceptible to the granting of a PATENT. A patent may be granted on an invention if it pertains to a new and useful process, machine, manufacture or composition of matter, 35 U.S.C. § 101, is timely filed in the United States Patent and Trademark Office, 35 U.S.C. § 102, and is nonobvious, 35 U.S.C. § 103(a). See Nash & Rawicz, INTELLECTUAL PROPERTY IN GOVERNMENT CONTRACTS, chap. 1 (6th ed. 2008).

INVENTORY   The portion of a financial statement reflecting the value of goods in stock and raw materials, work in process, and finished products used or consumed in a business. BLACK's LAW DICTIONARY 988 (11th ed. 2019). See CONTRACTOR INVENTORY and TERMINATION INVENTORY.

INVERTED DOMESTIC CORPORATION   *Official:* A foreign incorporated entity which is treated as an inverted domestic corporation under 6 U.S.C. § 395(b), i.e., a corporation that used to be incorporated in the United States, or used to be a partnership in the United States, but now is incorporated in a foreign country, or is a subsidiary whose parent corporation is incorporated in a foreign country, that meets the criteria specified in 6 U.S.C. § 395(b), applied in accordance with the rules and definitions of 6 U.S.C. § 395(c). An inverted domestic corporation as herein defined does not meet the definition of an inverted domestic corporation as defined by the Internal Revenue Code at 26 U.S.C. § 7874. *Source:* FAR 9.108-1. Inverted domestic corporations are also known as corporate expatriates. The reason for a domestic corporation to incorporate overseas is to avoid U.S. taxes on business income generated in foreign countries. The tax code has similar criteria for defining an inverted domestic corporation for federal income tax purposes at 26 U.S.C. § 7874. FAR 9.108-2 lists a number of APPROPRIATIONS ACTs that prohibit the awarding of contracts to inverted domestic corporations. However, FAR 9.108-4 allows any HEAD OF THE AGENCY to waive the prohibition if (1) it is determined, in writing, to be in the best interests of national security, (2) the determination is documents, and (3) the determination is reported to Congress. When these acts apply, contracting officers are required to use the

Prohibition on Contracting with Inverted Domestic Corporations—Representative solicitation provision in FAR 52.209-2, and the Prohibition on Contracting with Inverted Domestic Corporations clause in FAR 52.209-10. DHS is prohibited from contracting with an inverted domestic corporation absent a waiver. 48 C.F.R. § 3009.108-7001. See CONG. RESEARCH SERV., Report No. R43780, CONTRACTING WITH INVERTED DOMESTIC CORPORATIONS: ANSWERS TO FREQUENTLY ASKED QUESTIONS (May 11, 2015).

INVITATION FOR BIDS (IFB)   The solicitation document used in SEALED BIDDING procurements. IFBs must describe the government's requirements clearly, accurately, and completely. FAR 14.101. IFBs must also use the UNIFORM CONTRACT FORMAT to the maximum extent practicable. FAR 14.201-1. FAR 14.202 provides the general rules for solicitation of bids with the IFB. An IFB includes all documents needed by prospective bidders for the purpose of bidding plus all terms and conditions of the prospective contract (except price) so that all bidders will submit bids on the same basis and award can be made solely on the basis of PRICE and PRICE-RELATED FACTORS. IFBs must be publicized through distribution to prospective bidders, FAR 14.101(b), posting in public places, publication of a SYNOPSIS in the GOVERNMENTWIDE POINT OF ENTRY, and such other means as may be appropriate. FAR 14.203-2; FAR 5.101. They must not include unnecessarily RESTRICTIVE SPECIFICATIONS or requirements that might unduly limit the number of bidders. Publicizing must occur a sufficient time before bid opening to enable prospective bidders to prepare and submit bids. FAR 14.101. The government may amend IFBs by using Standard Form 30, Amendment of Solicitation/Modification of Contract, FAR 53.301-30. See Cibinic, Nash & Yukins, FORMATION OF GOVERNMENT CONTRACTS 503–05 (4th ed. 2011).

INVOICE   *Official:* A contractor's bill or written request for payment under the contract for supplies delivered or services performed (see also "PROPER INVOICE"). *Source:* FAR 2.101. Contractors also submit invoices to obtain PROGRESS PAYMENTS and reimbursement of costs under COST REIMBURSEMENT CONTRACTs. In order to receive interest for late payment under the PROMPT PAYMENT ACT, a contractor must submit a "proper" invoice meeting the requirements of FAR 32.905. See the Prompt Payment clauses in FAR 52.232-25 through FAR 52.232-27. Under the DISPUTEs clause in FAR 52.233-1, a VOUCHER, invoice, or other routine request for payment that is not in dispute when submitted is not a CLAIM starting the running of interest, although it may be converted to a claim. FAR 33.201. See Feldman, GOVERNMENT CONTRACT GUIDEBOOK § 10:8 (4th ed. 2019–2020); Cibinic, Nagle & Nash, ADMINISTRATION OF GOVERNMENT CONTRACTS 1028 (5th ed. 2016).

INVOICE PAYMENT   A government disbursement of monies, subject to the PROMPT PAYMENT ACT (PPA), to a contractor under a contract or other authorization for supplies or services that have been accepted by the government. The term encompasses payments for partial deliveries that have been accepted by the government and interim payments on COST-REIMBURSEMENT CONTRACTs when Alternate I of the Prompt Payment clause in FAR 52.232.25 is used. See Cibinic, Knight & Nash, COST-REIMBURSEMENT CONTRACTING 892 (4th ed. 2014). Under the PPA, invoice payments also include all PROGRESS PAYMENTs made under the Payments under Fixed-Price Construction Contracts clause at FAR 52.232-5, and the Payments under Fixed-Price Architect-Engineer Contracts clause at FAR 52.232-10. Invoice payments do not include contract CONTRACT FINANCING PAYMENTs. FAR 32.901(b). The due date for a designated payment office to make an invoice payment is generally the 30th day after the designated billing office has received a proper

INVOICE from the contractor, or the 30th day after the government's acceptance of supplies delivered or services performed by the contractor, whichever is later. However, earlier dates are used in a variety of circumstances. FAR 32.904. See 5 C.F.R. part 1315; Cibinic, Nagle & Nash, ADMINISTRATION OF GOVERNMENT CONTRACTS 1028–36 (5th ed. 2016).

IRREFRAGABLE PROOF   The level of evidence necessary to prove BAD FAITH in terminating a contract for the convenience of the government, *Kalvar Corp. v. United States*, 543 F.2d 1298 (Ct. Cl. 1976). In *Am-Pro Protective Agency, Inc. v. United States*, 281 F.3d 1234 (Fed. Cir. 2002), the Federal Circuit held that the correct standard for proving bad faith during contract administration was clear and convincing evidence of specific intent to harm the contractor. See Cibinic, Nagle & Nash, ADMINISTRATION OF GOVERNMENT CONTRACTS 274–83 (5th ed. 2016). See also Nash, *Postscript II: Breach of the Duty of Good Faith and Fair Dealing*, 26 N&CR ¶ 9 (Feb. 2012); McCaleb, *Court of Federal Claims Gives Last Rites to "Irrefragable Proof" Standard*, 8 Procurement Law Advisor 9 (Dec. 2005).

IRREVOCABLE LETTER OF CREDIT   *Official:* A written commitment by a federally insured financial institution to pay all or part of a stated amount of money, until the expiration date of the letter, upon the Government's (the beneficiary) presentation of a written demand for payment. Neither the financial institution nor the offeror/contractor can revoke or condition the letter of credit. *Source:* FAR 2.101. When an individual SURETY is required to provide a BOND on a contract, an irrevocable letter of credit may be furnished to satisfy the bond obligations. FAR 28.203-2(b)(5). Such letters of credit may also be submitted as one of the two forms of security on construction contracts greater than $35,000 but not greater than $150,000, FAR 28.102-1(b).

ISSUE IN CONTROVERSY   *Official:* A material disagreement between the government and a contractor that (1) may result in a CLAIM or (2) is all or part of an existing claim. *Source:* FAR 33.201. Agencies are encouraged to settle all issues in controversy by mutual agreement or to use ALTERNATIVE DISPUTE RESOLUTION procedures if that is not possible. FAR 33.204. Otherwise they are resolved following the procedures of the CONTRACT DISPUTES ACT.

ITAR   See INTERNATIONAL TRAFFIC IN ARMS REGULATIONS.

ITEM   *Official:* Any individual part, component, subassembly, assembly, or subsystem integral to a major system, and other property which may be replaced during the service life of the system, including spare parts and replenishment spare parts, but [does] not include packaging or labeling associated with shipment or identification of an item. *Source:* 41 U.S.C. § 108. This definition is used in the statutory statement of technical data policy in 10 U.S.C. § 2320 and 41 U.S.C. § 2302, which applies to TECHNICAL DATA pertaining to "items and processes." However, the DOD data policy in DFARS Subpart 227.71 still refers to "items, components and processes" when describing its applicability. See Nash & Rawicz, INTELLECTUAL PROPERTY IN GOVERNMENT CONTRACTS, chap. 4 (6th ed. 2008).

ITMRA   See INFORMATION TECHNOLOGY MANAGEMENT REFORM ACT.

J

JAG See JUDGE ADVOCATE GENERAL.

JAVITS-WAGNER-O'DAY ACT ("JWOD ACT") An Act, codified at 41 U.S.C. §§ 46–48c, which requires government entities to purchase certain supplies and services from workshops for the blind and other severely disabled people ("sheltered workshops") (See BLIND OR SEVERELY DISABLED), if the supplies or services are available when required. FAR Subpart 8.7 prescribes policies and procedures for implementing the Act following the rules of the Committee for the Purchase from People Who Are Blind Or Severely Disabled, 41 C.F.R. chap. 51. See Cibinic, Nash & Yukins, FORMATION OF GOVERNMENT CONTRACTS 361 (4th ed. 2011).

JEWEL BEARING A piece of synthetic corundum (sapphire or ruby) of any shape, except a phonograph needle, that has one or more polished surfaces to provide supporting surfaces or low-friction contact areas for revolving, oscillating, or sliding parts in an instrument, mechanism, subassembly, or part. The FAR previously required, with certain exceptions, that contractors purchase jewel bearings used in precision instruments and similar equipment acquired under a government contract from the government-owned, contractor-operated William Langer Plant in Rolla, North Dakota. This requirement was removed by Pub. L. No. 104-201, and the plant was given to the city of Rolla subject to the condition that the land and property be used "for economic development relating to the jewel bearing plant." See Cibinic, Nash & Yukins, FORMATION OF GOVERNMENT CONTRACTS 361 (4th ed. 2011).

JOB ORDER An order issued by a contracting agency for work to be performed under the terms and conditions of a BASIC ORDERING AGREEMENT or MASTER AGREEMENT FOR REPAIR AND ALTERATION OF VESSELS. Job orders are usually FIRM-FIXED-PRICE CONTRACTs for specific items of work. FAR 16.703(d) and DFARS 216.703(d) provide guidance on the procedures to be followed in issuing orders under basic ordering agreements. Separate guidance is provided for the issuance of TASK ORDERs and DELIVERY ORDERs.

JOB ORDER CONTRACT (JOC) *Official:* An indefinite-delivery indefinite quantity contract which is awarded on the basis of FULL AND OPEN COMPETITION and EFFECTIVE COMPETITION and is used to execute sustainment, restoration, and modernization projects at installation (post, camp, station) level. The JOC includes a comprehensive collection of detailed repair, maintenance and minor construction task descriptions or specifications, units of measure and pre-established unit prices for each of these discrete tasks. Each project or job ordered under a JOC is normally comprised of a number of pre-described and pre-priced tasks. *Source:* AFARS 5117.9001. The JOC unit prices include direct material, labor and equipment costs, but not indirect costs or profit which are addressed in the coefficient(s). Depending upon the source of the data base used, the Unit Price Base (UPB) may contain from 25,000-90,000 line items. See Farris, *Checking Your Indefinite Delivery/Indefinite Quantity (IDIQ) IQ,* 24 Fall Conslaw 24 (Fall 2002).

JOINT REQUIREMENTS OVERSIGHT COUNCIL (JROC)   A council within DOD which is responsible to the Chairman of the Joint Chiefs of Staff for identifying and assessing the priority of joint military requirements to meet the National Military Strategy. The Vice Chairman of the Joint Chiefs of Staff chairs the JROC and decides all matters before it. The permanent members include the Vice Chiefs of the Army and Air Force, the Vice Chief of Naval Operations, and the Assistant Commandant of the Marine Corps. The JROC directly supports the DEFENSE ACQUISITION BOARD through the review, validation, and approval of key cost, schedule, and performance parameters at the start of the ACQUISITION PROCESS, prior to each milestone review, or as requested by the Under Secretary of Defense for Acquisition and Technology. DAU GLOSSARY.

JOINT VENTURE   A legal entity in the nature of a partnership engaged in the joint prosecution of a particular transaction for mutual profit. It is a business undertaking by two or more persons engaged in a single defined project that requires an express or implied agreement, a common purpose the joint venture is meant to carry out, shared PROFITs and LOSSes, and that each member has equal voice in controlling the project. BLACK'S LAW DICTIONARY 1003 (11th ed. 2019). FAR 9.603 provides that the government will recognize the integrity and validity of joint ventures if the arrangement is identified and fully disclosed to the government. However, they are infrequently used, except in construction contracting and contracts with small businesses. FAR 19.101 sets forth rules for determining whether small business joint ventures cease to meet size standards requirements.

JUDGE ADVOCATE GENERAL (JAG)   A general officer or admiral who is the chief attorney for the Air Force, Army, Coast Guard, or Navy, and the commander of a military service's Judge Advocate General's Corp. Each of the military services also has a general counsel. In the Army and the Air Force, the JAG and the General Counsel share responsibility for procurement issues whereas in the Navy the JAG has no responsibility for procurement issues.

JUDGMENT FUND   A freestanding appropriation used to satisfy specified claims against the government. 31 U.S.C. § 1304. The judgment fund has no time duration or limit on the amount that can be paid. However, it does not cover a contract adjustment negotiated without litigation or the compromise settlement of a Contract Disputes Act claim that is not incorporated into a judgment or a board decision. The judgment fund is used to satisfy judgments or decisions rendered by the COURT OF FEDERAL CLAIMS and the BOARDs OF CONTRACT APPEALS against the government on contractor claims, judgments under the Federal Tort Claims Act, as well as various administrative and Small Claims Act awards against the United States. See CONG. RESEARCH SERV., Report No. R42835, THE JUDGMENT FUND: HISTORY, ADMINISTRATION, AND COMMON USAGE (Mar. 7, 2013).

JUDGMENT IN PRICING   A subjective factor used to estimate the cost of future work by projecting from the FACTs at the time of the estimate to the period of performance of the prospective contract. When a contractor submits CERTIFIED COST OR PRICING

DATA as a part of a contract pricing proposal pursuant to the TRUTH IN NEGOTIA-TIONS ACT (TINA), ¶ I.C.(2)(i) of Table 15-2, Instructions for Submitting Cost/Price Proposals When Certified Cost or Pricing Data Are Required, in FAR15.408, requires the submission of such judgments as part of the proposal. Thus, pricing proposals consist of verifiable facts (cost or pricing data) and judgments. In the application of TINA, it has proved to be very difficult to draw a firm line between facts and judgments. See Manos, 2 GOVERNMENT CONTRACT COSTS & PRICING §§ 84:09–84:13 (2d ed. 2009–2020); Cibinic, Nash & Yukins, FORMATION OF GOVERNMENT CONTRACTS 1494–1512, 1322–28 (4th ed. 2011).

JUDGMENT OF COURT   A decision issued by a court (an individual judge, a panel of judges, or the court sitting *en banc*) that resolves a case, as far as that court is concerned, by ruling on the issue in that case. Judgments of the COURT OF FEDERAL CLAIMS in contract matters are final and binding on the parties unless they are appealed within 60 days. 28 U.S.C. § 2107(b). See Feldman, GOVERNMENT CONTRACT GUIDEBOOK § 24:13 (4th ed. 2019–2020). Judgments of the COURT OF APPEALS FOR THE FEDERAL CIRCUIT are final and binding on the parties unless one of the parties files a petition for a writ of certiorari with the Supreme Court within 90 days. See Feldman, GOVERNMENT CONTRACT GUIDEBOOK § 24:21 (4th ed. 2019–2020).

JURY VERDICT METHOD   A technique used by BOARDs OF CONTRACT APPEALS (BCAs) and courts to arrive at an amount of compensation for a contractual adjustment when incomplete or conflicting evidence has been submitted. It is often viewed as a means of determining the amount in cases of conflicting testimony rather than a method of proof of quantum (see BIFURCATION OF ENTITLEMENT AND QUANTUM). The jury verdict represents a figure that, in the view of the trier of the facts, is fair in light of all the facts of the case or, put another way, is supported by consideration of the entire record. The technique is generally not permissible if the contractor could have collected actual cost information to prove the amount of the adjustment and some BCAs and courts have refused to use the technique when very little or no evidence has been submitted. See Manos, 2 GOVERNMENT CONTRACT COSTS & PRICING § 87:30 (2d ed. 2009–2020); Cibinic, Nagle & Nash, ADMINISTRATION OF GOVERNMENT CONTRACTS 634–40 (5th ed. 2016).

JUSTIFICATION AND APPROVAL (J&A)   The government document required by 10 U.S.C. § 2304(f)(1) and 41 U.S.C. § 3304(3) when an agency is going to award a contract without providing for FULL AND OPEN COMPETITION. In such a case, the contracting officer must justify the action in writing, certify the accuracy and completeness of the justification, and obtain the approval of appropriate individuals. FAR 6.303-1. The justification may be prepared and approved following CONTRACT AWARD in situations of UNUSUAL OR COMPELLING URGENCY if prior preparation and approval would have unreasonably delayed the acquisition. FAR 6.302-2 and 6.303-1(e). Justifications must (1) identify the agency, the contracting activity, the action being approved, the supplies or services sought, and the statutory authority permitting the action; (2) demonstrate that the proposed contractor's unique qualifications or the nature of the acquisition require the action; (3) describe efforts made to ensure that offers were solicited from as many potential sources as practicable; (4) determine that the anticipated cost will be fair and reasonable; (5) describe market surveys conducted; and (6) describe any other facts supporting the use of OTHER THAN FULL AND OPEN COMPETITION. FAR 6.303-2. Depending on the size and nature of the contract, justifications must be approved in writing by an official at a level above the contracting officer, by the COMPETITION ADVOCATE for the procuring activity, or by the SENIOR PROCUREMENT EXECUTIVE of the government agency conducting the acquisition. FAR 6.304. Justifications must be made available for public inspection and posted on SAM as required by 10 U.S.C. § 2304(l) and 41 U.S.C. § 3304(f). FAR 6.305. See Feldman, GOVERNMENT CONTRACT AWARDS: NEGOTIATION AND SEALED BIDDING § 3:47 (2019–2020 ed.); Cibinic, Nash & Yukins, FORMATION OF GOVERNMENT CONTRACTS 286–88 (4th ed. 2011).

JWOD   See JAVITS-WAGNER O'DAY ACT.

JWOD PARTICIPATING NONPROFIT AGENCIES   A qualified nonprofit agency employing people who are blind or who have other severe disabilities approved by the Committee for the Purchase from People Who Are Blind Or Severely Disabled, an independent government activity with members appointed by the President, to produce a commodity for or provide a service to the government under the JAVITS-WAGNER-O'DAY ACT, 41 U.S.C. §§ 8501–06. Such agencies are given preference for some procurements in accordance with the procedures in FAR Subpart 8.7.

K

KEY PERFORMANCE PARAMETER (KPP) "An attribute or characteristic of a system that is critical or essential to the development of an effective military capability and those attributes that make a significant contribution to the characteristics of a future joint force as defined in the *Capstone Concept for Joint Operations." Department of Defense Handbook, Systems Requirements Document Guidance* [MIL-HDBK-520 (USAF)] (2010). See also DAU GLOSSARY. For example, the joint key performance parameters of the F-35 Joint Strike Fighter were (a) radio frequency signature, (b) combat radius, (c) sortie generation, (d) logistics footprint, (e) mission reliability, and (f) interoperability. Key performance parameters are assigned two numerical values: (a) the threshold value and (b) the objective value. The threshold value is the lowest (minimum) value that is acceptable, because it is essential to acceptable system performance. The objective value is the value desired by the system user.

KEY PERSONNEL Contractor personnel that are evaluated in the source selection process and that may be required to be used in the performance of a contract by a Key Personnel clause. See, for example, NFS 1852.235-71. A CONTRACTING ACTIVITY uses such clauses to ensure that in performing the contract the winning contractor will not use personnel less qualified than those described and evaluated in the winning proposal. Such clauses generally permit substitution of personnel with the approval of the CONTRACTING OFFICER. When key personnel are used as an EVALUATION FACTOR in BEST VALUE PROCUREMENTs, offerors can be rejected if they do not have firm commitments from the persons that are listed in the proposal. See Feldman, GOVERNMENT CONTRACT AWARDS: NEGOTIATION AND SEALED BIDDING § 10:26 (2019–2020 ed.); Cibinic, Nash & Yukins, FORMATION OF GOVERNMENT CONTRACTS 827–28 (4th ed. 2011). See also Edwards, *Evaluating Key Personnel: The Importance Of Letters Of Commitment Or Intent*, 19 N&CR ¶ 31 (June 2005); Nash, *Key Personnel: Evaluation Factors And/Or Promises?*, 18 N&CR ¶ 47 (Nov. 2004).

KICKBACK *Official:* Any money, fee, commission, credit, gift, GRATUITY, thing of value, or compensation of any kind which is provided, directly or indirectly, to any PRIME CONTRACTOR, prime contractor employee, SUBCONTRACTOR, or subcontractor employee for the purpose of improperly obtaining or rewarding favorable treatment in connection with a prime contract or in connection with a subcontract relating to a prime contract. *Source:* FAR 3.502-1. Kickbacks have been prohibited by statute for many years, but new legislation was enacted in the ANTI-KICKBACK ACT OF 1986. See Manos, 3 GOVERNMENT CONTRACT COSTS AND PRICING §§ 91:22–91:24 (2d ed. 2009–2020); Cibinic, Nagle & Nash, ADMINISTRATION OF GOVERNMENT CONTRACTS 105 (5th ed. 2016); Cibinic, Nash & Yukins,

FORMATION OF GOVERNMENT CONTRACTS 174–75 (4th ed. 2011). Kickbacks by construction workers to contractors and subcontractors are prohibited by the COPELAND ANTI-KICKBACK ACT.

KNOW HOW   Special knowledge that permits a person to manufacture a product or perform a process or service in an effective manner. While such knowledge would frequently be a TRADE SECRET, this slang expression can include more elementary types of knowledge that may not meet the requirements of trade secret law.

L

LABOR Effort expended by people in exchange for wages or salary. DIRECT LABOR is one of the principal breakdowns used in costing, pricing, and profit determination. Indirect labor is an element of INDIRECT COST. FAR Part 22 sets forth the policies of the government regarding the application of labor laws to the ACQUISITION PROCESS. Subjects treated include convict labor (FAR Subpart 22.2); the CONTRACT WORK HOURS AND SAFETY STANDARDS ACT (FAR Subpart 22.3); the DAVIS-BACON ACT (FAR 22.403-1, 22.404); the COPELAND ANTI-KICKBACK ACT (FAR 22.403-2); the WALSH-HEALEY PUBLIC CONTRACTS ACT (FAR Subpart 22.6); EQUAL EMPLOYMENT OPPORTUNITY (FAR Subpart 22.8); the SERVICE CONTRACT ACT OF 1965 (FAR Subpart 22.10); and employment of the handicapped (FAR Subpart 22.14).

LABOR-HOUR CONTRACT A type of contract calling for the contractor to be paid for labor at fixed hourly rates for specified classes of LABOR. FAR 16.602 states that this is a type of TIME-AND-MATERIALS CONTRACT differing only in that materials are not supplied by the contractor. The hourly rate includes wages, overhead (see INDIRECT COST), GENERAL AND ADMINISTRATIVE EXPENSE, and PROFIT. FAR 16.602 states that the limitations on the use of time-and-materials contracts also apply to labor-hour contracts. FAR 12.207(b) provides detailed procedures that must be followed when labor-hour contracts are used to acquire COMMERCIAL ITEMs. See Feldman, GOVERNMENT CONTRACT AWARDS: NEGOTIATION AND SEALED BIDDING § 4:27 (2019–2020 ed.); Cibinic, Nash & Yukins, FORMATION OF GOVERNMENT CONTRACTS 1319–26 (4th ed. 2011).

LABOR RELATIONS The process of dealing with employees. FAR 31.205-21 states that the costs incurred by a contractor in conducting labor relations are ALLOWABLE COSTs. See Manos, 1 GOVERNMENT CONTRACT COSTS AND PRICING §§ 28:1–28:3 (2d ed. 2009–2020); Cibinic, Knight & Nash, COST-REIMBURSEMENT CONTRACTING 692 (4th ed. 2014). FAR 22.101-1 establishes the basic policy of procuring agencies to remain impartial concerning any dispute between LABOR and contractor management. It also states that government agencies should maintain sound relations with industry and labor to keep abreast of events that might adversely affect the government ACQUISITION PROCESS and to ensure that the government obtains needed supplies and services without DELAY. DFARS Part 222.1 and DOD PGI 222.101 provide guidance for when labor relations impact defense programs.

LABOR SURPLUS AREA (LSA) *Official:* A geographical area identified by the Department of Labor in accordance with 20 C.F.R. part 654, subpart A, as an area of concentrated unemployment or underemployment or an area of labor surplus. *Source:* FAR 2.101. 20 C.F.R. § 654.5 states that the basic criteria for a LSA is (1) an unemployment rate at least 120% of the national average unemployment rate for civilian workers, or (2) an unemployment rate of 10% or higher.

LABOR SURPLUS AREA CONCERN   *Official:* A concern that together with its first-tier subcontractors will perform substantially in LABOR SURPLUS AREAs (LSAs). Performance is substantially in LSAs if the cost incurred under the contract on account of manufacturing, production, or performance of appropriate services in LSAs exceed 50 % of the contract price. *Source:* FAR 2.101. In the case of equal low bid among SMALL BUSINESS CONCERNS, awards are required to be made first to small business concerns which are also labor surplus area concerns. FAR 19.202-3. Previously, LSA concerns received greater benefits such as price preferences and set-asides, but these were repealed with the Federal Acquisition Streamlining Act (FASA) of 1994. See Luckey, Cong. Research Serv., Report No. R41115, Location-Based Preferences in Federal and Federally Funded Contracting: An Overview of the Law (Oct. 1, 2010).

LABORERS OR MECHANICS   *Official:* (i) Workers, utilized by a contractor or subcontractor at any tier, whose duties are manual or physical in nature (including those workers who use tools or who are performing the work of a trade), as distinguished from mental or managerial; (ii) Apprentices, trainees, helpers, and, in the case of contracts subject to the CONTRACT WORK HOURS AND SAFETY STANDARDS ACT, watchmen and guards; (iii) Working foremen who devote more than 20% of their time during a workweek performing the duties of a laborer or mechanic, and who do not meet the criteria of 29 C.F.R. part 541, for the time so spent; and (iv) Every person performing the duties of a laborer or mechanic, regardless of any contractual relationship alleged to exist between the contractor and those individuals; and Does not include workers whose duties are primarily executive, supervisory (except as provided in paragraph (iii) of this definition), administrative, or clerical, rather than manual. Persons employed in a bona fide executive, administrative, or professional capacity as defined in 29 C.F.R. part 541 are not deemed to be laborers or mechanics. *Source:* FAR 22.401. The DAVIS-BACON ACT requires that construction contractors and subcontractors pay this class of workers the PREVAILING WAGE RATE in the locality. FAR 22.403-1. The Contract Work Hours and Safety Standards Act requires the payment of time-and-a-half wages for this class of workers if they work more than 40 hours in a workweek. FAR 22.403-3.

LAST IN, FIRST OUT (LIFO)   An INVENTORY costing method in which sales are recorded as having been made from the most recently acquired stock, leaving the earliest acquired items in stock. The LIFO method attempts to match the most recent costs of acquiring inventory with sales. CAS 411, Accounting for Acquisition Cost of Material, 48 C.F.R. § 9904.411, identifies LIFO as one of the inventory cost methods that a contractor must use in accounting for ACQUISITION COSTs of material.

LATE BID   A bid received in the office designated in the INVITATION FOR BIDS after the exact time for BID OPENING. FAR 14.304(b). A late bid, late modification of a bid, or late withdrawal of a bid will not be considered unless it is received before CONTRACT AWARD, and then only if the bid was (1) transmitted through an electronic commerce method authorized by the SOLICITATION and received by the government not later than 5:00 p.m. one working day before the date set for receipt of bids, or (2) received by the government installation designated for receipt of bids and was under the government's control prior to the time set for receipt of bids. Acceptable evidence of the time of receipt of bids includes the date/time stamp at the government installation, other documentary evidence maintained by the installation or a statement of a government employee. See Feldman, GOVERNMENT CONTRACT AWARDS: NEGOTIATION AND SEALED BIDDING § 27:12 (2019–2020 ed.).

LATE PROPOSAL   An offer received in the office designated in the REQUEST FOR PROPOSALS after the exact date specified for receipt of proposals. FAR 15.208(b). A late offer, late modification of an offer, late FINAL PROPOSAL REVISION, or late withdrawal of an offer will not be considered unless it is received before CONTRACT AWARD, and then only if the offer was (1) transmitted through an electronic commerce method authorized by the SOLICITATION and received by the government not later than 5:00 p.m. one working day before the date set for receipt of bids, (2) received by the government installation designated for receipt of bids and was under the government's control prior to the time set for receipt of bids, (3) was the only proposal received, or (4) delayed due to an emergency or unanticipated event which interrupts normal government processes. The late proposal rule is strictly enforced. Acceptable evidence of the time of receipt of proposals includes the date/time stamp at the government installation, other documentary evidence maintained by the installation or a statement of a government employee. Inconsistent decisions by the GAO and Court of Federal Claims in cases involving electronically submitted proposals have created confusion as to whether submission occurs when an email is received in the appropriate inbox or on the government server. In addition, the Court of Federal Claims has held that submission of a late proposal is equivalent to no proposal, leaving a contractor with a late submission no standing to make a bid protest. *Labatt Food Service v. United States*, 577 F.3d 1375, 1381 (Fed. Cir. 2009). See Feldman, GOVERNMENT CONTRACT AWARDS: NEGOTIATION AND SEALED BIDDING, chap. 8 (2019–2020 ed.).

LATENT   Not readily discoverable by observation or INSPECTION; hidden or concealed. "Latent" can refer to a type of deficiency potentially found in solicitations or contracts (a latent AMBIGUITY) or in contract performance (LATENT DEFECT). "Latent" is an antonym of PATENT.

LATENT AMBIGUITY   See AMBIGUITY.

LATENT DEFECT (1)   *Official:* A defect that exists at the time of acceptance but cannot be discovered by the use of a reasonable INSPECTION. *Source:* FAR 2.101. This definition refers to defects in the work performed by a contractor. Such latent defects overcome the finality of acceptance in the Inspection of Supplies—Fixed-Price clause, FAR 52.246-2, and the Inspection of Construction clause, FAR 52.246-12. See Cibinic, Nash & Nagle, ADMINISTRATION OF GOVERNMENT CONTRACTS 763–66 (5th ed. 2016). **(2)** A defect in the contract specifications or drawings that is not readily discoverable by offerors at the time they submit their bids or proposals. Contractors are entitled to compensation for such defects under the government's IMPLIED WARRANTY OF SPECIFICATIONS because they are not required to perform an analysis of the accuracy of the specifications and drawings at the time of computing their bid or offer. On the other hand, they cannot recover for defects that are obvious. See Cibinic, Nagle & Nash, ADMINISTRATION OF GOVERNMENT CONTRACTS 251–66 (5th ed. 2016); Nash, *Patent Defects vs. Patent Ambiguities: There's a Big Difference*, 18 N&CR ¶ 45 (Oct. 2004).

LEADER-COMPANY CONTRACTING   An acquisition technique used to establish a SEC-OND SOURCE for a product that is being or has been developed by a single contractor. It is often called "leader/follower" procurement. FAR 17.401 states that leader-company contracting is an extraordinary acquisition technique used only in special circumstances. Under this technique, a developer or sole producer of a product or system is designated to be the leader company and to furnish assistance and know-how to one or more designated follower companies, which subsequently become sources of supply. Leader-company contracting is intended to do one or more of the following: (1) reduce delivery time; (2) achieve geographic dispersion of suppliers; (3) maximize use of scarce tooling and equipment; (4) ensure uniformity and reliability in equipment, compatibility or standardization of components, and interchangeability of parts; (5) eliminate problems in use of PROPRIETARY DATA; and (6) facilitate the transition from development to production to subsequent competitive acquisition of end items or major components. FAR 17.401. Leader-company contracting should be used only when (1) the leader company has the necessary production know-how, (2) no other source can meet the government's requirements without assistance from a leader company, (3) the assistance is limited to that which is essential to produce the item, and (4) its use is authorized in accordance with agency procedures. FAR 17.402. This technique is unpopular with leader companies because it requires them to foster their own competition. See Feldman, GOVERNMENT CONTRACT AWARDS: NEGOTIATION AND SEALED BIDDING § 5:14 (2019–2020 ed.); Nash & Rawicz, INTELLECTUAL PROPERTY IN GOVERNMENT CONTRACTS, chap. 8 (6th ed. 2008).

LEADER/FOLLOWER   See LEADER-COMPANY CONTRACTING.

LEARNING CURVE   A technique for projecting the amount of direct LABOR that will be used to manufacture a product on a repetitive basis. The learning curve concept originated in the observation that organizations performing repetitive tasks tend to exhibit a rate of improvement due to increased manual dexterity and improved manufacturing methodology. (Thus, it is more aptly called an "improvement curve.") Learning or improvement curve theories include the "Boeing" or "unit curve" theory and the "Northrop" or "cumulative average" theory. The Boeing theory holds that as the total quantity of units produced doubles, the cost per unit decreases by some constant percentage (the rate of learning). The Northrop theory holds that as the total quantity of units produced doubles, the *average* cost per unit decreases by some constant percentage (the rate of learning). See DAU, *Contract Pricing Reference Guides* v. II (Feb. 22, 2012).

LEASE   A contract with the owner of real or personal property to permit another party to use that property for a specified period of time. Leases are contracts subject to the CONTRACT DISPUTES ACT OF 1978. 41 U.S.C. § 7102. FAR Subpart 7.4 provides guidance on the decision of a contracting officer whether to lease rather than purchase equipment. FAR Subpart 8.11 provides guidance on leasing of motor vehicles. See RENTAL COSTS for the treatment of the costs incurred by a contractor for leases.

LEGAL FEES   The amount paid to a lawyer for professional services. FAR 31.205-47 sets forth detailed rules governing whether such fees paid by contractors are ALLOWABLE COSTs. Generally, such fees are allowable when incurred in performing normal functions required for the performance or termination of a contract, but are unallowable in the PROSECUTION OF CLAIMS and in the defense of a number of specified claims. See Manos, 2 GOVERNMENT COST AND PRICING §§ 54:1–54:11 (2d ed. 2009–2020). However, small businesses can recover legal fees for prosecution of claims under the EQUAL ACCESS TO JUSTICE ACT (EAJA).

LEGAL PROCEEDING *Official:* Any civil judicial proceeding to which the government is a party or any criminal proceeding. The term includes appeals from such proceedings. *Source:* FAR 9.403. When an agency is considering whether to SUSPEND a contractor that has not been indicted and the contractor submits evidence that raises a genuine dispute over the facts, the agency must afford the contractor an opportunity to appear with counsel to present its position unless the Department of Justice advises that the government's position would be compromised in a pending or contemplated legal proceeding. FAR 9.407-3(b)(2). FAR 31.205-47 makes the costs of legal and other proceedings (see LEGAL PROCEEDING COSTS) unallowable unless specific conditions are met. Legal proceedings for which costs are unallowable include criminal proceedings, civil proceedings for FRAUD or similar misconduct, DEBARMENT and SUSPENSION proceedings, prosecution or defense of contract CLAIMs, merger and reorganization proceedings, antitrust suits (see ANTITRUST VIOLATIONS), and WHISTLEBLOWER suits.

LEGAL PROCEEDING COSTS *Official:* The costs incurred in LEGAL PROCEEDINGs including, but not limited to, administrative and clerical expenses; the cost of legal services, whether performed by in-house or private counsel; the cost of the services of accountants, consultants, or others retained by the contractor to assist it; the cost of employees, officers, and directors; and any similar costs that bear a direct relationship to the proceedings. *Source:* FAR 31.205-47. This cost principle was written with this broad definition to ensure that the full costs of legal proceedings were UNALLOWABLE COSTs when the proceeding fell within its coverage. See Cibinic, Knight & Nash, Cost-Reimbursement Contracting 694–96 (4th ed. 2014); Manos, *Allowability Of Legal Costs/Edition III*, Briefing Papers No. 16-13 (Dec. 2016); Willard, *Allowability of Legal Costs*, Briefing Papers No. 10-5 (Apr. 2010).

LETTER CONTRACT *Official:* A written preliminary contractual instrument that authorizes the contractor to begin immediately manufacturing supplies and performing services. *Source:* FAR 16.603-1. Letter contracts are a means of permitting contractors to commence work when the parties are unable to negotiate a firm contract. The Congressional term for letter contracts is UNDEFINITIZED CONTRACT ACTIONs. They are strongly disfavored (10 U.S.C. § 2326 places restrictions on their use) and may not be used unless the HEAD OF THE CONTRACTING ACTIVITY or a designee determines that no other instrument is suitable. FAR 16.603-3. A letter contract must specify the maximum liability of the government and must be superseded by a definitive contract within a specified time. Letter contracts contain a negotiated definitization schedule including (1) dates for submission of the contractor's price proposal and related information; (2) a date for the start of negotiations; and (3) a target date for definitization, which should be either within 180 days after the date of the letter contract or before completion of 40% of the work to be performed, whichever occurs first. FAR 16.603-2. See the Contract Definitization clause in FAR 52.216-25. The DOD follows DFARS 217.7404-3(a) to establish a definitization schedule, which requires definitization within 180 days after receipt of a qualified proposal or when the amount of obligated funds is more than 50% of the not-to-exceed price. See Feldman, Government Contract Awards: Negotiation and Sealed Bidding § 4:28 (2019-2020 ed.).

LETTER OF CREDIT An instrument, issued by a bank or other financing institution, permitting the government to withdraw funds up to a specified amount if a contractor does not meet its obligations under a contract. Contractors required to submit PERFORMANCE BONDs and PAYMENT BONDs on contracts over $150,000 can furnish bonds secured by IRREVOCABLE LETTERs OF CREDIT. FAR 28.204-3. For construction contracts from $35,000 to $150,000, FAR 28.102-1 permits the use of an irrevocable letter of credit to provide payment protection.

LETTER OF INTENT   A letter customarily employed as a preliminary understanding of parties that intend to enter into a contract. BLACK'S LAW DICTIONARY 1088 (11th ed. 2019). In government procurement, such instruments take the form of LETTER CONTRACTs in almost all cases.

LETTER OF OFFER AND ACCEPTANCE (LOA)   The instrument that creates a contractual relationship between the U.S. Government and a foreign purchaser in a FOREIGN MILITARY SALES transaction. The LOA lists supplies or services to be purchased, estimated costs, terms and conditions of the transaction, and payment schedules. The purchaser, an authorized representative of the foreign government, must sign, date, and return the LOA before its expiration date. If the LOA is implemented, it becomes official tender. See DOD 5105.38-M, *Security Assistance Management Manual*, chap. 5; DFARS 225.7301.

LETTER OF REQUEST (LOR)   The instrument used as the first step in initiating a FOREIGN MILITARY SALES transaction. The LOR is used to request defense articles and services, as well as planning and review data, price and availability data, or an actual LETTER OF OFFER AND ACCEPTANCE. It includes a statement of what is desired, with sufficient detail to enable DOD or another agency to provide a firm basis for a price estimate. The foreign government forwards the LOR through the U.S. Embassy, the designated Security Assistance Office, or the foreign government's in-country representative in the United States. See DOD 5105.38-M, *Security Assistance Management Manual*, chap. 5.

LEVEL OF CONFIDENCE ASSESSMENT RATING (LOCAR)   A technique used in SOURCE SELECTION to evaluate risk. It entails developing a numerical or adjectival adjustment factor based on assessments of offeror capability criteria such as experience, past performance, and key personnel, and applying it to source selection numerical scores or adjectival ratings. The product of that application is a risk-adjusted score or rating that reflects the expected value of the offeror's promises in light of its assessed capability. See Edwards, SOURCE SELECTION ANSWER BOOK 98 (2d ed. 2006). For examples of actual use see *AdapTech General Scientific*, Comp. Gen. Dec. B-293867, 2004 CPD ¶ 126 and *Colmek Systems Engineering*, Comp. Gen. Dec. B-291931.2, 2003 CPD ¶ 123.

LEVEL-OF-EFFORT CONTRACT   A type of contract stating the work in terms of an amount of effort (usually labor-hours or labor-years) to be performed by specified classes of employees over a given period of time. There are four types of level-of-effort contracts: the FIXED-PRICE LEVEL-OF-EFFORT CONTRACT, the TIME-AND-MATERIALS CONTRACT, the LABOR-HOUR CONTRACT, and the TERM CONTRACT. See Feldman, GOVERNMENT CONTRACT AWARDS: NEGOTIATION AND SEALED BIDDING § 4:12 (2019–2020 ed.).

LIABILITIES   Obligations of a business that have been incurred but not yet paid, such as notes payable and accounts payable. A company's BALANCE SHEET lists all ASSETs and liabilities in order to show the company's NET WORTH.

LICENSE   A legal instrument granting permission to do a particular thing, to exercise a certain privilege, to carry on a particular business, or to pursue a certain occupation. When granted by an appropriate government body, licenses are permits allowing a person, firm, or corporation to pursue some occupation or business, subject to regulation. BLACK'S LAW DICTIONARY 1104 (11th ed. 2019). Under the Permits and Responsibilities clause in FAR 52.236-7, construction contractors bear the responsibility for obtaining necessary licenses and permits and complying with any federal, state, and municipal laws, codes, and regulations applicable to the performance of the work on fixed-price construction or dismantling, demolition, or removal-of-improvements contracts. FAR 36.507. The TECHNICAL DATA and COMPUTER SOFTWARE policies of the government give the government a license (of varying scope depending on the circumstances) to use the data and software. See DFARS 227.7103-4; DFARS 227.7203-4. See also UNLIMITED RIGHTS; LIMITED RIGHTS; RESTRICTED RIGHTS; GOVERNMENT-PURPOSE RIGHTS. The standard Patents Rights clauses in FAR 52.227-11 and DFARS 252.227-7038 give the government a royalty-free license to use INVENTIONS made under the contract. See PATENT RIGHTS; PATENT LICENSE.

LICENSE RIGHTS   See GOVERNMENT-PURPOSE LICENSE RIGHTS; GOVERNMENT-PURPOSE RIGHTS; DIRECT LICENSE.

LICENSE TO USE INVENTION   See PATENT LICENSE.

LIFE-CYCLE COST   For a defense acquisition program, LCC consists of research and development (R&D) costs, investment costs, operating and support costs, and disposal costs over the entire life cycle. These costs include not only the direct costs of the acquisition program, but also include indirect costs that logically would be attributed to the program. In this way, all costs that are logically attributed to the program are included, regardless of funding source or management control. DAU GLOSSARY. See the DOD 5000 Series. See also DEFENSE ACQUISITION GUIDEBOOK, *Life-Cycle Cost Analysis*.

LIFE CYCLE MANAGEMENT [1]   A management process applied throughout the life of a system that bases all programmatic decisions on the anticipated mission-related and economic benefits derived over the life of the system. It includes the implementation, management, and oversight by the designated Program Manager (PM) of all activities associated with the acquisition, development, production, fielding, sustainment, and disposal of a DoD system across its life cycle. DAU GLOSSARY. **[2]** The designated program manager's implementation, management, and oversight of all activities associated with the acquisition, development, production, fielding, sustainment, and disposal of a DoD system across its life cycle. Under Life Cycle Management, the Program Manager, with support from the Product Support Manager for sustainment activities, is responsible for the development and documentation of an acquisition strategy to guide program execution from program initiation through re-procurement of systems, subsystems, components, spares, and services beyond the initial production contract award, during post-production support, and through retirement or disposal. DOD PRODUCT SUPPORT MANAGER GUIDEBOOK (Dec. 2019), para. 1.2.

LIFE CYCLE SUSTAINMENT   Translates force provider capability and performance requirements into tailored product support to achieve specified and evolving life cycle product support availability, reliability, and affordability parameters. Life cycle sustainment considerations include supply, maintenance, transportation, sustaining engineering, data management, Configuration Management (CM), Human Systems Integration (HSI), environment, safety (including explosives), and occupational health, protection of critical program information and anti-tamper provisions, supportability, and interoperability. Initially begun during Materiel Solution Analysis (MSA) phase and matured during the Technology Development (TD) phase, life cycle sustainment planning spans a system's entire life cycle from MSA phase to disposal. *Source*: DAU Glossary.

LIMITATION OF COST (LOC) CLAUSE   A key clause used in all fully funded COST-REIMBURSEMENT CONTRACTs to meet the requirements of the ANTI-DEFICIENCY ACT by limiting the OBLIGATION of the government to an amount no greater than the contract's ESTIMATED COST plus any required FEE, unless the contract is modified to state a greater amount. FAR 32.705-2(a). The clause requires the contractor to notify the contracting officer, in writing, whenever the contractor has reason to believe that (1) the costs the contractor expects to incur under the contract within a specified period (usually one to three months), when added to all costs previously incurred, will exceed a specified percentage (usually 75 to 85%) of the estimated cost; or (2) the total cost for the performance of the contract, exclusive of fee, will be either greater or substantially less than had been previously estimated. In the absence of the specified notice, the government is not obligated to reimburse the contractor for any costs in excess of the estimated cost specified in the schedule. FAR 32.704. The clause obligates the contractor to use its BEST EFFORTS to perform the work specified and all obligations under the contract within the estimated cost but provides that the contractor has no further obligation until the estimated cost is increased. The basic clause is set forth in FAR 52.232-20. See Manos, 2 GOVERNMENT COST AND PRICING § 85:7 (2d ed. 2009–2020); Cibinic, Knight & Nash, COST-REIMBURSEMENT CONTRACTING 763–64 (4th ed. 2014).

LIMITATION OF FUNDS (LOF) CLAUSE   A clause used in all incrementally funded COST-REIMBURSEMENT CONTRACTs. FAR 32.705-2(b). This type of clause prevents a violation of the ANTI-DEFICIENCY ACT by avoiding governmental open-ended liability. The clause requires the contractor to notify the contracting officer in writing when it appears that additional funds must be allotted to the contract to complete performance. The clause is set forth in FAR 52.232-22. The LOF clause and the LIMITATION OF COST CLAUSE are the basis for the contractor's freedom from performance risks. Even if the contract contains a completion-type STATEMENT OF WORK, with definitive performance requirements and fixed performance dates, these clauses operate to relieve the contractor from any legal obligation to complete the work when the funds are exhausted. See Manos, 2 GOVERNMENT CONTRACT COSTS & PRICING § 85:7 (2d ed. 2009–2020); Cibinic, Knight & Nash, COST-REIMBURSEMENT CONTRACTS 764-66 (4th ed. 2014).

LIMITATION OF GOVERNMENT'S OBLIGATION (LOGO) CLAUSE   A clause used by DOD in all incrementally fixed-price contracts. DFARS 232.705-70. This type of clause prevents a violation of the ANTI-DEFICIENCY ACT by avoiding governmental open-ended liability. The clause requires the contractor to notify the contracting officer in writing when it appears that additional funds must be allotted to the contract to complete performance. The clause also contains a prospective schedule providing the dates and amounts of funds that the parties contemplate will be allotted to the contract. The clause is set forth in DFARs 252.232-7007.

LIMITED RIGHTS   (1) Under the FAR: *Official:* The right of the government to reproduce and use TECHNICAL DATA with the express limitation that they will not, without written permission of the contractor, be used for purposes of manufacture nor disclosed outside the government; except that the government may disclose these data outside the government for the following purposes, if any; provided that the government makes such disclosure subject to prohibition against further use and disclosure. [*Agencies may list additional purposes as set forth in 27.404-2(c)(1) or if none, so* state]. *Source:* The Rights in Data—General clause in FAR 52.227-14. (2) Under the DFARS: Official: The rights to use, modify, reproduce, release, perform, display, or disclose technical data, in whole or in part, within the government. The government may not, without the written permission of the party asserting limited rights, release or disclose the technical data outside the government, use the technical data for manufacture, or authorize the technical data to be used by another party, except that the government may reproduce, release, or disclose such data or authorize the use or reproduction of the data by persons outside the government if—(i) The reproduction, release, disclosure, or use is—(A) Necessary for emergency repair and overhaul; or (B) A release or disclosure to—(1) A covered government support contractor, for use, modification, reproduction, performance, display, or release or disclosure to authorized person(s) in performance of a Government contract; or (2) A foreign government, of technical data other than detailed manufacturing or process data, when use of such data by the foreign government is in the interest of the government and is required for evaluational or informational purposes; (ii) The recipient of the technical data is subject to a prohibition on the further reproduction, release, disclosure, or use of the technical data; and (iii) The contractor or subcontractor asserting the restriction is notified of such reproduction, release, disclosure, or use. *Source:* The Rights in Technical Data—Noncommercial Items clause in DFARS 252.227-7013. Although the clause has not been updated, 10 U.S.C. § 2320 has been amended to require that LIMITED RIGHTS DATA be available to other contractors when it constitutes INTERFACE DATA necessary for "segregation" and "reintegration" of components of a system that are furnished with limited rights and components that are covered by unlimited rights or government purpose rights. 10 U.S.C. § 129d also requires that such data be available to "litigation support contractors" before or during litigation. These limited rights are basically designed to give the contractor protection against use of data DEVELOPED AT PRIVATE EXPENSE (FAR policy) or DEVELOPED EXCLUSIVELY AT PRIVATE EXPENSE (DOD policy) by competitors. See Nash & Rawicz, INTELLECTUAL PROPERTY IN GOVERNMENT CONTRACTS, chap. 4 (6th ed. 2008).

LIMITED RIGHTS DATA   *Official:* DATA (other than COMPUTER SOFTWARE) that embody TRADE SECRETs or are commercial or financial and confidential or privileged, to the extent that such data pertain to items, components, or processes DEVELOPED AT PRIVATE EXPENSE, including minor modifications thereof. *Source:* FAR 27.401. The FAR also contains an alternative, general definition that may be used in contracts for research work: "Data (other than computer software) developed at private expense that embody trade secrets or are commercial or financial and confidential or privileged." See FAR 27.404-2(b). Under the Rights in Data—General clause at FAR 52.227-14, the contractor may protect qualifying limited rights data and restricted computer software by withholding them from delivery to the government and delivering FORM, FIT, AND FUNCTION DATA instead. However, the government may use Alternate II to this clause requiring the delivery of limited rights data with appropriate legends. This term is not used in the DOD technical data regulation in DFARS Subpart 227.71.

LINE ITEM   See CONTRACT LINE ITEMS.

LIQUIDATED DAMAGES An express provision in a contract stating a sum for which one of the parties will be liable upon BREACH OF CONTRACT or failure to perform. FAR Subpart 11.5 contains the policies and procedures governing the use of liquidated damages to cover late performance of government contracts. FAR 11.502 states that liquidated damages clauses should be used only when both (1) the time of delivery or performance is such an important factor that the government can reasonably expect to suffer damage if delivery or performance is delinquent, and (2) the extent or amount of damage would be difficult or impossible to ascertain or prove. The rate of liquidated damages used must be reasonable because liquidated damages fixed without any reference to probable actual damages may be held to be a PENALTY and, therefore, unenforceable. In construction contracts, liquidated damages should be assessed for each day of DELAY; and the rate should, at a minimum, cover (1) the estimated cost of INSPECTION and superintendence for each day of delay in completion; and (2) specific losses due to the failure to complete the work, such as the cost of substitute FACILITIES, RENTAL COSTS, or continued payment of quarters allowance. FAR 11.502(b). 15 U.S.C. § 637(d)(4)(F) allows a CONTRACTING OFFICER to assess liquidated damages when a contractor fails to make a good-faith effort to comply with a subcontracting plan. FAR 19.705-7. See issued by the DOL, must be included in construction contracts for such projects. FAR 22.404-2. See Feldman, Government Contract Guidebook §§ 29:17–29:28 (4th ed. 2019–2020); Cibinic, Nagle & Nash, Administration of Government Contracts 919–38 (5th ed. 2016). See also Ewald, et al., *Contesting and Defending Liquidated Damages Provisions*, Constr. Briefings 2005-5 (May 2005).

LIST OF PARTIES EXCLUDED FROM PROCUREMENT AND NOPROCUREMENT PROGRAMS A list (formerly referred to as the Consolidated List of Debarred, Suspended and Ineligible Contractors), which contained the names of contractors proposed for DEBARMENT, debarred, or suspended (see SUSPENSION) by agencies, as well as contractors declared ineligible under other statutory or regulatory authority. This list was compiled, maintained, and distributed by the General Services Administration. It has been replaced by the electronic SAM Exclusions list in accordance with FAR 9.404.

LOADED LABOR RATE An hourly billing rate used in a contract that includes the contractor's direct costs, indirect costs, and profit. A loaded labor rate is a unit price for labor but it does not have the same effect as a FIRM-FIXED-PRICE CONTRACT because the contractor does not agree to perform a specified amount of work for the hours billed to the government.

LOADED HOURLY RATE See LOADED LABOR RATE.

LOAN GUARANTEE See GUARANTEED LOAN.

LOBBYING ACT See ANTI-LOBBYING ACT.

LOBBYING COSTS Costs incurred by a contractor to influence the outcome of legislation. Legislative lobbying costs are considered UNALLOWABLE COSTs if associated with any of the following: (1) attempts to influence the outcome of a federal, state, or local election, referendum, initiative, or similar procedure, through contributions, endorsements, publicity, or similar activities; (2) establishing, administering, contributing to, or paying the expenses of a political party, political campaign, or political action committee; (3) any attempt to influence the introduction of federal, state, or local legislation, or the enactment or modification of any pending federal, state, or local legislation (a) through communication with a member or employee of Congress or a state legislature, or with a government official or employee in connection with a decision to sign or veto enrolled legislation, (b) by preparing, distributing, or using publicity or propaganda, or (c) by urging the public to contribute to or participate in a mass demonstration, march, rally, fund-raising drive, lobbying campaign, or letter-writing or telephone campaign; (4) legislative liaison activities, gathering information regarding legislation, and analyzing the effect of legislation, when such activities are in support of, or in knowing preparation for, an effort to engage in unallowable activities, or (5) costs incurred in attempting to improperly influence an officer of the Executive Branch to give consideration to a regulatory or contract matter. FAR 31.205-22(a). Lobbying costs are considered ALLOWABLE COSTs, however, if they involve (1) presentation of technical and factual information on a topic directly related to contract performance, (2) efforts to influence state legislation to directly reduce contract cost or avoid impairment of contract performance, and (3) any activity specifically authorized by statute to be funded under the contract. FAR 31.205-22(b). See Manos, 1 GOVERNMENT CONTRACT COSTS AND PRICING §§ 29:1–29:4 (2d ed. 2009–2020); Cibinic, Knight & Nash, COST-REIMBURSEMENT CONTRACTING 659–60 (4th ed. 2014).

LOGISTICS   See ACQUISITION LOGISTICS.

LONG-LEAD ITEMS; LONG-LEAD-TIME MATERIALS   Those components of a system or piece of equipment for which the times to design and fabricate are the longest and, therefore, to which an early commitment of funds may be desirable in order to meet the earliest possible date of system completion. For planning purposes, long-lead items might be ordered during engineering development to arrive in time for the start of production. DAU GLOSSARY. In approving MULTIYEAR PROCUREMENTs, Congress occasionally approves the advance procurement of long-lead items to facilitate the procurement of an ECONOMIC ORDER QUANTITY. See DFARS 217.172(f)(2).

LONG-TERM CONTRACT   *Official:* For the purpose of small business status REREPRESENTATION, a contract of more than five years in duration, including options. FAR 19.301-2(a).

LOSS   The failure to earn a PROFIT on a contract because the costs of performance (both DIRECT COSTs and INDIRECT COSTs) have exceeded the amount paid to the contractor under the terms of the contract. FAR 31.205-23 states that losses on other contracts are UNALLOWABLE COSTs. See Manos, 1 GOVERNMENT CONTRACT COSTS AND PRICING § 30:1 (2d ed. 2009–2020); Cibinic, Knight & Nash, COST-REIMBURSEMENT CONTRACTING 734 (4th ed. 2014).

LOSS OF EFFICIENCY   A reduction in expected productivity that can result from a variety of causes such as adverse weather, a reduced amount of work, a crowded worksite, restricted access to the worksite, out-of-sequence work, and excess or unavailability of workers. A government contractor may use several clauses as a basis for a claim for loss of efficiency: the Changes clause, FAR 52.243-4, the DIFFERING SITE CONDITIONS clause, FAR 52.236-2, and the SUSPENSION OF WORK clause, FAR 52.242-14. See Cibinic, Nagle & Nash, ADMINISTRATION OF GOVERNMENT CONTRACTS 657–58 (5th ed. 2016). See also Nash, *Postscript: Measured Mile Computation of Loss of Productivity*, 22 N&CR ¶ 46 (Aug. 2008); Lee Davis, et al., *Does The "Measured Mile" Measure Up? When It Has, When It Hasn't, And What May Happen Under Daubert/Kumho*, CONSTR. BRIEFINGS No. 2007-04 (Apr. 2007).

LOSS OF PRODUCTIVITY   See LOSS OF EFFICIENCY.

LOSS OF USEFUL VALUE   An allowable termination cost, pertaining to SPECIAL TOOL-ING and special machinery and equipment, which is generally allowable provided that (1) the special tooling or special machinery and equipment is not reasonably capable of use in the contractor's other work, (2) TITLE is transferred to the government or the government's interest is protected by other means deemed appropriate by the contracting officer, and (3) "the loss of useful value for any one terminated contract is limited to that portion of the ACQUISITION COST that bears the same ratio to the total acquisition cost as the terminated portion of the contract bears to the entire terminated contract and other government contracts for which the special tooling or special machinery and equipment was acquired." FAR 31.205-42(d). See Manos, 1 GOVERNMENT CONTRACT COSTS AND PRICING § 49:6 (2d ed. 2009–2020); Cibinic, Nagle & Nash, ADMINISTRATION OF GOVERNMENT CONTRACTS 987 (5th ed. 2016); Cibinic, Knight & Nash, COST-REIMBURSEMENT CONTRACTING 750–51 (4th ed. 2014).

LOW-RATE INITIAL PRODUCTION (LRIP)   The initial stage of PRODUCTION AND DEPLOYMENT of a DOD product or system as prescribed in the DOD 5000 Series. In this stage a contract for the initial production of a minimum quantity is called for in order to complete manufacturing development and demonstrate an efficient manufacturing process.

LOWEST OVERALL COST   The least expenditure of funds over the life of a system or item. Lowest overall cost is calculated on the basis of purchase price, LEASE or rental prices, or service prices of the contract actions involved, as well as other identifiable and quantifiable costs directly related to the acquisition and use of the system or item (for example, personnel, maintenance and operation, site preparation, energy consumption, installation, conversion, system startup, contractor support, and the PRESENT VALUE discount factor). The quantifiable cost of conducting the contracting action and other administrative costs directly related to the ACQUISITION PROCESS are also included. The costs considered in deriving lowest overall cost for a telecommunication acquisition include such elements as personnel, purchase price or rentals, maintenance, site preparation and installation, programming, and training. See OMB Circular A-130, *Management of Federal Information Resources* (Nov. 28, 2000).

LOWEST PRICE TECHNICALLY ACCEPTABLE (LPTA)   A competitive negotiation source selection process where the non-price factors of a proposal are evaluated to determine which proposals are "technically acceptable" and award is made to the offeror of the technically acceptable proposal with the lowest price. FAR 15.101-2(a) states that this process is appropriate when BEST VALUE is expected to result from the use of this process. Thus, the "best value" decision is made in planning the procurement not in evaluating the proposals (as in the TRADEOFF PROCESS). In the lowest price technically acceptable process the non-price factors are all evaluated on an acceptable/unacceptable basis with no gradations or scores for higher levels of achievement. Thus, no tradeoffs are made in the source selection decision. Congressionally imposed limitations and prohibitions of the use of this technique are contained in DFARS 215.101-2-70. Similar limitations and prohibitions will also be added to FAR 15.101-2. See Cibinic, Nash & Yukins, FORMATION OF GOVERNMENT CONTRACTS 679–81 (4th ed. 2011). See also Nash, *Postscript V: Lowest Price Technically Acceptable*, 33 N&CR ¶9 (Feb. 2019); Nash & Edwards, *The "Tradeoff" Procurement Process: Is*

It Always the Best Way to Go?, 26 N&CR ¶ 66 (Dec. 2012); Edwards & Nash, *Streamlining Source Selection: A Labor-Saving Approach to Lowest Price Technically Acceptable Source Selection*, 23 N&CR ¶ 26 (May 2009).

LOWEST RESPONSIVE, RESPONSIBLE BIDDER   The bidder in a sealed bid procurement (see SEALED BIDDING) that is entitled to award of the contract. 10 U.S.C. § 2305(b)(3) and 41 U.S.C. § 3702, require award to the responsible source (see RESPONSIBILITY) whose bid conforms to the solicitation (see RESPONSIVENESS) and is most advantageous to the government, considering only PRICE and other PRICE-RELATED FACTORS included in the SOLICITATION. Detailed guidance is set forth in FAR Part 14. See Feldman, GOVERNMENT CONTRACT AWARDS: NEGOTIATION AND SEALED BIDDING §§ 27:16–27:21 (2019–2020 ed.); Cibinic, Nash & Yukins, FORMATION OF GOVERNMENT CONTRACTS 502-03, 598–610 (4th ed. 2011).

M

MAILBOX RULE   A common-law rule providing that an ACCEPTANCE OF an OFFER becomes effective (creates a binding contract) when it is transmitted rather than when it is received. RESTATEMENT (SECOND) OF CONTRACTS § 63 (1981). In government contracting, the time of acceptance is subject to the mailbox rule unless the SOLICITATION provides for a different time. However, there is some authority holding that acceptance is not binding until the document is received by the offeror. See Cibinic, Nash & Yukins, FORMATION OF GOVERNMENT CONTRACTS 244–46 (4th ed. 2011).

MAINTENANCE AND OPERATING CONTRACT   See MANAGEMENT AND OPERATING CONTRACT.

MAJOR AUTOMATED INFORMATION SYSTEM (MAIS) ACQUISITION PROGRAM   An automated information system (AIS) acquisition program specifically designated by the Under Secretary of Defense for Acquisition, Technology and Logistics, or estimated to require program costs in any single year in excess of $40 million in FY 2014 constant dollars, total program costs in excess of $165 million in FY 2014 constant dollars, or total LIFE-CYCLE COSTs in excess of $520 million in FY 2014 constant dollars. See the DOD 5000 Series.

MAJOR DEFENSE ACQUISITION PROGRAM (MDAP)   *Official:* A Department of Defense acquisition program that is determined by the Under Secretary of Defense for Acquisition, Technology and Logistics to require an eventual total expenditure for research, development, test, and evaluation of more than $480 million in FY 2014 constant dollars or a total expenditure for procurement of more than $2.79 million in FY 2014 constant dollars. *Source:* 10 U.S.C. § 2430. In accordance with this statute, the amounts have been adjusted to $365 million for research, development, test, and evaluation and $2.109 billion for total procurement (calculated in FY 2000 constant dollars). These programs are subject to the detailed reporting and management requirements in 10 U.S.C. chapter 144. See the DOD 5000 Series. See also ACQUISITION CATEGORIES.

MAJOR DISASTER   *Official:* As used in 6.208, 13.201, 13.500, 18.001, 18.202, 18.203, and subpart 26.2, any natural catastrophe (including any hurricane, tornado, storm, high water, wind-driven water, tidal wave, tsunami, earthquake, volcanic eruption, landslide, mudslide, snowstorm, or drought), or regardless of cause, any fire, flood, or explosion, in any part of the United States, which, in the determination of the President, causes damage of sufficient severity and magnitude to warrant major disaster assistance under the Stafford Act to supplement the efforts and available resources of States, local governments, and disaster relief organizations in alleviating the damage, loss, hardship, or suffering caused thereby (42 U.S.C. § 5122). *Source:* FAR 2.101. When there is a declaration of a major disaster, agencies can use EMERGENCY ACQUISITION FLEXIBILITIES and the other procedures in the FAR provisions cited above.

MAJOR DISASTER OR EMERGENCY AREA   *Official:* The area included in the official Presidential declaration(s) and any additional areas identified by the Department of Homeland Security. *Source:* FAR 26.201. Major disaster declarations and emergency declarations are published in the Federal Register and are available at http://www.fema.gov news/ disasters.fema. The Robert T. Stafford Disaster Relief and Emergency Assistance Act, 42 U.S.C. § 5150, gives a preference for local firms when EMERGENCY RESPONSE CONTRACTs are awarded to deal with work in these areas. See FAR Subpart 26.2 for mandatory procedures.

MAJOR HELIUM REQUIREMENT   *Official:* An estimated refined helium requirement greater than 200,000 standard cubic feet (measured at 14.7 pounds per square inch absolute pressure and 70 degrees Fahrenheit temperature) of gaseous helium or 7510 liters of liquid helium delivered to a helium use location per year. *Source:* FAR 8.501. Agencies and their contractors are required to purchase major helium requirements from FEDERAL HELIUM SUPPLIERs. FAR 8.502. When an agency contemplates the acquisition of such a requirement it must use the Required Sources for Helium and Helium Usage Data clause in FAR 52.208-8.

MAJOR SYSTEM   *Official:* that combination of elements that will function together to produce the capabilities required to fulfill a mission need. The elements may include hardware, equipment, software, or any combination thereof, but exclude construction or other improvements to real property. A system is a major system if-(1) The Department of Defense is responsible for the system and the total expenditures for research, development, test, and evaluation for the system are estimated to be more than $185 million based on Fiscal Year 2014 constant dollars or the eventual total expenditure for the acquisition exceeds $835 million based on Fiscal Year 2014 constant dollars (or any update of these thresholds based on a more recent fiscal year, as specified in the DOD Instruction 5000.02, "Operation of the Defense Acquisition System"); (2) A civilian agency is responsible for the system and total expenditures for the system are estimated to exceed $2.5 million or the dollar threshold for a "major system" established by the agency pursuant to Office of Management and Budget Circular A-109, entitled "Major System Acquisitions," whichever is greater; or (3) The system is designated a "major system" by the head of the agency responsible for the system (10 U.S.C. § 2302 and 41 U.S.C. § 109). *Source:* FAR 2.101. Special procedures are generally used for the procurement of major systems and they are subject to FAR Part 34. See MAJOR SYSTEM ACQUISITION.

MAJOR SYSTEM ACQUISITION   The process of acquiring a MAJOR SYSTEM. OMB Circular A-109, *Major systems Acquisitions* and FAR Part 34, *Major System Acquisition*, prescribe various top-level policies and procedures, but agencies prescribe their own in greater detail. See, for example, e.g., the DOD 5000 Series, the Coast Guard's MAJOR SYSTEMS ACQUISITION MANUAL, and NASA's Policy Directive 7120.4, *NASA Engineering and Program/Project Management Policy.* See Fox & Miller, CHALLENGES IN MANAGING LARGE PROJECTS DAU Press (2006). For background and history, see Peck & Scherer, *The Weapons Acquisition Process: An Economic Analysis* (Harvard, 1962); Sapolsky, *The Polaris System*

Development: Bureaucratic and Programmatic Success in Government (Harvard, 1972); Johnson, *The Secret of Apollo: Systems Management in American and European Space Programs* (Johns Hopkins, 2002); Rhodes, *The Making of the Atomic Bomb* (Simon & Schuster, 1987); Sheehan, *A Fiery Peace in a Cold War: Bernard Schriever and the Ultimate Weapon* (Random House, 2009).

MAJOR SYSTEM INTERFACE   *Official.* A shared boundary between a major system platform and a major system component, between major system components, or between major system platforms, defined by various physical, logical, and functional characteristics, such as electrical, mechanical, fluidic, optical, radio frequency, data, networking, or software elements; and is characterized clearly in terms of form, function, and the content that flows across the interface in order to enable technological innovation, incremental improvements, integration, and interoperability. *Source.* 10 U.S.C. § 2446a. In using the MODULAR OPEN SYSTEM APPROACH to the design phase of a MAJOR DEFENSE ACQUISITION PROGRAM, an agency must obtain the TECHNICAL DATA and COMPUTER SOFTWARE describing the interface. 10 U.S.C. § 2320(a)(2)(G) requires this information to be furnished with GOVERNMENT PURPOSE RIGHTS even if it describes an item or process that was developed at private expense or mixed funding. See INTERFACE DATA.

MAKE ITEM   *Official:* An item or work effort to be produced or performed by the PRIME CONTRACTOR or its AFFILIATES, subsidiaries, or divisions. *Source:* FAR 15.407-2(b). See also BUY ITEM. Such items are reviewed by the contracting officer when a contractor is required to submit a MAKE-OR-BUY PROGRAM under the requirements of FAR 15.407-2.

MAKE-OR-BUY PROGRAM   *Official:* That part of a contractor's written plan for a contract identifying those major items to be produced or work efforts to be performed in the prime contractor's FACILITIES (MAKE ITEMs) and those to be subcontracted (BUY ITEMs). *Source:* FAR 2.101. The government may reserve the right to review and agree on the contractor's make-or-buy program when necessary to ensure (1) negotiation of reasonable contract prices, (2) satisfactory performance, or (3) implementation of socioeconomic policies. FAR 15.407-2. Contracting officers may freely require prospective contractors to submit make-or-buy program plans on negotiated acquisitions estimated to be over $13.5 million requiring CERTIFIED COST OR PRICING DATA, except if it is a RESEARCH AND DEVELOPMENT CONTRACT and, if prototypes or hardware are involved, no significant follow-on production is anticipated. They may not require the submission of such plans for acquisitions under $13.5 million without determining the information is necessary and documenting the reason for such requirement. FAR 15.407-2(c). The minimum dollar amount for make-or-buy programs for contracts with the DOD is $1.5 million. DFAR 215.407-2.

MANAGEMENT AND OPERATING (M&O) CONTRACT   *Official:* An agreement under which the government contracts for the operation, maintenance, or support, on its behalf, of a government-owned or -controlled research, development, special production, or testing establishment wholly or principally devoted to one or more major programs of the contracting federal agency. *Source:* FAR 17.601. An M&O contract is characterized both by its purpose and by the special relationship it creates between the government and contractor. Certain criteria generally apply: (1) the situation requires the use of government FACILITIES (in the interest of NATIONAL DEFENSE or MOBILIZATION readiness, for example, or to perform the agency's mission adequately, or because private enterprise is unable or unwilling to use its own facilities for the work); (2) because of the nature of the work, or because it is to be performed in government facilities, the government must maintain a close relationship with the contractor and the contractor's personnel in such important areas as safety, security, cost control, and site conditions; (3) the conduct of the work is wholly or at least substantially separate from the contractor's other business, if any; and (4) the work is closely related to the agency's mission and is of a long-term or continuous nature, and there is a need to ensure its continuity and to have special protection covering the orderly transition of personnel and work in the event of a change in contractors. FAR17.604. The FAR coverage on this subject, Subpart 17.6, was written principally with the needs of DOE in mind; the subpart's provisions do not apply to DOD. DFARS Subpart 217.6. DOE has extensive supplementary regulations dealing with M&O contracts at DEAR Part 970. See also GOVERNMENT-OWNED CONTRACTOR-OPERATED PLANT.

MANAGEMENT AND PROFESSIONAL SUPPORT SERVICES   *Official:* Contractual services that provide assistance, advice or training for the efficient and effective management and operation of organizations, activities (including management and support services for R&D activities), or systems. These services are normally closely related to the basic responsibilities and mission of the agency originating the requirement for the acquisition of services by contract. Included are efforts that support or contribute to improved organization of program management, logistics management, project monitoring and reporting, data collection, budgeting, accounting, performance auditing, and administrative technical support for conferences and training programs. *Source:* FAR 2.101 (in definition of ADVISORY AND ASSISTANCE SERVICES). This is one of the three types of advisory and assistance services that are subject to statutory limitations.

MANAGEMENT PROPOSAL   In SOURCE SELECTION, a proposal or a part of a proposal that describes how an offeror will plan, organize, staff, direct, and control its performance of a prospective contract, including resumes of proposed key personnel. Information about experience and past performance might be included in a management proposal or in a separate proposal document. See FAR 15.204-5(b) suggesting that the SOLICITATION might call for the submission of a management proposal. The term is informal, and government instructions for the preparation of management proposals may vary significantly from one acquisition to another.

MANDATORY DISCLOSURE   A written report to an agency INSPECTOR GENERAL, with a copy to the contracting officer, whenever a contractor finds credible evidence that a principal, employee, agent, or subcontractor of the contractor has committed—(A) A violation of federal criminal law involving fraud, conflict of interest, bribery, or gratuity violations found in Title 18 of the United States Code; or (B) A violation of the Civil False Claims Act (31 U.S.C. §§ 3729–3733). This is a requirement of the Contractor Code of Business Ethics and Conduct clause in FAR 52.203-13 which is included in solicitations, contracts and subcontracts expected to exceed $5.5 million with a performance period exceeding 120 days. FAR 3.1004(a). All contractors, however, are subject to SUSPENSION or DEBARMENT if they fail to meet the mandatory disclosure requirement. FAR 3.1003(a)(2). See Canni, *Shoot First, Ask Questions Later: An Examination and Critique of Suspension and Debarment Practice Under the FAR, Including a Discussion of the Mandatory Disclosure Rule, the IBM Suspension, and Other Noteworthy Developments*, 38 Pub. Cont. L.J. 547 (2009).

MANUFACTURED END PRODUCT   *Official:* Any end product in product and service codes (PSC) 1000-9999, except—(1) PSC 5510, Lumber and Related Basic Wood Materials; (2) Product or service group (PSG) 87, Agricultural Supplies; (3) PSG 88, Live Animals; (4) PSG 89, Subsistence; (5) PSC 9410, Crude Grades of Plant Materials; (6) PSC 9430, Miscellaneous Crude Animal Products, Inedible; (7) PSC 9440, Miscellaneous Crude Agricultural and Forestry Products; (8) PSC 9610, Ores; (9) PSC 9620, Minerals, Natural and Synthetic; and (10) PSC 9630, Additive Metal Materials. *Source:* FAR 2.101. Manufactured end products are subject to the BUY AMERICAN ACT.

MANUFACTURING   The production of a product that is ready for sale. This term is not defined in the procurement regulations but is important in implementing the BUY AMERICAN ACT and the TRADE AGREEMENTS ACT. These acts give a preference for products that are manufactured in the United States. GAO has held that to meet this test under the Buy American Act the "essential nature" of the product must be altered, *TRS Research*, Comp. Gen. Dec. B-285514, 2000 CPD ¶ 128. However, the Federal Circuit has held that the test can be met even if the product is not substantially transformed in the United States, *Acetris Health, LLC v. U.S.*, 949 F.3d 719 (Fed. Cir. 2020).

MANUFACTURING ENGINEERING   Developing and deploying new or improved materials, systems, processes, methods, equipment, pilot production lines, plant layout, production scheduling, tools and techniques to be used in providing products or services. FAR 31.205-25 specifies that the costs of such work incurred by a contractor are ALLOWABLE COSTs. See Manos, 1 GOVERNMENT CONTRACT COSTS AND PRICING §§ 32:1–32:3 (2d ed. 2009–2020); Cibinic, Knight & Nash, COST-REIMBURSEMENT CONTRACTING 657–59 (4th ed. 2014). FAR 31.205-18(a) provides that such work is not a part of a contractor's INDEPENDENT RESEARCH AND DEVELOPMENT effort.

MANUFACTURING TECHNOLOGY   Activities whose objectives are (1) to establish or improve, in a timely manner, the manufacturing processes, techniques, or equipment required to support current and projected programs; and (2) to assure the ability to produce, reduce lead time, ensure economic availability of end items, reduce costs, increase efficiency, improve reliability, or enhance safety and anti-pollution measures. Brechtel, *Subcontracts: Government and Industry Issues* (NCMA 1989). 10 U.S.C. § 2521 requires DOD to establish a manufacturing technology program to develop advanced manufacturing technologies and processes to reduce the LIFE-CYCLE COSTs of weapon systems. See DOD Directive 4200.15, *Manufacturing Technology Program*, Sept. 19, 2002, ch. 1, Oct. 15, 2018.

MARCH-IN   The right of the government under 35 U.S.C. § 203 to require a contractor or subcontractor that has made a SUBJECT INVENTION to grant another party a LICENSE to use that invention if it is determined that the contractor has not achieved PRACTICAL APPLICATION of the invention or that a license is needed for public purposes. The conditions for exercising this right are set forth in the Patent Rights clauses in FAR 52.227-11 and -13, and DFARS 252.227-7038. This compulsory license right has not been exercised in any reported instance, but its exercise is subject to appeal in the COURT OF FEDERAL CLAIMS. 35 U.S.C. § 203(2). See Thomas, CONG. RESEARCH SERV., REPORT NO. R44597, MARCH-IN RIGHTS UNDER THE BAYH-DOLE ACT (Aug. 22, 2016).

MARKET ACCEPTANCE   of an ITEM by commercial buyers or other government agencies under current or recent contracts for the same or similar requirements. Section 8002(c) of the FEDERAL ACQUISITION STREAMLINING ACT OF 1994 provides that agencies may require offerors to demonstrate that offered products have achieved market acceptance or otherwise meet the contract SPECIFICATIONs. FAR 11.103 contains guidance on the use of this procedure.

MARKET ANALYSIS   The process of analyzing prices and trends in the competitive marketplace to compare product availability and offered prices with market alternatives and establish the reasonableness of offered prices. Market analysis is one of the elements of PRICE ANALYSIS that is undertaken by the contracting officer to ensure that the contract is being awarded at a FAIR AND REASONABLE PRICE. See FAR 15.404-1(b)(2)(ii). See also MARKET RESEARCH; MARKET SURVEY.

MARKET PRICE   *Official:* Current prices that are established in the course of ordinary trade between buyers and sellers free to bargain and that can be substantiated through competition or from sources independent of the offerors. *Source:* FAR 2.101 (in the definition of "commercial service"). Such a price permits an agency to treat a STAND-ALONE COMMERCIAL SERVICE as a COMMERCIAL SERVICE if other requirements are met. It is not clear whether a price established in a competition for a unique task of job (such as the cleaning or construction of a unique building) is such a market price. See Nash, *Postscript VI: Defining Commercial Services*, 16 N&CR ¶ 15 (Mar. 2002).

MARKET RESEARCH   *Official:* Collecting and analyzing information about capabilities within the market to satisfy agency needs. *Source:* FAR 2.101. The process is used by the contracting officer in order to take the most suitable approach to acquiring, distributing, and supporting supplies and services. FAR Part 10. Market research is required by 10 U.S.C. § 2305(a)(1)(A)(ii) and 41 U.S.C. § 3306(a)(1)(B). It involves determining if COMMERCIAL PRODUCTs, COMMERCIAL SERVICES or NONDEVELOPMENTAL ITEMs are available to meet the government's needs or could be modified to meet those needs. FAR 10.002(b). Techniques for conducting market research include: contacting knowledgeable individuals in industry and government; reviewing the results of recent market research; publishing formal requests for information; querying government databases; querying the governmentwide database of contracts and other procurement instruments intended for use by multiple agencies available at www.contractdirectory.gov/contractdirectory/ and other government and commercial databases that provide information relevant to agency acquisitions; participating in interactive, on-line communications among industry personnel, acquisition personnel, and customers; obtaining source lists from other contracting activities; reviewing catalogs and other product literature, and conducting interchange meetings and PRESOLICITATION CONFERENCEs. FAR 10.002(b)(2). For INDEFINITE QUANTITY CONTRACTs, the contracting officer should use market research to establish a MAXIMUM QUANTITY. FAR 16.504(a)(1). See Feldman, GOVERNMENT CONTRACT GUIDEBOOK § 3:2–3:3 (4th ed. 2019–2020); Cibinic, Nash & Yukins, FORMATION OF GOVERNMENT CONTRACTS 341–45 (4th ed. 2011).

MARKET SURVEY   An attempt by a contracting agency to ascertain whether there are unknown qualified sources capable of satisfying the government's requirements. This testing of the marketplace may range from written or telephone contact with federal and other experts regarding similar or duplicate requirements (and the results of any market test recently undertaken) to more formal "sources sought" announcements in scientific journals or the GOVERNMENTWIDE POINT OF ENTRY or SOLICITATIONS FOR

INFORMATION OR PLANNING PURPOSES. See MARKET RESEARCH. See Cibinic, Nash & Yukins, FORMATION OF GOVERNMENT CONTRACTS 341–45 (4th ed. 2011).

MARKETING CONSULTANT   *Official:* Any independent contractor who furnishes advice, information, direction, or assistance to an offeror or any other contractor in support of the preparation or submission of an OFFER for a government contract by that offeror. An independent contractor is *not* a marketing consultant when rendering—(1) Services excluded in FAR Subpart 37.2 (ADVISORY AND ASSISTANCE SERVICES); (2) Routine engineering and technical services (such as installation, operation, or maintenance of systems, equipment, software, components, or FACILITIES); (3) Routine legal, actuarial, auditing, and accounting services; and (4) Training services. *Source:* FAR 9.501. FAR 9.505-4(c) warns that contractors can improperly obtain proprietary or source selection information from marketing consultants. FAR Subpart 9.5 therefore directs contracting officers to address this type of ORGANIZATIONAL CONFLICT OF INTEREST in the procurement process.

MASTER AGREEMENT FOR REPAIR AND ALTERATION OF VESSELS   *Official:* A written instrument of understanding, negotiated between a contracting activity and a contractor that—(A) Contains contract clauses, terms, and conditions applying to future contracts for repairs, alterations, and/or additions to vessels; and (B) Contemplates separate future contracts that will incorporate by reference or attachment the required and applicable clauses agreed upon in the master agreement; and is not a contract. *Source:* DFARS 217.7101. This is a form of BASIC ORDERING AGREEMENT used for the repair and alteration of ships. It is not a contract but, rather, a written instrument of understanding that establishes in advance the terms and conditions on which a contractor will affect repairs, alterations, or additions to vessels, under the provisions of job orders awarded by contracting activities from time to time. JOB ORDERs (fixed-price contracts entered into with contractors that have previously executed master agreements) apply to specific acquisitions. They set forth the scope of work, price, delivery date, and additional matters peculiar to the acquisition, and they incorporate by reference or append the appropriate clauses from the master agreement. Guidance on the use of these master agreements is contained in DFARS Subpart 217.71.

MASTER SOLICITATION   *Official:* A document containing special clauses and provisions that have been identified as essential for the acquisition of a specific type of supply or service that is acquired repetitively. *Source:* FAR 2.101. This term is used in SEALED BIDDING procurements. The master solicitation may be requested by, and is provided to, potential sources who retain it for continued and repetitive use. FAR 14.203-3.

MATERIAL   *Official:* Property that may be consumed or expended during the performance of a contract, component parts of a higher assembly, or items that lose their individual identity through incorporation into an end ITEM. Material does not include equipment, SPECIAL TOOLING, SPECIAL TEST EQUIPMENT or REAL PROPERTY. *Source:* FAR 45.101. The term prior to the issuance of FAC 2005-17, May 15, 2007, FAR 45.303-1 provided that contractors ordinarily should be required to furnish all material necessary to perform their contracts but that the government should provide material when necessary to achieve significant economy, standardization, or expedited production. This guidance has been incorporated into the general guidance on government property in FAR 45.102. The new Government Property clause in FAR 52.245-1 contains requirements for contractor management and control of GOVERNMENT-FURNISHED MATERIAL, including material to which title has passed to the government as the result of the payment provisions of the contract. CAS 411, Accounting for Acquisition Cost of Material, 48 C.F.R. § 9904.411, sets forth rules that govern accounting for costs of material by charging it directly to a contract, allocating it to an INDIRECT COST POOL, or placing it in inventory (see MATERIAL INVENTORY RECORD).

MATERIAL COSTS [1]   *Official:* The costs of such items as raw materials, parts, subassemblies, components, and manufacturing supplies, whether purchased or manufactured by the contractor, which may include such collateral items as inbound transportation and in-transit insurance. In computing material costs, the contractor shall consider reasonable overruns, spoilage, or defective work (unless otherwise provided in any contract provision relating to inspecting and correcting defective work). *Source:* FAR 31.205-26. Such costs are generally ALLOWABLE COSTs subject to the requirements of FAR 31.205-26. See Manos, 1 GOVERNMENT CONTRACT COSTS AND PRICING §§ 33:1–33:5 (2d ed. 2009–2020). **[2]** Under a TIME-AND-MATERIALS CONTRACT: *Official:* (1) Direct materials, including supplies transferred between divisions, subsidiaries, or affiliates of the contractor under a common control); (2) Subcontracts for supplies and incidental services for which there is not a labor category specified in the contract; (3) Other direct costs (e.g., incidental services for which there is not a labor category specified in the contract, travel, computer usage charges, etc.); and (4) Applicable indirect costs. *Source:* FAR 16.601. In accordance with the Payment under Time-and-Materials and Labor-Hour Contracts clause in FAR 52.232-7, these costs are paid, subject to the application of the COST PRINCIPLES, under such contracts without profit except for commercial items transferred from another element of the contractor.

MATERIAL HANDLING COSTS   INDIRECT COSTS that are allocated to direct materials in accordance with a contractor's usual accounting practices. Such costs can be included in MATERIAL COSTS in TIME-AND-MATERIALS (T&M) CONTRACTs if they are clearly excluded from the labor-hour rate. FAR 16.601(c)(3). These costs were explicitly billable to T&M contracts under the Payment under Time-and-Materials and Labor-Hour Contracts clause in FAR 52.232-7 that was in effect until February 2007. Under the new clause, they are not dealt with explicitly but are still billable as "applicable indirect costs." See Edwards, *The New Clause for Payments Under Noncommercial Time-and-Materials and Labor-Hour Contracts: An End To the Confusion?*, 21 N&CR ¶ 15 (Apr. 2007).

MATERIAL INSPECTION AND RECEIVING REPORT (MIRR)   A DOD form (DD Form 250) used to document the INSPECTION and acceptance (see ACCEPTANCE OF WORK) of supplies and services. DFARS Appendix F sets forth procedures and instructions for using, preparing, and distributing (1) the MIRR and (2) suppliers' commercial shipping/ packing lists used as evidence of government procurement QUALITY ASSURANCE (QA). MIRRs are used to document QA, acceptance of supplies and services, and shipments. They are used by receiving, status control, technical, contracting, inventory control, requisitioning, and paying activities. The procedures of Appendix F apply to supplies or services procured by DOD when the contract includes the Material Inspection and Receiving Report clause at DFARS 252.246-7000.

MATERIAL INVENTORY RECORD   *Official:* Any record used for the accumulation of actual or STANDARD COSTs of a category of MATERIAL recorded as an ASSET for subsequent cost allocation to one or more COST OBJECTIVEs. *Source:* CAS 411, Accounting for Acquisition Costs of Material, 48 C.F.R. § 9904.411-30. CAS 411 provides that the cost used in this record will be the purchase price of the item of material adjusted by extra charges incurred or discounts earned. It then permits that one of the following methods must be used consistently to charge material costs to a contract: FIRST-IN, FIRST-OUT; MOVING AVERAGE COST; WEIGHTED AVERAGE COST; STANDARD COST; or LAST-IN, FIRST-OUT. See Cibinic & Nash, Cost Reimbursement Contracting 939–41 (3d ed. 2004).

MATERIAL MANAGEMENT AND ACCOUNTING SYSTEM (MMAS) *Official:* The contractor's system or systems for planning, controlling, and accounting for the acquisition, use, issuing, and disposition of MATERIAL. Material management and accounting systems may be manual or automated. They may be stand-alone systems or they may be integrated with planning, engineering, estimating, purchasing, INVENTORY, accounting, or other systems. *Source:* DFARS 252.242-7004. DOD policy requires that large contractors with cost-reimbursement contracts or fixed-price contracts with cost-based progress payments have a system that reasonably forecasts material requirements; ensures that the costs of purchased and fabricated material charged or allocated to a contract are based on VALID TIME-PHASED REQUIREMENTS; and maintains a consistent, equitable, and unbiased logic for costing of material transactions. DFARS Subpart 242.72. This policy is implemented by inclusion of the Material Management and Accounting System clause in DFARS 252.242-7004 in contracts. Detailed guidance on the audit of MMAS is contained in *DCAA Contract Audit Manual* ¶ 5-703. This is one of the six systems covered by the CONTRACTOR BUSINESS SYSTEM clause in DFARS 252.242-7005 that permits withholding of payments if there is a SIGNIFICANT DEFICIENCY in a system.

MATERIAL SOLUTION ANALYSIS PHASE The first phase in obtaining a new WEAPON SYSTEM in the DEPARTMENT OF DEFENSE following the procedures in the DOD 5000 Series. In this phase the agency assesses potential material solutions to meet an operational capability gap. The work focuses on identification and analysis of alternative technologies, measures of effectiveness, cost, schedule, concepts of operations, and overall risk. DAU Glossary.

MATRIX See PROVISION AND CLAUSE MATRIX.

MAXIMUM FEE Dollar amount negotiated at the inception of a COST-PLUS-INCENTIVE-FEE CONTRACT as the maximum amount of PROFIT that the contractor is entitled to receive. After contract performance the FEE payable to the contractor is determined in accordance with a contract-specified fee adjustment formula based on the relationship of total ALLOWABLE COST to total TARGET COST. When total allowable cost is *less* than the range of cost within which the fee adjustment formula operates (see RANGE OF INCENTIVE EFFECTIVENESS), the contractor is paid the total allowable cost plus the maximum fee. FAR16.405-1. See Cibinic, Knight & Nash, Cost-Reimbursement Contracting 55 (4th ed. 2014).

MAY *Official:* This term denotes the permissive. However, the words "no person may . . ." mean that no person is required, authorized, or permitted to do the act described. *Source:* FAR 2.101. The mandatory terms are SHALL or must. When the regulations state that an action may be performed, agencies have the discretion to not take that action.

MEASUREMENT OF COST   Accounting methods and techniques used in defining the components of cost, determining the basis for cost measurement, and establishing criteria for use of alternative cost measurement techniques. 48 C.F.R. § 9903.302-1(a). Such measurement is one type of COST ACCOUNTING PRACTICE. Examples of cost accounting practices that involve measurement of costs are (1) the use of HISTORICAL COST, MARKET VALUE, or PRESENT VALUE; (2) the use of STANDARD COST or ACTUAL COST; or (3) the designation of those items of cost that must be included in or excluded from TANGIBLE CAPITAL ASSET or PENSION PLAN costs. See Cibinic, Knight & Nash, COST-REIMBURSEMENT CONTRACTING 562 (4th ed. 2014).

MEDIATION   A voluntary, flexible technique for resolving DISPUTEs: the contracting parties present their positions to a mediator who then assists them to negotiate a settlement. Generally, each party appoints a PRINCIPAL with the authority to settle the dispute. The positions of the parties can be presented to the mediator separately or in a joint session. Similarly, the negotiation can be conducted between the principals, with the mediator assisting, or by the mediator walking offers of settlement back and forth between the parties. Mediation is now one of the most widely used ALTERNATIVE DISPUTE RESOLUTION methods. See Arnavas & Victorino, *Litigation or ADR: Choosing the Right Dispute Resolution Process*, BRIEFING PAPERS No. 09-8 (July 2009).

MEMORANDUM OF UNDERSTANDING (MOU)   An executive agreement with a foreign government. MOUs are used by DOD and NASA in situations where they have joint programs with foreign governments. Specific MOUs are negotiated with each country. They frequently contain provisions that waive the requirements of the BUY AMERICAN ACT to acquisitions of certain supplies mined, produced, or manufactured in designated foreign countries (because the agency has determined that it would be inconsistent with the public interest to apply its restrictions). See FAR Subpart 25.8. DOD policies for not applying the domestic preference laws and programs to offers of products from "qualifying" foreign countries can be found at DFARS Subpart 225.872.

MENTOR FIRM   See MENTOR-PROTÉGÉ PROGRAM.

MENTOR-PROTÉGÉ PILOT PROGRAM   A program that encourages large DOD contractors to act as "mentors" to SMALL BUSINESS CONCERNs. The program seeks to increase the participation of small businesses as subcontractors and suppliers under DOD contracts, other federal government contracts, and commercial contracts by furnishing them with assistance aimed at enhancing their performance. It provides mentor firms with incentives including reimbursement equal to the total amount of PROGRESS PAYMENTs made under the program to a Protégé firm, reimbursement for the costs of the assistance furnished, or recognition of costs as "credits" in lieu of subcontract awards toward subcontracting participation goals. The program was created by § 831 of the FY 1991 Defense Authorization Act, Pub.L.No.101-510, and is implemented by DFARS Subpart 219.71. DOD policy and procedures for implementation of the program are contained in DFARS Appendix I, Policies and Procedures for the DOD Pilot Mentor-Protégé Program. A mentor firm must have at least one active approved subcontracting plan. DFARS 219.7102(a). A protégé firm must be a SMALL DISADVANTAGED BUSINESS CONCERN, a qualified organization employing the severely disabled, a WOMEN-OWNED BUSINESS CONCERN, a SERVICE-DISABLED VETERAN-OWNED SMALL BUSINESS CONCERN, or a HUBZONE SMALL BUSINESS CONCERN. DFARS 219.7102(b). Section 872 of the

National Defense Authorization Act for FY 2020 extended the program until Sept. 30, 2024. See U.S. Gov't Accountability Office, SMALL BUSINESS CONTRACTING: DOD Should Take Actions to Ensure That Its Pilot Mentor-Prote ge Program Enhances the Capabilities of Prote ge Firms, GAO-17-172 (Apr. 2017).

MENTOR-PROTÉGÉ PROGRAM   A program of the SMALL BUSINESS ADMINISTRA-TION that encourages large contractors to act as "mentors" to SMALL BUSINESS CONCERNs. The program was established in 2016 pursuant to the Small Business Jobs Act of 2010 and the National Defense Authorization Act for Fiscal Year 2013. It is implemented at 13 C.F.R. parts 121, 124 and 125. Proteges must be a small business with industry experience, have a proposed mentor, and be organized as for profit or an agricultural cooperative. They may only have two mentors in the firm's lifetime. Mentors must be organized for profit and have no more than three protégés at a time. Mentor protege agreements are for three years (renewable) and are certified by the small business administration. The firms can then form joint ventures to compete for government contracts that are set aside for small businesses. The protege firm must own at least 51% of the joint venture and its employees must perform at least 40% of the work. Prior to this program, several other agencies had similar programs. See, for example, DOD's MENTOR-PROTÉGÉ PILOT PROGRAM. See NASA, Mentor-Protégé Program Guidebook (Mar. 2014).

MERGER   See BUSINESS COMBINATION.

MERGER GUIDELINES   See HORIZONTAL MERGER GUIDELINES.

MERIT BASED COMPETITIVE PROCEDURES   Official: Methods that encourage participation in DoD programs by a broad base of the most highly qualified performers. These procedures are characterized by competition among as many eligible proposers as possible, with a published or widely disseminated notice. Source: 32 C.F.R. 22.315. These procedures for DOD grants and cooperative agreements require obtaining competition by publicizing agency research opportunities using techniques such as BROAD AGENCY ANNOUNCE-MENTs. Detailed guidance is contained in 32 C.F.R. Subpart 22.3.

METHODS OF PROCUREMENT   A broad term describing the way the government procures supplies and services including construction. The government uses two basic methods of procurement: SEALED BIDDING (see FAR Part 14) and NEGOTIATION (see FAR Part 15). Also referred to as method of contracting or contracting method. Any contract awarded without using sealed bidding procedures is a negotiated contract. FAR 15.000. The SIMPLIFIED ACQUISITION PROCEDURES of FAR Part 13 are a subset of negotiation. Procurement methods can also be characterized as those meeting the statutory requirement for FULL AND OPEN COMPETITION and those not meeting this requirement. Those meeting the requirement are said to use COMPETITIVE PROCEDURES; those not meeting it include sole source acquisition (see SOLE SOURCE), use of UNSOLICITED PROPOSALs, and various other processes. FAR Part 17 discusses special contracting methods, including MULTIYEAR CONTRACTING (covering more than one year but not more than five years of requirements), OPTIONs (under which the government has the unilateral right to increase the quantity or extend the term of the contract), LEADER-COMPANY CONTRACTING (under which a developer or sole source contractor furnishes assistance and know-how to another contractor so that the latter can become a source of supply), and INTERAGENCY ACQUISITION.

METRIC CONVERSION ACT OF 1975   Pub. L. No. 94-168, 15 U.S.C. § 205a et seq. A law designating the metric system as the preferred system of weights and measures for United States trade and commerce and requiring all agencies to use the metric system in their acquisitions, unless it is impracticable to do so or is likely to cause significant inefficiencies or loss of markets to United States firms. Agencies are responsible for implementing this act in stating their requirements. FAR 11.002(b).

MICRO-PURCHASE   *Official:* An acquisition of supplies or services using SIMPLIFIED ACQUISITION procedures, the aggregate amount of which does not exceed the MICRO-PURCHASE THRESHOLD. *Source:* FAR 2.101. Micro-purchases may be made from any source using any simplified technique (they are not SET-ASIDE for SMALL BUSINESS). FAR 13.003(b). Agency heads are encouraged to delegate micro-purchase authority to individuals who will be using the supplies or services being purchased. FAR 13.201(a). They are also encouraged to use GOVERNMENT-WIDE COMMERCIAL PURCHASE CARDs in carrying out these purchases. FAR 13.201(b). See Feldman, GOVERNMENT CONTRACT GUIDE-BOOK § 3:14 (4th ed. 2019-2020).

MICRO-PURCHASE THRESHOLD   *Official:* $10,000, except it means—(1) For acquisitions of construction subject to the DAVISs-BACON ACT, $2,000; (2) For acquisitions of services subject to the SERVICE CONTRACT ACT, $2,500; and (3) For acquisitions of supplies or services that, as determined by the head of the agency, are to be used to support a contingency operation or to facilitate defense against or recovery from nuclear, biological, chemical, or radiological attack, as described in 13.201(g)(1), except for construction subject to the Davis-Bacon Act—(i) $20,000 in the case of any contract to be awarded and performed, or purchase to be made, inside the United States; and (ii) $35,000 in the case of any contract to be awarded and performed, or purchase to be made, outside the United States. *Source:* FAR 2.101. Acquisitions within the threshold should use MICRO-PURCHASE procedures. See Feldman, GOVERNMENT CONTRACT GUIDEBOOK § 3:14 (4th ed. 2019-2020).

MIDDLE TIER ACQUISITION PROCESS   *Official:* A streamlined and coordinated requirements, budget, and acquisition process that results in the development of an approved requirement for each program in a period of not more than six months from the time that the process is initiated. *Source:* § 804 of the National Defense Authorization Act for FY 2016, Pub. L. No. 114-92. This process is to be used for RAPID FIELDING and RAPID PROTOTYPING. The statute was implemented by the DOD 5000 series.

MILESTONE PAYMENTS   See PERFORMANCE-BASED PAYMENTS.

MILESTONES FOR THE ACQUISITION CYCLE   Designated steps of the planned acquisition identified in the ACQUISITION PLAN, including (1) acquisition plan approval; (2) STATEMENT OF WORK; (3) SPECIFICATIONs; (4) data requirements; (5) completion of acquisition-package preparation; (6) purchase request; (7) justification and approval for OTHER THAN FULL AND OPEN COMPETITION where applicable and/or any required DETERMINATION AND FINDING approval; (8) issuance of SYNOPSIS; (9) issuance of solicitation; (10) evaluations of proposals, AUDITs, and field reports; (11) beginning and completion of negotiations; (12) contract preparation, review, and clearance; and (13) CONTRACT AWARD. FAR 7.105(b)(21). See Cibinic, Nash & Yukins, FORMATION OF GOVERNMENT CONTRACTS 285 (4th ed. 2011).

MILITARY AND STATE SECRETS DOCTRINE   A privilege, belonging to the federal government, which must be formally asserted in court, that protects military and state secrets by protecting evidence containing information pertaining to national security from discovery in a litigation context. See *United States v. Reynolds*, 345 U.S. 1 (1953). The government was permitted to assert this privilege to keep a contractor from obtaining information to be used to assert that the government failed to disclose vital information as a defense to a TERMINATION FOR DEFAULT. *McDonnell Douglas Corp. v. United States*, 323 F.3d 1006 (Fed. Cir. 2003). See Nash, *Postscript III: The "A-12" Default Termination*, 17 N&CR ¶ 28 (May 2003). However, in *General Dynamics Corp. v. United States*, 563 U.S. 478 (2011), the Supreme Court held that the presence of evidence constituting a state secret precluded any contract litigation with the result that the parties were left in the position they found themselves prior to the government's default termination. See Nash, *More A-12 Litigation: The Supreme Court Speaks*, 25 N&CR ¶ 35 (July 2011).

MILITARY DEPARTMENT   See DEPARTMENT OF DEFENSE.

MILITARY-FEDERAL [CONTRACT ITEM]   With respect to contract QUALITY ASSURANCE, an item of supply that is described in government drawings and specifications. FAR 46.203(a)(2). Although this is identified as one of the criteria that are to be used to determine the extent of the government's quality assurance efforts, the key determinants are the complexity and criticality of an item. FAR 46.202-4 (establishing the criteria for using HIGHER-LEVEL CONTRACT QUALITY REQUIREMENTS).

MILITARY INTERDEPARTMENTAL PURCHASE REQUEST (MIPR)   An order issued by one military service to another to procure services, supplies, or equipment for the requiring service. The MIPR (DD Form 448) may be accepted on a direct citation or reimbursable basis. Guidance on the use of the form is in DFARS Subpart 208.70. Instructions in filling out the form are in DOD PGI 253.208-1. It is an ECONOMY ACT (31 U.S.C. § 1535) order subject to downward adjustment when the obligated appropriation is no longer valid for obligation. DOD *Financial Management Regulation* 7000.14-R (2019), Glossary.

MILITARY SPECIFICATIONS (MIL-SPECs) AND STANDARDS (MIL-STDs)   SPECIFICATIONs and STANDARDs, unique to DOD, that are prepared, maintained, and controlled by an element of DOD. In 1994, the Secretary of Defense issued a new DOD policy advocating a greater use of performance and commercial specifications in lieu of military specifications. The intent of the policy was not to eliminate military specifications altogether, but to curtail the automatic development and imposition of unique military specifications as the cultural norm at DOD. As a result, the order of precedence for contract specifications in FAR 11.101 is now (1) documents mandated by law; (2) performance-oriented documents; (3) detailed design-oriented documents; and (4) standards, specifications and related publications issued by the government outside the defense or federal series. To continue this process of reducing reliance on military specification and standards, DFARS 211.273 provides procedures to use other statements of requirements. See Cibinic, Nash & Yukins, FORMATION OF GOVERNMENT CONTRACTS 368-69 (4th ed. 2011). From 1994 to 1996, 2,676 military specifications and standards were canceled. See DOD, MilSpec Reform: Results of the First Two Years (1996). Unclassified MIL-SPECs and MIL-STDs, along with related standardization documents and VOLUNTARY STANDARDs adopted by DOD, are listed in the DOD INDEX OF SPECIFICATIONS AND STANDARDS (DODISS). The DODISS can be searched on assist.dla.mil.

MILITARY STANDARD REQUISITIONING AND ISSUE PROCEDURE (MILSTRIP)
A procedure used by the military departments to requisition material or place government material under supply control. When authorized by the terms of a contract, contractors may also use MILSTRIP, which uses uniform codes and punch-card formats to standardize procedures for requisitioning, receiving, and returning material, and permits the maximum utilization of AUTOMATIC DATA PROCESSING EQUIPMENT. MILSTRIP applies when DOD contractors requisition from General Services Administration supply sources. The Defense Logistics Standard Systems Office is responsible for MILSTRIP. See DOD Manual 4000.25-1, *Military Standard Requisitioning and Issue Procedures, Change 8,* Dec. 14, 2016.

MILLER ACT   Pub. L. No. 89-719, 40 U.S.C. § 3131 et seq., A 1935 law requiring the execution of separate PERFORMANCE BONDs and PAYMENT BONDs as a prerequisite to award of CONSTRUCTION contracts exceeding $150,000. See FAR 28.102. The Act protects the government by requiring the performance bond and gives some classes of persons furnishing LABOR and materials the right to recover under a payment bond. A performance bond SURETY under the Miller Act is liable for all monetary sums owed by the contractor to the government under the contract up to the bond's PENAL AMOUNT. Miller Act jurisdiction for laborers and materialmen suing for compensation under the payment bond is limited to actions against the contractor or its sureties and grants no right of action against a subcontractor. The FEDERAL ACQUISITION STREAMLINING ACT OF 1994 required that the FAR provide alternatives to payment bonds for contracts exceeding $25,000 but not greater than $100,000 (now $35,000 and $150,000). See FAR 28.102-1(b). See also DFARS 228.102-1 waiving bonding requirements for cost-reimbursement-type construction contracts but requiring payment protection for laborers and materialmen of fixed price subcontractors under cost-reimbursement contracts.

MINIMUM FEE   Dollar amount negotiated at the inception of a COST-PLUS-INCENTIVE-FEE CONTRACT as the minimum amount of PROFIT that the contractor is entitled to receive. After contract performance the FEE payable to the contractor is determined in accordance with a contract-specified fee adjustment formula based on the relationship of total ALLOWABLE COST to total TARGET COST. When total allowable cost is *greater* than the range of cost within which the fee-adjustment formula operates (see RANGE OF INCENTIVE EFFECTIVENESS), the contractor is paid the total allowable cost plus the minimum fee. FAR 16.405-1. The minimum fee is usually a positive number (i.e., the contractor is guaranteed to make a profit). However, if a high MAXIMUM FEE is negotiated, the contract must also provide for a low minimum fee. This low minimum fee may be zero (in which case the contractor would be paid total allowable cost only). In rare cases, it may be a negative fee (the contractor would be paid total allowable cost *minus* the negative minimum fee; in other words, its losses would be limited). FAR 16.405-1(b)(3). See Cibinic, Knight & Nash, Cost-Reimbursement Contracting 55 (4th ed. 2014).

MINIMUM NEEDS   A misnomer for the rule that contracting agencies may not use SPECIFICATIONs or conditions that are unduly restrictive (see RESTRICTIVE SPECIFICATIONS). See FAR 11.002(a)(1)(ii), which provides that plans, DRAWINGS, specifications, STANDARDs, or PURCHASE DESCRIPTIONs must include restrictive provisions only to the extent necessary to satisfy the needs of the agency and describe the supplies and/or services in a manner designed to promote FULL AND OPEN COMPETITION. The term is misleading because it suggests that government agencies must buy supplies and services that are minimally effective. This clearly is not so because agencies are generally entitled to buy supplies or services that provide the BEST VALUE, determined by the technical and economic judgment of the procuring agency. See Cibinic, Nash & Yukins, FORMATION OF GOVERNMENT CONTRACTS 370–73 (4th ed. 2011).

MINIMUM QUANTITY   A stated quantity (in dollars or amount of work) in an INDEFI-NITE QUANTITY CONTRACT (IDIQ) which is sufficiently large to constitute CON-SIDERATION given by the government to bind the contractor to the contract. The minimum quantity must be more than a nominal quantity but should not exceed the amount that the government is fairly certain to order. FAR 16.504(a)(2). The dollar amount of the minimum quantity must be OBLIGATED at the time of contract award. See Cibinic, Nash & Yukins, FORMATION OF GOVERNMENT CONTRACTS 1387–89 (4th ed. 2011).

MINITRIAL   A flexible, voluntary, and nonjudicial procedure wherein members of top management (called "PRINCIPALS") hear a short presentation of the factual and legal positions of the parties in a contract dispute and engage in nonbinding negotiations to resolve a CLAIM. In most cases they are aided by a NEUTRAL ADVISOR who acts as a mediator. This procedure permits either party to withdraw at any time without prejudicing the litigation process. Management officials of both parties meet to resolve the dispute rather than permit a third party—a judge or arbitrator—to control the process. This technique is expressly recognized by the ADMINISTRATIVE DISPUTE RESOLUTION ACT. The minitrial process is one of the more widely used ALTERNATIVE DISPUTE RESOLU-TION options in dealing with government contract claims. See FAR 33.201. See Arnavas & Victorino, *Litigation or ADR: Choosing the Right Dispute Resolution Process*, BRIEFING PAPERS No. 09-8 (July 2009).

MINOR INFORMALITIES OR IRREGULARITIES IN BIDS   *Official:* A minor informality or irregularity that is merely a matter of form and not of substance. It also pertains to some immaterial defect in a bid or variation of a bid from the exact requirements of the invitation that can be corrected or waived without being prejudicial to other bidders. The defect or variation is immaterial when the effect on price, quantity, quality, or delivery is negligible in comparison with the total cost or scope of the supplies or services being acquired. *Source:* FAR 14.405. Such defects or variations are of so little import that they do not keep a bid from being responsive (see RESPONSIVENESS). The contracting officer must give the bidder an opportunity to cure any DEFICIENCY resulting from a minor informality or irregularity, or must waive the deficiency, whichever is to the advantage of the government. FAR 14.405 contains several examples of minor informalities or irregularities including failure of a bidder to return the required number of copies of signed bids and failure to furnish required information concerning the number of the bidders' employees. See Feldman, GOVERNMENT CONTRACT AWARDS: NEGOTIATION AND SEALED BIDDING § 27:20 (2019–2020 ed.)

MINORITY INSTITUTION (MI)   *Official:* An institution of higher education meeting the requirements of Section 365(3) of the Higher Education Act of 1965 (20 U.S.C. § 1067k), including a Hispanic-serving institution of higher education, as defined in Section 502(a) of the Act (20 U.S.C. § 1101a). *Source:* FAR 2.101. 34 C.F.R. § 637.4 implements these statutes by defining a minority institution as an accredited college or university whose enrollment of a single minority group or a combination of minority groups exceeds 50% of the total enrollment. The Secretary (of Education) verifies this information from the data on enrollments (Higher Education General Information Surveys HEGIS XIII) furnished by the institution to the Office for Civil Rights, Department of Education. Executive Order No. 12928, Sept. 16, 1994, directs all agencies to promote participation of HISTORICALLY BLACK COLLEGEs OR UNIVERSITies. See FAR Subpart 26.3 for procedures to achieve this goal.

MISCHARGING   The improper charging of a cost to a government contract. FAR 31.205-15 makes such costs incurred by contractors—including the costs of identification, measurement, and correction—UNALLOWABLE COSTs. Mischarging can arise through improper ALLOCATION OF COSTs or through charging of EXPRESSLY UNALLOWABLE COSTs to a contract. It can constitute criminal conduct under the FALSE CLAIMS ACT. See Manos, 1 GOVERNMENT CONTRACT COSTS & PRICING § 22:4 (2d ed. 2009-2020); Cibinic, Nagle & Nash, ADMINISTRATION OF GOVERNMENT CONTRACTS 139 (5th ed. 2016).

MISREPRESENTATION   Either a FALSE STATEMENT of a substantive FACT or any conduct that intentionally deceives or misleads another person so that, with respect to a substantive fact material to proper understanding of the matter at hand, the other person believes what is not true. BLACK'S LAW DICTIONARY 1198 (11th ed. 2019). The normal remedies for misrepresentation are DISQUALIFICATION before the contract award or RESCISSION after the contract award. (See also FALSE STATEMENTS ACT.) See Cibinic, Nagle & Nash, ADMINISTRATION OF GOVERNMENT CONTRACTS 100–23 (5th ed. 2016).

MISREPRESENTATION OF FACT   *Official:* A false statement of substantive fact, or any conduct which leads to a belief of a substantive fact material to proper understanding of the matter in hand, made with the intent to deceive or mislead. *Source:* FAR 33.201. 41 U.S.C. § 7103(c)(2) provides that if any CLAIM under the CONTRACT DISPUTES ACT is unsupported because of misrepresentation, the contractor is liable to the government for the amount of the claim plus the cost to the government in reviewing the claim. See FAR 33.209 providing that the contracting officer shall refer such situations to the agency official responsible for investigating FRAUD. See Cibinic, Nagle & Nash, ADMINISTRATION OF GOVERNMENT CONTRACTS 1145–48 (5th ed. 2016); Nash, *Postscript II: Forfeiture of Claims*, 23 N&CR ¶ 15 (Apr. 2009).

MISTAKE   A belief that is not in accord with the existing facts (but not an error in business judgment). Mistakes made by contractors may be discovered either before or after contract awards. Before award, the CONTRACTING OFFICER has an obligation to examine all bids and then notify the offeror of any suspected mistake and to request verification that no mistake was made (see DUTY OF VERIFICATION). In SEALED BIDDING procurement, mistakes discovered before award entitle the contractor either to withdraw the bid or to correct bids that are responsive in accordance with the guidance in FAR 14.407-3. In negotiated procurement (see NEGOTIATION), mistakes may be corrected during the procurement process in accordance with the procedures in FAR 15.306. If a mistake is discovered after award, the contractor may receive REFORMATION if there was a MUTUAL MISTAKE or a UNILATERAL MISTAKE about which the contracting officer was or should have been on notice. FAR 14.407-4. See Feldman, GOVERNMENT CONTRACT AWARDS: NEGOTIATION AND SEALED BIDDING §§ 14:11–14:13 and 20:11–20:13 (2019–2020 ed.).

MISTAKE IN INTEGRATION   See MUTUAL MISTAKE.

MITIGATION OF DAMAGES   An obligation imposed on a party injured by BREACH OF CONTRACT or TORT to exercise reasonable diligence and ordinary care in attempting to minimize its damages or avoid aggravating the injury. In effect, this obligation limits the amount of an EQUITABLE ADJUSTMENT or damages to the amount that would have been suffered if they had been mitigated.

MIXED FUNDING   The situation where an ITEM, component, process, or COMPUTER SOFTWARE has been DEVELOPED partially at private expense and partially at government expense. 10 U.S.C. § 2320(a)(2)(E) provides that the rights to TECHNICAL DATA pertaining to items or processes developed with mixed funding should be negotiated as early as possible in the ACQUISITION PROCESS but that the government shall have GOVERNMENT PURPOSE RIGHTS unless other rights are in the best interest of the government. Under the 1988 DOD data policy, such rights were only negotiated when requested by the contractor. Under the 1995 DOD data policy, as well as the computer software policy, the government automatically obtains government purpose rights when development has been accomplished with mixed funding. Under the concept of SEGREGABILITY, it is likely that most technical data and computer software will not fall into the mixed funding category. This concept is not included in the FAR data policy. See Nash & Rawicz, INTELLECTUAL PROPERTY IN GOVERNMENT CONTRACTS, chaps. 4 and 5 (6th ed. 2008).

MIXED WORKFORCE   See BLENDED FEDERAL WORKFORCE.

MOBILIZATION   The initial effort to perform a CONSTRUCTION contract by hiring necessary personnel and moving the necessary equipment and facilities on to the site of the work. Contracting agencies frequently include a separate bid item for mobilization on major construction projects in order to permit the contractor to be paid promptly for this effort. When this is done, DFARS 236.570(b)(2) prescribes the use of the Payment for Mobilization and Preparatory Work clause in DFARS 252.236-7003 or the Payment for Mobilization and Demobilization clause in DFARS 252.236-7004.

MOBILIZATION BASE   See INDUSTRIAL MOBILIZATION.

MODEL PROCUREMENT CODE (MPC)   A model code containing basic rules for contracting by state and local governments that was adopted by the American Bar Association (ABA) in 1979. The MPC provides (1) the statutory principles and policy guidance for managing and controlling the procurement of supplies, services, and construction for public purposes; (2) administrative and judicial remedies for the resolution of controversies relating to public contracts; and (3) a set of ethical standards governing public and private participants in the procurement process. A revised code was adopted in 2000 and updated in 2002. Articles 1 through 10 cover basic procurement policies for supplies, services, construction and legal remedies; article 11 covers socioeconomic policies a state may wish to amplify; article 12 establishes ethical standards for governmental procurement. The MPC, which is based on established principles of state and federal law, is currently adopted, completely or partially, by 25 states and a large number of municipalities. See Miller, *The 2000 ABA Model Procurement Code*, 36 The Procurement Lawyer 4 (Fall 2000). The Model Procurement Code for State and Local Governments (with commentary) and the MODEL PROCUREMENT REGULATIONS are available at www.americanbar.org/content/dam/aba/administrative/public_contract_law/pcl-model-02-2000-code-procurement.pdf.

MODEL PROCUREMENT REGULATIONS   A set of regulations for use by state and local governments that adopt the MODEL PROCUREMENT CODE. These regulations were issued by the Public Contract Section and the State and Local Government Section of the American Bar Association in 2002.

MODIFICATION   See CONTRACT MODIFICATION; PROPOSAL MODIFICATION.

MODIFIED COVERAGE   A type of COST ACCOUNTING STANDARDS (CAS) coverage that requires only that the contractor comply with the following cost accounting standards: 48 C.F.R. § 9904.401, Consistency in Estimating, Accumulating, and Reporting Costs; 48 C.F.R. § 9904.402, Consistency in Allocating Costs Incurred for the Same Purpose; 48 C.F.R. § 9904.405, Accounting for Unallowable Costs; and 48 C.F.R. § 9904.406, Cost Accounting Standard—Cost Accounting Period. Modified coverage may be applied to a covered contract of less than $50 million awarded to a BUSINESS UNIT that received less than $50 million in net CAS-covered contract awards in the immediately preceding cost accounting period. However, if the business unit receives a contract for more than $50 million that contract and all subsequent CAS-covered contracts must be subject to FULL COVERAGE. 48 C.F.R. § 9903.201-2(b)(1)-(2). Contract clauses are specified in FAR 30.201-4. See Manos, 2 GOVERNMENT CONTRACT COSTS AND PRICING, chap. 60 (2d ed. 2009-2020); Cibinic, Knight & Nash, COST-REIMBURSEMENT CONTRACTING 527–28 (4th ed. 2014).

MODIFIED TOTAL COST METHOD   A variation of the TOTAL COST METHOD used to establish the amount of DAMAGES or EQUITABLE ADJUSTMENT due a contractor. The modified method results in the contractor being compensated for the difference between its actual expenses and its bid price, with modifications for possible inaccuracies or errors in bidding and for costs incurred that are the responsibility of the contractor. This method requires a contractor to demonstrate that proving actual losses is either impossible or highly impracticable, but prevents the government from obtaining a windfall when a contractor is unable to satisfy all elements of the total cost method. See Nash & Feldman, 2 GOVERNMENT CONTRACT CHANGES § 19:22 (3d ed. 2006–2020); Cibinic, Nagle & Nash, ADMINISTRATION OF GOVERNMENT CONTRACTS 633–34 (5th ed. 2016).

MODULAR CONTRACTING   *Official:* The use of one or more contracts to acquire INFORMATION TECHNOLOGY systems in successive, interoperable increments. *Source:* FAR 39.002. Section 35 of the CLINGER-COHEN ACT OF 1996, 41 U.S.C. § 1907-1908, 41 U.S.C. § 104 provides that this technique should be used to acquire a major system of information technology "to the maximum extent practicable." FAR 39.103(a) explains that buying an information technology system in discrete increments is intended to balance the need of the government for fast access to a rapidly changing technology with stability in program development and management of contract performance and risk. Guidance on the use of this type of contracting is contained in FAR Subpart 39.1.

MODULAR OPEN SYSTEM APPROACH   *Official* With respect to a MAJOR DEFENSE ACQUISITION PROGRAM, an integrated business and technical strategy that—(A) employs a modular design that uses MAJOR SYSTEM INTERFACEs between a major system platform and a major system component, between major system components, or between major system platforms; (B) is subjected to verification to ensure major system interfaces comply with, if available and suitable, widely supported and consensus-based standards; (C) uses a system architecture that allows severable major system components at the appropriate level to be incrementally added, removed, or replaced throughout the life cycle of a major system platform to afford opportunities for enhanced competition and innovation while yielding—(i) significant cost savings or avoidance; (ii) schedule reduction; (iii) opportunities for technical upgrades; (iv) increased interoperability, including system of systems interoperability and mission integration; or (v) other benefits during the sustainment phase of a major weapon system; and (D) complies with the technical data rights set forth in 10 U.S.C. § 2320. *Source.* 10 U.S.C. § 2446a(b). 10 U.S.C. § 2446a(a) requires the use of this design technique "to the maximum extent practicable." The goal of the technique is to ensure that major defense systems are designed in a way that allows their major components to be competitively acquired during the life of the system. In order to meet this goal, an agency must obtain RIGHTS IN TECHNICAL DATA and COMPUTER SOFTWARE describing the interface so that competitors can design a competitive component. See MAJOR SYSTEM INTERFACE. 10 U.S.C. § 2446b(c) contains a detailed description of the elements of this modular approach, and 10 U.S.C. § 2446c requires DoD to have the resources and training necessary to use the approach.

MONTE CARLO SIMULATION   (also Monte Carlo Method) A statistical decision making analysis used to predict results after considering sources of uncertainty. It can be used in MAJOR SYSTEM PROGRAMs to estimate costs and to predict cost overruns and can also be used to predict schedule overruns and system failures. It has many other applications in military and business affairs. The origin of the method has been traced to the Los Alamos Laboratory and the Manhattan program to develop the atomic bomb during World War II. See Methods and Models for Life Cycle Costing, Final Report of Task Group SAS-054, RTO-TR-SAS-054 (North Atlantic Treaty Organization, 2007), Ch. 7; Kochanski, Monte Carlo Simulation (2005); Tyson, et al., Support Costs and Reliability in Weapons Acquisition: Approaches for Evaluating New Systems, DTIC AD-A227 592 (Institute for Defense Analyses, 1990). Of historical interest is Dienemann, Estimating Cost Uncertainty Using Monte Carlo Techniques, Memorandum RM-4854-PR (Rand Corporation 1966).

MOST FAVORED CUSTOMER   The status that earns the largest discount that a contractor gives to its customers. The government expects contractors on the FEDERAL SUPPLY SCHEDULES to sell supplies to the government at prices not exceeding those given to a contractor's most favored customer. GSAR 538.270. However, contractors are permitted to identify specific customers instead of all customers for the purposes of applying this principle. In addition, contracting officers are permitted to award FSS contracts at more than the price of a most favored customer if the price is fair and reasonable. GSAR 538.270. The most favored customer requirement is implemented by including the Price Reductions clause in GSAR 552.238-81 in FSS contracts. This clause states that the government is entitled to receive a reduction in price (or an increase in discount) if during the term of the contract the contractor makes any changes in its discount or pricing practices which would result in a less advantageous relationship between the government and the customer or category of customers upon which the contract discount or price was predicated. Different procedures are applied if the contractor agrees to provide TRANSACTIONAL DATA. See Feldman, Government Contract Awards: Negotiation and Sealed Bidding §§ 23:1–23:21 (2019–2020 ed.).

MOVING AVERAGE COST   *Official:* An INVENTORY costing method under which an average unit cost is computed after each acquisition by adding the cost of the newly acquired units to the cost of the units of INVENTORY on hand and dividing this figure by the new total number of units. *Source:* FAR 31.001. This method is one of the acceptable methods of charging material in a contractor's inventory to contracts under CAS 411, Accounting for Acquisition Cost of Material, 48 C.F.R. § 9904.411.

MULTI-AGENCY CONTRACT (MAC)   *Official:* A TASK ORDER CONTRACT or DELIVERY ORDER CONTRACT established by one agency for use by government agencies to obtain supplies and services, consistent with the ECONOMY ACT (see 17.502-2). Multi-agency contracts include contracts for information technology established pursuant to 40 U.S.C. § 11314(a)(2). *Source:* FAR 2.101. When an agency awards such a contract, it must be listed on the government-wide database at www.contractdirectory.gov/contractdirectory/. FAR 5.601. The procedures to be followed in placing orders against such contracts are set forth in FAR 16.505(a)(8). Agencies must prepare a BUSINESS CASE analysis to establish MACs, which includes (1) strategies for small business participation; (2) details on administration of the contract, including DIRECT and INDIRECT COSTs; (3) a description of the impact the contract will have on the government's ability to leverage its purchasing power; (4) an analysis concluding there is a need for the MAC; and (5) documented roles and responsibilities in administration of the contract. FAR 17.502-2. See Cibinic, Nash & Yukins, FORMATION OF GOVERNMENT CONTRACTS, chap. 8 (4th ed. 2011). There has been considerable criticism of "interagency contracting" by the GAO. See U.S. GOV'T ACCOUNTABILITY OFFICE, INTERAGENCY CONTRACTING: FRANCHISE FUNDS PROVIDE CONVENIENCE, BUT VALUE TO DOD IS NOT DEMONSTRATED, GAO-05-456 (July 2005); U.S. GOV'T ACCOUNTABILITY OFFICE, INTERAGENCY CONTRACTING: PROBLEMS WITH DOD's AND INTERIOR'S ORDERS TO SUPPORT MILITARY OPERATIONS, GAO-05-201 (Apr. 2005).

MULTIPLE AWARD PREFERENCE   A statutory preference that DELIVERY ORDER CONTRACTs and TASK ORDER CONTRACTs be awarded to multiple contractors rather than a single contractor. 10 U.S.C. § 2304a(d)(3); 41 U.S.C. § 4103(d)(4)(A). The preference is implemented in FAR 16.504(c). It requires multiple awards to the maximum extent practicable unless (1) only one contractor is able to supply unique or specialized supplies or services, (2) more favorable terms can be obtained by a single award, (3) the expected cost of administering multiple awards outweighs the benefits of multiple awards, (4) tasks likely to be ordered are so integrally related that only one contractor can reasonably perform the work, (5) the total estimated value of the contract is less than the SIMPLIFIED ACQUISITION THRESHOLD, or (6) multiple awards would not be in the best interest of the government. The preference is especially strong for contracts for ADVISORY AND ASSISTANCE SERVICES that exceed three years and $12.5 million. FAR 16.504(c)(2). See Cibinic, Nash & Yukins, FORMATION OF GOVERNMENT CONTRACTS 1392–97 (4th ed. 2011); Nash, *Indefinite Delivery/Indefinite Quantity Contracts: The Multiple Award Preference*, 18 N&CR ¶ 33 (Aug. 2004).

MULTIPLE-AWARD SCHEDULE (MAS)   *Official:* Contracts awarded by GSA or the Department of Veterans Affairs (VA) for similar or comparable supplies, or services, established with more than one supplier, at varying prices. The primary statutory authorities for the MAS program are 41 U.S.C. § 152(3), Competitive Procedures, and 40 U.S.C. § 501, Services for Executive Agencies. *Source:* FAR 8.401. These FEDERAL SUPPLY SCHEDULE contracts cover items at either the same or different prices for delivery to a single geographic area. A MAS permits the government to use industry distribution FACILITIES effectively and to select among comparable supplies and services when there are no prescribed STANDARDs or SPECIFICATIONs. Agencies are expected to make a best value decision when ordering from these schedules. FAR 8.404(d). Because agencies may select from among several contractors, contractors do not know what volume of sales to expect; consequently, although the agencies benefit, the sources suffer because of the possibility that few, if any, orders might be placed with them. MAS contracts differ from most government contracts in that (1) items procured through them are not designed or manufactured to government specifications, nor are they produced exclusively or principally for government use; and (2) the government makes no commitment to purchase any items covered by them. The contractor must sell to any authorized user of the MAS at the prices and on the terms and conditions provided in the contract and government agencies may negotiate lower prices with MAS contractors. See Cibinic, Nash & Yukins, FORMATION OF GOVERNMENT CONTRACTS 1143–88 (4th ed. 2011). See also McCullough, Perry, and Aronie, *Multiple Award Schedule Protests*, BRIEFING PAPERS No. 18-7 (June 2018).

MULTIPLE INCENTIVE CONTRACT   See INCENTIVE CONTRACT.

MULTIPLE YEAR CONTRACTS   *Official:* Contracts having a term of more than 1 year regardless of fiscal year funding. The term includes MULTI-YEAR CONTRACTs (see FAR 17.103). *Source:* FAR 22.1001. Such contracts are commonly used by government agencies to obtain better prices by stabilizing workloads. They can be accomplished by the use of OPTIONS for additional years, multi-year contracts, or multiple year INDEFINITE-QUANTITY CONTRACTs. See the definition of multi-year contract in FAR 17.103 for an explanation of an official distinction between multiple year and multi-year contracts. See Cibinic, Nash & Yukins, FORMATION OF GOVERNMENT CONTRACTS 1363–64, 1397–99, 1407–10 (4th ed. 2011).

MULTIYEAR APPROPRIATION   See APPROPRIATION.

MULTI-YEAR CONTRACT   *Official:* A contract for the purchase of supplies or services for more than 1, but not more than 5, program years. A multiyear contract may provide that performance under the contract during the second and subsequent years of the contract is contingent upon the appropriation of funds, and (if it does so provide) may provide for a cancellation payment to be made to the contractor if appropriations are not made. The key distinguishing difference between multi-year contracts and multiple year contracts is that multi-year contracts, defined in the statutes cited at 17.101, buy more than 1 year's requirement (of a product or service) without establishing and having to exercise an option for each program year after the first. *Source:* FAR 17.103. This is a special type of REQUIREMENTS CONTRACT where the total funds to be obligated are not available at the time of CONTRACT AWARD. FAR 17.103. FAR 17.105-2 states that these contracts are intended to achieve—by permitting early planning and ECONOMIES OF SCALE— lower costs, STANDARDIZATION, administrative simplicity, and stability, among other things. Multi-year contracts may not cover more than five years of requirements unless authorized by statute. Each program year is annually budgeted and funded and, at the time of award, funds need only have been appropriated for the first year. The contractor is protected against loss resulting from cancellation by contract provisions that allow reimbursement of costs included in a CANCELLATION CEILING. If funds do not become available to support requirements for the succeeding years, the agency must cancel the contract. See FAR Subpart 17.1. Multi-year contracting authority can be used to make an "advanced procurement" of an ECONOMIC ORDER QUANTITY. See DFARS 217.174. Agencies must notify Congress of multi-year procurements over stated thresholds. FAR 17.108. See Feldman, GOVERNMENT CONTRACT AWARDS: NEGOTIATION AND SEALED BIDDING §§ 5:2–5:8 (2019–2020 ed.).

MUNITION LIST   See DEFENSE ARTICLE.

MUST An imperative word in the FAR addressing the mandatory obligations of government personnel. SHALL is more generally used for this purpose. See FAR 2.101 cross-referencing these terms.

MUTUAL MISTAKE A MISTAKE common to both parties to a contract. Mutual mistakes can occur when the parties include terms in the contract that do not conform to or express their actual intent or agreement (called mistakes in integration) or when the parties labor under the same misconception about a fundamental fact on which the contract is based (called mistakes in BASIC ASSUMPTION). See Nash, *Mutual Mistake of Basic Assumption: A Rare Beast*, 33 N&CR ¶ 57 (Oct. 2019); Cibinic, *Postscript III: Mutual Mistake of Basic Assumption*, 16 N&CR ¶ 28 (June 2002). Both types of mutual mistake have led to contract REFORMATION by the BOARDS OF CONTRACT APPEALS or the courts or through EXTRAORDINARY CONTRACTUAL ACTIONs. Mutual mistakes are also grounds for avoiding the binding effect of a CONTRACT MODIFICATION. FAR 33.205 states that such mistakes should now be dealt with under the DISPUTEs procedures. See Cibinic, Nagle & Nash, ADMINISTRATION OF GOVERNMENT CONTRACTS 296–302 (5th ed. 2016).

N

NAFTA See NORTH AMERICAN FREE TRADE AGREEMENT.

NASA See NATIONAL AERONAUTICS AND SPACE ADMINISTRATION.

NASA FAR SUPPLEMENT (NFS) The NASA acquisition regulation, which establishes agency-wide policies and procedures for implementing and supplementing the FEDERAL ACQUISITION REGULATION, designated 48 C.F.R. chap. 18. All agency-wide policies and procedures that govern the contracting process, control contracting relationships, or require publication in the FEDERAL REGISTER for public comment are included in the NFS. NFS 1801.105-1. The NFS is amended by the issuance of procurement notices which are analogous to FEDERAL ACQUISITION CIRCULARS. NFS 1801.270. The NFS cites or incorporates provisions of some of NASA's nonprocurement documents and handbooks. The NFS is available at https://www.acquisition.gov/nfs/nasa-far-supplement-0.

NASA PROCUREMENT REGULATION (NPR) The original regulation issued under the ARMED SERVICES PROCUREMENT ACT to govern NASA procurement practices. It was based on and very similar to the ARMED SERVICES PROCUREMENT REGULATION and was in effect from the inception of NASA until April 1, 1984, the beginning of the FEDERAL ACQUISITION REGULATIONS SYSTEM.

NASA RESEARCH ANNOUNCEMENT (NRA) A BROAD AGENCY ANNOUNCEMENT used to announce NASA research interests and solicit proposals reflecting those interests. The NRA process is oriented to those research procurements for which it would be impossible to draft a sufficiently detailed REQUEST FOR PROPOSAL without constraining the technical responses. Special preparation and evaluation procedures apply. NFS 1835.016-71. See Cibinic, Nash & Yukins, FORMATION OF GOVERNMENT CONTRACTS 1083 (4th ed. 2011).

NATIONAL AERONAUTICS AND SPACE ADMINISTRATION (NASA) An independent civilian agency of the U.S. Government, established by the National Aeronautics and Space Act of 1958, 42 U.S.C. § 2452. Its basic mission is to conduct aeronautic and space activities for peaceful purposes in conjunction with the scientific and engineering communities and to widely disseminate information on the results of those efforts. NASA consists of a headquarters in Washington, DC, and a number of research and engineering field installations throughout the country. NASA contracts fall under the ARMED SERVICES PROCUREMENT ACT as implemented in the FEDERAL ACQUISITION REGULATION (FAR) and the NASA FAR SUPPLEMENT (NFS). There are no lower-level acquisition regulations of general applicability. Before the FAR and the NFS went into effect in April 1984, NASA contracts were governed by the NASA PROCUREMENT REGULATION.

NATIONAL CONTRACT MANAGEMENT ASSOCIATION (NCMA) An organization composed of individuals who are engaged in public and commercial contracting through government agencies and companies or are in related fields of endeavor. NCMA's mission is to increase the effectiveness of public contract management by (1) helping members improve their skills through educational programs and contact with knowledgeable persons in the field; (2) establishing a uniform code of ethics; (3) providing a forum for the interchange of ideas; (4) introducing new literature, ideas, and improvements; (5) encouraging a professional attitude toward contract management and procurement; and (6) enabling members to share in the range of experience and knowledge represented by the membership as a whole. NCMA publishes the monthly *Contract Management* magazine, and it administers a certification program for contract professionals. [NCMA, 21740 Beaumeade Circle, Suite 125, Ashburn, VA 20147, 571-382-0082, www.ncmahq.org]

NATIONAL DEFENSE *Official:* Any activity related to programs for military or atomic energy production or construction, military assistance to any foreign nation, stockpiling, or space, except that for use in Subpart 11.6, see the definition in 11.601. *Source:* FAR 2.101. For purposes of PRIORITIES AND ALLOCATIONS, the term "national defense" includes emergency preparedness activities conducted pursuant to title VI of The Robert T. Stafford Disaster Relief and Emergency Assistance Act (42 U.S.C. § 5195 et seq.) and critical infrastructure protection and restoration (50 U.S.C. App. § 2152), FAR 11.601. The Space Act, 42 U.S.C. § 2452, does not give the NATIONAL AERONAUTICS AND SPACE ADMINISTRATION a military role in space.

NATIONAL DEFENSE INDUSTRIAL ASSOCIATION (NDIA) A nonpartisan, nonprofit, nonlobbying, educational association that drives strategic dialogue in national security by identifying key issues and leveraging the knowledge and experience of its military, government, industry, and academic members to address them. NDIA has over 1,600 corporate members and 70,000 individual members. [NDIA, 2101 Wilson Boulevard, Suite 700, Arlington, VA 22201-3061; (703) 522-1820] NDIA's Internet site is located at www.ndia.org.

NATIONAL DEFENSE PROJECTS RATING PLAN (NDPRP) A RISK-POOLING arrangement. Specifically, an insurance plan designed to apply to eligible defense projects from inception to cancellation or expiration. See DFARS 228.304. The plan covers workers' compensation, general liability, automobile liability and employer's liability claims asserted against the contractor and subcontractors at insured projects. The NDPRP was established in 1951 to minimize the cost to the government of purchasing workers' compensation and liability insurance for defense projects. The NDPRP uses the services and organizations of the insurance industry, at a minimum cost to the government, for safety engineering and handling of claims arising out of eligible defense contracts. The NDPRP is intended to provide this insurance to an eligible contractor at lower costs. Policies issued under the NDPRP are for a term of one year, but provide for automatic renewal at each anniversary date unless notice of unwillingness to renew is served. Endorsements are attached to all renewal policies to tie renewals together and make the NDPRP applicable on an overall basis from inception to cancellation or expiration of the plan. See *Johnson Controls World Services, Inc. v. U.S.*, 48 Fed. Cl. 479, 482 (2001); DOD PGI 228.304—Insurance.

NATIONAL INDUSTRIAL SECURITY PROGRAM   A program, established by Exec. Order No. 12829, 58 Fed. Reg. 3479 (Jan. 8, 1993), for the purpose of safeguarding CLASSIFIED INFORMATION released to contractors, licensees, or grantees of government agencies. The Executive Order provided for the issuance and maintenance of a manual. See DOD Instruction 5220.22, *National Industrial Security Program* (Mar. 18, 2011), chap. 1, May 1, 2018, and the *National Industrial Security Program Operation Manual*, DOD 5220.22-M (Feb. 1995), chap. 2, May 18, 2016, and updated with periodic Industrial Security letters. The manual sets out the specific requirements, restrictions, and other safeguards necessary to protect classified information.

NATIONAL INDUSTRIES FOR THE BLIND (NIB)   A CENTRAL NONPROFIT AGENCY, headquartered in Vienna, Virginia, that operates under the Javits-Wagner-O'Day Act, 41 U.S.C. § 8501-06, to provide employment opportunities for persons who are blind or severely disabled. FAR Subpart 8.7. NISH is the coordinating agency for this program giving preference to organizations employing such persons. See https://www.nib.org.

NATIONAL INSTITUTE OF STANDARDS AND TECHNOLOGY (NIST)   The organization (formerly known as the Bureau of Standards) responsible for establishing technical standards for products manufactured and sold in the United States. 15 U.S.C. § 272 et seq. NIST operates certain FEDERAL TECHNOLOGY TRANSFER programs, such as the Regional Centers for the Transfer of Manufacturing Technology. These programs transfer know-how and technologies developed by NIST and other federal organizations to small- and mid-sized manufacturing companies.

NATIONAL PERFORMANCE REVIEW   An initiative of the Clinton-Gore Administration created in 1993 "to reform the way the Federal Government works." Headed by Vice President Gore, National Performance Review's interagency task force examined the problems of government agencies and published reports containing hundreds of proposed recommendations. The task force then began to implement many initiatives contained in the reports. The major efforts were to focus attention of federal agencies on "customer satisfaction" and to reduce the number of federal employees.

NATIONAL SECURITY INDUSTRIAL ASSOCIATION (NSIA)   A not-for-profit, nonpolitical, nonlobbying association established in 1944 to foster a close working relationship and effective two-way communication between government (primarily defense) and its supporting industry. Conceived by James Forrestal, the first Secretary of Defense, NSIA was an association of some 400 industrial, research, legal, and educational organizations of all sizes and representing all segments of industry interested in and related to national security. In 1997, NSIA merged with the American Defense Preparedness Association (ADPA). It is now known as the NATIONAL DEFENSE INDUSTRIAL ASSOCIATION.

NATIONAL SECURITY SYSTEM   *Official:* Any telecommunications or information system operated by the United States Government, the function, operation, or use of which (1) Involves intelligence activities, (2) Involves cryptologic activities related to national security, (3) Involves command and control of military forces, (4) Involves equipment that is an integral part of a weapon or WEAPON SYSTEM, or (5) Is critical to the direct fulfillment of military or intelligence missions. This does not include a system that is to be used for routine administrative or business applications, such as payroll, finance, logistics, and personnel management applications. *Source:* FAR 39.002. These systems are not subject to the procedures of the CLINGER-COHEN ACT OF 1996 pertaining to the acquisition of INFORMATION TECHNOLOGY, except for the provisions of § 5141(b) of that Act. Acquisitions of national security systems are conducted in accordance with 40 U.S.C. § 11302, with regard to requirements for performance- and results-based management, the role of the agency chief information officer in acquisitions, and accountability. FAR 39.001; OMB Circular No. A-130, *Management of Federal Information Resources*, Dec. 12, 1985; Exec. Order No. 13011, 61 Fed. Reg. 37657 (July 16, 1996).

NATIVE AMERICAN PREFERENCE The rebuttable presumption that NATIVE AMERICANS are SOCIALLY DISADVANTAGED INDIVIDUALS for the purpose of determining the ownership of a SMALL DISADVANTAGED BUSINESS CONCERN. 13 C.F.R. § 124.103. They must then demonstrate to the SMALL BUSINESS ADMINISTRATION that are ECONOMICALLY DISADVANTAGED INDIVIDUALS. Businesses owned by such individuals are given special preferences in government procurement. See SMALL DISADVANTAGED BUSINESS CONCERN.

NATIVE AMERICANS *Official:* Alaska Natives, Native Hawaiians, or enrolled members of a Federally or State recognized Indian Tribe. *Source:* 13 C.F.R. § 124.103. See NATIVE AMERICAN PREFERENCE.

NEGATIVE INSTANT CONTRACT SAVINGS *Official:* The increase in the INSTANT CONTRACT cost or price when the acceptance of a VALUE ENGINEERING CHANGE PROPOSAL results in an excess of the contractor's allowable development and implementation costs over the product of the INSTANT UNIT COST REDUCTION multiplied by the number of instant contract units affected. *Source:* FAR 48.001. The Value Engineering clause in FAR 52.248-1 provides that the contract price will be increased when such negative savings (increased costs) occur. See Nash & Feldman, 1 GOVERNMENT CONTRACT CHANGES § 9:11 (3d ed. 2006–2020); Cibinic, Nagle & Nash, ADMINISTRATION OF GOVERNMENT CONTRACTS 374 (5th ed. 2016).

NEGLIGENCE The failure to use such care as a reasonably prudent and careful person would use under similar circumstances. Generally, all persons, including contractors, are liable for personal injury or property damage that occurs because of the negligence of their employees. Similarly, the government is liable for the negligence of its employees under the FEDERAL TORT CLAIMS ACT unless they are performing a DISCRETIONARY FUNCTION. Most contractors protect against claims for negligence of their employees by INSURANCE, but FAR 28.308 permits SELF-INSURANCE under prescribed circumstances. The government does not carry insurance but utilizes self-insurance for the negligence of its employees.

NEGOTIATED CONTRACT *Official:* A contract awarded using a procedure other than SEALED BIDDING. *Source:* FAR 15.000. Procedures for awarding negotiated contracts are in FAR Part 15. Negotiated contracts may be awarded on a competitive or SOLE SOURCE basis. Smaller negotiated contracts are awarded using the SIMPLIFIED ACQUISITION PROCEDURES in FAR Part 13. Contracts for COMMERCIAL ITEMS are awarded using the procedures in FAR Part 12. See Cibinic, Nash & Yukins, FORMATION OF GOVERNMENT CONTRACTS 334–37, 673–994 (4th ed. 2011).

NEGOTIATION   A method of contracting that uses either competitive or other-than-competitive procedures that permits BARGAINING with the offerors after receipt of PROPOSALs. Contracting by negotiation is a flexible process that includes the receipt of proposals from offerors, discussion of deficiencies or weaknesses with the offeror, and usually affords offerors an opportunity to revise their offers before award of a contract. In negotiation, award can be made on the basis of technical excellence, management capability, personnel qualifications, prior experience, PAST PERFORMANCE, and other factors bearing on quality, as well as cost. It is distinguished from SEALED BIDDING where only PRICE and PRICE-RELATED FACTORS are considered. Negotiation also permits the use of COST-REIMBURSEMENT CONTRACTs, which provide for payment to the contractor of allowable incurred costs. Prior to the passage of the COMPETITION IN CONTRACT-ING ACT, negotiation had to be justified. It is now an equally acceptable method of contracting as long as FULL AND OPEN COMPETITION is achieved, in which case it is called the COMPETITIVE PROPOSALS method of contracting. FAR 6.102. See generally Cibinic, Nash & Yukins, FORMATION OF GOVERNMENT CONTRACTS, chap. 6 (4th ed. 2011); Nash, *Postscript: Negotiation Instead of Sealed Bidding*, 23 N&CR ¶56 (Oct. 2009); Edwards, *The Decision to Use Negotiation Instead of Sealed Bidding: Is It Entirely Discretionary?*, 21 N&CR ¶73 (Dec. 2007).

NET ACQUISITION SAVINGS   *Official:* The total ACQUISITION SAVINGS, including instant, concurrent, and future contract savings, less government costs. *Source:* FAR 48.001. This is the base for calculation the price adjustment that is required when the government adopts a VALUE CHANGE ENGINEERING PROPOSAL. See FAR 48.104-2. See Nash & Feldman, 1 GOVERNMENT CONTRACT CHANGES § 9:7 (3d ed. 2006–2020); Cibinic, Nagle & Nash, ADMINISTRATION OF GOVERNMENT CONTRACTS 372–74 (5th ed. 2016).

NET BOOK VALUE   The stated value of a TANGIBLE CAPITAL ASSET after subtracting DEPRECIATION from the cost of the asset. Net book value of assets is used to compute the COST OF CAPITAL COMMITTED TO FACILITIES under CAS 414, 48 C.F.R. § 9904.414. It is also used in computing the "facilities capital employed" element of the WEIGHTED GUIDELINES METHOD used by DOD to compute the profit objective when profit is negotiated. DFARS 215.404-71-4. See Cibinic, Nash & Yukins, FORMATION OF GOVERNMENT CONTRACTS 1555–59 (4th ed. 2011).

NET WORTH   The amount stated on a company's BALANCE SHEET when LIABILITIES are subtracted from ASSETs. This amount provides a rough appraisal of the amount of funds a company has retained in its business and thus gives an indication of the financial capability of the company. It is used in making the determination of whether the company is a responsible contractor (see RESPONSIBILITY).

NETWORK ANALYSIS SYSTEM   A recognized scheduling system, such as the CRITICAL PATH METHOD, that shows the duration, sequential relationships, and interdependence of various work activities. While many construction projects make use of this system, it is not required by the standard Schedule for Construction Contracts clause in FAR 52.236-15, which only requires the contractor to prepare a "practicable schedule." However, FAR 36.515 identifies the fact that agencies can use alternate clauses that identify "other management approaches for ensuring that a contractor makes adequate progress" and these approaches would generally require a network analysis system.

NEUTRAL   and **NEUTRAL ADVISOR**. See NEUTRAL PERSON.

NEUTRAL PERSON   *Official:* An impartial third party, who serves as a mediator, fact finder, or arbitrator, or otherwise functions to assist the parties to resolve the issues in controversy. A neutral person may be a permanent or temporary officer or employee of the federal government or any other individual who is acceptable to the parties. A neutral person must have no official, financial, or personal CONFLICT OF INTEREST with respect to the issues in controversy, unless the interest is fully disclosed IN WRITING to all parties and all parties agree that the neutral person may serve (5 U.S.C. § 583). *Source:* FAR 2.101. A shorter definition is contained in 5 U.S.C. § 571(9). FAR 33.214(d) permits the use of neutral persons in the ALTERNATIVE DISPUTE RESOLUTION process. Neutral advisors have been used extensively in MINITRIALs. The ADMINISTRATIVE DISPUTE RESOLUTION ACT contains detailed provisions regarding the use of a "neutral" at 5 U.S.C. § 573. These provisions require an interagency committee established by the President to develop procedures that permit agencies to obtain the services of neutrals on an expedited basis. The Act also permits agencies to enter into contracts with neutrals.

NO-SETOFF COMMITMENT   *Official:* A contractual undertaking that, to the extent permitted by the Assignment of Claims Act, 31 U.S.C. § 3727, payments by the designated agency to the ASSIGNEE under an ASSIGNMENT OF CLAIMS will not be reduced to liquidate the indebtedness of the contractor to the government. *Source:* FAR 32.801. Without such an agreement, the government has the right to SETOFF any claims that it has against the contractor from contract payments. The Act authorizes such a commitment during a war or other national emergency by DOD, the General Services Administration, the Department of Energy, or any other agency designated by the President. FAR 32.803(d). When this commitment is made, Alternate I to the Assignment of Claims clause in FAR 52.232-23 is included in the contract. FAR 32.806(a)(2). See Cibinic, Nagle & Nash, Administration of Government Contracts 1071–72 (5th ed. 2016).

NO-YEAR APPROPRIATION   See APPROPRIATION.

NOLO CONTENDERE   A Latin phrase meaning "I will not contest it." As a plea in a criminal proceeding, it has an effect similar to pleading guilty; however, in pleading *nolo contendere*, the defendant neither admits nor denies the charges, and the plea cannot be used against the defendant in a civil action based on the same acts. Black's Law Dictionary 1259 (11th ed. 2019). A plea of *nolo contendere* is treated as a conviction for the commission of a crime and can be used as a cause for DEBARMENT. See FAR 2.101 including pleas of nolo contendere in the definition of CONVICTION. If legal proceedings for a contractor's violation of law or regulation result in a conviction entered upon a plea of *nolo contendere*, costs related to the proceedings are unallowable. FAR 31.205-47.

NONAPPROPRIATED FUNDS   Monies derived from sources other than congressional APPROPRIATIONs. An example would be funds derived from the sale of supplies and services to military and civilian personnel and their dependents and used to support or provide recreational, religious, or educational programs or programs to improve welfare or morale. The Department of the Treasury's fiscal records do not account for nonappropriated funds. See DAU Glossary; Manos, 3 Government Contract Costs and Pricing § 90:7 (2d ed. 2009–2020).

NONAPPROPRIATED FUNDS INSTRUMENTALITY (NAFI)   An organization operated with NONAPPROPRIATED FUNDS. Such instrumentalities may include post or base exchanges, officers and noncommissioned officers clubs, theaters, bowling alleys, and similar facilities at military installations. Their procurements are not subject to the FEDERAL ACQUISITION REGULATION but frequently follow procedures essentially the same as those set forth in that regulation. See Zoldan, *All Roar and No Bite: Lion Raisins and the Federal Circuit's First Swipe at the NAFI Doctrine*, 36 PUB. CONT. L.J. 153 (2007).

NONCOMMON CARRIER   See CARRIER (TELECOMMUNICATIONS).

NONCOMPENSABLEDELAY   See DELAY.

NONCOMPLEX ITEM   An item of supply that has quality characteristics for which simple measurement and test of the end item are sufficient to determine conformance to contract requirements. FAR 46.203(b)(2). In determining the contract quality assurance requirements, noncomplex items do not warrant the use of HIGHER-LEVEL CONTRACT QUALITY REQUIREMENTS. FAR 46.202-4.

NONCOMPLIANCE   *Official:* A failure in estimating, accumulating, or reporting costs to— (1) Comply with applicable COST ACCOUNTING STANDARDS; or (2) Consistently follow disclosed or established cost accounting practices. *Source:* FAR 30.001. When it is determined that a contractor has a noncompliance, the government official administering the cost accounting standards must determine whether it is material or immaterial. FAR 30.602. If a noncompliance is material, the contractor is subject to a PRICE ADJUSTMENT. See Cibinic & Nash, COST REIMBURSEMENT CONTRACTING 666–68 (3d ed. 2004).

NONCRITICAL APPLICATION [OF AN ITEM]   A use of an item of supply in which the failure of the item could not injure personnel or jeopardize a vital agency mission. FAR 46.203(c)(2). In determining the contract quality assurance requirements, items with noncritical applications do not warrant the use of HIGHER-LEVEL CONTRACT QUALITY REQUIREMENTS. FAR 46.202-4.

NONDEVELOPMENTAL ITEM (NDI)   *Official:* (1) Any previously developed item of supply used exclusively for government purposes by a federal agency, a state or local government, or a foreign government with which the United States has a mutual defense cooperation agreement; (2) Any item described in paragraph (1) that requires only minor modification or modifications of a type customarily available in the commercial marketplace in order to meet the requirements of the procuring department or agency; or (3) Any item of supply being produced that does not meet the requirements of paragraphs (1) or (2) solely because the item is not yet in use. *Source:* FAR 2.101. 10 U.S.C. § 2377 and 41 U.S.C. § 2645 state the congressional preference for the acquisition of commercial and nondevelopmental items by the DOD and other agencies. These statutes are implemented in FAR 7.102(a)(1), 7.103(b), and 11.002(a)(2). Nondevelopmental items can be COMMERCIAL PRODUCTs if they meet the more restrictive requirements of that definition. See also OFF-THE-SHELF PRODUCT.

NONDISCLOSURE AGREEMENT   An agreement by the recipient of proprietary TECHNICAL DATA or COMPUTER SOFTWARE not to disclose the data or software to others or use it for purposes other than those for which it was furnished. DFARS 227.7103-7 provides a standard form agreement and requires that third parties sign such an agreement prior to the receipt of technical data or computer software subject to restrictions. The agreement permits use only for government purposes and prohibits use for commercial purposes. The agreement makes the contractor whose data or software is being furnished a THIRD-PARTY BENEFICIARY to the agreement—giving that party the right to sue to enforce the agreement. FAR 9.505-4(b) requires that contractors performing ADVISORY AND ASSISTANCE SERVICES sign such an agreement if they obtain access to proprietary information of other contractors. See Nash & Rawicz, INTELLECTUAL PROPERTY IN GOVERNMENT CONTRACTS, chaps. 4 & 5 (6th ed. 2008); Nash, *Enforcing A Nondisclosure Agreement*, 26 N&CR ¶ 38 (July 2012); Nash, *Nondisclosure Agreements: A Variety of Approaches*, 24 N&CR ¶ 58 (Dec. 2010); Nash, *Postscript II: Mixed Workforce Questions*, 21 N&CR ¶ 3 (Feb. 2007).

NONMANUFACTURER RULE *Official:* A contractor under a small business set-aside or 8(a) contract shall be a small business under the applicable size standard and shall provide either its own produce or that of another domestic small business manufacturing or processing concern (see 13 C.F.R. § 121.406). *Source:* FAR 19.001. This rule, promulgated by the SMALL BUSINESS ADMINISTRATION, applies in the procurement of manufactured products under a small business set-aside or 8(a) acquisition, and allows a firm that does not manufacture the product to be acquired to meet the limitations on subcontracting if it obtains the product from another small business. FAR 19.102(f) and 13 C.F.R. § 121.406. See https://www.sba.gov/document/support–non-manufacturer-rule-class-waiver-list.

NONMONETARY CLAIM A claim under the CONTRACT DISPUTES ACT that does not request the payment of money. The most common nonmonetary claims are appeals of a TERMINATION FOR DEFAULT and accounting issues. Although claims seeking CONTRACT INTERPRETATION are permitted, they are discretionary in nature and are generally not accepted by the COURT OF FEDERAL CLAIMS or the BOARDs OF CONTRACT APPEALS. See Cibinic, Nagle & Nash, ADMINISTRATION OF GOVERNMENT CONTRACTS 1137–41 (5th ed. 2016); Nash, *Postscript: Nonmonetary Claims*, 19 N&CR ¶ 38 (Aug. 2005).

NONPERSONAL HEALTH CARE SERVICES Services of physicians, dentists, and other health care providers obtained by the government through NONPERSONAL SERVICE CONTRACTs. FAR 37.400. Under contracts for these services, the government may evaluate the quality of the professional and administrative services provided, but retains no control over the medical aspects of the services, such as professional judgments, diagnosis for specific medical treatments. FAR 37.401(b). Contractors are required to indemnify the government from liability for act of the contractor or its employees during contract performance in accordance with the Indemnity and Medical Liability Insurance clause in FAR 52.237-7. See FAR Subpart 37.4.

NONPERSONAL SERVICES CONTRACT *Official:* A contract under which the personnel rendering services are not subject, either by the contract's terms or by the manner of its administration, to the supervision and control usually prevailing in relationships between the government and its employees. *Source:* FAR 37.101. Such contracts are not subject to the restrictions imposed on PERSONAL SERVICES CONTRACTS. See Nash, *Personal Services Contracts: Is the Federal Acquisition Regulation Guidance Valid?*, 21 N&CR ¶ 16 (Apr. 2007).

NONPROCUREMENT COMMON RULE *Official:* The procedures used by federal executive agencies to suspend, debar, or exclude individuals or entities from participation in nonprocurement transactions under Executive Order 12549. Examples of nonprocurement transactions are grants, cooperative agreements, scholarships, fellowships, contracts of assistance, loans, loan guarantees, subsidies, insurance, payments for specified use, and donation agreements. *Source:* FAR 9.403. Organizations or persons suspended, debarred, or excluded under this rule are included in the EXCLUDED PARTIES LIST SYSTEM which bars them from obtaining contracts unless a waiver is issued. FAR 9.404(b).

NONPROFIT AGENCY SERVING PEOPLE WHO ARE BLIND or NONPROFIT AGENCY SERVING PEOPLE WITH OTHER SEVERE DISABILITIES   *Official:* A qualified nonprofit agency employing people who are blind or have other severe disabilities approved by the COMMITTEE FOR PURCHASE FROM PEOPLE WHO ARE BLIND OR SEVERELY DISABLED to furnish a commodity or a service to the government under the Javits-Wagner-O'Day Act. *Source:* FAR 8.701. These agencies are referred to jointly as ABILITYONE participating nonprofit agencies. Such agencies are given preferences in accordance with FAR Subpart 8.7.

NONPROFIT ORGANIZATION   *Official:* A university or other institution of higher education or an organization of the type described in section 501(c)(3) of the Internal Revenue Code of 1954 (26 U.S.C. § 501(c)) and exempt from taxation under section 501(a) of the Internal Revenue Code (26 U.S.C. § 501(a)), or any nonprofit scientific or educational organization qualified under a state nonprofit organization statute. *Source:* FAR 27.301. Such organizations are entitled to have a PATENT RIGHTS clause in their contracts that permits them to retain TITLE to SUBJECT INVENTIONs (giving the government a LICENSE) in accordance with 35 U.S.C. §§ 200–212. See FAR Subpart 27.3; Nash & Rawicz, INTELLECTUAL PROPERTY IN GOVERNMENT CONTRACTS, chap. 2 (6th ed. 2008). Prior to the issuance of FAC 2005-17, May 15, 2007, FAR 45.301 defined the term differently as any corporation, foundation, trust, or institution operated for scientific, educational, or medical purposes, not organized for profit, and no part of the net earnings of which inures to the benefit of any private shareholder or individual. This definition determined when a nonprofit educational institution was entitled to be bound by a less stringent clause when accounting for FACILITIES. This guidance has now been removed from the FAR. See Manos, 1 GOVERNMENT CONTRACT COSTS AND PRICING § 6:8 (2d ed. 2009–2020).

NONRECURRING COSTS   *Official:* Costs which are generally incurred on a one-time basis and include such as costs of plant and equipment relocation, plant rearrangement, SPECIAL TOOLING and SPECIAL TEST EQUIPMENT, preproduction engineering, initial spoilage and rework, and specialized workforce training. *Source:* FAR 17.103. In MULTIYEAR CONTRACTING such costs are included in the CANCELLATION CEILING and are recoverable upon CANCELLATION of the multiyear contract up to the amount of the ceiling. FAR 17.106-1. When the government has paid NONRECURRING COSTs, they may be recovered through RECOUPMENT, in accordance with agency procedures, from contractors that sell, LEASE, or LICENSE the resulting products or technology to buyers other than the federal government. See FAR 35.001 and FAR 35.003.

NONSEVERABLE   *Official:* Property that cannot be removed after construction or installation without substantial loss of value or damage to the installed property or to the premises where installed. *Source:* FAR 45.101. While this term is defined in FAR Part 45, the part contains no guidance as to where it is applied. However, the Government Property clause in FAR 52.245-1(e) provides that government property shall not "become a fixture or lose its identity as personal property by being attached to any real property."

NONSEVERABLE DELIVERABLE   *Official:* A deliverable item [of supply or service] that is a single end product or undertaking, entire in nature, that cannot be feasibly subdivided into discrete elements or phases without losing its identity. *Source:* DFARS 204.7101. In general, DFARS Subpart 204.71 requires that such items be included in separate CONTRACT LINE ITEMs.

NONSEVERABLE PRODUCTION AND RESEARCH PROPERTY   Prior to the issuance of FAC 2005-17, May 15, 2007, this term defined GOVERNMENT PRODUCTION AND RESEARCH PROPERTY that could not be removed after erection or installation without substantial loss of value or damage to the property or to the premises where it was installed and the FAR stated that the government should not provide government production and research property to contractors when it would be installed or constructed on land not owned by the government in such a way that it became nonseverable. This guidance has now been removed from the FAR.

NONTRADITIONAL DEFENSE CONTRACTOR   *Official:* An entity that is not currently performing and has not performed any contract or subcontract for DOD that is subject to full coverage under the cost accounting standards prescribed pursuant to 41 U.S.C. § 1502 and the regulations implementing such section, for at least the one-year period preceding the solicitation of sources by DOD for the procurement (10 U.S.C. § 2302(9)). *Source:* DFARS 212.001. 10 U.S.C. § 2380a allows contracting officers to treat supplies and services provided by nontraditional defense contractors as COMMERCIAL PRODUCTs. See DFARS 212.102(a)(iii). A nontraditional defense contractor may be awarded a PROTO-TYPE OTHER TRANSACTION contract without cost-sharing. 10 U.S.C. § 2371b. Such a contractor may also be awarded a follow-on contract to a prototype other transaction contract using the procedures in FAR Part 15.

NORMAL WORKWEEK   *Official:* A workweek of 40 hours. Outside the United States and its outlying areas, a workweek longer than 40 hours may be considered normal if—(1) The workweek does not exceed the norm for the area, as determined by local custom, tradition, or law; and (2) The hours worked in excess of 40 in the workweek are not compensated at a premium rate of pay. *Source:* FAR 22.103-1. FAR 22.103 provides that it is the government's policy to encourage contractors to perform their contracts without the use of OVER-TIME and contains guidance on the approval of overtime when it is necessary.

NORTH AMERICAN FREE TRADE AGREEMENT (NAFTA)   An agreement between the United States, Canada, and Mexico to eliminate trade barriers, promote fair competition, protect intellectual property, and resolve disputes between the members. The agreement was entered into in 1992 and implemented by Pub. L. No. 103-182 to become effective on January 1, 1994, 19 U.S.C. § 3311 et seq. The Act was replaced by the UNITED STATES—MEXICO—CANADA AGREEMENT in 2020. NAFTA provided for waiver of the BUY AMERICAN ACT in certain situations. See FAR Subpart 25.4. This Act also made changes to COPYRIGHT law to conform to NAFTA. See Nash & Rawicz, INTELLEC-TUAL PROPERTY IN GOVERNMENT CONTRACTS, chap. 1 (6th ed. 2008); Eyester, *NAFTA and the Barriers to Federal Procurement Opportunities in the United States,* 31 PUB. CONT. L.J. 695 (2002).

NORTH AMERICAN INDUSTRY CLASSIFICATION SYSTEM (NAICS)   Adopted in 1997 to replace the old Standard Industrial Classification (SIC) system, NAICS is the industry classification system used by the statistical agencies of the United States. It is the first economic classification system to be constructed based on a single economic concept. The NAICS provides a consistent system for economic analysis across the three North American

Free Trade Agreement partners—Canada, Mexico, and the United States. A complete list of the 2017 NAICS hierarchy can be located on the NAICS website at www.census.gov/eos/www/naics. Small businesses are classified using this system, FAR 19.102(b), and contracting officers must include the appropriate NAICS code in solicitations, FAR 19.303.

NOTICE AND ASSISTANCE Notice by a contractor to the government of any claim for COPYRIGHT or PATENT INFRINGEMENT and assistance of the government in defending against such claim. FAR 27.201-2(b) requires that all contracts containing an AUTHORIZATION AND CONSENT clause include the Notice and Assistance Regarding Patent and Copyright Infringement clause at FAR 52.227-2. The clause provides that the government will pay the costs of any requested assistance unless the contractor has indemnified the government for the infringement. See Nash & Rawicz, INTELLECTUAL PROPERTY IN GOVERNMENT CONTRACTS, chap. 2 (6th ed. 2008).

NOTICE OF AWARD A method of ACCEPTANCE OF OFFER that the government uses to make an immediate award of a contract. FAR 14.408-1, FAR 15.504. A notice of award is usually given electronically or by FACSIMILE, and FAR 14.408-1(c)(2) requires that it be followed as soon as possible by the formal award using Standard Form 33, Solicitation, Offer, and Award, FAR 53.301-33, or Standard Form 26, Award/Contract, FAR 53.301-26. FAR 36.213-4 contains additional guidance on the use of notices of award in construction contracts. See Feldman, GOVERNMENT CONTRACT AWARDS: NEGOTIATION AND SEALED BIDDING, chap. 20 (2019–2020 ed.).

NOTICE OF CHANGES See NOTICE REQUIREMENTS.

NOTICE OF INTENT TO DISALLOW COSTS See DISALLOWANCE.

NOTICE OF INTENTION TO MAKE A SERVICE CONTRACT A notice that was submitted by contracting officers to the Wage and Hour Division of the DEPARTMENT OF LABOR (DOL), requesting a WAGE DETERMINATION under the SERVICE CONTRACT ACT OF 1965. This notice was required to be submitted on all service contracts and modifications over $2,500. FAR 22.1007 (prior to FAC 2005-10, 71 Fed. Reg. 36930, June 28, 2006). The notice is no longer used but wage determinations are still required. Contracting officers are required to search for the appropriate wage determination on the Department of Labor website (www.wdol.gov) and, if it is not posted, to request a wage determination electronically. FAR 22.1008-1.

NOTICE TO PROCEED A government notice that directs the contractor to proceed with the performance of the work called for by a contract. In CONSTRUCTION contracting, it is common practice to require completion of performance in a specified number of days after issuance of the notice to proceed. In such cases, the NOTICE OF AWARD must specify the date of commencement of work or advise that a notice to proceed will be issued. FAR 36.213-4.

NOTICE REQUIREMENTS Requirement that contractors notify the contracting agency that they have encountered a situation during the performance of a contract that will obligate the government to make an EQUITABLE ADJUSTMENT or a PRICE ADJUSTMENT to a contract. A number of the standard clauses, such as the CHANGEs clause, the DIFFERING SITE CONDITIONS clause, and the SUSPENSION OF WORK clause, contain such notice requirements. In addition, the courts and boards have denied the cost of dealing with such situations when notice from the contractor would have allowed the contracting agency to address the problem. See Cibinic, Nagle & Nash, ADMINISTRATION OF GOVERNMENT CONTRACTS 424–32, 477–78, 546 (5th ed. 2016); Cibinic, *Postscript: Notice of Changes*, 18 N&CR ¶25 (June 2004).

NOVATION AGREEMENT   *Official:* A legal agreement (1) Executed by the (i) Contractor (transferor); (ii) Successor in interest (transferee), and (iii) government; and (2) By which, among other things, the transferor guarantees performance of the contract, the transferee assumes all OBLIGATIONs under the contract, and the government recognizes the transfer of the contract and related ASSETs. *Source:* FAR 2.101. Under the common law, a novation is an agreement where a contracting party accepts a new party in place of the prior party (relieving the prior party of any further obligations). However, in government contracting a novation is merely an ASSIGNMENT OF CONTRACT (with the prior party retaining all obligations in the event the new party fails to perform). Although 41 U.S.C. § 6305 prohibits assignment of government contracts, the government may, in its interest, recognize a third party as the successor in interest to a government contract when the third party's interest in the contract arises out of the transfer of all the contractor's assets or the entire portion of the assets involved in performing the contract. FAR 42.1204. A format for novation agreements can be found at FAR 42.1204(i). There are now statutory limitations on the RESTRUCTURING COSTS that are permitted in novation agreements. 10 U.S.C. § 2324. See Dover, Horan & Overman, *Mergers & Acquisitions—Special Issues When Purchasing Government Contractor Entities/Edition II*, BRIEFING PAPERS No. 09-07 (June 2009).

NUMERICAL RATING (SCORING)   In SOURCE SELECTION, the practice of using numbers on a numerical scale of VALUE as shorthand expressions of the evaluated merits of offerors and their offers. A typical scale of value is 0 to 100 points, 100 being best. However, agencies have used scales of 0 to 10 points and 0 to 1,000 points. The use of numerical rating is often discouraged because some users misunderstand the nature of numerical subjectivity and mistakenly consider numerical ratings to be objective and precise expressions. However, the proper use of numerical ratings can greatly simplify and facilitate the aggregation and interpretation of complex and diverse evaluation findings. See Von Winterfeldt & Edwards, DECISION ANALYSIS AND BEHAVIORAL RESEARCH (Cambridge, 1986), p. 20, *Numerical Subjectivity*; Edwards, *Scoring and Rating in Source Selection: A Continuing Source of Confusion*, 20 N&CR ¶7 (Feb. 2006).

O

OBJECT CODE   The version of a COMPUTER PROGRAM that is built into or inserted into a COMPUTER to enable the computer to perform an operation or a series of operations. Object code is in a machine-readable form, usually magnetic or optical, and may be stored in the form of a disk, tape, compact disk, computer chip, etc. It is compiled from the SOURCE CODE. Under COPYRIGHT law, the object code generally may not be copied except for use in the computer for which it was bought or for archival purposes. 17 U.S.C. § 117. See Nash & Rawicz, Intellectual Property in Government Contracts, chap. 5 (6th ed. 2008); DeVecchio, *Copyright Protection Under Government Contracts*, Briefing Papers No. 06-05 (Apr. 2006).

OBLIGATION   A definite commitment by the government to spend APPROPRIATED FUNDS. A binding contract is an obligation. Obligations may not be made prior to the enactment of an APPROPRIATION or other statutory authority. The creation and recording of obligations is governed by 31 U.S.C. § 1501. See ANTI-DEFICIENCY ACT. See Cibinic, Nash & Yukins, Formation of Government Contracts 49–58 (4th ed. 2011); U.S. Gov't Accountability Office, Principles of Federal Appropriations Law: Annual Update to the Third Edition, chap. 7 (Washington, D.C.: Mar. 2015). See also Nash, *Unilaterally Changing the Government's Funding Obligation: A No-No*, 32 N&CR ¶ 31 (July 2018); Durkee, *The Proper Obligation and Use of Appropriated Funds in Interagency Contracting Under Non-Economy Act Authorities: Have We Got It Right Yet?*, 38 Pub. Cont. L.J. 317 (2009); Mansfield, *Appropriations Law: Obligations vs. Contingent Liabilities*, 22 N&CR ¶ 41 (July 2008).

OF VALUE   See THING OF VALUE.

OFF-LOADING   The abuse of the ECONOMY ACT and INTER-AGENCY CONTRACTING in order to avoid competition, improperly record OBLIGATIONs, and avoid oversight requirements. The practice of having another agency improperly procure supplies or services came to light in the early 1990s and sparked much congressional concern. See Cibinic, Nash & Yukins, Formation of Government Contracts 1123–26 (4th ed. 2011); Durkee, *The Proper Obligation and Use of Appropriated Funds in Interagency Contracting Under Non-Economy Act Authorities: Have We Got It Right Yet?*, 38 Pub. Cont. L.J. 317 (2009).

OFF-THE-SHELF ITEM   *Official:* An ITEM produced and placed in stock by a contractor, or stocked by a distributor, before receiving orders or contracts for its sale. The item may be commercial or produced to military or federal SPECIFICATIONs or description. *Source:* FAR 46.101. FAR 46.403(a) requires inspection at destination if supplies are purchased off-the-shelf and require no technical inspection. "Off-the-shelf" also refers to procurement of COMMERCIALLY AVAILABLE OFF-THE-SHELF (COTS) ITEMs, which can be acquired using more efficient procedures than noncommercial items.

OFFER   *Official:* A response to a SOLICITATION that, if accepted, would bind the OFFEROR to perform the resultant contract. Responses to INVITATIONs FOR BIDS (SEALED BIDDING) are offers called BIDs or "sealed bids"; responses to requests for proposals (negotiation) are offers called "proposals"; however, responses to a REQUEST FOR QUOTATIONS (simplified acquisition) are QUOTATIONs, not offers. For unsolicited proposals, see subpart 15.6. *Source:* FAR 2.101. While the FAR states that responses to a REQUEST FOR PROPOSALS, in NEGOTIATION, are offers that are called PROPO-SALs, this is inaccurate in that FAR Part 15 generally uses the term "proposal" to include requested information as well as the offeror's offer. Quotations cannot be accepted by the government to create a binding contract because they are informational in character and used for planning purposes. FAR 13.004. An offer may also take the form of an UNSOLICITED PROPOSAL, submitted upon the initiative of the submitter. Generally, the government structures each procurement so that offers are made by prospective contractors and ACCEP-TANCE OF AN OFFER is made by the government. However, in SIMPLIFIED ACQUI-SITION PROCEDURES, the offer is generally made by the government by sending the prospective contractor a PURCHASE ORDER. See Cibinic, Nash & Yukins, FORMATION OF GOVERNMENT CONTRACTS 232–37 (4th ed. 2011).

OFFER FACTORS   Attributes of an OFFER that the government will evaluate during SOURCE SELECTION and that will become part of the contract if the offer is accepted. They are specific promises, such as price or estimated cost and fee, features of proposed products and services, DELIVERY OR PERFORMANCE SCHEDULE, and warranties (see WARRANTY). See EVALUATION FACTOR; Cibinic, Nash & Yukins, FORMATION OF GOVERNMENT CONTRACTS 689–701 (4th ed. 2011).

OFFEROR   The party that makes an OFFER and looks for acceptance (see ACCEPTANCE OF OFFER) from the offeree. BLACK'S LAW DICTIONARY 1305 (11th ed. 2019). In government contracting offeror is the generic term for prospective contractors that submit BIDs or PROPOSALs. See FAR 2.101 stating that the term "offeror" includes BIDDERs.

OFFICE OF DISPUTE RESOLUTION FOR ACQUISITION (ODRA)   The Office in the FEDERAL AVIATION ADMINISTRATION that resolves DISPUTES and PROTESTS in that agency (www.faa.gov/about/office_org/headquarters_offices/agc/pol_adjudication/agc70/). This office was established when the agency was given the authority to conduct its procurement operations without following the FEDERAL PROPERTY AND ADMINIS-TRATIVE SERVICES ACT and the FEDERAL ACQUISITION REGULATION. See Department of Transportation Appropriations Act for FY 1996, Pub. L. No. 104-50, § 348 and 49 U.S.C. § 46101 et seq. The Office has a Director and three Dispute Resolution Officers but also uses ADMINISTRATIVE JUDGEs from other agencies as Special Masters to handle its cases. See Carey, Scalzo & Wiersum, *Flying in Friendly Skies: The Federal Aviation Administration's Unique Bid Protest Forum*, BRIEFING PAPERS No. 19-10 (Sept. 2019).

OFFICE OF FEDERAL PROCUREMENT POLICY (OFPP)   An office in the OFFICE OF MANAGEMENT AND BUDGET that was established in 1974 to provide overall direction of government-wide procurement policies, regulations, procedures, and forms for executive agencies and to promote economy, efficiency, and effectiveness in the procurement of property and services by the executive branch of the federal government. 41 U.S.C. § 1101. The Administrator of the office provides overall direction of procurement policy and leadership in the development of procurement systems of the executive agencies, 41 U.S.C. § 1121(a), and is charged with the responsibility to coordinate procurement policies and statutory changes and consult with federal agencies to achieve sound procurement practices. 41 U.S.C. § 1122. The Administrator also appoints the members and chairs the COST ACCOUNTING STANDARDS BOARD, 41 U.S.C. § 1501.

OFFICE OF FEDERAL PROCUREMENT POLICY ACT Pub. L. No. 93-400, 41 U.S.C. § 1101 through § 2313. A 1974 Act establishing the OFFICE OF FEDERAL PROCUREMENT POLICY. In addition to defining the functions of OFPP (§ 1121 through § 1131), the Act contains a number of substantive provisions affecting the entire government, including protecting the constitutional rights of contractors (§ 2309), determining the benchmark compensation amount for "SENIOR EXECUTIVEs" of contractors (§ 1127), discouraging the use of nonstandard clauses and restricting the use of CERTIFICATION requirements (§ 1304), establishing the COST ACCOUNTING STANDARDS BOARD (§ 1501), establishing policies for management of the ACQUISITION WORKFORCE (§ 1703), establishing COMPETITION ADVOCATEs (§ 1705), establishing CHIEF ACQUISITION OFFICERs and SENIOR PROCUREMENT EXECUTIVEs (§ 1702), requiring procurement notices (see SYNOPSIS) (§ 1708), limiting the use of contractors to perform ADVISORY AND ASSISTANCE SERVICES (§ 1709), requiring the use of a public-private competition before conversion of work to performance by a contractor (§ 1710), requiring the use of VALUE ENGINEERING (§ 1711), adopting SIMPLIFIED ACQUISITION PROCEDURES (§ 1901 and § 1905), adopting MICRO-PURCHASE procedures (§ 1902), adopting special, EMERGENCY PROCUREMENT authority (§ 1903), listing laws inapplicable to the procurement of COMMERCIAL ITEMs (§ 1906), requiring the FAR to contain a list of laws inapplicable to the procurement of COMMERCIALLY AVAILABLE OFF-THE-SHELF ITEMs (§ 1907), requiring inflation adjustments for ACQUISITION THRESHOLDs (§ 1908), adopting the PROCUREMENT INTEGRITY ACT (§§ 2101 through 2107), requiring the use of ELECTRONIC COMMERCE (§ 2301), requiring the use of MODULAR CONTRACTING in procuring INFORMATION TECHNOLOGY (§ 2308), allowing the use of commercial item procedures for PERFORMANCE-BASED SERVICE CONTRACTS not exceeding $25 million (§ 2310), and requiring the establishment of a CONTINGENCY CONTRACTING CORPS (§ 2312). The Act also contains requirements pertaining to RIGHTS IN TECHNICAL DATA for agencies subject to the FEDERAL PROPERTY AND ADMINISTRATIVE SERVICES ACT (§ 2302).

OFFICE OF FEDERAL PROCUREMENT POLICY (OFPP) POLICY LETTERS Policy guidance infrequently issued by the OFFICE OF FEDERAL PROCUREMENT POLICY to implement procurement policy in the form of letters that are numbered sequentially by the year of issuance (thus, 91-2 would be the second policy letter issued in 1991). These letters are usually implemented, subsequent to their issuance, in the FEDERAL ACQUISITION REGULATION. Policies letters that are still in effect are listed at www.whitehouse.gov/omb/procurement/index_policy.html.

OFFICE OF GOVERNMENT ETHICS (OGE) An office of the executive branch of the government with the responsibility for issuing uniform STANDARDS OF CONDUCT for all government employees. Exec. Order No. 12674, 54 Fed. Reg. 15159 (Apr. 12, 1989), as amended by Exec. Order No.12731, 55 Fed. Reg. 42547 (Oct. 17, 1990). The office promulgates broad guidance on the ethical conduct of executive branch employees at 5 C.F.R. part 2635.

OFFICE OF INFORMATION AND REGULATORY AFFAIRS (OIRA)   The office, within the OFFICE OF MANAGEMENT AND BUDGET, that oversees the federal regulations and information requirements and develops policies to improve government statistics and information management. Pursuant to the PAPERWORK REDUCTION ACT OF 1980 and the CLINGER-COHEN ACT OF 1996, the Administrator of OIRA is charged with providing leadership and oversight for the government's INFORMATION RESOURCES MANAGEMENT activities.

OFFICE OF MANAGEMENT AND BUDGET (OMB)   A government agency, in the Executive Office of the President, that serves as the President's principal arm for exercising the budgetary and managerial functions of the presidency. 31 U.S.C. § 501. OMB strives to improve government organization, information, and management systems and devises programs for developing career executive talent throughout the government. OMB assists the President in preparing the annual budget and in overseeing its execution. The PAPERWORK REDUCTION ACT OF 1980 imposes a requirement on federal agencies to obtain OMB's approval before collecting information from 10 or more members of the public. The information collection and record-keeping requirements contained in the FEDERAL ACQUISITION REGULATION have been approved by OMB. FAR 1.106.

OFFICE OF MANAGEMENT AND BUDGET (OMB) CIRCULARS   Policy guidelines issued by the OFFICE OF MANAGEMENT AND BUDGET to federal agencies to promote efficiency and uniformity in government activities. An indexed list of these circulars is at www.whitehouse.gov/omb/circulars/index.html. The contents of OMB Circulars are frequently incorporated into the FEDERAL ACQUISITION REGULATION, but the documents continue to remain in effect as circulars. Relevant OMB Circulars and their FAR references include A-76, *Policies for Acquiring Commercial or Industrial Products and Services Needed by the Government*, FAR Subpart 7.3; and A-109, *Major Systems Acquisitions*, FAR Part 34.

OFFICE OF RESEARCH AND TECHNOLOGY APPLICATION (ORTA)   An office within a federal laboratory that serves as a federal mechanism for FEDERAL TECHNOLOGY TRANSFER. Created by the STEVENSON-WYDLER ACT, ORTAs are responsible for identifying and assessing technologies, know-how, or ideas that may have commercial or other outside applications, as well as cooperating with state and local governments and other federal organizations involved in technology transfer (see FEDERAL TECHNOLOGY TRANSFER). See Nash & Rawicz, Intellectual Property in Government Contracts, chap. 7 (6th ed. 2008).

OFFICE OF SMALL AND DISADVANTAGED BUSINESS UTILIZATION (SADBU)   *Officia:* The Office of Small Business Programs when referring to the Department of Defense. *Source:* FAR 2.101. Each agency must appoint a SADBU who reports directly to the agency head or deputy head and is responsible for implementing the government's small business programs in the agency. The functions of SADBUs are set forth in FAR 19.201(c). See DFARS Part 219 for guidance on the coordination with SADBUs.

OFFICIAL   *Official:* An officer, as defined in 5 U.S.C. § 2104, an employee, as defined in 5 U.S.C. § 2105, a member of the uniformed services, as defined in 5 U.S.C. § 2101(3), or a special government employee as defined in 18 U.S.C. § 202. *Source:* FAR 3.104-1. This term is used in the PROCUREMENT INTEGRITY rules that went into effect on January 1, 1997 to define the class of government employers subject to the Act if they have participated in a procurement and have had access to CONTRACTOR BID OR PROPOSAL INFORMATION or SOURCE SELECTION INFORMATION. See Cibinic, Nash & Yukins, FORMATION OF GOVERNMENT CONTRACTS 163–65, 170–72, 212–16 (4th ed. 2011).

OFFSET   The right of a contractor to deduct the amount of understated COST OR PRICING DATA submitted in support of price negotiations on the same transaction from DEFECTIVE COST OR PRICING DATA for which the government has a claim. Offsets are permitted only when the government has a legitimate claim for PRICE REDUCTION and then only up to the amount of the government's claim. FAR 15.407-1. See Cibinic, Nagle & Nash, ADMINISTRATION OF GOVERNMENT CONTRACTS 674 (5th ed. 2016). The term offset is also used to mean SETOFF and to mean an amount that a foreign government requires to be spent in its country when it agrees to purchase United States products. See DFARS 202.101 for a detailed description of offsets in these foreign sales.

OFPP   See OFFICE OF FEDERAL PROCUREMENT POLICY.

OMB UNIFORM GUIDANCE   *Official:* The abbreviated title for Uniform Administrative Requirements, Cost Principles, and Audit Requirements for Federal Awards (2 C.F.R. part 200), which supersedes OMB Circulars A-21, A-87, A-89, A-102, A-110, A-122, and A-133, and the guidance in Circular A-50 on Audit Follow-up. *Source:* FAR 2.101. This document consolidated all of the guidance of the OFFICE OF MANAGEMENT AND BUDGET pertaining to the award and administration of GRANTs and COOPERATIVE AGREEMENTs that are not subject to the FEDERAL ACQUISITION REGULATION.

OMBUDSMAN   An employee of an agency with the authority to hear complaints from OFFERORs or CONTRACTORs, investigate the matter, and propose or implement a solution if the complaint is warranted or explain the matter if the complaint has no merit. 10 U.S.C. § 2304c(d) and 41 U.S.C. § 4106(g) require agencies to establish an ombudsman to hear complaints pertaining to the issuance of ORDERs on multiple award DELIVERY ORDER CONTRACTs and TASK ORDER CONTRACTs. See FAR 16.505(b)(6), which requires this ombudsman to be a senior agency official who is independent of the contracting officer and permits the COMPETITION ADVOCATE to serve in this position. While Executive Order No. 12979, 60 Fed. Reg. 55171, Oct. 25, 1995, requires agencies to establish agency protest procedures, it does not require that such protests be handled by the agency ombudsman. However, the DEPARTMENT OF STATE has created an ombudsman to hear complaints for contracts over the SIMPLE ACQUISITION THRESHOLD, 48 C.F.R. § 652.206-70. NASA has also created an agency ombudsman and an ombudsmen at each CONTRACTING ACTIVITY to hear any complaint related to a contract or proposed contract. NFS 1815.7001; NPR 5010.33A.

OMISSIONS AND MISDESCRIPTIONS   Omissions or erroneous descriptions of the details of the work in the contract SPECIFICATIONs and DRAWINGS. When the government provides detailed specifications and drawings to the contractor, it is frequently held liable for errors or misdescriptions under the IMPLIED WARRANTY OF SPECIFICATIONS. Some government agencies attempt to avoid this liability by including an EXCULPATORY

CLAUSE in the contract. See, for example, the Contract Drawings, Maps, and Specifications clause in DFARS 252.236-7001, which states that DOD is not liable for omissions and mis-descriptions of details of work that are "manifestly necessary to carry out the intent of the drawings and specifications, or which are customarily performed." Such clauses have been effective when the omission or misdescription is in the details of the work. See Nash & Feldman, 1 GOVERNMENT CONTRACT CHANGES § 13:27 (3d ed. 2006–2020); Cibinic, Nagle & Nash, ADMINISTRATION OF GOVERNMENT CONTRACTS 322 (5th ed. 2016).

OMNIBUS TRADE AND COMPETITIVENESS ACT OF 1988   Pub. L. No. 100-148, 15 U.S.C. § 205b. A law which amended the Metric Conversion Act of 1975 to designate the metric system of measurement as the preferred system of weights and measures for U.S. trade and commerce and to require that federal agencies use the metric system in its acquisitions "to the extent economically feasible." See FAR 11.002.

ON SALE BAR   The rule in 35 U.S.C. § 102(b) that prohibited the issuance of a PATENT if an INVENTION was on sale in the United States more than one year prior to the date of the patent application. An offer for sale made in a PROPOSAL fell within the rule if the proposal contained a description of the INVENTION. See Nash & Rawicz, INTELLECTUAL PROPERTY IN GOVERNMENT CONTRACTS, chap. 1 (6th ed. 2008). Pursuant to Pub. L. No. 112-29, effective March 16, 2013, 35 U.S.C. § 102(a)(1) removes this one-year grace period and provides that no patent can be issued if the invention was on sale before the patent application was filed, with exceptions in 35 U.S.C. § 102(b).

ON STANDBY   The requirement that a contractor must meet to recover UNABSORBED OVERHEAD. This requirement was adopted by *P.J. Dick, Inc. v. Principi*, 324 F.3d 1364 (Fed. Cir. 2003). It requires that (1) there was a nonconcurrent government-caused delay that "was not only substantial but of indefinite duration," (2) during the delay the contractor "was required to be ready to resume work on the contract, at full speed as well as immediately," and (3) "much, if not all, of the work" was suspended. See Nash & Feldman, 2 GOVERNMENT CONTRACT CHANGES § 17:13 (3d ed. 2006–2020); Cibinic, Nagle & Nash, ADMINISTRATION OF GOVERNMENT CONTRACTS 647–53 (5th ed. 2016). See also Nash, *Postscript: Unabsorbed Overhead and the "Eichleay" Formula*, 17 N&CR ¶ 33 (June 2003).

ONLINE REPRESENTATIONS AND CERTIFICATIONS APPLICATION (ORCA)   *Official:* The primary government repository for contractor submitted representations and certifications required for the conduct of business with the government. Access ORCA via http://www.acquisition.gov. *Source:* FAR 2.101. This application establishes an electronic system that contractors use to meet the numerous certification requirements to obtain government contracts. ORCAs are completed annually and must be updated when circumstances change. FAR 4.1201. Solicitations are required to include the Annual Representations and Certifications provision at FAR 52.204-8, which instructs offerors on the representations and certifications required for the procurement and the ORCA procedures. A separate provision in FAR 52.212-3 is used when the procurement is for a COMMERCIAL ITEM.

OPEN SOURCE SOFTWARE   COMPUTER SOFTWARE, including SOURCE CODE, provided to other parties without the enforcement of PATENT RIGHTS or COPYRIGHT if those parties agree to make any improvements to the software available to others on the same terms. In effect, the owner of the open source software copyrights the software but licenses all users on a royalty-free basis if they agree to participate in the arrangement. The goal is to allow a wide number of users to modify and improve the software in an expeditious manner. The use of open source software is promoted by the Open Source Initiative. See www.opensource.org. The NATIONAL AERONAUTICS AND SPACE ADMINISTRA-TION has promulgated a NASA Open Source Agreement at www.opensource.org/licenses/nasa1.3.php. DOD has endorsed the use of open source software. See *Open Systems Architecture and Data Rights Overview* (Nov. 2011). The Navy has also issued a *Naval Open Architecture Contract Guidebook for Program Managers* (Oct. 2013), calling for the use of open source software when feasible. See Nash & Rawicz, INTELLECTUAL PROPERTY IN GOVERNMENT CONTRACTS 688–93 (6th ed. 2008).

OPEN SYSTEM ARCHITECTURE   *Official.* A technical architecture that yields modular, interoperable systems allowing components to be added, modified, replaced, removed, and/or supported by different vendors throughout the life cycle in order to drive opportunities for enhanced competition and innovation. *Source.* DoD Open Systems Architecture: Contract Guidebook for Program Managers, v.1.1. (June 2013). The Guidebook contains detailed guidance on the acquisition of military products using open system architecture including obtaining the necessary rights to TECHNICAL DATA and COMPUTER SOFT-WARE. See MODULAR OPEN SYSTEM APPROACH.

OPERATING REVENUE   *Official:* Amounts accrued or charged to customers, clients, and tenants for the sale of products manufactured or purchased for resale, for services, and for rentals of property held primarily for leasing to others. It includes both reimbursable costs and fees under cost-type contracts and percentage-of-completion sales accruals except that it includes only the fee for management contracts under which the contractor acts essentially as an agent of the government in the erection or operation of government-owned facilities. It excludes incidental interest, dividends, royalty, and rental income, and proceeds from the sale of assets used in the business. *Source:* CAS 403, Allocation of Home Office Expenses to Segments, 48 C.F.R. § 9904.403-30. This term is used in connection with the COST ACCOUNTING STANDARDS in 48 C.F.R. chap. 99. CAS 403 provides that operating revenue (1) is used to determine how RESIDUAL EXPENSEs are allocated (see ALLOCA-TION) and (2) is part of a three-factor formula used to determine the allocation of such expenses when a certain threshold is met. See 48 C.F.R. § 403-50(c). See Manos, 2 GOVERN-MENT CONTRACT COSTS AND PRICING §§ 64:1–64:5 (2d ed. 2009–2020).

OPERATIONAL TEST AND EVALUATION   *Official:* The field test, under realistic combat conditions, of any ITEM of (or key component of) weapons, equipment, or munitions for the purpose of determining the effectiveness and suitability of the weapons, equipment, or munitions for use in combat by typical military users and the evaluation of the results of such test. *Source:* 10 U.S.C. § 139(a)(2)(A). 10 U.S.C. § 2399 requires the completion of operational test and evaluation before a MAJOR DEFENSE ACQUISITION PROGRAM can proceed beyond LOW-RATE INITIAL PRODUCTION. To ensure that this testing is carried out independently, 10 U.S.C. § 139 establishes a separate director of operational test and evaluation in DOD. The procedures for meeting these requirements are set forth in the DOD 5000 Series.

OPERATIONS AND SUPPORT   The fifth phase of a DOD acquisition program involving the use of new technology as prescribed in the DOD 5000 Series. In this phase the agency supports a product or system that has been deployed by conducting maintenance, sustaining engineering, data management, configuration management, training and other activities necessary to ensure its continued reliability and usability, while minimizing total LIFE-CYCLE COSTs.

OPTION   *Official:* A unilateral right in a contract by which, for a specified period, the government may elect to purchase additional supplies or services called for by the contract, or may elect to extend the term of the contract. *Source:* FAR 2.101. Options are the most frequently used technique in government contracting to buy goods and services over periods of time longer than the single year for which APPROPRIATIONs are normally made. Since they generally obligate the contractor to a firm pricing structure for a number of years, they are a useful means of preventing BUYING-IN. Options can be used for both SEALED BIDDING and NEGOTIATED CONTRACTs as long as the contracting officer finds the option is in the best interest of the government and not subject to a prohibition in FAR 17.202(c). When exercising an option, the contracting officer must provide the contractor written notice within the time period specified in the contract. The contracting officer may exercise an option only after determining that (1) funds are available, (2) the requirement covered by the option fulfills an existing government need, (3) exercise of the option is the most advantageous method of fulfilling the government's need, price, and other factors considered, (4) the option was synopsized (see SYNOPSIS) when required, and (5) the contractor is not listed in the EXCLUDED PARTIES LIST SYSTEM. FAR 17.207. See the contract clauses at FAR 52.217-3 through -9, which deal with evaluation exclusive of options, evaluation of options, options for increased quantity, and options to extend services or the term of the contract. See Feldman, Government Contract Awards: Negotiation and Sealed Bidding §§ 5:9–5:13 (2019–2020 ed.); Cibinic, Nash & Yukins, Formation of Government Contracts 1406–35 (4th ed. 2011). See also Nibley & Armstrong, *The Government's Exercise of Options*, Briefing Papers No. 13-8 (July 2013); Edwards, *Exercising Options: What Is "An Amount Specified"?*, 24 N&CR ¶ 36 (Aug. 2010); Edwards, *Exercising Options: An Unanticipated Issue*, 24 N&CR ¶ 30 (June 2010); Edwards, *Postscript: Options for Additional Years of Work*, 23 NC&R ¶ 21 (Apr. 2009); Nash, *Options for Additional Years of Work: Are They Overused?*, 23 N&CR ¶ 4 (Jan. 2009).

OPTIONAL FORMS (OFs)   Forms used in the procurement process that may be altered at the option of the agency. FAR 53.302 illustrates those few optional forms relevant to procurement, of which the most commonly used is OF 347, Order for Supplies and Services. FAR 53.302-347. OFs are distinguished from STANDARD FORMS by the fact that the latter cannot be altered or substituted for without receipt, in advance, of an exception (an approved departure from the established design, content, printing specifications, or conditions for use). FAR 53.103. Agencies may computer-generate OFs without exception approval, provided that there is no change to the name, content, or sequence of the data elements and that the form carries the OF number and edition date. FAR 53.105. Holders of the loose-leaf edition of the FAR may photocopy the sample OFs from FAR 53.302. OFs may be obtained through the GSA Forms Library at www.gsa.gov/portal/forms/type/TOP. See Forms Policy and Management Team, GSA Office of Governmentwide Policy *Standard and Optional Forms Procedural Handbook*, forms@gsa.gov (July 2009).

"OR EQUAL"   See BRAND-NAME-OR-EQUAL DESCRIPTION.

ORAL PRESENTATION   A presentation by an offeror during SOURCE SELECTION, usually in lieu of submission of a written technical proposal, to demonstrate its capability to perform a proposed contract. FAR 15.102. A common format for oral presentations is to have the OFFEROR present a summary of the methods it will use to perform the key requirements of the prospective contract, followed by questions and answers or the solution of a SAMPLE TASK. Another format is for agency personnel to conduct an interview of the offeror's KEY PERSONNEL. Some agencies have also used oral presentations to supplement written proposals. The advantage of the oral presentation is that it permits the agency evaluators to speak directly with the key personnel who will perform the contract if it is awarded to the offeror. See Cibinic, Nash & Yukins, FORMATION OF GOVERNMENT CONTRACTS 736–39, 775–78, 799–802 (4th ed. 2011); Nash, Oral Presentations: *A Flexible Tool*, 23 N&CR ¶ 27 (May 2009); *Postscript: Oral Presentations*, 23 N&CR ¶ 19 (Apr. 2009); Nash, *Oral Presentations: The Blind Leading the Blind*, 20 N&CR ¶ 11 (Mar. 2006).

ORDER   See DELIVERY ORDER, JOB ORDER, TASK ORDER.

ORDER OF PRECEDENCE   The hierarchy of various parts of the contract in the CONTRACT INTERPRETATION process. In the absence of a specific contract clause stating an order of precedence, the general rule of common law is that, when contracts contain inconsistencies, specific provisions will prevail over general provisions and written or typed provisions will prevail over general provisions. This general rule does not apply, however, when a specific provision conflicts with a standard government contract clause required by statute or regulation. Cibinic, Nagle & Nash, ADMINISTRATION OF GOVERNMENT CONTRACTS 170–73 (5th ed. 2016). The Order of Precedence clauses in FAR 52.214-29 and FAR 52.215-33 state that inconsistencies in the SOLICITATION or CONTRACT are to be resolved by giving precedence in the following order: (1) the schedule (excluding the SPECIFICATIONs); (2) representations and other instructions; (3) contract clauses; (4) other documents, exhibits, and attachments; and (5) the specifications. See UNIFORM CONTRACT FORMAT. See Nash & Feldman, 1 GOVERNMENT CONTRACT CHANGES § 11:11 (3d ed. 2006–2020).

ORDERING ACTIVITY   *Official:* An activity that is authorized to place orders, or establish BLANKET PURCHASE AGREEMENTS (BPA), against the GSA MULTIPLE AWARD SCHEDULE contract. A list of eligible ordering activities is available at http://www.gsa.gov/schedules (click "For Customers Ordering from Schedules" and then "Eligibility to Use GSA Sources"). *Source:* FAR 8.401. Included are a wide variety of activities including government agencies, international agencies, and government contractors with COST-REIMBURSEMENT CONTRACTs (in accordance with FAR Subpart 51.1). See GSA Order ADM 4800.2E, Jan. 3, 2000. In FAR Subpart 17.5, dealing with INTERAGENCY ACQUISITION, agencies issuing orders are referred to as a REQUESTING AGENCY. See Cibinic, Nash & Yukins, FORMATION OF GOVERNMENT CONTRACTS, chap. 8 (4th ed. 2011).

ORDERING OFFICE   See ORDERING ACTIVITY.

ORGANIZATION COSTS   Costs of organization or reorganization of a business, including but not limited to incorporation fees and costs of attorneys, accountants, brokers, promoters, organizers, management consultants, and investment counselors, whether or not employees of the contractor. FAR 31.205-27. Organization costs in connection with the following are UNALLOWABLE COSTs: (1) planning or executing the organization or reorganization of the corporate structure of a business, including mergers and acquisitions; (2) resisting or planning to resist the reorganization of the corporate structure of a business or a change in the controlling interest in the ownership of a business; and (3) raising capital (NET

WORTH plus long-term LIABILITIES). Also unallowable are certain "reorganization" costs, including the cost of any change in the contractor's financial structure (except the administrative costs of short-term borrowings for working capital) resulting in alterations in the rights and interests of security holders, whether or not additional capital is raised. See *DCAA Contract Audit Manual* ¶7-1707; Manos, 1 GOVERNMENT CONTRACT COSTS AND PRICING §§ 34:1–34:4 (2d ed. 2009–2020); Cibinic, Knight & Nash, COST-REIMBURSEMENT CONTRACTING 735 (4th ed. 2014).

ORGANIZATIONAL CONFLICT OF INTEREST (OCI)   *Official:* Because of other activities or relationships with other persons, a person is unable or potentially unable to render impartial assistance or advice to the government, or the person's objectivity in performing the contract work is or might be otherwise impaired, or a person has an UNFAIR COMPETITIVE ADVANTAGE. *Source:* FAR 2.101. Guidance on dealing with OCIs is contained in FAR Subpart 9.5. The contracting officer is responsible for resolving any significant potential conflicts before the award is made. FAR 9.504 and FAR 9.507. The FAR coverage on OCI also implements OFPP Policy Letter No. 89-1, Conflict of Interest Policies Applicable to Consultants, Dec. 8, 1989. In addition, some agencies have unique or additional statutory OCI requirements. According to DOE's OCI regulations, an OCI exists when an offeror or a contractor has past, present, or currently planned interests that (1) either directly or indirectly, through a client relationship, relate to the work to be performed under a DOE contract; and (2) may diminish the offeror's or contractor's capacity to give impartial, technically sound assistance and advice or may give the offeror or contractor an UNFAIR COMPETITIVE ADVANTAGE. Offerors and contractors include chief executives and directors who will or do become involved in the contract performance and proposed consultants or subcontractors who may perform services similar to the services provided by the prime contractor. DEAR 909.570-3. GAO has classified organizational conflicts of interest as (1) IMPAIRED OBJECTIVITY, (2) BIASED GROUND RULES, and (3) UNEQUAL ACCESS TO NONPUBLIC INFORMATION. See Feldman, GOVERNMENT CONTRACT AWARDS: NEGOTIATION AND SEALED BIDDING §§ 18:34–18:41 (2019–2020 ed.). See also Geldon & Conroy, *Organizational Conflicts Of Interest/Edition VI: Is the OCI Pendulum Swinging Back at the GAO?*, BRIEFING PAPERS NO. 18-13 (Dec. 2018).

ORIGINAL COMPLEMENT OF LOW-COST EQUIPMENT   *Official:* A group of items acquired for the initial outfitting of a TANGIBLE CAPITAL ASSET or an operational unit, or a new addition to either. The items in the group individually cost less than the minimum amount established by the contractor for CAPITALIZATION for the classes of assets acquired but in the aggregate they represent a material investment. The group, as a complement, is expected to be held for continued service beyond the current period. Initial outfitting of the unit is completed when the unit is ready and available for normal operations. *Source:* FAR 31.001. These costs must be capitalized if in total they exceed the threshold in the contractor's capitalization policy, CAS 404.40. See Cibinic, Knight & Nash, COST-REIMBURSEMENT CONTRACTING 709–10 (4th ed. 2014).

ORIGINAL EQUIPMENT MANUFACTURER (OEM)   *Official:* A company that manufactures products that it has designed from purchased components and sells those products under the company's brand name. *Source:* DFARS 202.101. This term commonly is used to refer to a company that has developed a WEAPON SYSTEM under a development contract and has thereby gained an almost insurmountable advantage in obtaining contracts for the production of the system.

ORIGINAL SOURCE *Official:* An individual who either (1) prior to a public disclosure under subsection (e)(4)(A), has voluntarily disclosed to the government the information on which allegations or transactions in a claim are based, or (2) who has knowledge that is independent of and materially adds to the publicly disclosed allegations or transactions, and who has voluntarily provided the information to the government before filing an action under this section. *Source:* 31 U.S.C. § 3730(e)(4)(B). Persons that qualify as an original source can file a qui tam action (see QUI TAM PROCEEDING) under the FALSE CLAIMS ACT. Courts have no jurisdiction over qui tam actions based on public disclosure of allegations or transactions unless the action is brought by a person who is an original source. 31 U.S.C. § 3730(e)(4)(A). See Boese, CIVIL FALSE CLAIMS AND QUI TAM ACTIONS (5th ed. 2020).

OSTENSIBLE SUBCONTRACTOR *Official:* A subcontractor that is not a similarly situated entity, as that term is defined in § 125.1 of this chapter, and performs primary and vital requirements of a contract, or of an order, or is a subcontractor upon which the prime contractor is unusually reliant. All aspects of the relationship between the prime and subcontractor are considered, including, but not limited to, the terms of the proposal (such as contract management, technical responsibilities, and the percentage of subcontracted work), agreements between the prime and subcontractor (such as bonding assistance or the teaming agreement), and whether the subcontractor is the incumbent contractor and is ineligible to submit a proposal because it exceeds the applicable size standard for that solicitation. *Source:* 13 C.F.R. § 121.103(h)(4). If a large business meets this test, it will be held to be affiliated with a SMALL BUSINESS CONTRACTOR with the result that generally the small business will not be eligible to be awarded a set-aside contract.

OTHER THAN FULL AND OPEN COMPETITION Conducting a procurement without meeting the statutory requirement in 10 U.S.C. § 2304(c) and 41 U.S.C. § 3304, to use COMPETITIVE PROCEDURES. FAR Subpart 6.3 describes this process as "other than full and open competition" and provides for seven circumstances permitting contracting without FULL AND OPEN COMPETITION: (1) only one responsible source; (2) UNUSUAL AND COMPELLING URGENCY; (3) INDUSTRIAL MOBILIZATION, or the need to maintain engineering, developmental, or research capability; (4) international agreement; (5) statutory authorization or requirement; (6) risk of compromising the national security; and (7) protecting the public interest. Agencies must justify the use of these procedures by writing a justification (FAR 6.303), obtaining higher level approvals (FAR 6.304), and publicly posting the justification (FAR 6.305). See Feldman, GOVERNMENT CONTRACT AWARDS: NEGOTIATION AND SEALED BIDDING §§ 3:35–3:51 (2019–2020 ed.); Cibinic, Nash & Yukins, FORMATION OF GOVERNMENT CONTRACTS 286–88 (4th ed. 2011). See also Manuel, CONG. RESEARCH SERV., Report No. R40516, COMPETITION IN FEDERAL CONTRACTING: AN OVERVIEW OF THE LEGAL REQUIREMENTS (Aug. 20, 2009); U.S. GOV'T ACCOUNTABILITY OFFICE, FEDERAL CONTRACTING: OPPORTUNITIES EXIST TO INCREASE COMPETITION AND ASSESS REASONS WHEN ONLY ONE OFFER IS RECEIVED, GAO-10-833 (July 2010).

OTHER TRANSACTIONS A form of CONTRACT, originally described in the National Aeronautics and Space Act, 42 U.S.C. § 2473(c)(5), as a permissible form of contract. Since it is not a PROCUREMENT CONTRACT, GRANT, or COOPERATIVE AGREEMENT, it is not subject to many of the statutes and regulations governing those types of instruments. This authority was given to DOD in 1990 for basic, applied, and advanced research projects, 10 U.S.C. § 2371, and subsequently for prototypes, 10 U.S.C. § 2371b.

See PROTOTYPE OTHER TRANSACTIONS. The DEPARTMENT OF HOMELAND SECURITY has the same authority, 6 U.S.C. § 391(a). The Department of Energy has the authority for research, development and demonstration projects, 42 U.S.C. § 7256. These contracts are covered by regulations applying to TECHNOLOGY INVESTMENT AGREEMENTS. See the DOD "Other Transactions Guide," Nov. 2018. See also Nash, *Postscript: Protesting Other Transactions*, 33 N&CR ¶ 59 (Oct. 2019); Nash, *Postscript: Other Transactions*, 33 N&CR ¶ 1 (Jan. 2019); Kelly, *IP Rights Under NASA and DOD "Other Transaction" Agreements-Inventions and Patents*, BRIEFING PAPERS No. 18-9 (Aug. 2018); Vadiee & Garland, *The Federal Government's "Other Transaction" Authority*, BRIEFING PAPERS No. 18-5 (Apr. 2018); Dunn, *Other Transaction Agreements: What Applies?*, 32 N&CR ¶ 22 (May 2018); Nash, *Other Transactions: A Preferred Technique?*, 32 N&CR ¶ 8 (Feb. 2018).

OTHER TRANSACTIONS CONSORTIUM   A group of companies and universities working in a field of technology that enter into another transaction agreement with a government organization to pursue prototype projects. When the government organization identifies a requirement, the consortium establishes a team of organizations best qualified to perform the work. DOD and the military services all have a number of consortia. A list of active consortia is at https://aida.mitre.org/ota/existing-ota-consortia.

OUTCOME   (also Result) In PERFORMANCE-BASED ACQUISITION a level of quality, timeliness, quantity, etc., that is achieved by a CONTRACTOR in the performance of a service. According to FAR 37.601(b)(2), the outcomes desired by the government are to be specified as measurable standards in PERFORMANCE WORK STATEMENTs. See *Guidebook for Performance-Based Services Acquisition (PBSA) in the Department of Defense*, Dec. 2000. See PERFORMANCE-BASED ACQUISITION.

OUTCOME PREDICTION   An ALTERNATE DISPUTE RESOLUTION technique used by the GOVERNMENT ACCOUNTABILITY OFFICE to assist in resolving PROTESTs. See 4 C.F.R. § 21.10. An outcome prediction conference is generally held after submission of the AGENCY REPORT and the protester's comments. If a party requests outcome prediction and the GAO attorney has a high degree of confidence regarding the outcome, the attorney will inform the parties of the likely outcome of the protest. When informed that they are likely to lose the protest, agencies almost always take CORRECTIVE ACTION.

OUTSOURCING   The transfer of activities that are being performed by federal employees at federal facilities to private contractor employees at federal or private facilities. Outsourcing decisions are governed by the policies and procedures contained in OMB Circular No. A-76 (revised), *Performance of Commercial Activities*, Aug. 4, 1983, most recently amended May 29, 2003 (https://obamawhitehouse.archives.gov/omb/circulars/a076/a076fedr); and its *Revised Supplemental Handbook* (June 14, 1999). Circular A-76 requires federal agencies to compare the cost of contracting and the cost of in-house performance to determine whether commercial activities should be outsourced. Very limited guidance is contained in FAR Subpart 7.3. Outsourcing is limited to those activities that are not defined as INHERENTLY GOVERNMENTAL FUNCTIONS. Such activities are those that are so intimately related to the public interest that they must be performed by government employees. They typically involve the discretionary exercise of government authority or the performance of monetary transactions for the government. Detailed guidance is provided by OFPP Policy Letter No. 11-01, *Performance of Inherently Governmental and Critical Functions*, 76 Fed. Reg. 56227, Sept. 12, 2011, and FAR Subpart 7.5. See Grasso, CONG.

RESEARCH SERV., Report No. RL30392, DEFENSE OUTSOURCING: THE OMB CIRCULAR A-76 POLICY (June 30, 2005); Braziel, *Contracting Out Contracting*, 38 PUB. CONT. L.J. 857 (2009).

OVERHEAD   See INDIRECT COST.

OVERHEAD RATE   A percentage rate that is derived by dividing a contractor's INDIRECT COST POOL for an accounting period by the ALLOCATION BASE in order to allocate INDIRECT COSTs to contracts performed during the period (see ALLOCATION OF COST). CAS 418, Allocation of Direct and Indirect Costs, 48 C.F.R. § 9904.418, provides guidance on the selection of allocation bases that equitably allocate indirect costs. See Manos, 2 GOVERNMENT CONTRACT COSTS AND PRICING §§ 79:1–75:4 (2d ed. 2009–2020).

OVERRUN   An amount by which the ACTUAL COST of performance exceeds the amount budgeted for the work. Programs are said to be overrun when the original budget is exceeded. Contracts are said to be overrun when the original price or cost estimate is exceeded or when the total costs incurred exceed the price or estimated cost as adjusted in accordance with contract clauses (depending on the usage of the term). The procedures for dealing with COST OVERRUNs on COST-REIMBURSEMENT CONTRACTs are set forth in the LIMITATION OF COST CLAUSE. See Cibinic, Knight & Nash, COST-REIMBURSEMENT CONTRACTING 761–64 (4th ed. 2014). See also Nash, *Funding Overruns: The Evolving Bona Fide Needs Rule*, 23 N&CR ¶ 52 (Oct. 2009); Mateer, *The Cost Overrun Dilemma: In Search of a Solution*, 4 CP&A Rep. ¶ 21 (May 2009); Edwards, *Cost Overrun vs. Cost Growth: Is There a Difference? Does It Matter?*, 22 N&CR ¶ 37 (June 2008).

OVERTIME   *Official:* Time worked by a contractor's employee in excess of the employee's normal workweek. *Source:* FAR 2.101. "Normal workweek" means, generally, a workweek of 40 hours. FAR 22.103-2 provides that contractors must perform government contracts, so far as is practicable, without using overtime, particularly as a regular employment practice, except when lower overall costs to the government will result or when overtime is necessary to meet urgent program needs. Any approved overtime, extra-pay shifts, and multishifts should be scheduled to achieve these objectives. FAR 22.103-2. The contracting officer must review and approve any contractor requests for overtime on contracts where the OVER-TIME PREMIUM will be charged to the government. FAR 22.103-4. The CONTRACT WORK HOURS AND SAFETY STANDARDS ACT requires that LABORERS OR MECHANICS employed by construction contractors be paid premium wages (not less than one-and-one-half times the basic rate) for overtime hours. See FAR Subpart 22.3. This requirement is implemented by including the Contract Work Hours and Safety Standards Act—Overtime Compensation clause in FAR 52.222-4 in such contracts.

OVERTIME PREMIUM   *Official:* The difference between the contractor's regular rate of pay to an employee for the shift involved and the higher rate paid for OVERTIME. It does not include SHIFT PREMIUM, i.e., the difference between the contractor's regular rate of pay to an employee and the higher rate paid for extra-pay-shift work. *Source:* FAR 2.101. In order to charge the costs of these premiums to the government on COST-REIMBURSEMENT CONTRACTs or TIME-AND-MATERIAL CONTRACTs or LABOR-HOUR CONTRACTs, approval of the procuring agency must be obtained. FAR 22.103-4(b) and (c).

OZONE-DEPLETING SUBSTANCE   *Official:* Any substance the ENVIRONMENTAL PROTECTION AGENCY designates in 40 C.F.R. part 82 as (1) Class I, including, but not limited to, chlorofluorocarbons, halons, carbon tetrachloride, and methyl chloroform; or (2) Class II, including, but not limited to, hydrochlorofluorocarbons. *Source:* FAR 2.101. The government's policy to encourage contractors to minimize the use of these substances is set forth in FAR Subpart 23.8. DFARS 223.803 prohibits DOD contracts from requiring the use of class I ozone-depleting substances unless specifically authorized by no one lower than a general, flag officer, or member of the Senior Executive Service of the requiring activity.

P

PACKAGING   See BUNDLING.

PACKARD COMMISSION   The popular name of the President's Blue Ribbon Commission on Defense Management, which published its final report, *A Quest for Excellence*, in June 1986. Chaired by David Packard, the commission made a number of significant recommendations on reorganizing the Joint Chiefs of Staff, the defense command structure, and the defense acquisition process, including creating the position of Under Secretary of Defense for Acquisition. The commission's acquisition task force suggested (1) streamlining acquisition organization and procedures, (2) using technology to reduce costs, (3) balancing cost and performance, (4) stabilizing programs, (5) expanding the use of COMMERCIAL PRODUCTs, and (6) enhancing the quality of acquisition personnel. The commission's preliminary report was called *A Formula for Action: A Report to the President on Defense Acquisition* (Apr. 1986).

PAPERWORK REDUCTION ACT OF 1980   Pub. L. No. 96-511, 44 U.S.C. § 3501 et seq. An Act whose major purpose is to minimize the federal paperwork burden for individuals, small businesses, state and local governments and other persons. The Act created the OFFICE OF INFORMATION AND REGULATORY AFFAIRS in the OFFICE OF MANAGEMENT AND BUDGET which must approve all efforts to collect information from 10 or more persons. See FAR 1.106 for all current approvals. Among other objectives, the Act sought to "ensure that automatic data processing and telecommunications technologies are acquired and used by the federal government in a manner which improves service delivery and program management," and to "implement policies and oversee, review, and approve the acquisition and use of automatic data processing telecommunications and other technology for managing information." The Act also directed each EXECUTIVE AGENCY to designate a senior official (see DESIGNATED SENIOR OFFICIAL) to ensure that all automatic data processing and telecommunications acquisitions are conducted properly. The functions addressing oversight of information technology usage and acquisition have now been assigned to the Office of Electronic Government in OMB, 44 U.S.C. § 3601 et seq. and the senior officials in each agency are now called CHIEF INFORMATION OFFICERs, 44 U.S.C. § 3506(a)(2). See Nash, *The Public Protection Provision of the Paperwork Reduction Act: Could It Apply in Bid Protests?*, 33 N&CR ¶ 56 (Oct. 2019).

PARALLEL PROCEEDING   A simultaneous proceeding, whether administrative, civil, or criminal, brought by the government in another forum against a contractor litigating a contract CLAIM before a BOARD OF CONTRACT APPEALS (BCA). This situation raises complex strategic decisions for both the government and the contractor. For example, when the contractor is litigating an affirmative claim before a BCA, government counsel may move to stay the BCA action pending the outcome of a criminal action. See Nash, *Stay of Board Proceedings Based on Fraud Investigations: A Toss Up*, 23 N&CR ¶ 7 (Feb. 2009).

PARAMETRIC COST ESTIMATE   An estimating methodology using statistical relationships between historical costs and other program variables, such as system physical or performance characteristics, contractor output measures or manpower loading. DAU GLOSSARY. This technique can be used (1) to estimate costs associated with the development, manufacturing, or modification of an end item, see *DCAA Contract Audit Manual* ¶ 9-1002.1; and (2) to perform a PRICE ANALYSIS. See FAR 15.404-1(b)(2)(iii). See Cibinic, Nash & Yukins, FORMATION OF GOVERNMENT CONTRACTS 1483–84 (4th ed. 2011).

PARENT   An organizational element of a company that has a controlling interest in a SUBSIDIARY. The term is variously referred to for regulatory purposes as: COMMON PARENT, parent corporation, parent company, parent organization, parent concern, or simply parent.

PAROL EVIDENCE RULE   A rule of evidence that prohibits the introduction of EXTRINSIC EVIDENCE to contradict terms of an INTEGRATED AGREEMENT. Thus, in the absence of FRAUD, DURESS, MUTUAL MISTAKE, or something of the kind, the parol evidence rule will preclude a party from presenting prior written or oral agreements to prove that the words of a contract have a meaning contrary to their clear meaning. RESTATEMENT (SECOND) CONTRACTS § 215 (1981). If the agreement is found to be completely integrated, additional terms will be barred even if they are consistent with the agreement. RESTATEMENT (SECOND) CONTRACTS § 216 (1981). While the rule does not prevent the use of extrinsic evidence in government contract controversies to interpret ambiguous language, the judicial decisions appear to hold that the rule prevents the use of extrinsic evidence to prove an AMBIGUITY (see PLAIN MEANING). See Nash & Feldman, 1 GOVERNMENT CONTRACT CHANGES § 11:16 (3d ed. 2006–2020); Cibinic, Nagle & Nash, ADMINISTRATION OF GOVERNMENT CONTRACTS 190–97 (5th ed. 2016); Nash, *Postscript VI: Identifying What's in the Contract*, 19 N&CR ¶ 53 (Nov. 2005).

PARTIAL PAYMENT   A payment made, as authorized by the contract, upon delivery and government acceptance (see ACCEPTANCE OF WORK) of one or more complete units (or one or more distinct items of service), even though other quantities remain to be delivered. Partial payments are permitted on any contract where the unit of work is priced in a separate CONTRACT LINE ITEM. Although partial payments are not generally considered FINANCING PAYMENTs, they can help contractors participate in government contracts without, or with only minimal, contract financing. FAR 32.102(d). A payment made against a termination claim before final settlement of the total termination claim is also called a "partial payment." Under contracts authorizing partial payments on termination SETTLEMENT PROPOSALs before settlement, contractors may request partial payment at any time after submission of interim or final settlement proposals. FAR 49.112-1. FAR 49.602-4 prescribes use of Standard Form 1440, Application for Partial Payment, in FAR 53.301-1440. See also TERMINATION FOR CONVENIENCE. See Cibinic, Nagle & Nash, ADMINISTRATION OF GOVERNMENT CONTRACTS 1017 (5th ed. 2016).

PARTIAL SET-ASIDE   See SET-ASIDE (n).

PARTIAL TERMINATION   *Official:* The termination of a part, but not all, of the work that has not been completed and accepted under a contract. *Source:* FAR 2.101. Under the government's rights to TERMINATE FOR DEFAULT and TERMINATE FOR CONVENIENCE, it is entitled to terminate only part of the work and require the contractor to complete unterminated work. When this occurs on a termination for convenience, the contractor is entitled to an equitable adjustment in the price of the unterminated work. FAR 49.208. When a COST-REIMBURSEMENT CONTRACT is partially terminated for convenience, the SETTLEMENT PROPOSAL is to be only for an appropriate reduction in the fee. FAR 49.304. Model language for partial terminations is provided in FAR 49.603-2; FAR 49.603-5; FAR 49.603-7. See Cibinic, Nagle & Nash, ADMINISTRATION OF GOVERNMENT CONTRACTS 1006 (5th ed. 2016). The deletion of relatively minor work items can be accomplished by a DEDUCTIVE CHANGE instead of partial termination. See Feldman, GOVERNMENT CONTRACT GUIDEBOOK § 20:30 (4th ed. 2019–2020); Nash & Feldman, 2 GOVERNMENT CONTRACT CHANGES § 18:24 (3d ed. 2006–2020).

PARTICIPATED PERSONALLY AND SUBSTANTIALLY IN A FEDERAL AGENCY PROCUREMENT   *Official:* (1) Active and significant involvement of an official in any of the following activities directly related to that procurement: (i) Drafting, reviewing, or approving the SPECIFICATION or STATEMENT OF WORK for the procurement. (ii) Preparing or developing the SOLICITATION. (iii) Evaluating BIDs or PROPOSALs, or selecting a source. (iv) Negotiating price or terms and conditions of the contract. (v) Reviewing and approving the award of the contract. (2) Participating personally means participating directly, and includes the direct and active supervision of a subordinate's participation in the matter. (3) Participating substantially means that the official's involvement is of significance to the matter. Substantial participation requires more than official responsibility, knowledge, perfunctory involvement, or involvement on an administrative or peripheral issue. Participation may be substantial even though it is not determinative of the outcome of a particular matter. A finding of substantiality should be based not only on the effort devoted to a matter, but on the importance of the effort. While a series of peripheral involvements may be insubstantial, the single act of approving or participating in a critical step may be substantial. However, the review of procurement documents solely to determine compliance with regulatory, administrative, or budgetary procedures, does not constitute substantial participation in a procurement. (4) Generally, an official will not be considered to have participated personally and substantially in a procurement solely by participating in the following activities: (i) Agency-level boards, panels, or other advisory committees that review program milestones or evaluate and make recommendations regarding alternative technologies or approaches for satisfying broad agency-level missions or objectives. (ii) The performance of general, technical, engineering, or scientific effort having broad application not directly associated with a particular procurement, notwithstanding that such general, technical, engineering, or scientific effort subsequently may be incorporated into a particular procurement. (iii) Clerical functions supporting the conduct of a particular procurement. (iv) For procurements to be conducted under the procedures of OMB Circular A-76, participation in management studies, preparation of in-house cost estimates, preparation of "most efficient organization" analyses, and furnishing of data or technical support to be used by others in the development of PERFORMANCE STANDARDs, STATEMENTs OF WORK, or SPECIFICATIONs. *Source:* FAR 3.104-1. Under the PROCUREMENT INTEGRITY provisions of 41 U.S.C. § 2103, persons that meet this test are barred from having employment discussions with a contractor and must follow the procedures in FAR 3.104-3(c) if contacted by a contractor. See Cibinic, Nash & Yukins, Formation of Government Contracts 170–72 (4th ed. 2011).

PARTIES EXCLUDED FROM FEDERAL PROCUREMENT AND NONPROCUREMENT PROGRAMS See LIST OF PARTIES EXCLUDED FROM FEDERAL PROCUREMENT AND NONPROCUREMENT PROGRAMS.

PARTNERING A procedure, adopted at the beginning of performance of a contract, to encourage the employees of the contractor and the government to work together to achieve the contract objectives. Partnering involves the development of a cooperative management team, representing both the government and the contractor that seeks to identify common goals and objectives. Both sides work to bring about a "mutual win" situation and discourage an "us against them" attitude. The goal is to avoid litigation that involves unnecessary expense, delay, and disruption. See Cibinic, Nagle & Nash, Administration of Government Contracts 9 (5th ed. 2016); Edelman, et al., Updated By Carr, *Partnering Guide Partnering: A Tool for USACE, Engineering, Construction, and Operations*, Army Corps of Engineers Pamphlet IWR Pamphlet 91-ADR-P-4 (Dec. 1991; revised May 2010).

PAST PERFORMANCE An EVALUATION FACTOR used to assess an offeror's capability, comprising of three elements: "(1) observations of the historical facts of a company's work experience—what work it did, when and where it did it, whom it did it for, and what methods it used; (2) qualitative judgments about the breadth, depth, and relevance of that experience based on those observations; and (3) qualitative judgments about how well the company performed, also based on those observations." Edwards, *How to Evaluate Past Performance: A Best Value Approach* (The Geo. Wash. Univ. Law School, Government Contract Program 1996). FAR 15.304(c)(3) makes past performance a mandatory evaluation factor for negotiated competitive acquisitions expected to exceed the SIMPLIFIED ACQUISITION THRESHOLD. The solicitation must describe the approach for evaluating past performance, including evaluating offerors with no relevant performance history, and provide offerors an opportunity to identify past contracts (including federal, state, and local government and private) for efforts similar to the government requirement. A contractor's past performance is evaluated on the basis of PAST PERFORMANCE INFORMATION that is obtained by checking references on single procurements or from data banks. FAR 15.305(a)(2). Firms lacking relevant performance history or for whom no information is available may not be evaluated favorably or unfavorably on this factor. FAR 15.305(a)(2)(iv); 41 U.S.C. § 1126. See Office of Federal Procurement Policy Guide, *Best Practices for Collecting and Using Current and Past Performance Information* (May 2000); Office of the Under Secretary of Defense for Acquisition, Technology and Logistics, *A Guide to Collection and Use of Past Performance Information* (May 2003). See Feldman, Government Contract Awards: Negotiation and Sealed Bidding § 6:12 (2019–2020 ed.). See also Nash, *Postscript IX: Past Performance Evaluations*, 33 N&CR ¶ 2 (Jan. 2019); Edwards, *Past Performance: Has Bureaucratization Crippled A Useful Policy?*, 30 N&CR ¶ 1 (Jan. 2016); Cong. Research Serv., Report No. R41562, Manuel, Evaluating the "Past Performance" of Federal Contractors: Legal Requirements and Issues (Feb. 5, 2015).

PAST PERFORMANCE INFORMATION *Official:* Relevant information, for future SOURCE SELECTION purposes, regarding a contractor's actions under previously awarded contracts. It includes, for example, the contractor's record of (1) conforming to contract requirements and to standards of good workmanship; (2) forecasting and controlling costs; (3) adherence to contract schedules, including the administrative aspects of performance; (4) reasonable and cooperative behavior and commitment to customer satisfaction; (5) reporting into databases (see subparts 4.14 and 4.15), and reporting requirements in the solicitation provisions and clauses referenced in 9.104-7; (6) integrity and business ethics; and (7) business-like concern for the interest of the customer. *Source:* FAR 42.1501(a). FAR 42.1502 requires agencies to collect this information on contracts and task or delivery orders over the SIMPLIFIED ACQUISITION THRESHOLD, on construction contracts of $700,000 or more, and on architect-engineer contracts of $35,000 or more. Agency evaluations of a contractor's past performance must be provided to the contractor as soon as practicable after completion of the evaluation. The contractor will then be given at least 30 days to submit comments, rebutting statements, or additional information. FAR 42.1503(b). FAR 42.1503(c) requires agencies to submit the data to the CONTRACTOR PERFORMANCE ASSESSMENT REPORTING SYSTEM. See PAST PERFORMANCE. See Cibinic, Nash & Yukins, Formation of Government Contracts 704–08, 845–58 (4th ed. 2011). See also Cong. Research Serv., Report No. R41562, Manuel, Evaluating the "Past Performance" of Federal Contractors: Legal Requirements and Issues (Feb. 5, 2015).

PAST PERFORMANCE INFORMATION RETRIEVAL SYSTEM (PPIRS)   The electronic system that the government used to collect and distribute PAST PERFORMANCE INFORMATION. This was replaced by the CONTRACTOR PERFORMANCE ASSESSMENT REPORTING SYSTEM.

PATENT (adj)   Readily discoverable by observation or inspection. The adjective "patent" can refer to an AMBIGUITY that an offeror found or should have found in a solicitation or contract or a defect in a contract specification (PATENT DEFECT). Patent means "open or manifest" and is an antonym for LATENT.

PATENT (n)   An instrument by which the government grants or conveys to an inventor the right to exclude others from making, using, offering for sale, or selling an INVENTION in the United States or importing an invention into the United States for 20 years from the date of filing with the Patent Office. 35 U.S.C. § 154(a)(1). FAR 27.104(g) states that the government honors rights in patents and complies with the stipulations of law in using or acquiring such rights. However, 28 U.S.C. § 1498(a) provides that the government or its contractors with AUTHORIZATION AND CONSENT can use any patent after which the government will be liable to pay reasonable compensation. In effect, this gives the government and its contractors the right of EMINENT DOMAIN with regard to patents. FAR Subpart 27.2 prescribes policy with respect to PATENT RIGHTS in inventions made during the performance of government contracts, the granting of authorization and consent to infringe patents, patent infringement liability of contractors through PATENT INDEMNIFICATION, royalties payable in connection with performing government contracts, and security requirements covering patent applications containing classified subject matter filed by contractors. See issued by the DOL, must be included in construction contracts for such projects. FAR 22.404-2. See Feldman, Government Contract Guidebook §§ 11:2–11:10 (4th ed. 2019–2020); Nash, *Postscript II: Forfeiture of Title to Patent*, 26 N&CR ¶7 (Feb. 2012); Nash, *Ownership of Patents: The Inventor Or the Employer?*, 25 N&CR ¶ 39 (Aug. 2011); Nash, *Government Use of Patents: A License to Steal*, 24 N&CR ¶ 12 (Mar. 2010); Wyatt, *In Search of "Reasonable Compensation": Patent Infringement by Defense Contractors with the Authorization and Consent of the U.S. Government*, 20 Fed. Circuit B.J. 79

(2010). FAR 31.205-30 makes the costs of obtaining patents that are required by a contract ALLOWABLE COSTs. See Manos, 1 Government Contract Costs and Pricing §§ 37:1–37:3 (2d ed. 2009–2020).

PATENT AMBIGUITY See AMBIGUITY.

PATENT DEFECT *Official:* Any defect which exists at the time of acceptance and is not a LATENT DEFECT. *Source:* FAR 46.101. Patent defects in the contract work are those that are discoverable by the government by the use of reasonable INSPECTION methods. In accordance with the Inspection of Supplies—Fixed-Price clause in FAR 52.246-2 and the Inspection of Construction clause in FAR 52.246-12, government ACCEPTANCE OF WORK containing patent defects is conclusive on the government—with the result that the government cannot require the contractor to correct such defective work at the contractor's own expense unless the contract contains a WARRANTY clause giving it that right. The fact that the government did not inspect the work is not relevant to the determination of whether a defect was patent. The issue is whether the defect *could have been discovered* had the government conducted a reasonable inspection. See Cibinic, Nagle & Nash, Administration of Government Contracts 762–67 (5th ed. 2016).

PATENT INDEMNIFICATION The promise of a contractor to reimburse the government for any amount the government is required to pay an owner of a PATENT for use of that patent during performance of the contract. FAR 27.201-2(c) states the policy of the government to obtain patent indemnification from all contractors furnishing COMMERCIAL ITEMs unless the contracts are awarded under FAR Part 12 or SIMPLIFIED ACQUISITION PROCEDURES. FAR 27.201-2(d) requires patent indemnification on construction contracts but provides for exclusion of noncommercial elements of a construction project. Such indemnification is necessary because the government is primarily liable for paying compensation to the owner of a patent under 28 U.S.C. § 1498(a). See AUTHORIZATION AND CONSENT. The government obtains patent indemnification by using the Patent Indemnification clauses in FAR 52.227-3 and -4. If the contract work contains some commercial supplies and services and some work made to the design of the government, the FAR requires the contracting officer to segregate the commercial work and to provide for indemnification for that work only. See Nash & Rawicz, Intellectual Property in Government Contracts, chap. 8 (6th ed. 2008).

PATENT INFRINGEMENT Selling, making, using, or importing a patented invention without the consent of the owner of the PATENT. Under the patent laws, the owner of a patent can usually obtain an injunction against patent infringement or damages for infringement. Such injunctions are not permitted against the government because the only remedy for infringement by the government or its contractors with AUTHORIZATION AND CONSENT is reasonable compensation under the provisions of 28 U.S.C. § 1498(a). See Nash & Rawicz, Intellectual Property in Government Contracts, chap. 10 (6th ed. 2008); Wyatt, *In Search of "Reasonable Compensation": Patent Infringement by Defense Contractors with the Authorization and Consent of the U.S. Government*, 20 Fed. Circuit B.J. 79 (2010).

PATENT LICENSE An agreement of the owner of a PATENT to permit another party to make, use, sell, or import an invention to the extent the owner has such a right. Technically, a patent license is an agreement not to sue the licensee for PATENT INFRINGEMENT because the owner of the patent may not have the right to make, use, sell, or import the invention (generally when it is an invention that makes an improvement to another patented invention). The government obtains a license in all SUBJECT INVENTIONs under its policy on PATENT RIGHTS. In addition, 10 U.S.C. § 2386 gives DOD the right to acquire patent licenses. FAR 31.205-30 makes the costs incurred by contractors for licenses ALLOWABLE COSTs unless the government has license rights or the patent is invalid, unenforceable, or expired. See Nash & Rawicz, INTELLECTUAL PROPERTY IN GOVERNMENT CONTRACTS, chap. 2 (6th ed. 2008).

PATENT RIGHTS   The rights of the government in PATENTs resulting from inventions made during the performance of government contracts (see SUBJECT INVENTION). 35 U.S.C. § 202 requires the government to permit all SMALL BUSINESS CONCERNs and NONPROFIT ORGANIZATIONs to take TITLE to all subject inventions and provides that the government will have, at a minimum, a nonexclusive, nontransferable, irrevocable, paid-up LICENSE to practice the invention on its own behalf. See BAYH-DOYLE ACT. This, in effect, divides the rights in a patent—giving the contractor commercial rights and the government the right to use the invention for government purposes. A presidential memorandum "Government Patent Policy," Feb. 18, 1983, requires that this policy be followed with regard to large contractors to the extent authorized by law, which excludes DOE (see DEAR 927.300) and NASA (see NFR 1827.302) which are required to take title but can waive this automatic right to title. This policy is implemented in FAR Subpart 27.3. See Nash & Rawicz, INTELLECTUAL PROPERTY IN GOVERNMENT CONTRACTS, chap. 2 (6th ed. 2008); Greene, *Patent Law in Government Contracts: Does It Serve the Department of Defense's Mission?*, 36 PUB. CONT. L.J. 331 (2007); DeVecchio, *Patent Rights Under Government Contracts*, BRIEFING PAPERS No. 07-7 (June 2007).

PAY-AS-YOU-GO   See BUDGET ENFORCEMENT ACT OF 1990.

PAY-AS-YOU-GO COST METHOD   *Official:* A method of recognizing pension cost only when benefits are paid to retired employees or their beneficiaries. *Source:* FAR 31.001. For pay-as-you-go PENSION PLANs, the entire cost assignable to a cost accounting period may be assigned to the COST OBJECTIVEs of that period only if the payment of benefits can be compelled. Otherwise, the assignable cost is limited to the amount of benefits actually paid. CAS 412, Cost Accounting Standard for Composition and Measurement of Pension Costs, 48 C.F.R. § 9904.412-40(c). See Manos, 2 GOVERNMENT CONTRACT COSTS AND PRICING § 73-75 (2d ed. 2009–2020).

PAYING OFFICE CONTRACT FILE   An organized collection of documents maintained by a government paying office that includes a copy of the contract and all modifications; bills, invoices, vouchers, and supporting documents; records of payments and receipts; and any other pertinent records. FAR 4.803(c). This is one of the mandatory CONTRACT FILEs which government agencies must compile and retain. See FAR 4.801.

PAYMENT   The satisfaction of the government's OBLIGATION to compensate the contractor in accordance with the terms of a contract. The government's payment obligation is not dealt with in any single part of the FAR but is scattered through various parts. Most of the clauses setting forth the requirements for payment are contained in FAR 52.216 or FAR 52.232. See, for example, the standard Allowable Cost and Payment clause in FAR 52.216-7, which is used in cost-reimbursement contracts; the Payments clause in FAR 52.232-1, which is used in fixed-price supply contracts; and the Payments under Fixed-Price Construction Contracts clause in FAR 52.232-5. Payment may be made in the form of PROGRESS PAYMENTs, PARTIAL PAYMENTs, and FINAL PAYMENTs. The

PROMPT PAYMENT ACT uses the terms INVOICE PAYMENTs and FINANCING PAYMENTs. See Cibinic, Nagle & Nash, ADMINISTRATION OF GOVERNMENT CONTRACTS, chap. 12 (5th ed. 2016); Chierichella & Gallacher, *Financing Government Contracts/Edition II – Part II*, BRIEFING PAPERS No. 04-13 (Dec. 2004); Chierichella & Gallacher, *Financing Government Contracts/Edition II – Part I*, BRIEFING PAPERS No. 04-12 (Nov. 2004).

PAYMENT BOND   A promise of a SURETY ensuring payment to all persons supplying LABOR or MATERIAL in the prosecution of the work provided for in a contract. See the definition of BOND in FAR 28.001. This bond is purchased by a prospective contractor in accordance with the requirement of the government. The MILLER ACT requires such bonds for construction contracts exceeding $150,000, and they may occasionally be required for other contracts as well. FAR 28.102-1, FAR 28.103. The PENAL AMOUNT of Miller Act payment bonds must be 100% of the contract price plus 100% of any price increases. FAR 28.102-2(b)(2). For construction contracts, the bond is furnished on Standard Form 25-A, FAR 53.301-25-A. For nonconstruction contracts, the bond is furnished on Standard Form 1416, FAR 53.301-1416. In lieu of furnishing a payment bond a contractor may deposit securities. FAR 28.204. A payment bond is only required when a PERFORMANCE BOND is required and it is in the government's interest. FAR 28.103-3.

PAYMENT DATE   *Official:* The date on which a check for payment is dated or, for an ELEC-TRONIC FUNDS TRANSFER, the settlement date. *Source:* FAR 32.902. This is the date that cuts off interest that is due under the PROMPT PAYMENT ACT when the government fails to make payment within the required period. The government establishes a SPEC-IFIED PAYMENT DATE in order to endeavor to ensure timely payment to its contractors.

PEER OR SCIENTIFIC REVIEW   A process of proposal review that utilizes a group of experts in the field to evaluate the proposal for merit. FAR 6.102(d)(2) provides that the award of basic and applied research contracts in response to a BROAD AGENCY ANNOUNCEMENT using a peer or scientific review is one of the COMPETITIVE PRO-CEDURES. FAR 35.016(d) requires the evaluation of such proposals using a peer or scientific review process. See NFS Subpart 1872.4.

PEER REVIEW   A DOD procedure that establishes a team of senior contracting officials and attorneys to review acquisitions as they proceed through the acquisition process. For acquisitions of $1 billion or more the team was established by the Director of Defense Pricing and Contracting (DPC) and was composed of officials from agencies other than the contracting agency. For acquisitions under $1 billion the team was established by the contracting agency. DFARS 201.170. Detailed procedures that are required to be followed are set forth in DOD PGI 201.170. DPC peer reviews were limited to major weapon system acquisitions and special interest programs by a class deviation issued on August 20, 2019.

PENAL AMOUNT   *Official:* The amount of money specified in a BOND (or a percentage of the bid price in a BID BOND) as the maximum payment for which the SURETY is obligated or the maximum amount of security required to be pledged to the government in lieu of a corporate or individual surety for the bond. *Source:* FAR 28.001. For example, on CONSTRUCTION contracts, the penal amount of performance and payment bonds must normally be 100% of the original contract price, unless the contracting officer determines that a lesser amount would be adequate for the protection of the government. FAR 28.102-2. See Gallagher & McCallum, *The Importance of Surety Bond Verification*, 39 PUB. CONT. L.J. 269 (2010).

PENAL SUM   See PENAL AMOUNT.

PENALTY   A punishment for the commission of a criminal act or the violation of a law or regulation. FAR 31.205-15(a) makes the costs of penalties resulting from contractor violations of, or failure to comply with, federal, state, local, or foreign laws and regulations unallowable (see UNALLOWABLE COST) unless they are incurred as a result of compliance with specific TERMS AND CONDITIONS of a contract or written instructions from a contracting officer. See Manos, 1 GOVERNMENT CONTRACT COSTS AND PRICING §§ 22:1–22:2 (2d ed. 2009–2020); Cibinic, Knight & Nash, COST-REIMBURSEMENT CONTRACTING 727–28 (4th ed. 2014). FAR 31.205-47, dealing with the allowability of the costs of legal and other proceedings, states that penalties do not include restitution, reimbursement, or compensatory damages. If LIQUIDATED DAMAGES are found to constitute a penalty, the government may not enforce them. See Cibinic, Nagle & Nash, ADMINISTRATION OF GOVERNMENT CONTRACTS 920–22 (5th ed. 2016). Contracting officers are not authorized to resolve CLAIMs for penalties prescribed by statute or regulation that another agency is specifically authorized to administer, settle, or determine. FAR 33.210.

PENSION PLAN   *Official:* A DEFERRED COMPENSATION plan established and maintained by one or more employers to provide systematically for the payment of benefits to plan participants after their retirements, provided that the benefits are paid for life or are payable for life at the option of the employee. Additional benefits, such as permanent and total disability and death payments, and survivorship payments to beneficiaries of deceased employees, may be an integral part of a pension plan. *Source:* FAR 31.001. Pension plans are generally either the insured type (insured under a contract with a life insurance company) or the trustee type (self-insured under a formal trust agreement with a trustee). The allowability of costs (see ALLOWABLE COST) incurred by a contractor to fund pension plans is governed by FAR 31.205-6(j). The allocability of such costs (see ALLOCABLE COST) is covered in CAS 412 and CAS 413, 48 C.F.R. § 9904.412 and 48 C.F.R. § 9904.413. See Manos, 2 GOVERNMENT CONTRACT COSTS AND PRICING, chaps. 73 & 74 (2d ed. 2009–2020); Cibinic, Knight & Nash, COST-REIMBURSEMENT CONTRACTING 678–83 (4th ed. 2014); *DCAA Contract Audit Manual* ¶ 7-600.

PERFORMANCE-BASED ACQUISITION (PBA)   *Official:* An acquisition structured around the results to be achieved as opposed to the manner by which the work is to be performed. *Source:* FAR 2.101. FAR Subpart 37.6 contains policies and procedures pertaining to the acquisition of services using PBA methods. See PERFORMANCE-BASED SERVICES ACQUISITION. FAR 37.002 states that PBA is the preferred method for the acquisition of services and it must be used to the maximum extent practicable except for ARCHITECT-ENGINEER SERVICES, CONSTRUCTION, utility services, and services that are incidental to supply purchases. If PBA is not the method used for service contracts, the ACQUISITION PLAN must provide a rationale for using a different method. See Office of Federal Procurement Policy, *Report of the Acquisition Advisory Panel*, 15–17 (2007); Econom, *Confronting the Looming Crisis in the Federal Acquisition Workforce*, 35 PUB. CONT. L.J. 171 (2006).

PERFORMANCE-BASED CONTRACTING   *Official:* Structuring all aspects of an acquisition around the purpose of the work to be performed as opposed to either the manner by which the work is to be performed or broad and imprecise statements of work. *Source:* FAR 37.101. FAR Part 37 requires the use of "performance-based acquisitions" to the maximum extent practicable and provides minimal guidance on this type of contracting. See PERFORMANCE-BASED SERVICES ACQUISITION.

PERFORMANCE-BASED LOGISTICS (PBL) A strategy for weapon system product support that employs the purchase of support in long-term performance agreements as an integrated performance package designed to bring higher levels of system readiness. PBL is the DOD preferred approach for implementing product support. PBL delineates outcome performance goals of weapon systems; ensures that responsibilities are assigned; and provides incentives for attaining those goals for the overall life-cycle management of system reliability, supportability, and total ownership cost. See DOD Performance Based Logistics (PBL) Guidebook (Mar. 2016); U.S. Gov't Accountability Office, Opportunities To Enhance the Implementation of Performance-Based Logistics, GAO-04-715 (Aug. 2004).

PERFORMANCE-BASED PAYMENTS CONTRACT FINANCING PAYMENTS on fixed-price-type contracts that are not payments for accepted items but are based on objective performance measures, the accomplishment of specified activities (milestones), or other quantifiable measures of results. FAR 32.1002. FAR 32.1001(a) states that these are the preferred financing method when they are practical and the contractor agrees to use them (in contrast to PROGRESS PAYMENTS BASED ON COSTS). Guidance on the use of these payments is set forth in FAR Subpart 32.10. These payments may not be used on COST-REIMBURSEMENT CONTRACTS (FAR 32.1001(e)(1)), contracts for construction, architect-engineer services, or shipbuilding (FAR 32.1001(e)(2)), or contracts awarded using sealed bidding procedures (FAR 32.1001(e)(3)). When used, they may not exceed 90% of the contract price of the entire contract or an item delivered under the contract. FAR 32.1004(b)(2). DOD follows unique policies that are set forth in DFARS Subpart 232.10. See Cibinic, Nagle & Nash, Administration of Government Contracts 1062–64 (5th ed. 2016).

PERFORMANCE-BASED PROCUREMENT (PBP) A competitive procurement process used by the WORLD BANK resulting in a contract that requires payments to a contractor for measured outputs. PBP, also known as output-based procurement, differs from more traditional payment schemes by emphasizing outputs instead of focusing on inputs; PBP articulates the desired outcomes without prescribing how the outcomes must be achieved. SPECIFICATIONS define the desired result; which outputs are to be measured (those that aim at satisfying a functional need in terms of quantity, quality, and reliability); and how those outputs will be measured. The bidding documents do not prescribe input specifications; the contractor is free to propose the most appropriate solution for meeting the output requirements. Payment is made in accordance with the delivered outputs, subject to quality standards. Reductions in payment can be made for lower-quality level of outputs and, in some cases, premiums may be paid for outputs of higher quality. When PBP is used for design, supply, and/or CONSTRUCTION, prequalification and TWO-STAGE BIDDING is normally required. World Bank Borrowers, *Guidelines: Procurement of Goods, Works, and Non-Consulting Services Under IBRD Loans and IDA Credits & Grants* 35–36 (Jan. 2011). See PERFORMANCE BASED SERVICES ACQUISITION.

PERFORMANCE-BASED SERVICE ACQUISITION (PBSA) An approach to service contracting in which the government specifies the results that it wants the contractor to achieve instead of specifying the manner or method of performance or a number of labor hours. Alternatively called PERFORMANCE-BASED CONTRACTING, it was established as the preferred way to contract for services in Office of Federal Procurement Policy (OFPP) Letter 91-2 on service contracting that was issued on April 9, 1991. OFPP PBSA policy was subsequently incorporated into FAR Subpart 37.6, which requires (1) a PERFOR-MANCE WORK STATEMENT, (2) measurable performance standards and methods of assessing compliance, and (3) performance incentives when appropriate. See also Seven Steps to Performance-Based Services Acquisition at https://www.acquisition.gov/comp/seven_steps/home.html. Although PBSA became government-wide policy in 1991, the method had been in use since 1979, when the Air Force issued its regulation (AFR) 400-28, *Base Level Service Contracts*, which introduced the concept of the PERFORMANCE WORK STATEMENT. Earlier attempts to take a performance-based approach to specifying services date to 1971, when the now-defunct Office of Economic Opportunity conducted experiments in "performance contracting" for educational services. See Nash, *Performance Based Service Contracting: It's All About Productivity*, 24 N&CR ¶ 20 (Apr. 2010); Edwards & Nash, *A Proposal for a New Approach to Performance-Based Services Acquisition*, DEFENSE ACQUISITION REV. J. 352 (2007); Edwards, *The Acquisition Advisory Panel and Performance-Based Contracting*, 20 N&CR ¶ 32 (July 2006); Edwards, A *Chance To Fix Performance-Based Contracting*, 19 N&CR ¶ 18 (Apr. 2005).

PERFORMANCE-BASED SERVICE CONTRACTING (PBSC)   See PERFORMANCE-BASED SERVICE ACQUISITION.

PERFORMANCE BOND   A promise of a SURETY, sometimes referred to as a "completion bond," assuring the government that once the contract is awarded, the contractor will perform its OBLIGATIONs under the contract. See BOND. This bond is purchased by a prospective contractor in accordance with the requirements of the government. The MILLER ACT generally requires performance bonds for construction contracts exceeding $150,000, and they may occasionally be required for other contracts as well. FAR 28.102-1, 28.103. The PENAL AMOUNT of a Miller Act performance bond must be 100% of the original contract price plus 100% of any price increases, unless the contracting officer determines that a smaller amount will adequately protect the government. FAR 28.102-2. Contractors may furnish an annual performance bond, which is a single bond that secures the fulfillment of the contractor's obligations under nonconstruction contracts in a specific FISCAL YEAR. FAR 28.001. In lieu of a performance bond a contractor may deposit securities. FAR 28.204. See Nash & Cibinic, *Postscript: The Rights of Performance Bond Sureties*, 19 N&CR ¶ 34 (July 2005).

PERFORMANCE EVALUATION   The evaluation of the performance of a contractor in carrying out its obligations on government contracts. Performance evaluations are required at the time of completion of all contracts that exceed the SIMPLIFIED ACQUISITION THRESHOLD. FAR 42.1502(a). See PAST PERFORMANCE INFORMATION.

PERFORMANCE EVALUATION AND MEASUREMENT PLAN   A plan unilaterally established by the government to be used in determining the amount of AWARD FEE earned by the contractor in MANAGEMENT AND OPERATING CONTRACTS. The plan sets forth the criteria on which the contractor will be evaluated for performance relating to any technical, schedule, management, and COST OBJECTIVEs selected for evaluation. The plan includes the criteria to be considered under each area evaluated and includes the percentage of award fee available for each area. These plans are prescribed by the Total Available Fee: Base Fee Amount and Performance Fee Amount clause in DEAR 970.5215-1. This clause may also be used in other DOE contracts that contain COST-PLUS-AWARD-FEE provisions. DEAR 970.1504-5(a).

PERFORMANCE INCENTIVE　A contractual provision that provided for increases or decreases in profit or fee if the contractor meets or fails to meet specified performance targets. Such targets include delivery or test schedules, quality controls, maintenance requirements, and achievement of design specification requirements for reliability and maintainability. See DOD PGI 216.402-2. Guidance on the use of such incentives is contained in FAR 16.402-2 through 16.402-4. This regulation states that these incentives may be "particularly appropriate" in major systems contracts and warns that performance tests must generally be specified in order to ensure that the parties have agreed on how performance will be measured. See Cibinic, Nash & Yukins, FORMATION OF GOVERNMENT CONTRACTS, 1276–88 (4th ed. 2011).

PERFORMANCE OUTCOME　The desired result achieved through successful completion of a contractor's work. This term is used in PERFORMANCE-BASED SERVICES ACQUISITION. See Seven Steps to Performance-Based Services Acquisition at https://www.acquisition.gov/comp/seven_steps/index.html.

PERFORMANCE REQUIREMENTS　Statements describing the required services in terms of output in clear, concise, commonly used, easily understood, measurable terms. Detailed procedures should not be included that dictate how the work is to be accomplished; rather, the requirements should allow the contractor the latitude to work in a manner best suited for innovation and creativity. See PERFORMANCE WORK STATEMENT; Seven Steps to Performance-Based Services Acquisition at https://www.acquisition.gov/comp/seven_steps/index.html.

PERFORMANCE REQUIREMENTS SUMMARY　A summary of the elements in the PERFORMANCE WORK STATEMENT. It is presented as a matrix that includes performance objectives, associated PERFORMANCE STANDARDs, acceptable quality levels, method(s) of surveillance to determine adherence to the standard(s), and positive and negative incentives for meeting, exceeding, or failing to meet the standard(s). See Seven Steps to Performance-Based Services Acquisition at https://www.acquisition.gov/comp/seven_steps/index.html.

PERFORMANCE SCHEDULE　See DELIVERY OR PERFORMANCE SCHEDULE.

PERFORMANCE SPECIFICATIONS　Technical requirements that set forth the operational characteristics desired for an ITEM. They indicate what the final product must be capable of accomplishing rather than how the product is to be built or what its measurements, tolerances, or other design characteristics must be. When the contract contains performance specifications, the contractor accepts general responsibility for product design and engineering and for achieving the stated performance requirements. See Cibinic, Nash & Yukins, FORMATION OF GOVERNMENT CONTRACTS 365–66 (4th ed. 2011). Performance specifications are preferred over DESIGN SPECIFICATIONS. FAR 11.101(a).

PERFORMANCE STANDARD　The target level of performance, stated as a tangible, measurable objective against which actual achievements can be compared (quality, timeliness, accuracy, completeness, reliability, cost, etc.) that is required by the government to meet contract requirements. See FAR 37.603. Such standards can be proposed by an offeror in response to a STATEMENT OF OBJECTIVES; however, agencies must determine that such proposals meet agency needs. Performance at a level below a standard is generally unacceptable. These standards may be objective (e.g., response time) or subjective (e.g., customer satisfaction), but must reflect the level of service required by the government to meet mission objectives. Standards must enable assessment of contractor performance to determine whether contract results and objectives are being met. See Seven Steps to Performance-Based Services Acquisition at https://www.acquisition.gov/comp/seven_steps/index.html.

PERFORMANCE UNDER PROTEST   The performance by one party to a contract in accordance with a demand from the other party, despite a disagreement between the parties about the contractual legitimacy of the demand, while expressly asserting or reserving the right to seek an EQUITABLE ADJUSTMENT or pursue a remedy for BREACH OF CONTRACT. This is an alternative to refusing to perform on the grounds that the other party's demand is a material breach of contract, which is a risky course of action. An example would be a contractor's agreement under protest to accelerate its performance in response to the government's demand that it meet a specified delivery or completion date, despite the contractor's assertion of entitlement to a time extension due to an EXCUSABLE DELAY. Performance under protest reserves the performing party's right to seek relief. Performance without protest might result in a decision by the COURT OF FEDERAL CLAIMS or a BOARD OF CONTRACT APPEALS that the performing party has waived its rights. See *E. Walters & Co. v. United States*, 217 Ct. Cl. 254 (1978). The Disputes clause, FAR 52.233-1, requires a CONTRACTOR to perform under protest pending resolution of a CLAIM ARISING UNDER A CONTRACT. Alternate I of the clause, when included in a contract, requires the CONTRACTOR to perform under protest pending resolution of a claim RELATING TO A CONTRACT. See FAR 33.213.

PERFORMANCE WORK STATEMENT (PWS)   *Official:* A STATEMENT OF WORK for PERFORMANCE-BASED ACQUISITIONs that describes the results that the contractor must produce in clear, specific and objective terms as measurable outcomes. *Source:* FAR 2.101. According to FAR 37.602, agencies must, to the maximum extent practicable: (1) describe the work in terms of the purpose of the work to be performed rather than either "how" the work is to be accomplished or the number of hours to be provided and (2) enable assessment of work performance against measurable performance standards. Although the term came into general use during the late 1990s, the concept had been developed by the Air Force in the late 1970s and was first described in its regulation (AFR) 400-28, *Base Level Service Contracts* (1979).

PERSONAL CONFLICT OF INTEREST   A number of types of conduct prescribed by law and regulation, on grounds that the conduct would compromise or appear to compromise the complete impartiality of the procurement process. Prohibitions apply to government employees, former government employees, and members of Congress. As a rule, no government employee may solicit or accept a GRATUITY (18 U.S.C. § 201(c); 10 U.S.C. § 2207; 5 U.S.C. § 7353; 5 C.F.R. § 2635, Subpart B) or solicit or accept a bribe (see BRIBERY) 18 U.S.C. § 201(b). Nor, as a rule, may a government employee have a financial interest in an organization with which he or she is dealing (18 U.S.C. § 208; 5 C.F.R. § 2635, Subpart D). Discussion of future employment or business opportunities with a contractor seeking a government contract is considered a financial interest under 18 U.S.C. § 208, 5 C.F.R. § 2635.603(b), and is also dealt with in FEDERAL AGENCY PROCUREMENTs by 41 U.S.C. § 2103, FAR 3.104-3(c), 3.105. Award of a contract to a government employee or to a business substantially owned or controlled by a government employee is also prohibited by FAR 3.601. Post-employment restrictions are contained in 18 U.S.C. § 207 and 41 U.S.C. § 2104 (see REVOLVING DOOR). As a rule, no member of Congress may be awarded a government contract or personally benefit from award of a contract (41 U.S.C. § 6306). See DOD Directive 5500.07, Standards of Conduct, Nov. 29, 2007, and DOD 5500.07-R, Joint Ethics Regulation, Nov. 17, 2011. See also PROCUREMENT INTEG-RITY. See Cibinic, Nagle & Nash, ADMINISTRATION OF GOVERNMENT CONTRACTS 91–104 (5th ed. 2016). When contractors perform acquisition functions closely associated with INHERENTLY GOVERNMENTAL FUNCTIONS, FAR Subpart 3.11 requires them to adopt procedures that ensure that their employees do not have a personal conflict of interest. The Preventing Personal Conflicts of Interest clause at FAR 52.203-16 contains a detailed description of the types of activity that constitute a personal conflict of interest. See Kathuria, *Best Practices for Compliance with the New Government Compliance and Ethics Rules Under the Federal Acquisition Regulation*, 38 PUB. CONT. L.J. 803 (2009). Nash, *Postscript III: Mixed Workforce Questions*, 22 N&CR ¶ 30 (May 2008).

PERSONAL IDENTITY VERIFICATION   A requirement that contractor or subcontractor personnel with access to a FEDERALLY CONTROLLED FACILITY or a FEDERALLY CONTROLLED INFORMATION SYSTEM have a badge or other identification that entitles them to access. See FAR Subpart 4.13 and the Personal Identification of Contractor Personnel clause in FAR 52.204-9.

PERSONAL PROPERTY   *Official:* Property of any kind, or interest in it except REAL PROP-ERTY, RECORDS of the federal government, and naval vessels of the following categories: (1) battleships; (2) cruisers; (3) aircraft carriers; (4) destroyers; and (5) submarines. *Source:* FAR 2.101. Any moveable or intangible thing that is the subject of ownership and not clas-sified as real property. BLACK'S LAW DICTIONARY 1472 (11th ed. 2019). Instructions on con-tractor reporting of excess personal property are set forth in FAR Subpart 45.6. Such reports, when required by the contract, are submitted on Standard Form 120, Report of Excess Per-sonal Property, FAR 53.301-120. Navin, *Herding Cats II: Disposal of DoD Personal Property*, THE ARMY LAWYER (Apr. 2010), at 25.

PERSONAL SERVICES CONTRACT   *Official:* A contract that, by its express terms or as administered, makes the contractor personnel appear to be, in effect, government employees. *Source:* FAR 2.101. Government agencies may not award personal services contracts unless specifically authorized by statute to do so, because such contracts tend to circumvent the civil service laws requiring the government to obtain its employees by direct hire using established competitive procedures. FAR 37.104(b). FAR 37.104(c) provides that the key indicator of a personal services contract is "relatively continuous supervision and control" of contractor employees by government officials. FAR 37.104(d) provides a list of other elements that may indicate that a personal services contract exists. See also DFARS 237.104. For an analy-sis of the legal validity of these policies see *Report of the Acquisition Advisory Panel*, 400–04 (2007); Nash, *Personal Services Contracts: Is the Federal Acquisition Regulation Guidance Valid?*, 21 N&CR ¶ 16 (Apr. 2007).

PERSONALLY IDENTIFIABLE INFORMATION   *Official:* Information that can be used to distinguish or trace an individual's identity, either alone or when combined with other infor-mation that is linked or linkable to a specific individual. (See Office of Management and Budget (OMB) Circular No. A-130, Managing Federal Information as a Strategic Resource.) *Source:* FAR 24.101. This information is subject to protection under the PRIVACY ACT, 5

U.S.C. § 552a, in accordance with the procedures in FAR Subpart 24.1. If a contract will involve the design, development, or operation of a system of records on individuals to accomplish an agency function, solicitations and contracts must include the clauses at FAR 52.224-1 and -2.

PETTY CASH   See IMPREST FUND.

PHYSICAL CONFIGURATION AUDIT (PCA)   A review that "examines the actual configuration of an item being produced. It verifies that the related design documentation matches the item as specified in the contract. In addition to the standard practice of assuring product verification, the PCA confirms that the manufacturing processes, quality control system, measurement and test equipment, and training are adequately planned, tracked, and controlled. The PCA validates many of the supporting processes used by the contractor in the production of the item and verifies other elements of the item that may have been impacted/redesigned after completion of the System Verification Review. A PCA is normally conducted when the government plans to control the detail design of the item it is acquiring via the TECHNICAL DATA PACKAGE. When the government does not plan to exercise such control or purchase the item's Technical Data Package (e.g., performance based procurement), the contractor should conduct an internal PCA to define the starting point for controlling the detail design of the item and establishing a product baseline. The PCA is complete when the design and manufacturing documentation match the item as specified in the contract. If the PCA was not conducted before the Full-Rate Production Decision, it should be performed as soon as production systems are available." DOD, Defense Acquisition Guidebook 263 (Jan. 2012).

PHYSICALLY COMPLETED CONTRACT   *Official:* A contract is considered to be physically completed when (1) the contractor has completed the required deliveries and the government has inspected and accepted the supplies, or the contractor has performed all services and the government has accepted those services, and all option provisions, if any, have expired, or (2) the government has given the contractor a notice of complete contract termination. Rental, use, and storage agreements are physically completed when the government has given the contractor a notice of complete contract termination or the contract period has expired. *Source:* FAR 4.804-4. FAR 4.804-1 calls for CLOSEOUT of contract files within specified times after contracts are physically completed.

PILOT MENTOR-PROTÉGÉ PROGRAM See MENTOR-PROTÉGÉ PILOT PROGRAM.

PLAIN MEANING   The meaning attributed to a document by a court or BOARD OF CONTRACT APPEALS after giving the words their ordinary sense and without referring to EXTRINSIC EVIDENCE. The courts have been placing increasing reliance on ascertaining plain meaning as the paramount way to interpret contract language. See Nash & Feldman, Government Contract Changes § 11:5 (3d ed. 2006–2020); Cibinic, Nagle & Nash, Administration of Government Contracts 164 (5th ed. 2016). See also Nash, *Postscript XII: The Plain Meaning Rule*, 32 N&CR ¶ 17 (Apr. 2018).

PLAINTIFF   The party bringing suit in a court. In the COURT OF FEDERAL CLAIMS, the contractor is always the plaintiff even though the suit may be based on a government CLAIM under the CONTRACT DISPUTES ACT OF 1978. In such cases, the government is referred to as the DEFENDANT. (If such a case were appealed to a BOARD OF

CONTRACT APPEALS, the contractor would be referred to as the appellant and the government would be called the respondent.)

PLANNING, PROGRAMMING, BUDGET, AND EXECUTION (PPBE) PROCESS An annual, formal, systematic structure used by the Department of Defense for making decisions on policy, strategy, and the development of forces and capabilities to accomplish anticipated missions. Each year the process produces planning guidance, approved PROGRAM OBJECTIVES MEMORANDUMs for the Military Departments and Defense Agencies covering the base year and four additional years, and the DOD portion of the President's Budget covering the base year. The process also calls for an annual review of how well the programs have been executed. Guidance is provided in DOD Directive 7045.14(D) CE-01, *The Planning, Programming, Budgeting and Execution (PPBE) Process*, Aug. 29, 2017.

PLANT CLEARANCE All actions relating to the reporting, screening, reutilization, and disposal of government property excess to contracts and TERMINATION INVENTORY under fixed-price contracts from a contractor's plant or work site. FAR Subpart 45.6 contains guidance on the procedures to be followed in the plant clearance process. See also DFARS Subpart 245.6. For this function, government agencies normally appoint a PLANT CLEARANCE OFFICER.

PLANT CLEARANCE OFFICER *Official:* An authorized representative of the contracting officer, appointed in accordance with agency procedures, responsible for screening, redistributing, and disposing of contractor inventory from a contractor's plant or work site. The term "Contractor's plant" includes, but is not limited to, Government-owned contractor-operated plants, Federal installations, and Federal and non-Federal industrial operations, as may be required under the scope of the contract. *Source:* FAR 2.101. FAR Subpart 45.6 and DFARS Subpart 245.6 contain guidance on the procedures to be followed in the PLANT CLEARANCE process.

PLANT EQUIPMENT Personal property of a capital nature (including equipment, machine tools, test equipment, furniture, vehicles, and accessory and auxiliary items) for use in manufacturing supplies, in performing services, or for any administrative or general plant purpose. It does not include SPECIAL TEST EQUIPMENT or SPECIAL TOOLING. This definition was in FAR 45.101 prior to the issuance of FAC 2005-17, May 15, 2007, which revised the GOVERNMENT PROPERTY regulations. The pre-2007 FAR Part 45 contained special procedures dealing with plant equipment. Under the new FAR Part 45 plant equipment is not distinguished from other types of GOVERNMENT PROPERTY and there are no special procedures for such equipment.

PLEA OF NOLO CONTENDERE See NOLO CONTENDERE.

POINT OF TOTAL ASSUMPTION (PTA) The level of cost in a FIXED-PRICE INCENTIVE CONTRACT where the contractor bears all of the additional costs of performance because the CEILING PRICE overrides the sharing formula. In effect, at this point the contract becomes a FIRM-FIXED PRICE CONTRACT. See Cibinic, Nash & Yukins, FORMATION OF GOVERNMENT CONTRACTS 1272–75 (4th ed. 2011).

POLLUTION PREVENTION *Official:* Any practice that (1)(i) reduces the amount of any hazardous substance, pollutant, or contaminant entering any waste stream or otherwise released into the environment (including fugitive emissions) prior to recycling, treatment, or disposal; and (ii) reduces the hazards to public health and the environment associated with the release of such substances, pollutants, and contaminants; (2) reduces or eliminates the creation of pollutants through increased efficiency in the use of raw materials, energy, water, or other resources; or (3) protects natural resources by conservation. *Source:* FAR 2.101. The policies of the government to encourage contractors to engage in practices that prevent pollution are set forth in FAR Subpart 23.9.

POOL *Official:* A group of concerns (see 19.001) that have—(1) Associated together in order to obtain and perform, jointly or in conjunction with each other, defense production or research and development contracts; (2) Entered into an agreement governing their organization, relationship, and procedures; and (3) Obtained approval of the agreement by either— (i) The Small Business Administration (SBA) under section 9 or 11 of the Small Business Act (15 U.S.C. § 638 or § 640) (see 13 C.F.R. part 125); or (ii) A designated official under Part V of Executive Order 10480, August 14, 1953 (18 FR 4939, August 20, 1953) and section 708 of the Defense Production Act of 1950 (50 U.S.C. App. § 2158). *Source:* FAR 9.701. With minor exceptions, pools are treated as if they were individual contractors. FAR 9.702(a). However, contracting officers are required to obtain certified powers of attorney from each pool member identifying the person empowered to serve as the agent for the pool. FAR 9.702(e). See DEFENSE PRODUCTION POOL and RESEARCH AND DEVELOPMENT POOL.

POOL OF CONTRACTORS See POOL.

POSITIVE LAW As used in connection with the UNITED STATES CODE, positive law consists of the statutes (public laws) enacted by Congress in accordance with the U.S. Constitution. Public laws are published by the Office of the Federal Register in the National Archives and Records Administration in pamphlets called "slip laws." The statutes are collected annually in volumes of the U.S. STATUTES AT LARGE. General and permanent laws are then collected into topical sets ("codified") by the Office of the Law Revision Council of the House of Representatives as the United States Code. The topical sets in the U.S.C. are called "titles." The purpose of codification is to make the law about a particular matter easier to find. The text in the titles of the U.S.C. is only prima facie evidence of the law and subject to comparison with the text in the Statutes at Large until Congress enacts a title into positive law and repeals the text in the Statutes at Large. In enacting a title into positive law Congress generally announces that the enactment is intended to preserve the policy, intent, and purpose of the original enactment. See Office of the Law Revision Council, Positive Law Codification in the United States Code, available at http://uscode.house.gov, and Whisner, *The United States Code, Prime Facie Evidence, and Positive Law*, 101 LAW LIBR. J. 545 (2009). The 111th Congress enacted Title 41, Public Contracts, into positive law on January 4, 2011, Pub. L. No. 111-350, replacing the text of the relevant laws enacted before December 31, 2008. In so doing, Congress renumbered the sections of the title. As used in legal philosophy and theory, the term positive law has a broader meaning. See Nonet, *What Is Positive Law?*, 100 YALE L.J. 667 (1990) and Hall, *Concerning the Nature of Positive Law*, 58 YALE L.J. 545 (1949).

POST-AWARD DEBRIEFING See DEBRIEFING.

POST CONSUMER FIBER *Official:* (1) Paper, paperboard, and fibrous materials from retail stores, office buildings, homes, and so forth, after they have passed through their end-usage as a consumer item, including: used corrugated boxes; old newspapers; old magazines; mixed waste paper; tabulating cards; and used cordage; or (2) All paper, paperboard, and fibrous materials that enter and are collected from municipal solid waste; but not (3) Fiber derived from printers' over-runs, converters' scrap, and over-issue publications. *Source:* FAR 52.204-4(a). The Printed or Copies Double-Sided on Recycled Paper clause in FAR 52.204-4 is required to be included in all contracts over the SIMPLIFIED ACQUISITION THRESHOLD. It requires contractors to submit paper documents, such as offers, letters, and reports, printed double-sided on paper containing at least 30% post-consumer fiber whenever practicable if not using electronic means to submit information to the government. See FAR Subpart 4.3. Agencies are required to purchase and use at least 30% post-consumer fiber content paper if it is available, meets the agency's reasonable performance requirements, and available at a reasonable price. FAR 11.303.

POST CONSUMER MATERIAL   *Official:* A material or finished product that has served its intended purpose and has been discarded for disposal or recovery, having completed its life as a consumer item. Postconsumer material is part of the broader category of RECOVERED MATERIAL. For paper and paper products, post-consumer material means POST CON-SUMER FIBER. *Source:* FAR 11.301. The government's policy on the use of such material in products that it acquires is contained in FAR Subpart 11.3.

POTENTIALLY RESPONSIBLE PARTY (PRP)   *Official:* Any individual(s), or company(ies) identified as potentially liable under CERCLA [Comprehensive Environmental Response, Compensation, and Liability Act, 42 U.S.C. § 9601 et seq.] for cleanup or payment for costs of cleanup of hazardous substance sites. PRPs may include individual(s), or company(ies) identified as having owned, operated, or in some other manner contributed wastes to Hazardous Substance sites. *Source:* 40 C.F.R. § 35.6015(a). Such parties are required to share in payment of the costs of cleaning up sites where they have been responsible for placing hazardous materials in the site.

POWER OF ATTORNEY   *Official:* The authority given one person or corporation to act for and obligate another, as specified in the instrument creating the power; in corporate suretyship, an instrument under seal that appoints an attorney-in-fact to act in behalf of a surety company in signing bonds (see also "attorney-in-fact" at 28.001). *Source:* FAR 2.101. Guidance on proof of this power to sign a BID BOND is contained in FAR 28.101-3.

PRACTICAL APPLICATION   *Official:* To manufacture, in the case of a composition or product; to practice, in the case of a process or method; or to operate, in the case of a machine or system; and, in each case, under such conditions as to establish that the invention is being utilized and that its benefits are, to the extent permitted by law or government regulations, available to the public on reasonable terms. *Source:* FAR 27.301. The Patent Rights clauses in FAR 52.227-11, and -13 and DFARS 252.227-7038 provide that the government, pursuant to its MARCH-IN rights, may require the contractor to LICENSE others to use a SUBJECT INVENTION, to which it has obtained TITLE, if it does not bring the invention to the point of practical application. See Nash & Rawicz, INTELLECTUAL PROPERTY IN GOVERNMENT CONTRACTS, chap. 2 (6th ed. 2008).

PREAWARD DEBRIEFING   See DEBRIEFING.

PREAWARD SURVEY   *Official:* An evaluation of a prospective contractor's capability to perform a proposed contract. *Source:* FAR 2.101. A preaward survey is normally conducted by the cognizant CONTRACT ADMINISTRATION OFFICE and is required when the information on hand or readily available to the contracting officer is not sufficient to make a determination regarding RESPONSIBILITY. FAR 9.106-1(a). The surveying activity begins by checking whether the prospective contractor is debarred, suspended, or ineligible (see PARTIES EXCLUDED FROM FEDERAL PROCUREMENT AND NONPRO-CUREMENT PROGRAMS), in which case the surveying activity notifies the contracting officer and does not proceed with the preaward survey. FAR 9.106-1(c). The following standard forms (SFs) are used for preaward surveys: SF 1403 (General), SF 1404 (Technical), SF 1405 (Production), SF 1406 (Quality Assurance), SF 1407 (Financial Capability), and SF 1408 (Accounting System). FAR 53.301-1403 through 1408.

PRE-BID CONFERENCE A meeting of the contracting officer with prospective bidders during the SOLICITATION period of a SEALED BIDDING procurement. FAR 14.207 provides that such conferences may be used, usually in complex acquisitions, as a means of briefing prospective bidders and explaining complicated specifications and requirements to them as early as possible after the INVITATION FOR BIDS (IFB) has been issued and before bids are submitted. They are not to be used, however, as a substitute for amending a defective or ambiguous IFB. Notice of the conference must be provided to all prospective bidders.

PRECONTRACT COSTS *Official:* Costs incurred before the effective date of the contract directly pursuant to the negotiation and in anticipation of the contract award when such incurrence is necessary to comply with the proposed contract delivery schedule. *Source:* FAR 31.205-32. This regulation specifies that such costs are ALLOWABLE COSTs if they would have been allowable after the date of the contract. See Manos, 1 GOVERNMENT CONTRACT COSTS AND PRICING §§ 39:1–39:6 (2d ed. 2009–2020); Cibinic, Knight & Nash, COST-REIMBURSEMENT CONTRACTING 738–41 (4th ed. 2014).

PREDETERMINED, FORMULA-TYPE INCENTIVE See INCENTIVE CONTRACT.

PREEMPTION The situation where federal law overrides and supersedes state or local law. 17 U.S.C. § 301 states that the Copyright Act preempts state law with regard to any of the exclusive rights within the general scope of the Act. The patent laws also preempt state law. In contrast, state law governs TRADE SECRETs because there is no overriding federal law on that subject. See Nash & Rawicz, INTELLECTUAL PROPERTY IN GOVERNMENT CONTRACTS, chap. 1 (6th ed. 2008).

PREJUDICE A showing of harm. Prejudice is an essential element in every viable PROTEST. To prevail in a protest, the protester must not only show a significant error in the procurement process but also that the error prejudiced it. See *LaBarge Products, Inc. v. West*, 46 F.3d 1547 (Fed. Cir. 1995). To establish prejudice the protester must demonstrate some probability that it would have received the award. See Cibinic, Nash & Yukins, FORMATION OF GOVERNMENT CONTRACTS 1735–40, 1787–90 (4th ed. 2011); Nash, *Standards of Review in Bid Protests: The GAO's Competitive Prejudice Rule*, 25 N&CR ¶ 12 (Mar. 2011).

PRELIMINARY DESIGN REVIEW (PDR) A review, conducted during SYSTEMs acquisition, of each configuration item to (1) evaluate the progress, technical adequacy, and risk resolution of the selected design approach; (2) determine the item's compatibility with the performance and engineering requirements of the development SPECIFICATION; and (3) establish the existence and compatibility of the physical and functional interfaces among the item and other items of equipment, FACILITIES, computer programs, and personnel. DOD 5000 Series, calls for a PDR at the end of the TECHNOLOGY DEVELOPMENT

PHASE of a weapon system acquisition to determine if the system should proceed to the ENGINEERING AND MANUFACTURING DEVELOPMENT PHASE.

PRELIMINARY INJUNCTION   An interim remedy granted by a court ordering a party not to proceed with a proposed action. The COURT OF FEDERAL CLAIMS may use this remedy in a BID PROTEST to afford a party temporary relief. 28 U.S.C. § 1491(b)(2). Such relief generally is not granted unless the court determines that the protester is likely to succeed on the merits. In granting such relief, the court is required to consider the interests of NATIONAL DEFENSE and national security. See Cibinic, Nash & Yukins, FORMATION OF GOVERNMENT CONTRACTS 1791–93 (4th ed. 2011).

PRENEGOTIATION OBJECTIVE   A plan that documents the government's initial negotiation position before entering into price negotiation, as established through cost or price analysis. FAR 15.406-1. Contracting officers are required to establish such objectives based on an analysis of a contractor's proposal and considering the information in FIELD PRICING ASSISTANCE and technical analysis.

PREPONDERANCE OF THE EVIDENCE   *Official:* Proof by information that, compared with that opposing it, leads to the conclusion that the fact at issue is more probably true than not. *Source:* FAR 2.101. This is the standard of proof in almost all issues litigated under the CONTRACT DISPUTES ACT. It is the standard used in determining to void or rescind a contract pursuant to the PROCUREMENT INTEGRITY ACT when there has been no conviction (FAR 3.703(b)(2) and 3.704(c)), or to debar a contractor when there has been no conviction (FAR 9.406-2(b) and 9.406-3(d)(3)).

PREPRODUCTION TESTING   See FIRST ARTICLE TESTING.

PREPROPOSAL CONFERENCE   A meeting of the contracting officer with prospective offerors during the SOLICITATION period of a procurement by NEGOTIATION. Such conferences are one form of exchanges with prospective offerors that are encouraged by FAR 15.201. Prior FAR guidance indicated that adequate notice of the conference should be given to all prospective offerors, technical and legal personnel should be invited to attend and prospective offerors should be invited to submit questions in advance. See Cibinic, Nash & Yukins, FORMATION OF GOVERNMENT CONTRACTS 397–99 (4th ed. 2011). See also PRE-SOLICITATION CONFERENCE.

PREQUALIFICATION   Determination of the RESPONSIBILITY of an OFFEROR prior to SOLICITATION; in other words, determination of an offeror's eligibility to *compete* for a government contract. In early decisions of GAO, prequalification was held to be improper because it was an undue restriction on FULL AND OPEN COMPETITION. However, in 1984 Congress enacted 41 U.S.C. § 3311 and 10 U.S.C. § 2319, which set forth conditions that agencies must meet in establishing a prequalification system. See FAR Subpart 9.2. Agencies have also adopted less formal prequalification systems that have not been challenged as unduly restricting competition. See Nash & Feldman, GOVERNMENT CONTRACT CHANGES §§ 3:28–3:35 (3d ed. 2006–2020).

PRESENT VALUE   The value in current dollars of work to be performed in the future. See BLACK'S LAW DICTIONARY 1433 (11th ed. 2019). This value is determined by discounting the price of work to be paid for in the future by a rate commensurate with the interest rate on the funds for the period before payment is required. Making a determination of present value is a beneficial way of comparing competing offers that call for payment by the government at varying times. Thus, it is a way of dealing with UNBALANCED BIDs. OMB Circular No. A-94, *Guidelines and Discount Rates for Benefit-Cost Analysis of Federal Programs*, Oct. 29, 1992 (with annual revised discount rates in Appendix C), contains tables of present value calculations in another context.

PRESIDENT'S BLUE RIBBON COMMISSION ON DEFENSE MANAGEMENT   See PACKARD COMMISSION.

PRESOLICITATION CONFERENCE   A meeting held by the contracting officer with prospective offerors as a preliminary step in negotiated acquisitions (see NEGOTIATION) in order to develop or identify interested sources, request preliminary information based on a general description of the supplies or services involved, explain complicated SPECIFICA-TIONs and requirements, and aid prospective contractors in preparing proposals without undue expenditure of effort, time, and money. Such conferences are one form of exchanges with prospective offerors that are encouraged by FAR 15.201.

PRESOLICITATION NOTICE   A notice of a proposed contract action published on the GOVERNMENT POINT OF ENTRY. In many procurement situations such notice must be given 15 days before issuance of a solicitation. See 15 U.S.C. § 637(e) and 41 U.S.C. § 1708. The requirement for a presolicitation notice is implemented in FAR Subpart 5.2. In negotiated procurements (see NEGOTIATION), a presolicitation notice is one of the forms of exchange with prospective contractors that are discussed in FAR 15.201. Instructions on the content of such notices are contained in FAR 5.207. See FAR 36.213-2 regarding the use of presolicitation notices in construction contracting. See also Cibinic, Nash & Yukins, FORMATION OF GOVERNMENT CONTRACTS 390–99 (4th ed. 2011).

PRESUMPTION OF GOOD FAITH   The legal presumption that government officials act in good faith in carrying out their obligations during the performance of a contract. See *Tecom, Inc. v. United States*, 66 Fed. Cl. 736 (2005), for an extensive analysis of the wide application of this presumption by the courts and appeals boards and its impact in limiting contractor recovery for government actions. The Report of the Acquisition Advisory Panel (January 2007) recommended that legislation be enacted extending this presumption of good faith to contractor officials in order to place the contracting parties on an equal footing.

PREVAILING PARTY   A party that succeeds on any significant issue in litigation and thereby achieves some of the benefit sought by the individual or corporation bringing the suit. Under the EQUAL ACCESS TO JUSTICE ACT (EAJA), courts and BOARDs OF CONTRACT APPEALS award fees and other expenses to small businesses that are prevailing parties in adversary adjudications if the government position is not SUBSTANTIALLY JUSTIFIED. A party may be deemed to have prevailed even if it recovers on only a portion of its claim but it cannot be a prevailing party if it obtains a settlement of the dispute without the aid of a court or board. See 28 U.S.C. § 2412, 5 U.S.C. § 504. See Nash & Feldman, GOVERN-MENT CONTRACT CHANGES § 16:38 (3d ed. 2006–2020); Cibinic, Nagle & Nash, ADMINIS-TRATION OF GOVERNMENT CONTRACTS 684 (5th ed. 2016); Nash, *Postscript II: Prevailing Party*, 16 N&CR ¶ 42 (Aug. 2002).

PREVAILING WAGE RATE   The rate of wages, including fringe benefits, paid to a majority of the workers in a geographic area for the same type of work on similar projects. DOL ascertains the prevailing wage rates in order to establish WAGE DETERMINATIONs for construction contracts in excess of $2,000 under the DAVIS-BACON ACT and for service contracts in excess of $2,500 under the SERVICE CONTRACT ACT. See 29 C.F.R. § 1.2 and 29 C.F.R. § 4.3; FAR 22.404 and 22.1002-2. See also Cibinic, Nash & Yukins, FORMATION OF GOVERNMENT CONTRACTS 1650–52, 1657–60 (4th ed. 2011).

PRICE   *Official:* COST plus any FEE or PROFIT applicable to the contract type. *Source:* FAR 15.401. This definition is anachronistic because it treats the sum of the cost and fee on a COST-REIMBURSEMENT CONTRACT as a price when the term is usually associated with a FIXED-PRICE CONTRACT, which calls for the payment of a negotiated amount, established at the outset or by redetermination, for satisfactorily completed work.

PRICE ADJUSTMENT   An adjustment to the price that is called for by the terms of a contract. Most price adjustments are EQUITABLE ADJUSTMENTs that contain an adjustment of PROFIT as well as an amount commensurate with the change in costs that has occurred. However, the Suspension of Work clause in FAR 52.242-14 and the Government Delay of Work clause in FAR 52.242-17 call for price adjustments that exclude profit and reflect only the costs incurred by the contractor during the time the contracting officer unreasonably delayed performance. Price adjustments to reflect changed economic conditions are also called for in a FIXED-PRICE CONTRACT WITH ECONOMIC PRICE ADJUSTMENT. Price adjustments (excluding indirect costs and profit) are also required when wage rates are increased on service contracts. See the Fair Labor Standards Act and Service Contract Act—Price Adjustment (Multiple Year and Option Contracts) clause in FAR 52.222-43 and the Fair Labor Standards Act and Service Contract Act—Price Adjustment clause in FAR 52.222-44. See Nash & Feldman, 1 GOVERNMENT CONTRACT CHANGES, chap. 16 (3d ed. 2006–2020); Cibinic, Nagle & Nash, ADMINISTRATION OF GOVERNMENT CONTRACTS, chap. 8 (5th ed. 2016).

PRICE ANALYSIS   *Official:* The process of examining and evaluating a proposed PRICE without evaluating its separate cost elements and proposed PROFIT. *Source:* FAR 15.404-1(b). This is the minimum analysis a contracting officer must use when acquiring commercial items. FAR 15.403-3(c). It is also the type of analysis used in most instances when the contracting officer is prohibited from obtaining CERTIFIED COST OR PRICING DATA. Price analysis may be accomplished by (1) comparing offers with one another; (2) comparing prior proposed prices and contract prices with current proposed prices for the same or similar end items; (3) using PARAMETRIC ESTIMATING METHODs (dollars per pound or per horsepower, or other units) to highlight significant inconsistencies that warrant additional inquiry; (4) comparing offers with competitive published price lists, published market prices of commodities, similar indexes, and discount or rebate arrangements; (5) comparing proposed prices with independently developed government estimates; (6) comparing proposed prices with prices of the same or similar items obtained through MARKET RESEARCH; or (7) analyzing DATA OTHER THAN CERTIFIED COST OR PRICING DATA. FAR 15.404-1(b)(2). The contracting officer is responsible for selecting and using whatever price analysis techniques will ensure a FAIR AND REASONABLE PRICE. Price analysis, with or without competition, may provide the basis for selecting the contract type, but particular attention must be paid to the ability of the analysis to provide a realistic pricing standard. FAR 16.104(b). See Manos, 2 GOVERNMENT CONTRACT COSTS AND PRICING § 84:20 (2d ed. 2009–2020); Cibinic, Nash & Yukins, FORMATION OF GOVERNMENT CONTRACTS 1476–87 (4th ed. 2011).

PRICE COMPETITION   The competition that is achieved on a government procurement when price will be a significant element in the SOURCE SELECTION. FAR 16.104 states that, normally, effective price competition usually results in realistic pricing and a FIXED-PRICE CONTRACT is ordinarily in the government's interest. CERTIFIED COST OR PRICING DATA may not be required to be submitted by contractors when there is ADEQUATE PRICE COMPETITION. FAR 15.403-1.

PRICE NEGOTIATION MEMORANDUM (PNM)   A government document that summarizes the process of negotiating a contract's price and the outcome of that process and that serves as a record of the decisions made in determining a price to be fair and reasonable. FAR 15.406-3 requires the government's contracting officer to prepare a PNM promptly at the conclusion of each negotiation of an initial or revised PRICE. The memorandum, which is included in the contract file, must (1) document the purpose of the negotiation, (2) describe the acquisition, (3) give information on participants in the negotiation, (4) give the status of the contractor's purchasing system, (5) if CERTIFIED COST OR PRICING DATA were not required, state the exemption used, (6) if certified cost or pricing data were required, give a statement about reliance, (7) summarize the contractor's proposal and any field pricing assistance recommendations, (8) state the most significant facts or considerations controlling the establishment of the prenegotiation objectives, (9) discuss and quantify the impact of direction given by Congress, (10) state the basis for the PROFIT or FEE, and (11) provide documentation of fair and reasonable pricing. See Cibinic, Nash & Yukins, FORMATION OF GOVERNMENT CONTRACTS 1568–70 (4th ed. 2011).

PRICE REALISM ANALYSIS   The evaluation of each offeror's prices to determine if they are sufficiently high to permit successful performance of the proposed contract or if they are so low that they indicate that the offeror does not understand the work. This technique is not addressed in FAR Part 15 but is widely used by agencies to ensure that they do not award a contract to a contractor that will fail to perform because of insufficient resources. The technique can only be used when the RFP informs offerors that there will be such an evaluation. In making the evaluation, the contracting officer cannot adjust the offered price but may evaluate an unduly low price entails a performance risk or a lack of understanding of the work when it is determined that the low price is not based on a more efficient method of performing the work. See Nash, *Postscript IV: Price Realism*, 33 N&CR ¶ 37 (June 2019).

PRICE REASONABLENESS   See FAIR AND REASONABLE PRICE.

PRICE REDETERMINABLE CONTRACT   See FIXED-PRICE REDETERMINATION—PROSPECTIVE CONTRACT; FIXED-PRICE REDETERMINATION—RETROACTIVE CONTRACT.

PRICE REDUCTION   The amount by which the government is entitled to adjust a contract formed by NEGOTIATION if CERTIFIED COST OR PRICING DATA required under the TRUTH IN NEGOTIATIONS ACT are found not to be ACCURATE, COMPLETE, AND CURRENT. This adjustment consists of any significant amount by which the negotiated price, including PROFIT or FEE, was increased because of the DEFECTIVE COST OR PRICING data. In arriving at this price reduction, the contracting officer is to consider the time when the cost or pricing data became reasonably available to the contractor and the extent to which the government relied on the defective data. FAR 15.407-1(b)(2). OFFSETs against the amount of the reduction are required for understated cost or pricing data up to (but not exceeding) the amount of the reduction. FAR 15.407-1(b)(4). Price reductions are required by the Price Reduction for Defective Certified Cost or Pricing Data clause at FAR 52.215-10. See Cibinic, Nagle & Nash, ADMINISTRATION OF GOVERNMENT CONTRACTS 670–74 (5th ed. 2016); Howell, *A Clause in Search of Meaning: A Critical Dissection of the Price Reductions Clause (Plus Suggestions for Reform)*, 37 PUB. CONT. L.J. 337 (2008).

PRICE-RELATED FACTORS   EVALUATION FACTORS other than price that affect a contract's overall cost to the government and can be quantified in dollars. The term is used mainly in the context of SEALED BIDDING procurements, which must be awarded solely on the basis of price and the price-related factors included in the SOLICITATION. See FAR 14.101(e). Price-related factors are added to the price to determine the low bidder. Examples of price-related factors that may be applicable in evaluating bids are (1) foreseeable costs or DELAYs to the government resulting from such factors as differences in INSPECTION procedure, locations of supplies, and transportation costs; (2) changes made or requested by a bidder in any of the provisions of the INVITATION FOR BIDS, if the changes do not constitute grounds for rejection; (3) advantages or disadvantages to the government that might result from making more than one award ($500 is assumed to be the administrative cost to the government for issuing and administering each contract awarded under a solicitation); (4) the applicability of federal, state, and local taxes; and (5) the origin of supplies and, if foreign, the application of the BUY AMERICAN ACT or any other factor affecting foreign purchases. FAR 14.201-8. See Cibinic, Nash & Yukins, FORMATION OF GOVERNMENT CONTRACTS 591–97 (4th ed. 2011).

PRICING   *Official:* The process of establishing a reasonable amount or amounts to be paid for supplies or services. *Source:* FAR 2.101. See CONTRACT PRICING.

PRICING ARRANGEMENT   A basis agreed to by contractual parties for the payment of amounts for specified performance. Such an arrangement is determined by the TYPE OF CONTRACT. See FAR Part 16 and Cibinic, Nash & Yukins, FORMATION OF GOVERNMENT CONTRACTS, chap. 9 (4th ed. 2011); Edwards, *Contract Pricing Arrangements: A Primer-Part II*, BRIEFING PAPERS No. 09-12 (Nov. 2009); Edwards, *Contract Pricing Arrangements: A Primer-Part II*, BRIEFING PAPERS No. 09-11 (Oct. 2009).

PRIME CONTRACT   *Official:* A contract or contractual action entered into by the United States for the purpose of obtaining SUPPLIES, materials, equipment, or SERVICES of any kind. *Source:* FAR 3.502-1. The term is used in FAR Subpart 3.5 dealing with KICKBACKs but is not used in the balance of the FAR which generally uses the term CONTRACT. "Prime" is used to distinguish that contract from any SUBCONTRACT entered into between the PRIME CONTRACTOR and a supplier or vendor called a subcontractor, or between such a subcontractor and another, lower-level subcontractor. There is PRIVITY OF CONTRACT between the government and prime contractors, but not between the government and subcontractors.

PRIME CONTRACTOR   *Official:* A person who has entered into a PRIME CONTRACT with the United States. *Source:* FAR 3.502-1. The term is used in FAR Subpart 3.5 dealing with KICKBACKs but is not used in the balance of the FAR which generally uses the term CONTRACTOR. In construction contracting, the prime contractor is usually called the GENERAL CONTRACTOR.

PRIME VENDOR   A supplier of a wide variety of products within a specific industry/sector, which along with supplying those products provides additional capabilities such as warehousing and distribution. The additional capabilities are evaluated as part of the best value decision-making process. Examples are the Medical/Surgical, Pharmaceutical, and Garrison Feeding PV contracts. DLAD 17.9501. Contracts with Prime Vendors are long-term INDEFINITE DELIVERY CONTRACTs with commercial distributors, ORIGINAL EQUIPMENT MANUFACTURERs, or third-party logistics providers for integrated logistics support that may include forecasting, inventory management, distribution, engineering support, technical services or other services to support customer needs. Such contracts enable DLA to quickly support U.S. combat operations without maintaining large inventories on hand and are a part of its SURGE AND SUSTAINMENT PROGRAM. See DLAD Subpart 17.93.

PRINCIPAL   *Official:* An officer, director, owner, partner, or a person having primary management or supervisory responsibilities within a business entity (e.g., general manager; plant manager; head of a division or business segment; and similar positions). *Source:* FAR 2.101. A more general definition would be a person with authority to act for an organization. In agency law, principals are those who delegate authority to agents to act on their behalf. In ALTERNATIVE DISPUTE RESOLUTION proceedings, principals are the representatives of the parties with the authority to negotiate a binding settlement of the matter in DISPUTE. See Yukins, *A Versatile Prism: Assessing Procurement Law Through the Principal–Agent Model*, 40 Pub. Cont. L.J. 63 (2010).

PRINTED OR COPIED DOUBLE-SIDED   Printing or reproducing a document so that information is on both sides of a sheet of paper. FAR 4.302 requires contractors to submit documents to the government printed or copied double-sided on recycled paper. This policy is implemented through inclusion of the Printed or Copied Double-Sided on Recycled Paper clause in FAR 52.204-4 in SOLICITATIONS and CONTRACTS for acquisitions in excess of the SIMPLIFIED ACQUISITION THRESHOLD.

PRIOR COURSE OF DEALING   The dealings between the contracting parties on transactions prior to the current contract. Under U.C.C. § 1-205(1), "prior course of dealing" or "course of dealing" refers to a sequence of interactions between parties to a particular transaction that may fairly be regarded as establishing a basis for interpreting their statements and other conduct. The concept is similar to, yet more specific than, "course of business," which refers to what is usually and normally done in the management of trade or business. When the parties to a contract interpretation dispute have interpreted ambiguous provisions of a similar, previously performed contract, the courts and boards of contract appeals frequently conclude that the parties intended the same meaning for the provisions in the disputed contract. See Cibinic, Nagle & Nash, Administration of Government Contracts 205–11 (5th ed. 2016).

PRIORITIES AND ALLOCATIONS   A method for implementing the DEFENSE PRIORITIES AND ALLOCATIONS SYSTEM (DPAS), which ensures that critical materials and facilities are to be used for national defense in the event of an emergency. FAR Subpart 11.6. Certain contracts and orders are accorded preferential treatment by being designated as RATED ORDERS under the DPAS regulation that guides the DEPARTMENT OF COMMERCE's Office of Industrial Resource Administration in developing, coordinating, and administering a system of priorities and allocations with respect to industrial resources, pursuant to Title I of the Defense Production Act of 1950, 50 U.S.C. App. § 2061 et seq.

PRISON INDUSTRIES   See FEDERAL PRISON INDUSTRIES, INC.

PRIVACY ACT   An Act, 5 U.S.C. § 552a, prohibiting the disclosure, except pursuant to a written request by, or with the prior written consent of, the individual to whom the record pertains, about a person's education, financial transactions, medical history, and criminal or employment history that contains his name, or the identifying number, symbol, or other identifying particular assigned to the individual, such as a finger or voice print or a photograph. The Act is implemented in FAR Subpart 24.1. See PERSONALLY IDENTIFIABLE INFORMATION and SENSITIVE INFORMATION.

PRIVATE EXPENSE   See DEVELOPED AT PRIVATE EXPENSE.

PRIVATELY OWNED U.S.-FLAG COMMERCIAL VESSEL   *Official:* A vessel that is (1) registered and operated under the laws of the United States, (2) used in commercial trade of the United States, and (3) owned and operated by U.S. citizens, including a vessel under voyage or time charter to the government; and a government-owned vessel under bareboat charter to, and operated by, U.S. citizens. *Source:* FAR 47.501. Such vessels are included in the definition of U.S.-FLAG VESSELs for purposes of the cargo preference regulations in FAR Subpart 47.5.

PRIVATIZATION   The process of changing a public entity or enterprise to private control and ownership. It does not include a determination as to whether a support service should be obtained through public or private resources when the government retains full responsibility and control over the delivery of those services. OMB Circular No. A-76, *Revised Supplementary Handbook*, Mar. 1996. It is a form of OUTSOURCING that usually involves the actual transfer of ownership or control of ASSETs, such as land, FACILITIES, or equipment from the federal government to private entities. See OMB Circular No. A-76, *Performance of Commercial Activities*, May 29, 2003, revised by OMB Memorandum M-07-02, Oct. 31, 2006, and its *Revised Supplemental Handbook* (June 14, 1999); OFPP Policy Letter No. 11-01, *Performance of Inherently Governmental and Critical Functions*, Sept. 12, 2011; Cibinic, Nash & Yukins, Formation of Government Contracts 345–53 (4th ed. 2011).

PRIVILEGED INFORMATION   Information not subject to the disclosure requirements of the FREEDOM OF INFORMATION ACT or subject to disclosure under a PROTECTIVE ORDER in litigation. The most commonly used privileges include the ATTORNEY WORK-PRODUCT PRIVILEGE, the EXECUTIVE PRIVILEGE, and the TRADE-SECRET PRIVILEGE. See Nash & Rawicz, Intellectual Property in Government Contracts, chap. 9 (6th ed. 2008); Cox, *Is the Procurement Integrity Act "Important" Enough for the Disclosure Rule? A Case for Inclusion*, 40 Pub. Cont. L.J. 347 (2011).

PRIVITY OF CONTRACT   The legal relationship and responsibilities between parties to the same contract. The government has privity of contract with the PRIME CONTRACTOR; the prime contractor has privity of contract with the first-tier SUBCONTRACTOR, but there is generally no privity of contract between the government and subcontractors. The result is that CLAIMs of subcontractors against the government under the CONTRACT DISPUTES ACT OF 1978 must be asserted by the prime contractor or in the name of the prime contractor, unless the subcontractor can show that it was a THIRD-PARTY BENEFICIARY of the prime contract. This can prove problematic because the Act requires prime contractors to certify claims of more than $100,000 submitted by their subcontractors. Thus, under this "sponsorship" system, contract disputes are certified by the prime contractor, even though it may take a passive role in litigating the dispute. See SPONSORSHIP OF SUBCONTRACTOR CLAIMS. See Cibinic, Nagle & Nash, Administration of

GOVERNMENT CONTRACTS 1151 (5th ed. 2016); Feldman, *Subcontractors in Federal Procurement: Roles, Rights and Responsibilities*, BRIEFING PAPERS No. 03-02 (Jan. 2003).

PRIZE COMPETITION *Official:* One or more of the following types of activities: (1) A point solution prize that rewards and spurs the development of solutions for a particular, well-defined problem, (2) An exposition prize competition that helps identify and promote a broad range of ideas and practices that may not otherwise attract attention, facilitating further development of the idea or practice by third parties, (3) Participation prize competitions that create value during and after the competition by encouraging contestants to change their behavior or develop new skills that may have beneficial effects during and after the competition, or (4) Such other types of prize competitions as each head of an agency considers appropriate to stimulate innovation that has the potential to advance the mission of the respective agency. *Source:* 15 U.S.C. § 3719(c). Agencies are permitted to award cash or non-cash prizes to winners of these competitions. The rules for conducting such competitions are set forth in 15 U.S.C. § 3719. See also Challenge.gov where agencies can post competitions, and 10 U.S.C. § 2374a giving DOD the authority to conduct prize competitions. These competitions have been widely used to induce multiple private organizations and individuals to address challenging technological problems.

PROBABLE COST The government's best estimate of the costs that a contractor will incur in performing a COST-REIMBURSEMENT CONTRACT. FAR 15.404-1(d)(2). The probable cost must be ascertained by making a COST REALISM ANALYSIS during the evaluation of each proposal and must be used in making the source selection decision. It is determined by adjusting each offeror's proposed cost to reflect any additions or reductions in cost elements to realistic levels based on the results of cost realism analysis. Proposed costs should not be adjusted if the seemingly low cost estimate is based on a more efficient method of performing the required work. See Cibinic, Knight & Nash, COST-REIMBURSEMENT CONTRACTING 307, chap. 7 (4th ed. 2014); Cibinic, Nash & Yukins, FORMATION OF GOVERNMENT CONTRACTS 1516–30 (4th ed. 2011).

PROCEDURES, GUIDANCE AND INFORMATION (DOD PGI) *Official:* A companion resource to the DFARS that—(1) Contains mandatory internal DoD procedures. The DFARS will direct compliance with mandatory procedures using imperative language such as "Follow the procedures at . . ." or similar directive language; (2) Contains non-mandatory internal DoD procedures and guidance and supplemental information to be used at the discretion of the contracting officer. The DFARS will point to non-mandatory procedures, guidance, and information using permissive language such as "The contracting officer may use . . ." or "Additional information is available at . . ." or other similar language; (3) Is numbered similarly to the DFARS, except that each DOD PGI numerical designation is preceded by the letters "PGI"; and (4) Is available electronically at http://www.acq.osd.mil/dpap/dars/index.htm. *Source:* DFARS 202.101. DOD personnel and contractors dealing with DOD agencies should check the FAR, the DFARS and DOD PGI to ensure that they are aware of all of the mandatory requirements and guidance on an issue.

PROCUREMENT *Official:* All stages of the process of acquiring property or services, beginning with the process for determining a need for property or services and ending with contract completion and closeout. *Source:* 41 U.S.C. § 111. The synonymous term ACQUISITION is usually used in the FEDERAL ACQUISITION REGULATIONS

SYSTEM, whereas "procurement" is used in the United States Code. Contracting is a subset of procurement.

PROCUREMENT ADMINISTRATIVE LEAD TIME (PALT)   *Official:* The time between the date on which an initial solicitation for a contract or order is issued by a Federal department or agency and the date of the award of the contract or order. *Source:* Section 878 of the National Defense Authorization Act for FY 2018, Agencies will be required to report the PALT on contracts and orders above the SIMPLIFIED ACQUISITION THRESHOLD. See the OFPP ANPR of January 21, 2020, soliciting comments on a proposed regulation implementing this requirement.

PROCUREMENT CENTER REPRESENTATIVE (PCR)   An official of the SMALL BUSINESS ADMINISTRATION assigned to a CONTRACTING ACTIVITY. 15 U.S.C. § 644(l) requires PCRs to review procurements and advocate increasing SMALL BUSINESS CONCERN participation in federal procurement through traditional SET-ASIDEs. The responsibilities of CONTRACTING OFFICERs to work with PCRs are set forth in FAR 19.402.

PROCUREMENT CONTRACT   A contract between the government and a private party to provide supplies or services (including construction). 31 U.S.C. § 6301 et seq. distinguishes between procurement contracts, GRANTs, and COOPERATIVE AGREEMENTs and contains guidance as to when each type of instrument should be used. 31 U.S.C. § 6303 calls for the use of a procurement contract when (1) the principal purpose of the instrument is to acquire (by purchase, lease, or barter) property or services for the direct benefit or use of the United States Government; or (2) the agency decides in a specific instance that the use of a procurement contract is appropriate. Procurement contracts are those instruments governed by the FEDERAL ACQUISITION REGULATION. The coverage of the CONTRACT DISPUTES ACT OF 1978 is also limited to procurement contracts and contracts for the disposal of PERSONAL PROPERTY.

PROCUREMENT EXECUTIVE   See SENIOR PROCUREMENT EXECUTIVE.

PROCUREMENT FOR EXPERIMENTAL PURPOSES   *Official:* Procurement of ordnance, signal, chemical activity, transportation, energy, medical, space-flight, telecommunications, and aeronautical supplies, including parts and accessories, and designs thereof, that the Secretary of Defense or the Secretary concerned considers necessary for experimental or test purposes in the development of the best supplies that are needed for the national defense. *Source:* 10 U.S.C. § 2373. These purchases may be made without using COMPETITIVE PROCEDURES as long as the quantities are no greater than necessary for experimentation, technical evaluation, assessment of operational utility, or safety or to provide a residual operational capability.

PROCUREMENT INSTRUMENT IDENTIFICATION (PII) NUMBERS   Numbers that are assigned to DOD SOLICITATIONs, contracts, and related instruments based on a prescribed uniform format. DFARS 204.7000. The basic PII number remains unchanged throughout the life of the instrument; it consists of 13 alphanumeric characters. The first six positions begin with the capital letters assigned to the department preparing the instrument (e.g., "DA" for Department of the Army, "AF" for Air Force) and identify the activity preparing the instrument. The seventh and eighth positions contain the last two digits of the fiscal year in which the PII number is assigned. The ninth position contains a capital letter indicating the type of instrument code (e.g., "A" for blanket purchase agreement, "B" for invitation for bids, etc.). Finally, the 10th through the 13th positions represent the serial number of the instrument. DFARS 204.7003. NASA has a similar system, called ACQUISITION INSTRUMENT IDENTIFICATION.

PROCUREMENT INTEGRITY   Rules of conduct, contained in the 1989 amendments to the OFFICE OF FEDERAL PROCUREMENT POLICY ACT, 41 U.S.C. §§ 2101–2107, that were formalized for the purpose of upholding the integrity of the government procurement process. These rules were revised by § 4304 of the CLINGER-COHEN ACT OF 1996, Pub. L. No. 104-106. The rules (1) prohibit disclosure of CONTRACTOR BID OR PROPOSAL INFORMATION or SOURCE SELECTION INFORMATION before the award of a FEDERAL AGENCY PROCUREMENT contract, (2) prohibit obtaining such information, (3) require agency OFFICIALs to report contacts by bidders or offerors relating to non-federal employment and reject such possibility or disqualify themselves from further work on the procurement, and (4) prohibit a limited group of employees who have participated in actions over $10 million from accepting compensation from the contractor for one year after their participation. They also remove all prior certification requirements. FAR 3.104. See Manos, 3 GOVERNMENT CONTRACT COSTS AND PRICING §§ 91:15–91:19 (2d ed. 2009–2020); Cibinic, Nagle & Nash, ADMINISTRATION OF GOVERNMENT CONTRACTS 91–104, 143–48 (5th ed. 2016); Cibinic, Nash & Yukins, FORMATION OF GOVERNMENT CONTRACTS 170–72, 212–16 (4th ed. 2011); Tillipman & Mahini, *Government Lawyering*, BRIEFING PAPERS No. 11-3 (Feb. 2011); Cox, *Is the Procurement Integrity Act "Important" Enough for the Mandatory Disclosure Rule? A Case for Inclusion*, 40 PUB. CONT. L.J. 347 (2011); Kathuria, *Best Practices for Compliance with the New Government Contractor Compliance and Ethics Rules under the Federal Acquisition Regulation*, 38 PUB. CONT. L.J. 803 (2009); Briggerman & Bateman, *Handling Procurement Information*, BRIEFING PAPERS No. 05-9 (Aug. 2005).

PROCUREMENT LIST   *Official:* A list of SUPPLIES (including military resale commodities) and services that the Committee (for Purchase from People Who Are Blind or Severely Disabled) has determined are suitable for purchase by the government under the JAVITS-WAGNER-O'DAY ACT. *Source:* FAR 8.701. Agencies must purchase supplies or services on the list from ABILITYONE if they are available within the time required. FAR 8.704. See Cibinic, Nash & Yukins, FORMATION OF GOVERNMENT CONTRACTS 361 (4th ed. 2011).

PROCUREMENT OFFICIAL   Any civilian or military official or employee of an agency who, as defined under the original PROCUREMENT INTEGRITY prohibitions of the OFFICE OF FEDERAL PROCUREMENT POLICY ACT, 41 U.S.C. § 423, had "PARTICIPATED PERSONALLY AND SUBSTANTIALLY" in the conduct of the relevant agency procurement, including all officials and employees responsible for reviewing or approving the procurement. The term included participation in the following activities: (1) developing ACQUISITION PLANs; (2) developing specifications, STATEMENT OF WORK, purchase descriptions, or purchase requests; (3) developing solicitation or contract provisions; (4) evaluating or selecting a contractor; and (5) negotiating or awarding a contract or a MODIFICATION to a contract. This term is not used in the revised procurement integrity rules that became effective on January 1, 1997. The term was defined in FAR 3.104-4 prior to its revision on January 2, 1997 and is operative for contracts entered into prior to the revision of the Act.

PROCUREMENT SYSTEM *Official:* The integration of the PROCUREMENT process, the professional development of procurement personnel, and the management structure for carrying out the procurement function. *Source:* 41 U.S.C. § 112. This term is used in Subtitle I of Title 41 of the U.S. Code covering general policies applicable to all agencies (Part B) and procurement policies applicable to agencies other than DOD, NASA, and the Coast Guard (Part C). The FAR uses the term "acquisition" rather than "procurement."

PROCURING ACTIVITY *Official:* A component of an EXECUTIVE AGENCY having a significant acquisition function and designated as such by the head of the agency. Unless agency regulations specify otherwise, the term "procuring activity" is synonymous with "CONTRACTING ACTIVITY." *Source:* FAR 2.101.

PROCURING CONTRACTING OFFICER (PCO) A contracting officer in a government buying office who enters into contracts and signs them on behalf of the government. This term is used by DOD and other major agencies. In such agencies, after contract execution, an ADMINISTRATIVE CONTRACTING OFFICER typically assumes responsibility for CONTRACT ADMINISTRATION. Generally, a PCO is responsible for creating and publicizing the SOLICITATION, determining whether CERTIFIED COST OR PRICING DATA must be submitted, selecting the source, negotiating and executing the contract, negotiating and executing certain contract MODIFICATIONs, and settling certain defective pricing issues. A PCO is not normally involved in contract terminations, which are usually handled by a TERMINATION CONTRACTING OFFICER. In many agencies, particularly those with decentralized contracting offices, all of the contracting officer functions are handled by the same person. See Nash & Feldman, 1 GOVERNMENT CONTRACT CHANGES §§ 5:2–5:8 (3d ed. 2006–2020); Cibinic, Nash & Yukins, FORMATION OF GOVERNMENT CONTRACTS 81–92 (4th ed. 2011).

PRODUCIBILITY REVIEW A review of the design of a specific hardware item or system to determine the relative ease of producing it using available production technology considering the elements of fabrication, assembly, inspection, and test. DAU GLOSSARY. A review of this type is required at the end of the DOD ENGINEERING AND MANUFACTURING DEVELOPMENT PHASE to demonstrate that the system is ready to proceed to the PRODUCTION AND DEPLOYMENT PHASE.

PRODUCT SUPPORT MANAGEMENT The development and implementation of product support strategies, and the planning and management of cost and performance across the product support value chain, from design through disposal, to ensure supportability is considered throughout the system life cycle. This is accomplished by balancing the performance outcomes of reliability, availability, maintainability, and reduced total ownership cost. The scope of product support management planning and execution includes the enterprise level integration of all 12 Integrated Product Support elements throughout the life cycle commensurate with the roles and responsibilities of the Product Support Manager. DAU GLOSSARY.

PRODUCTION AND DEPLOYMENT PHASE The fourth phase of a DOD acquisition program involving the use of new technology as prescribed in the DOD 5000 Series. In this phase the agency awards a contract for the production of the initial quantity of a product or system that has demonstrated its full capability. This phase may be initiated by the award of a contract for LOW-RATE INITIAL PRODUCTION of a minimum quantity.

PRODUCTION ENGINEERING See MANUFACTURING ENGINEERING.

PRODUCTION READINESS REVIEW [1]   A formal examination of a program to determine if the design is ready for production and if the prime contractor and major subcontractors have accomplished adequate production planning without incurring unacceptable risks that will breach thresholds of schedule, performance, cost, or other established criteria. PRRs are normally performed as a series of reviews toward the end of Engineering and Manufacturing Development (EMD) phase. A final PRR should occur at the completion of the EMD phase and assess the manufacturing and quality risk as the program proceeds into Low Rate Initial Production (LRIP). Under some circumstances, a PRR may also be appropriate during the LRIP effort to assess manufacturing risk for full-rate production. DAU GLOSSARY.

PRODUCTION SURVEILLANCE   *Official:* A function of CONTRACT ADMINISTRATION used to determine contractor progress and to identify any factors that may delay performance. Production surveillance involves government review and analysis of (a) contractor performance plans, schedules, controls, and industrial processes, and (b) the contractor's actual performance under them. *Source:* FAR 42.1101. Although the contractor is responsible for timely contract performance, the government maintains surveillance as necessary to protect its interests. FAR 42.1103. The office administering the contract determines the extent of surveillance on the basis of the criticality (degree of importance to the government) of the supplies or services and consideration of the following factors: (1) contract requirements for reporting production progress and performance, (2) the contractor performance schedule, (3) the contractor's production plan, (4) the contractor's history of contract performance, (5) the contractor's experience with the contract supplies or services, (6) the contractor's financial capability, and (7) any supplementary written instructions from the contracting office. FAR 42.1104.

PRODUCT SUBSTITUTION   Delivery to the government of a product that does not meet the contract requirements. Such substitution can occur by mismarking products, deviation from specifications, and other types of conduct that indicate an intention to deceive the government in the performance of the contract. Such conduct subjects contractors to criminal and civil sanctions under the FALSE CLAIMS ACT. See SEYFARTH SHAW LLP, THE GOVERNMENT CONTRACT COMPLIANCE HANDBOOK, chap. 15 (5th ed. 2014–2019); Cibinic, Nagle & Nash, ADMINISTRATION OF GOVERNMENT CONTRACTS 138–39 (5th ed. 2016); Cibinic, Nash & Yukins, FORMATION OF GOVERNMENT CONTRACTS 205–07 (4th ed. 2011).

PROFESSIONAL AND CONSULTANT SERVICES   *Official:* Those services rendered by persons who are members of a particular profession or possess a special skill and who are not officers or employees of the contractor. Examples include those services acquired by contractors or subcontractors in order to enhance their legal, economic, financial, or technical positions. Professional and consultant services are usually acquired to obtain information, advice, opinions, alternatives, conclusions, recommendations, training or direct assistance, such as studies, analyses, evaluations, liaison with government officials, or other forms of representation. *Source:* FAR 31.205-33(a). This COST PRINCIPLE specifies that the costs of contracting for such services incurred by contractors are generally ALLOWABLE COSTs subject to specified conditions. See Manos, 1 GOVERNMENT CONTRACT COSTS AND PRICING §§ 40:1–40:6 (2d ed. 2009–2020); Cibinic, Knight & Nash, COST-REIMBURSEMENT CONTRACTING, 692–94 (4th ed. 2014). The government may contract for such services with the individual professionals or with organizations, but such contracts may be subject to the rules governing PERSONAL SERVICES CONTRACTS. 10 U.S.C. § 2331 states a preference that DOD contracts for professional services be for stated tasks rather than for hours of services provided. If the professional services are ARCHITECT-ENGINEER SERVICES, special contracting procedures must be used. All other types of professional services are subject to the normal procurement rules.

PROFESSIONAL EMPLOYEE   *Official:* Any person meeting the definition of "employee employed in a bona fide... professional capacity" given in 29 C.F.R. part 541. The term embraces members of those professions having a recognized status based upon acquiring professional knowledge through prolonged study. Examples of these professions include accountancy, actuarial computation, architecture, dentistry, engineering, law, medicine, nursing, pharmacy, the sciences (such as biology, chemistry, and physics), and teaching. To be a professional employee, a person must not only be a professional but must also be involved essentially in discharging professional duties. *Source:* FAR 22.1102. These employees are not subject to the SERVICE CONTRACT ACT OF 1965. FAR 22.1101. However, FAR 22.1103 states that it is the government's policy that these employees be compensated fairly and properly. When the amount of a SERVICE CONTRACT formed by NEGOTIATION is expected to exceed $700,000 and the contract work will require meaningful numbers of professional employees, offerors must submit for evaluation a total compensation plan for those employees. FAR 22.1103.

PROFIT   The amount realized by a contractor after the costs of performance (both direct and indirect) are deducted from the amount to be paid under the terms of the contract. On an annual basis, profit is computed by subtracting total costs of a contractor from the total amount received from sales. In procurements by NEGOTIATION where there is COST ANALYSIS, the government negotiates a projected amount of profit in accordance with FAR 15.404-4. FAR 15.404-4(a)(2) states that it is in the government's interest to offer contractors opportunities for financial rewards sufficient to (1) stimulate efficient contract performance, (2) attract the most capable and qualified contractors, and (3) maintain a viable industrial base. Just as actual costs may differ from estimated costs, the contractor's actual realized profit may differ from the negotiated profit because of such factors as efficiency of performance and incurrence of costs not allowed by the government (see ALLOWABLE COST and TYPE OF CONTRACT). In COST-REIMBURSEMENT CONTRACTs, the amount of projected profit included in the contract by negotiation is called FEE. FAR 15.404-4(c)(4) imposes limitations on negotiated FIXED FEEs on COST-PLUS-FIXED-FEE CONTRACTs. See Manos, 2 Government Contract Costs and Pricing § 84:23 (2d ed. 2009–2020); Cibinic, Nash & Yukins, Formation of Government Contracts 1534–65 (4th ed. 2011).

PROFIT CENTER   *Official:* The smallest organizationally independent segment of a company charged by management with PROFIT and LOSS responsibilities. *Source:* FAR 31.001. INDIRECT COSTs are normally accumulated and reported for each profit center. See Cibinic, Knight & Nash, Cost-Reimbursement Contracting 615 (4th ed. 2014).

PROFIT OBJECTIVE   The amount that the contracting officer, in preparing to negotiate PRICE based on COST ANALYSIS, concludes is the appropriate negotiated PROFIT or FEE for a procurement. FAR Subpart 15.404-4 provides overall guidance to agencies in establishing profit objectives and FAR 15.404-4(b)(1) requires each agency making noncompetitive awards over $100,000 totaling $50 million or more a year to have a structured approach to establishing such objectives. The DOD uses three different structured approaches to developing profit objectives on all negotiated contracts, except for COST-

PLUS-AWARD-FEE CONTRACTs, when COST OR PRICING DATA is obtained: (1) the WEIGHTED GUIDELINES APPROACH, (2) the modified weighted guidelines approach, and (3) an alternate structured approach. DFARS 215.404-4. In establishing a profit objective for a prospective CONTRACT AWARD, the contracting officer must consider all pertinent information (including audit data) available before negotiation. The profit objective need not be computed using precise mathematical calculations, however, particularly with respect to sub-elements of the major profit factors. *DCAA Contract Audit Manual* ¶ 9-902. See Cibinic, Nash & Yukins, FORMATION OF GOVERNMENT CONTRACTS 1534–65 (4th ed. 2011).

PROGRAM **(n.)** A defined effort funded by Research, Development, Test and Evaluation (RDT&E) and/or procurement appropriations with the express objective of providing a new or improved capability in response to a stated mission need or deficiency. Programs are generally a set of interrelated projects. **(v.)** To schedule funds to meet requirements and plans. "Programing" is a financial process used by agencies to allocate funds to elements of the agency. See DAU GLOSSARY.

PROGRAM ASSESSMENT RATING TOOL (PART) A methodology devised by the OFFICE OF MANAGEMENT AND BUDGET in 2002 to rate the effectiveness of federal programs. This effort was undertaken to carry out the goals of the Government Performance and Results Act of 1993, Pub. L. No. 103-62. See 31 U.S.C. §§ 1115, 1116. The ratings are now used in the formulation of the president's budget.

PROGRAM DECISION MEMORANDUM (PDM) A memorandum, issued as the last step in the programming phase of PLANNING, PROGRAMMING, BUDGET AND EXECUTION PROCESS. PDMs recorded the program review decisions of the Defense Resources Board and were signed by the Secretary of Defense and distributed to DOD components and the OFFICE OF MANAGEMENT AND BUDGET. This document is no longer identified in DOD Directive 7045.14(D) CE-01, *The Planning, Programming, Budgeting and Execution (PPBE) Process*, Aug. 29, 2017.

PROGRAM EXECUTIVE OFFICER (PEO) The government official in DOD with immediate supervisory authority over PROGRAM MANAGERs. PEOs report directly to the COMPONENT ACQUISITION EXECUTIVE of the procuring agency. They were established to ensure that the reporting chain between program managers and senior procurement executives was not excessive. See 10 U.S.C. § 1733(b)(1)(B)(i). PEOs must meet specific experience and training requirements including 10 years' experience in an acquisition position. 10 U.S.C. § 1735(c). Their responsibilities are set forth in the DOD 5000 Series.

PROGRAM FRAUD CIVIL REMEDIES ACT A 1986 Act, 31 U.S.C. § 3801 et seq., that allows federal agencies to adjudicate small-dollar cases, arising out of FALSE CLAIMS and FALSE STATEMENTS made to the government, that previously would have required court litigation. Agencies may assess civil penalties of up to $5,000 per false claim or false statement, as well as double damages for those claims that the government has paid. Liability for false claims requires the establishment of four elements: (1) there must be a claim, (2) the claim must be made to an authority, (3) the claim must be false, and (4) the defendant must know or have reason to know that the claim is false. 31 U.S.C. § 3802(a)(1). There is a ceiling of $150,000 on claims that can be resolved under the Act. 31 U.S.C. § 3803(c)(1). See Manos, 3 GOVERNMENT CONTRACT COSTS AND PRICING § 91:10 (2d ed. 2009–2012); Davidson, *Combating Small-Dollar Fraud Through a Reinvigorated Program*

Fraud Civil Remedies Act, 37 PUB. CONT. L.J. 213 (2008). See also FALSE CLAIMS ACT; FALSE STATEMENTS ACT.

PROGRAM MANAGEMENT   The process whereby a single leader exercises centralized authority and responsibility for planning, organizing, staffing, controlling, and leading the combined efforts of participating/assigned civilian and military personnel and organizations, for the management of a specific defense acquisition program or programs, throughout the system life cycle. DAU GLOSSARY. Generally, the management of interrelated projects.

PROGRAM MANAGER (PM)   In DOD, the designated individual with responsibility for and authority to direct the development, production, and deployment of new defense systems and to achieve the cost, schedule, and performance parameters specified in the approved program baseline. *Source:* DAU GLOSSARY.

PROGRAM OBJECTIVES MEMORANDUM (POM)   The final product of the programming process within DoD, a Component's POM displays the resource allocation decisions of the military department in response to, and in accordance with the Defense Planning Guidance (DPG). The POM shows programmed needs five years hence (e.g., in FY 2016, POM 2018–2022 will be submitted). *Source:* DAU GLOSSARY. See also, DOD 7000.14-R, DOD FINANCIAL MANAGEMENT REGULATION, Vol. 2A.

PROGRAM OPPORTUNITY NOTICE (PON)   A type of BROAD AGENCY ANNOUNCEMENT used by DOE to inform potential offerors of scientific and technological areas in which DOE wants to accelerate demonstration of the technical, operational, economic, and commercial feasibility and environmental acceptability of particular energy technologies, systems, subsystems, and components. DEAR 917.7201-1(a). At a minimum, each PON must include the goal of the demonstration effort, the time schedule for award, evaluation criteria, PROGRAM POLICY FACTORS, amount of cost detail required, and proposal submission information. DEAR 917.7201-1(b).

PROGRAM RESEARCH AND DEVELOPMENT ANNOUNCEMENT (PRDA)   A type of BROAD AGENCY ANNOUNCEMENT used by DOE to inform potential offerors of DOE's interest in entering into arrangements for research, development, and related activities in specific areas of interest in the energy field. DEAR 917.7301-1(a). PRDAs may not be used when a requirement can be sufficiently defined for solicitation under standard advertised or negotiated acquisition procedures or to inhibit or curtail the submission of unsolicited proposals. DEAR 917.7301-1(b).

PROGRESS PAYMENT   A payment made on a fixed-price type contract during the performance of the work but before completion of the contract. Progress payments are made on the basis of either a percentage of completion of the work, FAR 32.102(e), or the incurrence of costs, FAR 32.102(b). Progress payments made on the basis of percentage of completion to construction contractors and architect-engineers are considered to be INVOICE PAYMENTs, which are subject to the PROMPT PAYMENT ACT. FAR 31.001 (in the definition of INVOICE PAYMENT). PROGRESS PAYMENTS BASED ON COSTS and PERFORMANCE-BASED PAYMENTS are considered to be CONTRACT FINANCING PAYMENTS which are not subject to the PROMPT PAYMENT ACT. FAR 32.102(b) and (f). The Progress Payment Not Included clause at FAR 52.232-15 is used to warn offerors that no progress payments will be included in the contract. See Cibinic, Nagle & Nash,

ADMINISTRATION OF GOVERNMENT CONTRACTS 1118–21 (5th ed. 2016). See also FINANCING.

PROGRESS PAYMENTS BASED ON COSTS CONTRACT FINANCING PAYMENTS on fixed-price-type contracts that are not payments for accepted items but are based on a percentage of costs incurred in performing the contract. FAR 32.501-1. Guidance on the use of these payments is set forth in FAR Subpart 32.5. The percentage has varied from time to time and is currently 80% for large business and 85% for small business. The Progress Payments clause in FAR 52.232-16 is used when these payments are agreed to and may be used in both negotiated and sealed bidding contracts. These payments may not be used on COST-REIMBURSEMENT CONTRACTS (FAR 32.500(a)), or contracts for construction or shipbuilding (FAR 32.500(b)). As the government pays for completed contract items, the progress payments previously paid are "liquidated" at rates provided for in the clause. FAR 32.503-8, -9 and -10. The payments can be suspended or reduced if the contractor does not make the progress anticipated when the contract was awarded, FAR 32.503-6. Progress payments based on costs that do not use the CUSTOMARY PROGRESS PAYMENTs rate, the cost base and frequency of payment established in the contract's Progress Payments clause, and either the ordinary liquidation method (see FAR 32.503-8) or the alternate method (see FAR 32.503-9) are considered UNUSUAL PROGRESS PAYMENTs and may be used only when authorized in exceptional cases. See FAR 32.501-1 and -2. See Cibinic, Nagle & Nash, ADMINISTRATION OF GOVERNMENT CONTRACTS 1018 (5th ed. 2016).

PROJECT A planned undertaking having a finite beginning and ending, involving definition, development, production, and logistics support of a major weapon or weapon support system or systems. A project may be the whole or a part of a program. DAU GLOSSARY. This term is frequently synonymous with PROGRAM.

PROJECT MANAGER (PM) An official responsible for planning and controlling assigned projects to achieve program goals. Typical duties that relate to the government procurement process include establishing program objectives; developing requirements, including PURCHASE REQUESTs containing SPECIFICATIONs and STATEMENTS OF WORK; obtaining required approvals; scheduling, estimating, budgeting, and controlling projects; coordinating project planning with the contracting officer; and functioning as the CONTRACTING OFFICER REPRESENTATIVE or CONTRACTING OFFICER TECHNICAL REPRESENTATIVE. See also PROGRAM MANAGER.

PROJECT ON GOVERNMENT OVERSIGHT (POGO) "A nonpartisan independent watchdog that investigates and exposes waste, corruption, abuse of power, and when the government fails to serve the public or silences those who report wrongdoing." POGO Mission Statement, http://www.pogo.org/ about. Located in Washington, DC, the organization issues reports about what it perceives to be corruption, misconduct, and conflicts of interest. See, e.g., *Smaller Budgets Will Result in a More Effective Military* (Apr. 10, 2019), https://www.pogo.org/testimony/2019/04/smaller-budgets-will-result-in-a-more-effective-military/.

PROJECT WAGE DETERMINATION See WAGE DETERMINATION.

PROJECTED AVERAGE LOSS *Official:* The estimated long-term average loss per period for periods of comparable exposure to risk of loss. *Source:* FAR 2.101. When a contractor has a SELF-INSURANCE program, costs of actual losses are ALLOWABLE COSTs unless they exceed projected average losses. FAR 31.205-19. See CAS 416, Accounting for Insurance

Costs, 48 C.F.R. § 9904.416. See Cibinic, Knight & Nash, Cost-Reimbursement Contracting 728–30 (4th ed. 2014).

PROMISSORY ESTOPPEL   A legal doctrine binding a person to a promise when another party has relied on the promise to its detriment and the person making the promise could have reasonably foreseen the reliance. Restatement (Second) of Contracts § 90 (1981). Courts usually award damages for breach of the promise commensurate with the costs incurred in reliance on the promise. The COURT OF FEDERAL CLAIMS and the BOARDs OF CONTRACT APPEALS have ruled that they have no jurisdiction over claims of BREACH OF CONTRACT based on promissory estoppel by the government. See Cibinic, Nash & Yukins, Formation of Government Contracts 275–77 (4th ed. 2011).

PROMPT PAYMENT ACT (PPA)   A 1983 Act, 31 U.S.C. § 3901 et seq., requiring solicitations and contracts to specify payment procedures, payment due dates, and INTEREST penalties for late INVOICE PAYMENTs. The Act is implemented by FAR Subpart 32.9 and OMB regulations at 5 C.F.R. § 1315. The government must make invoice payments and CONTRACT FINANCING PAYMENTs as close as possible to, but not later than, the due dates specified in the contract (generally no longer than 30 days after receipt of a PROPER INVOICE). The detailed procedures followed are set forth in the Prompt Payment clause in FAR 52.232-25, the Prompt Payment for Fixed-Price Architect-Engineer Contract clause in FAR 52.232-26, and the Prompt Payment for Construction Contracts clause in FAR 52.232-27. Determination of the date of payment is based on receipt of a proper invoice or contract financing request and satisfactory contract performance. Checks are mailed and electronic funds transfers are made on or about the same day the payment action is dated. Agencies pay an interest penalty for late invoice payments or improperly taken discounts for prompt payment. There is no interest penalty for late contract financing payments. See Cibinic, Nagle & Nash, Administration of Government Contracts 1039–48 (5th ed. 2016); McClure, *The Application of the Prompt Payment Act to Commercial Item Acquisitions: Contractors Are Not Entitled to Interest on Late Commercial Interim Payments*, 29 Pub. Cont. L.J. 269 (2000).

PROPER INVOICE   *Official:* An invoice that meets the minimum standards specified in 32.905(b). *Source*: FAR 2.101. The submission of a proper invoice starts the period for computing the due date for payment under the PROMPT PAYMENT ACT. FAR 32.905(b) requires a proper invoice, except in the case of COST-REIMBURSEMENT CONTRACTs, to contain: (i) Name and address of the contractor. (ii) Invoice date and invoice number. (Contractors should date invoices as close as possible to the date of mailing or transmission.) (iii) Contract number or other authorization for supplies delivered or services performed (including order number and contract line item number). (iv) Description, quantity, unit of measure, unit price, and extended price of supplies delivered or services performed. (v) Shipping and payment terms (e.g., shipment number and date of shipment, discount for prompt payment terms). Bill of lading number and weight of shipment will be shown for shipments on government bills of lading. (vi) Name and address of contractor official to whom payment is to be sent (must be the same as that in the contract or in a proper notice of assignment). (vii) Name (where practicable), title, phone number, and mailing address of person to notify in the event of a defective invoice. (viii) Taxpayer Identification Number (TIN). The contractor must include its TIN on the invoice only if required by agency procedures. (See 4.9 TIN requirements.) (ix) Electronic funds transfer (EFT) banking information. (A) The contractor must include EFT banking information on the invoice only if required by agency procedures. (B) If EFT banking information is not required to be on the invoice, in order for the invoice to be a proper invoice, the contractor must have submitted correct EFT banking information in accordance with the applicable solicitation provision (e.g., 52.232-38, Submission of Electronic Funds Transfer Information with Offer), contract clause (e.g., 52.232-33, Payment by Electronic Funds Transfer-Central Contractor Registration, or 52.232-34, Payment by Electronic Funds Transfer-Other Than System for Award Management), or applicable agency procedures. (C) EFT banking information is not required if the Government waived the requirement to pay by EFT. (x) Any other information or documentation required by the contract (e.g., evidence of shipment). See INVOICE.

PROPERTY   *Official:* All tangible property, both real and personal. *Source:* FAR 45.101. FAR 45.102 states that the policy is to provide GOVERNMENT PROPERTY to contractors only in very limited circumstances. Thus, most government property held by contractors is CONTRACTOR ACQUIRED PROPERTY. See Cibinic, Nagle & Nash, ADMINISTRATION OF GOVERNMENT CONTRACTS, chap. 7 (5th ed. 2016).

PROPERTY ADMINISTRATOR   *Official:* An AUTHORIZED REPRESENTATIVE of the contracting officer appointed in accordance with agency procedures, responsible for administering the contract requirements and obligations relating to GOVERNMENT PROPERTY in the possession of a contractor. *Source:* FAR 45.101. In general, property administrators oversee the contractor's compliance with the property management requirements in FAR Part 45. Their most important function is analysis of the compliance of a contractor's PROPERTY MANAGEMENT SYSTEM.

PROPERTY MANAGEMENT SYSTEM   A CONTRACTOR BUSINESS SYSTEM that contemplates a system or systems for managing and controlling GOVERNMENT PROPERTY. DFARS 252.245-7003. However, FAR 45.103(b) provides that agencies generally will not require contractors to establish property management systems that are separate from a contractor's established procedures, practices, and systems used to account for and manage contractor-owned property. Paragraph (b) of the Government Property clause at FAR 52.245-1 requires a contractor to have a system (including processes, procedures, records and methodologies) to control, use, preserve, repair, protect, and maintain government property in the contractor's possession. The contractor's responsibilities extend from the initial acquisition of property though stewardship and use, until formally relieved of responsibility by authorized means. DOD can withhold payment if there is a SIGNIFICANT DEFICIENCY in this system.

PROPOSAL   *Official:* An OFFER in a negotiated procurement (see NEGOTIATION). *Source:* FAR 2.101 (in the definition of "offer"). Proposals for new contracts are submitted in response to a REQUEST FOR PROPOSALS (RFPs) or a BROAD AGENCY ANNOUNCEMENT. In spite of the definition in FAR 2.101 stating that a proposal is an offer, the term "proposal" is generally used in FAR Part 15 to mean not only the offer submitted by an offeror in a negotiated procurement but also all of the information that the RFP requires to be submitted with the offer. Thus, FAR 15.102(b) states that an ORAL PRESENTATION can be part of a proposal. Proposal is also defined in FAR 31.001 as "any offer or other submission used as a basis for pricing a contract, contract MODIFICATION, or termination settlement (see TERMINATION FOR CONVENIENCE) or for securing payments thereunder." Proposals for contract modifications or termination settlements are submitted pursuant to clauses of the contract. When proposals are submitted without prior request from a government agency they are called UNSOLICITED PROPOSALs.

PROPOSAL EVALUATION   *Official:* An assessment of the PROPOSAL and the offeror's ability to perform. *Source:* FAR 15.305(a). In contracting by NEGOTIATION, this is the process by which the government assesses both the OFFER and the other information submitted in response to the REQUEST FOR PROPOSALS to determine the relative merits of the offer and the offeror's ability to successfully accomplish a prospective contract. The government conducts both a cost or price evaluation (using COST ANALYSIS or PRICE ANALYSIS), a PAST PERFORMANCE evaluation, and a TECHNICAL EVALUATION. FAR 15.305. 10 U.S.C. § 2305(b)(1) and 41 U.S.C. § 3701(a) require agencies to evaluate competitive proposals solely on the basis of factors specified in the SOLICITATION. 10 U.S.C. § 2305(a)(2)(A) and 41 U.S.C. § 3306(b) require that the solicitation describe the SOURCE SELECTION system to be used by listing all significant EVALUATION FACTORS and stating their RELATIVE IMPORTANCE. This statutory language essentially leaves procuring agencies free to use any proposal evaluation system they choose, and a wide variety of systems have been adopted. The agency manuals, handbooks, and documents that provide instructions on proposal evaluation demonstrate that there is no consensus on the procedures to be followed or the scoring systems to be used. Some call for evaluation by individual evaluators, while others require evaluation by teams. As to the scoring systems, agencies use numerical scoring, adjectival scoring, color coding or ratings. The relative STRENGTHs, DEFICIENCYs, SIGNIFICANT WEAKNESSes, and risks supporting proposal evaluation must be documented in the contract file. See Feldman, GOVERNMENT CONTRACT AWARDS: NEGOTIATION AND SEALED BIDDING, chap. 12 (2019–2020 ed.).

PROPOSAL MODIFICATION   *Official:* A change made to a PROPOSAL before the SOLICITATION closing date and time, made in response to an AMENDMENT, or made to correct a MISTAKE at any time before award. *Source:* FAR 15.001. Proposal modifications other than corrections of a mistake must be submitted by the time specified for the submission of the PROPOSAL or they will be treated as LATE PROPOSALs. However, a modification submitted after the closing date and time of an otherwise successful proposal that makes its terms more favorable to the government will be considered at any time and may be accepted. FAR 15.208. See Cibinic, Nash & Yukins, FORMATION OF GOVERNMENT CONTRACTS 760–67 (4th ed. 2011). The definition of proposal modification in FAR 15.001 has been cited as authority for a contracting officer to correct a mistake during CLARIFICATIONs but GAO has ruled otherwise. See Nash, *Postscript: Mistakes in Negotiated Procurement,* 20 N&CR ¶ 52 (Nov. 2006).

PROPOSAL REVISION   *Official:* A change to a PROPOSAL made after the SOLICITATION closing date, at the request of or as allowed by the contracting officer, as a result of NEGOTIATIONs. *Source:* FAR 15.001. Proposal revisions are made to document understandings reached during negotiations, FAR 15.307(b), but offerors are not prohibited from revising other aspects of their proposal. At the conclusion of discussions, each offeror still in the COMPETITIVE RANGE must be given the opportunity to submit a FINAL PROPOSAL REVISION. Proposal revisions generally must be submitted by the specified time for their receipt, unless the criteria in FAR 15.208(b)(1) are met. See Feldman, GOVERNMENT CONTRACT AWARDS: NEGOTIATION AND SEALED BIDDING §§ 17:1–17:7 (2019–2020 ed.).

PROPOSED REGULATION A proposed revision to the FAR or a FAR Supplement issued in accordance with the procedures prescribed in 41 U.S.C. § 1707. Proposed regulations must be published in the FEDERAL REGISTER and allow 60 days for public comment before a FINAL REGULATION is issued. Regulations are subject to these requirements if they relate to the expenditure of appropriated funds; and **(i)** have a significant effect beyond the internal operating procedures of the agency issuing the policy, regulation, procedure, or form; or **(ii)** have a significant cost or administrative impact on contractors or offerors. The requirements can be waived in urgent circumstances.

PROPRIETARY DATA TECHNICAL DATA submitted to the government under a contract and subject to protection by the contractor. Under FAR Subpart 27.4 and DFARS Subpart 227.71 such data are subject to LIMITED RIGHTS if they are DEVELOPED AT PRIVATE EXPENSE or DEVELOPED EXCLUSIVELY AT PRIVATE EXPENSE, respectively. Under the DFARS the data can also be delivered subject to GOVERNMENT PURPOSE RIGHTS. See Nash & Rawicz, INTELLECTUAL PROPERTY IN GOVERNMENT CONTRACTS, chap. 4 (6th ed. 2008). Restrictions on disclosure of proprietary data by government employees are set forth in the PROCUREMENT INTEGRITY provisions (which now call it CONTRACTOR BID OR PROPOSAL INFORMATION) and the TRADE SECRETS ACT. See Nash, *Protesting Stolen Proprietary Data: A Lost Cause*, 33 N&CR ¶ 20 (Apr. 2019).

PROPRIETARY INFORMATION Information contained in a bid or proposal, COST OR PRICING DATA, or any other information submitted to the government by a contractor and designated as proprietary. This term was used in the PROCUREMENT INTEGRITY ACT, 41 U.S.C. §§ 2101–2107, prior to its amendment by the CLINGER-COHEN ACT OF 1996, to identify a class of information that could not be disclosed. The amended act uses the term CONTRACTOR BID OR PROPOSAL INFORMATION. Paragraph (e) of the Instructions to Offerors—Competitive Acquisition solicitation provision in FAR 52.215-1 provides that all information in a PROPOSAL may be marked as proprietary information. FAR 15.609 provides that all information in UNSOLICITED PROPOSALS may be marked as proprietary information. This information is also subject to protection from release in accordance with the FREEDOM OF INFORMATION ACT. See Nash, *Nondisclosure Agreements: A Variety of Approaches*, 24 N&CR ¶ 58 (Dec. 2010).

PROSECUTION OF CLAIMS The assertion by a contractor of a CLAIM for additional compensation or other benefit from the government in a court or BOARD OF CONTRACT APPEALS. FAR 31.205-47(f) provides that costs of legal, accounting, and consulting services and directly associated costs incurred by contractors for such efforts are UNALLOWABLE COSTs. See Manos, 1 GOVERNMENT CONTRACT COSTS AND PRICING §§ 54:1–54:11 (2d ed. 2009–2020). The major exception to this rule is that small companies can recover if they qualify under the EQUAL ACCESS TO JUSTICE ACT. See also PROFESSIONAL AND CONSULTANT SERVICES.

PROSPECTIVE PRICING Pricing of a contract before the work is begun. It is the policy of the government to use prospective pricing whenever possible. See FAR 16.603-3 limiting the use of LETTER CONTRACTs and FAR 43.102(b), stating that CONTRACT MODIFICATIONs should be priced before they are executed. See also UNDEFINITIZED CONTRACTUAL ACTION.

PROTECTIVE ORDER   An order of a court or administrative tribunal limiting the scope of the disclosure of PRIVILEGED INFORMATION. Protective orders are used to ensure that information obtained in DISCOVERY is not improperly used. They are issued under Rule 26(c) of the Federal Rules of Civil Procedure, Rule 14 of the UNIFORM RULES (in cases before the BOARDs OF CONTRACT APPEALS), and Rule 21.4 of the GOVERNMENT ACCOUNTABILITY OFFICE (in PROTESTs). See Cibinic, Nash & Yukins, FORMATION OF GOVERNMENT CONTRACTS 1725–27, 1782–83 (4th ed. 2011).

PROTÉGÉ   FIRM See MENTOR-PROTÉGÉ PROGRAM.

PROTEST   *Official:* A written objection by an INTERESTED PARTY to any of the following: (1) A solicitation or other request by an agency for offers for a contract for the procurement of property or services. (2) The cancellation of the solicitation or other request. (3) An award or proposed award of the contract. (4) A termination or cancellation of an award of the contract, if the written objection contains an allegation that the termination or cancellation is based in whole or in part on improprieties concerning the award of the contract. *Source:* FAR 33.101. Protests are also known as "bid protests," "award protests," or "protests against award." Protests can be made to (1) the procuring agency, before or after award, FAR 33.103; (2) the GOVERNMENT ACCOUNTABILITY OFFICE, within 10 calendar days after the grounds for the protest are known or should have been known, see GAO Bid Protest Regulations for detailed timing rules, 4 C.F.R. part 21, FAR 33.104; or (3) the COURT OF FEDERAL CLAIMS, 28 U.S.C. § 1491(b)(1). The clauses in FAR 52.233-2 and -3 inform offerors and winning contractors of mandatory protest procedures. See Feldman, GOVERNMENT CONTRACT GUIDEBOOK, §§ 7:5–7:15 (4th ed. 2019–2020); Cibinic, Nash & Yukins, FORMATION OF GOVERNMENT CONTRACTS, chap. 12 (4th ed. 2011). See also Manual & Schwartz, CONG. RESEARCH SERV., Report No. R40228, GAO BID PROTESTS: AN OVERVIEW OF TIME FRAMES AND PROCEDURES (Jan. 19, 2016); Rector, Jorgensen & Cook, *To File Or Not To File: Key Issues When Deciding To Protest*, BRIEFING PAPERS No. 15-3 (Feb. 2015); Edwards, *Pathologies of the Protest System: Recommendations for a Cure*, 25 N&CR ¶ 32 (July 2011); Nash, *Standards of Review in Bid Protests: The GAO's Competitive Prejudice Rule*, 25 N&CR ¶ 12 (Mar. 2011); Kipa, Szeliga & Madon, *Identifying Viable Preaward Bid Protest Allegations at the GAO*, BRIEFING PAPERS No. 10-6 (May 2010); Schaengold, Guiffré & Gill, *Choice of Forum for Federal Government Contract Bid Protests*, 18 FED. CIR. B.J. 243 (2009).

PROTOTYPE OTHER TRANSACTION   An OTHER TRANSACTION used to acquire prototypes. Temporary authority to award this type of CONTRACT was originally given to DOD by § 845 of the National Defense Authorization Act for FY 1994, Pub. L. No. 103-160. After being extended repeatedly, the authority was made permanent in 10 U.S.C. § 2371b. The DEPARTMENT OF HOMELAND SECURITY has the same authority, 6 U.S.C. § 391(a). The DEPARTMENT OF ENERGY has similar authority to contract for "demonstration projects," 42 U.S.C. § 7256(g). Guidance on prototype other transactions is contained in DOD's "*Other Transaction Guide*" (Nov. 2018). See Nash & Rawicz, INTELLECTUAL PROPERTY IN GOVERNMENT CONTRACTS, chap. 7 (6th ed. 2008); Modeszto, *The Department of Defense's Section 845 Authority: An Exception for Prototypes or a Prototype for Revised Government* Procurement, 34 PUB. CONT. L.J. 211 (2004).

PROVISION   See SOLICITATION PROVISION.

PROVISION AND CLAUSE MATRIX   A comprehensive chart in FAR Subpart 52.3 that provides menus of the solicitation PROVISIONs and contract CLAUSEs suitable for contracts of various types and purposes. The matrix (1) lists all FAR-prescribed provisions and clauses by number and title; (2) tells users where in the FAR each provision or clause is prescribed; (3) distinguishes provisions from clauses; (4) codes all the provisions and clauses to indicate whether they can be incorporated by reference or must be set forth in full text; (5) designates the section of the UNIFORM CONTRACT FORMAT in which each provision or clause should appear; and (6) categorizes the provisions and clauses as *required*, *required when applicable*, or *optional* in terms of each applicable type or purpose of contract.

PROVISIONAL PAYMENT   An interim payment made by the government to a contractor to provide compensation during the negotiation and settlement of CLAIMs or EQUITABLE ADJUSTMENT proposals. The FAR contains no guidance on such payments, but they are used by agencies to provide financing to contractors that have incurred substantial costs in performing work not covered by the contract because the contract has not been modified to reflect the value of the claim or adjustment. Provisional payments are made pursuant to MODIFICATIONs that generally limit such payments to an amount commensurate with the government's evaluation of the value of the claim or proposal. See DFARS 232.102-70 providing guidance on "provisional delivery payments" for UNDEFINITIZED CONTRACT ACTIONs. See Cibinic, Nagle & Nash, ADMINISTRATION OF GOVERNMENT CONTRACTS 1025–27 (5th ed. 2016). Payments of this nature on contracts that have been terminated are called PARTIAL PAYMENTs. FAR 49.112-1.

PROVISIONING   *Official:* The process of determining and acquiring the range and quantity of spare and repair parts, and support and test equipment required to operate and maintain an end item for an initial period of service. *Source:* DOD PGI 217.7601. DOD contracts frequently contain provisions calling for provisioning during performance of the contract. The procedures to be followed when a contract contains such a requirement are set forth in DOD PGI Subpart 217.76.

PUBLIC INTEREST   In the interest of the United States. This term is frequently used when broad authority is granted to an officer of the government. For example, 10 U.S.C. § 2304(c)(7) and 41 U.S.C. § 3304(a)(7) permit award of contracts without FULL AND OPEN COMPETITION when the HEAD OF THE AGENCY determines that such action would be in the public interest. Further, FAR 14.209 instructs that invitations for bids should not be cancelled unless cancellation is clearly in the public interest, and FAR 25.102 explains that the BUY AMERICAN ACT requires purchase of domestic end products except where the agency head determines that domestic preference would be inconsistent with the public interest.

PUBLIC LAW 85-804   See EXTRAORDINARY CONTRACTUAL ACTION.

PUBLIC-PRIVATE PARTNERING   A long-term business relationship between the government and one or more firms to perform government work jointly or using leased or purchased government facilities and equipment. The relationship can be one or a combination of several forms, including teaming arrangements, contracts, memoranda of agreements, and sales or leases of government facilities. The DEPARTMENT OF DEFENSE has made extensive use of public private partnerships for the performance of depot maintenance. See Office of the Secretary of Defense, *Public-Private Partnerships for Depot-Level Maintenance through the End of Fiscal Year 2005* (May 2006); U.S. GOV'T ACCOUNTABILITY OFFICE, DEPOT MAINTENANCE: PUBLIC-PRIVATE PARTNERSHIPS HAVE INCREASED, BUT LONG-TERM GROWTH AND RESULTS ARE UNCERTAIN, GAO-03-423 (Apr. 2003).

PUBLIC RELATIONS   *Official:* All functions and activities dedicated to (1) maintaining, protecting, and enhancing the image of a concern or its products; or (2) maintaining or promoting reciprocal understanding and favorable relations with the public at large, or any segment of the public. The term public relations includes activities associated with areas such as ADVERTISING, customer relations, etc. *Source:* FAR 31.205-1. Public relations costs are ALLOWABLE COSTs only in specified circumstances. See FAR 31.205-1(d) and (e). See Manos, 1 GOVERNMENT CONTRACT COSTS AND PRICING §§ 8:1–8:2 (2d ed. 2009–2020); Cibinic, Knight & Nash, COST-REIMBURSEMENT CONTRACTING 641–44 (4th ed. 2014).

PUBLICIZING CONTRACT ACTIONS   The dissemination to the public of information about proposed contract actions and awards. The primary purposes of making such information available are to enhance competition and to improve small business access to acquisition opportunities. Contracting officers are required by 15 U.S.C. § 637(e) and 41 U.S.C. § 1708 to disseminate information on proposed contract information by (1) synopsizing proposed contract actions expected to exceed $25,000 (see SYNOPSIS); and (2) for contract actions between $10,000 and $25,000, displaying in a public place, including an electronic bulletin board or other electronic means, a notice or copy of the solicitation. In addition, other methods of publicizing contract actions which the contracting officer may use include (1) preparing and displaying periodic handouts listing proposed contracts, (2) assisting local trade associations in disseminating information to their members, (3) making brief announcements of proposed contracts to newspapers, trade journals, magazines or other mass media outlets, and (4) placing paid advertisements in newspapers or other communications media. See FAR Part 5. See Feldman, GOVERNMENT CONTRACT AWARDS: NEGOTIATION AND SEALED BIDDING § 3:2 (2019–2020 ed.).

PUNCH LIST   A list of defects found on inspection of a construction project when the contractor asserts that the work has reached the stage of SUBSTANTIAL COMPLETION. Government inspectors compile this list during their inspection and the contractor is expected to correct any significant defects on the list in order to earn FINAL PAYMENT.

PUNITIVE DAMAGES   Damages that are awarded in a civil action, in addition to COMPENSATORY DAMAGES, to punish a DEFENDANT for gross or willful misconduct. Punitive damages are generally not recoverable in BREACH OF CONTRACT actions. RESTATEMENT (SECOND) OF CONTRACTS § 355 (1981). They are recoverable in TORT actions between private parties but not in actions against the government under the FEDERAL TORT CLAIMS ACT.

PURCHASE CARD   See GOVERNMENT-WIDE COMMERCIAL PURCHASE CARD.

PURCHASE DESCRIPTION   A description of the essential physical characteristics and functions required to meet the government's requirements. When used in a general sense, the term embraces SPECIFICATIONs, STANDARDs, and other means of describing the government's requirements. It can be used more narrowly, however, to denote a description developed for a given procurement when no existing specification is appropriate. Purchase descriptions must describe the supplies or services to be acquired in a manner designed to permit FULL AND OPEN COMPETITION. A BRAND NAME OR EQUAL DESCRIPTION must include the SALIENT CHARACTERISTICS of the product. FAR 11.104(b). Purchase descriptions must not specify a product or feature of a product peculiar to one manufacturer, thereby precluding consideration of products from other companies, unless the particular product or feature is essential to the government's requirements and other companies' similar products or products lacking the particular feature would not meet the government's needs. FAR 11.105. See FAR 11.106 for drafting requirements of purchase descriptions for service contracts.

PURCHASE ORDER (PO)   *Official:* An OFFER by the government to buy supplies or services, including construction and research and development, upon specified terms and conditions, using SIMPLIFIED ACQUISITION PROCEDURES. *Source:* FAR 2.101. Procedures for issuing purchase orders are set forth in FAR 13.302. A binding contract may be formed upon either (1) written acceptance of the purchase order by the contractor (see BILATERAL CONTRACT) or (2) the contractor's undertaking performance of the work (see UNILATERAL CONTRACT). FAR 13.302-3. Standard Form 44 can be used for small, over-the-counter purchases. FAR 13.306. Standard Form 1449 or Optional Form 347, Order for Supplies or Services, FAR 53.302-347 may also be used as a purchase order, or an agency form/format may be used. FAR 13.307. Purchase orders are generally issued on a FIRM-FIXED-PRICE CONTRACT basis; but they may provide for ECONOMIC PRICE ADJUSTMENT when used to buy COMMERCIAL ITEMS. FAR 12.207(a). They should reflect any trade or prompt payment discounts that are offered. FAR 13.302-1(a)(5). Unpriced purchase orders may be used in limited circumstances. FAR 13.302-2. Guidance on the modification of purchase orders is set forth in FAR 13.302-3. See Cibinic, Nash & Yukins, FORMATION OF GOVERNMENT CONTRACTS 235–37 (4th ed. 2011); Nash, *Unilateral Purchase Orders: When Are They Binding?*, 21 N&CR ¶ 11 (Mar. 2007).

PURCHASE REQUEST   A document that, when submitted to a contracting office, officially initiates a particular procurement action; sometimes called a procurement request, requisition or request for contract. Purchase requests provide the official basis for deciding how a procurement will be conducted and how a contract will be awarded. They contain a description of the requirement, required authorizations, and necessary administrative details that enable the contracting officer to prepare and issue a SOLICITATION and develop a contract document. The heart of the purchase request is the SPECIFICATION, STATEMENT OF WORK, or PURCHASE DESCRIPTION, which tells what must be delivered or accomplished.

PURCHASING SYSTEM   *Official:* The contractor's system or systems for purchasing and subcontracting, including make-or-buy decisions, the selection of vendors, analysis of quoted prices, negotiation of prices with vendors, placing and administering of orders, and expediting delivery of materials. *Source:* DFAR 252.244-7001. This is one of the six CONTRACTOR BUSINESS SYSTEMs where the contractor is subject to withholding of payment if the system has a SIGNIFICANT DEFICIENCY. A contracting officer can use a CONTRACTOR PURCHASING SYSTEM REVIEW to evaluate the efficiency and effectiveness with which the contractor spends government funds and to approve the contractor's purchasing system. FAR 44.301.

Q

QUALIFICATION REQUIREMENT *Official:* A government requirement for testing or other quality assurance demonstration that must be completed before award of a contract. *Source:* FAR 2.101. FAR Subpart 9.2 sets forth policies and procedures regarding qualification requirements. See PREQUALIFICATION. An agency can also qualify a produce after contract award by requiring FIRST ARTICLE TESTING AND APPROVAL.

QUALIFIED BIDDERS LIST (QBL) *Official:* A list of bidders who have had their products examined and tested and who have satisfied all applicable QUALIFICATION REQUIREMENTs for that products or have otherwise satisfied all applicable qualification requirements. *Source:* FAR 9.201. These lists are used infrequently in the procurement process. FAR Subpart 9.2 sets forth the procedures that must be used to establish QBLs and to use them in the procurement process. See also PREQUALIFICATION.

QUALIFIED MANUFACTURERS LIST (QML) *Official:* A list of manufacturers who have had their products examined and tested and who have satisfied all applicable QUALIFICATION REQUIREMENTs for those products. *Source:* FAR 9.201. These lists are used when an agency determines that manufacturers must have special capabilities to enable them to meet the government requirements. FAR Subpart 9.2 sets forth the procedures that must be used to establish QMLs and to use them in the procurement process. See also PREQUALIFICATION.

QUALIFIED PENSION PLAN *Official:* A pension plan comprising a definite written program communicated to and for the exclusive benefit of employees that meets the criteria deemed essential by the Internal Revenue Service as set forth in the Internal Revenue Code for preferential tax treatment regarding contributions, investments, and distributions. Any other plan is a nonqualified pension plan. *Source:* FAR 31.001. The costs of such plans are ALLOWABLE COSTs. FAR 31.205-6(j). See Cibinic, Knight & Nash, COST-REIMBURSEMENT CONTRACTING 678–83 (4th ed. 2014).

QUALIFIED PRODUCTS LIST (QPL) *Official:* A list of products that have been examined, tested, and have satisfied all applicable QUALIFICATION REQUIREMENTs. *Source:* FAR 2.101. These lists are used on procurements to restrict offerors to those products on the lists. FAR Subpart 9.2 sets forth the procedures that must be used to establish QPLs and to use them in the procurement process. See also PREQUALIFICATION.

QUALITY ASSURANCE (QA) *Official:* The various functions, including inspection, performed by the government to determine whether a contractor has fulfilled the contract obligations pertaining to quality and quantity. *Source:* FAR 46.101 (in the definition of GOVERNMENT CONTRACT QUALITY ASSURANCE). These policies and procedures are set forth in FAR Part 46 and include INSPECTION, ACCEPTANCE, WARRANTY, and other measures associated with QUALITY REQUIREMENTS. See also DFARS Part 246 containing additional requirements applicable to DOD contracts. The basic government QA policy is to require contractors to perform sufficient testing and inspection to ensure that quality requirements are met in order to limit government efforts to those necessary to ensure that quality requirements are met. The term QUALITY CONTROL is sometimes used interchangeably with quality assurance. See Cibinic, Nagle & Nash, ADMINISTRATION OF GOVERNMENT CONTRACTS, chap. 9 (5th ed. 2016).

QUALITY ASSURANCE SURVEILLANCE PLAN (QASP)   A plan describing how the agency will survey, observe, test, sample, evaluate, and document the contractor's performance in meeting critical PERFORMANCE STANDARDs identified in the contract. The QASP and the STATEMENT OF WORK should be developed concurrently because of their influence on one another. The plan should specify which work requires surveillance, the method of surveillance and the place where surveillance will take place (at source or destination). FAR 46.401.

QUALITY CONTROL (QC)   Tasks performed by contractors to improve the quality of the organization's output. FAR 46.105 states the government policy that contractors have the fundamental responsibility for control of the quality of the work they perform. The INSPECTION requirements of most government contracts call for the contractor to provide a QC system that ensures that the work meets contract requirements. FAR Subpart 46.3. However, FAR 46.202-4 permits the imposition of HIGHER-LEVEL CONTRACT QUALITY REQUIREMENTS when necessary. QC can be seen as consisting of four steps: (1) setting cost, performance, safety, and reliability standards (or noting the standards that apply to a given contract); (2) comparing the offered product or service with those standards; (3) taking corrective action when necessary; and (4) planning for improvements. See Cibinic, Nagle & Nash, ADMINISTRATION OF GOVERNMENT CONTRACTS 717–19 (5th ed. 2016).

QUALITY CONTROL PLAN   A contractor's internal quality assurance procedures for measuring, tracking, reporting, and analyzing contract performance. A contractor's quality control plan is separate from the government's QUALITY ASSURANCE SURVEILLANCE PLAN.

QUALITY REQUIREMENT   The contract provisions specifying the level of QUALITY ASSURANCE or QUALITY CONTROL. FAR Subpart 46.201. FAR 46.202 describes four general categories of quality requirements: (1) existing contractor procedures for COMMERCIAL ITEMs, (2) reliance solely on contractor inspection for SIMPLIFIED ACQUISITIONS, (3) inclusion of standard INSPECTION clauses, or (4) inclusion of a clause calling for HIGHER LEVEL CONTRACT QUALITY REQUIREMENTS. Solicitations may provide for alternative quality requirements to achieve wide competition and low cost. FAR 46.201(b).

QUANTUM   The amount owed by one party to the other party as a result of a CLAIM on the contract. This amount is generally determined by computing the EQUITABLE ADJUSTMENT or PRICE ADJUSTMENT called for by a contract clause. On occasion, it is determined by computing DAMAGES for BREACH OF CONTRACT. BOARDS OF CONTRACT

APPEALS frequently delay the determination of quantum until they have decided whether the claim has merit. See BIFURCATION OF ENTITLEMENT AND QUANTUM.

QUANTUM MERUIT   A Latin expression meaning "as much as he deserves." Quantum meruit is an equitable doctrine, and it implies a promise to pay the reasonable value of work completed or materials or services provided. The doctrine is based on the concept that there should not be unjust enrichment by one contracting party for the labor and materials expended by the other party. BLACK'S LAW DICTIONARY 1498 (11th ed. 2019). Although this is a restitutionary cause of action in commercial law, the government has never waived its SOVEREIGN IMMUNITY for such a cause of action (see RESTITUTION). However, this measure of compensation has been used to compensate contractors that have proved that they had an implied-in-fact contract (see IMPLIED CONTRACT). See Cibinic, Nagle & Nash, ADMINISTRATION OF GOVERNMENT CONTRACTS 618 (5th ed. 2016). See also QUANTUM VALEBANT.

QUANTUM VALEBANT   A Latin expression meaning "as much as they were worth." BLACK'S LAW DICTIONARY 1499 (11th ed. 2019). The term is traditionally used by the courts to describe an action for the value of goods delivered. The term QUANTUM MERUIT is more commonly used in government contract litigation.

QUASI-CONTRACT   A synonym for an implied-in-law contract. See IMPLIED CONTRACT and RESTITUTION.

QUI TAM PROCEEDINGS   A legal procedure named for a Latin phrase meaning (in its entirety) "who sues for the king as well as for himself in the matter." Under the 1986 amendments to the FALSE CLAIMS ACT, any person may bring a civil action under the Act "for the person and for the United States," and the action is brought "in the name of the United States." 31 U.S.C. § 3730(b). The qui tam plaintiff files a civil complaint, typically against an employer/contractor. If DOJ intervenes, it bears primary responsibility for prosecuting the action. If DOJ fails to intervene, the qui tam plaintiff may continue the suit to conclusion. Qui tam plaintiffs are given a share of the government's monetary recovery against the contractor and are granted WHISTLEBLOWER protection. 31 U.S.C. § 3730(d) and (h). See Boese, CIVIL FALSE CLAIMS AND QUI TAM ACTIONS (5th ed. 2020); Cibinic, Nagle & Nash, ADMINISTRATION OF GOVERNMENT CONTRACTS 115–19 (5th ed. 2016).

QUOTATION   A statement of current prices for items being procured under SIMPLIFIED ACQUISITION PROCEDURES, made in response to Standard Form 18, Request for Quotations, FAR 53.301-18, or to an oral request for quotations. FAR 13.106-1(c). Quotations are also solicited from contractors holding FEDERAL SUPPLY SCHEDULE contracts when an agency is procuring services that require a STATEMENT OF WORK. FAR 8.405-2(c). They are also solicited under TASK ORDER CONTRACTs and DELIVERY ORDER CONTRACTs. A quotation does not constitute a binding OFFER; therefore, issuance by the government of an order in response to a supplier's quotation does not establish a contract. FAR 13.004(a). See Cibinic, Nash & Yukins, FORMATION OF GOVERNMENT CONTRACTS 234–37 (4th ed. 2011).

R

RACKETEER INFLUENCED AND CORRUPT ORGANIZATIONS (RICO) ACT   Pub. L. No. 91-452, 18 U.S.C. §§ 1961–1968. A law that does not penalize on the basis of a specific crime, but imposes additional criminal and civil penalties on persons who engage in a pattern of racketeering activity, defined as the violation of two or more of more than 30 specified federal and state statutes during a 10-year period. Crimes that can serve as predicates for a RICO violation include BRIBERY, the furnishing of an illegal GRATUITY, and mail and wire FRAUD, but not false claims or false statements (see FALSE CLAIMS ACT and FALSE STATEMENTS ACT). To establish a RICO criminal violation, the government must prove the existence of an enterprise that affected interstate or foreign commerce and employed an individual who knowingly and willfully participated, directly or indirectly, in the affairs of the enterprise through a pattern of racketeering activity. See Manos, 3 GOVERNMENT CONTRACT COSTS AND PRICING § 91:11 (2d ed. 2009–2020).

RAND CORPORATION   A nonprofit research organization that serves as a "think tank" for government agencies, especially the military services. Its staff has included many great names and Nobel Prize winners in chemistry, economics, and physics. The company made major contributions to the use of SYSTEMS ANALYSIS, decision analysis, and other analytical techniques and contributed greatly to strategic thinking and weapons development during the Cold War. Its work has also included research in education, finance, and politics. Its research has produced many influential papers, such as: *Preliminary Design of an Experimental World-Circling Spaceship* (1946), one of the earliest scientific studies of the possibility of man-made satellites; Williams, *The Compleat Strategyst: Being a Primer on the Theory of Games of Strategy* (1954); Buchheim, *Space Handbook: Astronautics and Its Applications* (1958); Bordie, *Strategy in the Missile Age* (1959); Dole & Asimov, *Planets for Man* (1964). It has produced many papers about a wide range of topics in contracting and logistics. Its publications are available at its website, www.rand.org. See Abella, *Soldiers of Reason: The Rand Corporation and the Rise of the American Empire* (Harcourt, Inc. 2008), and Campbell, *How RAND Invented the Postwar World, Invention & Technology*, Summer 2004, http://www.rand.org/content/dam/rand/www/external/about/history/Rand.IT.Summer04.pdf.

RANDOLPH SHEPPARD ACT   20 U.S.C. § 107 et seq. A socio-economic statute that establishes a program that grants a preference to blind persons licensed by a state government to operate vending facilities and cafeterias under contract on federal property. The Department of Education, Office of Special Education and Rehabilitative Services, implements the program. The implementing regulations are in 34 C.F.R. part 395 and in the Federal Property Management Regulation, 41 C.F.R. § 102-74.40 et seq.

RANGE OF INCENTIVE EFFECTIVENESS (RIE)   Under a COST-PLUS-INCENTIVE-FEE CONTRACT, the dollar range of possible cost outcomes under which the contractor has a monetary incentive to control costs. The contract specifies a MAXIMUM FEE and a MINIMUM FEE which place limits on the sharing required by the incentive formula. The RIE is the range of costs within these limits. If the ALLOWABLE COSTS incurred falls outside of the RIE, the contract becomes, in effect, a COST-PLUS-FIXED-FEE CONTRACT. See Cibinic, Knight & Nash, Cost-Reimbursement Contracting 57–59 (4th ed. 2014); Cibinic, Nash & Yukins, Formation of Government Contracts 1266–67 (4th ed. 2011).

RAPID FIELDING   *Official:* The use of proven technologies to field production quantities of new or upgraded systems with minimal development required. The objective of an acquisition program under this pathway shall be to begin production within six months and complete fielding within five years of the development of an approved requirement. *Source:* § 804 of the National Defense Authorization Act for FY 2016, Pub. L. No. 114-92. This is one of the DoD acquisition techniques authorized as part of the MIDDLE TIER ACQUISITION PROCESS. § 804 calls for a "merit-based process for the consideration of existing products and proven technologies" to meet operational needs taking into consideration life-cycle costs and logistics support. *DoD Acquisition Reform: Leadership Attention Needed to Effectively Implement Changes to Acquisition Oversight*, GAO-19-439 (June 2019), indicates that the military services have used this authority on four programs as of March 2019.

RAPID PROTOTYPING   *Official:* The use of innovative technologies to rapidly develop fieldable prototypes to demonstrate new capabilities and meet emerging military needs. The objective of an acquisition program under this pathway shall be to field a prototype that can be demonstrated in an operational environment and provide for a residual operational capability within five years of the development of an approved requirement. *Source:* § 804 of the National Defense Authorization Act for FY 2016, Pub. L. No. 114-92. This is one of the DoD acquisition techniques authorized as part of the MIDDLE TIER ACQUISITION PROCESS. § 804 calls for a "merit-based process for the consideration of innovative technologies" with cost-sharing, operational demonstration of the prototypes, and a process for transitioning to production using RAPID FIELDING. The Secretary of Defense is required to establish a special rapid prototyping fund to support these programs. *DoD Acquisition Reform: Leadership Attention Needed to Effectively Implement Changes to Acquisition Oversight*, GAO-19-439 (June 2019), indicates that the military services have used this authority on 31 programs as of March 2019.

RATED ORDER   *Official:* A prime contract, a SUBCONTRACT, or a PURCHASE ORDER in support of an approved program issued in accordance with the provisions of the DPAS regulation (15 C.F.R. part 700). *Source:* FAR 11.601. The DPAS regulation is issued by the DEPARTMENT OF COMMERCE which operates the DEFENSE PRIORITIES AND ALLOCATIONS SYSTEM. Rated orders are issued by agencies that have been delegated the authority by the department. FAR 11.603(b); 50 U.S.C. App. § 2061 et seq. Rated orders receive ratings of DX and DO; DX ratings have priority. Contractors and suppliers may be directed to accept rated orders, rearrange production or delivery schedules to accommodate them, or improve shipments against them. See FAR 11.603.

RATIFICATION   *Official:* The act of approving an UNAUTHORIZED COMMITMENT by an official who has the authority to do so. *Source:* FAR 1.602-3(a). Unless a higher-level official is designated by the agency, the HEAD OF THE CONTRACTING ACTIVITY may ratify any unauthorized commitment if (1) supplies or services have been provided to and accepted by the government, (2) the official has the authority to enter into the unauthorized commitment, (3) the contract would have been proper if made by an appropriate contracting officer, (4) the contracting officer reviewing the unauthorized commitment determines the price to be fair and reasonable, (5) the contracting officer recommends payment and legal counsel concurs, (6) funds are available and were available at the time the unauthorized commitment was made, and (7) the ratification is in accordance with any other limitations prescribed under agency procedures. FAR 1.602-3(c). This authority may be delegated to an official no lower than the chief of the contracting office. Ratification can also be accomplished outside of the FAR procedures. Courts and boards of contract appeals also have found that ratification has occurred in the course of contract performance. See Nash & Feldman, GOVERNMENT CONTRACT CHANGES §§ 5:18–5:21 (3d ed. 2006–2020); Cibinic, Nagle & Nash, ADMINISTRATION OF GOVERNMENT CONTRACTS 45–51 (5th ed. 2016).

RATING (SCORING)   In SOURCE SELECTION, the practice of using numbers, adjectives, or symbols as shorthand expressions in order to communicate the merits of offerors and their offers as evaluated in SOURCE SELECTION and facilitate comparisons and tradeoff analyses. Think of the Amazon.com star rating system. The purpose of ratings is to covert voluminous, diverse evaluation findings to a common scale of VALUE, such as 0 to 100 points, in order to simplify and aggregate them into a summary assessment of overall value. The FAR does not require the use of ratings and permits the use of any rating system or combination of systems. See FAR 15.305(a). The system used by most agencies is ADJECTIVAL RATING. Some agencies, such as NASA, use NUMERICAL RATING. Ratings are generally assigned on the basis of both objective and subjective assessments of how well offerors and their offers perform on the nonprice EVALUATION FACTORS FOR AWARD.

RCRA   See RESOURCE CONSERVATION AND RECOVERY ACT.

READILY AVAILABLE PRODUCTS AND SERVICES   *Official:* Any product or service that requires no customization by the vendor and can be ordered directly by customers, to include products and services that only governments buy. *Source:* SECTION 809 PANEL Report, Volume 3. The panel's recommendation 35 calls for new streamlined procedures for these products and services to replace the current procedures for COMMERCIAL ITEMS. No steps have been taken to implement this recommendation.

READILY AVAILABLE WITH CUSTOMIZATION   *Official:* Includes the products and services that are sold in the private sector, including to other public-sector customers, for which customization or manufacturing that is consistent with existing private sector practices is necessary to meet DoD's needs. *Source:* SECTION 809 PANEL Report, Volume 3. The panel's recommendation 35 calls for new streamlined procedures for these products and services to replace the current procedures for COMMERCIAL ITEMS. No steps have been taken to implement this recommendation.

REAL PROPERTY   *Official:* (1) Any interest in land, together with the improvements, structures, and fixtures located thereon (including prefabricated movable structures, such as Butler-type storage warehouses and Quonset huts, and house trailers with or without undercarriages), and appurtenances thereto, under the control of any Federal agency, except—(i) The public domain; (ii) Lands reserved or dedicated for national forest or national park purposes; (iii) Minerals in lands or portions of lands withdrawn or reserved from the public domain that the Secretary of the Interior determines are suitable for disposition under the public land mining and mineral leasing laws; (iv) Lands withdrawn or reserved from the public domain but not including lands or portions of lands so withdrawn or reserved that the Secretary of the Interior, with the concurrence of the Administrator of General Services, determines are not suitable for return to the public domain for disposition under the general public land laws because such lands are substantially changed in character by improvements or otherwise; and (v) Crops when designated by such agency for disposition by severance and removal from the land. (2) Improvements of any kind, structures, and fixtures under the control of any Federal agency when designated by such agency for disposition without the underlying land (including such as may be located on the public domain, on lands withdrawn or reserved from the public domain, on lands reserved or dedicated for national forest or national park purposes, or on lands that are not owned by the United States) excluding, however, prefabricated movable structures, such as Butler-type storage warehouses and Quonset huts, and house trailers (with or without undercarriages). (3) Standing timber and embedded gravel, sand, or stone under the control of any Federal agency, whether designated by such agency for disposition with the land or by severance and removal from the land, excluding timber felled, and gravel, sand, or stone excavated by or for the government prior to disposition. *Source:* 41 C.F.R. § 102-71.20. This definition describes the property that is subject to the policies of the General Services Administration, set forth in 41 C.F.R. parts 102-71 through 102-82. Real property is a component of GOVERNMENT PROPERTY and is therefore subject to FAR Part 45 when it is furnished to a contractor. Purchases of real property are not covered by the FEDERAL ACQUISITION REGULATION or the CONTRACT DISPUTES ACT OF 1978. However, construction contracts are not considered real property for this purpose.

REASONABLE COMPENSATION   *Official:* With respect to a regularly employed officer or employee of any person, compensation that is consistent with the normal compensation for such officer or employee for work that is not furnished to, not funded by, or not furnished in cooperation with the federal government. *Source:* FAR 3.801. When reasonable compensation is paid to an employee of a contractor for rendering professional or technical services rendered directly in the preparation, submission, or negotiation of a bid or proposal, such payments are not subject to the prohibitions on payments for influencing federal transactions in 31 U.S.C. § 1352. FAR 3.803(a)(2).

REASONABLE PRICE   See FAIR AND REASONABLE PRICE.

REASONABLENESS OF COST   One of the elements in the determination of whether a cost is an ALLOWABLE COST. A cost is reasonable if, in its nature and amount, it does not exceed that which would be incurred by a prudent person in the conduct of competitive business. The government attaches no presumption of reasonableness to the incurrence of costs by a contractor. If an initial review of the facts results in the challenge of a specific cost by the contracting officer or the contracting officer's representative, the burden of proof is on the contractor. What is reasonable depends on a variety of considerations and circumstances, including (1) the type of cost generally recognized as ordinary and necessary for the conduct of the contractor's business or the performance of the contract; (2) generally accepted sound business practices, arm's-length bargaining, and federal and state laws and regulations; (3) the contractor's responsibilities to the government, other customers, the owners of the business, employees, and the public at large; and (4) any significant deviations from the contractor's established practices. FAR 31.201-3. See Cibinic, Knight & Nash, Cost-Reimbursement Contracting 570–90 (4th ed. 2014).

RECEIVING REPORT *Official:* Written evidence that indicates government ACCEPTANCE of supplies delivered or services performed (see subpart 46.6). Receiving reports must meet the requirements of 32.905(c). *Source:* FAR 2.101. These reports are prepared by agency officials receiving the supplies or services and forwarded to the DESIGNATED PAYMENT OFFICE by the fifth working day after acceptance or approval. FAR 32.905(c). Generally, INVOICE PAYMENTs are not made until they are supported by a receiving report or other similar documentation. See Cibinic, Nagle & Nash, Administration of Government Contracts, 1031–32 (5th ed. 2016).

RECERTIFICATION (ALSO, RE-CERTIFICATION) See REREPRESENTATION

RECONDITIONED *Official:* Restored to the original normal operating condition by readjustments and material replacement. *Source:* FAR 11.001. When contracting for other than COMMERCIAL ITEMs, agencies must require offerors to identify reconditioned supplies and such supplies may not be furnished unless authorized by the contracting officer. FAR 11.302(b)(1). The Material Requirements solicitation provision in FAR 52.211-5 alerts offerors to this requirement. When contracting for commercial items, agencies have more flexibility in dealing with reconditioned supplies. FAR 11.302(b)(2).

RECORD *Official:* Any item, collection, or grouping of information about an individual that is maintained by an agency, including, but not limited to, education, financial transactions, medical history, and criminal or employment history, and that contains the individual's name, or the identifying number, symbol, or other identifying particular assigned to the individual, such as a fingerprint or voice print or a photograph. *Source:* FAR 24.101. This definition pertains to the Privacy Act of 1974, 5 U.S.C. § 552a which protects against the disclosure of such records. See FAR Subpart 24.1. For the purpose of the Records Disposal Act, "records" also denotes books, papers, maps, photographs, machine-readable materials, or other documentary materials, regardless of physical form or characteristic, made or received by an agency of the government under federal law or in connection with the transaction of public business, and preserved or appropriated for preservation by that agency or its legitimate successor either as evidence of the organization, functions, policies, decisions, procedures, operations, or other activities of the government or because of the informational value of the data in them. Library and museum material made or acquired and preserved solely for reference or exhibition purposes, extra copies of documents preserved only for convenience of reference, and stocks of publications and of processed documents are not included. 44 U.S.C. § 3301. See FAR Subpart 4.7 regarding contractor records and FAR Subpart 4.8 regarding contractual records created by government agencies. The term AGENCY RECORDS is used in conjunction with the FREEDOM OF INFORMATION ACT.

RECORD DRAWINGS *Official:* Drawings submitted by a contractor or subcontractor at any tier to show the CONSTRUCTION of a particular structure or work as actually completed under the contract. *Source:* FAR 36.102. Such drawings are necessary to serve as a basis for any future work on the structure or work. When these drawings are required to be prepared, FAR 36.521 requires the use of alternate versions of the Specifications and Drawings for

Construction clause in FAR 52.236-21. Record drawings are frequently called "as-built drawings." They are often used, in conjunction with AS-PLANNED DRAWINGS, to prove DELAY.

RECORDS DISPOSITION   *Official:* Any activity with respect to (a) disposal of temporary RECORDs no longer necessary for the conduct of business by destruction or donation; (b) transfer of records to federal agency storage facilities or records centers; (c) transfer to the National Archives of the United States of records determined to have sufficient historical or other value to warrant continued preservation; or (d) transfer of records from one federal agency to any other federal agency. *Source:* 44 U.S.C. § 2901(5). Agencies are required to establish records disposition programs, 36 C.F.R. § 1224.10, in accordance with the guidance in 36 C.F.R. § 1220.30 through .34. Guidance is provided in FAR 4.805. See RECORDS MANAGEMENT and RECORDS RETENTION.

RECORDS MANAGEMENT   *Official:* The planning, controlling, directing, organizing, training, promoting, and other managerial activities involved in RECORDs creation, records maintenance and use, and RECORDS DISPOSITION in order to achieve adequate and proper documentation of the policies and transactions of the federal government, and effective and economical management of agency operations. *Source:* 44 U.S.C. § 2901(2). The HEAD OF THE AGENCY is responsible for complying with the records management policies and guidance provided by the Administrator of the General Services Administration and the Archivist of the United States for all media (paper, electronic, or other). See 44 U.S.C. § 2904. Regulations on records management are contained in 36 C.F.R. chap. XII, subchapter B. See RECORDS RETENTION and the National Archives *Records Management Handbook* at https://www.archives.gov/files/records-mgmt/pdf/dfr-2000.pdf.

RECORDS RETENTION   Preserving records for a period of time to ensure that they are available for contractual purposes. The policy on retention of records by contractors and subcontractors is set forth in FAR Subpart 4.7. Specific retention periods are prescribed in FAR 4.705. The policy on retention of contract records by government agencies with specific retention periods is set forth in FAR 4.805.

RECOUPMENT   *Official:* The recovery by the government of government-funded NONRECURRING COSTS from contractors that sell, LEASE, or LICENSE the resulting products or technology to buyers other than the federal government. *Source:* FAR 35.001. FAR 35.003(c) states that recoupment should be "in accordance with agency procedures." Contract clauses calling for recoupment were widely used on DOD contracts in the 1970s and 1980s but are no longer used except on FOREIGN MILITARY SALES (FMS) contracts. Section 4303 of the CLINGER-COHEN ACT amended the Arms Export Control Act, 22 U.S.C. § 2761(e)(2), to permit the President to waive recoupment on foreign military sales. DOD Directive 2140.02, *Recoupment of Nonrecurring Costs (NC) on Sales of U.S. Items*, May 22, 2018. See Cibinic, Knight & Nash, COST-REIMBURSEMENT CONTRACTING 98–99 (4th ed. 2014).

RECOVERED MATERIAL   *Official:* Waste materials and by-products recovered or diverted from solid waste, but the term does not include those materials and by-products generated from, and commonly reused within, an original manufacturing process. For use in subpart 11.3 for paper and paper products, see the definition in 11.301. *Source:* FAR 2.101. The official definition for paper products in FAR 11.301 is: The following materials: (1) Postconsumer fiber. (2) Manufacturing wastes such as—(i) Dry paper and paperboard waste generated after completion of the papermaking process (that is, those manufacturing operations up to and including the cutting and trimming of the paper machine reel into smaller rolls or rough sheets) including: envelope cuttings, bindery trimmings, and other paper and paperboard waste resulting from printing, cutting, forming, and other converting operations; bag, box, and carton manufacturing wastes; and butt rolls, mill wrappers, and rejected unused stock; and (ii) Repulped finished paper and paperboard from obsolete inventories of paper and paperboard manufacturers, merchants, wholesalers, dealers, printers, converters, or others. FAR Subpart 23.4 sets forth the government policy to encourage contractors to use such materials in the performance of their contracts. See RESOURCE CONSERVATION AND RECOVERY ACT.

RECRUITMENT COSTS   The costs of locating and hiring new employees necessary for the performance of the contractor's work. FAR 31.205-34 specifies that such costs, typically including help-wanted ADVERTISING, operating costs of an employment office, aptitude and testing programs, recruiter and prospective employee travel costs, and fees paid to employment agencies, are ALLOWABLE COSTs with certain specified limitations. See Manos, 1 GOVERNMENT CONTRACT COSTS AND PRICING §§ 41:1–41:3 (2d ed. 2009–2020); Cibinic, Knight & Nash, COST-REIMBURSEMENT CONTRACTING 705–06 (4th ed. 2014).

RECURRING COSTS   *Official:* Costs that vary with the quantity being produced, such as LABOR and materials. *Source:* FAR 17.103. Such costs are distinguished from NONRECURRING COSTS. The inclusion of recurring costs in the CANCELLATION CEILING of a MULTI-YEAR CONTRACT awarded by DOD, NASA or the Coast Guard must be approved by the HEAD OF THE AGENCY. FAR 17.106(e). See Cibinic, Nash & Yukins, FORMATION OF GOVERNMENT CONTRACTS 1380–82 (4th ed. 2011).

RED BOOK (Redbook)   A nickname for PRINCIPLES OF FEDERAL APPROPRIATIONS LAW, a multi-volume treatise on fiscal and appropriations law prepared and published by the GOVERNMENT ACCOUNTABILITY OFFICE and available online at https://www.gao.gov/legal/appropriations-law/red-book. The nickname is inspired by the red three-ring binders in which the publication was sold in hard copy by the GOVERNMENT PRINTING OFFICE. This publication contains the most authoritative guidance that is available on the fiscal requirement that pertain to government contracts.

REDETERMINABLE CONTRACT   See FIXED-PRICE REDETERMINATION—PROSPECTIVE CONTRACT and FIXED-PRICE REDETERMINATION—RETROACTIVE CONTRACT. See Cibinic, Nash & Yukins, FORMATION OF GOVERNMENT CONTRACTS 1239–42 (4th ed. 2011).

REDUCTION TO PRACTICE   See FIRST ACTUAL REDUCTION TO PRACTICE.

REFORMATION   An equitable remedy used to alter the language of a written contract to reflect the real agreement between contracting parties when, through either MUTUAL MISTAKE or UNILATERAL MISTAKE coupled with actual or equitable FRAUD by any party, the writing fails to represent the contract the parties made. If the writing does not conform to the parties' agreement, by mistake of fact as to the writing's contents or by mistake of law with regard to the writing's legal effect, the writing can be reformed to accord with the agreement. BLACK'S LAW DICTIONARY 1533 (11th ed. 2019). Contracting agencies can reform their contracts when they have discovered a mistake after award. See FAR 14.407-4 for the procedures to be followed. See also FAR 15.508. Usually a court will not grant reformation unless it can determine from the conduct of the parties the terms of the agreement that they would have agreed to but for the mistake. See, however, *National Presto Industries, Inc. v. United States*, 167 Ct. Cl. 749, 338 F.2d 99 (1964), *cert. denied*, 380 U.S. 962 (1965), where the court granted reformation in the contract price without clear evidence of the price that would have been agreed to. See Cibinic, Nagle & Nash, ADMINISTRATION OF GOVERNMENT CONTRACTS 313–14 (5th ed. 2016).

REGISTERED IN THE SYSTEM FOR AWARD MANAGEMENT (SAM)	*Official:* (1) The Contractor has entered all mandatory information, including the unique entity identifier and the Electronic Funds Transfer indicator (if applicable), the Commercial and Government Entity (CAGE) code, as well as data required by the Federal Funding Accountability and Transparency Act of 2006 (see subpart 4.14), into SAM; (2) The Contractor has completed the Core, Assertions, Representations and Certifications, and Points of Contact sections of the registration in SAM; (3) The Government has validated all mandatory data fields, to include validation of the Taxpayer Identification Number (TIN) with the Internal Revenue Service (IRS). The contractor will be required to provide consent for TIN validation to the Government as a part of the SAM registration process; and (4) The Government has marked the record "Active." *Source:* FAR 2.101. Such registration is required before the submission of a BID or PROPOSAL unless one of the exceptions in FAR 4.1102 applies. See CENTRAL CONTRACTOR REGISTRATION.

REINSTATEMENT OF TERMINATED CONTRACT	The reestablishment, in whole or in part, by mutual consent of the parties, of a contract that was terminated for convenience or default. FAR 49.102(d) and 49.401(e) permit reinstatement if circumstances clearly indicate a requirement for the terminated items and it is advantageous to the government. See Cibinic, Nagle & Nash, ADMINISTRATION OF GOVERNMENT CONTRACTS 870–71 (5th ed. 2016).

REINSURANCE	*Official:* A transaction which provides that a surety, for a consideration, agrees to indemnify another surety against loss which the latter may sustain under a BOND which it has issued. *Source:* FAR 28.001. If the PENAL AMOUNT of a required bond exceeds the underwriting limit of a corporate surety, the bond of that surety will be acceptable if it obtains reinsurance of the excess amount from an acceptable surety. FAR 28.202(a).

REINTEGRATION DATA	See SEGREGATION AND REINTEGRATION DATA

REJECTION OF BID	The determination by the contracting officer that a bid does not conform to the essential requirements of an INVITATION FOR BIDS. Such bids must be rejected as being non-responsive (see RESPONSIVENESS). FAR 14.404-2. However, rejection is not proper if there is only a MINOR INFORMALITY. FAR 14.405. Bids may also be rejected if the BIDDER is found to lack RESPONSIBILITY. All bids may be rejected, and the invitations for bids cancelled before award but after BID OPENING, for reasons including, but not limited to, the following: (1) cancellation is in the public interest, (2) bids were collusive or submitted in bad faith, (3) the supplies or services being procured are no longer needed, or (4) the SPECIFICATIONs have been revised. FAR 14.404-1(c). See Cibinic, Nash & Yukins, FORMATION OF GOVERNMENT CONTRACTS 527–73, 610–24 (4th ed. 2011).

REJECTION OF WORK	The government's refusal to accept work that does not conform to the requirements of a contract. The right of rejection is the initial right granted to the government in the standard INSPECTION clauses used in government contracts. FAR 46.407 states that contracting officers should reject supplies or services not conforming in all respects to contract requirements, but contractors ordinarily should be given an opportunity to correct or replace nonconforming supplies or services when correction or replacement can be accomplished within the required delivery schedule. FAR 46.407(d) permits contracting officers to decide not to reject work when the nonconformance is minor, but FAR 46.407(f) requires that an EQUITABLE ADJUSTMENT reducing the price or other CONSIDERATION be obtained when this is done. See Cibinic, Nagle & Nash, ADMINISTRATION OF GOVERNMENT CONTRACTS 732–46 (5th ed. 2016).

RELATIONAL CONTRACT A nontraditional contract that describes the obligations and rights of the parties in broad terms, with the parties agreeing to work out the details during the course of performance. Instead of detailed and strict terms and conditions, as are found in TRANSACTIONAL CONTRACTS, relational contracts are grounded in a business relationship that is based on trust and a commitment to mutual cooperation. See Macneil, *The Many Futures of Contracts*, SOUTH. CALIF. LAW REV., No. 47, pp. 691–816 (1974); Macneil, THE NEW SOCIAL CONTRACT: AN INQUIRY INTO MODERN CONTRACTUAL RELATIONS (Yale, 1980); Jennings, *The True Meaning of Relational Contracts: We don't Care About the Mailbox Rule, Mirror Images, or Consideration Anymore—Are We Safe?*, DENVER UNIV. LAW REV., No. 73; Campbell, ed., THE RELATIONAL THEORY OF CONTRACT: SELECTED WORKS OF IAN MACNEIL (Sweet & Maxwell, 2001); *Symposium: Relational Contracting in a Digital Age*, TEXAS WESLEYAN LAW REV. 675 (Spring 2005); Edwards & Nash, *A Proposal for a New Approach to Performance-Based Services Acquisition*, Vol. 14, No. 2, p. 353 (Sept. 2007). See also Newman, ed., THE NEW PALGRAVE DICTIONARY OF ECONOMICS AND THE LAW, Vol. 3, *Relational Contracts* (Palgrave Macmillan, 2002).

RELATING TO THE CONTRACT Having a connection with a contract. This term of art is used in the CONTRACT DISPUTES ACT OF 1978 to broaden the scope of the DISPUTEs process to include claims that cannot be resolved through a contract clause providing for the type of relief sought, such as claims for BREACH OF CONTRACT or for correction of MISTAKEs. Prior to the Act, the disputes process covered only claims ARISING UNDER THE CONTRACT. The effect of this broadened scope is to make the current Disputes clause in FAR 52.233-1 an ALL DISPUTES CLAUSE. FAR 33.205 emphasizes the all-encompassing scope of the current clause by stating that many claims previously submitted under Pub. L. No. 85-804 should be handled through the disputes procedures. See Cibinic, Nagle & Nash, ADMINISTRATION OF GOVERNMENT CONTRACTS 1135–36 (5th ed. 2016).

RELATIVE IMPORTANCE The relationship of the EVALUATION FACTORS and subfactors in a competitive NEGOTIATED CONTRACT using the TRADEOFF PROCESS. The REQUEST FOR PROPOSALS must state the relative importance of the evaluation factors and significant subfactors in order to provide prospective offerors with information on which evaluation factors the agency believes to be most important in satisfying the agency's procurement objectives. FAR 15.304(d). There is also a statutory requirement that the RFP state the relative importance of the cost or price factors versus the non-cost or price factors. FAR 15.304(e). The statement of relative importance does not control the ultimate source selection decision because that is made on the basis of trade-offs between the proposals received. See Cibinic, Nash & Yukins, FORMATION OF GOVERNMENT CONTRACTS 720–27 (4th ed. 2011); Edwards, *The Relative Importance of Source Selection Evaluation Factors:*

Analysis of a Misunderstood Rule, 10 N&CR ¶ 34 (July 1996); Nash, *Postscript II: Relative Importance of Evaluation Factors,* 19 N&CR ¶ 1 (Jan. 2005).

RELEASE An agreement of a contracting party that the other party will not be liable if CLAIMs are asserted in the future. An unconditional general release by a contractor bars all existing contractor claims, including pending claims as well as known and unknown claims. The contractor, however, may preserve its rights to specific claims by expressly excepting those claims when the release is executed. The contract may require the contractor to give a release of claims and liabilities before the government makes final payment. FAR 43.204(c)(2) states that contracting officers should insert releases in SUPPLEMENTAL AGREEMENTs settling claims. See Nash & Feldman, GOVERNMENT CONTRACT CHANGES § 22:13 (3d ed. 2006–2020); Cibinic, Nagle & Nash, ADMINISTRATION OF GOVERNMENT CONTRACTS 1107–11 (5th ed. 2016).

RELIANCE DAMAGES A monetary measure of DAMAGES awarded for losses incurred by the plaintiff in reliance on the contract. This type of damages is rarely claimed in litigation regarding PROCUREMENT CONTRACTs because EXPECTANCY DAMAGES generally yield a higher recovery. See Cibinic, Nagle & Nash, ADMINISTRATION OF GOVERNMENT CONTRACTS 616 (5th ed. 2016); Posner, ECONOMIC ANALYSIS OF LAW 130–40 (7th ed. 2007); Cibinic, *Postscript II: Remedies for Faulty Estimates in Requirements Contracts,* 18 N&CR ¶ 11 (Mar. 2004).

RELOCATION COSTS *Official:* The costs incident to the permanent change of work location (for a period of 12 months or more) of an existing employee or upon recruitment of a new employee. *Source:* FAR 31.205-35(a). This regulation specifies that such costs incurred by contractors are ALLOWABLE COSTs if specified limitations are met. Allowable relocation costs include travel and transportation costs, cost of finding a new home, closing costs, mortgage interest differential payments, rental differential payments, and the cost of canceling an unexpired lease. See Manos, 1 GOVERNMENT CONTRACT COSTS AND PRICING §§ 42:1–42:3 (2d ed. 2009–2020); Cibinic, Night & Nash, COST-REIMBURSEMENT CONTRACTING 706–07 (4th ed. 2014).

REMANUFACTURED *Official:* Factory rebuilt to original SPECIFICATIONs. *Source:* FAR 11.001. When contracting for other than COMMERCIAL ITEMs, agencies must require offerors to identify remanufactured supplies and such supplies may not be furnished unless authorized by the contracting officer. FAR 11.302(b)(1). The Material Requirements solicitation provision in FAR 52.211-5 alerts offerors to this requirement. When contracting for commercial items, agencies have more flexibility in dealing with remanufactured supplies. FAR 11.302(b)(2).

REMEDY The right of a contracting party when the other party does not fulfill its contractual obligations. In general, contracting parties have remedies for BREACH OF CONTRACT by the other party. However, in government contracts most of the remedies available to the parties are spelled out in contract clauses. Thus, the government has remedies for non-performance under the TERMINATION FOR DEFAULT clause and for defective performance under the INSPECTION clause of the contract. The contractor's remedies are generally for EQUITABLE ADJUSTMENT or PRICE ADJUSTMENT under a variety of clauses. Prospective contractors also have remedies against the government through the PROTEST procedures.

REMEDY COORDINATION OFFICIAL (RCO)   *Official:* The person or entity in the agency who coordinates within that agency the administration of criminal, civil, administrative, and contractual remedies resulting from investigations of FRAUD or corruption related to procurement activities. *Source:* FAR 32.006-2. The term was created by § 836(a) of the FY 1991 National Defense Authorization Act, Pub. L. No. 101-510. If an agency RCO in DOD or NASA finds substantial evidence that a contractor's request for advance, partial, or PROGRESS PAYMENT under a contract is based on fraud, the RCO must recommend that the head of the agency reduce or suspend further payments to that contractor. 10 U.S.C. § 2307(h)(1). The procedures for this process, which can be used only by DOD and NASA, are in FAR 32.006.

REMEDY GRANTING CLAUSE   A CONTRACT CLAUSE that stipulates the ENTITLEMENT (right) of one party when there is a specified act or failure to act by the other party, or when there is a specified change in the conditions of performance. For example, the Changes clauses, FAR 52.243-1 through -5, stipulate that the contractor will be entitled to an EQUITABLE ADJUSTMENT to the contract price or delivery schedule if the government changes the contract specification and the contractor's cost and/or the time required for performance are increased as a result. The Differing Site Conditions clause, FAR 52.236-2, stipulates that the contractor will be entitled to an equitable adjustment if conditions at the site of the work are found to differ from expectations in specified ways. When a CLAIM can be resolved pursuant to the terms of a remedy granting clause, the claim is said to be a claim ARISING UNDER THE CONTRACT, as distinguished from a claim RELATING TO THE CONTRACT. See Cibinic, Nagle & Nash, ADMINISTRATION OF GOVERNMENT CONTRACTS 1136 (5th ed. 2016).

RENEGOTIATION   The recovery from a contractor of an amount determined to reflect "excessive profits" made in the performance of defense contracts. 50 U.S.C. § 1213 et seq. Renegotiation began in 1942 and ended in 1976 and was carried out, after 1950, by an independent government agency known as the Renegotiation Board. Essentially covering defense and space-related contracts, renegotiation considered a contractor's business in a single, composite assessment each fiscal year. In most cases, the most difficult and complex part of renegotiation was determining the extent to which the contractor's PROFITs were excessive. Contractors were entitled, under the statute, to DE NOVO review of the Renegotiation Board's decision in the Court of Claims.

RENEWABLE ENERGY   *Official:* Energy produced by solar, wind, geothermal, and biomass, landfill gas, ocean (including tidal, wave, current, and thermal), municipal solid waste, or new hydroelectric generation capacity achieved from increased efficiency or additions of new capacity at an existing hydroelectric project (Energy Policy Act of 2005, 42 U.S.C. § 15852). *Source:* FAR 2.101. It is the government's policy to acquire products that use RENEWABLE ENERGY TECHNOLOGY. FAR 23.200(a). See FAR 23.203 calling for the use of ENERGY-EFFICIENT PRODUCTs. FAR 23.205 also calls for making the maximum use of ENERGY-SAVINGS PERFORMANCE CONTRACTs.

RENEWABLE ENERGY TECHNOLOGY   *Official:* Technologies that use RENEWABLE ENERGY to provide light, heat, cooling, or mechanical or electrical energy for use in facilities or other activities; or the use of integrated whole-building designs that rely upon renewable energy resources, including passive solar design. *Source:* FAR 2.101. It is the government's policy to acquire supplies and services that foster markets for this type of technology. FAR 23.200(a). See FAR 23.203 calling for the use of ENERGY-EFFICIENT PRODUCTs. FAR 23.205 also calls for making the maximum use of ENERGY-SAVINGS PERFORMANCE CONTRACTs.

RENTAL COSTS   The costs paid to the owner of real or personal property for the use of that property. FAR 31.205-36 sets forth the rules on when such costs incurred by a contractor are ALLOWABLE COSTs. The cost principle focuses on the reasonableness of the rental costs, considering the following factors: (1) rental costs of similar property; (2) market conditions in the area; (3) type, estimated life, and value of the property; (4) alternatives to the leased asset; and (5) the provisions of the lease. See Manos, 1 GOVERNMENT CONTRACT COSTS AND PRICING §§ 43:1–43:5 (2d ed. 2009–2020); Cibinic, Knight & Nash, COST-REIMBURSEMENT CONTRACTING 717–19 (4th ed. 2014).

RENTAL EQUIVALENT   An evaluation factor, equal to the amount of rent that would normally be charged, that is added to a competitor's offered price to overcome the UNFAIR COMPETITIVE ADVANTAGE gained from the rent-free use of GOVERNMENT PROPERTY. Although FAR 45.202(a) requires the use of such a factor, FAR 45.301(d) requires contractors to pay rent on government property that will be used on fixed price contracts. Such rent is computed in accordance with the Use and Charges clause in FAR 52.245-9 and a rental equivalent could also be computed using this methodology.

REPAIRS AND MAINTENANCE   *Official:* The total endeavor to obtain the expected service during the life of TANGIBLE CAPITAL ASSETs. Maintenance is the regularly recurring activity of keeping assets in normal or expected operating condition while repair is the activity of putting them back into such condition. *Source:* CAS 404, Capitalization of Tangible Assets, 48 C.F.R. § 9904.404-30. Under CAS 409, Depreciation of Tangible Capital Assets, 48 C.F.R. § 9904.409, the costs of repairs and maintenance must be taken into account in estimating the service life of a TANGIBLE CAPITAL ASSET and determining appropriate DEPRECIATION charges. 48 C.F.R. § 9904.409-50(a). See Cibinic, Knight & Nash, COST-REIMBURSEMENT CONTRACTING 708–12 (4th ed. 2014).

REPLACEMENT CONTRACT   A contract issued after a TERMINATION FOR DEFAULT to repurchase the work from another contractor. See FAR 49.402-6. If the amount paid is higher than the price of the terminated contract, the government is entitled to collect the EXCESS COSTS OF REPROCUREMENT from the original contractor. FAR 49.402-6(c). In awarding a replacement contract the contracting officer does not have to obtain FULL AND OPEN COMPETITION because the procurement is on behalf of the defaulted contractor. See Cibinic, Nagle & Nash, ADMINISTRATION OF GOVERNMENT CONTRACTS 899–914 (5th ed. 2016).

REPLACEMENT CONTRACT RULE   In federal appropriations law, a rule which provides that when a contract is terminated for default, the funds obligated under the original contract are available beyond their original period of obligational availability for the purpose of contracting for the completion of the unfinished work. It is an exception to the BONA FIDE NEEDS RULE. GAO, PRINCIPLES OF FEDERAL APPROPRIATIONS LAW: ANNUAL UPDATE TO THE THIRD EDITION, chap. 5, GAO-15-303SP (Washington, D.C.: Mar. 2015). See EXCESS COSTS OF REPROCUREMENT. See Cibinic, Nagle & Nash, ADMINISTRATION OF GOVERNMENT CONTRACTS 918–19 (5th ed. 2016).

REPLENISHMENT PARTS   *Official:* Repairable or consumable parts acquired after the initial provisioning process. *Source:* DFARS 217.7501. The policies on acquisition of replenishment parts by DOD agencies are set forth in DFARS Subpart 217.75. Full and open competition is required unless data are not available—in which case, detailed policies are prescribed to obtain competition whenever possible. DFARS 217.7502(b). Price increases by sole source contractors of 25% or more above the prior year price are subject to special procedures set forth in DFARS 217.7505. See Nash & *Rawicz*, Intellectual Property in Government Contracts 1149–82 (6th ed. 2008).

REPOSITORY   See DATA REPOSITORY.

REPUDIATION   Rejection, disclaimer, or renunciation. Repudiation of a contract is the refusal to perform a duty or obligation owed to the other party. It may consist of words or actions. Repudiation of a contract before the performance is due serves as an anticipatory BREACH OF CONTRACT but does not constitute a breach unless the other party elects to treat it as such. Black's Law Dictionary 1559 (11th ed. 2019). If the contractor, at any time, repudiates the contract, the government can terminate the contract for default (see TERMINATION FOR DEFAULT). Repudiations may be withdrawn, however, if the withdrawal occurs before the termination action. U.C.C. § 2-611. Repudiation is sometimes called ANTICIPATORY REPUDIATION. See Cibinic, Nagle & Nash, Administration of Government Contracts 835–42 (5th ed. 2016).

REPURCHASE AGAINST CONTRACTOR'S ACCOUNT   See EXCESS COSTS OF REPROCUREMENT and REPLACEMENT CONTRACT.

REQUEST FOR CONTRACT   See PURCHASE REQUEST.

REQUEST FOR EQUITABLE ADJUSTMENT (REA)   A request by one of the contracting parties for an EQUITABLE ADJUSTMENT under a contract clause providing for such adjustment. Contractors frequently submit an REA to indicate to the contracting officer that they want to avoid litigation by negotiating a settlement. Most REAs are submitted by contractors under the CHANGEs clause of the contract, which generally requires that the assertion of the right to an adjustment must be submitted within 30 days of receipt of a CHANGE ORDER. However, this time limitation is enforced only when the government has been prejudiced by late submission of the request. REAs exceeding the SIMPLIFIED ACQUISITION THRESHOLD submitted to DOD agencies must be certified that the request is made in good faith and that the supporting data are accurate and complete, DFARS 243.204-71. The Requests for Equitable Adjustment clause in DFARS 252.243-7002 is included in contracts to alert contractors to this requirement. If a contractor calls a submission an REA but it has the indicia of a CLAIM, it will be treated as a claim by a BOARD OF CONTRACT APPEALS or the COURT OF FEDERAL CLAIMS. See Nash & Feldman, Government Contract Changes § 16:32 (3d ed. 2006–2020); Cibinic, Nagle & Nash, Administration of Government Contracts, chap. 8 (5th ed. 2016). The government can also submit an REA to a contractor when the CONTRACTING OFFICER determines that a downward adjustment in the price is warranted. See Zupa, *When Is A Claim Not A Claim?*, Pub. Cont. L.J. 22 (Summer 1993); Johnson, *A Retrospective on the Contract Disputes Act*, Pub. Cont. L.J. 28 (Summer 1999); Nash & Edwards, *Requests for Equitable Adjustments vs. Claims: Is There a Difference?* 26 N&CR ¶ 10 (Feb. 2012); Nash & Edwards, *Postscript: Requests for Equitable Adjustments vs. Claims*, 26 N&CR ¶ 42 (Aug. 2012); Nash & Edwards, *Postscript II: Requests for Equitable Adjustments vs. Claims*, 26

N&CR ¶ 51 (Oct. 2012); Nash, *Postscript III: Requests for Equitable Adjustments vs. Claims* (Nov. 2012); Nash, *Postscript IV: Requests for Equitable Adjustments vs. Claims*, 30 N&CR ¶ (Feb. 2016); Nash, *Postscript V: Requests for Equitable Adjustment vs. Claims*, 33 NCR-NL ¶ 58 (Oct. 2019); Edwards, *Postscript VI: Request for Equitable Adjustment vs. Claim*, 33 NCR-NL ¶ 65 (Nov. 2019).

REQUEST FOR INFORMATION (RFI)   A request for information used when the government does not presently intend to award a contract but needs to obtain price, delivery, other market information, or capabilities for planning purposes. Responses to these notices are not OFFERs and cannot be accepted by the government to form a binding contract. There is no required format for RFIs. FAR 15.201(e). RFIs are one of the recommended techniques to improve communication between an agency and its potential contractors. FAR 15.201(c).

REQUEST FOR PROPOSALS (RFP)   A SOLICITATION document used in negotiated procurements (see NEGOTIATION) to communicate government requirements to prospective contractors and to solicit PROPOSALs from them. RFPs must contain the information necessary to enable prospective contractors to prepare proposals properly. FAR 15.203. RFPs generally contain essentially all the terms and conditions of the prospective contract, except price or estimated cost, and are prepared using the UNIFORM CONTRACT FORMAT shown at FAR 15.204-1. When an RFP so states, the government reserves the right to award a contract on the basis of initial offers received, without any written or oral DISCUSSION with offerors. An RFP can be compared with a REQUEST FOR QUOTATIONS (RFQ), the other type of solicitation document used in negotiated procurement. An RFP solicits a binding OFFER, whereas an RFQ solicits information rather than binding offers. Compare Standard Form 33, Solicitation, Offer and Award, FAR 53.301-33 with Standard Form 18, Request for Quotations, FAR 53.301-18. See Cibinic, Nash & Yukins, FORMATION OF GOVERNMENT CONTRACTS 727–49 (4th ed. 2011).

REQUEST FOR QUOTATIONS (RFQ)   A solicitation document (usually Standard Form 18, FAR 53.301-18) used in SIMPLIFIED ACQUISITIONs to communicate government requirements to prospective contractors and to obtain pricing and other information regarding a prospective procurement. FAR 13.307(b)(1). As it is merely a request for information, QUOTATIONs submitted in response to it are not OFFERs, and consequently may not be accepted by the government to form a binding contract. (A contract comes into being only when the supplier accepts the government's order in response to its quotation or the parties mutually agree to a subsequent contract.) FAR 13.004. An RFQ is also used when procuring services that require a STATEMENT OF WORK from FEDERAL SUPPLY SCHEDULE contractors. FAR 8.405-1(d) and 8.405-2(c). RFQs are also used to obtain information for orders under TASK ORDER CONTRACTs and DELIVERY ORDER CONTRACTs. For simplified acquisitions, quotations may be solicited orally rather than in writing whenever economical and practical. FAR 13.106-1(c). See Cibinic, Nash & Yukins, FORMATION OF GOVERNMENT CONTRACTS 234–36, 1172–75 (4th ed. 2011).

REQUEST FOR TECHNICAL PROPOSALS (RFTP)   A solicitation document used in the first step of TWO-STEP SEALED BIDDING to determine the acceptability of the supplies or services offered. FAR 14.501(a). FAR 14.503-1 requires that RFTPs include, at a minimum, the following: (1) a description of the supplies or services required; (2) a statement of intent to use the two-step method; (3) the requirements of the proposal; (4) the evaluation factors; (5) a statement that proposals are not to include prices or pricing information;

(6) the time by which proposals must be received; (7) a statement that, in the second step, only bids based on proposals determined to be acceptable, either initially or as a result of discussions, will be considered for award, and that each bid in the second step must be based on the bidder's own proposal; (8) a statement that offerors should submit proposals acceptable without additional explanation, and that proposals may be evaluated as submitted or after discussion; (9) a statement that a notice of unacceptability will be forwarded to unsuccessful offerors following proposal evaluation; and (10) a statement about whether multiple proposals may be submitted. See Cibinic, Nash & Yukins, FORMATION OF GOVERNMENT CONTRACTS 656–68 (4th ed. 2011).

REQUESTING AGENCY   *Official:* The agency that has a requirement for an INTER-AGENCY ACQUISITION. *Source:* FAR 2.101. Requesting agencies can use an ASSISTED ACQUISITION or a DIRECT ACQUISITION. FAR 17.502-1. Procedures for making such requests are set forth in FAR Subpart 17.5. See Cibinic, Nash & Yukins, FORMATION OF GOVERNMENT CONTRACTS, chap. 8 (4th ed. 2011).

REQUIRED IN THE PERFORMANCE OF A CONTRACT   A term used in FAR 31.205-18 requiring that costs "required in the performance of a contract" not be treated as INDEPENDENT RESEARCH AND DEVELOPMENT. The courts have reached different conclusions as to the meaning of the term—some holding that the terms covers costs *explicitly* required to be incurred by the terms of a contract and others holding that costs can be *implicitly* required if the costs necessarily must be incurred in order to complete the contract work. See Nash & Rawicz, INTELLECTUAL PROPERTY IN GOVERNMENT CONTRACTS 512–14 (6th ed. 2008). See also Manos, *Postscript: Independent Research and Development Costs*, 20 N&CR ¶2 (Jan. 2006); Nash, *Independent Research and Development Costs: Distinguishing Direct Costs*, 18 N&CR ¶39 (Sept. 2004).

REQUIRED SOURCES OF SUPPLIES AND SERVICES   Mandatory sources from which the government must (frequently in accordance with statutory requirements) buy specific products or services. Such sources are designated in FAR Part 8. Agencies must satisfy requirements for supplies and services from or through the following sources, listed in descending order of priority. **Supplies**—from (1) agency inventories; (2) EXCESS PERSONAL PROPERTY from other agencies; (3) FEDERAL PRISON INDUSTRIES, INC.; (4) procurement lists of products available from the Committee for Purchase from PEOPLE WHO ARE BLIND OR SEVERELY DISABLED; (5) wholesale supply sources, such as stock programs of the General Services Administration, the Defense Logistics Agency, the Department of Veterans Affairs, and military inventory control points; (6) mandatory FEDERAL SUPPLY SCHEDULES (FSS); (7) optional FSS; and (8) commercial sources. **Services**—from (1) procurement lists of services available from the Committee for Purchase from People Who Are Blind or Severely Disabled; (2) mandatory FSS; (3) optional FSS; (4) Federal Prison Industries, Inc. or commercial sources. FAR 8.001. See Cibinic, Nash & Yukins, FORMATION OF GOVERNMENT CONTRACTS 356–61 (4th ed. 2011).

REQUIREMENT   A statement of an agency need for supplies or services. FAR 11.002 encourages agencies to establish their requirements so that they allow full and open competition and can be met with commercial supplies or services, to allow potential offerors to comment on the requirements, and to modify requirements to achieve these goals. FAR Part 11 contains guidance on the drafting and maintenance of REQUIREMENTS DOCUMENTs.

See Cibinic, Nash & Yukins, FORMATION OF GOVERNMENT CONTRACTS 362–85 (4th ed. 2011).

REQUIREMENTS CONTRACT   *Official:* A contract that provides for filling all actual purchase REQUIREMENTs of designated government activities for supplies or services during a specified contract period (from one contractor), with deliveries or performance to be scheduled by placing orders with the contractor. *Source:* FAR 16.503(a). The contractor is legally bound to such a contract because the government's promise to buy its requirements constitutes CONSIDERATION. A requirements contract may be used when the government anticipates recurring requirements but cannot predetermine the precise quantities of supplies or services that designated government activities will need. FAR 16.503(b). Funds are obligated by each order, not by the contract itself. Requirements contracts are a type of INDEFINITE-DELIVERY CONTRACT. They may permit faster deliveries than the other two types—DEFINITE-QUANTITY CONTRACTs and INDEFINITE-QUANTITY CONTRACTs—when production lead time is involved, because a contractor is usually willing to maintain limited stocks when the government will obtain all of its actual purchase requirements from the contractor. In spite of the definition that requirements contracts call for purchasing *all* of an agency's requirement from a single contractor, such contracts have been used to purchase all supplies and services in excess of those that can be provided by a government activity or to purchase a stated percentage of the activity's requirements. See the Requirements clause in FAR 52.216-21 (for purchasing all requirements), Alternate I (for purchasing requirements in excess of agency capability), Alternate II (allowing purchase of brand name products from other sources), Alternate III (for shared requirements between set-aside and non-set-aside contractors), Alternate IV (for both brand name and set-aside situations). See Cibinic, Nash & Yukins, FORMATION OF GOVERNMENT CONTRACTS 1336–63 (4th ed. 2011); Nash, *Requirements Contracts: Now You See Them, Now You Don't,* 25 N&CR ¶ 33 (July 2011).

REQUIREMENTS DOCUMENT   A government document that states a government REQUIREMENT in terms that make it suitable for use in an ACQUISITION. Such documents are stated in terms of functions to be performed, performance required or essential physical characteristics and must define requirements to allow the furnishing of COMMERCIAL ITEMs when feasible. FAR 11.002(a)(2). Performance-oriented documents are preferred over detailed design-oriented documents. FAR 11.101(a). Guidance on the drafting and maintenance of requirements documents is contained in FAR Part 11. See Cibinic, Nash & Yukins, FORMATION OF GOVERNMENT CONTRACTS 362–85 (4th ed. 2011).

REQUIREMENTS-TYPE CONTRACTS   Two or more contracts that provide that all actual purchase requirements of designated government activities for specific supplies or services during a specified contract period will be obtained from the holders of these contracts. As in a REQUIREMENTS CONTRACT, deliveries are scheduled as orders are placed and funds are obligated by each order, not by the contract itself. These contracts are not described in the FAR but have been recognized by the courts. See *Ace-Federal Reporters, Inc. v. Barram,* 226 F.3d 1329 (Fed. Cir. 2000). They provide an effective way to obtain commitments from a group of contractors when the government has a recurring need for supplies or services that can be furnished by a large number of contractors. See Cibinic, Nash & Yukins, FORMATION OF GOVERNMENT CONTRACTS 1344–47 (4th ed. 2011).

REQUIRING AGENCY *Official:* The agency needing the supplies or services. *Source:* FAR 8.401. This is the REQUESTING AGENCY that orders supplies or services from the FEDERAL SUPPLY SCHEDULE.

REQUISITION See PURCHASE REQUEST.

REREPRESENTATION The requirement that a contractor rerepresent (recertify) its small business size and socioeconomic status as prescribed in FAR 19.301-2, *Rerepresentation by a contractor that represented itself as a small business concern,* or FAR 19.301-3, *Rerepresentation by a contractor that represented itself as other than a small business concern.* See 13 C.F.R. § 121.404, *When is the size status of a business concern determined?* See also Chudd & Specht, *Small Business Issues in Government Contracts Mergers & Acquisitions,* BRIEFING PAPERS NO. 14-9 (Aug. 2014).

RESCISSION OF BUDGET AUTHORITY An action by the president that rescinds all or part of any BUDGET AUTHORITY. 2 U.S.C. § 683. A rescission is a type of presidential IMPOUNDMENT. This action is taken whenever the president determines that all or part of any budget authority will not be required to carry out the full objectives or scope of programs for which it is provided or that such budget authority should be rescinded for fiscal policy or other reasons, or whenever all or part of budget authority provided for only one fiscal year is to be reserved from obligation for such FISCAL YEAR. A rescission must be communicated to the Congress by the president in a special message. Any amount of budget authority proposed to be rescinded must be made available for obligation unless, within the prescribed 45-day period, the Congress has completed action on a rescission bill rescinding all or part of the amount proposed to be rescinded. Funds made available for obligation under this procedure may not be proposed for rescission again. See DEFERRAL OF BUDGET AUTHORITY.

RESCISSION OF CONTRACT The relieving of a party from all obligations under a contract. Rescission is a remedy for MUTUAL MISTAKE, when REFORMATION is not possible, and for other defects in contract formation such as DURESS, FRAUD, MISREPRESENTATION, and UNCONSCIONABILITY. AVOIDANCE is used to mean rescission when the party to the contract exercises the right on its own initiative. See Cibinic, Nagle & Nash, ADMINISTRATION OF GOVERNMENT CONTRACTS 314 (5th ed. 2016).

RESEARCH Effort directed toward increasing knowledge by study and experimentation. Research is generally divided into BASIC RESEARCH and APPLIED RESEARCH. FAR Part 35 provides guidance on contracting for research. Research is also supported by GRANTs and COOPERATIVE AGREEMENTs. See also RESEARCH AND DEVELOPMENT.

RESEARCH AND DEVELOPMENT (R&D) Effort that constitutes either RESEARCH or DEVELOPMENT or both. FAR Part 35 prescribes policies and procedures that apply government-wide to R&D contracting and the PROVISION AND CLAUSE MATRIX in FAR 52.300 provides guidance on the solicitation provisions and contract clauses to be used in R&D contracts. R&D contracts are to be used only to acquire supplies or services for the direct benefit or use of the federal government. If the goal is to stimulate or support R&D for some other public purpose, GRANTs or COOPERATIVE AGREEMENTs are appropriate. Further, it is important to distinguish R&D contracting from INDEPENDENT RESEARCH AND DEVELOPMENT, which is defined and discussed at FAR 31.205-18.

In many agencies, the funds to support R&D are contained in a separate APPROPRIATION (such as the research, development, test, and evaluation appropriation for DOD). See Szeliga, *Alternative Agreements for Research and Development With NASA*, BRIEFING PAPERS No. 18-4 (Mar. 2018).

RESEARCH AND DEVELOPMENT POOL   A group of concerns that have associated together in order to obtain and perform, jointly or in conjunction with each other, research and development contracts and that meet the requirements for a POOL. With minor exceptions, these pools must be treated in the same manner as a single contractor when contracting for RESEARCH AND DEVELOPMENT. FAR 9.702. FAR Subpart 9.7 contains the rules governing contracting with these pools.

RESEARCH ANNOUNCEMENT   A NASA BROAD AGENCY ANNOUNCEMENT informing researchers of areas of interest to the agency. For guidance on responses see the NASA Guidebook for Proposers, Mar. 2018 (http://www.hq.nasa.gov/office/procurement/nraguidebook/proposer2018.pdf). See 48 C.F.R. § 1835.016-71.

RESEARCH, DEVELOPMENT, TEST, AND EVALUATION (RDT&E)   One of the major APPROPRIATION categories that is used to furnish funds to DOD. See RESEARCH AND DEVELOPMENT; TEST AND EVALUATION.

RESEARCH OPPORTUNITY   An area of RESEARCH for which an agency has issued a BROAD AGENCY ANNOUNCEMENT. NASA issues RESEARCH ANNOUNCEMENTs. Similar announcements are issued by the National Science Foundation (www.nsf.gov/funding), and the Environmental Protection Agency (www.epa.gov/epahome/grants.htm).

RESEARCH TAX CREDIT   A tax credit against corporate income taxes in the various amounts up to 20% of additional costs of research funded by a company. 26 U.S.C. § 41. Costs incurred on COST-REIMBURSEMENT CONTRACTs are not funded by a company, but costs incurred on a FIXED-PRICE CONTRACT have been held to be funded by a company. See U.S. GOV'T ACCOUNTABILITY OFFICE, TAX POLICY: THE RESEARCH TAX CREDIT'S DESIGN AND ADMINISTRATION CAN BE IMPROVED, GAO-10-136 (Nov. 2007).

RESIDUAL POWERS   The power to take any EXTRAORDINARY CONTRACTUAL ACTION under Pub. L. No. 85-804 other than agreeing to a CONTRACT ADJUSTMENT or an ADVANCED PAYMENT. FAR 50.104. The procedures to be followed in exercising these broad, essentially undefined, powers are described in FAR 50.104-1 through -4. The major use of these powers is to agree to INDEMNIFICATION of a contractor when it is entering into a contract involving unusually hazardous or nuclear risks, FAR 50.104-3.

RESIDUAL VALUE   *Official:* The proceeds, less removal and disposal costs, if any, realized upon disposition of a TANGIBLE CAPITAL ASSET. It usually is measured by the net proceeds from the sale or other disposition of the ASSET, or its fair value if the asset is traded in on another asset. The estimated residual value is a current forecast of the residual value. *Source:* FAR 2.101. CAS 409, Depreciation of Tangible Capital Assets, 48 C.F.R. § 9904.409, requires that DEPRECIATION be computed on the acquisition cost of an asset, less its estimated residual value. See FAR 31.205-11(a) stating that the estimated residual value need not be deducted from the cost of the asset unless it exceeds 10%. See Cibinic, Knight & Nash, COST-REIMBURSEMENT CONTRACTING 708–13 (4th ed. 2014).

RESOURCE CONSERVATION AND RECOVERY ACT (RCRA)   42 U.S.C. § 6962. A 1976 Act that establishes government policy on conservation of resources. The Act requires agencies responsible for drafting or reviewing SPECIFICATIONs to ensure that government specifications and STANDARDs do not exclude the use of RECOVERED MATERIALS, do not require the item to be manufactured from virgin materials, but do require the use of recovered materials to the maximum extent possible without jeopardizing the intended end use of the item. The Act is implemented in FAR Subpart 23.4. The government's policy is to acquire items composed of the highest percentage of recovered materials practicable, consistent with maintaining a satisfactory level of competition, without adversely affecting performance requirements or exposing suppliers' employees to undue hazards from the recovered materials. FAR 23.403.

RESPONDENT   In a contract DISPUTE, the party that must file an ANSWER to a COMPLAINT presented by an APPELLANT before a BOARD OF CONTRACT APPEALS. The contracting agency is always the respondent because the contractor is required to initiate appeals before the boards of contract appeals.

RESPONSIBILITY   The status of a prospective contractor determining that it has the capability, tenacity, and perseverance to perform a contract. 10 U.S.C. § 2305(b) and 41 U.S.C. § 3702(b) and § 3703(c) require that contracts be awarded to responsible contractors only. FAR 9.103(b) implements this requirement by stating that contracting officers should make an "affirmative determination" of responsibility before making an award. The contracting officer's signature on a contract constitutes a determination that the prospective contractor is responsible with respect to that contract. If a contracting officer makes a determination of nonresponsibility, a written statement must be included in the contract file giving the reasons for such determination. FAR 9.105-2. FAR 9.104-1 lists the general standards a contractor must meet to be considered responsible: (1) have or be able to obtain adequate financial resources to perform the contract; (2) be able to comply with the required or proposed delivery or performance schedule, taking into consideration all existing commercial and government business commitments; (3) have a satisfactory performance record; (4) have a satisfactory record of integrity and business ethics; (5) have or be able to obtain the necessary organization, experience, accounting and operational controls, and technical skills; (6) have or be able to obtain the necessary production, construction, and technical equipment and facilities; and (7) be otherwise qualified and eligible to receive an award under applicable laws and regulations. A PREAWARD SURVEY can be used when the information available is insufficient to permit the contracting officer to make a determination regarding responsibility. FAR 9.105-1. If the prospective contractor is a SMALL BUSINESS CONCERN, the SMALL BUSINESS ADMINISTRATION can issue a CERTIFICATE OF COMPETENCY overriding a determination of nonresponsibility in almost all procurements. FAR Subpart 19.6. See Cibinic, Nash & Yukins, FORMATION OF GOVERNMENT CONTRACTS 409–38 (4th ed. 2011). See also Manuel, CONG. RESEARCH SERV., Report No. R40633, RESPONSIBILITY DETERMINATIONS UNDER THE FEDERAL ACQUISITION REGULATION: LEGAL STANDARDS AND PROCEDURES (Aug. 18, 2010); Nash, *Challenging Affirmative Responsibility Determinations: A Rare Animal*, 22 N&CR ¶ 70 (Dec. 2008); Nash, *Responsibility vs. Qualification: A Close Distinction*, 20 N&CR ¶ 47 (Oct. 2006).

RESPONSIBLE AUDIT AGENCY   *Official:* The agency that is responsible for performing all required contract audit services at a business unit. *Source:* FAR 2.101. For contractors other than educational institutions and nonprofit organizations, the DEFENSE CONTRACT AUDIT AGENCY is generally the responsible audit agency. FAR 42.101(b). See FAR Subpart 42.1 for guidance on contract audit services. See Cibinic, Knight & Nash, COST-REIMBURSEMENT CONTRACTING 850–51 (4th ed. 2014).

RESPONSIBLE PROSPECTIVE CONTRACTOR   *Official:* A contractor that meets the standards in 9.104. *Source:* FAR 2.101. These standards are the detailed guidance on the RESPONSIBILITY determination.

RESPONSIVENESS   An objective, nondiscretionary determination by the contracting officer, at the time of opening of sealed bids (see SEALED BIDDING), that a bid conforms to the INVITATION FOR BIDS (IFBs). 10 U.S.C. § 2305(b)(3) and 41 U.S.C. § 3702(b) require a bid to conform in all material respects to the IFB in order to be considered for award. This requirement for compliance ensures that all bidders stand on an equal footing and maintains the integrity of the sealed bidding system. FAR 14.301. Any bid that fails to conform to the IFB's essential requirements must be rejected. FAR 14.404-2. Bids should be filled out, executed, and submitted in accordance with the IFB's instructions. If a bidder uses its own bid form or a letter to submit a bid, the bid may be considered only if (1) the bidder accepts all the terms and conditions of the IFB and (2) award on the bid would result in a binding contract with terms and conditions that do not vary from those of the IFB. FAR 14.301(d). Bids are still considered responsive if they contain MINOR INFORMALITIES—variations from the exact requirements of the IFB that can be corrected or waived without being prejudicial to other bidders. FAR 14.405. The concept of responsiveness does not apply to procurements by NEGOTIATION. See Cibinic, Nash & Yukins, FORMATION OF GOVERNMENT CONTRACTS 527–73 (4th ed. 2011).

REPROCUREMENT   See EXCESS COSTS OF REPROCUREMENT.

REQUIREMENTS ANALYSIS   The formal, systematic process of defining user needs and objectives in the context of planned use, environments, and identified system characteristics to determine requirements for systems functions. DAU, SYSTEMS ENGINEERING FUNDAMENTALS, chap. 4 (2001). More generally, any process used to determine the essential attributes of supplies or services to be acquired. Guidance on establishing requirements documents for acquisitions is found in FAR Subparts 11.1, 11.2, and 11.3.

RESTATEMENT OF THE LAW OF CONTRACTS   A methodical summary of the common law of contracts, prepared and adopted by the American Law Institute. The first RESTATEMENT was adopted in 1932, the second in 1981. THE RESTATEMENT is composed of statements of each legal rule, followed by comments and factual examples. It attempts to state the current legal rules being applied by the courts of the various states. The RESTATEMENT is frequently cited by the courts and either followed or distinguished. [American Law Institute, 4025 Chestnut St., Philadelphia, PA 19104; www.ali.org.]

RESTITUTION   A cause of action against a party that has been "unjustly enriched" at the expense of the party filing the action. This cause of action should be distinguished from an action for BREACH OF CONTRACT because there is no promise that has been breached when there has merely been unjust enrichment. Actions of this nature are frequently called actions for "quasi-contracts" or "contracts implied in law." The COURT OF FEDERAL CLAIMS has no jurisdiction over contracts for restitution. 28 U.S.C. § 1491(a)(1). The BOARDs OF CONTRACT APPEALS have also held that they have no jurisdiction over such actions. See Cibinic, Nash & Yukins, FORMATION OF GOVERNMENT CONTRACTS 252–56 (4th ed. 2011). See also RESTITUTIONARY DAMAGES.

RESTITUTIONARY DAMAGES   A remedy for BREACH OF CONTRACT in which damages are measured on the basis of the benefit that a breach confers on the breaching party, instead of the effect of the breach on the injured party. This measure of damages is rarely used in government breaches of PROCUREMENT CONTRACTs.

RESTRICTED COMPUTER SOFTWARE   *Official:* COMPUTER SOFTWARE DEVELOPED AT PRIVATE EXPENSE and that is a TRADE SECRET, that is commercial or financial and confidential or privileged, or is copyrighted computer software, including minor modifications of the computer software. *Source:* FAR 27.401. Under the Rights in Data—General clause in FAR 52.227-14, the contractor is entitled to assert RESTRICTED RIGHTS in such software if it is required to be delivered to the government. The term is not used in the DOD computer software policies but the same rights apply. See Nash & Rawicz, INTELLECTUAL PROPERTY IN GOVERNMENT CONTRACTS, chap. 5 (6th ed. 2008).

RESTRICTED DATA   *Official:* All data concerning (1) the design, manufacture, or utilization of atomic weapons; (2) the production of special nuclear material; or (3) the use of special nuclear material in the production of energy, except for data declassified or removed from the restricted data category, pursuant to Section 142, as amended, of the Atomic Energy Act of 1954 (42 U.S.C. § 2162). *Source:* 42 U.S.C. § 2014(y); 48 C.F.R. § 904.401. 42 U.S.C. § 2161 et seq. provides rules on the handling and declassification of such data. Severe penalties are imposed on persons disclosing restricted data, 42 U.S.C. § 2274 et seq. The DOE regulations on restricted data are in 10 C.F.R. part 1045.

RESTRICTED RIGHTS   *Official:* The rights of the government in RESTRICTED COMPUTER SOFTWARE as set forth in a RESTRICTED RIGHTS NOTICE. *Source:* FAR 27.401. In ¶(a) of the Rights in Data—General clause in FAR 52.227-14 the term restricted rights is defined as: "The rights of the government in restricted computer software, as set forth in a Restricted Rights Notice of ¶(g), or as otherwise may be provided in a collateral agreement incorporated in and made part of this contract, including minor modifications of such computer software." The Notice states that restricted right computer software: "May be—(1) Used or copied for use with the computer(s) for which it was acquired, including use at any Government installation to which the computer(s) may be transferred; (2) Used or copied for use with a backup computer if any computer for which it was acquired is inoperative; (3) Reproduced for safekeeping (archives) or backup purposes; (4) Modified, adapted, or combined with other computer software, provided that the modified, adapted, or combined portions of the derivative software incorporating any of the delivered, restricted computer software shall be subject to the same restricted rights; (5) Disclosed to and reproduced for use by support service Contractors or their subcontractors in accordance with paragraphs (b)(1) through (4) of this notice; and (6) Used or copied for use with a replacement computer." In DOD contracts ¶(a)(15) of the Rights in Noncommercial Computer Software and Noncommercial Computer Software Documentation clause at DFARS 252.227-7014, defines the term restricted rights as: "The Government's rights to—(i) Use a computer program with one computer at one time. The program may not be accessed by more than one terminal or central processing unit or time shared unless otherwise permitted by this contract; (ii) Transfer a computer program to another Government agency without the further permission of the Contractor if the transferor destroys all copies of the program and related computer software documentation in its possession and notifies the licensor of the transfer. Transferred programs remain subject to the provisions of this clause; (iii) Make the minimum number of copies of the computer software required for safekeeping (archive), backup, or modification purposes; (iv) Modify computer software provided that the Government may—(A) Use the modified software only as provided in paragraphs (a)(15)(i) and (iii) of this clause; and (B) Not release or disclose the modified software except as provided in paragraphs (a)(15)(ii), (v), (vi), and (vii) of this clause; (v) Permit contractors or subcontractors performing service contracts (see 37.101 of the Federal Acquisition Regulation) in support of this or a related contract to use computer software to diagnose and correct deficiencies in a computer program, to modify computer software to enable a computer program to be combined with, adapted to, or merged with other computer programs or when necessary to respond to urgent tactical situations, provided that— (A) The Government notifies the party which has granted restricted rights that a release or disclosure to particular contractors or subcontractors was made; (B) Such contractors or subcontractors are subject to the use and non-disclosure agreement at 227.7103-7 of the Defense Federal Acquisition Regulation Supplement (DFARS) or are Government contractors receiving access to the software for performance of a Government contract that contains the clause at DFARS 252.227-7025, Limitations on the Use or Disclosure of Government-Furnished Information Marked with Restrictive Legends; (C) The Government shall not permit the recipient to decompile, disassemble, or reverse engineer the software, or use software decompiled, disassembled, or reverse engineered by the Government pursuant to paragraph (a)(15)(iv) of this clause, for any other purpose; and (D) Such use is subject to the limitation in paragraph (a)(15)(i) of this clause; (vi) Permit contractors or subcontractors performing emergency repairs or overhaul of items or components of items procured under this or a related contract to use the computer software when necessary to perform the repairs or overhaul, or to modify the computer software to reflect the repairs or overhaul made, provided that—(A) The intended recipient is subject to the use and non-disclosure agreement at DFARS 227.7103-7 or is a Government contractor receiving access to the software for performance of a Government contract that contains the clause at DFARS 252.227-7025, Limitations on the Use or Disclosure of Government-Furnished Information Marked with Restrictive Legends; and (B) The Government shall not permit the recipient to decompile, disassemble, or reverse engineer the software, or use software decompiled, disassembled, or reverse engineered by the Government pursuant to paragraph (a)(15)(iv) of this clause, for any other purpose; and (vii) Permit covered Government support contractors to use, modify, reproduce, perform, display, or release or disclose the computer software to authorized person(s) in the performance of Government contracts that contain the clause at 252.227-7025, Limitations on the Use or Disclosure of Government-Furnished Information Marked with Restrictive Legends." These broad rights pertain to computer software DEVELOPED AT PRIVATE EXPENSE or DEVELOPED EXCLUSIVELY AT PRIVATE EXPENSE. (The comparable term relating to TECHNICAL DATA is LIMITED RIGHTS). See Nash & Rawicz, INTELLECTUAL PROPERTY IN GOVERNMENT CONTRACTS, chap. 5 (6th ed. 2008); DeVecchio, *Technical Data & Computer Software After Night Vision: Marking, Delivery & Reverse Engineering*, BRIEFING PAPERS No. 06-05 (Apr. 2006); DeVecchio, *Copyright Protection Under Government Contracts*, BRIEFING PAPERS No. 05-06 (May 2005).

RESTRICTIVE LEGENDS Markings on TECHNICAL DATA or COMPUTER SOFTWARE that restrict the rights of the government to use such data or software. Under the policy in FAR Subpart 27.4, the contractor may use either a LIMITED RIGHTS legend or a RESTRICTED RIGHTS legend in appropriate circumstances. Under the 1995 DOD policy, the legends can be limited rights, restricted rights, GOVERNMENT-PURPOSE RIGHTS or SPECIFICALLY NEGOTIATED LICENSE RIGHTS. If any technical data or computer software delivered under the contract are marked with these notices and use of the notices is not authorized by the contract, or if the data bear any other restrictive or limiting markings not authorized by the contract, the contracting officer may, at any time, either return the data to the contractor or cancel and ignore the markings subject to the VALIDATION procedures in 10 U.S.C. § 2321 and 41 U.S.C. § 4703. See FAR 27.404(h); DFARS 227.7103-12 and 227.7203-12. See Nash & Rawicz, INTELLECTUAL PROPERTY IN GOVERNMENT CONTRACTS, chaps. 4 & 5 (6th ed. 2008); DeVecchio, *Technical Data & Computer Software After Night Vision: Marking, Delivery & Reverse Engineering*, BRIEFING PAPERS No. 06-05 (Apr. 2006).

RESTRICTIVE SPECIFICATIONS   Specifications that exclude a potential contractor from competing for a procurement. 10 U.S.C. § 2305(a)(1)(B)(ii) and 41 U.S.C. § 3306(a)(2)(B) permit restrictive provisions or conditions only to the extent necessary to satisfy the needs of the agency—prohibiting UNDULY RESTRICTIVE specifications. Thus, the specifications must, whenever possible, describe the supplies or services in a manner designed to promote FULL AND OPEN COMPETITION. PERFORMANCE SPECIFICATIONS containing unnecessary design requirements, specifications including arbitrary requirements not related to the government's needs, and specifications written around a specific product are examples of unduly restrictive specifications. See Cibinic, Nash & Yukins, FORMATION OF GOVERNMENT CONTRACTS 370–73 (4th ed. 2011).

RESTRUCTURING ACTIVITIES   *Official:* Nonroutine, nonrecurring, or extraordinary activities to combine facilities, operations, or workforce in order to eliminate redundant capabilities, improve future operations, and reduce overall costs. Restructuring activities do not include routine or ongoing repositionings and redeployments of a contractor's productive facilities or workforce (e.g., normal plant rearrangement or employee relocation), nor do they include other routine or ordinary activities charged as indirect costs that would otherwise have been incurred (e.g., planning and analysis, contract administration and oversight, or recurring financial and administrative support). *Source:* DFARS 231.205.70(b)(3). The allowability of the costs of these activities are governed by the rules on RESTRUCTURING COSTS.

RESTRUCTURING COSTS   *Official:* The costs, including both direct and indirect, of RESTRUCTURING ACTIVITIES. *Source:* DFARS 231.205-70(b)(4). Allowable restructuring costs may include severance pay, early retirement incentive payments, employee retraining costs, employee relocation expense, and relocation and rearrangement of plant and equipment. Restructuring costs are either internal or external. Internal restructuring costs are those that involve the facilities or workforce of only one of the companies involved in a business combination or, when there has been no business combination, the costs of restructuring a single company. The allowability of internal restructuring costs are governed by the FAR Part 31 COST PRINCIPLES. External restructuring costs are costs incurred as a result of external restructuring activities that result from a business combination that affects the operations of companies not previously under common ownership or control. External restructuring costs are allowable only when audited savings for DOD resulting from the restructuring will exceed the costs allowed by a margin of at least two to one, or the business combination will result in the preservation of a critical capability that might otherwise be lost to DOD. DFARS 231.205.70(c).

RESULT   See OUTCOME.

RETAINAGE   A percentage of the PROGRESS PAYMENT due under a CONSTRUCTION contract that is retained either routinely or because the contractor failed to make satisfactory progress. Such retainage is permitted by ¶ (e) of the Payments under Fixed-Price Construction Contracts clause in FAR 52.232-5. FAR 32.103 provides that retainage should not be used as a substitute for good contract management and the contracting officer should not withhold funds without cause. Determinations of whether and how much to retain are made on a case-by-case basis and are based on the contracting officer's assessment of the contractor's performance and of the likelihood that such performance will continue. The amount of retainage withheld may not exceed 10% of the amount due in accordance with the terms of the contract and may be adjusted as the contract approaches completion to recognize better than expected performance, the ability to rely on alternative safeguards, and other factors. Upon completion of all contract requirements, retained amounts must be paid promptly.

RETENTION OF RECORDS   Retention by contractors of documents connected with government contracts. Such retention is required by various contract clauses, including the Audit and Records—Negotiation clause in FAR 52.215-2 and the Audit and Records—Sealed Bidding clause in FAR 52.214-26. FAR Subpart 4.7 gives guidance on the requirements for records retention and the methods that may be used to satisfy these requirements.

RETENTION PERIOD   The period of time during which a contractor is obligated to retain records developed under government contracts that include either the clause at FAR 52.214-26, Audit and Records—Sealed Bidding, or FAR 52.215-2, Audit and Records—Negotiation. Policies regarding contractor records retention are set forth in FAR Subpart 4.7. Retention periods for specific types of records are specified in FAR 4.705.

REVERSE AUCTION   A competitive negotiation procedure in which prospective contractors compete by offering prices for specified supplies or services that are disclosed publicly (without disclosure of the vendor submitting the price) for a specified period of time within which they can lower their prices. The contract is awarded to the responsible offeror whose price is lowest at the auction closing time. Unlike a traditional auction, in which there is one seller and many buyers, in a reverse auction there is one buyer and many sellers. The process is said to be "reverse" because it is the seller who bids by lowering its proposed price in response to competition. The procedure is usually conducted online. Although frequently used by federal agencies, the FAR does not mention reverse auctions. DFARS 217.7801 prohibits the use of reverse auctions to procure personal protective equipment or an aviation critical safety item. Many companies provide reverse auction software and services.

REVERSE ENGINEERING   The process of developing DESIGN SPECIFICATIONS by inspection and analysis of a product. The UNIFORM TRADE SECRETS ACT provides that reverse engineering is a proper means of obtaining a person's TRADE SECRETs. DOD PGI 217.7504(4) provides that reverse engineering can be used, but is the "last alternative," to obtain competition for REPLENISHMENT PARTS. See Nash & Rawicz, INTELLECTUAL PROPERTY IN GOVERNMENT CONTRACTS, chaps. 4 & 8 (6th ed. 2008); Nash, *Reverse Engineering: A Way to Obtain Competition on Proprietary Items*, 33 N&CR ¶ 67 (Nov.

2019); DeVecchio, *Technical Data & Computer Software After Night Vision: Marking, Delivery & Reverse Engineering*, BRIEFING PAPERS No. 06-05 (Apr. 2006).

REVOLVING DOOR   The practice of government employees leaving government service to join private industry. Restrictions on the activities of such employees are contained in 18 U.S.C. § 207. These provisions are amplified and interpreted by regulations issued by the OFFICE OF GOVERNMENT ETHICS at 5 C.F.R. § 2637 and § 2641. They deal primarily with any former government employee representing companies with which the employee has dealt and assisting foreign entities before the government or any companies in trade negotiations. They also bar senior-level employees, for one year, from communicating with or making an appearance before the agency for which he or she worked. Restrictions barring employment of specified individuals, are contained in the PROCUREMENT INTEGRITY rules. The revolving-door problem is especially serious when it involves the employment of any former government employee by a contractor seeking that individual's knowledge about specific procurements or seeking to obtain an advantage by that employee's special contacts. See Covington, *"Don't Let the Door Hit You on the Way Out": A Primer on Revolving Door Restrictions* (May 21, 2018).

RIGHTS IN COMPUTER SOFTWARE   The government's rights to make various uses of COMPUTER SOFTWARE. Very broadly speaking, if the government has funded or will fund development of software, the government generally obtains UNLIMITED RIGHTS in the software. If, in contrast, a contractor or subcontractor developed the software at PRIVATE EXPENSE, the government generally obtains only RESTRICTED RIGHTS in the software. The distinction is important because software delivered with unlimited rights may be disclosed to competing contractors, whereas RESTRICTED RIGHTS DATA are considered proprietary and must be protected to the extent provided by the contract clauses. DOD also obtains GOVERNMENT-PURPOSE RIGHTS to software pertaining to software developed with MIXED FUNDING and can negotiate SPECIFICALLY NEGOTIATED LICENSE RIGHTS in some situations. DFARS 227.7203-5. All of these rights are license rights with the contractor retaining title to the software. DFARS 227.7203-4(a). See Nash & Rawicz, INTELLECTUAL PROPERTY IN GOVERNMENT CONTRACTS, chap. 5 (6th ed. 2008); Nash, *Software Licenses: Seller Beware!*, 33 N&CR ¶ 68 (Nov. 2019); DeVecchio, *Licensing Commercial Software to the Government: Notice, Subcontracting & Pricing Issues*, BRIEFING PAPERS No. 15-6 (May 2015); DeVecchio, *Rights in Technical Data & Computer Software Under Government Contracts: Key Questions & Answers*, BRIEFING PAPERS No. 10-10 (Sept. 2010).

RIGHTS IN TECHNICAL DATA   The government's rights to make various uses of TECHNICAL DATA. Very broadly speaking, if the government has funded or will fund development of an item, component, or process, the government generally obtains UNLIMITED RIGHTS in the technical data. If, in contrast, a contractor or subcontractor developed the item, component, or process at PRIVATE EXPENSE, the government generally obtains only LIMITED RIGHTS in the technical data. The distinction is important because data delivered with unlimited rights may be disclosed to competing contractors, whereas LIMITED RIGHTS DATA are considered proprietary and may be disclosed to parties outside of the government only under conditions specified in contract clauses. DOD also obtains GOVERNMENT-PURPOSE RIGHTS to technical data pertaining to items, components, or processes developed with MIXED FUNDING and can negotiate SPECIFICALLY NEGOTIATED LICENSE RIGHTS in some situations. DFARS

227.7103-5. All of these rights are license rights with the contractor retaining title to the technical data. DFARS 227.7103-4(a). See Nash & Rawicz, INTELLECTUAL PROPERTY IN GOVERNMENT CONTRACTS, chap. 4 (6th ed. 2008); Nash, *Postscript II: Protecting Unlimited Rights Data*, 33 N&CR ¶ 4 (Jan. 2019); DeVecchio, *Taking The Mystery Out Of Data Rights*, BRIEFING PAPERS No. 18-8 (July 2018); Nash, *New Technical Data Legislation: Revisions to the DOD Statutes*, 26 N&CR ¶ 18 (Apr. 2012); DeVecchio, *Rights in Technical Data & Computer Software Under Government Contracts: Key Questions & Answers II*, BRIEFING PAPERS No. 12-6 (May 2010); DeVecchio, *Rights in Technical Data & Computer Software Under Government Contracts: Key Questions & Answers I*, BRIEFING PAPERS No. 10-10 (Sept. 2010); Nash, *Subcontractor Rights to Technical Data: A Little Known Problem*, 23 N&CR ¶ 42 (Aug. 2009).

RISK   The assumption of responsibility for possible monetary loss or gain in view of the job or work to be done. FAR 16.103 indicates that risk is a major consideration in determining the TYPE OF CONTRACT under which performance will occur. The contractor's assumption of greater cost risks should result in a proportionate increase in compensation. The contractor assumes the greatest cost risk in a FIRM-FIXED-PRICE CONTRACT, in which the contractor has full responsibility for the performance costs and the resulting profit or loss. Under a COST-PLUS-FIXED-FEE CONTRACT, the contractor bears minimal risk because the government is responsible for the increased performance costs. FAR 15.404-4(d)(1)(ii) requires that this risk also be assessed in negotiating the contractor's PROFIT. Complex requirements, particularly those unique to the government, usually lead to the government's assuming greater risk. FAR 16.104(d). See Cibinic, Nash & Yukins, FORMATION OF GOVERNMENT CONTRACTS 1201–06, 1552–54 (4th ed. 2011).

RISK ALLOCATION   The apportionment of the risk of financial loss on a contract by the TYPE OF CONTRACT or the contract clauses. FAR 16.103 calls for the use of a type of contract that does not allocate undue risks to the contractor. The standard contract clauses also balance the allocation of risk by providing that the government will grant EQUITABLE ADJUSTMENTs or PRICE ADJUSTMENTs upon the occurrence of specified events. The term "risk allocation" is also used to denote the resolution of a contractual DISPUTE by apportioning the damages incurred by one party to the contractual parties in accordance with each share of the risk of the occurrence that led to the assessment of damages. This has occurred when there was joint fault, joint negligence, or concurrent delays. See Cibinic, Nagle & Nash, ADMINISTRATION OF GOVERNMENT CONTRACTS, chap. 3 (5th ed. 2016).

RISK ANALYSIS   The activity of examining each identified risk to refine the description of the risk, isolate the cause, and determine the effects and aiding in setting risk mitigation priorities. It refines each risk in terms of its likelihood, its consequence, and its relationship to other risk areas or processes. Office of the Deputy Assistant Secretary of Defense for Systems Engineering, RISK, ISSUE, AND OPPORTUNITY MANAGEMENT GUIDE FOR DEFENSE ACQUISITION PROGRAMS, DOD ACQUISITION (Jan. 2017). Risk analysis is an element of RISK MANAGEMENT in DOD system acquisitions.

RISK MANAGEMENT   Generally, all plans and actions taken to identify, assess, mitigate, and continuously track, control, and document program risks. DAU GLOSSARY. Risk management is an overarching process that encompasses identification, analysis, mitigation, planning, mitigation plan implementation, and tracking of future root causes and their consequences. Office of the Deputy Assistant Secretary of Defense for Systems Engineering, RISK, ISSUE,

AND OPPORTUNITY MANAGEMENT GUIDE FOR DEFENSE ACQUISITION PROGRAMS, DOD ACQUISITION (Jan. 2017). See also the DOD 5000 Series, which contains procedures for managing the risks in the acquisition of weapon systems. The OFFICE OF MANAGEMENT AND BUDGET calls for risk management throughout the life cycle of a system addressing the following risk areas: schedule risk; cost risk; technical feasibility; risk of technical obsolescence; dependencies between a new project and other projects or systems; procurement and contract risk; and resources risks. Appendix I.5.5, of OMB Circular A-11, *Preparation, Submission and Execution of the Budget*, July 2016. FAR Part 39 discusses risk management in the context of INFORMATION TECHNOLOGY procurements, suggesting that reasonable risk-taking is appropriate as long as risks are controlled and mitigated. Appropriate risk management and mitigation techniques include prudent project management, use of MODULAR CONTRACTING, thorough ACQUISITION PLANNING tied to budgeting planning, continuous collection and evaluation of risk-based assessment data, prototyping prior to implementation, post-implementation reviews, and focusing on risks and returns using quantifiable measures. FAR 39.102.

RISK-POOLING   An insurance arrangement in which participants pool their individual liability risks and redistribute them in a way that benefits them all. FAR 28.304 authorizes agencies to establish risk-pooling arrangements, pursuant to which the DEPARTMENT OF DEFENSE has established the National Defense Projects Rating Plan (NDPRP), which is a risk-pooling arrangement. DFARS 228.304. For a detailed explanation of the NDPRP see *Johnson Controls World Services, Inc. v. United States*, 48 Fed. Cl. 479 (2001); DOD PGI 228.304.

ROYALTY   Compensation for the use of property. In government procurement, royalties are generally paid by contractors for the use of PATENTs or COPYRIGHTs. FAR 31.205-37 provides that patent royalties are ALLOWABLE COSTs if they are arrived at through arm's-length bargaining, unless the government has a LICENSE in the patent. See Manos, 1 GOVERNMENT CONTRACT COSTS AND PRICING §§ 44:1–44:3 (2d ed. 2009–2020). To ascertain whether a contractor has licensed a patent to which the government has rights, FAR 27.204 requires the reporting of royalties on most contracts. See the Royalty Information clause in FAR 52.227-6. There are no similar provisions with regard to contractor payment of royalties for the use of copyrights. 10 U.S.C. § 2320(a)(1) prohibits any provision in procurement regulations that precludes a contractor from charging another company a royalty for the use of TECHNICAL DATA to which it has rights. The government also assesses royalties against contractors as part of its RECOUPMENT policy.

RULE 4 FILE   See APPEAL FILE.

RULE OF TWO   A judgmental rule that requires a small business SET-ASIDE on contracts over the SIMPLIFIED ACQUISITION THRESHOLD when the contracting officer determines that there is a reasonable expectation that (1) offers will be obtained from at least two responsible (see RESPONSIBILITY) SMALL BUSINESS CONCERNS offering the products of different small business concerns, and (2) award will be made at FAIR MARKET PRICEs. FAR 19.502-2(b). This rule is based on the assumption that two competing concerns will provide sufficient competition to ensure a FAIR AND REASONABLE PRICE. The rule generates considerable controversy in the acquisition community. Critics have asserted that it is unfair to reserve a contract or all contracts in a given category for small business whenever only two small business offerors express an interest, with no regard to whether the contract could be awarded at a lower price to a large firm or to what effect this has on the overall percentage of the contracts set aside in a particular industry. See Cibinic, Nash & Yukins, FORMATION OF GOVERNMENT CONTRACTS 1590–93 (4th ed. 2011); Edwards, *Postscript: The Rule of Two*, 23 N&CR ¶ 13 (Mar. 2009); Nash & Edwards, *The "Rule of Two:" It's Applicable to Task and Delivery Orders*, 22 N&CR ¶ 75 (Dec. 2008).

RULE 12 PROCEDURES   See EXPEDITED PROCEDURES.

S

SAFETY ACT   See SUPPORT ANTI-TERRORISM BY FOSTERING EFFECTIVE TECHNOLOGIES ACT OF 2000.

SALIENT CHARACTERISTICS   Those qualities of an ITEM that are essential to ensure that the intended use of the item can be satisfactorily realized. The term is mainly used in connection with describing a government requirement with a BRAND-NAME-OR-EQUAL DESCRIPTION. FAR 11.104(b) requires that such descriptions contain a statement of the salient physical, functional, and other characteristics of the referenced product that an equal product must have in order to meet the government's needs.

SALVAGE   Property that, because of its worn, damaged, deteriorated, or incomplete condition or specialized nature, has no reasonable prospect of sale or use as serviceable property without major repairs, but has some value in excess of its SCRAP value. This term was defined in FAR 45.501 prior to the issuance of FAC 2005-17, May 15, 2007. It is no longer used in FAR Part 45 but FAR Subpart 45.6 contains general guidance on reporting, reutilization, and disposal of GOVERNMENT PROPERTY.

SAMPLE TASK   A hypothetical task that is given to offerors during SOURCE SELECTION to evaluate their understanding of the work and ability to perform the work. Sample tasks are given in the solicitation with written solutions to be submitted with the proposal or are given during ORAL PRESENTATIONs with verbal solutions to be given during the presentation. FAR 15.102(c). Agencies are not required to identify WEAKNESSes or deficiencies (see DEFICIENCY) that they detect in the responses to sample tasks. Sample tasks are most frequently used in IDIQ contract competitions. See Cibinic, Nash & Yukins, FORMATION OF GOVERNMENT CONTRACTS 1400 (4th ed. 2011).

SARA PANEL   See ACQUISITION ADVISORY PANEL.

SBIR/STTR DATA   *Official:* All Data developed or generated in the performance of an SBIR or STTR award, including Technical Data and Computer Software developed or generated in the performance of an SBIR or STTR award. The term does not include information incidental to contract or grant administration, such as financial, administrative, cost or pricing, or management information. *Source:* SBIR/STTR Policy Directive, May 2, 2019. Even though such data are produced with government funds, they are entitled to special protection in the form of SBIR/STTR DATA RIGHTS.

SBIR/STTR DATA RIGHTS   *Official:* The Government's license rights in properly marked SBIR/STTR Data during the SBIR/STTR PROTECTION PERIOD as follows:

SBIR/STTR Technical Data Rights in SBIR/STTR Data that are Technical Data or any other type of Data other than Computer Software and SBIR/STTR Computer Software Rights in SBIR/STTR Data that is Computer Software. Upon expiration of the protection period for SBIR/STTR Data, the Government has a royalty-free license to use, and to authorize others to use on its behalf, these Data for Government Purposes, and is relieved of all disclosure prohibitions and assumes no liability for unauthorized use of these Data by third parties, except that any such Data that is also protected under a subsequent SBIR/STTR award shall remain protected through the protection period of that subsequent award. The Government receives Unlimited Rights in all Form, Fit, and Function Data, OMIT Data, and unmarked SBIR/STTR Data. *Source:* SBIR/STTR Policy Directive, May 2, 2019. This definition has not yet been incorporated in the FAR or DFARS clauses. Thus, the Rights in Noncommercial Technical Data and Computer Software—Small Business Innovation Research (SBIR) Program clause in DFARS 252.227-7018 defines SBIR data rights as—A royalty-free license for the government, including its support service contractors, to use, modify, reproduce, release, perform, display, or disclose technical data or computer software generated and delivered under this contract for any United States Government purpose. *Source:* Under this clause, the government has these rights for five years after acceptance of all items on the contract. The comparable term under the FAR is SBIR rights, defined in ¶ (d) of the Rights in Data—SBIR Program clause in FAR 52.227-20 which states that for a period of four years after the acceptance of all items to be delivered under the contract: "The government will use these data for government purposes only, and they shall not be disclosed outside the government (including disclosure for procurement purposes) during such period without permission of the contractor, except that, subject to the foregoing use and disclosure prohibitions, these data may be disclosed for use by support contractors. After the protection period, the government has a paid-up license to use, and to authorize others to use on its behalf, these data for government purposes, but is relieved of all disclosure prohibitions and assumes no liability for unauthorized use of these data by third parties. This notice shall be affixed to any reproductions of these data, in whole or in part." These rights give small businesses performing SMALL BUSINESS INNOVATIVE RESEARCH (SBIR) CONTRACTs the right to limit, for the specified periods of time, the government's use, and disclosure of TECHNICAL DATA or COMPUTER SOFTWARE produced in the performance of the contract to internal use and disclosure to support service contractors. The rights do not appear to attach to any product resulting from such a contract with the result that the government can give competitors the product but not the technical data describing the product. See Nash & Rawicz, Intellectual Property in Government Contracts, chap. 4 (6th ed. 2008); Nash, *SBIR/STTR Data Rights: A New Policy Directive*, 33 N&CR ¶ 38 (July 2019).

SBIR/STTR PROTECTION PERIOD   *Official:* The period of time during which the government is obligated to protect SBIR/STTR Data against unauthorized use and disclosure in accordance with SBIR/STTR DATA RIGHTS. The SBIR/STTR Protection Period begins at award of an SBIR/STTR Funding Agreement and ends not less than 20 years from that date. (See § 8(b)(4) of this Policy Directive.) *Source:* SBIR/STTR Policy Directive, May 2, 2019. This is a major change from the prior four or five year periods that began with each new SBIR contract. The FAR and DFARS clauses have not been amended to reflect this new period.

SCANWELL ACTION A PROTEST filed in a U.S. District Court. The case *Scanwell Laboratories, Inc. v. Shaffer*, 424 F.2d 859 (D.C. Cir. 1970), established that an unsuccessful offeror could challenge the award of a government procurement contract on the grounds of arbitrary or capricious action not in compliance with the Administrative Procedure Act, 5 U.S.C. § 552. The district courts were deprived of jurisdiction over these actions by the ADMINISTRATIVE DISPUTE RESOLUTION ACT OF 1996. These actions may be available to challenge the award of an OTHER TRANSACTIONS agreement.

SCHEDULE Part I of the UNIFORM CONTRACT FORMAT, which includes contract sections A through H. FAR 14.201-2 and 15.204-2.

SCHEDULE CONTRACT; SCHEDULES See FEDERAL SUPPLY SCHEDULES.

SCHEDULES E-LIBRARY *Official:* The on-line source for GENERAL SERVICES ADMINISTRATION and VETERANS ADMINISTRATION FEDERAL SUPPLY SCHEDULE contract award information. Schedules e-Library may be accessed at http://www.gsa.gov/elibrary. *Source:* FAR 8.401.

SCRAP *Official:* PERSONAL PROPERTY that has no value except its basic metallic, mineral, or organic content. *Source:* FAR 2.101. FAR Subpart 45.6 contains general guidance on reporting, reutilization, and disposal of GOVERNMENT PROPERTY. FAR 45.602 provides that its reutilization requirements for government property that is no longer needed for the performance of a contract do not apply to scrap except for scrap aircraft parts.

SCREENING The process used by the FEDERAL AVIATION ADMINISTRATION to determine which offeror provides the BEST VALUE to the government. For less complex procurements, screening is done in a single step, soliciting offers from all vendors (essentially the same as the solicitation of COMPETITIVE PROPOSALs in a competitive negotiation). In more complex procurements, screening can be done in three steps, soliciting qualification information in the first step, soliciting screening information from qualified vendors in the second step, and soliciting offers from the remaining vendors in the third step. See FAA Acquisition Management Policy 3.2.2.3.1.2 (fast.faa.gov/). See Cibinic, Nash & Yukins, FORMATION OF GOVERNMENT CONTRACTS 1111–14 (4th ed. 2011).

SCREENING INFORMATION REQUEST (SIR) A request by the FEDERAL AVIATION ADMINISTRATION for documentation, information, presentations, proposals, or binding offers. The SIR is used in each step of the SCREENING process for a different purpose and will solicit different information depending on that purpose. When it is used to obtain qualification information, it is tailored to obtain all information necessary to determine that the potential vendor is qualified to perform the work to be procured. When it is used to obtain screening information, it is tailored to obtain information about the key discriminators that will be used to select the winning contractor. When it is used to obtain offers, it is written as a solicitation of a binding offer. FAA Acquisition Management Policy 3.2.2.3.1.2.1 (fast.faa.gov/). See Cibinic, Nash & Yukins, FORMATION OF GOVERNMENT CONTRACTS 1111–14 (4th ed. 2011).

SCIENTIFIC AND TECHNICAL REPORTS Reports documenting the work accomplished under a RESEARCH AND DEVELOPMENT (R&D) contract. FAR 35.010 provides that such reports must be required in order to make a permanent record of the work accomplished. Agencies are encouraged to make R&D contract results available to other government activities and to the private sector, and R&D contracts should require that contractors send copies of scientific and technical reports to the Defense Technical Information Center (DTIC) or the National Technical Information Service. See FAR 35.010 and DFARS 235.010. The DTIC provides DOD information to qualified requesters. See DOD PGI 235.010(b).

SCOPE OF THE COMPETITION   All work that was contemplated by the competitors when the contract was first competed. When competitors protest that they should have been allowed to compete for work added to a contract, the test is whether the added work is within the scope of the original competition. This is determined by looking at the entire solicitation to determine if its terms include the added work. See Nash & Feldman, GOVERNMENT CONTRACT CHANGES §§ 3:7–3:13 (3d ed. 2006–2020); Cibinic, Nagel & Nash, ADMINISTRATION OF GOVERNMENT CONTRACTS 350–54 (5th ed. 2016).

SCOPE OF THE CONTRACT   All work that was fairly and reasonably within the contemplation of the parties at the time the contract was made. Nearly all government contracts contain a Changes clause that permits the contracting officer to make unilateral changes in designated areas, within the general scope of the contract. FAR 43.201. Changes beyond the scope of the contract are CARDINAL CHANGEs. The determination of whether changes lie beyond the contract's general scope typically entails comparing the total work performed by the contractor with the work called for by the original contract. If the function of the work as changed is generally the same as the work originally called for, the changes fall within the contract's general scope. See Nash & Feldman, GOVERNMENT CONTRACT CHANGES §§ 4:2–4:9 (3d ed. 2006–2020); Cibinic, Nagel & Nash, ADMINISTRATION OF GOVERNMENT CONTRACTS 347–49 (5th ed. 2016).

SCRAP   *Official:* Personal property that has no value except for its basic metallic, mineral, or organic content. *Source:* FAR 2.101. FAR 45.606 provides procedures for the disposal of scrap.

SEALED BIDDING   A method of contracting that, through an INVITATION FOR BIDS, solicits the submission of competitive bids, followed by a public opening of the bids (see BID OPENING). A contract is awarded to the responsive and responsible bidder (see RESPONSIVENESS; RESPONSIBILITY) whose bid is most advantageous to the government, considering price and PRICE-RELATED FACTORS. FAR 14.103-2. Prior to the COMPETITION IN CONTRACTING ACT, sealed bidding was called "formal advertising" and was the preferred method of contracting. Under CICA, it is merely one of the COMPETITIVE PROCEDURES that meets the requirement to obtain FULL AND OPEN COMPETITION. 10 U.S.C. § 2304(a)(2)(A) and 41 U.S.C. § 3301(b)(1). Sealed bidding is a highly structured form of procurement that is governed by the rules in FAR Part 14. See Manos, 1 GOVERNMENT CONTRACT COSTS AND PRICING § 5:2 (2d ed. 2009–2020); Cibinic, Nash & Yukins, FORMATION OF GOVERNMENT CONTRACTS, chap. 5 (4th ed. 2011).

SECOND SOURCE   An alternative source for a supply or service, obtained to foster competition. When quantities of work are sufficient to permit economical performance by two sources, it is the government's policy to obtain second sources. See DUAL SOURCE. Agencies are permitted to exclude the original source from a competition to establish a second source. FAR 6.202. FAR Subpart 17.4 provides a means of obtaining a second source called LEADER COMPANY CONTRACTING.

SECRECY ORDER   An order imposed by the United States Patent and Trademark Office blocking the issuance of a PATENT and prohibiting the publication of the patent application because it would be detrimental to the national security. 35 U.S.C. § 181. Patent applications dealing with national security are sent to procuring agencies to be screened to determine if a secrecy order should be imposed. If an INVENTION is disclosed after the imposition of an order, it will be held to be abandoned. 35 U.S.C. § 182, and criminal prosecution can be pursued, 35 U.S.C. § 186. The owner of the invention is entitled to damages caused by the order or compensation if the government uses the invention. 35 U.S.C. § 183. The term of the patent, after the lifting of the secrecy order, is extended to reflect the time the order has been in effect, 35 U.S.C. § 154(b)(1)(C)(ii).

SECRETARY   The head of an agency with cabinet status. Exceptions are DOJ, whose head is called the Attorney General, and DOD, where there is a Secretary of Defense (with cabinet status) as well as Secretaries of the Departments of the Army, Navy, and Air Force (without cabinet status). The term is similar to the broader term HEAD OF THE AGENCY. It is used primarily in statutes governing the activities of a single cabinet-level department. Some decisions are permitted to be made only by the Secretary or at the "secretarial level." When handling extraordinary contractual actions to facilitate the national defense, "secretarial level" means a level at or above the level of a deputy or assistant agency head, or a CONTRACT ADJUSTMENT BOARD. FAR 50.001; DFARS 250.001. Acquisitions conducted without providing for FULL AND OPEN COMPETITION because it is not in the public interest, under the authority of 10 U.S.C. § 2304(c)(7) or 41 U.S.C. § 3304(a)(7), require a written determination by the Secretary of Defense, the Secretary of the Army, the Secretary of the Navy, the Secretary of the Air Force, the Secretary of Homeland Security for the Coast Guard, the Administrator of NASA, or the head of any other EXECUTIVE AGENCY. This authority may not be delegated. FAR 6.302-7.

SECTION 8(A)   See 8(a) PROGRAM.

SECTION 508   A provision of the Rehabilitation Act, as amended by the Workforce Investment Act of 1998, 29 U.S.C. § 794d, that requires federal agencies developing, procuring, maintaining, or using electronic and information technology, to ensure that the electronic and information technology allows federal employees with disabilities to have access to and use of information and data that is comparable to the access to and use of information and data by federal employees who are not individuals with disabilities, unless an undue burden would be imposed on the agency. Section 508 also requires that individuals with disabilities, who are members of the public seeking information or services from a federal agency, have access to and use of information and data that is comparable to that provided to the public who are not individuals with disabilities. Section 508(a)(2)(A) requires the Architectural and Transportation Barriers Compliance Board (Access Board) to publish standards setting forth a definition of electronic and information technology and the technical and functional performance criteria necessary for accessibility for such technology. If an agency determines that meeting the standards, when procuring electronic and information technology, imposes an undue burden, it must explain why meeting the standards creates an undue burden. The Act is implemented in FAR Subpart 39.2. See www.Section508.gov. See Stark, *The Role of Section 508 in Federal Procurement*, BRIEFING PAPERS No. 02-03 (Feb. 2002).

SECTION 800 PANEL   A committee of 13 members established by DOD as directed by § 800 of the National Defense Authorization Act for FY 1991, Pub. L. No. 101-510. The panel was charged with the task of reviewing all laws affecting DOD procurement "with a view toward streamlining the defense acquisition process." The panel submitted its report in January 1993, recommending amendment of 163 statutes and repeal of 135 statutes. This report contained a detailed analysis of the recommendations and served as the basis for the FEDERAL ACQUISITION STREAMLINING ACT OF 1994 and the CLINGER-COHEN ACT OF 1996. Among the more important recommendations were raising the threshold for SIMPLIFIED ACQUISITION from $25,000 to $100,000, broadening the definition of COMMERCIAL ITEMs, and making many of the socioeconomic statutes inapplicable to simplified acquisitions and purchases of commercial items. See Manos, 1 GOVERNMENT CONTRACT COSTS & PRICING § 2:13 (2d ed. 2009–2020).

SECTION 807 PANEL   A committee of government and industry members established by DOD in accordance with § 807 of the National Defense Authorization Act for FY 1992 and 1993, Pub. L. No. 102-190. This panel was given the task of negotiating a DOD technical data policy that complied with 10 U.S.C. § 2320. The panel's report was forwarded to Congress in April 1994 and served as the basis for the new DOD technical data and computer software policy that was adopted in 1995. See Nash & Rawicz, INTELLECTUAL PROPERTY IN GOVERNMENT CONTRACTS, chap. 4 (6th ed. 2008).

SECTION 809 PANEL   A committee of government and industry members established by DOD as directed by § 809 of the National Defense Authorization Act for FY 2016, Pub. L. No. 114-92. The panel was charged with the task of reviewing all acquisition regulations affecting DOD procurement "with a view toward streamlining and improving the effectiveness of the defense acquisition process and maintaining defense technology advantage." The panel submitted its report in three volumes from January 2018 to January 2019. The panel made 98 recommendations for statutory and regulatory changes, 15 of which have been adopted by Congress. See Nash, *Postscript: The Section 809 Panel*, 32 N&CR ¶ 15 (Mar. 2018); Nash & Edwards, *The Section 809 Panel Interim Report: Strong on Analysis, Short on Solutions*, 31 N&CR ¶ 41 (July 2017).

SECTION 813 PANEL   A committee of government and industry members established by DOD in accordance with § 813 of the National Defense Authorization Act for FY 2016, Pub. L. No. 114-92. This panel was given the task of studying technical data and computer software issues and making recommendations to Congress. The panel's report was issued in November 2018, containing a large number of recommendations for both Congressional and regulatory changes which are in the process of being considered. The most important recommendations relate to the need for sufficient technical data and computer software with necessary rights to allow for competition during the SUSTAINMENT of DoD systems. See Nash, *The 813 Panel Report: Some Interesting Recommendations*, 33 N&CR ¶ 11 (Feb. 2019).

SEGMENT   *Official:* One of two or more divisions, product departments, plants, or other subdivisions of an organization reporting directly to a HOME OFFICE, usually identified with responsibility for PROFIT and/or producing a product or service. The term includes—(1) government-owned contractor-operated (GOCO) facilities; and (2) JOINT VENTUREs and subsidiaries (domestic and foreign) in which the organization has—(i) A majority ownership; or (ii) Less than a majority ownership, but over which it exercises control. *Source:* FAR 2.101. A contractor's cost accounting system must, to the maximum extent practicable, allocate HOME OFFICE expenses directly to segments, based on the relationship between the expenses and the segments that incur them or benefit from them. See CAS 403, 48 C.F.R. § 9904.403. See Manos, 2 GOVERNMENT CONTRACT COSTS & PRICING § 64:1–64:5 (2d ed. 2009–2020); Cibinic, Knight & Nash, COST-REIMBURSEMENT CONTRACTING 615–18 (4th ed. 2014).

SEGMENT CLOSING *Official:* A SEGMENT that has (1) been sold or ownership otherwise transferred, (2) discontinued operations, or (3) discontinued doing or actively seeking government business under contracts subject to CAS 413. *Source:* 48 C.F.R. § 9904.413-30. If a segment is closed, the contractor is required to adjust previously determined PENSION COSTS by determining the difference between the actuarial accrued liability for the segment and the market value of the assets allocated to the segment. 48 C.F.R. § 9904.413-50. See Manos, 2 GOVERNMENT CONTRACT COSTS & PRICING § 74:1–74:5 (2d ed. 2009–2020).

SEGREGABILITY The ability to segregate TECHNICAL DATA or COMPUTER SOFTWARE to a low level in order to determine whether it was DEVELOPED AT PRIVATE EXPENSE, DEVELOPED AT GOVERNMENT EXPENSE, or developed with MIXED FUNDING. DFARS 227.7103-4(b) requires that such segregation be made for technical data "at any practical sub-item or subcomponent level or for any segregable portion of a process." DFARS 227.7203-4(b) requires that such segregation be made for computer software "at the lowest practical segregable portion of the software or documentation (e.g., a software subroutine that performs a specific function)." The FAR is silent on this technique but the concept is implied. This concept reduces the possibility that technical data or computer software will meet the mixed funding test. See Nash & Rawicz, INTELLECTUAL PROPERTY IN GOVERNMENT CONTRACTS, chaps. 4 & 5 (6th ed. 2008). See also Nash, *Postscript: Segregation/Reintegration Data*, 31 N&CR ¶ 11 (Feb. 2017).

SEGREGATION AND REINTEGRATION DATA TECHNICAL DATA or COMPUTER SOFTWARE that is more detailed than FORM, FIT AND FUNCTION DATA and that is necessary for the segregation of an item or process from, or the reintegration of that item or process (or a physically or functionally equivalent item or process) with, other items or processes. (1) Unless agreed otherwise by the Government and the contractor, the nature, quality, and level of technical detail necessary for these data or software shall be that required for persons reasonably skilled in the art to perform such segregation or reintegration activities. (2) The segregation or reintegration of any such an item or process may be performed at any practical level, including down to the lowest practicable segregable level, *e.g.*, a subitem or subcomponent level, or any segregable portion of a process, computer software (*e.g.*, a software subroutine that performs a specific function), or documentation. (3) The term— (i) Includes data or software that describes in more detail (than form, fit, and function data) the physical, logical, or operational interface or similar functional interrelationship between the items or processes; and (ii) May include, but would not typically require, detailed manufacturing or process data or computer software source code to support such segregation or reintegration activities. This definition was included in the proposed rule in 81 C.F.R. 39,483 implementing § 815 of the FY 2016 National Defense Authorization Act. 10 U.S.C. § 2320(a)(2)(D)(i)(II) was subsequently amended to permit the government to release this type of data, when it constituted INTERFACE DATA, outside of the government even though it is subject to LIMITED RIGHTS. This statute has not been implemented in the DFARS and there were public comments on the proposed rule objecting to this definition.

SELECTED ACQUISITION REPORTS (SARs)   Standard, comprehensive summary status reports on selected DOD ACQUISITION PROGRAMs, required by 10 U.S.C. § 2432 to be submitted by DOD to Congress. SARs provide key cost, schedule, and technical information in a concise, summary form, generally limited to no more than 20 pages. They are required for MAJOR DEFENSE ACQUISITION PROGRAMs in which the eventual expenditure for research, development, test, and evaluation will exceed $300 million or the total expenditure will exceed $1.8 billion. (Both thresholds are calculated in FY90 constant dollars.) In addition to an initial filing, programs may require quarterly or annual submission of SARs.

SELECTED COSTS   A type of cost, incurred by a contractor, that is dealt with specifically in the FAR COST PRINCIPLES. FAR 31.205 discusses the allowability (see ALLOWABLE COST) or unallowability (see UNALLOWABLE COST) of 46 selected costs: PUBLIC RELATIONS and ADVERTISEMENT costs; BAD DEBTS; BONDING COSTS; compensation for personal services (see PERSONAL SERVICES CONTRACT); contingencies (see CONTINGENCY); contributions or DONATIONs; cost of money (see COST OF MONEY FACTORS); DEPRECIATION; ECONOMIC PLANNING COSTS; employee morale, health, welfare, food service, and dormitory costs and credits; ENTERTAINMENT costs; FINEs, penalties, and MISCHARGING costs; gains and losses on disposition of depreciable property or other capital ASSETs; IDLE CAPACITY and IDLE FACILITIES costs; INDEPENDENT RESEARCH AND DEVELOPMENT costs and BID AND PROPOSAL COSTS; INSURANCE and INDEMNIFICATION; INTEREST and other financial costs; LABOR RELATIONS costs; legislative LOBBYING COSTS; LOSSes on other contracts; manufacturing and production engineering costs (see MANUFACTURING ENGINEERING); MATERIAL costs; ORGANIZATION COSTS; other business expenses; plant protection costs; PATENT costs; plant reconversion costs; PRECONTRACT COSTS; PROFESSIONAL AND CONSULTANT SERVICES costs; RECRUITMENT COSTS; RELOCATION COSTS; RENTAL COSTS; ROYALTY and other costs for use of patents; SELLING costs; service and WARRANTY costs; SPECIAL TOOLING and SPECIAL TEST EQUIPMENT costs; TAXES; termination costs (see TERMINATION FOR CONVENIENCE and TERMINATION FOR DEFAULT); TRADE, BUSINESS, TECHNICAL, AND PROFESSIONAL ACTIVITY COSTS; TRAINING AND EDUCATION COSTS; TRAVEL COSTS; costs related to legal and other proceedings (see LEGAL FEES); RESEARCH AND DEVELOPMENT costs; GOODWILL; costs of alcoholic beverages; and asset valuations resulting from BUSINESS COMBINATIONs. See Manos, 1 GOVERNMENT CONTRACT COSTS & PRICING, Part II (2d ed. 2009–2020); Cibinic, Knight & Nash, COST-REIMBURSEMENT CONTRACTING, chap. 10 (4th ed. 2014).

SELECTIVE APPLICATION   See TAILORING.

SELF-CERTIFICATION   The certification by a firm that it qualifies as a SMALL BUSINESS CONCERN. This is the initial step in determining whether a contractor is a small business. The contracting officer is bound to accept the self-certification unless another offeror or INTERESTED PARTY challenges the contractor's small business representation in a SIZE PROTEST, or the contracting officer has reason to question the representation. FAR 19.301(b). See SIZE STATUS.

SELF-INSURANCE *Official:* The assumption or retention of the risk of loss by the contractor, whether voluntarily or involuntarily. Self-insurance includes the deductible portion of purchase insurance. *Source:* FAR 2.101. CAS 416, 48 C.F.R. § 9904.416, which contains rules governing the accounting for insurance costs, provides that self-insurance costs will generally be measured on an actuarial basis rather than an actual-loss basis. See Manos, 2 GOVERNMENT CONTRACT COSTS & PRICING §§ 77:1–77:7 (2d ed. 2009–2020). FAR 28.308 requires that the contractor submit information on any proposed self-insurance program to the ADMINISTRATIVE CONTRACTING OFFICER and obtain approval of the program when it is anticipated that (1) 50% or more of the self-insurance costs to be incurred at a SEGMENT of a contractor's business will be allocable (see ALLOCABLE COST) to negotiated government contracts and (2) self-insurance costs at the segment for the fiscal year will be $200,000 or more. To qualify for a self-insurance program, a contractor must demonstrate its ability to sustain the potential losses involved. See also INSURANCE. See Cibinic, Knight & Nash, COST-REIMBURSEMENT CONTRACTING 728–30 (4th ed. 2014).

SELLING COSTS The cost of all efforts to market a contractor's products or services. FAR 31.205-38. Selling costs are generally unallowable under FAR 31.205-38, unless they constitute "direct selling efforts" or are made allowable by other COST PRINCIPLES of FAR 31.205. The principle activities that fall under the generic term "selling" include (1) advertising (see ADVERTISEMENT) (FAR 31.205-1); (2) corporate image enhancement, including broadly targeted sales efforts, other than advertising (includes PUBLIC RELATIONS, FAR 31.205-1, and ENTERTAINMENT, FAR 31.205-14); (3) BID AND PROPOSAL COSTS (FAR 31.205-18); (4) market planning (FAR 31.205-12); and (5) direct selling (FAR 31.205-38). See Manos, 1 GOVERNMENT CONTRACT COSTS AND PRICING §§ 45:1–45:3 (2d ed. 2009–2012); Cibinic, Knight & Nash, COST-REIMBURSEMENT CONTRACTING 637–40 (4th ed. 2014); Masiello & Bareis, *A User's Guide to Selling Costs: Cost Classification & Common Problems*, BRIEFING PAPERS NO. 13-10 (Sept. 2013).

SEMICONDUCTOR CHIP PRODUCT *Official:* The final or intermediate form of any product—(A) having two or more layers of metallic, insulating, or semiconductor material, deposited or otherwise placed on, or etched away or otherwise removed from, a piece of semiconductor material in accordance with a predetermined pattern; and (B) intended to perform electronic circuitry functions. *Source:* 17 U.S.C. § 901. See SEMICONDUCTOR MASK WORKS.

SEMICONDUCTOR MASK WORKS A series of related images representing the pattern of layers of a SEMICONDUCTOR CHIP PRODUCT. Such works are subject to special protection under the Semiconductor Chip Protection Act of 1984, 17 U.S.C. § 901 et seq. Under the Act, the owner of the mask work has the exclusive right to reproduce the layers of a chip except for the purpose of teaching or analysis. This permits REVERSE ENGINEERING but prohibits copying of the layers by photographic means or otherwise. See Nash & Rawicz, INTELLECTUAL PROPERTY IN GOVERNMENT CONTRACTS, chap. 1 (6th ed. 2008).

SENIOR EXECUTIVE *Official:* (A) Prior to January 2, 1999—(1) The Chief Executive Officer (CEO) or any individual acting in a similar capacity at the contractor's headquarters; (2) The four most highly compensated employees in management positions at the contractor's headquarters, other than the CEO; and (3) If the contractor has intermediate home offices or segments that report directly to the contractor's headquarters, the five most highly compensated employees in management positions at each such intermediate home office or segment. (B) Effective January 2, 1999, the five most highly compensated employees in management positions at each home office and each segment of the contractor, whether or not the home office or segment reports directly to the contractor's headquarters. *Source:* FAR 31.205-6(p)(1)(ii). The total compensation of these executives that can be treated as an ALLOWABLE COST is limited to the BENCHMARK COMPENSATION AMOUNT established annually by the Administrator of the OFFICE OF FEDERAL PROCUREMENT POLICY in accordance with 41 U.S.C. § 1127.

SENIOR PROCUREMENT EXECUTIVE　*Official:* The individual appointed pursuant to 41 U.S.C. § 1702(c), who is responsible for management direction of the acquisition system of an EXECUTIVE AGENCY, including implementation of the unique acquisition policies, regulations, and standards of the executive agency. *Source:* FAR 2.101. Each agency must appoint a SENIOR PROCUREMENT EXECUTIVE to ensure that there is clear authority for carrying out efficient and effective procurement policies. An agency may either appoint its CHIEF ACQUISITION OFFICER as the senior procurement executive or have the senior procurement report directly to the chief acquisition officer. 41 U.S.C. § 1702(c)(3).

SENSITIVE INFORMATION　*Official:* Any information the loss, misuse, or modification of which, or unauthorized access to, could adversely affect the national interest or the conduct of federal programs, or the privacy to which individuals are entitled under the PRIVACY ACT, 5 U.S.C. § 552a, but which has not been specifically authorized, under criteria established by an executive order or act of Congress, to be kept secret in the interest of national defense or foreign policy. *Source:* DFARS 252.239-7016. Contractors must agree to secure such information during telecommunications. DFARS 239.7402(b). See CONTROLLED UNCLASSIFIED INFORMATION.

SENSITIVE PROPERTY　*Official:* Property potentially dangerous to the public safety or security if stolen, lost, or misplaced, or that shall be subject to exceptional physical security, protection, control, and accountability. Examples include weapons, ammunition, explosives, controlled substances, radioactive materials, hazardous materials or wastes, or precious metals. *Source:* FAR 45.101. If this property is excess, it can be abandoned under the procedures set forth in FAR 45.603(b).

SERVICE　Work done by one party, a service provider, for another party, a service recipient, in order to change some state of affairs with respect to a person, a group of persons, an organization, personal or real property, or information. The result of a service is a new state of affairs. The basic component of a service is a TASK, which is a discrete unit of work that produces a specific result. A service may consist of a single task, a series of tasks, or a system of tasks. The result of any single task may be complete, in and of itself, or an input to another task. See Hill, *On Goods and Services*, 23 Rev. Income & Wealth 315 (Dec. 1977); Edwards, *The Service Contracting Policy Mess*, 15 N&CR ¶ 55 (Nov. 2001); Edwards, *Service Contracting: Three Unsolved Problems*, 25 N&CR ¶ 56 (Nov. 2011).

SERVICE CONTRACT　*Official:* A contract that directly engages the time and effort of a contractor whose primary purpose is to perform an identifiable task rather than to furnish an end item of supply. A service contract may be either a nonpersonal or personal contract. It can also cover services performed by either professional or nonprofessional personnel whether on an individual or organizational basis. Some of the areas in which service contracts are found include the following: (1) Maintenance, overhaul, repair, servicing, rehabilitation, salvage, modernization, or modification of supplies, systems, or equipment. (2) Routine recurring maintenance of real property. (3) Housekeeping and base services. (4) ADVISORY AND ASSISTANCE SERVICES. (5) Operation of Government-owned equipment, real property, and systems. (6) Communications services. (7) Architect-Engineering (see subpart 36.6). (8) Transportation and related services (see part 47). (9) RESEARCH AND DEVEL-OPMENT (see part 35). *Source:* FAR 37.101. Guidance on service contracting is contained in FAR Part 37. See also and Edwards, *Non-conforming Services: What are the Government's Rights Under Fixed Price Service Contracts?*, 22 N&CR ¶ 22 (Apr. 2008).

SERVICE CONTRACT ACT (SCA) OF 1965   41 U.S.C. §§ 6701–6707. A law requiring that contractors pay not less than the PREVAILING WAGE RATE and provide safe conditions of work under contracts for the performance of services in the United States through the use of SERVICE EMPLOYEEs. Prevailing wage rates are established by DOL on the WDOL website or at the request of a contracting officer using the e98 process on the website (see www.wdol.gov). FAR 22.1008-1. Examples of services subject to the Act include (1) motor pool operation, parking, taxicab, and ambulance services; (2) packing, crating, and storage; (3) custodial, janitorial, housekeeping, and guard services; (4) food service and lodging; (5) laundry, dry cleaning, linen supply, clothing alteration, and repair services; (6) snow, trash, and garbage removal; (7) aerial spraying and aerial reconnaissance for fire detection; (8) some support services at installations, including grounds maintenance and landscaping; (9) certain specialized services requiring specific skills, such as drafting, illustrating, graphic arts, stenographic reporting, or mortuary services; (10) electronic equipment maintenance and operation and engineering support services; (11) maintenance and repair of all types of equipment, such as aircraft, engines, electrical motors, vehicles, and electronic, office and related business and construction equipment; (12) operation, maintenance, or logistics support of a federal facility; and (13) data collection, processing, and analysis services. FAR 22.1003-5. Service contracts over $2,500 must contain provisions regarding minimum wages and fringe benefits, safe and sanitary working conditions, notification to employees of the minimum allowable compensation, and equivalent federal employee classifications and wage rates. FAR Subpart 22.10. See Cibinic, Nash & Yukins, FORMATION OF GOVERNMENT CONTRACTS 1653–64 (4th ed. 2011); Tompkins, Gill & Weber, *The Service Contract Act: A Primer for the New Decade,* 57 FED. LAW. 58 (Oct. 2010).

SERVICE-DISABLED VETERAN   *Official:* A veteran, as defined in 38 U.S.C. § 101(2), with a disability that is service-connected, as defined in 38 U.S.C. § 101(16). *Source:* FAR 2.101; 13 C.F.R. § 125.8(f). A "veteran" is a person who has served in the active military, naval, or air service and who was discharged or released on conditions other than dishonorable. A "service-connected" disability is one that was incurred or aggravated in the active military, naval, or air service. When such veterans own and control a SMALL BUSINESS, they are entitled to the preference given to a SERVICE-DISABLED VETERAN-OWNED SMALL BUSINESS.

SERVICE-DISABLED VETERAN-OWNED SMALL BUSINESS CONCERN   *Official:* A SMALL BUSINESS CONCERN (1) Not less than 51% of which is owned by one or more SERVICE-DISABLED VETERANs or, in the case of any publicly owned business, not less than 51% of the stock of which is owned by one or more service-disabled veterans; and (2) The management and daily business operations of which are controlled by one or more service-disabled veterans or, in the case of a service-disabled veteran with permanent and severe disability, the spouse or permanent caregiver of such veteran. *Source:* FAR 2.101.

The status of such a business is determined by the SMALL BUSINESS ADMINISTRA-TION in accordance with the provisions of 13 C.F.R. parts 125.8 through 125.13. FAR Subpart 19.14 contains procedures for giving preference to these firms including SET-ASIDES and sole source contracts that can be awarded at a FAIR AND REASONABLE PRICE. FAR Subpart 19.7 requires that such firms be included in SUBCONTRACTING PLANs. See Cibinic, Nash & Yukins, FORMATION OF GOVERNMENT CONTRACTS 1611–12 (4th ed. 2011). See also Korsak, *The Service-Disabled Veteran-Owned Small Business in the Federal Marketplace*, 2008 ARMY LAW. 45 (July 2008); Sherman, *Paved with Good Intentions: Obstacles to Meeting Federal Contracting Goals for Service-Disabled Veteran-Owned Small Businesses*, 36 PUB. CONT. L.J. 125 (2006).

SERVICE EMPLOYEE   *Official:* Any person engaged in the performance of a SERVICE CONTRACT other than any person employed in a bona fide executive, administrative, or professional capacity, as those terms are defined in part 541 of title 29, Code of Federal Regulations. The term service employee includes all such persons regardless of any contractual relationship that may be alleged to exist between a contractor or subcontractor and such persons. *Source:* FAR 22.1001. The term includes employees of SUBCONTRACTORs. Service employees are those employees given the protection of the SERVICE CONTRACT ACT OF 1965. See Cibinic, Nash & Yukins, FORMATION OF GOVERNMENT CONTRACTS 1653–64 (4th ed. 2011).

SERVICE LEVEL AGREEMENT   A SPECIFICATION of performance requirements in a contract for services to operate and maintain an INFORMATION TECHNOLOGY system. Some typical requirements include: system availability, interactive responsiveness, batch processing time, transaction rates, and security. In a government contract, these requirements are usually included in the STATEMENT OF WORK or PERFORMANCE WORK STATEMENT, or in a separate attachment to the contract.

SERVICES ACQUISITION REFORM ACT of 2003 (SARA)   Title XIV of the National Defense Authorization Act for Fiscal Year 2004, Pub. L. No. 108-136. The law included provisions for: (1) acquisition workforce recruitment and training, (2) the creation of CHIEF ACQUISITION OFFICERs in federal agencies and a Chief Acquisition Officers Council, (3) the creation of an ACQUISITION ADVISORY PANEL, (4) the use of time-and-materials and labor-hour contracts to acquire commercial items, and (5) emergency procurements. See Doke & Shager, *2003 Procurement Review*, BRIEFING PAPERS No. 04-02 (Jan. 2004).

SERVICING AGENCY   *Official:* The agency that will conduct an ASSISTED ACQUISI-TION on behalf of the REQUESTING AGENCY. *Source:* FAR 2.101. See FAR Subpart 17.5. Servicing agencies performing acquisitions under the ECONOMY ACT must have (1) an existing contract, (2) capability and expertise that is not available in the requesting agency, or (3) specific authority to purchase on behalf of other agencies. FAR 17.502-2(c)(1)(iii). The servicing agency must concur that it will provide the required assistance, FAR 17.502-1(a)(1), and enter into an INTERAGENCY AGREEMENT with the requesting agency establishing their relationship. FAR 17.502-1(b)(1). See Cibinic, Nash & Yukins, FORMATION OF GOVERNMENT CONTRACTS, chap. 8 (4th ed. 2011).

SET-ASIDE(n)   An acquisition exclusively or partially reserved for the participation of SMALL BUSINESS CONCERNs pursuant to the SMALL BUSINESS ACT, 15 U.S.C. § 644. A set-aside restricts the competition to small business concerns that qualify under the applicable standards. A total set-aside restricts the entire procurement, whereas a partial set-aside restricts only a stated portion of the procurement. The contracting officer makes the initial determination of whether an acquisition should be set aside and must document why a set-aside is inappropriate when the procurement is not set aside. FAR 19.501(c). The RULE OF TWO requires that a procurement be set aside when there are two responsible small business concerns. FAR 19.502-2(b)(1). FAR 19.502-6 provides that the following, in and of themselves, do not make a set-aside inappropriate: (1) a large percentage of previous contracts for the required items have been with small business concerns, (2) the item is on an established planning list under the Industrial Readiness Planning Program, (3) the item is on the QUALIFIED PRODUCTS LIST, (4) a period of less than 30 days is available for receipt of offers, (5) the contract is classified, (6) small businesses are already receiving a fair portion of the agency's contracts, (7) a class set-aside has been made by another contracting activity, and (8) a BRAND NAME OR EQUAL product description will be used. See Feldman, GOVERNMENT CONTRACT GUIDEBOOK §§ 8:3–8:5 (4th ed. 2019–2020); Cibinic, Nash & Yukins, FORMATION OF GOVERNMENT CONTRACTS 1589–96 (4th ed. 2011).

SET ASIDE (v)   To reserve an acquisition exclusively or partially for the participation of a special class of contractors The SMALL BUSINESS ACT, at 15 U.S.C. § 644, authorizes procuring agencies to set aside procurements or portions of procurements for the exclusive participation of SMALL BUSINESS CONCERNs. See also SET-ASIDE (n). Sakallaris, *Questioning the Sacred Cow: Reexamining the Justifications for Small Business Set Asides*, 36 PUB. CONT. L.J. 685 (2007).

SETOFF   The reduction of contract payments by the amount of a contractor's indebtedness to the government. The government's right of setoff applies to debts arising from unrelated as well as related transactions and to non-contractual as well as contractual debts. There is no requirement that the government's claim be judged by a court before setoff may be used. See U.S. GOV'T ACCOUNTABILITY OFFICE, PRINCIPLES OF FEDERAL APPROPRIATIONS LAW: ANNUAL UPDATE TO THE THIRD EDITION, chap. 13, GAO-15-303SP (Washington, D.C.: Mar. 2015). However, it has been held that setoff (but not WITHHOLDING) can only be made in accordance with the procedures of the DEBT COLLECTION ACT and the CONTRACT DISPUTES ACT OF 1978. See Cibinic, Nagle & Nash, ADMINISTRATION OF GOVERNMENT CONTRACTS 1070–73 (5th ed. 2016). See also NO-SETOFF COMMITMENT.

SETTLEMENT AGREEMENT   *Official:* A written agreement in the form of a CONTRACT MODIFICATION settling all or a severable portion of a SETTLEMENT PROPOSAL. *Source:* FAR 49.001. Contracting officers are authorized to enter into these agreements. FAR 49.101(a).

SETTLEMENT AUTHORITY   The authority to settle contractual DISPUTEs by agreement. FAR 33.210 provides that the contracting officer has the authority to settle all CLAIMs arising under or related to the contract that are subject to the CONTRACT DISPUTES ACT OF 1978. Exceptions are (1) claims involving penalties or forfeitures prescribed by statute or regulation that another federal agency is specifically authorized to administer, settle, or determine; and (2) claims involving FRAUD. If a contracting officer is unable to settle a claim but renders a decision, the settlement authority varies thereafter. If the DECISION OF THE CONTRACTING OFFICER on a claim is the subject of an appeal to an agency BOARD OF CONTRACT APPEALS (BCA), the contracting officer retains settlement authority and may not delegate that authority to a government trial attorney. If the decision of the contracting officer is appealed to the COURT OF FEDERAL CLAIMS or the decision of a BCA is appealed to the COURT OF APPEALS FOR THE FEDERAL CIRCUIT, settlement authority resides with the Attorney General and is normally delegated to DOJ attorneys. See Cibinic, Nagle & Nash, ADMINISTRATION OF GOVERNMENT CONTRACTS 1189–92 (5th ed. 2016).

SETTLEMENT DATE   *Official:* As it applies to ELECTRONIC FUNDS TRANSFER, the date on which an electronic funds transfer payment is credited to the contractor's financial institution. *Source:* FAR 32.902. If the settlement date for an INVOICE PAYMENT is later than the DUE DATE, the government payment office is required to add interest to the payment in accordance with the requirements of the PROMPT PAYMENT ACT. FAR 32.907. To avoid such interest payments, the payment office is required to give the appropriate Federal Reserve Bank a SPECIFIED PAYMENT DATE.

SETTLEMENT EXPENSES   The costs incurred by a contractor in carrying out a termination including (1) accounting, legal, clerical, and similar costs reasonably necessary for—(A) the preparation and presentation, including supporting data, of settlement claims to the contracting officer; and (B) the termination and settlement of subcontracts; (2) reasonable costs for the storage, transportation, protection, and disposition of property acquired or produced for the contract; and (3) indirect costs related to salary and wages incurred as settlement expenses in (1) and (2) (normally, such indirect costs are limited to payroll taxes, fringe benefits, occupancy costs, and immediate supervision costs). FAR 31.205-42(g). These expenses are ALLOWABLE COSTs. See Manos, 1 GOVERNMENT CONTRACT COSTS AND PRICING § 49.8 (2d ed. 2009–2020); Cibinic, Nagle & Nash, ADMINISTRATION OF GOVERNMENT CONTRACTS 994 (5th ed. 2016); Cibinic, Knight & Nash, COST-REIMBURSEMENT CONTRACTING 752 (4th ed. 2014).

SETTLEMENT PROPOSAL   *Official:* A proposal for effecting settlement of a contract terminated in whole or in part, submitted by a contractor or subcontractor in the form, and supported by the data, required by this part. A settlement proposal is included within the generic meaning of the word CLAIM under the FALSE CLAIMS ACT (see 18 U.S.C. § 287 and 32 U.S.C. § 3729). *Source:* FAR 49.001. Settlement proposals are submitted by contractors in TERMINATIONs FOR CONVENIENCE, as well as by cost-reimbursement contractors in TERMINATIONs FOR DEFAULT. In the case of a termination for default, however, the costs of preparing the proposal are not ALLOWABLE COSTs. FAR 49.403(b)(1). FAR 49.602 discusses the forms and procedures necessary for settling terminated contracts. See Cibinic, Nagle & Nash, ADMINISTRATION OF GOVERNMENT CONTRACTS 969–74 (5th ed. 2016). Termination claims supported by SETTLEMENT PROPOSALs submitted more than one year after termination have been held to have been forfeited. See Nash, *Postscript II: Late Convenience Termination Settlement Proposals*, 20 N&CR ¶ 30 (June 2006).

SEVERANCE PAY   *Official:* A payment in addition to regular salaries and wages by contractors to workers whose employment is being involuntarily terminated. *Source:* FAR 31.205-6(g)(1). Severance pay, or dismissal wages, must meet the requirements of FAR 31.205-6(g) to be an ALLOWABLE COST. See Manos, 1 GOVERNMENT CONTRACT COSTS & PRICING § 13.9 (2d ed. 2009–2020). The FAR distinguishes between normal turnover severance pay, which is allowable, and mass severance pay, which is unallowable but is to be considered on a case-by-case basis. See Cibinic, Knight & Nash, COST-REIMBURSEMENT CONTRACTING 673 (4th ed. 2014).

SEVERE FORMS OF TRAFFICKING IN PERSONS   *Official:* (1) SEX TRAFFICKING in which a commercial sex act is induced by force, fraud, or coercion, or in which the person induced to perform such act has not attained 18 years of age; or (2) The recruitment, harboring, transportation, provision, or obtaining of a person for labor or services, through the use of force, fraud, or coercion for the purpose of subjection to involuntary servitude, peonage, debt bondage, or slavery. *Source:* FAR 22.1702. 22 U.S.C. § 7104 prohibits contractors from engaging in this type of conduct. All contracts are required to contain the Combating Trafficking in Persons clause in FAR 52.222-50. Guidance on this policy is contained in FAR Subpart 22.17. See also OMB Memorandum, *Anti-Trafficking Risk Management Best Practices & Mitigation Considerations* (Oct. 21, 2019).

SEVERELY DISABLED   See BLIND OR SEVERELY DISABLED.

SEVERIN DOCTRINE   A legal rule preventing contractors from recovering damages on behalf of subcontractors for BREACH OF CONTRACT by the government if the contractor has no liability to the subcontractor. The rule originated with the case of *Severin v. United States*, 99 Ct. Cl. 435 (1943), which held that a clause in a subcontract completely exculpating the contractor from liability barred any CLAIM on behalf of the subcontractor against the government because the contractor could not prove that it (rather than the subcontractor) had suffered any damages. The doctrine does not apply if a subcontract contains a clause that provides that the contractor is liable only if it recovers from the government. The rule does not apply to claims for compensation under contract clauses. See Cibinic, Nagle & Nash, ADMINISTRATION OF GOVERNMENT CONTRACTS 1155 (5th ed. 2016); Feldman, *Subcontractors in Federal Procurement: Roles, Rights & Responsibilities*, BRIEFING PAPERS No. 03-03 (Feb. 2003).

SEX TRAFFICKING   *Official:* The recruitment, harboring, transportation, provision, or obtaining of a person for the purpose of a commercial sex act. *Source:* FAR 22.1702. 22 U.S.C. § 7104 prohibits contractors from engaging in this type of conduct. See SEVERE FORMS OF TRAFFICKING IN PERSONS.

"SHALL"   *Official:* The imperative. *Source:* FAR 2.101. When the FEDERAL ACQUISITION REGULATION uses the term "shall," it denotes that the regulation must be followed unless the contracting officer has obtained a DEVIATION. The alternate mandatory word is "must." If a mandatory clause that implements fundamental procurement policy is omitted from the contract without a deviation, it is included in the contract by operation of the CHRISTIAN DOCTRINE.

SHARE-IN-SAVINGS CONTRACTING   An acquisition method under which an agency enters into a contract turning over the operation of an agency function to a contractor with the payment to be based on a share of the reduced costs incurred by the agency. This type of contract relieves the agency from the necessity of making capital expenditures and induces the contractor to provide a more efficient method of operation. It has been used extensively with ENERGY-SAVINGS PERFORMANCE CONTRACTS. See also SHARED-SAVINGS PROJECT. See Cibinic, *Share-In Savings Contracts: An Update*, 18 N&CR ¶ 43 (Oct. 2004); Nash, *Postscript: Share-In-Savings Contracts*, 17 N&CR ¶ 12 (Feb. 2003); U.S. GOV'T ACCOUNTABILITY OFFICE, CONTRACT MANAGEMENT: COMMERCIAL USE OF SHARE-IN SAVINGS CONTRACTING, GAO-03-327 (Jan. 2003); Nash, *Share-In-Savings Contracts: A Non-FAR Type of Contract*, 14 N&CR ¶ 63 (Dec. 2000).

SHARE RATIO   Under a fixed-price incentive or cost-plus-incentive-fee INCENTIVE CONTRACT, the contract stipulation of how the government and the contractor will share the amount of a cost underrun or overrun when determining the contractor's final profit or fee. The contract stipulates only the contractor's share, in the form of a number of cents of each dollar of cost incurred above or below the target cost, which is the dollar amount to be added to or deducted from the contractor's target profit or target fee. In speech, the share ratio is commonly expressed in the form "seventy-thirty" or "sixty-forty," and in writing extrinsic to the contract it is expressed in the form "70/30" or "60/40," in which expressions, by convention, the first number is the government's share. The sum of the shares must equal $1.00. Thus, if the share ratio is 75/25, the government keeps $.75 of each dollar of a cost underrun or pays $.75 of each dollar of a cost overrun, the contractor keeps or pays $.25 as an increase or reduction in profit or fee. A contract may have different share ratios for different cost outcomes. The FAR does not mention this term. DFARS 216.402-1(b) states that a 50/50 share should be the "point of departure" for negotiating a FIXED-PRICE INCENTIVE CONTRACT. See Cibinic, Nash & Yukins, FORMATION OF GOVERNMENT CONTRACTS 1258–67, 1270–75 (4th ed. 2011); Cibinic, Knight & Nash, COST-REIMBURSEMENT CONTRACTING 56 (4th ed. 2014); DAU, *Contract Pricing Reference Guides* v. IV.

SHARED-SAVINGS PROJECT   A project where an agency enters into a contract to achieve energy savings by permitting the contractor to make energy audits, install energy saving equipment, and train personnel in exchange for a share of the energy savings resulting from such measures. This type of contract is permitted by 42 U.S.C. § 8287, which contains quite detailed guidance on their form. Such contracts may be for periods up to 25 years. FAR 23.205 encourages agencies to make "maximum use" of such ENERGY-SAVINGS PERFORMANCE CONTRACTs. FAR 41.102(b)(7) states that FAR Part 41, providing guidance on acquisition of utilities, does not apply to such contracts. See SHARE-IN-SAVINGS CONTRACTING.

SHARING ARRANGEMENT   The method by which an agency determines a contractor's fair share of ACQUISITION SAVINGS resulting from the application of an accepted VALUE ENGINEERING CHANGE PROPOSAL. The contractor is entitled to a percentage share of any net acquisition savings realized on the instant contract, concurrent contracts, and future contracts (see CONCURRENT CONTRACT SAVINGS and FUTURE CONTRACT SAVINGS). FAR 48.104 provides guidance for determining the government/contractor shares of such savings. See Nash & Feldman, GOVERNMENT CONTRACT CHANGES, chap. 9 (3d ed. 2006–2020); Cibinic, Nagle & Nash, ADMINISTRATION OF GOVERNMENT CONTRACTS 372–74 (5th ed. 2016).

SHARING BASE   *Official:* The number of affected end items on contracts of the contracting office accepting a VALUE ENGINEERING CHANGE PROPOSAL. *Source:* FAR 48.001. The sharing base is one of the elements in the computation of ACQUISITION SAVINGS.

SHARING PERIOD   *Official:* The period beginning with acceptance of the first unit incorporating the VALUE ENGINEERING CHANGE PROPOSAL and ending at a calendar date or event determined by the contracting officer for each VECP. *Source:* FAR 48.001. The sharing period is one of the elements in the computation of FUTURE CONTRACT SAVINGS. Guidance on the determination of this period is contained in FAR 48.104-1. See Cibinic, Nagle & Nash, ADMINISTRATION OF GOVERNMENT CONTRACTS 374 (5th ed. 2016).

SHELTERED WORKSHOP See BLIND OR SEVERELY DISABLED.

SHIFT PREMIUM *Official:* The difference between the contractor's regular rate of pay to an employee and the higher rate paid for extra-pay-shift work. *Source:* FAR 2.101 (in the definition of OVERTIME PREMIUM). Shift premiums are not subject to the stringent requirements governing the use of OVERTIME.

SHOP DRAWINGS *Official:* Drawings submitted by the construction contractor or a subcontractor at any tier or required under a construction contract, showing in detail either or both of the following: (1) The proposed fabrication and assembly of structural elements. (2) The installation (i.e., form, fit, and attachment details) of materials or equipment. *Source:* FAR 2.101. The standard Specifications and Drawings for Construction clause in FAR 52.236-21 contains detailed procedures for the submission of shop drawings when they are required by the contract. These procedures require the contracting officer to give approval or disapproval of such drawings, but the clause states that approval does not relieve the contractor of the responsibility for errors or omissions in the drawings (see OMISSIONS AND MISDESCRIPTIONS). See Parrott, *The Shop Drawing Submittal Process*, CONSTR. BRIEFING No. 96-9 (Aug. 1996).

SHOULD *Official:* An expected course of action or policy that is to be followed unless inappropriate for a particular circumstance. *Source:* FAR 2.101. This term is used in the FAR when a nonmandatory procedure is described.

SHOULD-COST ANALYSIS See SHOULD-COST REVIEW.

SHOULD-COST REVIEW A technique aimed at establishing a PRICE on the basis of what it *should* cost the contractor to produce, assuming reasonable economy and efficiency of operation. It is a specialized form of COST ANALYSIS that does not assume that a contractor's historical costs reflect efficient and economical operation, but instead evaluates the economy and efficiency of the contractor's existing workforce, methods, materials, facilities, operating systems, and management. A should-cost review is performed at the contractor's plant, employing a multi-functional team of government procurement, contract administration, pricing, AUDIT, and engineering representatives. The objective is to reduce the cost of performance of government contracts by promoting both short- and long-range improvements in the contractor's economy and efficiency; quantifying the findings in terms of their impact on cost; and developing a realistic price objective for negotiation. The scope of a should-cost review can range from a large-scale review of the contractor's entire operation, including plantwide overhead and major subcontractors, to a small-scale tailored review examining specific contractor operations. FAR 15.407-4. In establishing a should-cost review, the contracting officer should identify the specific elements of a contractor's operations that have the greatest potential for cost savings. DOD suggests a should-cost review before award of a major systems contract and an overhead should-cost review for contractor business units with large sales to DOD. DOD PGI 215.407-4. See Cibinic, Knight & Nash, COST-REIMBURSEMENT CONTRACTING 478 (4th ed. 2014); Cibinic, Nash & Yukins, FORMATION OF GOVERNMENT CONTRACTS 1531–32 (4th ed. 2011).

SHOULD-COST REVIEW TEAM An integrated team of government procurement, contract administration, pricing, AUDIT, and engineering representatives formed to conduct a coordinated, in-depth SHOULD-COST REVIEW at the contractor's plant. The team normally consists of a team leader, a deputy team leader, a DEFENSE CONTRACT AUDIT

AGENCY representative, an operations and administration officer, and three subteams—technical, management, and pricing. See *DCAA Contract Audit Manual* ¶ 9-1303 and ¶ 9-1304.

SHOW CAUSE NOTICE   A preliminary written notice given to the contractor by the contracting officer when TERMINATION FOR DEFAULT appears to be appropriate. FAR 49.402-3(e)(1). It (1) notifies the contractor of the possibility of termination, (2) indicates the contractual liabilities of default termination, and (3) asks the contractor to show cause why the contract should not be terminated for default. A major purpose of the notice is to determine whether the contractor is entitled to any EXCUSABLE DELAYs. The notice may state that failure of the contractor to show cause may be taken as admission that there is no valid cause. The notice may also invite the contractor to discuss the matter at a meeting or conference. A suggested format for a show cause notice is set forth in FAR 49.607(b). See Cibinic, Nagle & Nash, ADMINISTRATION OF GOVERNMENT CONTRACTS 878 (5th ed. 2016). See also CURE NOTICE.

SHRINK WRAP LICENSE   A license to use a COMPUTER PROGRAM that is entered into by opening the package containing the program. The terms of the license usually provide that the user is not the owner of the copy of the OBJECT CODE in the package, that title to the object code is retained by the program proprietor, and that the user will not reverse engineer, decompile or disassemble the object code. Such provisions give the purchaser of the license fewer rights than would be obtained under the Copyright Act if the purchaser was the owner of the program. A similar form of license entered into when a program is obtained through the internet is a CLICK WRAP LICENSE. This form of license has been held to be a valid contract in *ProCD v. Zeidenberg*, 86 F.3d 1447 (7th Cir. 1996). See Nash & Rawicz, INTELLECTUAL PROPERTY IN GOVERNMENT CONTRACTS, chap. 5 (6th ed. 2008).

SIGNATURE   *Official:* The discrete, verifiable symbol of an individual which, when affixed to a writing with the knowledge and consent of the individual, indicates a present intention to authenticate the WRITING. This includes electronic symbols. *Source:* FAR 2.101. Only CONTRACTING OFFICERs can sign contracts. FAR 4.101. Guidance on the signature required by various types of contractors is set forth in FAR 4.102. Electronic signatures are permitted by FAR 4.502(d). See Cibinic, Nash & Yukins, FORMATION OF GOVERNMENT CONTRACTS 257–62 (4th ed. 2011); Nash, *The Contracting Officer's Signature: When Is It Binding?*, 22 N&CR ¶ 3 (Jan. 2008).

SIGNED   See SIGNATURE.

SIGNIFICANT REVISIONS   *Official:* Revisions that alters the substantive meaning of any coverage in the FEDERAL ACQUISITION REGULATION SYSTEM having a significant cost or administrative impact on contractors or offerors, or a significant effect beyond the internal operating procedures of the issuing agency. This expression, for example, does not include editorial, stylistic, or other revisions that have no impact on the basic meaning of the coverage being revised. *Source:* FAR 1.501-1. Public comments must be solicited on proposed revisions to the FAR system unless the proposed coverage does not constitute a significant revision. FAR 1.501-3.

SIGNIFICANT WEAKNESS   *Official: A* flaw in a PROPOSAL that appreciably increases the risk of unsuccessful contract performance. *Source:* FAR 2.101 (in the definition of WEAKNESS). Significant weaknesses must be discussed with offerors in the COMPETITIVE

RANGE. FAR 15.306(d)(3). See Feldman, GOVERNMENT CONTRACT GUIDEBOOK, §§ 6:18–6:23 (4th ed. 2019–2020); Cibinic, Nash & Yukins, FORMATION OF GOVERNMENT CONTRACTS 892–96 (4th ed. 2011).

SIMPLIFIED ACQUISITION PROCEDURES *Official:* The methods prescribed in Part 13 for making purchases of supplies and services. *Source:* FAR 2.101. These simplified procedures are intended to (1) reduce administrative costs, (2) improve opportunities for SMALL BUSINESS CONCERNS and SMALL DISADVANTAGED BUSINESS CONCERNs, (3) promote efficiency and economy in contracting, and (4) avoid unnecessary burdens for agencies and contractors. FAR 13.002. Simplified purchases may be made using IMPREST FUNDS, FAR 13.305; PURCHASE ORDERS, FAR Subpart 13.302; BLANKET PURCHASE AGREEMENTs, FAR Subpart 13.303; GOVERNMENT-WIDE COMMERCIAL PURCHASE CARDs, FAR 13.301; or any other authorized method. These procedures must be used to the maximum extent practicable for all purchases not exceeding the SIMPLIFIED ACQUISITION THRESHOLD, unless requirements can be met by using required sources of supply or existing IDIQ contracts. FAR 13.003(a). The contracting officer is required to SET ASIDE all purchases exceeding $10,000 but not exceeding $250,000 (except foreign purchases) for SMALL BUSINESS CONCERNS. Since 1996, simplified acquisition procedures have been available for contracts for the purchase of COMMERCIAL ITEMS whose expected value exceeds the simplified acquisition threshold but is below $7.5 million (or $15 million in the case of goods or services purchased in support of contingency operations, or for defense against or recovery from cyber, nuclear, biological, chemical, or radiological attack). FAR Subpart 13.5. See Feldman, GOVERNMENT CONTRACT GUIDEBOOK §§ 3:8–3:14 (4th ed. 2019–2020); Cibinic, Nash & Yukins, FORMATION OF GOVERNMENT CONTRACTS 1027–59 (4th ed. 2011); Manuel, CONG. RESEARCH SERV., Report No. R40516, COMPETITION IN FEDERAL CONTRACTING: AN OVERVIEW OF THE LEGAL REQUIREMENTS (Jan. 10, 2011); Edwards, *Simplified Acquisition Procedures: Why Can't We Keep Them Simple?*, 21 N&CR ¶ 31 (July 2007).

SIMPLIFIED ACQUISITION THRESHOLD *Official:* $250,000, except for (1) Acquisitions of supplies or services that, as determined by the head of the agency, are to be used to support a contingency operation or to facilitate defense against or recovery from cyber, nuclear, biological, chemical, or radiological attack (41 U.S.C. § 1903), the term means—(i) $800,000 for any contract to be awarded and performed, or purchase to be made, inside the United States; and (ii) $1.5 million for any contract to be awarded and performed, or purchase to be made, outside the United States; and (2) Acquisitions of supplies or services that, as determined by the head of the agency, are to be used to support a humanitarian or peacekeeping operation (10 U.S.C. § 2302), the term means $300,000 for any contract to be awarded and performed, or purchase to be made, outside the United States. *Source:* FAR 2.101. This is the maximum dollar value of an acquisition that may use SIMPLIFIED ACQUISITION PROCEDURES. The threshold was established at $100,000 by the FEDERAL ACQUISITION STREAMLINING ACT OF 1994 and has been periodically increased.

SIMPLIFIED CONTRACT FORMAT A standardized format used in lieu of the UNIFORM CONTRACT FORMAT when obtaining supplies or services using a FIRM-FIXED-PRICE CONTRACT or a FIXED-PRICE CONTRACT WITH ECONOMIC PRICE ADJUSTMENT in SEALED BID procurements. The recommended format is the Solicitation/Contract form (Standard Form 1447), followed by the contract schedule, clauses, a list of documents and attachments (if necessary), and representations and instructions. The contracting officer, however, has flexibility in organizing and preparing the documentation. See FAR 14.201-9.

SIMPLIFIED PROCEDURES FOR CERTAIN COMMERCIAL ITEMS The use of SIMPLIFIED ACQUISITION PROCEDURES for contracts for the purchase of COMMERCIAL ITEMS whose expected value exceeds the simplified acquisition threshold but is below $7.5 million (or $15 million in the case of goods or services purchased in support of contingency operations, or for defense against or recovery from cyber, nuclear, biological, chemical, or radiological attack which are deemed to be commercial items). FAR Subpart 13.5. See Cibinic, Nash & Yukins, FORMATION OF GOVERNMENT CONTRACTS 1027–59 (4th ed. 2011).

SINGLE-AWARD BPA A BLANKET PURCHASE AGREEMENT awarded to a single contractor holding a FEDERAL SUPPLY SCHEDULE contract. FAR 8.405-6 contains detailed guidance on the circumstances that permit single-award BPAs. If a single-award BPA will have an estimated value exceeding $112 million, it must be approved by the HEAD OF THE AGENCY. FAR 8.405-3(a)(3)(ii).

SINGLE-AWARD IDIQ CONTRACT An INDEFINITE DELIVERY/INDEFINITE QUANTITY CONTRACT that is awarded only to a single contractor. While there is a MULTIPLE AWARD PREFERENCE, FAR 16.504(c)(ii)(B) calls for single awards if (1) only one contractor is capable of providing performance at the level of quality required because the supplies or services are unique or highly specialized; (2) based on the contracting officer's knowledge of the market, more favorable terms and conditions, including pricing, will be provided if a single award is made; (3) the expected cost of administration of multiple contracts outweighs the expected benefits of making multiple awards; (4) the projected orders are so integrally related that only a single contractor can reasonably perform the work; (5) the total estimated value of the contract is less than the simplified acquisition threshold; or (6) multiple awards would not be in the best interests of the government. Single awards over $112 million must be approved by the HEAD OF THE AGENCY, who must notify Congress and prepare a detailed DETERMINATION AND FINDING. FAR 16.504(c)(ii)(D). These single award contracts provide an agency with the greatest flexibility to establish the requirements for services by issuing TASK ORDERs as a project progresses. These contracts have been used extensively.

SINGLE GOVERNMENT WIDE POINT OF ENTRY *Official:* The one point of entry to be designated by the Administrator of the OFFICE OF FEDERAL PROCUREMENT POLICY that will allow the private sector to electronically access procurement opportunities governmentwide. *Source:* FAR 2.101. This is the major means that government agencies publish a required SYNOPSIS informing potential contractors of upcoming procurements (FAR 5.203) and SOLICITATIONs (FAR 5.102(a)). FAR 5.201(d) specifies that the point of entry is www.beta.SAM.gov. See Cibinic, Nash & Yukins, FORMATION OF GOVERNMENT CONTRACTS 390–403 (4th ed. 2011).

SINGLE PROCESS INITIATIVE A DOD policy designed to implement a single process in a contractor's plant or facility in order to reduce the cost of performance of all DOD contracts at that plant or facility. See SPI PROCESS. A single process is implemented by processing a "block change" modification to all contracts with the plant or facility consolidating or eliminating multiple processes, specifications, and standards. Guidance on acceptance of contractor requests for a single process is set forth in DFARS Subpart 211.273 and the Substitutions for Military or Federal Specifications and Standards clause at DFARS 252.211-7005.

SINGLE SOURCE   See SOLE SOURCE.

SITE OF THE WORK   *Official:* (1)(i) The primary site of the work. The physical place or places where the construction called for in the contract will remain when work is completed; and (ii) The secondary site of the work, if any. Any other site where a significant portion of the building or work is constructed, provided that such site is—(A) Located in the United States; and (B) Established specifically for the performance of the contract or project; (2) Except as provided in paragraph (3) of this definition, includes fabrication plants, mobile factories, batch plants, borrow pits, job headquarters, tool yards, etc., provided—(i) They are dedicated exclusively, or nearly so, to performance of the contract or project; and (ii) They are adjacent or virtually adjacent to the "primary site of the work" as defined in paragraphs (1)(i) and of "the secondary site of the work" as defined in paragraph (1)(ii) of this definition; (3) Does not include permanent home offices, branch plant establishments, fabrication plants, or tool yards of a contractor or subcontractor whose locations and continuance in operation are determined wholly without regard to a particular Federal contract or project. In addition, fabrication plants, batch plants, borrow pits, job headquarters, yards, etc., of a commercial or material supplier, which are established by a supplier of materials for the project before opening of bids and not on the project site, are not included in the "site of the work." Such permanent, previously established facilities are not a part of the "site of the work," even if the operations for a period of time may be dedicated exclusively, or nearly so, to the performance of a contract. *Source:* FAR 22.401. The DAVIS-BACON ACT is applicable only to LABORERS OR MECHANICS employed directly on the site of work. FAR 22.404.

SIZE APPEAL   See SIZE PROTEST.

SIZE PROTEST   The protest by an offeror or interested party challenging another offeror's representation of itself as a SMALL BUSINESS CONCERN. Such protests must be filed within five days after BID OPENING or receipt of notice of an apparent successful offeror. FAR 19.302(d)(1). Size protests are referred to the SMALL BUSINESS ADMINISTRATION (SBA) regional office where the principal office of the challenged offeror is located. FAR 19.302(c). Once the contracting officer receives a protest, he or she may not award the contract until SBA makes a size determination or 10 business days transpire after SBA's receipt of the protest, whichever occurs first. When the contracting officer determines in writing that award must be made to protect the PUBLIC INTEREST, the award need not be stayed, although the contracting officer must notify the SBA. FAR 19.302(h). The contracting officer may stay the award longer than 10 days, until SBA's determination is received, unless the delay would prove disadvantageous to the government. Appeals from adverse size determinations by the SBA must be filed with the SBA Office of Hearings and Appeals in Washington, DC. FAR 19.302(i). See Greenspahn, *Small Business Size Protests & Appeals: Trends & Analysis*, BRIEFING PAPERS No. 12-7 (June 2012). See also SIZE STATUS.

SIZE STANDARDS   See SMALL BUSINESS CONCERN.

SIZE STATUS   The characteristics of a firm that qualify it to obtain the benefits of being a SMALL BUSINESS CONCERN. The size status of a concern is determined, in the first instance, by SELF-CERTIFICATION that a firm meets size standards established by the SMALL BUSINESS ADMINISTRATION. Guidance on the application of size standards is set forth in FAR 19.102. If the status is challenged, the size is determined through the SIZE PROTEST procedures.

SLIP LAW   A pamphlet containing the text of an individual PUBLIC or PRIVATE LAW that is published after enactment by the OFFICE OF THE FEDERAL REGISTER in the NATIONAL ARCHIVES AND RECORDS ADMINISTRATION. The slip law is the first publication of a law that is made available to the public. See *How Are Laws are Made*, available at https://www.usa.gov/how-laws-are-made.

SMALL AND DISADVANTAGED BUSINESS UTILIZATION SPECIALIST (SADBUS)   A government employee with the responsibility of ensuring the utilization of SMALL BUSINESS CONCERNs and SMALL DISADVANTAGED BUSINESS CONCERNs (SDBCs) in accordance with agency regulations. FAR 19.201(d). Agencies frequently use titles such as "small business specialist" or "small business/disadvantaged business specialist" in lieu of SADBUS. The duties assigned to this function vary from agency to agency. Within DOD, DOD PGI 219.201(d) specifies that the SADBUS must (1) make sure that programs affecting small business concerns, HISTORICALLY BLACK COLLEGES AND UNIVERSITIES (HBCUs), MINORITY INSTITUTIONs (MIs), and LABOR SURPLUS AREA (LSA) CONCERNs are implemented; (2) advise contracting, program, and requirements personnel on all matters affecting small businesses, HBCUs, MIs, and LSA concerns; (3) advise and inform small businesses, SDBCs, HBCUs, MIs, and LSA concerns about acquisition procedures and proposed acquisitions and instruct them in preparing proposals and interpreting solicitation provisions and contract clauses; (4) maintain outreach programs designed to locate small businesses, SDBCs, HBCUs, and MIs and to develop information on their technical competence; (5) ensure that small business concerns are offered financial assistance available under existing regulations and that they obtain payment under their contracts; (6) help contracting officers determine when subcontracting plans are needed, whether they are acceptable, and whether they are being complied with; and (7) monitor performance against small and disadvantaged business program goals and recommend action to correct deficiencies.

SMALL BUSINESS ACT   A 1963 Act, 15 U.S.C. § 631 et seq., that created the SMALL BUSINESS ADMINISTRATION (SBA). The SBA is jointly responsible with the federal procuring agencies for promoting policies and taking actions to ensure that SMALL BUSINESS CONCERNs and SMALL DISADVANTAGED BUSINESS CONCERNs obtain their fair share of government procurements. The Act has been amended periodically to add to the powers and functions of the SBA. See Cibinic, Nash & Yukins, FORMATION OF GOVERNMENT CONTRACTS 1573–1614 (4th ed. 2011). See also CONG. RESEARCH SERV., Report No. R45576, AN OVERVIEW OF SMALL BUSINESS CONTRACTING (Aug. 14, 2020).

SMALL BUSINESS ADMINISTRATION (SBA)   A government agency that aids, counsels, assists, and protects the interests of small business; ensures that SMALL BUSINESS CONCERNs receive a fair portion of government purchases, contracts, and subcontracts, as well as of the sales of government property; makes loans to small business concerns, State and local development companies, and the victims of floods or other catastrophes, or of certain types of economic injury; and licenses, regulates, and makes loans to small business investment companies. Office of the Federal Register, National Archives and Records Administration, *U.S. Government Manual* (2011 ed.). The SBA is authorized to (1) define specific small business size standards; (2) make loans; (3) enter into contracts with the government and arrange for performance by subcontracting to small business (see 8(a) PROGRAM); (4) engage in determinations that certain interests would be served by awarding all or part of a contract to small business; (5) determine the SIZE STATUS of small business concerns; (6) certify the competency, including capacity and credit, of small businesses to perform particular contracts (see CERTIFICATE OF COMPETENCY); and (7) assist and encourage small business to undertake joint research and development programs (see SMALL BUSINESS INNOVATIVE RESEARCH CONTRACT). SBA regulations are at 13 C.F.R. parts 101 through 140. See www.sba.gov.

SMALL BUSINESS COMPETITIVENESS DEMONSTRATION PROGRAM A program to improve the small business policies of the government, enacted by the Business Opportunity Development Reform Act of 1988, 15 U.S.C. § 644. This program became effective as a temporary program on January 1, 1989 and was made permanent in 1997 (Pub. L. No. 105-135, § 421). It was repealed by § 1335 of the Small Business Jobs Act of 2010, Pub. L. No. 111-240.

SMALL BUSINESS CONCERN *Official:* A CONCERN, including its affiliates, that is independently owned and operated, not dominant in the field of operation in which it is bidding on government contracts, and qualified as a small business under the criteria and size standards in 13 C.F.R. part 121 (see 19.102). Such a concern is "not dominant in its field of operation" when it does not exercise a controlling or major influence on a national basis in a kind of business activity in which a number of business concerns are primarily engaged. In determining whether dominance exists, consideration must be given to all appropriate factors, including volume of business, number of employees, financial resources, competitive status or position, ownership or control of materials, processes, patents, license agreements, facilities, sales territory, and nature of business activity. (See 15 U.S.C. § 632.) *Source:* FAR 2.101. The definition of a small business varies by industry. To qualify, a contractor must fall within the size standard applicable to the industry as classified in the NORTH AMERICAN INDUSTRY CLASSIFICATION SYSTEM (NAICS). 13 C.F.R. § 121.201. Depending on the industry in question, the standard applied is based on either dollar volume (average ANNUAL RECEIPTS for the preceding five fiscal years) or the number of employees. Contracting officers are required to include the applicable NAICS code in each solicitation. FAR 19.303. See also SIZE STATUS; SIZE PROTEST.

SMALL BUSINESS INNOVATIVE RESEARCH (SBIR) CONTRACT A contract issued pursuant to the Small Business Innovation Development Act of 1982, 15 U.S.C. § 638(f). This act requires agencies with a budget for "extramural" research and development of more than $100 million to expend a prescribed percentage of such budget with small businesses on SBIR contracts (from 2.7% in FY 2013 to 3.2% in FY 2017). These contracts are issued in two phases: Phase I in an amount up to $150,000 to demonstrate the feasibility of the innovation and Phase II in a "guideline amount" of $1,000,000, up to $1,500,000 for development of the innovation. A second Phase II contract can be awarded if necessary to further the effort. Agencies are also directed to issue, to the extent practicable, Phase III contracts for further development or production of the technology developed under the program. However, these contracts must be funded with non-SBIR funds. Procedures for these contracts are contained in the SBIR/STTR Policy Directive, May 2, 2019. Contracts issued under the SBIR program meet the COMPETITIVE PROCEDURES requirement of the COMPETITION IN CONTRACTING ACT. 10 U.S.C. § 2302(2); 41 U.S.C. § 152(4). These contracts must also provide SBIR/STTR DATA RIGHTS. See Cibinic, Nash & Yukins, FORMATION OF GOVERNMENT CONTRACTS 1093–1101 (4th ed. 2011); Nash & Rawicz, INTELLECTUAL PROPERTY IN GOVERNMENT CONTRACTING, chap. 4 (6th ed. 2008); Metzger, et al., *How SBIR/STTR Regulation Will Impact Investment Firms*, Government Contracts Law 360 (May 23, 2012); Nash, *Small Business Innovative Research: Does Successful Performance Lead To More Work?*, 21 N&CR ¶ 65 (Jan. 2007); DeVecchio, *Technical Data & Computer Software After Night Vision: Marking, Delivery & Reverse Engineering*, BRIEFING PAPERS No. 06-05 (Apr. 2006); Nash, *Proprietary Rights in Products: A Conundrum?*, 20 N&CR ¶ 3 (Jan. 2006); Nash, *Small Business Innovation Research Contracts: A Regulatory Gap*, 19 N&CR ¶ 27 (June 2005).

SMALL BUSINESS INNOVATIVE RESEARCH DATA RIGHTS   See SBIR/STTR DATA RIGHTS.

SMALL BUSINESS SUBCONTRACTING PROGRAM   A program, also known as the SUBCONTRACTING ASSISTANCE PROGRAM, established by the SMALL BUSINESS ACT which requires that SMALL BUSINESS CONCERNS, SMALL AND DISADVANTAGED BUSINESS CONCERNS, HUBZONE businesses, WOMEN-OWNED SMALL BUSINESSES, SERVICE-DISABLED VETERAN-OWNED SMALL BUSINESS CONCERNS, and VETERAN-OWNED SMALL BUSINESS CONCERNs have the maximum practicable opportunity to participate as subcontractors in federal procurement. 15 U.S.C. § 637(d). Prime contractors holding contracts exceeding the SIMPLIFIED ACQUISITION THRESHOLD are required to agree to give such small businesses the maximum opportunity to participate in the performance of the contract. The program requires contractors to submit SUBCONTRACTING PLANS in contracts valued at greater than $750,000 (or $1.5 million for construction). FAR 19.702. 15 U.S.C. § 637(d)(4)(F) directs that a contractor's failure to make a good faith effort to comply with the requirements of the subcontracting plan must result in the imposition of LIQUIDATED DAMAGES. The SMALL BUSINESS ADMINISTRATION has authority to oversee and monitor the program which it does through its COMMERCIAL MARKET REPRESENTATIVES. The program is implemented in FAR Subpart 19.7. See Chudd & Specht, *Small Business Issues in Government Contracts Mergers & Acquisitions*, BRIEFING PAPERS. No. 14-9 (Aug. 2014); Hewitt, *Small Business Contracting Programs: An Update*, BRIEFING PAPERS. No. 12-8 (July 2012); Hewitt, Williams & Alba, *Small Business Contracting Programs-Part II*, BRIEFING PAPERS. No. 10-13 (Dec. 2010); Hewitt, Williams & Alba, *Small Business Contracting Programs-Part I*, BRIEFING PAPERS. No. 10-11 (Oct. 2010).

SMALL BUSINESS SUBCONTRACTOR   *Official:* A CONCERN that does not exceed the size standard for the North American Industry Classification Systems code that the prime contractor determines best describes the product or service being acquired by the subcontract. *Source:* FAR 2.101. Contractors holding contracts for more than the SIMPLIFIED ACQUISITION THRESHOLD are required to give small business subcontractors the maximum practicable opportunity to participate in the performance of their contracts. FAR 19.702. Such subcontractors are eligible to participate in the SMALL BUSINESS SUBCONTRACTING PROGRAM, also known as the subcontracting assistance program in FAR Subpart 19.7 if they meet the other requirements for being a SMALL BUSINESS

CONCERN. See Cibinic, Nash & Yukins, Formation of Government Contracts 1596–99 (4th ed. 2011); Manuel, Cong. Research Serv., Report No. R41230, Legal Protections for Subcontractors on Federal Prime Contracts (Oct. 6, 2010); Manuel, Cong. Research Serv., Report No. R40998, The Inapplicability of Limitations on Subcontracting to "Preference Contracts" for Small Businesses: Washington Harris Group (Oct. 6, 2010).

SMALL BUSINESS TEAMING ARRANGEMENT *Official:* (1) An arrangement where— (i) Two or more SMALL BUSINESS CONCERNs have formed a joint venture; or (ii) A small business offeror agrees with one or more other small business concerns to have them act as its subcontractors under a specified government contract. A Small Business Teaming Arrangement between the offeror and its small business subcontractor(s) exists through a written agreement between the parties that—(A) Is specifically referred to as a "Small Business Teaming Arrangement"; and (B) Sets forth the different responsibilities, roles, and percentages (or other allocations) of work as it relates to the acquisition; (2) (i) For civilian agencies, may include two business concerns in a mentor-protege relationship when both the mentor and the protege are small or the protege is small and the concerns have received an exception to affiliation pursuant to 13 C.F.R. § 121.103(h)(3)(ii) or (iii). (ii) For DoD, may include two business concerns in a mentor-protege relationship in the Department of Defense Pilot Mentor-Protege Program (see section 831 of the National Defense Authorization Act for Fiscal Year 1991 (Pub. L. No. 101-510; 10 U.S.C. § 2302 note)) when both the mentor and the protege are small. There is no exception to joint venture size affiliation for offers received from teaming arrangements under the Department of Defense Pilot Mentor-Protege Program. See 13 C.F.R. § 121.103(b)(9) regarding the exception to affiliation for offers received from Small Business Teaming Arrangements in the case of a solicitation of offers for a bundled contract with a reserve. *Source:* FAR 2.101. These teaming arrangements between small business contractors allow them jointly to meet the rules regarding the amount of work that must be performed by small businesses under set aside contracts. See 13 C.F.R. § 125.6. When they meet these rules, some of the work can be subcontracted to large businesses. See OSTENSIBLE SUBCONTRACTOR: Jones & Habsham, *Limitations on Teaming Arrangements in Small Business Set-asides*, 45 The Procurement Lawyer 3 (2010).

SMALL BUSINESS TECHNOLOGY TRANSFER PROGRAM (STTR) 15 U.S.C. § 638(n). A program instituted pursuant to the Small Business Technology Transfer Act of 1992. This act requires agencies with a budget for "extramural" research and development of more than $1 billion to expend a prescribed percentage of such budget with small businesses on STTR contracts (from 0.35% in FY 2013 to 0.45% in FY 2017). These contracts are issued in two phases: Phase I for one year not to exceed $150,000 to demonstrate the feasibility of the innovation and Phase II in a "guideline amount" of $1,000,000, up to $1,500,000 for development of the innovation. Agencies are also directed to issue, to the extent practicable, Phase III contracts for further development or production of the technology developed under the program. However, these contracts must be funded with non-STTR funds. Procedures for these contracts are contained in the SBIR/STTR Policy Directive, May 2, 2019. See Nash, *SBIR/STTR Data Rights: A New Policy Directive*, 33 N&CR ¶ 38 (July 2019); Metzger, et al., *How SBIR/STTR Regulation Will Impact Investment Firms*, Government Contracts Law 360 (May 23, 2012).

SMALL CLAIMS PROCEDURES See EXPEDITED PROCEDURES.

SMALL DISADVANTAGED BUSINESS CONCERN (SDBC)   *Official:* Consistent with 13 C.F.R. § 124.1002, a small business concern under the size standard applicable to the acquisition, that (1) Is at least 51 percent unconditionally and directly owned (as defined at 13 C.F.R. § 124.105) by—(i) One or more SOCIALLY DISADVANTAGED (as defined at 13 C.F.R. § 124.103) and ECONOMICALLY DISADVANTAGED (as defined at 13 C.F.R. § 124.104) individuals who are citizens of the United States; and (ii) Each individual claiming economic disadvantage has a net worth not exceeding $750,000 after taking into account the applicable exclusions set forth at 13 C.F.R. § 124.104(c)(2); and (2) The management and daily business operations of which are controlled (as defined at 13 C.F.R. § 124.106) by individuals who meet the criteria in paragraphs (1)(i) and (ii) of this definition. *Source:* FAR 2.101. These SMALL BUSINESS CONCERNs can participate in the 8(a) PROGRAM and the SMALL BUSINESS SUBCONTRACTING PROGRAM. Joint ventures of such firms are also included in this definition if they are certified by the SMALL BUSINESS ADMINISTRATION. 13 C.F.R. § 124.1002(f). See Cibinic, Nash & Yukins, FORMATION OF GOVERNMENT CONTRACTS 1600–08 (4th ed. 2011).

SMALL PURCHASE PROCEDURES   See SIMPLIFIED ACQUISITION PROCEDURES.

SOCIALLY DISADVANTAGED INDIVIDUALS   *Official:* Individuals who have been subjected to racial or ethnic prejudice or cultural bias within American society because of their identities as members of a group and without regard to their individual qualities. The social disadvantage must stem from circumstances beyond their control. *Source:* 13 C.F.R. § 124.103(a). Individuals who certify that they are members of named groups (Black Americans, Hispanic Americans, NATIVE AMERICANS, ASIAN-PACIFIC AMERICANS, SUBCONTINENT—ASIAN AMERICANS) are presumed to be socially disadvantaged. 13 C.F.R. § 124.103(b). Businesses owned by such individuals that are also ECONOMICALLY DISADVANTAGED INDIVIDUALS are given special preferences in government procurement as SMALL DISADVANTAGED BUSINESS CONCERNs.

SOCIOECONOMIC PROGRAMS   Programs that are incorporated into the procurement process to foster the achievement of national goals. Although federal procurement policy endeavors to obtain supplies and services economically, efficiently, and in a timely manner, the government also utilizes its purchasing power as a means of promoting public policies. Government contracts attempt to further such national goals as fostering small business, overcoming regional unemployment, assisting minority workers, giving preference to domestic and other special sources, ensuring fair treatment of employees, maintaining integrity and fair competitive practices, and protecting the environment. See FAR Part 19, Small Business and Small Disadvantaged Business Concerns; FAR Part 22, Application of Labor Laws to Government Acquisitions; FAR Part 23, Environment, Conservation, Occupational Safety, and Drug-Free Workplace; FAR Part 24, Protection of Privacy and Freedom of Information; and FAR Part 25, Foreign Acquisition. See Cibinic, Nash & Yukins, FORMATION OF GOVERNMENT CONTRACTS, chap. 11 (4th ed. 2011).

SOFTWARE   See COMPUTER SOFTWARE.

SOFTWARE DOCUMENTATION   See COMPUTER SOFTWARE DOCUMENTATION.

SOFTWARE RESOURCES DATA REPORTING (SRDR) SYSTEM.   One element of the COST AND SOFTWARE DATA REPORTING (CSDR) SYSTEM that is required for use in MAJOR SYSTEM ACQUISITION programs and major automated information system programs by the DOD 5000 Series. Guidance on this reporting is contained in DOD Manual 5000.04, *Cost and Software Data Reporting (CSDR) Manual*, Apr. 18, 2018. Contractors are required to establish metrics based on the technique that will be used to develop software and to report progress against these metrics.

SOFTWARE RIGHTS   See RIGHTS IN COMPUTER SOFTWARE

"SOLD IN SUBSTANTIAL QUANTITIES TO THE GENERAL PUBLIC"   See COMMERCIAL, OFF-THE-SHELF.

SOLE SOURCE ACQUISITION   *Official:* A contract for the purchase of SUPPLIES or services that is entered into or proposed to be entered into by an agency after soliciting and negotiating with only one source. *Source:* FAR 2.101. A sole source acquisition ordinarily is justified when there is only one responsible source (see RESPONSIBILITY) and no other supplies or services will satisfy agency requirements. FAR 6.302-1. Note that an acquisition in which an agency solicits bids or proposals from more than one source but receives only one response is not a sole source acquisition. The general competition requirements (restricting sole source acquisitions) are contained in FAR Part 6 and require that sole source acquisitions must be supported by a JUSTIFICATION AND APPROVAL (J&A), and the agency must publish a SYNOPSIS of its intent to procure on a sole source basis and must consider any bids or proposals received in response to the synopsis, unless the acquisition is authorized or required by statute. FAR 6.302-1(d)(1); 6.302-5. Less stringent competition requirements apply to special categories of acquisitions such as acquisitions made pursuant to GSA's FEDERAL SUPPLY SCHEDULE program (see FAR 8.405-1(c) and 8.405-2(c)); simplified acquisitions (see FAR 13.106-1); and acquisitions using SIMPLIFIED PROCEDURES FOR CERTAIN COMMERCIAL ITEMS. See Cibinic, Nash & Yukins, FORMATION OF GOVERNMENT CONTRACTS 300–13 (4th ed. 2011). See also Edwards, *Sole Source Acquisitions: What Are The Proper Procedures?*, 26 N&CR ¶ 12 (Mar. 2012); Edwards, *Sole-Source ("No Bid") Contracting*, BRIEFING PAPERS No. 08-6 (May 2008).

SOLICITATION   *Official:* Any request to submit OFFERs or QUOTATIONS to the government. Solicitations under sealed bid procedures are called "INVITATIONs FOR BIDS." Solicitations under negotiated procedures are called "REQUESTs FOR PROPOSALS." Solicitations under SIMPLIFIED ACQUISITION PROCEDURES may require submission of either a quotation or an offer. *Source:* FAR 2.101. The term is also used to denote the process of issuing such documents and obtaining responses. See Cibinic, Nash & Yukins, FORMATION OF GOVERNMENT CONTRACTS, chaps. 5 & 6 (4th ed. 2011).

SOLICITATION PROVISION   *Official:* A term or condition used only in SOLICITATIONs and applying only before contract award. *Source:* FAR 2.101. Solicitation provisions are distinguished from CLAUSEs, which are terms and conditions in contracts. FAR Subpart 52.2 sets forth the text of all FAR provisions and clauses (as do DFARS Subpart 252.2 and NFS Subpart 1852.2 for DFARS and NASA provisions and clauses, respectively), each in its own separate subsection. The subpart is arranged by subject matter in the same order as, and keyed to, the parts of the FAR. All FAR provision numbers begin with "52.2." The next two digits correspond with the number of the FAR subject part in which the provision is prescribed. The number is completed by a hyphen and a sequential number assigned within each section of FAR Subpart 52.2. For example, FAR 52.225-1 contains the Buy American Act—Supplies clause prescribed at FAR 25.1101(a)(1), whereas FAR 52.225-2 contains the

Buy American Act Certificate provision prescribed at FAR 25.1101(a)(2). The FAR provision number will be followed by the provision's title and its effective date. FAR Subpart 52.1 contains instructions for using provisions, and FAR Subpart 52.3 contains an extensive PROVISION AND CLAUSE MATRIX.

SOURCE   A firm that can furnish required SUPPLIES or services, as in "source selection."

SOURCE CODE   The version of a COMPUTER PROGRAM that is written in a human-readable programming language. In order to be used in a COMPUTER, the program must be converted into OBJECT CODE. Creation of the source code is the initial step in writing a computer program after its design has been formulated. Modifications or adaptations of the program are also generally made to the source code initially and then converted to object code. See Nash & Rawicz, Intellectual Property in Government Contracting, chap. 5 (6th ed. 2008).

SOURCE SELECTION   The selection of a contractor and AWARD of a contract through COMPETITIVE NEGOTIATION. The process is used for most large and complex competitive acquisitions. The principal rules for conducting source selections are in FAR Subpart 15.3, *Source Selection*, but many agencies have published additional rules and procedures in their FAR supplement or in INTERNAL AGENCY GUIDANCE. According to FAR 15.302, the objective of source selection is to obtain BEST VALUE. There are two primary methods of conducting source selections—the TRADEOFF PROCESS, described in FAR 15.101-1, and the LOWEST PRICE TECHNICALLY ACCEPTABLE process, described in FAR 15.101-2, but agencies may use a combination of processes. According to FAR 15.303(a), AGENCY HEADS are responsible for source selection, and a contracting officer is the designated SOURCE SELECTION AUTHORITY unless the agency head designates someone else. Source selection typically entails the following main steps: (1) developing a SOURCE SELECTION PLAN, including EVALUATION FACTORS, (2) appointing a team of proposal evaluators (SOURCE SELECTION BOARD), (3) preparing and issuing a REQUEST FOR PROPOSALS (RFP), (4) receiving and safeguarding PROPOSALS, (5) evaluating proposals, (6) selecting a contractor *or* establishing a COMPETITIVE RANGE, conducting DISCUSSIONs, soliciting and evaluating FINAL PROPOSAL REVISIONS, and *then* selecting a contractor, and (7) awarding a contract. See generally Cibinic, Nash & Yukins, Formation of Government Contracts, chap. 6 (4th ed. 2011), Feldman, Government Contract Awards—Negotiation and Sealed Bidding (2020–2021 ed.), and Edwards, *Competitive Processes in Government Contracting: The FAR Part 15 Process Model and Process Inefficiency* (2003), https://www.wifcon.com/anal/analcomproc.htm.

SOURCE SELECTION ADVISORY COUNCIL (SSAC)   A panel of senior government personnel appointed by a SOURCE SELECTION AUTHORITY to advise on the conduct of the source selection process and prepare a comparative analysis of the evaluation results on a competitively negotiated procurement (see NEGOTIATION). SSACs are used on major procurements under agency policies, which are generally promulgated by handbooks or regulations outside of the FAR system.

SOURCE SELECTION AUTHORITY (SSA)   The government official in charge of selecting a source or sources in a competitive negotiated acquisition (see NEGOTIATION). The title is most often used in the FORMAL SOURCE SELECTION process, when the official is someone other than the contracting officer. FAR 15.303. The agency head or a designee formally designates the source selection authority, who (1) establishes an evaluation group structure, (2) approves a SOURCE SELECTION PLAN, and (3) considers the recommendations of evaluation and advisory groups in making the source selection decision. In smaller procurements, the contracting officer is the source selection authority.

SOURCE SELECTION BOARD (SSB)   A panel of agency officials that oversees the evaluation of PROPOSALs submitted on competitively negotiated procurements. SSBs are generally responsible for ensuring that the evaluations submitted to the SOURCE SELECTION AUTHORITY are consistent and represent a fair evaluation of the proposals submitted. SSBs are used most frequently on major procurements, and the procedures that they follow vary in accordance with agency procedures, which are generally found in handbooks or regulations outside the FAR system.

SOURCE SELECTION EVALUATION BOARD (SSEB)   A synonym for SOURCE SELECTION BOARD.

SOURCE SELECTION INFORMATION   *Official:* Any of the following information that is prepared for use by an agency for the purpose of evaluating a BID or PROPOSAL to enter into an agency procurement contract, if that information has not been previously made available to the public or disclosed publicly: (1) Bid prices in response to an agency INVITATION FOR BIDS, or lists of those bid prices before bid opening; (2) Proposed costs or prices submitted in response to an agency SOLICITATION, or lists of those proposed costs or prices; (3) SOURCE SELECTION PLANs; (4) TECHNICAL EVALUATION plans; (5) Technical evaluations of proposals; (6) Cost or price evaluations of proposals; (7) COMPETITIVE RANGE determinations that identify proposals that have a reasonable chance of being selected for award of a contract; (8) Rankings of bids, proposals, or competitors; (9) Reports and evaluations of source selection panels, boards or advisory councils; and (10) Other information marked as "Source Selection Information—See FAR 2.101 and 3.104" based on a case-by-case determination by the head of the agency or the contracting officer, that its disclosure would jeopardize the integrity or successful completion of the federal agency procurement to which the information relates. *Source:* FAR 2.101. This information may not be disclosed pursuant to the PROCUREMENT INTEGRITY provisions of the OFFICE OF FEDERAL PROCUREMENT POLICY ACT, 41 U.S.C. § 2102. The definition was slightly different in the statute and regulations in effect prior to January 1, 1997. FAR 3.104-4 provides guidance on the treatment of this information. See Cibinic, Nagle & Nash, ADMINISTRATION OF GOVERNMENT CONTRACTS 144 (5th ed. 2016); Cibinic, Nash & Yukins, FORMATION OF GOVERNMENT CONTRACTS 212–16 (4th ed. 2011). See also Briggerman & Bateman, *Handling Procurement Information*, BRIEFING PAPERS No. 05-09 (Aug. 2005).

SOURCE SELECTION OFFICIAL (SSO)   A synonym for SOURCE SELECTION AUTHORITY.

SOURCE SELECTION PLAN   A plan formulated by an agency to specify the key elements of a proposed SOURCE SELECTION. The source selection plan must identify those milestones at which a decision should be made. The plan should address all technical, business management, and other significant considerations that will control the procurement. The specific content of plans can vary, depending on the nature, circumstances, and stage of the acquisition. FAR 7.105. See Nash, *Postscript II: Source Selection Plans*, 24 N&CR ¶ 44 (Sept. 2010).

SOVEREIGN ACT   A public and general act of the government (frequently a law or regulation) that impacts a broad class of citizens or companies. Under the SOVEREIGN ACTS DOCTRINE, the government is not required to compensate contractors for extra costs of performance because of such acts. See Cibinic, Nagle & Nash, ADMINISTRATION OF GOVERNMENT CONTRACTS 330–36 (5th ed. 2016).

SOVEREIGN ACTS DOCTRINE   A defense employed by the federal government to avoid liability when a government SOVEREIGN ACT affects a contractor's performance of a government contract. The doctrine does not apply if the government action is directed solely at a single contractor or a specified group of contractors. See Cibinic, Nagle & Nash, ADMINISTRATION OF GOVERNMENT CONTRACTS 330–36 (5th ed. 2016).

SOVEREIGN IMMUNITY   A legal doctrine that precludes a litigant from asserting an otherwise meritorious cause of action against a sovereign or a party with sovereign attributes unless the sovereign consents to suit. Sovereignty is the supreme, absolute, and uncontrollable power by which any independent state is governed. Sovereignty entails the power to make laws, regulate, collect taxes, wage war, or make peace. Historically, governments (whether federal, state, city, or other) have been immune from TORT (injury to person or property) liability arising from activities that were governmental in nature. BLACK'S LAW DICTIONARY 899 (11th ed. 2019). The federal government has waived its sovereign immunity to permit certain types of actions against the government through a wide variety of statutes, such as the FEDERAL TORT CLAIMS ACT (tort actions), the TUCKER ACT (actions based on the Constitution, statutes, regulations, or contracts, express or implied in fact), the CONTRACT DISPUTES ACT OF 1978 (disputes concerning claims arising under or relating to contracts), 28 U.S.C. § 1498 (use of PATENTs and COPYRIGHTs), and the EQUAL ACCESS TO JUSTICE ACT (recovery of ATTORNEY'S FEES by SMALL BUSINESSes).

SPARES ACQUISITION INTEGRATED WITH PRODUCTION (SAIP)   *Official:* A technique used to acquire REPLENISHMENT PARTS concurrently with parts being produced for the end item. *Source:* DOD PGI 217.7503. SAIP minimizes the cost of spares by avoiding the charges normally associated with separate material orders and manufacturing actions. SAIP is appropriate where ECONOMIES OF SCALE achieved by combining spares orders with installation orders substantially exceed any added administrative costs.

SPEARIN DOCTRINE   A rule creating an IMPLIED WARRANTY OF SPECIFICATIONS when the government furnishes detailed specifications that are not suitable for their intended purpose or are defective. The doctrine is one of the most common bases for government liability under either a CONSTRUCTIVE CHANGE or BREACH OF CONTRACT theory. *United States v. Spearin*, 248 U.S. 132 (1918). See Nash & Feldman, 1 GOVERNMENT CONTRACT CHANGES § 13:2 (3d ed. 2006–2020); Cibinic, Nagle & Nash, ADMINISTRATION OF GOVERNMENT CONTRACTS 251–72 (5th ed. 2016). See also Tramountanas, *Affirmative Defenses to the Spearin Doctrine: Government Attempts to Avoid the Implied Warranty of Specifications*, CONSTR. BRIEFINGS No. 2003-5 (May 2003).

SPECIAL COMPETENCY   *Official:* A special or unique capability, including qualitative aspects, developed incidental to the primary functions of the FEDERALLY FUNDED RESEARCH AND DEVELOPMENT CENTER to meet some special need. *Source:* FAR 2.101. Work should not be placed with a FFRDC unless it is within its special competency. FAR 35.017-3.

SPECIAL EMERGENCY PROCUREMENT AUTHORITY   Authority in 41 U.S.C. § 1903 raising the thresholds for MICRO-PURCHASEs and SIMPLIFIED ACQUISITIONs for procurements (1) in support of a contingency operation (as defined in section 101(a) of title 10 [10 U.S.C.S. § 101(a)]); (2) to facilitate the defense against or recovery from cyber, nuclear, biological, chemical, or radiological attack against the United States; (3) in support of a request from the Secretary of State or the Administrator of the United States Agency for International Development to facilitate the provision of international disaster assistance pursuant to chapter 9 of part I of the Foreign Assistance Act of 1961 (22 U.S.C. § 2292 et seq.); or (4) in support of an emergency or major disaster (as those terms are defined in section 102 of the Robert T. Stafford Disaster Relief and Emergency Assistance Act (42 U.S.C. § 5122)). This authority is implemented in the definitions of SIMPLIFIED ACQUISITION THRESHOLD and MICRO-PURCHASE THRESHOLD and in FAR Subpart 19.5.

SPECIAL ITEM NUMBER (SIN)   *Official:* A group of generically similar (but not identical) supplies or services that are intended to serve the same general purpose or function. *Source:* FAR 8.401. Items of supplies and services are listed on and ordered from FEDERAL SUPPLY SCHEDULES by special item number.

SPECIAL STANDARDS OF RESPONSIBILITY   Standards of RESPONSIBILITY established by the government for a particular acquisition or class of acquisitions. FAR 9.104-2 states that such standards may be particularly desirable when experience has demonstrated that unusual expertise or specialized facilities are needed to ensure contract performance. See Cibinic, Nash & Yukins, Formation of Government Contracts 428–34 (4th ed. 2011).

SPECIAL TEST EQUIPMENT   *Official:* Either single or multipurpose integrated test units engineered, designed, fabricated, or modified to accomplish special purpose testing in performing a contract. It consists of items or assemblies of equipment including foundations and similar improvements necessary for installing special test equipment, and standard or general purpose items or components that are interconnected and interdependent so as to become a new functional entity for special testing purposes. Special test equipment does not include MATERIAL, SPECIAL TOOLING, REAL PROPERTY, and equipment items used for general testing purposes or property that with relatively minor expense can be made suitable for general purpose use. *Source:* FAR 2.101. Prior to the issuance of FAC 2005-17, May 15, 2007, FAR 45.307 permitted agencies to provide existing special test equipment to contractors. This guidance has been removed from the FAR and replaced by general guidance on the furnishing of GOVERNMENT PROPERTY in FAR Subparts 45.1 and 45.3. It has traditionally been the policy of the government to permit contractors to include the full cost of special test equipment needed for a specific contract in the price of that contract. FAR 31.205-40 specifies that such costs incurred by a contractor are ALLOWABLE COSTs. See Manos, 1 Government Contract Costs and Pricing §§ 47:1–47:3 (2d ed. 2009–2020).

SPECIAL TOOLING   *Official:* Jigs, dies, fixtures, molds, patterns, taps, gauges, and all components of these items including foundations and similar improvements necessary for installing special tooling, and which are of such a specialized nature that without substantial modification or alteration their use is limited to the development or production of particular supplies or parts thereof or to the performance of particular services. Special tooling does not include MATERIAL, SPECIAL TEST EQUIPMENT, REAL PROPERTY, equipment, machine tools, or similar capital items. *Source:* FAR 2.101. Prior to the issuance of FAC 2005-17, May 15, 2007, FAR 45.306 permitted agencies to provide existing special tooling to contractors and provided guidance on when contractors should be permitted to retain title to special tooling required for contract performance. This guidance has been removed from the FAR and replaced by general guidance on the furnishing of GOVERNMENT PROPERTY in FAR Subparts 45.1 and 45.3. When existing government tooling is not available, it has traditionally been the policy of the government to include the full cost of special tooling in the contract price. FAR 31.205-40 specifies that such costs incurred by a contractor are ALLOWABLE COSTs. See Manos, 1 GOVERNMENT CONTRACT COSTS AND PRICING §§ 47:1–47:3 (2d ed. 2009–2020); Cibinic, Nagle & Nash, ADMINISTRATION OF GOVERNMENT CONTRACTS 563–65 (5th ed. 2016).

SPECIAL WORKS   WORKS that are produced under contract for the government's own use, or when there is a specific need to limit distribution and use of the data and/or to obtain indemnity for liabilities that may arise out of the content, performance, or disclosure of the data. FAR 27.405(a). See also DFARS 227.7106(d) giving the following examples: audiovisual works, computer data bases, computer software documentation, scripts, soundtracks, musical compositions, and adaptations; histories of departments, agencies, services or units thereof; surveys of government establishments; instructional works or guidance to government officers and employees on the discharge of their official duties; reports, books, studies, surveys, or similar documents; collections of data containing information pertaining to individuals that, if disclosed, would violate the right of privacy or publicity of the individuals to whom the information relates; or investigative reports. Such works are procured using the Rights in Data—Special Works clause in FAR 52.227-17 and the Rights in Special Works clause in DFARS 252.227-7020. These clauses severely restrict the contractor's ability to assert copyright for such works. They also require the contractor to indemnify the government from a variety of claims that might arise from the use of such work. See Nash & Rawicz, INTELLECTUAL PROPERTY IN GOVERNMENT CONTRACTS, chap. 4 (6th ed. 2008).

SPECIALLY NEGOTIATED LICENSE RIGHTS   Rights of the government in TECHNICAL DATA or COMPUTER SOFTWARE that differ from the standard rights in the Rights in Technical Data—Noncommercial Items (June 1995) clause in DFARS 252.227-7013 or the Rights in Noncommercial Computer Software and Noncommercial Computer Software Documentation (June 1995) clause in DFARS 252.227-7014. These clauses permit the negotiation of such rights and guidance on their use is in DFARS 227.7103-5(d) and DFARS 227.7203-5(d). Their use is preferred in DoD contracts that obtain TECHNICAL DATA to support the product support strategy of a MAJOR WEAPON SYSTEM or subsystem of a major weapon system. 10 U.S.C. § 2320(f). They were also recommended to facilitate contracting with commercial companies in the DOD training guide, *Intellectual Property: Navigating Through Commercial Waters*, Oct. 2001. See Nash & Rawicz, INTELLECTUAL PROPERTY IN GOVERNMENT CONTRACTS, chaps. 4 & 5 (6th ed. 2008).

SPECIALTY METALS   *Official:* (1) Steel—(i) With a maximum alloy content exceeding one or more of the following limits: Manganese, 1.65%; silicon, 0.60%; or copper, 0.60%; or (ii) Containing more than 0.25% of any of the following elements: Aluminum, chromium, cobalt, molybdenum, nickel, niobium (columbium), titanium, tungsten, or vanadium; (2) Metal alloys consisting of—(i) Nickel or iron-nickel alloys that contain a total of alloying metals other than nickel and iron in excess of 10%; or (ii) Cobalt alloys that contain a total of alloying metals other than cobalt and iron in excess of 10%; (3) Titanium and titanium alloys; or (4) Zirconium and zirconium alloys. *Source:* DFARS 225.7003-1. 10 U.S.C. § 2533b contains detailed restrictions on the inclusion of these metals in products acquired by DOD. The statute is implemented in DFARS Subpart 225.7003. Contractors are informed of these restrictions by the inclusion in contracts of the Restriction on Acquisition of Specialty Metals clause in DFARS 252.225-7008, and the Restriction on Acquisition of Certain Articles Containing Specialty Metals clause in DFARS 252.225-7009.

SPECIFIC APPROPRIATION   See APPROPRIATION.

SPECIFICATION   A description of the technical requirements for a material, product, or service that includes the criteria for determining whether these requirements are met. Specifications may be prepared to cover a group of products, services, or materials, or a single product, service, or material. Specifications should be designed to promote FULL AND OPEN COMPETITION and should not contain UNDULY RESTRICTIVE requirements, with due regard to the nature of the supplies or services to be acquired. FAR 11.002. For some purposes, specifications are classified as FUNCTIONAL SPECIFICATIONS, DESIGN SPECIFICATIONS, and PERFORMANCE SPECIFICATIONS. See Cibinic, Nash & Yukins, FORMATION OF GOVERNMENT CONTRACTS 362–79 (4th ed. 2011). See also STANDARD; MILITARY SPECIFICATIONS AND STANDARDS.

SPECIFIED PAYMENT DATE   A date specified by a government payment office, for the purposes of the PROMPT PAYMENT ACT, when the payment is to be made by ELECTRONIC FUNDS TRANSFER (EFT). This date is given to the Federal Reserve System as the date on which the funds are to be transferred to the contractor's account by the financial agent. FAR 32.906. Specifying this date does not relieve the government from liability for late payment if the SETTLEMENT DATE when funds are actually transferred to the contractor's financial institution is not within the time permitted by the Act.

SPI PROCESS   *Official:* A management or manufacturing process that has been accepted previously by the Department of Defense under the SINGLE PROCESS INITIATIVE for use in lieu of a specific military or federal SPECIFICATION or standard at specific facilities. Under SPI, these processes are reviewed and accepted by a Management Council, which includes representatives of the contractor, the Defense Contract Management Agency, the Defense Contract Audit Agency, and the military departments. *Source:* DFARS 252.211-7005. Guidance on acceptance of contractor requests for a single process is set forth in DFARS Subpart 211.273 and the Substitutions for Military or Federal Specifications and Standards clause at DFARS 252.211-7005.

SPIRAL APPROACH   A risk-driven controlled prototyping approach that develops prototypes early in the development process to specifically address risk areas followed by assessment of prototyping results and further determination of risk areas to prototype. Areas that are prototyped frequently include user requirements and algorithm performance. Prototyping continues until high risk areas are resolved and mitigated to an acceptable level. *Source:* DAU GLOSSARY.

SPONSORSHIP OF SUBCONTRACTOR CLAIMS   A process of permitting SUBCONTRACTORs to appeal adverse DECISIONs OF THE CONTRACTING OFFICER wherein the prime contractor permits the subcontractor to use the prime's name or agrees to appeal for the benefit of the subcontractor. The sponsorship system is a means of preserving the technical concept of PRIVITY OF CONTRACT by permitting appeals and suits to be brought by or in the name of the prime contractor even though the prime has no real interest in the matter and plays a passive role. Sponsorship means that the subcontractor may have its attorney prosecute the appeal, but the paperwork must be done in the name of the prime contractor and the prime contractor must certify the claim as required by the CONTRACT DISPUTES ACT OF 1978. See *United States v. Johnson Controls, Inc.*, 713 F.2d 1541 (Fed. Cir. 1983). If sponsorship occurs in a claim for BREACH OF CONTRACT, the SEVERIN DOCTRINE will bar the claim if the contractor is totally absolved of liability to the subcontractor. See Cibinic, Nagle & Nash, Administration of Government Contracts 1153 (5th ed. 2016).

SPOON FEED   In SOURCE SELECTION, telling an offeror what it must state in its PROPOSAL in order to receive the highest possible RATING or SCORE. While contracting officers must conduct meaningful discussions with offerors within a competitive range, they need not spoon feed offerors by telling them what to propose in order to win. The term is used by the GAO and the U.S. COURT OF FEDERAL CLAIMS in their protest decisions. See, e.g., *CRAssociates, Inc. v. United States*, 102 Fed. Cl. 698 (2011), and *Unisys Corp.*, Comp. Gen. Dec. B-406326, 2012 CPD ¶153.

SPREAD-GAIN ACTUARIAL COST METHOD   *Official:* Any of the several projected benefit actuarial cost methods under which actuarial gains and losses are included as part of the current and future normal costs of a PENSION PLAN. *Source:* FAR 31.001. Actuarial gains and losses under a pension plan whose costs are measured by this actuarial cost method must be included as part of current and future normal cost and spread over the remaining average working lives of the workforce. 48 C.F.R. § 9904.413-50.

STAFFORD ACT   42 U.S.C. § 5121 et seq. The Robert T. Stafford Disaster Relief and Emergency Assistance Act authorizes the president to issue major disaster and emergency declarations and federal agencies to provide assistance to states. Section 5150 of the statute requires agencies to show a preference for contracting with local organizations, firms, and individuals when contracting to provide for disaster or emergency assistance. The Act is implemented in FAR Subpart 26.2.

STAND-ALONE COMMERCIAL SERVICE   A service that is defined as a COMMERCIAL ITEM (¶(6)) in FAR 2.101. Such services may be procured using the procedures of FAR Part 12 if they are of a type offered and sold competitively in substantial quantities in the commercial marketplace based on established CATALOG PRICEs or MARKET PRICEs for specific tasks performed or specific outcomes to be achieved and under standard commercial terms and conditions. FAR 2.101. See Cibinic, Nash & Yukins, Formation of Government Contracts 1001–03 (4th ed. 2011). See also Seidman, et al., *Service Contracting in the New Millennium—Part I*, Briefing Papers No. 02-11 (Oct. 2002); Nash, *Postscript VI: Defining Commercial Services*, 16 N&CR ¶15 (Mar. 2002).

STANDARD   A document that establishes engineering and technical limitations and applications of items, materials, processes, methods, designs, and engineering practices. It includes any related criteria deemed essential to achieve the highest practical degree of uniformity in materials or products, or interchangeability of parts used in those products. FAR Subpart 11.1 provides guidance on the use of standards. Standards may be used in SPECIFICATIONs, INVITATIONs FOR BIDS, REQUESTs FOR PROPOSALS, and contracts. A voluntary standard is a standard established by a private-sector body and available for public use. The term does not include private standards of individual firms. See OMB Circular No. A-119, *Federal Participation in the Development and Use of Voluntary Consensus Standards and in Conformity Assessment Activities*, Jan. 27, 2016.

STANDARD COST *Official:* Any cost computed with the use of preestablished measures. *Source:* FAR 31.001. A standard cost is a goal or baseline cost that is used to expedite the costing of transactions; it is determined from historical experience or derived from the best information available. Except for costs attributable to precise and highly predictable operations, ACTUAL COSTs will almost always vary from standard costs due to factors that affect performance, such as employee fatigue, unforeseen interruptions, and other delays (called VARIANCEs). See DAU, *Contract Pricing Reference Guides* v. III. Guidance on the use of standard costs for estimating, accumulating, and reporting costs of direct material and direct LABOR is contained in CAS 407, 48 C.F.R. § 9904.407. See Manos, 1 GOVERNMENT CONTRACT COSTS AND PRICING §§ 68:1–68:2 (2d ed. 2009–2020).

STANDARD FORMS (SFs) Forms prescribed by the FAR for use throughout the government in the contracting process. FAR Part 53 illustrates SFs for government procurement prescribed elsewhere in the FAR and contains requirements and information generally applicable to SFs, OPTIONAL FORMS, and agency-prescribed forms. Unless provided in the FAR instructions for use of a standard form, agencies may not alter any standard form prescribed by the FAR, or use any form other than the standard form prescribed by the FAR for a particular purpose, without receiving, in advance, an exception (an approved departure from the form's established design, content, printing specifications, or conditions for use). SFs may be obtained through the GSA Forms Library at www.gsa.gov/reference/forms. See Forms Policy and Management Team, GSA Office of Governmentwide Policy, *Standard and Optional Forms Procedural Handbook*, forms@gsa.gov (July 2009).

STANDARD INDUSTRIAL CLASSIFICATION (SIC) A system once used for classifying industries into major groups and subgroups and which was the basis for establishing SMALL BUSINESS SIZE STANDARDS. It has been replaced by the NORTH AMERICAN INDUSTRIAL CLASSIFICATION SYSTEM (NAICS).

STANDARD OF PROOF The amount, degree, or level of proof required in a legal action to convince a judge or jury about an allegation. In criminal trials, the standard is *beyond a reasonable doubt.* In civil trials, the standard is either *clear and convincing evidence* or *preponderance of the evidence.* The clear and convincing evidence standard is higher than the preponderance of the evidence standard, but the nature of the distinction is not always clear. In SEALED BIDDING, when a bid is transmitted by ELECTRONIC DATA INTERCHANGE and is unreadable, FAR 14.406 requires "clear and convincing evidence" (a) of the content of the original bid and (b) that the unreadable condition of the bid was caused by government software or hardware error, malfunction, or other government mishandling. FAR 14.407-4(c) requires "clear and convincing evidence" of a mistake in bid when the contractor claims after award that it made a mistake and seeks correction by contract modification. "Clear and convincing evidence" is also the standard in disputes in which the contractor accuses the government of BAD FAITH, but there it must be proof of "specific intent to injure" the contractor. *Am-Pro Protective Agency, Inc. v. United States*, 281 F.3d 1234 (Fed. Cir. 2002). See Nash, *Special Treatment of the Sovereign?*, 17 N&CR ¶ 55 (Oct. 2003); Cibinic, *Bad Faith: Searching For Meaning*, 14 N&CR ¶ 35 (July 2000).

STANDARDIZATION   The adoption of a single product or group of products to be used by different organizations or all parts of one organization. Agencies are required to select existing requirements documents or develop new requirements documents that permit standardization. FAR 11.102. This regulation contains a list of the government publications that promote standardization. Standardization of weapons has been the DOD policy for many years. It is also the policy of DOD and the North Atlantic Treaty Organization to (1) achieve the closest practicable cooperation among forces; (2) facilitate the most efficient use of research, development, and production resources; and (3) agree to adopt on the broadest possible basis the use of (a) common or compatible operational, administrative, and logistic procedures and criteria, (b) common or compatible technical procedures and criteria, (c) common, compatible, or interchangeable supplies, components, weapons, or equipment, and (d) common or compatible tactical doctrines with corresponding organizational compatibility. DAU GLOSSARY.

STANDARDS OF CONDUCT   The rules applicable to government employees and individuals dealing with the government. The primary standards are set forth in the following sections of title 18 U.S.C. § 201, BRIBERY and Gratuities (see GRATUITY); § 202, Definitions; § 203, Compensation of Members of Congress and Government Officers; § 204, Practice in U.S. Claims Court and Court of Appeals for the Federal Circuit by Members of Congress; § 205, Activities of Officers and Employees in Claims Against and Other Matters Affecting Government; § 206, Exemption of Retired Officers of the Uniformed Services; § 207, Post-Employment Restrictions (see REVOLVING DOOR); § 208, Acts Affecting a Personal Financial Interest (see PERSONAL CONFLICT OF INTEREST); § 209, Supplementation of Salary of Government Employees; § 210, Offer to Procure Appointive Public Office; § 211, Acceptance or Solicitation to Obtain Appointive Public Office; § 212, Offer of Loan or Gratuity to Bank Examiner; § 213, Acceptance of Loan or Gratuity by Bank Examiner; § 214, Offer for Procurement of Federal Reserve Bank Loan and Discount of Commercial Paper; § 215, Receipt of Commissions or Gifts for Procuring Loans; § 216, Penalties and Injunctions; § 217, Acceptance of Consideration for Adjustments of Farm Indebtedness; and § 218, Voiding Contracts Violating These Criminal Provisions. Other standards are set forth in other parts of the criminal code (see, particularly, the FALSE CLAIMS ACT and the FALSE STATEMENTS ACT). Guidance on these standards is set forth in the regulations of the Office of Government Ethics, 5 C.F.R. § 2600 et seq. See Cibinic, Nagle & Nash, ADMINISTRATION OF GOVERNMENT CONTRACTS 75–149 (5th ed. 2016); Cibinic, Nash & Yukins, FORMATION OF GOVERNMENT CONTRACTS 136–219 (4th ed. 2011). See also PROCUREMENT INTEGRITY.

STANDBY   See ON STANDBY

STANDING PRICE QUOTATIONS   A method of obtaining prices for simplified acquisitions or COMMERCIAL ITEMs where contractors hold open prices that the government can accept without obtaining individual quotations for each purchase. FAR 13.103. This technique reduces paperwork in that authorized individuals merely issue a PURCHASE ORDER against such standing price quotations. Standing price quotations may be used if the pricing information is current and the government obtains the benefit of maximum discounts before award. This procedure is used extensively by the Department of Veterans Affairs. See Cibinic, Nash & Yukins, FORMATION OF GOVERNMENT CONTRACTS 1039 (4th ed. 2011).

STATE AND LOCAL TAXES   *Official:* TAXES levied by the states, the District of Columbia, outlying areas of the United States, or their political subdivisions. *Source:* FAR 2.101. Such taxes include income taxes, sales and use taxes, franchise taxes, EXCISE TAXes, and property taxes. FAR 31.205-41 specifies the rules governing whether such taxes paid by contractors are ALLOWABLE COSTs. See Manos, 1 GOVERNMENT CONTRACT COSTS AND PRICING §§ 48:1–48:6 (2d ed. 2009–2020). Contractors are frequently not subject to such taxes when working on federal contracts. See FAR Subpart 29.3. Contractors normally bear the risk of determining what taxes of this nature apply to their contracts but are given PRICE ADJUSTMENTs for changes in such taxes under the Federal, State, and Local Taxes clause in FAR 52.229-3.

STATE SECRETS DOCTRINE   See MILITARY AND STATE SECRETS DOCTRINE.

STATEMENT OF OBJECTIVES (SOO)   *Official:* A government-prepared document incorporated into the SOLICITATION that states the overall performance objectives. It is used in solicitations when the government intends to provide the maximum flexibility to each offeror to propose an innovative approach. *Source:* FAR 2.101. SOOs identify the broad, basic, top-level objectives of the acquisition and are used as a focusing tool for both the government and offerors. FAR 37.601 permits the use of a SOO in solicitations for a PERFORMANCE-BASED ACQUISITION. FAR 37.602 indicates that when a SOO is used, the contractor should respond by submitting a PERFORMANCE WORK STATEMENT. See Seidman, et al., *Service Contracting in the New Millennium—Part I*, BRIEFING PAPERS No. 02-11 (Oct. 2002).

STATEMENT OF WORK (SOW)   The generic term for the description in a SOLICITATION of the work that will be required to be performed. The SOW is frequently called the SPECIFICATION. The SOW is set forth in Section C of the UNIFORM CONTRACT FORMAT. It plays a key role in the solicitation because it serves as the basis for the contractor's response. It also serves as a baseline against which progress and subsequent contractual changes are measured during contract performance. The FAR uses the term WORK STATEMENT in referring to the SOW for a RESEARCH AND DEVELOPMENT contract. FAR 35.005. See Cibinic, Nash & Yukins, FORMATION OF GOVERNMENT CONTRACTS 362–79 (4th ed. 2011).

STATUTE OF LIMITATIONS   A law prescribing limitations to the right of action on certain described causes of action, declaring that no suit may be maintained on such causes of action unless brought within a specified period of time after the right accrued. BLACK'S LAW DICTIONARY 1707 (11th ed. 2019). Under 28 U.S.C. § 2501, the limitation period for CLAIMs against the government in the COURT OF FEDERAL CLAIMS is six years after the right of action accrues. Under 28 U.S.C. § 2415(a), the limitation period for claims filed by the government is six years after the right of action accrues, or one year after the final decision in any applicable administrative proceeding required by contract or law, whichever is later. Under the CONTRACT DISPUTES ACT OF 1978, 41 U.S.C. § 7103(a)(4), the limitation period for claims by both the contractor and the government is six years after the accrual of the claim. See Manos, 3 GOVERNMENT CONTRACT COSTS AND PRICING § 89:15 (2d ed. 2009–2020). See also U.S. GOV'T ACCOUNTABILITY OFFICE, PRINCIPLES OF FEDERAL APPROPRIATIONS LAW: ANNUAL UPDATE TO THE THIRD EDITION, chap. 13, GAO-15-303SP (Washington, D.C.: Mar. 2015); Pompeo, Casimir & Samuels, *The Statute Of Limitations Under The Contract Disputes Act: Recent Developments*, BRIEFING PAPERS No. 17-4 (Mar. 2017).

STATUTES AT LARGE   (also, the United States Statutes at Large) A multi-volume publication that is the official source of the texts of all of the laws ever enacted by Congress. It is published by the Government Printing Office. It also contains the texts of the Declaration of Independence, the Articles of Confederation, the Constitution, amendments to the Constitution, treaties with Indian and foreign nations, Congressional resolutions, and presidential proclamations. Abbreviated Stat. for legal citation. The Statutes at Large are referred to as "session laws," because each volume contains the laws enacted during a specific session of a Congress. See *How Our Laws Are Made*, available at the Library of Congress website, http://thomas.loc.gov/home/lawsmade.toc.html.

STEVEDORING   *Official:* Loading cargo from an agreed point of rest on a pier or lighter and its storage aboard a vessel; or breaking out and discharging of cargo from any space in the vessel to an agreed point of rest dockside or in a lighter. *Source:* DFARS 247.270-2. DFARS Subpart 247.2 contains general guidance on the award of stevedoring contracts but DFARS 247.270-2 states that it is impracticable to prescribe standard technical provisions covering all phases of stevedoring operations.

STEVENSON-WYDLER ACT   A series of statutes with the goal of promoting the transfer of technology from the government to state and local governments and private organizations. 15 U.S.C. § 1510a. The Act consists of the Stevenson-Wydler Technology Innovation Act of 1980, Pub. L. No. 96-480, the Federal Technology Transfer Act of 1986, Pub. L. No. 98-462, the National Competitiveness Technology Transfer Act, National Defense Authorization Act for FYs 1990, 1991, §§ 3131–3133, Pub. L. No. 101-189, the Technology Transfer Improvements Act of 1995, Pub. L. No. 104-113, and the Technology Transfer Commercialization Act of 2000, Pub. L. No. 106-404. See FEDERAL TECHNOLOGY TRANSFER. See Nash & Rawicz, INTELLECTUAL PROPERTY IN GOVERNMENT CONTRACTS, chap. 7 (6th ed. 2008).

STOCK OPTION   An option to buy stock in a corporation. FAR 31.205-6(i) provides that the costs of such options, when given by contractors to employees as compensation, are ALLOWABLE COSTs only when they meet the rules governing DEFERRED COMPENSATION. See Manos, 1 GOVERNMENT CONTRACT COSTS AND PRICING § 13:14 (2d ed. 2009–2020); Cibinic, Knight & Nash, COST-REIMBURSEMENT CONTRACTING 683 (4th ed. 2014). See also Johnson, *A Critical Look at the Compensation Cost Principle—Stock Options and Restricted Stock*, 34 PUB. CONT. L.J. 103 (2004).

STOP-WORK ORDER   A unilateral order of the contracting officer requiring the contractor to stop all or any part of the work called for under the contract. Stop-work orders may be issued if the contract contains the Suspension of Work clause in FAR 52.242-14 (mandatory in fixed-price construction and architect-engineer contracts) or the Stop-Work Order clause in FAR 52.242-15 (optional in contracts for supplies, services, or research and development (R&D)). These clauses give the contractor an adjustment in the price to compensate for costs incurred because of the order (plus profit under the Stop-Work Order clause). FAR 42.1303 provides that stop-work orders may be used in negotiated, fixed-price or cost-reimbursement supply, R&D, or service contracts if work stoppage is required for reasons such as advancements in the state-of-the-art, production or engineering breakthroughs, or realignment of programs. Generally, a stop-work order will be issued only if it is advisable to suspend work pending a decision by the government but a supplemental agreement providing for the suspension is not feasible. Issuance of a stop-work order must be approved at a level higher than the contracting officer. A stop-work order may not be used in place of a TERMINATION

NOTICE after a decision to proceed with a TERMINATION FOR DEFAULT has been made. See Cibinic, Nagle & Nash, ADMINISTRATION OF GOVERNMENT CONTRACTS 523–25 (5th ed. 2016).

STRATEGIC SOURCING [1]   A governmental approach to contracting out described in official documents as follows: "The collaborative and structured process of critically analyzing an organization's spending and using this information to make business decisions about acquiring commodities and services more effectively and efficiently." OFFICE OF MANAGEMENT AND BUDGET Memorandum, *Improving Acquisition through Strategic Sourcing* (Dec. 5, 2012). This approach is intended to provide contracts that meet the needs of a number of different agencies or different offices within an agency in order to obtain lower prices from vendors. See GSA's Federal Strategic Sourcing Initiative which has contracts for building maintenance and operations, maintenance repair facility supplies, maintenance, repair, and operations, janitorial and sanitation, domestic delivery services, wireless communications, office supplies, and print management, htpp://www.gsa.gov/portal/content/112561. **[2]** Generally, the practice of making strategic decisions about purchasing by identifying those functions that are a firm's "core competencies," which are the sources of the firm's competitive advantage in the marketplace, and contracting out non-core functions on a long-term basis. See: *Category Management and Strategic Sourcing*, https://www.dau.edu/cop/ace/Pages/Category-Management.aspx; Gottfredson, Puryear & Phillips, *Strategic Sourcing: From Periphery to the Core*, HARV. BUS. REV. (Feb. 2005); Venkatesan, *Strategic Sourcing: To Make or Not to Make*, HARV. BUS. REV. (Nov.–Dec. 2002); U.S. GOV'T ACCOUNTABILITY OFFICE, BEST PRACTICES: TAKING A STRATEGIC APPROACH COULD IMPROVE DOD'S ACQUISITION OF SERVICES, GAO-02-230 (Jan. 2002).

STREAMLINED PROCEDURES FOR COMMERCIAL ITEMS   Procedures in FAR Subpart 12.6 that allow agencies to issue a combined SYNOPSIS/SOLICITATION as a single document with a shortened response time that is of sufficient length to permit the submission of meaningful proposals. The procedure avoids the need for a separate synopsis with its required waiting period. FAR 12.603 contains detailed guidance on the contents of these documents. This procedure is not appropriate if the agency's requirements are complex in nature.

STRENGTH   An aspect of a PROPOSAL that is identified during PROPOSAL EVALUATION as providing some benefit to the government. This term is not defined in the FAR but strengths must be discussed with offerors in the COMPETITIVE RANGE. FAR 15.306(d)(3). See Cibinic, Nash & Yukins, FORMATION OF GOVERNMENT CONTRACTS 892–96 (4th ed. 2011).

STRUCTURED PROFIT APPROACH   A method used by the government to establish the initial negotiating position of the contracting officer on the amount of profit to include in the negotiated price when it is based on COST ANALYSIS. FAR 15.404-4(b) requires agencies making noncompetitive contract awards over $100,000 totaling $50 million or more a year to adopt a structured approach. This involves the creation of a formula considering (1) contractor effort, (2) contract cost risk, (3) Federal socioeconomic programs, (4) capital investments, (5) cost control and other past accomplishments, and (6) independent development. DOD does not comply with this guidance but use its own WEIGHTED GUIDELINES METHOD. See Cibinic, Knight & Nash, COST-REIMBURSEMENT CONTRACTING

481 (4th ed. 2014); Cibinic, Nash & Yukins, FORMATION OF GOVERNMENT CONTRACTS 1534–65 (4th ed. 2001).

STUDIES, ANALYSIS, AND EVALUATIONS *Official*: Contracted services that provide organized, analytical assessments/evaluations in support of policy development, decision-making, management, or administration. Included are studies in support of R&D activities. Also included are acquisitions of models, methodologies, and related software supporting studies, analyses, or evaluations. *Source*: FAR 2.101 (in definition of ADVISORY AND ASSISTANCE SERVICES). This is one of the three types of advisory and assistance services that are subject to statutory limitations.

SUBCONTINENT-ASIAN AMERICANS United States citizens whose origins are in India, Pakistan, Bangladesh, Sri Lanka, Bhutan, the Maldives Islands, or Nepal. 13 C.F.R. § 124.103(b). These persons are presumed to be socially disadvantaged individuals for the purpose of determining the ownership of a SMALL DISADVANTAGED BUSINESS CONCERN. They must then demonstrate to the SMALL BUSINESS ADMINISTRATION that they are ECONOMICALLY DISADVANTAGED INDIVIDUALS. Businesses owned by such individuals are given special preferences in government procurement. See SMALL DISADVANTAGED BUSINESS CONCERN.

SUBCONTRACT The FAR contains several slightly different definitions of this term with the result that the correct definition must be used as applicable. **[1]** In the context of the application of civil and criminal penalties under the ANTI-KICKBACK ACT OF 1986: *Official*: A CONTRACT or contractual action entered into by a prime contractor or SUBCONTRACTOR for the purpose of obtaining SUPPLIES, MATERIALS, equipment, or services of any kind under a prime contract. *Source*: FAR 3.502-1. **[2]** In the context of the requirement for formal SUBCONTRACTING PLANs under the SMALL BUSINESS SUBCONTRACTING PROGRAM: *Official*: Any agreement other than one involving an employer-employee relationship entered into by a government prime contractor or subcontractor calling for supplies and/or services required for performance of the contract, contract modification, or subcontract. *Source*: FAR 19.701. **[3]** In the context of the application of EQUAL EMPLOYMENT OPPORTUNITY requirements: *Official*: Any agreement or arrangement between a contractor and any person in which the parties do not stand in the relationship of an employer and an employee (a) for the purchase, sale, or use of personal property or NONPERSONAL SERVICES that, in whole or in part, are necessary to the performance of any one or more contracts, or (b) under which any portion of the contractor's obligation under any one or more contracts is performed, undertaken, or assumed. *Source*: FAR 22.801. **[4]** In the context of the requirements for ADVANCE NOTIFICATION of the award of subcontracts and CONSENT TO SUBCONTRACT: *Official*: Any contract as described in Subpart 2.1 entered into by a subcontractor to furnish supplies or services for performance of a prime contract or a subcontract. It includes but is not limited to PURCHASE ORDERS, and changes and MODIFICATIONs to purchase orders. *Source*: FAR 44.101. FAR 12.001 and 15.401 state that the term includes INTERORGANIZATIONAL TRANSFERS. See FAR 31.205-26(e). Although a subcontractor lacks PRIVITY OF CONTRACT with the federal government, prime contractors pass on significant government requirements to subcontractors, such as the requirements for submission of CERTIFIED COST OR PRICING DATA and the TERMINATION FOR CONVENIENCE clause. See Nash, *Subcontractor Rights to Technical Data: A Little Known Problem*, 23 N&CR ¶ 42 (Aug. 2009); Solomson & Handwerker, *Subcontractor*

Challenges to Federal Agency Procurement Actions, BRIEFING PAPERS No. 06-3 (Feb. 2006); Masiello & Seckman, *Managing Subcontract Defective Pricing Liability*, BRIEFING PAPERS No. 04-10 (Sept. 2004); Meagher & Bingham, *Administering Subcontracts After a Termination for Convenience*, BRIEFING PAPERS No. 04-4 (Mar. 2004).

SUBCONTRACT APPROVAL The contracting officer's written consent for the contractor to enter into a particular subcontract. FAR 44.201-1(b) requires consent to specified subcontracts awarded under COST-REIMBURSEMENT CONTRACTs, TIME-AND-MATERIALS or LABOR-HOUR CONTRACTs, LETTER CONTRACTs and UNPRICED ACTIONs under FIXED-PRICE CONTRACTs over the SIMPLIFIED ACQUISITION THRESHOLD when the contractor does not have an approved purchasing system (see CONTRACTOR PURCHASING SYSTEM). When the contractor has an approved purchasing system, consent may be required at the discretion of the contracting officer when the subcontract work is complex, the dollar value is substantial, or the government's interest is not adequately protected by competition and the type of prime contract or subcontract. FAR 44.201-1(a). Consent requirements are imposed by using the Subcontracts clause at FAR 52.244-2.

SUBCONTRACTING ASSISTANCE PROGRAM See SMALL BUSINESS SUBCONTRACTING PROGRAM.

SUBCONTRACTING PLAN A plan, adopted by a contractor, to further the government's program under the SMALL BUSINESS ACT by subcontracting parts of the contract work to SMALL BUSINESS CONCERNs. Successful offerors under both negotiated and sealed bidding acquisitions that are expected to exceed $750,000 (or $1.5 million for construction) and that have subcontracting possibilities must provide formal subcontracting plans. 15 U.S.C. § 637(d); FAR 19.702(a). Subcontracting plans are not required (a) from SMALL BUSINESS CONCERNs; (b) for personal service contracts; (c) for contracts that will be performed entirely outside of the United States; or (d) for modifications to contracts that do not contain the Utilization of Small Businesses clause. FAR 19.702(b). FAR 19.704 provides that the subcontracting plans must include (1) percentage goals for using SMALL BUSINESS CONCERNs (including ANCs and Indian tribes), VETERAN-OWNED SMALL BUSINESS CONCERNs, SERVICE-DISABLED VETERAN-OWNED SMALL BUSINESS CONCERNs, HUBZONE concerns, SMALL DISADVANTAGED BUSINESS CONCERNs, and WOMEN-OWNED SMALL BUSINESS CONCERNs as subcontractors; (2) a statement of the dollars and types of work planned for each category, (3) a description of the methods to be used to develop the goals and identify potential sources, (4) a statement of how indirect costs were included in the calculations, (5) the name of an individual who will administer the offeror's subcontracting program; (6) a description of the efforts the offeror will make to ensure that small business has an equitable opportunity to compete for subcontracts; (7) assurances that the offeror will include the clause at FAR 52.219-8, Utilization of Small Business Concerns, in all subcontracts; (8) assurances that the offeror will (a) cooperate in studies or surveys, (b) submit periodic reports, (c) submit the Individual Subcontractor Report (ISR) and the Summary Subcontract Report (SSR) through the electronic Subcontracting Reporting System (eSRS) at http://www.esrs.gov, and (d) require that each subcontractor with a subcontracting plan provide the prime contract number, its unique identity identifier and the email address of the subcontractor's official responsible for acknowledging receipt of or rejecting the ISRs, to its subcontractor with subcontracting plans; (9) a description of the records the offeror will maintain to demonstrate procedures adopted to comply with the plan; (10) assurances that the offeror will make a good faith effort to use the subcontractors described in its bid or proposal and will explain its failure to do so; (11) assurances that the offeror will not prohibit its subcontractors from discussing payment issues with the contracting officer; and (12) assurances that the offeror will make timely payments to its subcontractors. FAR 19.704(b) provides that contractors can provide master plans for a division and FAR 19.704(d) encourages the submission of "commercial plans" for divisions selling COMMERCIAL ITEMs. 15 U.S.C. § 637(d)(4)(F) directs that a contractor's failure to make a good faith effort to comply with the requirements of the subcontracting plan must result in the imposition of LIQUIDATED DAMAGES. This is implemented in FAR 19.705-7. The contracting officer is required to review the subcontracting plan for adequacy, ensuring that the required information, goals, and assurances are included. FAR 19.705-4. See Hewitt, *Small Business Contracting Programs-Part II*, BRIEFING PAPERS No. 10-13 (Oct. 2010); Nash, *Small Business Subcontracting Plans: An Evaluation Factor?*, 21 N&CR ¶ 39 (Aug. 2007).

SUBCONTRACTOR   The FAR contains several slightly different definitions of this term with the result that the correct definition must be used as applicable. **[1]** In the context of the application of civil and criminal penalties under the ANTI KICKBACK ACT OF 1986: *Official:* Any person, other than the prime contractor, who offers to furnish or furnishes any supplies, materials, equipment, or services of any kind under a prime contract or a subcontract entered into in connection with such prime contract, and any person who offers to furnish or furnishes general supplies to the prime contractor or a higher tier subcontractor. *Source:* FAR 3.502-1. **[2]** In the context of the requirement to provide EQUAL EMPLOYMENT OPPORTUNITY: *Official:* Any person who holds, or has held, a subcontract subject to E.O. 11246. The term first-tier subcontractor means a subcontractor holding a subcontract with a prime contractor. *Source:* FAR 22.801. **[3]** In the context of advance notification and consent to subcontract (see SUBCONTRACT APPROVAL): *Official:* Any supplier, distributor, vendor, or firm that furnishes supplies or services to or for a prime contractor or another subcontractor. *Source:* FAR 44.101. **[4]** In the context of the Vietnam Era Veterans Readjustment Act of 1974, as amended, 38 U.S.C. § 4212, and the affirmative action and nondiscrimination obligations of contractors and subcontractors regarding "special disabled veterans," "veterans of the Vietnam era," "recently separated veterans," and "other protected veterans": *Official:* Any person holding a subcontract of $25,000 or more, and for the purposes of subpart D of 41 C.F.R. Subtitle B, any person who has had a subcontract subject to the Act. *Source:* 41 C.F.R. § 60-250.2. When the term "subcontractor" is used in a contract clause, the context of the clause must be analyzed to determine whether the term means only first-tier subcontractors or subcontractors at every tier. See Nash, *Commercial Item Subcontractors: Confusing Rules*, 32 N&CR ¶ 19 (Apr. 2018); Edwards, *What Is a Subcontract? Who Is a Subcontractor?: Confusion Prevails*, 26 N&CR ¶ 19 (Apr. 2012); Edwards, *Time-And-Materials Contract Payments: What Rate for Subcontractor Employees?*, 25 N&CR ¶ 23 (May 2011); Nash, *Postscript II: Subcontractor Delays Under Commercial Item Contracts*, 22 N&CR ¶ 51 (Aug. 2008); Solomson & Handweker, *Subcontractor Challenges to Federal Agency Procurement Actions*, BRIEFING PAPERS No. 06-03 (Feb. 2006).

SUBCONTRACTOR CLAIMS   See SPONSORSHIP OF SUBCONTRACTOR CLAIMS.

SUBJECT INVENTION   *Official:* An invention of the contractor made in the performance of work under a government contract. *Source:* 35 U.S.C. § 201(e); FAR 27.301. For the purpose of this definition "made" is defined as: (1) When used in relation to any invention other than a plant variety, the CONCEPTION or FIRST ACTUAL REDUCTION TO

PRACTICE of the invention; or (2) When used in relation to a plant variety means that the contractor has at least tentatively determined that the variety has been reproduced with recognized characteristics. Under its PATENT RIGHTS policy, the government generally obtains a LICENSE to use such inventions, although TITLE is obtained in some circumstances. The determination of whether an invention is a subject invention is not dependent on the relative financial contributions of the parties in funding the work that led to the invention; rather, it depends on whether either of two events—conception or first actual reduction to practice—occurred during performance of the work called for by the contract. See Nash & Rawicz, INTELLECTUAL PROPERTY IN GOVERNMENT CONTRACTS, chaps. 2 & 3 (6th ed. 2008).

SUBLINE   *Official:* A subset of a line item. *Source:* FAR 2.101. See CONTRACT LINE ITEM.

SUBROGATION   The substitution of one person in the place of another with reference to a lawful claim, demand, or right, so that the one substituted succeeds to the rights of the other in relation to the debt or claim and its rights, remedies, and securities. BLACK'S LAW DICTIONARY 1726 (11th ed. 2019). A SURETY that carries out its obligation under the BOND and pays for the completion of the work after the contractor has been unable to perform is entitled to the rights of subrogation. The surety's right to recover under the doctrine of subrogation is limited to the contract balance at the time the government was notified of the surety's interest. In view of the surety's right of subrogation, agencies frequently negotiate a SURETY TAKEOVER AGREEMENT when a contract is in default.

SUBSIDIARY   A firm that is owned by another firm, which is called the PARENT COMPANY. A subsidiary is an AFFILIATE of the parent and of other firms owned by the parent. See BLACK'S LAW DICTIONARY 1728 (11th ed. 2019).

SUBSTANTIAL COMPLETION   SUBSTANTIAL PERFORMANCE of contract requirements in a construction contract, though not complete performance. Substantial completion is often found when the contractor completes construction of the structure but fails to complete PUNCH LIST items, install ornamental features, finish site cleanup, etc. The doctrine of substantial completion bars the government from assessing LIQUIDATED DAMAGES or terminating the contract without providing a reasonable period of time to correct the deficiencies. The doctrine does not bar the government, however, from insisting on strict compliance and full completion of the work or from obtaining an EQUITABLE ADJUSTMENT in the contract price if strict compliance is not attained. The term has also been used to decide DISPUTEs under contracts for services. See Cibinic, Nagle & Nash, ADMINISTRATION OF GOVERNMENT CONTRACTS 737–40 (5th ed. 2016).

SUBSTANTIAL COMPLIANCE   The timely delivery of supplies on a supply contract that substantially comply with the contract requirements. When a contractor has met the test of substantial compliance, the government may not issue a summary TERMINATION FOR DEFAULT but must give the contractor a reasonable period to correct the deficiency. In order to meet the test of substantial compliance, (1) the supplies must have been delivered within the contract schedule, (2) the contractor must demonstrate that it had reasonable grounds to believe that the delivery would conform to the contract requirements, and (3) any defects must be minor in nature and extent and susceptible to correction within a reasonable time. Other relevant considerations include the usability of the items, the nature of the product, and the urgency of the government's requirement. See Cibinic, Nagle & Nash, ADMINISTRATION OF GOVERNMENT CONTRACTS 800–04 (5th ed. 2016).

SUBSTANTIAL EVIDENCE   *Official:* Information sufficient to support the reasonable belief that a particular act or omission has occurred. *Source:* FAR 2.101. This is the standard of proof for reduction or suspension of payments on a contract under FAR Part 32.

SUBSTANTIAL PERFORMANCE   Performance short of full performance but nevertheless performance in good faith and in compliance with the contract, except perhaps for minor and relatively unimportant deviations. BLACK'S LAW DICTIONARY 1373 (11th ed. 2019). This term is not used in government contracting but it can be taken as synonymous with SUBSTANTIAL COMPLETION.

SUBSTANTIALLY AS FOLLOWS   Official: When used in the prescription and introductory text of a provision or clause, means that authorization is granted to prepare and utilize a variation of that provision or clause to accommodate requirements that are peculiar to an individual acquisition; provided that the variation includes the salient features of the FAR provision or clause, and is not inconsistent with the intent, principle, and substance of the FAR provision or clause or related coverage of the subject matter. *Source:* FAR 2.101. The same meaning is given to "substantially the same as."

SUBSTANTIALLY JUSTIFIED   A position of the government regarding a DISPUTE that is clearly reasonable. Under the EQUAL ACCESS TO JUSTICE ACT (EAJA), a court or an agency must award ATTORNEY'S FEES and other expenses to individuals with net worth of no more than $2 million, profit-making small businesses with no more than $7 million net worth or 500 employees, and tax-exempt organizations that prevail in adversary adjudications in which the government's position during settlement negotiations or litigation was not substantially justified. In determining substantial justification, the courts and boards of contract appeals evaluate the issue of reasonableness of the government's position based on what support in law and fact the government offers in defending its case. See Nash & Feldman, GOVERNMENT CONTRACT CHANGES § 16:39 (3d ed. 2006–2020); Cibinic, Nagle & Nash, ADMINISTRATION OF GOVERNMENT CONTRACTS 686 (5th ed. 2016).

SUBSTITUTED CONTRACT   A method of resolving a disputed issue under a contract whereby the parties agree to discharge all obligations under the original contract and substitute a new contract in its place. If the performance is not rendered under the new contract, the nonbreaching party may sue only for breach of the new contract. RESTATEMENT (SECOND) OF CONTRACTS § 279 (1981). This should be contrasted with an ACCORD AND SATISFACTION where the nonbreaching party has the election of suing for breach of the original contract if the other party breaches the accord. Substituted contracts are normally accomplished by execution of a bilateral MODIFICATION. The distinction between substituted contracts and accords and satisfaction is rarely recognized in government contract litigation. See Cibinic, Nagle & Nash, ADMINISTRATION OF GOVERNMENT CONTRACTS 1113–15 (5th ed. 2016).

SUCCESSOR IN INTEREST   See NOVATION AGREEMENT.

SUITABLE FOR INTENDED USE   The condition of property such that it can be used by a contractor in a manner that facilitates expeditious and economical performance. GOVERNMENT PROPERTY furnished to a contractor need not be perfect, but it must be given to the contractor in a condition suitable for its intended use under the contract. See ¶ (d) of the

Government Property clause in FAR 52.245-1. To recover an EQUITABLE ADJUSTMENT for defective GOVERNMENT-FURNISHED PROPERTY (GFP), the contractor must demonstrate that (1) the property was furnished as GFP, (2) the property was unsuitable, (3) the unsuitability related to the property's intended purpose, and (4) the unsuitability caused the contractor's injury (cost overrun, late delivery, etc.). See Cibinic, Nagle & Nash, ADMINISTRATION OF GOVERNMENT CONTRACTS 559–72 (5th ed. 2016).

SUM CERTAIN   The monetary amount being claimed by a contractor under the CONTRACT DISPUTES ACT OF 1978. Under this act a CLAIM entails, among other things, a written demand for the payment of money in a "sum certain." FAR 2.101 (in the definition of CLAIM). When the recovery of money is the essence of the contractor's request for relief, the contracting officer need not issue a final decision (see DECISION OF THE CONTRACTING OFFICER) unless the contractor's claim specifies the amount of recovery sought—a sum certain—in a finite amount not subject to qualification or conditions. The reasoning behind this rule is that the contracting officer cannot determine whether the Act's requirement for certification of claims of $100,000 or more applies to the contractor's claim unless the claim is made in a specific dollar amount. See Nash & Feldman, 2 GOVERNMENT CONTRACT CHANGES § 16:27 (3d ed. 2006–2020); Cibinic, Nagle & Nash, ADMINISTRATION OF GOVERNMENT CONTRACTS 1167 (5th ed. 2016). See also Nash, *Contract Disputes Act Claims: The "Sum Certain" Requirement*, 26 N&CR ¶ 41 (Aug. 2012).

SUPERIOR KNOWLEDGE   A legal rule providing that a contracting party has an obligation to disclose vital information to the other party. Generally, the government must disclose to offerors or contractors information it possesses that (1) is relevant to contradictory information in the solicitation or contract and should be disclosed to keep the offeror or contractor from being misled; or (2) may materially affect an offer, and the offeror lacks the information or is relying on erroneous assumptions; and (3) it knows the contractor does not know. Failure to disclose such information may result in the government's assuming responsibility for the contractor's increased costs through the CONSTRUCTIVE CHANGE doctrine. To establish that the government breached its duty to disclose its superior knowledge, the contractor must prove that the government possessed such knowledge, that the knowledge was vital to contract performance, that the information was unknown and not reasonably available to the contractor, and that the contractor was misled by the nondisclosure. See Nash & Feldman, GOVERNMENT CONTRACT CHANGES § 14:3 (3d ed. 2006–2020); Manos, 2 GOVERNMENT CONTRACT COSTS AND PRICING § 87:8 (2d ed. 2009–2020); Cibinic, Nagle & Nash, ADMINISTRATION OF GOVERNMENT CONTRACTS 249–51 (5th ed. 2016). See also Nash, *Postscript II: Nondisclosure of Superior Knowledge*, 20 N&CR ¶ 25 (May 2006).

SUPPLEMENTAL AGREEMENT   *Official:* A contract MODIFICATION that is accomplished by the mutual action of the parties. *Source:* FAR 2.101. FAR 43.103 includes supplemental agreements in its discussion of bilateral modifications.

SUPPLIES   *Official:* All property except land or interest in land. It includes (but is not limited to) public works, buildings, and facilities; ships, floating equipment, and vessels of every character, type, and description, together with parts and accessories; aircraft and aircraft parts, accessories, and equipment; machine tools; and the alteration or installation of any of the foregoing. *Source:* FAR 2.101. This FAR definition is misleading in that it includes public works, buildings, and facilities within the scope of the term. However, the PROVISION AND CLAUSE MATRIX in FAR 52.300 provides separate provisions and clauses for supply contracts and construction contracts. The Inspection of Supplies—Fixed Price clause in FAR 52.246-2 defines supplies as including, but not limited to, raw materials, components, intermediate assemblies, end products, and lots of supplies. However, the Inspection of Supplies—Cost-Reimbursement clause in FAR 52.246-3 defines supplies to include data if the contract does not include a Warranty of Data clause. The term "supplies" is a term used primarily in government contracting; the synonymous term in commercial contracting is GOODS.

SUPPLY CHAIN **[1]**   Generally, a network between a company and its suppliers to produce and distribute a specific product. More broadly, an organized system of people, organizations, facilities, processes, activities, and technology needed to bring a product or service to customers. **[2]** Within DOD, weapon system support contractors, retail supply activities, distribution depots, transportation networks including contracted carriers, Military Service and Defense Logistics Agency (DLA) integrated materiel managers (IMMs), weapon system program offices, commercial distributors and suppliers including manufacturers, commercial and organic maintenance facilities, and other logistics activities (e.g., engineering support activities (ESAs), testing facilities, cataloging services, reutilization and marketing offices). See DOD Manual 4240.01 *DoD Supply Chain Materiel Management Procedures: Operational Requirements*, chap. 2, Feb. 10, 2014.

SUPPORT ANTI-TERRORISM BY FOSTERING EFFECTIVE TECHNOLOGIES ACT OF 2003 (SAFETY ACT)   Part of the Homeland Security Act of 2002, 6 U.S.C. §§ 441–444, that provides "risk management" and "litigation management" protections for sellers of qualified anti-terrorism technologies and others in the supply and distribution chain. The aim of the Act is to encourage the development and deployment of anti-terrorism technologies that will substantially enhance the protection of the nation. Specifically, the Act creates certain liability limitations for "claims arising out of, relating to, or resulting from an act of terrorism" where qualified anti-terrorism technologies have been deployed. The Act's "Designation" and "Certification" are designed to support effective technologies aimed at preventing, detecting, identifying, or deterring acts of terrorism, or limiting the harm that such acts might otherwise cause, and which also meet other prescribed criteria. The Act also allows contractors with certified technologies to assert the GOVERNMENT CONTRACTOR DEFENSE. The Act is implemented in 6 C.F.R. part 25. See Levin, *The Safety Act of 2003: Implications for the Government Contractor Defense*, 34 Pub. Cont. L.J. 175 (2004); Zenner, Handwerker & Catoe, *Fundamentals of Contracting With the Department of Homeland Security*, Briefing Papers No. 03-04 (Mar. 2003).

SURETY   *Official:* An individual or corporation legally liable for the debt, default, or failure of a principal to satisfy a contractual obligation. The types of sureties referred to are as follows: (1) An individual surety is one person, as distinguished from a business entity, who is liable for the entire PENAL AMOUNT of the bond. (2) A corporate surety is licensed under various insurance laws and, under its charter, has legal power to act as surety for others. (3) A co-surety is one of two or more sureties that are jointly liable for the penal amount of the bond. A limit of liability for each surety may be stated. *Source:* FAR 2.101. Contractors purchase BONDs from sureties when such bonds are specified by the government to be a condition of award. FAR 28.201 requires agencies to obtain adequate security for bonds (including coinsurance and reinsurance agreements) required or used with a contract for supplies or services (including construction). The FAR contains guidance on the use of corporate sureties (FAR 28.202), individual sureties (FAR 28.203), and alternatives in lieu of sureties (FAR 28.204). See Standard Form 28, Affidavit of Individual Surety, FAR 53.301-28; SF 1414, Consent of Surety, FAR 53.301-1414; and Standard Form 1415, Consent of Surety and Increase of Penalty, FAR 53.301-1415. See Bezer, *The Inadequacy of Surety Bid Bonds in Public Construction Contracting*, 40 PUB. CONT. L.J. 87 (2010); Gallagher & McCallum, *The Importance of Surety Bond Verification*, 39 PUB. CONT. L.J. 269 (2010).

SURETY TAKEOVER AGREEMENT   An agreement between the government and a SURETY that fixes the surety's rights when it agrees to complete performance of a contract, for which it has given a PERFORMANCE BOND, that the contractor is unable to complete. When a surety elects to complete a defaulted contract, contracting officers are authorized to enter into takeover agreements following the guidance in FAR 49.404.

SURGE AND SUSTAINMENT PROGRAM   A program of the DEFENSE LOGISTICS AGENCY that is designed to enable it to quickly support military operations without maintaining large inventories of supplies. The program is carried out through the establishment of various kinds of long-term PRIME VENDOR relationships. The prime vendors provide DLA with a full range of logistics support services and access to commercial inventories and production capabilities. See DLAD Subpart 19.3.

SURPLUS PROPERTY   *Official:* PERSONAL PROPERTY not required by any federal agency as determined by the Administrator of the General Services Administration. *Source:* FAR 2.101. FAR 45.604 sets forth the procedures to be followed in disposing of surplus property resulting from government contracts.

SURPLUS STRATEGIC AND CRITICAL MATERIALS   Inventories of metals and ores, such as cobalt, industrial diamond stones, lead, nickel, tin, and zinc, that exceed Defense National Stockpile requirements. FAR 8.003 requires government agencies to satisfy their requirements for such materials from or through surplus holdings that are maintained by the Defense National Stockpile Center.

SURVEYING ACTIVITY   *Official:* The cognizant contract administration office or, if there is no such office, another organization designated by the agency to conduct PREAWARD SURVEYs. *Source:* FAR 9.101. FAR 9.106 provides guidance on the functions of surveying activities.

SUSPENDED COST   An indirect or direct cost under a COST-REIMBURSEMENT CONTRACT that lacks adequate explanation or documentary support for definitive AUDIT approval or disapproval, and that is not paid until the required data is received and a determination is made as to its allowability. Audit guidance and procedures on suspension of costs are provided in *DCAA Contract Audit Manual* ¶ 6-900. DCAA Form 1, Notice of Contract Costs Suspended And/Or Disapproved, is used by the AUDITOR to indicate a suspended cost. The procedures for cost DISALLOWANCE (not including suspension of costs) are contained in FAR 42.803. See Cibinic, Knight & Nash, COST-REIMBURSEMENT CONTRACTING 586 (4th ed. 2014).

SUSPENDING OFFICIAL   *Official:* An AGENCY HEAD or a designee authorized by the agency head to impose SUSPENSION. *Source:* FAR 9.403. FAR 9.407 states the rules and procedures guiding the conduct of suspending officials. See Cibinic, Nash & Yukins, FORMATION OF GOVERNMENT CONTRACTS 470–96 (4th ed. 2001).

SUSPENSION *Official:* An action taken a SUSPENDING OFFICIAL under 9.407 to disqualify a contractor temporarily from government contracting and government-approved subcontracting; a contractor that is disqualified is "suspended." *Source:* FAR 2.101. Causes for suspension include adequate evidence of or INDICTMENT for (1) commission of a FRAUD or criminal offense related to obtaining or performing a public contract; (2) violation of antitrust statutes; (3) commission of embezzlement, theft, forgery, BRIBERY, falsification of destruction of records, making FALSE STATEMENTs, tax evasion or receiving stolen property; (4) violation of the Drug-Free Workplace Act of 1988, 41 U.S.C. § 701 et seq.; (5) intentionally affixing a "Made in America" label to a product sold or shipped to the United States, but not made in the United States; (6) commission of an unfair trade practice; (7) delinquent federal taxes; (8) knowing failure to meet MANDATORY DISCLOSURE requirements or disclose significant overpayments; and (9) commission of any other offense indicating a lack of business integrity or business honesty that seriously and directly affects the present RESPONSIBILITY of a government contractor or subcontractor. FAR 9.407-2. Suspension can occur without prior notice to the contractor, but notice must be given after the decision to suspend has been made. FAR 9.407-3. No suspension can exceed 18 months unless legal proceedings are initiated within that time. FAR 9.407-4. See Cibinic, Nash & Yukins, FORMATION OF GOVERNMENT CONTRACTS 470-96 (4th ed. 2011). See also West, Ludwiszewski, Meunier & Fenton, *The Environmental Protection Agency's Suspension and Debarment Program*, BRIEFING PAPERS No. 13-12 (Nov. 2013); Wilson, *Changing the Balance of Power in Debarments, Suspensions*, Law360 (July 24, 2012); U.S. GOV'T ACCOUNTABILITY OFFICE, SUSPENSION AND DEBARMENT: SOME AGENCY PROGRAMS NEED GREATER ATTENTION, AND GOVERNMENTWIDE OVERSIGHT COULD BE IMPROVED, GAO-11-739 (Aug. 2011).

SUSPENSION OF WORK Government DELAY, either by order or constructively, of the work of a construction contractor or an architect-engineer. The Suspension of Work clause in FAR 52.242-14 is required to be included in fixed-price construction and ARCHITECT-ENGINEER CONTRACTs. FAR 42.1305. It permits the contracting officer to order the contractor, in writing, to suspend, delay, or interrupt performance of all or any part of the work for the period of time that the contracting officer determines appropriate for the convenience of the government. It also gives the contractor rights if performance is suspended, delayed, or interrupted for an unreasonable period of time by (1) an act of the contracting officer in the administration of the contract or (2) the contracting officer's failure to act within the time specified in the contract. In both cases a PRICE ADJUSTMENT is required to be made for any increase in the cost of performance of the contract (excluding PROFIT) that necessarily results from an unreasonable delay. See Cibinic, Nagle & Nash, ADMINISTRATION OF GOVERNMENT CONTRACTS 523–25 (5th ed. 2016).

SUSTAINABLE ACQUISITION *Official:* Acquiring goods and services in order to create and maintain conditions—(1) Under which humans and nature can exist in productive harmony; and (2) That permit fulfilling the social, economic, and other requirements of present and future generations. *Source:* FAR 2.101. The federal government has adopted policies requiring that procurements advance sustainable acquisition. Guidance is provided in FAR Subpart 23.1.

SUSTAINMENT See LIFE CYCLE SUSTAINMENT.

SWEEP A precautionary procedure in which, after the conclusion of price negotiations with the government, but prior to the offeror's execution of a CERTIFICATE OF CURRENT COST

OR PRICING DATA, an offeror notifies its executives, managers, and employees of the status of negotiations and calls upon them to notify the offeror's negotiators of any information in their possession that might constitute CERTIFIED COST OR PRICING DATA which should be submitted to the government. This procedure is followed in order to ensure that the contractor has met the requirement that certified cost or pricing data be "current."

SYNOPSIS   A notice of contract awards and proposed contract actions published in the GOVERNMENTWIDE POINT OF ENTRY as required by 15 U.S.C. § 637(e) and 41 U.S.C. § 1708. Guidance on synopsis requirements is contained in FAR Subpart 5.2 and FAR Subpart 5.3. When a synopsis of a proposed contract action is required, it must be published 15 days before issuance of the SOLICITATION. FAR 5.203. However, when buying COMMERCIAL ITEMs, the agency may combine the synopsis with the solicitation (see COMBINED SYNOPSIS/SOLICITATION). FAR 12.603. The format for the synopsis of proposed contract actions is contained in FAR 5.207. FAR 5.206 also encourages contractors to place synopses of subcontract opportunities in the Governmentwide Point of Entry.

SYSTEM DEVELOPMENT AND DEMONSTRATION   The third phase of a DOD acquisition program involving the use of new technology as prescribed in the DOD 5000 Series. In this phase, the agency awards a development contract calling for full development of the product or system including the production of prototypes to demonstrate its success. This effort was previously called ENGINEERING AND MANUFACTURING DEVELOPMENT.

SYSTEM FOR AWARD MANAGEMENT (SAM)   Official: The primary government repository for prospective Federal awardee and Federal awardee information and the centralized government system for certain contracting, grants, and other assistance-related processes. It includes—(1) Data collected from prospective Federal awardees required for the conduct of business with the government; (2) Prospective contractor-submitted annual representations and certifications in accordance with FAR Subpart 4.12; and (3) Identification of those parties excluded from receiving Federal contracts, certain subcontracts, and certain types of Federal financial and non-financial assistance and benefits. Source: FAR 2.101. SAM is the consolidated electronic database containing information regarding prospective contractors and contracting opportunities. Prospective contractors are required to register in SAM in order to be awarded contracts by the federal government. See FAR Subpart 4.11. FAR 4.1102(a) contains a list of contractors that need not register in SAM, such as PURCHASE CARD sellers, contractors with classified contracts, foreign contractors and contractors performing military, contingency or emergency operations, and MICRO-PURCHASE contractors. Registrants must update or renew their registration annually to maintain an active status. See Richard, Whiteman & Gleich, *Contractor Reporting Requirements in the Wake of Implementation of the System for Award Management*, BRIEFING PAPERS No. 13-6 (May 2013).

SYSTEM OF RECORDS ON INDIVIDUALS   *Official:* A group of any records under the control of any agency from which information is retrieved by the name of an individual or by some number, symbol, or other identifying particular assigned to the individual. *Source:* FAR 24.101. The Privacy Act of 1974, 5 U.S.C. § 552a, requires that contracts for the maintenance of such systems must comply with its provisions. FAR Subpart 24.1 provides guidance on the implementation of this requirement. NFS 1824.102 provides examples of systems of records to which the Privacy Act does not apply.

SYSTEMS ANALYSIS   "A management planning technique that applies scientific methods of many disciplines to major problems or decisions. The list of disciplines includes, but is not limited to, traditional military planning, economics, political science and social sciences, applied mathematics, and the physical sciences." DAU GLOSSARY. The technique is an offshoot of operations research, which was developed and used extensively during World War II in the solutions of many kinds of military problems. RAND CORPORATION prepared many studies and papers about systems analysis during the 1950s and 1060s. Today, the method is taught in many universities and numerous textbooks have been written. In ACQUISITION it is used extensively in the development of weapon systems and information systems, but it has been used in the development of solutions to many other kinds of economic, social, and political problems. Systems analysis is used in the REQUIREMENTS ANALYSIS process.

SYSTEMS ENGINEERING   A logical sequence of activities and decisions that transforms an operational need into a description of system performance parameters and a preferred system configuration. Systems engineering is a disciplined approach to coordinating all aspects of a system, ensuring that its individual parts will function as intended in the operational environment and meet contract requirements. It is a process for identifying and assessing each technical and other variable involved in total system design. A contractor that performs systems engineering is barred from contracting for manufacturing work on that system by the ORGANIZATIONAL CONFLICT OF INTEREST rules. FAR 9.505-1.

T

TAILORING   The process by which individual sections, paragraphs, or sentences of the SPECIFICATIONs, STANDARDs, and related documents selected for use in a procurement are reviewed and modified so that each one that is selected contains an accurate statement of the government's needs, is not unduly restrictive (see RESTRICTIVE SPECIFICATIONS), and incorporates COMMERCIAL ITEMs or NONDEVELOPMENTAL ITEMs. FAR 11.002(c) encourages agencies to allow prospective contractors to assist in tailoring requirements documents. Selective application is the process of reviewing and choosing from the many available specifications, standards, and related documents only those relevant to a particular acquisition. FAR 11.101. FAR 12.302 also permits tailoring of SOLICITATION PROVISIONs and contract clauses used in the procurement of COMMERCIAL ITEMs. However, FAR 12.302(b) contains a list of contract clauses that may not be tailored and FAR 12.302(c) prohibits tailoring that is inconsistent with commercial practice unless the contracting officer obtains a waiver. FAR 15.304(a) calls for EVALUATION FACTORs to be tailored to each acquisition.

TAKEOVER AGREEMENT   An agreement, between the government and the SURETY that has furnished a PERFORMANCE BOND, that the surety will complete the performance of a contract that has been terminated for default (see TERMINATION FOR DEFAULT). Guidance on entering into such an agreement is contained in FAR 49.404. Since the surety is liable to the government for the consequences of the contractor's default, it is not required to enter into a takeover agreement. However, FAR 49.404(c) provides that the contracting officer will normally enter into such an agreement if the surety offers to complete the contract. If a surety enters into a takeover agreement, it gives up any financial protection that it has pursuant to the ceiling amount in the bond (see PENAL AMOUNT) but it gains access to the COURT OF FEDERAL CLAIMS and the BOARDs OF CONTRACT APPEALS to pursue CLAIMs against the government.

TANGIBLE CAPITAL ASSET   *Official:* An ASSET that has physical substance, more than minimal value, and is expected to be held by an enterprise for continued use or possession beyond the current accounting period for the services it yields. *Source:* FAR 31.001. Such assets may take the form, for example, of cash, land, or buildings. Rosenberg, DICTIONARY OF BANKING AND FINANCE (2d ed. 1985). CAS 404, 48 C.F.R. § 9904.404, sets forth criteria that contractor policies on the CAPITALIZATION of tangible assets must meet. CAS 409, 48 C.F.R. § 9904.409, provides guidance on the DEPRECIATION of tangible capital assets. See Cibinic, Knight & Nash, COST-REIMBURSEMENT CONTRACTING 709–11 (4th ed. 2014).

TANKER   *Official:* A vessel used primarily for the carriage of bulk liquid cargoes such as liquid petroleum products, vegetable oils, and molasses. *Source:* FAR 47.501. Under the Preference for Privately Owned U.S.-Flag Commercial Vessels clause in FAR 52.247-64, contractors must compute shipments in these vessels separately in determining whether they have met the requirement of the CARGO PREFERENCE ACTS that at least 50% of the gross tonnage shipped be in U.S.-FLAG VESSELs.

TARGET COST   The negotiated amount of cost included in INCENTIVE CONTRACTs. See FAR Subpart 16.4. The target cost serves as the baseline for adjusting the contractor's TARGET PROFIT (in a FIXED-PRICE-INCENTIVE CONTRACT) or TARGET FEE (in a COST-PLUS-INCENTIVE-FEE CONTRACT). In these types of contracts, the negotiated PROFIT or FEE will be adjusted, upon completion of the contract, by a formula based on the relationship of total ALLOWABLE COSTs to total target costs. The formula provides, within limits, for increases in profit or fee when total allowable costs are less than target costs, and decreases in profit or fee when total allowable costs exceed target costs. The adjustment is intended to provide an incentive for the contractor to manage the contract effectively. FAR 16.401(a)(2). Before this adjustment is made, the parties must adjust the target cost to reflect all EQUITABLE ADJUSTMENTs and PRICE ADJUSTMENTs called for by the contract. See Cibinic, Knight & Nash, Cost-Reimbursement Contracting 53 (4th ed. 2014); Cibinic, Nash & Yukins, Formation of Government Contracts 1261–62, 1272–75 (4th ed. 2011).

TARGET FEE   The amount of FEE the contractor will receive if its total ALLOWABLE COSTs equal total TARGET COSTs in a COST-PLUS-INCENTIVE-FEE CONTRACT. In this type of contract, under the contract SHARING ARRANGEMENT, the final fee paid to the contractor is adjusted downward if actual costs exceed the target costs and upward if actual costs are less than target costs. This adjustment is limited, however, by the RANGE OF INCENTIVE EFFECTIVENESS resulting from the MINIMUM FEE and MAXIMUM FEE contained in the contract. FAR 16.405-1. See Cibinic, Knight & Nash, Cost-Reimbursement Contracting 54 (4th ed. 2014); Cibinic, Nash & Yukins, Formation of Government Contracts 1263 (4th ed. 2011).

TARGET PRICE   The sum of the TARGET COST and the TARGET PROFIT in a FIXED-PRICE-INCENTIVE CONTRACT.

TARGET PROFIT   The amount of PROFIT the contractor will receive if its total ALLOWABLE COSTs equal total TARGET COSTs in a FIXED-PRICE-INCENTIVE (FPI) CONTRACT. In FPI contracts with a firm target, the incentive formula also contains a target cost and CEILING PRICE. The target profit is adjusted in accordance with the contract SHARING ARRANGEMENT until the target cost and target profit reach the ceiling price (the POINT OF TOTAL COST ASSUMPTION), at which point the contractor absorbs all additional costs. FAR 16.403-1. In FPI contracts with successive targets, the parties negotiate at the outset the production point at which a firm target cost and target profit will be negotiated. FAR 16.403-2. The target profit is either established in the competitive process or negotiated, with the government's position being based on a structured profit formula, following agency guidance such as the WEIGHTED GUIDELINES METHOD in DFARS 215.404-71. See Cibinic, Nash & Yukins, Formation of Government Contracts 1272–76 (4th ed. 2011).

TASK   A discrete unit of work that is expected to produce a specific result. The result may be complete, in and of itself, and the object of inspection and acceptance, or an input to another task. FAR 37.102 provides that SERVICE CONTRACTs should specify tasks in PERFORMANCE WORK STATEMENTs. FAR 37.602(b) explains that this means specifying tasks in terms of the result required rather than the processes to be used.

TASK ORDER   *Official:* An order for services placed against an established contract or with government sources. *Source:* FAR 2.101. When such orders are issued under multiple award INDEFINITE DELIVERY/INDEFINITE QUANTITY contracts, each awardee must be given a FAIR OPPORTUNITY to be considered. FAR 16.505(b). PROTESTs of task order competitions may be taken to the GOVERNMENT ACCOUNTABILITY OFFICE (but not to the COURT OF FEDERAL CLAIMS) if the order has a value in excess of $25,000,000 for DOD, NASA and the Coast Guard, 10 U.S.C. § 2304c(e), or $10,000,000 for other agencies, 41 U.S.C. § 4106(f). However, protests may be taken to either forum, without regard for the dollar value of the task order, to contest whether the order increases the scope, period, or maximum value of the contract under which the order is issued. Protests of task orders of any size may be referred to the agency OMBUDSMAN. 10 U.S.C. § 2304c(f) and 41 U.S.C. § 4106(g). Task orders are also issued against FEDERAL SUPPLY SCHEDULE contracts. Protests of these task order competitions can be taken to either forum, without regard to the dollar value of the task order. See Cibinic, Nash & Yukins, FORMATION OF GOVERNMENT CONTRACTS 1165–84, 1401–06 (4th ed. 2011). See also Nash, *Task and Delivery Orders: Applying Part 15 Protest Rules*, 33 N&CR ¶ 14 (Mar. 2019); Nash, *Sample Task "Prices" in IDIQ Contracting: Valid Only With "Binding" Rates?*, 25 N&CR ¶ 20 (Apr. 2011).

TASK-ORDER CONTRACT   *Official:* A contract for services that does not procure or specify a firm quantity of services (other than a minimum or maximum quantity) and that provides for the issuance of orders for the performance of tasks during the period of the contract. *Source:* FAR 16.501-1. 10 U.S.C. § 2304a and 41 U.S.C. § 4106 contain special rules for task order contracts requiring that they include (1) the period of the contract, including options; (2) the maximum quantity or dollar value of the services that may be procured; and (3) a STATEMENT OF WORK that reasonably describes the general scope, nature, complexity, and purposes of the services to be procured under the contract. 10 U.S.C. § 2304a(d) and 41 U.S.C. § 4106(d) establish a preference for multiple award contracts (see MULTIPLE AWARD PREFERENCE). These requirements are implemented in FAR 16.504. See Cibinic, Nash & Yukins, FORMATION OF GOVERNMENT CONTRACTS 1121–43, 1189–97, 1386–1406 (4th ed. 2011).

TASK STATEMENT   The fundamental component of a PERFORMANCE WORK STATEMENT or STATEMENT OF WORK. A task statement specifies what the contractor must do, the object of the contractor's effort, and the result that the contractor must produce. When written for a performance work statement, a task statement does not describe the process that the contractor must use to produce the result, leaving that choice to the contractor's discretion.

TAXES   Mandatory amounts paid to governments to support their operation. Guidance on taxes is contained in FAR Part 29. See EXCISE TAXes and STATE AND LOCAL TAXES. Most general taxes, other than federal income and excess profits taxes and taxes related to refinancing or reorganization, are allowable costs under FAR 31.205-41. However, this provision contains a number of specific rules. See Cibinic, Knight & Nash, COST-REIMBURSEMENT CONTRACTING 741–45 (4th ed. 2014); Feldman, *Contractor Liability for Taxes Under FAR 52.229-3: When are Equitable Adjustments Permissible?*, 44 THE PROCUREMENT LAWYER 1 (Summer 2009); Pereira, Note, *Withholding Taxes: Too Taxing on Government Procurement*, 38 PUB. CONT. L.J. 451 (2009).

TAXPAYER IDENTIFICATION NUMBER (TIN)   *Official:* The number required by the Internal Revenue Service to be used by the OFFEROR in reporting income tax and other returns. The TIN may be either a Social Security Number or an Employer Identification Number. *Source:* FAR 2.101. FAR 4.903 and 4.904 require agencies to report certain contract and payment information to the Internal Revenue Service on Form 1099. The TIN is obtained from the contractor through the SYSTEM FOR AWARD MANAGEMENT or by having the contractor complete the certification in the required Taxpayer Identification solicitation provision at FAR 52.204-3.

TEAM AGREEMENT   An agreement in which (1) two or more companies form a partnership or JOINT VENTURE to act as a potential PRIME CONTRACTOR, or (2) a potential prime contractor agrees with one or more other companies to have them act as SUBCONTRACTORs under a specified government contract or ACQUISITION PROGRAM. FAR 9.601 (calling this a "contractor team arrangement"). Team agreements enable the companies to complement each other's capabilities and offer the government the best combination of performance, cost, and delivery for the system or product being acquired. The agreements prove particularly appropriate in complex RESEARCH AND DEVELOPMENT acquisitions. Companies normally form a team agreement before the offer is submitted. FAR 9.602. It is the government's policy to recognize the integrity and validity of team agreements if they are disclosed in an OFFER or before the agreement becomes final. FAR 9.603. See Koehler, *Teaming Agreements: The Proverbial "Wolf in Sheep's Clothing"*, BRIEFING PAPERS No. 14-6 (May 2014); Humphries & Irwin, *Teaming Agreements/Edition III*, BRIEFING PAPERS No. 03-10 (Sept. 2003).

TECHNICAL ANALYSIS   The examination and evaluation—by personnel having specialized knowledge, skills, experience, or capability in engineering, science, or management—of proposed quantities and kinds of materials, LABOR, processes, SPECIAL TOOLING, FACILITIES, and associated factors set forth in a PROPOSAL, in order to determine and report on the need for and reasonableness of the proposed resources, assuming reasonable economy and efficiency. FAR 15.404-1(e). This analysis is required when offerors for NEGOTIATED CONTRACTs are required to submit TECHNICAL PROPOSALs. FAR 15.404-1(e)(2) states that, at a minimum, a technical analysis of proposals should assess (1) the quantities and kinds of materials proposed, and (2) the need for the number and kinds of labor hours and the labor mix.

TECHNICAL DATA   *Official:* Recorded information (regardless of the form or method of the recording) of a scientific or technical nature (including COMPUTER DATABASEs and COMPUTER SOFTWARE DOCUMENTATION). This term does not include COMPUTER SOFTWARE or financial, administrative, cost or pricing, or management data or other information incidental to contract administration. The term includes recorded information of a scientific or technical nature that is included in computer databases (see 41 U.S.C. § 116). *Source:* FAR 2.101. Contracts containing the Rights in Data—General clause in FAR 52.227-14 prior to December 2007 had a narrower definition of technical data because under the earlier FAR data policy the term "computer software" includes COMPUTER PROGRAMs, COMPUTER DATABASEs, and COMPUTER SOFTWARE DOCUMENTATION. The current definition was added by FAC 2005-21, 723 Fed. Reg. 63045, Nov. 7, 2007, to conform to the 1995 DOD policy where the term "technical data" is described as—"Recorded information, regardless of the form or method of the recording, of a scientific or technical nature (including computer software documentation). The term does not include computer software or data incidental to contract administration, such as financial or management information." See Nash & Rawicz, INTELLECTUAL PROPERTY IN GOVERNMENT CONTRACTS, chap. 4 (6th ed. 2008). The government obtains LIMITED RIGHTS, UNLIMITED RIGHTS, GOVERNMENT-PURPOSE RIGHTS, or SPECIFICALLY NEGOTIATED LICENSE RIGHTS to technical data in accordance with the clauses used. See DeVecchio, *Taking the Mystery Out of Data Rights*, BRIEFING PAPERS No. 18-8 (July 2018).

TECHNICAL DATA PACKAGE (TDP)   A relatively complete package of design and manufacturing information adequate for supporting an ACQUISITION STRATEGY, production, engineering, and logistics support. The description, typically incorporated into the contract, defines the required design configuration and procedures to ensure adequacy of item performance. It consists of all applicable TECHNICAL DATA, such as drawings, associated lists, SPECIFICATIONs, STANDARDs, performance requirements, quality assurance provisions, and packaging details. The TDP is one of the traditional logistic support elements. DAU GLOSSARY.

TECHNICAL DIRECTION   Government guidance of a contractor's effort toward certain areas of endeavor or lines of inquiry that fall within the contract STATEMENT OF WORK. Technical direction is frequently called for on COST-REIMBURSEMENT CONTRACTs. Technical direction is generally provided in writing by the CONTRACTING OFFICER TECHNICAL REPRESENTATIVE (COTR), with a copy to the contracting officer. The COTR coordinates such direction with the contractor to ensure that it does not impose work beyond the contract requirements. The FAR contains no standard technical direction clause, but a number of agencies have adopted agency clauses. See Nash & Feldman, GOVERNMENT CONTRACT CHANGES §§ 8:9–8:12 (3d ed. 2006–2020); Cibinic, Knight & Nash, COST-REIMBURSEMENT CONTRACTING 796–801 (4th ed. 2014).

TECHNICAL EVALUATION   The evaluation of the technical aspects of a PROPOSAL submitted in a COMPETITIVE PROPOSALS procurement or a TWO-STEP SEALED BIDDING procurement. Such evaluation is conducted by government employees (or occasionally by contractor employees) skilled in the fields of technology addressed in the proposal. FAR 15.305(a)(3) contains minimal guidance on evaluation of proposals in competitive negotiations. FAR 14.503-1(e) discusses evaluation of technical proposals in two-step sealed bidding procurements. Evaluation must be done against the criteria contained in the solicitation. See Cibinic, Nash & Yukins, FORMATION OF GOVERNMENT CONTRACTS 663–68, 804–26 (4th ed. 2011).

TECHNICAL LEVELING   A practice of helping (such as by pointing out weaknesses resulting from an offeror's lack of diligence, competence, or inventiveness in preparing the proposal) an offeror to bring its PROPOSAL up to the level of other proposals through one or more rounds of DISCUSSION. Prior to FAC 97-02, September 30, 1997, FAR 15.610(d) prohibited the contracting officer and other government procurement personnel from engaging in technical leveling. FAR 15.306(e)(1) now merely prohibits favoring one offeror over another in the conduct of discussions (in effect eliminating the prohibition of technical leveling). Furthermore, FAR 15.306(d)(4) suggests giving specific suggestions to offerors as to potential improvements in their proposals. See Cibinic, Nash & Yukins, FORMATION OF GOVERNMENT CONTRACTS 890–91, 919 (4th ed. 2011); Nash, *Technical Leveling: Its Reincarnation As Fair Treatment*, 17 N&CR ¶ 21 (Apr. 2003). See also AUCTION; SOURCE SELECTION; TECHNICAL TRANSFUSION.

TECHNICAL PROPOSAL   A proposal submitted in response to a REQUEST FOR PROPOSALS. This ambiguous term is used in FAR Part 15 in different ways. In FAR 15.204-5(b), it appears to mean a proposal solely on the technical aspects of the work. In FAR 15.101-2, discussing lowest price technically acceptable, the technical proposal appears to cover all types of information from proposed plans for performing a proposed contract to mere information relating to an offeror's PAST PERFORMANCE or experience. FAR 15.204-5(b) permits the RFP instructions in Section L to call for the submission of technical proposals in separate volumes. Technical proposals are frequently used to assess an offeror's understanding of the work. See Nash, *Postscript III: The Technical Proposal*, 18 N&CR ¶ 23 (June 2004).

TECHNICAL TRANSFUSION   Government disclosure of technical information pertaining to a PROPOSAL that results in improvement of a competing proposal. Prior to FAC 97-02, September 30, 1997, FAR 15.610(e)(1) prohibited such conduct. FAR 15.306(e)(3) does not use this term but prohibits revealing an offeror's technical solution, including unique technology, innovative and unique uses of COMMERCIAL ITEMs, or any other information that would disclose an offeror's intellectual property to another offeror. See Cibinic, Nash & Yukins, FORMATION OF GOVERNMENT CONTRACTS 211–16, 919–20 (4th ed. 2011). See also AUCTION; SOURCE SELECTION.

TECHNOLOGY INVESTMENT AGREEMENT   A DOD agreement to stimulate or support research issued either as a COOPERATIVE AGREEMENT or an OTHER TRANSACTION. 32 C.F.R. § 37.110. Guidance on the use of these agreements is contained in the DOD Grant and Agreement Regulations, 32 C.F.R. part 21 through part 37. DOE also has regulations on Technology Investment Agreements in 10 C.F.R. part 603. See Nash & Rawicz, INTELLECTUAL PROPERTY IN GOVERNMENT CONTRACTS, chap. 7 (6th ed. 2008).

TECHNOLOGY MATURATION AND RISK REDUCTION (TMRR) PHASE   The second phase of a DOD acquisition program involving the use of new technology as prescribed in the DOD 5000 Series. In this phase, the agency reduces the risk of the program by identifying technologies that are sufficiently mature to ensure the likelihood of success of the development process. Two or more contracts are to be awarded calling for the companies to submit COMPETITIVE PROTOTYPES of the systems or subsystems that are not sufficiently mature. The goal is to demonstrate that segments of technology are sufficiently mature in order to proceed to the ENGINEERING AND MANUFACTURING DEVELOPMENT PHASE.

TECHNOLOGY TRANSFER   See FEDERAL TECHNOLOGY TRANSFER.

TELECOMMUNICATIONS   *Official:* The transmission, emission, or reception of signals, signs, writing, images, sounds, or intelligence of any nature, by wire, cable, satellite, fiber optics, laser, radio, or any other electronic, electric, electromagnetic, or acoustically coupled means. *Source:* DFARS 239.7401. For guidance on the acquisition of telecommunications see TELECOMMUNICATIONS SERVICES.

TELECOMMUNICATIONS SERVICES *Official:* The services acquired, whether by lease or contract, to meet the government's TELECOMMUNICATIONS needs. The term includes the telecommunications facilities and equipment necessary to provide such services. *Source:* DFARS 239.7401. The General Services Administration provides both local and long distance telecommunications service for federal agencies, including service at locations where consolidation can bring better prices or where meeting a common need (for example, national security) cannot be cost justified by individual agencies. The objective is to have a single telecommunications service to meet the needs of all agencies at a location. See www.gsa.gov/telecommunications. DOD has been delegated authority to enter into contracts for telecommunications services for its own use. DFARS 239.7405. DOD's policy is to acquire telecommunications services from both common and noncommon carriers (see CARRIER (TRANSPORTATION)), normally on a competitive basis. DFARS 239.7402.

TENDER OFFICIAL   See AGENCY TENDER OFFICIAL.

TERM CONTRACT   A type of COST-PLUS-FIXED-FEE CONTRACT in which the scope of work is described in general terms and the contractor's obligation is stated in terms of a specified level of effort for a stated period of time. FAR 16.306(d)(2). This is contrasted to a COMPLETION FORM CONTRACT in which the scope of work is stated as a definite goal or target with a specified end product. In the term-type contract, the contractor earns the fixed fee when the level of effort has been completed—without regard to the work accomplished. In the completion form contract, the fixed fee is not earned until the end result is accomplished. While this term is defined in the FAR as applying to cost-plus-fixed-fee contracts, it is also relevant in describing other types of COST-REIMBURSEMENT CONTRACTS.

TERM OF ART   A word or phrase having a specific, precise meaning in a given specialty, apart from its general meaning in ordinary contexts. BLACK'S LAW DICTIONARY 1774 (11th ed. 2019). CERTIFIED COST OR PRICING DATA and EQUITABLE ADJUSTMENT are examples of terms of art used in government contracting. Terms of art play an important role in CONTRACT INTERPRETATION. See Nash & Feldman, 1 GOVERNMENT CONTRACT CHANGES § 11:10 (3d ed. 2006–2020); Cibinic, Nagle & Nash, ADMINISTRATION OF GOVERNMENT CONTRACTS 156–63 (5th ed. 2016).

TERMINATED PORTION OF THE CONTRACT   *Official:* The portion of a contract that the contractor is not to perform following a PARTIAL TERMINATION. For construction contracts that have been completely terminated for convenience, it means the entire contract, notwithstanding the completion of, and payment for, individual items of work before termination. *Source:* FAR 2.101. Contractors are entitled to an EQUITABLE ADJUSTMENT for the continuing portion of a fixed-price contract that is terminated for convenience but contracting officers must ensure that this amount is not included in the TERMINATION SETTLEMENT covering the terminated portion of the contract. FAR 49.208.

TERMINATION CONTRACTING OFFICER (TCO)   A CONTRACTING OFFICER (CO) who settles terminated contracts. After the CO issues a notice of termination, the TCO is responsible for negotiating any settlement with the contractor, including a no-cost settlement if appropriate. FAR 49.101(d). See TERMINATION FOR CONVENIENCE;

TERMINATION FOR DEFAULT. In accordance with the termination clause and the notice of termination, the TCO (1) directs the action required of the contractor; (2) examines the SETTLEMENT PROPOSAL of the contractor and, when appropriate, the settlement proposals of the subcontractors; (3) promptly negotiates settlement with the contractor and enters into a settlement agreement; and (4) if a complete settlement cannot be negotiated, promptly settles the contractor's settlement proposal by determination for the elements that cannot be agreed upon. FAR 49.105. In DOD, TCOs are frequently specialists with no other responsibilities. In other agencies, the TCO functions are usually handled by the CO who was responsible for initiation of the procurement. See Cibinic, Nagle & Nash, ADMINIS-TRATION OF GOVERNMENT CONTRACTS 967 (5th ed. 2016).

TERMINATION COSTS   Costs incurred by a contractor attributable to the termination, such as termination settlement expenses and subcontractor claims, or costs which the contractor incurred planning to charge them to the contract or amortize them over the life of the contract. FAR 31.205-42 provides detailed regulations on the allowability of such costs. These costs are included in termination settlements on COST-REIMBURSEMENT CONTRACTs and FIXED-PRICE CONTRACTs terminated for convenience. FAR 49.103. See Manos, 1 GOVERNMENT CONTRACT COSTS AND PRICING §§ 49:1–49:9 (2d ed. 2009–2020); Feldman, GOVERNMENT CONTRACT GUIDEBOOK §§ 20:13–20:28 (4th ed. 2019–2020); Cibinic, Nagle & Nash, ADMINISTRATION OF GOVERNMENT CONTRACTS 966–1004 (5th ed. 2016); Cibinic, Knight & Nash, COST-REIMBURSEMENT CONTRACTING 746–59 (4th ed. 2014). See also Seidman & Seidman, *Maximizing Termination for Convenience Settlements/Edition II—Part II*, BRIEFING PAPERS No. 08-5 (Apr. 2008); Seidman & Seidman, *Maximizing Termination for Convenience Settlements/Edition II—Part I*, BRIEFING PAPERS No. 08-3 (Feb. 2008); Nash, *Postscript II: Late Convenience Termination Settlement Proposals*, 21 N&CR ¶ 13 (Apr. 2007).

TERMINATION FOR CAUSE   The term used in a contract for COMMERCIAL ITEMS for TERMINATION FOR DEFAULT. See FAR 12.403(c) and ¶ (m) of the Contract Terms and Conditions–Commercial Items clause in 52.212-4. The term is also used in conjunction with GSA FEDERAL SUPPLY SCHEDULE contracts. See FAR 8.406-4.

TERMINATION FOR CONVENIENCE   *Official:* The exercise of the government's right to completely or partially terminate performance of work under a contract when it is in the government's interest. *Source:* FAR 2.101. This long-standing right allows the government to withdraw from a contract without having to pay the contractor the profit and fixed overhead it would have earned had the contract gone to completion. The courts have placed limits on this right, but there is considerable confusion as to the extent of these limits. The right to terminate for convenience is made a part of almost all government contracts by inclusion of the standard Termination for the Convenience of the Government clauses in FAR 52.249-1 through -5. The parties may settle cost-reimbursement and fixed-price contracts terminated for the convenience of the government by negotiated agreement, determination of the TER-MINATION CONTRACTING OFFICER (only when settlement cannot be reached by agreement), costing out (in cost-reimbursement contracts), or a combination of these methods. FAR 49.103. If the parties are unable to agree on a settlement, the government must pay the contractor the costs incurred in performing the terminated work, the costs of settling and paying SETTLEMENT PROPOSALs under terminated subcontracts, and a fair and reasonable PROFIT on work performed (but not on terminated work). The contracting officer is required to enter into a no-cost settlement if it is known the contractor will accept one,

GOVERNMENT PROPERTY was not furnished, and the contractor does not have any outstanding payments, debts or obligations due to the government. FAR 49.101. See Feldman, GOVERNMENT CONTRACT GUIDEBOOK, chap. 20 (4th ed. 2019–2020); Cibinic, Nagle & Nash, ADMINISTRATION OF GOVERNMENT CONTRACTS, chap. 11 (5th ed. 2016). See also Seidman, *Postscript III: Termination for Convenience of FAR Part 12 Commercial Item Contracts*, 33 N&CR ¶ 26 (May 2019); Meagher, Bingham, Zamaray & DuVal, *Termination for Convenience of the Government: Key Issues for Contractor Recovery*, BRIEFING PAPERS No. 14-10 (Sept. 2014); Nash, *Postscript: Termination for Convenience of FAR Part 12 Commercial Item Contracts*, 25 N&CR ¶ 37 (Aug. 2011); Nash, *Termination for Convenience of FAR Part 12 Commercial Items: Is Fair Compensation Required?*, 24 N&CR ¶ 37 (Aug. 2010); Seidman & Seidman, *Maximizing Termination for Convenience Settlements/Edition II—Part II*, BRIEFING PAPERS No. 08-5 (Apr. 2008); Seidman & Seidman, *Maximizing Termination for Convenience Settlements/Edition II—Part I*, BRIEFING PAPERS No. 08-3 (Feb. 2008); Nash, *Retroactive Termination for Convenience: When Is It Possible?*, 21 N&CR ¶ 10 (Mar. 2007).

TERMINATION FOR DEFAULT *Official:* The exercise of the government's right to completely or partially terminate a contract because of the contractor's actual or anticipated failure to perform its contractual obligations. *Source:* FAR 2.101. This type of termination is also called a "default termination." This right is included in almost all government contracts by the inclusion of the standard default clauses in FAR 52.249-8 through -10. See FAR 49.504 for guidance on the use of these clauses. Procedures for administering default terminations are set forth in FAR Subparts 49.1 and 49.4. Under fixed-price supply and service contracts, the government has the right, subject to the CURE NOTICE requirements for certain situations, to terminate the contract if the contractor fails to (1) deliver the supplies or perform the services within the time specified; (2) perform any other provisions of the contract; or (3) make sufficient progress, if that failure endangers performance of the contract. FAR 49.402-1. The contractor is liable to the government for any excess costs incurred in acquiring supplies or services similar to those terminated for default and for any other damages, whether or not repurchase is affected (see EXCESS COSTS OF REPROCUREMENT). See FAR 49.402-2, FAR 49.402-6, FAR 49.402-7. If the contractor can establish, or it is otherwise determined, that the contractor was not in default or that the failure to perform is excusable, the default clauses provide that a termination for default will be considered to have been a TERMINATION FOR CONVENIENCE, and the rights and obligations of the parties will be governed accordingly. FAR 49.401. See Feldman, GOVERNMENT CONTRACT GUIDEBOOK, chap. 19 (4th ed. 2019–2020); Cibinic, Nagle & Nash, ADMINISTRATION OF GOVERNMENT CONTRACTS, chap. 10 (5th ed. 2016). See also Feldman, *Reprocurement and Termination for Default*, BRIEFING PAPERS No. 17-5 (Apr. 2017).

TERMINATION INVENTORY *Official:* Any property purchased, supplied, manufactured, furnished, or otherwise acquired for the performance of a contract subsequently terminated and properly allocable to the terminated portion of the contract. It includes GOVERNMENT-FURNISHED PROPERTY. It does not include any facilities, material, or items of SPECIAL TEST EQUIPMENT or SPECIAL TOOLING that are subject to a separate contract or to a special contract requirement governing their use or disposition. *Source:* FAR 2.101. After termination the contractor prepares schedules of all termination inventory in accordance with FAR Subpart 45.6, the contracting officer decides on the disposition of the inventory (FAR 49.105(b)(4)), and the contractor disposes of the inventory as directed by the contracting officer (FAR 49.104(i)). See Cibinic, Nagle & Nash, ADMINISTRATION OF GOVERNMENT CONTRACTS 993–94 (5th ed. 2016); Cibinic, Knight & Nash, COST-REIMBURSEMENT CONTRACTING 747 (4th ed. 2014).

TERMINATION LIABILITY *Official:* A contingent government obligation to pay a utility supplier the unamortized portion of a connection charge and any other applicable nonrefundable service charge as defined in the contract in the event the government terminates the contract before the cost of connection facilities has been recovered by the utility supplier (see "Connection charge"). *Source:* FAR 41.101. Guidance on dealing with these liabilities in UTILITY SERVICE contracts is set forth in FAR 41.205. A more generic meaning of the term "termination liability" is the maximum cost the government would incur if a contract is terminated. Paragraph (f) of the Termination for Convenience of the Government (Fixed-Price) clause in FAR 52.249-2 limits the termination liability to the contract price plus SETTLEMENT EXPENSES. Paragraph (d)(2) of the Limitation of Cost clause in FAR 52.232-20 implies that the termination liability in cost-reimbursement contracts is limited to the ESTIMATED COST or TARGET COST. When a multiyear contract (see MULTIYEAR CONTRACTING) is terminated before completion of the work on the current year, the amount includes the current year termination charges plus cancellation charges for the unfunded years. FAR 17.106-1(h).

TERMINATION NOTICE A notice from the contracting officer to the contractor stating that the contract is partially or completely terminated under either a TERMINATION FOR CONVENIENCE or a TERMINATION FOR DEFAULT. FAR 49.601-1 provides recommended formats for notices of termination for convenience and suggests that an electronic notice be used. FAR 49.402-3 contains guidance on the issuance of notices of termination for default. In such cases, DELINQUENCY NOTICEs may be required or desirable prior to the issuance of the termination notice. The default termination notice is a final DECISION OF THE CONTRACTING OFFICER, which is subject to immediate appeal under the CONTRACT DISPUTES ACT OF 1978. FAR 49.402-3(g)(7). See Cibinic, Nagle & Nash, ADMINISTRATION OF GOVERNMENT CONTRACTS 959 (5th ed. 2016).

TERMS AND CONDITIONS All the provisions of a contract. FAR 14.201-1 and FAR 15.204-1 require that the terms and conditions follow the UNIFORM CONTRACT FORMAT, with exceptions listed in FAR 14.201-1(a) and FAR 15.204. Standard terms and conditions are set forth in FAR Part 52. See also GENERAL PROVISIONS.

TEST AND EVALUATION (T&E) A process by which a SYSTEM or components are compared with requirements and SPECIFICATIONs through testing. The government evaluates the results to assess the progress of design, performance, supportability, and the like. During the ACQUISITION PROCESS, T&E can be any of three types: DEVELOPMENT TEST AND EVALUATION (DT&E), which assists the engineering design and development phase and verifies attainment of technical performance specifications and objectives; OPERATIONAL TEST AND EVALUATION (OT&E), which estimates a system's operational effectiveness and suitability, identifies needed modifications, and provides information on tactical, organizational, and personnel requirements; and production acceptance test and evaluation (PAT&E), which demonstrates that the items meet the requirements and specifications of the contract. DAU GLOSSARY. 10 U.S.C. § 2399 requires DOD to conduct OT&E on all MAJOR DEFENSE ACQUISITION PROGRAMs.

TESTING   *Official:* That element of INSPECTION that determines the properties or elements, including functional operation of supplies or their components, by the application of established scientific principles and procedures. *Source:* FAR 46.101. Testing is part of the QUALITY CONTROL and the QUALITY ASSURANCE processes. It is done by both the contractor (and its subcontractors) and the government to ensure that supplies meet contract requirements.

THE AEROSPACE CORPORATION   A private, non-profit corporation that has operated a FEDERALLY FUNDED RESEARCH AND DEVELOPMENT CENTER (FFRDC) for the United States Air Force since 1960. The Aerospace FFRDC provides scientific and engineering support for launch, space, and related ground systems. As the FFRDC for national-security space Aerospace works closely with organizations such as the U.S. Air Force Space and Missile Systems Center and the National Reconnaissance Office to provide "objective technical analyses and assessments for space programs that serve the national interests." [www.aero.org.]

THING OF VALUE   A cash payment, a gift, or any variety of benefits including automobiles, cameras, clothing, food, loans, prostitutes, vacations, or promises of future employment. An element in finding the existence of either BRIBERY or a GRATUITY is that something of value is given, offered, promised, solicited, or received. Generally, the term is broadly construed and encompasses more than just items of substantial value. See Cibinic, Nagle & Nash, ADMINISTRATION OF GOVERNMENT CONTRACTS 86–89 (5th ed. 2016); Cibinic, Nash & Yukins, FORMATION OF GOVERNMENT CONTRACTS 149–55 (4th ed. 2011).

THIRD-PARTY BENEFICIARY   An entity that is not a party to a contract but has rights under the contract because the contracting parties have designated it to have benefits flowing from the contract. Courts are reluctant to find this relationship without explicit contract language. The PATENT RIGHTS clauses state that they create such an agreement between subcontractors and the government. In addition, the Rights in Technical Data— Noncommercial Items (June 1995) clause in DFARS 252.227-7013 and the Rights in Noncommercial Computer Software and Noncommercial Computer Software Documentation (June 1995) clause in DFARS 252.227-7014 appear to create a third-party beneficiary relationship between subcontractors and the government. However, subcontractors are rarely found to be third-party beneficiaries in other circumstances. See Nash, *Postscript VI: Subcontractors as Third-Party Beneficiaries*, 26 N&CR ¶ 37 (July 2012).

THIRD-PARTY DRAFT   *Official:* An agency bank draft, similar to a check, that is used to acquire and to pay for supplies and services. *Source:* FAR 13.001; Treasury Financial Manual Section 3040.70. Third-party drafts may be used to acquire and pay for MICRO-PURCHASEs of supplies and services. FAR 13.305. However, FAR 13.201(b) states that use of the GOVERNMENT-WIDE COMMERCIAL PURCHASE CARD is the preferred method of obtaining such supplemental services.

THIRD-PARTY LIABILITY   Liability to parties other than the government and the contractor (third persons) arising from contract performance. Such liability arises when either the government or a contractor injures a person or destroys or damages the property of another party. In such cases, the third party may have a TORT claim against the government or the contractor, whichever performed the act causing the injury, destruction, or damage. Contractors normally carry INSURANCE against such claims. See FAR Subpart 28.3 providing guidance on such insurance. FAR 28.307 prescribes insurance requirements for COST

REIMBURSEMENT CONTRACTs and FAR 28.311-1 requires the use of the Insurance–Liability to Third Persons clause in FAR 52.228-7 in such contracts (making the amount of third-party liability above insurance coverage a reimbursable cost subject to the availability of appropriations). See Cibinic, Knight & Nash, Cost-Reimbursement Contracting 842–47 (4th ed. 2014).

THRESHOLD   A dollar amount establishing a limit to the use of a specific technique or action or an amount over which a specific technique must be used. For example, SIMPLIFIED ACQUISITION PROCEDURES may be used if the procurement does not exceed $250,000 (or other amounts for different types of actions—see SIMPLIFIED ACQUISITION THRESHOLD) and CERTIFIED COST OR PRICING DATA must be obtained on procurements that exceed $2,000,000 (unless an exception applies).

TIERED EVALUATION OF OFFERS   *Official:* A procedure used in negotiated acquisitions, when market research is inconclusive for justifying limiting competition to small business concerns, whereby the contracting officer—(1) Solicits and receives offers from both small and other than small business concerns; (2) Establishes a tiered or cascading order of precedence for evaluating offers that is specified in the solicitation; and (3) If no award can be made at the first tier, evaluates offers at the next lower tier, until award can be made. *Source:* DFARS 202.101. Guidance on use of this procedure is set forth in DFARS 215.203-70. See CASCADING SET-ASIDE.

TIME-AND-MATERIALS (T&M) CONTRACT   A type of contract providing for the acquisition of supplies or services on the basis of (1) direct LABOR hours at specified fixed hourly rates that include wages, overhead, GENERAL AND ADMINISTRATIVE EXPENSEs, and PROFIT; and (2) materials at cost including, if appropriate, indirect costs. FAR 16.601. Subcontracted work can be treated as direct labor with fixed hourly rates specified in the contract or as material if no rates are specified. A T&M contract may be used only if (1) at the time of placing the contract it is not possible to estimate accurately the extent or duration of the work or to anticipate costs with any reasonable degree of confidence; (2) the contracting officer executes a DETERMINATION AND FINDINGS concluding that no other contract type is suitable; and (3) the contract includes a CEILING PRICE that the contractor exceeds at its own risk (such a ceiling price is not a true ceiling because the contractor has no obligation to continue performance without further funding when the ceiling is reached). FAR 16.601(d). A T&M contract provides no positive profit incentive to the contractor for cost control or labor efficiency. See Cibinic, Nash & Yukins, Formation of Government Contracts 1319–26 (4th ed. 2011). See also Edwards, *Time-and-Materials Contract Payments: What Rate for Subcontractor Employees?*, 25 N&CR ¶ 23 (May 2011); Edwards, *Postscript: Time-and-Materials and Labor-Hour Contracts for Commercial Items*, 22 N&CR ¶ 59 (Oct. 2008); Edwards, *The New Clause for Payments Under Time-and-Materials and Labor-Hour Contracts: An End to the Confusion?*, 21 N&CR ¶ 15 (Apr. 2007); Edwards, *Time-and-Materials and Labor-Hour Contracts for Commercial Items: A Significant Departure from Tradition*, 21 N&CR ¶ 5 (Feb. 2007); Edwards, *Clarifying the Time-and-Materials Payment Clause: A Lost Cause?*, 19 N&CR ¶ 54 (Nov. 2005); Nash, *Payment Under Time-and-Materials Contracts: What Is an Hourly Rate?*, 17 N&CR ¶ 49 (Oct. 2003).

TIMELY DECISION   A DECISION OF THE CONTRACTING OFFICER under the CONTRACT DISPUTES ACT that is issued within the time limitations that are imposed by the CONTRACT DISPUTES ACT OF 1978. FAR 33.211(c) calls for a decision within

60 days of receipt of a CLAIM for $100,000 or less. FAR 33.211(d) calls for a decision within 60 days of receipt of a CERTIFIED CLAIM for over $100,000, unless the contracting officer notifies the contractor that a decision will be issued in a reasonable time. See Feldman, Government Contract Guidebook, §§ 22:8–22:12 (4th ed. 2019–2020); Cibinic, Nagle & Nash, Administration of Government Contracts 1193 (5th ed. 2016).

TITLE (code)   As used in connection with the UNITED STATES CODE and the CODE OF FEDERAL REGULATIONS, an organized collection of the laws and regulations pertaining to a particular topic. A title is one part of a CODE, such as the United States Code. For example, Title 10 of the United States Code, Armed Forces, contains the laws pertaining to management of the military departments, including its acquisition functions, and Title 41, Public Contracts, contains laws pertaining to acquisition throughout the government and laws applicable to the civilian agencies. Title 13 of the Code of Federal Regulations contains the regulations pertaining to small business programs, and Title 48 contains regulations pertaining to acquisition. Title is not synonymous with volume, and a title may occupy one or more volumes depending upon the edition of the code. The United States Code contains 51 titles, and the Code of Federal Regulations contains 50. See *How Our Laws Are Made*, available at the Library of Congress website, https://www.usa.gov/how-laws-are-made.

TITLE (ownership)   The paramount right to property. Title to property is commonly called ownership, giving the owner the right to exclude others from the use of the property or to grant others a LICENSE to use the property. The government claims title to all property bought by the contractor during the performance of a contract when the PROGRESS PAYMENTs clause in FAR 52.232-16 or the Performance-Based Payments clause in FAR 52.232-32 is included in fixed-price contracts, or when the Government Property clause in FAR 52.245-1 is included in cost-reimbursement contracts, time-and-materials contracts, or fixed-price contracts with cost-reimbursable line items. However, *Marine Midland Bank v. United States*, 231 Ct. Cl. 496, 687 F.2d 395 (1982), holds that the government right is not title but rather a lien with priority over all other claims against the property. See also FAR 32.503-15, which gives the contractor considerable control over the property during performance of the contract. With regard to PATENTs, TECHNICAL DATA, and COMPUTER SOFTWARE, the contractor generally retains title to the intellectual property rights when they are created in the performance of the contract, but the government is given a LICENSE, of varying scope, to use the rights. See FAR 27.302(b); DFARS 227.7103-4 and DFARS 227.7203-4.

TORT   Injury to a person by NEGLIGENCE or through committing an act that is proscribed by community standards. Tort is one of the common causes of action that can be used to recover DAMAGES. The FEDERAL TORT CLAIMS ACT permits persons injured by negligent conduct of the government to sue for damages in a U.S. District Court.

TOTAL COST   *Official:* The sum of the direct and indirect costs allocable (see ALLOCABLE COST) to the contract, incurred or to be incurred, plus any allocable cost of money (see COST OF MONEY FACTORS), less any allocable credits. *Source:* FAR 31.201-1(a). This amount includes STANDARD COSTs adjusted for applicable VARIANCEs. The amount that is reimbursable by the government under COST-REIMBURSEMENT CONTRACTs or is accepted in pricing of FIXED-PRICE CONTRACTs is only the ALLOWABLE COST not the total cost. FAR 31.201-1(b).

TOTAL COST METHOD   A method of establishing the amount of DAMAGES or EQUITABLE ADJUSTMENT that results in the contractor's being compensated for the difference between its actual expenses and its bid or originally estimated costs. The courts and boards of contract appeals look on this method of proving damages with disfavor, tolerating its use only when no other method of calculating damages is available. Acceptability of the method requires a demonstration that (1) the nature of the particular losses makes it impossible or highly impracticable to determine them with a reasonable degree of accuracy, (2) the contractor's bid or estimate was realistic, (3) the actual costs expended were reasonable, and (4) the contractor was not responsible for the added expenses. See Nash & Feldman, 2 GOVERNMENT CONTRACT CHANGES §§ 19:17–19:22 (3d ed. 2006–2020); Manos, 2 GOVERNMENT CONTRACT COSTS AND PRICING § 87:27 (2d ed. 2009–2020); Cibinic, Nagle & Nash, ADMINISTRATION OF GOVERNMENT CONTRACTS 629–33 (5th ed. 2016); Hess, *The Total Cost Method of Proving Damages*, CONSTR. BRIEFINGS No. 2007-02 (Feb. 2007).

TOTAL SET-ASIDE   See SET-ASIDE (n).

TRADE AGREEMENTS ACT OF 1979   U.S.C. §§ 2501–2582. A law requiring agencies to evaluate offers from contractors from designated countries without regard to the restrictions of the BUY AMERICAN ACT. The exemption applies only to procurements at or over the dollar equivalent of 150,000 SPECIAL DRAWING RIGHTS units. FAR Subpart 25.4 contains guidance and procedures implementing this Act. Exceptions to the Trade Agreements Act, under which the Buy American Act does apply, are found at FAR 25.401. See Cibinic, Nash & Yukins, FORMATION OF GOVERNMENT CONTRACTS 1624–31 (4th ed. 2011). See also Nibley, Hoang & Bakies, *Real Steps Towards "Buy American" Compliance*, BRIEFING PAPERS No. 19-06 (May 2019); Grier, *Trade Agreements Open Foreign Procurements Market*, BRIEFING PAPERS No. 17-10 (Sept. 2017).

TRADE, BUSINESS, TECHNICAL, AND PROFESSIONAL ACTIVITY COSTS   Costs incurred by a contractor as a result of membership in trade, business, technical, and professional organizations. FAR 31.205-43 makes the following costs allowable: membership costs; subscriptions to trade, business, professional, or other technical periodicals; and costs associated with meetings, conferences, symposia, or seminars, as specified below, when their principal purpose is the dissemination of trade, business, technical, or professional information or the stimulation of production or improved productivity. Allowable meeting costs are the costs of organizing, setting up, and sponsoring the meetings, symposia, etc., including rental of meeting facilities, transportation, subsistence, and incidental costs; the costs of attendance by contractor employees, including travel costs; and the costs of attendance by individuals who are not employees of the contractor, provided such costs are not also reimbursed to the individual by the employing company or organization and provided the individual's attendance is essential in achieving the purpose of the conference, meeting, symposium, or seminar. See also ALLOWABLE COST. See Manos, 1 GOVERNMENT CONTRACT COSTS AND PRICING §§ 50:1–50:3 (2d ed. 2009–2020); Cibinic, Knight & Nash, COST-REIMBURSEMENT CONTRACTING 661 (4th ed. 2014).

TRADEMARK   Distinctive symbols, pictures or words affixed to a product to distinguish and identify its origin. Under the Lanham Act, 15 U.S.C. §§ 1051–1127, marks are protected upon registration in the United States Patent and Trademark Office. See 37 C.F.R. parts 1–7. There are no regulations covering the relationship of trademarks to federal procurement.

TRADEOFF ANALYSIS   The analysis by the SOURCE SELECTION OFFICIAL in a competitive negotiation of the differences in the prices and non-price EVALUATION FACTORs of the competing offerors to determine which offer provides the BEST VALUE to the government. In a procurement for a COST-REIMBURSEMENT CONTRACT, the tradeoff analysis is between the PROBABLE COST plus FEE differences of the competing offerors and their differences on the non-cost evaluation factors. See FAR 15.308 requiring a "comparative assessment of proposals against all source selection criteria in the solicitation." Source selection officials may rely on the evaluations and recommendations of members of the source selection team but must vouch for the basic substance of the tradeoff analysis. See Cibinic, Nash & Yukins, FORMATION OF GOVERNMENT CONTRACTS 948–58 (4th ed. 2011).

TRADEOFF PROCESS   The competitive negotiation process where the government evaluates both cost/price and non-cost/price factors and awards the contract to the offeror proposing the combination of factors which offers the BEST VALUE to the government. FAR 15.101-1(a) states that this process is appropriate when it is in the best interest of the government to consider award to other than the lowest price offeror or the highest technically rated offeror. In making the award decision under this process, the government makes a TRADE-OFF ANALYSIS of the proposals, ascertaining which offers the best overall value. Prior to FAC 97-02, September 30, 1997, this process was widely described as the best value process. See BEST VALUE PROCUREMENT. See Cibinic, Nash & Yukins, FORMATION OF GOVERNMENT CONTRACTS 677–79 (4th ed. 2011); Nash, *Postscript: Best Value "Tradeoff" Procurements*, 25 N&CR ¶ 8 (Feb. 2011).

TRADE PRACTICE   See TRADE USAGE.

TRADE SECRET   *Official:* Information, including a formula, pattern, compilation, program, device, method, technique, or process, that (1) derives independent economic value, actual or potential, as a result of not being generally known to and not being readily ascertainable by proper means by other persons who can obtain economic value from its disclosure or use, and (2) is the subject of efforts that are reasonable under the circumstances to maintain its secrecy. *Source:* Uniform Trade Secrets Act § 1(4). The government is generally barred from disclosing trade secrets under the TRADE SECRETS ACT, the PROCUREMENT INTEGRITY ACT, and the FREEDOM OF INFORMATION ACT. The Economic Espionage Act of 1996, 18 U.S.C. § 1832, makes it a federal crime to steal a trade secret for the purpose of placing a product in interstate commerce. See Nash & Rawicz, INTELLECTUAL PROPERTY IN GOVERNMENT CONTRACTS, chaps. 1 & 9 (6th ed. 2008); Nash, *Damages for Destroying Trade Secrets: Some Rare Guidance*, 25 N&CR ¶ 27 (June 2011); Briggerman & Bateman, *Handling Procurement Information*, BRIEFING PAPERS No. 05-09 (Aug. 2005).

TRADE SECRETS ACT   18 U.S.C. § 1905. A law making it a crime for an employee of the United States to publish or disclose TRADE SECRETs and other confidential information obtained as a result of government employment. The Act has not led to any significant amount of criminal prosecution, but it is important in establishing a standard barring disclosure of information under the FREEDOM OF INFORMATION ACT. See Nash & Rawicz, INTELLECTUAL PROPERTY IN GOVERNMENT CONTRACTS, chap. 9 (6th ed. 2008); Briggerman & Bateman, *Handling Procurement Information*, BRIEFING PAPERS No. 05-09 (Aug. 2005); Nash, *Trade Secrets: Overly Broad Claims*, 17 N&CR ¶ 8 (Fed. 2003).

TRADE SECRETS EXEMPTION   An exemption under the FREEDOM OF INFORMATION ACT from the disclosure of TRADE SECRETS. 5 U.S.C. § 552(b)(4). See Nash & Rawicz, INTELLECTUAL PROPERTY IN GOVERNMENT CONTRACTS, chap. 9 (6th ed. 2008); Nash, *Postscript IV: Exemption 4 of the Freedom of Information Act*, 33 N&CR ¶ 47 (Aug. 2019). See also PRIVILEGED INFORMATION.

TRADE USAGE   A use of language with such regularity of observance in a place, vocation, or trade as to justify an expectation that it will be observed with respect to a particular agreement. Trade usage is distinguished from common usage or normal dictionary definitions. Evidence of trade usage, typically in conjunction with industry or trade custom or practice, may be used to interpret vague contract language. As a general rule, trade usage and trade practice or custom will not prevail over clear and unambiguous contractual language. See Cibinic, Nagle & Nash, ADMINISTRATION OF GOVERNMENT CONTRACTS 160 (5th ed. 2016); Nash & Feldman, GOVERNMENT CONTRACT CHANGES § 11:10 (3d ed. 2006–2020); RESTATEMENT (SECOND) CONTRACTS § 222 (1981); Nash, *Trade Practice: The Most Difficult Contract Interpretation Issues*, 32 N&CR ¶ 30 (July 2018).

TRAINING COSTS   Costs of providing training intended to increase the skills of a contractor's employees. FAR 31.205-44 specifies that such costs are ALLOWABLE COSTs, with some limitations. See Manos, 1 GOVERNMENT CONTRACT COSTS AND PRICING §§ 51:1–51:3 (2d ed. 2009–2012); Cibinic, Knight & Nash, COST-REIMBURSEMENT CONTRACTING 707 (4th ed. 2014).

TRANSACTIONAL CONTRACT   A traditional contract, characterized by detailed terms that specify the obligations and rights of the parties and that is based on a philosophy of "sharp in by clear agreement, sharp out by clear performance." Macneil, *The Many Futures of Contracts*, 47 S. CAL. L. REV. 691–816, 738 (1974). See RELATIONAL CONTRACT.

TRANSACTIONAL DATA   *Official:* The historical details of the products or services delivered by the Contractor during the performance of task or delivery orders issued against this contract. *Source:* The Transactional Data Reporting clause in GSAR 552.216-75. This clause is intended to obtain data on all sales of the contractor over the duration of a contract. The clause can be included in GSA-awarded GWACs and MACs but may not be included in FEDERAL SUPPLY SCHEDULE contracts. GSAR 516.506(e). The clause requires reporting of the following data: (i) Contract or Blanket Purchase Agreement (BPA) Number. (ii) Delivery/Task Order Number/Procurement Instrument Identifier (PIID). (iii) Non Federal Entity. (iv) Description of Deliverable. (v) Manufacturer Name. (vi) Manufacturer Part Number. (vii) Unit Measure (each, hour, case, lot). (viii) Quantity of Item Sold. (ix) Universal Product Code. (x) Price Paid per Unit. (xi) Total Price.

TRANSPARENCY   An attribute of the conduct of a contract action (or any other government action) that permits the public to see how it was done and to ascertain whether it was conducted in compliance with law and regulation. It is achieved by publishing information about contracting processes and results or by otherwise making the information available upon request and without undue delay. Transparency is thought to greatly reduce corruption and lawlessness in government. In 2006, Congress enacted and the president approved the Federal Funding Accountability and Transparency Act of 2006, Pub. L. No. 109-282, which requires the creation of a publicly searchable database of federal contracts and grants. In addition, in 2011 Congress enacted Pub. L. No. 111-350 requiring the adoption of the FEDERAL AWARDEE PERFORMANCE AND INTEGRITY INFORMATION

SYSTEM, which includes a broad variety of data on contractors. See 41 U.S.C. § 2313 and FAR 9.104-6. Subsequently, Congress enacted 41 U.S.C. § 2311 requiring the contract and grant database to include data on interagency contracting and OTHER TRANSACTIONS. See Yukins, *The Gathering Winds of Reform: Congress Mandates Sweeping Transparency for Federal Grants and Contracts*, 48 GOV'T CONTRACTOR ¶ 318 (Sept. 2006); Kinsey, *Transparency in Government Procurement: An International Consensus?*, 34 PUB. CONT. L.J. 155 (2004).

TRANSPORTATION   The shipment of material, parts, components, or end items in the procurement of supplies. FAR Part 47 deals with policies and procedures for applying transportation and traffic management considerations in the acquisition of transportation or transportation-related services by contract methods other than BILLS OF LADING, transportation requests, transportation warrants, and similar transportation forms. The preferred method of transporting supplies for the government is by commercial carrier (see CARRIER TRANSPORTATION). However, government-owned, leased, or chartered vehicles, aircraft, and vessels may be used if they are available and not fully utilized, if their use will result in substantial economies, and if their use is in accordance with all applicable statutes, policies, and regulations. FAR 47.101.

TRANSPORTATION SECURITY ADMINISTRATION (TSA)   An agency established by the Aviation and Transportation Security Act of 2001, 49 U.S.C. § 44901 et seq. to protect the nation's transportation systems. TSA was originally in the DEPARTMENT OF TRANSPORTATION but is now part of the DEPARTMENT OF HOMELAND SECURITY. The Act made the FAA's Acquisition Management System applicable to TSA acquisitions and allowed TSA to modify that system for its particular purposes. In 2008, Pub. L. No. 110-161 changed this and made TSA acquisitions subject to the FAR and the regulations of the DEPARTMENT OF HOMELAND SECURITY.

TRANSPORTATION TERM CONTRACTS   INDEFINITE DELIVERY/INDEFINITE QUANTITY CONTRACTs for transportation or transportation-related services. See FAR 47.205. Such contracts are generally used for the transportation of household goods, office furniture, and other general freight. FAR Subpart 47.2 provides guidance on the use of such contracts. See also INDEFINITE-DELIVERY CONTRACT.

TRAVEL COSTS   The cost of transportation, lodging, subsistence, and incidental expenses. FAR 31.205-46 specifies that such costs incurred by a contractor are ALLOWABLE COSTs, with some limitations, if they are incurred on official company business. See Manos, 1 GOVERNMENT CONTRACT COSTS AND PRICING §§ 53:1–53:6 (2d ed. 2009–2020); Cibinic, Knight & Nash, COST-REIMBURSEMENT CONTRACTING 689–92 (4th ed. 2014).

TREASURY INTEREST RATE   The interest rate set by the Secretary of the Treasury for each six-month period on a calendar year basis. The rate is published in the FEDERAL REGISTER and is used to calculate the amount of INTEREST payable by the government under the PROMPT PAYMENT ACT and the CONTRACT DISPUTES ACT OF 1978.

TRUTH IN NEGOTIATIONS ACT (TINA)   10 U.S.C. § 2306a, 41 U.S.C. §§ 3501–3509 (renamed TRUTHFUL COST OR PRICING DATA). A law that was added to the ARMED SERVICES PROCUREMENT ACT in 1963 to enhance the government's ability to negotiate fair prices by ensuring that the contracting officer has the same factual information that is available to the contractor at the time of price negotiations. TINA requires contractors to submit COST OR PRICING DATA and certify of their accuracy, complete-ness, and currency for the award of any negotiated contract expected to exceed $2,000,000. However, requiring such data is prohibited when SIMPLIFIED ACQUISITION PROCEDURES are used, when there is ADEQUATE PRICE COMPETITION, when the agency is procuring a COMMERCIAL ITEM, when the price is established by law or regulation, when a waiver is obtained, and when the agency exercises an OPTION or funds an OVERRUN. FAR 15.403-1 and 15.403-2 (see CERTIFIED COST OR PRICING DATA). It also provided for contract price adjustment as a result of submission of DEFECTIVE COST OR PRICING DATA. In 1984, the COMPETITION IN CONTRACTING ACT added these requirements to the FEDERAL PROPERTY AND ADMINISTRATIVE SERVICES ACT OF 1949 at 41 U.S.C. § 254b. Subsequently, in 1986, TINA was greatly expanded and codified at 10 U.S.C. § 2306a. The FEDERAL ACQUISITION STREAMLINING ACT OF 1994, Pub. L. No. 103-355, further modified and refined TINA requirements. TINA is not the only remedy available to the gov-ernment for defective data; a contractor may be found liable for civil fraud under the FALSE CLAIMS ACT, 31 U.S.C. §§ 3729–3732, for knowingly submitting defective data. Certification under the Act is accomplished by the Certificate of Current Cost or Pricing Data in FAR 15.506-2. The Act is implemented by the Price Reduction for Defective Cost or Pricing Data clauses at FAR 52.215-22 and -23. The data are submitted in accordance with Table 15-2, FAR 15.408. See Manos, 2 GOVERNMENT CONTRACT COSTS AND PRICING §§ 84:2–84:18 (2d ed. 2009–2020); Feldman, GOVERNMENT CONTRACT GUIDEBOOK §§ 9:63–9:76 (4th ed. 2019–2020). See also Bodenheimer, *Litigation & Proof in Defective Pricing Cases*, BRIEFING PAPERS No. 15-5 (Apr. 2015).

TRUTHFUL COST OR PRICING DATA   The name given to the TRUTH IN NEGOTIATIONS ACT when Title 41 of the United States Code was recodified in 2011 by Pub. L. No. 211-350. The act is in 41 U.S.C. §§ 3501–3509.

TUCKER ACT   An Act, 28 U.S.C. §§ 1346(a) and 1491(a), that waives SOVEREIGN IMMUNITY from suit for all CLAIMs founded upon the Constitution, statutes, regula-tions, or any contract, express or implied, against the U.S. Government. Originally passed in 1855 and enacted in its present form in 1887, the Tucker Act made the Court of Claims the major court resolving government contract DISPUTEs, but gave federal district courts jurisdiction up to $10,000. The CONTRACT DISPUTES ACT OF 1978 repealed the part of the Tucker Act that gave the federal district courts jurisdiction over claims under that Act (leaving the district courts with jurisdiction over claims up to $10,000 asserted under other types of contracts) and gave contractors direct access to the Court of Claims to challenge contracting officer decisions on contract disputes. The FEDERAL COURTS IMPROVEMENT ACT further altered the process by creating the COURT of FEDERAL CLAIMS (originally named the Claims Court) and the COURT OF APPEALS FOR THE FEDERAL CIRCUIT out of the former Court of Claims.

TURN KEY   See DESIGN-BUILD.

TWO-PHASE DESIGN-BUILD SELECTION PROCEDURES   *Official:* A selection method in which a limited number of offerors (normally five or fewer) is selected during Phase One to submit detailed proposals for Phase Two. *Source:* FAR 6.102. This DESIGN BUILD selection procedure was authorized by the CLINGER-COHEN ACT OF 1996, 10 U.S.C. § 2505a and 41 U.S.C. § 3309. It is implemented in FAR Subpart 36.3. It may be used when it is determined that three or more offers are anticipated and significant design work will be required in order to select the design-build contractor. In making this determination, the following criteria must be considered: (1) the adequacy of the definition of project requirements, (2) the time constraints for delivery of the project, (3) the capability and experience of potential contractors, (4) the suitability of the project for the two-phase method, (5) the capability of the agency to manage the project, and (6) other criteria established by the contracting activity. FAR 36.301. See Nash, *Design-Build Contracting: Are "Bridging Documents" Necessary?*, 20 N&CR ¶ 5 (Jan. 2006).

TWO-STEP SEALED BIDDING   A method of procurement that combines competitive procedures in order to obtain the benefits of SEALED BIDDING when adequate SPECIFICATIONs are not available. FAR 14.501. One objective of this process is to permit the development of a sufficiently descriptive and not unduly restrictive statement of the government's requirements, including an adequate TECHNICAL DATA PACKAGE, so that subsequent acquisitions can be made by conventional sealed bidding. This method is especially useful in acquisitions requiring technical proposals, particularly those for complex items. Step One consists of the request for and submission, EVALUATION, and DISCUSSION of technical proposals; no pricing is involved. FAR 14.503-1. Step Two involves the submission of sealed bids by offerors that submitted acceptable technical proposals in Step One. FAR 14.503-2. See Feldman, Government Contract Awards: Negotiation and Sealed Bidding §§ 27:32–27:35 (2019–2020 ed.); Cibinic, Nash & Yukins, Formation of Government Contracts 656–72 (4th ed. 2011).

TYPE OF CONTRACT   Categories of contracts that are differentiated according to the risk imposed on the contractor and the time the work is defined. FAR Part 16 describes and states the policies governing the various types of contract. Contracts dealing with firmly established work requirements are of three basic types: FIXED-PRICE CONTRACTs, INCENTIVE CONTRACTs, and COST-REIMBURSEMENT CONTRACTs. Within these three basic families are a sizable number of specific types. The major difference in these contract types is the degree of risk of higher costs than anticipated assumed by the contractor—with major risk being imposed by fixed-price type contracts, very limited risk being imposed by cost-reimbursement type contracts and risk being shared in incentive contracts. FAR Part 16 also describes another set of types of contracts that provide for defining the amount of and ordering work after the contract is awarded. These contract types include INDEFINITE-DELIVERY CONTRACTs, TIME-AND-MATERIALS CONTRACTs, LABOR-HOUR CONTRACTs, and LETTER CONTRACTs. These types of contract impose varying degrees of risk on the contractor. For discussion of the various contract types, see Feldman, Government Contract Guidebook §§ 4:17–4:33 (4th ed. 2019–2020); Cibinic, Knight & Nash, Cost-Reimbursement Contracting, chap. 2 (4th ed. 2014); Cibinic, Nash & Yukins, Formation of Government Contracts, chap. 9 (4th ed. 2011); Edwards, *Contract Types: There are More Things in Heaven and Earth, Judge, than are Dreamt of in the FAR*, 32 N&CR ¶ 3 (Jan. 2018); Nash, *Selection of Contract Type*, 25 N&CR ¶ 55 (Nov. 2011); Nash, *Selecting the Type of Contract: A Critical Decision*, 24 N&CR ¶ 4 (Jan. 2010); Manuel, Cong. Research Serv., Report No. R41168 Contract Types: An Overview of the Legal Requirements and Issues (Oct. 1, 2010); Edwards, *Contract Pricing Arrangements: A Primer—Part II*, Briefing Papers No. 09-12 (Nov. 2009); Edwards, *Contract Pricing Arrangements: A Primer—Part I*, Briefing Papers No. 09-11 (Oct. 2009).

U

UNABSORBED OVERHEAD   Overhead (see INDIRECT COST) that cannot be charged to a contract as originally anticipated because the direct costs of performance have been stopped due to a delay. During periods of government DELAY in or SUSPENSION of a particular contract, there is a marked decrease in or cessation of DIRECT COSTs incurred for that contract. Consequently, the HOME OFFICE costs that would otherwise have been charged to that contract by means of applying the home office overhead rate to direct costs cannot be "absorbed" by that contract during the period of the delay and must be borne by the contractor's other work. The EICHLEAY FORMULA is the prevalent method for calculating unabsorbed and extended overhead. The COURT OF APPEALS FOR THE FEDERAL CIRCUIT has held that a contractor must be ON STANDBY in order to recover unabsorbed overhead. *P.J. Dick, Inc. v. Principi*, 324 F.3d 1364 (Fed. Cir. 2003). See Nash & Feldman, GOVERNMENT CONTRACT CHANGES §§ 17:9–17:16 (3d ed. 2006–2020); Cibinic, Nagle & Nash, ADMINISTRATION OF GOVERNMENT CONTRACTS 647–52 (5th ed. 2016).

UNALLOWABLE COST   *Official:* Any cost that, under the provisions of any pertinent law, regulation or contract, cannot be included in prices, cost-reimbursements, or settlements under a government contract to which it is allocable. *Source:* FAR 2.101. Unallowable costs must be identified and excluded from any billing, claim, or proposal applicable to a government contract. FAR 31.201-6. CAS 405, 48 C.F.R. § 9904.405, provides guidance in accounting for such costs. 10 U.S.C. § 2324 and 41 U.S.C. § 4308 call for severe sanctions for claiming costs that are expressly unallowable pursuant to statute or regulation. See Manos, 2 GOVERNMENT CONTRACT COSTS & PRICING, chap. 66 (2d ed. 2009–2020); Cibinic, Knight & Nash, COST-REIMBURSEMENT CONTRACTING, chaps. 9 & 10 (4th ed. 2014). See also ALLOWABLE COST and EXPRESSLY UNALLOWABLE COST.

UNAUTHORIZED COMMITMENT   *Official:* An agreement that is not binding solely because the government representative who made it lacked the authority to enter into that agreement on behalf of the government. *Source:* FAR 1.602-3(a). HEADs OF CONTRACTING ACTIVITIES may ratify such commitments and this authority may be delegated to an official no lower than the chief of the contracting office. FAR 1.602-3(b). See RATIFICATION. See Cibinic, Nagle & Nash, ADMINISTRATION OF GOVERNMENT CONTRACTS 45–52 (5th ed. 2016); Cibinic, Nash, & Yukins, FORMATION OF GOVERNMENT CONTRACTS 46–53 (4th ed. 2011).

UNBALANCED BID   A BID that states nominal or low prices for some work and enhanced prices for other work. For the bid to be deemed nonresponsive (see RESPONSIVENESS), it must be both mathematically unbalanced and materially unbalanced. FAR 14.404-2(g). A determination of mathematical unbalance asks whether each bid item carries its share of the cost of the work plus profit or whether the bid is based on nominal or low prices for some work and enhanced prices for other work. A determination of material unbalance asks whether there is reasonable doubt that award to the bidder submitting the mathematically unbalanced bid ultimately will result in the lowest cost. See ¶ (e) of the Contract Award—Sealed Bidding solicitation provision in FAR 52.214-10. FAR 15.404-1(g) gives the contracting officer more discretion in dealing with UNBALANCED PRICING in negotiated procurements. See Cibinic, Nash & Yukins, FORMATION OF GOVERNMENT CONTRACTS 578–87 (4th ed. 2011).

UNBALANCED PRICING   Pricing of a negotiated contract where the price of one or more contract line items is significantly over or understated as indicated by the application of cost or price analysis techniques. FAR 15.404-1(g) indicates that such pricing may increase performance risk or result in unreasonably high prices. Contracting officers are therefore directed to analyze all line item prices to determine if they are unbalanced and to reject the offer if the unbalancing poses an unacceptable risk to the government. This regulation rejects the mathematical/material analysis used to deal with UNBALANCED BIDs in favor of granting the contracting officer discretion to deal with this issue on a case-by-case basis.

UNCONSCIONABILITY   A bargain or contract that no person in possession of his or her senses—that is to say, not under a delusion—would make and that no fair and honest person would accept. The basic test of unconscionability is whether, under circumstances existing when the contract was made and in light of general commercial background and commercial needs of the particular trade or case, the contract clauses are so one-sided as to oppress or unfairly surprise a party. Unconscionability generally implies an absence of meaningful choice on the part of one of the parties. Moreover, the one-sidedness often obtains when the imbalance is buried in small print or couched in language unintelligible even to a person of moderate education. BLACK'S LAW DICTIONARY 1835 (11th ed. 2019). Unconscionability is grounds for contract AVOIDANCE. U.C.C. § 2-302. See Cibinic, Nagle & Nash, ADMINISTRATION OF GOVERNMENT CONTRACTS 311 (5th ed. 2016).

UNDEFINITIZED CONTRACT ACTION (UCA)   *Official:* Any contract action for which the contract terms, SPECIFICATIONs, or price are not agreed upon before performance is begun under the action. Examples are LETTER CONTRACTs, orders under basic ordering agreements, and provisioned item orders, for which the price has not been agreed upon before performance has begun. For policy relating to definitization of CHANGE ORDERs, see 243.204-70. *Source:* DFARS 217.7401. 10 U.S.C. § 2326 precludes DOD agencies, NASA and the Coast Guard from entering into undefinitized contractual actions without proper justification and provides that DEFINITIZATION should occur within 180 days of the contractor's proposal to definitize and before the expenditure of more than 50% of the funds to be used. Procedures for complying with this statute are contained in DFARS Subpart 217.74.

UNDEFINITIZED LINE ITEM   *Official:* A contract item for which a firm price has not been established in the basic contract or by MODIFICATION. *Source:* DFARS 204.7101. DFARS 204.7106 contains criteria on the use of CONTRACT LINE ITEMs when a CONTRACT MODIFICATION effects an undefinitized item. See UNIFORM CONTRACT LINE ITEM NUMBERING SYSTEM.

UNDULY RESTRICTIVE [OF COMPETITION]   An attribute of a SPECIFICATION, STATEMENT OF WORK, contract term, SOLICITATION, or acquisition practice that limits competition more than is necessary for the satisfaction of the government's requirements, thereby violating the COMPETITION IN CONTRACTING ACT mandate for FULL AND OPEN COMPETITION. See Cibinic, Nash & Yukins, FORMATION OF GOVERNMENT CONTRACTS 370–73 (4th ed. 2011); Nash, *Unduly Restrictive Requirements Protests*, 25 N&CR ¶3 (Jan. 2011).

UNEQUAL ACCESS TO NONPUBLIC INFORMATION   A type of ORGANIZATIONAL CONFLICT OF INTEREST where an organization has obtained information from the government that gives it an UNFAIR COMPETITIVE ADVANTAGE. FAR 9.505-4 calls for "restrictions" when a contractor "requires proprietary information from others to perform a Government contract and can use the leverage of the contract to obtain it." This is one of the categories of OCIs that GAO has identified in its protest decisions.

UNFAIR COMPETITIVE ADVANTAGE   An advantage of one competitor over another competitor that is derived from improper government action or is created by the government. An unfair competitive advantage exists when a contractor competing for the award of any federal contract possesses PROPRIETARY INFORMATION that was obtained from a government official without proper authorization or SOURCE SELECTION INFORMATION that is relevant to the contract but is not available to all competitors, and such information would assist that contractor in obtaining the contract. FAR 9.505-4. An unfair competitive advantage also exists when a contractor is permitted to use GOVERNMENT PROPERTY in a competitive procurement without payment of rent or addition of a RENTAL EQUIVALENT to its offered price. FAR 45.103(a)(2). Rent is required to be paid for the use of government property in accordance with the Use and Charges clause in FAR 52.245-9. However, contracting officers are allowed to use a rental equivalent in lieu of rent. FAR 45.202(a). Being the incumbent contractor is not an unfair competitive advantage.

UNFAIR TRADE PRACTICE   *Official:* The commission of any or the following acts by a contractor: (1) A violation of § 337 of the Tariff Act of 1930 (19 U.S.C. § 1337) as determined by the International Trade Commission. (2) A violation, as determined by the Secretary of Commerce, of any agreement of the group known as the "Coordination Committee" for purposes of the Export Administration Act of 1979 (50 U.S.C. App. § 2401 et seq.) or any similar bilateral or multilateral export control agreement. (3) A knowingly false statement regarding a material element of a certification concerning the foreign content of an item of supply, as determined by the Secretary of the Department or the head of the agency to which such certificate was furnished. *Source:* FAR 9.403. Such conduct is a cause for DEBARMENT or SUSPENSION of a contractor.

UNICOR   See FEDERAL PRISON INDUSTRIES, INC.

UNIFORM COMMERCIAL CODE (U.C.C.)   A uniform law governing commercial transactions such as sales of GOODS, commercial paper, bank deposits and collections, LETTERs OF CREDIT, bulk transfers, warehouse receipts, BILLs OF LADING, investment securities, and secured transactions. All states except Louisiana have adopted the U.C.C. The U.C.C. is one of the Uniform Laws drafted by the National Conference of Commissioners on Uniform State Laws. BLACK'S LAW DICTIONARY 1840 (11th ed. 2019). The U.C.C.'s underlying purposes and policies are to simplify, clarify, and modernize the law governing commercial transactions; permit the continued expansion of commercial practices through custom, usage, and agreement of the parties; and make the law uniform throughout the various jurisdictions. U.C.C. § 1-102. The U.C.C. is not directly applicable to government contracting, but it is used by analogy and for guidance when the terms of a contract or the regulations do not deal directly with a subject. See generally White & Summers, UNIFORM COMMERCIAL CODE HORNBOOK SERIES (Practitioner Treatise Series) (6th ed. 2012–2020).

UNIFORM CONTRACT FORMAT (UCF)   A standardized format for structuring government SOLICITATIONs and CONTRACTs. FAR 14.201-1; FAR 15.204-1. Its use facilitates preparation of the solicitation and contract as well as reference to and use of the documents in the solicitation and contract. Found on Standard Form 26—Award and Contract—and Standard Form 33—Solicitation, Offer and Award—the UCF is simply a table of contents for organizing contractual documents into four parts and 13 sections. In negotiated acquisitions, Part I, The Schedule, includes sections A, Solicitation/contract form; B, Supplies or services and prices/costs; C, Description/specifications/work statement; D, Packaging and marking; E, Inspection and acceptance; F, Deliveries or performance; G, Contract administration data; and H, Special contract requirements. Part II, Contract Clauses, consists of a single section I, Contract clauses. Part III, List of Documents, Exhibits, and Other Attachments, consists of a single section J, List of attachments. Part IV, Representations and Instructions, contains sections K, Representations, certifications, and other statements of offerors or quoters; L, Instructions, conditions, and notices to offerors or quoters; and M, Evaluation factors for award. In sealed bidding, the format is the same, with minor differences in language. See Feldman, GOVERNMENT CONTRACT AWARDS: NEGOTIATION AND SEALED BIDDING §§ 6:6–6:10 (2019–2020 ed.); Cibinic, Nash & Yukins, FORMATION OF GOVERNMENT CONTRACTS 504–05, 728–39 (4th ed. 2011).

UNIFORM CONTRACT LINE ITEM NUMBERING SYSTEM   *Official:* The DOD system for assigning CONTRACT LINE ITEMs in SOLICITATIONs and CONTRACTs. *Source:* DFARS Subpart 204.71. DFARS 204.7103-1 requires the use of separate line items unless it is not feasible and contains detailed criteria on when separate line items should be used. DFARS 204.7104-1 contains detailed criteria on when separate subline items should be used. DFARS 204.7106 contains guidance on the numbering of CONTRACT MODIFICATIONs.

UNIFORM RULES   A standardized set of rules of procedure for the various agency BOARDs OF CONTRACT APPEALS (BCAs). The CONTRACT DISPUTES ACT OF 1978 requires that the Administrator of the OFFICE OF FEDERAL PROCUREMENT POLICY (OFPP) issue guidelines with respect to the establishment, functions, and procedures of the agency BCAs. 41 U.S.C. § 607(h) (pre-2011 codification). OFPP issued "Uniform Rules of Procedure for Boards of Contract Appeals" in 1979. See 44 Fed. Reg. 12519, Mar. 7, 1979; 44 Fed. Reg. 34227, June 14, 1979. The rules have, in effect, been superseded by the uniform rules drafted by the National Conference of Boards of Contract Appeals Members (now called the Board of Contract Appeals Judges Association), with sections added to implement the Contract Disputes Act's small claims and subpoena provisions. OFPP intended that the various BCAs would adopt the Uniform Rules in place of their individual rules, except when a BCA's size or the nature of its docket justified a variance. Each BCA's "customized" version of the rules can be found in the loose-leaf advance sheet section of the *Board of Contract Appeals Decisions* available from Commerce Clearing House, Inc., 4025 West Peterson Avenue, Chicago, IL 60646.

UNILATERAL CHANGE   *Official:* A change in cost accounting practice from one compliant practice to another compliant practice that a contractor with a CAS-covered contract(s) or subcontract(s) elects to make that has not been deemed a desirable change by the cognizant federal agency official and for which the government will pay no aggregate increased costs. *Source:* FAR 30.001. Under the COST ACCOUNTING STANDARDS a contractor may make such a change but the government may not pay for any costs of the change. FAR 30.603-2. A more common meaning of unilateral change is a CHANGE ORDER issued by a contracting officer, without the need for agreement or acceptance by the contractor, under a Changes clause. Most government contracts contain a Changes clause permitting the contracting officer to make unilateral changes in designated areas, within the general SCOPE OF THE CONTRACT. FAR 43.201. The contractor is bound to proceed in accordance with such a change order even if it does not agree with it. It is the policy of the government to avoid issuing unilateral changes by attempting instead to price changes before they are issued and then issue a bilateral MODIFICATION. FAR 43.102(b). When this cannot be done, it is the policy of the government to negotiate a maximum price in the change order. See Nash & Feldman, GOVERNMENT CONTRACT CHANGES § 7:12 (3d ed. 2006–2020); Cibinic, Nagle & Nash, ADMINISTRATION OF GOVERNMENT CONTRACTS 364 (5th ed. 2016). Unilateral changes are issued on Standard Form 30, Amendment of Solicitation/Modification of Contract, FAR 53.301-30. FAR 43.201(a). See also UNILATERAL MODIFICATION.

UNILATERAL CONTRACT   A binding contractual agreement where the OFFER specifies that the ACCEPTANCE can be effective only if it is in the form of performance. *Restatement (Second) Contracts* § 45 (1981). In such instances, an attempted acceptance by communication or promise will be ineffective to form a contract. This is called a unilateral contract because the OFFEROR is bound while the other party is not (the offer being considered the giving of an OPTION under the *Restatement*). The term "unilateral contract" has frequently been thought to mean any contract formed by an offer from one party and acceptance in the form of performance by the other party. The contracting officer can issue a PURCHASE ORDER as this type of unilateral contract or as a BILATERAL CONTRACT. FAR 13.302-3. See Cibinic, Nash & Yukins, FORMATION OF GOVERNMENT CONTRACTS 246–47 (4th ed. 2011); Nash, *Unilateral Purchase Orders: When Are They Binding?*, 21 N&CR ¶ 11 (Mar. 2007).

UNILATERAL MISTAKE   A MISTAKE of only one party—generally the contractor. Relief for such mistakes may be given if they are alleged by the offeror before award, provided they are not mistakes in business judgment. See FAR 14.407. FAR 15.306 gives incomplete guidance on handling mistakes alleged before award by offerors in negotiated procurements. See Nash, *Postscript: Mistakes in Negotiated Procurement*, 20 N&CR ¶ 52 (Nov. 2006); Cibinic, *Mistakes in Negotiated Procurement: A Sensible Rule Mistakes in Negotiated Procurement*, 18 N&CR ¶ 17 (Apr. 2004); Nash, *Postscript: Verification of Proposals When Mistakes Are Suspected*, 17 N&CR ¶ 56 (Nov. 2003). No relief is given for such mistakes alleged by a contractor after award unless the contracting officer knew or should have known of the mistake before award or failed to ask for verification (see DUTY OF VERIFICATION). See FAR 14.407-4 and 15.508. See Cibinic, Nagle & Nash, ADMINISTRATION OF GOVERNMENT CONTRACTS 303–10 (5th ed. 2016).

UNILATERAL MODIFICATION   A MODIFICATION to a contract that is signed only by the contracting officer. Unilateral modifications are generally used to make

ADMINISTRATIVE CHANGEs, issue CHANGE ORDERs, make changes authorized by clauses other than a Changes clause, and issue TERMINATION NOTICEs. FAR 43.103. The alternative to a unilateral modification is a BILATERAL MODIFICATION. See Nash & Feldman, Government Contract Changes, chap. 7 (3d ed. 2006–2020).

UNILATERAL PRICE DETERMINATION   A government-directed MODIFICATION to a contract that sets forth a presumptively fair price for the supplies or services that are at issue. This presumption is rebuttable upon a contractor showing that the unilaterally determined price is either not fair or not reasonable, or both, based on certain facts, cost or price principles or assumptions, or legal theories. Such determinations are most frequently used when the parties cannot agree on the definitization of a LETTER CONTRACT, FAR 16.603-2(c), or a termination settlement, FAR 49.109-7. If a contractor does not sign the unilateral price determination but fails to object in a timely manner, the modification may have the force and effect of a bilateral agreement and may not be susceptible to subsequent legal challenge. See also UNILATERAL CHANGE. See Nash & Feldman, Government Contract Changes, chap. 7 (3d ed. 2006–2020).

UNIQUE AND INNOVATIVE CONCEPT   *Official:* When used relative to an unsolicited research proposal, means that—(1) In the opinion and to the knowledge of the government evaluator, the meritorious proposal—(i) Is the product of original thinking submitted confidentially by one source; (ii) Contains new, novel, or changed concepts, approaches, or methods; (iii) Was not submitted previously by another; and (iv) Is not otherwise available within the federal government. (2) In this context, the term does not mean that the source has the sole capability of performing the research. *Source:* FAR 2.101. When such a concept is included in an UNSOLICITED PROPOSAL, a contracting agency may award a contract to the offeror without obtaining FULL AND OPEN COMPETITION. 10 U.S.C. § 2304(d)(1) and 41 U.S.C. § 3304(b)(1). Guidance is provided in FAR Subpart 15.6. See Cibinic, Nash & Yukins, Formation of Government Contracts 309–11 (4th ed. 2011).

UNIQUE ENTITY IDENTIFIER   *Official:* A number or other identifier used to identify a specific commercial, nonprofit, or Government entity. See www.sam.gov for the designated entity for establishing unique entity identifiers. *Source:* FAR 2.101. This number must be included when a contractor registers in the SYSTEM FOR AWARD MANAGEMENT. It also must be included in each OFFER made to the government. See the Unique Entity Identifier provision in FAR 52.204-5. Any changes to the number must be communicated promptly to the government. See the Unique Entity Identifier Maintenance clause in FAR 52.204-12.

UNIT COST REDUCTION   See INSTANT UNIT COST REDUCTION.

UNITED STATES   *Official:* The 50 States and the District of Columbia, except as follows: (1) For use in Subpart 3.10, see the definition at 3.1001. (2) For use in subpart 22.8, see the definition at 22.801. (3) For use in subpart 22.10, see the definition at 22.1001. (4) For use in subpart 22.12, see the definition at 22.1201. (5) For use in subpart 22.13, see the definition at 22.1301. (6) For use in subpart 22.16, see the definition at 22.1601. (7) For use in Subpart 22.17, see the definition at 22.1702. (8) For use in Subpart 22.18, see the definition at 22.1801. (9) For use in part 23, see definition at 23.001. (10) For use in part 25, see definition at 25.003. (11) For use in Part 27, see the definition at 27.001. (12) For use in subpart 47.4, see the definition at 47.401. *Source:* FAR 2.101. The varying definitions of United States broaden the definition by adding territories, possessions and other outlying areas, defined more specifically in each case. The definitions do not include areas under United States jurisdiction in foreign countries.

UNITED STATES AGENCY FOR INTERNATIONAL DEVELOPMENT (USAID) An agency that provides economic, development and humanitarian assistance around the world in support of the foreign policy goals of the United States. The AIDAR is USAID's Acquisition Regulation supplementing the FAR and is published as Chapter 7 of 48 C.F.R. [USAID, Ronald Reagan Building, 1300 Pennsylvania Avenue, NW, Washington, D.C. 20523. 202-712-0000. www.USAID.gov.]

UNITED STATES CODE (U.S.C.) A consolidation and codification of all the general and permanent laws of the United States. The code is prepared by the Office of the Law Revision Counsel, U.S. House of Representatives. When a bill becomes law it is published in a pamphlet called a "slip law." Thereafter, it is published in the STATUTES AT LARGE. Subsequently, it is codified, which may entail minor textual revisions. The STATUTES AT LARGE continue to be the official text of the law until Congress establishes a title of the code as positive law. The code provides an organized system for finding federal laws by title (50 headings, primarily alphabetical) and section. For example, Title 41, Public Contracts, contains many of the basic laws governing the procurement process. Within Title 41, §§ 251 through 266a contained the procurement parts of the FEDERAL PROPERTY AND ADMINISTRATIVE SERVICES ACT OF 1949, §§ 403 through 438 contained the OFFICE OF FEDERAL PROCUREMENT POLICY Act, and §§ 601 through 613 contained the CONTRACT DISPUTES ACT OF 1978. In 2011, Title 41 was recodified with subtitle I covering "Federal Procurement Policy," subtitle II covering "Other Advertising and Contract Provisions," subtitle III covering "Contract Disputes," and subtitle IV covering "Miscellaneous." Note, however, that the ARMED SERVICES PROCUREMENT ACT is codified in Title 10, Armed Forces. Whereas bills passed by Congress are sequentially numbered as public laws or statutes, the code organizes the laws by subject matter, often placing portions of new statutes in multiple U.S.C. titles. Current versions of the code are published by commercial vendors such as Thomson-West (United States Code Annotated or U.S.C.A.) and LexisNexis (United States Code Service or U.S.C.S.).

UNITED STATES-MEXICO-CANADA AGREEMENT (USMCA) A free trade agreement between these three countries that replaced the NORTH AMERICAN FREE TRADE AGREEMENT. The agreement was negotiated in 2018 and ratified in 2020. Compared to NAFTA, USMCA increases environmental and working regulations, and incentivizes more domestic production of cars and trucks. The agreement also provides updated intellectual property protections, gives the United States more access to Canada's dairy market, imposes a quota for Canadian and Mexican automotive production, and increases the duty-free limit for Canadians who buy U.S. goods online from $20 to $150.

UNITED STATES MUNITION LIST See DEFENSE ARTICLE.

UNLIMITED RIGHTS *Official:* The rights of the government to use, disclose, reproduce, prepare DERIVATIVE WORKS, distribute copies to the public, and perform publicly and display publicly, in any manner and for any purpose, and to have or permit others to do so. *Source:* FAR 27.401. This definition pertains to the FAR policy on TECHNICAL DATA and COMPUTER SOFTWARE. Such rights give the government a very broad LICENSE except with regard to COPYRIGHT where the government has only the right for government purposes, FAR 27.404(f). Under the Rights in Data—General clause in FAR

52.227-14, the government acquires unlimited rights in (1) data first produced in the performance of a contract; (2) FORM, FIT, AND FUNCTION DATA delivered under contract; (3) data that constitute manuals or instructional and training material for installation, operation, or routine maintenance and repair of items, components, or processes delivered or furnished for use under a contract; and (4) all other data delivered under a contract, other than LIMITED RIGHTS DATA or restricted COMPUTER SOFTWARE. FAR 27.404. Under the DOD policy, the Rights in Technical Data—Noncommercial Items (June 1995) clause in DFARS 252.227-7013 and the Rights in Noncommercial Computer Software and Noncommercial Computer Software Documentation (June 1995) clause in DFARS 252.227-7014 define unlimited rights as the right to use, modify, reproduce, release, perform, display, or disclose [technical data or computer software or computer software documentation, as appropriate] in whole or in part, in any manner, and for any purpose whatsoever, and to have or authorize others to do so. This DOD policy takes unlimited rights in a slightly broader set of situations than does the FAR policy. See Nash & Rawicz, INTELLECTUAL PROPERTY IN GOVERNMENT CONTRACTS, chaps. 4 & 5 (6th ed. 2008). See also Nash, *Postscript II: Protecting Unlimited Rights Data*, 33 N&CR ¶4 (Jan. 2019).

UNMISTAKABILITY DOCTRINE   The legal doctrine that contracts that limit the government's sovereign power to exercise its regulatory authority in the future are strongly disfavored and will be recognized only rarely and only when they do so in unmistakable terms. Contracts that merely make the government liable to pay damages for breach are not subject to the doctrine. See Lee, *Does Mobil Oil Weaken the Sovereign Defenses of Government Breach of Contract Claims? An Analysis of the Unmistakability Doctrine & the Sovereign Acts Doctrine*, 31 PUB. CONT. L.J. 559 (2002).

UNPRICED PURCHASE ORDER   *Official:* An order for supplies or services, the PRICE of which is not established at the time of issuance of the order. *Source:* FAR 13.302-2(a). An unpriced PURCHASE ORDER may be used only when (1) the transaction is not expected to exceed the SIMPLIFIED ACQUISITION THRESHOLD; (2) it is impractical to obtain pricing before issuing the purchase order; and (3) the purchase is for repairs to equipment requiring disassembly to determine the nature and extent of repairs, or for material that is available from only one source and for which the cost cannot be readily established, or for supplies or services for which prices are known to be competitive but exact prices are not known (for example, miscellaneous repair parts or maintenance services). FAR 13.302-2(b). These orders must have a realistic monetary limitation. FAR 13.302-2(c).

UNSETTLED CONTRACT CHANGE   *Official:* Any contract change or contract term for which a definitive modification is required but has not been executed. *Source:* FAR 49.001. All such changes must be settled in order to reach a final settlement of a terminated contract. FAR 49.114. If the contract is only partially terminated, this is usually done by the contracting officer handling the contract modification rather than a TERMINATION CONTRACTING OFFICER.

UNSOLICITED PROPOSAL   *Official:* A written proposal for a new and innovative idea that is submitted to an agency on the initiative of the offeror for the purpose of obtaining a contract with the government, and that is not in response to a REQUEST FOR PROPOSALS, a BROAD AGENCY ANNOUNCEMENT, Small Business Innovation Research topic, Small Business Technology Transfer Research topic, Program Research and Development Announcement, or any other government-initiated SOLICITATION or program. *Source:*

FAR 2.101. Unsolicited proposals are a means for government agencies to obtain innovative or unique methods or approaches to accomplishing their missions from sources outside the government but the basic policy of the government is to encourage the submission of such methods or approaches in response to broad agency announcements. FAR 15.603. 10 U.S.C. § 2304(d)(1) and 41 U.S.C. § 3304(b)(1) provide that agencies may enter into contracts based on unsolicited RESEARCH proposals without obtaining FULL AND OPEN COMPETITION. A valid unsolicited proposal must contain a UNIQUE AND INNOVATIVE CONCEPT; be independently originated and developed; be prepared without government supervision; and be sufficiently detailed for government review, but must not be an advance proposal for a known agency requirement. FAR 15.603. Agencies are to encourage potential offerors to make preliminary contacts with appropriate agency personnel before the offerors expend extensive effort on detailed unsolicited proposals or submit PROPRIETARY DATA to the government. Potential offerors' preliminary contacts should include inquiries into the general need for the type of effort contemplated and discussions with agency technical personnel for the limited purpose of obtaining an understanding of the agency's mission and responsibilities in relation to the contemplated effort. FAR 15.604. FAR 15.609 permits proprietary legends on unsolicited proposals and directs government personnel to attempt to protect data in such proposals even if proprietary legends are not applied. Proprietary legends are used to restrict the proposal if the offeror does not want data included in the proposal disclosed for any purpose other than evaluation. See Feldman, GOVERNMENT CONTRACT AWARDS: NEGOTIATION AND SEALED BIDDING §§ 9:1–9:7 (2019–2020 ed.); Cibinic, Nash & Yukins, FORMATION OF GOVERNMENT CONTRACTS 309–11 (4th ed. 2011).

UNUSUAL AND COMPELLING URGENCY   A condition that will lead to serious injury if a procurement is not undertaken immediately. 10 U.S.C. § 2304(c)(2) and 41 U.S.C. § 3304(a)(2) permit the award of a contract without FULL AND OPEN COMPETITION when such urgency exists. However, 10 U.S.C. § 2304(f)(5)(A) and 41 U.S.C. § 3304(e)(5)(A)(i) preclude the use of this exception to full and open competition if the urgency is created by lack of ACQUISITION PLANNING or concerns over the amount of funds available for the procurement. FAR 6.302-2 provides guidance on the use of this exception. Examples of unusual and compelling urgencies are provided in DOD PGI 206.302-2. See Cibinic, Nash & Yukins, FORMATION OF GOVERNMENT CONTRACTS 313–17 (4th ed. 2011).

UNUSUAL CONTRACT FINANCING   *Official:* Any financing not deemed CUSTOMARY CONTRACT FINANCING by the agency. Unusual contract financing is financing that is legal and proper under applicable laws, but that the agency has not authorized contracting officers to use without specific reviews or approvals by higher management. *Source:* FAR 32.001. Such financing can be used only if approved by the head of the agency or in agency regulations. FAR 32.114.

UNUSUAL PROGRESS PAYMENT   Any PROGRESS PAYMENT based on cost that provides payment not in accord with the guidance on CUSTOMARY PROGRESS PAYMENTs in FAR Subpart 32.5. FAR 32.501. The contracting officer may provide unusual progress payments only if (1) the contract necessitates predelivery expenditures that are large in relation to contract price and in relation to the contractor's working capital and credit; (2) the contractor fully documents an actual need to supplement any private financing available, including GUARANTEED LOANs; and (3) the contractor's request is approved by the HEAD OF THE CONTRACTING ACTIVITY or a designee. FAR 32.501-2. The excess of the unusual progress payment rate approved over the customary progress payment rate should be the smallest amount possible under the circumstances. Progress payments are not considered unusual merely because they are on LETTER CONTRACTs or the definitive contracts that supersede letter contracts.

UNUSUALLY SEVERE WEATHER Adverse weather that is at variance with normal weather conditions at the time of year it occurs for the place in which it occurs. Unusually severe weather is a cause for an EXCUSABLE DELAY if it impacts a contractor's ability to make normal progress. See Cibinic, Nagle & Nash, ADMINISTRATION OF GOVERNMENT CONTRACTS 495 (5th ed. 2016).

URGENCY See UNUSUAL AND COMPELLING URGENCY.

U.S.-FLAG AIR CARRIER *Official:* An air carrier holding a certificate under section 401 of the Federal Aviation Act of 1958 (49 U.S.C. § 41102). *Source:* FAR 47.401. FAR 47.402 requires that contractors use such carriers for government-financed international air travel and transportation of their personal effects. This policy is implemented by the Preference for U.S.-Flag Air Carriers clause in FAR 52.247-63, which implements the Air Transportation Fair Competitive Practices Act of 1974, 49 U.S.C. § 40118.

U.S.-FLAG VESSEL *Official:* Either a GOVERNMENT VESSEL or a PRIVATELY OWNED U.S.-FLAG COMMERCIAL VESSEL. *Source:* FAR 47.501. FAR 47.502 requires that contractors and subcontractors give preference to the use of such vessels in the performance of their contracts under the terms of the Preference for Privately Owned U.S.-Flag Commercial Vessels clause in FAR 52.247-64, which implements the policies of the CARGO PREFERENCE ACTS and the Merchant Marine Act of 1936, 46 U.S.C. § 1101.

U.S.-MADE END PRODUCT *Official:* An article that is mined, produced, or manufactured in the United States or that is substantially transformed in the United States into a new and different article of commerce with a name, character, or use distinct from that of the article or articles from which it was transformed. *Source:* FAR 25.003. Such products may be acquired in accordance with the provisions of the TRADE AGREEMENTS ACT of 1979, FAR 25.403(c). See Cibinic, Nash & Yukins, FORMATION OF GOVERNMENT CONTRACTS 1624–31 (4th ed. 2011).

UTILITY SERVICE *Official:* A service, such as furnishing electricity, natural or manufactured gas, water, sewerage, thermal energy, chilled water, steam, hot water, or high temperature hot water. The application of part 41 to other services (e.g., rubbish removal, snow removal) may be appropriate when the acquisition is not subject to the Service Contract Act of 1965 (see 37.107). *Source:* FAR 41.101. FAR Part 41 contains policies and procedures that address the procurement of utility services—attempting to allow the government to obtain such services using competitive techniques even though they are regulated by state authorities. FAR 41.102 states that Part 41 does not apply to utility services marketed by a federal agency or a federal power or water marketing agency, telecommunication services, acquisitions of gas when purchased as a commodity, acquisitions of utility services in foreign countries, acquisition of real property of facilities, or SHARED-SAVINGS CONTRACTs.

V

V-LOAN See GUARANTEED LOAN.

VA See DEPARTMENT OF VETERANS AFFAIRS.

VALID TIME-PHASED REQUIREMENTS *Official:* MATERIAL that is—(1) Needed to fulfill the production plan, including reasonable quantities for scrap, shrinkage, yield, etc.; and (2) Charged or billed to contracts or other COST OBJECTIVEs in a manner consistent with the need to fulfill the production plan. *Source:* DFARS 252.242-7004. DOD policy requires contractors to have a MATERIAL MANAGEMENT AND ACCOUNTING SYSTEM that reasonably forecasts material requirements, ensures that the costs of purchased and fabricated material charged or allocated to a contract are based on valid time-phased requirements, and maintains a consistent, equitable, and unbiased logic for the costing of material transactions. DFARS 242.7202. This is implemented by the inclusion of the Material Management and Accounting System clause in DFARS 252.242-7004 in contracts over the SIMPLIFIED ACQUISITION THRESHOLD that are not for COMMERCIAL ITEMs.

VALIDATION The checking of all TECHNICAL DATA submitted by a contractor with RESTRICTIVE LEGENDS to ensure that such legends are properly applied. Validation procedures are prescribed by 10 U.S.C. § 2321 and 41 U.S.C. § 4703; they are implemented by FAR 27.404-5(a) and DFARS 227.7103-4. The procedures are contained in ¶ (e) of the Rights in Data—General clause in FAR 52.227-14 and the DOD Validation of Restrictive Markings on Technical Data (June 1995) clause in DFARS 252.227-7037. They permit a contractor to appeal any challenges of a legend through the DISPUTEs procedure and preclude the government from removal of the legend until the appeal is resolved. DOD also uses a Validation of Asserted Restrictions—Computer Software clause, DFARS 252.227-7019, containing the same procedures.

VALUE ENGINEERING (VE) *Official:* An analysis of the functions of a program, project, system, product, item of equipment, building, facility, service, or supply of an EXECUTIVE AGENCY, performed by qualified agency or contractor personnel, directed at improving performance, reliability, quality, safety, and LIFE-CYCLE COSTs (41 U.S.C. § 1711). For use in the clause at 52.248-2, see the definition at 52.248-2(b). *Source:* FAR 2.101. The Value Engineering–Architect-Engineer clause in FAR 52.248-2 defines value engineering as "An organized effort to analyze the functions of systems, equipment, facilities, services, and supplies for the purpose of achieving the essential functions at the lowest life cycle cost consistent with required performance, reliability, quality, and safety." FAR 48.101(a) describes value engineering as a formal technique by which contractors may (1) voluntarily suggest methods for performing more economically and may share in any resulting savings or (2) be required to establish a program or identify and submit to the government methods for performing more economically. Value engineering attempts to eliminate, without impairing essential functions or characteristics, anything that increases acquisition, operation, or support costs. FAR Part 48 contains guidance on VE. The government encourages VE by including one of the Value Engineering clauses in FAR 52.248-1 through -3 in almost all government contracts. These clauses contain one of two approaches to submission of VALUE ENGINEERING CHANGE PROPOSALs (VECPs): an incentive or voluntary approach or a mandatory program in which the government pays for a specific VE effort. In either case, the contractor is motivated to submit VECPs by being paid for INSTANT CONTRACT SAVINGS, CONCURRENT CONTRACT SAVINGS, FUTURE CONTRACT SAVINGS, and/or COLLATERAL SAVINGS in accordance with the provisions of the specific clause used in the contract. FAR 48.104-1. See Nash & Feldman, GOVERNMENT CONTRACT CHANGES, chap. 9 (3d ed. 2006–2020); Cibinic, Nagle & Nash, ADMINISTRATION OF GOVERNMENT CONTRACTS 371–78 (5th ed. 2016).

VALUE ENGINEERING CHANGE PROPOSAL (VECP)   *Official:* (1) A proposal that— (i) Requires a change to the INSTANT CONTRACT to implement; and (ii) Results in reducing the overall projected cost to the agency without impairing essential functions or characteristics, provided that it does not involve a change—(A) In deliverable end item quantities only; (B) In research and development (R&D) items or R&D test quantities that are due solely to results of previous testing under the instant contract; or (C) To the contract type only. (2) For use in the clauses at—(i) 52.248-2, see the definition at 52.248-2(b); and (ii) 52.248-3, see the definition at 52.248-3(b). *Source:* FAR 2.001. In the Value Engineering–Construction clause in FAR 52.248-3, a VECP is defined as: "A proposal that—(1) Requires a change to this, the instant contract to implement; and (2) Results in reducing the contract price or estimated cost without impairing essential functions or characteristics; provided, that it does not involve a change—(A) In deliverable end item quantities only; or (B) To the contract type only." The Value Engineering–Architect-Engineer clause in FAR 52.248-2 substitutes the term VALUE ENGINEERING PROPOSAL. See Nash & Feldman, GOVERNMENT CONTRACT CHANGES §§ 9:2–9:3 (3d ed. 2006–2020); Cibinic, Nagle & Nash, ADMINISTRATION OF GOVERNMENT CONTRACTS 371–78 (5th ed. 2016).

VALUE ENGINEERING PROPOSAL   *Official:* In connection with an A-E contract, a change proposal developed by employees of the federal government or contractor value engineering personnel under contract to an agency to provide value engineering services for the contract or program. *Source:* FAR 48.001. This term is used when the Value Engineering–Architect-Engineer clause in FAR 52.248-2 is included in a contract. The definition is slightly different than the definition of VALUE ENGINEERING CHANGE PROPOSAL because in architect-engineer contracts VALUE ENGINEERING suggestions can be made by both contractor and government employees.

VARIABLE COSTS   Costs of an organization that vary with the amount of work performed. Variable costs are usually contrasted with FIXED COSTs in analyzing a contractor's INDIRECT COSTs. If variable costs are a small percentage of a contractor's indirect costs, then the contractor's OVERHEAD RATEs can be expected to increase more sharply with a decrease in volume of work than would be the case if fixed costs were a small percentage of the contractor's indirect costs.

VARIANCE   *Official:* The difference between a preestablished measure and an actual measure. *Source:* FAR 31.001. The term most frequently is used to describe the amount that a contractor's ACTUAL COSTs deviate from its STANDARD COSTs. Variances are normally recorded for each unit of a contractor's manufacturing operation and are used to compute actual costs and to estimate future costs. They must be allocated at least annually and may be included in INDIRECT COST POOLs if they are immaterial. See CAS 407, 48 C.F.R. § 9904.407-50.

VARIATION IN QUANTITY   A variation in the quantity of supplies delivered or services performed from the amount ordered or estimated to be required in the performance of a contract. FAR 11.701(a) requires the use of the Variation in Quantity clause in FAR 52.211-16 in supply contracts when an agency decides to permit such variation. This clause provides for specified variations in quantity when such variation will meet the needs of the government. FAR 11.702 requires the use of the Variation in Estimated Quantity clause in FAR 52.211-18 in construction contracts calling for the furnishing of work to be paid for at unit prices. This clause provides for price adjustments if the quantity of actual work varies from the estimated quantity by more than 15%. See Cibinic, Nash & Yukins, FORMATION OF GOVERNMENT CONTRACTS 1355–58 (4th ed. 2011).

VENDOR   A seller of goods. In government contracting, the term "vendor" generally refers to a person or organization selling goods to contractors, but can also mean a person or organization selling to the government under SIMPLIFIED ACQUISITION PROCEDURES.

VERIFICATION   See DUTY OF VERIFICATION.

VETERAN   *Official:* A person who served in the active military, naval, or air service, and who was discharged or released therefrom under conditions other than dishonorable. *Source:* 38 U.S.C. § 101(2).

VETERAN-OWNED SMALL BUSINESS CONCERN   *Official:* A SMALL BUSINESS CONCERN—(1) Not less than 51% of which is owned by one or more VETERANs or, in the case of any publicly owned business, not less than 51% of the stock of which is owned by one or more veterans; and (2) The management and daily business operations are controlled by one or more veterans. *Source:* FAR 2.101. FAR 19.201(a) states that veteran-owned small businesses, among other designated small businesses, must have the "maximum practicable opportunity" to participate as contractors and as subcontractors in the contracts awarded by any agency. The FAR contains no special procedures to carry out this goal but FAR Subpart 19.14 contains procedures to direct work to SERVICE-DISABLED VETERAN-OWNED SMALL BUSINESSes. The DEPARTMENT OF VETERANS AFFAIRS is required to set aside its procurements for veteran-owned small business concerns if the RULE OF TWO applies, 38 U.S.C. § 8127(d). Contracting officers must insert in most contracts the Utilization of Small Business Concerns clause in FAR 52.219-8, which requires contractors to provide veteran-owned small businesses the "maximum practicable opportunity" to participate in SUB-CONTRACTs. FAR 19.702. See U.S. GOV'T ACCOUNTABILITY OFFICE, VETERANS FIRST PROGRAM: VA NEEDS TO ADDRESS, GAO-19-432 (May 2019).

VETERANS BENEFITS ACT OF 2003   15 U.S.C. § 657f. A procurement program for SERVICE-DISABLED VETERAN-OWNED SMALL BUSINESS CONCERNs which provides that federal contracting officers may restrict competition to these firms and award a sole source or set-aside contract where certain criteria are met. See FAR Subpart 19.14.

VIRGIN MATERIAL   *Official:* Previously unused raw material, including previously unused copper, aluminum, lead, zinc, iron, other metal or metal ore; or any undeveloped resource that is, or with new technology will become, a source of raw materials. *Source:* FAR 2.101. Agencies are prohibited from requiring virgin materials unless compelled by regulation or such material is vital for safety or meeting performance requirements. FAR 11.302(a).

VOIDABLE CONTRACT   See AVOIDANCE OF CONTRACT.

VOLUNTARY CONSENSUS STANDARDS   *Official:* Common and repeated use of rules, conditions, guidelines or characteristics for products, or related processes and production methods and related management systems. Voluntary Consensus Standards are developed or adopted by domestic and international voluntary consensus standard making bodies (e.g., International Organization for Standardization (ISO) and ASTM-International). See OMB Circular A-119. *Source:* FAR 2.101. Such standards must, if practicable, be used in lieu of government-unique standards to describe supplies or services being procured by the government. FAR 11.101(b). When an agency uses a government-unique standard, it must use, in specified cases, the Alternatives to Government-Unique Standards solicitation provision in FAR 52.211-7 allowing contractors to propose the use of a voluntary consensus standard, FAR 11.107(b).

VOLUNTARY REFUND   *Official:* A payment or credit (adjustment under one or more contracts or subcontracts) to the government from a contractor or subcontractor that is not required by any contractual or other legal obligation. *Source:* DFARS 242.7100. It may be unsolicited or it may be made in response to a request by the government. In most cases, voluntary refunds are requested after it has been determined that no contractual REMEDY is readily available for the government to obtain the amount sought from the contractor. Acceptance of a voluntary refund does not prejudice remedies otherwise available to the government. The refund should be made by CONTRACT MODIFICATION, if possible. Otherwise, it is made by check, which is credited to the appropriation or account for the contract. DOD PGI 242.7100.

VOUCHER   A document recording a business transaction, such as an expense voucher that records expenses incurred by an employee or in relation to a certain transaction. FAR 4.705-1 requires that financial and cost accounting records such as vouchers be retained by contractors for four years.

W

WAGE DETERMINATION *Official:* A determination of minimum wages or fringe benefits made under 41 U.S.C. § 6703 or § 6707(c) applicable to the employment in a given locality of one or more classes of service employees. *Source:* FAR 22.1001. These are determinations of DOL that a certain scale of WAGES is the PREVAILING WAGE in a locality. Wage determinations are issued under the DAVIS-BACON ACT and the SERVICE CONTRACT ACT OF 1965 and establish the minimum wages that government contractors must pay their employees. Under the Davis-Bacon Act, wage determinations are either "general wage determinations"—issued periodically with no expiration date—or "project wage determinations"—issued for a specific project at the request of the procuring agency and expiring in 180 days. FAR 22.404-1. General wage determinations are posted on the Internet at www.wdol.gov. The procedures for requesting project wage determinations are contained in FAR 22.404-3. Under the Service Contract Act, wage determinations are based on either prevailing rates or collective bargaining agreements. FAR 22.1002. Many prevailing rate wage determinations are posted at www.wdol.gov. If there is no such posted wage determination, a new wage determinations can be requested on that website. FAR 22.1008-1. The procedures for determining the minimum wages applicable to a service contract when there is a collective bargaining agreement are in FAR 22.1012-2. See Cibinic, Nash & Yukins, Formation of Government Contracts 1650–52, 1657–60 (4th ed. 2011).

WAGES *Official:* The basic hourly rate of pay; any contribution irrevocably made by a contractor or subcontractor to a trustee or to a third person pursuant to a bona fide fringe benefit fund, plan, or program; and the rate of costs to the contractor or subcontractor which may be reasonably anticipated in providing bona fide fringe benefits to laborers and mechanics pursuant to an enforceable commitment to carry out a financially responsible plan or program, which was communicated in writing to the laborers and mechanics affected. The fringe benefits enumerated in the DAVIS-BACON ACT include medical or hospital care, pensions on retirement or death, compensation for injuries or illness resulting from occupational activity, or insurance to provide any of the foregoing; unemployment benefits; life insurance, disability insurance, sickness insurance, or accident insurance; vacation or holiday pay; defraying costs of apprenticeship or other similar programs; or other bona fide fringe benefits. Fringe benefits do not include benefits required by other Federal, State, or local law. *Source:* FAR 22.401. This is the definition applicable to the DAVIS-BACON ACT. See FAR 22.406 for guidance on administering construction contractors' meeting of the requirement to pay the wages required by WAGE DETERMINATIONs.

WAIVER   The intentional or voluntary relinquishment of a known right, or conduct that warrants an inference that the right has been relinquished. Waiver entails the renunciation, REPUDIATION, abandonment, or surrender of some claim, right, or privilege, or of the opportunity to take advantage of some defect, irregularity, or wrong. BLACK'S LAW DICTIONARY 1894 (11th ed. 2019). If for example, the government fails within a reasonable period to issue a TERMINATION FOR DEFAULT based on late delivery of supplies, and the contractor relies on that failure to terminate the contract and continues performance, the government has waived its right to terminate the contract for the contractor's failure to meet the delivery date. See Cibinic, Nagle & Nash, ADMINISTRATION OF GOVERNMENT CONTRACTS 843–47 (5th ed. 2016). Waiver of a SPECIFICATION entails written authorization to accept an item that departs from specified requirements but is nevertheless considered suitable either "as is" or after rework by an approved method. DAU GLOSSARY. The parties may also waive contract requirements, such as delivery dates, testing requirements, and PERFORMANCE STANDARDs, or may waive potential rights regarding future claims, interest on claims, ATTORNEY'S FEES, appeal, and so forth.

WALSH-HEALEY PUBLIC CONTRACTS ACT   41 U.S.C. §§ 6501–6511. A 1936 law requiring that contracts over $15,000 for the manufacture or furnishing of materials, supplies, articles, or equipment include or incorporate by reference the stipulations required by the Act pertaining to such matters as minimum wages, maximum hours, child labor, convict labor, and safe and sanitary working conditions. FAR 22.602. DOL does not issue WAGE DETERMINATIONS under this Act; all contractors subject to the act must pay the minimum wages specified in the FAIR LABOR STANDARDS ACT. The Act is implemented by using the Walsh-Healey Public Contracts Act clause in FAR 52.222-20. When a contract subject to the act is awarded, the contracting officer must furnish to the contractor DOL Publication WH-1313, *Notice to Employees Working on Government Contracts*. FAR 22.608(a). See Feldman, GOVERNMENT CONTRACT GUIDEBOOK, §§ 8:26–8:27 (4th ed. 2019–2020); Cibinic, Nash & Yukins, FORMATION OF GOVERNMENT CONTRACTS 1665–66 (4th ed. 2011).

WARRANT   The CONTRACTING OFFICER's (CO's) certificate of authority to enter into, administer, or terminate contracts and make related DETERMINATIONS AND FINDINGS. COs may bind the government only to the extent of the authority delegated to them. Information about the limits of the contracting officer's authority must be readily available to the public and to agency personnel. FAR 1.602-1. COs are appointed in writing on Standard Form 1402, Certificate of Appointment, FAR 53.301-1402, which states any additional limitations on the scope of authority to be exercised beyond those contained in applicable laws or regulations. Appointing officials must maintain files containing copies of all certificates of appointment that have not been terminated. FAR 1.603-3. See Cibinic, Nagle & Nash, ADMINISTRATION OF GOVERNMENT CONTRACTS 31 (5th ed. 2016); Cibinic, Nash & Yukins, FORMATION OF GOVERNMENT CONTRACTS 81–92 (4th ed. 2011).

WARRANTY   *Official:* A promise or affirmation given by a contractor to the government regarding the nature, usefulness, or condition of the supplies or performance of services furnished under the contract. *Source:* FAR 2.101. The principal purpose of a warranty in a government contract is to relieve the government of the conclusiveness of ACCEPTANCE OF WORK, which would otherwise preclude it from imposing the liability for PATENT DEFECTs on the contractor. Other purposes of warranties are to delineate the rights and obligations of the contractor and the government for defective items and services and to foster quality performance. Generally, a warranty should provide a contractual right to correct defects, notwithstanding any other contract requirement pertaining to government acceptance of the supplies or services. It should also specifically state the period of time after acceptance during which the government may assert its right to have defects corrected. The benefits to be derived from a warranty must be commensurate with the cost of the warranty to the government. FAR 46.702. In determining whether a warranty is appropriate for a specific acquisition, the contracting officer considers (1) the nature and use of the supplies or services, (2) warranty cost, (3) the feasibility of administration and enforcement, (4) whether warranty is customary in the trade, and (5) whether warranty costs can be offset by reduced QUALITY ASSURANCE requirements. FAR 46.703. In DOD, the chief of the contracting office must approve the use of a warranty, with certain exceptions. See DFARS 246.704. Standard warranty clauses are included in FAR 52.246-17 through -21. See Cibinic, Nagle & Nash, ADMINISTRATION OF GOVERNMENT CONTRACTS 776–84 (5th ed. 2016).

WEAKNESS *Official:* A flaw in the proposal that increases the risk of unsuccessful contract performance. *Source:* FAR 15.001. Significant weaknesses must be discussed with offerors in the COMPETITIVE RANGE. FAR 15.306(d)(3). See Cibinic, Nash & Yukins, FORMATION OF GOVERNMENT CONTRACTS 892–912 (4th ed. 2011).

WEIGHTS (WEIGHTING) In SOURCE SELECTION, statements of RELATIVE IMPORTANCE or numerical importance "weights" that are assigned to EVALUATION FACTORS as required by FAR 15.304(d) and (e). See Edwards, *The Relative Importance of Source Selection Evaluation Factors: Analysis of a Misunderstood Rule*, 10 N&CR ¶ 34 (July 1996).

WEIGHTED GUIDELINES METHOD DOD's STRUCTURED PROFIT APPROACH for establishing the contracting officer's negotiating position on PROFIT. See DFARS 215.404-71. The weighted guidelines method ensures consideration of the relative value of appropriate profit factors, including the contractor's degree of performance risk, the risk imposed on the contractor by the type of contract, facilities investment, and working capital. The contracting officer uses DD Form 1547, Record of Weighted Guidelines Application, DFARS 253.303-1547, in computing profit. See DFARS 215.404-70. FAR 15.404-4 requires other agencies to have a structured system similar to the weighted guidelines method, including the profit factors discussed in FAR 15.404-4(d) (which are somewhat different from the current DOD factors but which use earlier factors from the older weighted guidelines methods). DOE provides extensive guidance on its weighted guidelines at DEAR 915.404-4-70. See Cibinic, Nash & Yukins, FORMATION OF GOVERNMENT CONTRACTS 1535–65 (4th ed. 2011).

WHISTLEBLOWER An employee who discloses to an outside person or entity an activity by his or her employer that the employee characterizes as illegal, immoral, or otherwise improper. The Defense Acquisition Improvement Act of 1986 provides that no contractor or subcontractor employee may be discharged, demoted, or otherwise discriminated against as a reprisal for disclosing to a member of Congress or to an authorized DOD or DOJ official information about a substantial violation of law related to a defense contract. 10 U.S.C. § 2409. See DFARS Subpart 203.9. The CIVIL FALSE CLAIMS ACT provides relief for employees that file QUI TAM suits against their employers. 31 U.S.C. § 3730(h). See U.S. GOV'T ACCOUNTABILITY OFFICE, WHISTLEBLOWERS: KEY PRACTICES FOR CONGRESS TO CONSIDER WHEN RECEIVING THE REFERRING INFORMATION, GAO-19-432 (May 2019).

WIFCON.COM Where In Federal Contracting? http://www.wifcon.com. An informational website devoted to government contracting.

WILL-COST MANAGEMENT   "Using historically informed independent cost estimation to inform managing of programs to cost objectives," Under Secretary of Defense, Acquisition, Technology and Logistics, *Memorandum for Acquisition Professionals—Better Buying Power: Mandate for Restoring Affordability and Productivity in Defense Spending* (June 28, 2010). See also Under Secretary of Defense, Acquisition, Technology and Logistics, *Memorandum for Acquisition and Logistics Professionals—Implementation of Will-Cost and Should-Cost Management* (Apr. 22, 2011). Will-cost management is expected to develop a system within a program's independent cost estimate. This is distinct from should-cost management, which is designed to reduce system development cost to below the will-cost estimate through cost saving measures.

WILLFUL MISCONDUCT   Prior to the issuance of FAC 2005-17, May 15, 2007, this term was defined in the Government Property clause for cost-reimbursement, time-and-materials, and labor-hour contracts, FAR 52.245-5, ¶ (g)(2)(iv) (May 2004), as conduct marked by a "knowing disregard for greatly unreasonable risks." This definition was removed from the FAR by FAC 2005-17 but ¶ (h) of the Government Property clause in FAR 52.245-1 still makes the contractor liable if such misconduct on the part of the contractor's managerial personnel results in the loss, theft, damage, or destruction of government property. In COST-REIMBURSEMENT CONTRACTs, the costs of correcting defective supplies or paying third-party claims for damages are ALLOWABLE COSTS unless there is such misconduct on the part of the contractor's managerial personnel, FAR 52.246-3, 52.228-7.

WITHHOLDING   The nonpayment of contract amounts by the contracting officer because the contractor failed to carry out some obligation under the contract. This term is sometimes used more broadly to denote SETOFF (the nonpayment of contract amounts because of debts of the contractor outside of the contract). Withholding is permitted by a number of contract clauses such as the Withholding of Funds clause in FAR 52.222-7, under which the government may withhold funds necessary to pay contractor employees the full amount of wages required by the contract. However, withholding is a general right of the government, even without such a clause. The amount withheld should be commensurate with the anticipated amount of damage the government will suffer as a result of the nonperformance. See Cibinic, Nagle & Nash, ADMINISTRATION OF GOVERNMENT CONTRACTS 1065–69 (5th ed. 2016). DOD allows contracting officers to withhold a percentage of payments, under certain conditions, when a contractor's business system contains significant deficiencies. See DFARS Subpart 242.70; DOD CONTRACTOR BUSINESS SYSTEMS.

WOMEN-OWNED SMALL BUSINESS CONCERN   *Official:* (1) A SMALL BUSINESS CONCERNs (i) That is at least 51% owned by one or more women; or, in the case of any publicly owned business, at least 51% of the stock of which is owned by one or more women; and (ii) Whose management and daily business operations are controlled by one or more women; or (2) A small business concern eligible under the Women-Owned Small Business Program in accordance with 13 C.F.R. part 127 (see subpart 19.15). *Source:* FAR 2.101. FAR 19.201 states that women-owned small businesses must have the "maximum practicable opportunity" to participate as contractors and as subcontractors in the contracts awarded by any agency. This is implemented in FAR Subpart 19.15 permitting set-asides for such concerns. Contracting officers must insert in most contracts the Utilization of Small Business Concerns clause in FAR 52.219-8, which requires contractors to provide women-owned small businesses the "maximum practicable opportunity" to participate in SUBCON-TRACTs. FAR 19.702. The Women's Business Ownership Act of 1988, 15 U.S.C.

§ 631(h), makes an affirmative finding of discrimination in entrepreneurial endeavors based on gender and establishes a National Women's Business Council. This council makes annual recommendations to the Interagency Committee on Women's Business Enterprise and reports and makes recommendations, as it deems appropriate, to Congress and the President. See Cibinic, Nash & Yukins, FORMATION OF GOVERNMENT CONTRACTS 1612–14 (4th ed. 2011). See also U.S. GOV'T ACCOUNTABILITY OFFICE, WOMEN-OWNED SMALL BUSINESS PROGRAM: ACTIONS NEEDED TO ADDRESS ONGOING OVERSIGHT ISSUES, GAO-19-168 (Mar. 2019); Beede & Rubinovitz, *Utilization of Women-Owned Small Businesses in Federal Prime Contracting*, a report prepared for the Small Business Administration (Washington, D.C.: Economics and Statistics Administration, Department of Commerce, Dec. 31, 2015).

WORK A work of authorship that under the Copyright Act, Title 17 of the United States Code, is a (1) literary work, (2) musical work, (3) dramatic work, (4) pantomime or choreographic work, (5) pictorial, graphic, or sculptural work, (6) motion picture or other audiovisual work, (7) sound recording, or (8) architectural work. 17 U.S.C. § 102(a). To obtain a COPYRIGHT an author must demonstrate that his or her product is a work of one of these types. See Nash & Rawicz, INTELLECTUAL PROPERTY IN GOVERNMENT CONTRACTS, chap. 1 (6th ed. 2008).

WORK BREAKDOWN STRUCTURE (WBS) A hierarchical breakdown of a project into its component tasks, displayed either graphically or in textual outline. Alternatively, "A product-oriented family tree composed of hardware, software, services, data, and facilities." DOD, *Department of Defense Standard Practice: Work Breakdown Structures for Defense Materiel Items* (MIL-STD-881D, Apr. 9, 2018). WBSs are important project planning and management tools. In large and complex system development programs, they are the product of systems analysis accompanied by a WBS dictionary, which defines the various work elements. The WBS serves as the framework for project organization, work planning and management, and product specification. When project work is contracted out, WBSs are further broken down into contract WBSs, which become the basis for development of STATEMENTs OF WORK. WBSs are essential to EARNED VALUE MANAGEMENT.

WORK-IN-PROCESS Material that has been released to manufacturing, engineering, design, or other services under the contract and includes undelivered manufactured parts, assemblies, and products, either complete or incomplete. This definition was included in FAR 45.501 prior to the issuance of FAC 2005-17, May 15, 2007 and prior FAR 45.505-3 required contractors to keep records of such material. This specific requirement has been deleted from the FAR, but contractors are still required to have appropriate systems to manage property. FAR 45.105.

WORK MADE FOR HIRE *Official:* (1) A WORK prepared by an employee within the scope of his or her employment; or (2) a work specially ordered or commissioned for use as a contribution to a collective work, as a part of a motion picture or other audiovisual work, as a translation, as a supplementary work, as a compilation, as an instructional text, as a test, as answer material for a test, or as an atlas, if the parties expressly agree in a written instrument signed by them that the work shall be considered a work made for hire. For the purpose of the foregoing sentence, a "supplementary work" is a work prepared for publication as a secondary adjunct to a work by another author for the purpose of introducing, concluding, illustrating, explaining, revising, commenting upon, or assisting in the use of the other work, such as forewords, afterwords, pictorial illustrations, maps, charts, tables, editorial notes, musical arrangements, answer material for tests, bibliographies, appendixes, and indexes, and an "instructional text" is a literary, pictorial, or graphic work prepared for publication and with the purpose of use in systematic instructional activities. *Source:* 17 U.S.C. § 101. Under 17 U.S.C. § 201(b), the employer is the author of a work for hire and therefore is the owner of the COPYRIGHT in the work. See Nash & Rawicz, Intellectual Property in Government Contracts, chap. 1 (6th ed. 2008).

WORK OF THE UNITED STATES GOVERNMENT *Official:* A WORK prepared by an officer or employee of the United States Government as part of that person's official duties. *Source:* 17 U.S.C. § 101. Such works are not entitled to protection under the COPYRIGHT law. 17 U.S.C. § 105. This statutory limitation does not apply to works of contractors or grantees to which the government obtains rights pursuant to contract clauses. See Nash & Rawicz, Intellectual Property in Government Contracts, chap. 1 (6th ed. 2008).

WORK STATEMENT The description of the work to be performed on a contract. FAR 35.005 provides that in RESEARCH AND DEVELOPMENT contracts, a clear and complete work statement concerning the area of exploration (for BASIC RESEARCH) or the end objectives (for DEVELOPMENT and APPLIED RESEARCH) is essential. The work statement should allow contractors to be innovative and creative; it must be individually tailored by technical and contracting personnel for this purpose. In basic research, the emphasis is on achieving specified objectives and knowledge rather than achieving predetermined end results prescribed in a statement of specific performance characteristics. In reviewing work statements, contracting officers should ensure that language suitable for a level-of-effort approach is not intermingled with language suitable for a task-completion approach. A level-of-effort approach requires the furnishing of technical effort and a report on the results; a task-completion approach often requires the development of a tangible end item designed to achieve specific performance characteristics. The wording of the work statement should also be consistent with the type and form of contract to be negotiated. FAR 37.602 calls for the use of a PERFORMANCE WORK STATEMENT when an agency is acquiring services. See also STATEMENT OF WORK.

WORKERS ADJUSTMENT AND RETRAINING NOTIFICATION (WARN) ACT 29 U.S.C. § 2101 et seq. A law that provides that employers must give employees advance warning of plant closings or mass layoffs. Implementation of the Act requires no action by government contracting activities. However, the Act might apply to some contracts (such as on-site support service contracts), and some of the costs of a contractor's noncompliance with the Act could be subject to reimbursement by the government. See Levine, Cong. Research Serv., Report No. RL31250, The Worker Adjustment and Retraining Notification Act (WARN) (Feb. 20, 2004).

WORKING CAPITAL ADJUSTMENT FACTOR Under the DOD WEIGHTED GUIDELINES METHOD, an adjustment added to the profit objective for contract-type risk for the purpose of giving general recognition to the contractor's cost of working capital under varying contract circumstances, financing policies, and the economic environment. It applies only to fixed-price contracts that provide for progress payments. Although a formula approach is used, it is not intended to be an exact calculation of the cost of working capital. See DFARS 215.404-71-3(a). DFARS 215.404-71-3(b) explains the determination of the adjustment. See Cibinic, Nash & Yukins, Formation of Government Contracts 1559–61 (4th ed. 2011).

WORLD TRADE ORGANIZATION (WTO)   An organization established in 1995 under GATT to administer trade agreements, serve as a forum for trade negotiations and handle trade disputes. The organization is located in Geneva, Switzerland, and has 164 members. The World Trade Organization Government Procurement Agreement (WTO GPA) provides for waiver of the BUY AMERICAN ACT in certain situations. See http://www.wto.org/.

WORLD TRADE ORGANIZATION GOVERNMENT PROCUREMENT AGREEMENT (WTO GPA) COUNTRY   *Official:* Any of the following countries: Armenia, Aruba, Australia, Austria, Belgium, Bulgaria, Canada, Croatia, Cyprus, Czech Republic, Denmark, Estonia, Finland, France, Germany, Greece, Hong Kong, Hungary, Iceland, Ireland, Israel, Italy, Japan, Korea (Republic of), Latvia, Liechtenstein, Lithuania, Luxembourg, Malta, Moldova, Montenegro, the Netherlands, New Zealand, Norway, Poland, Portugal, Romania, Singapore, Slovak Republic, Slovenia, Spain, Sweden, Switzerland, Taiwan, Ukraine, or the United Kingdom. *Source:* FAR 25.003. These countries are entitled to the special treatment accorded by the TRADE AGREEMENTS ACT. See FAR Subpart 25.4.

WTO GPA COUNTRY END PRODUCT   *Official:* An article that—(1) Is wholly the growth, product, or manufacture of a WTO GPA country; or (2) In the case of an article that consists in whole or in part of materials from another country, has been substantially transformed in a WTO GPA country into a new and different article of commerce with a name, character, or use distinct from that of the article or articles from which it was transformed. The term refers to a product offered for purchase under a supply contract, but for purposes of calculating the value of the end product includes services (except transportation services) incidental to the article, provided that the value of those incidental services does not exceed that of the article itself. *Source:* FAR 25.003. These articles are subject to the special requirements of the TRADE AGREEMENTS ACT. See FAR Subpart 25.4. See Cibinic, Nash & Yukins, Formation of Government Contracts 1624–31 (4th ed. 2011). See also U.S. Gov't Accountability Office, INTERNATIONAL TRADE: Government Procurement Agreements Contain Similar Provisions, but Market Access Commitments Vary, GAO 16-272 (Sept. 2016).

WRITING   See IN WRITING.

WRITTEN   See IN WRITING.

WRITTEN INTERROGATORY   See INTERROGATORY.

WRITTEN OR ORAL DISCUSSIONS   See DISCUSSION.

WUNDERLICH ACT   Pub. L. No. 83-356, prior 41 U.S.C. §§ 321–322. A 1954 law that precluded contract clauses from preventing judicial review of agency decisions on DISPUTEs. The Act codified the "arbitrary and capricious" standard of review for administrative decisions and permitted the courts to overrule administrative decisions that were not supported by "substantial evidence." The Act also provided that contractors could bargain away their right to full-scale judicial review of administrative decisions on questions of law. The purpose of the legislation was to overcome the effect of the Supreme Court decision in the case of *United States v. Wunderlich,* 342 U.S. 98 (1951), under which the decisions of government officers rendered pursuant to the Disputes clause were held to be final in the absence of FRAUD on the part of the government officers. The Act has been subsumed by the CONTRACT DISPUTES ACT OF 1978, which incorporates judicial review of agency decisions in the DISPUTEs process.